P9-DHQ-717

Using MS-DOS® 6.2 Special Edition

Allen L. Wyatt Sr.
W. Edward Tiley
Jon Paisley

que

Using MS-DOS 6.2, Special Edition

Copyright © 1993 by Que® Corporation

All rights reserved. Printed in the United States of America. No part of this book may be used or reproduced in any form or by any means, or stored in a database or retrieval system, without prior written permission of the publisher except in the case of brief quotations embodied in critical articles and reviews. Making copies of any part of this book for any purpose other than your own personal use is a violation of United States copyright laws. For information, address Que Corporation, 201 W. 103rd St., Suite 300, Indianapolis, IN 46290.

Library of Congress Catalog No.: 93-86565

ISBN: 1-56529-646-x

This book is sold *as is*, without warranty of any kind, either express or implied, respecting the contents of this book, including but not limited to implied warranties for the book's quality, performance, merchantability, or fitness for any particular purpose. Neither Que Corporation nor its dealers or distributors shall be liable to the purchaser or any other person or entity with respect to any liability, loss, or damage caused or alleged to be caused directly or indirectly by this book.

96 95 94 10 9 8 7 6 5

Interpretation of the printing code: the rightmost double-digit number is the year of the book's printing; the rightmost single-digit number is the number of the book's printing. For example, a printing code of 93-1 shows that the first printing of the book occurred in 1993.

Screens reproduced in this book were created using Collage Plus from Inner Media, Inc., Hollis, NH.

Publisher: David P. Ewing

Director of Publishing: Michael Miller

Managing Editor: Corinne Walls

Marketing Manager: Ray Robinson

The text in this book is printed on recycled paper.

Dedication

For Allen Wyatt, who hired me to write my first book.

—Ed Tiley

Credits

Publishing Manager
Brad R. Koch

Acquisitions Editor
Thomas F. Godfrey, III

Product Director
Steven M. Schafer

Production Editor
Jodi Jensen

Editors
Cheri Clark
Charles A. Hutchinson
Heather Kaufman
Chris Nelson
Virginia Noble
Susan Pink

Technical Editors
Bruce Meyer
Michael Watson

Book Designer
Amy Peppler-Adams

Cover Designer
Jay Corpus

Production Team
Angela Bannan
Danielle Bird
odie Cantwell
Paula Carroll
Laurie Casey
Charlotte Clapp
Anne Dickerson
Meshell Dinn
Karen Dodson
Brook Farling
Michelle Greenwalt
Carla Hall
Bob LaRoche
Shelly Palma
Caroline Roop
Amy L. Steed
Tina Trettin
Michelle Worthington
Lillian Yates

Indexers
Joy Dean Lee
Michael Hughes

Editorial Assistant
Jill Stanley

Composed in *Stone Serif* and *MCPdigital*
by Que Corporation

About the Authors

Allen L. Wyatt, Sr. has been working with small computers for more than a dozen years and has worked in virtually all facets of programming and computer publishing. He has written more than 15 books related to computing, programming, and programming languages. He is president of Discovery Computing Inc., a microcomputer consulting and services corporation. Allen likes to spend his spare time doing "family stuff" with his wife, Debra, and his three children.

Ed Tiley lives and teaches in Tallahassee, Florida. He is the founder of Data-Train, a vertical market software house. His other books include *Using Clipper*, Special Edition, *Windows After Hours, PCs After Hours,* and *Windows Stuff Microsoft Forgot,* all published by Que Corporation. Additionally, he has written *Tricks of the Windows 3.1 Masters,* published by Sams Publishing, and *Tricks of the Nintendo Masters,* published by Hayden Books.

Jon Paisley is a freelance writer, computer consultant, and audio systems engineer working in the performance business. He is currently working for Thoughtful Designs, a small audio engineering firm in Las Vegas, Nevada, which specializes in show control automation systems. He has been involved with MS-DOS-based computers—teaching, training, troubleshooting, and programming—since the early 1980s.

Acknowledgments

Special thanks from Que to Allen Wyatt for his commitment to completing this project and, as always, for doing it so well.

Trademarks

All terms mentioned in this book that are known to be trademarks or service marks have been appropriately capitalized. Que cannot attest to the accuracy of this information. Use of a term in this book should not be regarded as affecting the validity of any trademark or service mark.

MS-DOS is a registered trademark and Microsoft Windows is a trademark of Microsoft Corporation.

Contents at a Glance

Introduction 1

DOS Fundamentals 11

1 DOS and the Personal Computer 13
2 Starting DOS 29
3 Using DOS Commands 47
4 Using the DOS Shell 67

DOS Fundamentals

Files and Directories 111

5 Understanding Files and Directories 113
6 Understanding Disks and Disk Drives 149
7 Preparing and Maintaining Disks 167
8 Working with Files 201
9 Managing Your Files 225
10 Protecting Your Data 253
11 Emergency Procedures 289

Files and Directories

Controlling DOS 307

12 Working with System Information 309
13 Controlling Your Environment 331
14 Controlling Devices 347

Controlling DOS

Maximizing DOS 375

15 Using the DOS Editor 377
16 Understanding Batch Files 411
17 Mastering Doskey and Macros 443
18 Configuring Your Computer 455
19 Getting the Most from Your Hard Drive 491

Maximizing DOS

Customizing DOS 523

20 Understanding ANSI.SYS 525
21 Understanding the International Features of DOS 539

Customizing DOS

Command Reference 559
A Files Supplied with MS-DOS 6 967
B DOS Environment Variables 995
C DOS Messages 1005
D DOS and DOS Utility Programs, Keyboard Commands 1051
E ASCII and Extended ASCII Codes 1063
F ANSI Control Codes 1073
G International Country Codes 1081
Glossary 1087
Index 1095

Reference

Contents

Introduction **1**

Who Should Read This Book? 1
What Hardware Do You Need? 2
What Versions Are Covered? 2
What Is Not Covered? 2
How Is This Book Organized? 3
Part I: DOS Fundamentals 3
Part II: Files and Directories 4
Part III: Controlling DOS 5
Part IV: Maximizing DOS 5
Part V: Customizing DOS 6
Command Reference 6
Appendixes 7
Glossary 7
Conventions Used in This Book 8
For More Help 9

I DOS Fundamentals **11**

1 DOS and the Personal Computer **13**

PC Hardware 13
The PC Architecture 14
Computer Memory 15
Peripheral Devices 17
What Happens When the Power Is Turned On? 18
DOS and Random-Access Memory 20
Conventional Memory 21
Expanded Memory 23
Extended Memory 25
DOS and Disks 26
Summary 28

2 Starting DOS **29**

Booting Your Computer 29
Understanding the Boot Disk 30
Booting from a Floppy or a Hard Disk 31
System Configuration 33
CONFIG.SYS 33
AUTOEXEC.BAT 36

Controlling the Boot Process 38
Creating Multiple Configurations 40
Creating a Default Configuration 42
Displaying Color Menus 42
Using the Configuration Menu as a System Menu 44
Summary 46

3 Using DOS Commands **47**

Understanding DOS Commands 47
Internal vs. External 48
Making Sure DOS Can Find External Commands 48
Understanding the Elements of a DOS Command 49
The Command Syntax 50
The Command-Line Parameters 52
The Optional Switches 52
Getting Help 53
Using the Command-Line Help Switch 53
Issuing DOS Commands 60
Editing and Canceling Commands 61
Using Scroll Control 63
Using Wildcards in DOS Commands 63
Summary 64

4 Using the DOS Shell **67**

What Is the DOS Shell? 68
Starting the DOS Shell 69
Using the Shell Interface 70
Selecting an Area 72
Moving Around an Area 73
Using the DOS Shell Menus 74
Using the Menu Bar 74
Using Pull-Down Menus 75
Using Keystroke Commands 77
Using Dialog Boxes 78
Modifying the View 81
Using the Shell Screen Modes 87
Using the Help System 88
Using the Program List 90
Working with Program Groups 91
Working with Program Items 95
Working with Directories and Files 97
Expanding and Collapsing Branches 98
Creating Directories 100
Selecting Files in the DOS Shell 101
Selecting a Single File 101
Selecting Multiple Files 102
Selecting All Files 103
Deselecting All Files 103
Selecting Files across Directories 104

Using the Shell to View a File 104
Associating Files with Programs 105
Using the Task Swapper 106
Copying Files in the Shell 107
Moving a File in the Shell 109
Summary 110

II Files and Directories 111

5 Understanding Files and Directories 113

Introducing the DOS File System 113
- Understanding Files 114
- Understanding File Names 116
- Observing File-Naming Conventions 120
- Avoiding Bad File Names 124
- Understanding File Attributes 124

Understanding the Role of Directories 128
Expanding the File System through Subdirectories 131
- Understanding Path Name Expressions 133
- Creating Directories with MKDIR (MD) 137
- Changing the Current Directory with CHDIR (CD) 138
- Deleting Directories with RMDIR (RD) 140
- Using DELTREE to Delete Directories 140
- Renaming Directories 142

Helping DOS Find Files with PATH 143
Listing Directories with TREE 145
Using a Temporary Directory 145
Summary 147

6 Understanding Disks and Disk Drives 149

Opening and Retrieving Files 149
Understanding the Disk's Magnetic Storage Technique 150
Understanding Disk Drives 151
- Hard Disk Drives 152
- Floppy Disk Drives 154
- Write-Protecting a Floppy Disk 155

Understanding the Dynamics of the Disk Drive 156
- Disk Drive Heads 157
- Disk Tracks 157
- Disk Cylinders 158
- Disk Sectors 160

Understanding Disk Formats 162
- Floppy Disk Formats 162
- Raw Capacity and Usable Capacity 164
- Hard Disk Drive Formats 165

Summary 166

7 Preparing and Maintaining Disks 167

Understanding Disk Preparation 167
Preparing Floppy Disks with the FORMAT Command 170
Formatting Floppy Disks 171
FORMAT's Other Tasks 174
Using FORMAT's Switches 176
Preparing the Hard Disk 180
Dividing a Hard Disk with FDISK 180
Formatting a Hard Disk 188
Related Commands 189
Naming Disks with LABEL 189
Examining Volume Labels with VOL 190
Using SYS to Transfer the DOS System 190
Analyzing a Disk with CHKDSK 192
Analyzing a Disk with the ScanDisk Utility 196
Summary 199

8 Working with Files 201

Using DOS to Work with Files 201
Listing Files with DIR 202
Issuing the DIR Command 203
Understanding the Operation of DIR 205
Displaying a Screen of Information with DIR 206
Searching for Files with the DIR Command 209
Customizing the DIR Command 210
Viewing Files 211
Understanding Types of Files 211
Using the TYPE Command to View Files 212
Searching for Text with FIND 214
Using Interlnk to Share Another Computer's Resources 215
Setting Up Interlnk 215
Loading INTERLNK.EXE 217
Loading the Server 219
Establishing the Interlnk Connection 220
Using Interlnk to Transfer Files 220
Using a Remote Printer 221
Installing Interlnk Remotely 221
Running Programs Remotely 222
Summary 223

9 Managing Your Files 225

Copying Files 225
Using the COPY Command 226
Copying Groups of Files 228
Combining Text Files 228
Renaming Files with COPY 229
Copying from a Device to a File 229

Using the MOVE Command 231
Moving Directories and Files 232
Renaming Directories with MOVE 233
Renaming Files 233
Combining Copying and Directory Management with XCOPY 234
Understanding the Operation of XCOPY 236
Using XCOPY Effectively 237
Disk Duplication with XCOPY 238
Duplicating a Directory Branch 238
Setting Defaults for COPY, MOVE, and XCOPY 239
Comparing Files with FC 240
Understanding the Operation of FC 242
Using FC to Compare a Copied File to Its Original 243
Comparing Two Text Files 243
Copying Entire Disks with DISKCOPY 245
Comparing Disks with DISKCOMP 247
Deleting Files 248
Understanding the Delete Operation 249
Deleting Files from the Command Line 250
Deleting Unwanted Files 250
Summary 251

10 Protecting Your Data 253

Avoiding Data Loss 253
Preventing Software Failures 254
Preventing Mistakes 255
Understanding Microsoft Backup 256
Configuring the Backup Programs 258
Understanding Microsoft Backup Functions 260
Setting Up a Backup Policy 262
Issuing the MSBACKUP Command 263
Using Microsoft Backup 264
Performing a Full Backup 264
Performing Intermediate Backups 267
Special-Purpose Backups 268
Using Other Backup Options 274
Restoring Backup Files 275
Understanding Computer Viruses 280
Understanding How Viruses Spread 280
Fighting Viruses with Microsoft Anti-Virus 281
Using the Windows Version of Microsoft Anti-Virus 285
Guarding against Infection 286
Summary 286

11 Emergency Procedures 289

Unformatting a Disk 289
Recovering from an Accidental Format 291
Recovering from an Accidental Format without a MIRROR Image File 292
Rebuilding a Partition Table 294
Recovering Deleted Files with UNDELETE 295
Using UNDELETE from the Command Line 295
Recovering Files with UNDELETE 297
Using the DOS Directory to Recover a File 300
Using the Microsoft Undelete Program for Windows 301
Configuring Microsoft Undelete 301
Selecting Files to Recover 302
Recovering Files 303
Using Other Options 304
Summary 305

III Controlling DOS 307

12 Working with System Information 309

Changing the Date and Time 310
Issuing the DATE Command 311
Issuing the TIME Command 313
Displaying the Version with VER 314
Setting the Version with SETVER 315
Displaying the Amount of Free and Used Memory 319
Issuing the MEM Command 319
Understanding the Operation of MEM 320
Loading a Secondary Command Processor 325
Issuing the COMMAND Command 326
Understanding the Operation of COMMAND 326
Using EXIT to Leave the Current Copy of the Command Processor 328
Uses for a Secondary Command Processor 328
Summary 329

13 Controlling Your Environment 331

Changing DOS Variables 332
Issuing the SET Command 332
Changing Environment Variables with SET 332
Defining Your Own Environmental Variables with SET 333
Changing the User Interface 334
Changing the Command Prompt with PROMPT 334
Altering the Look of the Screen with MODE 337

Changing Disk Drives 342
The ASSIGN Command 342
The JOIN Command 342
The SUBST Command 343
Summary 345

14 Controlling Devices 347

The CLS Command 348
The GRAPHICS Command 349
Issuing the GRAPHICS Command 349
Using GRAPHICS to Print a Screen Image 351
The PRINT Command 352
Issuing the PRINT Command 353
Using PRINT to Print Several Files 354
General Rules for Using PRINT 356
The CTTY Command 356
The MODE Command 358
Using MODE to Change Parallel Port Settings 358
Using MODE to Change Serial Port Settings 360
Using MODE to Redirect a Parallel Port to a Serial Port 363
Issuing the MODE Command to Redirect Ports 363
Using MODE to Redirect Ports 363
Using MODE to Change the Typematic Rate 364
The Redirection Commands 365
Issuing the Redirection Operators 365
General Rules for Using Redirection 367
The MORE Filter 367
Issuing the MORE Filter 368
Using MORE to Pause the Screen 368
General Rules for Using MORE 368
The FIND Filter 369
Issuing the FIND Filter 369
Using FIND to Find Files on Disk 370
General Rules for Using FIND 370
The SORT Filter 371
Issuing the SORT Filter 371
Using SORT to Sort Subdirectory Listings 372
General Rules for Using SORT 373
Summary 373

IV Maximizing DOS 375

15 Using the DOS Editor 377

Understanding the DOS Editor 377
Uses for the DOS Editor 377
Files Required to Run the DOS Editor 378

Starting the DOS Editor 378
Getting Acquainted with the Initial Editor Screen 379
Navigating the DOS Editor 380
Understanding the Menu System 380
Understanding Dialog Boxes 381
Using Shortcut Keys 382
Using a Mouse 383
Mastering Fundamental Editing Techniques 385
Moving the Cursor 385
Scrolling 386
Inserting Text into a Line 387
Deleting Text from a Line 387
Splitting and Joining Lines 388
Inserting and Deleting an Entire Line 388
Overtyping 388
Learning Special Editing Techniques 388
Using Automatic Indent 389
Using Tab 389
Using Place Markers 390
Block Editing 390
Selecting Text 390
Understanding the Clipboard 391
Working with Text Blocks 392
Searching and Replacing 393
Using the Find Command 394
Using the Change Command 396
Managing Files 397
Introducing the File Menu 397
Saving a File 398
Using the Save As Command 399
Using the Open Command to Load a File 400
Loading a File When You First Start the DOS Editor 401
Using the New Command 402
Printing a File 402
Exiting the DOS Editor 403
Starting the DOS Editor with Optional Switches 403
Customizing the DOS Editor Screen 404
Changing Colors and Removing Scroll Bars 404
Saving Customized Settings 405
Using the Help System 406
Summary 409

16 Understanding Batch Files 411

Introducing Batch Files 411
Understanding the Contents of Batch Files 413
Creating a Simple Batch File 414
Understanding Replaceable Parameters 416
Using Batch File Commands 421

Displaying Messages and Inserting Comments 422
Branching with GOTO 423
Using the IF Command 424
Using IF to Test ERRORLEVEL 424
Using IF to Compare Strings 427
Using IF to Look for Files 429
Pausing for Input in a Batch File 430
Making a Two-Way Choice 430
Creating a Simple Menu 431
Creating a Simple Display Menu 432
Using FOR..IN..DO 433
Using a FOR..IN..DO Batch File 434
Using FOR..IN..DO at the DOS Prompt 435
Using FOR..IN..DO with Other Commands 435
Moving Parameters with SHIFT 436
Running Batch Files from Other Batch Files 437
Shifting Control Permanently to Another Batch File 438
Calling a Batch File and Returning Using CALL 438
Using COMMAND.COM to Execute a Batch File 441
Summary 441

17 Mastering Doskey and Macros 443

Using Doskey 443
Loading Doskey 443
Editing the Command Line 444
Reusing Commands 446
Creating and Using Macros 449
Creating Macros 450
Running Macros 453
Deleting Macros 454
Summary 454

18 Configuring Your Computer 455

Getting the Most from Your Computer Resources 456
Understanding Device Drivers 456
Optimizing Your Computer's Memory 459
Using Extended Memory and HIMEM.SYS 460
Loading DOS into High Memory 464
Using Expanded Memory and EMM386.EXE 465
Loading Device Drivers and TSRs into Upper Memory 468
Displaying the Amount of Free and Used Memory 470
Configuring Memory with MemMaker 473
Increasing Hard Disk Performance 480
Fine-Tuning Your Computer with CONFIG.SYS and AUTOEXEC.BAT 482
Accessing Files through FCBS 482
Using the FILES Command 483
Using LASTDRIVE to Change the Number of Disk Drives 483

Using the SHELL Command 484
Using the INSTALL Command 486
Using the REM Command 487
Using the SWITCHES Command 488
Telling DOS When to Break 488
Using the DOS Pretender Commands 489
Using Other Device Control Commands 489
Summary 490

19 Getting the Most from Your Hard Drive 491

Getting the Most Speed from Your Hard Disk 492
Using a Disk Cache (SMARTDrive) 492
Using FASTOPEN 497
Using a RAM Disk 498
Defragmenting Your Disk 502
Getting the Most Space from Your Hard Disk 508
Freeing Up Disk Space 509
Deleting Unnecessary Files 509
Using File Compression 510
Archiving Files 510
Understanding DoubleSpace 511
Installing DoubleSpace 513
Controlling the Operation of DoubleSpace 513
Displaying Compressed Drive Information 514
Changing the Size of a Compressed Drive 514
Changing the Compression Ratio 515
Formatting a Compressed Drive 517
Deleting a Compressed Drive 517
Creating a New Uncompressed Drive 517
Using Other DoubleSpace Features 519
Summary 521

V Customizing DOS 523

20 Understanding ANSI.SYS 525

Installing ANSI.SYS 525
Using ANSI.SYS 526
Issuing ANSI.SYS Codes in Batch Files 527
Issuing ANSI.SYS Codes in Text Files 528
Issuing ANSI.SYS Codes with the PROMPT Command ... 529
Controlling Your Screen with ANSI.SYS 530
Cursor Movement 530
Cursor Positioning 531
Setting the Screen Mode 531

Setting the Text Attributes 532
Screen Control 533
Customizing Your Keyboard with ANSI.SYS 534
Summary 536

21 Understanding the International Features of DOS 539

Understanding COUNTRY.SYS 540
Understanding KEYB.COM 543
Considering Keyboard Remappings 545
Understanding Code Page Switching 546
Checking Your Hardware for Code Page Switching 547
Installing Code Page Switching 548
Loading the Code Page Tables 551
Switching the Code Page 552
Exploring More Uses for MODE and CODEPAGE 553
Using Dead Keys to Cope with the Changed Keyboard 554
Summary 557

MS-DOS 6 Command Reference 559

DOS Commands by Function 559
Batch File Commands 560
CONFIG.SYS Commands 561
CONFIG.SYS DEVICE= Drivers 562
Directory Commands 563
Disk Commands 563
File Commands 564
Full-Screen DOS Applications 564
Help Commands 565
International Commands and Device Drivers 565
Memory and System Performance Commands 566
Miscellaneous Commands 566
Windows Applications 567
Conventions Used in This Command Reference 568
Icons Used in This Command Reference 570
File Names and Path Names 571
Legal File Name Characters 571
DOS Reserved Names 572

A Files Supplied with MS-DOS 6 967

B DOS Environment Variables 995

C DOS Messages 1005

D DOS and DOS Utility Programs' Keyboard Commands 1051

E ASCII and Extended ASCII Codes **1063**

F ANSI Control Codes **1073**

G International Country Codes **1081**

Glossary **1087**

Index **1095**

Introduction

Since its introduction in 1981, MS-DOS has grown to become the most widely used operating system in the world. Hundreds of thousands of programs have been written for MS-DOS. And with more than 40 million users worldwide, DOS affects more people than any software product ever written.

Using MS-DOS 6.2, Special Edition, represents Que Corporation's continuing commitment to provide the best microcomputer books in the industry. Over the years, this book has evolved as DOS has evolved, culminating in what you are reading right now. Keeping pace with technology and explaining it clearly, simply, and completely has been Que's goal. This book is a comprehensive learning tool and reference volume for users of MS-DOS and PC DOS. This Special Edition reflects the maturity of DOS and the far-reaching impact that DOS-based microcomputing has had on the way people work.

DOS is the operating system of choice for the majority of personal computer users. *Using MS-DOS 6.2,* Special Edition, offers DOS users a comprehensive source of information that can help them organize their work with the PC more effectively and make their hardware respond more efficiently.

Who Should Read This Book?

This book is written and organized to meet the needs of a large group of readers. This book is suited for readers who have a basic familiarity with DOS, but need more information to increase their knowledge and sharpen their skills. *Using MS-DOS 6.2,* Special Edition, is also a comprehensive reference on DOS for the more advanced user.

Maybe you have just learned to use your PC and are looking to move beyond the basics. Perhaps you have upgraded your hardware to a more powerful PC, with more memory and disk capacity. Or maybe you have upgraded your version of DOS and want to take advantage of its new or expanded features. If you find that you fit into any of these categories, this comprehensive edition is a "must have" volume.

What Hardware Do You Need?

This book applies to the family of IBM personal computers and their close compatibles—those that operate using the Intel family of microprocessors—such as the IBM PS/1 and PS/2 series, COMPAQ, Hewlett-Packard, Gateway, Zeos International, Packard Bell, Tandy, Dell, Northgate, CompuAdd, Epson, Leading Edge, and Zenith Data Systems, to name a few. There is no way that this list can be complete; there literally are thousands of computer brands that run MS-DOS. Suffice it to say that if your computer runs the MS-DOS operating system, you have the necessary hardware.

What Versions Are Covered?

We have discovered that the vast majority of readers are using DOS 5, 6, or now 6.2. This book is focused on these DOS versions, although there is limited information available for those using an older DOS version. (The best advice we can offer is to recommend upgrading. If you are using a version of DOS older than 5.0, upgrade right away; you will find it well worth the time and effort.) Throughout this book, specific versions of DOS are indicated. When a particular reference applies to both DOS 6.0 and 6.2, however, the more generic *DOS 6* designation is used.

What Is Not Covered?

This book does not include the DEBUG or LINK commands, nor does it include a technical reference to the applications programming interface that DOS provides for programmers. If you are interested in programming at the operating system level, Que offers a complete line of books dealing with DOS programming: *DOS Programmer's Reference,* 4th Edition; *Using Assembly Language,* 3rd Edition; and *Advanced Assembly Language.*

For information on how to install or upgrade your version of DOS, you should refer to a separate book—your MS-DOS manual. *Using MS-DOS 6.2,* Special Edition, assumes that you already have DOS installed and are using it.

Also not included in this book are computer-specific setup or configuration commands, such as IBM's SETUP for the PS/2 and Toshiba's CHAD for laptop displays. Although these commands often are distributed with the same disks as DOS, they are too variable to be covered adequately here. Your computer-supplied manual and your PC dealer are the best sources of information about these machine-specific features.

How Is This Book Organized?

You can flip quickly through this book to get a feeling for its organization. *Using MS-DOS 6.2,* Special Edition, approaches DOS in a logical, functionally defined way. The material in this book is arranged in five main parts, a Command Reference, a set of appendixes, and a Glossary.

Part I: DOS Fundamentals

Part I, "DOS Fundamentals," is devoted to explaining the fundamental role of DOS in a working PC.

Chapter 1, "DOS and the Personal Computer," takes a look at today's PCs. The chapter explores the major components of the PC and addresses the use of system and peripheral hardware. In this chapter, you get a feel not only for your system but also for systems with different keyboards, displays, and peripherals. You also learn the role of DOS in relation to your system.

Chapter 2, "Starting DOS," steps through the process of booting DOS and explains important concepts along the way. You also learn how you can control the booting process through setting up multiple configurations.

Chapter 3, "Using DOS Commands," introduces and explains how to use DOS commands. You learn the concepts behind issuing commands at the DOS command line. The chapter explains syntax, parameters, and switches in an easy-to-learn fashion. Important keys and various examples of the DOS command are also covered, along with information on how to access the DOS built-in help system.

Chapter 4, "Using the DOS Shell," gets you up and running with the DOS Shell. This chapter explores the DOS Shell screen and discusses aspects of the Shell common to all its commands.

Part II: Files and Directories

Part II, "Files and Directories," covers everything you need to know about the heart of DOS—working with disks and the files stored on them.

Chapter 5, "Understanding Files and Directories," recognizes the important job DOS performs in managing your files. This chapter defines files and clearly explains file-naming conventions. Also explored is the tree-structured directory system used by DOS to organize your files. You learn how to use commands that create, change, remove, and display directories.

Chapter 6, "Understanding Disks and Disk Drives," provides the framework you need to better understand how DOS stores information on your disk. You discover what disks are, how information is recorded on them, as well as some of the technological issues related to disks.

Chapter 7, "Preparing and Maintaining Disks," builds on the information presented in Chapter 6. Here you learn what formatting does and how DOS uses formatted disks to store your files. You also learn how to partition a hard disk into sections that DOS can use as logical disks. Also presented are two DOS commands, CHKDSK and SCANDISK, which analyze disks for damage.

Chapter 8, "Working with Files," is the first of two chapters devoted to managing your files. Here you learn how to examine directory listings, view the contents of files, and use the Interlnk program to transfer files between a laptop and your desktop computer.

Chapter 9, "Managing Your Files," illuminates the file-level DOS commands. Because you probably spend most of your time with DOS working with files, this chapter offers an in-depth view of the file-level commands. Each command includes examples that help you appreciate the full power of these important commands.

Chapter 10, "Protecting Your Data," covers the important issues involved with safeguarding the most important part of your computer system—your computer data. You learn common-sense solutions to data protection, as well as how to use the backup programs supplied with DOS. This chapter concludes with a discussion of computer viruses and tells you how to use the Microsoft Anti-Virus program to stop them.

Chapter 11, "Emergency Procedures," discusses how you can recover from catastrophic errors or events. You learn how to undelete files, unformat a drive, and recover data on your hard disk. When you find yourself in a situation that requires this information, you'll probably agree that this chapter alone is worth the price of this book.

Part III: Controlling DOS

Part III, "Controlling DOS," covers the DOS commands and concepts that enable you to change how DOS does its work. The information covered in Part III lets you use DOS effectively to reflect the way you do your work.

Chapter 12, "Working with System Information," covers the commands that set and retrieve system information in your DOS-based computer. These commands often are neglected, but they key you into the control panel of DOS. These commands are helpful whether you oversee one PC or help other users with their PCs.

Chapter 13, "Controlling Your Environment," discusses how you can set system variables and change the DOS prompt. You also learn how you can use the MODE command to change how DOS displays information on your screen, as well as how you can use DOS to change your disk drive configuration.

Chapter 14, "Controlling Devices," explains the DOS commands that control the behavior of logical DOS devices. By using these commands, you can control the way DOS sees your system's drives and directories. You learn how to use your printer while doing other computer work, and you see how to use effectively the DOS pipes and filters.

Part IV: Maximizing DOS

Part IV, "Maximizing DOS," provides the information you need to tap the expanded power available with DOS. This part of the book helps you use the many features provided with DOS and helps you customize your computer system.

Chapter 15, "Using the DOS Editor," provides a tutorial approach to the built-in text-file editor that comes with DOS. The examples developed in this chapter show you how to use the DOS Editor as a day-to-day utility. With the careful attention given to the Editor's practical use, you learn the skills needed to quickly compose a text file. Practical examples, using the DOS Editor to create memos and batch files, also are presented.

Chapter 16, "Understanding Batch Files," guides you through the process of creating batch files and keystroke macros. The commands related to batch files are explained in a tutorial style. Useful examples make it easier to master the basics of batch files.

Chapter 17, "Mastering Doskey and Macros," covers an alternative to batch files. You can use the Doskey program to create simple macros that quickly accomplish a series of tasks. You learn how to use Doskey to make entering DOS commands easier and faster, as well as how to record commonly used commands as macros.

Chapter 18, "Configuring Your Computer," is a comprehensive collection of DOS commands and directives that can help you get the best performance from your PC. In this chapter, you learn to use Microsoft MemMaker, a utility that automatically, and optimally, configures the way your PC uses RAM. You also learn how to set up your CONFIG.SYS and AUTOEXEC.BAT files to provide the best overall system configuration.

Chapter 19, "Getting the Most from Your Hard Drive," describes how you can keep your hard disk at its most efficient level. This chapter describes SMARTDrive, a disk cache that increases the speed with which you can access data on your hard disk. You also learn about Microsoft Defrag, a utility that keeps your files in proper order. Additionally, you explore the use of DoubleSpace—the DOS program that lets you virtually double the amount of information you can store on your disk drives.

Part V: Customizing DOS

Part V, "Customizing DOS," tops off your understanding of DOS. In this part, you learn about controlling and programming your screen and keyboard, as well as how to use international character sets.

Chapter 20, "Understanding ANSI.SYS," shows you how to make DOS screens look colorful and controlled. The details of the ANSI.SYS driver are presented in workshop fashion. You learn how to reassign keys, control the cursor's position on-screen, display the date and time, and more.

Chapter 21, "Understanding the International Features of DOS," steps you through the complicated, but sometimes necessary, configuration of a PC to various international language standards.

Command Reference

In the Command Reference, all the commands that DOS provides for use at the DOS prompt or in your CONFIG.SYS file are arranged in alphabetical order. For each command, the purpose, proper syntax, and notes concerning its use are provided. In many cases, examples and error messages are included to help you use the command correctly. If you are unsure of how to use a particular DOS command, or if you would like to know more about it, check the entry for the command in this section. The Command Reference is a complete, easy-to-use, quickly accessed resource on the proper use of DOS commands.

Appendixes

Using MS-DOS 6.2, Special Edition, also includes seven appendixes containing useful information.

Appendix A, "Files Supplied with MS-DOS 6," lists the files that are provided with MS-DOS 6 and includes a brief description of what each file is used for. The information in this appendix can help you determine if it is safe to remove some of the files installed by DOS.

Appendix B, "DOS Environment Variables," describes the environment variables that are used by DOS and its utility programs, which you can use to control the way DOS operates on your computer.

Appendix C, "DOS Messages," lists and explains screen messages you may see while you are using DOS.

Appendix D, "DOS and DOS Utility Programs' Keyboard Commands," lists the various keyboard commands available at the DOS prompt or when you are using utility programs, such as EDIT and DOSSHELL.

Appendix E, "ASCII and Extended ASCII Codes," lists the 256 characters defined by the American Standard Code for Information Interchange (ASCII), which is the characer set that DOS uses on PC-compatible computers.

Appendix F, "ANSI Control Codes," describes the ANSI commands that you can use with the ANSI.SYS device driver provided by DOS. ANSI commands enable you to control how information is displayed on your screen.

Appendix G, "International Country Codes," lists the various code pages and values you can use when configuring DOS for international use.

Glossary

Finally, this book wraps up with a Glossary that offers definitions for many of the new terms you were introduced to in this book.

Conventions Used in This Book

Certain conventions are followed in this edition to help you more easily understand the discussions.

UPPERCASE letters are used to distinguish file names and DOS commands. Please note, however, that although uppercase letters are used in the examples, you can type commands in either upper- or lowercase letters.

In most cases, keys are represented as they appear on your keyboard, and key combinations are connected by hyphens. For example, Ctrl-Break indicates that you press and hold the Ctrl key while you press the Break key. Other hyphenated key combinations, such as Ctrl-Z or Alt-F1, are activated in the same manner.

Words or phrases defined for the first time appear in *italics*. Words or phrases that you are asked to type appear in **boldface**. Screen displays and on-screen messages appear in a special `monospace` typeface.

Throughout the chapters of this book, syntax lines appear in `monospace` type and use the conventions shown in the following example:

```
dc:pathc\CHKDSK filename.ext /V /F /?
```

In any syntax line, not all elements can be represented in a literal manner. For example, *`filename.ext`* can represent any file name with any extension. It also can represent any file name with no extension at all. However, command names (such as CHKDSK) and switches (such as /V, /F and /?) are represented in a literal way.

To activate the command CHKDSK.EXE, you first must type the command name **CHKDSK.** Any literal text (text you type letter for letter) in a syntax line appears in UPPERCASE letters. Any variable text (text that acts as a placeholder for other text) is shown in *`lowercase italic`* letters.

In addition to the conventions just mentioned, this icon is used throughout the book to point out features that are new in MS-DOS 6.2.

Note

The conventions used for syntax lines in the Command Reference are slightly different from those used in the chapters of this book. Please refer to the section "The Conventions Used in This Command Reference" near the beginning of the Command Reference for more information on how syntax lines are presented in that section.

For More Help

If you have additional questions about any of the MS-DOS commands, or if you need help with other aspects of MS-DOS, you can contact Microsoft directly as follows:

Microsoft Corporation
One Microsoft Way
Redmond, WA 98052
Phone: (206) 882-8080
Fax: (206) 93MSFAX
CompuServe Forum for DOS support: MSDOS

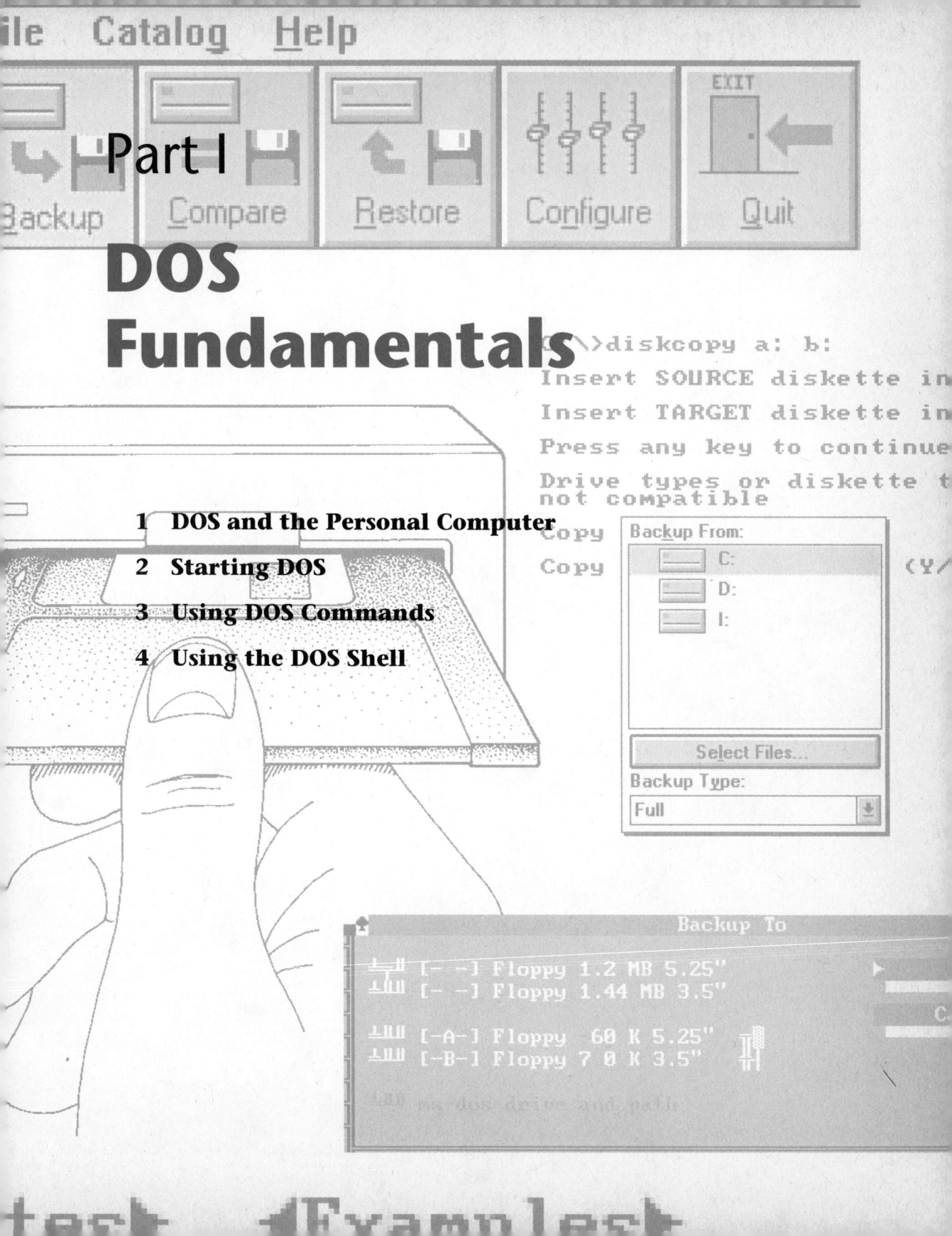

Part I

DOS Fundamentals

1 DOS and the Personal Computer

2 Starting DOS

3 Using DOS Commands

4 Using the DOS Shell

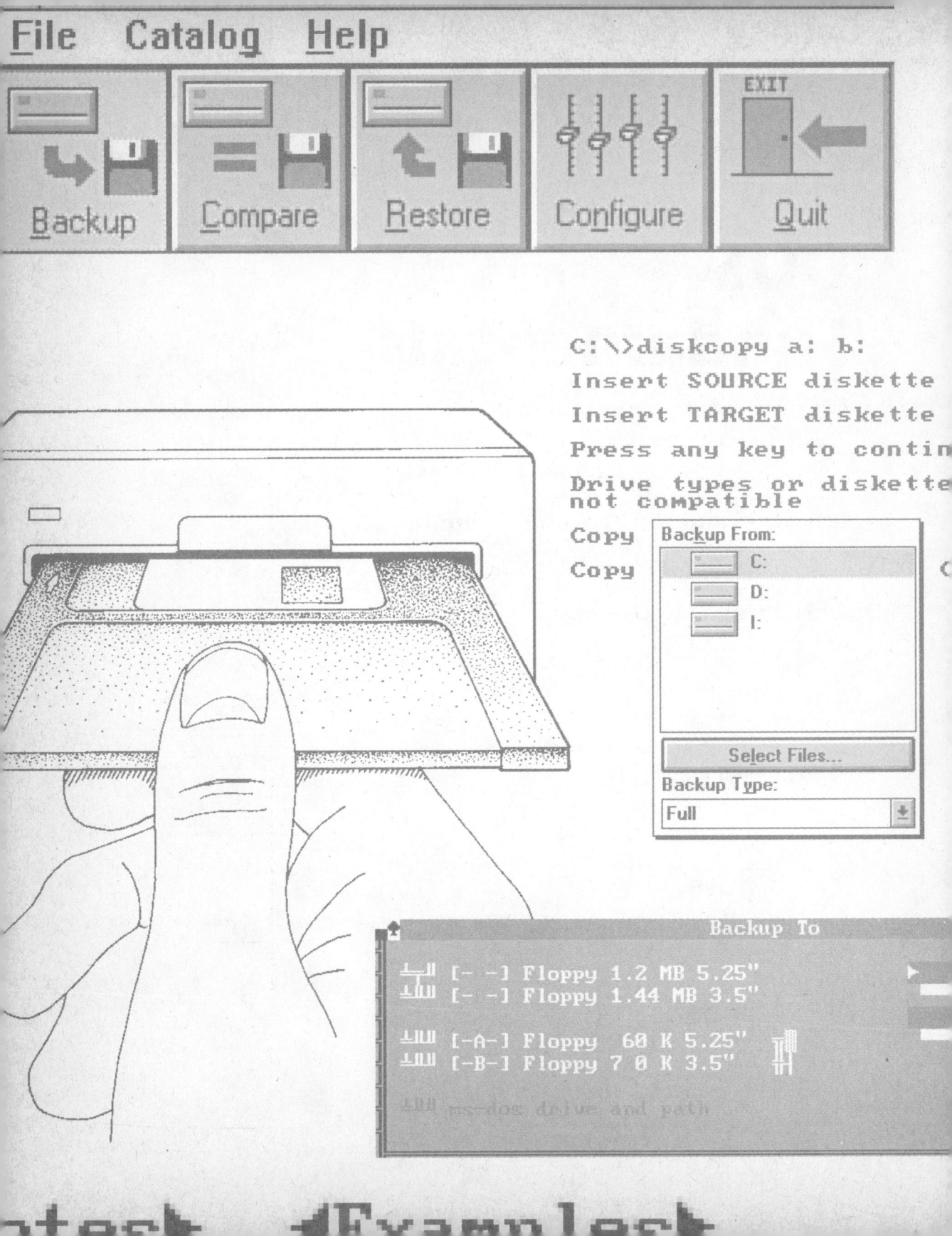
File Catalog Help
Backup
Compare
Restore
Configure
EXIT
Quit
C:\>diskcopy a: b:
Insert SOURCE diskette
Insert TARGET diskette
Press any key to contin
Drive types or diskette
not compatible
Copy
Copy
Backup From:
C:
D:
I:
Select Files...
Backup Type:
Full
Backup To
[- -] Floppy 1.2 MB 5.25"
[- -] Floppy 1.44 MB 3.5"
[-A-] Floppy 60 K 5.25"
[-B-] Floppy 7 0 K 3.5"
ms-dos drive and path

Chapter 1

DOS and the Personal Computer

You may find it hard to believe, but the personal computer is now a teenager and so is its cousin MS-DOS. Since the first release of the IBM PC, more than 95 percent of all the tens of millions of personal computers sold have used MS-DOS as the operating system. The objective of this chapter is to familiarize those of you who are less experienced computer users with the inner workings of your system. If you are "an old hand" and already familiar with the way your computer and DOS interact, you may want to skim through this chapter on your way to Chapter 2, "Starting DOS."

For those readers who have been using computers only a short time or who have never checked out the inner workings of your PC, this chapter provides a quick introduction that gives you the basics. Knowing this information enables you to better exploit the features of DOS and gives you more control over your computing environment.

PC Hardware

In 1981, IBM introduced the IBM PC, which became the worldwide standard for personal computers. This standard endures to this day—even through all the subsequent upgrades in technology.

In the early 1980s, IBM manufactured and sold more than half of all the personal computers sold. As the decade wore on, however, IBM's grip on computer sales weakened and scores of manufacturers introduced models of their own. All of these manufacturers have adopted the basic hardware architecture that made the original IBM computers a de facto standard. In fact, the question most asked by prospective buyers these days isn't "Is it IBM compatible?" The question is "Is it DOS compatible?"

The PC Architecture

The heart and soul of any personal computer is its central processing unit (CPU). The CPU is a microprocessor chip capable of receiving input, processing data, and producing the results as output. DOS-compatible personal computers have long been based on the Intel family of microprocessors and their clones.

Everything in your computer is designed around the needs of the CPU. The CPU is plugged or soldered into the main circuit board of your system, which is where the term *motherboard* comes from. The motherboard also contains the core group of components needed to build a complete computer system. Figure 1.1 shows the typical layout of a PC motherboard.

Your system's CPU is *hardwired* (physically connected) to memory chips and the system bus. The system bus provides a communications highway where the CPU can "talk to" memory chips as well as peripheral devices installed in the expansion slots along the bus.

Note

The word *peripheral* comes from the Greek language and means *around the center.* As used in computer jargon today, a peripheral is any device that is connected to your computer's CPU, either by an expansion slot card or plugged into a port.

In your system, DOS plays the role of the traffic cop, organizing the flow of data in the computer and offering services that programs can use. DOS directs the activities of your system's CPU and helps the CPU to communicate instructions and receive information from other parts of the system. In other words, DOS makes all the separate components inside your computer system work together as if they were all one single machine.

When you install a video card or a modem into an expansion slot in your computer, it must conform to certain standards. These standards ensure that both DOS and the CPU know how to interface with the device.

It is not unusual for some peripheral devices, such as parallel and serial communications ports, to be built directly onto the motherboard of the computer. These devices also must conform to the standards that let DOS and the CPU control them.

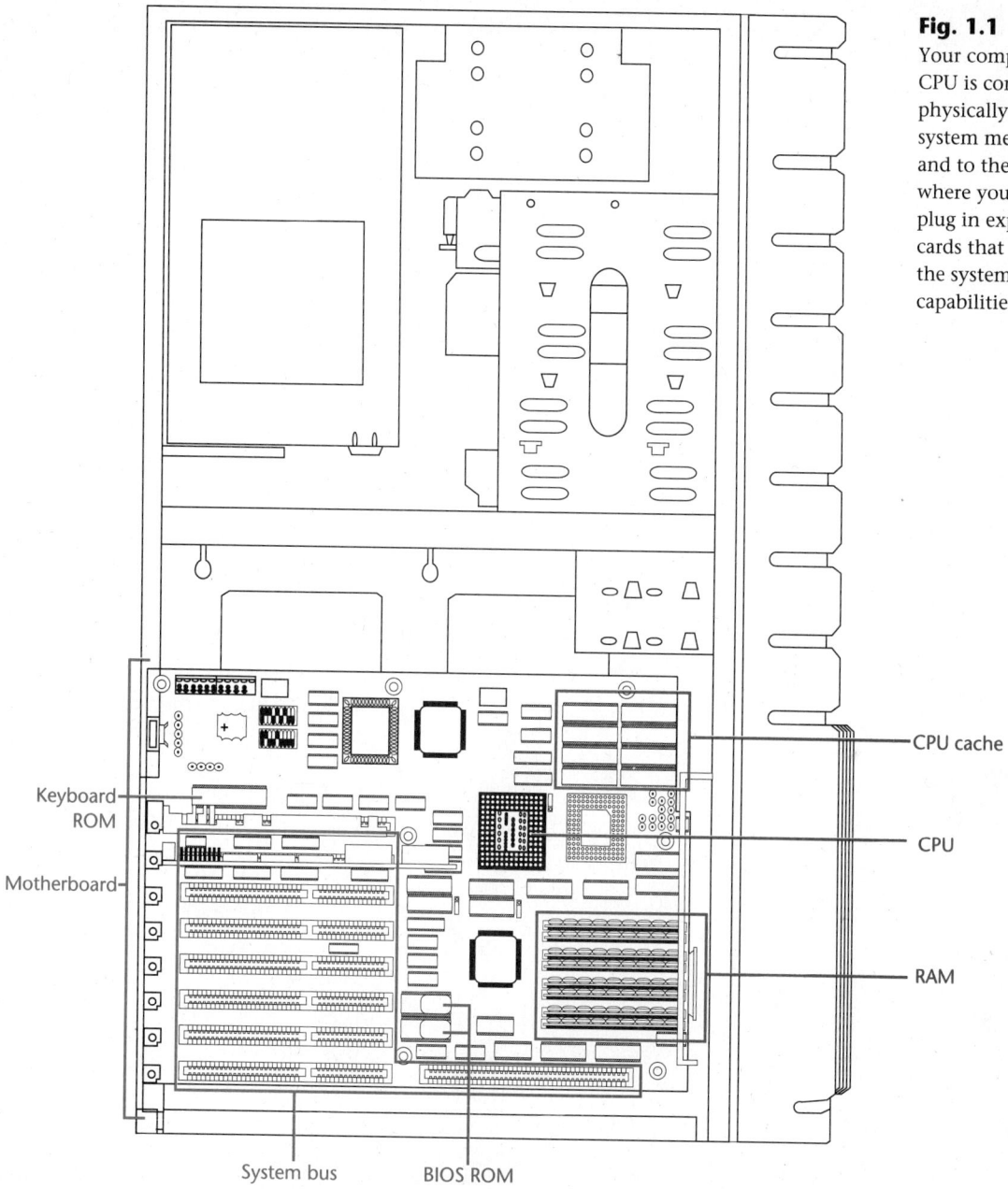

Fig. 1.1
Your computer's CPU is connected physically to system memory and to the bus where you can plug in expansion cards that add to the system's capabilities.

Computer Memory

To perform operations, your computer uses binary numbers to represent both data and program instructions. Binary numbers use the binary digits 0 and 1 in various combinations to represent everything you do with your computer. Binary digits usually are called *bits*, which is an abbreviation of *binary digits*.

Computer memory is nothing more than thousands or millions of individual switches that can have one of two conditions: on or off. The binary digit 0 represents off, whereas 1 represents the on condition. Eight bits arranged together form a byte; the arrangement of bits within the byte can produce one of 256 (2^8) possible values.

Each of the 256 possible values of a byte are arranged into an extension of the ASCII (American Standard Code for Information Interchange) code. The original ASCII code used 7 bits to represent 128 different characters. After the eighth bit was added, ASCII could represent up to 256 characters. Officially, this set is called the PC 8 Symbol Set but has come to be known—somewhat inaccurately by computerists all over the world—as the ASCII Extended character set.

The first 32 ASCII codes represent common commands used by the CPU and peripherals for such activities as making the speaker beep, telling a printer to use compressed print, controlling data transmissions, and so on. The rest of the ASCII codes represent letters, numerals, and graphics characters. A method, therefore, is needed to store this information and make it available to the CPU.

To store information, your computer typically uses three kinds of memory: random-access memory (RAM), read-only memory (ROM), and disk-based storage. Each type of memory has a different role to play in your system.

Random-access memory, RAM for short, is a volatile form of memory. *Volatile* means that it can hold information only when electrically powered. If you turn off the power, all the information stored in RAM chips is lost. Think of RAM as an electronic chalkboard where information can be written and erased at will. When you turn off the computer, RAM is erased automatically. As you see later in this chapter, RAM is broken down into three categories determined by the way the computer addresses memory.

Read-only memory, ROM for short, is a close cousin to RAM, with one important exception: the information stored on ROM is non-volatile. The information is permanently recorded on the circuits of the chip during manufacture and cannot be erased. When you turn off the power on your computer, this information is not lost. When you once again turn on the computer, the information stored in ROM is once again available to the CPU and to DOS.

Your computer uses ROM to store instructions and programming, as you see later in this chapter.

The third type of computer memory is disk storage. If you have the "typical" computer system, you can use both floppy disks and a hard disk (often called a hard drive) to store information while the computer is turned off. Disk storage uses metal or plastic disks coated with a magnetic material to record and play back information in much the same way as your stereo system uses magnetic tapes to record and play back music. Disk storage comes in a sometimes bewildering array of formats. Later in this chapter, you find the information you need to demystify disk storage.

Peripheral Devices

Although you may think of your computer system as a single machine, it actually is made up of many discrete peripheral devices. Strictly speaking, your computer is the CPU and its attached RAM. By themselves, the CPU and RAM can do nothing useful because there is no way to provide input for the CPU to work with, and no way for the CPU to provide output in a form you can understand and use. Without peripheral devices, a computer is worthless. Without DOS, your computer would be the modern equivalent of the Tower of Babel.

Everything in your computer except the CPU and memory is a peripheral device. Keyboards, disk drives, printers, and monitors are all examples of peripheral devices. One of the most basic jobs DOS performs for you is to provide the standards and programming necessary to add peripheral devices to your system so that you can get some work done.

Back in the wild and woolly days of personal computers before the IBM PC, each computer maker employed its own standards and peripheral devices. If you had an Apple II computer, you couldn't share disks with anyone who didn't have an Apple II. If the keyboard for your TRS-80 broke, you couldn't replace it with a keyboard from any other machine. Worst of all, if you went from an Apple II to another kind of computer, you had to learn a whole new set of commands.

One of the ancestors of DOS was an operating system called CP/M (Control Program for Microcomputers). CP/M standardized the commands needed to use a computer, many of which you still use in DOS, but each different computer manufacturer still used different standards for peripheral devices and disk formats. According to legend, IBM investigated using CP/M as its operating system for the first PCs. As the rumor goes, there were differences in time frames, engineering, and personalities, so IBM turned to a small, upstart company called Microsoft. If things had gone differently, this book might have been titled *Using CP/M*!

The simultaneous introduction of the IBM Personal Computer and DOS changed the computing world forever. For the first time, you were able, because of standardization, to walk into a computer store and buy disk drives, video cards, keyboards, and other peripherals made by other companies to put into your IBM or compatible computer.

Peripherals for personal computers sold today adhere to two standards: hardware and software. The hardware standards ensure that peripherals can fit into your system without doing damage and that they can communicate with the CPU. The software standards imposed by DOS ensure that the peripheral becomes an integral, functioning part of your computer system.

What Happens When the Power Is Turned On?

When you flip the power switch on your computer system, you set into motion a series of steps that must occur before you can see the DOS prompt, which signals that your computer is ready to use. No doubt you have seen these steps performed, possibly without realizing their significance. This set of steps is called *booting the computer*. This phrase refers to the old saying "pull yourself up by the bootstraps," meaning to make of yourself something from nothing. That's exactly what booting does; it makes that $2,000 paperweight on your desk into a fully functional computer.

The first of these steps is the activation of the Power On Self Test (POST). The Power On Self Test is a program that has been recorded on a ROM chip located on the motherboard of your system. This program gets the ball rolling. First, it loads instructions into RAM for the CPU to follow. These instructions tell the computer to perform a quick self-diagnostic check of the hardware. One of the first things you see when you turn on the computer, therefore, is the system counting and testing the installed RAM.

Next, the POST checks to see that the system setup is still valid. Your system contains a special kind of chip called a Complimentary Metal Oxide Semiconductor, or CMOS, that stores information about your system's configuration.

CMOS chips are used because they need only a trickle of power, which can be supplied by a battery, to retain the stored information for several years. Your system's date and time settings are stored on this chip, along with information about installed floppy disk drives, hard disk configuration, and other system configuration information that can vary from manufacturer to manufacturer. If the system setup is okay, the POST passes on to the next step, loading DOS.

When the self test is satisfied that everything about your system is in order, it is time to load DOS using another program found on your system's ROM chips—the bootstrap loader. This program's job is simple and to the point: find the operating system's loader on the disk and cause it to run. By default, the first place it searches is drive A to see whether you have a bootable floppy disk inserted into the drive. If the program fails to find a disk in drive A, it next looks to your hard disk. When the loader finds a valid operating system (in this case DOS), it starts the program found on the boot sectors of the disk.

Describing completely all the steps involved in booting DOS would take several pages and bore you to tears, so the following description is somewhat simplified. When the ROM bootstrap loader finds a disk with a bootable copy of DOS, it transfers control to that disk's boot sectors where the DOS loading program takes over.

The first file loaded is IO.SYS. IO.SYS places into memory the basic input/output services DOS provides. After this file is loaded, the second file, MSDOS.SYS, is loaded. Between these two files, DOS sets up the many services it offers to programs such as file handling, printer handling, and so on.

IO.SYS and MSDOS.SYS

If you look at a directory of your boot disk, you normally do not see the IO.SYS and MSDOS.SYS files listed. Both of these files have the hidden attribute, which prevents the DIR command from listing them in the directory.

Also, because hardware manufacturers sometimes alter portions of DOS to meet specific hardware needs, these files may have slightly different names. IBMIO.SYS and IBMDOS.SYS are common variations, for example.

MSDOS.SYS completes the foundation for providing DOS services to your system. After it is loaded, it checks the disk's boot directory (normally C:\) to see whether a file named CONFIG.SYS is present. If this file is found, it is loaded into memory, converted to all uppercase letters, and interpreted. Each line of CONFIG.SYS specifies some type of configuration information such as a device driver to be loaded or a system setting to be made. After these settings are established, COMMAND.COM is loaded.

COMMAND.COM is the user interface to DOS. Its job is to evaluate whether commands presented to DOS from the keyboard or from batch files are legal. If the commands are legal, they are run. If a command is not legal, COMMAND.COM is responsible for issuing one of those error messages that can prove so frustrating to new users.

For Related Information

■ "Booting Your Computer," p. 29

Just before COMMAND.COM turns the computer over to you, the user, it checks to see whether a file called AUTOEXEC.BAT is present in the boot directory. AUTOEXEC.BAT is a standard batch file that usually contains commands to customize your DOS installation. The only thing special about AUTOEXEC.BAT is that it gets run automatically during boot-up.

DOS and Random-Access Memory

To understand the memory issues that surround DOS and your computer system, you first need to know a bit of history. When Intel designed the 8088 and 8086 processors on which the first generation of DOS computers (PCs and XTs) were based, Intel thought that no user would ever need more than one megabyte (1M) of memory. Most of the computers then in use had only 64 kilobytes (64K) of memory, so this speculation might have been reasonable at the time. The problem is that this speculation was wrong—very wrong.

Real Mode versus Protected Mode

When Intel developed the 80286 processor, it created a new mode of operation that let the CPU address memory above 1M. Additionally, more than one program was able to run at the same time, with each program protected from the actions of other programs. This mode of operation was called *protected mode.*

To differentiate this new capability from the limited capabilities of the 8088 and 8086 processors, the term *real mode* was coined. Not until the release of the 80386 generation of processors did protected mode software begin to appear. Even today, the vast majority of commercial software applications continue to use real mode operations.

For most computer users, the first taste of protected mode operation comes when you fire up Windows in the 386 Enhanced mode.

Shortly after the release of the IBM PC, Lotus released a hot new spreadsheet program called 1-2-3. Soon businesses were buying PCs by the carload just to run Lotus 1-2-3. It wasn't long before users found they could build large spreadsheets that exceeded the memory limits of their computers.

A few years later, IBM introduced the PC-AT, based on Intel's 80286 processor. The AT's processor was faster than those used in PC and XT machines, and it had the capability to access up to 16M of memory using a new processor feature called *protected mode*. Unfortunately, DOS was never enhanced to take advantage of this capability, so software developers never used the full capabilities of the 80286 chip. Many ATs lived and died without ever running protected mode software.

Later still, Intel developed the 80386 and 80486 chips that addressed up to 4 gigabytes (4G) of memory. Until Windows 3.0 came on the scene, precious little software was able to run the computer's protected mode. Instead, users simply used these machines as fast PCs. Users who needed more memory than the original 1M had to rely on a memory scheme called *expanded memory*, which was created collectively by Lotus, Intel, and Microsoft.

Today, computer RAM is classified in three ways: conventional memory, expanded memory, and extended memory. Understanding the distinctions can be quite useful.

Conventional Memory

As you've already learned, the generation of personal computers that preceded DOS and the IBM PC used, at most, 64K of random-access memory. The Intel 8088 processor addressed up to 1M—at the time a significant advance. Of this 1M, 640K was made available for DOS and applications programs to use. The remaining 384K was reserved for system use. Figure 1.2 shows the way conventional memory is used.

As you can see in the figure, DOS places a table of available services into memory beginning at byte 0. When DOS loads the rest of itself into memory, it occupies memory addresses beginning at 1K. The space from 1K to 640K is reserved for DOS and whatever programs you may run. Addresses above 640K (the infamous 640K barrier) are reserved for addresses for ROMs and for accessing video card memory.

In DOS, memory addresses use a segment:offset notation to pinpoint an exact location where data or program instructions can be stored. These address locations are always specified using the hexadecimal number system.

Each segment is 64K bytes in length, but each segment begins only 16 bytes up from its neighbor. The offset portion of the address specifies how many bytes the address is from the beginning of the segment. (For more information, see *DOS Programmer's Reference*, 4th Edition, by Que Corporation.)

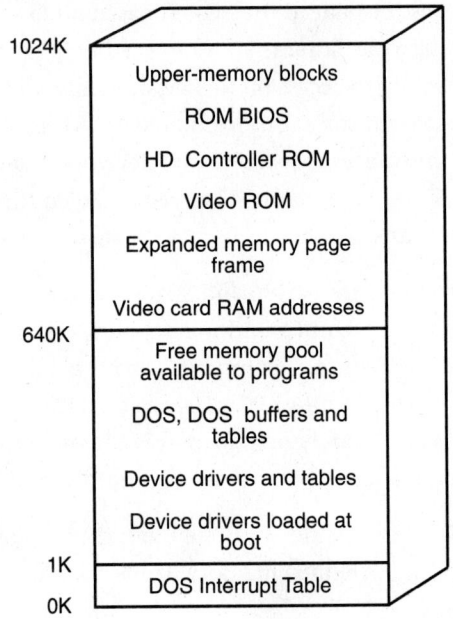

Fig. 1.2
Conventional memory is restricted to 1M.

Programmers soon discovered that you can get an extra block of usable memory by specifying the last possible segment in the 1M area in the segment portion of the address. Using this trick opens up an extra 64K (minus the 16 bytes that fall below the 1M line) of memory above 1M that can be addressed without sending DOS and the processor into Never Never Land. Thus, the *high memory area* was born.

This newly discovered high memory area was almost immediately grabbed by network designers. They saw this area as a safe place to put their data buffers which didn't take away RAM from running programs that already were beginning to feel the squeeze of the 640K barrier.

Beginning with the release of DOS 5.0, you can make use of unused addresses between 640K and 1M to run DOS, programs, and device drivers by using HIMEM.SYS and EMM386.EXE to make this space available. You use the LOADHIGH and DEVICEHIGH DOS commands to place programs, device drivers, and even portions of DOS itself into the *upper memory area*.

You can find more information about using upper memory blocks in Chapter 18, "Configuring Your Computer."

Expanded Memory

When Lotus 1-2-3 users and others began demanding a way to access more than the 640K memory provided by the conventional memory scheme, Lotus, Intel, and Microsoft put their heads together to come up with the Expanded Memory Specification (EMS), also known as the LIM 3.2 specification. This specification was adopted before the Intel 80286 processor hit the market. EMS was an immediate hit, which in part accounts for the fact that few software companies even tried to exploit the enhanced memory addressing capabilities of the 80286 processor. Programs that needed more than 640K memory easily could be modified to adhere to the EMS system, so there was no great push for DOS to use the chip's protected mode that could address up to 16M of RAM.

The Expanded Memory Specification makes more memory available to processors running in real mode, the name given to the mode of operation that mimics the original 8088 processor used in PCs and XTs. The LIM specifications reserve a 64K area of memory in the upper memory block (the area between 640K and 1M) for use as a page frame. Figure 1.3 shows how expanded memory is situated in a computer system. As you can see, the page frame can accommodate up to four 16K pages that show the contents of memory chips on the EMS memory board.

You can install up to 16M of memory on a special memory board and plug it into an expansion slot in the system. Information stored in these memory addresses can be swapped from the memory board to the page frame and back again as needed. In effect, the page frame acts as a window into the expanded memory.

Shortly after the EMS specification was adopted, several companies, including AST Research, who was at the time the largest seller of add-on memory boards, came up with an Enhanced Expanded Memory Specification (EEMS). This new expanded memory scheme used a backfilling technique that eliminated the need for the page frame in upper memory and let expanded memory reside inside the 640K range. In fact, some early EEMS products required users to remove any RAM in their system above the 256K mark, which provided 384K of expanded RAM to be situated within conventional memory addresses. Figure 1.4 shows how you can use the Enhanced Expanded Memory Specification, also called LIM 4.0, to eliminate the page frame.

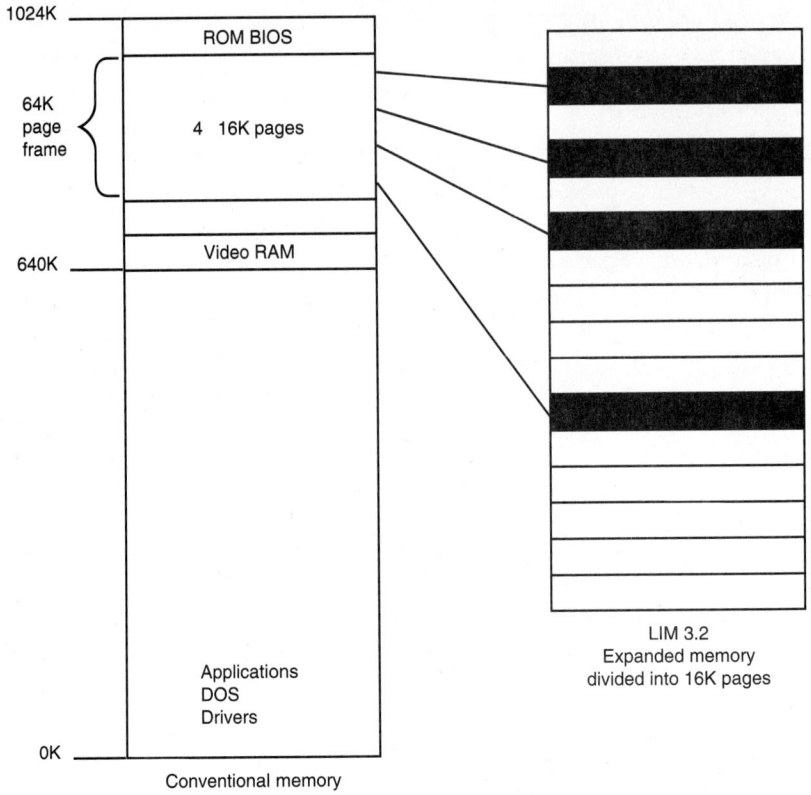

Fig. 1.3
Expanded memory resides on a special memory board and is swapped into the page frame when needed.

The Expanded Memory Specification has always been, and will always be, a kludge. Life today would be much simpler for those folks who support computer users if the hardware and software manufacturers had taken a "bite the bullet" attitude when the 80286 processor became available and built systems to use extended memory.

Fortunately, the number of programs that use the EMS scheme are dying off as Windows is used more frequently. Today, most new software that requires huge amounts of memory is written for the Windows environment. The only DOS programs that use expanded memory, for the most part, are "the old chestnuts" such as Lotus 1-2-3 and AutoCAD, whose roots go back to the early days of PCs. Windows 3.1 uses DOS's EMM386 utility to create expanded memory, even for older DOS programs that require EMS, so no need exists for special EMS memory boards.

The DOS Expanded Memory Manager (EMM386) makes old-fashioned EMS boards obsolete because it can simulate expanded memory using the extended memory found in most modern computers. In fact, you would be hard pressed to find a computer store that still stocks expanded memory boards.

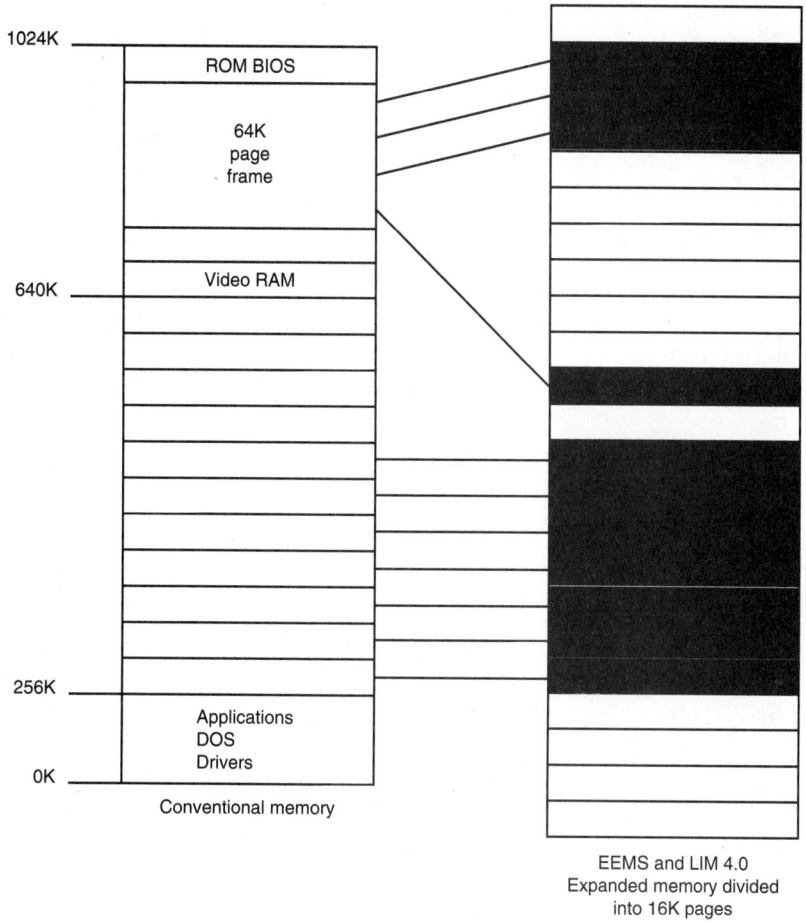

Fig. 1.4
EEMS memory can be mapped into conventional memory addresses, eliminating the need for a page frame in the system area.

Extended Memory

The Extended Memory Specification (XMS) is a simpler way of making memory addresses above 1M available to your programs. Extended memory is simply an extension of conventional memory addresses. The 384K system memory area is still present under XMS, so programs can use the conventional 640K memory area and addresses greater than 1M.

To implement extended memory, the protected mode operations of the processor (80286, 80386, 80486, or higher) are turned on. DOS accomplishes this task by loading HIMEM.SYS at boot-up from the CONFIG.SYS file. HIMEM, which is an extended memory manager, enables DOS to address memory above the conventional 1M mark.

For Related Information

■ "Optimizing Your Computer's Memory," p. 459

To date, few DOS programs take advantage of the availability of extended memory. Windows and Windows programs, however, routinely use extended memory.

DOS and Disks

RAM is volatile storage. As soon as the power goes off, RAM goes to sleep. ROMs provide a permanent storage medium, but you can't write files to ROM. What is needed is a third method of storing data and programs. DOS stands for disk operating system, so if you get the notion that disks are used for permanent storage of data and programs, give yourself the afternoon off.

One of the major functions of DOS is to facilitate the reading and writing of data stored on disks. Disks are circular platters of plastic or metal coated with a magnetic emulsion similar to those used to produce cassette tapes or video tapes. Optical disks also use a process similar to CD technology, but they are still expensive and thus not yet in common use.

By offering standardized disk services, DOS saves programmers uncounted hours of work because their programs can simply ask DOS to read or write a disk. The programmer is spared the task of writing code to store data. There is an added benefit to computer users from these DOS file services. Because DOS takes care of placing files onto disks, any file created by a DOS program can reside on the same disk as any other DOS file.

When a program writes to a disk, DOS ensures that the data is stored as a named collection of information called a *file*. DOS rules determine naming conventions. A legal DOS file name can be from one to eight characters, followed by an optional period and one- to three-character extension. A file name's extension is most often used to indicate the type of file being stored.

Floppy disks are wafer-thin plastic disks coated with a magnetic emulsion and encased within a protective sleeve. The original IBM PC used floppy disks measuring 5 1/4 inches across. In the last few years 3 1/2-inch floppies have become more common. The advantages of the 3 1/2-inch format are its greater data density (it holds considerably more information than the physically larger 5 1/4-inch disks) and the hard plastic sleeve that better protects them from damage.

Floppy disks most commonly are used to store data to be archived or transferred to another computer. The biggest disadvantages of floppy disks are that reading and writing on floppies is relatively slow, and they do not hold enough information to accommodate today's larger programs and data files.

Hard disks are nonremovable, high-capacity, rigid platters sealed inside a dust-free casing. For increased storage capacity, several platters can be stacked within a single hard disk drive where multiple pickup heads are used to read and write the stored information. You can find more detailed information about magnetic disks in Chapter 7, "Preparing and Maintaining Disks."

Nonmagnetic Disks

Increasingly, software companies are using CD-ROMs to distribute their wares. CD-ROMs are 4 1/2-inch hard plastic disks containing an embedded sheet of metal foil. A laser scans the surface of the metal foil, which is covered with pits or indentations. When the laser strikes a smooth area of the disk, the laser is reflected back up to an optical sensor. When the laser strikes a pit, the light is diffused, causing the light to miss the sensor. In this manner, the zeros and ones that make up computer data can be embedded on the surface of the CD.

CDs have the advantages of being nearly indestructible and of holding large amounts of data in a small space. When not acting as a DOS disk drive, most CD-ROM drives also have the advantage of being able to play normal music CDs. If a headphone jack is on the face of the drive, you can assume that it can play audio CDs as well as act as a disk drive. Plug in a pair of speakers or headphones, and you can groove to your favorite tunes while you work.

In the last few years, a great deal of research and development has gone into creating optical disk drives that can both read and write data. Unlike magnetic technology, optical disks cannot be erased or written over. Most optical disks available today are of the Write Once, Read Many (WORM) variety and are used to archive important data. The expense of these drives—and the cost of the optical disks—has kept these disks from entering the mainstream.

Recently, however, advances in optical storage technology have made the day when a read/write optical disk may be installed in your computer a not-too-distant probability. Within the next five to seven years, optically stored data will largely replace today's magnetic media.

For Related Information

- "Getting the Most Speed from Your Hard Disk," p. 492
- "Getting the Most Space from Your Hard Disk," p. 508

Summary

In this chapter, you explored some of the fundamental concepts concerning the way DOS makes your computer work. Understanding these concepts is necessary to understand fully how to take advantage of the features of DOS 6.2. Following are the main points covered in this chapter:

- MS-DOS (Microsoft Disk Operating System) provides the software support necessary to make your computer operate efficiently and to enable other software to be run.
- The central processing unit (CPU) is the brain of your computer system. All other devices attached to the system are peripherals and are controlled by DOS and the CPU.
- Most DOS software operates within the 640K barrier. Unused addresses from 640K to 1M are known as upper memory blocks and can be used to run programs and device drivers. Major portions of DOS itself can be loaded into the upper memory area.
- The LIM 3.2 and LIM 4.0 Expanded Memory Specifications (EMS and EEMS) can use conventional memory addresses (those below 1M) to act as a window into added memory of up to 16M.
- The Extended Memory Specification (XMS) is a linear extension of memory addresses above the 1M mark. Few DOS programs currently can use extended memory, but Windows and Windows programs routinely load into extended memory addresses.
- Floppy disks and hard disks use a magnetic technology similar to cassette recorders and VCRs to store data permanently as named files. CD-ROMs and optical drives someday will be the dominant method for storing files.

In Chapter 2, "Starting DOS," you learn a bit more about the process DOS goes through whenever you turn on your computer or reboot your system.

Chapter 2

Starting DOS

In Chapter 1, "DOS and the Personal Computer," you got an overview of DOS and of the PC. By now you are ready to start your PC and to learn more about the practical operation of DOS. This chapter is an overview of the start-up process. In this chapter, you learn how to control the boot process, how to load device drivers, and how to control the environment of your PC.

With the introduction of DOS 6.0, and continued in DOS 6.2, you have access to a powerful feature that enables you to have multiple configurations on the same system. Power users of PCs have long used crude tricks to achieve multiple configurations. You no longer have to worry about using these tricks.

Booting Your Computer

In Chapter 1, you read a description of the steps taken when you boot up your computer. In fact, two types of booting are available. The first is known as a *cold boot*. This term comes from the fact that the computer's power is off and that the unit is not yet warm. As you might guess, the second type of boot is the *warm boot*.

A cold boot occurs when you turn on the power switch to your system. Some systems also have a reset button. Pressing this button also triggers a cold boot. The difference between a cold and a warm boot is simple. A cold boot begins at the absolute beginning, using the POST (Power On Self Test) to check the condition of the system's major components and of RAM.

A warm boot, on the other hand, bypasses the preliminary self test, moving directly to the loading of DOS. A warm boot is triggered when you press the Ctrl-Alt-Del keys all at the same time. This combination of keys was chosen because on most keyboards it is almost impossible to press these three keys simultaneously by accident.

The Big Red Button

Although the general population may believe differently, computer users have a tremendous sense of humor. This sense of humor has introduced two slang terms to differentiate between cold and warm boots. Because early PCs had a large red power switch on the side of the case, cold booting has been dubbed "Big Red Button Time," or BRB for short. A BRB is usually necessary only when your system is so thoroughly hung up and confused that it fails to respond to the Ctrl-Alt-Del key combination. Pressing these three keys normally triggers a warm boot, so some anonymous wag named a warm boot "the three finger salute."

The net effect of either a cold or warm boot is to wipe the slate clean and start the computer out fresh. Being the sophisticated computer user that you are, of course, you should realize that rebooting the computer on a whim can be a dangerous proposition. Triggering a boot when a file is open and in the process of editing can cause you to lose valuable data because you don't have an opportunity to save the file to disk before the boot takes place.

Understanding the Boot Disk

In the preceding chapter, you learned that during the booting process three files are loaded into memory: IO.SYS, MSDOS.SYS, and COMMAND.COM. You also learned that two other files, CONFIG.SYS and AUTOEXEC.BAT, are used in the boot process as well. The reason for recalling this information to your attention is to point out that DOS is not some monolithic creation. Rather, DOS is composed of many modular components working together.

DOS is not, however, a mind reader, so you are required to specially prepare bootable disks capable of starting your computer. You can create bootable disks in two ways: you can use the FORMAT command, with the /S switch, or you can use the SYS command.

When you use the FORMAT command to create a bootable disk, using the /S switch causes the newly formatted disk to contain the disk portion of the bootstrap loader in the boot sector, IO.SYS, MSDOS.SYS, and COMMAND.COM. If any of these four conditions is not satisfied, you cannot use the disk to start DOS.

Using the SYS command to make a disk bootable requires you to know a few undocumented facts about the way boot disks are constructed. For a disk to be bootable, the following conditions must be met:

- IO.SYS must be the first directory entry in the root directory of the disk.
- MSDOS.SYS must be the second entry in the root directory.
- IO.SYS must be the first physical file on the disk.

Knowing these three rules, you now can understand more readily why the SYS command so often reports the `No room for system on destination disk` error message even though the disk has plenty of free space. If files already are written on the disk, chances are that the first directory entry in the root is taken.

Many years ago, when DOS was well on the way to becoming the number one bootlegged bit of software of all time, the DOS development team came up with the /B switch to the FORMAT command. Sending someone a bootable disk is a violation of your DOS software license because that disk enables the person to start up a computer with software for which he or she hasn't paid. The idea behind the /B switch is to reserve space on the disk so that you can use the SYS command later to make the disk bootable.

In practice, the /B switch of the FORMAT command simply copies IO.SYS and MSDOS.SYS to the newly formatted disk, leaving off COMMAND.COM and the bootstrap loader. This restriction ensures that the SYS command can come along later and finish the job of making the disk bootable. You may only ever need the /B switch once every five years, but it can come in handy.

Booting from a Floppy or a Hard Disk

These days, finding a computer system lacking a hard disk is unusual. The single major exception to this rule is a network workstation where the file server provides all the hard disk storage needed. Because the boot process must be local to the workstation on a standard PC, booting from a floppy in this case is a no-brainer.

Booting from the computer's hard disk is, in general, more efficient. Hard disk drives are faster than floppy drives, so booting from the hard disk gets you to a DOS prompt more quickly. There are times, however. . . .

Okay, so there you are late one Saturday night; your buddy from Chicago, who has recently been learning to program, is staying with you. He wants to show you his latest creation. You plug in the disk, start up the program, and it bombs. Worse than that, though, his baby trashes your drive C. No matter what you try, you can't get the system to reboot. You have a recent backup, but you can't get the computer to boot. And you can't get to the tape backup program. A brilliant flash of inspiration sends you digging for your original DOS disks, but you have an upgrade version, so none of the disks are bootable. What do you do?

If you are properly prepared (most people aren't), you reach into your floppy disk box and pull out your emergency boot disk. Ten or fifteen minutes later, you are back in business. If, like most people, you aren't prepared, you turn off the computer and hope the boot disk you make at the office on Monday will do the trick.

You can cut downtime from days or hours to just a few minutes by being prepared. Just follow these steps:

1. Format a floppy disk in drive A using the /S (System) switch to make it a bootable disk. If you have compressed your drive with DoubleSpace, FORMAT automatically copies DBLSPACE.BIN to the new floppy as a hidden system file.
2. Copy AUTOEXEC.BAT and CONFIG.SYS to the new boot disk.
3. Copy all the files you need for a clean boot to the floppy. Include DBLSPACE.SYS if you have compressed disks. Copy any other drivers you absolutely need. Leave off the drivers such as MSCDEX that you don't need just to repair the disk.
4. Mark the label clearly *DOS 6.2 BOOT DISK*.
5. If your boot floppy is a 5 1/4-inch disk, stick a write-protect tab over the notch. If the boot disk is a 3 1/2-inch disk, slide the write-protect tab so that the hole is open.
6. Put your emergency boot disk in a safe place, but don't forget where you put it. As your system configuration changes, remember to update your emergency boot disk.

For Related Information

■ "What Happens When the Power Is Turned On?," p. 18

System Configuration

If you are not a long-time computer user, or if you have always had someone else maintain your system configurations for you, you may not be familiar with the roles played by two important files during start-up. The CONFIG.SYS and AUTOEXEC.BAT files customize the way your computer is configured. These files load drivers, set options, and tweak the DOS environment.

Note

The *DOS environment* is a space in memory reserved for creating variables that can be looked at by programs running on your system. The default size of the DOS environment is only 256 bytes in length. Some programs make extensive use of the DOS environment to store customization settings. Use the SHELL command to increase the size of the environment.

CONFIG.SYS

During the boot process, as soon as IO.SYS and MSDOS.SYS are loaded into memory and before COMMAND.COM is loaded, a search is made of the root directory of the boot disk to see whether the CONFIG.SYS file exists. On 99 percent of the computers in use today, the file is available.

When CONFIG.SYS is found, its contents are read into memory, and the file is acted upon line by line. Each line in CONFIG.SYS contains a DOS command that tells DOS to enhance the DOS configuration.

A number of DOS commands are valid in CONFIG.SYS. Table 2.1 gives a quick rundown of those commands. For detailed information, refer to the Command Reference section of this book.

Table 2.1 Commands Often Used in CONFIG.SYS

Command	Meaning
BREAK	Determines how DOS reacts to the Ctrl-Break or Ctrl-C keystrokes.
BUFFERS	Sets the number of file buffers DOS uses in transferring data to and from disk.
COUNTRY	Configures language-dependent features.

(continues)

Table 2.1 Continued

Command	Meaning
DEVICE	Loads a device driver (special software to control your computer's configuration) in conventional memory.
DEVICEHIGH	Loads a device driver into upper memory (above 640K).
DOS	Determines whether DOS is loaded into the high memory area and whether DOS maintains links to upper memory blocks.
DRIVPARM	Modifies the parameters for an existing drive by specifying information about tracks, sectors, heads, and so on.
FCBS	Determines the number of file control blocks that can be open simultaneously. Needed only for ancient software compatibility.
FILE	Sets the number of files that can be open simultaneously.
INSTALL	Loads a memory-resident (TSR) program.
LASTDRIVE	Specifies the highest valid disk drive letter.
NUMLOCK	Specifies the initial setting of the NUMLOCK key.
REM	Creates a remark. Nothing following REM on the same line is acted upon by DOS during booting.
SET	Creates and sets values for environment variables.
SHELL	Informs DOS what command processor should be used. SHELL also is used to increase the default size of the DOS environment.
STACKS	Sets the number and size of stacks used to process hardware interrupts.
SWITCHES	Specifies special DOS options.

Figure 2.1 shows the contents of a typical CONFIG.SYS file. In all likelihood, the DOS installation program either created or modified your CONFIG.SYS file.

As you can see in this figure, a great deal is going on. Following is a quick play-by-play of each line. If you want more in-depth information about one of the commands discussed here, check the Command Reference section of the book.

```
DEVICE=C:\DOS\HIMEM.SYS
DEVICE=C:\DOS\EMM386.EXE NOEMS HIGHSCAN NOVCPI WIN=B500-B7FF WIN=B200-
➥B4FF
DOS=UMB, HIGH
BUFFERS=15,0
FILES=49
LASTDRIVE=N
STACKS=9,256
SWITCHES=/k /f
SHELL=C:\DOS\COMMAND.COM C:\DOS\ /e:512 /p
DEVICEHIGH /L:2,12048 =C:\DOS\SETVER.EXE
DEVICEHIGH /L:2,10928 =C:\DOS\SBPCD.SYS /D:MSCD001 /P:220
DEVICEHIGH /L:2,44784 =C:\DOS\DBLSPACE.SYS /MOVE
```

Fig. 2.1
A typical CONFIG.SYS file.

The first line in figure 2.1 uses the DEVICE command to load HIMEM.SYS, the Extended Memory Manager. HIMEM accesses memory addresses above 1M, including the high memory area from 1024K to 1088K. This file must be loaded before EMM386.

The second line also uses DEVICE to load EMM386.EXE, the Expanded Memory Manager. The parameters shown on this line (from left to right) specify no EMS memory, check availability of upper memory blocks, disable VCPI support, and reserve areas in upper memory for Windows. You must load EMM386 to get access to upper memory (640K to 1024K).

The third line uses the DOS command to specify that upper memory be used and to load portions of DOS into the high memory area (1024K to 1088K). The fourth line sets up 15 buffers for transferring files, with no secondary cache buffers created.

The fifth line in figure 2.1 specifies that DOS make 49 file handles available so that many files can be open at a time. The sixth line uses LASTDRIVE to specify that drive N is the highest drive present in the system. This setting should include drives created by DoubleSpace and any drives used by your network if you are connected to one.

The STACKS line specifies that nine stacks of 256 bytes each are used to handle hardware interrupts. The SWITCHES line disables extended keyboard support with the /K switch. The /F switch dispenses with the default two-second delay after the `Starting MS-DOS...` message appears during boot-up.

The SHELL line increases the size of the DOS environment to 512 bytes. Don't forget to use the /P switch if you use this command; otherwise, DOS ignores AUTOEXEC.BAT at boot time.

The last three lines of this typical CONFIG.SYS file are DEVICEHIGH commands. These commands load the specified driver files into upper memory. If upper memory is not available, DOS loads drivers into conventional memory as though the DEVICE command were used.

You easily can customize your CONFIG.SYS file using the EDIT command. Exercise caution, however, because you accidentally can alter commands that screw up your configuration. Using the following command to make a backup of the file before editing is always a good idea:

```
COPY CONFIG.SYS CONFIG.OLD
```

That way, you can restore the old settings if something goes wrong.

AUTOEXEC.BAT

After COMMAND.COM is loaded into memory during the boot process, the system is ready for you to use. The last task the boot process performs is to look in the boot directory for the AUTOEXEC.BAT file. If found, this file is fed to COMMAND.COM's batch-file processor.

AUTOEXEC.BAT can contain almost any legal DOS command, except those commands such as DEVICE and SHELL, which are reserved for use in CONFIG.SYS. AUTOEXEC.BAT is used mostly to run commands that further configure the DOS session and to run those commands that need to be run only once when the computer is started up.

Although DOS now enables you to use the SET command in either CONFIG.SYS or AUTOEXEC.BAT, traditionally you found these SET commands exclusively in AUTOEXEC.BAT or in batch files run later for special purposes. There is one good reason to continue this practice. If you have your initial SET commands split between CONFIG.SYS and AUTOEXEC.BAT, you possibly can create the same variable twice by using different values. If CONFIG.SYS contains the line SET TEMP=C:\TEMP, and AUTOEXEC.BAT contains the line SET TEMP=C:\MYTEMP, for example, the value of the TEMP variable is MYTEMP after AUTOEXEC.BAT is run.

In effect, AUTOEXEC.BAT is nothing but a regular batch file, as discussed in Chapter 16, "Understanding Batch Files." Two things make it special, however. The first (and most important item) is that it is executed automatically each time your computer is booted. The second is that because AUTOEXEC.BAT is considered part of the booting process, DOS 6.2 enables you to step interactively through each command in AUTOEXEC.BAT, just as you can through CONFIG.SYS. This capability is discussed in more detail in the next section.

To better understand your AUTOEXEC.BAT file, look at figure 2.2. It lists the contents of a typical AUTOEXEC.BAT file.

```
@ECHO OFF
CLS
PROMPT $P$G
PATH C:\DOS;D:\WINDOWS;C:\;C:\NU
SET PCPLUS-F:\PROCOMM
SET TEMP=C:\TEMP
SET BLASTER=A220 I5 D1 T2
SET SOUND=G:\SBPRO
LH /L:0;1,42432 /S C:\DOS\SMARTDRV.EXE
LH /L:1,56928 C:\DOS\MOUSE.COM /Y
LH /L:1,13984 C:\DOS\SHARE /L:500
LH /L:1,6400 C:\DOS\DOSKEY.COM
LH /L:1,46576 C:\DOS\MSCDEX /d:MSCD001 /M:15 /V
SET WINPMT=Running Windows $P$G
WIN
```

Fig. 2.2
A sample AUTOEXEC.BAT file.

The first line in figure 2.2 uses the ECHO OFF command to suppress the display of the commands as they are processed. (The @ symbol at the beginning of the line suppresses display of the command line.) The second line, CLS, clears the screen.

In the third line, the PROMPT command alters the way the DOS prompt is displayed. The PG portion of the line causes the prompt to show the currently logged drive and path, followed by a greater-than sign (>). You can use the PROMPT command to turn the DOS prompt into anything you want it to be.

The fourth line in figure 2.2 uses the PATH command to specify where and in what order DOS should search directories when a command is entered at the DOS prompt or in a batch file. DOS looks in these directories for a .COM, .EXE, or .BAT file having the same name as the command. Only after these directories have been searched does DOS return the dread `Bad Command or File Name` error message.

The three lines following the PATH command use the SET command to place variables in the DOS environment. Environment variables can contain character strings, which programs can use to determine parameters. The SET BLASTER variable, for example, documents Sound Blaster Pro card's installation parameters. Programs that play sounds routinely rely on this variable to provide information they need.

The next five lines use the LH command, an abbreviated form of LOADHIGH, to run software and drivers needed each time the system starts up. Using LH is the best way to load utilities such as SMARTDrive, the mouse driver, the CD-ROM driver, and DosKey. It saves you from having to start these programs manually each time the system boots. Besides, you forget to type these commands about half the time, not realizing something isn't loaded until you try to use it.

The last two lines in figure 2.2 are Windows oriented. SET WINPMT creates an environment variable that specifies how the DOS prompt should be displayed when you're running a DOS session under Windows. The last line launches Windows automatically every time the computer boots.

For Related Information

- "Fine-Tuning Your Computer with CONFIG.SYS and AUTOEXEC.BAT," p. 482

Remember, nothing is sacred or untouchable about AUTOEXEC.BAT; it's just another batch file. Use the EDIT command to add and delete entries to create the exact start-up configuration you want to have each time you use your computer. Creating a backup of the file before you edit it is always a good idea, of course. Use the following:

```
COPY AUTOEXEC.BAT AUTOEXEC.OLD
```

By creating a backup, you can restore the previous version if you accidentally mess up your configuration.

Controlling the Boot Process

Users who practice safe computing should make sure that they have a floppy-based boot disk before messing with either CONFIG.SYS or AUTOEXEC.BAT. Fortunately, the DOS development team has made this practice less necessary. Beginning with DOS 6.0, a new feature was introduced that enables you to use function keys to exercise control over the boot.

Imagine, for example, that you have just edited AUTOEXEC.BAT to load a program during boot-up. For whatever reason, this program is incompatible with your system, and the computer just freezes each time the command is run. You can never get to a DOS prompt to edit the file because the machine hangs every time. You can boot off your floppy boot disk, of course, but now you have an easier way.

When the `Starting MS-DOS...` message appears on-screen during the boot process, you know that IO.SYS and MSDOS.SYS are about to be loaded. At this point, you can press two keys or key combinations that modify the boot process. If you are using DOS 6.0, you can use the F5 and F8 keys; with DOS 6.2, you can use these two keys plus Ctrl-F5 and Ctrl-F8.

If you press the F5 key when the message appears, DOS bypasses loading and processing both CONFIG.SYS and AUTOEXEC.BAT. You boot up as if you had a floppy boot disk that didn't contain these files.

If you have installed DoubleSpace, you also can press Ctrl-F5. This key combination not only skips CONFIG.SYS and AUTOEXEC.BAT, but it also skips the loading of DoubleSpace. This practice is great if you have programs (such as the latest high-performance games) that do not work with disk-compression programs such as DoubleSpace.

If you press the F8 key when the `Starting MS-DOS...` message appears, DOS displays the following message:

```
MS-DOS will prompt you to confirm each CONFIG.SYS command.
```

Each line in CONFIG.SYS then is displayed along with a [Y,N] prompt. To execute the displayed command, press either **Y** or Enter (not both). To bypass the command, press **N**.

After you have dealt with all the lines in CONFIG.SYS, you see the following message:

```
Process AUTOEXEC.BAT [Y,N]?
```

DOS is giving you the option of bypassing the execution of AUTOEXEC.BAT. Answer this query as you did the earlier ones. If you press **N**, the AUTOEXEC.BAT file is skipped entirely. If you are using DOS 6.2 and you press **Y**, each line in your AUTOEXEC.BAT file is displayed, in turn, and you can choose whether you want it executed.

The final key combination you can use to modify the boot process is Ctrl-F8. If you press this combination, you can process CONFIG.SYS and AUTOEXEC.BAT interactively, but DoubleSpace is not loaded. Understand that if you choose this option, drivers or programs that you attempt to load (which are normally stored on a compressed drive) are not accessible.

After you have broken through to the DOS prompt, you then can use the EDIT command to rectify whatever problem keeps your system from successfully booting.

By default, there is a two-second delay between the time the `Starting MS-DOS...` message appears and the loading of DOS system files begins. If you eliminate this delay with the SWITCHES=/F command in CONFIG.SYS, DOS still can recognize the F5, Ctrl-F5, F8, or Ctrl-F8 keystrokes. Even on a fast hard disk, it takes a second or two for IO.SYS and MSDOS.SYS to be loaded. You should be able to break in with a keystroke before CONFIG.SYS is processed.

Creating Multiple Configurations

Being able to boot your computer into one of several configurations is often handy. You might have a DOS program that you run which requires expanded memory, for example, but nothing else you do requires EMS. If you run Windows and Windows programs most of the time, the 64K page frame in upper memory can be a drag on performance, so doing without the EMS is better. Maybe you have reason to log into a network several times a day, but some of your programs object to having the network shell take up memory that they want to use. You may have any number of reasons to want different configurations at different times.

With earlier versions of DOS, you had to jump through hoops if you needed to have more than one standard configuration. A common trick was to have two or more versions of CONFIG.SYS tucked away in subdirectories or written in the boot directory with alternate names. When you needed a configuration different from your normal working environment, you had to copy one of these alternate CONFIG.SYS files into the boot directory and reboot. Changing back to your normal configuration was just as complex. No more!

A new DOS feature lets you create multiple configurations within your CONFIG.SYS file and display a menu of the available options. To create a boot menu, all you have to do is divide your CONFIG.SYS files into sections by naming each section. A section name consists of a word inside brackets, as in [menu]. Two section names have special meanings.

The [menu] section creates the menu of options displayed at boot time. Each menu item is created with a line similar to

```
menuitem=Normal,Everyday Configuration
```

where the word to the right of the equal sign is the name of the section you want to use for your configuration, and the words following the comma make up the menu prompt. If you omit the description, the section name is used as the menu prompt.

The [common] section enters lines that should be used in all your various configurations. You can have more than one section named [common]. DOS executes these sections in the order in which they appear in the file.

Microsoft recommends that multiple configuration CONFIG.SYS files end with a [common] section, even if it is empty. You end the file with a [common] section to accommodate programs that create entries in CONFIG.SYS. Usually, programs append their entries to the end of CONFIG.SYS. By having a [common] section at the end of your file, you ensure that new entries are always executed.

Figure 2.3 shows a multiple configuration CONFIG.SYS file. When the computer on which this CONFIG.SYS file resides boots up, a menu appears offering you two different configurations. If you select Work, the network and mouse drivers are loaded. If you select Games, no network or mouse driver is loaded. Instead, the ANSI.SYS driver is loaded. In all other respects, the configurations are the same because those aspects of the DOS session are controlled by the entries in the [common] sections.

```
[menu]
menuitem=Work
menuitem=Games

[common]
DEVICE=C:\DOS\HIMEM.SYS
DEVICE=C:\DOS\EMM386.EXE NOEMS
BUFFERS =15,0
FILES=49
DOS=UMB,HIGH

[work]
DEVICE=C:\DOS\NET.SYS
DEVICE=C:\DOS\MOUSE.SYS

[games]
DEVICE=C:\DOS\ANSI.SYS

[common]
```

Fig. 2.3
A multiple configuration CONFIG.SYS file.

Creating a Default Configuration

You can include a line in the [menu] section of CONFIG.SYS to create a default configuration that is used if a selection is not made from the menu within a specified number of seconds. For example:

```
menudefault=work,5
```

Placing this line in the [menu] section causes DOS to default to the `work` configuration if a menu selection is not made within five seconds after the menu is displayed.

Displaying Color Menus

Another command enables you to specify screen colors for displaying the boot menu. For example:

```
menucolor=15,1
```

Placing this line in the [menu] section of CONFIG.SYS causes DOS to display the menu using bright white letters on a blue background. The first parameter supplies the color code for the foreground color; the second parameter specifies the background color and is optional. If you do not specify the background color, the default value of 0 (black) is used. Table 2.2 shows the valid color codes you can use.

Table 2.2 CONFIG.SYS Menu Colors

Number	Color
0	Black
1	Blue
2	Green
3	Cyan
4	Red
5	Magenta
6	Brown
7	White
8	Gray
9	Bright Blue
10	Bright Green

Number	Color
11	Bright Cyan
12	Bright Red
13	Bright Magenta
14	Yellow
15	Bright White

You can pull an undocumented trick when you're specifying menu colors. Most video cards are not capable of displaying bright colors (8 through 15) as the background color. If you specify a bright background color on most video cards, the foreground color is set to blink. Thus, the following line produces a blinking yellow foreground on a standard blue background:

```
menucolor=14,9
```

Figure 2.4 shows how you edit the sample CONFIG.SYS file shown in figure 2.3 to display a menu in color. The foreground is yellow and the background is blue. Descriptive menu prompts and a default configuration also have been added.

```
[menu]
menuitem=work,Normal Configuration
menuitem=games,Let's Play Games
menucolor=14,1
menudefault=work,10

[common]
DEVICE=C:\DOS\HIMEM.SYS
DEVICE=C:\DOS\EMM386.EXE NOEMS
BUFFERS =15,0
FILES=49
DOS=UMB,HIGH

[work]
DEVICE=C:\DOS\NET.SYS
DEVICE=C:\DOS\MOUSE.SYS

[games]
DEVICE=C:\DOS\ANSI.SYS

[common]
```

Fig. 2.4
Displaying a configuration menu in color with descriptive prompts and a default configuration.

The CONFIG.SYS file shown in figure 2.4 renders the menu shown in figure 2.5. Notice that DOS precedes each menu choice with a number.

You can select a menu prompt in one of two ways. The first method is to press the number key corresponding to the prompt you want to select. The second method is to highlight the desired prompt and press Enter.

Fig. 2.5
The DOS 6.2 Startup menu.

```
MS-DOS 6.2 Startup Menu
=======================

   1. Normal Configuration
   2. Let's Play Games

Enter a choice: 1       Time remaining: 10



F5=Bypass startup files F8=Confirm each line of CONFIG.SYS and AUTOEXEC.BAT [N]
```

Using the Configuration Menu as a System Menu

Almost everyone who is computer literate knows someone who just will never get the hang of working with computers. These same people are the ones who you give the exact syntax of the COPY command letter by letter every time they call you with a problem. These users figure out just enough about one or two programs to get their work done and to be dangerous. Sadly, even DOSSHELL is a mystery to them.

You can employ a trick using DOS environment variables to turn the CONFIG.SYS configuration menu into a system menu that runs a particular program each time the computer is booted. When a particular configuration is chosen, DOS automatically creates an environment variable named CONFIG. As its value, this variable is given the name of the configuration section chosen. If you choose to have a section called [net] as your configuration, for example, the value of CONFIG is net.

You can use the value of CONFIG to branch off within the AUTOEXEC.BAT file to run commands specific to that configuration. Assume that CONFIG.SYS has three sections that offer you a choice in the configuration menu between Windows, WordPerfect, and Lotus 1-2-3. Also assume that these sections are named WINDOWS, WP, and LOTUS.

In batch files, you can create sections similar to the sections that you can create in CONFIG.SYS. In batch files, however, you name sections by using the colon (:), as in the following:

```
:labelname
```

You can execute a specific section of commands by using the GOTO command inside the batch file. Because AUTOEXEC.BAT is a batch file like any other, you can use the value of the CONFIG variable to branch off in AUTOEXEC.BAT. Figure 2.6 shows how you might construct such an AUTOEXEC.BAT file.

```
ECHO OFF
CLS
PROMPT $P$G
PATH C:\DOS;D:\WINDOWS;C:\;C:\NU
SET PCPLUS-F:\PROCOMM
SET TEMP=C:\TEMP
SET BLASTER=A220 I5 D1 T2
SET SOUND=G:\SBPRO
LH /L:0;1,42432 /S C:\DOS\SMARTDRV.EXE
LH /L:1,56928 C:\DOS\MOUSE.COM /Y
LH /L:1,13984 C:\DOS\SHARE /L:500
LH /L:1,6400 C:\DOS\DOSKEY.COM
REM  Commands above are common to all configurations.
GOTO %CONFIG%

:WINDOWS
SET WINPMT=Running Windows $P$G
WIN
GOTO END

:WP
C:\WP\WP
GOTO END

:LOTUS
CD 123
123
GOTO END

:END
REM Check once in a while to make sure you haven't
REM installed any programs that put lines here that
REM need to be moved to the common lines at the top.
```

Fig. 2.6
Using the CONFIG variable to run configuration-specific commands.

As you can see in the figure, AUTOEXEC.BAT is divided into five sections. The first section contains all the commands common to all configurations. This section isn't named because DOS begins executing lines at the top. The last line of this section uses GOTO to branch directly to one of the three choices on the CONFIG.SYS menu.

Three named sections occupy the middle of the file. Because they each finish with a GOTO command that directs the batch file to the :END section, only those commands in the chosen section execute.

The :END section is necessary to let DOS skip over the sections that haven't been chosen and to let any commands added by software installation take effect. The problem is that commands in the :END section do not take effect until you exit from whatever program is called by one of the named sections above :END. When you install new software, always check AUTOEXEC.BAT if you use this technique because you may have to move entries up into the first section of commands common to all configurations.

A drawback to using this technique is that when you exit the program, you don't have any way to loop back into the menu except to reboot the computer. Also, the start-up menu always advertises the availability of the F5 and F8 keys.

For Related Information

- "Fine-Tuning Your Computer with CONFIG.SYS and AUTOEXEC.BAT," p. 482

Make sure not to simply reboot the computer while you're still in an application program; otherwise, you lose data. Similarly, avoid using the F5 or F8 keys, or you may think the menu is broken.

Summary

In this chapter, you learned the steps your computer goes through each time you boot the computer. As part of the boot process, you learned the following key points:

- To boot a computer, you can use only disks (floppy or hard) that you have formatted with the /S switch of the FORMAT command or that you have made bootable by using the SYS command.
- Booting from a hard disk is usually more efficient than booting from a floppy disk, but sometimes you need a bootable floppy disk.
- The CONFIG.SYS file configures your computer's DOS session.
- You can create menus by adding to CONFIG.SYS and AUTOEXEC.BAT sections that allow for multiple configurations.
- AUTOEXEC.BAT is a normal batch file that is run each time the computer boots. This file further refines the computer's configuration by running commands that need to be entered only once.

In the next chapter, you learn how you can use the DOS Shell to gain computing power quickly.

Chapter 3

Using DOS Commands

DOS is made up of hundreds of small modules that provide needed services such as accessing disks, displaying output on-screen, and so on. These services are available to programs by way of a mechanism called an *interrupt*. When a program calls a DOS interrupt, the computer (under DOS's direction) literally interrupts whatever program it is running, performs the service, and then returns control of the computer to the original program. Users get access to the various DOS interrupts by entering commands.

This chapter introduces you to the elements that make up DOS commands and teaches you how to issue commands correctly at the DOS prompt. Unless you plan to become a programmer, you don't have to worry about the DOS interrupt system. All you have to know is that when you issue a command, you cause a program to be run that accesses the DOS interrupts to provide you with the action you want carried out.

Understanding DOS Commands

In Chapter 2, "Starting DOS," you learned that COMMAND.COM is one of the files loaded into memory when DOS boots up. COMMAND.COM is a command interpreter that acts as your interface to DOS services. COMMAND.COM displays the DOS prompt used to indicate that the computer is ready for you to use. COMMAND.COM takes the characters you type at the DOS prompt and turns them into an action. And COMMAND.COM is responsible for painting that most frustrating of messages on-screen: `Bad command or file name`. The more you understand the mechanics of how DOS offers its services, the less often you will see this message.

When you want your computer to perform an action, you communicate this request for service by entering commands at the DOS prompt. All DOS commands begin with a word, sometimes called a *keyword*, that identifies the action you want to take. Most DOS commands can accept parameters that serve to refine the scope of the command. The DIR command, for example, tells DOS to show you a list of files written on a disk. Adding parameters to this command enables you to specify exactly the files you want listed.

Internal versus External

DOS recognizes and responds to over 80 commands. The programming to provide the most commonly used commands is contained within the DOS command interpreter, COMMAND.COM. You use commands such as DIR and COPY so frequently that making them available on demand whenever the computer is displaying a DOS prompt saves time. Because DOS does not have to *launch* (start) any program to provide the service, the commands provided by COMMAND.COM are called *internal commands*. You can tell which commands are internal by looking in the directory where DOS is installed. You never find COPY.COM or COPY.EXE, so you know that the COPY command is internal.

Other commands are stored as utility programs in a directory on your hard disk. Because these commands are not built into the command processor, they are called *external commands*. When you type a command that COMMAND.COM does not recognize as one of its internal commands, COMMAND.COM responds by looking on disk for a program file having the same name as the command. The FORMAT command, for example, is provided by programming found in the file FORMAT.COM, which is located in the DOS directory.

Whether a command is internal or external, all DOS commands conform to rules that provide a grammar or syntax that is consistent throughout DOS. As a user, you need to make sure only that DOS can find the program files for external commands.

Making Sure DOS Can Find External Commands

When you install DOS on your system, by default the program files for external commands are written to a directory named DOS on the drive letter that your computer boots from. Because most systems boot from drive C, most of the time you find that the DOS directory is called C:\DOS.

If you look into the AUTOEXEC.BAT file, you probably find a command line that begins with PATH, followed by a list of directories. This command tells

DOS where to search for program files when it is trying to run a command. If your DOS directory is listed in the PATH command line, COMMAND.COM can find the program files for external commands no matter what disk drive or directory you are logged onto.

For Related Information

- "Helping DOS Find Files with PATH," p. 143

Understanding the Elements of a DOS Command

To begin to understand DOS commands, you first need to know a few fundamental facts:

- DOS requires that you use a specific set of rules, or syntax, when you issue commands.
- All DOS commands begin with a *keyword* that identifies the action you want performed.
- Parameters, which are a part of a command's syntax, refine the way a command is executed.

Syntax is the order in which you type the elements of the DOS command—its grammar. If you say, "Ball red choose I," people probably will not understand that you are trying to say, "I choose the red ball." Some people may understand what you are trying to say, but not many. A computer, on the other hand, has no intelligence or imagination; it can interpret commands only according to its programming. To program several optional syntaxes for commands requires using a great deal of extra memory and disk space, which cuts down on the resources available to do real work. That's why you have to supply the intelligence and imagination and why you must enter DOS commands precisely according to the rules of command syntax.

You can think of the command keyword as the action part, or verb, of a DOS command. In addition to the keyword, many commands require or allow further directions. You supply these directions as parameters and switches. *Parameters* tell DOS what action to take or how to apply the action. Using DOS commands is easy as long as you follow the rules of order and use the correct parameters. After you know the basic rules, you often can figure out parameters for commands that you don't use on a regular basis.

Note

Applications software—such as word processors or drawing programs—is run by entering a command at the DOS prompt. The command you use to start an application is the name of the program file (.COM or .EXE) in which the programming for the software is stored.

Most applications software incorporates the issuing of commands as part of the software's operation. The commands discussed in this book are DOS commands. Be sure that you know the difference between DOS commands, which you issue at the DOS command line, and the commands you learn to use with your applications software.

If you are unsure whether a command you have been taught to use is part of DOS, look in the Command Reference section later in this book. If that command is not listed, it is an application program command, not a DOS command.

The Command Syntax

The syntax for most DOS commands can be boiled down to one of two simple formats:

```
KEYWORD Drive\Files Switches
```

or

```
KEYWORD SourceFiles TargetFiles Switches
```

A DOS command always begins with the keyword, which is the name of the command, followed by a space. If you use the language metaphor, the keyword is the verb that specifies the action to be taken.

The first example shows the common form for DOS commands that don't change files in some way. The *Drive\Files* portion of the example is a parameter that specifies what drive and/or files on which the command is supposed to act. This parameter is analogous to a noun in English. In other words, the parameter is the thing on which the verb acts. This portion of the syntax is in italics to show that the parameter is optional.

The parameter also can be followed by command-line switches. To extend the language metaphor, switches are like adverbs; they modify the verb. They change the action to be done.

The second example here is typical of the syntax for most DOS commands that operate on groups of files. The keyword, of course, specifies the action, followed by two parameters that indicate the disk and/or files that provide the data source for the action. The second parameter indicates the target disk and/or files. To copy a group of files from one disk or directory to another, for example, you can use the following command:

```
COPY A:Myfile.TXT B:Yourfile.TXT
```

This command copies a file having the name MYFILE.TXT on drive A into the memory of your computer and then writes the contents of the file onto drive B using the name YOURFILE.TXT.

Note

Some parameters or switches are optional, meaning that some parts of the command syntax, such as the keyword, are mandatory. When you enter only the mandatory command elements, DOS (in most cases) uses default parameters for other elements.

A good example is the COPY command. If the command is

```
COPY A:MyFile.TXT
```

the default target is the currently logged disk and directory. If you're in C:\TEMP, the file is copied to that directory, and the current file name, MYFILE.TXT, is the target file name as well.

As you can see, having defaults makes commands easier to use, shorter, and gives you less opportunity to make mistakes.

Because many DOS commands have several parameters, switches, and defaults, different forms of these commands may be correct. You seldom, if ever, use all the optional syntax for any command. Some switches actually are mutually exclusive. You cannot format a floppy disk as both high density and low density, for example.

To find out what options are available for any given command, you should look up the command in the Command Reference section later in this book. The first time you look up a complex command, don't let the sheer volume of optional parameters and switches throw you for a loop. Even the simplest of DOS commands has several options.

The way the syntax is presented often is called the *paradigm*. Even the simple DOS commands have an imposing paradigm. A good example is the DIR command, a real workhorse of a command. Its paradigm looks something like the following:

```
DIR filespec /P /W /S /B /L /C /CH /O:sortorder  /A:attributes
```

You use the DIR command to display a directory of one or more files stored on a disk. This command may look formidable, but it is much easier to understand if you break down the individual components.

The Command-Line Parameters

In addition to the command's name, a DOS command contains syntax elements known as *parameters*. Parameters (sometimes called arguments) are the parts of a command line that provide DOS with the objects of the command's action. The objects may be files, system settings, or hardware devices.

In the DIR example in the preceding section, *filespec* is the complete file name, including any drive, path, and wildcards that you want the DIR command to use. In some commands, you may see the *filespec* spelled out, as in the following:

```
d:path\filename.ext
```

Don't be confused by this formal rendering of the *filespec*; it simply states that the *filespec* can contain a drive letter, a path name, a file name, and an extension.

The Battle of the Slashes ///// \\\\\

Many new users are confused about the way slashes and backslashes are used in commands. In actuality, their uses are stated simply in two rules:

Backslashes (\) are used as separators (delimiters) when specifying directory and file information.

Slashes (/), sometimes called forward slashes, are used as signals to DOS that the next character is a command-line switch.

A good mind association to use is that a backslash connects one name back to the name that comes before it, whereas a slash connects to the character in front of it.

The Optional Switches

A switch is a parameter that turns on an optional function of a command. Switches are special parameters because they usually are not the objects of a command's action; rather, switches modify the command's action. You can use the /W switch with the DIR command, for example, to display a wide directory of files instead of the usual single-column list. Switches can make a basic command more versatile and powerful. In the DIR example, /P, /W, /S, /B, /L, /O, /C, /CH, and /A are switches.

Usually, you can use a command's switches in any order or any combination. Not all DOS commands have switches, however. Also, the letter used for a switch in one DOS command may have a different meaning in another DOS command. In addition, some switches require a parameter. You usually attach switch parameters to the switch using a colon (:); for example:

```
FORMAT A: /F:360 /S
```

In this example, the /F switch specifies that a 360K floppy disk be formatted in a disk drive that normally uses high-density (1.2M) disks.

For Related Information

- "Copying Files," p. 225
- "Listing Files with DIR," p. 202

Getting Help

These days, the manuals supplied with DOS don't provide all the information they did in previous versions. They no longer contain a complete printed reference for all the DOS commands. To get the official Microsoft syntax for every DOS command, you have to pony up extra dollars to buy the MS-DOS Technical Reference. Because you already have this book, you probably don't want or need the Technical Reference. The Command Reference section at the back of this book contains a wealth of information about undocumented switches and parameters.

In place of the printed manual that used to come with DOS, Microsoft has opted instead to supply you with an on-line command reference. It falls short of the reference in the back of this book, of course, because it doesn't include the undocumented information; but most of the time, you will find the on-line reference to be adequate and handy.

To access on-line help for the use of a particular command, use one of the following procedures from the DOS prompt:

- Type the DOS command, followed by the switch /?.

or

- Type **HELP**, followed by the DOS command.

The following sections describe each method in detail.

Using the Command-Line Help Switch

One DOS command-line switch is never documented in the syntax examples, but you can use this switch with any DOS command. The /? switch is universal to all DOS commands.

After you enter a DOS command followed by the /? switch, DOS prints to the screen a summary of the command syntax. In some cases, the sample syntax is simplified by omitting options not available to you at the command line. A good example is the EMM386 command. Usually, EMM386 is loaded via CONFIG.SYS. After DOS is running, only those parts of the command that are accessible during a DOS session are displayed, omitting the parameters that can be given only at boot time.

The handy thing about using the /? switch is that it gives you a short summary of the command, leaving enough room on-screen for a DOS prompt. This way, you can refer to the syntax and type the command without taking your attention away from the screen.

To get a command summary of the DIR command, for example, type the following command and then press Enter:

```
DIR /?
```

DOS displays the command summary help screen shown in figure 3.1.

Fig. 3.1
Using the DOS command summary help.

```
Displays a list of files and subdirectories in a directory.

DIR [drive:][path][filename] [/P] [/W] [/A[[:]attribs]] [/O[[:]sortord]]
    [/S] [/B] [/L] [/C[H]]

  [drive:][path][filename]   Specifies drive, directory, and/or files to list.
  /P       Pauses after each screenful of information.
  /W       Uses wide list format.
  /A       Displays files with specified attributes.
  attribs    D  Directories    R  Read-only files          H  Hidden files
             S  System files   A  Files ready to archive   -  Prefix meaning "not"
  /O       List by files in sorted order.
  sortord    N  By name (alphabetic)        S  By size (smallest first)
             E  By extension (alphabetic)   D  By date & time (earliest first)
             G  Group directories first     -  Prefix to reverse order
             C  By compression ratio (smallest first)
  /S       Displays files in specified directory and all subdirectories.
  /B       Uses bare format (no heading information or summary).
  /L       Uses lowercase.
  /C[H]    Displays file compression ratio; /CH uses host allocation unit size.

Switches may be preset in the DIRCMD environment variable.  Override
preset switches by prefixing any switch with - (hyphen)--for example, /-W.
```

Using the On-Line Help System

The second method for obtaining help is to use HELP followed by the keyword you want information about. If you don't know the keyword you are looking for, just type **HELP** and you are presented with a list of command keywords from which to choose.

The on-line help system displays a detailed description of the command's function, correct syntax, available switches, and a detailed explanation of the effect of each switch.

The on-line help system also contains special notes and examples related to each command and enables you to view information on related commands or topics by using only a few keystrokes. If you have a mouse, using the on-line help system is a snap. You even can print information on selected commands.

To get the complete on-line help for the DIR command, for example, type the following and then press Enter:

```
HELP DIR
```

DOS displays the on-line help screen shown in figure 3.2.

```
File  Search                                                    Help
                          MS-DOS Help: DIR
<Notes>  <Examples>

                                  DIR

Displays a list of the files and subdirectories that are in the directory
you specify.

When you use DIR without parameters or switches, it displays the disk's
volume label and serial number; one directory or filename per line,
including the filename extension, the file size in bytes, and the date and
time the file was last modified; and the total number of files listed, their
cumulative size, and the free space (in bytes) remaining on the disk.

Syntax

    DIR [drive:][path][filename] [/P] [/W]
    [/A[[:]attributes]][/O[[:]sortorder]] [/S] [/B] [/L] [/C]

Parameters

[drive:][path]
<Alt+C=Contents> <Alt+N=Next> <Alt+B=Back>                  N 00001:002
```

Fig. 3.2
The DOS on-line help facility shows syntax, notes, and examples about each DOS command.

Navigating the Help System. The on-line help system contains a great deal of information and provides several ways for you to locate, view, and print topics of interest to you. You can use either a mouse or the keyboard to issue commands in the on-line help system; this section describes both methods. Most of the keystrokes and mouse movements are the same for the help system as they are for the DOS Shell program. For more detailed information about moving around a window, refer to Chapter 4, "Using the DOS Shell."

Because the HELP command provides such complete information, information about a topic or command usually requires more than one screen. To view all the information about a topic, you must scroll the display forward and backward.

To scroll through the text one line at a time, use one of the following methods:

- Click the downward pointing scroll arrow in the scroll bar at the right edge of the screen to move forward one line. To move backward, click the upward pointing scroll arrow.

or

- Press the Ctrl-down arrow key combination to move forward; press the Ctrl-up arrow key combination to move backward.

To scroll through the text one screen at a time, use one of these methods:

- Click the scroll bar below the scroll box to move forward one screen; click above the scroll box to move backward.

or

- Press the PgDn key to move forward one whole screen; press the PgUp key to move backward.

In figure 3.2, notice the words `Notes` and `Examples` near the top-left corner of the screen. Each word is enclosed within solid, triangular characters. Each of these specially marked words is a jump. A *jump* provides a link to additional information on the currently selected topic or to related topics.

Jumps in the body of the help system's text are marked with angle brackets (<>). The brackets are colored to help you more easily see them if your video card and monitor support color. Although not shown in figure 3.2, the word `<TREE>` at the end of the DIR help text is another example of a jump.

When you select a jump, the on-line help system displays the text related to the topic named by the jump word. To select a jump, use one of the following methods:

- Click the jump with the mouse.

or

- Move the cursor over the jump and then press Enter.

If you select the <Examples> jump shown in figure 3.2, the help system displays a screen containing examples of the DIR command and explanations of each example. Selecting a jump such as <TREE> causes the help system to display the help for the TREE command.

In figure 3.2, the solid bar across the top of the screen with the words File and Search is the help system's menu bar. You use the help system's pull-down menus in the same way you use the pull-down menus in the DOS Shell. Refer to Chapter 4, "Using the DOS Shell," for a discussion of pull-down menus if you are unfamiliar with using menus.

The choices on the File menu enable you to print a topic or to exit the on-line help system. The choices on the Search menu enable you to search for a topic, word, or phrase, and to repeat the last search.

Another solid bar appears at the bottom of the screen (refer again to fig. 3.2). The bottom-right corner of this area of the help screen displays numbers indicating the current line and column number of the cursor. In figure 3.2, the cursor is at line 1, column 2 of the help text for the DIR command.

At the left edge of this area, three keystroke combinations and their functions are displayed:

```
<Alt+C=Contents> <Alt+N=Next> <Alt+B=Back>
```

Each of the labels enclosed in brackets also doubles as a command button if you have a mouse. You can click the command button or press the key combination to select the action.

The Contents command, Alt-C, causes the on-line help system to display its table of contents. Each item in the table of contents is a jump. The Next command, Alt-N, causes the on-line help system to display the next topic. The Back command, Alt-B, causes the on-line help system to display the last topic you looked at.

Table 3.1 summarizes the command keys, and their actions, available in the on-line help system.

Table 3.1 On-Line Help Command Keys

Key	Action
Alt	Activates the help system menu
Alt-B	Returns to the last topic you viewed
Alt-C	Displays the list of topics covered in the help system
Alt-F	Opens the File menu
Alt-S	Opens the Search menu
Alt-N	Moves to the next topic
Ctrl-down arrow	Scrolls the screen down one line
Ctrl-up arrow	Scrolls the screen up one line
Ctrl-Home	Moves to the beginning of the current topic
Ctrl-End	Moves to the end of the current topic
Enter	Selects a menu command or selects the jump under the cursor (the DOS help system displays the text for the jump topic.)
Esc	Cancels a command; closes a menu or dialog box without making a selection or carrying out the action
F1	Displays context-sensitive help on using the on-line help system
F3	Repeats the last search
A-Z	Moves to the next jump beginning with the letter pressed
Shift-letter	Moves to the previous jump beginning with the letter pressed
PgUp	Scrolls the text up one screen
PgDn	Scrolls the text down one screen
Shift-Ctrl-F1	Moves to the preceding topic
Tab	Moves clockwise to the next jump
Shift-Tab	Moves counterclockwise to the next jump

Printing a Topic. The on-line help system enables you to print the text for the currently displayed topic. You may optionally send the output to a file on your disk instead of to the printer. The Print command is located on the File menu.

When the help system displays the File menu, click the Print command. The help system opens the Print dialog box shown in figure 3.3. (For information on using dialog boxes, option buttons, text boxes, and command buttons, refer to Chapter 4, "Using the DOS Shell.")

To print the current topic on your printer, simply press Enter or click the OK

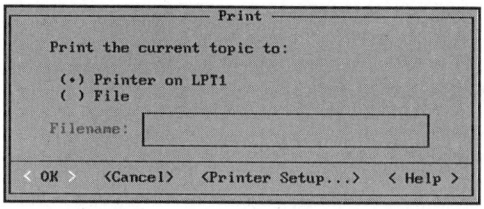

Fig. 3.3
The on-line help system's Print dialog box.

command button. To send the text for the current topic to a disk file, select the File option button; then, in the text box, enter the name of the file to which you want to send the output. Finally, press Enter or click the OK command button.

Searching for a Topic. You use the Find command to search for a specific topic, word, or phrase. The Find command is located on the Search menu.

When the help system opens the Find dialog box, you see a screen similar to the one shown in figure 3.4.

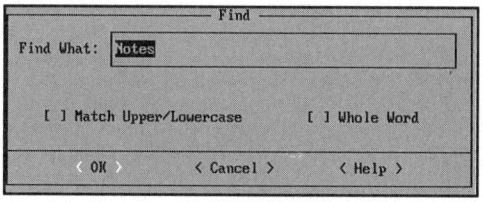

Fig. 3.4
The on-line help system's Find dialog box.

When the Find dialog box first opens, the Find What text box contains the word that the cursor was on when you selected the Find command. In figure 3.4, the cursor was on the word *Notes* when the Find command was selected, so the Find What text box contains the word *Notes*.

Enter the topic, word, or phrase that you want to search for in the Find What text box, or use the word already in the text box. Then select which of the two Find options you want to use. You can use one, both, or neither of these options.

If you check the Match Upper/Lowercase option check box, the search is case sensitive. If you check the Whole Word option check box, it is assumed that you are searching for a whole word; partial word matches will be ignored.

You can repeat any search by selecting the Repeat Last Find command on the Search menu or by pressing F3.

Exiting the Help System. To exit the on-line help system using the mouse, pull down the File menu and click Exit. To exit the help system using the keyboard, press Alt-F followed by X.

Issuing DOS Commands

When you enter a DOS command, two sets of parameters determine how the command is carried out. Any parameters or switches that you explicitly type take precedence, of course, but unless you override them the default values for a command are used.

Throughout this chapter, you've seen the DIR command used as an example. Here's one more:

```
DIR /P
```

When you issue the DIR command to see the files on a disk, the currently logged directory is used unless you specify otherwise. Also, all the files in the directory are shown unless you somehow override the default by explicitly specifying a file or group of files. By default, the display of files scrolls to the end without stopping. In the preceding example, the display of all files in the current directory (the default) is used, but the /P switch, which makes the listing pause after each page of file names, overrides the default behavior of scrolling to the end of the list without stopping.

Figure 3.5 breaks down the different elements that make up the DIR command. As you can see, only two of the switches (/P and /W) are illustrated.

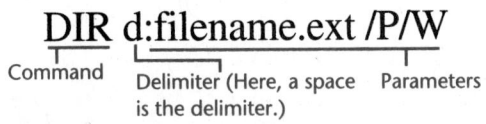

Fig. 3.5
The syntax of the DIR command.

Figure 3.6 is a diagram of the DIR command as you might use it. If you are unfamiliar with the anatomy of a command, the following sections explain each of the different parts.

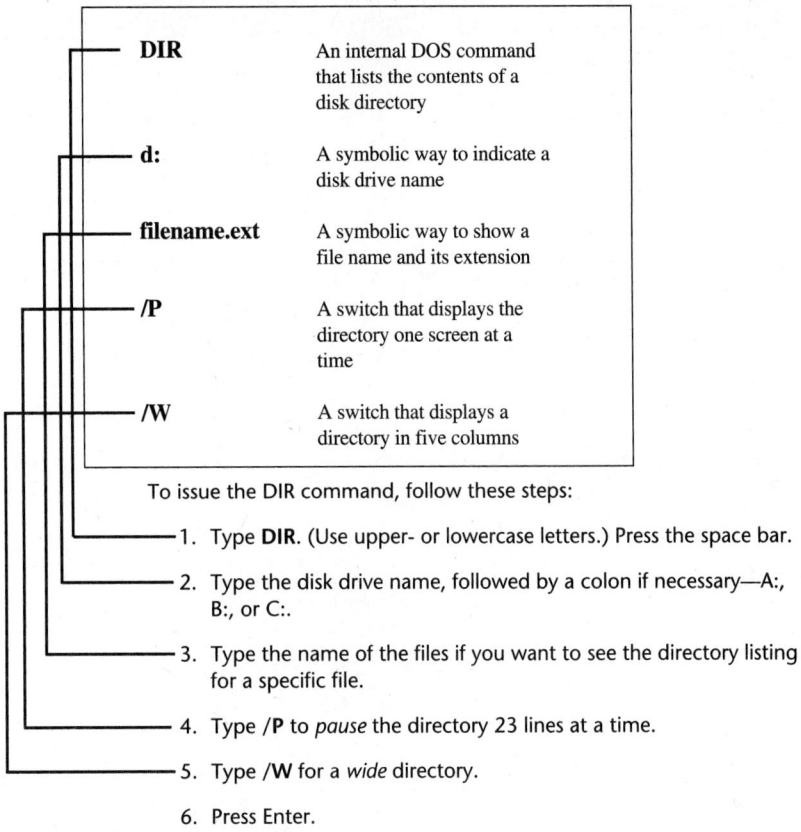

Fig. 3.6
Issuing the DIR command.

Editing and Canceling Commands

You occasionally may make a mistake when you are entering a command. Because DOS does not act on the command until you press Enter, you can correct a mistake by using the arrow keys or the Backspace key to reposition the cursor and type over your entry. If you need to insert characters into the command line, press the Ins key to turn on the insert mode. After you press Enter, DOS automatically returns to the overtype mode.

If, however, you have gotten way off track and want to cancel what you have and start over, you can press the Esc key, Ctrl-C, or Ctrl-Break. The Break key is found on late-model computer systems that can accept the enhanced keyboards introduced with the IBM AT.

DOS stores keystrokes that have not yet been displayed in a type-ahead buffer. The idea of the type-ahead buffer is to keep keystrokes from being lost when entered by fast typists, or when a prolonged operation takes the computer's focus away from the keyboard for a moment. If the type-ahead buffer gets filled with keystrokes, your PC beeps when you press an additional keystroke, warning you that you are losing keystrokes. The buffer storage areas also give DOS some special editing capabilities.

Each time you complete a command by pressing Enter, the command is stored in another buffer, the last command buffer. Using the DOS editing keystrokes, you can recall the last command, or you can pull the preceding command line from the buffer and use it again. This feature is helpful when you want to issue a command that is similar to the last command you used or when you mistyped a parameter. Table 3.2 lists the keys you use to edit the input buffer.

Table 3.2 DOS Command-Line Editing Keys

Key	Action
Tab	Moves the cursor to the next tab stop
Esc	Cancels the current line and does not change the last command buffer
Ins	Enables you to insert characters into the line
Del	Deletes a character from the line
F1 or right arrow	Copies the next single character from the last command buffer
F2	Copies all characters from the last command buffer up to, but not including, the next character you type
F3	Copies all remaining characters from the preceding command line
F4	Deletes all characters from the last command buffer up to, and including, the next character typed (opposite of F2)
F5	Moves the current line into the buffer but does not allow DOS to execute the line
F6	Produces an end-of-file marker (^Z) when you copy from the console to a disk file

These editing keystrokes come from the earliest versions of DOS. Beginning with version 5.0, there is a better way. The DOSKEY command, usually entered via AUTOEXEC.BAT, loads into memory a program that creates a much larger buffer to store previous command lines. (Refer to the Command Reference section for the DOSKEY listing.) You can recall these commands by pressing the up-arrow key. The DOSKEY buffer is 512 bytes by default, which is enough on average to store the last 20 commands executed.

For a complete reference source for DOS editing keystrokes, see Appendix D, "DOS and DOS Utility Programs' Keyboard Commands."

Using Scroll Control

The term *scrolling* describes what happens as a DOS screen fills with information. When DOS displays text in response to your typing or as a result of a DOS command, the text fills the screen from left to right and top to bottom. As the screen fills, information scrolls off the top of the display. To stop a scrolling screen, press Ctrl-S (hold down the Ctrl key and then press S). Press any key to restart the scrolling. On enhanced keyboards, press the Pause key to stop scrolling.

Using Wildcards in DOS Commands

Almost everyone has at one time played a game such as poker that employs wildcards. If you hear the dealer say, "Deuces are wild!" you know that cards having the number 2 printed on the face can be substituted for any other card in the deck.

DOS uses wildcards too. When you're entering DOS commands, you can use wildcards to specify groups of files. DOS recognizes two wildcard characters: the question mark (?) and the asterisk (*), also called *star* ("star dot star" means *.*).

In DOS commands, the ? represents any single character. The command

```
DIR LTR???.TXT
```

produces a directory listing of any files in the currently logged directory that have a file name beginning with the letters LTR followed by up to three characters. Also, only those files bearing the extension .TXT match and are listed. Thus, LTR.TXT, LTR0.TXT, LTR01.TXT, LTR001.TXT, LTRMOM.TXT, LTR_32.TXT, and LTR999.TXT are listed but not LTRPOPS.TXT or LTR1001.TXT.

The * represents any string of characters. For example, *.* represents all file names with any extension, the default scope of the DIR command. The command

```
DIR *.DOC
```

lists all files in the currently logged directory having the extension .DOC.

The following command lists all the files listed by the DIR LTR???.TXT example, as well as file names not matched by that form of the command:

```
DIR LTR*.TXT
```

You should look out for one thing when you're using the * wildcard, however. The following command does *not* produce the result you might expect:

```
DIR *LTR.TXT
```

This example does not list all the .TXT files whose names end in LTR. Rather, it lists all the files having the extension .TXT. The reason is deceptively simple. Because the * can represent up to eight characters in a file name, any string of characters matches *LTR.

After you get the hang of using wildcards to refine the scope of command parameters that supply file names, you will find that you are well on your way to becoming a DOS power user.

Summary

In this chapter, you learned the underlying logic behind issuing DOS commands. Although the DIR command is used for examples in this chapter because of its typical syntax, the thrust of this chapter is to provide you with general concepts that you can apply to all DOS commands.

Even though each DOS command has its own characteristics, it also has a defined syntax that may or may not include parameters and switches. The basic knowledge of how to issue DOS commands is an important ingredient in your mastery of DOS. These concepts are assumed beginning with Chapter 5, "Understanding Files and Directories," so take a moment to review the following major concepts covered in this chapter:

- Commands that you enter at the DOS prompt are your way of requesting and receiving operating system services.
- The proper phrasing of each DOS command is called the command's syntax.
- In addition to the name of the command, a syntax line can contain parameters and switches.

- You can use the /? command-line switch or the HELP command to get help on any DOS command.
- You can edit a DOS command line by using special DOS editing keys.
- Commands that take file name specifications as parameters accept wildcard characters (? and *) as substitutes for position-matching in file name parameters.

The next chapter introduces the DOS Shell, a visually oriented program that gives you, if you're a new DOS user, a set of "training wheels" you can use until you become comfortable with issuing DOS commands.

Chapter 4

Using the DOS Shell

The DOS Shell, introduced with DOS 4.0, is no longer a primary part of DOS. With the advent of DOS 6.2, it has been relegated to the status of a supplemental program, and is thus included on the Supplemental Disk. If you are upgrading from an earlier version of DOS, however, the older version of the DOS Shell remains on your disk, ready and available to work.

The DOS Shell is a mildly controversial feature of DOS. Praised by some as a kinder and gentler way of using DOS, others deride it as a crutch and a crippled imitation of Windows. In fact, there is truth to both opinions.

The DOS Shell has features that are strikingly familiar to Windows users. The point-and-click interface, disks and directories displayed in tree format, the capability to associate file name extensions with the program that produced them so that selecting a file also starts the program—these features are all hallmarks of the popular Windows operating environment. In fact, if your video card permits (EGA and higher), you can run the Shell in graphics mode.

Still, to perform complex tasks, you are often required to enter command lines using the Run option of the File menu. For anything but the most rudimentary tasks, you still are required to know the syntax of DOS commands.

Unlike Windows, which was built from the ground up to be used as a graphical interface, the DOS Shell is mostly textbound. Using the extended ASCII drawing characters, the DOS Shell simulates a *graphical user interface* (GUI). Even when it's run in graphics mode, the interface changes only slightly.

Many longtime DOS users find the DOS Shell to be restrictive, even though many tasks are easier and quicker when you use the Shell. On the other side of the coin, many new computer users, especially those with less than one year's experience, find the Shell easier to work with than the bare DOS prompt.

Most users who begin their computer careers working with the DOS Shell usually end up doing one of two things. They either discard the Shell, like a worn out pair of training wheels, or they move on to the Windows environment.

In practice, the DOS Shell has become a tool used by PC support specialists when training newer users. Many MIS departments and support consultants find that if they teach new users the ins and outs of the DOS Shell, they end up fielding fewer support calls from inexperienced users.

It is assumed that many of the readers of this book fall into the category of support specialist or office computer guru. Although you may not want to use the DOS Shell in your own work, you may want to use it as training wheels for users that you must support. In this chapter, you find a great deal of information about the DOS Shell that you can use to further these activities.

Now that the Windows environment has begun to spread like wildfire, Microsoft has downplayed the importance of the DOS Shell. The DOS 6.2 manual devotes only two and a half pages to the Shell, whereas the more detailed DOS 6.2 Technical Reference devotes even less space. You may find this chapter to be the most extensive documentation of the DOS Shell currently available.

What Is the DOS Shell?

The DOS Shell program is a visually oriented user interface that replaces the DOS command line with easy-to-use and easy-to-understand menus. It enables you to use a mouse (or other pointing device) to perform many common DOS tasks.

With the DOS Shell, you can select many commands from a menu instead of typing the commands on the DOS command line. More significantly, with the DOS Shell many tasks are greatly simplified. You can search quickly through directories or an entire hard disk for files or groups of files. Using a mouse, you can select and copy files between directories or between disks using a Windows-like drag-and-drop feature.

The DOS Shell also provides features not available at the DOS prompt. You can start one applications program, for example, and then switch to a second application without exiting from the first. Unlike other environments, such as those provided by Windows, QEMM, or 386MAX, however, programs in the background cannot remain active.

The Shell enables you to view the contents of files in ASCII or hexadecimal formats without opening applications programs. Another feature associates specific file name extensions with a particular applications program so that selecting a file causes DOS to start the associated program.

Note

To utilize the Shell effectively, a mouse and mouse driver must be present on the system. Although you can stumble through the Shell using keystrokes, using a mouse can reduce frustration and save time.

For the mouse to be available, the mouse device driver must be loaded into memory before you run the DOS Shell. DOS 6.0 includes a generic mouse device driver called MOUSE.COM, which can usually be found in the DOS directory. The mouse driver usually is loaded with a line in the AUTOEXEC.BAT file using the LOAD or LOADHIGH command.

Remember that some mice are not MS Mouse-compatible and may not work properly with the generic DOS mouse driver. Manufacturers of such mice normally include a special mouse driver for you to use. See the mouse manual for details.

Starting the DOS Shell

When you install DOS 6.0, you are prompted for whether you want the DOS Shell to be started automatically. If you select this option, you need merely to turn on the computer to reach the DOS Shell screen.

If your computer does not display the DOS Shell automatically when you turn on your computer, type the following at the DOS prompt to load the DOS Shell into memory:

```
DOSSHELL
```

The DOS Shell first displays a copyright notice and then displays the full-screen DOS Shell window.

When the Shell first loads, it also displays a message box in the center of the screen containing the message `Reading Disk Information`. The Shell scans the currently logged drive for the directory structure and file information. After the drive is scanned, the Shell creates a display similar to the one shown in figure 4.1.

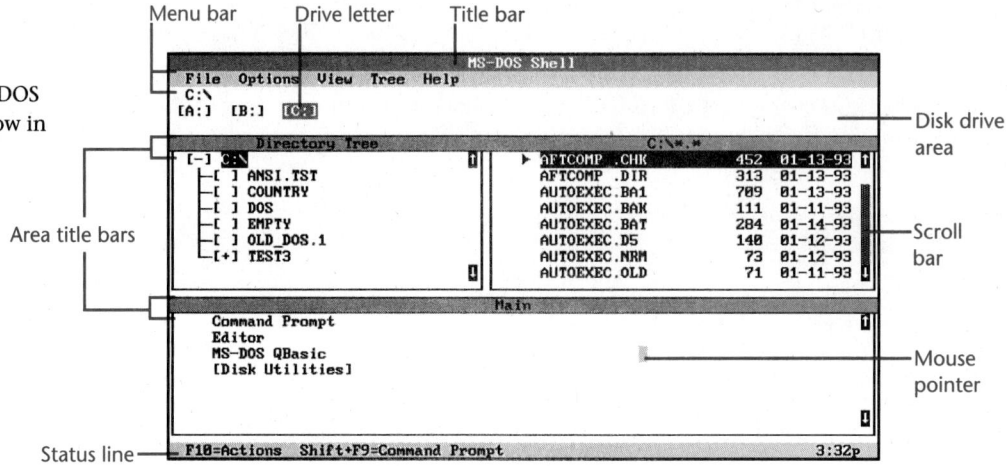

Fig. 4.1
The initial DOS Shell window in text mode.

Using the Shell Interface

When you start the DOS Shell, the top line of the screen, the *title bar*, displays the program name, MS-DOS Shell. The second line of the screen, the *menu bar*, lists the names of available menus. You can choose all DOS Shell commands from menus that pull down from the menu bar.

Just below the menu bar, the available disk drives are listed along with a prompt showing the current drive and directory. All types of drives, including CD-ROMs and DBLSPACE drives, are listed.

Initially, the DOS Shell window appears in text mode, as shown in figure 4.1. See the "Shell Screen Modes" later in this chapter for information on switching to graphics mode. Figure 4.2 shows the 34-line graphics mode available for VGA displays.

Note that the bitmap icons used to indicate drives also indicate drive types. The icons for a hard disk differ from the icons used to indicate a floppy disk or CD-ROM.

The last line of the DOS Shell window is the *status line*. The status line usually displays two messages: `F10=Actions` and `Shift+F9=Command Prompt`. At the right side of the status line, the Shell displays the current time. Occasionally, the status line also displays other messages related to the command you are executing.

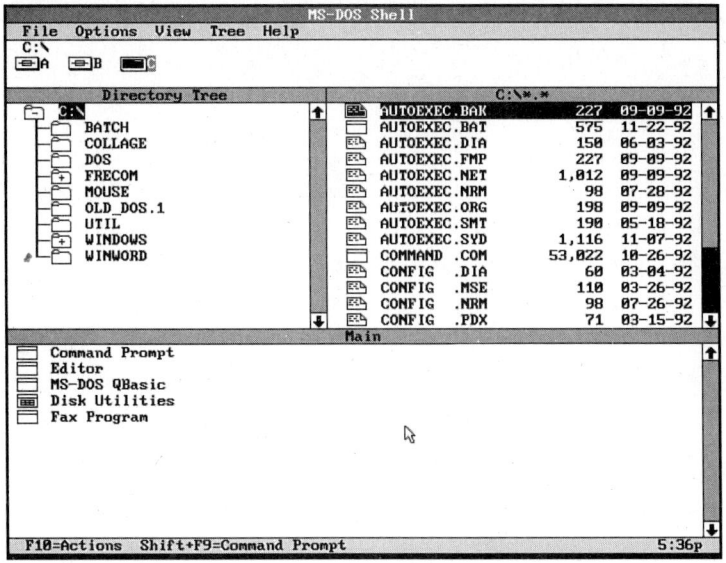

Fig. 4.2
The DOS Shell window displayed in graphics screen mode.

Caution

Using Shift-F9 to get a DOS prompt is completely safe when you are working only in DOS. If, however, you want to run the DOS Shell in a DOS session launched under Windows, do not use Shift-F9 to get to a command prompt; otherwise, you may corrupt memory.

The terminology may be confusing, but many programs enable you to "shell out to DOS" or launch a "DOS Shell." These terms have been in use since early versions of DOS that did not include the DOSSHELL program. DOSSHELL uses different terminology, but the effect is the same.

Programs that shell out to a DOS prompt do so by launching COMMAND.COM as a second application. Launching COMMAND.COM in this fashion is dangerous under Windows because the normal safeguards Windows uses to ensure memory integrity are bypassed.

Programs that are run under this second COMMAND.COM in a Windows DOS session may allocate memory that is never reclaimed after the program terminates. Worse, programs may try to use memory already in use by Windows or a Windows application. These conditions may cause the computer to hang and unsaved data to be lost.

If you need a DOS prompt while you're working in Windows, always launch a separate DOS session from the Windows Program Manager.

Between the drive area and the status line, the DOS Shell divides the screen into rectangular windows, each of which is headed by an *area title bar*. When there is more information than can be displayed in the window, you can scroll up and down using either the keyboard or the mouse.

When a window is active, at least one item is highlighted for selection. At the right edge of these windows you find *scroll bars*. If you press the arrow keys or the PgUp/PgDn keys to move the active highlight bar, the scroll bars are relegated simply to showing you the relative position (top to bottom) of the currently highlighted area. Using the mouse is quicker and more efficient. See the section "Moving Around an Area" later in this chapter for details about using the mouse interface.

Drive information is displayed in a pair of windows. The left window displays the directory structure of the disk, and the right window displays the files found in the currently highlighted directory.

Using the View menu, you can choose to view two disk drive windows, or you can choose to view Program/File Lists. In this view, the bottom window of the display serves as a menu for starting DOS applications and for accessing DOS utility programs. This area lists a group of programs, called a *program group*. The name of the currently listed program group appears in the area title bar. In text mode, group names are shown enclosed in brackets (refer to fig. 4.1). In graphics mode, icons indicate single programs and groups. Notice how the icon for Disk Utilities differs from the other icons shown in figure 4.2. To switch to a group, double-click its icon or highlight the group using the arrow keys and press Enter.

When you choose Enable Task Swapper from the Options menu, a fourth area, the *active task list area*, is displayed in the DOS Shell window. The active task list area displays the names of DOS applications you have activated through the DOS 6.0 task swapper. Figure 4.3 shows the DOS Shell window with the active task list displayed.

Selecting an Area

Although several windows can be displayed in the DOS Shell, at any given moment only one area is *selected* (active) at a time. The selected area is indicated by a highlighted area title bar. An area must be selected before you can perform any operation in that area.

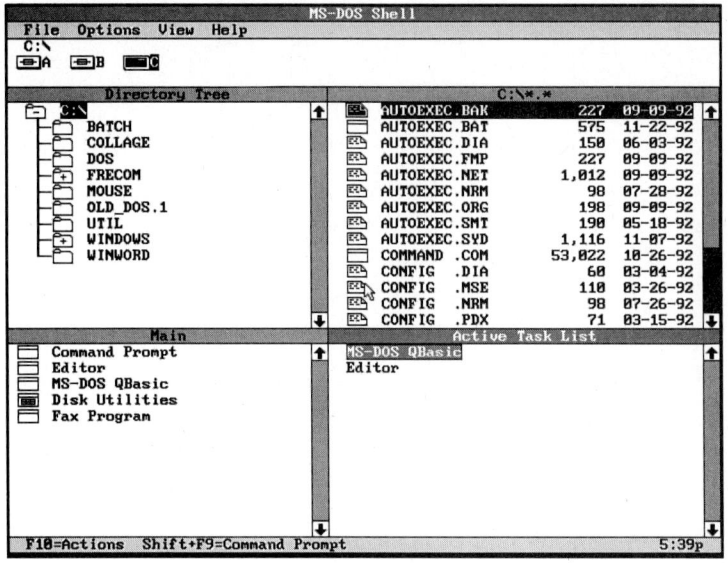

Fig. 4.3
The DOS Shell window with the active task list displayed.

You can use either of two methods to select an area in the Shell window:

- Move the mouse pointer into the area you want to activate and click the left button. The Shell highlights the area's title bar.
- Press the Tab key to cycle through the areas that are currently displayed in the window.

Moving Around an Area

After you select an area, the Shell highlights one of the items listed in the area. This highlight is called the *selection cursor*. To move the selection cursor within the selected area, use one of the following methods:

- Use the cursor-movement keys on the keyboard. Press the up- or down-arrow key to move up or down one item at a time. Press PgUp or PgDn to move up or down one page at a time. Press Home or End to go to the beginning or end of the list.
- Use the mouse and the scroll bar, shown in figure 4.4, to scroll up or down. You learn how to use the scroll bars in the following paragraphs.

The scroll bar has the following components:

- A scroll arrow at the top and bottom of the bar. By clicking the scroll arrow, you scroll text up or down one line at a time. Click the scroll arrow and hold down the mouse button to scroll continuously in the direction of the arrow.

- A scroll box, sometimes called a *thumb,* is located on the scroll bar between the up-scroll arrow and the down-scroll arrow. The position of the box on the scroll bar indicates the relative position of the selection cursor with respect to the entire list of items in the selected area.

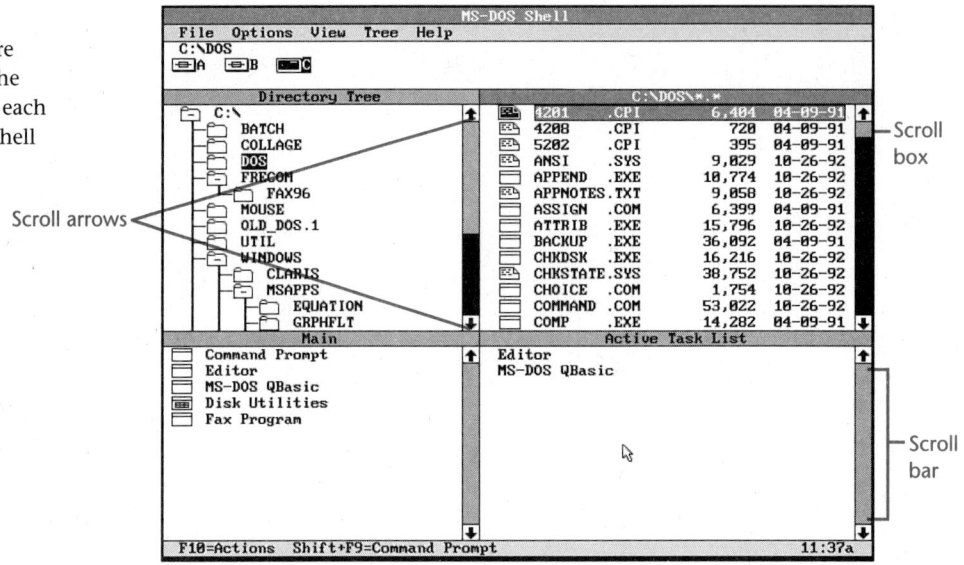

Fig. 4.4
Scroll bars are located on the right side of each area of the Shell window.

Click the scroll bar above the scroll box to move the selection cursor up one page at a time. Click below the scroll box to move down one page at a time.

You can scroll quickly through the list in either direction by clicking the scroll box, holding down the left mouse button, and dragging the box in the direction you want the selection cursor to move.

Using the DOS Shell Menus

You can initiate virtually every DOS Shell operation by choosing options from menus. These DOS Shell menus fall into two categories: the menu bar and pull-down menus.

Using the Menu Bar

When the disk drive area, directory tree area, or file list area is active, the menu bar lists five menu names: File, Options, View, Tree, and Help. The Tree menu name does not appear when the program list or active task list is the active area. Choosing a menu name displays a pull-down menu.

You can choose a menu option from the menu bar in one of three ways:

- Move the mouse pointer to an option and click the left button.
- Press the F10 key or the Alt key to activate the menu bar. The Shell underlines one letter in each menu name and places a selection cursor on the menu name **F**ile at the left end of the menu bar. Press the key that corresponds to the underlined letter in the menu name you want to choose. To choose **V**iew from the menu bar, for example, press F10 or Alt and then press V.
- Press F10 or Alt to activate the menu bar, use the right- or left-arrow key to move the selection cursor to your choice, and press Enter. This method is sometimes called the *point-and-shoot method.*

Even after you choose a menu name, you still can choose another menu name by clicking the name with the mouse or by using the right- or left-arrow key.

Using Pull-Down Menus

When you choose a menu name from the menu bar, the Shell displays a pull-down menu, which displays a list of items below the menu bar. If you choose **F**ile, for example, while the file list is the active area, the Shell displays the **F**ile pull-down menu shown in figure 4.5. The items listed in the menu depend on which area is active.

To choose an item from a pull-down menu, use one of the following methods:

- Move the mouse pointer to a menu item and click the left button.
- The Shell underlines one letter in each menu item. Press the key that corresponds to the underlined letter in the item you want to choose. To choose **V**iew File Contents from the **F**ile menu in figure 4.5, for example, press V.
- The Shell places the selection cursor on the first item at the top of the pull-down menu. Use the up- or down-arrow keys to move the selection cursor to your choice and then press Enter.

When a menu is pulled down, you can display an adjacent menu by pressing the left- or right-arrow key. To cancel a pull-down menu without making a selection, click the menu name, an area outside the menu, or press Esc. The Shell returns to the preceding window display. You also can press Alt or F10 to cancel a pull-down menu while maintaining an active menu bar so that you can choose another menu name. The DOS Shell uses the following conventions when it lists menu items:

- A menu item that displays a dialog box, which is discussed later in this chapter, ends with an ellipsis (...).
- A menu item that is dimmed, such as the Create Directory item shown in figure 4.5, is not a valid option in the current context.
- Some menu items toggle between two states—on or off. A menu item that is toggled on displays a small diamond to the left of the item name. The diamond is absent when the item is turned off.
- Some commands that you can select through menu items have shortcuts in the form of key combinations or keystroke commands. When a keystroke command shortcut is available for a command, the Shell lists the keystroke in the menu, to the right of the command. Five of the commands in the File menu, for example, list shortcut keystroke commands (refer to fig. 4.5).

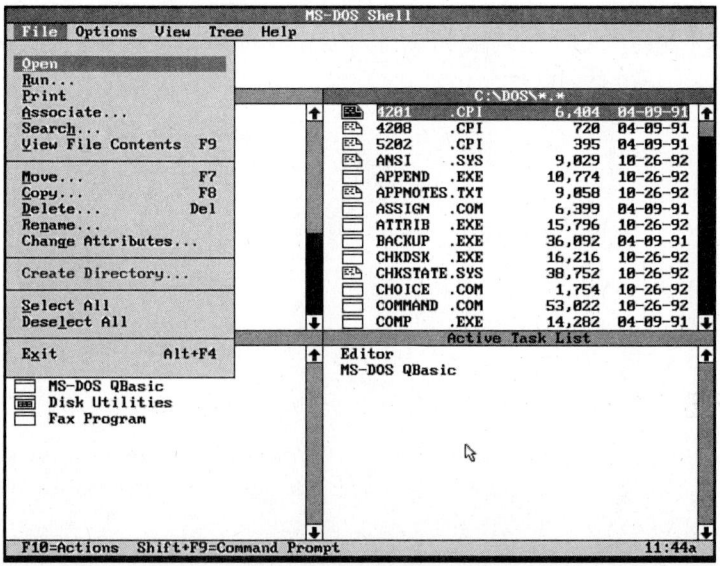

Fig. 4.5
The File pull-down menu displayed when the file list area is active.

Using Keystroke Commands

The DOS Shell provides many keystroke command shortcuts, called *hot keys*. Many of these commands are listed in pull-down menus. Two such commands, F10 and Shift-F9, are listed in the Shell window status line.

Table 4.1 lists all DOS Shell hot-key commands for DOS 6. After you learn these keystroke commands, you may find them quicker to use than any equivalent menu items. Using menus requires that you use multiple keystrokes or that you take one hand from the keyboard to use the mouse. To perform a command by using the hot keys, you press a single keystroke or keystroke combination. Windows users will find many of these hot keys familiar.

Table 4.1 DOS Shell Shortcut Commands

Key	Function
F1	Displays context-sensitive help
F3	Exits the DOS Shell, returns to the command line, and removes the DOS Shell from memory (same as Alt-F4)
Alt-F4	Exits the DOS Shell, returns to the command line, and removes the DOS Shell from memory (same as F3)
F5	Refreshes the file list(s)
Shift-F5	Repaints the screen
F7	Moves selected file(s)
F8	Copies selected file(s)
Shift-F8	Extends selection in Add mode
F9	Views file contents
Shift-F9	Accesses the command line without removing the DOS Shell from memory (Do not use under Windows!)
F10	Activates the menu bar (same as Alt)
Alt	Activates the menu bar (same as F10)
Del	Deletes selected file(s)
+	Expands one level of the current branch in the directory tree
*	Expands all levels of the current branch in the directory tree

(continues)

Table 4.1 Continued

Key	Function
Ctrl-*	Expands all branches in the directory tree
– (hyphen)	Collapses the current branch in the directory tree
Alt-Tab	Cycles through active tasks, if Task Switching is enabled
Alt-Esc	Switches between active task and the DOS Shell, if Task Switching is enabled
Shift-up arrow	Extends selection up
Shift-down arrow	Extends selection down
Shift-left arrow	Extends selection left
Shift-right arrow	Extends selection right
Esc	Cancels current function
Tab	Cycles forward through areas (left to right, top to bottom)
Shift-Tab	Cycles backward through areas (right to left, bottom to top)
Ctrl-/	Selects all files in the selected directory
Ctrl-F5	Refreshes the selected directory
Ctrl-\	Cancels file selections

Using Dialog Boxes

As you work with the DOS Shell, the program routinely displays messages and prompts in pop-up boxes, called *dialog boxes*, on-screen. Any menu item that ends with an ellipsis (...) displays a dialog box when you choose the item. When you choose **C**opy from the **F**ile menu, for example, the Copy File dialog box, shown in figure 4.6, appears.

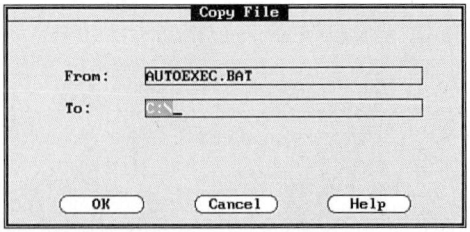

Fig. 4.6
The Copy File dialog box.

Dialog boxes fall into two general categories: those that request information and those that provide information. The Copy File dialog box in figure 4.6 is an example of a dialog box that requests information. Pressing F1, by contrast, displays a dialog box that provides information and is titled MS-DOS Shell Help. This help screen, shown in figure 4.7, assists you in learning the Shell.

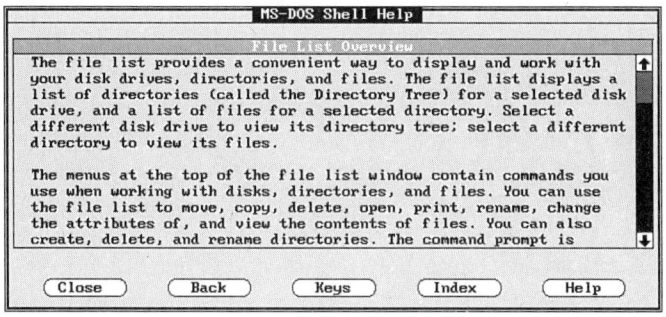

Fig. 4.7
The MS-DOS Shell Help dialog box.

All dialog boxes are built from a standard set of elements: text boxes, list boxes, option buttons, option check boxes, and command buttons. The following sections explain how to use each element.

Using a Text Box. When you need to type information in a dialog box, the Shell includes one or more rectangular fields known as *text boxes*. The Copy File dialog box shown in figure 4.6 contains two text boxes, one labeled From and one labeled To.

To make an entry in a text box, you first highlight the box. Using the mouse, move the mouse pointer to the box and click the left button. Alternatively, you can press Tab or Shift-Tab repeatedly until the text box is highlighted.

Often the Shell provides a default value in each text box. The text boxes in figure 4.6, for example, include the default values AUTOEXEC.BAT and C:\. When you select a text box, the Shell highlights any default contained in that text box. Typing new text in the text box replaces the default value.

Sometimes you don't want to replace the entire default value in a text box. When you want to edit the value, press the right- or left-arrow key to cause the Shell to remove the highlighting. You then can edit the existing entry.

After you make the desired entry or change the value in the text box, press Enter to accept the value that is displayed in the text box. When you press Enter, the Shell also closes the dialog box and executes the command, if any, with which the dialog box is associated.

Using a List Box. Some dialog boxes contain information or a list of choices displayed in a rectangular area, referred to in this book as a *list box*. A title bar appears at the top of each list box, as well as a scroll bar on the right side of the list box. Refer to figure 4.7, which shows a help dialog box containing a list box entitled File List Overview.

Often the text or list is too long to fit in the list box, so the Shell enables you to scroll vertically through the contents of the box. To scroll through a list box, use your mouse and the scroll bar, or use the cursor-movement keys.

Using Option Buttons. Some dialog boxes require that you use *option buttons* (also called radio buttons) to select command settings. Each option button is a circle (a pair of parentheses if your screen is in text mode) followed by a command setting. Option buttons always occur in groups—never alone. The buttons in each group are mutually exclusive; only one button can be selected at a time.

The File Display Options dialog box shown in figure 4.8, for example, contains option buttons listed on the right side of the dialog box, beneath the label Sort By. Displayed file names can be sorted by name, extension, date, size, or disk order, but the Shell does not sort files by more than one of these parameters at a time.

To select a different option button, use the mouse to click the desired option button. Alternatively, use the Tab or Shift-Tab key to move the underscore (cursor) to the group of option buttons. Then use the up- or down-arrow key to move the dot to the desired button. Press the space bar to select the new option. Press Enter to close the dialog box and execute the command, if any, with which the dialog box is associated.

Using Option Check Boxes. Some Shell dialog boxes enable you to select the desired command settings by "checking" the appropriate *option check boxes*. An option check box is a pair of brackets followed by a command setting. The File Display Options dialog box in figure 4.8, for example, contains the following check boxes:

- Display hidden/system files
- Descending order

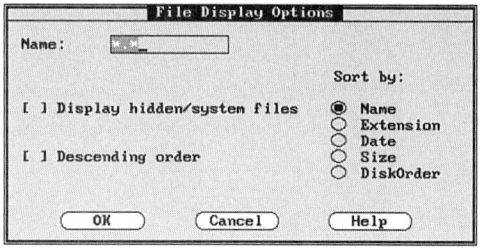

Fig. 4.8
The File Display Options dialog box.

An option check box turns a command setting on or off. The setting is checked (or on) when an X appears between the brackets. The setting is off when the space between the brackets is blank. To toggle the setting on or off, use the mouse to click between the brackets. Alternatively, use the Tab or Shift-Tab key to move the cursor to the option check box and then press the space bar. Each time you click the box or press the space bar, the option toggles on or off.

Using Command Buttons. After you make any desired entries in text boxes, select appropriate option buttons, and check the correct check boxes, you are ready to execute the DOS Shell command. To do so, choose one of the *command buttons*. Most dialog boxes in the DOS Shell contain three command buttons: OK, Cancel, and Help (refer to fig. 4.8). The OK command button activates the choices you made in the dialog box and executes the command, if any, with which the dialog box is associated. The Cancel command button aborts any changes you made in the dialog box and returns to the DOS Shell window. The Help command button accesses the Shell's on-line help facility.

To execute a command button, use one of the following methods:

- Move the mouse pointer to the desired command button and click the left mouse button.
- Press Tab or Shift-Tab to move the cursor to the desired command button and press Enter.

Tip
You can execute the command associated with a dialog box by pressing Enter, even though the cursor is not in the OK command button (as long as the cursor is not on one of the other command buttons).

Modifying the View

The DOS Shell is quite flexible. In the directory tree area and file list area, you can display directories and file names from any of your computer's disk drives, including directories and file names from two disks at one time. You also can display just the program list, change the entire screen to a graphics mode, and show as many as 60 lines of information on a single screen (depending on the capability of your computer's monitor).

The following sections describe how to modify the display to list directories and files from other disks, to display files from two disks at one time, and to change the amount of information displayed about each file. In addition, the following sections show you how to display the program list full-screen and how to change the number of lines that appear on-screen.

Logging on to a Different Disk. As you learned in Chapter 2, "Starting DOS," each time you turn on your computer, the operating system (DOS) is loaded from one of your computer's disks. This disk is the boot disk. If your system is configured to start the DOS Shell immediately after your computer boots up, the Shell window lists directories and file names found on the boot disk. Often, you may need to display the directories and file names on a disk other than the boot disk. Figure 4.2, for example, shows three drive letters: A, B, and C. Drive C is the boot disk; therefore, the directories found in drive C are shown in the directory tree. Drive C's icon is highlighted, indicating that C is the currently selected disk drive.

To display the directories found on another disk, move the mouse pointer to the drive icon of the desired disk and click the left mouse button. Alternatively, press the left- or right-arrow key until the Shell highlights the drive letter you want and then press Enter.

The Shell displays a message that it is reading the disk information and then displays in the directory tree and file list areas of the DOS Shell window the directories and file names from the target disk. Figure 4.9, for example, shows file names from a disk in drive B.

Because the DOS Shell enables you to start other programs that may create, modify, or delete files on your disk, the list of files in the DOS Shell window may at times be inaccurate. If you suspect that the directory tree area or file list area does not reflect the actual contents of the disk, use the Shell's Refresh command. To refresh the file list, press F5 or choose **R**efresh from the **V**iew menu (see fig. 4.10).

Note

When DOS Shell is run in text mode, there is no visual differentiation between file types. Running the Shell using one of the graphics modes, however, causes file lists to show icons to the left of the listed files. These icons differentiate between executable files and document files. If you look closely at the icons in figure 4.9, you see that document files are represented as dog-eared pages and that executable files (.EXE, .COM, and .BAT) have a rectangular icon that represents a running program.

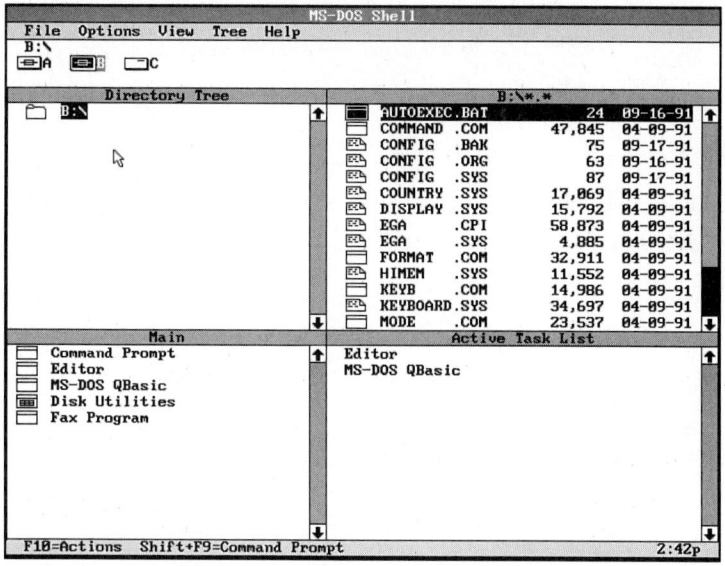

Fig. 4.9
Displaying the directories and file names from the disk in drive B.

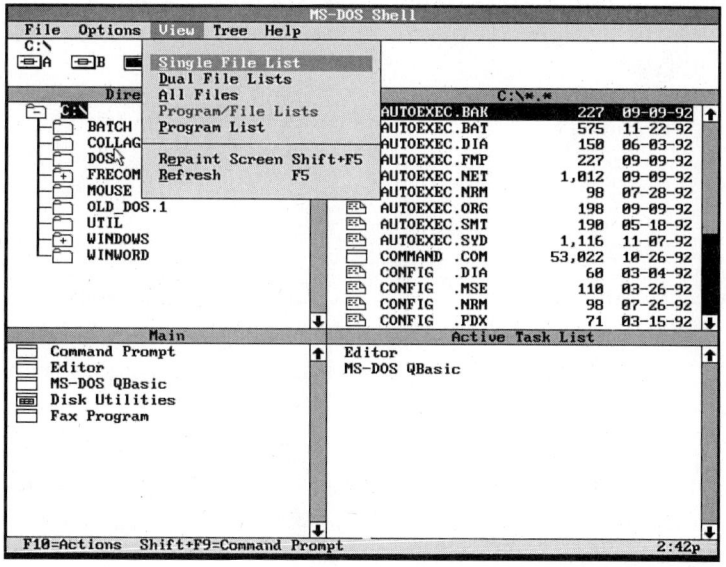

Fig. 4.10
The View menu.

The Shell displays the message `Reading Disk Information` and then returns to the DOS Shell window and displays the updated list of directories and files in the directory tree and file list areas.

Switching between Dual and Single File Lists. From time to time, you may want the convenience of seeing lists of directories and files from two disks simultaneously. Perhaps you want to copy a file from one disk to another, or maybe you want to compare the list of files on one disk to the list of files on another disk.

The DOS Shell enables you to display two file lists on the same screen. To do so, choose **D**ual File Lists from the **V**iew menu (refer to fig. 4.10).

The Shell replaces the program list area, at the bottom of the window, with a second disk drive area, directory tree area, and file list area showing the directory tree and file list from the current disk drive (see fig. 4.11). This view is called a *dual file list.*

Fig. 4.11
A dual file list.

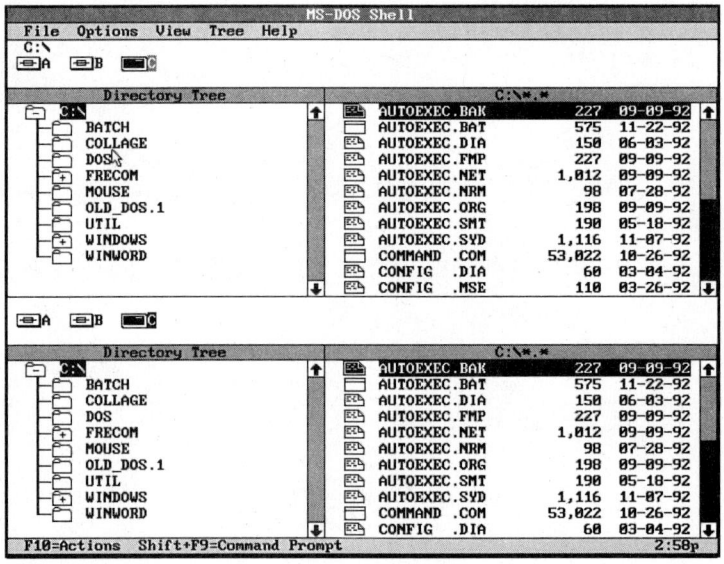

Even though the initial display of the second file list is a duplicate of the top window, each file list is independent of the other. Note that each file list has its own set of disk drive icons. To select a second disk drive in the bottom portion of the window, click the icon in the bottom disk drive area for the drive for which you want to list directories and files.

Alternatively, use Tab or Alt-Tab to cycle the selection cursor until it highlights the drive icon of the currently selected drive in the bottom disk drive area. Then use the left- or right-arrow key to highlight the desired drive icon and press Enter.

The Shell lists directories and file names from the second disk in the lower set of directory tree and file list areas (see fig. 4.12). You can switch between the two lists by using the mouse or the Tab key.

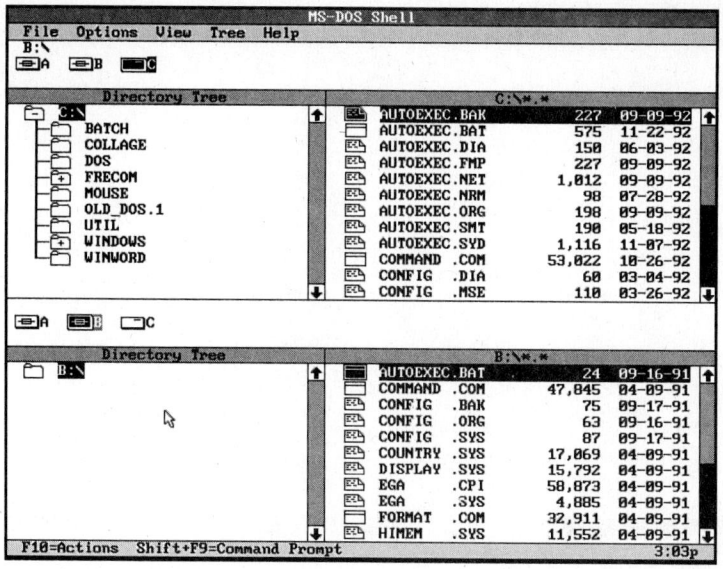

Fig. 4.12
Viewing directories and file names from two disks at one time.

At times, especially when a directory contains many files, you need a single full-screen file list. Choose **S**ingle File List from the **V**iew menu to see a list, called a *single file list,* similar to the one shown in figure 4.13.

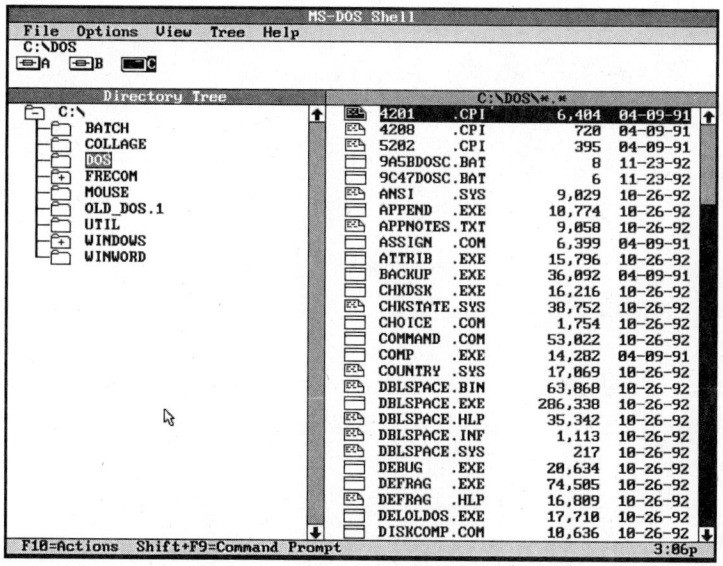

Fig. 4.13
Viewing a single file list.

Note

When you exit from the DOS Shell, it remembers the changes you made using the View menu. The next time you start the Shell, it will have the same appearance.

Displaying All Files. Occasionally, you may want the Shell window to display all files on a disk, regardless of the directory. To display all files in a single list, choose **A**ll Files from the **V**iew menu.

In the All Files view, the Shell displays a window on the right side of the screen listing the names of all files on the disk in alphabetical order. To the left of this window is an area that displays information about the currently highlighted file. Figure 4.14 shows the All Files view.

Fig. 4.14
The All Files view.

```
MS-DOS Shell
File  Options  View  Tree  Help
C:\DOS
A  B  C

File
  Name   : HELP.COM
  Attr   : ...a
Selected        B      C
  Number:       1      1
  Size   :            437
Directory
  Name   : DOS
  Size   :     6,057,622
  Files  :           126
Disk
  Name   : EAGLE_AT
  Size   :    42,366,976
  Avail  :     4,222,976
  Files  :           872
  Dirs   :            19

                                  *.*
GENI     .PAL          410  08-01-91   6:21p
GLOSSARY.DOC         1,965  10-07-91   9:01p
GLOSSARY.HLP        46,570  03-10-92   3:10a
GORILLA .BAS        29,434  04-09-91   5:00a
GOTH    .CHR         8,560  08-29-88   2:00a
GOTHIC  .FOT         1,324  04-22-92  10:57a
GOTHIC  .TTF        54,200  03-09-92  12:00a
GOTHICB .FOT         1,326  04-22-92  10:57a
GOTHICB .TTF        47,912  03-09-92  12:00a
GOTHICBI.FOT         1,340  04-22-92  10:57a
GOTHICBI.TTF        50,244  03-09-92  12:00a
GOTHICI .FOT         1,330  04-22-92  10:57a
GOTHICI .TTF        54,964  03-09-92  12:00a
GRAFTABL.COM        11,205  04-09-91   5:00a
GRAMMAR .DLL       311,808  10-17-91  12:00p
GRAPH   .EXE       546,304  09-24-91   3:45p
GRAPH   .HLP       296,643  09-24-91   3:45p
GRAPHICS.COM        19,694  10-26-92   6:00a
GRAPHICS.COM        19,694  04-09-91   5:00a
GRAPHICS.DOC        29,846  10-21-91  12:00p
GRAPHICS.PRO        21,232  10-26-92   6:00a
GRAPHICS.PRO        21,232  04-09-91   5:00a
GREP    .COM         7,029  10-23-90   6:00a
GR_AM   .LEX       780,688  10-17-91  12:00p
HANDOUT .DOT         2,974  03-22-92   1:54p
HELP    .COM           413  10-26-92   6:00a
HELP    .EXE        11,473  04-09-91   5:00a
F10=Actions  Shift+F9=Command Prompt                3:11p
```

Switching between the Program List and the Program/File Lists. The first time you start the DOS Shell, the DOS Shell window displays the directory tree area, the file list area, and the program list area. Some users prefer to use the Shell primarily as a menu for starting applications programs and thus don't want to view the directory tree and file list every time. The Shell, therefore, provides a view that displays only the program list. To select this view, shown in figure 4.15, choose **P**rogram List from the **V**iew menu.

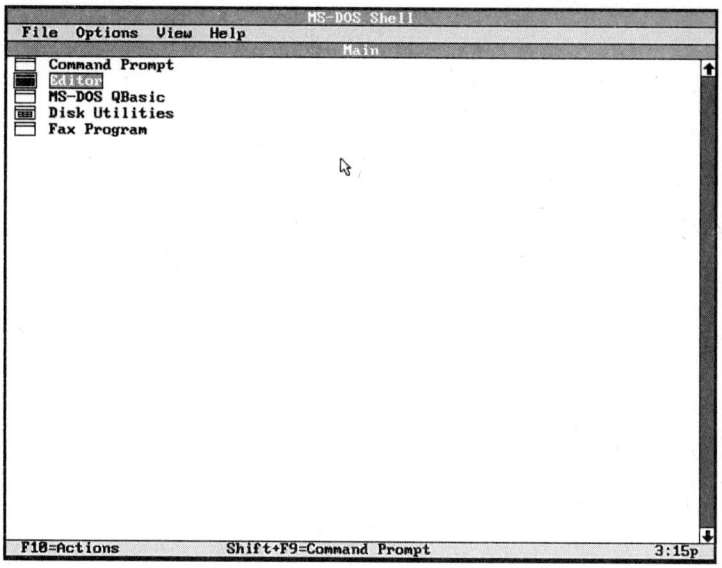

Fig. 4.15
The full-screen program list area.

If you decide later that you want to display the directory tree and file list areas on-screen along with the program list area, you need only choose Program/**F**ile Lists from the **V**iew menu. The Shell then returns to the original view, with the disk drive area, directory tree area, and file list area in the top half of the screen and program list area in the bottom half of the screen.

Using the Shell Screen Modes

As you learned previously in this chapter, the Shell window can be displayed as a text representation of a GUI (graphical user interface) or in graphics mode. The number of available screen modes depends on the type of display adapter and monitor you have.

When you launch DOSSHELL the first time, the Shell window appears in the default 25-line low-resolution text mode. If your video card permits, and most modern ones do, you can choose **D**isplay from the **O**ptions menu to select from a variety of modes.

If you have a system with video cards that can support more text and graphic modes, you can choose from an array of modes ranging from the default 25-line text mode up to high-resolution graphics modes that display 60 lines of information on-screen. Table 4.2 shows the full list of display modes available.

Table 4.2 Available Video Modes in the DOS Shell		
Text	25 lines	Low Resolution
Text	43 lines	High Resolution 1
Text	50 lines	High Resolution 2
Graphics	25 lines	Low Resolution
Graphics	30 lines	Medium Resolution 1
Graphics	34 lines	Medium Resolution 2
Graphics	43 lines	High Resolution 1
Graphics	60 lines	High Resolution 2

To change the screen mode, first select the **O**ptions menu (see fig. 4.16) and then choose **D**isplay. The Screen Display Mode dialog box appears (see fig. 4.17). Next, highlight a choice in the dialog box, and click OK or press Enter. If you are unsure about your video card's support for a particular mode, you can choose the Preview button to see what results from that choice.

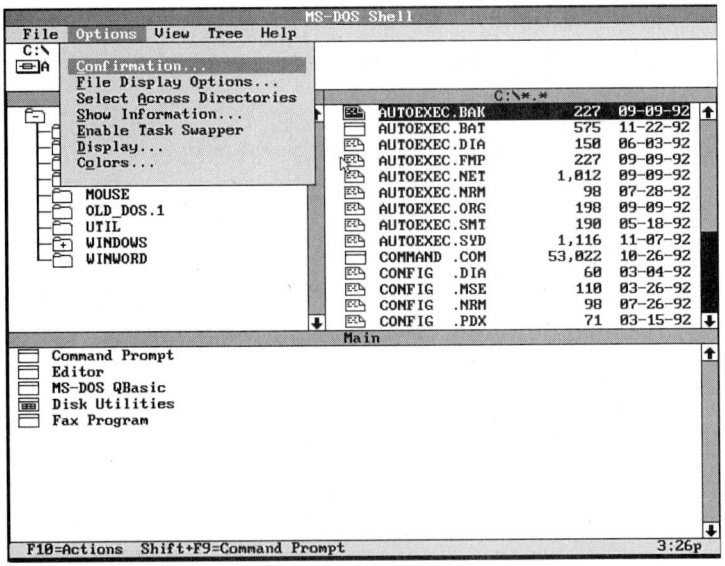

Fig. 4.16
The Options menu.

Using the Help System

At any time during a DOS Shell session, pressing F1 causes a help window to appear. On-line help assists you with the current selection or action so that you can make an informed selection.

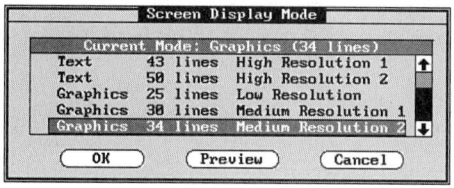

Fig. 4.17
The Screen Display Mode dialog box.

The Shell's help system is *contextual,* meaning that DOS looks at the menu item currently highlighted and provides information about that selection. You can go from that help screen to other help screens to get help on additional topics. Figure 4.18 shows a typical help screen.

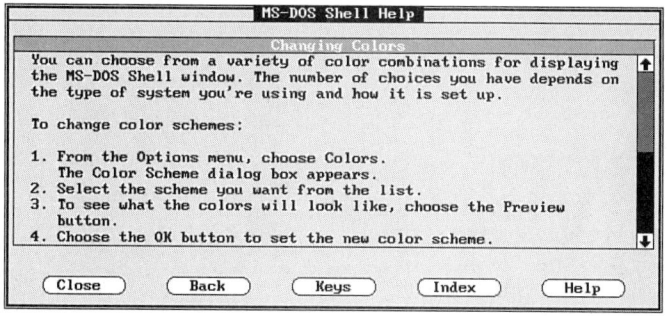

Fig. 4.18
The Changing Colors help screen.

Five command buttons appear at the bottom of a help screen:

- *Close* returns you to the screen from which you pressed F1.
- *Back* returns to the preceding help screen.
- *Keys* displays an index of help information on keystroke commands.
- *Index* displays the DOS Shell help index, a list of topics on which you can receive help.
- *Help* displays information on how to use the help system. Use the mouse and scroll bar or the cursor-movement keys to display the information in which you are interested.

Additional related topics are listed in a different color on the help screen. Use the Tab key to highlight the related topic and press Enter, or click the topic. The Shell displays another help screen.

Choose the Close command button or press Esc to return to the screen from which you pressed F1.

Using the Program List

In addition to providing an alternative DOS interface to the command line, the DOS Shell also provides a convenient method for running all the other programs stored in your computer. A program that performs this function is sometimes called a *menuing program*. The Shell's program list area provides menuing capability.

Items listed in the program area of the DOS Shell window fall into two categories: program items and program groups. A *program item* starts a specific software application on your hard disk; a *program group* is a collection of program items or other program groups.

Program groups enable you to group your applications programs by category. You may create a Word Processing group, a Database group, and a Spreadsheet group, for example. By default, the initial list of program items, which you see when you first start the DOS Shell, are in the Main program group. The Main group includes another program group named Disk Utilities, which includes program items that perform disk-related DOS commands.

You can easily tell whether an option listed in the program list area is a program item or a program group. When the DOS Shell window is in text screen mode, program group names are enclosed in brackets. For example, the Disk Utilities program group appears as `[Disk Utilities]` when the screen is in text mode.

In graphics mode, the Shell uses special icons to distinguish between program items and program groups. The following icon appears to the left of program item names:

The following icon appears to the left of program group names:

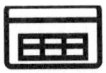

When you first install the DOS Shell, the program list area lists the program group Main. This group includes the program items Command Prompt, Editor, and MS-DOS QBasic. Selecting a program item starts the selected program. Also included in the main program group is the program group Disk Utilities. Selecting Disk Utilities causes the Shell to display another group of program items, the Disk Utilities group, which consists of DOS utility programs that enable you to copy, back up, restore, format, and undelete disks (see fig. 4.19). You can press Esc to return to the preceding program group or select the Main program group, which appears at the top of the program list.

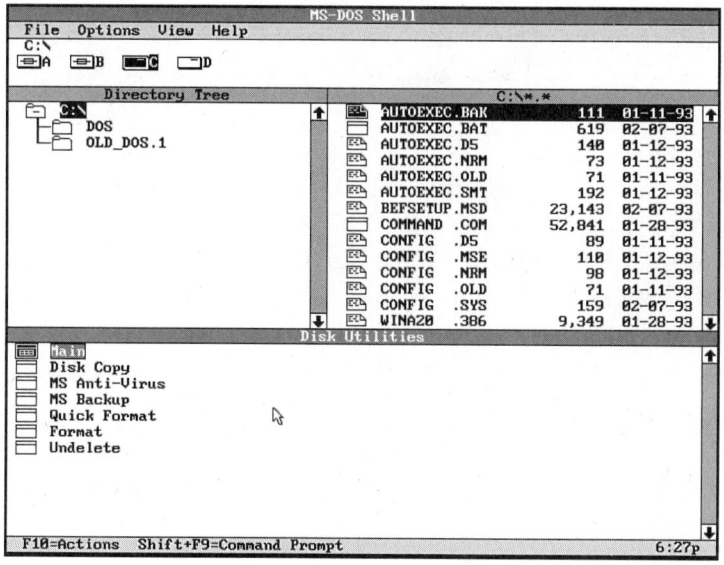

Fig. 4.19
Disk Utilities program items.

To run a program item or to select an alternate program group, highlight your choice and press Enter, or simply double-click on your choice. If you choose to run a program, you are returned to the DOS Shell when that program terminates.

Working with Program Groups

Now that you know what programs groups are, it is necessary to learn how you can work with them. The following sections teach you how to add, modify, and delete program groups.

Adding a Program Group. To add a new program group, make the program list area the active area of the DOS Shell window and display the program group to which the new group is to be added. If you want to add a new program group to the Main program group, for example, press Esc until the title bar of the program list area displays the title Main. When you want to add a program group to a different program group, use the mouse or cursor-movement keys to select the intended "parent" group in the program list area.

When the program group you want is displayed, complete the following steps:

1. Choose **N**ew from the **F**ile menu. The New Program Object dialog box appears (see fig. 4.20). This dialog box contains two option buttons: Program Group and Program Item.

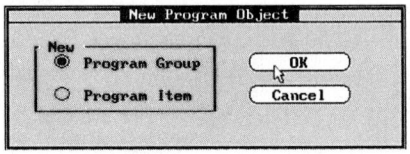

Fig. 4.20
The New Program Object dialog box.

2. Click the Program Group option button, and then click the OK command button or press Enter. The Add Group dialog box appears (see fig. 4.21). This dialog box contains three text boxes: Title, Help Text, and Password. You must type an entry in the Title text box to supply the group name. Entries in the Help Text and Password text boxes are optional.

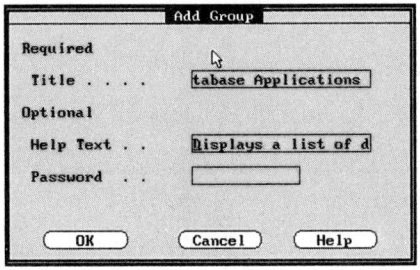

Fig. 4.21
The Add Group dialog box.

3. Type a program group title in the Title text box. (You can use up to 23 characters, including spaces.) This title will be the name, or menu option, that appears in the program list area when the parent program group is displayed.

   If you are creating a program group for your database applications, for example, you might type **Database Applications** in the Title text box. This title appears not only in the program list area, but also in that area's title bar when a program group is activated.

4. Type a help message, if you choose, in the Help Text text box. (The message can be up to 255 characters long, even though the Shell can display only 20 characters at a time in the text box; the text in the text box scrolls to the left as you type past the 20th character.)

For a Database Applications group, for example, you might type the help message **Displays list of database applications**. Afterward, whenever you press F1 while the Database Applications item is highlighted, the help message appears.

The Shell displays help messages in the Shell Help dialog box and formats the help message to fit in the dialog box. If you want a line to break at a particular point, type the characters **^m** (or **^M**) at that point. Any following text starts on the next line when the help message is displayed in the Help dialog box.

5. Type a password, if you choose, in the Password text box. (The password can be up to 20 characters long, including spaces.)

Caution

Using a password to limit access to a DOS Shell program group provides only minimal security. Any user with access to your computer easily can bypass the Shell and start programs from the DOS command line instead.

6. Click the OK command button or press Enter. The Shell adds the new program group to the selected program group. Now, if you select the new program group, the Shell opens an empty file list area so that you can add program items.

Modifying Program Group Properties. After you create a program group, you can change the parameters that define it—its *properties*—through the Shell File menu. To change a program group's properties, highlight the group's name in the file list area and choose **P**roperties from the **F**ile menu. The Program Group Properties dialog box appears (see fig. 4.22).

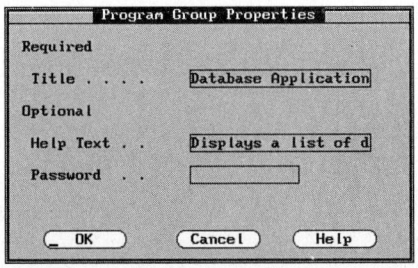

Fig. 4.22
The Program Group Properties dialog box.

This dialog box essentially is a copy of the Add Group dialog box, except that the title, help message, and password (if you supplied one) for the selected group already appear in the text boxes. Make any changes you want; then click OK or press Enter. Clicking Cancel returns you to the Shell window without changing any of the program group's properties.

Deleting a Program Group. Through the File menu, you also can remove a program group. Before you delete a program group, make sure that all items in the group are deleted (see the section "Deleting a Program Item" later in this chapter).

To delete a program group, select the group name and choose Delete from the File menu or press the Del key. The Delete Item dialog box appears (see fig. 4.23). Select Delete This Item, and click OK or press Enter.

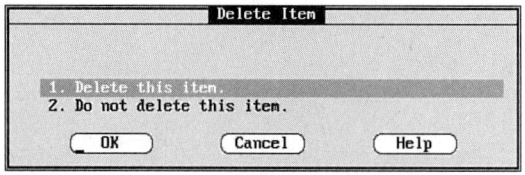

Fig. 4.23
The Delete Item dialog box.

Note

If you attempt to delete a program group before it is empty, the Shell displays an error message box.

Changing the Order of a Group's Listings. Placing the groups that you use most frequently near the top of the group listing is convenient, enabling you to find these groups quickly. You can place groups in any order you want. To move a group from one place to another in the menu list, follow these steps:

1. Move the selection bar to the group that you want to move.
2. Choose Reorder from the File menu. The Shell displays the following message in the status line:

   ```
   Select location to move to, then press Enter. Esc to cancel.
   ```

3. Use the cursor-movement keys to move the selection bar to the desired new location for the selected group and then press Enter. The Shell moves the group to the new position.

You can repeat these steps as often as necessary to produce the order you want for your groups.

Working with Program Items

After you create program groups, you may next want to add program items. The following sections describe how to add program items, as well as how to modify and delete existing program items in the program group. (To reorder program items, follow the procedure described in the preceding section.)

Adding a Program Item. Adding a program item is similar to adding a program group. When you want to add a program item to a particular group, make the program list area the active area of the DOS Shell window and then display the program group to which you want to add the program item. If you want to add a program item to the Database Applications program group, for example, press Esc until Main appears in the title bar of the program list area and then use the mouse or cursor-movement keys to highlight Database Applications.

After you've selected the program group, choose **N**ew from the **F**ile menu and select Program Item from the dialog box. The Add Program dialog box appears (see fig. 4.24).

This dialog box contains five text boxes: Program Title, Commands, Startup Directory, Application Shortcut Key, and Password. You must type entries in the Program Title and Commands text boxes, but entries in the Startup Directory, Application Shortcut Key, and Password text boxes are optional. All entries in the Add Program dialog box are referred to collectively as the program item's *properties*.

You also can click the Advanced command button to add a help message, to specify special memory or video requirements, or to select other advanced options.

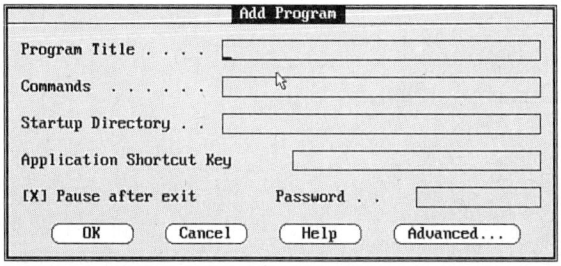

Fig. 4.24
The Add Program dialog box.

Modifying Program Items. Modifying the properties of a program item is fairly easy and straightforward. To modify properties, you follow these steps:

1. Activate the program list area. If the group that contains the program item that you want to modify is not included in the selected group, select the program group that includes the item.
2. Use the mouse or cursor-movement keys to move the selection bar to the name of the program item that contains the properties you want to modify.
3. Choose **P**roperties from the **F**ile menu. The Program Item Properties dialog box appears.
4. Make the desired changes in the values in the text boxes. Then click OK or press Enter to confirm your choices.

Deleting a Program Item. You may want to delete a program item that you no longer use. The program itself is not deleted—only the program item. To remove a program from your computer, you must delete that program's files from the disk.

To delete a program item, follow these steps:

1. Move the selection bar to the name of the item that you want to delete.
2. Choose **D**elete from the **F**ile menu or press Del. The Delete Item dialog box appears.
3. Select `1. Delete this item`. Then click OK or press Enter. The Shell deletes the program item from the selected program group list.

Using Shortcut Keys. You can specify shortcut keys to start applications. When you specify these key combinations, the Shell displays them in the Application Shortcut Key text box in the Add Program dialog box. If you press and hold down Ctrl and Alt simultaneously and then press **P**, for example, the Shell displays `ALT+CTRL+P` in the text box.

A specified shortcut-key combination starts the program only if the following three conditions are met:

- The DOS 6.0 task swapper is enabled.
- You started the program through the DOS Shell's program list area.
- You used one of the task-swapper keystrokes (Alt-Tab, Alt-Esc, or Ctrl-Esc) to switch to another program or back to the Shell.

Suppose that you first enable the DOS Shell task swapper and then start Paradox from the program item in the Database Applications program group. You then switch back to the Shell by pressing Alt-Tab and start WordStar. To return to Paradox quickly, you simply press the shortcut key you defined (for example, Ctrl-Alt-P). The task swapper quickly swaps WordStar to disk and displays the Paradox screen.

When you return to the DOS Shell window while the program you were using earlier is swapped out to disk, the Shell lists the shortcut in parentheses to the right of the program item title in the active task list area.

Working with Directories and Files

DOS manages files on your disks by maintaining file information in a hierarchical directory structure. The directory tree area, in the upper-left quadrant of the window, graphically depicts this directory structure. At the top of this area, the root directory of the logged disk is shown as a folder-shaped icon, or as a pair of brackets ([ ]) if the DOS Shell is in text mode. All other directories are shown as folder-shaped icons (or pairs of brackets). These other directories are listed below the root icon and connected to the root icon by a vertical line. The name of each directory is listed to the right of its icon.

At any time during a session with the DOS Shell, one directory name is highlighted. This highlighted directory is referred to as the *selected directory*. When you first start the Shell, the directory that is current when you start the program is the selected directory (usually the root directory of the boot disk). The file list area of the DOS Shell window, in the upper-right quadrant of the screen, lists the file names in the selected directory.

Expanding and Collapsing Branches

As you know, the DOS directory structure is tree-like. The root directory is like the trunk of a tree, with all other directories growing out like branches of a tree. The DOS Shell graphically represents this tree-like nature in the directory tree area of the DOS Shell window as an upside-down tree.

The DOS directory structure can have multiple levels, but initially the Shell shows only the first level of the tree. Each first-level directory—a directory attached directly to the root—is depicted as a branch of the tree. Just as branches of a real tree can have offshoot branches, each DOS directory can contain offshoot directories. The Shell indicates that a directory contains other directories by placing a plus sign (+) in the directory icon. Figure 4.25 shows plus signs in the directory icon for the following first-level directories:

DV

OLD_DOS.1

OPTQEMM

To *expand* (show the directories subordinate to) by one level a directory tree branch that shows a + in its directory icon, click the + in the directory icon or do the following:

1. Select the directory tree area that contains the target directory icon.
2. Move the selection cursor to the directory name.
3. Press the + key, or choose Expand One Level from the **T**ree menu.

The Shell then shows the next level of directories beneath the selected directory. Figure 4.25, for example, shows the expanded DATABASE directory containing three second-level directories: ACCESS, DBASE, and PARADOX.

Offshoot directories can contain more offshoots. The relationship among directory levels is analogous to a family tree—child, parent, grandparent, and so on. When a second-level directory contains one or more third-level directories, the Shell shows a plus sign (+) in the second-level directory icon. The directory icon of the PARADOX directory shown in figure 4.25, for example, indicates that this branch of the DATABASE directory also contains at least one directory. To expand one level of the PARADOX branch, follow the procedure you used to expand one level of the DATABASE branch.

If you do not remember precisely where a directory is located in the directory tree, expanding branches one level at a time may become tedious. When you want to expand all levels beneath a particular directory branch, use the following procedure:

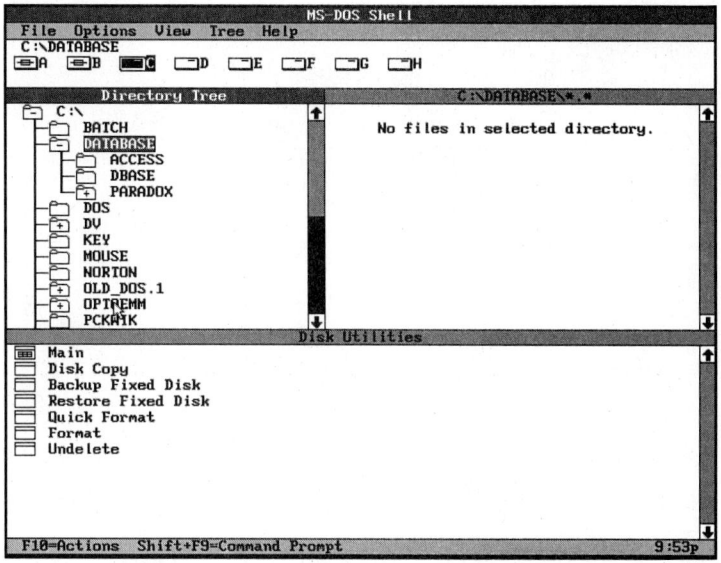

Fig. 4.25
Expanding a directory tree branch.

1. Use the mouse to click the directory name or use the arrow keys to move the selection cursor to the directory name.
2. Press the * key, or choose Expand **A**ll from the **T**ree menu.

The Shell expands all levels of the tree below the currently selected directory. Figure 4.26, for example, shows the fully expanded DATABASE branch of drive C's directory tree.

The opposite of expanding a directory branch in the directory tree area is *collapsing* a branch. When you first start the DOS Shell, you may notice that a root directory's icon contains a minus sign (–). After you expand a directory branch, the icon for the expanded branch also contains a minus sign. These minus signs are a reminder that you can collapse the branch. To collapse a branch whose icon contains a –, click the directory icon with your mouse or use the following procedure:

1. Select the directory name.
2. Press the – (hyphen) key or choose **C**ollapse Branch from the **T**ree menu.

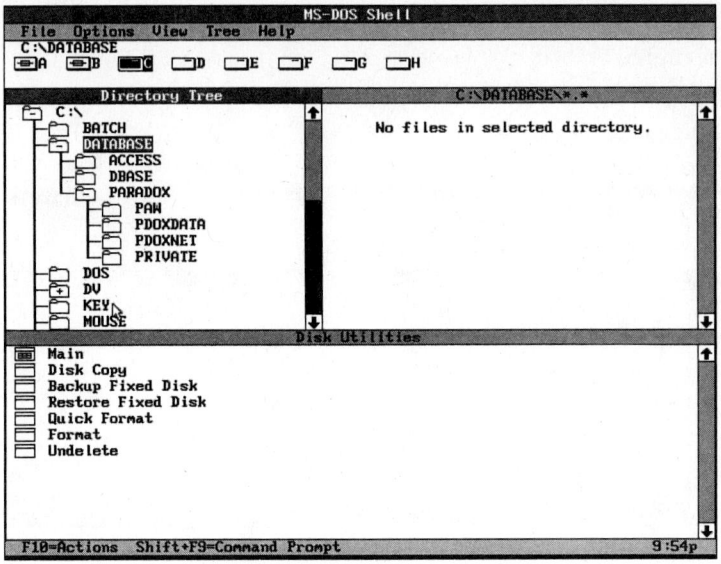

Fig. 4.26
The fully expanded DATABASE branch.

To collapse the entire tree, click the root directory icon or do the following:

1. Select the root directory name at the top of the directory tree.
2. Press the – (hyphen) key or choose **C**ollapse Branch from the **T**ree menu.

The Shell collapses the entire tree down to the root level and places a + in the root directory icon.

Creating Directories

Because the only automatically available directory on a DOS disk is the root, you must add any additional directories. Even after you establish a workable directory structure for your computer, you occasionally need to create new directories on your disks. DOS enables you to add directories to a disk through the DOS Shell.

To create a new directory using the DOS Shell, do the following:

1. Select the directory tree area of the DOS Shell window.
2. Select the directory to be the parent of the new directory.
3. Select **F**ile from the menu bar to display the File menu.
4. Choose Cr**e**ate Directory from the **F**ile menu.

The Shell displays the Create Directory dialog box shown in figure 4.27. This dialog box indicates the name of the parent directory, C:\SPREADSH.

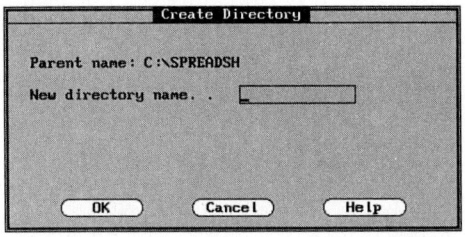

Fig. 4.27
The Create Directory dialog box.

5. Type the name of the new directory, and press Enter or click OK.

The Shell creates the new directory and returns to the directory tree area of the DOS Shell window. The Shell also adds to the tree an icon for the new directory.

Selecting Files in the DOS Shell

In the DOS Shell, you perform file-management operations primarily through the **F**ile menu. The active menu options displayed in the File menu, however, vary according to which area of the window is active. Although the menu options displayed when the directory tree is active are the same as the options displayed when the file list is active, many of these menu options are dimmed (not valid) when the directory tree is active.

The DOS Shell's file-management commands operate on all selected files. At any time, you can select any number of files. The Shell displays both the name and the file-list icon of each selected file in reverse video. Selected files need not be from the same directory.

Selecting a Single File

To select a single file, follow these steps:

1. Activate the directory tree area.
2. Use the mouse and scroll bar or the cursor-movement keys to scroll through the directory tree until the name of the directory containing the files you want to select appears.
3. Use the mouse or the arrow keys to move the selection cursor to the target directory.
4. Activate the file list area.

5. Use the mouse and scroll bar or the cursor-movement keys to scroll the file list until the name of the file you want to select appears.
6. Click the name of the file to be selected (the target file). Alternatively, use the cursor-movement keys to move the selection cursor to the target file and then press the space bar.

To indicate that a file is selected, DOS displays the file name and file list icon in reverse video.

Note

A file is not selected until the icon is displayed in reverse video. Simply highlighting the file name with the selection cursor is not sufficient to select the file.

Selecting Multiple Files

If you want to apply a DOS Shell command to several files, applying the command simultaneously to all the files is more efficient than applying it to one file at a time. After you select the first file, you can select the other files in either of the following ways. This procedure is referred to in the DOS Shell as *extending the selection*:

- Hold down the Ctrl key and click the name of the file that you want to select.

or

- Press Shift-F8. When the message ADD appears in the status bar, move the selection cursor to the name of the file you want to select and then press the space bar. Press Shift-F8 again to turn off the ADD message.

The icon and file name of each selected file appear in reverse video (see fig. 4.28).

Frequently, you may want the Shell to work on several files that are listed one after the other in the list area. To select contiguous files, you can select each file individually, using the previously discussed method. But the Shell provides an easier way to select files as a group.

To select contiguous files in the DOS Shell, follow these steps:

1. Select the first file.
2. Use one of the following procedures to select the remaining files:

Use the mouse to position the pointer on the last file you want to select, press the Shift key, and click the left mouse button.

or

While holding the Shift key, use the cursor-movement keys to move the selection bar to the last file.

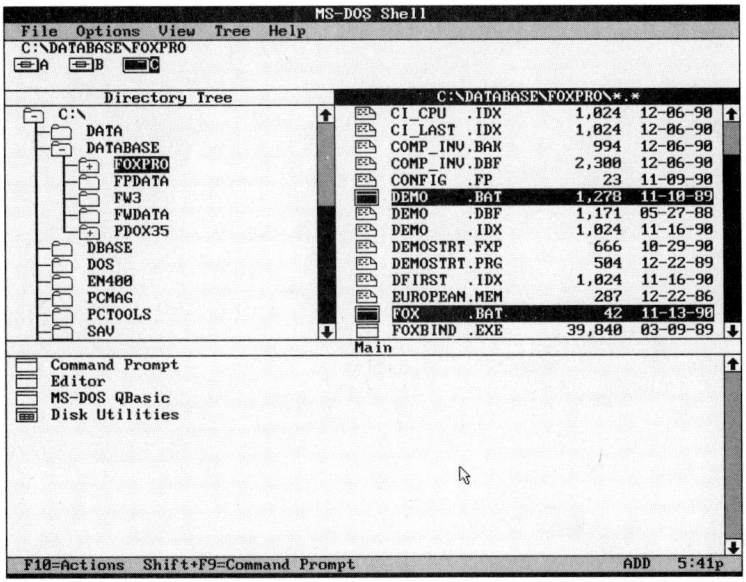

Fig. 4.28
Selecting several files in the DOS Shell.

The Shell selects all the files. To indicate that these files are selected, the Shell displays the file names and their icons in reverse video.

Selecting All Files

To select all the files in a directory, follow these steps:

1. Select the directory in the directory tree area.
2. Activate the file list area.
3. Press Ctrl-/, or choose **S**elect All in the **F**ile menu.

Deselecting All Files

After you select files, you may decide that you don't want to perform a DOS Shell operation on that group of files. Perhaps you want to start a fresh selection process by *deselecting* all selected files. Normally, selecting a different directory also deselects all selected files.

You also can deselect all selected files in one procedure. Use the mouse to click anywhere in the file area or press the space bar. Alternatively, choose Deselect All from the **F**ile menu.

Selecting Files across Directories

By default, the DOS Shell enables you to select files in only one directory at a time. By selecting a different directory, you deselect all selected files. Occasionally, however, you may want to perform a file-management operation on files from several directories. You may want to copy to a floppy disk, for example, one file from each of three directories on your hard disk.

Before you can select files in several directories, you must choose Select **A**cross Directories in the **O**ptions menu.

To copy files from three directories to a floppy disk in one procedure, first select the directories and then the files, one at a time. Then use the **C**opy command in the **F**ile menu to copy all the selected files to the floppy disk.

Using the Shell to View a File

When you want to view the contents of a file from within the DOS Shell, follow these steps:

1. Select the target file in the file list area.
2. Choose **V**iew File Contents from the **F**ile menu.

When the file you want to view contains only ASCII characters, the Shell displays the ASCII file viewer. One of the files distributed with DOS 6.0, for example, is named APPNOTES.TXT and contains only ASCII text. To view the contents of APPNOTES.TXT, select its name in the file list area, and then choose **V**iew File Contents from the **F**ile menu. The Shell displays the file in the ASCII viewer (see fig. 4.29).

To scroll through the file, use the cursor-movement keys or use the mouse to click the labels PgUp, PgDn, ↑, or ↓, which are displayed near the top of the window.

When the file you want to view contains data other than ASCII characters, the Shell uses the hexadecimal (base 16, often referred to as *hex*) viewer. If you select the DOS command processor file, COMMAND.COM, and press F9, for example, the Shell displays the contents of the file as four columns of hexadecimal codes and one column of ASCII characters. (This information normally has meaning only to programmers and to the computer.) As in the ASCII viewer, you can scroll through the file by using the cursor-movement keys or the mouse.

```
MS-DOS Shell - APPNOTES.TXT
 Display  View  Help
   To view file's content use PgUp or PgDn or ↑ or ↓.

APPNOTES.TXT

NOTES ON USING APPLICATIONS WITH MS-DOS VERSION 6.0
===================================================

This document provides important information not included in
the Microsoft MS-DOS User's Guide or in online Help.

Look through the following table of contents to determine
whether your application is included.

ATTENTION CODEVIEW AND INTEL ABOVEBOARD USERS
+++++++++++++++++++++++++++++++++++++++++++++
Sections 1 and 5 contain critical information
about using Intel Above Board and CodeView with
MS-DOS 6.0.
+++++++++++++++++++++++++++++++++++++++++++++

For information about installing MS-DOS 6.0 and using
hardware and networks with MS-DOS 6.0, see the README.TXT
file.

The following topics are discussed in this file:

1. Above Board 286 and Above Board Plus Installation
   Programs
2. Amload
3. AutoCAD release 10
 <┘=PageDown  Esc=Cancel  F9=Hex/ASCII                    1:25p
```

Fig. 4.29
The ASCII viewer.

Associating Files with Programs

Many programs create and work with files that have distinctive file name extensions. Lotus 1-2-3 files have the extensions WKS, WK1, or WK3; Microsoft Word document files have the extension DOC; and dBASE database files have the extension DBF. The DOS Shell enables you to associate particular extensions with a specific program so that you can start the program and load a file with an associated extension in one step.

The easiest method of associating a file extension with a program is to follow these steps:

1. In the file list area, select a file whose extension you want the Shell to associate with a specific program.

2. Choose **A**ssociate from the **F**ile menu. The Shell displays the Associate File dialog box, containing a text box in which you can type the program's directory path and file name. If the current file extension already is associated with a program, the Shell displays the program's path and file name in the text box.

3. In the text box, type the program's complete file name, including the extension. If the file is in a directory that's not included in the PATH statement, type the directory path as well as the file name.

4. Click OK or press Enter.

Note

Program associations are stored in an ASCII file called DOSSHELL.INI. You can use any text editor, including the DOS Editor, to edit this file.

Using the Task Swapper

The DOS Shell also has the capability to load more than one program at a time. DOS accomplishes this feat through a technique called *task swapping*. To activate this feature, choose **E**nable Task Swapper from the **O**ptions menu. The Shell adds an active task list area to the window (see fig. 4.30). Initially, nothing is listed in this area because no program (other than the Shell) is active.

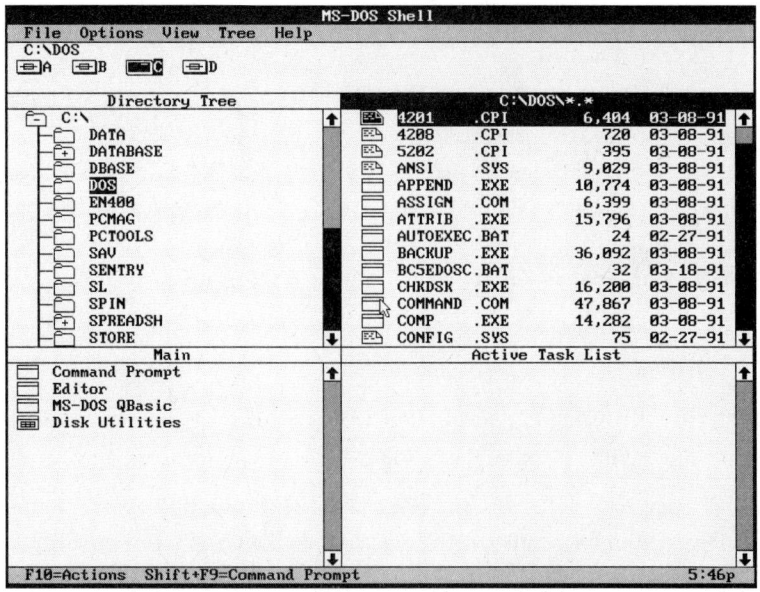

Fig. 4.30
The DOS Shell window with an active task list area.

With the task swapper enabled, you still start programs by using any of the methods described earlier in this chapter. But after you start a program, you can jump back to the DOS Shell instantly without exiting the program. Simply press Alt-Esc or Alt-Tab, and the screen returns to the DOS Shell window, where the program (or associated data file) is listed in the active task list area. DOS has swapped the contents of memory (RAM) to disk, freeing space in memory so that you can run another program.

The fastest way to switch between active tasks is to hold down the Alt key and tap the Tab key. *Do not release the Alt key.* The Shell displays the name of the task at the top of the screen. Still holding down the Alt key, press the Tab key again to see the name of the next task. Repeat this keystroke until the target task name appears. Finally, release the Alt key. The Shell switches to the target task.

Copying Files in the Shell

With the DOS Shell, you can copy one or more files in a directory, between directories, or between disks, using any of several approaches. The approach described in this section—the dual file list method—is the quickest and easiest to learn and use.

To perform the copy operation using the dual file list method, you first must select the source and target drive and directory and create a dual file list. Complete the following steps:

1. Select the source drive and directory (those that contain the files you want to copy).
2. Choose **D**ual File Lists from the **V**iew menu to switch to the dual file list.

Note

Under certain specific circumstances, you can skip step 2. For example, you can drag selected files to another directory on the same disk without opening a dual file list. Completing this step, however, always produces the result that you want.

3. Use the mouse or the cursor-movement keys to select the target drive and directory in the second directory tree.
4. Use the mouse or keyboard to select, in the first (upper) file list, the files that you want to copy.

The remaining steps for completing the copy operation differ, depending on whether you want to use the mouse or the keyboard. If you use a mouse, complete the following steps:

1. Position the mouse pointer on a selected file in the upper file list. Hold down the Ctrl key while you press and hold the left mouse button. While holding down both the Ctrl key and the mouse button, drag the mouse pointer to the target drive letter in the lower drive area or, alternatively, to the target directory's name in the lower directory tree.

   When you begin to drag the mouse, the pointer changes from an arrow (or a block, in text mode) to a circle (or two exclamation-point symbols, in text mode). When the pointer enters the second directory tree, the circle becomes a file icon (or a diamond, in text mode). If you are copying several files, the file icon resembles a stack of three papers. Figure 4.31 shows how you should have the dual file lists set up before dragging the file names to copy them to the target disk.

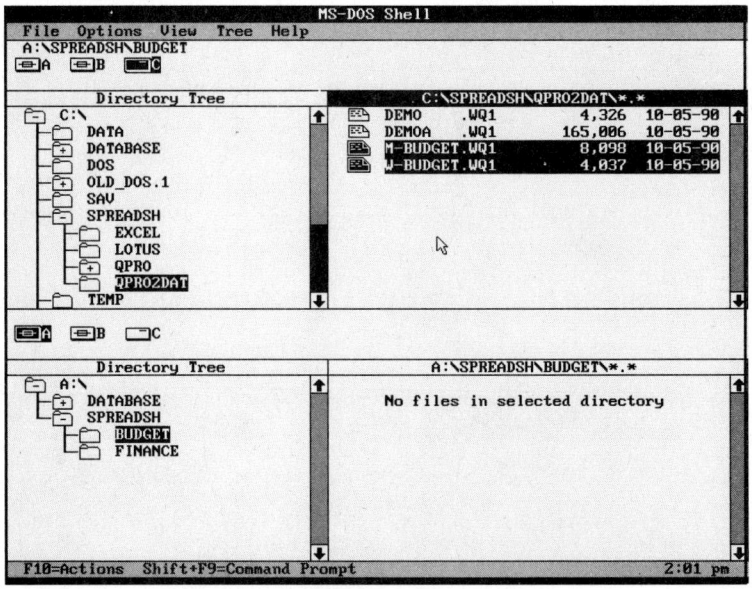

Fig. 4.31
Using the dual file list display to copy files.

Note

When you are copying files to a different disk, you don't have to hold down the Ctrl key; holding down the mouse button is enough. If you drag files to another directory on the same disk without holding down the Ctrl key, however, the Shell assumes that you want to *move* the files rather than *copy* them.

Depending on the selections you have made in the Confirmations item dialog box of the Options menu, you may be asked to confirm the Copy operation.

2. To confirm that the Copy should take place, click Yes.

To copy files using the keyboard only, complete the copy procedure by following these steps:

1. Choose **C**opy from the **F**ile menu or press F8. The Shell displays the Copy File dialog box. This dialog box contains the From and To text boxes. The Shell lists the source files in the From text box and the source directory in the To text box.

2. Type the target drive and directory name in the To text box and then press Enter. The Shell copies the files to the target directory and displays a message to that effect in the center of the screen.

Moving a File in the Shell

When the Shell moves a file, the program copies the file from one storage location to another and then deletes the file from its original location. Therefore, the steps for moving one or more files with the DOS Shell are nearly the same as those for copying files. When you want to move one or more files, select the files to be moved just as you do if you are going to copy them.

If you are using a mouse, position the mouse pointer on one of the selected files in the upper file list. Hold down the Alt key while you press and hold down the left mouse button. While holding both the Alt key and the mouse button, drag the mouse pointer to the target drive letter in the lower drive area or to the target directory's name in the lower directory tree.

To move files using only the keyboard, follow these steps:

1. Choose **M**ove from the **F**ile menu or press F7. The Shell displays the Move File dialog box. This dialog box contains two text boxes, one labeled From and another labeled To. The Shell lists the source files in the From text box and the source directory in the To text box.

2. Type the target drive and directory name in the To text box, and then click OK or press Enter. The Shell moves the files to the target directory and displays a message to that effect in the center of the screen.

Summary

The DOS Shell adds a new dimension to using DOS. Even if you are comfortable using DOS at the DOS prompt, you should explore the DOS Shell. Important points covered in this chapter include the following:

- The DOS Shell provides a visual interface that enables you to operate your computer quickly and easily without having to type commands at the DOS prompt.
- You can use the DOS Shell without a mouse, but using a mouse or other pointing device makes your actions go quickly, easily, and intuitively.
- Windows users may find many of the keystrokes and features of the DOS Shell to be familiar.
- You access DOS Shell features through a menu. When you choose the main menu prompts, a pull-down menu containing that menu's options appears.
- Some options in the DOS Shell's menus display a dialog box to enable you to specify parameters and options needed for the option.
- The DOS Shell's Task Swapper enables you to move easily from program to program with just a few keystrokes.
- You can associate programs with their data files, and you can start programs using hot keys.
- You can add or change the program groups and program items that appear in the Shell's program list area.
- You can use the Shell to manipulate files and directories quickly and easily.

In the next chapter, you learn how to manage files and directories effectively.

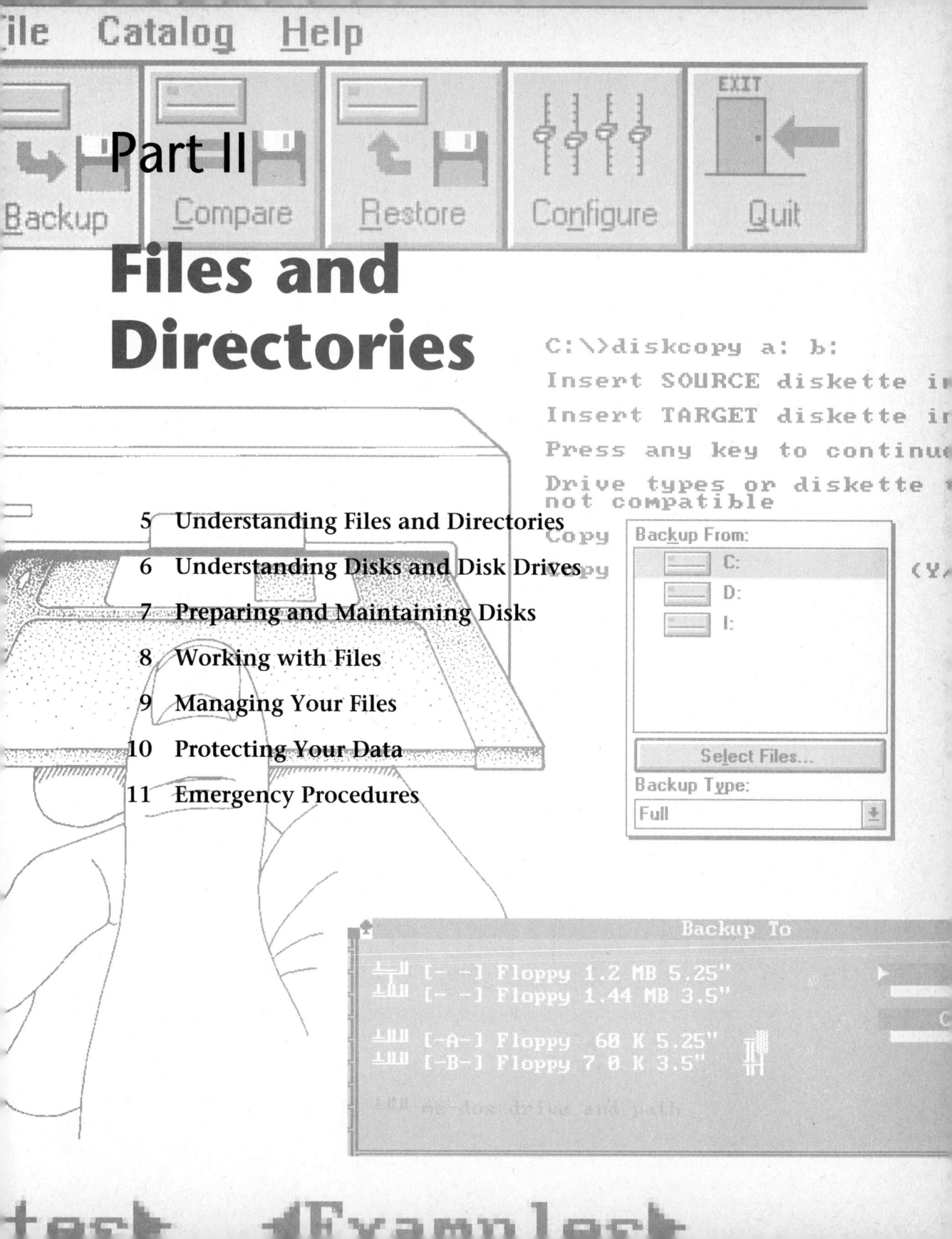

Part II

Files and Directories

5 Understanding Files and Directories

6 Understanding Disks and Disk Drives

7 Preparing and Maintaining Disks

8 Working with Files

9 Managing Your Files

10 Protecting Your Data

11 Emergency Procedures

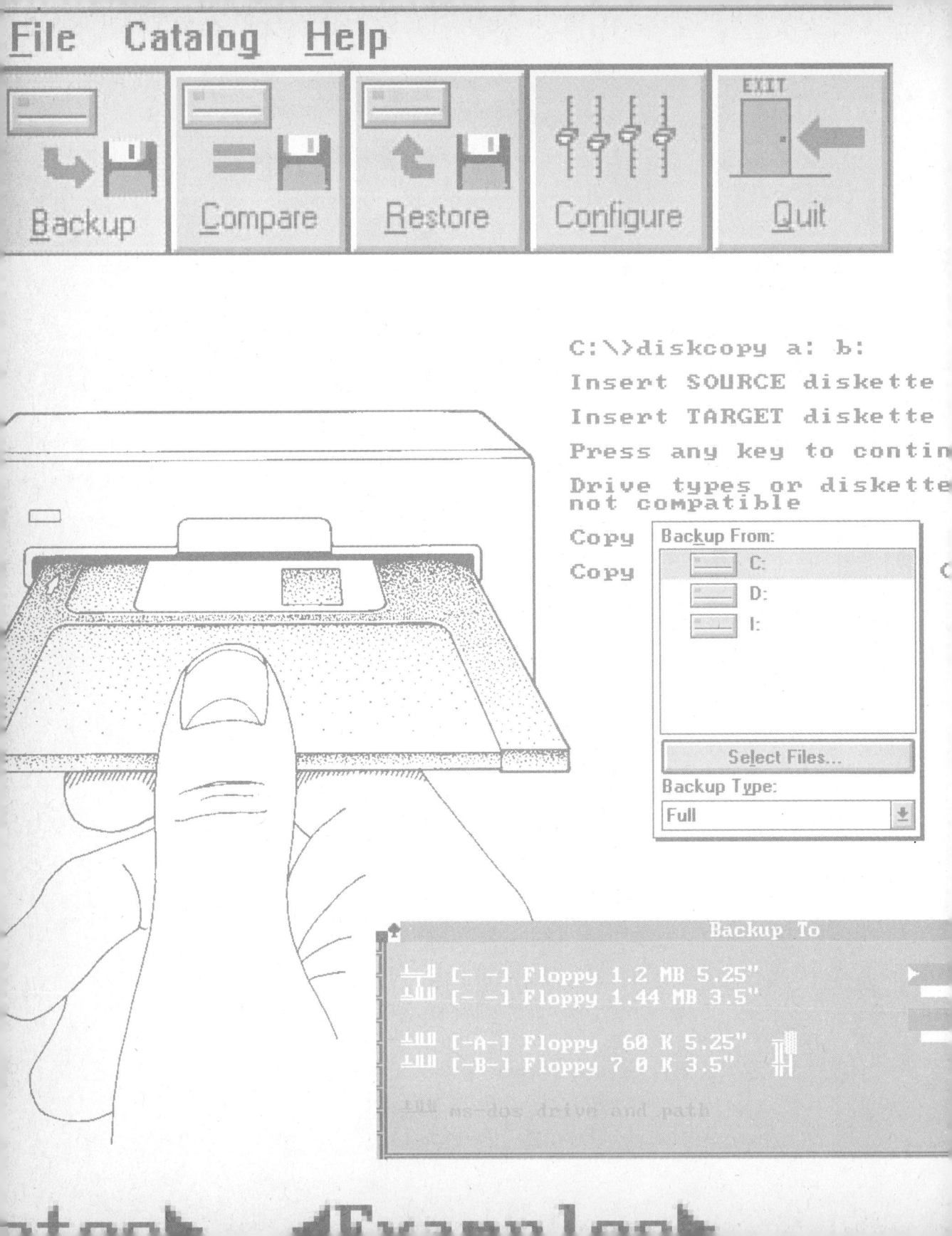
File Catalog Help
Backup
Compare
Restore
Configure
EXIT
Quit
C:\>diskcopy a: b:
Insert SOURCE diskette
Insert TARGET diskette
Press any key to contin
Drive types or diskette
not compatible
Copy
Copy
Backup From:
C:
D:
I:
Select Files...
Backup Type:
Full
Backup To
[- -] Floppy 1.2 MB 5.25"
[- -] Floppy 1.44 MB 3.5"
[-A-] Floppy 60 K 5.25"
[-B-] Floppy 7 0 K 3.5"

Chapter 5

Understanding Files and Directories

Two of the primary roles of a disk operating system are storing and retrieving data. This chapter introduces you to the fundamental ways in which DOS handles these roles. To provide data storage and retrieval, the operating system must provide a common method for file storage and retrieval so that any software package can access information easily and quickly. It is also important that DOS provide these services without your having to know the internal details of how the disk works and why.

DOS generally insulates you from the technical details involved in storing and retrieving data on your computer. You must, however, prepare disks by formatting them, and you may occasionally have to repair them. In this chapter, you learn information about the most basic part of DOS—the file and directory system. After you've mastered this information, you will have a firm footing for understanding DOS completely.

Introducing the DOS File System

Ask almost any non-computer user what a file is and he or she almost invariably describes a collection of papers wrapped in a manila folder. Such files are stored in file cabinets like the one pictured in figure 5.1. They are familiar and comfortable.

On a computer, a *file system* is an organized collection of files that has a direct parallel to the old, familiar file cabinet. The hard disk and floppy disks you use to store data electronically use many of the same conventions. Each file on a disk has a unique name, just as each file folder in a file cabinet is labeled for identification. Files are arranged on your disks in directories (discussed later in this chapter) to make them easier to find, just as sections in a file cabinet are organized to group file folders that have a common purpose.

Fig. 5.1
The trusty, familiar, old file cabinet.

Understanding Files

A *file* is a variable length collection of related information that is referenced by a name. Just as a file folder can be filled with various papers that contain information in the form of writing, an electronic file can contain various pieces of related information wrapped up in an electronic file folder referenced by the file's name.

Files written to disk can serve many purposes. A word processor file might hold all the sentences in a letter or a book chapter. A database file might contain the names and addresses of all the members of a club or all the invoices for a store. Just as a good secretary uses color-coded labels and different markings on file folders to indicate the type of information in a file, DOS file names most often indicate what kind of information they hold.

Often the way data is written in a file depends on the software that creates it. You can type the same letter, using all the same words and punctuation, using Microsoft Word and WordPerfect. When printed, the letters are identical, yet the format of the files created by these two programs is very different. You can, with a little work, use Lotus 1-2-3 to store the same letter in yet another file format.

Although many programs recognize each other's file formats and convert them for you, DOS cares little about the format of a file's content. DOS doesn't bother trying to decipher the contents of a file. Its job is to wrap the information in a file folder (the file's name) and put it where you can find it later. Your job is to know what the file contains and which program you need to use to access correctly the data contained in the file.

In a computer setting, a file can contain data (information), programs (instructions that guide computer tasks), or both. A file can exist on a disk, on magnetic tape, on CD ROMs, or even in a computer's memory. Files are made up of elements of data or programs. The individual elements can be stored as patterns of holes in a paper tape, as patterns of magnetic fields on the surface of a disk, and in many other ways.

Fortunately, unless you write programs for a living, you usually can ignore the technical aspects of how a file is stored. After all, you don't have to know how a fuel injector works to drive a fuel-injected car.

Physical storage techniques for files vary greatly, but on PCs a few file storage methods dominate. On PCs, floppy disks are used primarily for distributing files to other computers. Hard disks provide long-term and working storage. CD ROMs often are used for storing files that do not need to be edited or altered, and tape drives and floppy disks are used to make backup copies of files for safekeeping.

Regardless of the actual media (floppy, hard disk, tape, and so on), DOS uses *file names* to identify files. As you may remember from an earlier chapter, a full file name consists of one to eight characters followed by a period (.) and up to three characters called the *extension*. The period and extension are optional but are used almost universally.

The *name* portion of a file name (before the period) usually provides a mind association or description of the contents of the file. Extensions, on the other hand, traditionally describe the *type* of file—its format.

If you're using a word processing application to write a memo, you might use as the name portion of a file name the name (or a close approximation) of the person who will receive the memo. You then can use the extension .MEM to indicate that the file is a memo. You can call a memo to Mr. Fleenor, for example, FLEENOR.MEM. Similarly, you can use the extension .DOC for office-policy document files. A monthly policy statement for January can be named JAN.DOC.

DOS enables you to use a wide variety of file names. You are free to develop your own file-naming conventions, provided that you stay within the character limits imposed by DOS and the requirements of the software you use to create the file. Although most software packages are lenient in the file names they can use, many programs require a file to have a specific extension before they recognize the file as one of their own.

Understanding File Names

DOS ensures that every one of your files has a name. In fact, DOS does not provide a way to put file data on a disk without a file name. When a file is created, either by your software or a DOS file service routine, information about the physical location of the file is stored in a *File Allocation Table* (FAT), which is similar to a book's table of contents. DOS places the name of each file and its attributes in a special structure called a *directory*, which you can think of as the chapter headings of a book. Using this analogy, you can think of files as the pages in each chapter.

For now, however, you need only concern yourself with the names of files. You learn more about the other parts of the DOS file system later in this chapter. Keep in mind that a directory is a special structure used to store file names and files. Later in this chapter, you learn more information about the directory.

Creating File Names. The characters you see on your computer screen are the ASCII code representations of bytes of data. One character is stored in one byte. In a disk directory, each slot where a file name can be stored reserves a space 11 bytes long (8 for the first part of the file name plus 3 for the extension). DOS accepts for file names most characters that you use for "everyday" names. You can use the uppercase and lowercase letters *A* through *Z*; DOS automatically stores letters in uppercase in a directory entry. You also can use the numeric characters *0* through *9* and many punctuation characters not used as separators in the file system.

Following are the rules for creating legal file names:

- Each file name on a disk must be unique.
- File names, even though they are not always expressed that way, include the drive letter and directory path of the file. In practical terms, this naming convention means that each file in a directory must have a unique name because the difference in directory names adds to a file name's uniqueness.
- A file name consists of the following items:
  - A name of one to eight characters
  - An optional extension of one to three characters
  - A period between the name and the extension (if an extension is used)
- The following characters are allowed in a file name:
  - The letters *A* through *Z* (lowercase letters are transformed into uppercase automatically)
  - The numerals 0 through 9
  - The following special characters and punctuation marks:

    $ # & @ ! ( ) - { } ' _ ~ ^ '
- DOS reserves certain ASCII codes for other uses and does not let them be a part of the file name. The following characters are not allowed in a file name:
  - Any control character (ASCII codes used as commands)
  - The space character
  - The following special characters and punctuation symbols:

    + = / [ ] " : ; , ? * \ < > |

To understand why DOS disallows the use of some characters in file names, you must look below the surface of DOS. Certain characters are not allowed because DOS does not pass those characters from the keyboard to the command or external command program that controls a file's name. You cannot, for example, use the Ctrl-G (^G) character in a file name because Ctrl-G tells an input device to sound the computer's bell or beep signal. DOS does not accept the Escape character, produced by the Esc key, as part of a file name because DOS interprets the Esc key as your request to cancel the command line and start again.

Another example of an unacceptable character is Ctrl-S (^S), which DOS and other operating systems use to stop the flow of characters from the input device to the output device. Ctrl-S stops screen scrolling, for example. If you press Ctrl-S while entering a file name, DOS assumes that you are entering an input-stopping character, not part of a file name.

You cannot use in a file name any characters that COMMAND.COM and external command programs use to divide the parameters and switches from the command in a command line. Because DOS must break out, or *parse* (distinguish the various components of), the command line, DOS sees certain characters as delimiters of parameters or as parts of a parameter. The backslash character (\), for example, separates directory names in a path specifier. DOS always reads a backslash in a command line as part of a path.

Avoiding Reserved Names. One of the ways in which DOS is able to control so many different types of devices is by using a *logical device*. It is important to understand that each of these devices has a name that is reserved and cannot be used for other purposes.

In theory, DOS treats all the input and output devices it controls as if they were made out of software. Such devices include almost everything you think of as belonging to a computer system—disks, printers, keyboards, screens, and modems.

The hardware manufacturers are responsible for accepting and generating data in a fashion that conforms to DOS standards. The actual control over the actions of a device (print heads, disk drive motors and heads, and so on) is left to programming contained on ROM chips incorporated into the devices. Thus, DOS needs to know only that a printer exists and that the printer is connected to the system in a specific way, normally via a parallel or serial port.

To you, a parallel port is a hardware connector where you plug in a cable. To DOS, the parallel port is simply an address in memory where it sends and receives data. Each of these addresses is called a *logical device* and is given a name. By default, DOS expects to see a printer connected to the first parallel port, which it calls LPT1:.

The first available disk is A:. By convention, B: is reserved for the second floppy disk, and C: is reserved for the first hard disk volume. The keyboard and video card are combined to create a logical device named CON:.

Notice that all of these logical device names end with the colon (:). The colon signifies that something is a DOS logical device. In some contexts, however, the colon is omitted. For example:

```
COPY CON SUMFILE.TXT
```

This variation on the COPY command tells DOS to take input from the console (CON:) and save it to the currently logged drive and directory as a file having the name SUMFILE.TXT.

What has all this talk of logical devices got to do with file names? Simply, DOS's internal routines treat logical devices like files in many ways. That's why when you try to name a file with a name for a logical device, DOS gets confused and weird things can happen, such as losing data or sending a file to a printer.

For this reason, DOS reserves names for its logical devices. DOS can treat some of these logical PC devices in a high-level way by accepting their names as input or output parameters in a command line, as in the preceding example. Before it uses the file name parameters in a command line to look for a file, DOS checks to see whether the file name is a device name. Table 5.1 lists the major logical DOS input and output device names and their purposes.

Table 5.1 DOS Device Names

Device Name	Purpose
COM*x* or AUX	Identifies a serial communication port (*x* may be the number 1, 2, 3, or 4).
LPT*x* or PRN	Identifies a parallel printer port (*x* may be the number 1, 2, 3, or 4).

(continues)

Table 5.1 Continued

Device Name	Purpose
CON	Identifies the screen and keyboard.
NUL	Identifies the "do nothing" device, also called a bit bucket. Output sent to NUL is neither displayed, stored, nor acted on in any way.
CLOCK$	Provides date and time services.

Never attempt to write a disk file with a name that is the same as one of the device names listed in table 5.1. DOS intercepts the device name, even if you add an extension, and tries to use the device—not the file you intend—to complete the command. Use a device name only as a device parameter in a command.

Observing File-Naming Conventions

A *convention* is an informal rule that is not explicitly enforced. DOS file names often follow certain conventions. Although you can use any file name that follows DOS's character and device-name rules, observe DOS file-naming conventions whenever possible. You can, for example, name a memo file and give it a .BAT extension, but this extension has a special meaning to DOS because all batch files have the extension .BAT. As long as you do not try to execute the memo as a batch file, DOS is happy. If you try to execute the memo file, however, DOS sees the .BAT extension and tries to execute it. Of course, the memo cannot be executed because it probably isn't made up of legal DOS commands.

You can name an .EXE file with a .COM extension. Although both files are executable, they have internal differences. DOS does not take the extension's name to mean that the file is indeed an .EXE or .COM file; DOS inspects a key part of the file before deciding how to load and execute the program file. If you name a spreadsheet file as an .EXE or .COM file, for example, DOS is not fooled into executing the nonprogram file. In all likelihood, your system simply will lock up, and you will have to perform a warm boot to begin again.

Many software manufacturers use certain extensions for special file formats created by their applications. To avoid confusion about the contents of a file, avoid using those extensions. Table 5.2 lists some conventional file name extensions and their meanings. Multiple programs can use the same extensions in their file-naming conventions.

Table 5.2 Common File Name Extensions

Extension	Common Use
ARC	Archive (compressed file)
ASC	ASCII text file
ASM	Assembler source file
BAK	Backup file
BAS	BASIC program file
BAT	DOS batch file
BGI	Borland Graphics Interface file (Quattro, Paradox)
BIN	Binary program file
BMP	Windows bitmap file
C	C source file
CPP	C++ source file
CBL	COBOL source file
CFG	Program configuration information
CHP	Chapter file (Ventura Publisher)
CHR	Character file (Quattro, Paradox)
CNF	Program configuration information
COM	Program file
CPI	Code page information file (DOS)
DAT	Data file
DB	Database file (Paradox)
DBF	Database file (dBASE)
DCT	Dictionary file
DEV	Program device driver file
DIF	Data Interchange Format file
DIR	A program data file used as a directory
DLL	Windows Dynamic Link Library

(continues)

Tip
You don't have to memorize all the file-naming conventions. The documentation supplied with your program describes the file-naming conventions used by that program.

Table 5.2 Continued

Extension	Common Use
DOC	Document file (used by many word processors)
DOT	Word for Windows template file
DRV	Program device driver file
DTA	Data file
EPS	Encapsulated PostScript file
EXE	Executable program file
FNT	Font file
GIF	Graphics Interchange Format file (CompuServe)
GRP	Windows Program Group
H	A header file for a C program
HLP	Help file
IDX	Index file (Q&A)
IMG	GEM image (graphics) file
INF	Information file
INI	Initialization files (Windows and other programs)
LET	Letter
LHA	Compressed file (LHARC)
LIB	Program library file
LOG	File logging actions
LST	Listing of a program (in a file)
MAK	A programmer's make file
MAP	Linker map file
MSG	Program message file
NDX	Index file (dBASE)
OBJ	Intermediate object code (program) file
OLD	Backup file

Extension	Common Use
OVL	Program overlay file
OVR	Program overlay file
PAK	Packed (archive) file
PAS	Pascal source file
PCX	Picture file for PC Paintbrush
PIF	Program Information File (TopView/Windows)
PM4	PageMaker 4 data file
PM5	PageMaker 5 data file
PRN	Program listing for printing
PRO	Profile (configuration file)
PS	PostScript program file
RFT	Revisable Form Text (Document Content Architecture)
RPT	A report file
RTF	Rich Text Format, a Microsoft document exchange format
SAM	Ami-Pro document
SAV	Backup file
STY	Style sheet (Ventura Publisher, Microsoft Word)
SYS	System or device driver file
TIF	Picture file in Tagged Image File Format (TIFF)
TMP	Temporary file
TST	Test file
TXT	Text file
WK1	Worksheet file (Lotus 1-2-3 Release 2)
WK2	Quattro Pro 5.0 spreadsheet file
WK3	Worksheet file (Lotus 1-2-3 Release 3)
WKQ	Quattro spreadsheet file

(continues)

Table 5.2 Continued

Extension	Common Use
WKS	Worksheet file (Lotus 1-2-3, Releases 1 and 1A)
WQ1	Quattro Pro spreadsheet file
XLM	Excel macro file
XLS	Excel spreadsheet file
ZIP	Compressed file (PKZIP)

Avoiding Bad File Names

When you enter a file name in a command, DOS may not simply reject a bad file name; in certain cases, DOS takes some unusual actions. The following example uses the COPY command to show what can happen:

```
COPY TEST.TXT 123456789.1234
```

Notice that both the file name and the extension given for the destination file name contain an extra character: the file name has the extra character *9*, and the extension has the extra character *4*. You might predict that DOS will issue a message warning that the file name and extension are too long. No such luck! DOS simply truncates the file name to eight characters and the extension to three characters to create a legal file name (12345678.123), and then it completes the COPY operation.

Illegal characters in a file name can prevent DOS from carrying out a command. For example:

```
COPY 12345678.123 1[3.123
```

This command causes DOS to display the following message:

```
File creation error
```

Few experienced DOS users purposely use illegal characters in a file name, but typos easily can creep into your DOS commands and introduce illegal characters into file name parameters. Type commands carefully, remembering that DOS's reaction to an illegal file name isn't always predictable.

Understanding File Attributes

As you will learn later in this chapter, DOS tracks each file on a disk through a *directory entry*. This entry maintains critical information about the file and where it is stored on disk. One of the pieces of information maintained in the directory entry is called the *file attribute field*. This one-byte field stores a number of characteristics about each file but is not displayed in a normal directory listing. Each characteristic stored in the file attribute field is called a *file attribute*, and each file can have more than one file attribute. Each file attribute is represented in the attribute byte by a single bit, often called an *attribute bit*. Table 5.3 lists the attributes and their purposes in DOS. You can view and modify most attribute bits by using the ATTRIB command; DOS manages some attribute bits directly.

Table 5.3 File Attributes and Their Meanings

Attribute Bit	Meaning
Archive	When DOS writes to a file, it sets the Archive attribute on. Some DOS commands such as MSBACKUP and XCOPY remove this attribute from files. Files having the Archive attribute have been altered or created since the last time they were archived.
Hidden	This file is bypassed by most DOS file-management commands and does not appear in a directory listing. Hidden files, however, are listed by the DOS Shell in the file list area.
Read-only	This file can be accessed for information but cannot be erased or modified. (Note that you can erase a read-only file by using the DOS Shell.)
Subdirectory	This attribute identifies the entry as a directory rather than a standard file.
System	This file is a DOS system file.
Volume label	This entry is the volume label for a disk. The entry does not identify an actual file.

The Archive attribute works with DOS file-management commands to determine which files the commands process. The MSBACKUP command resets the Archive attribute of any file it copies to disk. As you work with the files on your disk, each file on which DOS performs a write operation gets flagged with the Archive attribute, which signals that the file has changed since it was last archived. If you have a recent full-disk backup, you can create a backup of only the files that have changed since the last backup by telling MSBACKUP that you want to copy only files having the Archive attribute.

A file entry with the Hidden attribute turned on is "invisible" to most DOS file-management commands. Hidden files have file names and extensions like normal user files but are not processed by the DIR and COPY commands. The two DOS system files on the boot disk are examples, as are the files that manage a DoubleSpace drive.

You can detect the presence of hidden files using the ATTRIB or CHKDSK command. Using ATTRIB, you also can list hidden files. CHKDSK merely indicates the number of hidden files on the disk.

The Subdirectory attribute indicates to DOS that the entry is not intended for a user file but for an additional directory called a subdirectory. When it carries out file-management commands, DOS knows to bypass a file with the Subdirectory attribute turned on.

The System attribute indicates that a file is an operating system file. The two DOS system files have this attribute in addition to the Hidden attribute. You need not worry about the System attribute; it does not affect your DOS work.

The Volume Label attribute indicates that the directory entry involved is to be used as the name of the volume, not as a file name. DOS then combines the file name and extension fields to provide an 11-character volume label for the disk. Only a volume label entry can have this attribute set (turned on).

The Archive, Hidden, Read-only, and System attributes are the only attributes you can change directly through DOS. DOS controls the other attributes without your intervention.

Changing File Attributes with the ATTRIB Command. DOS's ATTRIB command provides the means to change the settings of the Archive, Read-only, Hidden, and System attributes. The syntax of the ATTRIB command is

```
ATTRIB [+R¦-R] [+A¦-A] [+S¦-S] [+H¦-H] filespec [/S]
```

If you issue the ATTRIB command with no parameters, you get a list of all the files in the current directory, along with a showing of their attribute status. Figure 5.2 shows a typical result.

As you can see in the figure, all the files have the Archive attribute set on. Also, all the files beginning with the letters R and G are marked as Read-only.

To change the attributes of files, use the first letter of each attribute's name and a plus (+) sign to set the attributes on or a minus (–) sign to set the attributes off. You can have any logical combination on one command line. For example:

```
ATTRIB -A +R
```

The preceding example turns off the Archive attribute and turns on the Read-only attribute for every file in the current directory. You can narrow the scope of the ATTRIB command by specifying a path name expression (drive, path, and wildcards are honored) on the command line. For example:

```
ATTRIB -R G*.*
```

This example removes the Read-only attribute from only those files whose names begin with G. (You get a heavy dose of path name expressions later in this chapter.)

```
H:\TEST>ATTRIB
  A          H:\TEST\CONFIG.MEM
  A          H:\TEST\FM_LETS.DBF
  A          H:\TEST\FM_LETS.DBT
  A    R     H:\TEST\GROUND.DBF
  A    R     H:\TEST\GROUP.DBF
  A    R     H:\TEST\GUEST.DBF
  A    R     H:\TEST\GUEST.LBL
  A          H:\TEST\HOTEL.DBF
  A          H:\TEST\HOT_COMM.DBF
  A          H:\TEST\LIST.DBF
  A          H:\TEST\PASSW.DBF
  A          H:\TEST\PAYMTS.DBF
  A          H:\TEST\PAY_VEND.DBF
  A    R     H:\TEST\RES_AIR.DBF
  A    R     H:\TEST\RES_CAR.DBF
  A    R     H:\TEST\RES_GROU.DBF
  A    R     H:\TEST\RES_HOT.DBF
  A    R     H:\TEST\RES_TOUR.DBF
  A          H:\TEST\SEMI_4.DBF
  A          H:\TEST\TOUR.DBF
  A          H:\TEST\TRANS.MEM

H:\TEST>
```

Fig. 5.2
The ATTRIB display when no parameters are given.

You also can widen the scope of the ATTRIB command by using the /S switch. If you give ATTRIB a path name expression as a parameter, by default the actions are limited only to the specified path. Giving no path name expression to ATTRIB limits its action to the currently logged directory. Using the /S switch widens the scope of the ATTRIB command to include any directories under the directory where ATTRIB begins its actions.

Establishing Read-Only Files. The ATTRIB command gives you control over file attributes. In particular, the Read-only attribute makes DOS unable to overwrite a file. DOS commands such as EDIT, COPY, DEL, and XCOPY are capable of changing the data contained in a file. Files with the Read-only attribute cause a message to appear, telling you that the command you have tried to use cannot provide the service you are wanting.

In practice, however, the Read-only attribute has become little more than a confirmation flag to many modern programs. Both the DOS Shell and the Windows File Manager can erase files having the Read-only attribute, for example, but only after you confirm that it is okay.

For Related Information

- "Using Wildcards in DOS Commands," p. 63
- "Analyzing a Disk with CHKDSK," p. 192

To give files the Read-only attribute, use the +R parameter, as in the following:

```
ATTRIB +R F:\WSTAR\*.TXT
```

Using the –R parameter has exactly the opposite effect, that of removing the Read-only flag.

Caution

The FDISK and FORMAT commands do not observe the read-only status of a file. FDISK and FORMAT are disk-level commands; therefore, they don't look at disk directories when they are doing their jobs. Don't rely on the Read-only attribute of a file to protect the file from a disk-level command. Use the disk's write-protect tab to prevent floppies from being destroyed with FDISK and FORMAT.

Understanding the Role of Directories

To this point in the chapter, you have read many references to the directory. These references, while necessary for the explanations of files at the time, did not provide a great deal of information about directories. Now that you know all about files, however, it is time to turn your attention to the method used by DOS to organize files—directories.

In many homes, flatware is stored in a drawer in the kitchen. In some homes, the forks and knives and spoons are laid in a jumble, all mixed up. In other homes, a plastic tray that has compartments for each type of utensil is used. Forks stay with forks, salad forks have their own compartment, and so on. The capacity of the drawer to store flatware is not affected, but the drawer stays more organized. So it is with directories. DOS directories have the same purpose: they keep your files organized.

The *root directory* is an important table created by the FORMAT command on every disk it touches. It is called the root directory because it is the root, or beginning, of the disk's file system. DOS uses the directory as a kind of index system for finding files. The file names and subdirectory names in this index system are called *directory entries*. DOS allows for a fixed number of directory entries in the root directory. This number is the same for disks with the same format but varies with different formats. Disks with larger capacities allow for more root directory entries. Although limited, the number of entries is generous. If you properly organize your disks, you will never even come close to this limit.

The DIR command is a window into the structure of a DOS directory. The DIR command accesses and displays selected parts of directory entries, as in this example:

```
C:\>dir ??.bat

 Volume in drive C is DATA-TRAIN
 Volume Serial Number is 1A9A-BEDA
 Directory of C:\

D4        BAT        39 09-18-90  12:51a
EE        BAT        34 04-23-92   4:05p
G         BAT        31 05-03-92   3:35a
HJ        BAT        28 12-10-92   6:34p
SK        BAT        26 08-27-90   3:23p
T         BAT        53 06-04-92   1:01a
W         BAT       128 05-25-92  10:49a
WP        BAT        16 08-27-91   3:46a
WS        BAT        35 12-05-90   2:40p
DP        BAT        37 09-06-91  10:37a
       10 file(s)        427 bytes
                 16,437,248 bytes free

C:\>
```

As you can see, DIR lists the file names, extensions, the number of bytes in the file, the date it was last written to disk, and the time of the last write. The DIR command, however, does not display all the elements of a directory entry. Table 5.4 lists the components of a directory entry.

Table 5.4 The Main Features of DOS Directories

Feature	Example	What Is Stored
File name	THANKYOU	Eight-character file prefix
File name extension	DOC	Three-character file suffix

(continues)

Table 5.4 Continued

Feature	Example	What Is Stored
File attributes	R (read-only)	Special status information about this file used by DOS
Time	10:22	The time of creation or last modification
Date	11-14-91	The date of creation or last modification
Starting cluster	576	The number of the first cluster allocated to this file by DOS in the FAT
File size	1024 bytes	The number of bytes in this file

You undoubtedly recognize the file name, extension, time, and date components of a directory entry as the ones displayed by the DIR command. DIR also displays the file size. These components, or fields, of a directory entry contain information useful to you as well as to DOS (see fig. 5.3). DIR displays this information to assist your file-management activities.

Fig. 5.3
The fields of a directory entry.

File Name	Extension	Attributes	Reserved	Time	Date	Starting Cluster	Size

Note

DOS also stores volume labels in directory entries, using the combined file name and extension fields to form an 11-byte (11-character) field just like a file name. DOS knows that the directory entry is a volume label—not a file name—because the volume label attribute for the entry is set.

The starting cluster and file attribute fields, shown in table 5.4 and in figure 5.3, are not included in the DIR command's displayed output. The starting cluster field contains the cluster number of the first cluster DOS has allocated for a particular file's storage.

Chaining through a File

The starting cluster field of a file's directory entry is the key to the file's storage allocation as tracked in the FAT. You recall that DOS creates a FAT for each disk during formatting. The FAT indicates whether each cluster on the disk is allocated to a file. Much as a restaurant hostess looks at a table chart for a place to seat you, DOS looks at the FAT for available clusters when a file is created or enlarged. When you arrive early at a restaurant, it is nearly empty, and the hostess seats you in the general vicinity of other guests, leaving other sections of the restaurant unused. When DOS allocates files on a freshly formatted disk, DOS uses the first cluster and sequences through a connected series of clusters, leaving many clusters unused at the end of the FAT. When you leave the restaurant, the hostess marks your table as being available. Likewise, when you erase or shorten a file, DOS marks the released clusters in the FAT as being available to store another file.

You may have had a dining experience in which the hostess did not have enough adjacent tables to seat your entire party. Your group is fragmented across two or more tables, with other parties seated at tables between the parts of your group. Your group is fragmented, but you can remain connected as a group by telling the waiter, "We're with those people over there," as you point to the other table.

When a DOS command or applications program asks DOS to store a file on the disk, DOS checks the FAT, finds the next available cluster, and stores a portion of the file there. If that cluster cannot accommodate the entire file, DOS finds the next available cluster and stores part of the file there. DOS does not look for the largest available block of clusters, so the entire file may not fit in the first group of available clusters. As with the large party in the restaurant, your file becomes fragmented across the disk.

In Chapter 19, "Getting the Most from Your Hard Drive," you learn more about fragmentation. There you also learn how you can correct this condition and improve your disk performance.

Expanding the File System through Subdirectories

Earlier in this chapter, disk directories were likened to the plastic trays that many households use to organize eating utensils. The metaphor is not outlandish. This plastic tray separates like utensils to make them easier to find, takes up very little room, and generally simplifies the storage of forks, spoons, knives, and so on. The DOS directory structure simplifies the storage of program and data files and makes them easier to find when needed.

When you use FORMAT to prepare a disk, it creates a root directory structure. The number of entries that this directory can contain is limited. On most floppy disk formats, the number of entries is limited to 512. On hard disks, the capacity is proportional to the size of the volume (logical disk) being created. There is very little chance that you will ever exceed the capacity, unless you try to store all the files on your hard disk in the root directory.

Imagine what chaos might reign if all your files were lumped together in one single directory. You would never be able to tell what files belonged with what program. Your data files from your word processor would all be scrambled up with files created by other programs, and every time you wanted to locate a file, the directory listing would go on for screen after screen.

To avoid these problems, DOS employs a method of creating *subdirectories* that branch off from the root directory. Subdirectories can in turn branch off into subordinate subdirectories. Figure 5.4 shows part of the display generated by the TREE command, which is used to represent the directory of a disk graphically.

Figure 5.4 shows the directory structure of a working disk drive. At the top of the tree, the E: represents the root directory. The vertical line that aligns with the E: shows the first level of directories, those that appear in the root directory. Two subdirectories, BRIEF and CLIPPER5, branch off from the root. The BRIEF directory in turn branches off four times to create four subdirectories to hold files associated with Brief, a programmer's editor. One of these subordinate directories contains Help files, another contains macro files, and so on. If you want to find a file containing a Brief macro, you use the DIR file to generate a listing, as in the following:

```
DIR E:\BRIEF\MACROS
```

It is unlikely that a Brief macro can work its way into the CLIPPER5\LIB directory, so you can see that creating and maintaining directories enables you to pinpoint easily the files you need to work with. In Chapter 14, "Controlling Devices," you learn about the FIND command, which helps track down files that are not stored where you think they should be stored.

A good general system for creating directory structures is to have each application you install on your hard disk be contained within its own directory. The directory should have a name that tells you immediately what program resides in the directory. A good name for a WordPerfect directory is WP, for instance.

```
Directory PATH listing for Volume MAXTOR_E
Volume Serial Number is 07FF-1544
E:.
├───BRIEF
│   ├───BRIEF
│   ├───DBRIEF
│   ├───HELP
│   └───MACROS
├───CLIPPER5
│   ├───BIN
│   │   └───BACKUP
│   ├───INCLUDE
│   │   └───BACKUP
│   ├───LIB
│   │   └───BACKUP
│   ├───OBJ
│   ├───PLL
│   ├───SOURCE
│   │   ├───DBU
│   │   ├───PE
│   │   ├───RL
│   │   ├───SAMPLE
│   │   └───SYS
│   ├───TILEY
│   │   └───STUFF
│   └───TBLUIZ
│       ├───ARRAYS
│       ├───DATABASE
│       ├───GENERAL
│       ├───GUIDE
│       ├───INCLUDE
│       ├───LIB
│       ├───MAKE
│       ├───NET
│       ├───SKIPDBF
│       ├───SPRDSHT
│       └───TEXT
```

Fig. 5.4
Directories are used to organize the files on a disk.

Installation programs for software applications often install files into directory structures created during installation. The Clipper programming language automatically creates a directory called CLIPPER5 and then places library, object, and binary files into subdirectories called LIB, OBJ, and BIN. It also creates other directories, but you get the idea.

Files associated with the main application can be made to reside in subdirectories that hold groups of files of the same types. The Clipper installation routine puts all the library files into the LIB directory. If later you create or buy other libraries from another source, you can copy them into the library directory, or you can create a directory that branches off the LIB directory to hold these files. You should do whatever makes them easiest for you and your software to find them.

Understanding Path Name Expressions

A *path name expression* indicates the path that DOS must traverse to find a specified file, or group of files. A path name expression has three components: drive, directories, and files.

The drive component identifies the disk drive used to store the files. The drive component is made up of three characters: the drive letter, followed by a colon (:) and a backslash (\). For example:

```
C:\
```

DOS uses the backslash character to separate the directories within a path name expression. The preceding example is a path name expression that indicates the root directory of drive C because the backslash immediately follows the colon.

The directory component of the path name expression is a list of all the directories that must be traversed to get to the last named directory or the file component. For example:

```
C:\WINDOWS\SYSTEM\GAMES
```

In this example, the path name expression tells DOS to look for files by starting at the root directory of C:, moving into the WINDOWS directory, through the SYSTEM directory that branches from the WINDOWS directory, and then into the GAMES directory. Simply stated, a path name expression gives DOS directions to directories, just like you might give a friend directions to your house.

The third portion of a path name expression specifies a single file explicitly, or it uses wildcards to specify a group of files. For example:

```
C:\WINDOWS\SYSTEM\GAMES\SOL.EXE
C:\DOS\*.COM
```

The first example specifies a single file in the GAMES directory, whereas the second example specifies a group of files using a wildcard. Path name expressions can use ?, *, ., and .. as valid wildcard characters.

DOS requires each file on a disk to have a unique name. For this reason, DOS considers a file's full name to be the path name expression that explicitly identifies that one file. For example:

```
C:\DOS\GO.BAT
```

is not the same as the following:

```
C:\TEMP\GO.BAT
```

Yes, two files have the name GO.BAT, but they are in different directories, so both files have a unique name.

If you issue the command

```
TYPE GO.BAT
```

which file's contents are displayed depends on what directory you are currently logged into. If you are logged into either the DOS or TEMP directories of drive C, you see the contents of the file named GO.BAT found in that directory. If you are logged into the GRAPHIC directory, you may get a `file not found` message.

The trick to using path name expressions effectively is knowing when to use the full formal path name and when to use a less specific path name expression.

People, like files, can be called either by a formal title, such as William Jefferson Clinton, President of the United States, or by a less formal form of address, such as President Bill Clinton. Mr. Clinton, Bill, and Dad are other examples of names that identify the President. Path name expressions can likewise be formal or informal.

New Directories

Newcomers to DOS often are puzzled to see directory listings that contain file names that look like periods. Many people, afraid to appear silly, never ask what the periods mean.

When you create a new directory in DOS, it adds two entries to the new directory. The name of the first entry is always . (called "dot"). The second entry is always named .. (called "dot-dot"). The dot entry in a directory refers, or points, to the directory that contains it. You can think of the dot entry as an alias for the current directory's name, analogous to the pronoun *me*. Although no DOS manual documents this fact, you also can use the dot as a wildcard character in most commands. For example:

```
DEL .
```

is the same as

```
DEL *.*
```

DOS uses the dot-dot entry to point to the parent of the current directory. This entry is an alias for the parent directory's name and is analogous to the names *Mom* or *Dad*. For example:

```
DIR ..
```

lists all the files in the current directory's parent directory. In the root directory, .. has no meaning because the root directory has no parent.

The full formal path name expression for a file expresses the location of a file or group of files explicitly without regard to the currently logged directory. This type of path name expression is sometimes called an *absolute path*. For example:

```
TYPE C:\AUTOEXEC.BAT
```

This command displays the contents of your AUTOEXEC.BAT file on-screen no matter what drive or directory is currently logged. If, however, you currently are logged into the root directory of C:, typing the C:\ portion of the path name expression becomes optional because DOS always looks for a specified file in the current directory. Therefore, the following finds the proper file if you are logged into C:\:

```
TYPE AUTOEXEC.BAT
```

This path name expression uses a *relative path* to locate the file. Specifying a relative path involves giving directions to DOS, based on its currently logged directory. For example:

```
DIR ..
DIR C:
DIR SAMPLES\*.DOC
```

Each of these three examples uses a relative path as its path name expression. The first uses .. to cause DIR to show all files in the directory from which the current directory branches out. The second example lists all files in whatever directory is currently logged on drive C. The third example lists all the .DOC files in the SAMPLES directory, which branches off from the current directory.

Path name expressions can range from the very simple to the very complex. Keep in mind two rules when you're creating directories on your system:

- DOS path name expressions cannot exceed 63 characters in length, including the implicit backslash DOS adds internally.
- Typing long strings of directory names is both a pain in the neck and an invitation to typing errors.

If you really understand the second rule, you will never have a problem with the first rule. When you're creating directory structures on hard disks, keep the depth of directories to a minimum. When you are tempted to create a path name that exceeds three directories deep, stop and think. At least half the time, you can come up with a better way to arrange directories so that you don't end up typing path name expressions that sprawl across half the screen.

As complex as path name expressions can become, most new users are surprised to find that they need only learn three simple commands to create and maintain DOS directories. The following sections provide a rundown of each command.

Creating Directories with MKDIR (MD)

DOS provides the internal MKDIR command to create directories. You can abbreviate the name of the command as MD for convenience. Because MD, make directory, is easier to remember, this form is used in this chapter. Anywhere you see a reference to the MD command, you can substitute MKDIR.

The syntax for the MD command is as follows:

```
MD d:\path\dirname
```

The command uses a path name to explicitly describe the drive and pathway to the new directory to be created. You learn more about path names in the following paragraphs. For now, consider the following line:

```
MD E:\BRIEF\MACROS\OLDMACS
```

This example creates the OLDMACS directory branching from the BRIEF\MACROS directory. Subdirectory names are just directory entries in the parent directory. For example, MACROS is just an entry in the BRIEF directory. What differentiates a subdirectory name from a file name is the Directory attribute. The starting cluster associated with the directory name is the first cluster on the disk where that directory's entries are written.

DOS naming rules allow a directory name to be up to 11 characters long. You can create a directory named STUFF.OLD, but by convention, DOS users have largely agreed to keep directory names to eight characters or less. When the DIR command lists a directory, subdirectories are marked with a <DIR> in the column where the size of a file is normally shown. Figure 5.5 illustrates how directory names are listed by DIR.

As you can see, the DIR listing shows the directory structure for the root directory of E:. It contains several entries for subdirectories as well as three text files.

When you use the MD command, follow these guidelines:

- The specified or implied parent directory of the intended directory must exist. If the JILL directory doesn't exist, MD JILL\JACK fails.
- MD cannot make more than one directory at a time.
- MD does not change the current directory to the new directory. To change to the new directory, you must use CHDIR (CD).

Fig. 5.5
Directory names are marked with <DIR> to show that they are not files.

```
E:\>dir

 Volume in drive E is MAXTOR_E
 Volume Serial Number is 07FF-1544
 Directory of E:\

BRIEF        <DIR>     03-31-92  10:09a
CLIPPER5     <DIR>     06-26-93   3:20a
FAST     TXT       809 07-30-93   1:03a
ME           <DIR>     03-10-93   4:37p
WAV          <DIR>     03-31-92  10:11a
WINWORD      <DIR>     03-31-92  10:13a
WORD         <DIR>     03-31-92  10:11a
SLOW     TXT       878 07-30-93   1:03a
MEDIUM   TXT       793 07-29-93  11:57p
        9 file(s)       2480 bytes
                  14,737,408 bytes free

E:\>
```

If, for example, your current directory is \DOS and you want to add the directory \DOS\DRIVERS, you can issue the following command:

```
MD DRIVERS
```

Notice that no backslash appears in front of the new directory name. DOS interprets this path to be a relative path, and it adds the current directory path to the path name expression on the command line.

Changing the Current Directory with CHDIR (CD)

As you work with drives and files in DOS, you can consider each directory to be a location and the path name expression of the directory to be its map. DOS keeps in memory your current location on each drive of your machine.

Use the CHDIR command to change from one directory to another. The short form of CHDIR is CD, meaning change directory. If you are in the

WINDOWS directory and you want to work in the SYSTEM directory that branches off the WINDOWS directory, you issue the following command:

```
CD SYSTEM
```

The WINDOWS\SYSTEM directory then becomes your currently logged directory. DOS remembers which directory is current for each drive in your system. When you switch to another drive, DOS automatically retains a memory of where you were working last. For example:

```
C:
CD \DOS\UTILS
F:
COPY *.BAT C:
```

In this example, you move onto drive C and change directories to the DOS\UTILS directory. The next command moves you to drive F and copies all the batch files in the current directory of F: to the current directory of C:. In this case, the files are copied to C:\DOS\UTILS.

Tip

You also can use the MOVE command in certain circumstances to create new directories. Information about MOVE is presented later in this chapter and in Chapter 9, "Managing Your Files."

Note

To change directly to the root directory of the currently logged disk from any directory on the disk, issue the following command:

```
CD \
```

Do not pass GO. Do not collect $200.

Also, if you are not sure what directory you are currently logged into, issuing the CD command with no path name expression causes DOS to display the full path name expression for the current directory.

You can use either a relative path or an absolute path to specify what directory to change into. Assume you are currently logged into C:\DOS\UTILS, for example, and issue the following command:

```
CD ..\STUFF
```

This example uses a relative path to log you into the C:\DOS\STUFF directory. You also can log into the same directory by issuing this command:

```
CD \DOS\STUFF
```

When you're using the CD command, follow these guidelines:

- The drive and path parameters in the command line must be valid.
- If the path parameter begins with \, CD assumes that the directory specified in the path is absolute—from the root.
- If the path parameter does not begin with \, CD assumes that the directory given in the path is relative to the current directory.
- When you specify a drive parameter but no path parameter, CD reports the current working directory for the specified disk.
- When you omit the path parameter and the drive parameter from the command line, CD reports the current working directory of the currently logged drive.

Deleting Directories with RMDIR (RD)

Just as you occasionally need to add a directory to a disk, you may need to delete a directory. DOS enables you to remove empty directories at the end of a directory branch in the directory tree with the RMDIR command, RD for short.

When you're working with the RD command, remember that RD can delete only empty directories. If a directory contains files or has another directory branching from it, RD fails. To delete a directory using RD, use a command similar to the following:

```
RD \COLD\HOT\WARM
```

If the WARM directory is empty, RD removes it from the directory tree.

Note

The easiest way to cause DOS to display the names of the current drive and directory is to place the following line in your AUTOEXEC.BAT file:

```
PROMPT $p$g
```

This line alters the default DOS prompt to show you the current path name expression. For more information about PROMPT, see Chapter 13, "Controlling Your Environment."

Using DELTREE to Delete Directories

The DELTREE command, new in DOS 6.0, makes the RD command obsolete. DELTREE enables you to delete directories that contain files—even complete branches of a directory tree. This command removes the directory you specify and everything in it—subdirectories, files, and files in subdirectories. In addition, attributes of files in the subdirectories are ignored. You do not need to use ATTRIB to clear attributes such as Read-only or Hidden before you delete them.

The syntax for DELTREE is as follows:

```
DELTREE /Y d:path
```

The optional *d:* parameter specifies the disk that contains the directory branch to be removed. If you omit *d:* from the command line, DOS assumes that the current (logged) disk holds the directory to be removed.

The required path name expression specifies the topmost level of the directory branch to be removed. If the path begins with a backslash (\), DOS assumes that the path to the directory name is absolute from the root. If the path parameter does not begin with a backslash, DOS assumes that the path to the directory name is relative from the current directory of *d:*.

The /Y parameter is optional. Because DELTREE is a potentially dangerous command, capable of wiping out hundreds of files at a time, DOS normally displays the following message:

```
Delete d:path and all its subdirectories? [Y/N]
```

If you type **Y** and press Enter, the command proceeds; if you type **N** and press Enter, the operation stops. If you use the /Y parameter, however, the message does not appear, and DELTREE proceeds as though you had typed **Y**.

Caution

DELTREE deletes everything in its path. As with anything in computing, a feature that gives you a great deal of power also gives you the ability to shoot yourself in the foot. Be sure you no longer need anything in any of the directories subordinate to the one you name before proceeding. To make sure, first issue the DIR command (with the /S parameter) or the TREE command, which is discussed later in this chapter.

Assume, for example, that your hard disk has a string of directories branching off from the root directory of C:. The path name expression that specifies the lowest level directory is C:\HOT\COLD\WARM\TEPID\ICY. If you issue the command

```
DELTREE /Y C:\HOT\COLD\WARM
```

all of the files and directories in the WARM directory are deleted regardless of file attributes. Any directories that may branch off from WARM, TEPID, or ICY are also deleted, along with any files they contain.

As you can see, DELTREE is a powerful command. Always double-check your command line for errors before you press Enter to activate the command.

Remember, too, that you can use wildcards in the path name expression of the command line, but use them only with caution. If a wildcard in a path name expression matches both directory names and file names, both are deleted. It is often a good idea to use the DIR command first to see what files the path name expression affects before using that path name expression with DELTREE.

Renaming Directories

Having to change the name of a directory is not uncommon. This need may arise because you misspell the name of the directory during creation or because you have upgraded software and want the upgrade to be reflected in the directory name.

The MOVE command enables you to rename directories from the command line and also moves files from one directory to another. The syntax of the MOVE command for renaming directories is as follows:

```
MOVE d:oldpath d:newpath
```

The optional *d: parameter* specifies the disk that contains the directory branch to be removed. If you omit *d:* from the command line, DOS assumes that the current (logged) disk holds the directory to be removed.

This command requires two path name expressions. The first specifies the directory you want to move and/or rename. The second path name expression specifies the new name of the target directory or the name of a directory to be created as a result of the command's actions. If the directory does not exist, MOVE prompts you to ask whether the directory should be created. Answer **Y**, and the new directory is created.

To rename a directory, use the MOVE command as in the following example:

```
MOVE C:\TEMP\BAK C:\TEMP\BACKUP
```

For Related Information

■ "Using the MOVE Command," p. 231

Helping DOS Find Files with PATH

When you issue a DOS command, COMMAND.COM, the command interpreter, looks first to see whether the command is internal to DOS. If the command is not internal, DOS looks on the disk for a file name having the same name as the command.

In this regard, both external DOS commands and other executable files have equal status. Files having the extensions .EXE, .COM, and .BAT are all considered by DOS to be executable program files. DOS simply looks for any executable file having the same name as the command line keyword. It then runs the first file it finds.

Note

The DOS search path works only with executable files. If a program uses auxiliary files such as overlays and data files, an error may occur unless the program is written to search its own directory, not just the currently logged directory.

None of DOS's external commands use auxiliary files, so you never have a "file not found" problem as long as the DOS directory is included in the search path. To run applications that use auxiliary files, you should log into the directory where the application is written to disk to ensure error-free operation.

You have three ways to make sure DOS finds an external program file. You can do any of the following:

- Log on to the disk and directory that contains the command
- Supply the path in the command line
- Establish a DOS search path to the command's directory

The PATH command places a path search string in the DOS environment. DOS uses the contents of this environment variable to determine where on the system it should look for program files.

Normally, the PATH command is included as a statement in the AUTOEXEC.BAT file, so it takes effect even before the first DOS prompt is displayed. Using the PATH command, however, is not restricted to lines in AUTOEXEC.BAT. You can type a new search string at any DOS prompt.

Whether it is in a batch file or typed at a DOS prompt, the PATH command is used the same way. For example:

```
PATH C:\;C:\DOS;D:\WINDOWS;E:\BRIEF
```

If you enter a command at the DOS prompt and COMMAND.COM does not recognize it as an internal DOS command, DOS always looks first in the currently logged directory. If the file cannot be found there, DOS uses the PATH information to first search the root directory of drive C, then the \DOS directory of C:, then the WINDOWS directory on D:, and finally the BRIEF directory on E:. Only after searching all five directories for an executable file, and not finding it, does DOS give you the dread `Bad command or file name` message.

The directories you want searched are listed on the command line separated by semicolons (;). The order in which the directories are listed is the order in which they are searched. For this reason, it is prudent to keep the DOS directory and other heavily utilized directories at the front of the search string.

In the preceding sample PATH command, DOS is directed to first look in the root directory of drive C. This directory is traditionally a favorite repository for batch files that automate the launching of applications. The second directory specified is the DOS directory. The DOS directory should always be at or near the beginning of the search path because files in this directory are constantly being called upon. Having the DOS directory at the head of the search path cuts down on the time spent searching for external DOS commands. Exceedingly long search paths can dramatically slow down your computer's response time.

The order of the search path is important for another reason as well. If two directories have executable programs with the same names, the program that is run is the one whose directory is specified closest to the beginning of the search path.

Although the maximum length of the search path is 127 characters, avoid creating long search paths. Traditionally, search paths are used mainly to allow DOS to find often-used utilities without having to change logged drives or directories. Having too many directories in the search path slows down system performance because it takes DOS longer to determine if a command is valid. Some software applications, such as Windows, require an entry in the search path for efficient operation, however. In general, if you seldom use the executable files in a directory, it is better to leave that directory out of the search path.

Listing Directories with TREE

DOS provides an external command—TREE—that lists all the directories of a disk as a tree structure similar to the DOS Shell's directory display. Figure 5.4 shows the TREE command's output. The TREE command also can list the files in the directories. TREE is especially useful when you're working with hard disks because it visually maps out the directory structures of disks.

The TREE command syntax is as follows:

```
TREE d:path  /F/A
```

d: is an optional parameter that indicates the drive whose directories you want to list. If you omit *d:*, TREE lists the directories on the current disk drive.

The *path* expression names the directory where TREE is to start processing the listing. If you omit this parameter, TREE begins processing from the root directory.

TREE accepts two switches. The /F switch instructs TREE to display the files contained within directories as part of the visual tree. The /A switch instructs TREE to use printable characters instead of the line-drawing characters normally used to indicate branching of directories. Use the /A switch when you're directing output to an older printer that cannot print graphics characters or when using a text-only video adapter.

Using a Temporary Directory

Many programs and some DOS operations use a directory as a temporary location to store scratchpad files. A *scratchpad file* is a file that is created as a buffer to store information temporarily before a permanent file is created. A good example of a program that uses temporary storage space is Windows. Windows creates .TMP files in the temporary directory to hold swapping information. Also, the Windows Print Manager uses the temporary directory to create files to hold print jobs. Other programs use temporary space as a place to store sorting information, backup copies of files being processed, and so on.

Traditionally, DOS users have created a directory called TEMP that branches off the root directory of C:. In fact, if this directory doesn't exist when you install DOS 6.2 using the Setup program, it is created for you automatically.

The SET command, which creates DOS environment variables, normally is used in AUTOEXEC.BAT to create a variable called TEMP. For example:

```
SET TEMP=C:\TEMP
```

Redirecting Your Output

Like DIR and TYPE, TREE is one of those DOS commands that can produce many pages of output. DOS offers two features to enable you to capture screen output in a more usable form.

You can use the MORE command to capture screen output from other commands and present the screens one at a time, pausing for a keystroke as each screen is displayed. MORE is unusual because you enter it on the command line of another command using the pipe (¦) symbol, which is found on the same key as the backslash on most keyboards. For example:

```
TREE /F ¦ MORE
```

The preceding command captures the output of the tree command and passes it to the MORE command. The MORE command breaks up the output into single screen portions. As each single screenful of the output is displayed, MORE waits for you to press a key before it displays the next screenful.

The problem with MORE is that you cannot go backward. Once a screenful of output has been replaced with another, the first screenful is lost. To see it again, you must repeat the command that called MORE.

You also can use the DOS redirection feature to capture long output to a file or send it directly to a printer using the output redirection symbol >. For example:

```
TREE /F >TREE.TXT
```

or

```
TREE /F >PRN
```

The first example directs the output to be saved in a file named TREE.TXT. You then can use an editor to view the output of the TREE command. If your editor has problems displaying graphic characters, use the /A switch to get readable output.

The second example directs the output of the TREE command to the printer. Make sure the printer is on-line and ready before you put the TREE command into action.

For more information on DOS's redirection features, see Chapter 14, "Controlling Devices."

When DOS or another program needs to create temporary files, it looks in the environment to see whether a TEMP variable exists. This way, you can direct DOS to use a specific directory. If you don't have a TEMP directory, most software uses the currently logged directory to create scratchpad files. You should always make sure that the TEMP directory resides on a disk with plenty of free space. Lack of scratchpad space can make programs run much slower than normal or display an error message.

Caution

Most programs that create scratch files do a good job of cleaning up after themselves by deleting any files they may create when the files are no longer needed.

It is a good idea to check the TEMP directory every few days just to make sure that no scratchpad files have been orphaned by a power failure or untimely reboot. If you find files in the TEMP directory, you should delete them.

Be careful, however, not to delete files in the TEMP directory while you're running Windows or when you're shelled out to a DOS session from within a running application. Under these circumstances, the files still may be active and in use. Never delete files from the TEMP directory unless you are at a DOS prompt with no other programs running.

For Related Information

■ "Using a RAM Disk," p. 498

Summary

In this chapter, you learned about DOS file requirements and directories. Following are the key points covered in this chapter:

- DOS organizes files into a file system that DOS manages.
- Disks are the main storage medium for DOS-based PCs.
- Files are the storage units of disks.
- File names consist of name portions (up to eight characters to the left of the period) and extensions (up to three characters to the right of the period).
- File name characters must be "legal" to DOS.
- DOS tracks file names in a disk directory. Each file name in a directory must be unique.
- By convention, certain file names refer to specific types of files. You can override file-naming conventions, but observing these conventions makes file names more meaningful.

- DOS uses one of its standard devices when you use a file name that contains the device name. Avoid using the names PRN, CON, NUL, LPT, and COM in file names.
- Directories organize files and are a primary management tool you can use to make your work productive.
- The primary commands for working with directories are MD (create a directory), CD (change to a directory), and RD (remove a directory).
- You can rename a directory by using the MOVE command.
- A path is a unique address that identifies where a file is located. The path is composed of all the directories that must be traversed to reach a given file.
- The PATH command can help you access commonly used programs.
- The TREE command helps you get a better picture of your directory structure.

Indeed, you have learned quite a bit of information in this chapter. This information is essential, however, to a complete understanding of how DOS works. In the next chapter, you learn about the physical disks and disk drives that hold your files and directories.

Chapter 6

Understanding Disks and Disk Drives

In Chapter 5, "Understanding Files and Directories," you learned about the basis of the DOS system—files and directories. This chapter takes you deeper into DOS to learn about the underlying concepts that permit DOS to store your files. Here you learn about different types of disks and drives.

Early computer hobbyists used everything from discarded paper tape drives to cassette tapes to store files. For a while, Radio Shack sold cassette tapes that didn't have the normal plastic leader at the head of the tape so that computer users didn't have to wind tapes past the leader by hand.

Fortunately, the fastest advances in computer science have revolved around memory and storage. The original IBM PC had two single-sided 5 1/4-inch (160K) floppy disk drives, period. Hard drives weren't supported by the IBM PC BIOS until the 10M hard disk became the standard in the early XTs.

Floppy disks have evolved to a point where four standard sizes are in common use. A fifth size—Extra High Density—is available, but few manufacturers support it yet. You learn more about these sizes later in this chapter.

Hard disks have changed the most. A number of technology standards have come and gone as hard disks have steadily gotten larger and faster. Drives capable of storing more than two gigabytes (two billion bytes) now cost less than $2,500.

CD-ROM drives, which can hold more than 900M of data, are becoming commonplace as the price drops on both the hardware and diskware. The major weakness of current CDs, however, is their read-only capability. CDs will remain a publisher's medium. Optical read/write drives, while available, have yet to become common due to costs and competing technologies. Within the next few years, however, drives that will both read CD formats and read and write optical formats will begin to become available and affordable.

For the time being, at least, magnetic media is king. Magnetic media comes in two basic flavors: floppy and hard. The following sections of this chapter give you the technical background on how disks work.

Although this material doesn't make using the COPY or FORMAT commands any more or less effective, knowing this information can save your data. Magnetic disks, like all humans, are mortal; they sometimes suddenly drop dead. Usually, users make mistakes that wreck disks, but sometimes disks just give up the ghost unexpectedly or get trapped in a lightning zap. Disks generally are prone to hazard. This problem is, of course, why backups are so important. Highly specialized disk-editing software such as Norton Disk Doctor and others of its ilk can help you to revive and resurrect lost data, but only if you know how disks are formatted and how data is stored.

Understanding the Disk's Magnetic Storage Technique

Almost everyone is familiar with the way audio tape recorders work. Because tape recorders and computer disks use similar technologies, take a moment to review the form of the technology you are probably most familiar with.

In a cassette tape, a long thin ribbon of plastic is coated with an emulsion of ferrous oxides (magnetic coatings), enclosed in a protective plastic case, and passed through a tape transport. The transport mechanism pulls the ribbon of tape through at a controlled speed and brings the tape into contact with three magnetic tape heads.

Most tape recorders use an erase head, a record head, and a playback head. On some inexpensive tape recorders, a single head is used for both playback and recording. This setup doesn't, by itself, lower sound quality; it means only that you can't listen to the tape as it is recorded.

When you're recording a tape, the erase head randomizes the magnetic particles in the oxide emulsion, effectively erasing any previously stored information (sound).

The stereo record head actually has two heads, one for the left channel and one for the right. Sounds are converted into electrical fields. As the tape passes across the record head, it passes through these fields, and the random magnetic particles align into replicas of the field through which it passes.

When the tape passes over the playback head, the magnetic patterns on the tape are picked up much like a microphone's diaphragm picks up sound waves. The magnetic images create electrical fields that then can be turned back into sound waves with a speaker.

A standard stereo cassette tape has four tracks of sound information, two in each playback direction. The ribbon of tape has four discrete stripes of magnetic information.

Now imagine that you make a cassette tape several inches in width. Cut circular discs out of the tape, enclose them in a plastic casing, and build a machine that locks onto the center of the disc and rotates it like a potter's wheel. To the machine, add a magnetic tape head mounted on an arm that can float over the surface of the disc. As the magnetic disc rotates, the head can be positioned to create magnetic stripes in concentric rings just like the rings in a tree trunk, only symmetrical and evenly spaced.

Voilà! You have just invented the *floppy disk*!

Understanding Disk Drives

Actually, you have a few steps to complete before you have a *floppy disk drive*. First, discard the record head. Because all you are recording are the ones and zeros of binary numbers (the bits in a byte), you simply can record over previously recorded information. Because there are only two possible signals, not varying shades of musical nuance, when you write a one or a zero, it effectively overwrites the previous character. You need only a single read/write head for each side of the disk, so your floppy disk needs two head assembly units to be double sided.

You also need to record a formatting track to parallel or interweave with the data tracks so that a computer can say, "Record this group of bytes in this location, and then read the bytes on that other location." Provide internal programming on a ROM chip so that DOS needs to send instructions only to the disk drive to read and write data from any location at any time. Oh, yes, and hide all this complexity from computer users. Now you have invented the usable floppy disk!

Take one step further. Coat a stack of ceramic or metal disks with a much denser magnetic material, mount them on a spindle, and spin them much faster than before. Then mount multiple high-density read/write heads, one for each platter side. Beef up the response times and speeds for all the moving components. Seal all these components into a dust free can, and now you have invented the *hard disk*, also called a *fixed disk* because the platters cannot be removed without the user damaging them.

The mechanical parts and electrical circuits of disk drives are complex. Although a disk drive is part of a PC system, the drive is a machine in its own right. DOS relies on the driver programs of the BIOS (Basic Input Output System found on ROMs inside your computer) and on ROMs within the drive to handle the low-level control of the drive's mechanical components.

All disk drives have certain common components: read/write heads, head-positioner mechanisms, and disk-spinning motors. All disk drives record on disks. Some disks are removable; some are built into the drive. Both fixed disks and removable disks spin on a center spindle within the disk drive.

Today, most PCs incorporate both fixed disks and removable disks. The BIOS extensions of DOS make provisions for both types of drives. Even with their common features, fixed and floppy disk drives have some important differences, which the following sections describe. Knowing these distinctions helps you understand how each type of drive operates in your system.

Hard Disk Drives

Drives with built-in disks are called *fixed disk drives* or, because their disks are made of rigid material, *hard disk drives*. You can shorten these terms to fixed disk and hard disk.

A hard disk drive can contain more than one hard disk, or *platter*. Multiple platters are arranged in a stack, with space between the individual platters. Hard disk drives have great storage capacity; these drives can hold anywhere from a few million to a few billion bytes of data.

Figure 6.1 shows a cutaway view of a typical older hard disk. The platters are the drive's magnetic disks. A head-positioner arm holds the read/write heads above and below each surface of each platter. When the drive leaves the factory, the components are not exposed, as they are in this figure; the drive is sealed to keep dust, hair, dirt, smoke, and other contaminants out of the delicate mechanical parts.

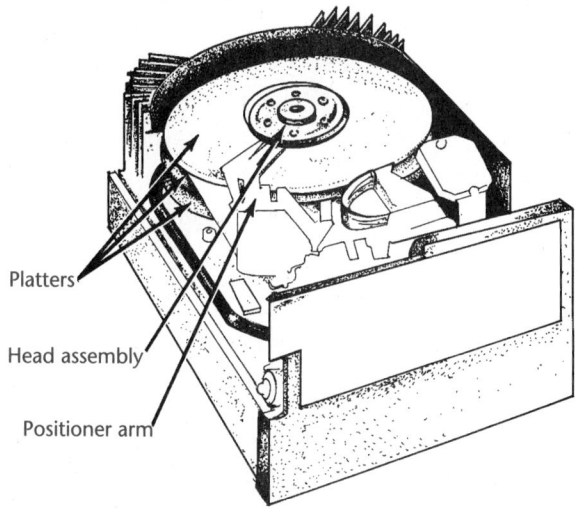

Fig. 6.1
An inside view of the main components of a hard disk.

These parts are delicate because the read/write heads must float very close to the surface of the platter without actually touching them. A single hair on the surface produces a reaction similar to driving the family car over a fallen tree trunk.

Hard disks have the advantages of quick operation, high reliability, and large storage capacity. Hard disks have the disadvantage of tying the data stored on the disk to the PC in which the drive is installed. Because the hard disk's platters cannot be removed, the data is tied to the drive. Moving an entire hard disk to another computer simply to use the hard disk's data is impractical.

One way of sharing files among many computers is to run wire or fiber optical cables between machines and let a single computer offer file services for all the connected workstations. In this idea, you find the genesis of computer networking.

Floppy Disk Drives

In a PC system, the disadvantage of tying data to the hard disk is counterbalanced by the PC's floppy disk drive. Floppy disks are protected by a permanent jacket, which encloses the flexible disk. The flexible disk inside the jacket is made of Mylar and is coated with sensitive magnetic film.

The first floppy disks were 8 inches in diameter. By today's standards, the early 8-inch floppy disks didn't store much data.

A smaller version of the 8-inch floppy—the 5 1/4-inch minifloppy—quickly became the floppy of choice for PC designers because of its smaller size. The 3 1/2-inch microfloppy is yet another departure from its larger, older cousins because it incorporates a rigid plastic case (its jacket) as a protective cover. The 3 1/2-inch-diameter Mylar disk inside the microfloppy disk is flexible, like the media in 8-inch and 5 1/4-inch floppies.

Not surprisingly, given the history of computer development, each new generation of floppy has gotten smaller in physical size. What does surprise many new users is that the physically smaller disks each have greater storage capacity than their larger ancestors. If some hardware manufacturers have their way, a very high capacity 2-inch floppy disk is in your future.

The original IBM PCs used a single-sided 5 1/4-inch floppy disk that stored only 160K of data. Later drive mechanisms in both PCs, XTs, and their clones added a second read/write head assembly to access the other side, and the double-sided, double-density 5 1/4-inch floppy disk that could store 360K was born. Available advances in drive technology enabled IBM to introduce the double-sided, high-density 5 1/4-inch floppy with the AT generation of computers. These new disks could store 1.2M, almost quadruple the storage of the double-sided variety.

Modern 5 1/4-inch drives almost universally support the high-density disks. The cost of the double-density disk is about half the cost of the high-density disk, so many people continue to use the lower cost disks when distributing smaller amounts of data. High-density drives easily read and write double-density disks, but double-sided drives do not support high-density disks. Figure 6.2 shows both vertical and horizontal mounting of the typical 5 1/4-inch floppy drive.

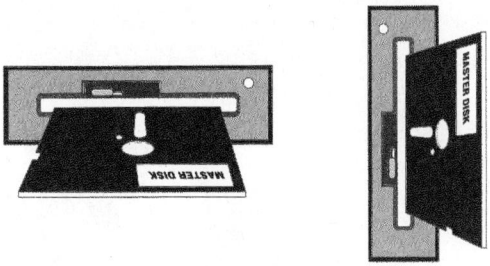

Fig. 6.2
When you're inserting 5 1/4-inch disks, the label should be towards the drive's closing mechanism.

When IBM introduced the PS/2 computer models, it used a disk drive type that had been pioneered on the Apple Macintosh. A 3 1/2-inch floppy disk capable of storing 720K of data was the standard drive on early PS/2s. Because 720K was a step down from the 1.2M available on 5 1/4-inch disks, development of a 3 1/2-inch high-density format was accelerated. Most of today's 3 1/2-inch drives are high density, but like their 5 1/4-inch cousins they also can read and write double-density disks. Figure 6.3 shows the 3 1/2-inch disk drive.

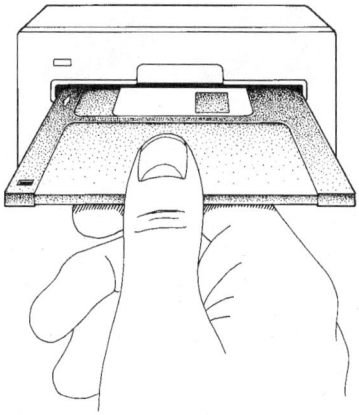

Fig. 6.3
You should insert the metal shutter on a 3 1/2-inch disk first.

You easily can tell just by comparing 3 1/2-inch disks with 5 1/4-inch disks that you cannot insert them into the other's drive. You cannot tell just by looking, however, whether a given drive is double density or high density. Only trying to read high-density disks tells you that information.

Write-Protecting a Floppy Disk

You often store data on floppy disks that should not be erased. To ensure that the files on a floppy disk do not get erased accidentally, write-protect the disk.

To write-protect a 3 1/2-inch disk, locate the plastic write-protect shutter and slide it so that the window is open (see fig. 6.4). To write-protect a 5 1/4-inch floppy disk, locate the write-protect notch and cover the notch with a write-protect tab so that the notch is covered (see fig. 6.5).

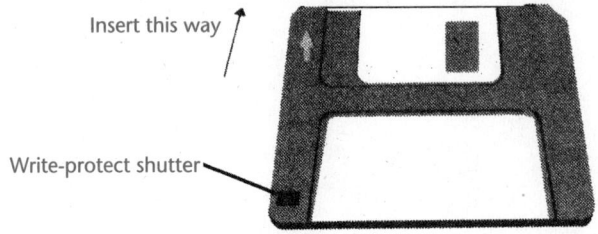

Fig. 6.4
A 3 1/2-inch floppy disk showing a built-in write-protect shutter.

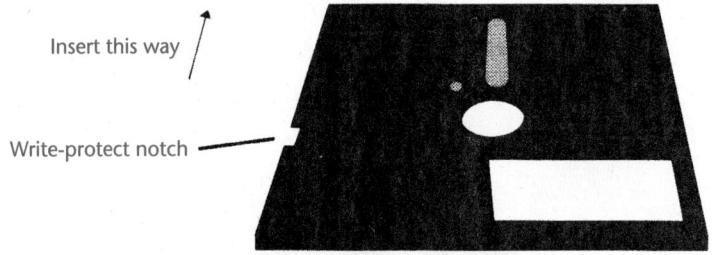

Fig. 6.5
A 5 1/4-inch disk showing a write-protect notch.

Note

Most packages of 5 1/4-inch disks contain both labels for marking the contents of the disk and a sheet of write-protect tabs. If these write-protect tabs are misplaced, you can improvise a write-protect tab with a piece of masking tape or some other opaque tape. Just make sure that the heat generated inside a computer does not cause your improvised write-protect tab to peel off and get stuck inside the drive.

When a disk is write-protected, the drive cannot write new information on the disk even if you inadvertently issue a command that attempts to write data to the disk.

Understanding the Dynamics of the Disk Drive

Thus far, the discussion of the mechanics of magnetic disk technology has centered on the physical. The following sections of this chapter introduce you to the logical aspects of how drives are constructed and used.

Disk Drive Heads

The read/write heads used in magnetic disk drives bear little resemblance to the heads in a tape recorder because they must be mounted in such a way that they can cover the entire radius of a disk. Figure 6.6 shows the hardware for read/write heads.

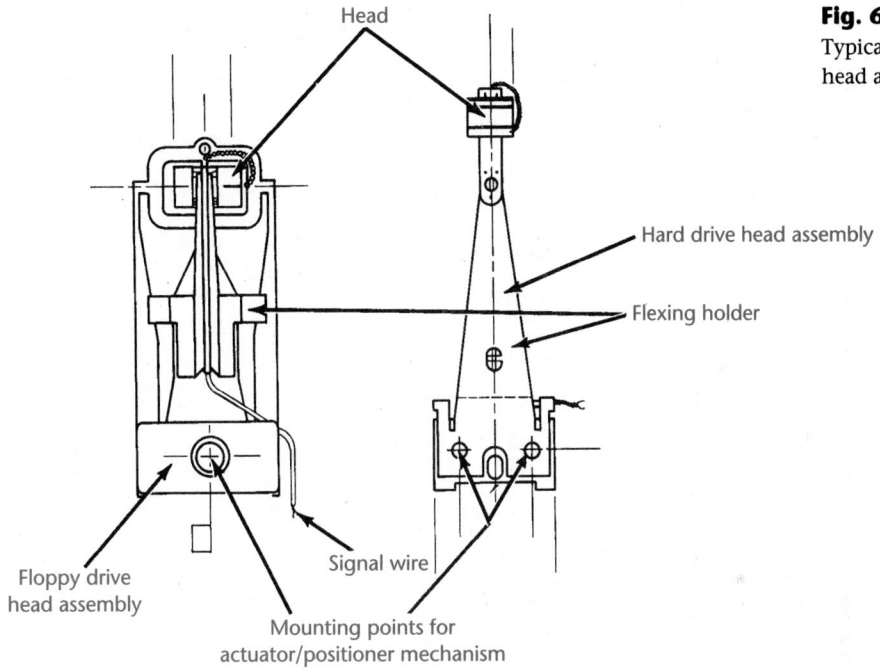

Fig. 6.6
Typical disk drive head assemblies.

As you can see, the heads are held in place on flexible metal assemblies. A set of wires carrying electrical signals connect to a flexible ribbon cable. The ribbon cable absorbs wire movements when the head assembly moves back and forth from track to track.

Disk Tracks

Regardless of the type of disk drive, all disks spin on a center axis just like a CD spins in your stereo system. A floppy disk spins at 360 revolutions per minute; the rotational speed of a hard disk is 10 times greater (approximately 3,600 rpm). The heads, which are positioned above the spinning surface of the disk, are held and moved in distinct steps by an actuator arm and head positioner.

The actuator arm and positioner move the heads over the tracks, thin stripes of magnetically recorded information. Magnetic disk tracks are concentric circles, not a spiraling groove. Each track is broken up into areas called *sectors*. As you can see by the illustration in figure 6.7, sectors are all the same size physically. At the inside track, the sectors are very close together, but at the outermost track the edges of the sectors are spaced farther apart.

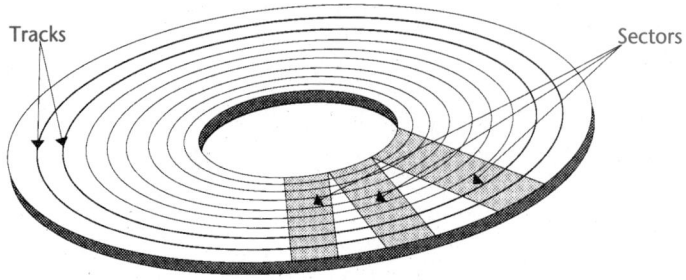

Fig. 6.7
Concentric tracks on a disk's surface; each track is segmented into areas called sectors.

Disk Cylinders

A disk drive's multiple heads are affixed to a single positioner mechanism, which can move only in a straight line. When one head moves one track in or out on its side of a platter (or floppy), the other heads all move one track on their respective sides of their respective platters.

If the disk has more than one platter, and most hard disks do, all the heads are positioned on the same track on each of the platters. This alignment of heads on the same track position on different sides of the platters is called a *cylinder* (see fig. 6.8), a term derived from the imaginary shape of the stacked circular tracks at any one stopping point of the positioner mechanism.

On most drives, only one head can be active at one time; the drive must activate all its heads in sequence to write (or read) all tracks across the platters at a particular cylinder position. To fill a cylinder, a four-head drive writes a track with Head 1, then Head 2, then Head 3, and finally Head 4. The head positioner moves one cylinder, and the sequence repeats. Processing all tracks of a cylinder before moving to the next cylinder is efficient because all heads already are in new track positions. As you can see, the data for a file is spread across all the platters of a hard disk and on both sides of a floppy.

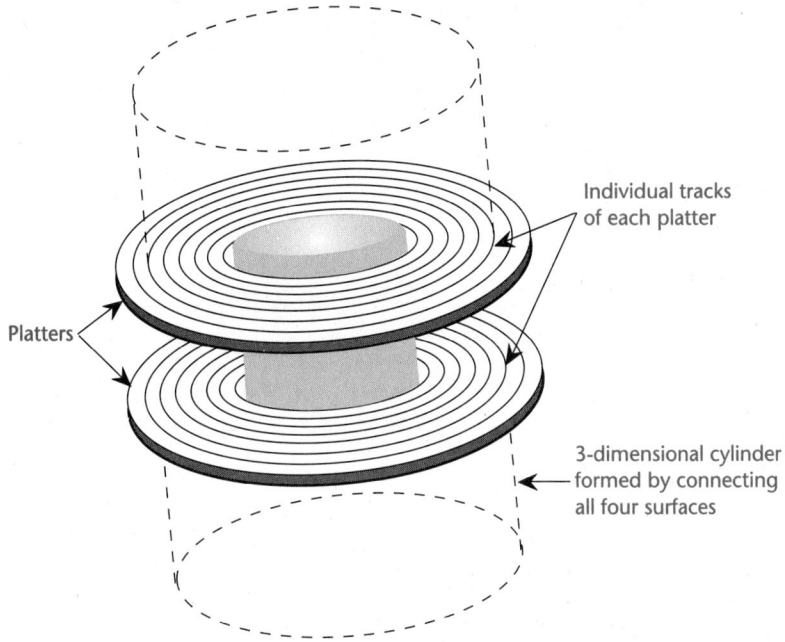

Fig. 6.8
Tracks, platters, and cylinder.

Another factor that spreads files across disks is *sector interleaving*. Hard disks spin quickly—so quickly that some hard disk mechanisms cannot write a sector and be ready to write the next sector as it spins under the head. If the drive waits for a full revolution of the platter, however, too much time is wasted. For this reason, hard disks use an interleave; that is, they write a sector and then skip two before writing to the third. Interleaves are expressed in ratios, so a hard disk that writes one and skips two has a 1:3 interleave. Some fast drives do not have to wait; they easily can write to the next sector, giving the drive a 1:1 ratio.

When you create files, DOS writes to all the empty sectors on a cylinder and then moves to the closest cylinder with empty sectors. As you use a disk over a period of time, you naturally create and destroy many files.

DOS creates on the outer tracks of a disk a table called the *File Allocation Table* (FAT). When you delete a file, DOS simply changes the FAT to mark as vacant the tracks and sectors that the file occupied, and the file's directory information is similarly voided. Remember, drives do not have an erase head, so even "erased" files are still present on the disk until written over. If you erase a file accidentally, you can use the UNDELETE command or a commercial program such as PC Tools or the Norton Utilities to get it back. Just make sure nothing writes to the drive before you unerase the file; otherwise, the "empty" sectors may get used for another file. For more information on UNDELETE, see Chapter 11, "Emergency Procedures."

Imagine for a moment that you create a bunch of files on a disk. Some are small and some are large. Use the DOS DEL command to delete only the smallest files, and you may free up enough room to store another large file. The "empty" spaces on the disk are distributed across the disk much like the holes in a slice of Swiss cheese. When you tell DOS to create a new large file, the first cylinder to be written to is the one closest to the current head position having available sectors.

When all the sectors on that cylinder are full, the drive moves the heads to another track and fills all the available space on that cylinder. The process continues until all the data in a file is written. The FAT is updated to show the locations of the data. This process of writing data on widely dispersed cylinders is called *file fragmentation.*

File fragmentation is not a dangerous condition, but the constant repositioning of the heads slows the operations of the drive and puts extra strain on the actuator mechanism. For these reasons, DOS offers the DEFRAG command, which rearranges files on the disk so that they are contiguous. For more information on improving your system's performance with DEFRAG, see Chapter 19, "Getting the Most from Your Hard Drive."

Disk Sectors

When a disk is blank, as it is when it comes from the factory, the disk contains no tracks and, therefore, no information. DOS has to prepare the disk to accept data. The preparation process is known as *formatting.*

Formatting, as the name implies, places a uniform pattern of format information in all tracks of the disk. The format information in each track enables DOS to slice each track into smaller, more manageable components of fixed size. These components are called *sectors.*

Figure 6.9 shows the sectors of a floppy disk represented as slices of a disk's surface. The figure shows the boundaries for every other sector. The concentric arcs between the indicated sectors are the disk's tracks. Notice that each track has the same number of sector boundaries (and, therefore, sectors).

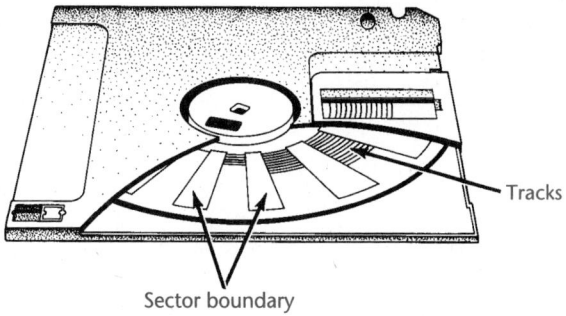

Fig. 6.9
A visual representation of sectors.

As you can see in figure 6.9 and in figure 6.7, the arrangement of sectors creates V-shaped areas of the disk that remain unused; these areas are *sector boundaries*. Although you might consider this construction a waste, it makes the mechanics of drives easier to work with because sectors are all a uniform size. Having a uniform size for sectors provides DOS with a standard unit of data transmission.

DOS reads and writes disk data one sector at a time. Some of DOS's internal file-system bookkeeping is performed by sectors. To DOS, a sector is the disk's most manageable block of data. By default, DOS uses 512-byte sectors.

The number of sectors formatted into each track is tied to the data density the drive uses when reading or writing data. The more dense the recording in a track, and the more tracks on a disk, the more sectors DOS can format. Designers select the number of tracks and the number of sectors per track with reliability in mind. Floppy disk drives are designed with more margin for error than are hard disk drives. You easily can see why some margin for error is desirable for a drive that must ensure the mechanical alignment of disks that users simply shove into the drive door. Floppy disk drives also must read disks that may have been stored in a place where magnetic fields weakened the disk's magnetic imprint.

Despite the protective disk jacket, the magnetic-coated surfaces of many floppy disks can be contaminated by smoke, dust, or fingerprints. A drive must be able to tolerate some disk contamination and still perform without errors. Clearly, no disk drive can avoid errors if the disks it uses are abused. Drive heads cannot read through liquid spills, for example, or through dents made by a ballpoint pen.

For Related Information

- "Preparing Floppy Disks with the FORMAT Command," p. 170
- "Preparing the Hard Disk," p. 180
- "Getting the Most Speed from Your Hard Disk," p. 492

Hard disk drives have greater data-storage capacity than their floppy cousins. This capacity is due in large part to the precision with which the drive's critical components work with the special oxides that magnetically coat the platters. In addition, the working parts of the drive are sealed at the factory in a way that protects the platters, positioners, and heads from contamination. With outside influence on these critical components sealed out, a hard disk drive can offer more tracks and sectors in the same space that a floppy drive occupies. When you consider the fact that most hard disks have more than one platter, each of which is capable of two-sided operation and each of which provides more tracks than a floppy disk can, you begin to see how hard disks get their large storage capacities.

Understanding Disk Formats

Disk drives have a universal way to divide a disk's available physical space. The number of platters, the number of sides, the number of tracks, the number of bytes per sector, and the number of sectors per track are the specific details that factor into this logical division of disk space. The specification for a disk's use of its physical space is called the disk's *format*.

PCs use a variety of disk drive sizes and formats. Some PCs, for example, have both 5 1/4-inch and 3 1/2-inch floppy drives that can handle both double-density and high-density disks.

Most PC users and software manuals differentiate one format from other formats by using the byte-capacity figure for the desired format. Each new version of DOS has maintained support for the disk formats supported by its predecessors. This support ensures that disks made with older drive formats can be used with current versions of DOS.

Floppy Disk Formats

The first DOS-supported disk drives allowed for twice as many tracks on a 5 1/4-inch floppy disk as the standard 5 1/4-inch disk formats of the time could accommodate. These DOS formats were called *double-density* formats. The original PC disk size and format was 5 1/4-inch, single-sided, 40 tracks, with 8 sectors per track and 512 bytes per sector. These disks are called *single-sided, double-density* (SSDD) disks. The capacity of this 8-sector, single-sided format is 160K (K equals 1,024 bytes).

Note

Computers generally store data in groups of 8 bits. An 8-bit group of data is called a byte. By design, digital computers are most efficient when working with numbers as some power of 2. Numbers that are powers of 2 can be represented directly in binary notation.

Computer programmers and designers apply this power-of-2 convention to the expression of a quantity of bytes. A kilobyte, for example, is 1,024 bytes; 2 kilobytes is 2,048 bytes, or 2K. A megabyte, or 1M, equals 1,024K. A gigabyte (G) is 1,024M.

You don't have to know about the use of numbers in the power of 2 except to note that capacity expressed in kilobytes, megabytes, or gigabytes uses 1,024 as the multiplier rather than 1,000. Why? Because a byte has eight bits, and 1,000 is not evenly divisible by eight. For scaling purposes, however, you can think of 1K as representing approximately 1,000 bytes.

The capacity of disk drives is stated in kilobytes, megabytes, or gigabytes. The storage capacity of a modern hard disk drive is usually anywhere from 40 megabytes on up to 2 gigabytes. The typical capacity of floppies ranges from hundreds of thousands of bytes to more than 2 megabytes, so a floppy drive's capacity can be described in either kilobytes or megabytes.

As you learned earlier, 5 1/4-inch floppies have two types with different storage capacities, either 360K or 1.2M. Similarly, a 3 1/2-inch disk can store either 720K or 1.44M. Still another standard format for 3 1/2-inch disks was introduced a few years ago, offering 2.88M of storage. To date, this format has not widely caught on because you must have a floppy disk drive and disks manufactured specifically to achieve 2.88M storage capacity.

Table 6.1 summarizes the common floppy disk formats.

Table 6.1 DOS Floppy Disk Formats

Format	Tracks	Sectors/Track	Total Sectors	Usable Capacity
SSDD	40	8	320	160K
DSDD	40	8	640	320K
SSDD-9	40	9	360	180K
DSDD-9	40	9	720	360K

(continues)

Table 6.1 Continued

Format	Tracks	Sectors/Track	Total Sectors	Usable Capacity
DSDD-9	80	9	1420	720K*
DSHD-15	80	15	2400	1.2M
DSHD-18	80	18	2880	1.44M*
HD-36	80	36	5760	2.88M**

** 3 1/2-inch formats*
*** Requires special disk and disk drive*

Raw Capacity and Usable Capacity

For Related Information

- "Understanding Disk Preparation," p. 167
- "Preparing Floppy Disks with the FORMAT command," p. 170

The process of formatting a blank disk places on the disk some data that is not part of the disk's total capacity. A 1.44M disk, for example, actually holds more than 1.44M bytes of information. You cannot use this extra space, however; the space is reserved for sector-identification and error-checking information. If you buy disks for a 1.44M drive, the identification label may say that the disks have 2M capacity; disks for a 720K drive may indicate 1M capacity. To understand this apparent discrepancy, you need to understand the difference between total (or raw) capacity and usable (or formatted) capacity. The larger of the two numbers for the same disk is considered to be the *raw capacity* of the disk.

Raw capacity includes the space that the formatting information will occupy. The smaller of the two numbers for the same disk is the *usable capacity* of the disk. This number of bytes is available for storing files after the formatting information has been put on the disk.

Hard disk manufacturers sometimes advertise the raw capacity of their drives instead of the usable capacity. Your 80M drive, therefore, may give you only 78M when formatted. Fortunately, most manufacturers of hard disks state the capacity of their drives as formatted capacity. Hard disks also lose some overhead space. If you have any doubt as to the meaning of a hard disk's stated capacity, ask the dealer whether the capacity is determined before or after formatting. In this book, disk capacity refers to usable capacity after formatting.

Hard Disk Drive Formats

Formats for hard disks nearly always employ 512-byte sectors, usually with 17 sectors per track. There is an alphabet soup of hard drive types: MFM, IDE, RLL, ESDI, SCSI, and so on. Each type of hard disk uses different numbers of sectors per track. You have to worry about these differences only when you are installing a hard disk drive. The manufacturer of the drive provides you with head, sector, and track information specific to your drive.

You can understand the concept of hard disk capacity by remembering the concept of cylinders. Hard disks, you may recall, have two or more heads. Remember that a cylinder is the alignment of all the heads on the same track on both sides of each platter. A disk with 306 tracks on one side of one platter has 306 cylinders. The total number of tracks on the disk is the number of cylinders times the number of heads. The disk's capacity in bytes is the number of tracks times the number of sectors per track times the number of bytes per sector. To obtain the capacity in kilobytes, divide the result by 1,024. To obtain the capacity in megabytes, divide the kilobyte total by 1,024. For approximations of capacity in megabytes, you can divide by a rounded 1,000.

DOS does not provide low-level format data for a hard disk, as it does for a floppy disk. Hard disks normally are given a low-level format at the factory, so you seldom need to initiate a low-level format on a hard disk. DOS uses the low-level format as a base upon which to perform its high-level format.

In a discussion of hard disk formatting, the term *format* refers to the high-level format initiated by the DOS FORMAT command. During the formatting of a hard disk, DOS initializes its bookkeeping tables and then writes "dummy" data into the disk's tracks. From your point of view, formatting a hard disk is the same basic operation as formatting a floppy. DOS keeps the details of the low-level format hidden and out of your way.

For Related Information

- "Understanding Disk Preparation," p. 167
- "Getting the Most Space from Your Hard Disk," p. 508

Note

Sometimes the alignment of a hard drive's read/write heads drifts slightly after continual use of the drive. Drift can also be detected when you remount the drive or stand the computer on its side like a tower. This drifting does not affect the information that has been written to the disk, but the heads may have difficulty locating the information because the low-level format identification information, which is needed to find the data, no longer is aligned beneath the heads. You can eliminate this problem by performing a low-level format of the disk to align the low-level disk tracks with the current location of the heads. Also, magnetic signals recorded on disks lose strength over the years, so the manufacturer's low-level format may fade to a point where the heads cannot reliably read format information.

Normally, a low-level format of your hard disk erases all existing data. Certain types of third-party software, however, can perform a low-level format without data loss. The best-known product of this type is SpinRite II (Gibson Research Corporation, Laguna Hills, California).

Summary

In this chapter, you learned about the physical devices used to store information in your computer—the disk drives. You also learned about the various disks you can use and a bit about the commands to make those disks usable. In particular, you learned the following:

- During formatting, DOS divides disks into tracks, cylinders, and sectors. A disk's storage capacity is governed by the number of sectors on the disk.
- Typical floppy-disk storage capacities are 360K, 720K, 1.2M, 1.44M, and 2.88M. Each floppy drive is designed to work optimally at one of these capacities.
- Hard disk capacities are determined by the number of platters and the number of sectors per track. Sectors, by default, hold 512 bytes of information.

In the next chapter, you learn the specifics about how to prepare disks for use.

Chapter 7

Preparing and Maintaining Disks

In Chapter 6, "Understanding Disks and Disk Drives," you learned the basic concepts of how disks are used by DOS. This chapter builds on that knowledge by giving you the information you need in order to put the theory into practice. You learn how to prepare blank floppy disks and hard disks, assign volume labels, transfer the system files, and analyze disks for problems.

This chapter covers the following commands:

- FORMAT
- FDISK
- VOL
- SYS
- CHKDSK
- SCANFIX

Understanding Disk Preparation

Both floppy disks and audiocassette tapes use magnetic media to store information, but they're different in other ways. You cannot just drop a blank disk into a drive and use the disk in the same way that you can record on a blank tape.

Why? Because the disk's recorded areas (sectors) can be accessed in any order randomly. The tape, however, is sequential. As it plays, the tape recorder doesn't jump around from place to place—unless, of course, it is being operated by a teenager.

To implement random access on a disk, you must first lay down information that can be used to find small sections of the disk quickly. In some ways, it's like drawing the lines on a sheet of notebook paper to show where the writing should be done (see fig. 7.1). This preparation process is called formatting. The DOS FORMAT command performs this process for disks; you do nothing more than enter the command. FORMAT analyzes a disk for defects, generates a root directory, sets up a storage table, and makes other technical modifications.

Fig. 7.1
Formatted disks are comparable to paper that has had lines drawn on it.

When you format a disk, DOS creates data-storage divisions on the disk's surface. As you learned in Chapter 5, "Understanding Files and Directories," these divisions are concentric circles called tracks (see fig. 7.2). DOS decides what type of drive you have and then positions the tracks accordingly.

You probably already know that with computers, items that are numbered often begin with 0 rather than 1. It's the same way with tracks on the disk—they're numbered beginning with track 0. DOS uses this first track (track 0) to record vital information about the disk's format. Later, by checking this information on track 0, DOS can quickly determine how to work with the disk.

As you can see in figure 7.2, each track is divided into segments called sectors, which are the smallest divisions of a disk. When you issue the FORMAT command, DOS creates a special disk table called the file allocation table (FAT).

The FAT, which is always located on track 0, monitors every sector on a disk as groups of clusters. DOS stores data in the clusters and uses the track number and cluster number to retrieve the data.

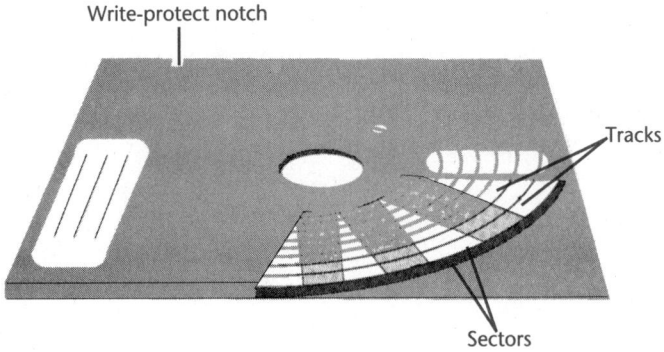

Fig. 7.2
Anatomy of a floppy disk.

A cluster is the smallest unit of storage that DOS allocates for file storage at one time unless you are using DoubleSpace, or a similar file-compression utility. DoubleSpace drives have storage allocated in smaller units, but this doesn't affect the way DOS views the disk. DOS hands data to be written to DoubleSpace in the standard way.

In the preceding chapter, you learned about cylinders. A cylinder is formed by stacking tracks on top of each other. For example, a cylinder on a floppy disk is made by stacking two tracks, the front and back of the disk. The two read/write heads in the floppy drive are positioned over two tracks. Tracks are broken up into sectors, so the read/write heads are positioned over two sectors.

DOS will not write one file on the front sector and one file on the back sector. Doing so would create a situation in which the read/write heads would have to move around too much and would slow down operations. To prevent this problem, DOS looks at the two sectors under the floppy drive's heads as a single unit, a cluster. Thus, if you write a file containing only six bytes onto a floppy disk, DOS reserves a cluster (two 512-byte sectors) for the file to reside in.

On hard disks, the number of sectors in a cluster is also equal to the number of read/write heads. Thus, a disk with four platters would group eight sectors into a cluster, so writing a six-byte file would actually take 4K of free space.

For Related Information
- "Understanding Disk Drives," p. 151
- "Understanding Disk Formats," p. 162

This might at first seem like a great deal of wasted space, but look at any disk and see how many files are only six bytes long. Data files are seldom static because information is constantly being added or removed. Chances are that the file won't stay six bytes long. Also, when you think that most files are thousands and hundreds of thousands of bytes long, a couple of unused sectors represent a very small percentage of total used disk space.

All DOS commands use tracks and clusters as road maps that enable them to carry out their operations. When a disk is formatted, DOS creates a FAT and root directory suited to the capacity of the disk.

Preparing Floppy Disks with the FORMAT Command

The FORMAT command prepares disks for use. All disks to be used by DOS must be formatted by DOS to be treated as valid DOS disks. Both floppies and hard disks must be formatted before they can be used. If you try to use a disk that has not been formatted, DOS will report a `General failure`, which sounds cataclysmic. All it really means is that the disk you are trying to read does not have valid format information. If the disk you are trying to read has been formatted, and you know that it has been formatted, then a problem exists. If that drive is your C: drive, you do have a cataclysmic experience to endure. Most of the time, however, a general failure just means that somebody has handed you an unformatted disk.

Note

When you issue the FORMAT command with its required parameters, DOS presents you with a prompt, requiring you to answer a question before the command actually begins its work. In the case of a floppy, DOS prompts you to insert the proper disk into the drive. On a hard disk, DOS reminds you that you are about to wipe out everything on the disk.

In either case, the tendency of experienced users is just to hit the key and go. *Don't!* Take a deep breath and read the prompt. You may have accidentally specified C: when you really meant B:. Take a moment to be sure; the data you save may be your own.

Reformatting an old disk also can be an efficient way to delete the contents without the hassle of dealing with individual files and directories.

Before DOS 5.0, reformatting a disk in effect erased the data stored on the disk with no way of getting it back. Starting in DOS 5.0, however, the FORMAT command first determines whether the disk contains data. If the disk contains data, FORMAT saves a copy of the boot sector, the FAT, and the root directory in a safe place on the disk where UNFORMAT can find the information if you need to unformat the disk. You can unformat a disk only if you have not created or copied other files onto the disk.

In DOS 5.0 (or later), the FORMAT command clears the disk's FAT and the first character of each file name in the root directory but does not erase any data. (The program also scans the entire disk for bad sectors.) FORMAT then saves the first letter of each file name in a safe place on the disk.

Caution

FORMAT is a DOS command that can quickly wipe out the contents of a disk. Even though the FORMAT command is now safer than it used to be, before you use this command, make sure that you are familiar with its syntax and the way it works. FORMAT issues warning messages on-screen and prompts you for verification before formatting a hard disk. Take care when you use FORMAT, read the screen prompts, and, most importantly, keep good backups of your data.

Also, the FORMAT command cannot format a disk that has been write-protected. If the command fails for this reason, determine what the disk contains before simply unprotecting the disk and proceeding with the format.

Formatting Floppy Disks

Unless you pay a small premium for preformatted disks, the disks you buy come unformatted. Before you can use these disks, they must be formatted by DOS. Some commands, such as DISKCOPY and BACKUP, stop and format disks if they're given unformatted disks to work with, but few DOS commands are so accommodating.

The following line shows the syntax for the FORMAT command:

```
FORMAT d:  /Q /V:label  /F:size  /S /B /C /U /1 /4 /8 /N:sectors  /T:tracks
```

This syntax shows all the switches available with the FORMAT command, but you normally use only a few of them at a time. (All the FORMAT switches are discussed in the section "Using FORMAT's Switches," later in this chapter.)

The simplest version of the FORMAT command is used when you are formatting a floppy disk that has the maximum capacity the drive is capable of, as in the following:

```
FORMAT A:
```

This command formats a nonbootable disk in the A: drive. If you are formatting a 360K disk in a drive whose maximum capacity is 360K, or formatting a 1.2M floppy in a high-density drive, fine. If, however, you are formatting a 360K disk in a 1.2M drive, you have to give the FORMAT command that information. To tell the FORMAT command the desired format size of the disk, use the /F switch. The /F switch is followed by a colon (:) and the size of the disk to be formatted, as in this line:

```
FORMAT A: /F:360
```

This command formats a double-density 5 1/4-inch disk in a high-density drive. Similarly,

```
FORMAT A: /F:720
```

formats a double-density 3 1/2-inch disk in a high-density drive. Remember, if you are formatting a high-density disk in a high-density drive, you do not have to give FORMAT the /F switch. Table 7.1 provides the valid values you can enter as part of the /F switch.

Table 7.1 Acceptable /F Switch Settings for Floppy Disks of Various Capacities

Size	Can Be Entered As (Select One)					
160K	160	160K	160KB			
180K	180	180K	180KB			
320K	320	320K	320KB			
360K	360	360K	360KB			
720K	720	720K	720KB			
1.20M	1200	1200K	1200KB	1.2	1.2M	1.2MB
1.44M	1440	1440K	1440KB	1.44	1.44M	1.44MB
2.88M	2880	2880K	2880KB	2.88	2.88M	2.88MB

Telling the Capacity of Disks by Sight

For 5 1/4-inch disks, you can easily tell the difference between a 360K disk and a 1.2M high-density disk. The 360K disks have a plastic reinforcement ring around the large hole in the center of the disk. High-density disks do not have a hub ring. Other than that small difference, however, they look the same.

When looking at 3 1/2-inch disks, you can easily tell a 1.44M high-density disk because it has a second square hole on the edge opposite the write-protect tab's hole. On a 720K double-density disk, there is only one hole, for the write-protect tab.

You cannot arbitrarily decide to format a double-density disk as a high-density disk. If you try to format a 720K disk as a high-density 1.44M disk, DOS tells you where to get off, as shown here:

```
D:\>format b: /F:1440
Insert new diskette for drive B:
and press ENTER when ready...

Checking existing disk format.
Existing format differs from that specified.
This disk cannot be unformatted.
Proceed with Format (Y/N)?y
Formatting 1.44M
Invalid media or Track 0 bad - disk unusable.
Format terminated.
Format another (Y/N)?
```

At least DOS is gracious enough to ask you whether you want to format another disk. Just make sure that it is a disk with a capacity matching the /F switch's value.

Similarly, you cannot format a 2.88M disk if your floppy drive doesn't support it, even if you have 2.88M disk in hand. If you attempt this action, you will see the following messages:

```
D:\>format b: /F:2880
Insert new diskette for drive B:
and press ENTER when ready...

Checking existing disk format.
Existing format differs from that specified.
This disk cannot be unformatted.
Proceed with Format (Y/N)?y
Formatting 2.88M
Parameters not supported by drive.
```

Other switches can be added to the command line to provide other formatting services. For example, this would be the command line to format a bootable 720K disk in a 1.44M drive:

```
FORMAT B: /F:720 /S
```

When you add the /S (System) switch, FORMAT creates a bootable disk.

FORMAT's Other Tasks

The primary task of the FORMAT command is to divide the disk into logical storage sectors, but this task is not the command's only purpose. FORMAT gives each disk a unique serial number and prompts you for a volume label (name) for the disk. As the formatting proceeds, FORMAT provides a continual update of what percentage of the disk has been formatted.

Assume for the moment that you have issued the command in the preceding section to format a 720K bootable disk. The following lines show the FORMAT dialog from start to finish:

```
C:\>FORMAT B: /F:720 /S
Insert new diskette for drive B:
and press ENTER when ready...

Checking existing disk format.
Formatting 720K
Format complete.
System transferred

Volume label (11 characters, ENTER for none)? bootable

      730,112 bytes total disk space
      199,680 bytes used by system
      530,432 bytes available on disk

        1,024 bytes in each allocation unit.
          518 allocation units available on disk.

Volume Serial Number is 1F44-0EE0

Format another (Y/N)?
```

When you press Enter to begin formatting, FORMAT first displays a two-line prompt telling you to enter a disk in drive A. Always make certain that this is what you intend. Next, several steps are performed.

The first of these steps is to check the disk format and preserve the FAT and directory structures in case you need to use the UNFORMAT command. Formatting then begins, and FORMAT ticks off the percentage of completion until the format is finished. You are told that the format is complete and nominally error free. If you have used the /S switch, the boot sector is prepared and the DOS system files are transferred to the disk.

You then are prompted to provide a volume label. Most users simply press Enter to bypass this option, but you can use the volume label to advantage in creating a cataloging system for your disks. You might want to name floppy disks according to categories such as budget, correspondence, backups, and so on.

When you press Enter to leave the Volume label prompt, FORMAT displays some relevant numbers about the disk. The first line is the total capacity of the disk. If you have created a bootable disk, the second line shows the amount of space taken up by the DOS system files. You also are shown the amount of remaining free space on the disk.

Note

As you can tell by examining the information provided by FORMAT, the DOS system files take up almost 200K of space on a newly formatted disk. Don't use the /S switch carelessly. This switch is intended only for disks that you plan to start the computer with. Unnecessarily making disks bootable is a major waste of space.

FORMAT then provides you with numerical data on what it calls allocation units. In this context, saying *allocation unit* is just a fancy way of saying *clusters*. Each sector is 512 bytes, and a floppy disk has two read/write heads; therefore, a cluster is 1024 bytes in length. The second line tells you that 532 clusters are available. Multiply 532 and 1024, and you get 544,768, exactly the amount of free space shown by FORMAT.

Note

As reliable as floppy disks are, they sometimes have flaws. If you hear an unusual grinding or churning noise while formatting a disk, probably the disk is damaged or has an excessive number of flaws. Any bad sectors found by FORMAT will be reported as part of the numerical data.

Depending on the number of flaws found, you might want to reformat the disk, throw it away, or use it only for noncritical storage.

Cleanliness Is Next to Godliness

Just as you must occasionally clean the heads in a cassette deck or VCR, you should clean the read/write heads in your floppy drives every once in a while. How often depends on whether you are getting errors on the drive, the environment your computer lives in, and how much you use the floppy drive.

Problems reading a nearly full disk almost always indicate the need to clean the drive. Sectors near the hub are much closer together than the sectors of Track 1, and these will be the first to display errors related to unclean heads.

Computer retailers sell various disk drive cleaning products. Most have a cleaning pad encased in a floppy disk jacket. You squeeze a few drops of an alcohol-based cleaning fluid onto the cleaning pad and insert the "disk" into the drive. To begin cleaning, you issue a command like DIR A: that causes DOS to try to read the disk, and the heads are scraped clean. Check with your computer supply vendor for more information on floppy drive cleaning.

Because your hard disk is sealed at the factory, you *never* have to clean its heads. Don't even think about it.

The last thing the FORMAT routine does is to assign a serial number to the disk. The idea behind a serial number is to enable programs to determine whether you have switched disks. The serial number, which is assigned automatically during formatting, uses the time and date of the format to create a hexadecimal number to be used as the serial number. No two disks from the same machine should ever have the same serial number, assuming that the system clock is properly set.

Finally, FORMAT offers to process another disk. This enables you to format more than one disk at a time. If you answer yes to the prompt by pressing Y and then Enter, FORMAT prompts you to place another disk in the drive. Any subsequently formatted disks will have the same attributes as the command-line parameters you entered to start the command. Only the serial numbers will be different.

Using FORMAT's Switches

The FORMAT command responds to several switches that modify its behavior. Table 7.2 gives a quick rundown on the available switches in the FORMAT syntax. Detailed information is also available in the Command Reference at the back of this book.

A True Story

Computer retailers have many wonderful stories to tell. This incident happened in Florida.

A woman called the computer store and asked to speak to the manager. She was connected to the owner, who asked how he could help her. The following conversation ensued:

"I was just in a different store and bought a box of floppy disks."

"Yes, ma'am."

"Well, the salesman there suggested that I format all the disks in the box so that they would all be formatted when I need one."

"That's not a bad idea. Is there a problem?"

"Well, I don't know. I barely got the third one in. I can't imagine getting the fourth one in; it's too tight, and there are ten disks in the box."

"Can you hold on?"

Somehow the owner of the store managed to get the phone on hold before rolling out of his chair to the floor in a laughing fit. Needless to say, all activity in the store stopped as employees and customers gathered around the owner to hear the resolution.

In the end, a service technician was dispatched to her place of business. The mangled disks were successfully removed without damaging the drive, and the owner charged her only half the normal service charge out of pity.

The moral of this story is that when you read that you can format more than one disk at a time, don't take it too literally.

Table 7.2 Commonly Used FORMAT Switches

Switch	Action
/B	Allocates space on the formatted disk for system files by creating hidden files of the same name and size on track 0. Used to create disks that can be made bootable with DOS 4.01 and earlier versions.
/F:*size*	Specifies the size of the floppy disk to be formatted (such as 160, 180, 320, 360, 720, 1.2, 1.44, and 2.88). You can specify kilobytes or megabytes if you prefer, but doing so is not necessary because DOS understands all the parameters shown here.

(continues)

Table 7.2 Continued

Switch	Action
/Q	Performs a quick format on a previously formatted disk. This switch effectively and quickly erases the contents of a disk so that it can be used again.
/S	Copies the system files and COMMAND.COM to the formatted disk, creating a bootable disk.
/U	Performs an unconditional format so that the disk cannot be unformatted with UNFORMAT.
/N:*sectors*	Enables you to specify the number of sectors per track (between 1 and 99). This switch is obsolete and has been replaced with the /F:*size* switch.
/T:*tracks*	Specifies the number of tracks per disk side (between 1 and 999). This switch is obsolete and has been replaced with the /F:*size* switch.
/V:*label*	Enables you to specify the volume label without waiting for a prompt.
/C	Retests a block previously marked as bad.
/1	Creates single-sided disks. This switch is obsolete.
/4	Provides a shortcut way of formatting a 5 1/4-inch 360K floppy disk in a high-density drive. It does the same thing as specifying f:360.
/8	Creates disks compatible with early versions of DOS that used 8 sectors per track rather than the 9 or 15 used today. This switch is obsolete.

The following sections describe some of the ways you can use FORMAT's switches.

Performing a Quick Format /Q. One way to clear all data from a disk is to format the disk. Because the formatting procedure can be relatively slow, the Quick Format feature was introduced.

Using a Quick Format saves you the hassle of changing the attributes of read-only files so that they can be deleted. A Quick Format also gets rid of directories without the laborious process of deleting all subordinate files and directories.

To clear data from a disk, type the command FORMAT /Q and then press Enter. If FORMAT cannot give a disk a Quick Format, a prompt appears asking whether you want to do a regular format.

Performing an Unconditional Format /U. Unless you use the /U switch, the FORMAT command performs a safe format of previously formatted disks. FORMAT first determines whether the disk has been formatted. If the disk has been formatted, FORMAT clears the FAT, boot record, and root directory but does not erase any data. FORMAT then scans the entire disk for bad sectors and saves a copy of the FAT, boot record, and root directory to a MIRROR image file where the UNFORMAT command can find them. If the disk has not been formatted previously, FORMAT overwrites every data byte with the hexadecimal value F6.

If you want DOS to overwrite all data on a previously formatted floppy disk (a procedure called unconditional formatting), use the /U switch. The following command, for example, unconditionally formats a disk in drive A:

```
FORMAT A: /U
```

Adding System Files /S. If you want to be able to use a disk to start your computer, the disk must contain hidden DOS system files as well as the command processor (COMMAND.COM). One way to install these system files on a disk is to use the /S switch during the formatting procedure. The /S switch reduces the disk's available storage capacity by about 185K.

For details on the /S switch, see Chapter 2, "Starting DOS."

Caution

Don't use the /S switch with FORMAT unless you plan to create a disk from which you can boot. Having at least one bootable system disk as a backup is important in case the disk that contains your working copy of DOS fails or your hard drive develops errors.

For Related Information

- "Unformatting a Disk," p. 289
- "Formatting a Compressed Drive," p. 517

Preparing the Hard Disk

Quite apart from the normal formatting that must be done to any DOS disk, hard disks require a little bit of extra work to get them ready for use. DOS provides the FDISK command to prepare a hard disk to be formatted.

The following sections explain how DOS divides and formats a hard disk. If you are relatively inexperienced, be sure to heed all warnings and read all explanations carefully. You are moving into potentially dangerous waters when you start playing around with FDISK. If you are determined to experiment with FDISK, make sure that you have a good backup of everything on the disk.

Caution

Many computer dealers pre-install DOS, Windows, and other programs you purchase. In all cases you should have copies of these programs on their original floppy disks. Without such disks, you do not have a legal copy of the program. If your dealer has installed an application, such as a word processing program, do not format the hard disk unless you also have a copy of the program on floppy disks. If you reformat your hard disk, all programs and data are erased.

Dividing a Hard Disk with FDISK

Before you can format a hard disk, you must partition it—that is, divide the hard disk logically into one or more areas called partitions. A partition is simply a section of the storage area of a hard disk. Many operating systems, including DOS, can use disk partitions, and most systems have some utility program that creates and manages partitions. In DOS, that utility program is the external command FDISK.

Note

Many computer dealers use FDISK on a system's hard disk before delivering the system to the user. In addition, FDISK is executed automatically by the DOS 6.2 Setup command during installation. If your hard disk contains files, it already has been partitioned with FDISK and formatted. If you have any questions about the state of your hard disk's preparation, consult your dealer.

Most hard-disk users choose a DOS partition size encompassing the entire hard disk. In other words, the one physical hard disk appears to DOS to be one logical hard disk. In this day of rapid growth in the sizes of the ordinary hard disk, you might want to rethink the idea of making a single volume out of a disk that might span many hundreds of megabytes. You might find it more manageable to have several partitions of smaller size.

DOS uses a partition table to store how the space on a hard disk is arranged. FDISK is the command that manipulates the information in the table.

Some PC users want to have both DOS and another operating system on their hard disk. Different operating systems use file systems that might not be compatible with DOS. Some operating systems can use file systems compatible with DOS—OS/2 and Windows NT, for instance. Some operating systems that have DOS-compatible file structures can use multiboot routines that give the user the opportunity to select which operating system to boot. The incompatibility comes into play only when you are using totally foreign operating systems that must reside in different partitions. FDISK, however, can only create DOS partitions and reserve spaces on the disk, whereas another operating system's equivalent utility can be used to prepare the partition for its own file scheme.

The partition table can be arranged so that DOS can use one partitioned section while the other operating system, such as UNIX, uses the other partitioned section. Through separation, each operating system sees its partition as being its own hard disk. Only one of these partitions, however, can be bootable. To use a partition with another operating system, you have to boot from a floppy when using the other operating system.

Fortunately, those DOS installations requiring a second operating system are rare. The rest of this chapter will speak to the 99.9 percent of installations in which DOS is the only operating system in use.

As you remember from an earlier chapter, DOS looks at disk drives as logical devices. A by-product of this arrangement is the fact that you can use FDISK to carve up a single large hard disk into smaller, more manageable volumes. Each volume has its own drive letter and for all practical purposes becomes a separate hard disk.

Note

Although making a large hard disk into a single logical drive might seem tempting, doing so might create some disadvantages. If your hard drive is especially large, any command that scans the entire drive, such as DIR or CHKDSK, might take an inordinately long time to complete execution. Files might become harder to find due to their sheer numbers. Unless you work with very large data files, you might prefer to limit your logical drives to 120M or less.

The FDISK command has no parameters. To start this utility, you simply type **FDISK** and press Enter.

In DOS 3.3 and later versions, you can use FDISK to create more than one DOS partition. After you create a primary DOS partition (or boot disk) with FDISK, you can create an extended DOS partition, which you divide into one or more logical drives.

After you have created your partitions, you must use the FORMAT command to format all DOS partitions and logical drives before you can use them.

Caution

You can use the FDISK command to delete an existing partition from the disk partition table. If you delete an existing partition, you lose all data in the files contained in that partition. Be sure that you have backed up or copied any data from a partition that you want to delete. FDISK is not a command to experiment with unless your hard disk contains no data.

There are two types of partitions: the primary partition, which the computer can boot from, and an extended partition, which you can divide into logical drives. The primary DOS partition normally is assigned the drive name C. The extended partition can be used to create drives D, E, F, and so on.

After you partition the hard disk, DOS treats the logical drives as separate drives and creates a file system for each when the drive is formatted. Figure 7.3 shows the opening screen that appears when you run FDISK.

As you can see, the Create option is the offered default; it appears within the brackets following the Enter choice prompt. You won't destroy the data on your disk if you accidentally choose this option. FDISK will simply beep and inform you that you already have partitions created.

```
                    MS-DOS Version 6.2
              Fixed Disk Setup Program
        Copyright Microsoft Corp. 1983 - 1993

                    FDISK Options

Current fixed disk drive: 1

Choose one of the following:

1. Create DOS partition or Logical DOS Drive
2. Set active partition
3. Delete partition or Logical DOS Drive
4. Display partition information
5. Change current fixed disk drive


Enter choice: [1]


Press Esc to exit FDISK
```

Fig. 7.3
FDISK partitions your hard disk so that DOS can use it efficiently.

Caution

The third choice offers to delete partitions. Unless there is something wrong with your system, or you are deliberately reconfiguring a drive, leave this one alone! Deleting partitions results in data loss.

To see how your hard disk is partitioned, press 4 to select Display partition information, and then press Enter. FDISK presents a screen similar to the one shown in figure 7.4. Of course, the information shown by your computer will be different.

Figure 7.4 shows the FDISK display output for the hard disk used in writing this chapter. Note that there are two partitions, both dedicated to DOS format. The first acts as the C: drive. The A under status indicates that it is the active partition and can be used for booting. This drive—drive C—is 23 megabytes in size, uses the standard DOS FAT 16-bit architecture, and takes up only 10 percent of the hard disk's available space.

Figure 7.4 also shows that there is an extended partition of 289M that takes up the rest of the drive. As the bottom of the FDISK display indicates, this partition is used to create logical drives. To see what logical drives have been created in the extended partition, you only have to press Enter, because Y, the default value, is already displayed. To return to the main FDISK screen, press Esc. Figure 7.5 shows the makeup of the extended DOS partition.

Fig. 7.4
Partition information as displayed by FDISK.

```
                    Display Partition Information

Current fixed disk drive: 1

Partition  Status   Type    Volume Label  Mbytes   System   Usage
 C: 1        A    PRI DOS   DATA-TRAIN      32    FAT16      10%
    2             EXT DOS                  289               90%


Total disk space is  321 Mbytes (1 Mbyte = 1048576 bytes)


The Extended DOS Partition contains Logical DOS Drives.
Do you want to display the logical drive information (Y/N).....?[Y]



Press Esc to return to FDISK Options
```

Fig. 7.5
Extended partitions can be used to carve the hard disk into logical drives.

```
                    Display Logical DOS Drive Information

Drv Volume Label  Mbytes  System  Usage
D:  MAXTOR_D        100   FAT16    35%
E:  MAXTOR_E         50   FAT16    17%
F:  MAXTOR_F         50   FAT16    17%
G:  MAXTOR_G         50   FAT16    17%
H:  MAXTOR_H         38   FAT16    13%


Total Extended DOS Partition size is  289 Mbytes (1 MByte = 1048576 bytes)


Press Esc to continue
```

The logical drive information shown in figure 7.5 indicates that the 289M contained in the partition is divided into five logical drives, D: through H:. The size of each of the logical drives is shown and marked as having the standard DOS File Allocation Table. The usage column indicates the relative sizes in relation to the partition, not the disk as a whole. Sharp-eyed readers will notice that the usage numbers add up to only 99 percent. FDISK rounds off fractional percentages.

By digesting the information in figures 7.4 and 7.5, you can tell that the drive has 321M of usable capacity broken into six drive letters, C: through H:. The rationale behind these settings and the relative sizes of the drives is as follows.

Drive C takes the biggest pounding. Because it is the boot drive, almost every commercial software package you install wants to make changes or install drivers on the C: drive. C: is also the traditional home of the DOS directory where DOS's external command program files are written. It is also the traditional home of directories used to store utility programs such as Norton Utilities and PC Tools. Plus, C: usually houses a TEMP directory where many software packages look for disk resources to use as a scratch pad. Windows Print Manager, for example, uses the TEMP directory to spool printing jobs into a file so that it can send data to the printer in the background. The drive is just large enough to accommodate all these uses and allow space to install software for testing, yet it's small enough to back up easily. Unproven software sometimes eats the disk it's installed on, so easy restoration of backup files is the key factor in the size of the C: drive.

Drive D on the hard disk is the Windows drive. Windows software tends to be large, as is Windows itself. When you use DoubleSpace, the 100M of reported space becomes closer to 200M—almost enough to do the job. Drives E and F are used to store applications and the overflow from drive D. On drives E and F you would find word processors, programming editors, communications programs, and the like. Drive G is given over to graphics programs and files. Drive H is a programming disk where source code to programs is written. *Source code* is the term used for the files containing programming language statements that are compiled into working .EXE and .COM files.

As you can see, the partitions of this hard disk have been well thought out in advance. Utilizing disk space effectively is the first step in optimizing DOS's efficiency. Before partitioning a hard disk, analyze the ways you use a computer. If you do desktop publishing, use Windows, or do database work on large files, you might want to partition the disk into fewer drives with larger capacities. One key point to keep in mind is that partitions should be small enough to enable you to make backups easily.

Checking Partition Status. You can check the status of your partition table by using the FDISK command's /STATUS switch:

```
FDISK /STATUS
```

FDISK shows a table of your hard disk's partition information (see fig. 7.6) without starting the FDISK program.

Fig. 7.6
Displaying disk partition information.

```
                    Fixed Disk Drive Status
Disk   Drv   Mbytes   Free   Usage
   1            321      0    100%
         C:      32
         D:     100
         E:      50
         F:      50
         G:      50
         H:      38

   (1 MByte = 1048576 bytes)
```

Caution

The next section of this chapter contains specific information on creating partitions with FDISK. Performing the steps given in the example will destroy the data on your hard disk. Do not practice these steps unless you have reliable backups of all the data on all the drives of your hard disk. If you can, practice first on a hard disk that is not currently loaded with data.

Partitioning a Drive. The steps required for partitioning a hard disk for the first time and those for repartitioning a drive to change the structures of the logical drives are very similar.

If you are repartitioning an existing hard disk structure, you will want to make sure that you have a rock-solid backup of all the files on the disk. If you are going to change the sizes of logical drives, you will want to back up individual directories rather than perform a whole-drive backup.

The actions shown in this section should be done only by experienced users of DOS. Not knowing what you are doing can cost you all the files on your hard disk.

After you have your backups safely stored away and have a bootable floppy containing FDISK and FORMAT, follow these steps to repartition your hard disk:

1. *Plan the partitions.* Decide how you want the partitioning to be done. Create a chart on paper, and apportion the available disk space among the partitions you want to create.

2. *Start FDISK.* If you are repartitioning a drive that is currently partitioned, Choose to delete existing partitions from the main FDISK menu. After the existing partitions have been deleted, the drive will be unusable until you repartition and reformat.

3. *Create the primary partition.* Select Create DOS Partition from the FDISK main screen. If there are no existing partitions, you get a menu. Choose 1 to create the partition to act as drive C. By default, FDISK offers the entire disk capacity for the primary partition. If you want to break the hard drive into multiple logical drives, answer N to the confirmation prompt and press ENTER.

   FDISK enables you to enter capacities for partitions as megabytes or as a percentage. Choose one method or the other, then assign the amount of space you want C: to have and return to the main FDISK menu.

4. *Make the primary partition the active partition.* Choose Set Active Partition from the FDISK main menu to make C: the active partition that can be made bootable.

5. *Create the extended partition.* Again choose Create from the main menu, but this time choose to Create Extended DOS partition. Again FDISK will offer to make the remaining disk space the size of the partition. If you want to have just C: and D:, accept the default. If you want to create more than one logical drive, reject the default and follow the prompts to specify the size of the partition to be used for D:.

6. *Create logical drives.* If you finish creating a partition and there are still disk sectors not assigned to a partition, FDISK loops around to create another logical drive. It offers all remaining space to be used for the logical drive. If you want to break the remaining space into more than

one drive, answer N to reject the default, and enter a value manually. When you create the last logical drive, accept the default to make sure that no usable cylinders are left out of the partition table.

7. *Format each logical drive.* After you have set up the partitions the way you want them, exit FDISK and save the partition table. Reboot the computer using your bootable floppy, and then format each of the logical drives you have created. Remember to format C: using the /S switch to make it bootable.

8. *Reboot and check the drives.* After you have formatted each of the logical drives, reboot the computer from the hard disk and run directories of all the logical drives to make sure that they are created the way you intended, and that they are recognized as valid DOS drives.

9. *Install files.* If you are repartitioning a drive or installing a new hard disk on an existing system, you will want to restore all the backups you made, including the DOS files on the boot drive, and the files in the DOS directory.

   If you are installing a new system, you will want to install DOS, then begin installing any software packages that have to reside on the hard disk of the computer.

10. *Test, test, test.* Before you pronounce the job finished, reboot from the hard disk, test all the software installed, and make sure that configuration files, drivers, and the like are actually written at the locations specified by entries in CONFIG.SYS and AUTOEXEC.BAT.

Formatting a Hard Disk

Simply stated, you format a hard disk or logical drive just like you format a floppy disk.

Assume that the hard disk (or logical disk) you are going to format is drive C. (If you are formatting another drive, use its drive letter in place of C in the example.) If your drive is not the primary DOS partition, you don't have to use the /S switch; DOS boots only from the primary DOS partition. To format drive C, follow these steps:

1. Insert your working copy of the DOS Start-up disk, or any bootable disk that contains FORMAT.COM, into drive A.

2. Switch to that drive by typing A: and pressing Enter.

3. Type the following command and press Enter:

   FORMAT C:/S

   FORMAT issues the following warning message and confirmation prompt:

   ```
   WARNING, ALL DATA ON NON-REMOVABLE DISK
   DRIVE C: WILL BE LOST!
   Proceed with Format (Y/N)?
   ```

   This prompt is extremely important. When the prompt appears on-screen, examine it carefully to confirm the disk-drive name (letter) before you press Y. If you make a habit of pressing Y in response to the confirmation prompts of less dangerous commands, you might make a serious mistake with this final FORMAT confirmation prompt.

4. If the specified drive is the one you want to format, press Y; if not, press N to terminate FORMAT. If you press Y, FORMAT updates the display with progress reports on the formatting operation. Depending on the size of the disk being formatted, the process can take from a few minutes to more than half an hour. The greater a disk's capacity, the longer the process takes.

For Related Information

- "Understanding Disk Formats," p. 162
- "Getting the Most Space from Your Hard Disk," p. 508

All the normal `Format complete` and `System transferred` messages that you see when formatting floppies are presented when you are formatting a hard disk.

Related Commands

Several useful DOS commands help you prepare and maintain disks. The following sections are devoted to these commands.

Naming Disks with LABEL

The external command LABEL adds, modifies, or changes a disk's volume label. In DOS, a volume label is a name given to a physical or logical disk.

If a disk's volume label is blank (if you or another user pressed Enter when FORMAT or LABEL prompted for the label), you can use the LABEL command to add a volume label or change the current volume label.

DOS displays the volume label when you issue commands such as VOL, CHKDSK, DIR, and TREE. Giving each disk (physical and logical) a volume label is a good idea. A disk with a unique volume label is easier to identify than one that doesn't have a label.

The syntax for the LABEL command is shown in the following line:

```
LABEL d:label
```

d: is the name of the drive that holds the disk you want to label.

label, the optional label text that you supply as the new volume label, can include up to 11 characters. (The acceptable characters for a volume label are listed in the section "Adding a Volume Label" earlier in this chapter.) DOS immediately updates the specified or default drive's label with no warning prompt. If you do not supply the label parameter, LABEL automatically goes into an interactive mode that prompts you for a new label.

Keep in mind this special restriction: You cannot use the LABEL command in a networked drive.

Examining Volume Labels with VOL

The internal command VOL is convenient when you want to view a disk's volume label or verify that a label exists. VOL accesses the disk's volume label from the root directory and then displays the label created during the disk's formatting or modified by a subsequent LABEL command.

You can use VOL freely because it is a display-only command; it does not change any files or the label name.

The syntax of the VOL command is simple:

```
VOL d:
```

d: is the optional name of the drive whose volume label you want to see. If you omit a value for *d:*, DOS displays the label for the default drive.

Using SYS to Transfer the DOS System

All DOS disks have a DOS file system, but only disks with the DOS system files and COMMAND.COM can be used to start the computer. The external command SYS transfers (copies) the hidden system files necessary to make a disk bootable.

As explained earlier in this chapter, you can make a disk bootable by using the /S switch with the FORMAT command. You can use the SYS command when you need to make an already formatted disk bootable. The disk must have room for the system files that SYS intends to transfer, and those system files must be compatible with your version of DOS.

To use SYS successfully, observe the following rules:

- The destination disk must be formatted.
- The destination disk must contain sufficient free space for the two hidden system files and COMMAND.COM (just over 133K for DOS 6.2 system files; over 197K if you use DoubleSpace), it must already contain earlier versions of the system files, or it must have been formatted with the /B switch.
- You cannot use SYS in a networked drive. If you want to use SYS in a networked drive, you must log off the network or pause your drive. (For the exact restrictions, consult your system's network documentation.)
- You must include the destination-drive parameter in the SYS command. SYS will not transfer a copy of the system to the current drive; the destination must be a different drive.

The syntax for the SYS command is shown in the following line:

```
SYS ds: dd:
```

dd: is the target, or destination, drive for the system files. You must specify a drive name (letter) for drive *dd:*. The drive specified by *ds:* is the drive used for the source of the system files.

Suppose that you are using DOS 6.2 with a hard disk and have an empty disk you want to make bootable for use with another computer. Follow these steps:

1. Insert the formatted disk (the one you want to transfer system files onto) into drive A.
2. Type the following command:

```
SYS C: A:
```

SYS replies with the message `System transferred`. The system files now are on the disk in drive A. You now can use this disk to boot your computer.

Note

The C: in step 2 is optional, depending on whether drive C is current. If you are logged onto drive C, C: already is the default source for the system files, and therefore, you don't have to add it to the command line.

Analyzing a Disk with CHKDSK

The external command CHKDSK analyzes a floppy or hard disk. CHKDSK checks a disk's FAT, directories, and if you want, the fragmentation of the files on the disk. Fragmentation is the scattering of parts of a file across a disk.

CHKDSK is DOS's self-test command. CHKDSK makes sure that the internal tables that keep files in control are in order.

Although the technical details of how CHKDSK performs its analysis are beyond the interest of most casual DOS users, the better you understand CHKDSK, the more comfortable you will be when the command uncovers problems. Just because you don't understand exactly how CHKDSK works doesn't mean that you must avoid using it.

CHKDSK checks for the following problems in the FAT:

- Unlinked cluster chains (lost clusters)
- Multiply-linked clusters (cross-linked files)
- Invalid next-cluster-in-chain values (invalid cluster numbers)
- Defective sectors where the FAT is stored

CHKDSK checks for the following problems in the directory system:

- Invalid cluster numbers (out of range)
- Invalid file attributes in entries (attribute values that DOS does not recognize)
- Damage to subdirectory entries (CHKDSK cannot process them)
- Damage to a directory's integrity (its files cannot be accessed)

Note

CHKDSK is meant to work with normal DOS volumes; it does not work with DoubleSpace disk volumes. If you want to analyze both DOS and DoubleSpace volumes, use the SCANDISK command, discussed later in this chapter.

Optionally, CHKDSK repairs problems in the FAT caused by lost clusters and writes the contents of the lost clusters to files. CHKDSK also can display all files and their paths. (Paths are discussed in Chapter 5, "Understanding Files and Directories.")

Note

Running CHKDSK periodically on your hard disk and on important floppies is good practice. Because the FAT and the hierarchical directory system work together to track file names and locations, a problem in the FAT or one of the directories is always a serious problem. In all likelihood, CHKDSK can find and correct most problems in a disk's internal bookkeeping tables.

The CHKDSK command uses the following syntax:

```
CHKDSK filespec /F/V
```

The optional *filespec* parameter is the drive, path, and file name of the file to be analyzed for fragmentation. If you don't include a *filespec*, CHKDSK does not check for fragmentation.

/F is the optional fix switch, which instructs CHKDSK to repair any problems it encounters.

/V is the verbose switch, which instructs CHKDSK to provide file names on-screen as it analyzes the files.

When the process is complete, CHKDSK displays a screen report of its findings. This report summarizes disk and system memory usage. Figures 7.7 and 7.8 show typical CHKDSK reports.

Note

Take advantage of the CHKDSK command's capability to make a "dry run" of its checking routines. You can use this feature to assess reported problems. Before issuing CHKDSK with the /F switch, for example, issue the command without the switch. CHKDSK without /F prompts you if the command finds a problem (as though you had used the /F switch). After you have assessed the findings of CHKDSK and have taken remedial actions (such as those that follow), you can issue CHKDSK with the /F switch so that the command can fix the problems it finds.

Fig. 7.7
A typical report produced by CHKDSK with no parameters.

```
C:\>chkdsk

Volume DCI 3       created 09-13-1993 5:30a
Volume Serial Number is 1B2B-392C

  340,746,240 bytes total disk space
   21,094,400 bytes in 6 hidden files
      884,736 bytes in 107 directories
  199,917,568 bytes in 3,195 user files
  118,849,536 bytes available on disk

        8,192 bytes in each allocation unit
       41,595 total allocation units on disk
       14,508 available allocation units on disk

      655,360 total bytes memory
      570,528 bytes free

Instead of using CHKDSK, try using SCANDISK.  SCANDISK can reliably detect
and fix a much wider range of disk problems.  For more information,
type HELP SCANDISK from the command prompt.
```

Fig. 7.8
The report produced when CHKDSK is issued with a path.

```
C:\>chkdsk \umsd\*.doc

Volume DCI 3       created 09-13-1993 5:30a
Volume Serial Number is 1B2B-392C

  340,746,240 bytes total disk space
   21,094,400 bytes in 6 hidden files
      851,968 bytes in 103 directories
  199,409,664 bytes in 3,188 user files
  119,390,208 bytes available on disk

        8,192 bytes in each allocation unit
       41,595 total allocation units on disk
       14,574 available allocation units on disk

      655,360 total bytes memory
      570,528 bytes free

C:\UMSD\UMD03.DOC Contains 3 non-contiguous blocks

Instead of using CHKDSK, try using SCANDISK.  SCANDISK can reliably detect
and fix a much wider range of disk problems.  For more information,
type HELP SCANDISK from the command prompt.
```

DOS stores every file as a chain of *clusters*. Each cluster is a group of sectors; clusters are also referred to as *allocation units*. Each entry in the disk's directory points to the entry in the FAT that contains the list of clusters allocated to a file.

Caution

Use CHKDSK /F only when you are running at the DOS prompt. Other programs should not be running because CHKDSK expects the DOS file system to be dormant while CHKDSK does its work. If you are shelled out to a DOS prompt from within an application, or running a DOS session under Windows, CHKDSK can damage your files.

CHKDSK processes each directory, starting at the root and following each subdirectory. CHKDSK checks the cluster chain by using the directory entry's FAT pointer and then compares the size of the file (in bytes) with the size of the FAT's allocation (in clusters). CHKDSK expects to find enough chained clusters in the FAT to accommodate the file, but not more than are necessary. If CHKDSK finds too many clusters, it displays the following message:

```
Allocation error,
size adjusted
```

The file is truncated (excess clusters are deallocated) if you use the /F switch.

CHKDSK makes sure that each of the FAT's clusters is allocated only once. In rare circumstances—for example, if power problems or hardware failures occur—DOS can give two different files the same cluster. By checking each cluster chain for cross-linked files, CHKDSK can report mixed-up files. Each time you see the message `filename is cross-linked on cluster nnnnn`, copy the file reported in `filename` to another disk. When CHKDSK reports another file with the same message, copy the second file to another disk also. Chances are good that the contents of the two files are mixed up, but you have a better chance of recovering the files if you save them to another disk before CHKDSK "fixes" the problem.

CHKDSK expects every cluster in the FAT to be available for allocation, part of a legitimate directory-based cluster chain, or a marked bad cluster. If CHKDSK encounters any clusters or cluster chains that are not pointed to by a directory entry, CHKDSK issues the message `lost clusters in XXX chains`. CHKDSK then asks

```
Convert lost chains to files (Y/N)?
```

This message appears even if you didn't use the /F switch.

If you used the /F switch and you press Y, CHKDSK turns each cluster chain into a file in the root directory. Each file created has the name

FILE*nnnn*.CHK. (*nnnn* is a number, starting with 0000, that increments by 1 for each file created by CHKDSK.) If you did not use the /F switch and you press Y, nothing happens. CHKDSK, however, does tell you what it would have done had you used the /F switch.

Note

You can use the TYPE command to examine the contents of a text file, and you might be able to use the DOS EDIT command to put the text back into its original file. The TYPE or EDIT commands don't do you any good, however, for a binary (program or data) file. If the problem is with a program file, you might have to use the DOS COMP or FC command to compare your disk's binary files with their counterparts from your master disks.

Of course, the disk does not lose any sectors physically. A lost-cluster report does not indicate that the clusters are bad; lost clusters indicate only that DOS made a bookkeeping error in the FAT, which makes some clusters appear to DOS to be lost. The clusters are not tied to a directory entry, yet they're marked as being in use.

The lost-cluster problem is most likely to occur when a program you are running crashes due to an error while files are being manipulated.

Remember that CHKDSK reports problems found during operation but does not repair the problems unless you include the /F switch in the command line. You'll find that it's a good idea to run CHKDSK at least once a week. Run CHKDSK daily during periods of extreme file activity.

Analyzing a Disk with the ScanDisk Utility

You might already know a bit about DoubleSpace, introduced with DOS 6.0. DoubleSpace enables you virtually to double the amount of information that can be stored on your disk. To accomplish this compression, however, information must be stored in a nonstandard manner. This means that the CHKDSK cannot provide correct information about a disk volume that uses DoubleSpace.

Beginning with DOS 6.2, however, there is a solution: the SCANDISK command. This command works with either regular or DoubleSpace disk volumes, and it provides greater functionality than the older CHKDSK command. In fact, whenever you use CHKDSK, you see this message at the bottom of any display:

```
Instead of using CHKDSK, try using SCANDISK.  SCANDISK can reliably
detect and fix a much wider range of disk problems.  For more
information, type HELP SCANDISK from the command prompt.
```

SCANDISK can detect and resolve all the problems that can be handled by CHKDSK. In addition, it can detect and correct the following problems:

- MS-DOS boot sector errors
- Defective clusters
- Problems in a DoubleSpace volume header
- Structure problems in the file structures of a DoubleSpace volume
- Errors in the DoubleSpace compression structure
- Errors in DoubleSpace volume signatures

There are two possible syntaxes for the SCANDISK command. If you want it to check a file or group of files, use the following syntax:

```
SCANDISK /FRAGMENT filespec
```

If you want SCANFIX to analyze an entire drive, use this syntax:

```
SCANDISK switches d:
```

In this syntax, *d:* is the drive you want to check; if you do not supply a drive, it is assumed that you want to check the current drive. Many more switches can be used with SCANDISK than with CHKDSK. These switches are detailed in table 7.3.

Table 7.3 Possible Switches for Use with SCANDISK

Switch	Meaning
/ALL	Checks all local drives.
/AUTOFIX	Fixes any problems encountered, without asking first.
/CHECKONLY	Analyzes the disk, but does not fix any problems.
/CUSTOM	Uses the SCANDISK settings contained in the file SCANDISK.INI.
/FRAGMENT	Checks a file for fragmentation. You must specify the full file name after the switch.

(continues)

Table 7.3 Continued

Switch	Meaning
/MONO	Forces display settings for a monochrome monitor.
/NOSAVE	Doesn't save lost cluster chains into files; simply frees them up (used only with /AUTOFIX).
/NOSUMMARY	Indicates that SCANDISK should not stop at summary screens (used only with /AUTOFIX or /CHECKONLY).
/SURFACE	Performs a surface scan.
/UNDO	Undoes previous repairs. You must have an undo disk, and you must specify the drive on the command line.

Caution

Use SCANDISK only at the DOS prompt. SCANDISK does not work properly if you are operating under a multitasking shell, such as DESQview, Windows, or the DOS Shell. Exit these programs before you attempt to use SCANDISK.

You might have already noted, from the information in table 7.3, that you can store your SCANDISK parameters in the file SCANDISK.INI. This file, which is stored in the DOS directory, is used to specify how you want SCANDISK to operate. For more information on this file, use a text editor to load the file. It contains extensive comments on how you can modify the file to change the behavior of SCANDISK.

As an example of how SCANDISK operates, enter SCANDISK at the DOS prompt. You will see a screen similar to that shown in figure 7.9.

Each of the five listed areas is analyzed, in turn, by SCANDISK. The first four areas are processed very quickly. The final area takes more time; thus, you will be prompted before SCANDISK actually performs a surface test. For instance, on a 340M hard drive, a surface scan can take up to 35 minutes to complete. This amount of time is necessary because every sector on the disk is read and analyzed to make sure that it is correct.

```
Microsoft ScanDisk
-----------------------------------------------------------------

ScanDisk is now checking the following areas of drive C:

   √    Media descriptor
   √    File allocation tables
   »    Directory structure
        File system
        Surface scan



< Pause >   < More Info >   < Exit >

-----------------------------------------------------------------
```

Fig. 7.9
The SCANDISK screen.

Summary

This chapter presented important information about formatting disks with FORMAT, partitioning hard disks with FDISK, and carrying out other disk-level DOS commands. The chapter covered the following key points:

- You must format both hard and floppy disks before you use them to store files.
- Formatting sets up a directory for file name and status information, and also creates a file-allocation table (FAT) that tracks the availability of storage space on the disk.
- Before you can format a hard disk, you must partition it by using FDISK.
- Disk partitions can be DOS partitions or partitions of another operating system.
- DOS partitions are either primary (bootable) partitions or extended partitions divided into one or more logical drives.
- The LABEL command adds or changes a disk's volume label.
- The VOL command displays a disk's volume label.

- You can use the SYS command to transfer system files to a floppy disk.
- CHKDSK is a disk-level command that finds and fixes problems. CHKDSK analyzes a disk's FAT and directory system.
- SCANDISK is an enhanced version of CHKDSK that works with both regular and DoubleSpace disk volumes.

The next chapter introduces the DOS commands you can use to manage files on your hard disk.

Chapter 8

Working with Files

After you have installed DOS on your computer, created your directories, and installed programs, in a sense you have set up housekeeping on your PC.

Most programs generate files as you work with them. You begin to accumulate files on your computer's disks in much the same way that you accumulate possessions in your home or office. Fortunately, DOS provides useful file-management commands that help you keep file clutter to a minimum. This chapter covers file-management techniques.

Using DOS to Work with Files

Personal computers commonly have storage media that can hold millions of bytes of information in hundreds or even thousands of files. By creating a directory structure that segregates groups of files according to their uses, you can keep the files on your computer's hard disk organized and cataloged. The adage "A place for everything, and everything in its place" was never more true than when you're storing files on a large hard disk.

It is important that you understand the distinction between utility programs and applications when devising a strategy to manage files using DOS. A utility is generally regarded as a single-purpose program that performs one specific task and then gets out of your way. Applications generally provide a working environment capable of providing all the services required to perform general tasks such as word processing and creating pictures.

DOS's external commands are perfect examples of utilities. Each external command serves a specific purpose, such as sorting lists or formatting disks. You usually run a utility program by typing a command line at the DOS prompt. It does its work and then terminates, giving you another DOS prompt to work from. Utilities usually have all their programming contained in a single .EXE or .COM file, and they seldom use auxiliary files. It therefore is most often convenient to place utility programs into directories that are part of the search path so that they are available no matter what directory you are logged into. By default, most utilities act on files in the currently logged directory.

Applications, even though they might be dedicated to a single activity such as word processing or database management, have a much broader scope. Unlike utilities, which do their job and terminate to a DOS prompt, applications create a working environment where users can access the features of the application. Only when you exit the application do you get another DOS prompt.

Applications are usually installed into a directory of their own. They often use auxiliary files such as overlays—a special type of file that contains the programming code necessary to provide a subset of the application's features. These auxiliary files often make it necessary or convenient to log into an application's home directory before running the application. This isn't a hard-and-fast rule, because some utilities create files too. But the most notable feature of an application, in the context of this discussion, is that it most often creates files having a specific format unique to the application. WordPerfect creates WordPerfect files, Lotus 1-2-3 creates 1-2-3 files, and so on.

For Related Information

- "Introducing the DOS File System," p. 113
- "Selecting Files in the DOS Shell," p. 101

In terms of working with files, the distinction between a utility and an application is simple. Utilities most often work with files in place, that is, in the location (directory) where they were created. Applications, on the other hand, usually work with files in specific directories created to store files that have the native format particular to that application.

When you're creating directory structures on your hard disk, it is usually a good idea to create dedicated directories for your applications where those applications can store the files you create. Doing so makes it much easier to find a particular file when you need it.

Listing Files with DIR

The DIR command is one of the first commands most DOS users learn. It is also the most used command in the DOS inventory. The command quickly gives you a list of your files, along with the date and time you created them, and the file sizes. If you type only DIR, you are using only a fraction of the command's full power. The following sections will help you to unlock the power of the DIR command.

Note

Many applications, when installed, by default create files in the application's home directory. Many applications have dozens of auxiliary files (overlays, printer drivers, video drivers, and so on). For this reason, it is a good idea to create one or more directories branching off the application's home directory where files created by the application are stored.

Many applications have settings that can specify which directory newly created files should be written in. Check the documentation for your applications to find out how to set up default directories for newly created files.

Issuing the DIR Command

DIR is an internal command. All the programming for this command is contained in COMMAND.COM, so you will never find DIR.EXE in your DOS directory. The syntax of the DIR command is shown here:

```
DIR FileNameExp /P /W /A:attributes /O:order /S /B /L
```

FileNameExp is a file name expression that can contain the drive, path, and file specification. Of course, the file name expression can include wildcards.

The DIR command also uses seven switches. These switches and their definitions are shown in table 8.1.

Table 8.1 DIR Switches

Switch	Action
/P	Displays one screen of information and then pauses. Pressing any key causes DIR to continue the listing.
/W	Displays only the file names, without the size, date, or modification time of the files. Files are listed in columns across the screen, rather than Switch Action one file name per line.

(continues)

Table 8.1 Continued

Switch	Action
/A:*attributes*	Displays only files that have, or lack, file attributes you specify, such as read-only, hidden, or system files.
/O:*order*	Lists files in a different sorted order, such as alphabetical order by name.
/S	Lists the contents of subdirectories.
/B	Lists file names only, one per line.
/L	Lists all file names in lowercase.
/C	Displays file compression ratio.
/CH	Displays file compression ratio using host allocation unit size.

The /A:*attributes* switch enables you to list only the files that have at least one attribute you specify. Substitute one or more of the following codes for the *attributes* parameter:

Attribute	Description
A	Archive attribute
D	Directory attribute
H	Hidden attribute
R	Read-only attribute
S	System attribute

The /O:*order* switch enables you to choose the sorted order in which DOS lists file names. To cause DOS to sort the file list in a particular order, substitute one of the following sort codes for the sort *order* parameter:

Attribute	Description
C	Sorts files by compression ratio
D	Sorts files chronologically by date and time
E	Sorts files alphabetically by file extension

Attribute	Description
G	Groups directories first before showing files
N	Sorts files alphabetically by name
S	Sorts files numerically by file size

When you issue the DIR command and any parameters are missing, DOS uses default values. If you omit the file name expression, DIR uses the currently logged directory. Unless you use the /O switch, files and directories are listed in their regular, unsorted order.

Understanding the Operation of DIR

When you issue the DIR command, the volume label and serial number of the disk are displayed along with a file name expression that specifies what directory is being displayed. Files and subdirectories are then displayed in the following format unless you specify the /W switch:

```
CIS       ZIP     55,029 08-01-93  11:47p
DISCPASS     <DIR>      06-16-93   3:10a
```

The first line of the example shows the standard format for files. Directory information is divided into five columns. From left to right they are as follows:

- File name
- Extension
- Size of the file in bytes
- The last date the file was edited
- The time of day the file was last edited

The second line of the example shows how directories are displayed. The <DIR> symbol indicates that the entry is a directory and thus doesn't have a byte count.

The information displayed by DIR includes most of the data stored in the directory table. The file attributes do not appear, but DOS uses them to determine whether to display a file. By default, hidden files are not included in this list. The location of the first cluster in the file allocation table (FAT) for the file also is not displayed because knowing the file's starting cluster is of little use to you as a user.

At the end of the listing, DOS indicates the total number of files in the directory, the total number of bytes used by the listed files, and the total number of bytes free on the current disk. The DIR report for C:\DOS, for example, might show the following information:

```
157 file(s)     6,455,328 bytes
              119,504,896 bytes free
```

If you add the size of each of the listed files on the disk and subtract the result from the total disk capacity, that number and the number of free bytes shown in the directory listing probably do not match, but the directory listing is correct. Remember that hidden files are not shown, and more important, the size of the file is not necessarily the same as the amount of disk space it occupies.

You might remember from earlier chapters that a cluster is the smallest possible chunk of disk space that can be allocated. When you create a file, no matter how small, DOS allocates at least one cluster to store the file. The directory listing shows the length of the data stored in bytes and calculates the free space, based on the number of free clusters on the disk. These free clusters are remaining positions on the disk not yet allocated to another file.

The free space reported by DIR is the number of unallocated clusters (also called allocation units) multiplied by the size of a cluster (1,024 bytes on most hard disks). You can also use CHKDSK to get a report of the total number of allocation units available on the disk.

Displaying a Screen of Information with DIR

If you add the /P switch to the DIR command, DOS pauses the scrolling of the screen at the end of each screen of information. Pressing any key displays the next page of information.

To see more file names, use the /W switch. When you use this switch, a directory listing like the one shown in figure 8.1 appears.

With hierarchical directories, your directory listing includes subdirectory names and files. In the wide listing, directory names are enclosed in brackets ([ ]). Because the file names are grouped so closely together, a wide listing can be useful when you want to see the types of files in a directory.

```
Volume in drive C is DCI 3
 Volume Serial Number is 1B2B-392C
 Directory of C:\DOS

[.]             [..]            CHOICE.COM      COUNTRY.SYS     GORILLA.BAS
MONEY.BAS       NIBBLES.BAS     REMLINE.BAS     DBLSPACE.BIN    ASSIGN.COM
KEYB.COM        KEYBOARD.SYS    MSD.EXE         NLSFUNC.EXE     README.TXT
DOSSHELL.COM    SCANDISK.EXE    ATTRIB.EXE      GRAFTABL.COM    CHKDSK.EXE
DEBUG.EXE       DEFRAG.EXE      DEFRAG.HLP      MIRROR.COM      EMM386.EXE
SCANFIX.EXE     EXPAND.EXE      MSHERC.COM      FDISK.EXE       FORMAT.COM
HELP.COM        MEM.EXE         4201.CPI        4208.CPI        5202.CPI
MORE.COM        LCD.CPI         SCANDISK.INI    SYS.COM         XCOPY.EXE
ANSI.SYS        APPEND.EXE      DBLWIN.HLP      DELTREE.EXE     DISKCOMP.COM
DISKCOPY.COM    DISPLAY.SYS     DOSHELP.HLP     DOSKEY.COM      DRIVER.SYS
FASTHELP.EXE    FASTOPEN.EXE    COMP.EXE        FC.EXE          FIND.EXE
SCANFIX.INI     WHATSNEW.TXT    GRAPHICS.COM    DOSSHELL.EXE    DOSSWAP.EXE
EDLIN.EXE       HIMEM.SYS       EXE2BIN.EXE     INTERLNK.EXE    INTERSVR.EXE
MOUSE.COM       MOVE.EXE        POWER.EXE       SMARTMON.EXE    SMARTMON.HLP
VFINTD.386      JOIN.EXE        CHKSTATE.SYS    DBLSPACE.EXE    DBLSPACE.HLP
DBLSPACE.INF    DBLSPACE.SYS    MEMMAKER.EXE    MEMMAKER.HLP    MEMMAKER.INF
RAMDRIVE.SYS    SIZER.EXE       SMARTDRV.EXE    MWBACKUP.EXE    EDIT.COM
EDIT.HLP        MWBACKF.DLL     MWBACKR.DLL     RECOVER.EXE     NETWORKS.TXT
OS2.TXT         QBASIC.EXE      QBASIC.HLP      HELP.HLP        MWBACKUP.HLP
EGA.SYS         WNTOOLS.GRP     LOADFIX.COM     MODE.COM        MSTOOLS.DLL
DOSSHELL.GRB    PRINT.EXE       SHARE.EXE       SUBST.EXE       MSBACKDB.OVL
MSBACKDR.OVL    DOSSHELL.HLP    MSBACKFB.OVL    MSBACKFR.OVL    MSBACKUP.HLP
MSBACKUP.EXE    MSBACKUP.OVL    MSBCONFG.HLP    MSBCONFG.OVL    MONOUMB.386
MWGRAFIC.DLL    MWUNDEL.EXE     MWUNDEL.HLP     SORT.EXE        UNDELETE.EXE
DOSSHELL.INI    MOUSE.INI       MSAV.INI        MSAV.EXE        PACKING.LST
CHKLIST.MS      MSAV.HLP        MSAVHELP.OVL    MSAVIRUS.LST    MWAV.EXE
MWAV.HLP        MWAVABSI.DLL    MWAVDLG.DLL     MWAVDOSL.DLL    MWAVDRVL.DLL
MWAVMGR.DLL     MWAVSCAN.DLL    MWAVSOS.DLL     MWAVTSR.EXE     DELOLDOS.EXE
EGA.CPI         EGA2.CPI        GRAPHICS.PRO    PRINTER.SYS     KEYBRD2.SYS
SMARTDRV.SYS    APPNOTES.TXT    LABEL.EXE       MSCDEX.EXE      REPLACE.EXE
DOSSHELL.VID    RESTORE.EXE     SETVER.EXE      TREE.COM        UNFORMAT.COM
VSAFE.COM       COMMAND.COM
      157 file(s)     6,455,328 bytes
                    119,504,896 bytes free
```

Fig. 8.1
Using the /W switch to see file names presented in wide format.

Using the Attributes Switch (/A). When you specify the /A switch, only those files having the attributes you include on the command line are listed in the DIR display. The /A switch uses one or more of the following codes for the *attributes* parameter:

D	Directory attribute
R	Read-only attribute
H	Hidden attribute
A	Archive attribute
S	System attribute

If you include the /A switch with no *attributes* parameter, DOS lists all file names—even the file names of hidden and system files—regardless of file attribute. To see only a listing of all hidden files in the current directory, enter the following command and press Enter:

```
DIR /AH
```

You can use attribute codes in any combination and in any order. You can list all file names with the read-only attribute and the archive attribute, for example, by issuing the following command:

```
DIR /ARA
```

DOS lists only file names that have both attributes.

To list only file names that do not have a certain attribute, insert a minus sign (–) before the attribute code. To see all files that are not directories and that don't have the archive bit, for example, type the following command at the command line and press Enter:

```
DIR /A-A-D
```

Using the Order Switch (/O). As mentioned earlier, the /O switch enables you to choose the order in which DOS lists file names. When you want DOS to sort the file list in a particular order, use the /O switch with the following sort codes:

C	Sorts files by compression ratio
D	Sorts files chronologically by date and time
E	Sorts files alphabetically by file extension
G	Groups directories first before showing files
N	Sorts files alphabetically by name
S	Sorts files numerically by file size

You can include sort codes in any combination. The order of the sort codes determines the final sorted order. For example /OEN sorts the file names first by name and then by extension. The command DIR /OEN sorts files by extension (for example, grouping all .COM files together and all .EXE files together) and then sorts the files by name. If you include the /O switch in a DIR command without specifying a sort code, DOS sorts the files alphabetically by name.

DOS assumes that all sorting should be done in ascending order—A through Z, smallest to largest, earliest to latest. DOS uses these criteria (the default setting) unless you precede your sort codes with a minus sign (–) to force the sort into reverse order—Z through A, largest to smallest, latest to earliest.

Using the /B and /L Switches. You can use the /B switch to display a "bare" file list—a list of file names without information about file size and the date and time the file was last changed. For example:

```
DIR A: /B
```

DOS lists all file names of files in the current directory of the floppy disk in drive A. DOS does not list file size or file date and time. If you want to capture the file list to a file, issue a command similar to this:

```
DIR A: /B >FILES.TXT
```

You can use the /L switch with the DIR command if you want the file names to appear in lowercase letters.

Searching for Files with the DIR Command

No matter how carefully you construct your directory structures, occasionally you will lose a file. Most of the time it is simply because you forgot where you put a particular file. Sometimes, however, it is because you have mistyped a file name expression. When you look in the directory you think a file should reside in, it is missing. Other times you simply have forgotten the exact name of the file you are looking for.

The DIR command is an effective tool for finding "lost" files when you use the /S switch. Entering the command

```
DIR C:\ /S
```

causes DOS to display every file written to drive C:. You can, of course, use file name expressions and other DIR switches to narrow the scope of the search. For example:

```
DIR C:\WP\*.DOC /S
```

This example lists all the .DOC files in the WordPerfect directory, and all the directories that branch off the WP directory.

Assume for the moment that you have created budget spreadsheets using your spreadsheet software and have saved these spreadsheets on your hard disk. You want to make a copy of the budget spreadsheet files, but you cannot remember the directory where they are located. However, you do remember that all the files start with the letters BUDG. You can use the DIR command to search the hard disk for the location of the files. Change to the root directory of your hard disk, and type the following command:

```
DIR BUDG*.* /S
```

When you press Enter, DOS displays a listing similar to this:

```
 Volume in drive C is DCI 3
 Volume Serial Number is 1B2B-392C

Directory of C:\SPREADSH\QPRO4DAT

BUDGET   WQ1       4,037 10-05-92   2:00a
        1 files(s)       4,037 bytes

Directory of C:\WORD_PRO\ENDATA

BUDGET   WK1       5,120 04-07-92   8:51p
        1 files(s)       5,120 bytes

Total files listed:
        2 files(s)       9,157 bytes
                   119,504,896 bytes free
```

Customizing the DIR Command

If you find that you continually use one or more of the seven switches with the DIR command, you can avoid typing them repeatedly by creating an environment variable named DIRCMD, using the following command:

```
SET DIRCMD=switches
```

For the *switches* parameter, substitute the switch or switches you want DOS to use automatically. If, for example, you want DOS to sort file names alphabetically and to pause scrolling after each screenful of information, include the following command in your AUTOEXEC.BAT:

```
SET DIRCMD=/ON/P
```

Reboot the computer. DOS creates the environment variable DIRCMD and gives it the value /ON/P. Each time you issue the DIR command, DOS adds these two switches automatically.

You can override a switch that is recorded in the DIRCMD by preceding the switch with a minus sign (–). For example, to override the /P switch currently recorded in DIRCMD so that DOS lists all file names without pausing at the end of each screen of information, issue the DIR command shown here:

```
DIR /-P
```

Viewing Files

After you have found a file, it is often necessary to peek into the file to find out what it contains. Knowing what a file contains is crucial to knowing how best to work with the file. DOS provides tools to enable you to look into files.

A previous chapter mentioned that DOS stores files on disks in binary format—zeros and ones. You also read that these binary digits, grouped in bundles of eight, form bytes and that each byte can form one of 256 values called the ASCII code, which is used to represent letters, numbers, computer commands, and so on. That's fine as far as it goes, but it is a simplistic view that doesn't present the whole picture.

Bits and bytes are used in many ways by a computer. The microprocessor in your computer is designed to use binary digits in groups of eight, true. But those binary digits can be used in different contexts. Each bit in a byte might be used to indicate the status of a condition, with 1 meaning on and 0 meaning off. Large numeric values, such as a spreadsheet might use, might be stored in two or four bytes, which get translated into decimal numbers that users understand. Bytes are also used to deliver instructions (program code) to your computer's microprocessor.

It isn't at all important for you to understand these contexts to be able to work with your computer, but knowing that these contexts exist makes it much easier to work with files. When it comes to viewing the contents of files, having this knowledge is essential.

Understanding Types of Files

From a user's point of view, files fall into two categories: binary and ASCII. Binary files are not understandable by humans. When you try to look into them, they appear to be gibberish. Strings of smiley faces, hearts, and a slew of weird-looking symbols are interspersed with letters and numbers to produce an unintelligible display. When you see this kind of display, you know you have opened a binary file.

ASCII files use bytes to represent the symbols we use to communicate every day: letters, numerals, punctuation marks, and so on. An ASCII file is the simplest file format used by DOS. When DOS displays or prints an ASCII file, the groupings of binary digits are directly translated into a human readable format. ASCII files are also referred to as DOS text files, or simply text files.

Unless you are programming, binary files should be of little interest. DOS does provide the DEBUG command to view and edit binary files, but you had better know what you are doing. The DEBUG command is documented in the Command Reference of this book for the sake of completeness, but its use is far beyond the scope of this book. It is enough for you to know that if you open a binary file, you can look all you want, but under no circumstances should you change anything or do a disk save on the file, even by accident. Changing even one byte in an executable file can render a program useless, or can even be dangerous to your data.

Caution

Some files contain a mixture of binary and ASCII data. Almost all modern applications store data and documents in proprietary file formats that contain binary elements. Many of these proprietary formats use a binary header. A header is a block of information at the beginning of a file that is used by a program as a map to the contents of the file.

Editing these types of files with a tool other than the program that created it can be dangerous. You can change the file so that the parent program will no longer recognize the file as being in the proper format.

If you know that a file was created by a specific application, use that application to view and edit the file. The parent application usually has a method of turning data into ASCII format, either with a conversion utility or by a special file save feature built into the application. See the documentation of your application for details.

DOS provides two commands for viewing the contents of ASCII files: EDIT and TYPE. The EDIT command enables you to view and edit files. For complete information on EDIT, see Chapter 15, "Using the DOS Editor."

Using the TYPE Command to View Files

When you need to see the contents of an ASCII text file, you can use the TYPE command. By redirecting the output of TYPE, you can print a hard copy of the file.

The syntax for the TYPE command is shown in the next line:

```
TYPE filename.ext
```

Replace *filename.ext* with the name of the file you want DOS to display. (Remember to include a disk drive and path name, if necessary.) A file name is not optional. Wildcard characters are not permitted because TYPE can display the contents of only one file at a time.

TYPE is designed to display the contents of a text file that contains ASCII characters. When you issue a TYPE command, DOS opens the specified file and sends the file's contents to the screen as ASCII characters. When DOS encounters a Ctrl-Z character (ASCII decimal 26; the end-of-file character), it stops displaying the contents of the file and returns to the command prompt.

When you use TYPE to view a text file, the file's contents can fill and begin to scroll off the screen faster than you can read the text. You can press Ctrl-S or the Pause key (available only on the Enhanced Keyboard) to stop scrolling, but the text you want to see might already have scrolled off the screen. The MORE filter displays a screenful of a command's output and then pauses until you press a key. You can use MORE with the TYPE command as shown in the following example:

```
TYPE AUTOEXEC.BAT ¦ MORE
```

The ¦ character in this command is the DOS pipe character, which instructs DOS to send a command's output to the filter that follows the pipe character. Piping to MORE causes DOS to pause the scrolling of the screen when the screen fills. Press any key to display the next screenful.

Note

An even easier way to display an ASCII file one screen at a time is to redirect a file into the MORE command without using the TYPE command. Use the following syntax:

```
MORE < d:path\filename.ext
```

The < symbol causes DOS to use the specified file parameter as input to the MORE filter. DOS displays the file, one page at a time, displaying the message — `More` — at the end of each page. To display a file in the C:\DOS directory, for example, type the following command (replacing *filename.ext* with the file name and extension of the file you want to view), and press Enter:

```
MORE < C:\DOS\filename.ext
```

For detailed information on DOS redirection and MORE, see Chapter 14, "Controlling Devices."

If you want a simple printed copy of the contents of a text file, you can redirect the output of the TYPE command to the printer by using the special redirection character, the greater-than sign (>). To print the contents of the README.TXT file, for example, make sure that your printer is on-line, and then issue the following command:

```
TYPE README.TXT >PRN
```

Your printer prints the file. (Because TYPE does not format the text into pages, the printed output might not break at page boundaries.)

When you use the TYPE command, remember the following guidelines:

- The output of TYPE stops when the command encounters the first Ctrl-Z in the file.
- Because TYPE does not accept wildcards in the file name parameter, use of the command is limited to one file at a time.
- TYPE tries to interpret any file as an ASCII text file, even if the file contains non-ASCII data. If you use a binary file (such as a .COM or .EXE file) as the file parameter, TYPE's output might produce graphical characters, control-character sequences, and beeps. TYPE's output might even lock up your computer, forcing you to reboot.
- You can pause TYPE's output by pressing Ctrl-S or Pause. Press any key to resume scrolling.
- You can terminate TYPE's output by pressing Ctrl-C or Ctrl-Break.

Searching for Text with FIND

As you saw earlier in this chapter, you can use the DIR command to locate files if you know something about their file name. But what do you use if you know only that somewhere in the file it says, "Meet me in St. Louis, Louie," and that the string is to be found in one of three files? You use the FIND command. Because FIND is useful in various situations, it is covered in detail in Chapter 14, "Controlling Devices."

Using Interlnk to Share Another Computer's Resources

More and more DOS users in the past few years have come to own more than one computer. Often they have a desktop machine in the office and a notebook or laptop computer they use when they travel. Although having two computers extends your computing power to places other than your office, having two computers can also make it difficult to keep data in both places up-to-date. And it is not uncommon for two users in an office to need to share files and maybe even a printer at times.

A relatively new DOS feature, Interlnk, enables you to access drives and printers on a remote computer as though they were part of your computer. You can use this feature to transfer files from a laptop or notebook computer to your desktop computer, to print files located on your portable computer on a printer attached to your desktop computer, and even to run programs directly from the remote computer.

When you use Interlnk, one computer—the server—becomes the completely passive "slave" of the other. Before you start, decide which computer you want to work on. The server should be the computer with the resources—files or printers—that you want to use remotely.

Setting Up Interlnk

Interlnk uses two executable files. INTERLNK.EXE is used to make a machine the client. This file must be loaded into the computer using the DEVICE command in CONFIG.SYS. After the Interlnk client software is loaded, it remains in memory as a terminate-and-stay-ready (TSR) application that responds to a set of commands not normally available in DOS.

INTERSVR.EXE is a command run from the DOS prompt. It completely takes over the system to act as an extension to the client computer running INTERLNK.EXE. You can run INTERSVR in a Windows-hosted DOS session, but while INTERSVR is running, all multitasking activities in Windows are suspended.

Note

Interlnk is the name given to the features provided by INTERLNK.EXE and INTERSVR.EXE. INTERLNK and INTERSVR are commands provided by Interlnk. You can tell by the capitalization whether the following sections are speaking of Interlnk features or the INTERLNK command.

Tip
To make Interlnk services available, you must load INTERLNK.EXE in CONFIG.SYS using the DEVICE command. This loads Interlnk's client features as a TSR, which occupies memory that might be better used for other things when you are not using Interlnk.

Use DOS's multiple configuration feature to enable your computer to boot with or without INTERLNK.EXE loaded. For information on multiple configurations, see Chapter 2, "Starting DOS."

You need to have a special cable built for use with Interlnk. The cable is used to connect one machine to the other and can use either a serial or a parallel connection. A standard printer cable cannot be used because the connector pins of an Interlnk cable must follow the configuration shown in table 8.2.

Table 8.2 Cable Configurations for Use with Interlnk

Pin Connections for Serial Port Connections

9 Pin	25 Pin		25 Pin	9 Pin
5	7	↔	7	5*
3	2	↔	3	2
7	4	↔	5	8
6	6	↔	20	4
2	3	↔	2	3
8	5	↔	4	7
4	20	↔	6	6

* *Ground wire*

Pin Connections for Parallel Port Connections

25 Pin		25 Pin
2	↔	15
3	↔	13
4	↔	12
5	↔	10

Pin Connections for Parallel Port Connections		
25 Pin		**25 Pin**
6	↔	11
15	↔	2
13	↔	3
12	↔	4
10	↔	5
11	↔	6
25	↔	25

Note

You can use either a serial or a parallel connection to wire the two computers together, but only a serial connection using all 7 wires is capable of using the /RCOPY switch of INTERSVR. The /RCOPY switch enables you to connect to computers that do not have Interlnk already installed by copying INTERSVR.EXE to the remote computer and running it.

If you have only a 3 wire, or NULL modem, serial cable, or parallel cable, you need to carry floppy disks to put INTERSVR.EXE on the slave machine.

Loading INTERLNK.EXE

Interlnk uses a client-server metaphor to divide up the responsibilities of the software. INTERLNK.EXE provides the client portion of Interlnk. The client module takes complete control of the server machine. Disks on the server appear to the client as if they were part of the client machine. Printers on the server are likewise made to appear as if they were attached to the client. INTERLNK.EXE is loaded at boot time via CONFIG.SYS. The syntax to load the Interlnk client portion, INTERLNK.EXE is shown here:

```
DEVICE=d:path\INTERLNK.EXE /DRIVES:n /NOPRINTER /COM:n ¦
   address /LPT:n¦ address /AUTO /NOSCAN /LOW /BAUD:rate /V
```

The file name expression indicates the drive and directory where INTERLNK.EXE is written to disk.

/DRIVES specifies the number of redirected drives. The default is 3.

/NOPRINTER specifies that printers are not to be redirected. By default, all printers are redirected.

/COM specifies a serial port to be used for data transfer. The port can be specified as either *n*, the port number, or the address of the port. If you specify the /COM switch without an accompanying /LPT switch, no parallel port is used. By default, Interlnk scans all available serial ports and uses the first port it finds connected to the server.

/LPT specifies a parallel port to be used for data transfer. The port can be specified as either *n*, the port number, or the address of the port. By default, the first port found connected to the server is used. If you specify the /LPT switch without an accompanying /COM switch, no serial port is used. By default, all COM and LPT ports are scanned.

/AUTO causes Interlnk to be loaded only when a connection is detected. By default, Interlnk is loaded even when no client/server connection is detected.

/NOSCAN causes Interlnk to be loaded into memory but not activated until you issue the INTERLNK command. DOS will not recognize the INTERLNK command, however, unless the device driver has been loaded.

/LOW specifies that Interlnk is to be installed in conventional memory. By default, Interlnk is loaded into an Upper Memory Block if space is available.

/BAUD is used only in serial communications to set the speed at which the two computers communicate through the serial cable. Valid rates are 9600, 19200, 38400, 57600, and the default, 115200. If you find serial communications unreliable, try lowering the baud rate to eliminate transmission errors.

/V is used for serial communications to prevent conflicts with the computer's timer. If one of the computers hangs up when you try to communicate, try the /V switch.

Normally, Interlnk scans all your drives and all your ports when this device driver loads. If you have a serial mouse and plan to run Microsoft Windows, add a parameter that tells Interlnk which port is connected to the remote computer. If you are using a second printer port for your connection, for example, type the following line:

```
DEVICE=C:\DOS\INTERLNK.EXE /LPT2
```

This command prevents Interlnk from examining all your serial and parallel ports (and from disrupting your mouse operations in the process).

Loading the Server

INTERSVR is an executable file, loaded from the command line, that suspends all the operations of the computer and gives control over the computer's resources to INTERLNK running on the client computer. You do not have to load INTERLNK.EXE on the server to make an Interlnk connection.

If you load INTERSVR on a machine that is running a multitasking system such as Windows or QEMM, all background operations are suspended until you exit INTERSVR. The syntax to load the server portion of Interlnk, INTERSVR.EXE is shown here:

```
INTERSVR.EXE /X=drives /COM:n ¦ address /LPT:n¦ address
   /BAUD:rate /B /V /RCOPY
```

/X specifies the letter or letters of drives that will be excluded from redirection. By default, all drives are redirected. If /X is used, any drives listed are unavailable to the client.

/COM specifies a serial port to be used for data transfer. The port can be specified as either *n*, the port number, or the address of the port. If you specify the /COM switch without an accompanying /LPT switch, no parallel port is used. By default, Interlnk scans all available serial ports and uses the first port it finds connected to the client.

/LPT specifies a parallel port to be used for data transfer. The port can be specified as either *n*, the port number, or the address of the port. By default, the first port found connected to the client is used. If you specify the /LPT switch without an accompanying /COM switch, no serial port is used. By default, all COM and LPT ports are scanned.

/BAUD is used only in serial communications to set the speed at which the two computers communicate through the serial cable. Valid rates are 9600, 19200, 38400, 57600, and the default, 115200. If you find serial communications unreliable, try lowering the baud rate to eliminate transmission errors.

/B causes the Interlnk screen to be displayed in monochrome.

/V is used for serial communications to prevent conflicts with the computer's timer. If one of the computers hangs up when you try to communicate, try the /V switch.

/RCOPY is used to copy the Interlnk files from one computer to another. You must be using a fully pinned serial cable, and the MODE and CTTY commands must be available on the computer where Interlnk is being installed.

Establishing the Interlnk Connection

After you have loaded INTERLNK on the client machine, all you have to do is load INTERSVR on the server machine, and you're in business. When you issue the INTERSVR command on the server, you see a screen similar to the one shown in figure 8.2.

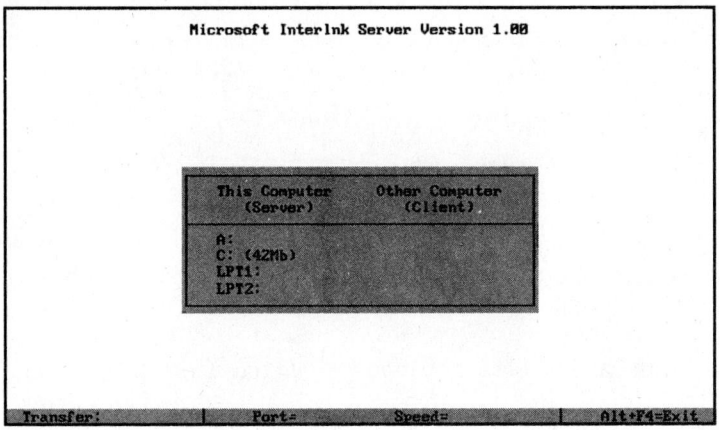

Fig. 8.2 INTERSVR, activated and waiting for INTERLNK.

After you have INTERSVR working on the server, return to the client machine and issue the command

```
INTERLNK
```

This command activates the connection. A message similar to the one shown in figure 8.3 appears, telling you how you can access the server's resources.

Fig. 8.3 Establishing the Interlnk connection.

```
Scanning

Port=LPT2

This Computer          Other Computer
  (Client)                (Server)
------------    -----------------------
D:          equals    A:
E:          equals    C:(42Mb)
LPT1:       equals    LPT2:
```

This message tells you that drive A of the remote computer now is available to you as drive D of your local computer, and drive C of the remote computer now is drive E of your local computer.

Using Interlnk to Transfer Files

After you have Interlnk running on both computers, you can use standard DOS commands to gain access to the server's resources.

Using the values shown in figure 8.3, if you want to see a directory on drive C of the remote computer, type the command

```
DIR E:
```

To copy files from one computer to the other, issue a COPY (or XCOPY) command, with a drive of one computer as the source and a drive of the other computer as the target. To copy C:\SPREADSH\BUDGET.WQ1 from your local computer to the server, for example, you would issue a command such as this:

```
COPY C:\SPREADSH\BUDGET.WQ1 E:\SPREADSH
```

Using a Remote Printer

Suppose that your remote computer is connected to a laser printer and your local computer isn't. The status report indicates that LPT1 of your computer is linked to LPT2 of the remote computer. Assuming that the laser printer is attached to LPT2 on that computer, you install your program to print its file to LPT2. Interlnk takes care of redirecting the print job to the server.

Installing Interlnk Remotely

If one of your computers is running DOS 6.2 and the other is running a version of DOS older than DOS 6.0, Interlnk will not be installed. Interlnk can install itself on the remote computer, however, if Interlnk is running on the local computer and if the computers are connected via a serial cable using all 7 pins. A parallel cable will not suffice. Also, the MODE command must be available on the remote unit. On the local computer, issue the following command:

```
INTERLNK /RCOPY
```

You are prompted to select the serial port to be used. After you indicate that port, go to the remote computer and type the following commands:

```
MODE COMn:2400,N,8,1,P
CTTY COMn:
```

In these commands, *n* represents the number of the serial port you are using on the remote computer. This parameter forces the remote computer to accept input from the specified serial port. When you finish typing these commands, return to the computer on which Interlnk is installed, and press Enter. Messages on both computers tell you that INTERLNK.EXE and INTERSVR.EXE are being copied. On the receiving computer, the message looks like the following example:

Tip
Interlnk is usable for occasional resource sharing. If you constantly must interrupt someone's work, however, to use their printer, you should consider investing in a printer sharing device or installing a small network, such as LANtastic or Netware Lite.

```
Loading bootstrap

Receiving INTERSVR.EXE (37266) 100%

Receiving INTERLNK.EXE (17133) 100%
```

The files are placed in the current directory of the receiving computer. Both computers then return to DOS. You can use either computer as the client or the server, provided that you install the device driver in the server's CONFIG.SYS. If the remote computer is running an early version of DOS, however (3.3 or earlier, for example), you might not be able to access files on the server that were created under a version of DOS greater than DOS 5.0, especially if those files are larger than 32M.

Running Programs Remotely

After you are linked to another computer by Interlnk, you can use that computer's drives as though they were part of your local computer. Thus, you can run a program on the remote computer from the command line as you would run one on your local computer.

Because programs on the remote computer do not appear on your local computer's PATH, you must either log onto the drive and directory where the program resides or enter a PATH command to extend the client's path to a remote directory on the server.

Which technique is appropriate depends on how the program works. If, for example, the program must be run from its home directory when it is not on the path, use the first option. Otherwise, you can use the second technique.

The preceding techniques actually just load the program from the remote computer and run it on your local computer. Consequently, you might encounter problems if the program is set up to use specific aspects of the remote computer's hardware that the local computer lacks. Suppose, for example, that the two computers have different types of screens. The program might be set up to display text and graphics on the remote computer's screen and might be unable to display anything on your local computer.

Another problem occurs if the program expects to find specific files on a particular drive but cannot access the drive because the drive names have been changed. Drive C still is drive C of your local computer, but drive C of the remote computer now is known to DOS as drive E of your local computer. If the program needs to find certain files in drive C, it cannot find those files unless they also exist in the same directory of your local computer. (In such a case, don't run the program from the remote computer; use the version on your local computer instead.)

Summary

DOS offers many useful commands for working with files. Use these commands to arrange your files and to keep your computer's disks well-organized and accessible. As you gain experience with file-management commands, you probably will want to incorporate additional switches or take advantage of more of the DOS defaults.

In this chapter, you learned the following key points:

- The end-of-file character ^Z marks the end of ASCII files.
- The TYPE command displays an ASCII file's contents.
- The DIR command, using the /S switch, can be used to search an entire disk, or any branch of subdirectories, to find files.
- The display produced by DIR lists information about file attributes, sizes, and so on. You can use the DIR command's switches and parameters to sort file names, include hidden files, and customize the functionality of DIR.
- Interlnk provides a method to connect two computers. One computer acts as the server, and the other client computer controls both machines. Interlnk is useful for copying files to and from notebook computers. Interlnk also enables you to use the server's printer as if it were attached to the client.

In the next chapter, you learn about managing files using commands to copy, move, delete, undelete, and compare files.

Chapter 9

Managing Your Files

This chapter concentrates on those DOS commands used to perform housekeeping functions on your files. As you work with applications software (word processors, spreadsheets, presentation graphics, and so on), you will begin building a large number of files that contain data. To effectively manage these files, you need to know the ins and outs of copying, moving, deleting, and undeleting files, both individually and in groups.

Copying Files

Probably the most common file-related function is copying files from one disk or directory to another. Copying files is a fundamental job for disk operating systems. MS-DOS provides the internal COPY command for use at the command line. Copying files via the DOS Shell was covered in Chapter 4, "Using the DOS Shell."

The DOS COPY command enables you to copy files as well as copy data to and from logical devices. Figure 9.1 diagrams the copy operation used with several possible inputs and two possible outputs. Three of the possible inputs consist of more than one file or logical device. DOS can join two or more inputs into one output in a process called combining. You might never need to use all these inputs and outputs, but they're available.

When you perform a copy operation, remember the following guidelines:

- The source parameter must contain at least one of the following parameters: path, file, or device.
- If the file specification portion of a file name expression is omitted, all files in the specified directory and drive are copied. This situation is equivalent to supplying *.* as the source-file parameter.

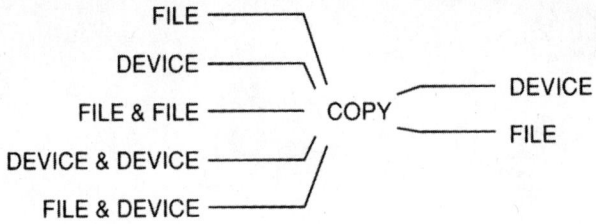

Fig. 9.1
Possible inputs and outputs in a copy operation.

- You can specify additional source-file parameters by using the + operator to combine the files.
- If the source-file parameter contains a wildcard and the destination parameter is a file name, the destination file will be the combination of source files that matches the source-file parameter.
- If COPY detects an attempt to copy a single source file to itself (same drive, directory, file name, and extension), the copy operation is aborted.
- The optional destination parameter consists of a combination of drive, path, and file name parameters. If you don't provide a drive or path, DOS uses the current drive or path for the destination. If you don't specify a destination file name, DOS uses the source file's name as the destination parameter.
- COPY definitely is a versatile file-management workhorse, but you do have to be careful. An incorrect COPY operation can do nearly as much damage as an incorrect DEL command because the destination file's entries in the FAT and in the directory are not saved as they were, making file recovery all but impossible. Be sure to treat COPY with respect. Many programs include warning messages as part of their internal file copying commands. The COPY command gives no warning when it is about to overwrite existing files.

Using the COPY Command

A COPY command line can be created in various ways. All the variations say the same thing to DOS: "COPY THIS THERE." The THIS represents the source—the files to be copied. The THERE represents the target—the disk location or device you want the files to be copied to.

In a COPY command, the order of the parameter requirements always moves from the source to the destination, or target. The full syntax for the COPY command is shown here:

```
COPY SourceExpression TargetExpression /V/A/B/Y
```

The *SourceExpression* and *TargetExpression* parameters specify either a file name expression that specifies one or more files, or a DOS device. For example:

```
COPY STUFF.TXT PRN
```

In this example, the file STUFF.TXT (an ASCII text file) is copied to the printer to produce a hard copy of the file's contents. Use COPY to print ASCII files only, because files containing word processor codes, graphics, or file headers don't result in clean reproductions of the file's content.

For combining files, the source expression can be two or more file name expressions that specify a single file, joined with the + symbol. For example:

```
COPY MEMO1.TXT + B:\MEMOS\MEMO2.TXT  H:\MYMEMO.TXT
```

In this example, the file MEMO1.TXT, located in the currently logged directory, will be combined with a file found in the MEMOS directory of drive B to create a file on drive H having the name MYMEMO.TXT.

The COPY command has three switches you can use: /V, /A, and /B. The /A and /B switches can be applied to individual file name expressions in both the source and the target expressions. The following list details the uses of the COPY switches:

- The /V switch verifies that the copy has been recorded correctly.
- When /A is used in a *SourceExpression*, files are treated as ASCII; that is, COPY copies all the information in the file up to, but not including, the first end-of-file marker (ASCII decimal 26). DOS ignores anything after the end-of-file marker.

  When /A is used in a *TargetExpression*, an end-of-file marker is added to the end of the ASCII file after it is copied.
- When /B is used in a *SourceExpression*, COPY copies the entire file (based on its size, as listed in the directory) as if the copied file were a program file (binary). Any end-of-file markers are copied.

When used in a *TargetExpression*, /B does not add the end-of-file marker to the end of the copied data.

- The /Y switch is used to indicate whether you want COPY to overwrite files with the same name without prompting. You can also use the /-Y switch to indicate that you want to be prompted.

Copying Groups of Files

Suppose that you have 20 files you want to copy to a floppy disk or to another directory on your hard disk. You can use wildcards in the file name expression to specify a subset of the files in a directory. For example:

```
COPY C:\ROCCANTI\*.TXT B:
```

This example finds all the .TXT files in the ROCCANTI directory and copies them onto the floppy disk in drive B. You will, of course, have to make sure that there is enough room on the disk in drive B to receive the files. Use the DIR command to find out how many bytes the files to be copied will require and to make sure that at least that much space is available on drive B.

If you want to copy all the files in a directory to another disk or to another directory, use a command similar to this:

```
COPY E:\CLIPPER5\INVNTRY\*.* H:\TEST
```

In this example, the *.* wildcard expression is used to specify that all files in the INVNTRY directory are to be copied to the TEST directory on drive H.

Some keyboards do not have a conveniently placed key for the asterisk. You might want to use the . wildcard to specify all files in the directory, as in this line:

```
COPY E:\CLIPPER5\INVNTRY\. H:\TEST
```

This command is functionally equivalent to the preceding example.

Combining Text Files

Although you can use COPY to combine any files, the combine operation is most effective when the files are ASCII text files. In most cases, combining binary files results in an unusable destination file.

For the following examples, assume that the current directory contains three text files, all with .TXT extensions. The files and their contents are listed here:

File	Contents
INTRO.TXT	Combining is
BODY.TXT	the joining of files
ENDING.TXT	into a new file.

To join the three files into a fourth file, type the following command:

```
COPY INTRO.TXT+BODY.TXT+ENDING.TXT ALL.TXT
```

The resulting file, ALL.TXT, contains the text from the three source files. To verify ALL.TXT, issue the following command:

```
TYPE ALL.TXT
```

TYPE sends the contents of ALL.TXT to the screen. DOS displays the following output:

```
Combining is the joining of files into a new file.
```

Note

If you omit the target expression, or specify only drive and path information in the file name expression, the file created by combining files will have the same name as the first file name specified in the source expression.

Renaming Files with COPY

As you might guess from the examples in the preceding section, you can change the name of a file or group of files with COPY. For example:

```
COPY *.TXT *.ASC
```

This example copies all the files in the current directory having the extension .TXT. Each .TXT file is copied to an .ASC file. The .ASC files have the same names as the original .TXT files. The contents are the same and the names are the same—only the extensions are altered.

Copying from a Device to a File

A common and handy use of the COPY command is copying to a file keystrokes entered from the keyboard or console device. (CON is the device name for console, a device constructed using your keyboard and monitor.) You can use the resulting text file as a batch file, a configuration file, a memo, and so on.

To practice copying from the keyboard to a file, you can create a simple batch file that changes the current directory to \123R3 and starts Lotus 1-2-3 Release 3. The command that creates the batch file is shown here:

```
COPY CON C:\DOS\RUN123.BAT
```

When you press Enter, DOS displays the cursor on the next line; the DOS prompt does not appear. You can type the file by following these steps:

1. Type **C:** and press Enter. The cursor drops to the next line.
2. Type **CD\123R3** and press Enter. The cursor drops to the next line.
3. Type **LOTUS** and press Enter. The cursor drops to the next line.
4. Press the F6 function key or Ctrl-Z to indicate the end of the file. DOS displays the end-of-file marker (^Z).
5. Press Enter. The ^Z code indicates to DOS that you are finished entering data into the file. DOS responds with the message `1 file(s) copied.`

To confirm that the new file is the way you want it, you can use the TYPE command to review the contents of the file.

Note

If you try this example on your system, be sure to use the appropriate directory names for DOS and Lotus 1-2-3.

For Related Information

- "Expanding the File System Through Subdirectories," p. 131
- "Creating a Simple Batch File," p. 414

Knowing how to use COPY CON can be both a lifesaver and a pain in the neck. A lifesaver because COPY CON will enable you to create a text file on any DOS system. A pain in the neck because after you have pressed Enter to go to the next line, there is no way to go back and edit previous lines. If you make a mistake, you must start over again.

If the DOS EDIT command, found only in Version 5.0 and later, is available, or if some other ASCII editor is available, use it. You will be much better off using the editor than the COPY command because you will be able to more easily correct any typos you find.

Using the MOVE Command

In early versions of DOS, if you wanted to move a file from one place to another, you had to first copy the file, then delete the original. Now DOS enables you to move files from one location to another using the MOVE command.

The MOVE command's syntax is similar to the syntax for COPY. In effect, the syntax of the MOVE command says, "MOVE THIS THERE."

In a MOVE command, the order of the parameter requirements always moves from the source to the destination, or target. The full syntax for the MOVE command is as shown here:

```
MOVE SourceExpression(s) TargetExpression /Y
```

Caution

If you omit a path parameter from both the source and the target, you either copy or rename the source file, depending on whether the specified target file name exists. If the name exists, you copy the source file over the target file, eliminating the target file. If the name does not exist, you rename the source file.

If your source parameter includes only one file, you can rename the file as you move it by specifying a new file name or extension as part or all of the target parameter. If your source parameter includes more than one file, you cannot use a file name and extension parameter as part of the target parameter. If you do so, however, DOS assumes that you want the target file to be the target for all the files to be moved, and the message `Cannot move multiple files to a single file` appears. You must, however, specify either a drive or a directory as the target.

The /Y switch is used to indicate whether you want MOVE to overwrite files with the same name without prompting. You can also use the /-Y switch to indicate that you want to be prompted.

As an example of how to use MOVE, suppose you want to move a file called BUDGET.WQ1 from a directory called C:\SPREADSH\QPRO4DAT to a directory called D:\OLDFILES (assuming neither directory is current). In this case, you enter this command:

```
MOVE C:\SPREADSH\QPRO4DAT\BUDGET92.WQ1 D:\OLDFILES
```

If the move is successful, DOS displays the following message:

```
c:\spreadsh\qpro4dat\budget92.wq1 => d:\oldfiles\budget92.wq1 [ok]
```

Caution

If the source and target parameters represent the same file, DOS erases the file without warning you.

Moving Directories and Files

You can use MOVE to move files from one directory to another. If the target directory doesn't exist, the MOVE command creates it. Figure 9.2 shows the MOVE command moving all the files in H:\TEST to a new TEST directory on drive G.

Fig. 9.2
Moving all the files in a directory.

```
H:\>rd g:\test

H:\>move h:\test\*.* g:\test
Make directory "g:\test"? [yn] y
h:\test\ground.dbf => g:\test\ground.dbf [ok]
h:\test\group.dbf => g:\test\group.dbf [ok]
h:\test\guest.dbf => g:\test\guest.dbf [ok]
h:\test\passw.dbf => g:\test\passw.dbf [ok]
h:\test\paymts.dbf => g:\test\paymts.dbf [ok]
h:\test\pay_vend.dbf => g:\test\pay_vend.dbf [ok]
h:\test\res_air.dbf => g:\test\res_air.dbf [ok]
h:\test\res_car.dbf => g:\test\res_car.dbf [ok]
h:\test\res_grou.dbf => g:\test\res_grou.dbf [ok]
h:\test\res_hot.dbf => g:\test\res_hot.dbf [ok]
h:\test\res_tour.dbf => g:\test\res_tour.dbf [ok]
h:\test\semi_4.dbf => g:\test\semi_4.dbf [ok]
h:\test\tour.dbf => g:\test\tour.dbf [ok]
h:\test\trans.mem => g:\test\trans.mem [ok]

H:\>
```

As you can see in the figure, the source expression specifies that all the files in the TEST directory on drive H are to be moved to a directory called TEST on drive G. Because the directory doesn't exist on drive G, MOVE prompts you to make sure that you intend to create a new directory to hold the moved files. As each file is moved, MOVE displays the original name, a => symbol, and the new name of each file.

The MOVE command has no effect on H:\TEST other than to remove the files from the directory. The source directory is not deleted from drive H.

Also, the MOVE command pays no attention to the Read Only file attribute. Even files marked Read Only are moved.

Renaming Directories with MOVE

Another use for the MOVE command is to rename a directory. For example:

```
MOVE C:\MEMOS  C:\LETTERS
```

The effect of the example command is to rename the MEMOS directory as LETTERS without affecting the files contained in the directory.

Renaming Files

If copying files is the most common file-related function of DOS, renaming files probably follows close on its heels. The reasons for renaming a file are many. You might want to use the current file name for another file, or perhaps you want to create a name that better describes the contents of the current file. Whatever the reason, DOS enables you to rename a file using the internal command RENAME. Like some other DOS commands, RENAME also has a short form, REN. Which form you use depends on how you feel about typing three extra letters.

The DOS rename operation changes the name in a file's directory entry, but the file and its physical location on the disk remain unchanged. Because two files in the same directory cannot have the same name, DOS will not change a file name if the new file name already exists.

When you use RENAME, remember the following guidelines:

- You can use the commands REN and RENAME interchangeably at the command line. Both commands produce identical results.
- You must supply both an old file name and a new file name. The file names can contain wildcards for DOS to use in pattern matching.
- You cannot use the RENAME operation to move a file from one directory or disk to another directory or disk.

This is the syntax for RENAME:

```
RENAME OldExpression NewExpression
```

or

```
REN OldExpression NewExpression
```

The REN command requires two parameters. *OldExpression* is a file name expression that specifies the files to be renamed. *NewExpression* is a file name expression that specifies what the new names of the files will be. For example:

```
REN MEMO.TXT MEMO12.TXT
```

This example renames the file MEMO.TXT as MEMO12.TXT.

You can also use wildcards to specify groups of files to be renamed. Suppose, for example, that you have a group of files in a directory named MEMO1.TXT, MEMO2.TXT, and so on. Issue this command:

```
REN MEMO?.TXT LTR?.DOC
```

The result is that MEMO1.TXT is renamed as LTR1.DOC, MEMO2.TXT becomes LTR2.DOC, and so on.

Note

If you are not sure which files a wildcard parameter will match, issue the DIR command, using the wildcard pattern that you plan to use in the file name parameter. DIR lists the matching file names. Study these names carefully to see whether using the wildcard pattern with the RENAME command will produce the result you expect.

Combining Copying and Directory Management with XCOPY

The external command XCOPY is an enhanced version of COPY that, among other capabilities, can copy whole directories and their subdirectories while creating directories on the destination disk.

Using XCOPY, you can exercise much more control over the files to be copied. For example, you can copy only those files with the archive attribute set, or only those files with a date stamp on or after a specified date. The syntax of XCOPY is similar to that of COPY, but the switches are more complex. The XCOPY syntax is as follows:

```
XCOPY SourceExpression  TargetExpression  /V/P/W/S/E/A/M/Y/D:date
```

Just like the COPY command, XCOPY takes file name expressions to specify the source files and the target files for the operation. Unlike COPY, XCOPY has several switches that enable you to finely control how the copy is done. Here is a rundown of the available switches:

- /V verifies the accuracy of the copy operation by comparing each file as it is written to the original file.
- /P displays a prompt to confirm whether you want to create each destination file. Using /P, you can specify a group of files with a wildcard, and then decide which files you actually want to copy. If, for example, you want to copy several files in a directory but don't want to do five separate COPY commands, you can use

  ```
  XCOPY *.TXT B: /P
  ```

  As each file is about to be copied, XCOPY prompts you to see whether that file should be copied. Answer **Y** and the file is copied; answer **N** and it is skipped.
- /W causes XCOPY to pause before copying any files, displaying the prompt `Press any key to begin copying file(s)`. You can use the pause to change disks.
- /S causes XCOPY to copy the files found in any directories that branch off from the source directory. Empty directories are ignored.
- /E causes XCOPY to copy even empty directories.
- /A causes XCOPY to copy only files with the archive attribute set without modifying the file's attributes.
- /M causes XCOPY to remove the archive bit from any files copied.
- The /Y switch is used to indicate whether you want XCOPY to overwrite files with the same name without prompting. You can also use the /–Y switch to indicate that you want to be prompted.
- /D enables you to specify a date parameter. XCOPY copies only files with a date attribute on or after the specified date. Which date format you use depends on the country setting you use.

In an XCOPY operation, DOS might not always recognize whether a particular parameter refers to a file or to a directory. When ambiguity arises, XCOPY asks whether the destination is a file name or path name.

Tip
All files created by XCOPY have the archive attribute set automatically, even if the original source file does not have the archive attribute.

Consider the following command:

```
XCOPY C:\WORDS\*.* A:\WORDS
```

If no directory named WORDS exists on the destination disk, DOS cannot determine whether you intend to create a file or a directory named WORDS on the A disk.

XCOPY displays the following message:

```
Does WORDS specify a file name
or directory name on the target
(F = file, D = directory)?
```

Press **F** when the destination (target) is a file name; **D** when the destination is a directory. Unlike COPY, XCOPY creates directories on the destination disk as needed.

If you append a backslash to the name of the target directory, XCOPY automatically assumes that the target is a directory, not a file. In the preceding example, if you use the command

```
XCOPY C:\WORDS\*.* A:\WORDS\
```

you will not have to specify that the target is a directory. XCOPY creates the \WORDS directory if it does not exist.

Understanding the Operation of XCOPY

XCOPY is best described as a hybrid between COPY and BACKUP/RESTORE. XCOPY and COPY duplicate files between directories and disks. Unlike COPY, however, XCOPY does not copy files to a nondisk device, such as the printer (PRN) or the console (CON). Like BACKUP and RESTORE, XCOPY can copy files selectively and traverse the directory tree to copy files from more than one directory. XCOPY also can make a destination directory when one does not exist. This directory capability makes XCOPY useful for duplicating a directory branch onto another disk.

Like COPY but unlike BACKUP, XCOPY copies files that are directly usable. (You cannot use files processed by BACKUP until you have processed them with RESTORE.)

When using the XCOPY command, consider the following guidelines:

- XCOPY cannot copy hidden source files.
- XCOPY does not overwrite read-only destination files.

- If a file parameter is omitted in the XCOPY syntax, XCOPY assumes the *.* full wildcard pattern as the default file parameter.
- If you include the /D switch, the date parameter must be entered in the format of the system's DATE command or in the format indicated by the latest COUNTRY command.
- The /V switch performs the same read-after-write checking as the SET VERIFY ON global verify flag.

To use XCOPY to copy empty source subdirectories, you must specify both the /S and the /E switches.

Using XCOPY Effectively

Using XCOPY, you can control by date or archive attribute the files copied, you can copy complete subdirectory trees, and you can confirm which files to copy. The command has several ideal uses: copying files selectively between disks or directories, performing a quick hard disk backup (backing up only a few critical files in several subdirectories), and keeping the directories of two or more computers synchronized.

With COPY, your control is limited. COPY duplicates all files that match the given name—an all-or-nothing approach. If you use the /P switch with XCOPY, however, DOS asks whether you want to copy each file.

XCOPY is practical to use if you want to make backup copies of less than a disk full of files from several directories. Rather than BACKUP, you might prefer to use the command XCOPY /A to select files that have changed since the last backup. Keep the following points in mind when you use XCOPY to back up a disk:

- If you suspect that the files cannot fit on one disk, be sure to use the /M switch. As XCOPY copies each file, the command resets the file's archive attribute bit. When the destination disk fills, XCOPY stops. Change disks and restart the XCOPY command, again using the /M switch. XCOPY copies the files whose archive bit has not yet been reset.
- XCOPY cannot break a large source file between destination disks. If you need to back up a file that doesn't fit on a single floppy disk, you must use BACKUP.
- A favorite use of XCOPY is to synchronize the contents of the hard disks of two computers. Many people have one computer at work and

another at home. If both computers have hard disks, keeping the copies of programs and data files current is a major task. Which files did you change today? Which machine has the more current version?

- When you want to keep separate hard disks synchronized, you might find XCOPY's /A, /D:*date*, and /S switches especially useful. The /S switch forces XCOPY to traverse your disk's directory structure, playing a hunting game for source files. Whether you use /A or /D depends on how often you copy files between the machines. If you copy files between the machines frequently, you might prefer the /A switch. If you let many days pass between synchronizing your computers' contents, you might find that the /D switch works better. Use /D if you have run BACKUP on the source machine since you last used XCOPY. BACKUP resets the archive attribute so that XCOPY's /A switch does not catch all files changed between XCOPY backups.

Disk Duplication with XCOPY

The XCOPY command can be used to create duplicate floppy disks, even when the disks are different sizes or formats. Of course, you can't make a disk hold more than its capacity, so you can't XCOPY a full 1.44M floppy onto a 720K disk. But you can transfer the contents and directory structures of a 1.2M 5 1/4-inch disk to a 1.44M 3 1/2-inch floppy, or a 720K 3 1/2-inch to a 1.2M or a 1.44M. For example, assume that you have a 720K disk with several levels of directories in drive B, and you want to copy it to a 1.2M disk in drive A. You issue the following command:

```
XCOPY B: A: /S
```

Duplicating a Directory Branch

For this example, assume that your hard disk has a subdirectory named \WPFILES that contains a few word processing files. \WPFILES also has two subdirectories. The first, \WPFILES\MEMOS, contains your current memos. The second, \WPFILES\DOCS, contains your document files. You want to keep a current set of the files in these three directories stored on a floppy disk. To copy all the files in this directory branch to the floppy, issue the following command:

```
XCOPY C:\WPFILES A:\WPFILES\ /S
```

XCOPY immediately begins to read the source directories. DOS displays the following messages:

```
Reading source file(s)...
C:\WPFILES\LET9_1.WP
C:\WPFILES\LET9_2.WP
C:\WPFILES\LET9_3.WP
C:\WPFILES\LET9_4.WP
C:\WPFILES\LET9_5.WP
C:\WPFILES\DOCS\SCHEDULE.DOC
C:\WPFILES\MEMOS\SALES.MEM
     7 File(s) copied
```

Because you included the /S switch, XCOPY copied the files in C:\WPFILES, C:\WPFILES\MEMOS, and C:\WPFILES\DOCS. The A:\WPFILES path parameter causes XCOPY to ask whether the name specifies a directory or a file. \WPFILES conceivably could be a user file in the root directory. The full path name of each file is echoed to the screen as the file is copied to drive A. When the command finishes, the \WPFILES directory branch has been copied to drive A.

As another example, assume that your PC experiences a hardware failure and needs to go to the shop for repairs. You want to use your floppy disk that contains the \WPFILES directory branch to place the \WPFILES directory branch on a second computer's hard disk. Enter the following command:

```
XCOPY A: C: /S
```

XCOPY reverses the copy process described in the preceding paragraphs by copying all the files on drive A to corresponding subdirectory locations on drive C.

Setting Defaults for COPY, MOVE, and XCOPY

If you are using DOS 6.2, you can use a new environment variable to specify how you want all three file-management commands to work. The COPYCMD environment variable is similar to the DIRCMD environment variable discussed in Chapter 8, "Working with Files"; it is used to set default switches that DOS will use whenever you issue the COPY, MOVE, or XCOPY commands.

The command to set the COPYCMD environment variable is as follows:

```
SET COPYCMD=switches
```

For the *switches* parameter, substitute the switch or switches you want DOS to use automatically. If, for example, you want DOS to never prompt you when it is about to overwrite a destination file, include the following command in your AUTOEXEC.BAT:

```
SET COPYCMD=/Y
```

Reboot the computer. DOS creates the environment variable COPYCMD and gives it the value /Y. Each time you issue the DIR command, DOS adds this switch automatically.

You can override a switch that is recorded in the COPYCMD by preceding the switch with a minus sign (–). For example, to override the /Y switch that is currently recorded in COPYCMD (so that DOS tells you when it will overwrite a file), issue the COPY command as shown here:

```
COPY /-Y
```

Comparing Files with FC

The external command FC (meaning file comparison) compares two files or two sets of files to find differences in the files. Any differences are reported on-screen. When a copied file is extremely important, you can use FC to compare the file with the original. If differences are found, you know that a problem might exist with the copy. Normally, DOS detects data integrity errors while reading and writing files, but if you want to be sure that two files are the same, you can ease your mind by using FC.

Note

PC DOS Versions 1.0 through 5.0 and MS-DOS Versions 3.3 through 5.0 include a simpler file comparison command, COMP. This command, however, is less versatile than FC, provides less information, has fewer options, and cannot compare files of different lengths.

The FC command has two general syntax forms. One form uses the /B switch for a forced binary comparison; the other form uses the remaining switches in an ASCII comparison. The two forms of syntax are shown next:

```
FC /B SourceExpression TargetExpression
```

and

```
FC /A/C/L/LBn/N/nnnn/T/W SourceExpression TargetExpression
```

The source expression specifies the originals of files to be compared. If you use wildcard characters in this parameter, all files matching this parameter are compared with the second file.

The target expression specifies the files to be compared to the originals. Usually, you need only specify the drive and directory part of a file name expression. FC compares those files specified in the source expression that can be found in the target directory.

Note

If you use wildcard characters in both the source and the target expressions, FC compares the files as sets. That is, only those files whose names match in other respects are compared.

If you use the command FC *.WK1 *.BAK, for example, FC compares each worksheet file having the extension .WK1 with the worksheet file having the same base name and the extension .BAK. For example, AUGSEPT.WK1 will be compared with AUGSEPT.BAK. FC does not compare every worksheet file with every backup file.

The switches used by FC enable you to control the operations of the command more tightly. The switches are as shown here:

- /A instructs FC to abbreviate its output (DOS 3.2 and later versions), displaying only the first and last lines of each set of differences separated by an ellipsis (...).
- /B performs a binary (byte-by-byte) comparison, showing the hexadecimal address and value of every differing byte.
- /C causes FC to ignore the case of alphabetic characters when making comparisons. Thus c = C.
- /L instructs FC to compare the files in ASCII mode, even when the files have .EXE, .COM, .SYS, .OBJ, .LIB, or .BIN extensions (DOS 3.2 and later versions).
- /LB*n* sets the number of lines in FC's buffer to *n*. The default number is 100 (DOS 3.2 and later versions). If the number of consecutive nonmatching lines exceeds the buffer size, FC aborts the compare operation.
- /N instructs FC to include the line numbers of lines reported in the output (DOS 3.2 and later versions).

- /*nnnn* establishes the number of lines that must match after a difference in order to resynchronize FC.
- /T instructs FC to view tab characters as literal characters rather than tab-expanded spaces (DOS 3.2 and later versions).
- /W instructs FC to compress whitespace—tabs, empty lines, and spaces—into a single space for purposes of file comparison.

Understanding the Operation of FC

FC works in two modes: ASCII and binary. FC defaults to ASCII mode comparison when the files to be compared do not have extensions (.EXE, .COM, .SYS, .OBJ, .LIB, or .BIN) that traditionally indicate binary files.

In ASCII mode, FC compares two files line-by-line. Lines from both files are held in a line buffer. FC uses the lines in the buffer to compare the first file to the second.

If FC detects a difference, it displays the first file name followed by the last matching line and the mismatching line or lines from the first file. FC then displays the next line to match in both files.

After displaying mismatch information about file 1, FC repeats the same sequence for file 2. The file 2 name is displayed first, followed by the last matching line and the mismatching lines from file 2, ending on the next line that matches in both files, thus synchronizing the two files.

FC can help you determine whether the contents of two files are different by showing you the extent and location of any mismatch FC finds. You can use this output as an alternative to a side-by-side comparison of the file contents.

Tip
If you are comparing two files that are not the same, you can quickly stop the reporting of differences by pressing Ctrl-C or Ctrl-Break.

In binary mode, FC compares two files byte for byte. At the first difference, the byte offset position in the first file is reported along with the value of the two files' bytes at that position. The offset and byte values are reported in hexadecimal (base 16) form. This form of FC is essentially equivalent to the older COMP command.

In binary mode, FC does not attempt to resynchronize the two files by finding an adjusted point of byte agreement. If one file has an additional byte at one place in the file, FC reports the additional byte and all subsequent bytes of the file as mismatches.

If one file is longer than its comparison file, the binary mode compares as many bytes as are present and then reports that one file is longer. When a binary file comparison results in a long listing of differences, you might want to stop the FC operation by pressing Ctrl-C or Ctrl-Break.

Only one switch is available in the binary mode. The /B switch causes the comparison to be binary even if file extensions indicate that the files are not binary. Use the /B switch to compare two text files in binary mode. You might find situations in which you would rather have the binary-mode output format of FC than the ASCII mode format. Binary mode format reports differences as pairs of hexadecimal values. You then can see the values of characters, such as Ctrl-G (bell), that do not produce printed output.

When you use FC, keep in mind that the default number of lines that must match in an ASCII comparison after a difference has ended is two. The files then are considered resynchronized. The number of "must match" lines can be changed using the */nnnn* switch by setting *nnnn* to the desired value.

Using FC to Compare a Copied File to Its Original

Suppose that you are copying the ANSI.SYS file from your hard disk to a floppy disk to use for an important demonstration on another PC. When the copy completes, you set the disk on the edge of your desk and go to the break room to get coffee. When you return, you notice that the disk has fallen off your desk and landed against the small transformer that runs your cassette recorder. You are worried that the magnetic field from the transformer has damaged ANSI.SYS. To verify that the copied ANSI.SYS is good, you can compare it to the original by using the following command:

```
FC A:ANSI.SYS C:\DOS\DRIVERS\ANSI.SYS
```

After a few seconds, FC reports `FC: No differences encountered`. The copy of ANSI.SYS seems to be good.

Comparing Two Text Files

Suppose that two similar text files, ORIGINAL.TXT and ANOTHER.TXT, are located in the default directory of the current drive. ORIGINAL.TXT contains the following text:

```
This is the first line.
This is the second line.
1
2
3
4
5
This is the last line.
```

ANOTHER.TXT contains the following text:

```
This is the first line.
This is not the third line.
1
2
3
4
5
6
7
8
9
This is the last line.
```

Note that ANOTHER.TXT has four more lines than ORIGINAL.TXT, and that the second lines of the files contain differing text. These simple files illustrate how FC reports differences. You can use the principles illustrated here to understand the result of comparisons of more complex files. If, for example, you want to compare the two files that are in the same directory, you issue the following command:

```
FC ORIGINAL.TXT ANOTHER.TXT
```

FC makes the following report:

```
Comparing files ORIGINAL.TXT and ANOTHER.TXT ***** ORIGINAL.TXT
This is the first line.
This is the second line.
1
***** ANOTHER.TXT
This is the first line.
This is not the third line.
1
*****


***** ORIGINAL.TXT
5
This is the last line.
***** ANOTHER.TXT
5
6
7
8
9
This is the last line.
*****
```

FC displays the lines before and after the mismatched line, if any exist. FC also finds mismatches that are not on equivalent lines so that it can match text even when one file contains material not found in the other. The second report concerning ANOTHER.TXT shows all the lines between the one containing the numeral 5 and the one containing the text `This is the last line`. Only these two matching lines appear in the report concerning ORIGINAL.TXT.

Copying Entire Disks with DISKCOPY

The external DISKCOPY command is used to make exact duplicates of a disk. Duplication is so complete that even file fragmentation is preserved. If the target disk has not yet been formatted, DISKCOPY automatically formats it before performing the duplication.

DISKCOPY does have one major limitation. You can copy only like media to like media. For example, a 1.2M diskette can be successfully copied only to another 1.2M disk. You cannot use DISKCOPY to duplicate a 720K floppy on a 1.44M diskette. See the section on using XCOPY to duplicate disks earlier in this chapter for information on duplicating unlike diskettes.

The syntax for DISKCOPY is as shown here:

```
DISKCOPY SourceDisk TargetDisk  /1 /V /M
```

The source disk is the drive letter that holds the original disk to be duplicated. The target disk is the optional name of the drive that holds the disk to receive the copy. This destination drive sometimes is called the target drive. If you don't specify a drive name for the target, DOS assumes that you want to use the current drive and prompts you to insert and remove source and destination disks as necessary.

Only three switches are recognized by DISKCOPY. The /1 switch causes DOS to copy only the first side of a double-sided disk. This switch is a holdover from very old versions of DOS that enables you to copy single-sided disks. Chances are you will never need the /1 switch.

The /V switch instructs DOS to verify that the copy and the original are identical. This switch slows down operations by adding the extra comparison step. You would use this switch only when you are working with disks that you will never have an opportunity to copy again and you need to make absolutely sure you got a clean copy.

The /M switch forces DISKCOPY to work in memory only. Using this switch means that DISKCOPY will not use temporary files on your hard disk to aid in duplication. Instead, all operations will be done in memory. This effectively forces you to swap disks during the copy, as was required in older versions of DOS.

Note

If you leave out the drive names in the DISKCOPY command line, DOS uses the current drive as the specifier. If you have a system with only one disk drive, or if the second disk drive supports only different formats, you can simply issue the command

```
DISKCOPY
```

Remember to log onto the drive you want to use before issuing the command. DOS prompts you to insert the source disk and the target disk at the appropriate times.

This is the classic example of the DISKCOPY command:

```
DISKCOPY A: B:
```

This example assumes that both drive A and drive B contain diskettes having the same capacity. After you issue the DISKCOPY command, DOS prompts you to insert the disks into the proper drives. Make sure that you insert the disks into the correct drives. Write-protect the source disk to safeguard its contents in case of a disk mix-up.

When the disks are in place, you are ready to continue. Press any key to start the DISKCOPY process. When the process is complete, DOS asks whether you want to make another copy. Press **Y** to copy another disk or **N** to exit the command (see fig. 9.3). If the drives or disks are not compatible, an error message appears, and nothing is copied (see fig. 9.4).

```
C:\>DISKCOPY A: B:

Insert SOURCE diskette in drive A:

Insert TARGET diskette in drive B:

Press any key to continue . . .

Copying 80 tracks
9 sectors per track, 2 side(s)

Volume Serial Number is 1EEA-0431

Copy another diskette (Y/N)? N

C:\>
```

Fig. 9.3
A typical DISKCOPY command sequence and messages from DOS.

```
C:\>diskcopy a: b:
Insert SOURCE diskette in drive A:
Insert TARGET diskette in drive B:
Press any key to continue . . .
Drive types or diskette types
not compatible
Copy process ended
Copy another diskette (Y/N)?
```

Fig. 9.4
An error message produced by the DISKCOPY command.

Comparing Disks with DISKCOMP

You can confirm that two disks are identical by using the external command DISKCOMP, which compares each track of one disk to each track of another disk sector by sector. Like DISKCOPY, DISKCOMP is a floppy-only command; you cannot use DISKCOMP to compare two hard disks. Further, the disk types and capacities must be the same for both disks in the comparison; any difference in disks made with DISKCOPY is a sign of a problem disk.

One practical use of DISKCOMP is comparing a master disk included with a software package to a working copy of that disk. DISKCOMP confirms whether the working copy is good.

Normally, you use DISKCOMP to test disks that were made from originals with the DISKCOPY command. Because DISKCOMP doesn't write any information to either disk, both disks can be write-protected. If the disks are identical, DOS displays the message `Compare OK`.

The syntax for DISKCOMP is similar to that for DISKCOPY. The syntax for DISKCOMP is as follows:

```
DISKCOMP SourceDisk TargetDisk /1 /8
```

The source disk is the original, and the target disk is the copy. DISKCOMP recognizes only two switches. The /1 switch causes DOS to compare only the first sides of the disks. The /8 switch compares only the first 8 sectors of each track on the disks. Both of these switches provide backward compatibility for testing floppy disks made with very old versions of DOS.

An example of the DISKCOMP command is as follows:

```
DISKCOMP A: B:
```

When the first DISKCOMP operation is complete, DOS asks whether you want to compare another disk.

In the sequence shown in figure 9.5, a working copy of a master disk is being compared to the original master. Notice the comparison errors. The working copy no longer is reliable, or other files have been added to the disk since DISKCOPY was used to make a working copy from the master. The best way to solve the problem is to make a new working copy.

Fig. 9.5
Comparing a working copy of a master disk to the original disk.

```
C:\>DISKCOMP A: B:

Insert FIRST diskette in drive A:

Insert SECOND diskette in drive B:

Press any key to continue . . .

Comparing 80 tracks
9 sectors per track, 2 side(s)

Compare error on
side 0, track 0

Compare error on
side 0, track 22

Compare another diskette (Y/N) ?N

C:\>
```

If you issue the DISKCOMP command with no drive parameters, DOS uses only one drive to carry out the comparison and prompts you to insert the first and second disks alternately. Depending on your system's memory, you will swap disks once or several times. By entering DISKCOMP alone, without parameters, you tell DOS to use the current floppy drive even if your system has two floppy drives. Make sure that you don't mix up the disks when you're swapping them. If you don't keep track of which disk DOS wants in the drive, you might end up comparing part of a disk to itself.

Deleting Files

Because no disk has unlimited storage space and because nearly every file eventually becomes obsolete, DOS provides a way to erase or delete files from your disks. The internal ERASE command enables you to delete files you no longer need.

Unlike other DOS commands' short forms, the ERASE command's short form is not simply an abbreviation of the keyword. The short form of ERASE is DEL. Because the short form is shorter, thus quicker to type, it is generally used rather than ERASE.

When you delete files, DOS locates the file in the directory and marks the directory entry with a special internal indicator. DOS considers this space to be available for reassignment when a new file is being added to the directory. By reclaiming a deleted file's directory entry, DOS can control the expansion of a subdirectory or reclaim one of the limited root directory entries.

Understanding the Delete Operation

The delete operation does not affect the contents of a file's allocated clusters. Deleting a file does not record over the file's data in the way erasing a cassette tape records over existing audio. Rather, DOS alters its bookkeeping records in the directory and in the file allocation table (FAT). The directory entry for the file is "deleted" by changing the first character of the file name to an unprintable character (E5 hex), and the FAT cluster chain for the file is deallocated. DOS marks the file's clusters as being "free."

The DOS bookkeeping records for the deleted file remain relatively intact until another file is added to the directory or until another file is expanded or added in any directory. The UNDELETE utility (discussed in Chapter 11, "Emergency Procedures") takes advantage of the fact that DOS does not erase a file's content when you delete the file. UNDELETE "fixes" the deleted file's directory entry and reconstructs the deleted file's cluster chain. If another file has been added, however, the UNDELETE command might not be able to recover the deleted file because DOS might have reallocated some or all of the storage space assigned to the deleted file.

When you are executing a delete operation, remember the following guidelines:

- At the command line, the DEL (or ERASE) command does not erase files marked with the read-only attribute, the hidden attribute, or the system attribute.
- The delete operation does not remove a directory, erase a volume label, or erase a hidden or system file.
- If you specify a directory name as the file name expression on the DEL command line, DOS tries to delete all the files in the specified subdirectory.

Deleting Files from the Command Line

The internal DEL and ERASE commands remove files from the disk, returning to the disk the space occupied by the deleted files. When you use DEL or ERASE to erase a file, DOS no longer can access the file. The erased file's directory entry and storage space become available to DOS for storage of another file.

Caution

Because DEL (or ERASE) deletes files from your disk, use the command with caution. DEL accepts wildcards in the file parameter. A momentary lapse of your attention while you use DEL can wipe out important data in the blink of an eye.

Here is the syntax for deleting files:

```
DEL FileNameExpression /P
```

or

```
ERASE FileNameExpression /P
```

The file name expression specifies the drive, the directory, and/or the name of the files to be deleted. You can use wildcards to specify multiple files.

Using the optional /P switch causes DEL (or ERASE) to prompt you for confirmation before DOS deletes each file. Press **Y** to instruct DOS to delete a file, or press **N** to skip the file without erasing it.

Deleting Unwanted Files

Suppose that you have completed and delivered a series of memos composed in your word processing program. That program automatically creates in the C:\WP directory a backup file, with a .BAK extension, for each memo. You want to keep the memo files on disk so that you can refer to them, but after the memos are safely delivered, you do not need the .BAK files. You can erase the files with .BAK extensions one at a time, or you can issue the DEL command as follows:

```
DEL C:\WP\*.BAK
```

In this command line, the *.BAK file name parameter instructs DOS to delete all the files with the .BAK extension. When the DEL command completes its work, all files with .BAK extensions are removed from the directory. Because this command line includes drive and path parameters, you can issue the command from any logged disk and current directory and still erase the .BAK files in C:\WP.

For Related Information

- "Recovering Deleted Files with UNDELETE," p. 295
- "Freeing Up Disk Space," p. 509

Summary

In this chapter, you have learned about DOS commands used to copy, move, compare, and delete files. The main points in this chapter are reviewed here.

- DOS's COPY command is used to make copies of files on other drives, or in other directories.
- The COPY command can be used to give new names to files as they're being copied. Groups of files can be copied at one time using wildcards in the command line.
- The MOVE command copies a file to a new location, then deletes the original file. The MOVE command can also be used to rename directories.
- The REN or RENAME command can be used to give files another name. Each name must be unique. Groups of files can be renamed using wildcards.
- The XCOPY command is used to copy both files and directory structures. The XCOPY command can be used to duplicate floppy disks when the disks have different capacities.
- The DISKCOPY command is used to make exact duplicates of floppy disks. Both disks must have the same capacity.
- The FC and DISKCOMP commands are used to compare files and floppy disks to make sure that good copies have been made. FC is used to compare individual files or groups of individual files. DISKCOMP is used to compare one floppy disk against another for accuracy.
- The DEL or ERASE command is used to "delete" files no longer needed. Files are not actually erased until DOS uses the directory entry or disk space for another file.

In the next chapter, you will learn how to protect your data from loss. Covered topics include making backups and protecting your system from damage from computer viruses.

Chapter 10

Protecting Your Data

Desktop computers commonly contain hard disk drives that can store thousands of pages of information. If your computer contains a hard disk, it almost certainly contains millions of bytes of software—the programs that run your computer. The hard disk probably also contains thousands or even millions of bytes of data—the information you or someone else has typed into the system. The software and data represent a significant investment in money and effort that would be lost if your hard disk were damaged or erased.

This chapter explains how to protect your computer files from various menaces such as static electricity, excessive heat, and erratic electrical power. Most important, in this chapter, you learn how to use the two hard disk backup programs, MSBACKUP and Microsoft Backup for Windows, to back up the files on your system and then restore those files in the event of damage to or erasure of your hard disk.

Note

If you have never learned how to back up your disk files or produce duplicates, now is the time to learn. If you use the ideas covered in this chapter, you can avoid the sinking feeling that comes from losing a significant amount of hard work to a hard disk crash, accidental disk format, or accidental file erasure.

Avoiding Data Loss

Today's personal computers are reliable and economical data processing machines. Like all machines, however, computers are subject to failures and operator errors. Table 10.1 lists some hardware and software problems discussed in this chapter and suggests ways to prevent these problems.

Table 10.1 Hardware and Software Problems and Prevention Techniques

Problem	Prevention
Static electricity	Use antistatic liquid or floor mat; place a "touch pad" on desk.
Overheating	Clean clogged air vents; remove objects that block vents; use air-conditioned room during the summer.
Damaged disks	Don't leave disks to be warped by the sun; use protective covers; avoid spilling liquids on disks; store disks in a safe place; avoid magnetic fields from appliances (televisions, microwave ovens, and so on); do not use a ball-point pen to write on flexible disk labels.
Data loss	Keep current backups of your hard disk and any floppy disks that contain important data; scan for viruses; use delete-tracking.
Viruses	Always scan a questionable disk for viruses before copying any files from it to your hard disk.

Always be cautious about your computer's environment. If your power fluctuates and the lights flicker, you might have to purchase a line voltage regulator from your computer dealer.

Your computer might perform erratically when it is too hot. Because circuits are not reliable when they overheat, you might get jumbled data. Make sure that your computer has room to breathe by cleaning the air vents.

You generate static electricity on your body when humidity is low, when you wear synthetic fabrics, or when you walk on carpet. Just by touching your keyboard while carrying a static charge, you can send an electrical shudder through your computer, causing a data jumble or circuit failure. Fortunately, you can avoid static problems by touching your grounded system cabinet before touching the keyboard. If static electricity is a serious problem for you, ask your dealer about antistatic products, which are inexpensive and easy to use.

Preventing Software Failures

A minority of software packages have flawed instructions called *bugs*. Software bugs are usually minor and rarely cause greater problems than keyboard lockups or jumbled displays. The potential does exist for a software bug to cause your disk drive to operate in an erratic way, however. Fortunately, most companies test and debug their software before marketing the packages. Performing a backup of your disks is your best insurance against damage caused by bugs.

Software viruses are purposely created software bugs with the potential to cause a great deal of damage to your files. Most viruses are additional program codes hidden in a .COM file such as COMMAND.COM. A virus most often does its damage by altering the disk's file allocation table (FAT) and marking clusters as bad or unavailable. A virus also has the capability of initiating a FORMAT or destroying a disk partition table.

Viruses "multiply" through the exchange of software between users. If you load an infected .COM file onto your PC, the virus can quickly infect other files on your system. Unfortunately, you can back up an infected file, and when the file is restored, the virus continues to do its dirty work. Your best defense against a virus is to install only reputable software from a source who can attest to the program's operation. If a virus infects your system, you might have to fall back to your write-protected master DOS disks and rebuild your system from the ground up.

DOS includes a pair of programs—Microsoft Anti-Virus (MSAV.EXE) and Windows Anti-Virus (MWAV.EXE)—that can monitor your system constantly to detect viruses. If necessary, these programs can also remove any viruses they find. Details of this software are covered later in this chapter.

Preventing Mistakes

As you gain skill, you might use DOS commands that can result in the accidental loss of files. When you use commands such as COPY, ERASE, and FORMAT, you might inadvertently remove important data. For this reason, study what you typed before you press Enter. It is easy to develop a typing rhythm that carries you straight through confirmation prompts into the clutches of disaster.

Although you can use Ctrl-C, Ctrl-Break, and if necessary, Ctrl-Alt-Del to abandon commands, you are only stopping what is already underway. These "panic buttons" might only limit the damage, not stop it completely. Because you are likely to make mistakes at one time or another, always have a backup copy of all important data.

DOS versions since 5.0 are more forgiving than previous versions. These DOS versions include a safe, reversible FORMAT command, as well as an UNDELETE command that you can use to recover from an accidental DEL or ERASE command.

Understanding Microsoft Backup

Compared to floppy disks, hard disks have many advantages. Hard disks are faster, have larger storage capacities and root directories, support multiple partitions, and never require a disk swap. A file on a hard disk can be many times the size of a file on a floppy disk. Commands such as COPY and XCOPY enable you to keep a few duplicate files on a floppy for backup purposes, but DOS provides a pair of special programs specifically designed for the big jobs: Microsoft Backup (MSBACKUP.EXE) and Microsoft Backup for Windows (MWBACKUP.EXE).

By default, the Setup program installed one of these programs when you installed DOS on your computer. If your system has Microsoft Windows, however, you have the option of installing both programs. As you might expect, Microsoft Backup for Windows can be used only within Microsoft Windows. The DOS version, however, can be used either at a command prompt or in a DOS window within Microsoft Windows.

Note

If you do not now use Microsoft Windows but plan to add that operating environment to your system later, you must reinstall DOS to install the Windows version of the backup program.

Both backup programs are full-featured programs that enable you to perform the following tasks:

- Copy files from a hard disk to another disk, usually a floppy disk
- Restore the copied files to their original location or to another disk of your choice
- Compare files on your backup copies with the originals to ensure their validity

Both programs have several types of menus and many options to enable you to copy only those files you want to copy and to ease the process of making backups regularly. Because the programs are similar, this chapter focuses on MSBACKUP. Relevant differences in the Windows version are noted.

Note

The files copied to the backup disk do not have the same format as files on your hard disk or files copied with the COPY or XCOPY commands. The directories of disks written by the backup programs show only one file per disk, taking all the available space, as in the following example:

```
Volume in drive A is DEFAULT FUL
 Directory of A:\

CC30914A 001   1,457,664 09-14-93   6:02a
        1 file(s)    1,457,664 bytes
                             0 bytes free
```

These files might actually contain the data that originally appeared in many files on your hard disk, along with information about their original location. Before you can use these files, they must be restored, using the Restore portion of one of the Backup programs.

Both versions of the Backup program can read backup disks created by the other version. You need not worry, therefore, about losing access to backup data if you switch from one version of the program to the other.

Backup disks contain not only special copies of files but also directory information about each file. This information enables the programs to copy the backup files to their original locations in the directory tree.

The Backup programs can spread a single file across more than one floppy disk. This capability enables you to copy to multiple disks files that are too big to fit on a single disk. If a backup operation uses more than one disk, each disk is linked internally to the next disk to form a backup set.

During the backup operation, each disk in a set is filled to capacity before the next disk is requested. If a file is only partially written to a backup disk when the disk reaches full capacity, the remainder of the file is written to the next disk in the set.

Like XCOPY, the Backup programs can copy files selectively. You can specify a directory or branch of directories, a file name, a file name patterned after a wildcard, and additional selection switches. By taking advantage of the programs' selectivity, you can maintain more than one set of backup disks, each set having its own logical purpose.

You can, for example, keep one backup set that contains every file on your hard disk. This set is insurance against data loss resulting from a hard disk failure or crash. You might have another backup set that contains only the files that have their archive attributes turned on. With an archive set for each day of the week, you can recover a week's worth of data between complete backups. When your hard disk fails, you replace it, restore using the full set, and then update with the daily sets.

You can lose the data on your hard disk in many ways. If you have not replicated the data, you might be forced to re-create the data and suffer the consequences of permanent data loss if you cannot re-create the data. If you have never experienced a disk-related failure, don't be overconfident. With 10 million hard disk users working on their computers for an average of eight hours per day, more than 250,000 people will experience a hard-disk-related failure this year. You could be next.

Configuring the Backup Programs

Before you can create backups of your data with either backup program, you must first test the program for compatibility. The test is performed automatically the first time you run the program. A special program runs through some of the backup program's menus, making selections as though you were running the program yourself. This program tests your floppy disk drives and the speed of your processor chip and hard disk. Periodically, dialog boxes appear and ask you for permission to continue. You respond by selecting "buttons" similar to those you might have seen in dialog boxes in the DOS Shell and the DOS Editor. You select options in the same way: by pressing the highlighted letter, by moving the highlight to the desired button with the Tab or Shift-Tab key, or by clicking the desired button with the mouse. In the DOS version, a highlighted button has pointers at its left and right ends and is a different color from the other buttons. In the Windows version, the highlighted button is simply a different color.

The program then displays a dialog box that gives you the option of choosing the drive and medium you want to use for the compatibility test (see fig. 10.1). To select a different capacity disk, move the highlight to the appropriate entry with the cursor keys; then press the space bar. Choose OK when the setting conforms to your choice. (If you have only one low-density drive, this option is not available.) If you have two drives of the same type, the program uses both, alternating backup disks between the drives.

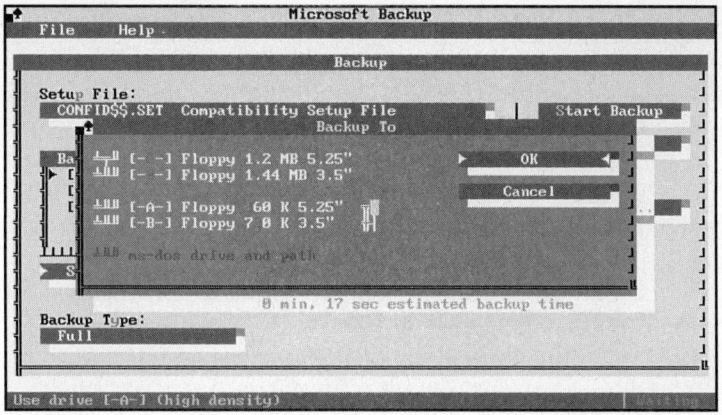

Fig. 10.1
Choosing a disk drive and capacity for backups.

The program then selects a group of files to back up and completes a backup. This procedure requires two floppy disks of the type you selected. Make sure that these do not contain any data you want to save because the disks will be erased completely. The program instructs you when to insert the disks. When the backup is complete, the program compares the data on the backup disks with the source files to verify that the backup is accurate.

Note

Even after you configure one of the backup programs, you still have to configure the second program. However, the backup files that either program creates can be read by the other program.

Your computer will probably pass the compatibility test. If it does, you can proceed to make backups with the program. However, the program might display the following warning message:

```
DMA Buffer size too small. You will not be able to perform a backup,
compare, or restore until the DMA buffer size is increased. See
'Troubleshooting' in your MS-DOS manual.
```

If this message appears, and you have an 80386 or 80486 microprocessor, use the DEVICE command to load the memory manager EMM386.EXE in your CONFIG.SYS file. Add the parameter D=64 to the command, as shown in the following line:

```
DEVICE:C:\DOS\EMM386.EXE D=64
```

Tip
Most commercial expanded memory managers include a parameter that you can use to enlarge the DMA buffer. If you use an expanded memory manager other than EMM386.EXE, consult the documentation for details.

If you have an 8088 or 80286 microprocessor and do not use an expanded memory manager, you will not encounter this problem; but the program might still fail the compatibility test. (See Chapter 18, "Configuring Your Computer," for details on EMM386.EXE and the CONFIG.SYS file.)

When you finish running the tests, the programs save your configuration information to disk so that it can be used whenever you run the backup program again.

Understanding Microsoft Backup Functions

Both the DOS and Windows backup programs have five basic functions: Backup, Compare, Restore, Configure, and Quit. In the DOS version, the dialog box shown in figure 10.2 contains buttons representing each function. In the Windows version, the functions are represented by a series of icons near the top of the screen (see fig. 10.3).

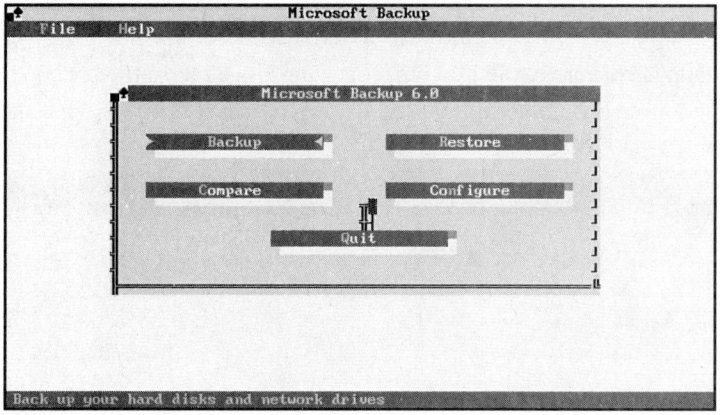

Fig. 10.2
The opening DOS Backup dialog box.

The functions are listed here:

- **B***ackup* duplicates all or selected files from your hard disk onto floppy disks.
- **C***ompare* compares the files in a set of backup floppy disks to their source on the hard disk to verify that the copies are accurate.
- **R***estore* copies the files on your backup floppy disks to the hard disk, in either their original location or a new location, or to another floppy disk in usable form.
- *Co***n***figure* enables you to select default settings for the program. In the DOS version, you can choose the following actions:

Change the number of rows of text shown on the screen

Switch to a display using normal text characters rather than the graphics characters shown in the illustrations here

Adjust the way your mouse behaves

Change the screen colors

- ***Quit*** enables you to exit the program.

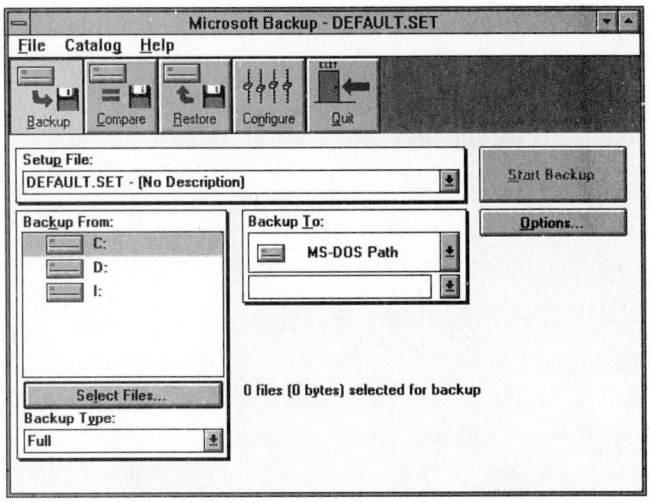

Fig. 10.3
The opening Backup for Windows screen.

The Configure options, which appear in figure 10.4, are similar to the options found on the DOS Shell's Options menu. You can also select a different drive or disk capacity for your backups or send your backups to a DOS path—that is, a directory on your hard disk.

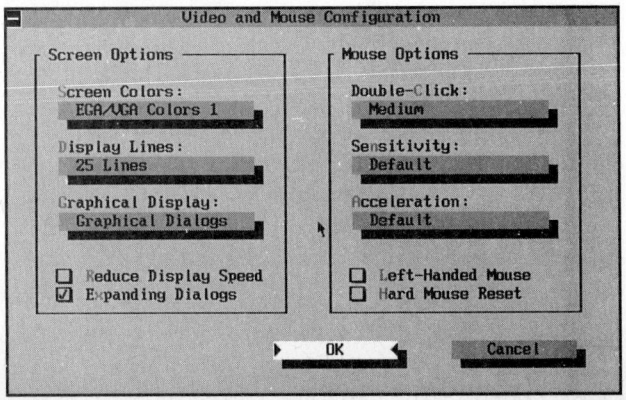

Fig. 10.4
Changing DOS Backup's display and mouse options.

Both programs have pull-down menus at the top of the screen. The File menu enables you to load and save setup files—files that contain all the settings you will use for a particular type of backup or restore. The File menu also enables you to print catalog files containing a list of the files that have been backed up. Both backup programs have a Help menu as well, which explains techniques and procedures. The Windows Backup program has a third menu, a Catalog menu, which enables you to select catalog files for restoration or comparison. This menu does not appear in the DOS version; however, you can select catalog files after you have chosen to perform a restore or compare.

Setting Up a Backup Policy

Every PC user should develop a backup policy—a defined method of backing up data regularly. Your policy might include making and keeping more than one backup set. The backup programs allow for three basic types of backups:

- A full backup copies every file on your hard disk. Keep at least two full backup sets so that you can re-create your system if your hard disk is destroyed; you need not make both copies at the same time.
- An incremental backup copies only new files or files that have been changed since the last full backup was performed. You use an additional set of disks for the incremental backup set. You might complete several backups between full backups, depending on how many files you work with and how large the files are. Each time you perform an incremental backup, you add any files that are new or have been modified since the previous new or incremental backup.
- A differential backup, like a partial backup, copies only files that are new or have been changed since the last full backup and requires a separate set of disks from the full backups. With a differential backup, however, you reuse the same floppy disks for each backup until you perform your next full backup.

The distinction between incremental and differential backups lies with the archive bit. When you perform a full backup, the backup programs turn off the archive attribute for any file that is backed up. When you modify or create a file, DOS turns on the new or modified file's archive attribute.

When you perform an incremental backup, the backup programs turn off the archive bit so that each incremental backup includes only files created or modified since the previous incremental backup. When you perform a differential backup, however, the backup programs do not turn off the archive bit.

Therefore, every file modified or created since the previous full backup is copied. The differential backup is appropriate if you work with the same few files daily and do not need several generations of each file.

Tip
You can use the ATTRIB command to determine the current archive attribute setting for each file on your system. If you want to make sure that a particular file is backed up by an incremental backup procedure, use ATTRIB to turn on the archive attribute.

You can perform a full backup weekly, monthly, or at some other interval. The intervening (incremental or differential) backup intervals reduce your risk of data loss between full backups. The time between performing intermediate backups depends on the amount of risk to your data you are willing to take. In a business setting, you might reduce your risk to an acceptable level by performing an intermediate backup every other day. If your PC activity level is high, you might have to perform an incremental backup daily. If your PC activity is minimal, a differential backup once every two weeks might be frequent enough to reduce your risk to a manageable level.

In addition to these three types of backups, you can create backup sets for special purposes. You can select files to include in, or exclude from, the backup. You can select these files individually, by directory, according to a wildcard pattern, by date, or by attribute, and save the selections in a setup file. You learn how to select files for backups later in this chapter.

Issuing the MSBACKUP Command

The syntax for the MSBACKUP command is shown in the following line:

```
MSBACKUP  filename  /video
```

Both switches are optional. *filename* is the name of a setup file. If you created setup files for different types of backups, you can load one automatically by specifying the file on the command line. If you do not specify a setup file, MSBACKUP loads DEFAULT.SET and applies the settings to the drive specified in that file. If no drive is specified, MSBACKUP applies the settings to the default drive.

/*video* specifies the type of video display to be used. Use /LCD for laptops or other LCD screens, /BW for black and white, or /MDA for monochrome displays, including those attached to Hercules-type adapters. Do not specify a video type for a color display.

By default, MSBACKUP uses the path contained in the MSDOSDATA environment variable to determine where to look for configuration information. If this environment variable does not exist, the program searches the directory from which MSBACKUP was started. If it is not located there, MSBACKUP uses default values and creates a configuration information file in that directory. To add this environment variable, add the following line to your AUTOEXEC.BAT file:

```
SET MSDOSDATA=C:\DOS
```

The path to the right of the equal sign can be changed to any other valid directory you want to use for your backup configuration information.

For Related Information
- "CONFIG.SYS," p. 33
- "Fine-Tuning Your Computer with CONFIG.SYS and AUTOEXEC.BAT," p. 482

Using Microsoft Backup

Now that you understand how Microsoft Backup (MSBACKUP.EXE) and Microsoft Backup for Windows (MWBACKUP.EXE) work, it is time to see how to use them to perform your backup procedures. The following sections explain how to perform these tasks.

Performing a Full Backup

In this section, you learn how to complete a full backup. First you learn how to use MSBACKUP and Microsoft Backup for Windows.

Performing a Full Backup with MSBACKUP. To perform a full backup in DOS, follow these steps:

1. Enter the following command:

   ```
   MSBACKUP
   ```

   The program scans drive C (unless you specified a different drive and saved the information in the default setup file, DEFAULT.SET), reads its directories, and then presents its opening screen.

2. Choose the **B**ackup button. As shown in figure 10.5, the default setup file is loaded, and the selected backup type is Full. To perform a full backup, select the drive to back up from the Bac**k**up From list by double-clicking the appropriate drive, or by using the cursor-movement keys to move the highlight to the drive and pressing the space bar. You might choose more than one drive. Each time you choose a drive, Backup scans the drive and adds the selected files to the totals.

   As you select files to back up, the Backup screen shows you exactly what is required. A message similar to this one appears:

   ```
   1,316 files (with catalog) selected for backup
   24 1.44 MB 3.5" floppies needed (maximum)
   15 min, 50 sec estimated backup time
   ```

Backup formats any target disks that are not formatted and compresses the data on the backup disks so that the capacity of the disks required might be less than the amount of data you need to back up.

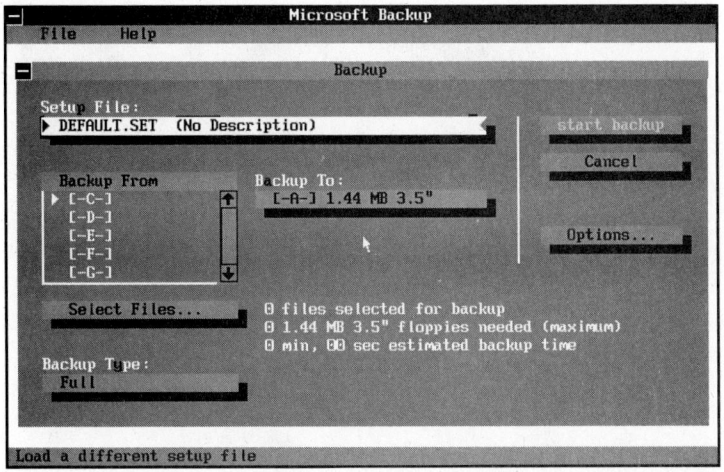

Fig. 10.5
The Backup screen.

Note

The Windows Backup program indicates how many bytes of data are selected for backup and compresses the files so that fewer backup disks and less time are required to complete a backup.

3. Choose **S**tart Backup. The program begins by creating a backup catalog, listing the files to be backed up and the options chosen. The following message appears:

```
Insert diskette #1 in drive A:
```

As the backup progresses, a display similar to figure 10.6 appears.

4. When the disk is full, the program prompts you to insert the next disk, and so on until the backup is complete.

As you remove each disk, label the disk "Full Backup #*nn*," in which *nn* is the number of the disk in the series. Date the label also. When the backup is complete, the opening screen reappears.

Comparing the Backup to the Original Files. The first time you use a series of disks for a backup, compare the backups to the originals to verify that the disks are readable and accurate. You don't want to discover that your backup is unusable when you want to use it to recover a hard disk!

Fig. 10.6
Viewing the progress of a backup.

```
Backup 2.09.14
C:\

C:\                          ✓ dsvxd    .386     5,741  10-26-92
 ├─▶BATCH                    ✓ evrxscan.sys      4,535  12-19-88
 ├─DDRIVE                    ✓ evx45    .sys     3,941   3-16-89
 │  └─WINDOWS                ✓ lastbkup             13  11-28-92
 ├─▶DOS                      ✓ loadhi   .sys    18,692   3-28-92
 ├─▶DV                       ✓ mouse    .sys    37,056   4-09-92
 │  └─▶DVC                   ✓ pckwin   .sys     3,024   3-03-92
 ├─EDRIVE                      qemm386  .sys    91,207   3-28-92

Diskette Progress            Backup Set Information

Drive A:                     Catalog: CC21130A Type   : Full
Track  :                     Name   : DEFAULT  Verify: Off

Drive B:      [              ]   Estimated              Actual
Track  :  9                      ──────────────────────────────
                                       100 ◀ Disks ▶          1
Your Time   :  0:11  % Complete:     %       1,321 ◀ Files ▶         16
Backup Time:  0:04  DOS Index :   38%  30,849,594 ◀ Bytes ▶    106,095
Compression:        Kbytes/Min:             37:40 ◀ Time ▶       0:15
```

To perform a compare, follow these steps:

1. Choose **C**ompare. A screen similar to the main Backup screen appears.
2. Choose Bac**k**up Set Catalog, and select the setup file you used for the backup. (If you haven't saved any setup files, this will be DEFAULT.SET.)
3. Select the drive or drives from the Compare From list; the number of files to compare changes from 0 to the number of files you backed up.
4. The program prompts you to insert each disk in turn, and a progress screen keeps you apprised of events.

At the end of the process, the dialog box indicating that no errors were found or that the errors were corrected will probably appear. If this is not the case, you might want to discard the disks that contain the errors, replace them with new ones, and repeat the backup.

Note

When you quit the program, you might be told that you have not saved your changes in the DEFAULT.SET setup file. In this case, you are asked whether you want to save your changes or discard them. You might find it more helpful to save your settings explicitly to other files, which you can load either from within the program or from the command line. To save a backup setup, choose Save **A**s from the **F**ile menu, and specify a file name and, optionally, a drive and directory where the setup file should be stored. The program automatically supplies the extension .SET.

Performing a Full Backup in Windows. The procedure for performing a full backup in Windows is essentially the same as for DOS. The primary difference is the appearance of the screen. When the program loads, you see a message warning you not to use your disk drives while a backup, restore, or compare operation is in progress. You can prevent this message from reappearing each time you load the program by checking the Disable This Message box. Otherwise, you proceed the same way you would in DOS. You can work in other programs while the backup is proceeding. A beep informs you when you must change disks.

Performing Intermediate Backups

Two types of intermediate backups are possible: incremental and differential. The difference depends on the status of the archive bit for selecting files. The incremental backup resets the archive bit after completion, and the differential backup does not reset it.

Performing an Incremental Backup. To perform an incremental backup, choose Backup T**y**pe, and then choose **I**ncremental from the dialog box. The backup proceeds in the same way that the full backup proceeds. Mark each disk in the set with the number and the date belonging to the increment for this backup. Store the completed set in a safe place, and avoid mixing the disks with disks from another backup set.

For example, you might perform an incremental backup every Tuesday and Friday and run a full backup every two weeks. Under this plan, you accumulate four incremental backup sets before you have to repeat the backup cycle and reuse the disks.

Note

No matter what type of backup you perform, the backup programs erase the target disks; therefore, each incremental backup must start on a new target disk. You cannot add backup files to disks that have been used as part of a set. By default, the backup programs warn you when the disk you are using is part of an existing backup set and give you the options of overwriting the disk, placing a different disk in the drive, or canceling the backup.

Performing a Differential Backup. If you use the differential backup method, you have just one intermediate backup set. The first time you do an intermediate backup in a backup cycle after a full backup, start with disk number 01 in your intermediate backup set. You might need more than one disk to complete the backup. Because the differential method does not reset the archive bit, the next intermediate backup set includes all the files included in the first intermediate backup set. Consequently, you can reuse the same backup disks for each intermediate backup set. To perform a differential backup, select **D**ifferential from the Bac**k**up Type dialog box, and proceed as you would with a full backup.

The differential method has the advantage of using fewer backup disks than the incremental method. On the other hand, you retain only one intermediate copy of your files that have been modified or created since the previous full backup. If you think you might need to examine successive iterations of a file, use the incremental method.

Special-Purpose Backups

You are not limited to full and intermediate backups of entire disks. You can specify any file or group of files to be included in a backup. When you complete a project, for example, you might want to back up all the files associated with that project in a special series for archival purposes. Or you might want to back up such files daily in a series of incremental or differential backups. Both backup programs provide the means to make any number of special-purpose backups.

To select a group of files for a special backup, first make sure that your backup type is Full. Otherwise, you cannot include files that do not have their archive bit set. Next, choose Se**l**ect Files. The backup program scans the default (or selected) drive to see how many files and directories are on it and displays a screen similar to the DOS Shell, with drives at the top, directories at the left, and files at the right (see fig. 10.7). The status line displays the following message:

```
Select entire directories with right mouse button or Spacebar
```

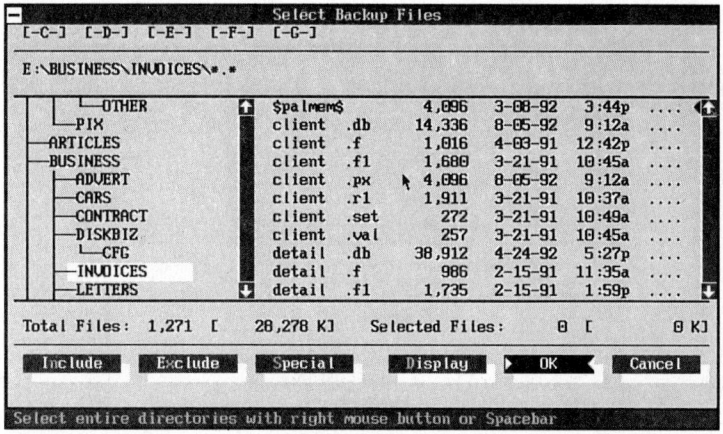

Fig. 10.7
Selecting files to back up.

You also see a series of buttons at the bottom of the screen. The Shell-like window and the buttons provide two different (although complementary) ways to select files for backing up. These procedures differ somewhat in the two backup programs.

Selecting Files Manually. When you choose Select Files and go to the selection screen, you see that the root directory of the current drive is highlighted. To select an entire directory, move the highlight to it; then double-click, press the space bar, or click once with the right mouse button. A pointer appears next to the root directory, and check marks appear next to the file names. To select only some of the files in a directory, select the files individually in the file window, or select the directory containing them and then deselect the files you want to exclude. To select or deselect a file, follow the same procedure you use to select a directory.

When only some of the files in a directory are selected, the pointer next to the directory name changes to this symbol: >.

Press Alt-N to select the Include button, and then choose OK. This action selects all the files in all the subdirectories of the root directory—that is, the entire drive. Choose OK; the Backup screen reappears.

You select files and directories for backup in Microsoft Backup for Windows the same way as in MSBACKUP. The main difference is the manner in which selection information is displayed. A series of symbols lets you know in detail which directories have some or all files selected and whether some or all of the selected files will be backed up. (Files might be selected and not backed up if you have chosen an intermediate type of backup, or if you have given the program explicit instructions not to back up some of the selected files, as described in the next section.) Choosing the **L**egend button displays the description of the symbols, as shown in figure 10.8.

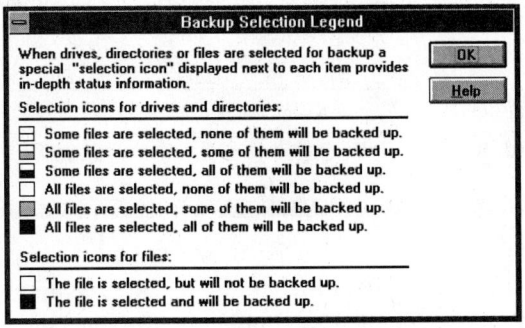

Fig. 10.8
File selection legend in Microsoft Backup for Windows.

If you want to reuse the selections you have made, be sure to save the selections in a setup file; if you don't do this, your selections are saved in the DEFAULT.SET file. To save your selections in a setup file, choose Save Setup **A**s from the **F**ile menu. The Save Setup File dialog box appears, enabling you to give the backup set a name and a description (see fig. 10.9). You can optionally choose a different drive and directory for the setup file. (The default is C:\DOS.) Figure 10.9 shows the Windows version of the dialog box, but the DOS version is very similar.

The next time you want to perform a backup of this type, load the setup file. In the DOS version, you can load the setup file from the command line or by choosing Open Setup from the File menu. In the Windows version, you can load the setup file from within the program using the same command. (The Open Setup File dialog box is similar to the Save Setup File dialog box.) Under some mysterious circumstances, you sometimes have to choose the appropriate drive from the Backup From list to activate your selections; usually, however, you do not.

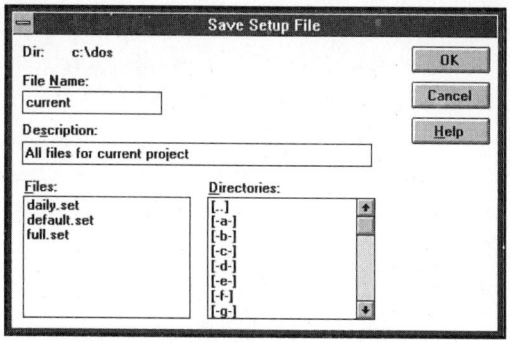

Fig. 10.9
The Save Setup File dialog box.

Choosing Files Using Selection Criteria. The buttons at the bottom of the file selection screen give you many ways to select files to include in or exclude from a backup. These buttons also control other aspects of the program:

- ***Include*** (**I**nclude in Microsoft Backup for Windows) and ***Exclude*** enable you to specify a path to include or exclude, and a file name. The file name might include a wildcard pattern. You can optionally check a box to include all subdirectories of the specified path.

  In addition to selecting files to include, you might want to exclude the following types of files, even from a full backup:

  > Configuration files that are regenerated and updated every time you use an applications program.
  >
  > Backup files created by applications programs (usually having the extension .BAK, or some other extension including the characters *B* and *K*).
  >
  > Temporary files (usually having the extension .TMP or an extension including the $ sign).

- ***Special*** enables you to exclude read-only, hidden, system, or copy-protected files, or select files by date.

- ***Display*** enables you to determine whether the files appear in the file window sorted by name, extension, size, date, or attribute, and whether selected files appear before unselected files when the screen is refreshed.

The Display button in Microsoft Backup for Windows, in addition to the functions available in MSBACKUP, enables you to determine which of the directory data appears in the file window. You can selectively exclude the file date, file time, file size, and file attributes. You can also rearrange the display so that the directory window appears above the file window rather than to its left.

Microsoft Backup for Windows includes two other buttons:

- ***Legend*** displays the Backup Selection Legend window (refer to fig. 10.8).
- ***Print*** enables you to print a list of the files selected for backup, either to the printer or to a file. (You can print the contents of the setup file from either program by choosing Print from the File menu.)

Editing the Include/Exclude List in MSBACKUP. When you choose Include or Exclude, the dialog box contains a button labeled Edit Include/Exclude List. Choosing this button produces the dialog box shown in figure 10.10. You can select an entry to copy, delete, or edit.

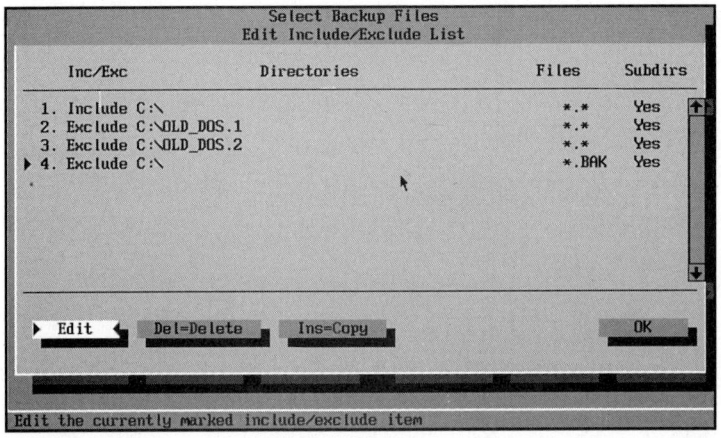

Fig. 10.10
The MSBACKUP Edit Include/Exclude List.

To edit a selection, choose **E**dit. This command displays the Edit dialog box shown in figure 10.11. In this dialog box, you can specify a drive, path, and file name, including wildcard patterns. You can choose whether to include or exclude the specified files and whether to apply the selection to subdirectories of the current directory.

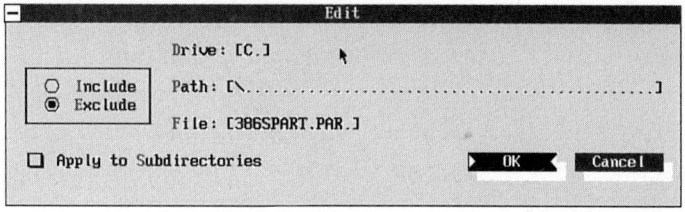

Fig. 10.11
Editing file specifications.

To use the Edit dialog box effectively, you first must copy an existing specification in the Edit Include/Exclude List dialog box (refer to fig. 10.10). Then select one of the copies, and choose **E**dit. After you enter the Edit dialog box, you can enter any specifications you want.

Note

In MSBACKUP, you need not include a drive name in a specification for inclusion or exclusion. By not specifying a drive name, you can apply the same specifications to any or all drives and select the drives from the Backup From list. In Microsoft Backup for Windows, you must include a drive name. However, you can load a setup file created by MSBACKUP in Microsoft Backup for Windows.

Editing the Include/Exclude List in Microsoft Backup for Windows. In Microsoft Backup for Windows, a single dialog box contains the list of included and excluded file specifications and the fields for editing specifications (see fig. 10.12). You do not have to edit existing specifications. You can just enter your criteria (which must include a drive name) and choose **A**dd.

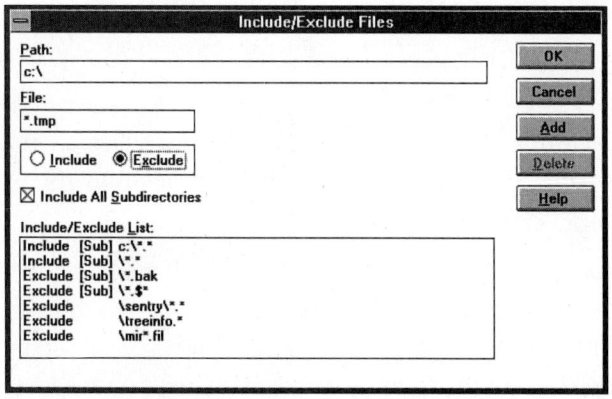

Fig. 10.12
Including and excluding files in Microsoft Backup for Windows.

Using Other Backup Options

Both backup programs give you additional options concerning their behavior. To view or change these options, use the **O**ptions button on the Backup screen. Figure 10.13 shows the resulting dialog box in Microsoft Backup for Windows, with the default options selected. The options—and the defaults—are the same in MSBACKUP.

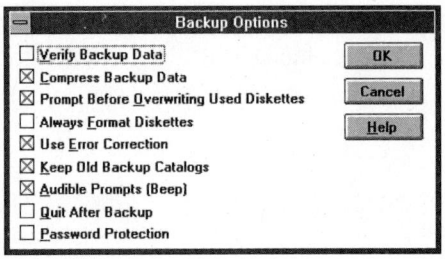

Fig. 10.13
The Backup Options dialog box.

The Backup Options dialog box contains the following options:

- ***V**erify Backup Data* forces the backup program to read the file from the backup disk after it is written and compare it to the original file. This process ensures that the backup is safe and accurate. When you use this option, however, the backup takes nearly twice as long.
- ***C**ompress Backup Data* causes the program to compress the data before writing it to the backup disk. Compression results in the backup requiring fewer disks and might reduce the time required.
- *Prompt Before **O**verwriting Used Diskettes* causes the program to display a warning before writing backup data on a used disk. You can then choose to overwrite the files on the backup disk or use a different disk.
- *Always **F**ormat Diskettes* forces the program to format every backup disk before writing to it so that the backup programs always format an unformatted disk or a badly formatted disk. Choosing this option increases the time required for a backup.
- *Use **E**rror Correction* adds special coding to each backup disk to make recovering the data easier if the backup disks become damaged or worn out. This option decreases the amount of data you can fit on each backup disk, but the extra margin of safety is worth the loss.

- ***K**eep Old Backup Catalogs* prevents the programs from erasing the previous catalog when you perform a full backup. If, as suggested, you have two separate full backup series, leave this option selected so that you can use the catalogs to locate files to be restored.
- ***A**udible Prompts (Beep)* causes the computer to beep every time a prompt appears.
- ***Q**uit After Backup* automatically closes the program when your backup procedure is complete. This option is useful when you are running MSBACKUP from a batch file or running Microsoft Backup for Windows in the background.
- ***P**assword Protection* enables you to enter a password, which will thereafter be required to access the backup data or the catalog.

Restoring Backup Files

Performing a backup operation is akin to buying an insurance policy. You hope you never have to use it, but if disaster strikes, you have a way to replace the loss. To reinstate lost data onto your hard disk, choose the **R**estore button in either program.

Note

The DOS backup programs can restore only data backed up with one of these programs or with one of the Norton backup programs, published by Symantec Corporation. DOS includes an external RESTORE command, which is the only command that can read files copied to a backup set by the BACKUP command from earlier versions of DOS. Consult the Command Reference later in this book for details on the use of this command.

The Restore option enables you to restore an individual file, selected files, or an entire hard disk.

Both backup programs provide the same facilities when restoring files, but they're arranged somewhat differently. When you choose Restore, the program loads the most recent backup set catalog and displays the Restore screen shown in figure 10.14. The catalog's name appears in the Backup Set Catalog field. The drive and capacity used for the backup appear in the Restore From field, and Original Locations appears in the Restore To (or Restore To in the Windows version) field.

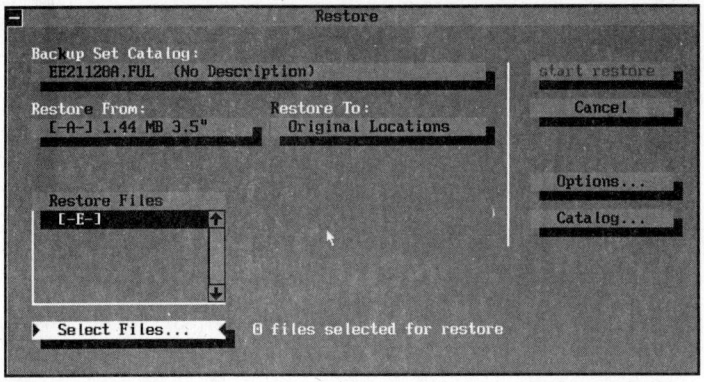

Fig. 10.14
The Restore screen.

To choose another backup set for restore, select Bac**k**up Set Catalog, and choose one of the other files listed. If the file is not in the default catalog directory (C:\DOS), choose Catalo**g** and then choose **L**oad; then select the drive and directory from the appropriate list before choosing the catalog file.

If your hard disk contains no catalog file for the backup series from which you want to restore, choose Catalo**g** and then **R**etrieve. The program asks you to place the last disk of the backup series in your drive, and the backup program reads the catalog from the disk. If the program cannot read the catalog, the catalog is missing, or the disk is damaged, choose Catalo**g** and then Re**b**uild. The program asks you to insert each backup disk from the series beginning with disk 01. The backup program reconstructs the catalog from the data on the backup disks.

Note

The Catalog command appears on a button in MSBACKUP and on the menu bar in Microsoft Backup for Windows.

By default, the programs restore files to their original locations. If the file's original directory is no longer on the destination disk, the program creates the directory before restoring the file. The programs make directory entries for files that are no longer on the destination disk and allocate the next available space in the FAT for the restored file's allocation.

You can restore to other drives or other directories. To do so, choose **R**estore To (or Restore **T**o in the Windows version), and select Othe**r** Drives or Other **D**irectories. You might want to use this option to restore an older version of a file without destroying your current version. By default, the programs automatically overwrite existing files of the same name in the same location. If you choose either of the alternative locations, you have a chance to enter both a drive name and a directory path after you begin the restore.

You can restore all or only some of the files in a backup set. To restore all the files, select the drive or drives in the Restore Files list. This action selects all the files in the backup set that were originally on the selected drive.

To select individual files to restore, choose Select Files. You again see a screen similar to the DOS Shell screen. However, only those drives included in the backup appear on the drive bar, and no file names appear in the file window if the current directory did not include any files that were backed up. In Microsoft Backup for Windows, directories that contain no files in the backup set appear in light gray. You select files and directories to restore in the same way you selected files and directories for backup.

When the correct entries appear in all fields of the Restore screen, choose Start Restore. Like the Backup module, the Restore module prompts you for the disks of the backup set.

Note

Restoring a full backup set to a freshly formatted disk eliminates any file fragmentation that might have existed on the disk when you backed up the files. Restoring an incremental backup set, however, might result in fragmented destination files. As you might recall, fragmentation doesn't affect the file's integrity, but it might slow disk performance slightly.

When you restore files, keep the following guidelines in mind:

- The destination disk must already be formatted. The restore operation, unlike the backup operation, has no provision to format the destination disk.
- Files restored to a freshly formatted disk are not fragmented.

Restoring Files after a Disk Failure. This section presents an example of restoring files. Assume that you are using a backup policy that includes a weekly full backup on Friday and an incremental backup each Wednesday. You have two backup sets. The first set from Friday contains all files. The second set contains only files modified or created after Friday, but before Thursday.

Caution

If you have copy-protected files on your hard disk when you do a backup, they might not restore properly to a destination disk. Ideally, you uninstall copy-protected software using the manufacturer's suggested procedure prior to performing the backup; then you reinstall the copy-protected programs after the restore operation. This practice might not be practical, however. Keep in mind that you might have to reinstall copy-protected software after restoring a complete disk.

Now suppose that you are saving a worksheet file on Thursday morning when a workman begins to use a large drill next door. DOS reports the following message:

```
General Failure on drive C:
```

You abort the spreadsheet session and run CHKDSK or SCANDISK to ensure that your FAT and directory system are in order. (Chapter 7, "Preparing and Maintaining Disks," covers the operation of both CHKDSK and SCANDISK.) DOS reports hundreds of lost clusters.

You have had an electrical noise-induced hard disk failure. You have no choice but to reformat your hard disk and then fall back to your backup disks. This process requires the steps discussed in the following paragraphs.

You first have to reboot your computer with a DOS Start-up disk in drive A because the DOS utilities on your hard disk might be corrupt. After you format your hard disk, copy the external DOS commands back to the hard disk from the DOS master disks. You must use MSBACKUP for the restore because you have not yet restored Windows. Use the PATH command to set a search path to the DOS directory so that DOS can locate the MSBACKUP command.

In case of total disk failure, restore your backup sets in chronological order. Restore your latest full backup set first. Locate the disks from your full backup set and put them in their proper order. Then issue the MSBACKUP command. You probably will have to configure the program all over again. When you have completed this process, choose **R**estore.

Put the last disk into drive A, and choose Catalo**g** and then **R**etrieve. Select the appropriate drive or drives in the Restore Fi**l**es list. Choose **S**tart Restore.

DOS lists the full path and file names of the files being restored on the progress screen. When all the files from the first disk are restored to the hard disk, DOS prompts you for the next disk in the backup set. This cycle repeats until you have completed the restore operation.

After restoring the full backup set, you must restore the incremental backup set. Because you want to restore all the files in the incremental backup set, you use the same procedures you used to restore the full backup set. The operation proceeds in the same fashion.

After both backup sets are restored, run CHKDSK or SCANDISK to ensure that the hard disk is in order. Keep both backup sets intact until you have determined that your hard disk is performing correctly. Run CHKDSK or SCANDISK several times during the day. If all is in order, perform a full backup at the end of the day.

Performing a Selective Restore. This section discusses how to perform a selective restore operation. Assume that last week you accidentally deleted the database file CLIENT.DB from your INVOICES directory. You discovered the error today and have already tried, unsuccessfully, to use the UNDELETE command. Luckily, an up-to-date version of the CLIENT.DB file is on your most recent backup set.

To restore only the \BUSINESS\INVOICES\CLIENT.DB file from the backup set, load the backup program you use, choose **R**estore, select the appropriate backup set, and choose Se**l**ect Files.

You again see a tree and file window, as shown in figure 10.15. Select the file from the file window.

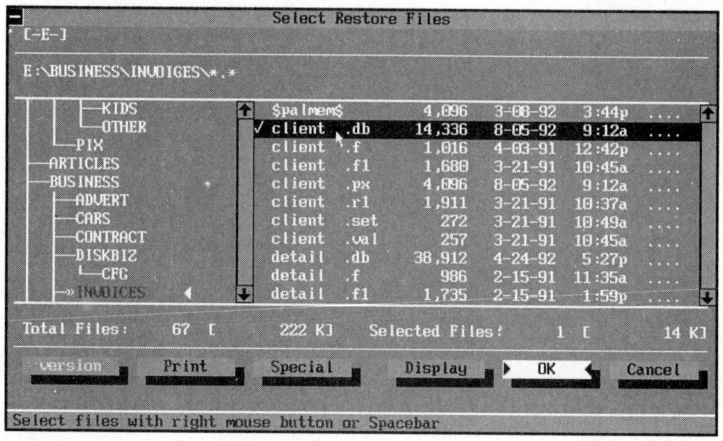

Fig. 10.15
Selecting a file to restore.

For Related Information

- "Analyzing a Disk with CHKDSK," p. 192
- "Analyzing a Disk with the ScanDisk Utility," p. 196

As in the complete restore example, RESTORE prompts you to insert the first disk. You can insert the first disk, or if you know the disk number that holds the CLIENT.DB file, you can insert that disk. RESTORE bypasses any files on the source disk that are not included in the destination parameter you gave in the command. When RESTORE encounters the file \BUSINESS\INVOICES\CLIENT.DB, the program lists the file name on the progress screen and copies the file to the destination disk.

Understanding Computer Viruses

In working with computers, you probably have encountered situations in which the computer didn't do what you wanted it to do. Frustrating as these situations can be, they simply represent a misunderstanding between you and your computer.

Computer viruses are quite different; viruses are supposed to do harm to your computer. Viruses are programs, written by unscrupulous programmers, designed to make copies of themselves and spread from one computer to another, just as a biological virus spreads in people. Usually, viruses also damage your computer by destroying legitimate data and programs. Creating a virus is against the law, but depraved programmers still spread viruses for the same reason that vandals throw bricks through windows—to cause senseless damage.

To protect yourself, you must understand how viruses work. The following sections explain computer viruses in detail.

Understanding How Viruses Spread

Computer viruses come in thousands of variations, each of which works a little differently. How viruses spread from one computer to another, and the damage they do, depends on how the virus is written.

A virus begins in the hands of an experienced but morally corrupt programmer who is either malicious or insensitive to the damage caused. The programmer usually starts with an existing program (anything from a game to a word processing program) and adds a few carefully crafted instructions that modify the workings of the program. This person then distributes the altered program to other users, either on a floppy disk or through an electronic bulletin board.

When the unsuspecting recipient runs the altered software, the program might appear to work correctly, but the added code—the virus—performs some type of operation that the victim doesn't want. This operation might delete important files or erase the hard disk entirely. The virus also might display a taunting message. The most dangerous viruses, however, do no immediate damage; they might alter the operating system by planting a kind of time bomb. Days, weeks, or months after the original infected program ran, the operating system might suddenly go wild, deleting files and destroying data.

Worse, most viruses are designed to spread to other computers. Between the time when a virus infects a computer and the time when it begins to damage that computer, the virus might copy itself onto every floppy that the victim inserts into the computer. Because the victim is unaware that the computer is infected until the virus begins to do damage, he or she might unwittingly spread hundreds of copies to friends.

Strange as it might seem, more than 1,000 viruses exist today. You should be concerned about computer viruses, and you should be serious about protecting your system. However, you might derive some comfort from knowing that your computer can become infected in only one of two ways:

- Loading and running infected software. Your chance of infecting your computer decreases greatly if you get software only from reputable software companies. When you load software from bulletin boards or from an illegal source, your chances of encountering a virus increase.
- Booting from an infected floppy disk. Many viruses spread when a computer boots from a floppy disk that carries the virus. Beware of disks that weren't formatted by you or by someone you trust.

Fighting Viruses with Microsoft Anti-Virus

Your best defense against viruses is a virus-scanning program. Such a program can scan files and disks, looking for telltale sequences of instructions that have been identified as parts of known viruses. Used correctly, a good virus program can protect you against the vast majority of known viruses before they damage your computer.

DOS includes two programs—Microsoft Anti-Virus (MSAV) and Microsoft Anti-Virus for Windows (MWAV)—that can scan your memory and disk for hundreds of known viruses. You can use these programs to detect and destroy viruses.

In its simplest use, you can start MSAV simply by typing MSAV at the DOS prompt. You can select the functions you want to perform from MSAV's menu. Figure 10.16 shows the main MSAV menu.

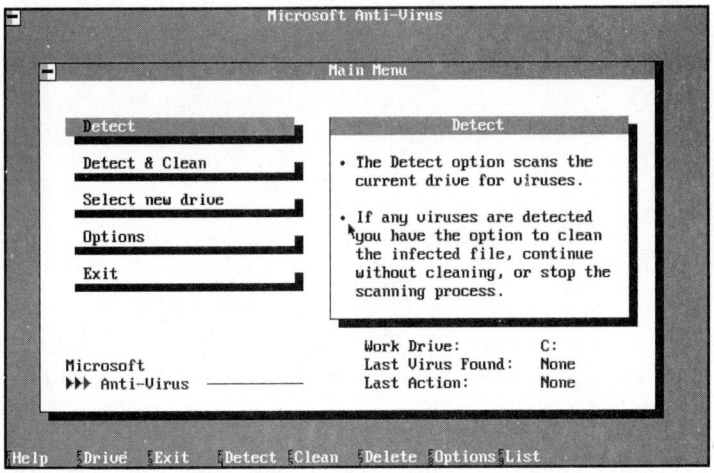

Fig. 10.16
The Microsoft Anti-Virus main menu.

The following list describes the options in this menu:

- **D***etect* looks for viruses and tells you what it finds, but it does not destroy viruses.
- *Detect* & **C***lean* looks for viruses and destroys any it finds.
- **S***elect new drive* enables you to specify the drive on which Detect or Detect & Clean runs.
- **O***ptions* enables you to configure various options that determine how MSAV works.
- **E***xit* terminates MSAV.

The most common operation you will perform is scanning for viruses. To scan the currently logged drive for viruses, select **D**etect (or press F4). MSAV scans the current drive for viruses and reports on how many files it searched and how many viruses it found (none, you hope). Figure 10.17 shows a sample report after MSAV has done its work.

Viruses Detected and Cleaned

	Checked	Infected	Cleaned
Hard disks :	1	0	0
Floppy disks :	0	0	0
Total disks :	1	0	0
COM Files :	25	0	0
EXE Files :	49	0	0
Other Files :	89	0	0
Total Files :	163	0	0
Scan Time :	00:00:09		

OK

Fig. 10.17
Typical MSAV report after a virus scan is completed.

With luck, you will never face the unpleasant prospect of finding a virus on your system. However, if MSAV finds a virus during its scan, it displays a dialog box telling you which virus it found and which file contained the virus, and asking what you want to do. If you select Continue, MSAV keeps looking for more viruses. If you select Clean, MSAV destroys the virus and then continues searching.

If you want to tell MSAV to scan your disk and clean any viruses it finds, select Detect & Clean. MSAV cleans any viruses it finds.

If you want to scan a different drive, select Select new drive (or press F2), and select the drive you want to scan.

The complete command-line syntax of the DOS version of Microsoft Anti-Virus is shown here:

```
MSAV drive: /S /C /R /A /L /N /P /F videoswitches /VIDEO
```

If you specify the drive parameter, MSAV scans the indicated drive; otherwise, it scans the currently logged drive.

The /S switch tells MSAV to immediately invoke the Detect function, causing it to scan the specified drive. However, with this option, MSAV doesn't remove any viruses it finds. The /C switch tells it to scan and remove the viruses it finds.

The /R switch tells MSAV to create a scan report. MSAV creates a file called MSAV.RPT, which lists the number of files MSAV scanned, the number of viruses detected, and the number of viruses removed. MSAV.RPT is always created in the drive's root directory.

The /A switch causes MSAV to scan all drives except A and B. The /L switch causes MSAV to scan all hard disks on your computer, but not drives on a network.

The /N switch causes MSAV to run without using the graphical user interface. If it detects a virus, it returns a special exit code (86). This switch is useful when you're scanning for viruses within a batch file.

The /P switch runs MSAV with a command-line interface rather than a graphical user interface. Normally, MSAV displays file names as it scans. The /F switch tells MSAV not to display file names. Use this switch only with the /N or /P switches.

MSAV also recognizes many switches that control how it uses the screen. These switches are shown in table 10.2. The /VIDEO switch can be used to display all these options.

Table 10.2 MSAV Options for Controlling Display

Switch	Meaning
/25	Sets screen to 25 lines (default)
/28	Sets screen to 28 lines (VGA only)
/43	Sets screen to 43 lines (EGA or VGA)
/50	Sets screen to 50 lines (VGA only)
/60	Sets screen to 60 lines (Video 7 display adapters only)
/BF	Uses the computer's BIOS for video display
/BT	Enables graphics mouse in Windows
/BW	Uses black-and-white scheme
/FF	Uses screen updating that works especially fast on CGA displays
/IN	Uses color scheme
/LCD	Uses a scheme that works well on LCD screens
/LE	Reverses left and right mouse buttons
/MONO	Uses monochromatic color scheme
/NF	Disables alternative fonts
/NGM	Uses the default mouse character rather than graphics mouse pointer
/PS2	Resets the mouse if the mouse pointer disappears

Understanding Checklists. After you have used MSAV to scan a drive, you might notice that each directory contains a file called CHKLIST.MS. This file contains identifying information (called *checksums*) about the files in that directory. Each time MSAV scans the files in that directory again, it can compare the current status of the file against information in the CHKLIST.MS file. If a file has become infected since the CHKLIST.MS file was created, the checksums indicate that a change has occurred.

The CHKLIST.MS files don't require much disk space, but if you want to free some disk space, you can start MSAV and press F7 to tell MSAV to delete all CHKLIST.MS files.

If you don't want MSAV to create CHKLIST.MS files in the future, start MSAV and select Options (or press F8), and turn off Create New Checksums.

Listing Virus. If you are interested in learning about the viruses known to MSAV, you can use MSAV's List feature to access its list of viruses. Start MSAV and press F9 to see MSAV's virus list.

You can use the scroll bars to scan through the list of known viruses, or you can search for a particular virus by entering its name in the blue box and selecting Find Next.

When you find a virus about which you would like more information, click the virus's name. MSAV displays information about the virus, such as the sample shown in figure 10.18.

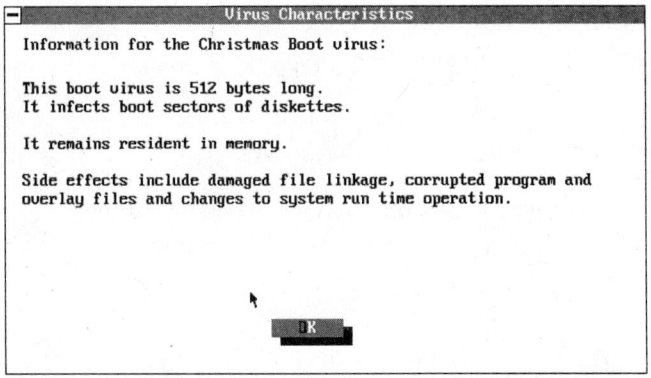

Fig. 10.18
Sample information about a virus.

Using the Windows Version of Microsoft Anti-Virus

The Windows version of Microsoft Anti-Virus, MWAV, is almost identical in its operation to the DOS version. When you invoke MWAV, you see the dialog box shown in figure 10.19. Select the drive you want to scan, and then click **D**etect to scan without removing viruses, or Detect and **C**lean to scan for viruses and remove any viruses found.

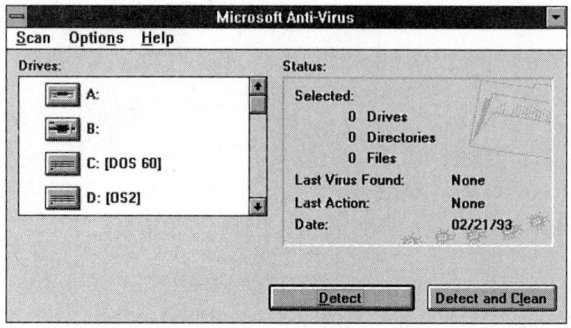

Fig. 10.19
Microsoft Anti-Virus for Windows main dialog box.

By selecting the Scan menu, you can access most of the other options described with MSAV in the preceding section. This menu includes Delete CHKLIST Files, which deletes all the CHKLIST.MS files on your disk, and Virus List, which enables you to access MWAV's virus list.

Guarding against Infection

Most users can protect themselves against viruses by following these steps:

1. Before you load any software from floppy disks, scan all the disks with MSAV or MWAV. Click **S**elect new drive, select your floppy disk drive, and execute **D**etect for each disk.
2. After you install new software and before you run it, run MSAV or MWAV on your hard disk.
3. If you download software from bulletin boards, run MSAV or MWAV on your hard disk before you run that software.
4. Never boot from a floppy disk that you have not scanned for viruses (with MSAV or MWAV) or that you did not format yourself.

Summary

This chapter covered the important DOS commands and procedures that enable you to ensure the integrity of your data and, even more important, protect yourself from data loss. These are the key points covered in this chapter:

- You can protect your computer hardware equipment by following common-sense safety precautions.
- The MSBACKUP command produces special copies of your program and data-file backup sets. Backup sets normally are used for recovering lost data.
- The RESTORE command reads files from backup sets and restores the files to their original directories on another disk.
- You can protect yourself from data loss by faithfully following a backup policy.
- Viruses can damage your system, but you can use the Microsoft Anti-Virus programs to protect yourself.
- You can protect yourself from computer viruses by purchasing only tested software and using MSAV or Microsoft Anti-Virus for Windows to check any new software.

In the next chapter, you learn what you can do to recover when disaster strikes.

Chapter 11

Emergency Procedures

We've all shared that sinking feeling before: you are just finishing up a tough work session, and you are in a hurry to leave. One more command, and you can be out the door and on your way. But before you know it, you type a command that deletes a file you didn't intend to delete or formats a disk you didn't want formatted.

The first reaction usually is panic. All my data! (All that work!) Fortunately, DOS provides some tools you can use to recover some of your data. It still takes some thought and work on your part, but generally you can turn a major catastrophe into a few minutes to a few hours of inconvenience.

In this chapter, you learn how to use the UNFORMAT and UNDELETE commands. Both of these can make your computer life safer; but you should remember that neither command is a substitute for regularly backing up your data.

Unformatting a Disk

Sooner or later, virtually all PC users format a disk accidentally. The UNFORMAT command is your best chance to undo the damage. UNFORMAT is designed to restore the previous format of hard and floppy disks. UNFORMAT also can help you recover from accidental change or damage to a hard disk's partition table.

The UNFORMAT command is one of those DOS commands that was originally part of commercial products. Microsoft has licensed the code for the UNFORMAT command from Central Point Software. UNFORMAT came to the DOS package from Central Point's PC Tools.

UNFORMAT has two primary uses:

- To recover files after an accidental format
- To rebuild a damaged partition table on your hard disk

Because UNFORMAT completely rebuilds a disk's FAT, root directory, and boot record, use this command only as a last resort. The degree of success you have in recovering all files depends on which version of DOS you used to format the disk, what switches you used, and what you have done to the disk since you reformatted it.

Caution

If the disk that you accidentally formatted is a hard disk, do not install DOS on it because the DOS files will overwrite files you want to recover. Do not copy or save files of any kind to the reformatted hard disk. If you have to reboot the computer, use a bootable floppy disk.

Note

The FORMAT commands create a MIRROR image file during the safe format procedure. The MIRROR image file contains a copy of the disk's FAT, root directory, and boot record. It saves this information in a normally unused portion of the disk. At the same time, FORMAT creates a hidden file named MIRORSAV.FIL, which contains information required by DOS to locate the MIRROR image file. The MIRORSAV.FIL file is given the hidden attribute so that it is not "visible" by the DIR command unless you use the /AH switch. If you use the /U switch with FORMAT, however, no MIRROR image file is created, and UNFORMAT will not work.

When you want to use UNFORMAT after an accidental format, use the following syntax:

```
UNFORMAT d: /J /L /P /TEST /U
```

d: is the drive that contains the disk to be unformatted.

/J causes UNFORMAT to verify that the MIRROR image file accurately reflects the current disk information.

/L searches a formatted disk and lists the file and directory names found.

/P sends all output to a printer.

/TEST provides a test run to indicate whether UNFORMAT can unformat a disk successfully.

/U attempts to unformat a disk without the benefit of a MIRROR image file.

When you want to use UNFORMAT to rebuild a hard-disk partition table, use the following syntax:

```
UNFORMAT /PARTN /L /P
```

/PARTN causes the command to try to rebuild the hard-disk partition tables.

/L displays the current partition table.

/P sends all output to a printer.

Recovering from an Accidental Format

Suppose that you just accidentally formatted a hard disk (or used the DOS RECOVER command incorrectly—see the Command Reference for a discussion of RECOVER). You need to use UNFORMAT, which uses the information stored in the MIRROR image file to restore the FAT, root directory, and boot record to their preformatting condition.

To unformat a disk that was safe-formatted, type the following command at the DOS prompt:

```
UNFORMAT d:
```

(Remember to replace the *d* with the letter of the drive that contains the disk you want to unformat.) UNFORMAT first tells you to insert a disk into the specified drive and press Enter. When you follow these instructions, the computer beeps and displays a screen similar to this:

```
Restores the system area of your disk with
the image file created by MIRROR

WARNING!            WARNING!

This should be used ONLY to recover from the inadvertent use
of the DOS FORMAT command or the DOS RECOVER command.
Any other use of UNFORMAT may cause you to lose data!
Files modified since the MIRROR file was created may be lost.
```

As you can see, the first thing UNFORMAT does is to try to scare the bejeebers out of you by giving you messages like `WARNING!` Then it settles down and searches the disk for the MIRROR file created the last time the disk was formatted. It then displays a message similar to the following one:

```
The last time MIRROR was used was at hh:mm on mm-dd-yy.
```

For the *hh:mm* and *mm-dd-yy* information in this message, UNFORMAT substitutes the time and date at which MIRROR.FIL was created. UNFORMAT again causes your computer to beep and then displays the following message, substituting the correct drive letter for *d:*

```
The MIRROR image file has been validated.

Are you SURE you want to update the SYSTEM area
of your drive d (Y/N)?
```

If you choose to use the MIRROR information, UNFORMAT restores the FAT, root directory, and boot record stored in the MIRROR file. Unfortunately, UNFORMAT might have problems fully restoring fragmented files. If UNFORMAT cannot restore a file due to fragmentation, it displays a prompt asking whether you want the file erased or truncated. This incapability to deal with file fragmentation severely limits the usefulness of UNFORMAT. Hard disks begin to fragment files from the first day you start using them.

Don't think of the UNFORMAT command as a magic bullet that will keep you and your disks from peril. Rather, think of it as a last-ditch chance to save you from a mistake that has only a 50/50 chance of being totally successful. Nothing will save you from data losses better than a rigorously applied system of disk backups.

Recovering from an Accidental Format without a MIRROR Image File

Even if a MIRROR image file is not available for a formatted disk, the UNFORMAT command might be able to recover most of the data. This process takes more time than if a MIRROR image file were available, however, and it does not recover files that were in the disk's root directory.

To use UNFORMAT to unformat a hard disk on which no current MIRROR image file exists, use the following syntax:

```
UNFORMAT d:  /U /L /TEST /P
```

Replace *d:* with the letter of the drive that contains the accidentally formatted disk.

The /U switch stands for "unformat" and tells UNFORMAT that you are not using a MIRROR image file created by FORMAT.

The optional /L parameter causes UNFORMAT to list all files and directories found during the UNFORMAT operation. Similarly, /P causes UNFORMAT to send the entire UNFORMAT process to your printer.

Use the /TEST option to run a simulation of the process so that you can see which files UNFORMAT can recover before any changes are written to the hard disk.

After you execute the command, UNFORMAT displays the following message:

```
CAUTION !!

This attempts to recover all files lost after a
FORMAT, assuming you've NOT been using MIRROR. This
method cannot guarantee complete recovery of your files.

The search-phase is safe: nothing is altered on the disk.
You will be prompted again before changes are written to
the disk.
Using drive d:
Are you SURE you want to do this?
If so, type Y; to cancel the operation, press any other key.
```

To continue with the unformat operation, press **Y** and then press Enter. Press any other key to cancel the process. While searching the disk, UNFORMAT displays the following message:

```
Searching disk
pp% searched, mm subdirectories found.
Files found in the root: 0
Subdirectories found in the root: mm
```

UNFORMAT does not find any root-level files, but it substitutes for *mm* the number of root-level subdirectories it finds. (Refer to Chapter 5, "Understanding Files and Directories," for a discussion of files and the root directory.) As UNFORMAT searches the disk, the command continually updates the last message, substituting the percentage of the disk read for *pp* and the number of subdirectories found for *mm*.

After UNFORMAT completes its search of the disk's data, the command lists the subdirectories found. Depending on which version of the FORMAT command was used, UNFORMAT might or might not be able to recover the names of subdirectories. If it cannot, UNFORMAT gives each subdirectory a name in the format SUBDIR.*nnn*, with *nnn* representing a number ranging from 1 to 512. If UNFORMAT can find the subdirectory names, it displays them and then displays a message similar to this one:

```
Walking the directory tree to locate all files_

Path=D:\
Path=D:\DIRNAME\
Path=D:\
```

In this message, *D* is the drive name, and *DIRNAME* is the subdirectory. This message is repeated for each subdirectory found. UNFORMAT then lists the number of files found, including subdirectories, and displays the following warning:

```
Files found: nn
Warning!  The next step writes changes to disk.
Are you sure you want to do this?

If so, type Y; to cancel the operation, press any other key.
```

To proceed with the unformat operation, press **Y** and then Enter. Again, UNFORMAT has problems dealing with fragmented files, so you will have to decide whether to truncate or delete fragmented files.

Rebuilding a Partition Table

UNFORMAT also enables you to recover from a corrupted hard-disk partition table. Such an error normally generates this DOS message:

```
Invalid drive specification
```

To recover from this problem, you first must issue the UNFORMAT command with the /PARTN switch and then use UNFORMAT without this parameter to restore the FAT, root directory, and boot sector.

To recover from a corrupted hard-disk partition table, follow these steps:

1. Boot your computer (with a floppy disk, if necessary), and display the DOS prompt.

2. Change to a drive that contains the UNFORMAT file, UNFORMAT.COM. If your only hard disk is inaccessible because of partition-table corruption, use a copy of DOS on a floppy disk. (UNFORMAT.COM is contained on the Start-up disk, one of the disks used during DOS installation.)

3. Type the following command at the DOS prompt:

   ```
   UNFORMAT /PARTN
   ```

   UNFORMAT prompts you to insert the disk containing the file PARTNSAV.FIL and to type the name of that disk drive.

4. Insert the disk that contains the copy of the partition table created by MIRROR.

5. Type the letter of this drive, and press Enter. MIRROR rebuilds the partition table from the file PARTNSAV.FIL found on the floppy disk. After

UNFORMAT has rebuilt the partition table, the program prompts you to insert a master DOS disk into drive A and press Enter. To complete this process, you need a bootable backup disk that contains your system files and the UNFORMAT command.

6. Insert a bootable DOS disk into drive A, and then press Enter. UNFORMAT causes your computer to reboot.

7. Use the copy of UNFORMAT on the floppy to restore the FAT, root directory, and boot record, following the steps described in "Recovering from an Accidental Format" earlier in this chapter.

For Related Information

- "Preparing Floppy Disks with the FORMAT Command," p. 170
- "Preparing the Hard Disk," p. 180

Recovering Deleted Files with UNDELETE

Because of the way DOS deletes files, reversing the process is relatively easy, but only if you act promptly. When DOS deletes a file, it changes the first character in the file name recorded in the directory area of the disk so that the target file no longer is listed. As far as DOS is concerned, the file is gone. DOS does not erase the file name entry completely, or overwrite any data in the file, until it needs the space for another file.

Eventually, as you add new files to the disk, DOS reallocates the disk space assigned to the deleted file, causing new data to overwrite the old data. Soon, the file and its data are gone permanently. But if you use the UNDELETE command before DOS has a chance to overwrite a deleted file's data, you can reverse the DELETE operation.

Tip
If you discover that you accidentally deleted a file, immediately try to recover it. The longer you wait, the less likely you are to recover the file completely by using the UNDELETE command.

Using UNDELETE from the Command Line

UNDELETE provides three levels of protection against losing accidentally deleted files: delete sentry, delete tracking, and standard. Both the delete sentry and the delete tracker options require you to load the memory-resident portion of UNDELETE, which requires just over 13K of memory.

Delete sentry gives you the highest level of protection by creating a hidden subdirectory called SENTRY. As files are deleted, the memory-resident portion of UNDELETE moves copies of the files into this directory without changing the FAT entry for the file. UNDELETE regulates the amount of disk space that can be taken up by files stored in the SENTRY directory to about 7 percent of the disk's total space. As files are deleted, and the SENTRY directory fills up, the oldest files in the directory are deleted for real to make room for recent additions.

Delete tracker's protection is one step down from the sentry. It uses a hidden file named PCTRACKER.DEL to record information about deleted files. When files are deleted, the delete tracker feature releases the file's FAT entry, making the disk space available to another file. You can undelete the file as long as no other file has been written to that location. Using delete tracker makes undelete operations easier because it stores the file's original names but does nothing to protect the file's location on the disk from being overwritten. Delete tracker, however, uses much less disk space.

The standard level of protection depends on a deleted file's directory entry and disk location remaining intact. If neither location has been overwritten, the standard undelete protection simply restores the directory entry as being no longer deleted. Despite the standard method's relative lack of protection, most DOS users rely on the standard method because there is no loss of memory due to loading the memory-resident version of UNDELETE, and there is no use of disk space to store deleted files or information about deleted files.

The UNDELETE command has two syntactical forms:

```
UNDELETE FileNameExpression  [/DS¦/DT¦/DOS]
```

and

```
UNDELETE /LIST¦/ALL¦/PURGE[drive]¦/STATUS¦/LOAD¦/UNLOAD
   ¦/S[drive]¦/Tdrive[-entries]]
```

The *FileNameExpression* of the first form specifies the file or files to be undeleted. You can use wildcards to indicate multiple files. By default, if you do not specify a file name, DOS attempts to undelete all deleted files in the current directory. If you do not specify a method using the three switches of the first form, DOS attempts to use delete sentry if available, then tracking if available, then DOS standard if neither of the other methods is available.

The /DS switch tells DOS to use the delete sentry method, recovering only files stored in the SENTRY directory. You are prompted to confirm undeletion of each file.

The /DT switch instructs DOS to use the delete tracking method of recovering the specified files. You are prompted to confirm undeletion of each file.

/DOS causes DOS, in its attempt to undelete files, to rely on the information still stored in the DOS directory instead of using one of the other more protective methods.

/LIST displays a list of the files that can be recovered without attempting to recover them.

The /ALL switch attempts to recover all deleted files without a confirmation prompt for each file. When used with this switch, UNDELETE first attempts to use the delete sentry method if available, then tries the delete tracking method, and finally if neither of these methods is available, uses information directly from the DOS directory.

/LOAD causes UNDELETE to install itself in memory. If no UNDELETE.INI file is found, it is created.

/UNLOAD removes the memory-resident portion of UNDELETE from your system's memory, disabling the delete sentry and delete tracking methods of file recovery.

/PURGE deletes the contents of the SENTRY directory on the specified drive. If no drive is specified, UNDELETE searches the current drive for the directory.

/STATUS lists the type of delete protection in effect for each of the drives currently protected with sentry or tracking.

/S enables delete sentry protection on the specified drives using the information found in UNDELETE.INI. If this file is not found, it is created. Normally, establishing delete sentry protection is done with a line in AUTOEXEC.BAT.

/T enables the delete tracking protection on the specified drives using information from UNDELETE.INI. If this file is not found, it is created. The ENTRIES portion of this parameter specifies the maximum number of files that can be tracked. Valid values range between 1 and 999. Normally, establishing delete tracking protection is done with a line in AUTOEXEC.BAT.

Tip
For details on the UNDELETE.INI file, its uses, and how it controls the UNDELETE command's operations, type HELP UNDELETE at a DOS prompt, and view the NOTES portion of the displayed information.

Recovering Files with UNDELETE

To install delete sentry or delete tracking, you will ideally put a command line in your AUTOEXEC.BAT file to load the UNDELETE command with its deletion-tracking option or its delete-sentry option. These options load a memory-resident portion of the regular UNDELETE command. You specify which option you want to use by including in the command-line switches that load UNDELETE as a resident program.

Suppose that you want to recover a file and have installed UNDELETE with the delete sentry option. Change to the directory that contains the deleted file, and then type the following command:

```
UNDELETE filename.ext
```

Be sure to substitute the name of the file that you want to recover for *filename.ext*. When you press Enter, DOS displays a message similar to this one:

```
UNDELETE - A delete protection facility

Copyright  1987-1993 Central Point Software, Inc.
All rights reserved.

Directory: C:\SPREADSH\QPRODAT
File Specifications: filename.ext
   Searching Delete Sentry control file...
    Delete Sentry control file contains    1 deleted files.
   Searching deletion-tracking file....
    Deletion-tracking file contains    0 deleted files.

    Of those,       0 files have all clusters available,
                    0 files have some clusters available,
                    0 files have no clusters available.

   MS-DOS directory contains    0 deleted files.
   Of those,        0 files may be recovered.

Using the Delete Sentry method.
   Searching Delete Sentry control file....
   filename.ext    4037   11-29-92    4:58p  ...A Deleted 12-5-92 1:32a

This file can be 100% undeleted. Undelete (Y/N)?n
```

This message indicates, in place of *filename.ext*, the name of the file you specified. The message then indicates the total number of deleted files by this name listed in the Delete Sentry directory; the total number of files by this name in the deletion-tracking file; the number of files by this name that have all clusters available and, therefore, are recoverable; the number of partially recoverable files; and the number of files that are not recoverable.

Next, the DELETE command's message might indicate that the deleted file still is listed in the MS-DOS directory. Such a file might have been deleted when UNDELETE was not resident in memory as well as when delete tracking was active.

Finally, the UNDELETE message lists the first file matching *filename.ext* that DOS found in the Delete Sentry directory. If this file is recoverable (that is, if the file's clusters have not yet been reallocated to another file), DOS asks whether you want to undelete the file. To recover the file, press **Y**. DOS recovers the file and displays the following message:

```
File successfully undeleted.
```

The UNDELETE message also lists any other files with the same name in the Delete Sentry directory. The files are listed one by one, starting with the most recently deleted files. For each file, UNDELETE asks whether you want to recover the file. If additional files with the same name are listed in the deletion-tracking file, UNDELETE repeats the procedure for each of these files.

If recovering a file creates a duplicate file name in the directory, UNDELETE displays the following message:

```
The filename already exists. Enter a different filename.

Press "F5" to bypass this file.

If you want to recover this file, type a unique file name (one that
does not already exist in the current directory). Otherwise, press F5
to skip this file.
```

Note

You might have created and deleted same-named files in a particular directory more than once. (In fact, every time you save a file on which you are working, you delete the preceding version and create a new one.) So don't be alarmed or confused if UNDELETE asks more than once whether you want to recover a particular file. Normally, you recover the most recently deleted version of the file and discard the others.

Occasionally, by the time you realize that you need to recover an accidentally deleted file, other files might have reused some of the file's clusters. In such a case, UNDELETE displays the following message:

```
Only some of the clusters for this file are available.
Do you want to recover this file with only the available clusters?
(Y/N)
```

Press **Y** to recover the available bytes or **N** to skip the file. If you wait too long before attempting to recover a file, you might not be able to recover the file because other files are using all its clusters. In this case, UNDELETE tells you so and displays this message:

```
Press any key to continue
```

Sometimes, even though most of a file still is on disk, the clusters in the first part of the file might have been reused by another file. In such a case, UNDELETE loses its "map" to the rest of the file and displays the following message:

```
Starting cluster is unavailable. This file cannot be recovered
with the UNDELETE command. Press any key to continue.
```

If you want to know which deleted files you still can recover, type the following command:

```
UNDELETE /LIST
```

UNDELETE displays, from the Delete Sentry directory, the deletion-tracking file, and/or the DOS directory, a list of deleted files from the current directory.

Note

If a deletion-tracking list is too long to fit in one screen, you can use Ctrl-S to pause the display. Press any key on the keyboard to resume scrolling. Do not use redirection or the MORE filter; these actions create disk files that might overwrite some or all of the data that you want to recover.

Caution

If you delete all the files in a directory and then delete the directory, you cannot recover any of the deleted files from that directory. UNDELETE cannot recover a deleted directory.

The UNDELETE command is a product of Central Point Software, licensed by Microsoft Corporation for distribution as part of DOS. Another Central Point Software product, PC Shell, can recover a deleted directory. (PC Shell is part of the PC Tools utility package.)

Using the DOS Directory to Recover a File

If you were not using UNDELETE's resident portion when you accidentally deleted the file that you want to recover, you can try to recover the file by using the information stored in the DOS directory. Type the following command:

```
UNDELETE filename.ext /DOS
```

Substitute for *filename.ext* the name of the file that you want to recover. UNDELETE displays a message similar to the following one:

```
Directory: C:\SPREADSH\QPRODAT
File Specifications: BUDGET.WQ1

      Delete Sentry Control file not found.
      Deletion-tracking file not found.
      MS-DOS Directory contains 1 deleted files.
      Of those,   1 files may be recovered.

Using the MS-DOS Directory.

  ?UDGET    WQ1    4037   11-29-92    4:58p   ...A
Undelete (Y/N)?
```

Press **Y** to recover the file or **N** to skip the file. After you press Y, UNDELETE displays the following prompt:

```
Enter the first character of the filename.
```

Because the DOS directory no longer has any record of this first character, you must supply the letter. Type the letter that you want UNDELETE to use as the beginning letter of the file name. UNDELETE recovers the file and displays the following message:

```
File successfully undeleted.
```

Using the Microsoft Undelete Program for Windows

If you use Microsoft Windows, the DOS Setup program probably installed the Windows utilities in their own program group in the Windows Program Manager. The Windows Tools group includes an Undelete program. When you open this program, Windows displays a screen similar to the one shown in figure 11.1, listing the deleted files in whatever directory was current when you started Windows. The following sections explain how to set up and use Microsoft Undelete for Windows.

Configuring Microsoft Undelete

If you have installed the DOS version of UNDELETE in your AUTOEXEC.BAT file, you need not configure Microsoft Undelete. If you have not installed UNDELETE, however, choose **C**onfigure Delete Protection from the **O**ptions menu. This command displays a dialog box in which you can choose one of the following options:

- Delete **S**entry
- Delete **T**racker
- St**a**ndard (no delete protection)

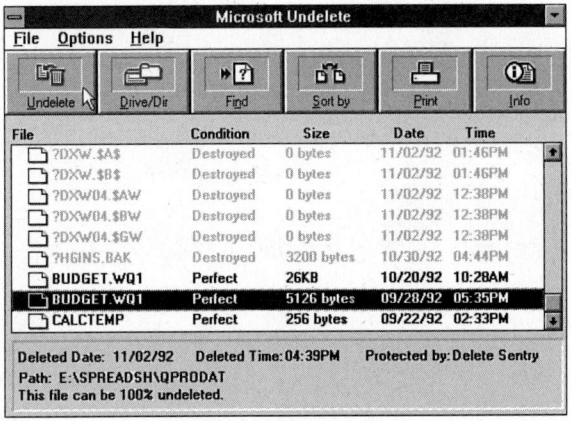

Fig. 11.1
Using the Windows Undelete program.

You already have seen what each of these options does. If you install Delete Protection through Windows, UNDELETE will be installed in your AUTOEXEC.BAT file automatically.

Selecting Files to Recover

If the default directory does not contain the file that you want to recover, click the **D**rive/Dir button or choose Change **D**rive/Directory from the **F**ile menu. A dialog box appears in which you can type the correct directory path in a text box or choose the directory from a list box. When you click OK, the main window shows the deleted file in your chosen directory (refer to fig. 11.1). When you select a file, Windows displays the following information below the directory window:

- The date and time when the file was deleted, if known (this information is available only if Delete Sentry is used)
- The protection method in use when the file was deleted, if any (if none, Windows displays the message `Protected by: DOS`)
- The current drive and directory
- The probability that the file can be recovered

If the directory in which the deleted file was stored is not current, click the **Find** button or choose **Find** Deleted File from the **File** menu. The Find Deleted Files dialog box appears (see fig. 11.2).

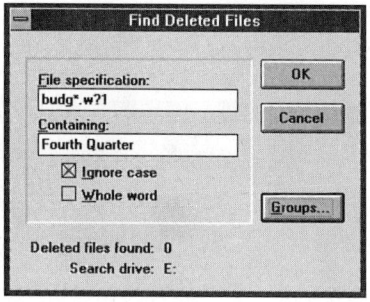

Fig. 11.2
The Find Deleted Files dialog box.

In this dialog box, you can type the name of the file that you want to find and also some text from the file; this information helps Undelete locate the correct version of the file. If you want to narrow the search further, click the **Groups** button to display a list of all the file types whose extensions are associated with a program in Windows. You can narrow the search more by clicking one or more of the listed groups. After you finish specifying what to search for, click OK.

If Undelete finds any matching files, it displays the files in the directory window.

Recovering Files

When you see the file that you want to recover, select it, and then perform one of the following actions:

- Click the **Undelete** button.
- Choose **Undelete** from the **File** menu.
- Choose Undelete **To** from the **File** menu.

You can select more than one file by clicking each file or by moving the selection bar to each file and pressing the space bar.

If you use either of the first two methods, Undelete simply recovers the file in its current location. If the prognosis for recovery is not good, however, you might want to use the Undelete To command so that you can recover the file to another drive.

You might have to search the disk to find the data that was in the file. If you're not successful the first time, Undelete To enables you to try again without disturbing the data on the original disk.

If you use the Undelete command and recover the file, the information in the Condition column changes to read `Recovered`, as shown in figure 11.3.

Fig. 11.3
Successfully undeleting files.

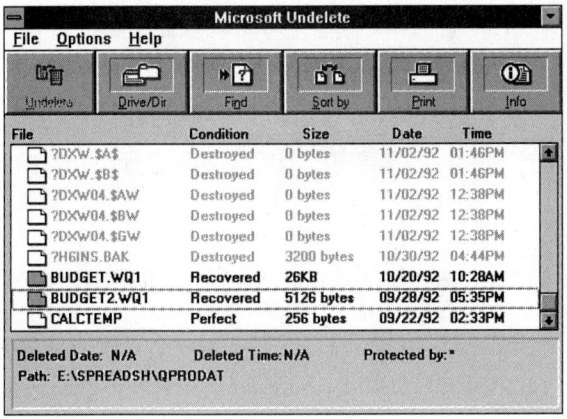

If you want to recover a file whose name is being used by another file, the message `File already exists` appears. Choose OK, and you see a dialog box in which you can enter a new name for the file. As you can see in figure 11.3, both files named BUDGET.WQ1 have been recovered, but one has been renamed.

Using Other Options

Microsoft Undelete includes several other options that are not available when you try to recover a deleted file from the DOS prompt:

- *Sorting.* The Sort By button and the Sort By command (Options menu) enable you to sort the file names displayed in the Undelete window by name, date, size, directory date and time, deletion date and time, or condition.
- *Printing.* You can group the files in the display by directory and then print them by clicking the Print button or choosing Print List from the File menu.
- *Displaying information.* Click the Info button or choose File Info from the File menu to display a box in which all the information about a deleted file is conveniently grouped in one place.

- *Selecting files.* The Options menu contains two commands that you can use to select groups of files for recovery. Choose Select by Name to display a dialog box in which you enter a file name. If you include a wildcard pattern in the file name, all matching files will be selected. You then can choose the Unselect by Name command to narrow the selection.

- *Deleting files.* If you installed the delete sentry option, you can choose Purge Delete Sentry File from the File menu to get rid of all the files—or selected files—in the Sentry directory. You might want to use this command if you are running low on disk space and need to install a new program.

For Related Information

- "Deleting Files," p. 248
- "Avoiding Data Loss," p. 253

Summary

This chapter has provided you with information you might never need. But if you are like most people, at some time you will need to undelete a file or unformat a disk. In this chapter, you have learned how to perform both of these procedures. In particular, you have learned the following information:

- You can use the UNFORMAT command to undo an accidental format. The efficiency of the command is increased if your newly formatted disk has a MIRROR file available on it.

- Deleted files can be restored to the disk using the UNDELETE command. UNDELETE offers three different methods for restoring deleted files. The delete sentry and delete tracker methods require the UNDELETE command to be loaded as a memory-resident program, whereas the standard method can be used without the overhead of a TSR program.

The next chapter starts a brand-new section of this book. In it, you will begin to learn how to make DOS work the way you do.

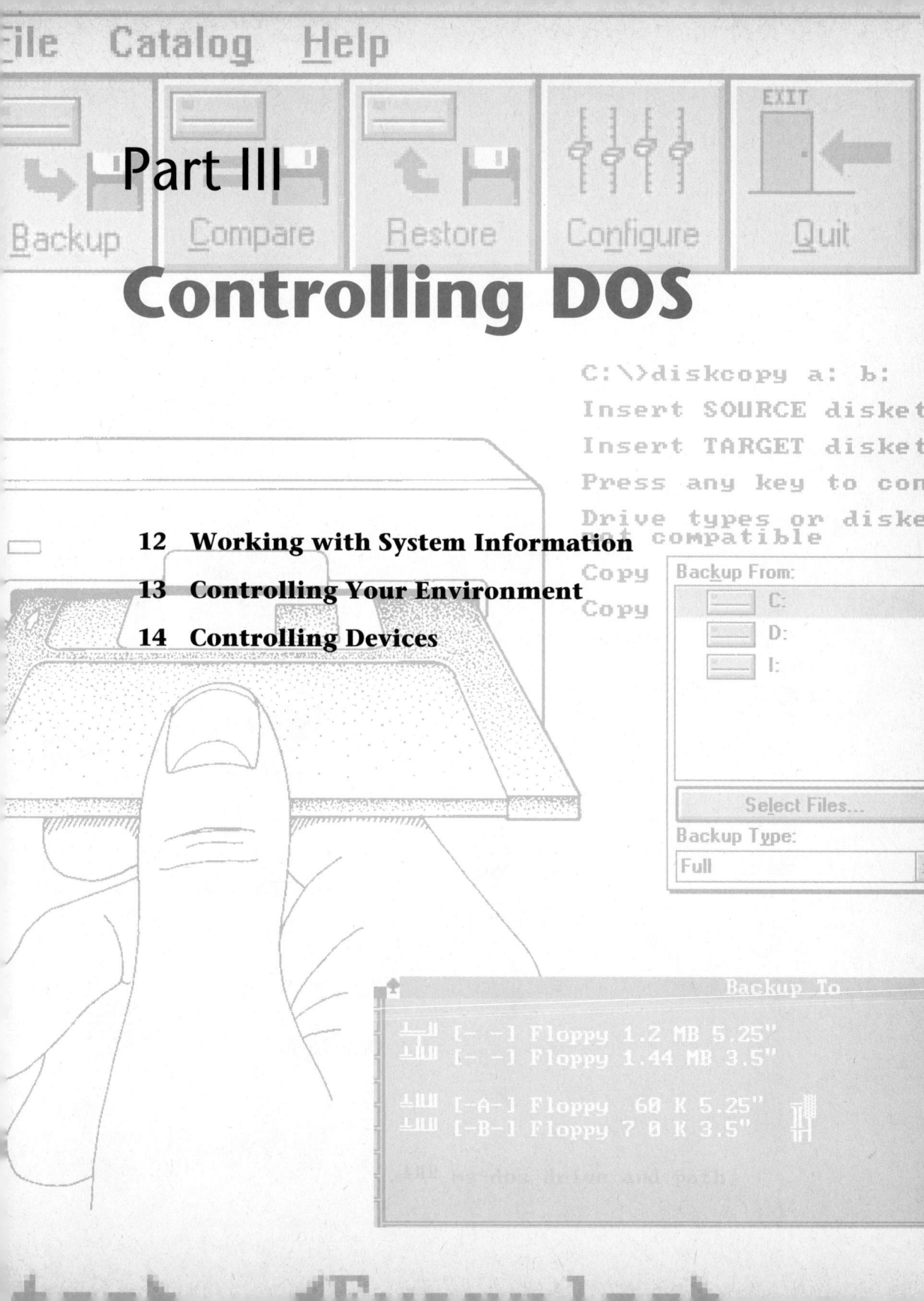

Part III

Controlling DOS

12 Working with System Information

13 Controlling Your Environment

14 Controlling Devices

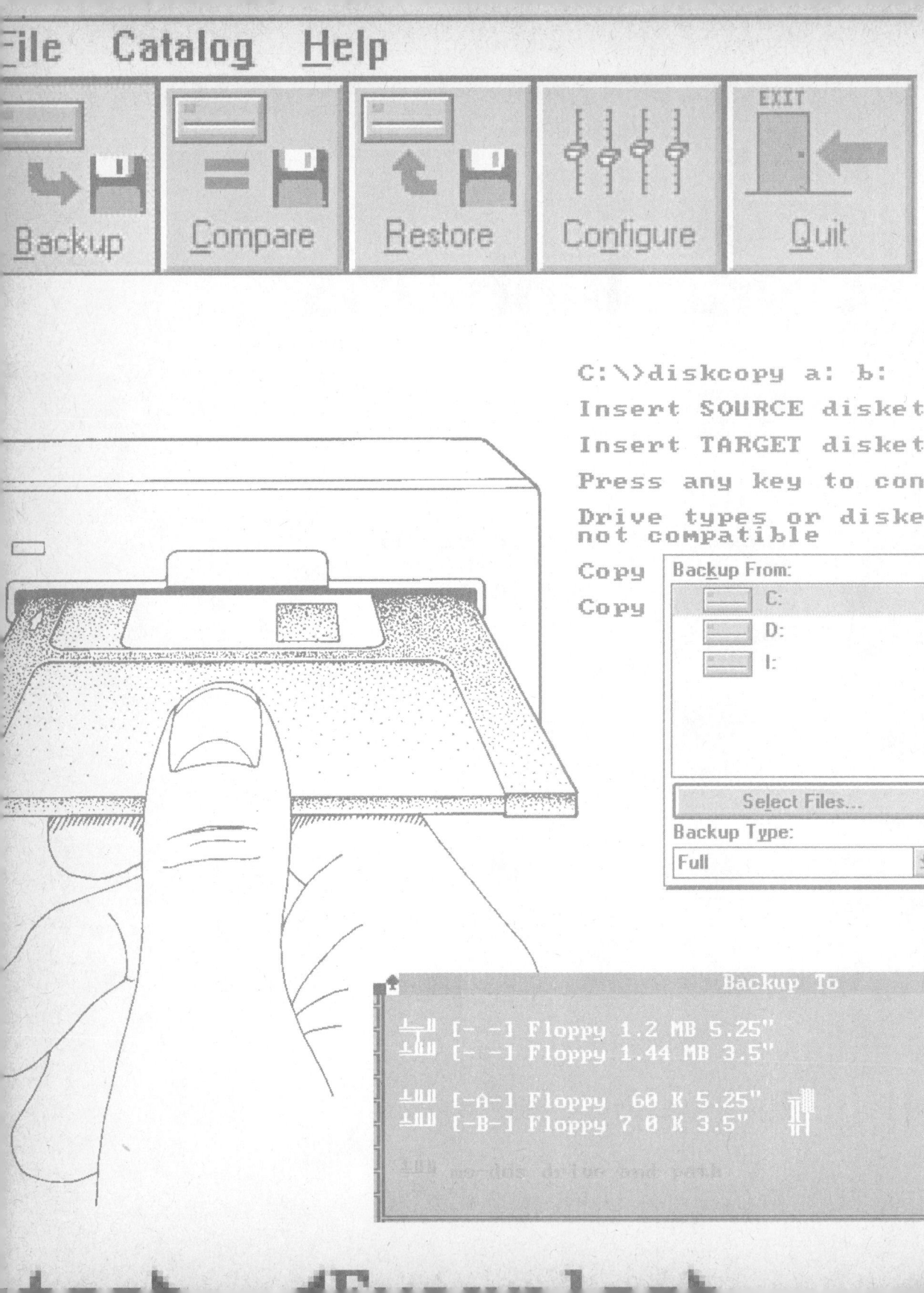
File Catalog Help
Backup
Compare
Restore
Configure
EXIT
Quit
C:\>diskcopy a: b:
Insert SOURCE diskette i
Insert TARGET diskette i
Press any key to continu
Drive types or diskette
not compatible
Copy
Copy
Backup From:
C:
D:
I:
Select Files...
Backup Type:
Full
Backup To
[- -] Floppy 1.2 MB 5.25"
[- -] Floppy 1.44 MB 3.5"
[-A-] Floppy 60 K 5.25"
[-B-] Floppy 7 0 K 3.5"

Chapter 12

Working with System Information

Chapters 1 through 4 of this book introduce the fundamentals of DOS and how these fundamentals relate to you and your hardware. Chapters 5 through 11 show you the commands associated with your disks, directories, and files. This chapter covers commands that provide information about your system. This information includes items such as the date and time maintained by your system and the appearance of the screen. It also includes commands that enable you to invoke secondary copies of DOS.

For lack of a better term, the commands covered in this chapter are collectively referred to as *system information commands*. This chapter covers the following commands:

DATE

TIME

VER

SETVER

MEM

COMMAND

EXIT

These commands, as well as their parameters and switches, are also described in the Command Reference.

Changing the Date and Time

In Chapter 5, "Understanding Files and Directories," you learned a bit about how DOS stores files using a directory. This directory maintains critical information about each file on your disk, including the file name, its attributes, its size, and where it is stored on the disk. It also contains date and time information that indicates when the file was last updated. This information is often referred to as a date and time stamp. This stamp is updated from the system date and time whenever you make changes to the file.

Unless your computer is an old IBM PC or PC/XT, it uses a battery-powered clock to maintain the date and time used by your system. Even when the computer is turned off, power from the battery goes to the chip containing the clock, and the date and time remain current. In an IBM PC or PC/XT, you can use an add-on, battery-backed clock for this purpose. When you have an add-on clock, you must run a special program (packaged with the clock) to transfer date and time information to DOS. Such a program is not necessary with the newer computers; these transfer the date and time to DOS automatically whenever you turn on the power to your machine.

Setting the date and time becomes increasingly important as you create more files on your computer. Because the DOS file-naming rules limit you to only eight characters in the root file name and three characters in the file extension (which is generally used to indicate the file type), the names of your files might not be very descriptive. In this situation, you might need to rely on the date and time stamp to tell which file is the most recent. On computers without a clock or with a clock that has a dead battery, however, the date and time are set to the same value each time you turn on the computer. This situation makes it difficult for you—or DOS—to tell the difference between an old file and a revised or new file. In addition, some DOS commands work by comparing file dates. If your system time and date are not correct, these commands will have little value to you.

Occasionally checking your computer's date and time is worthwhile. All batteries eventually fail and need replacing. All clocks in personal computers lose time. How much time your clock loses depends on the programs you run on your computer.

The clock that keeps the date and time in a PC is controlled by an electronic component in the computer—the system timer. This chip is the heartbeat of the computer. Everything the computer does takes a known amount of time.

The system timer provides a regular pulse that controls all the functions occurring in the computer.

One of these functions is to update the clock that DOS uses to tell the time (and consequently the date). Commands or other programs that cannot afford to be interrupted while they're working tell DOS not to interrupt them until they finish what they're doing. A typical example is a communications program that waits for a character to be sent from another computer. If DOS is busy performing other tasks, such as updating the clock, the program might miss the character. Consequently, this type of program disables the interrupts—the program tells DOS to do nothing else for the period that it needs full control. During these times, the clock is not updated. These periods are typically only a fraction of a second, but the effect is cumulative, and eventually the time loss is noticeable.

If you do not have an AUTOEXEC.BAT file (see Chapter 2, "Starting DOS"), DOS displays the current date and time when you start your computer and gives you the opportunity to change them. You should take a moment to check these settings. Make sure that you set the date and time correctly whenever you are prompted because both are used in many DOS operations.

Most people, however, use an AUTOEXEC.BAT file. This file seldom contains the commands necessary to change the date and time. In these instances, DOS uses its current settings. If you later notice that the date and time are incorrect (for instance, a newly created file might contain the wrong date and time), then you should change them using the DATE and TIME commands.

Issuing the DATE Command

DATE is an internal command that is very simple to use. There is only one possible parameter, as shown in the following syntax:

```
DATE today
```

If you type DATE at the DOS prompt and then press Enter, DOS shows you the date currently being used by your system, and then prompts you for a new date:

```
Current date is Tue 08-17-1993
Enter new date (mm-dd-yy):
```

The date that is displayed might or might not be correct; you can change it by entering a new date, or accept it by pressing Enter. Alternatively, if you don't want to see what the current date setting is, you can enter the DATE command followed by the date you want your system to use.

The exact format you should use for entering a date depends on the COUNTRY code set in your CONFIG.SYS file. (Chapter 21, "Understanding the International Features of DOS," includes a discussion of the country code settings.) The date format can be one of the following formats:

COUNTRY Code	Format
North America	*mm-dd-yy* *mm-dd-yyyy*
Europe	*dd-mm-yy* *dd-mm-yyyy*
East Asia	*yy-mm-dd* *yyyy-mm-dd*

mm is the month, *dd* is the day, and *yy* and *yyyy* are the year. For example, to set the date to December 23, 1993, on a machine configured for North America, you can enter the following line at the DOS prompt:

```
DATE 12-23-93
```

You also can type the year in its full form (1993, for example). If you use two digits, DOS assumes the 19. Rather than the hyphen, you can use periods or slashes as separators. Leading zeros are not required. If the month is January, for example, you can use 1 (instead of typing 01) for the month.

If you want to change the date, letting DOS prompt you is the best way to use this command. This is because the current date setting appears in the correct format, and you can copy this format rather than remember it. Here is an example of how the DOS screen might appear if you let DOS prompt you for the current date:

```
C:\>DATE
Current date is Tue 08-17-1993
Enter new date (mm-dd-yy): 12-23-1993
```

Pressing Enter when DOS prompts you for a new date retains the current setting. If you don't enter the date correctly or if you select a date that is outside of the range supported by DOS, you will see the error message `Invalid date`, after which you can again try to enter a date.

Issuing the TIME Command

Closely related to the DATE command is the internal TIME command. It also has only one possible parameter:

```
TIME now
```

As with DATE, if you type only TIME and press Enter at the DOS prompt, DOS shows you the current time setting and prompts you for a new one. You can change the time without being prompted by including the new time on the command line as a parameter.

When you enter a new time setting, you do so using hours, minutes, and seconds. The exact format you should use depends on the COUNTRY code setting in your CONFIG.SYS file.

You can use either a 12-hour or a 24-hour clock. The following line shows the format used for a 24-hour clock:

```
hrs:mins:secs.1/100secs
```

hrs is the hour, a number from 0 to 23; *mins* is the minutes, a number from 0 to 59; *secs* is the seconds, a number from 0 to 59; and *1/100secs* is the number of one-hundredth seconds, a number from 0 to 99. The 24-hour clock starts with midnight as 00:00.00. You can use a period rather than a colon when separating the hours, minutes, and seconds, or a comma in place of a period when separating the seconds from the hundredths of a second.

If you decide to enter the time using a 12-hour clock, the format is the same as for the 24-hour clock except that *hrs* is a number from 1 to 12, and you add *a* or *p* to signify a.m. or p.m. If you do not add an *a* or a *p*, DOS assumes a.m.

Just because DOS enables you to enter time to the nearest 1/100 of a second, you don't need to. In fact, you don't need to enter all the parts of the time. DOS sets any missing elements to zero (using the 24-hour clock notation). To set the time to 8:25 p.m., for example, you can enter one of the following lines at the DOS prompt:

```
TIME 20:25
```

or

```
TIME 8:25p
```

Either command sets the time to 8:25 p.m. The seconds and hundredths of a second are set to zero. To set the clock to 12:30 a.m., you can enter the following line:

```
TIME :30
```

As with the DATE command, letting DOS prompt you for the time is the easiest way to use this command. When DOS displays the current time, all you need to do is enter a new time using the same format. Following is an example of how the DOS screen might appear if you let DOS prompt you for the current time:

```
C:\>TIME
Current time is 2:35:07.23p
Enter new time: 2:40p
```

For Related Information

- "AUTOEXEC.BAT," p. 36
- "Understanding COUNTRY.SYS," p. 540

You can use the COUNTRY command to change the format DOS uses to display the time (see Chapter 21, "Understanding the International Features of DOS").

Displaying the Version with VER

DOS includes an internal command that displays the DOS version currently in use. Knowing how to use the VER command is invaluable if you ever work with an unfamiliar computer. Some commands, such as DISKCOMP, FORMAT, and XCOPY work differently or are not available with different DOS versions. If you do not know which version of DOS a computer is using, the VER command can tell you.

When you enter the VER command at the DOS prompt, you see a message similar to this one:

```
MS-DOS Version 6.20
```

This is the DOS version used to boot your computer. If a computer with a hard disk is booted from a floppy disk, the version of DOS might not be what you expected. Suppose that your hard disk is formatted for DOS 6.2, but you use a DOS 5.0 floppy disk to boot your computer. The Version 6.2 commands on your hard disk might not work while your computer is running a different version of DOS. In this instance, the following message appears when you try to use one of the DOS 6.2 commands:

```
Incorrect DOS Version
```

Sometimes DOS can be slightly different even within the same version. Some computer manufacturers supply DOS packages specially designed to work with their machines, so you might see a different message if you use a different product. COMPAQ Computer Corporation's version of DOS, for example, includes COMPAQ's name with the version number. Because of the differences between these versions, you might be able to track down problems on an unfamiliar computer more easily if you first determine the exact DOS version number and its manufacturer.

Setting the Version with SETVER

When a new version of DOS is released, some time passes before software manufacturers can upgrade popular applications programs to take full advantage of DOS's new features. Many programs ask the operating system to tell them which version of DOS the computer is running. If a program does not recognize the version of DOS in memory, it might refuse to run. One or more of your applications programs, therefore, might refuse to run because they have not been certified by the manufacturer to run properly with DOS 6.2.

You can get a reluctant program to run under DOS 6.2 in two ways:

- Contact the software manufacturer or your dealer to find out whether you need a program upgrade.
- Use the SETVER command to add the name of the program to DOS 6.2's version table. The version table is a list of programs with DOS version numbers listed next to them. When a program listed in the version table loads into memory and asks DOS for its version number, DOS reports the version number listed in the version table rather than the actual version number—6.2. The application is fooled into running under DOS 6.2.

The first option is the better choice. By checking with the manufacturer, you can determine whether the software has been tested in DOS 6.2.

Caution

If you use SETVER, you run the risk, however slight, that your program might become corrupted if it is incompatible with DOS 6.2.

The SETVER command operates as both a device driver and an executable command. Before DOS can use the version table, you must load SETVER.EXE as a device driver. Make sure that the command is included in your CONFIG.SYS file so that it executes every time you start your computer. If SETVER.EXE is not in your CONFIG.SYS file, you need to add it. Use the following syntax to add SETVER.EXE to your CONFIG.SYS file:

```
DEVICE=d:path\SETVER.EXE
```

The parameters *d:* and *path* are the disk and directory that contain the SETVER.EXE external program file. When you installed DOS, the installation program created a default CONFIG.SYS file for you, which includes the following command:

```
DEVICE=C:\DOS\SETVER.EXE
```

After the device driver SETVER.EXE is loaded into memory, DOS can use the version table to report different DOS versions to applications programs listed in the version table.

To see whether a particular program is already in the version table, use SETVER from the DOS command line. To do this, type **SETVER** at the DOS prompt; do not add switches, file names, or parameters. DOS displays a two-column listing with program names in the first column and the DOS version number the programs will work with in the second column. Microsoft has already tested the programs listed in the initial version table and determined that they operate properly in DOS 6.2. The version list that appears on your screen should resemble the following list:

```
KERNEL.EXE      5.00
NETX.COM        5.00
NETX.EXE        5.00
NET5.COM        5.00
BNETX.COM       5.00
BNETX.EXE       5.00
EMSNETX.EXE     5.00
EMSNET5.EXE     5.00
XMSNETX.EXE     5.00
XMSNET5.EXE     5.00
DOSOAD.SYS      5.00
REDIR50.EXE     5.00
```

```
REDIR5.EXE        5.00
REDIRALL.EXE      5.00
REDIRNP4.EXE      5.00
EDLIN.EXE         5.00
BACKUP.EXE        5.00
ASSIGN.COM        5.00
EXE2BIN.EXE       5.00
JOIN.EXE          5.00
RECOVER.EXE       5.00
GRAFTABL.COM      5.00
LMSETUP.EXE       5.00
STACKER.COM       5.00
NCACHE.EXE        5.00
NCACHE2.EXE       5.00
IBMCACHE.SYS      3.40
XTRADRV.SYS       5.00
2XON.COM          5.00
WINWORD.EXE       4.10
EXCEL.EXE         4.10
LL3.EXE           4.01
REDIR4.EXE        4.00
REDIR40.EXE       4.00
MSREDIR.EXE       4.00
WIN200.BIN        3.40
METRO.EXE         3.31
WIN100.BIN        3.40
HITACHI.SYS       4.00
MSCDEX.EXE        4.00
NET.EXE           4.00
NET.COM           3.30
NETWKSTA.EXE      4.00
DXMA0MOD.SYS      3.30
BAN.EXE           4.00
BAN.COM           4.00
DD.EXE            4.01
DD.BIN            4.01
REDIR.EXE         4.00
SYQ55.SYS         4.00
SSTDRIVE.SYS      4.00
ZDRV.SYS          4.01
ZFMT.SYS          4.01
TOPSRDR.EXE       4.00
```

When you run one of the programs listed in the first column of the version table, DOS reports to the program the DOS version number listed in the second column.

If you try to run a program and it displays an error message stating that you are using an incompatible version of DOS, you might want to try adding the program to the version table. Enter the SETVER command using the following syntax:

```
SETVER filespec n.nn
```

The *filespec* parameter indicates the full name of the file in question, including a path, a file name, and an extension. The *n.nn* parameter is a DOS version number that the program will recognize. Consult the program's documentation to determine with which versions of DOS the program can run. You can also use SETVER to delete program names. The syntax for using SETVER to delete programs from the version table is shown in the following line:

```
SETVER filespec  /DELETE /QUIET
```

The two switches—/DELETE and /QUIET—can be abbreviated as /D and /Q.

For an example of how you use SETVER, assume that you want to run a program called GOODPROG.EXE, but the program runs only with DOS Versions 3.0 to 3.3. To add GOODPROG.EXE to the version table, type the following command at the command prompt and press Enter:

```
SETVER GOODPROG.EXE 3.30
```

DOS displays the following series of messages, including an initial warning:

```
WARNING - The application you are adding to the MS-DOS version
table may not have been verified by Microsoft on this version of
MS-DOS. Please contact your software vendor for information on
whether this application will operate properly under this version
of MS-DOS. If you execute this application by instructing MS-DOS
to report a different MS-DOS version number, you may lose or
corrupt data, or cause system instabilities. In that circumstance,
Microsoft is not responsible for any loss or damage.

Version table successfully updated

The version change will take effect the next time you restart your
system.
```

To verify that the application has been added to the version table, execute SETVER again without switches or parameters. The added application appears at the end of the list. The modified table takes effect, however, only after you restart or reboot your computer.

If you later decide to delete a program from the version list, use the /D switch and the file-name parameter. To delete GOODPROG.EXE from the version table, for example, type one of the following commands at the command line, and press Enter:

```
SETVER GOODPROG.EXE /DELETE
```

or

```
SETVER GOODPROG.EXE /D
```

DOS deletes the application name from the version table and displays the message

```
Version table successfully updated
```

The version change takes effect the next time you start your system.

If you are using a batch file to delete a program name from the version table, you might want to suppress the preceding message. To prevent this message from appearing on-screen, add the /QUIET switch in addition to the /DELETE switch.

Displaying the Amount of Free and Used Memory

One of the handiest DOS commands is MEM. This external command enables you to determine how memory is being used on your system. (For a discussion of the types of memory in your system, see Chapter 1, "DOS and the Personal Computer.")

Issuing the MEM Command

The following line shows the syntax for the MEM command:

```
MEM /DEBUG /CLASSIFY /FREE /MODULE:programname /PAGE
```

All switches are optional, and you will find it handy to abbreviate each switch by typing only the first letter (/D, /C, /F, /M:*programname,* /P). Each switch is independent, meaning that you cannot use them together. The only exception to this is the /PAGE switch, which tells DOS to pause at the end of each screen it displays. This is a handy switch to use, because the output generated by MEM can easily run longer than a single screen.

The /DEBUG switch lists all the loaded programs and device drivers. This listing includes the name, size, position, and type of each item.

The /CLASSIFY switch lists the programs loaded into conventional memory as well as in upper memory—the 384K area of memory between 640K and 1M that is usually reserved for use by certain system devices, such as your monitor.

The /FREE switch lists the free areas of conventional and upper memory. The /MODULE:*programname* switch shows the way a program module is currently using memory. You must specify the program name after the /MODULE switch. The MEM /MODULE switch lists the areas of memory the program module is using and shows the address and size of each area.

Understanding the Operation of MEM

To see a "short" version of the memory report that indicates the amount of free conventional memory, EMS memory, and XMS memory, just enter MEM at the DOS prompt, without any switches. DOS displays a report similar to this one:

```
Memory Type         Total  =   Used  +   Free
----------------    -------   -------   -------
Conventional          640K       79K      562K
Upper                  71K       33K       38K
Reserved              384K      384K        0K
Extended (XMS)*     7,097K    2,537K    4,560K
----------------    -------   -------   -------
Total memory        8,192K    3,033K    5,159K

Total under 1 MB      711K      112K      599K

Total Expanded (EMS)                 7,488K (7,667,712 bytes)
Free Expanded (EMS)*                 4,800K (4,915,200 bytes)

* EMM386 is using XMS memory to simulate EMS memory as needed.
  Free EMS memory may change as free XMS memory changes.

Largest executable program size        561K (574,752 bytes)
Largest free upper memory block         22K  (22,016 bytes)
MS-DOS is resident in the high memory area.
```

This report gives you three types of information about every type of memory in your system, in three columns: the total amount, the amount currently being used, and the memory available for you to use for programs.

The first line describes the conventional memory: the total amount (generally 640K; 1K = 1,024 bytes), the amount of memory currently being used, and the amount of free memory. The next line shows you the amount of upper (reserved) memory and adapter RAM/ROM in the same format. These two amounts total 384K, which, in addition to the conventional memory, is the total amount of memory that DOS addresses—1,024K.

The MEM report then tells you the total amount of extended memory that has been mapped (converted) to XMS memory, the amount currently in use, and the amount available for use. In the example, 4,560K of XMS memory of the original 7,097K are available.

The next line shows the total amount of memory under 1M and the amount available to you for running programs. This amount may be misleading because the figure lumps together the amount of free conventional and free reserved memory. Most programs cannot use both of these types of memory as if they were contiguous.

The first two long lines below the totals show the total amount and free amount of expanded memory in your system. A footnote explains that the EMM386.EXE memory manager creates expanded memory from the pool of XMS memory as needed. Finally, MEM indicates whether MS-DOS currently is loaded in the high-memory area.

Sometimes, MEM's short report doesn't provide enough information to meet your needs. Understanding this, MEM provides three switches to produce longer versions of the report. Because these reports don't fit on a single screen, use the /PAGE switch to display one page of the report at a time.

The reports generated by MEM's /CLASSIFY and /DEBUG switches are highly technical in content. For example, to execute the MEM command with the /DEBUG switch, enter the following line at the DOS prompt:

```
MEM /DEBUG
```

A report similar to this one appears:

```
Conventional Memory Detail:

  Segment              Total        Name          Type
  -------              -----        ----          ----
   00000             1,039    (1K)                Interrupt Vector
   00040               271    (0K)                ROM Communication Area
   00050               527    (1K)                DOS Communication Area
   00070             2,752    (3K)  IO            System Data
                                       CON        System Device Driver
                                       AUX        System Device Driver
                                       PRN        System Device Driver
                                       CLOCK$     System Device Driver
                                       A: - D:    System Device Driver
                                       COM1       System Device Driver
                                       LPT1       System Device Driver
                                       LPT2       System Device Driver
                                       LPT3       System Device Driver
                                       COM2       System Device Driver
                                       COM3       System Device Driver
                                       COM4       System Device Driver
   0011C             5,600    (5K)  MSDOS         System Data
   0027A            49,712   (49K)  IO            System Data
                     1,152    (1K)      XMSXXXX0  Installed Device=HIMEM
                     3,104    (3K)      EMMXXXX0  Installed Device=EMM386
```

```
                    37,648   (37K)     DBLSYSH$  Installed Device=DBLSPACE
                     1,600   (2K)                FILES=32
                       256   (0K)                FCBS=4
                       512   (1K)                BUFFERS=10
                     2,288   (2K)                LASTDRIVE=Z
                     3,008   (3K)                STACKS=9,256
  00E9D                 80   (0K)  MSDOS        System Program
  00EA2              2,656   (3K)  COMMAND      Program
  00F48                 80   (0K)  MSDOS        -- Free --
  00F4D                528   (1K)  COMMAND      Environment
  00F6E                128   (0K)  MSDOS        -- Free --
  00F76             17,088  (17K)  MOUSE        Program
  013A2                160   (0K)  MEM          Environment
  013AC             88,992  (87K)  MEM          Program
  02966            485,776 (474K)  MSDOS        -- Free --

Upper Memory Detail:

  Segment  Region      Total        Name         Type
  -------  ------  --------------  ----------   --------
   0CD4A      1        800    (1K)  IO           System Data
                       768    (1K)     SETVERXX  Installed Device=SETVER
   0CD7C      1      4,224    (4K)  IO           System Data
                     4,192    (4K)     CON       Installed Device=ANSI
   0CE84      1         48    (0K)  MSDOS        -- Free --
   0CE87      1     29,024   (28K)  SMARTDRV     Program
   0D59D      1     16,432   (16K)  MSDOS        -- Free --
   0D9A0      1     22,016   (22K)  MSDOS        -- Free --

Memory Summary:

  Type of Memory       Total    =    Used    +    Free
  ---------------  ----------   ----------   ----------
  Conventional        655,360       80,384      574,976
  Upper                72,576       34,080       38,496
  Reserved            393,216      393,216            0
  Extended (XMS)*   7,267,456    2,598,016    4,669,440
  ---------------  ----------   ----------   ----------
  Total memory      8,388,608    3,105,696    5,282,912

  Total under 1 MB    727,936      114,464      613,472


  Handle      EMS Name      Size
  ------      --------      ----
       0                  060000

  Total Expanded (EMS)                 7,667,712 (7,488K)
  Free Expanded (EMS)*                 4,915,200 (4,800K)

  * EMM386 is using XMS memory to simulate EMS memory as needed.
    Free EMS memory may change as free XMS memory changes.

  Memory accessible using Int 15h              0     (0K)
  Largest executable program size        574,752   (561K)
```

```
Largest free upper memory block          22,016     (22K)
MS-DOS is resident in the high memory area.

XMS version  3.00; driver version  3.16
EMS version  4.00
```

The first column shows the starting address of each item that MEM found. The address is listed in hexadecimal (base 16) notation. The second column shows the size, in kilobytes, of each program or driver. The third column shows the name of the program or device driver loaded into memory. The final column includes the type of item listed. The types include the system files IO.SYS, MSDOS.SYS, and COMMAND.COM; programs; installed device drivers and system device drivers; environment; and any data areas the programs might need.

To see a listing of programs, drivers, and free space in conventional and upper memory, type the following command and press Enter:

```
MEM /C
```

DOS shows you a report similar to this one:

```
Modules using memory below 1 MB:

  Name           Total        =   Conventional    +   Upper Memory
  --------   ----------------   ----------------   ----------------
  MSDOS        18,029   (18K)     18,029   (18K)           0    (0K)
  HIMEM         1,168    (1K)      1,168    (1K)           0    (0K)
  EMM386        3,120    (3K)      3,120    (3K)           0    (0K)
  DBLSPACE     37,664   (37K)     37,664   (37K)           0    (0K)
  COMMAND       3,184    (3K)      3,184    (3K)           0    (0K)
  MOUSE        17,088   (17K)     17,088   (17K)           0    (0K)
  SETVER          816    (1K)          0    (0K)         816    (1K)
  ANSI          4,240    (4K)          0    (0K)       4,240    (4K)
  SMARTDRV     29,024   (28K)          0    (0K)      29,024   (28K)
  Free        613,472  (599K)    574,976  (562K)      38,496   (38K)

Memory Summary:

  Type of Memory        Total   =    Used    +    Free
  ---------------   ----------   ----------   ----------
  Conventional         655,360       80,384      574,976
  Upper                 72,576       34,080       38,496
  Reserved             393,216      393,216            0
  Extended (XMS)*    7,267,456    2,598,016    4,669,440
  ---------------   ----------   ----------   ----------
  Total memory       8,388,608    3,105,696    5,282,912

  Total under 1 MB     727,936      114,464      613,472

  Total Expanded (EMS)                  7,667,712 (7,488K)
  Free Expanded (EMS)*                  4,915,200 (4,800K)
```

```
* EMM386 is using XMS memory to simulate EMS memory as needed.
  Free EMS memory may change as free XMS memory changes.

Largest executable program size        574,752   (561K)
Largest free upper memory block         22,016    (22K)
MS-DOS is resident in the high memory area.
```

Note

Because some of the report scrolls off the screen before you can read it, you might want to use the /P switch to tell DOS to pause after each page. To do so, type the following line:

```
MEM /C /P
```

DOS displays the report one page at a time. Press any key when you are ready to display the next page.

The third and fourth columns of the report, titled `Conventional` and `Upper Memory`, show you how much memory is allocated to any particular driver or program. Use the `Upper Memory` column to determine whether any drivers or programs are loaded in upper memory, and use the `Memory Summary` at the end of the report to see how much upper memory is still free.

Before attempting to move a driver or program from conventional to upper memory (using DEVICEHIGH or LOADHIGH), compare the driver or program's size (in the `Conventional` memory size column) to the available upper-memory block (UMB) size shown at the bottom of the memory summary. The available UMB must be at least as big as the driver or program before you can load the driver or program into upper memory.

A quick way to see a listing of free memory space without searching through one of the longer reports is to use the /FREE switch, as shown in the following line:

```
MEM /F
```

If you use this switch, MEM lists the free areas of conventional and upper memory. This report shows you the segment address and size of each free area of conventional memory and the largest free block in each region of upper memory. The switch also summarizes your overall memory use. A sample of the report follows:

```
Free Conventional Memory:

  Segment         Total
  -------    ----------------
   00F48           80     (0K)
   00F6E          128     (0K)
   013A2          160     (0K)
   013AC       88,992    (87K)
   02966      485,776   (474K)

  Total Free: 575,136   (562K)

Free Upper Memory:

  Region   Largest Free      Total Free       Total Size
  ------  --------------  --------------  --------------
      1    22,016  (22K)   38,496  (38K)   72,576  (71K)
```

After you identify a driver or memory-resident program that appears to be the right size to fit in the available UMB, edit your CONFIG.SYS or AUTOEXEC.BAT to add DEVICEHIGH or LOADHIGH to the appropriate command or program file. Reboot your computer and issue the MEM /C command again to see whether the driver or program loaded.

To arrive at the best combination of device drivers and memory-resident programs loaded into upper memory, you might have to experiment a little. DOS loads programs into the largest available UMB first, so try loading the largest drivers and programs first by placing their start-up commands earliest in CONFIG.SYS or AUTOEXEC.BAT.

Tip

You can send the MEM report to your printer by using the following command:

```
MEM /C > PRN
```

This command redirects the report to the DOS device PRN, your computer's first printer port.

Loading a Secondary Command Processor

The COMMAND command enables you to load a second copy of COMMAND.COM, the system's command processor. Many programs do this automatically when they enable you to go to a DOS command prompt without exiting the program. Although you might not have much need to do this in your everyday use of DOS, you might want to load another command processor from within a batch file so that you can run another program in its own environment.

For Related Information

- "DOS and Random-Access Memory," p. 20
- "Optimizing Your Computer's Memory," p. 459

Issuing the COMMAND Command

The syntax for COMMAND is shown here:

```
COMMAND d:path\ /P /MSG /E:aaaaa /C string
```

For this command, *d:path* is the drive and the path position of the COMMAND.COM file you are loading. The other parameters are explained briefly in the list that follows and in more detail in the next section:

Parameter	Description
/P	Makes the second copy of the command processor permanent.
/MSG	Causes DOS to load DOS messages into memory instead of reading the messages from disk every time they are needed.
/E:*aaaaa*	Enables you to adjust the number of bytes of memory that the command processor reserves for its environment.
/C *string*	Enables you to pass a string of characters to the command processor being started.
/Y	Directs COMMAND.COM to step through the batch file specified by the /C switch.

Understanding the Operation of COMMAND

COMMAND.COM, your command processor, reserves a small amount of memory called the *environment*. COMMAND.COM uses this memory space to store variables, such as your PATH, PROMPT, and COMSPEC settings. If you load another copy of COMMAND.COM, but omit the *d:path* parameter, the second command processor inherits the contents of the first command processor's environment. If you include the *d:path* parameter, the second command processor does not inherit the old environment and only keeps the COMSPEC path specified by *d:path*.

After you have started a secondary command processor, you exit it and return to the first command processor by using the EXIT command. When you leave the second command processor, the first command processor's environment remains unchanged, even if you changed the second command processor's environment while you were working with it.

The optional /P switch makes the second copy of the command processor permanent. The first command processor is no longer available, and DOS runs your AUTOEXEC.BAT file if you have one. Remember, if you use the /P switch, you cannot use the EXIT command to exit the second copy of the command processor and return to the first one. You have to turn your computer off and reboot.

The /MSG switch causes DOS to load DOS messages into memory instead of reading the messages from the disk every time they are needed. Using this switch improves the performance of DOS, but you lose some memory space.

The /E:*aaaaa* switch enables you to adjust the number of bytes of memory that the command processor reserves for its environment. The minimum value for *aaaaa* is 160, and the maximum is 32768. The default is 256 bytes. (The recommended minimum value in a Windows environment is 512 bytes.) Each variable stored in the environment takes up space, and you might find that you run out of room in the environment. If, for example, the environment needs to store long settings (such as the long prompt used in the earlier PROMPT command example), you might have to adjust the size of the environment. If you see the message `Out of environment space`, enlarge the environment.

The /C *string* option enables you to pass a string of characters to the command processor you are starting. This option generally was used in batch files (see Chapter 16, "Understanding Batch Files") in DOS versions before 3.3 but is no longer needed with DOS 3.3 and later versions, in which it has been replaced by the CALL command.

If you are using DOS 6.2, and you use the /C switch to run a batch file under the new command processor, you can also use the /Y switch to instruct COMMAND.COM to single-step through the batch file. This procedure is similar to the single-stepping of AUTOEXEC.BAT you can do when you first boot DOS. For more information on how the single-stepping works, refer to Chapter 2, "Starting DOS."

For Related Information

- "Controlling the Boot Process," p. 38
- "Using COMMAND.COM to Execute a Batch File," p. 441

Using EXIT to Leave the Current Copy of the Command Processor

Use the EXIT command to leave the current copy of the command processor and return to the previously loaded copy. This is the syntax for the EXIT command:

```
EXIT
```

No options or switches exist for this command. You cannot use the EXIT command if the second command processor was started by using the /P switch.

Uses for a Secondary Command Processor

Used together, the COMMAND and EXIT commands provide two interesting uses. If you have specified an alternative location with the file COMMAND.COM, you use the COMMAND command to load the second processor. If, for example, the DOS command processor is in the root directory and another command processor is loaded in the OTHER subdirectory, you can enter the following command:

```
COMMAND C:\OTHER /E:320
```

This command loads the second COMMAND.COM and assigns it an environment size of 320 bytes. You can use the second command processor to execute commands using the 320-byte environment. When you are finished using the secondary command processor, type EXIT to return to the primary command processor.

The other use for this command pair is when you have set up a complex environment and you want to execute a command with a basic environment without changing the existing environment. In this case, you can start the second command processor with the *d:path*\ option. If necessary, you can change the environment by using the SET command (covered in the next chapter). Execute the desired commands in the altered environment, and then exit the second command processor.

If the command processor is in the root directory of drive C, enter the following command:

```
COMMAND C:\
```

This command loads a second copy of the command processor. The new environment includes only a setting for COMSPEC, showing that the command processor is loaded in C:\. The prompt does not have a setting and shows up in the form C>. You then execute any desired commands in the new environment. After you have finished issuing the commands, type EXIT to exit the second command processor and return to the first command processor. All the environment settings for the first command processor stay as they were originally.

The principles DOS uses to execute this command are also used by applications programs that enable you to suspend your program temporarily and go to DOS. When you select the DOSSHELL command within your word processor, for example, the program starts a second command processor. All the existing information is kept in memory with the first command processor. You execute DOS commands in the second command processor and type EXIT when the commands are complete. The first command processor is then active, and you return to your application program.

Summary

This chapter introduced the commands you use to see and change the DOS system information. The following key points were covered in this chapter:

- The DATE and TIME commands alter the date and time used by DOS when you save files to disk.
- The VER command displays the current booted version of DOS.
- The MEM command provides extensive information about the memory, programs, and devices currently running.
- The COMMAND command enables you to execute DOS commands in a different environment or temporarily suspend programs while you use DOS.
- The EXIT command returns you to your program or to the first copy of the command processor.

Chapter 13, "Controlling Your Environment," teaches you how you can change your environment and the DOS interface to reflect the work you want to do.

Chapter 13

Controlling Your Environment

MS-DOS has come a long way since Microsoft first introduced it in 1981. During the intervening years, many new commands and features have been added that make DOS more powerful than ever. In DOS, there are many commands that enable you to exercise control over your operating system environment. This chapter explores some of those commands. In particular, you learn about the following commands:

- SET
- PROMPT
- MODE
- ASSIGN
- JOIN
- SUBST

You can use each of these commands to effectively alter the way you work with DOS. For instance, you use the SET command to modify the variables used by many DOS commands and other programs running under DOS. You can use the PROMPT command to modify the DOS prompt, and MODE can alter the way your screen looks.

Finally, ASSIGN, JOIN, and SUBST are commands that can change how you address disk drives on your system.

Changing DOS Variables

The SET command enables you to adjust the DOS environment by changing the variables that are available to programs running under DOS. This command shows the current settings in the environment, or you can use the command to add or change environment variables.

Issuing the SET Command

The syntax for the SET command is shown in the following:

```
SET name=string
```

The variable *name=* is the name of the environment variable. The most frequently used environment variables are COMSPEC, PROMPT, and PATH. You can choose your own variable names in addition to these three, however. Many of the programs that you may use set their own environment variables, or require you to do so, before the program runs. These variables control the way the program works.

The parameter *string* is the value to which you want to set the variable. In the case of PATH, the string can be the list of directories through which you want DOS to search to find program files. If you use the *name=* parameter without a value for *string*, the variable specified is a null value (contains nothing). This effectively removes the environment variable, and DOS no longer keeps track of it.

You can also type SET at the command prompt without any variables. The command then lists all the current settings for environment variables.

Changing Environment Variables with SET

Typically, you use the SET command as part of a batch file to set variables to be used within your system. Most often, SET is part of the AUTOEXEC.BAT file, used to set the environment variables before any other programs are run.

If you examine your AUTOEXEC.BAT file, you may see some command lines similar to the following:

```
SET COMSPEC=C:\SYS\COMMAND.COM
PROMPT=$p$g
PATH=C:\;C:\DOS;C:\SYS;
```

These commands, even though they look a bit different from each other, accomplish the same thing—they assign values to system variables. The first command tells DOS that the command processor, COMMAND.COM, is in the SYS subdirectory of drive C. The second command sets the prompt to include the current path and a greater-than sign. The third command defines the root directory, the DOS directory, and the SYS directory of drive C as the search path for DOS to use.

Notice that the second and third command lines do not explicitly include the SET command. This is because neither of these variables require the SET command, although you can just as easily use these command lines:

```
SET PROMPT=$p$g
SET PATH=C:\;C:\DOS;C:\SYS;
```

What Is a COMSPEC?

COMSPEC is a reserved system variable name that defines your command processor's location. Typically, this is set to the complete path and file name for COMMAND.COM. If your command processor is not in the root directory of the boot drive, you must include an appropriate SHELL directive in CONFIG.SYS to inform DOS of the command processor's location. This command, in turn, automatically sets the COMSPEC variable correctly. Thus, you don't need to explicitly set the COMSPEC variable in your AUTOEXEC.BAT file if you use the SHELL directive. If you do not have the COMSPEC variable set on your system, it is possible for your system to hang when you boot your computer or when you leave an application program that needs to reload the command processor. This failure occurs because the system cannot find the command processor. Refer to Chapter 18, "Configuring Your Computer," for information on how to use the SHELL directive in CONFIG.SYS to tell the system where to find the command processor.

Defining Your Own Environmental Variables with SET

You also can use the SET command to set custom variables in the environment. These variables usually are the names of directories or switches that programs use. The programs know to look for particular variables in the environment, take the values assigned to those variables, and use them in the program.

For example, a word processing program may look for a dictionary file called DICT in the current directory. If you use the SET command, however, a different directory can contain the dictionary file. During installation, the program probably will insert a SET command in the batch file that invokes the program. This command may use the following form:

```
SET DICT=C:\WP\DICT
```

This command enables the program to look in the WP directory for the dictionary file instead of looking in the current directory. Setting a variable in the environment, however, is useful only to programs that know to look for that variable.

For Related Information

- "System Configuration," p. 33
- "Using the SHELL Command," p. 484

Each variable stored in the environment occupies space. If a program needs large variables set, you may have to increase the area of memory set aside for the environment when DOS boots. You make this change through the SHELL command in CONFIG.SYS (see Chapter 18, "Configuring Your Computer").

Changing the User Interface

The *user interface* is a term that is often overused in computer circles. However, it does describe an integral part of computers—how you (the user) interact with the computer. DOS provides what has come to be known as a text-based user interface, meaning that you communicate with DOS via a command line. In Chapter 4, "Using the DOS Shell," you learned about the DOS Shell, which provides a different user interface.

If you don't want to use the DOS Shell, you can still modify how you interact with DOS. Primarily, this is done through two commands: PROMPT and MODE. The PROMPT command enables you to change what the DOS command prompt looks like, and you use the MODE command to define how your system should work in conjunction with your video display.

Changing the Command Prompt with PROMPT

If you have ever booted a plain-vanilla version of DOS (one that does not have a CONFIG.SYS or AUTOEXEC.BAT file), you probably noticed the default command prompt used by DOS. It looks like this:

```
C>
```

This default command prompt shows the current drive and a greater-than sign—that's it. It is possible, however, to create a command prompt that is much more useful. This is done with the PROMPT command. For instance, if you look at your AUTOEXEC.BAT file, you may see a line that looks like this:

```
PROMPT $p$g
```

This line changes the default command line prompt to the following:

```
C:\>
```

While this may not look immediately more useful, the value of this prompt becomes apparent if you switch to another directory on your drive.

For example, if you use the CD command to switch to the DOS subdirectory, your command prompt looks like this:

```
C:\>cd\dos
C:\DOS>
```

It now shows the directory where you are located. This is of great value whenever you are issuing commands at the DOS prompt. If you use a hard disk, this display is the minimum recommended prompt setting because navigating subdirectories can be difficult if you don't know your current position. That is why you will find this use of the PROMPT command in many people's AUTOEXEC.BAT files.

The PROMPT command has many more settings that you can use to further refine your DOS prompt. Used to its fullest, the PROMPT command requires use of the ANSI.SYS device driver (see Chapter 20, "Understanding ANSI.SYS"). Even without using the ANSI.SYS device driver, however, you can choose from many different command prompts.

Issuing the PROMPT Command. The syntax for the PROMPT command is very simple:

```
PROMPT string
```

The *string* consists of text that defines how you want the command prompt to appear. This text can contain special pairs of characters, called *meta-strings*, which consist of a dollar sign followed by one of the following characters:

t d p v n g l b q h e _

The string can contain any text or any number of meta-strings in any order. Table 13.1 lists the meaning of the different meta-strings.

Table 13.1 Meta-strings for Use with the PROMPT Command

Meta-string	Displayed Information or Result
$_	Carriage return/line feed (moves the cursor to the beginning of the next line)
$b	Vertical bar character (|)
$d	Date
$e	Esc character

(continues)

Table 13.1 Continued

Meta-string	Displayed Information or Result
$g	Greater-than sign (>)
$h	Backspace (moves the cursor one space to the left)
$l	Less-than sign (<)
$n	Current drive
$p	Current path
$q	Equal sign (=)
$t	Time
$v	DOS version

Resetting the Default Prompt

If you don't like the current prompt and you want to reset it to the default originally used by DOS, you can enter the PROMPT command without any parameters. This causes DOS to reset the prompt to the current drive letter and a greater-than sign.

Understanding the Use of Meta-strings. Earlier in this chapter, you saw an example of how to use meta-strings in a PROMPT command:

```
PROMPT $p$g
```

This is just one possible use, albeit the most often used. You also can use other combinations, such as

```
PROMPT Date: $d Time: $t$_$p$g
```

After issuing this command, your command prompt would appear as follows:

```
Date: Mon 03-22-1993 Time: 2:35:07.23
C:\WP\MEMOS>
```

Notice that this creates a two-line command prompt which shows the current date and time, as well as the current directory. You can get as exotic as you want with your command prompts; it is entirely up to you.

It is not uncommon to change the command prompt based on certain configurations you may have within your system. For instance, suppose that you use several different DOS programs, each of which requires its own special setup. You may create a batch file (see Chapter 16, "Understanding Batch Files") that sets up the search paths and system variables necessary for properly using the program. If the name of this program is XYZ Spreadsheet, version 3.7, you may want to add the following line to the batch file that performs the configuration:

```
PROMPT Now using XYZ Spreadsheet, version 3.7$_$p$p
```

When this batch file executes, the command prompt becomes

```
Now using XYZ Spreadsheet, version 3.7
C:\SSDATA>
```

Now you can easily remember what configuration is active within your system. When you run another batch file to change the configuration again, a different prompt command that you have set up can indicate which configuration is in effect. Again, how you set up your command prompt is up to you and how you use your system.

Two of the meta-strings may require further explanation. You use the Esc character ($e) in association with the ANSI.SYS driver (see Chapter 20, "Understanding ANSI.SYS," for more information). In the same way that you use the dollar sign to indicate to DOS that the next character is a meta-string, you use the Esc character to signal ANSI.SYS that the next few characters are an ANSI.SYS command.

You can use the Backspace character ($h) to remove characters from the prompt. In the earlier PROMPT example that displayed the date and time, you may find the seconds and hundredths of a second in the displayed prompt are more of a distraction than they are helpful. You can alter the PROMPT command as follows:

```
PROMPT Date: $d Time: $t$h$h$h$h$h$h$_$p$g
```

The result is the following improved prompt, with everything after the minutes erased:

```
Date: Mon 03-22-1993 Time: 2:35
C:\WP\MEMOS>
```

For Related Information

- "Issuing ANSI.SYS Codes with the PROMPT Command," p. 529

Altering the Look of the Screen with MODE

You can use the external MODE command to customize the number of characters per line and the number of lines displayed on-screen. You can also use the MODE command to set the configuration of your computer ports (such as your printer port) and for code page switching.

What Are Code Pages?

Certain areas of memory in your system store the character tables for your video screen and your keyboard. By switching tables, you can configure DOS to use alternate character sets to suit your national language and customs. These tables are called *code pages*. For more information about code pages, see Chapter 21, "Understanding the International Features of DOS."

You may already know this, but it is possible to attach two types of video displays to your computer. For example, you can use a monochrome adapter and display for your word processing, and a color graphics adapter and display for a graphics program. You can switch between the displays by using the MODE command. When you type at the keyboard on a two-display system, you see the keystrokes only on one of the displays. This display is the *active display*. The keyboard and active display make up the *console*. As you learned in Chapter 5, "Understanding Files and Directories," DOS uses CON as the device name for the console.

Selecting the Display Type. To change display characteristics, you can use two forms of the MODE command. The following is the simplest form:

```
MODE dt
```

The abbreviation *dt* is the display type and mode. Available options are 40, 80, BW40, BW80, CO40, CO80, or MONO, as detailed in table 13.2. The 40 and 80 refer to the number of text columns displayed. What this setting means is that you can choose between 40 and 80 characters per line. BW stands for black and white; CO stands for color; and MONO refers to the monochrome display adapter.

Table 13.2 MODE Settings for Display Type

Command	Meaning
MODE 40	Sets the display to 40 characters per line
MODE 80	Sets the display to 80 characters per line
MODE BW40	Selects the color display in black-and-white mode, 40 characters per line
MODE BW80	Selects the color display in black-and-white mode, 80 characters per line

Command	Meaning
MODE CO40	Selects the color display, 40 characters per line
MODE CO80	Selects the color display, 80 characters per line
MODE MONO	Selects the monochrome display

Shifting the Screen on a Color Graphics Adapter. The second form of the MODE command is for use on a Color Graphics Adapter (CGA) only. This form, which does not work on an Enhanced Graphics Adapter (EGA) or a Video Graphics Array (VGA), enables you to configure your PC to work with a television instead of a specially designed computer monitor. It moves the horizontal position of the image on your screen. If you cannot see the far-left or far-right character on-screen, the following command corrects the problem:

```
MODE dt,dir,T
```

The *dt* parameter is the display type described in the preceding section. The *dir* parameter can have the value R to move the image to the right or L to move the image to the left. If the display is in 80-column mode, MODE moves the image two characters to the right or left. If in 40-column mode, MODE moves the image one character to the right or left.

The optional T parameter, when used, causes MODE to display a test pattern that you can use to align the display. For example, if you type

```
MODE CO80,R,T
```

a line of 80 characters appears across the screen, along with the following prompt:

```
Do you see the leftmost 0? (y/n)
```

If you respond **N** to the prompt, this image moves two positions to the right of its preceding position. If you respond **Y** to the prompt, the test is completed and the prompt is erased. Using the L option works in the same manner, but moves the image to the left.

If you operate your system after shifting the screen, you have a little less memory available for your use. To display the image in an adjusted position, DOS leaves a small portion of the MODE command in memory, occupying about 1K of memory. This program intercepts all output, adjusts it, and then sends it to the screen.

Using MODE to Adjust the Number of Columns or Lines On-Screen. You also can use MODE to adjust the number of columns or the number of lines displayed on-screen. You must install the ANSI.SYS device driver before MODE can adjust your screen, however.

One way you can use MODE to adjust screen size is the following:

```
MODE CON COLS=a LINES=b
```

COLS= sets the number of columns displayed on-screen to *a*, and LINES= sets the number of lines displayed on-screen to *b*. If you omit a setting for the number of columns or the number of lines, the current setting is preserved.

Valid numbers for *a* are 40 or 80. Valid numbers for *b* on a VGA screen are 25, 43, or 50; valid numbers for *b* on an EGA screen are 25 or 43.

If ANSI.SYS is loaded via the CONFIG.SYS file, typing the following command gives you a display mode 80 columns wide and 43 lines high on a computer with an EGA or VGA adapter and monitor:

```
MODE CON COLS=80 LINES=43
```

After you set the display mode, you can start your application program. The display mode remains, unless the application resets it. If you use the preceding MODE command on a computer with an EGA screen, for example, you can use WordPerfect in 43-line mode without adjusting any settings in WordPerfect.

Note

Not all applications can "see" that the extra lines are available. Try some MODE CON commands to determine whether you can use the extra lines. Using MODE CON to set your screen to 43 or 50 lines makes it easier to view long DIR listings, but the type is very small and may be difficult to read.

Another MODE command option enables you to alter the number of lines displayed without specifying that the screen is the console. This form, which is really a variation on the MODE CON format, is handy when you use an auxiliary console instead of CON. Chapter 14, "Controlling Devices," introduces the CTTY command, which is used to establish another device as the standard input-and-output device. The syntax for this form of the MODE command is shown in the following:

```
MODE dt,b
```

In this syntax, *dt* is the display type and *b* is the number of lines to be displayed. The acceptable values for *dt* and *b* are as previously described, but not all combinations of values for *dt* and *b* are possible. For example, you cannot adjust the number of lines on a monochrome or CGA monitor. Table 13.3 lists the workable combinations of parameters with the MODE command for setting the display type.

Table 13.3 Setting the Number of Lines by Display Type

Mode Option	MDA	CGA	EGA	VGA
CO40,25		4	4	4
CO40,43			4	4
CO40,50				4
CO80,25		4	4	4
CO80,43			4	4
CO80,50				4
BW40,25		4	4	4
BW40,43			4	4
BW40,50				4
BW80,25		4	4	4
BW80,43			4	4
BW80,50				4
MONO	4			

Using the information in table 13.3, you can determine that on a VGA system you can alter the display type to color with 40 columns and 50 lines by typing the following command:

```
MODE CO40,50
```

All forms of the MODE command that adjust the display are similar in syntax and purpose. An incorrect command does not damage anything, and DOS provides reasonably clear error messages. If the ANSI.SYS driver is required and not installed, for example, DOS displays the following error message:

```
ANSI.SYS must be installed to perform requested function
```

For Related Information

■ "The CTTY Command," p. 356

Changing Disk Drives

As you configure DOS to the environment you need, you may find times when you need to adjust how DOS treats your disk drives and directories. Three commands allow you to do just that. You use the ASSIGN command to redirect disk requests to different drives, the JOIN command to treat a disk drive as a subdirectory, and the SUBST command to treat a subdirectory as a disk drive.

The ASSIGN Command

You use the external command ASSIGN to redirect all DOS read-and-write (input-and-output) requests from one drive to another. Each drive is a DOS device. By using the ASSIGN command, DOS can interrogate a different disk than the one actually specified on a command line.

The syntax for the ASSIGN command is shown in the following:

```
ASSIGN d1=d2  .../STATUS
```

d1 is the drive letter for the original disk drive; *d2* is the drive letter for the reassignment. The ellipsis (...) indicates that you can reassign more than one drive on a single command line.

/STATUS, issued with no other parameters, displays a listing of current drive assignments.

The JOIN Command

You can use the JOIN command to add a disk drive to the directory structure of another disk. For example, the external command JOIN enables you to use a floppy disk in such a way that it appears to DOS to be part of a hard disk. You can also use JOIN if you have two hard disks: drive C and drive D. JOIN can attach drive D to a subdirectory on drive C, for instance.

The syntax for JOIN is shown in the following:

```
JOIN d1: d2:\path  /D
```

The directory structure of disk *d1* is added to the directory structure of hard disk *d2*. *d1:* is a valid disk drive name that becomes the alias or nickname. *d1:* may be a nonexistent disk drive. *d2:path* is the valid disk drive name and directory path that will be nicknamed *d1:*. If you use the /D switch, the alias is deleted.

When you use the JOIN command, DOS redirects any access to *d2:\path* to *d1:*. Thus, if you use the following command:

```
JOIN A: C:\SSDATA
```

then any time you access C:\SSDATA, you actually are accessing drive A. This is helpful if you have a program that can only look in a specific directory for data, and you actually want to keep the data elsewhere.

The SUBST Command

The external command SUBST is the inverse of the JOIN command. Instead of grafting a second disk onto the tree structure of your hard drive, the SUBST command splits a disk's directory structure in two. In effect, the SUBST command creates an alias disk drive name for a subdirectory.

Issuing the SUBST Command. You can use the SUBST command to perform different functions. To establish an alias, use the following syntax:

```
SUBST d1: d2:pathname
```

To delete an alias, use this form:

```
SUBST d1: /D
```

To see the current aliases, use the following form:

```
SUBST
```

The SUBST command replaces a path name for a subdirectory with a drive letter. After a SUBST command is in effect, DOS translates all I/O (input/output) requests to a particular drive letter back to the correct path name. The alias drive created by the SUBST command inherits the directory tree structure of the subdirectory reassigned to a drive letter.

Note

As the default, DOS assigns the LASTDRIVE= parameter (used in CONFIG.SYS) a value of E. You can make higher drive designators, however, by inserting a LASTDRIVE= parameter into the CONFIG.SYS file. DOS then establishes as DOS devices each of the drive letters up to and including the specified LASTDRIVE. When you use the SUBST command, DOS understands that you are referring to a device.

Using SUBST to Reference a Path with a Drive Letter. SUBST is commonly used in two different situations. If you want to run a program that does not support path names, you can use the SUBST command to assign a drive letter to a directory. The program then refers to the drive letter, and DOS translates the request into a path. If, for example, the data for a program is stored in C:\WORDPROC, you can use the following command so that you can refer to this subdirectory as drive E:

```
SUBST E: C:\WORDPROC
```

After the substitution is made, you can issue the following command:

```
SUBST
```

The following message appears:

```
E: => C:\WORDPROC
```

To disconnect the substitution of drive E for the C:\WORDPROC directory, type the following command:

```
SUBST E: /D
```

The other use for SUBST is to reduce typing long path names. When more than one person uses a PC, path names can become quite long because each user may use a separate section of the hard disk to store data files and common areas of the disk to store programs. If the paths \USER1\WORDDATA and \USER1\SSDATA exist on drive C, for example, you can reduce the typing required to reach files in the directories by using the following command:

```
SUBST E: C:\USER1
```

Issuing a directory command on drive E produces the following listing:

```
Volume in drive E is HARD DISK C
Volume Serial Number is 1573-0241
Directory of  E:\


.            <DIR>     05-02-92  12:07p
..           <DIR>     05-02-92  12:07p
WORDDATA     <DIR>     05-02-92   1:59p
SPREDATA     <DIR>     05-22-92   2:08p
        4 File(s)          0 bytes
                     3477824 bytes free
```

The volume label given is the label from drive C, but the directory itself is the contents of C:\USER1.

Note

Do not use the following DOS commands in conjunction with drives that you create with the SUBST command: ASSIGN, BACKUP, CHKDSK, DEFRAG, DISKCOMP, DISKCOPY, FDISK, FORMAT, LABEL, MIRROR, RECOVER, RESTORE, SCANFIX, and SYS. Some of these commands may refuse to work, and others may provide unwanted results.

As with JOIN and ASSIGN, you can use the SUBST command to fool software that insists on using an otherwise unusable drive. For example, a friend may have written an applications program that makes direct reference in its code to a directory on drive C. By using SUBST, you can have your friend's program attach drive D to a subdirectory on your drive C.

Understanding the General Rules for Using SUBST. As you are using the SUBST command, you must keep the following rules in mind:

- *d1:* and *d2:* must be different.
- You cannot specify a networked drive as *d1:* or *d2:*.
- *d1:* cannot be the current drive.
- *d1:* must have a designator less than the value in the LASTDRIVE statement of CONFIG.SYS. (See Chapter 18, "Configuring Your Computer," for more information on CONFIG.SYS.)
- Do not use SUBST with ASSIGN or JOIN.
- Remove all SUBST settings before you run ASSIGN, BACKUP, DEFRAG, DISKCOMP, DISKCOPY, FDISK, FORMAT, LABEL, MIRROR, PRINT, RECOVER, RESTORE, SCANFIX, or SYS.
- Beware of using APPEND, CHDIR, MKDIR, PATH, and RMDIR with any drives reassigned.

Summary

DOS is a full-featured environment that can be used on a variety of computers to run a vast number of software programs. Although many people never need to alter the default environment provided by DOS, you may be able to use the commands presented in this chapter to fine-tune DOS to your specific needs. In this chapter, you have learned the following:

- The SET command enables you to change individual environment variables. These variables include PROMPT, PATH, and COMSPEC.
- The PROMPT command alters the appearance of the command prompt. On systems that use hierarchical directories, changing the prompt setting to PROMPT pg is advisable because it results in the current path always being displayed.

- The MODE command can alter the appearance of the screen. You can alter the number of lines, the number of columns, and the current display.
- The ASSIGN, JOIN, and SUBST commands can redefine how DOS treats your disk drives and subdirectories.

In the next chapter, you learn how you can extend your control over DOS by using devices.

Chapter 14

Controlling Devices

Devices—hard disks, printers, video displays, keyboards, and modems, for example—can supply input to the computer, receive output from the computer, or both. This chapter discusses the commands that control the devices connected to your computer. You use these commands to redirect input and output, select alternate keyboards, and print graphics and text files.

DOS supplies many different commands to help you interact with devices. With three commands referred to as *filters,* DOS is responsible for channeling information between devices. You can use these filters—MORE, FIND, and SORT—to modify information as it passes from files to the screen. Table 14.1 lists and explains the functions of the commands and filters discussed in this chapter.

Table 14.1 Device Control Commands and Filters

Command	Function
CLS	Clears the screen.
GRAPHICS	Prints graphics screens.
PRINT	Prints in background.
CTTY	Selects a different console. Makes the serial port the console.
MODE	Controls device operations. Redirects a parallel port to a serial port. Changes the typematic rate.
MORE	Filter to control the display of text.

(continues)

Table 14.1 Continued

Command	Function
FIND	Filter to find strings of text.
SORT	Filter to sort information.

Table 14.2 lists and explains the functions of the redirection operators you use in conjunction with the device control commands and filters.

Table 14.2 Redirection Operators

Operators	Function
<	Redirects a command's input.
>	Redirects a command's output.
>>	Redirects a command's output and appends the output to the target, if one exists.
|	Passes the output from one command to another as input.

The CLS Command

The internal command CLS clears the screen, removing all visible text. CLS then displays the prompt so that you can continue to issue DOS commands. CLS clears only the on-screen display. If your system uses two screens, CLS clears only the active display, not both screens.

The CLS command, which has no switches, uses the following syntax:

```
CLS
```

Clearing the screen does not change the display mode. If, for example, you used the MODE command to change your screen display to 40 columns, the screen clears when you issue the CLS command; CLS then redisplays the DOS prompt in 40-column mode. All other attributes that you set previously—for example, if you define a background color and foreground color by using ANSI.SYS escape sequences—are also retained.

You frequently use the CLS command in batch files. By inserting a CLS command at the end of the AUTOEXEC.BAT file, for instance, you can remove all the messages that memory-resident programs may display as they load into your system.

For Related Information

- "Altering the Look of the Screen with MODE," p. 337
- "Understanding the Contents of Batch Files," p. 413
- "Controlling Your Screen with ANSI.SYS," p. 530

The GRAPHICS Command

You may have tried to use the Print Screen key (PrtSc on some keyboards) to print the contents of your screen to a printer. If so, you may have discovered that this key works properly only when your screen is in text mode.

If your monitor is a CGA, EGA, or VGA, the external command GRAPHICS enables you to use the Print Screen key to print graphics screens also. When you execute GRAPHICS, a portion of the program remains memory-resident. When you next press Print Screen, all ASCII code characters that would otherwise print as text are converted to graphics before the information is sent to the printer.

Issuing the GRAPHICS Command

Use the following syntax for the GRAPHICS command:

```
GRAPHICS printer d:path\filename /R /B /LCD /PRINTBOX:STD
```

printer is the type of printer you are using. Table 14.3 lists the values you can use for the *printer* parameter. If your printer is not listed, it may be compatible with one of the other printers on the list. Refer to your printer's instruction manual for details. If you do not specify a printer, DOS assumes the GRAPHICS printer type.

Table 14.3 List of Printer Types and Settings

Printer Type	Model Name
COLOR1	IBM PC Color Printer with black ribbon, which prints in gray scales
COLOR4	IBM PC Color Printer with RGB (red, green, blue) ribbon, which prints four colors (RGB plus black)
COLOR8	IBM Personal Computer Color Printer with CMY (cyan, magenta, yellow, and black) ribbon, which prints eight colors
DESKJET	Hewlett-Packard DeskJet printer

(continues)

Table 14.3 Continued

Printer Type	Model Name
GRAPHICS	IBM Personal Graphics Printer, IBM ProPrinter, or IBM Quietwriter printer
GRAPHICSWIDE	IBM Personal Graphics Printer with an 11-inch carriage, or IBM ProPrinters II and III
HPDEFAULT	Any Hewlett-Packard PCL printer
LASERJET	Hewlett-Packard LaserJet
LASERJETII	Hewlett-Packard LaserJet II
PAINTJET	Hewlett-Packard PaintJet printer
QUIETJET	Hewlett-Packard QuietJet printer
QUIETJETPLUS	Hewlett-Packard QuietJet printer
RUGGEDWRITER	Hewlett-Packard RuggedWriter printer
RUGGEDWRITERWIDE	Hewlett-Packard RuggedWriter wide printer
THERMAL	IBM PC-Convertible thermal printer
THINKJET	Hewlett-Packard ThinkJet printer

Tip
GRAPHICS.PRO is the profile file supplied with DOS. If you want to create a custom profile file for your printer, make a copy of the supplied GRAPHICS.PRO file and modify it. This exercise is also useful if you are interested in DOS programming. Modifying the GRAPHICS.PRO file is not necessary for most printers.

d:path\filename is the drive, path, and file name of a printer profile file that can be used by the GRAPHICS command for your printer. This file supports the printers of other manufacturers. If your printer doesn't fit into one of the categories supported by GRAPHICS, you can create a custom printer profile for use with GRAPHICS. The *\filename* parameter refers to the profile file, which specifies how graphics are translated for various printers. The profile file is an ASCII text file with two types of information for each printer in the file. A profile can include information about how the printer is controlled, such as selecting printer colors or adjusting the darkness of the printed piece. The second section of the profile lists the translation from the screen to the printer.

/R forces the printer to print a monochrome text screen as you see it—black background and white text. When you use the /R switch with a color screen, the darkest colors (black or blue) print as black; light colors appear as white or light gray; and other colors print as different shades of gray on a gray scale for contrast. If you don't use the /R switch, all on-screen information that is white prints as black, and all black on-screen information (usually the background) prints as white. The paper color in the printer is assumed to be white.

Tip
If the on-screen colors don't have a sharp enough contrast, the GRAPHICS command may "miss" the difference between colors and produce an all-white or all-black printout. If this problem occurs, try altering your screen colors before you print.

/B prints the background color. Use this switch only if you have a color printer and after you specify COLOR4 or COLOR8 as your printer type. If you try to use the /B switch with a black-and-white printer, DOS displays the following message:

```
The /B switch is invalid with black and white printers.
```

/LCD is a switch designed for use with the IBM PC-Convertible, which comes with a small liquid-crystal display (LCD) screen. /LCD forces the printer to print the screen as it appears, with the size of the screen and characters smaller than on normal monitors. You can also use this switch with any other laptop computer that has an old-style, smaller LCD screen like the IBM PC-Convertible. Most laptops now have a full-sized LCD screen and don't require the use of this switch.

/PRINTBOX:STD sets the printbox size to standard or normal size, as it appears on monochrome and VGA monitors of standard size and shape. You use this setting to print the screen when you work with Quattro Pro, Microsoft Word, or other programs in graphics mode. You also use this setting to print the contents of a narrow LCD screen if you want it to appear as if it were on a standard monitor. By typing /PRINTBOX:LCD, you can use this switch to force the printer to print in LCD mode (a longer form of the /LCD switch, shown above). You can abbreviate the /PRINTBOX switch to /PB.

Using GRAPHICS to Print a Screen Image

Suppose that you have an IBM ProPrinter printer. If you use a monochrome system and want to print a screen image with the background as black and the text as white, enter the following command at the DOS prompt:

```
GRAPHICS /R
```

After GRAPHICS loads into memory, you can create the screen of interest and press Print Screen to print to the printer.

To print eight-color images (including the background color) on an IBM Personal Computer Color Printer with a CMY ribbon installed, type the following command:

```
GRAPHICS COLOR8 /B
```

On the PC-Convertible with an attached full-sized monitor, you can send the screen image to the IBM PC-Convertible thermal printer by typing the following:

```
GRAPHICS THERMAL /PB:STD
```

Changing the command to either of the following prints the image as it normally appears on the liquid-crystal display:

```
GRAPHICS THERMAL /PB:LCD
GRAPHICS THERMAL /LCD
```

You should remember the following guidelines when using the GRAPHICS command:

- After you load GRAPHICS, you can press the Print Screen (Shift-PrtSc) key to print graphics screens on listed graphics printers.
- If you omit the /PB and /LCD switches, GRAPHICS uses the previous printbox setting.
- You can print up to eight colors on a color printer.
- You can print up to 19 shades of gray on a black-and-white printer.

The PRINT Command

In Chapter 9, "Managing Your Files," you learned that the COPY command can transfer information from one device to another. For example, the command

```
COPY LETTER.TXT PRN
```

copies the file named LETTER.TXT to the device PRN, the printer. During this copying process, the computer is not available for other use. If you are copying a large file to the printer, this can tie your computer up for a great while, depending on the speed of your printer.

You can make better use of your computer if you use the PRINT command. This command allows you to print in the background, thereby freeing up your computer for other tasks while you print a document. Printing occurs during the idle times—while the computer is waiting for you to type at the keyboard, for example. You also can *queue* files, which means send multiple files to the printer, each of which then prints in turn.

Issuing the PRINT Command

The external PRINT command uses the syntax

```
PRINT <switches> filename1 /P /T /C filename2 /P /T /C...
```

where you can replace *<switches>* with any of the switches listed in table 14.4. *filename1* is the drive, path, and file name of the first file you want to print, and *filename2* is the drive, path, and file name of the next file you want to print. The ellipsis (...) means that you can list more files. You can use wildcards in the file names.

Table 14.4 Switches for the PRINT Command

Switch	Meaning
/D:*device*	Names the serial or parallel port to which your output device is attached. Acceptable values include all DOS output devices and ports, such as LPT1, LPT2, LPT3, PRN, COM1, COM2, COM3, COM4, or AUX.
/Q:*qsize*	Specifies the maximum number of files—from 4 to 32—that can be queued at a time. If you omit the switch, 10 files is the default queue size.
/B:*size*	Determines the size of buffer used in the printing process. The data for printing is taken from the disk in chunks the size of the specified buffer. Increasing the buffer size causes the PRINT command to read data from the disk in bigger chunks. The minimum buffer size is 512 bytes; the maximum is 16K. If you don't specify the buffer size, the default size is 512 bytes. Remember that the larger you make the buffer, the less RAM you have for running applications programs.
/U:*ticks1*	Determines how long (in system clock ticks) the PRINT command waits for the printer to be available. In most cases, the PRINT command sends data to the printer faster than the printer can actually print. When the printer cannot accept anymore data, it sends a busy signal to the computer until it is ready to accept more data. The default setting for /U:*ticks1* is 1 clock tick, but you can set it as high as 255. If the printer is busy, PRINT waits the number of clock ticks set by this switch. If the printer is still busy, PRINT immediately transfers control back to DOS for other tasks without using the rest of the clock ticks set aside for it by the /S:*ticks3* switch.
/M:*ticks2*	Specifies the number of system clock ticks that the PRINT command waits for the printer to print a character. *ticks2* can be set to any value between 1 and 255; the default value is 2.

(continues)

Table 14.4 Continued

Switch	Meaning
/S:*ticks3*	Determines the number of clock ticks allocated to background printing. Too high a value for this switch causes the computer to respond sluggishly to other commands that you execute while you print in the background. A low value slows the printing process. The range of values is 1 to 255; the default value is 8.

Like GRAPHICS, PRINT leaves a portion of itself in memory after you issue the command, and the switches change how the PRINT command works. You can only specify the optional switches in table 14.4 when you first issue the PRINT command. The other switches (issued after the file names) can be issued at any time, however:

- The /P switch places a file in PRINT's queue. The preceding file and all subsequent files on the command line are printed.
- The /C switch cancels the printing of some files. The file name issued before the /C and all files after the /C on the same command line are removed from the print queue. (The printer alarm sounds if you cancel the currently printing file with the /C switch.) You must issue the /P switch to add files to the queue again.
- The /T switch terminates printing. All files are removed from the queue, including the file being printed. The printer alarm sounds, a file cancellation message prints, and the paper advances to the next page.

If you enter file names without a /P, /C, or /T switch, DOS uses the /P switch as a default so that all files are placed in the queue for printing. If, at the prompt, you type PRINT with no switches, a list of all files in the queue appears. This list includes the name of the file that is currently printing and the order of files yet to print. This command also displays any error messages. If, for example, you forget to turn on the printer, the following error message appears:

```
Errors on list device indicate that it may be off-line.
Please check it.
```

Using PRINT to Print Several Files

You do not have to enter the names of all the files to print at one time. You can issue the PRINT command several times to add or remove files from the print queue. You can specify the parameters that affect the way PRINT operates (those in table 14.4), however, only when you first issue the command. After you first issue the PRINT command, you use the command only to enter file names for printing or to cancel printing.

If you enter the PRINT command for the first time without specifying a device, PRINT prompts you for a device name. The default, PRN, is the first parallel port (LPT1) on your computer. Pressing Enter at the DOS prompt accepts the default.

If you are in no hurry to collect the printed output of files and want to use the computer while the printer prints your files, you can readjust the default installation settings for PRINT. By changing the /M:*ticks2* or /S:*ticks3* settings, you can give your computer better response time. To alter the default settings, you can type the following when you invoke the PRINT command for the first time:

```
PRINT /D:PRN /M:1 /S:25
```

If you are unconcerned about the sluggishness of the keyboard, you can improve the speed of the background printing by altering the buffer size, as well as by adjusting /M:*ticks2* and /S:*ticks3*. You might type in the following command, for example:

```
PRINT /D:PRN /B:16384 /M:1 /S:25
```

Experiment with these variables until you find a setting that is acceptable. A sluggish keyboard is not always tolerable. If the response time is too slow, you can make errors—for example, you may assume that a program didn't accept your keystrokes and try to retype the command, whereas the program was only waiting to regain control.

By using a combination of the /P, /T, and /C switches, you can adjust the order in which the files print. Suppose, for example, that you want to print four files: LETTER1.TXT, MEMO1.TXT, REPORT1.TXT, and REPORT2.TXT. Type the following on the command line:

```
PRINT /D:PRN LETTER1.TXT /P MEMO1.TXT REPORT1.TXT REPORT2.TXT
```

If you then decide that you want to print REPORT2.TXT before REPORT1.TXT, type the following command, which removes REPORT1.TXT from the print queue and adds the file to the end of the queue:

```
PRINT REPORT1.TXT /C REPORT1.TXT /P
```

You can cancel all files to be printed by typing the following command:

```
PRINT /T
```

General Rules for Using PRINT

As you are using PRINT, you should keep the following guidelines in mind:

- You can only specify the /D:*device*, /Q:*qsize*, /B:*size*, /S:*ticks3*, /U:*ticks1*, and /M:*ticks2* optional switches the first time that you issue the PRINT command.
- If you specify /D:*device*, you must type this switch first, before all other switches.
- If you issue /P, the preceding file and all subsequent files entered on the command line by the PRINT command print until a /T or /C switch is issued.
- If you issue /C, the preceding file and all subsequent files are canceled.
- The files print in the order that you enter them at the command line.
- A page-eject sequence is sent to the printer at the end of each file.
- You cannot use the printer for other purposes while PRINT is in operation. You cannot, for example, use Print Screen when PRINT is in effect.
- The files being printed must be on the same disk drive.
- You cannot alter files that are in the print queue or being printed.
- Specifying a nonexistent device causes unpredictable behavior by the computer.
- Tab characters in the printed file convert to blanks, up to the next 8-column boundary.

The CTTY Command

DOS can take information or data from and send it to different kinds of devices. Any device that you can use to give information to DOS is called an *input device*, and any device DOS can send information to is an *output device*. DOS uses your keyboard and screen as the standard input and output devices. Together, these two devices make up the *console*, known to DOS as the CON device. The internal command CTTY enables you to tell DOS that you want to use a different device for input and later enables you to restore the keyboard and screen as the console.

Use one of these syntax lines for the internal command CTTY

```
CTTY device
```

or

```
CTTY CON
```

where *device* is the name of a DOS device that you can use for input. CTTY causes DOS to intercept the I/O requests that normally come from the keyboard and go to the screen; the command redirects these calls to the device you specify.

For example, by typing the command

```
CTTY COM1
```

you designate COM1 as the device that sends and receives standard input and output. You use this command in association with specialized programs that need input from a different source than the keyboard. Later, typing

```
CTTY CON
```

from the auxiliary device restores the console to the keyboard and display.

You also can use CTTY if the computer is attached to an intelligent bar-code reader that collects information from packages. This reader, in association with a specialized program, may not need to use the display or keyboard.

You probably will not need to use the CTTY command. DOS usually can gather information through alternative devices without altering the standard input and output devices. Certain applications programs, however, benefit from your use of CTTY. One example is the DOS external program Interlnk, which requires the CTTY command in order to transfer itself to another computer (see Chapter 8, "Working with Files," for more information on Interlnk).

If you decide that you need to use CTTY, keep the following items in mind:

- You can use the character-based devices AUX, COM1, COM2, COM3, or COM4 as the alternative console.
- The physical device attached to the relevant AUX, COM1, COM2, COM3, or COM4 must be able to accept input and provide output.

For Related Information

- "Using Interlnk to Share Another Computer's Resources," p. 215

- Programs that do not use DOS function calls cannot make use of the alternative console.

The MODE Command

MODE is one of the more versatile external commands supplied with DOS. MODE sets the operational modes of serial and parallel ports and redirects information from parallel ports to serial ports. MODE also can set display modes, and you can use MODE with code pages. For more information about display modes and code pages, see Chapter 13, "Controlling Your Environment," and Chapter 21, "Understanding the International Features of DOS," respectively.

In this chapter, you learn how you can use the MODE command to control the parallel and serial ports, as well as to change how the keyboard acts. To read about all functions of the MODE command, turn to the Command Reference later in this book.

Using MODE to Change Parallel Port Settings

A parallel port transmits data by transferring an entire byte at one time. Because of this, parallel ports are typically used to send information to a printer. To help control your printer, you can use the MODE command to adjust the number of lines per inch and columns per line on your printer and to set the retry feature.

Issuing the MODE Command. Use the following syntax for the external MODE command, which changes the parallel printer characteristics:

```
MODE LPTn: cpl,lpi, P
```

LPT*n*: is the parallel port name, such as LPT1: or LPT2:. *cpl* is the number of characters per line. The default *cpl* setting is 80. *lpi* is the number of lines per inch. The default setting for *lpi* is 6. P specifies continuous retries on time-out or "busy" errors.

MODE also allows you to use an alternative format, as follows:

```
MODE LPTn: COLS=wid, LINES=lpi, RETRY=action
```

where *wid* is the number of columns per line, 80 or 132; *lpi* is the number of lines per inch, 6 or 8; and *action* is the message you want DOS to return or the action DOS should take when the printer port is busy.

When you use the MODE command to adjust the parallel port settings, this command alters only two items seen on the printout itself: the characters per line and the lines per inch. In general, printing is performed directly from an applications program, which is able to set many more parameters for a particular printer. The MODE command operates by sending Escape sequences to the printer that can adjust the printed output accordingly.

The retry setting is more significant than the other settings. When data is sent to the printer, the port expects to see return signals from the printer indicating that it received the data. If the port doesn't receive any signals within a particular period of time, a time-out error occurs. By default, DOS does not try to send information to the printer again and returns an error message to the screen. If you include the P option, DOS continuously tries to send the data; this prevents the error message from displaying. Pressing the Ctrl-Break key combination stops the retry process.

If you use the RETRY switch in the alternate MODE format, various retry options are available. If you don't specify a retry option, DOS doesn't continue trying to send data when a time-out error occurs. When you use the retry option, you can select from a list of options. The following list explains the various options:

- The B setting returns a busy signal to the device driver when the port is busy. This setting is not available with DOS 6.0.
- The R setting causes a ready signal to be returned from the port—even if the port is busy. Then, when the printer does become ready, the data is ready to send, and an error message does not appear on-screen.
- The E option is most commonly used when the printing is done in the background (by PRINT or a network print queue). The data is not transferred to the printer until the port is not busy.
- The N setting indicates that no retry action is taken.
- The P option causes DOS to try the printer continuously until the busy state ends.

Using MODE to Print a Large File. In some cases, you must use the P option to print a file. Consider a large DOS file that you want to copy to the printer. If the file is larger than the storage capacity of the printer, the printer port will be busy at some point during the data transfer. If the printer remains busy for too long, an error message appears on-screen; DOS thinks the printer is defective, and the printing process aborts. This is a particular concern when you are printing large, complex files such as those created by a PostScript program.

Specifying P in DOS 3.3 and earlier or RETRY=B in DOS 4.0 and 5.0 causes DOS to wait until the printer is ready to receive data. (The B option is not available in DOS 6.0, but you can use the P option for this purpose.) Use the following command for LPT1 in DOS 3.3:

```
MODE LPT1:,,P
```

For DOS 4.0, 4.01, 5.0, and 6.2, use the following command:

```
MODE LPT1 RETRY=B
```

For DOS 6.0 or 6.2, use the following command:

```
MODE LPT1 RETRY=P
```

If the file is large and you want to be able to fit more lines of text on a page, you can print the file with a higher number of lines per inch (8 instead of 6). Also, you can specify 132 columns per line instead of 80. This setting is not a problem for a wide-carriage printer, which accepts wide paper. If you are using a printer that accepts 8 1/2-inch paper, however, you must set the printer to print in a condensed character mode, which can fit 132 columns on a line of 8 1/2-inch paper.

When the printer is attached to LPT2, use the following command to fit as much information as possible on a page:

```
MODE LPT2:132,8
```

General Rules for Using MODE to Change Parallel Port Settings. When you are using the MODE command to change parallel port settings, you should keep the following items in mind:

- The default values of the port reset if you reset or initialize the printer.
- If you omit a parameter from the command line, the setting for that parameter does not change.
- Do not use any of the retry options when printers are being shared on an IBM PC network.

Using MODE to Change Serial Port Settings

You can use another option of the MODE command to alter the functions of the serial ports. This command works in a way similar to the parallel port adjustments. DOS changes the parameters that are sent to and from the device driver.

Issuing MODE to Adjust Serial Ports. The acceptable serial ports are COM1, COM2, COM3, and COM4. The serial port can receive and transmit data only one bit at a time. The signaling rate (the number of times per second that data is transmitted) is the *baud rate*. The amount of data transferred in a second is referred to as the *bps* (bits per second).

You can use the MODE command to adjust the baud settings and change the amount of data sent in a fixed time. Although it is called a baud setting, the numbers used are actually the number of bits transmitted per second. Acceptable baud settings are 110, 150, 300, 600, 1200, 2400, 4800, 9600, and 19200. You need to use only the first two digits of the number to set the baud rate.

The most common devices attached to a serial port that you need to set from DOS are serial printers and plotters. Although modems are serial devices, you usually don't adjust them from DOS. Communications programs, however, use the DOS functions to make adjustments to the serial ports.

Use the following syntax to change the serial port:

```
MODE COMy: baud,parity,databits,stopbits,P
```

The elements of the commands are as follows:

- COM*y*: is the name of the serial port device.
- *baud* is the baud rate. You must specify the baud rate for the serial port.
- *parity* is the parity. Parity is used in error-correction algorithms.
- *databits* is the number of data bits. The default number of data bits is 7.
- *stopbits* is the number of stop bits. Stop bits are used to mark the end of a character being transmitted. The default number of stop bits is 1 for all baud rates except 110, when 2 stop bits are set as the default.
- P specifies continuous retries on time-out errors.

You also can use the following syntax:

```
MODE COMy: BAUD=baud PARITY=parity DATA=databits STOP=stopbits
RETRY=action
```

All the variables in this version of the MODE command are the same as in the previous version. The only new one is *action*, which is the message you want DOS to return when the port is busy.

With versions of DOS prior to Version 4.0, the retry feature provided two choices when a time-out error occurred: no retry or continuous retries when you included the P option. When data is sent to the printer, the port expects to see signals from the printer indicating that it received the data. If the port doesn't receive any signals within a particular period of time, a time-out error occurs. By default, DOS does not try again to send information to the printer and returns an error message to the screen. If you include the P option, DOS continuously tries to send the data; this prevents the error message from displaying. The Ctrl-Break key combination stops the retry process.

With DOS 4.0 and later, more retry options are available. If you do not specify a retry option, DOS doesn't try again to send data when a time-out error occurs. When you use the retry option, you can select from the following four options:

- The R setting causes a ready signal to be returned from the port even if the port is busy. Then, when the printer does become ready, the data is ready to send and an error message does not appear on-screen.
- The E option is most commonly used when you are printing in the background (using PRINT or a network print queue). The data is not transferred to the printer until the port is not busy.
- The N option specifies no action; this setting is the default.
- The P action specifies continuous retry.

Using MODE to Set the Serial Port. To set the first serial port to communicate at 2400 bps, with 8 data bits, 1 stop bit, and no parity, you can type one of the following commands:

```
MODE COM1 2400,N,8,1
MODE COM1 24,N,8,1
```

If you are using DOS 3.3 or later, you can type the following instead to get the same settings:

```
MODE COM1 BAUD=24 DATA=8 STOP=1 PARITY=NONE
```

Note

The printer or plotter needs to be set to receive data in the same format in which the serial port is sending the data—that is, the same baud rate, parity, and so on.

General Rules for Using MODE with Serial Ports. When you are using the MODE command to change serial port settings, you should keep the following items in mind:

- If you set a retry option, a portion of MODE remains resident unless you use the DOS 4.0 RETRY=none option.
- The retry option slows the performance of foreground tasks when computers are being shared on an IBM PC network.
- DOS 4.0 and later can include Mark or Space parity settings. All versions of DOS support none, odd, and even parity settings.

Using MODE to Redirect a Parallel Port to a Serial Port

The final MODE setting you can use with ports is the command to redirect a parallel port to a serial port. Typically this is done if you want to redirect printer output to the serial port for use with a plotter or serial printer.

Issuing the MODE Command to Redirect Ports

Use the following syntax for the MODE command that changes the parallel printer to a serial printer:

```
MODE LPTn:=COMy:
```

where LPT*n*: is the name of the parallel printer port, and COM*y*: is the name of the serial port.

After you use MODE, DOS channels to the serial port all I/O requests that a program sends to the parallel port. The electronics associated with the port handles automatically the conversion of data from byte-wide to bit-wide.

Using MODE to Redirect Ports

Some early programs don't directly support serial printers. To use a serial printer, you can set a serial port and redirect a parallel port to that serial port. This process enables you to print when you use a serial printer and also use a program that doesn't directly support the printer.

Earlier in this chapter, you learned how to initialize a serial port using the MODE command. For example, you initialize a serial port with DOS 3.3 by using a command similar to the following:

```
MODE COM2 2400,E,7,2
```

With DOS 4.0 and later, you can type the following command instead:

```
MODE COM2 BAUD=24 DATA=7 STOP=2 PARITY=EVEN
```

You then follow the initialization command by typing the following command:

```
MODE LPT1=COM2
```

All data that normally goes to LPT1 is transmitted to COM2 at 2400 bps, with 7 data bits, 2 stop bits, and even parity.

General Rules for Using MODE to Redirect Ports. When you are using the MODE command to redirect ports, you should keep the following items in mind:

- You can redirect any parallel port to any serial port.
- You must initialize the serial port with both speed and data characteristics before the parallel port is redirected.
- The initialization of the serial port must include the retry option if the attached device is a printer.

Using MODE to Change the Typematic Rate

When you press a key on the PC keyboard, a character appears on-screen. If you continue to hold the key down, the pressed character repeats on-screen. The number of times a second the key repeats is known as the *typematic rate*.

The syntax for the MODE command that changes the typematic rate is

```
MODE CON RATE=rate DELAY=delay
```

where *rate* is the number of repetitions per second. The *rate* parameter can have values in the range 1 through 32. These values represent a repeat rate of from 2 to 30 characters per second (the higher the value, the faster the repeat rate). The default value is 20 for an IBM AT and 21 for an IBM PS/2, which is equivalent to approximately 10 characters per second.

The *delay* parameter is the time delay before DOS starts repeating a key. The delay is specified in .25-second intervals. The range for the delay is 1 through 4, making a total possible delay of 1 second.

To set the keyboard so that the delay before the key repeats is 0.75 seconds and the rate value is 24, type the following:

```
MODE CON RATE=24 DELAY=3
```

For Related Information

- "Altering the Look of the Screen with MODE," p. 337
- "Understanding Code Page Switching," p. 546

The Redirection Commands

DOS uses three standard devices: one for input, one for output, and one for errors. The main input/output device is the console, which is DOS's name for your keyboard and screen. The keyboard is the standard input device, and the display is the standard output and error device. In short, you type commands on the keyboard, and the commands and any error messages appear on-screen.

DOS enables you to choose the devices that you use to input and output information; this process is called *redirection*. (Error messages are always sent to the screen.)

Issuing the Redirection Operators

The redirection symbols are the greater-than and less-than signs. If you think about it, these symbols look like arrows (> or <) which show the input's source and destination. Use the following syntax for redirecting a program or command's input:

```
command < inputdevice
```

The syntax for redirecting a program or command's output is shown in the following:

```
command > outputdevice
```

The syntax for redirecting and appending to an existing file is shown in the following:

```
function command >> outputdevice
```

In each of these syntaxes, *inputdevice* is the source of the input; *outputdevice* is the destination of the output; and *command* can specify almost all applications programs or DOS commands. With the redirection command, you can use any DOS output device as an *outputdevice*, and you can use any DOS input device as an *inputdevice*.

Normally, redirected input comes from a file. Some devices, however, such as a mouse or a bar-code reader, can also be used as a source of input. For example, you can write a file that consists of the keystrokes used to operate a program, or you can use the output from a mouse as the input for a program.

Most DOS users redirect output more often than they redirect input. The two most common places to redirect output is to the printer or to a disk file. For example, the

```
DIR > PRN
```

command, which redirects the output of a directory to the printer, is a common example of redirection. When you issue this command, DOS redirects the output (the directory listing itself) to the PRN device instead of sending the listing to the screen. This command produces a hard copy listing of the directory.

Another common use is redirecting output to a file. To review the statistics of the MEM /C command, for example, type the following command:

```
MEM /C > CLASSIFY.MEM
```

When you use redirection commands with pipes and filters, discussed later in this chapter, the command becomes even more powerful.

Caution

Take care when you use the > operator to send output to a file. If you use > and refer to an existing file, DOS overwrites the existing file with the new output—*without warning*.

If you want to redirect to the printer a copy of your disk's directory structure and a list of the files on your hard disk, type the following:

```
TREE C:\ /F >PRN
```

The TREE command does not supply a directory listing that includes file sizes. If you want to create a full listing of all the directories on your hard disk by using redirection to append the output of the command, you specify that each directory be listed and then specify that the output be appended to a file. You then can print the full list. To perform this task, you type a command similar to the following for each directory:

```
DIR C:\ /S >> FULLIST.DIR
```

The DIR command lists the files in all the directories on drive C. The /S switch causes the DIR command to display all subdirectories. You can then substitute the names of other drives for C.

If you are testing programs that require a large amount of user input, the following redirection method is useful. For example, you can type the following:

```
PROGRAM < C:TESTPAT
```

This command results in the file TESTPAT supplying the input to PROGRAM. The redirection process enables you to construct a file that contains the correct keystrokes needed to operate a program. You then can test the program's basic operation before you include the error-trapping sequences. These sequences handle the situations when the user presses an incorrect key.

General Rules for Using Redirection

- Do not use redirection on a DOS batch file command line that includes CALL, FOR, or IF.
- Using > and referring to an existing file causes DOS to overwrite the existing file with the new output.
- Using >> adds the output to an existing file or creates a new file if the file does not exist.

The MORE Filter

DOS uses elements called *filters* to channel information between devices. You can use these filters to modify information as it passes from files to the screen. Filters, which work only on ASCII text files, are often used with the redirection symbols so that input can come from a source other than the keyboard or be sent to a device other than the screen.

Piping is another feature used with these commands. You use the pipe symbol (¦) to send output information that normally goes to the screen as input to another program. Piping, a form of redirection, diverts information destined for a device but then makes the information become the input from a device to another program.

The MORE filter buffers information from the input device or file and sends the data to the monitor one screen at a time.

Issuing the MORE Filter

The syntax for the MORE filter, which has no switches, is shown in the following:

```
MORE
```

MORE is commonly used in the following ways:

```
MORE < filename
```

where *filename* is the input file or

```
command | MORE
```

where *command* is any command or program.

MORE collects—and saves in a temporary disk file—information that normally goes to the screen. When a screen of input is obtained, MORE sends that information to the standard output device all at the same time. The text is channeled through the MORE filter until the end-of-file. Press any key when DOS displays the

```
-- More --
```

prompt; this action displays the next screen. After all the information has displayed on-screen, DOS erases the temporary file created by MORE.

Using MORE to Pause the Screen

When you use MORE to pause directory listings, the filter serves a function similar to the /P switch that is available with the DIR command.

The most common use of MORE, however, is to pause the TYPE command. To read the contents of a README.DOC file one page at a time, for example, type the following:

```
TYPE README.DOC | MORE
```

or

```
MORE <README.DOC
```

Both syntax forms work identically. To see the contents of a file, you can use the TYPE command. If the output of the file flows off the screen, reissue the command by pressing F3, and add the pipe character (|) and MORE.

General Rules for Using MORE

- Do not use MORE alone. MORE is a filter, which requires input to redirect or pipe.
- To view additional screens full of information, press any key when DOS displays the `-- More --` prompt.

- Ctrl-Break (and Ctrl-C) terminates the command without displaying any other screens.

The FIND Filter

The FIND filter finds strings of ASCII text in files. This filter is often used in association with redirection and piping.

Issuing the FIND Filter

Use the following syntax for the FIND Filter:

```
FIND /C /N /V /I "string" filename...
```

where *"string"* specifies the ASCII characters for which you want to search, and *filename* is the full file name of the file to search. The ellipsis (...) indicates that you can specify more than one file to search.

/C causes FIND to count all the lines that contain *"string"*. You use the /C switch to count the number of lines with the ASCII string; the text itself isn't passed to the screen.

/N causes FIND to include line numbers of the lines that contain the *"string"*. You use the /N switch to locate the line numbers within the text file. The line numbers listed are the line numbers in the original text file, not just sequential numbers. If the third, fifth, and sixth lines in the text file contain the string, for example, the line numbers displayed are 3, 5, and 6, not 1, 2, and 3.

/V causes FIND to search only for lines that do not contain the *"string"*. Only these lines are passed on to the screen.

/I makes FIND insensitive to case: upper- and lowercase letters are considered the same.

Note

You can use /C and /V together. The count displayed is the number of lines that do not contain *"string"*. You can also use /V and /N together. The lines that do not contain *"string"* display with their appropriate line numbers.

If you use FIND without options, the filter reads each of the files you specify and displays all lines that contain the ASCII string you are looking for.

DOS filters the information that normally goes to the output device. All lines that include the ASCII string display on-screen.

Like the other filter commands, FIND is often used with redirection and piping. If you search a text file for lines that include specific information, redirecting the output to a file may be helpful. You then can use the list as a reference while you look at the whole of the original file.

Using FIND to Find Files on Disk

You can use the FIND command to find on disk all files that have a certain extension. To find all files that have the extension .LET, for example, type the following command:

```
DIR /S /B ¦ FIND ".LET"
```

Because the /S switch is used with this DIR command, all files whose names contain LET—either in the root or extension—are listed under the name of the directory containing them. Because the /B switch is used, the file names are listed in the form FILENAME.EXT, with a period instead of spaces separating the file name and its extension. Therefore, you can search for .LET instead of LET. In this form, each file name is preceded by its directory path.

The DIR command with the /S option lists all the files on a disk. The output for DIR that normally goes to the screen is filtered through the FIND command. The output from FIND then displays on-screen.

You also can use the FIND filter with text files as a word-search utility. Suppose, for example, that you forget the name of the memo you sent to your boss, but you know that the file is either MEMO1, MEMO2, or MEMO3. You also know that you always use your boss's title, Supervisor, in memos. You can find the memo you need by typing the following:

```
FIND "Supervisor" MEMO1 MEMO2 MEMO3
```

When you issue this command, each line that contains *Supervisor* is listed. The listing appears in the following form:

```
---------- MEMO1
---------- MEMO2
Supervisor of Communications
---------- MEMO3
```

General Rules for Using FIND

- Use FIND only on ASCII text files.

- The "string" parameter is normally case-sensitive; that is, FIND regards the uppercase string *LOOK* as different from the lowercase string *look*. In DOS 5.0 and later, you can use the /I switch to make the search case-insensitive.
- To cause FIND to search for a quote in a string, type two quotation marks together (" "). FIND then searches for occurrences of ".
- If you do not specify a file name, FIND uses the standard input device.
- You cannot use wildcards in a file name.

The SORT Filter

The third DOS filter is SORT, which sorts the information from an ASCII file before displaying the result on-screen. Like FIND and MORE, SORT often is used with redirection and piping.

Issuing the SORT Filter

Use the following syntax for the SORT filter:

```
SORT /R /+n
```

where /R reverses the sort order, and *n* is the offset column for the sorting process.

The SORT filter processes information that normally goes to your screen or to another output device. The text from the input is analyzed on a line-by-line basis and sorted according to the ASCII binary values of the characters. This order is alphabetical, but SORT doesn't discriminate between upper- and lowercase letters.

When you use SORT with redirection or piping, more sophisticated sorting occurs. The most common use of SORT is to sort a directory listing into a text file, which you then can print.

The offset—the /+*n* option—in the command shows the leftmost column to be sorted. With a directory listing, you can sort by date or file size rather than by root name. Table 14.5 lists the offset values for a directory listing.

Table 14.5 Offset Values for SORT

Offset Value	Sorting By
1	Root name
10	File extension
14	File size
24	File date
34	File time

The sorted output appears on-screen; the original directory listing itself remains unchanged.

Note

This use of SORT is not as vital as it once was. Beginning with DOS 5.0, you can sort a directory listing by using the /O switch. To sort a directory by name, you can use the following command:

```
DIR \ /ON
```

Similarly, you can use /OE to sort by extension, /OS to sort by size, /OD to sort by date and time combined, and /OC to sort by compression ratio (for DoubleSpace volumes). You still need to use SORT if you want to sort the directory by time alone.

Using SORT to Sort Subdirectory Listings

You can use redirection and piping, as well as the FIND and SORT filters, in many ways. In DOS 4.0, 4.01, or 5.0, for example, you can create a sorted list of the subdirectories in the root directory by using the process outlined in the next paragraphs.

To create a sorted list of subdirectories in the root directory, follow these steps:

1. Type the following command:

   ```
   TREE C:\ /A ¦ FIND "-" ¦ SORT /+2 >TEMP.LST
   ```

   When issued with the /A switch, the TREE command produces a listing that utilizes the nongraphics character set. The FIND filter then removes all lines that are not subdirectory names. SORT sorts the output from FIND on column 2, and the output is redirected to a temporary file.

2. Use the temporary file as the input to the FIND filter, which removes all directories that are not in the root, by typing the following command:

```
FIND /V "¦" <TEMP.LST
```

The result is an alphabetical list of all subdirectories in the root directory.

Tip
Although the preceding commands work in all versions of DOS, you can perform essentially the same work with the DIR command, in a simpler manner. Combine switches /AD (directories only), /S (include subdirectories), and /ON (sort alphabetically by name), as shown in the following:

```
DIR /AD /S /ON
```

General Rules for Using SORT

- If *n* is not specified, DOS assumes column 1.
- Lines are sorted according to their ASCII binary values, with two exceptions. SORT is not case-sensitive; for example, the command sorts *A* and *a* as they occur in the source file. Additionally, SORT sorts characters with values over 127 in the order determined by the current COUNTRY code setting. (See Chapter 21, "Understanding the International Features of DOS," for more information.)
- The output file name must be different from the input file name when you use redirection.

Summary

This chapter discussed the commands associated with changing how DOS interacts with devices. These commands range from basic commands that clear a screen to advanced filtering and redirection commands. The chapter covered the following important points:

- Use the CLS command to clear the active display.
- Use the GRAPHICS command to print graphics screens on supported printers.
- The PRINT command is a background printing program.
- Use the CTTY command to change standard input and output devices.
- Use the options available with the MODE command to adjust settings for serial and parallel ports.

- You can use MODE with DOS 4.0, 5.0, and 6 to alter the keyboard typematic rate.
- You use the MORE, FIND, and SORT filters with text files. The filters are frequently used with redirection and piping.

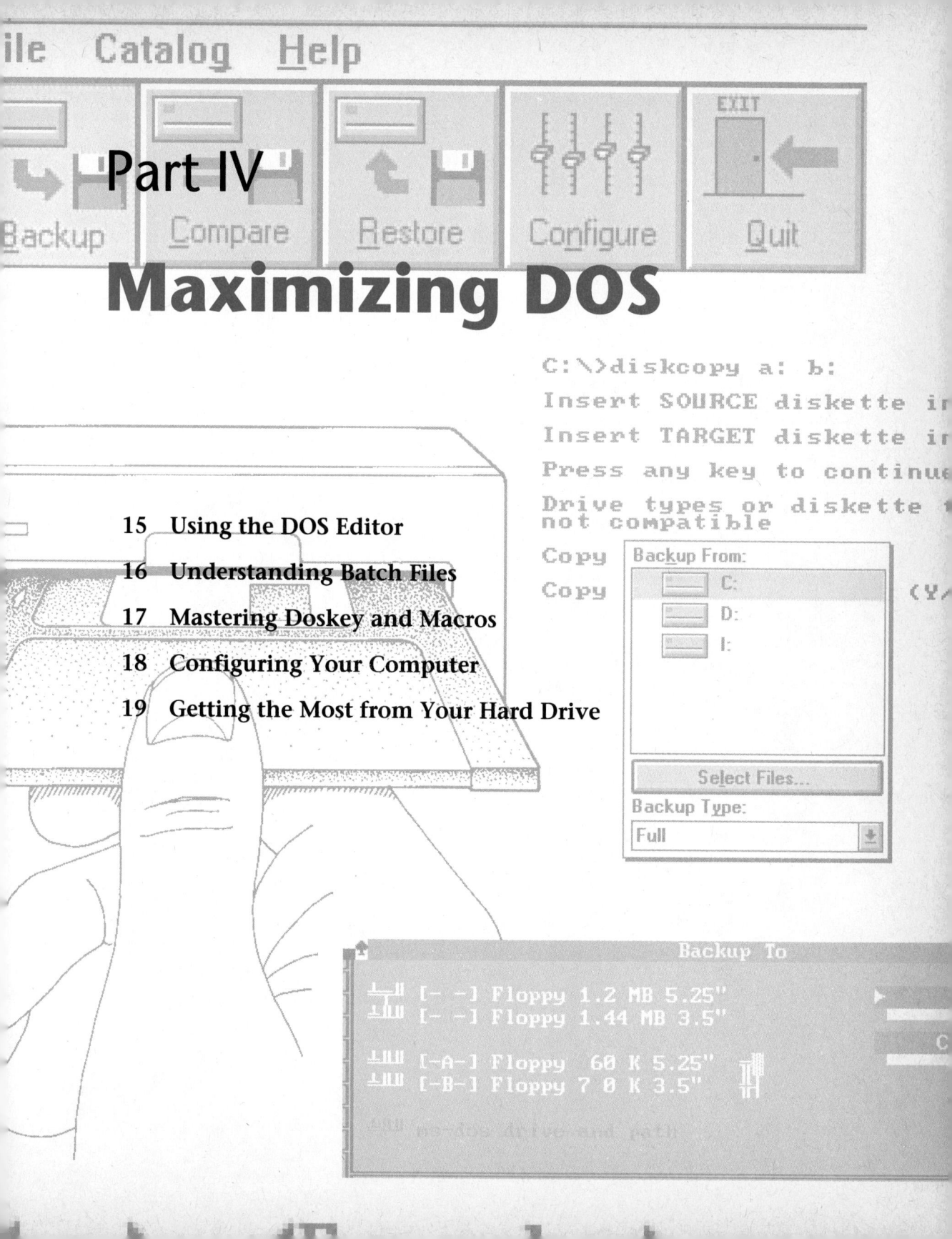

Part IV

Maximizing DOS

15 Using the DOS Editor

16 Understanding Batch Files

17 Mastering Doskey and Macros

18 Configuring Your Computer

19 Getting the Most from Your Hard Drive

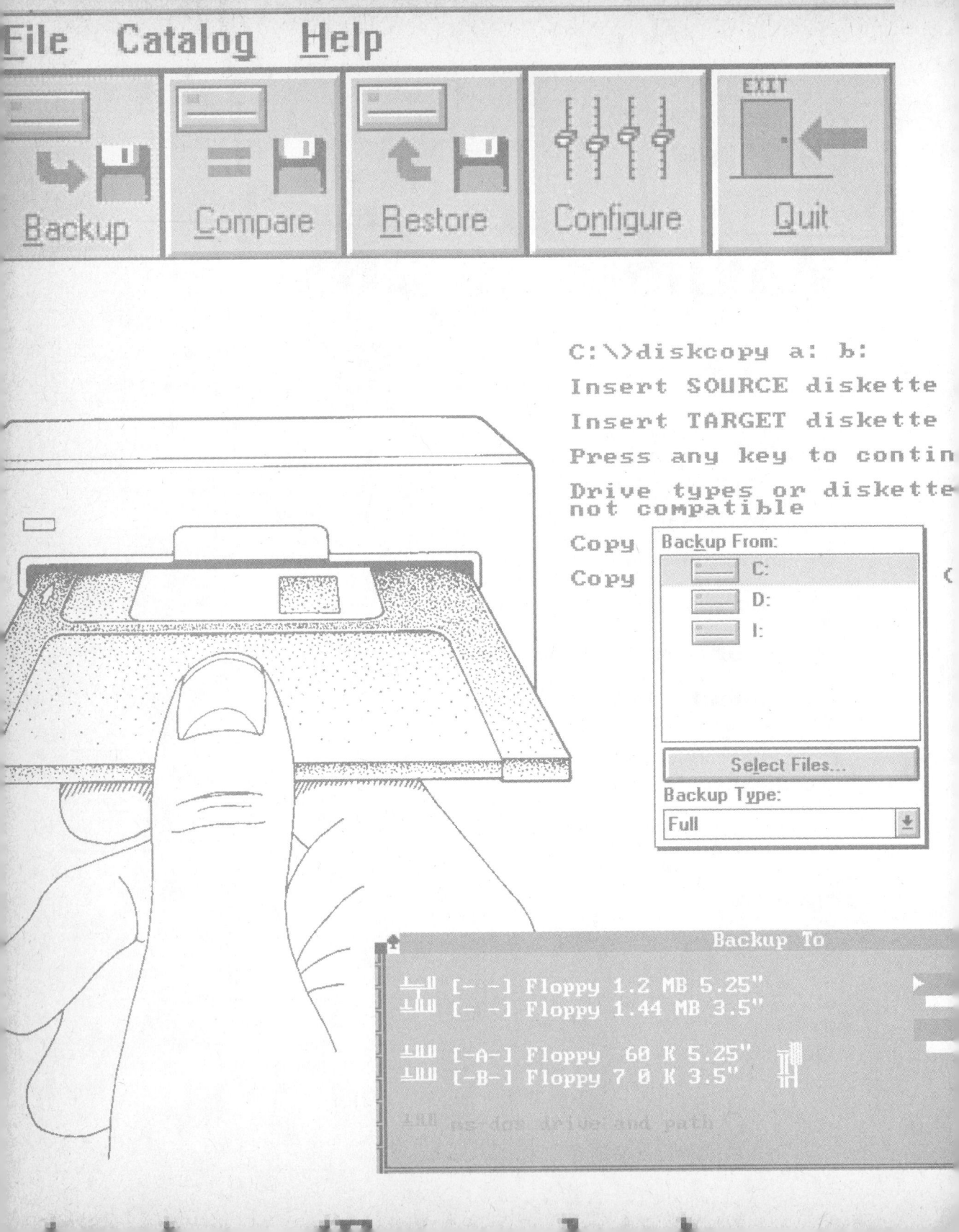
File Catalog Help
Backup
Compare
Restore
Configure
EXIT
Quit
C:\>diskcopy a: b:
Insert SOURCE diskette
Insert TARGET diskette
Press any key to contin
Drive types or diskette
not compatible
Copy
Copy
Backup From:
C:
D:
I:
Select Files...
Backup Type:
Full
Backup To
[- -] Floppy 1.2 MB 5.25"
[- -] Floppy 1.44 MB 3.5"
[-A-] Floppy 60 K 5.25"
[-B-] Floppy 7 0 K 3.5"

Chapter 15

Using the DOS Editor

The DOS Editor is a text processor, a kind of mini word processor. The Editor is the perfect tool for creating short text documents and editing text files. When you try the DOS Editor, you are in for a pleasant surprise. The Editor is so easy and intuitive to use that you will likely become a regular user.

This chapter explains how to use the basic features of the DOS Editor, including how to use its menus and shortcut commands and how to create, edit, save, and print text.

Understanding the DOS Editor

The DOS Editor falls into a class of programs known as *text editors*. As the name implies, a text editor works with files that contain pure text (as opposed to binary files, which contain programming instructions or formatted data).

Uses for the DOS Editor

Listed below are some of the typical tasks for which the DOS Editor is ideally suited:

- Creating, editing, and printing memos (and other text documents)
- Viewing text files whose contents are unknown
- Creating or modifying various system configuration files, such as AUTOEXEC.BAT and CONFIG.SYS
- Writing and modifying batch files (Batch files are discussed in Chapter 16, "Understanding Batch Files.")

- Writing and saving README files (Many computer users place a README file in a hard disk subdirectory, or on a floppy disk, to explain the contents of other files in the subdirectory or on the disk.)
- Creating and viewing files that are uploaded to or downloaded from electronic bulletin boards, such as CompuServe
- Writing programs for programming language environments that don't include a resident editor

For Related Information

- "Introducing Batch Files," p. 411
- "Creating a Simple Batch File," p. 414

Be aware that document files produced by some word processors aren't pure text files. The files may contain special formatting or printer-control characters. Most word processors can import the pure text files created with the DOS Editor. The Editor, however, may not successfully import word processor document files that contain certain formatting characters.

Files Required to Run the DOS Editor

The Editor is provided with DOS. It is invoked by the external command EDIT, which runs the program EDIT.COM. When you run the Editor, EDIT.COM calls on two other files: QBASIC.EXE and EDIT.HLP. Only QBASIC.EXE is required. EDIT.HLP contains the text of the help messages, but the Editor works without this file.

Starting the DOS Editor

You can start the DOS Editor from the DOS Shell or from the command line.

To start the DOS Editor, type

```
EDIT
```

at the DOS prompt, and press Enter. A preliminary screen appears (see fig. 15.1).

You now must press either Enter or Esc:

- Enter activates the Survival Guide. (The Survival Guide provides help about using the DOS Editor.)
- Esc clears the box in the center of the screen and prepares the Editor for working on a text file.

Press Esc. Now the DOS Editor screen is blank, and you can begin writing a text file. Your screen should look like the screen shown in figure 15.2.

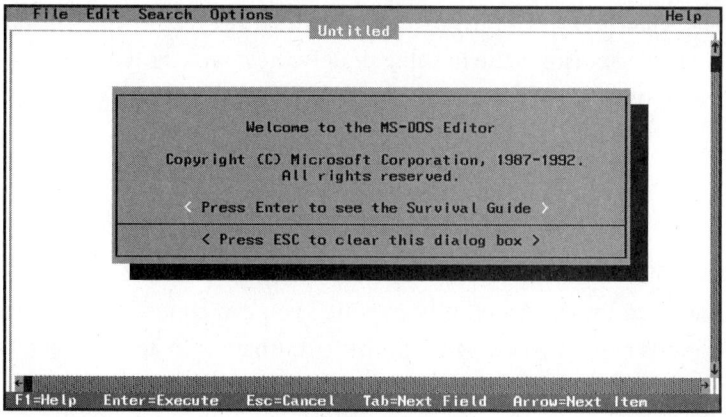

Fig. 15.1
The preliminary DOS Editor screen displays when you first use the EDIT command.

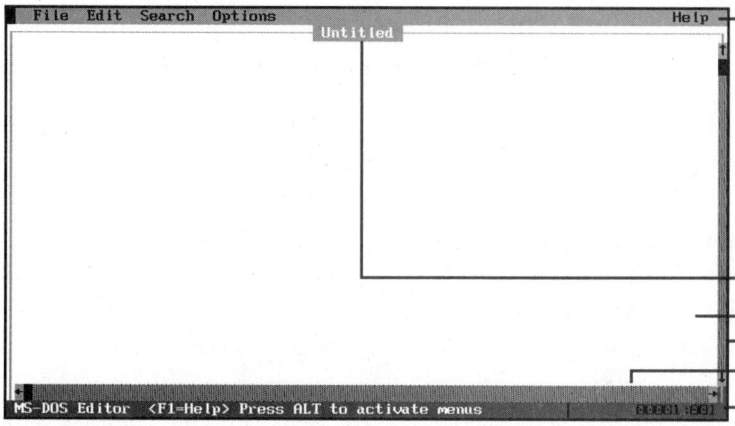

Fig. 15.2
The Editor screen, shown with a blank editing area, is ready for you to begin working on a file.

Getting Acquainted with the Initial Editor Screen

Take a moment to look at your screen (or refer to fig. 15.2). The screen consists of several elements:

- The *menu bar* lists the available menus: File, Edit, Search, Options, and Help. The title bar contains the name of the text file being edited (it is now Untitled).
- The *status bar* describes the current process and shows certain shortcut key options.
- *Scroll bars* are a vertical strip along the right edge and a horizontal strip just above the status bar. You use the scroll bars with a mouse to move through the file. (Mouse techniques are described in the section "Using a Mouse" later in this chapter.)

- The *Editor window* is the large area in which the text of your file appears. The cursor is the flashing underscore character that indicates where typed text will appear.

Navigating the DOS Editor

The DOS Editor provides several ways to perform most commands. The Editor has a user-friendly set of menus from which you can choose options. Many of these options require you to enter further information in an on-screen box known as a *dialog box*.

The Editor enables you to execute many commands by pressing special shortcut keys. You also can use a mouse to execute commands.

The sections that follow describe how to use menus, dialog boxes, shortcut keys, and a mouse in the DOS Editor.

Understanding the Menu System

The DOS Editor menu system provides many editing commands. The menu bar contains the following options: File, Edit, Search, Options, and Help. Choosing any of these options displays a pull-down menu. The File option displays a menu that enables you to load files, save files, and print files. You use the Edit menu to cut and paste text. You can use the Search menu for finding and replacing specified text. The Options menu can be used to reconfigure environment options, and the Help menu provides access to on-line help.

To activate the menu bar, press Alt. The first letter of each menu name is highlighted. Press the first letter of the menu name. For example, to activate the File menu press Alt and then F (Alt-F). Similarly, press Alt-E to display the Edit menu, Alt-S to display the Search menu, Alt-O to display the Options menu, or Alt-H to display the Help menu.

Every time you open a main menu, the first command on the menu is highlighted. You can move this highlight to the other commands by pressing the up- or down-arrow key. As you move the highlight, notice that the status bar displays a brief description of the highlighted command.

On a menu, one letter of each command is highlighted. On most systems, the highlighted letter appears in high-intensity white. To execute a command, move the highlight to that command and press Enter, or press the key that corresponds to the highlighted letter.

Depending on which editing commands you have executed previously, some commands in a menu may not be available. In such a case, the menu shows the command name in a dull color (usually gray), and no highlighted letter appears in the name. If you try to execute an unavailable command, the DOS Editor sounds a beep and refuses to execute the command.

The Esc key is the "oops" key. Pressing Esc closes the menu system and returns you to the Editor.

In the pull-down menus, an ellipsis (...) following the name of a command indicates that a dialog box opens when you issue that command. (Sometimes, depending on the circumstances, a command without an ellipsis also opens a dialog box.)

Understanding Dialog Boxes

When you execute a menu command, it may execute immediately or, depending on the command and the current context, a dialog box may pop up. A dialog box means that the DOS Editor needs more information before it can carry out the command. If, for example, you execute the command to save a new file, the Editor first needs to know what name to give the file. A dialog box prompts you for the necessary information.

For example, if you activate the Search menu and then choose Change, the DOS Editor displays the Change dialog box (see fig. 15.3).

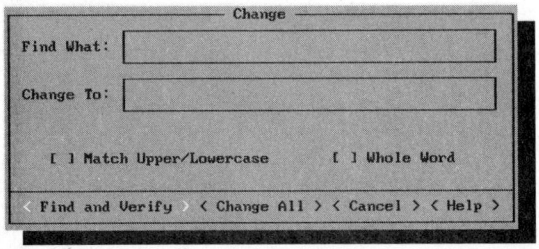

Fig. 15.3
The Change dialog box is used to indicate what you want to search and replace.

The DOS Editor uses dialog boxes to get a variety of information. Sometimes you must type something, such as a file name or a search string in a text box. Sometimes you must choose from a list of options. At other times, you select from a series of command buttons. (Refer to Chapter 4, "Using the DOS Shell," for a discussion of dialog boxes, text boxes, option buttons, and command buttons.)

When a DOS Editor dialog box opens, the following three keys have special significance:

- *Tab* moves the cursor from one area of the dialog box to the next area. After you specify information in one area, use Tab to move to the next area.
- *Esc* aborts the menu option and returns you to the Editor. Use Esc when you change your mind and decide against issuing a particular command.
- *Enter* is the "go ahead" key. Press it when all options in the dialog box are as you want them and you are ready to execute the command. You press Enter only once while you are working inside a dialog box. Use Tab, not Enter, to move the cursor from one area of the dialog box to the next area. (Be careful. Most people tend to press Enter after they type information, such as a file name. Remember that when you need to specify additional information inside the dialog box, press Tab, not Enter.)

In every dialog box, one command button is enclosed in highlighted angle brackets. The highlighted brackets identify the action that takes place when you press Enter.

To highlight the angle brackets of the command button you want, press Tab repeatedly. Be sure not to press Enter until you have specified everything satisfactorily.

When you are working with a dialog box, Alt is an "express" key. By pressing Alt and a highlighted letter, you activate an option even if the cursor is in another area.

Using Shortcut Keys

For convenience, many commonly used DOS Editor menu commands have an associated shortcut key. Pressing this shortcut key while you are working with the Editor executes the command directly, bypassing the menu system. Table 15.1 provides a complete list of shortcut keys.

Table 15.1 DOS Editor Keyboard and Mouse Shortcuts

Shortcut Key	Effect	Mouse
F1	View help on menu or command	Click right button on desired item
Shift-F1	View help on getting started	Click Getting Started (Help menu)
Ctrl-F1	View next help topic	Click Next (status bar)
Alt-F1	Review preceding help screen	Click Back (status bar)
Shift-Ctrl-F1	View preceding help topic	None
F3	Repeat the last Find	Click Repeat Last Find (Search menu)
F6	Move between help and desired window	Click in the desired window
Shift-F6	Make preceding window active	Click in the desired window
Shift-Del	Cut selected text	Click Cut (Edit menu)
Ctrl-Ins	Copy selected text	Click Copy (Edit menu)
Shift-Ins	Paste text from clipboard	Click Paste (Edit menu)
Del	Erase selected text	Click Clear (Edit menu)
Ctrl-Q, A	Change text	Click Change (Search menu)
Ctrl-Q, F	Search for text string	Click Find (Search menu)
Esc	Terminate Help System	Click Cancel (status bar)
Alt	Enter Menu-selection mode	None
Alt-Plus	Enlarge active window	Drag title bar up
Alt-Minus	Shrink active window	Drag title bar down

Using a Mouse

A mouse is an excellent pointing device for computer applications. The DOS Editor supports a mouse. You can execute menu commands and many editing tasks with a mouse. If your system is mouseless, you can get along fine; if you have a mouse, try it and see what you think.

Note

The DOS Editor works with any Microsoft-compatible mouse and driver. If you have a mouse, you presumably know how to install and activate your mouse driver. Microsoft supplies a mouse driver as part of the DOS package, but you should use it only if you have a Microsoft mouse.

When the mouse is active, you see a special mouse cursor on-screen. The mouse cursor is a small rectangle, about the size of one text character, that moves as you move the mouse. Notice that the regular blinking cursor remains active. You can continue to use all the keyboard commands and features. Refer to table 15.1 for a comprehensive list of mouse techniques.

Some additional mouse pointers follow:

- To open a menu, click the menu name in the menu bar.
- To execute a menu command, click the command name in the menu.
- To set an option in a dialog box, click that option.
- To abort a menu, click a location outside the menu.
- To move the cursor in the file, click at the location you want.
- To select text, drag the mouse over the text. That is, move the mouse pointer to one end of the text you want to select; then press and hold down the mouse button while you move the mouse, across the text, to the other end of the text you want to select.
- To activate the Editor window while a help screen is visible, click anywhere inside the Editor window.
- To expand or shrink the Editor window while a help screen is visible, drag the title bar of the Editor window up or down.
- To scroll the screen horizontally one character, click the left or right arrow at either end of the horizontal scroll bar.
- To scroll the screen vertically one character, click the up or down arrow at either end of the vertical scroll bar.
- To scroll text vertically to a specific position, move the mouse cursor to the scroll box (the inverse-video rectangle inside the vertical scroll bar). Then drag the scroll box along the scroll bar to the desired position.

- To scroll text one page at a time, click the vertical scroll bar somewhere between the scroll box and the top or bottom of the scroll bar.
- To scroll horizontally several positions at once, click the horizontal scroll bar somewhere between the scroll box and the left or right end of the scroll bar.
- To execute a dialog-box action enclosed in angle brackets, click the name between the brackets.
- To execute any keystroke action enclosed in angle brackets in the status bar, click the name inside the angle brackets.

For Related Information

- "Using Pull-Down Menus," p. 75
- "Using Dialog Boxes," p. 78

Mastering Fundamental Editing Techniques

Editing is a skill—almost an art. Some editing techniques are simple, others more complex. You can perform many editing tasks in more than one way. This section discusses the fundamental editing skills, which include moving the cursor, scrolling, and inserting and deleting text.

Moving the Cursor

With text in the DOS Editor, you can move the cursor around the text in several ways. The Editor provides two alternative cursor-movement interfaces:

- *Keypad interface.* The specialized IBM PC keys—the arrow keys, Ins, Del, and so on—govern most editing activities. To move the cursor up, for example, you use the up-arrow key.
- *Control-key interface.* Ctrl-key combinations govern most editing activities. To move the cursor up, for example, you press Ctrl-E. This interface is used in the word processing program WordStar.

Generally, the DOS Editor accommodates both camps. Most editing techniques are available with both the keypad and Control-key (WordStar-style) sequences. A few techniques, however, can be performed with only one method. This chapter focuses on the keypad style. The Control-key combinations are mentioned only when required by a particular editing technique.

Table 15.2 summarizes the cursor-movement commands.

Table 15.2 Cursor-Movement Commands

Effect	Keypad	Control-Key Style
Character left	Left arrow	Ctrl-S
Character right	Right arrow	Ctrl-D
Word left	Ctrl-left arrow	Ctrl-A
Word right	Ctrl-right arrow	Ctrl-F
Line up	Up arrow	Ctrl-E
Line down	Down arrow	Ctrl-X
First indentation level	Home	None
Beginning of line	None	Ctrl-Q, S
End of line	End	Ctrl-Q, D
Beginning of next line	Ctrl-Enter	Ctrl-J
Top of window	None	Ctrl-Q, E
Bottom of window	None	Ctrl-Q, X
Beginning of text	Ctrl-Home	Ctrl-Q, R
End of text	Ctrl-End	Ctrl-Q, C
Set marker	None	Ctrl-K, *n* (*n* equals 0—3)
Move to marker	None	Ctrl-Q, *n* (*n* equals 0—3)

Look at the far right end of the status bar, in the lower-right corner of the DOS Editor screen. You see two numbers, separated by a colon. The two numbers indicate the cursor's current location in your file. The first number is the current row; the second, the current column.

Use the arrow keys to move the cursor, and watch the numbers change. Press Num Lock; an uppercase `N` appears next to the location numbers to indicate that Num Lock is on. Press Num Lock a few more times to toggle the indicator on and off. Press Caps Lock; an uppercase `C` appears next to the location numbers, left of the `N`, to indicate that the Caps Lock key is on.

Scrolling

Scrolling is the movement of text inside the Editor window. When you scroll, you bring into view a portion of the file currently not visible in the Editor window. Scrolling, which can be horizontal as well as vertical, keeps the cursor at the same row and column number but moves the text in the window.

Table 15.3 summarizes the scrolling commands. For large-scale scrolling, you use the PgUp and PgDn keys. Try using these keys by themselves and with the Ctrl key.

Table 15.3 Scrolling Text

Effect	Keypad	Control-Key Style
One line up	Ctrl-up arrow	Ctrl-W
One line down	Ctrl-down arrow	Ctrl-Z
Page up	PgUp	Ctrl-R
Page down	PgDn	Ctrl-C
One window left	Ctrl-PgUp	None
One window right	Ctrl-PgDn	None

Inserting Text into a Line

You can insert text into an existing line. Move the cursor to the position at which you want to insert text. Type the text you want to insert. As you type, text to the right of the cursor moves right to accommodate the inserted text. You can move off the line by using any of the cursor-movement keys. Do not press Enter to move off the line. Pressing Enter splits the line in two.

Deleting Text from a Line

You can use one of the following two methods to delete a few characters from a line:

- Move the cursor to the character you want to delete. Press the Del key. To delete consecutive characters, continue pressing Del.
- Move the cursor to the character immediately to the right of the character you want to delete. Press the Backspace key.

Most people find the first method more natural. Try both methods and make your own choice.

Splitting and Joining Lines

Sometimes you need to split a line of text into two lines. Move the cursor so it is positioned under the character with which you want to begin the second line of text. Press Enter. The line splits in two, and the second half moves down to form a new line. Succeeding lines are pushed down to accommodate the new line.

Conversely, you can join two lines to form one line. Position the cursor in the second line, and press Home to move the cursor to the left end of the line. Press Backspace. The second line moves up to the right end of the first line. Lines beneath the split line move up one line.

Inserting and Deleting an Entire Line

To insert a blank line between two lines, move the cursor to column 1 in the lower of the two lines, and then press Ctrl-N or Home (to move the cursor to the left end of the current line), and press Enter. Then move the cursor up to the new blank line.

To delete an entire line, place the cursor anywhere on the line, and then press Ctrl-Y.

Overtyping

By default, the DOS Editor operates in Insert mode. If you type new text while the cursor is in the middle of a line, the Editor inserts that new text at the cursor location. If you prefer, you can choose Overtype mode, in which the new text replaces the former text.

To activate Overtype mode, press Ins. The cursor changes from a blinking line to a blinking box. The larger cursor signifies Overtype mode, in which any new character you type replaces the character at the cursor location.

To return to standard Insert mode, press Ins again. The Ins key acts as a toggle switch that alternates between Insert and Overtype modes.

Learning Special Editing Techniques

In addition to the basic editing techniques, the DOS Editor provides several special editing features. The sections that follow describe how to use the automatic indenting, tab, and place marker features.

Using Automatic Indent

When you type a line and press Enter, the cursor drops down one line but returns to the column where you began the preceding line. This feature is convenient when you want to type a series of indented lines.

For example, assume that you type the following line and press Enter:

```
This line is not indented
```

The cursor moves to the beginning of the next line. Then press the space bar three times to move the cursor to column 4 and type the following:

```
But this line is
```

Press Enter again. Note that the second time you press Enter, the cursor moves to the next row, but remains indented at column 4. Type

```
So is this one
```

and press Enter. The cursor remains indented.

Now, press the left-arrow key until the cursor returns to column 1. Type

```
Back to no indentation
```

and press Enter. The short text block you typed looks like the following:

```
This line is not indented
    But this line is
    So is this one
Back to no indentation
```

Using Tab

By default, tab stops are set every eight spaces. When you press the Tab key, the cursor moves to the right to the next tab stop. All text to the right of the cursor moves right when you press Tab. Additional tabbing techniques follow:

- To indent an existing line a full tab position, move the cursor to column 1 of the line, and press Tab.
- To remove leading spaces and move a line to the left, move the cursor anywhere on the line, and then press Shift-Tab.
- To indent or "unindent" an entire block of lines, select the lines by using one of the Shift keystrokes shown in table 15.4. Then press Tab to indent the entire block, or Shift-Tab to "unindent" the entire block.

- To change the number of default tab stops, first select Display from the Options menu. Press Tab several times to move the cursor to Tab Stops; type a new value for the number of characters per tab stop, and then press Enter to close the dialog box.

Using Place Markers

A place marker designates a specific location—a row and column—in your text. You can set as many as four place markers. After setting a place marker, you can move the cursor instantly from anywhere in the file to that marker's location. The markers are invisible; no character displays in the text to indicate a set marker.

You can set four markers, 0 through 3. To set a place marker, press and release Ctrl-K, and then press a number key from 0 through 3. This action associates the cursor's current position with the marker having the number whose key you pressed. To move the cursor to a previously set place marker, press and release Ctrl-Q, and then press the number of the marker (0 through 3).

You don't turn markers off; they are always set. You can reset them to a different location, but you cannot unset them. They are forgotten when you exit the program.

Block Editing

You can edit blocks of text as a single unit. Block editing requires that you understand two relevant concepts: *selecting text*, which identifies the block of text to be edited, and the *clipboard*, which temporarily stores a block of text in a reserved area of memory.

This section describes the following techniques:

- Selecting text for block operations
- Using the clipboard
- Cutting and pasting blocks of text

Selecting Text

A block of selected text is always one contiguous group of characters. The block may be one character, a few characters, a line, several lines, a paragraph, or even an entire file. Selected text appears in reverse video.

Follow these steps to select a block of text:

1. Move the cursor to one end of the block.
2. While you hold down the Shift key, use the cursor-movement keys to highlight the block.

Table 15.4 lists the keys used for selecting text. In general, the keys you use to select text are the same as those you use to move the cursor, but you also press Shift when using them to select text.

Table 15.4 Selecting Text

To Select	Use This Key Combination
Character left	Shift-left arrow
Character right	Shift-right arrow
To beginning of line	Shift-Home
To end of line	Shift-End
Current line	Shift-down arrow
Line above	Shift-up arrow
Word left	Shift-Ctrl-left arrow
Word right	Shift-Ctrl-right arrow
Screen up	Shift-PgUp
Screen down	Shift-PgDn
To beginning of text	Shift-Ctrl-Home
To end of text	Shift-Ctrl-End

After you have selected (highlighted) a block, you can deselect it by pressing any arrow key. (Do not use Shift, however; Shift expands or shrinks the selection.) The highlighting disappears, indicating that you have deselected the entire block.

Understanding the Clipboard

The clipboard is a text storage area in memory; it acts as a kind of halfway house for blocks of text. You can place a block of text into the clipboard and later retrieve the block. The clipboard has many uses. Its most common use is to cut and paste—to move or copy a block of text from one place in the file to another.

The clipboard stores only one block of text at a time. When you place text in the clipboard, the incoming text completely replaces the previous contents of the clipboard. Changing the block of text in the clipboard is always an all-or-nothing affair. You cannot add or subtract incrementally. Similarly, retrieval is all or nothing. You cannot move only part of the clipboard's contents into your file.

Working with Text Blocks

The DOS Editor supports four block-oriented editing techniques (see table 15.5). Each technique is available by using the Edit menu or by pressing the appropriate shortcut key. (Press Alt-E to activate the Edit menu.)

Table 15.5 Block-Editing Techniques

Menu Command	Shortcut Key	Description
Cut	Shift-Del	Deletes selected text from a file and places that text in clipboard.
Copy	Ctrl-Ins	Places in clipboard a copy of selected text from file; text in file remains selected.
Paste	Shift-Ins	Inserts contents of clipboard into the file at cursor; clipboard contents remain intact. If file currently has selected text, clipboard text replaces the selected text.
Clear	Del	Deletes selected text from file; contents of clipboard are not affected.

For example, to select the first three lines of text in a file, press Ctrl-Home to return the cursor to the beginning of the file. While holding down the Shift key, press the down-arrow key three times. This selects the first three lines of the file; they now display in reverse video (highlighted).

After the three lines are selected, you can use one of the block-editing commands. To activate the Edit menu, press Alt-E. The DOS Editor displays the Edit menu shown in figure 15.4. You can now use one of the menu commands. Alternatively, you can use one of the shortcut keys to operate on the selected block, even without displaying the Edit menu.

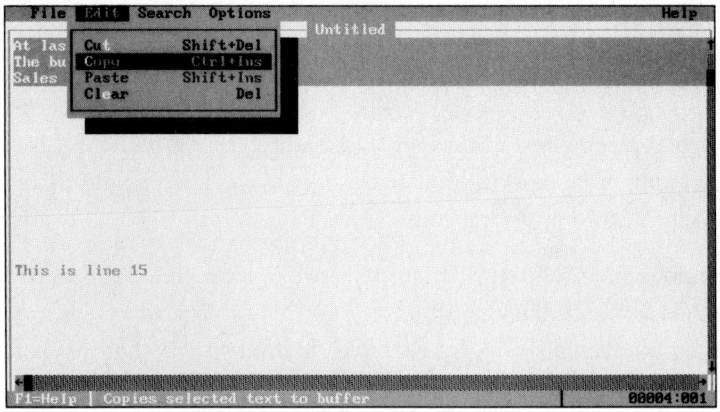

Fig. 15.4
The Edit menu, which allows you to cut, copy, paste, and clear text.

When you perform copy operations, a copy of the selected text moves to the clipboard but isn't deleted from the original location. If you perform a cut command, however, the DOS Editor removes the highlighted text from its original location and places it in the clipboard.

After text has been copied or cut to the clipboard, you can use the paste operation to copy the clipboard's contents to a new location in the file. Move the cursor to the desired target location and choose Paste from the Edit menu, or press Shift-Ins (the shortcut key for Paste). The Editor inserts a copy of the clipboard text at the cursor's location. (The clipboard still holds a copy of the pasted text. You can insert additional copies of the clipboard text at other locations in the file.)

Pressing Del or choosing the Clear command from the Edit menu permanently deletes the selected text from the file without placing a copy of it in the clipboard.

Searching and Replacing

The Search menu offers several options for searching for and replacing text. These capabilities are most useful in long files.

From the Search menu, you can perform the following actions:

- Find one or more occurrences of a designated text string

- Replace one or more occurrences of a designated text string with a second text string

A *text string* is a sequence of one or more consecutive text characters. These characters can be letters, digits, punctuation, or special symbols—any characters you can type from the keyboard.

Finding or replacing text always involves a search string, which is simply the text string being searched for. A search string can be a single character or, more likely, a word or several consecutive characters.

You cannot search for a string that spans two or more lines. The search string is confined to a group of characters on a single line. You can place some conditions on the search string. For example, you can specify that the search not discriminate between upper- and lowercase letters.

The search begins at the cursor's location and proceeds through the file. If the end of the file is reached before the search string is found, the search continues at the top of the file until the entire file has been traversed. Table 15.6 summarizes the three commands available from the **S**earch menu.

Table 15.6 Search Menu Commands

Command	Shortcut Key	Description
Find...	None	Opens a dialog box in which you specify the search string; finds the search string in your file.
Repeat Last Find	F3	Searches for the text specified in the last Find command.
Change...	None	Replaces one text string with another.

Using the Find Command

To use the Find command, first activate the **S**earch menu by pressing Alt-S. Your screen looks similar to figure 15.5.

Choose **F**ind. The Find dialog box opens, with the cursor on the Find What text box (see fig. 15.6). The word that is at the cursor's current location in the file (or the currently selected text) appears in the text box. If you want to search for this word, press Enter. Otherwise, type the correct search string, and then press Enter. The DOS Editor locates the first occurrence of the search string in your file and selects (highlights) the text found.

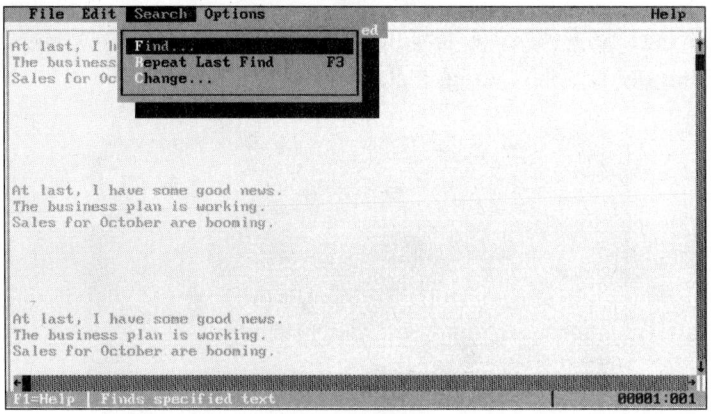

Fig. 15.5
The Search menu, which allows you to find text, repeat a find, and change text.

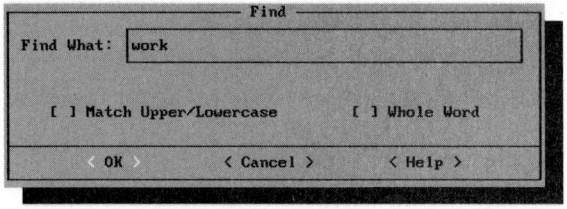

Fig. 15.6
The Find dialog box, which allows you to search for text.

You can press F3, or choose Repeat Last Find on the Search menu. The Editor moves to the next occurrence of the search string (if any).

As shown in figure 15.6, you can use the following check boxes in the dialog box to place conditions on the search:

- *Match Upper/Lowercase.* If you select this check box, a successful search occurs only when the upper- and lowercase letters in the text exactly match those in the search string. If this option is not selected, upper- and lowercase letters are considered the same.
- *Whole Word.* If you select this option, the search string must exist as an independent word and cannot be embedded inside a larger word. The character that immediately precedes and immediately follows the search string must be a space, a punctuation character, or one of the special characters (such as <, *, or [).

Using the Change Command

In addition to just searching for text, you can use the DOS Editor to search for specific text and then replace the text with other text.

Activate the **S**earch menu by pressing Alt-S. Choose the **C**hange command. The Editor displays the Change dialog box (see fig. 15.7).

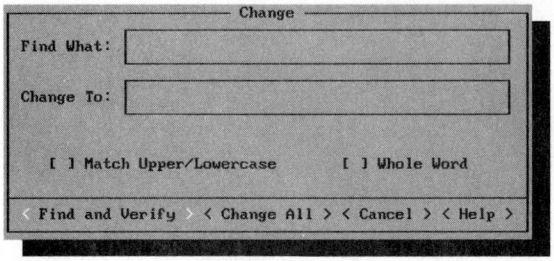

Fig. 15.7
The Change dialog box, which is used to search and replace text.

The first text box in the Change dialog box is labeled Find What. Type the text you want the Editor to find in this text box (the target text). The second text box is labeled Change To. Type the text you want entered. Figure 15.8 shows a completed Change dialog box.

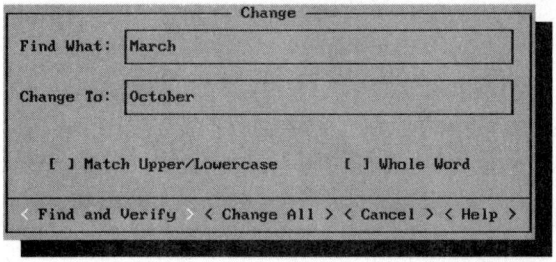

Fig. 15.8
The first step in performing a search-and-replace operation is to fill in the Find What and Change To boxes.

This dialog box contains two check boxes: Match Upper/Lowercase and Whole Word. Refer to the preceding section for a discussion of these check boxes.

After making the appropriate entries in the text boxes and selecting any desired check boxes, choose from among the following three command buttons:

- *Find and Verify*. Select this button to find each occurrence of the target string, one after another. (You specify the target string in the Find What dialog box.) As each occurrence of the target string is found, a second dialog box opens. This second box gives you the choice of making the substitution, skipping to the next occurrence, or canceling the remaining searches. Find and Verify is the default option, which you automatically choose by pressing Enter.

- *Change All* changes all occurrences of the target string to the string specified in the Change To box. The changes occur all at once. A dialog box informs you when the substitutions are complete.
- *Cancel* aborts the Change command, closing the dialog box without making any substitutions. This option is equivalent to pressing Esc.

After the DOS Editor finishes the find-and-replace operation, it displays a second dialog box. This second box contains the message `Change complete`. If no matching text can be found, the box displays the message `Match not found`. Choose the OK command button to return to the Editor window.

Managing Files

The DOS Editor includes many functions you can use to manage files. These functions, although primitive by the standards of today's full-blown word processors, enable you to perform the basics of file management. The following sections cover, in detail, the file-management operations you can perform using the DOS Editor.

Introducing the File Menu

The File menu is your command center for loading and saving files. Six commands are available on the File menu (see fig. 15.9).

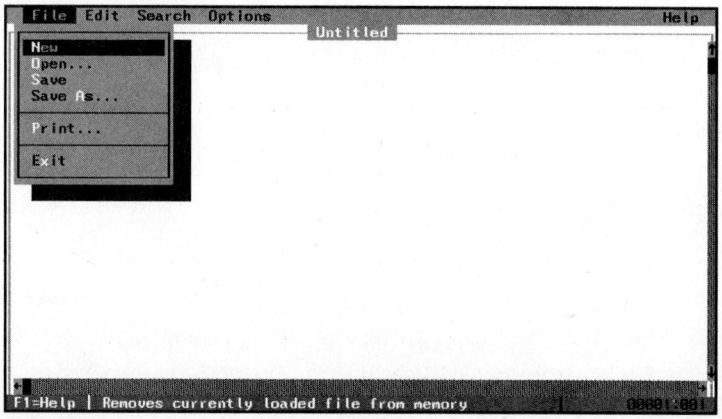

Fig. 15.9
The File menu, which enables you to access the file-management functions of the DOS Editor.

The following list explains the **File** menu commands:

- The *New* command clears the file currently in the DOS Editor. The result is a clean slate, as though you had just initialized the Editor. This command does not affect other copies of the file. If the file was saved on disk previously, for example, DOS does not erase the disk copy, but only the working copy in the Editor.
- *Open* loads a file from disk into the DOS Editor environment. You can use this command to see a list of file names in any directory.
- *Save* saves the current file to disk.
- *Save As* saves the current file to disk after prompting you for the file name.
- *Print* prints all or part of the text in the DOS Editor environment.
- *Exit* ends the editing session and returns you to the DOS Shell or the command-line prompt.

Note

When you are working with files, keep in mind these maxims:

1. Until you name a file, the Editor displays the temporary name Untitled in the title bar.
2. When you save a file, the Editor adds the extension .TXT to the file name if you don't specify another extension.
3. If you try to exit the Editor or open a new file without first saving a working file in the Editor, a dialog box opens to warn you.

Saving a File

When you save a file for the first time, you should specify two file attributes: the file path (the directory or disk on which to save the file) and the file name.

The DOS Editor stores files on disk in ASCII format. Such files are text files that most text editors and word processors can manipulate. You can view ASCII files directly from the DOS command line by using the TYPE command.

Using the Save As Command

Follow these steps to save the current Untitled file with a new file name:

1. Choose Save As from the File menu. In the dialog box that opens, the current path is shown below the words File Name (see fig. 15.10). A list box, below the label Dirs/Drives, lists the directories and disk drives available on your system.

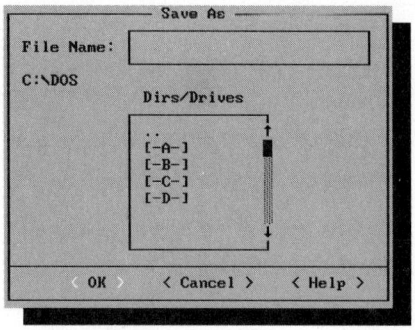

Fig. 15.10
The Save As dialog box is used when you first save a file or when you save a file under a new name.

2. Type the new file name in the File Name box. You may specify any file extension as part of the file name. Typical file extensions for ASCII text files are .TXT and .DOC.

3. Press Enter to save the file.

The DOS Editor saves the file to disk in the directory specified by the current path.

Save As is commonly used for storing a file the first time you create it and for saving a second version of a file in a different directory or with a name different from the first version. For example, assume that you are editing a file named MYWORK.TXT. After making a few changes, you decide to save the new version of the file under the name MEAGAIN.TXT. Display the File menu, and choose Save As. The DOS Editor displays the Save As dialog box.

The File Name text box contains the current file name, MYWORK.TXT. Type MEAGAIN.TXT and press Enter. The DOS Editor stores the file on disk as MEAGAIN.TXT, changing the name in the title bar accordingly. The file MYWORK.TXT remains stored on disk. Remember that if you continue editing the file on-screen, you are editing MEAGAIN.TXT (as indicated in the title bar), not MYWORK.TXT.

To store a file in a directory other than that specified by the current path, type the new directory path as part of the file name. For example, if you type the file name \MEMOS\PLAN.BID, the DOS Editor stores the file with the name PLAN.BID in the directory \MEMOS. After you save the file, the name PLAN.BID appears in the title bar. The next time you issue the Save As command, the default directory path is specified in the dialog box as C:\MEMOS. If you save a new file without including an explicit path, DOS saves the file in the C:\MEMOS directory.

You can use this technique to save files on different disk drives. To save a file named MYFILE.TXT in the root directory of the disk in drive A, for example, type the file name as A:\MYFILE.TXT.

Using the Save Command. Use Save to store a file you have already named. No dialog box appears. The current version of the file in the DOS Editor is saved to disk under the existing file name. As you edit a file, use Save periodically to update the file on disk.

Using Save on an unnamed (untitled) file has nearly the same effect as using Save As; the Editor opens a dialog box similar to that shown in figure 15.10 so that you can enter a file name.

Using the Open Command to Load a File

After text files are stored on disk, you can load a file into the DOS Editor with the Open command. Because this command lists files in any directory, you also can use Open to search your directories for specific file names. When you choose Open, the Open dialog box displays (see fig. 15.11).

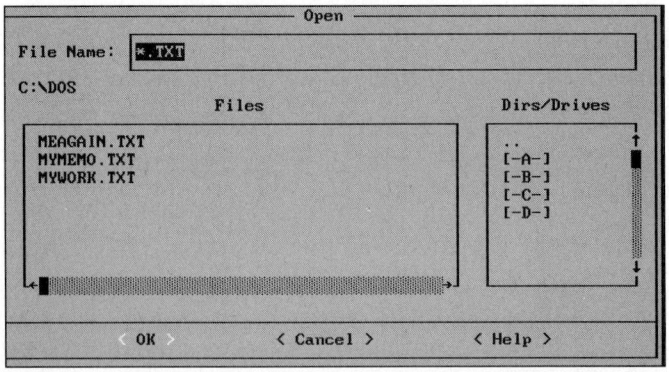

Fig. 15.11
The Open dialog box is used to load an existing disk file.

The Open dialog box contains the File Name text box. By default, this box contains *.TXT, the wildcard file name for all files with the extension .TXT.

The current directory path (C:\DOS in figure 15.11) appears below the File Name text box. In the File Name text box, type a file name, a directory path, or a name using the * and ? wildcard characters.

To change the default path, specify a path in the File Name text box, and press Enter. Otherwise, the DOS Editor looks in the current directory for files with the extension .TXT.

The Files list box contains the names of all files that satisfy the current directory, path, and file name specification. In figure 15.11, the Files box shows all files that satisfy the path and file name specification C:\DOS*.TXT.

The Dirs/Drives list box lists available directories and disks. You can move the cursor to the Dirs/Drives list box by pressing Tab repeatedly. Then press the up- and down-arrow keys to move the highlight to one of the directories or drives listed in the box. Press Enter to change the default path.

To load a specific file into the DOS Editor, you can use the File Name box or the Files box. To use the File Name box, type in the box the name of the specific file, including a path (or rely on the default path shown below the box). If you don't specify an extension, the Editor assumes the .TXT extension. For example, to load the file MYFILE.TXT, which is in the current directory, type **MYFILE**, and press Enter.

You also can select a file name from the Files list box if it contains the file name you want. First, press Tab to move the cursor to the Files list box. Then use the arrow keys to highlight the target file name. Alternatively, you can press the first letter of the file name to move the highlight. When the name you want is highlighted, press Enter.

The DOS Editor loads the file so that you can edit or view it.

Loading a File When You First Start the DOS Editor

You can load a file when you first start the DOS Editor. To do this, use the syntax

```
EDIT filename
```

where *filename* is the name of the file you want to edit. Include the path if the file isn't in the current directory. For example, to start the Editor with the file \SALES\MYFILE.TXT loaded, type the following line:

```
EDIT \SALES\MYFILE.TXT
```

The following notes apply when you load a file when you start the DOS Editor:

- The Editor does not assume the extension .TXT or any other extension if you don't specify an extension as part of the file name.
- The Editor initializes directly without taking the intermediate step of asking whether you want to see the help material in the on-screen Survival Guide.
- If the Editor cannot locate the specified file, the Editor assumes that you want to create a new file with that name. Accordingly, the Editor initializes with a fresh slate that includes your designated file name in the title bar. After you enter data into the file, you can save it directly with the Save command. (You don't have to use Save As and specify the file name a second time.)

Using the New Command

Use New when you want to stop work on one file and create a new file. If you haven't saved the old file, the DOS Editor opens a dialog box for confirmation. Otherwise, the old file clears, and the screen looks as though you had just initiated the Editor. You see a blank editing area with Untitled in the title bar.

Printing a File

Your computer system probably includes a printer. Whether you have a dot-matrix, daisywheel, or laser printer, follow these steps to print a copy of the file currently loaded in the Editor. You can print selected text or the complete file.

1. Activate the File menu.
2. Choose Print. This command opens the Print dialog box (see fig. 15.12).

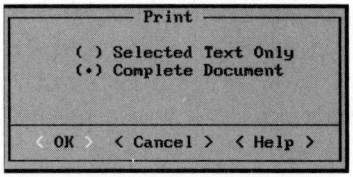

Fig. 15.12
The Print dialog box appears every time you choose the Print command from the File menu.

3. Choose one of the following option buttons:

- *Selected Text Only* prints only selected text, which appears in reverse video in the Editor. (Selecting text is explained earlier in this chapter.) This option is the default when a block of text is selected.
- *Complete Document* prints the entire file. This option is the default when no text is selected.

4. Press Enter to begin printing. Make sure that your printer is turned on and is on-line.

Exiting the DOS Editor

When you have finished editing files, you may want to leave the DOS Editor. Display the File menu and choose the Exit command. If the file already has been saved, the Editor returns to the DOS Shell or to the command line, depending on how you started the program.

If you try to quit without first saving the document you have been editing, the Editor opens a dialog box to ask whether you want to save the file. Choose the Yes command button to save the file and exit the Editor. Choose the No command button to exit from the Editor without saving any changes to the current file. Choose the Cancel button to close the dialog box and return to the Editor. To get help information about the dialog box, choose the Help button.

Starting the DOS Editor with Optional Switches

When you start the DOS Editor, four special parameter switches are available. These switches are listed in table 15.7.

Table 15.7 Optional Switches for the EDIT Command

Switch	Description
/B	Displays the DOS Editor in black and white, even when a color graphics adapter is present.
/G	Updates Editor screens as quickly as possible on systems with CGA (Color Graphics Adapter) video. (Note: Some computer systems cannot support this option. If screen flicker occurs when you choose /G, your hardware is not compatible with this option.)

(continues)

Table 15.7 Continued

Switch	Description
/H	Displays the maximum number of lines possible with your video hardware. EGA (Enhanced Graphics Adapter) and VGA (Video Graphics Array) systems can produce more than the standard number of lines on-screen.
/NOHI	Effectively displays the Editor on monitors that do not support high intensity.

To display the maximum number of lines when starting the DOS Editor, for example, use the following command:

```
EDIT /H
```

You can specify a file name with one of the command options, as in the following example:

```
EDIT \SALES\MYFILE /H
```

Use the /B switch if you run the DOS Editor on a computer system with a color video adapter but a black-and-white monitor. (Many laptop computers have this configuration.) At the DOS prompt, activate the Editor as follows:

```
EDIT /B
```

Customizing the DOS Editor Screen

Colors on the DOS Editor screen are preset. You can customize most of these colors and other attributes from the Options menu by using the Display command. If you have a color system, you may want different colors for the foreground and background text. If you don't use a mouse with the Editor, you may want to remove the scroll bars.

Changing Colors and Removing Scroll Bars

To change screen colors in the DOS Editor, display the **O**ptions menu and choose **D**isplay. A dialog box similar to figure 15.13 opens.

With the cursor on the Foreground box, you can select a new foreground text color by pressing the up- and down-arrow keys. The Foreground box cycles through the colors available with your video hardware. Notice that as you press the arrow keys, the text to the left of the dialog box (`Set colors for the text editor window`) shows the current foreground and background colors.

Select a new foreground color by moving the highlight to the color you want. Don't press Enter yet. You have more selections to make before closing this dialog box.

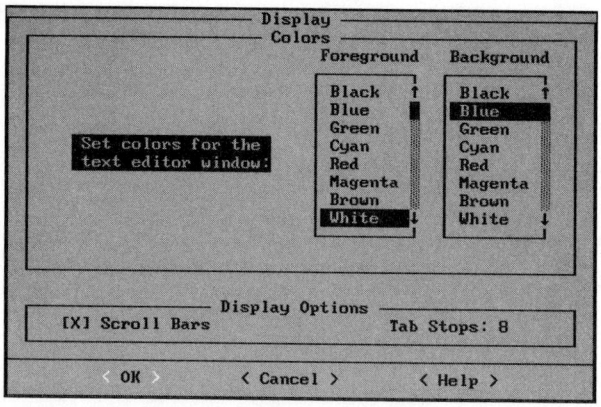

Fig. 15.13
The Display dialog box enables you to customize how the Editor screen appears.

Press Tab to move the cursor to the Background box. Select a new background color; the process is similar to the one you followed to select a new foreground color.

Now press Enter to return to the Editor screen. The new colors should be in use.

If you don't use a mouse, you may want to consider removing the scroll bars from your screen. Many users think that the screen looks less cluttered without the scroll bars. To see which you prefer, try the following exercise:

1. Reopen the dialog box by displaying the Options menu and choosing Display.
2. Press Tab several times to move the cursor to the Scroll Bars check box. The X inside the brackets indicates that scroll bars are displayed.
3. Press the space bar or *S* to deselect the check box. Removing the X indicates that you want to deselect the display of scroll bars.
4. Press Enter, and the scroll bars disappear (see fig. 15.14).

Saving Customized Settings

If you change one or more display options, the DOS Editor creates a file named QBASIC.INI and stores it in the directory containing the EDIT.COM and QBASIC.EXE files. (For most systems, this directory is \DOS.) The

QBASIC.INI file contains a record of the new screen configuration. When you later restart, the Editor uses QBASIC.INI to restore the screen with your customized settings.

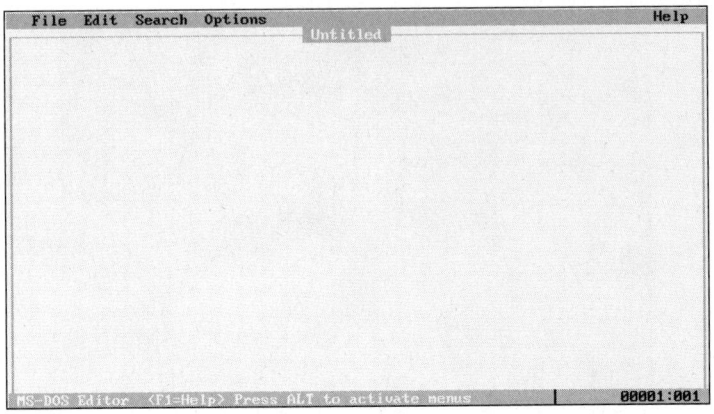

Fig. 15.14
An example of the Editor screen with the scroll bars removed.

Every time you start the Editor, it looks for QBASIC.INI in the default directory or in the directory chain established by the PATH statement in your AUTOEXEC.BAT file. If you restart from a different directory, be sure that the Editor has access to the QBASIC.INI file.

If you want to start the Editor with the original screen configuration, simply erase the QBASIC.INI file.

Note

The DOS Editor "borrows" the programming editor from the QBASIC.EXE file. Thus, the DOS Editor shares the editing environment found in the QBasic programming language. Similarly, the DOS Editor and QBasic share the initial configuration file (QBASIC.INI). Whether you run the DOS Editor or QBasic, the initial configuration is saved in the QBASIC.INI file.

Using the Help System

The DOS Editor provides on-line help through the Help menu (see fig. 15.15). Help screens include information about menus and commands, shortcut keys, dialog boxes, keyboard actions, and even about the help system itself.

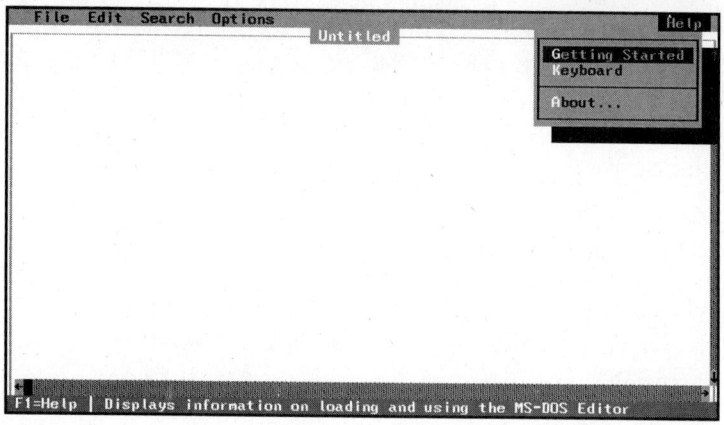

Fig. 15.15
The Help menu, which helps you learn to use the DOS Editor.

Three categories of information are available from the Help menu:

- *Getting Started* provides information about starting the Editor, using the menu and command system, and requesting help.
- *Keyboard* explains the different editing keystrokes and shortcuts for moving the cursor around your text file.
- *About* shows the Editor version number and copyright information.

The following are general notes on using the Help system:

- To activate the Help system at any time, press Alt-H.
- To move the cursor to the next help topic, press Tab. When the cursor is on the topic you want, press Enter to view the help screen.
- To activate the Getting Started help menu at any time, press Shift-F1.
- To close a help window and exit the help system, press Esc.
- A help screen opens in a separate window. The title bar of this window shows the help topic on display. For example, if you request help on the Save command from the File menu, the title bar of the help window reads HELP: Save command.
- The F1 key provides express help. To get help on any menu, command, or dialog box, press F1 when the cursor or highlight is on the desired item.
- For help when an error message occurs, move the cursor to the Help option in the error message box, and press Enter.

- Sometime, at your leisure, consider browsing through all the help screens. To browse, press Shift-F1, and then press Ctrl-F1 repeatedly.
- To scroll any particular help screen, press PgUp or PgDn.
- When help is active, a separate help window opens in addition to the Editor window. You can move the cursor between the help and the Editor windows by pressing F6 (or Shift-F6).
- When a help window and the Editor window are open simultaneously, you can enlarge or reduce the size of the active window by pressing Alt-plus or Alt-minus. (Here, *plus* and *minus* refer to the + and – keys on the numeric keypad.)
- To cut and paste text from a help screen into your file, first use the normal editing keys to select the text on the help screen. Copy the selected lines to the clipboard. Press F6 to activate the Editor window and then, using the normal editing keys, paste the help text into your file. Now reactivate the help screen by pressing F6 again.
- When the help system is active, as in all editing contexts, the status bar at the bottom of the screen displays useful keystrokes. If you want to execute a command shown enclosed in angle brackets, press the indicated keystroke or click the mouse when the mouse cursor is on the command name in the status bar.
- The Editor keeps track of the last 20 help screens you have viewed. To cycle back through previously viewed screens, press Alt-F1.
- When you start the Editor, the initial dialog box gives you the option of seeing the Survival Guide. If you press Enter to see the Guide, the help system is activated. A help screen displays information about getting started with the Editor and using the help system.
- The Editor stores the text of the help screens in a file named EDIT.HLP. To display any help screen, the Editor must have access to this file. The Editor searches for EDIT.HLP in the current directory or in directories specified by the PATH statement of your AUTOEXEC.BAT file. Normal DOS installation automatically places this file in the default \DOS directory. If for some reason, EDIT.HLP is located outside your PATH specifications, however, you can supply the Editor with the path to EDIT.HLP by choosing the Help Path command on the Options menu.

Summary

The DOS Editor is a text processor with which you can create, edit, and save text files. Among the Editor's features are full-screen editing, pull-down menus, shortcut keys, mouse support, and on-line help.

Although not in the same class as sophisticated word processors, the Editor is a considerable improvement from Edlin, the line-oriented editor (and the only text editor) supplied with earlier versions of DOS. The new Editor is easier to use and more powerful than Edlin.

The DOS Editor is perfectly suited for creating short text documents such as memos, README files, and batch files.

In this chapter, you have mastered the following concepts and skills:

- Navigating the menus and dialog boxes of the DOS Editor
- Basic editing techniques in the Editor
- Editing blocks of text
- Searching for and replacing selected text
- Managing files through the Editor
- Customizing your screen in the Editor

Chapter 16

Understanding Batch Files

When you discover that you're performing a certain task on your computer repeatedly, you should look for a way to get the computer to do more of the work. Your computer can perform most tasks faster than you can, and it doesn't make mistakes.

DOS has always enabled you to automate your use of DOS commands by creating *batch files*. A batch file is a text (ASCII) file containing a series of commands that you want DOS to execute. When you type the batch file name, DOS executes these commands in the order they occur within the batch file. This chapter explains how to create and use DOS batch files.

In Chapter 15, "Using the DOS Editor," you learned how to create text files with the Editor. In this chapter, you put the Editor to use creating batch files. You learn about batch file commands and the AUTOEXEC.BAT file, and you see some examples of batch files that you can modify to suit your needs.

Introducing Batch Files

The idea of getting a computer to do work in convenient, manageable batches predates the personal computer by several years. The earliest computers were large and expensive, and they could do only one job at a time. But even these early machines were fast. Making them wait for keyboard input between jobs was inefficient.

Batch processing was developed to make computers more productive. Collections of tasks to be carried out consecutively were put together off-line—that is, without using the computer's resources. The chunks, or batches, of tasks then were fed to the computer at a rate that kept the computer busy and productive.

Today, computers are less expensive than human resources. Batch processing enables computers to carry out a series of tasks automatically so that people don't have to waste time typing frequently used or complex commands.

A batch file is a text file that contains a series of DOS commands. Most commands used in batch files are familiar to you, having been explained in previous chapters of this book. Other commands, which control the flow of action in batch files, are available only in batch files. DOS executes the commands in a batch file one line at a time, treating each command as though you issued it individually.

You can use batch files to automate a DOS process. Using a set of commands in a batch file, you actually create a new, more powerful command. After a few experiments, you will find this DOS feature quite handy.

Recognizing a batch file in a directory listing is easy; batch files always have the file name extension .BAT. You can execute a batch file by typing the file name at the DOS prompt and then pressing Enter. To execute the batch file SAFE.BAT, for example, you type

```
SAFE
```

at the DOS prompt and press Enter. COMMAND.COM looks in the current directory for a file named SAFE.COM, then SAFE.EXE, and finally SAFE.BAT. When it finds the file, it reads it and executes the DOS commands that the file contains.

Batch files are useful for issuing frequently used commands whose parameters you have trouble remembering. For example, you can run the Backup program by typing MSBACKUP and then selecting options from the program. But what if you have saved several sets of options in setup files for different circumstances? You can create batch files to run MSBACKUP with the proper setup file when you issue a simple command such as DAILYBAK.

Batch files can echo (display) messages that you designate. This text-display capability is useful for presenting instructions or reminders on-screen. You can compose messages that describe how to execute a command or that contain syntax examples and reminders. Batch files also can use the TYPE command to display text from another file.

In some ways, batch files resemble computer programs. DOS has a host of special commands that are used primarily in batch files. Although you can type some of these commands at the DOS prompt, their main use is in batch files. These commands introduce flow-control and simple decision-making capabilities into a batch file.

Understanding the Contents of Batch Files

Batch files consist entirely of ASCII text characters. You can create batch files in the DOS Editor, in Edlin, and in nearly any other text-editing or word processing program. (If you use a word processing program, you must use a setting that omits the special formatting and control characters that many such programs use for internal purposes.)

The easiest way to create a short batch file, however, is to use the COPY command to redirect input from the keyboard (the CON device) to a file (see Chapter 9, "Managing Your Files," for more information).

When you create batch files, observe the following rules:

- Batch files must be ASCII files. If you use a word processing program, be sure that the program saves the file without formatting characters.
- The name of the batch file, which can be one to eight characters long, must conform to DOS's file name rules. Make batch file names meaningful so that they are easier to remember.
- The file name must end with the .BAT extension.
- The file name cannot be the same as a program file name (a file with an .EXE or .COM extension).
- The file name cannot be the same as an internal DOS command (such as COPY or DATE).
- The batch file can contain any valid DOS commands that you can enter at the DOS command line. (Typos cause errors.)
- You can include in the batch file any program name you usually type at the DOS command line. DOS executes the program as though you had entered its name at the command line.

- Use only one command or program name per line in the batch file. DOS executes batch files one line at a time.

You start a batch file by typing its file name (excluding the extension) at the DOS prompt and then pressing Enter. The following list summarizes the rules DOS follows when it executes a batch file:

- When DOS encounters a syntax error in a batch file's command line, DOS displays an error message, skips the incorrect command, and executes the remaining commands in the batch file.

For Related Information

- "Copying from a Device to a File," p. 229

- You can stop a batch file by pressing Ctrl-C or Ctrl-Break. DOS displays the following prompt:

```
Terminate batch job (Y/N)?
```

  Type **N** to skip the current command (the one being carried out) and proceed to the next command in the batch file. Type **Y** to abort execution of the batch file and return to the DOS prompt.

Creating a Simple Batch File

Tasks consisting of the same series of commands are ideal candidates for batch files. One task that you may perform repetitively is copying and comparing files.

In this section, you create a simple batch file, using the COPY command to redirect input from the keyboard (the CON device) in order to create an ASCII text file. (Remember that you also can use the DOS Editor, Edlin, or another text-editing or word processing program to create ASCII text files.)

Suppose that you often work with two spreadsheet files called SALES.WK1 and CUSTOMER.WK1. You frequently update these files and store them in the directory \STORE on drive C. After you update the files, you normally copy them to a disk in drive A and compare the copies on the floppy disk with the originals on the hard disk.

To begin creating a batch file that automates this process, type the following line at the DOS prompt and then press Enter:

```
COPY CON COPYCOMP.BAT
```

This COPY command redirects console (keyboard) input to the file COPYCOMP.BAT. After you press Enter, DOS drops the cursor to the line below the DOS prompt at the left of the screen and then waits for further instructions. Type the following three lines, pressing Enter after each line:

```
@ECHO OFF
COPY C:\STORE A:
FC C:\STORE A:/L
```

After you enter the last line in the file, press F6 or Ctrl-Z (both keys produce the characters ^Z on the screen). This sends a signal to DOS that the end of the file has been reached. Then press Enter. DOS copies the three lines into a file named COPYCOMP.BAT and displays the following message:

```
1 file(s) copied
```

Caution

When you use COPY CON to create a text file, check each line before pressing Enter. You can use Backspace and the DOS command-line editing keys (listed in Chapter 3, "Using DOS Commands") to edit the current line. After you press Enter, DOS moves the cursor down to the next line, and you cannot correct any errors in previous lines. You can abort the process without saving the file, however, by pressing Ctrl-C.

The first line of the COPYCOMP batch file, @ECHO OFF, instructs DOS not to display the batch file's commands as they are executed. In other words, when you run the batch file, you do not see the command lines themselves on-screen; you see only the results of their actions. The @ sign, just before the word ECHO, instructs DOS not to display that command line, either. Basically, all you need to remember is that @ stops display of the current line, while ECHO OFF stops display of all subsequent lines.

The second line of COPYCOMP.BAT copies the desired files from their source location in C:\STORE to the destination root directory of drive A.

The final line of the batch file uses FC.EXE, an external DOS command that compares the copied files with the originals. Although you can use the /V (verify) switch with COPY, using FC is more thorough.

Now that the COPYCOMP.BAT batch file is complete, you can run the file by typing the following command at the DOS prompt and then pressing Enter:

```
COPYCOMP
```

For Related Information

■ "Comparing Files with FC," p. 240

DOS first copies the two files from the C:\STORE directory to drive A and then compares the copies with the original files.

Understanding Replaceable Parameters

The batch files discussed so far in this chapter carry out exactly the same functions every time you use them. You may want a particular batch file to operate on different files each time you use it, even though the commands in the batch file are fixed. When you use replaceable parameters in a batch file, you can cause the same commands to do different things.

You already know that a parameter is an additional instruction that defines the task you want a DOS command to perform. When you type the name of the batch file at the DOS prompt, you can include up to nine parameters. DOS assigns a variable name to each parameter, starting with 1 and going up to 9. (DOS always assigns the variable name 0 to the name of the batch file itself.)

You can use each variable in your batch file by preceding the variable name with the percent sign (%). This combination of the percent sign and the variable name is called a *replaceable parameter.*

When used in a batch file, each replaceable parameter, numbered %0 through %9, holds the place for a parameter in one or more commands of a batch file so that you can provide the actual value of the parameter at the time you execute the batch file.

Consider the COPYCOMP.BAT batch file discussed earlier in this chapter:

```
@ECHO OFF
COPY C:\STORE A:
FC C:\STORE A:/L
```

Each time you execute this batch file, it copies all files from the C:\STORE directory to drive A and then compares the files. Suppose that you want to make this batch file more versatile so that you can use it to copy and compare the files in any directory. Revise COPYCOMP.BAT as follows:

```
@ECHO OFF
COPY %1 %2
FC %1 %2 /L
```

Notice that %1 and %2 replace C:\STORE and A:, respectively. These parameters are the replaceable parameters.

After making these changes in COPYCOMP.BAT, you can use the batch file to copy and compare the files from any directory to any disk or directory. To copy and compare the files in the \SPREADSH\QPRO2DAT directory on drive C with the files on a disk in drive B, for example, type the following command and then press Enter:

COPYCOMP C:\SPREADSH\QPRO4DAT B:

DOS copies all files from C:\SPREADSH\QPRO4DAT to the disk in drive B and then compares the original files with the copies to ensure that the copy procedure was effective.

To see how DOS replaces the parameters, create a batch file called TEST1.BAT which contains the following single line:

```
@ECHO %0 %1 %2 %3 %4 %5 %6 %7 %8 %9
```

After you create this file, type **TEST1,** followed by one space. Then type your first name, your last name, street address, city, state, ZIP code, and age, with each entry separated by spaces. Then press Enter. Your screen should look similar to the following:

```
C\:>TEST1 DAVID SMITH 1234 PINE STREET ANYTOWN IN 46032 39
TEST1 DAVID SMITH 1234 PINE STREET ANYTOWN IN 46032 39
C\:>
```

The batch file command instructs DOS to display the parameters 0 through 9. In the preceding example, these parameters are the following:

Parameter	Word
%0	TEST1
%1	DAVID
%2	SMITH
%3	1234
%4	PINE
%5	STREET

(continues)

Parameter	Word
%6	ANYTOWN
%7	IN
%8	46032
%9	39

Now try to "shortchange" DOS by not specifying a sufficient number of parameters to fill every variable marker. Run TEST1 again, but this time, type only your first name. Your screen should resemble the following example:

```
C>TEST1 DAVID
TEST1 DAVID
C>
```

DOS displays the batch file name and your first name. No other information is echoed to the screen. You specified fewer parameters, and DOS replaced the unfilled markers with nothing. In this case, the empty markers did no harm.

Some commands you use in a batch file, however, may require that a replaceable parameter not be empty. If you include DEL in a batch file with a replaceable parameter and the parameter is empty, you see the following error message:

```
Invalid number of parameters
```

You can use the IF command (discussed later in this chapter) to avert such errors. In the remainder of this section, you learn how to construct a batch file that takes advantage of replaceable parameters.

Suppose that you use several computers daily, but one of the hard disk systems is your "workhorse," where you store all the files you want to keep. You use floppy disks to move information from computer to computer. After copying a file back to a hard disk, you usually delete the file from the floppy disk. Deleting the file removes it from the process so that the file is not accidentally copied to the hard disk again later. You use the following steps to transfer data from a floppy disk to a hard disk:

1. Copy the file from the floppy disk to the hard disk with the verify switch on.

2. Erase the file from the floppy disk.

To simplify this process, you can create a batch file called C&E.BAT (copy and erase). Type the following commands in the file:

COPY A:%1 C:%2 /V
DEL A:%1

To use the C&E.BAT file, type the following command at the DOS prompt:

C&E *oldfilename newfilename*

The first parameter, *oldfilename*, represents the name of the file you want to copy from the floppy disk to the hard disk; *newfilename* is the new name for the copied file (if you want to change the file name as the file is being copied).

Suppose that you put a disk containing the file NOTES.TXT into drive A and want to copy the file to the hard disk. Type the following command at the DOS prompt:

C&E NOTES.TXT

The screen appears as follows:

```
C>COPY A:NOTES.TXT C: /V
1 file(s) copied
C>DEL A:NOTES.TXT
C>
```

Notice that even though you didn't type the parameter *newfilename*, DOS carried out the batch file, keeping the same file name during the copy. DOS copied NOTES.TXT from drive A to drive C and then deleted the file on the disk in drive A. The %2 parameter was dropped, and the file did not get a new name during the copy operation.

One benefit of creating a batch file that copies a file using parameters is that you can use a path name as the second parameter. By specifying a path name, you can copy the file from the floppy disk to a different directory on the hard disk. To copy NOTES.TXT to the WORDS directory, for example, type the following command:

C&E NOTES.TXT \WORDS

The screen display is as follows:

```
C>COPY A:NOTES.TXT C:\WORDS /V
1 file(s) copied
C>DEL A:NOTES.TXT
C>
```

Because \WORDS is a directory name, DOS copies the file NOTES.TXT into the directory \WORDS, following the rules of syntax for the COPY command. The batch file takes advantage of these syntax rules.

Note

Patience and persistence are important in understanding batch files. Many PC users who tried to avoid using batch files finally experimented with one or two examples; these users picked up the concept rapidly and now produce batch files that anyone would be proud to have created. Give yourself a chance to learn batch files by completing the exercises in this chapter. You can use the sample batch files as templates and apply them to specific situations. When you learn how to compose batch files, you have harnessed one of DOS's most powerful features.

Your use of batch files is not limited by your own imagination. If you pick up almost any personal-computer magazine, you can find a few useful batch files introduced in a feature or an article. You can use these featured batch files verbatim or modify them for your own special situation.

Even if you don't regularly create your own batch files, you can use your knowledge of batch file principles. Many programs are started by batch files rather than by the name of the actual program file. With your knowledge of batch files, you can use the TYPE command to display the contents of any batch file so that you can see what the batch operation is doing.

Many software programs use the commands in an installation batch file to install the main files. You can understand how an installation proceeds if you read the installation batch file. Knowing what the batch file does can help you avert installation conflicts. Suppose that you use drive B to install a program supplied on a 5 1/4-inch disk because your drive A is a 3 1/2-inch drive. Many installation batch files, however, assume that the files are to be installed from drive A. To prevent this conflict, you can modify a version of the installation batch file by changing all instances of A to B. When you run your modified installation batch file, you can install the new software without a hitch.

Working with batch files also can serve as a meaningful introduction to programming. The batch file commands covered in this chapter give batch files the kind of internal flow and decision-making capabilities that programming languages offer. Of course, don't expect batch files to equal the versatility of a full-featured programming environment. But batch files certainly can assume a programming flavor. By using batch files, you can increase DOS's usefulness significantly.

Using Batch File Commands

DOS includes special commands that often are used in batch files. Table 16.1 lists batch file commands.

Table 16.1 Batch File Commands

Command	Action
@	Suppresses the display of the command line on-screen
CALL	Runs another batch file and returns to the original batch file
CHOICE	Halts processing until a specified key is pressed (Use the IF ERRORLEVEL command to determine which key was pressed.)
ECHO	Turns on or off the display of batch commands as they execute; also can display a message on-screen
FOR..IN..DO	Permits the use of the same batch command for several files (the execution "loops")
GOTO	Jumps to the line following the specified label in a batch file
IF	Permits conditional execution of a command
PAUSE	Displays a message and halts processing until a key is pressed
REM	Enables you to insert comments into a batch file that describe the purpose of an operation
SHIFT	Shifts the command-line parameters one parameter to the left

You can use any of the commands listed in table 16.1 in a batch file; you can use some of them at the DOS system level, as well. For example, you can type

ECHO with or without an argument at the DOS prompt. DOS displays the string you type after ECHO or, if you provide no argument, tells you whether ECHO is ON or OFF. If you type PAUSE at the DOS prompt, DOS displays the message

```
Press any key to continue
```

and waits for a keystroke. Although these two commands are not very useful at the DOS prompt, the FOR..IN..DO command structure can be quite useful at the operating-system level to carry out repetitive commands.

The following sections explain the batch commands and their uses.

Displaying Messages and Inserting Comments

You already have had an introduction to the ECHO command earlier in this chapter. This command does two things: ECHO ON and ECHO OFF turn on and off the display of lines from batch files as commands are executed, and ECHO also displays messages.

ECHO can display a message up to 122 characters long (the 127-character DOS command-line limit, minus the length of the ECHO command and an additional space).

You can use REM (which stands for remark) in a batch file to remind you what the batch file does. When you review a batch file some time after you create it, you may no longer remember why you used certain commands or why you constructed the batch file in a particular way. Leave reminders in your batch file by using REM statements, which don't appear on-screen when ECHO is off. The REM comments make the batch file self-documenting, a feature that you and other users will appreciate later.

If you want the batch file to display particular messages, use ECHO. Messages set with ECHO appear on-screen whether or not you set ECHO OFF. To insert a blank line between messages, type a period (but no space) after the ECHO command, as follows:

```
ECHO.
```

Branching with GOTO

When you run a batch file, DOS normally processes commands one line at a time, from the beginning of the batch file to the end. When you use the GOTO command, however, you can change the order in which DOS executes batch commands by instructing DOS to branch to a specific line in the file.

The syntax of GOTO is as follows:

```
GOTO label
```

The GOTO command uses *label* to specify the place in the file to which DOS should branch. A batch file label is a separate line that is not a command, per se. A label consists of a colon followed by one to eight characters. The label name can be longer than eight characters, but DOS reads only the first eight characters.

When DOS encounters a GOTO command in the batch file, it starts at the beginning of the batch file and searches for a label matching the one specified by GOTO. DOS then branches to the batch file line following the label.

Consider the following batch file, LOOP.BAT. This file is similar to the TEST.BAT batch file you created previously, with the addition of the GOTO and PAUSE commands.

```
@ECHO OFF
:LOOP
   ECHO Hello, %1
   PAUSE
GOTO LOOP
```

To test the batch file, type

LOOP DAVID

and then press Enter. The screen shows the following message:

```
Hello, DAVID
Press any key to continue_
```

The batch file begins by echoing `Hello, DAVID` and then waits for you to press a key. After you press a key, DOS again displays the following message:

```
Hello, DAVID
Press any key to continue_
```

When you press a key again, DOS executes the GOTO LOOP command, causing execution of the batch file to return to the line labeled :LOOP at the beginning of the file. DOS again displays the message and pauses.

This batch file is an example of what programmers call an *infinite loop*. The program never stops on its own. To abort the batch file, you must press Ctrl-C or Ctrl-Break.

This simple example illustrates the operation of GOTO. You seldom will create infinite loops on purpose, but you should be able to use the GOTO command to control the order in which DOS executes batch file commands.

Using the IF Command

The IF command is a "test-and-do" command. When a given condition is true, the IF command executes a stated action. When the given condition is false, IF skips the action. If you are familiar with programming languages, such as BASIC, you should recognize the DOS IF command.

The IF command tests the following three conditions:

- The ERRORLEVEL of a program
- Whether a string is equal to another string
- Whether a file exists

The following sections explain these tests.

Using IF to Test ERRORLEVEL

The first condition that IF can test is ERRORLEVEL. The proper syntax for testing the ERRORLEVEL is as follows:

```
IF NOT ERRORLEVEL number command
```

ERRORLEVEL is a code left by a program when it finishes executing. A better name for this condition might be "exit level." This form of the IF command determines whether the value of ERRORLEVEL is greater than or equal to a number specified in the number parameter. Conversely, by adding the optional word NOT, you can determine whether the value of ERRORLEVEL is not greater than or equal to the value of the number parameter. If the specified condition is true, DOS executes the command specified in the command parameter. Otherwise, DOS skips to the next line in the batch file without executing the command.

The only DOS commands that leave an ERRORLEVEL (exit) code are BACKUP, DISKCOMP, DISKCOPY, FORMAT, GRAFTABL, KEYB, REPLACE, RESTORE, and XCOPY. Many other programs generate exit codes, however.

An exit code of zero (0) usually indicates that the command was successful. Any number greater than 0 usually indicates that something went wrong when the program executed. The following exit codes, for example, are generated by the DISKCOPY command:

Code	Meaning
0	The operation was successful.
1	A read/write error occurred that did not terminate the disk-copy operation.
2	The user pressed Ctrl-C.
3	A "fatal" read/write error occurred and terminated the copy procedure before it was completed.
4	An initialization error occurred.

An IF command in a batch file enables you to test for the exit code generated by a DOS command or program to determine whether the command or program worked properly.

When you use ERRORLEVEL to test exit codes, DOS tests whether the code is equal to or greater than the specified number. If the exit code is equal to or greater than the number, DOS executes the command parameter. If the code does not meet the condition, DOS skips the command parameter and executes the next command in the batch file. You can think of this condition as a BASIC-like statement, as follows:

```
IF exit code >= number THEN do command
```

The IF ERRORLEVEL command is most useful with the CHOICE command. When your batch file uses this utility, the file can pause for keyboard input. The utility puts a value in ERRORLEVEL related to the key pressed. You then can make your batch file branch or perform some other task based on the key pressed. A batch file otherwise does not accept keyboard input except when the input is provided on a batch-file command line. (For more information, see the section "Pausing for Input in a Batch File" later in this chapter.)

Suppose that you want to create a batch file named DCOPY.BAT that makes disk copies in your drive A, using the DISKCOPY command and the verify switch (see Chapter 9, "Managing Your Files"). If the disk-copy procedure terminates before completion, you want the batch file to inform you of the cause.

Create a batch file named DCOPY.BAT that contains the following lines:

```
@ECHO OFF
DISKCOPY A: A: /V
IF ERRORLEVEL 4 GOTO INIT_ERR
IF ERRORLEVEL 3 GOTO FATL_ERR
IF ERRORLEVEL 2 GOTO CTRL-C
IF ERRORLEVEL 1 GOTO NON_FATL
ECHO DISKCOPY successful and verified!
GOTO END
:INIT_ERR
   ECHO Initialization error!
   GOTO END
:FATL_ERR
   ECHO Fatal error! DISKCOPY stopped!
   GOTO END
:CTRL-C
   ECHO Someone pressed Ctrl-C!
   GOTO END
:NON-FATL
   ECHO A non-fatal error occurred. Check data!
:END
```

To run this batch file, type **DCOPY** at the command line, and then press Enter. DOS displays the following message:

```
Insert SOURCE diskette in drive A:
Press any key to continue_
```

When you press a key, DOS begins the disk-copy procedure. After the DISKCOPY command in the batch file executes, the batch file runs through a series of IF ERRORLEVEL tests. Based on what you already know, these tests are in descending order (4 to 1) because ERRORLEVEL considers any number equal to or greater than the specified number to be a match. Thus, if you were to check for 1 first, 4 would also be a match, and you would never get to the proper test.

First, the batch file tests for an initialization error (exit code = 4). If the exit code equals or is greater than 4, DOS skips to the line labeled :INIT_ERR. If the exit code is 3, execution of the batch file skips to the :FATL_ERR label. The batch file branches to the :CTRL_C label if an exit code of 2 is detected, and to the :NON_FATL label when the exit code is 1.

Finally, if no errors are detected by the series of IF ERRORLEVEL commands, the batch file displays the following message:

```
DISKCOPY successful and verified!
```

Using IF to Compare Strings

The second use for the IF command is to test whether string 1 equals string 2. The syntax of the batch command is as follows:

```
IF NOT string1==string2 command
```

This form of the IF command determines whether the first character string, *string1*, is the same group of characters as *string2*. Usually, one string is a replaceable parameter. If the two strings are identical, this condition is true and DOS executes the command specified in the command parameter. Otherwise, DOS skips to the next line in the batch file without executing the command. By adding NOT to the IF command, you can test for the condition when the two strings are not the same.

Assume that you want to create a batch file named DAYBACK.BAT that backs up your hard disk each day of the week. On Fridays, you want the batch file to perform a complete backup. On Mondays through Thursdays, you want the batch file to perform an incremental backup. Use the DOS Editor or another text editor to create the following batch file:

```
@ECHO OFF
CLS
IF "%1"==""  GOTO TRY_AGAIN
IF %1==FRI GOTO FULL
IF %1==MON GOTO ADD
IF %1==TUE GOTO ADD
IF %1==WED GOTO ADD
IF %1==THU GOTO ADD
:TRY_AGAIN
   ECHO Try again! Type DAYBACK and day of week (MON-FRI).
   GOTO END
:FULL
   ECHO Insert first disk of backup set.
   PAUSE
   C:
   CD \
   BACKUP C: A: /S
   GOTO END
:ADD
   ECHO Insert last disk of backup set.
   PAUSE
   C:
   CD \
   BACKUP C: A: /S/M/A
:END
```

To run this batch file, type **DAYBACK**, followed by the three-letter abbreviation for the day of the week (MON, TUE, WED, THU, or FRI), and then press Enter.

The first IF command in DAYBACK.BAT checks to make sure that you have typed the day of the week. If you don't provide enough parameters with the IF command, DOS replaces the replaceable parameter with a null value. (In batch files, null values must be enclosed in quotation marks to prevent a syntax error.)

The remaining IF commands determine whether you typed FRI or another day of the week. If you type FRI, the batch file branches to the :FULL label and performs a full backup. If you typed MON through THU, the file jumps to the :ADD label and performs an additive incremental backup. If you typed anything else, the batch file instructs you to try again.

Note

The :END label often is used to mark the end of the batch file. In the preceding batch file, execution branches to the :END label after a full backup, after an incremental backup, or after you are instructed to try again. When you use this technique, DOS executes only a portion of the batch file each time you run it, skipping the portions of the batch file that don't apply. Because the :END label is the last line in the batch file, the batch file ends at that point.

In the DAYBACK.BAT example, the replaceable parameter in the first IF command is enclosed in quotation marks because programmers commonly use quotation marks to delimit character strings. Actually, a comparison with any letter, number, or symbol can do the job. One common procedure is to use a single period instead of quotation marks, as shown in the following example:

```
IF %1. == . GOTO TRY_AGAIN
```

If you don't enter a parameter for %1, DOS interprets the line as follows:

```
IF . == . GOTO TRY_AGAIN
```

Use the syntax that is easiest for you to remember and understand.

If %1 equals nothing, DOS branches to the line following the label TRY_AGAIN and displays a message. If %1 equals something other than nothing, DOS does not branch to TRY_AGAIN; instead, it executes the second IF command in the batch file, which tests whether you typed DAYBACK FRI, and so on. Notice that GOTO statements are used to jump around the parts of the batch file that DOS should not execute.

When you use the IF command, DOS compares strings literally. Uppercase characters are different from lowercase characters. If you run DAYBACK by typing

DAYBACK Fri

DOS compares *Fri* with the uppercase *FRI* and decides that the two strings are not the same. The IF test fails, and DOS does not perform the backup operation.

Using IF to Look for Files

The third type of IF command tests whether a given file is on disk. The syntax for this form of the IF command is as follows:

```
IF NOT EXIST filename command
```

This form of the IF command determines whether the file specified in the *filename* parameter exists on your computer's disk (or doesn't exist, if you add NOT). If the file does exist, the IF command executes the command specified in the command parameter.

You can use IF EXIST when you start a word processing program. Perhaps you use a file called TEMP.TXT to store temporary files or to write blocks that are to be read into other documents. You can use IF EXIST to test for the existence of the file and to erase the file if it does exist.

Your batch file, called WORD.BAT, would look like the following example:

```
@ECHO OFF
CLS
CD \DOCUMENT
IF EXIST TEMP.TXT DEL TEMP.TXT
\WORDS\WP
CD \
```

This batch file turns off ECHO and clears the screen. The current directory changes to \DOCUMENT—the directory where you store your word processing documents.

Next, the IF command tests for the existence of TEMP.TXT. If the file does exist, DOS deletes the file. Finally, DOS starts your word processing program from the \WORDS subdirectory.

For Related Information

■ "Copying Entire Disks with DISKCOPY," p. 245

Notice the last line of the batch file: CD \. When your word processing program starts, the batch file is suspended temporarily. After you quit your word processing program, the batch file regains control. The batch file then executes its last line, CD \, which changes back to the root directory. The batch file ends.

Pausing for Input in a Batch File

Before DOS 6.0, the only way to affect the execution of a batch file after the file started was to press Ctrl-C or Ctrl-Break. These key combinations enabled you to cancel a single command or to end the entire operation. Starting with DOS 6.0, you get a means of temporarily halting the execution of a batch file and accepting limited user input. You can use this feature to decide whether to process certain commands, to branch to a different part of a batch file, or even to present a menu and accept any of a series of choices.

To employ this capability, you use the CHOICE command. The command's syntax is as follows:

```
CHOICE /C:choices  /N /S /T:c,nn message
```

Following are explanations of the components of this command:

- /C:*choices* lists the keys that can be pressed. If you don't specify choices, the default is YN.
- /N prevents the display of acceptable keys at the end of the prompt.
- /S instructs CHOICE to pay attention to the case of the key pressed; this feature enables you to use Y and y for different choices.
- /T:*c,nn* causes CHOICE to act as though you pressed the key represented by *c* if you don't make a choice within *nn* seconds.
- *message* is the optional prompt to display.

You respond to the key pressed by using a series of IF ERRORLEVEL commands. By default, the choices are Y and N. Y has the ERRORLEVEL code 2, and N has the ERRORLEVEL code 1.

Making a Two-Way Choice

If you don't specify which keys should be pressed, CHOICE assumes Y and N, and adds `[Y,N]?` to the end of whatever message you choose to include. This feature is extremely useful if you want to decide whether to load a certain program when your computer starts. For example, you might type the following commands near the end of your AUTOEXEC.BAT file:

```
CHOICE Back up hard disk
IF ERRORLEVEL 2 MSBACKUP
```

When the AUTOEXEC.BAT file reaches the first line, DOS displays the following message:

```
Back up hard disk[Y,N]?
```

If you have not yet backed up your hard disk today, you type **Y**, which generates the ERRORLEVEL code 2. DOS then executes the MSBACKUP program. If you have backed up your hard disk, type **N.** You need not test for this code, however, because it's the only other alternative. DOS then executes any commands following these lines in AUTOEXEC.BAT, but MSBACKUP doesn't run.

Creating a Simple Menu

Because you can specify any keys as choices, you can use CHOICE to create a simple menu, using the /C:*choices* parameter to specify the keys to be pressed. You might use a command such as the following:

```
CHOICE/c:swd Load Spreadsheet, Word Processor, or Database Manager
```

DOS displays the following message:

```
Load Spreadsheet, Word Processor, or Database Manager[S,W,D]?
```

The ERRORLEVEL codes for the specified keys read from left to right. Thus, pressing D generates a code 3; pressing W, a code 2; and pressing S, a code 1. These exit codes are then processed by batch file lines like the following:

```
IF ERRORLEVEL 3 DB
IF ERRORLEVEL 2 WP
IF ERRORLEVEL 1 SS
```

This assumes that your database program is named DB, your word processor is named WP, and your spreadsheet is named SS. There is a problem with this, however. The IF ERRORLEVEL command automatically assumes that all numbers higher than the one specified also are true. If you type **D**, for example, DOS loads your word processing program as soon as you exit from your database manager and your spreadsheet program as soon as you exit from your word processing program.

You can deal with this situation in either of two ways. One way is to add a second command that changes the flow of execution. Your file would have to resemble the following example:

```
CHOICE/C:swd Load Spreadsheet, Word Processor, or Database Manager
IF ERRORLEVEL 3 DB
IF ERRORLEVEL 3 GOTO END
IF ERRORLEVEL 2 WP
IF ERRORLEVEL 2 GOTO END
IF ERRORLEVEL 1 SS
:END
```

The second way to deal with the limitation of the ERRORLEVEL directive is to have each test execute a batch file instead of a program. (After you pass control to a second batch file, DOS does not return to the original file unless you use CALL or COMMAND /C.) For this command to work properly, the batch files must appear either in the current directory or in a directory in the path that precedes the directories containing the programs.

Always give a user a way to get out of a command without choosing any of the proffered alternatives. The user, of course, can break out of the CHOICE command by pressing Ctrl-C or Ctrl-Break. But you also can include a third alternative, such as Quit, as shown in the following example:

```
CHOICE /C:YNQ Back up hard disk
IF ERRORLEVEL 3 MSBACKUP
IF ERRORLEVEL 3 GOTO END
IF ERRORLEVEL 1 IF NOT ERRORLEVEL 2 GOTO END
other commands
:END
```

Creating a Simple Display Menu

You can use the other switches provided with CHOICE to create a display menu. You create text to explain the choices and suppress the display of characters at the end of the optional message. You might create a batch file called MENU.BAT and type the following commands:

```
@ECHO OFF
CLS
ECHO;
ECHO;
ECHO Press S to load Spreadsheet
ECHO Press W to load Word Processor
ECHO Press D to load Database Manager
ECHO Press Q to quit
ECHO;
CHOICE /C:SWDQ /N /T:Q,10 Your choice?
IF ERRORLEVEL 4 GOTO END
IF ERRORLEVEL 3 GOTO DB
IF ERRORLEVEL 2 GOTO WP
   ECHO Loading spreadsheet program_
   SS
   GOTO END
:WP
```

```
    ECHO Loading word processing program_
    WP
    GOTO END
:DB
    ECHO Loading database management program_
    DB
:END
```

Notice that there is no ERRORLEVEL choice for when the user presses S (the ERRORLEVEL would be 1). This is because there is no need to branch in this case. Instead, execution of the batch file falls through to the first line after the last ERRORLEVEL statement, which is the command for the spreadsheet section.

When you type the MENU command, DOS clears the screen and displays the following message:

```
Press S to load Spreadsheet
Press W to load Word Processor
Press D to load Database Manager
Press Q to quit
Your choice?
```

If no key is pressed within 10 seconds, the CHOICE command issues a Q, and the DOS prompt returns.

You can construct very elaborate menus by using the ASCII box-drawing characters, ANSI Escape sequences (to establish colors), and the CHOICE command. See Chapter 20, "Understanding ANSI.SYS," for a discussion of the uses of ANSI.SYS.

Using FOR..IN..DO

FOR..IN..DO is an unusual and extremely powerful batch command. The command's syntax is as follows:

```
FOR %%variable IN (set) DO command
```

variable is a one-letter name that takes on the value of each item in *set*. You can use this command from the DOS prompt as well as within a batch file. When you use the command at the DOS prompt, however, use only one percent sign (%) instead of two (%%) in front of *variable*. You must use two percent signs in a batch file so that DOS does not confuse *variable* with a replaceable parameter.

The *set* parameter is the list of items, commands, or disk files whose value you want variable to take. You can use wildcard file names with this parameter. You also can use drive names and paths with any file names you specify. If you have more than one item in the set, use a space or a comma between the names.

The *command* parameter is any valid DOS command that you want to perform for each item in *set*.

Using a FOR..IN..DO Batch File

An interesting example of the use of FOR..IN..DO is a batch file that compares file names found on a disk in drive A with the file names found on another disk and then produces a list of the files on both disks. Create the batch file CHECKIT.BAT, entering the following lines:

```
@ECHO OFF
CLS
IF "%1"==""  GOTO END
FOR %%a IN (B: C: D: E: b: c: d: e:) DO IF "%%a"=="%1" GOTO COMPARE
ECHO Syntax error: You must specify a disk to compare.
ECHO Be sure to leave a space before directory.
GOTO END
:COMPARE
   %1
   IF "%2"==""  GOTO SKIP
   CD %2
:SKIP
   ECHO The following files are on both disks:
   FOR %%a IN (*.*) DO IF EXIST A:%%a ECHO %%a
:END
```

Insert into drive A the disk that you want to compare, and then use the following syntax:

```
CHECKIT drive directory
```

drive is the drive that contains the other disk that you want to compare, and *directory* is the directory that you want to compare. This batch file substitutes the drive you specify for %1 in the batch file commands and substitutes any directory you specify for %2. The directory is optional; if you specify a drive and directory, separate their names with a space. Otherwise, the batch file treats the drive and directory as one replaceable parameter (%1). If you don't specify a directory name, DOS compares the current directory of the drive with the current directory of the disk in drive A.

Suppose that you want to compare the list of files in drive A with the list of files in the \GAMES directory in drive B. Type the following command at the command line:

```
CHECKIT B: \GAMES
```

The batch file determines which files in the \GAMES directory of the disk in drive B also are on the current directory of the disk in drive A.

When the CHECKIT batch file is called, DOS first determines whether %1 is empty. (%1 is empty if you typed no drive letter or directory after CHECKIT in the command line.) If %1 is empty, the batch file displays an error message, branches to the end of the file, and quits without performing a comparison.

If you specify a disk drive, DOS goes to the third line of the batch file and determines whether the drive letter is a valid drive letter. In this batch file, valid drive letters are B, C, D, E, b, c, d, and e. If no valid drive letter is found, or if you don't include a colon (:) and space after the drive letter, the batch file displays a message and branches to the end of the batch file.

If you specified a valid drive, CHECKIT branches to the :COMPARE section of the program. When executing the first line in this section, DOS logs onto the drive you specified in the command line (the drive designation replaces %1 in the batch file). The batch file determines whether you included a directory parameter; if you did include this parameter, DOS changes to that directory.

Finally, the batch file displays a message and then looks at all the file names in the current directory to see whether a file with the same name exists in drive A. For every match found, the batch file lists the file name.

Using FOR..IN..DO at the DOS Prompt

You may find that you want to issue commands such as the ones in CHECKIT at the DOS prompt. Instead of using the batch file for the preceding example, you can change subdirectories manually and then type the FOR..IN..DO line (the line that does all the work in the batch file) at the DOS prompt. If you do use FOR..IN..DO outside a batch file, DOS requires that you enter only one percent sign.

You also can use FOR..IN..DO if you copy files from a disk to the wrong subdirectory on a hard disk. Use this command to delete the files from the hard disk.

Using FOR..IN..DO with Other Commands

FOR..IN..DO works as well with commands as with file names. Instead of naming a set of files, you can name a series of commands that you want DOS to carry out. Consider the following example:

```
FOR %%a IN (COPY DEL) DO %%a C:*.*
```

In a batch file, this line first copies all the files on drive C to the current directory and then erases the files from drive C. Instead of specifying the drive and file, you can use a replaceable parameter in the line, as follows:

```
FOR %%a IN (COPY DEL) DO %%a %1
```

To use this batch file, you first must change to the destination directory (for example, D:\BAK). When you invoke this version of the batch file, you type the names of the files that you want to copy and remove. If you name the batch file MOVER.BAT, you can type the following command to invoke the file:

```
MOVER C:\WP
```

MOVER.BAT copies all the files in the subdirectory C:\WP to D:\BAK and then erases the files in C:\WP. This file works much like the C&E.BAT file you created earlier in this chapter.

Moving Parameters with SHIFT

The SHIFT command moves the parameters in the command line that invoked the batch file; each parameter moves one parameter to the left. SHIFT tricks DOS into accepting more than 9 replaceable parameters (10 if you include the batch file name, which is %0). The diagram of SHIFT is as follows:

```
%0  ←%1  ←%2  ←%3  ←%4  ←%5...
↓
bit bucket
```

In this diagram, parameter 0 is dropped. The old parameter 1 becomes parameter 0. The old parameter 2 becomes parameter 1; parameter 3 becomes 2; parameter 4 becomes 3; and so on. A command-line parameter that previously was 11th in line and not assigned a parameter number now becomes parameter 9.

The following batch file, SHIFTIT.BAT, is a simple example of the use of the SHIFT command:

```
@ECHO OFF
CLS
:START
ECHO %0 %1 %2 %3 %4 %5 %6 %7 %8 %9
SHIFT
PAUSE
IF NOT "%0"=="" GOTO START
```

Suppose that you type the following text:

```
SHIFTIT A B C D E F G H I J K L M N O P Q R S T U V W X Y Z
```

The screen shows the following message:

```
SHIFTIT A B C D E F G H I
Press any key to continue_
```

Notice that the batch file name is displayed because %0 holds the name of the batch file. Press a key to continue; DOS now displays the following message:

```
A B C D E F G H I J
Press any key to continue_
```

In this case, the file name has been dropped into the bit bucket. %0 now equals A. All the parameters have shifted one to the left. Each time you press a key to continue, SHIFT continues moving down the list of parameters you typed. When the left-most parameter (%0) is empty, the batch file ends.

SHIFT has many uses. You can use it to build a new version of the C&E.BAT file you created earlier in this chapter. The following modified version of the copy-and-erase batch file, called MOVE.BAT, shows a use for SHIFT:

```
@ECHO OFF
CLS
:LOOP
COPY %1 /V
ERASE %1
SHIFT
IF NOT "%1" == "" GOTO LOOP
```

This batch file copies and erases the specified file or files. The batch file assumes nothing about the files to be copied; you can specify a disk drive, a path, and a file name. The batch file copies the files to the current directory and then erases the files from the original disk or directory.

The last two lines shift the parameters to the left, determine whether any parameters remain, and then repeat the operation if necessary.

Running Batch Files from Other Batch Files

On some occasions, you may want to run a batch file from another batch file. Running batch files from within batch files is particularly useful when you want to create a menu batch file that can start several different programs.

This section discusses three ways to run batch files from other batch files. One method is a one-way transfer of control. The other two methods involve running a second batch file and returning control to the first batch file. These techniques are useful if you want to build menus with batch files or use one batch file to set up and start another batch file.

Shifting Control Permanently to Another Batch File

The first method of calling a second batch file is simple: include the root name of the second batch file as a line in the first batch file. The first batch file runs the second batch file as though you had typed the second batch file's root name at the DOS prompt.

To run BATCH2.BAT, for example, include in BATCH1.BAT the following line:

```
BATCH2
```

DOS loads and executes BATCH2.BAT. Control passes in only one direction: from the first batch file to the second. When BATCH2.BAT finishes executing, DOS displays the system prompt. Control goes to the second file but doesn't come back to the first file.

Calling a Batch File and Returning Using CALL

After your batch file is debugged, you can use the CALL statement to run a batch file and then return to the original one. The syntax of the CALL command is as follows:

```
CALL filename parameters
```

filename is the root name of the batch file. When you type the CALL command, you can specify any parameters that you want to pass to the batch file you are calling. You can place the CALL command anywhere in the first batch file.

When DOS executes a CALL command, DOS temporarily shifts execution to the called batch file. As soon as the called batch file is completed, DOS returns to the first batch file and continues execution with the line immediately following the CALL command.

The following three batch files demonstrate how CALL works:

BATCH1.BAT

```
@ECHO OFF
CLS
REM This file does the setup work for
```

```
REM demonstrating the CALL command.
ECHO This is the STARTUP batch file
ECHO The command parameters are %%0-%0 %%1-%1
CALL batch2 second
ECHO MEM from %0
MEM
ECHO Done!
```

BATCH2.BAT

```
ECHO This is the SECOND batch file
ECHO The command parameters are %%0-%0 %%1-%1
CALL batch3 third
ECHO MEM from %0
MEM
```

BATCH3.BAT

```
ECHO This is the THIRD batch file
ECHO The command parameters are %%0-%0 %%1-%1
ECHO MEM from %0
MEM
```

The first line of BATCH1.BAT sets ECHO OFF. The second line clears the screen. The next two lines in BATCH1 are remarks intended only to document the purpose of the batch file.

The two ECHO lines are similar for all three batch files. The first of the two lines identifies the batch file being used. The second ECHO line shows the 0 parameter (the name by which the batch file was invoked) and the first parameter (the first argument) for the batch file. Notice that to display the strings %0 and %1, you must use two percent signs (%%0 and %%1). If you use a single percent sign, DOS interprets the string as a replaceable parameter and does not display the actual percent symbol.

Each CALL statement in the first and second batch files invokes another batch file. BATCH1.BAT calls BATCH2.BAT, and BATCH2.BAT in turn calls BATCH3.BAT. In each case, a single argument passes to the batch file being called: second to BATCH2.BAT and third to BATCH3.BAT. Each batch file then displays its name (by using the %0 variable) and runs MEM. When DOS reaches the end of each called batch file, DOS returns to the calling batch file.

Check the printout or the screen display for the largest executable program size provided by the MEM command (in other words, the largest block of memory available for use by an executable program). This number grows larger after each batch file is executed and removed from memory. Figure 16.1 shows the output from a 486 computer when BATCH1 FIRST is typed.

Fig. 16.1
The output produced by issuing the BATCH1 FIRST on a 486 computer. Illustrates what happens when you use the CALL statement to switch between different batch files.

```
This is the STARTUP batch file.
The command parameters are %0-BATCH1 %1-FIRST.
This is the SECOND batch file.
The command parameters are %0-batch2 %1-second
This is the THIRD batch file.
The command parameters are %0-batch3 %1-third.

MEM from batch3.

Memory Type                    Total       =    Used        +    Free

Conventional                   640K             51K             589K
Upper                          0K               0K              0K
Adapter RAM/ROM                384K             384K            0K
Extended (XMS)                 7168K            1488K           5680K

Total memory                   8192K            1923K           6269K
Total under 1 MB               640K             51K             589K

      EMS is active.
      Largest executable program size   589K (603056
      bytes)
      Largest free upper memory block   0K (0 bytes)
      MS-DOS is resident in the high memory area.
      MEM from batch2.


Memory Type                    Total       =    Used        +    Free


Conventional                   640K             51K             589K
Upper                          0K               0K              0K
Adapter RAM/ROM                384K             384K            0K
Extended (XMS)                 7168K            1488K           5680K

Total memory                   8192K            1923K           6269K
Total under 1 MB               640K             51K             589K

      EMS is active.
      Largest executable program size   589K (603152
      bytes)
      Largest free upper memory block   0K (0 bytes)
      MS-DOS is resident in the high memory area.
      MEM from batch1.


Memory Type                    Total       =    Used        +    Free


Conventional                   640K             51K             589K
Upper                          0K               0K              0K
Adapter RAM/ROM                384K             384K            0K
Extended (XMS)                 7168K            1488            5680K
Total memory                   8192K            1923K           6269K
Total under 1 MB               640K             51K             589K

      EMS is active.
      Largest executable program size   589K (603152 bytes)
      Largest free upper memory block   0K (0 bytes)
      MS-DOS is resident in the high memory area.
      Done!
```

Each time you use the CALL command, DOS temporarily uses 80 bytes of RAM until the called batch file finishes running. Because DOS uses that much memory for each nested CALL command, you can run out of memory. (A nested CALL command is a CALL command from a called batch file.) Not many people nest CALL commands deeply in batch files. The accumulated memory-usage problem does not occur when a single batch file calls multiple other batch files. In that case, you can use the CALL command as many times as you want and use only the same 80 bytes of RAM for each call.

Using COMMAND.COM to Execute a Batch File

In all versions of DOS, you can call a second batch file from the first, execute the second batch file, and return to the first batch file. In DOS 3.0 through 3.2, you use COMMAND /C (discussed in Chapter 12, "Working with System Information"). In DOS 3.3 and later versions, you use the CALL command, discussed in the following section.

Although it may appear at first glance that there is no longer any need to use the COMMAND.COM method of running a batch file, beginning with DOS 6.2 there is a compelling new reason. That is, with DOS 6.2, you can use COMMAND.COM's /Y switch, in conjunction with /C, to single-step through a batch file. For instance, suppose you execute the following command line:

```
COMMAND /Y /C NEW.BAT
```

When you do this, DOS loads a copy of the command processor and executes NEW.BAT. As it executes, each line in the batch file displays, and you are asked whether you want to execute it. This is the same process used when you interactively execute the AUTOEXEC.BAT file, as described in Chapter 2, "Starting DOS."

This interactive execution capability is a great debugging tool for complex batch files. When the entire batch file is through running, DOS exits the command processor and returns to the original batch file.

For Related Information

- "Controlling the Boot Process," p. 38
- "Loading a Secondary Command Processor," p. 325

Summary

Batch files and macros can make your computer do the hard work for you, replacing repetitive typing with commands that execute automatically. As you work with batch files and macros, remember the following key points:

- You must give batch files the .BAT extension.
- You invoke batch files by typing the name of the batch file (without the extension) and pressing Enter. You can specify an optional drive name and path name before the batch file name.
- You can include in a batch file any command that you can type at the DOS prompt.
- Each word (or set of characters) in a command separated by a delimiter is a parameter. When you use a batch file, DOS substitutes the appropriate parameters for the variable markers (%0 through %9) in the file.
- You can use the ECHO command to turn on or off the display of DOS commands being executed by the batch file.
- The @ character suppresses the display of a single line from a batch file.
- The PAUSE command causes the batch file to suspend execution and then displays a message on-screen.
- Use the REM command to leave comments and reminders in your batch file; the comments do not appear on-screen when ECHO is off.
- You can use the GOTO command to change how a batch file executes.
- IF tests for a given condition.
- CHOICE enables you to prompt for input and create menus.
- FOR..IN..DO can repeat a batch file command for one or more files or commands.
- SHIFT moves command parameters to the left.
- COMMAND /C and CALL invoke a second batch file and then return control of the computer to the first batch file.

Chapter 17

Mastering Doskey and Macros

In Chapter 16, you learned how you can use batch files to simplify many of the repetitive tasks you perform with DOS. In addition to batch files, you can use the Doskey program to make the command line more efficient. Doskey remembers the commands you type at the DOS prompt, enabling you to use these commands again without retyping them. Doskey also enables you to store a series of commands in memory and assign them to a new command name called a *macro*. You can execute the stored commands simply by typing the name of the macro. This chapter teaches you how to use these Doskey features.

Using Doskey

Doskey is a program that enables you to edit and reuse DOS commands without retyping them. The program also enables you to create new commands, referred to as *macros*, that can take the place of several DOS commands. Yet Doskey occupies only about 4K of memory. The following sections explain how to load Doskey into your computer's memory and how to use the program's capabilities.

Loading Doskey

Doskey is a memory-resident program that was first available in DOS 5.0. This program enables you to easily edit what you enter at the DOS prompt. Doskey also maintains a running history of the commands you have entered. Doskey then enables you to reuse those commands without retyping them.

Before you can use Doskey's features, you must load the program into memory. To load Doskey, enter the following command at the DOS prompt:

```
DOSKEY
```

A message appears on-screen, letting you know that Doskey is installed. After this message appears, all Doskey features are available.

The most convenient way to load Doskey is to include a command in your AUTOEXEC.BAT file to start the program. In this way, Doskey loads every time you start your computer.

Tip
See Chapter 18, "Configuring Your Computer," for instructions on loading Doskey into upper memory blocks. This technique, which makes Doskey available without the use of any conventional memory, is available only on 386- or 486-based systems.

As is true of most DOS commands, Doskey has several available switches. The full syntax of the command to install Doskey is as follows:

```
DOSKEY /REINSTALL /BUFSIZE=size /MACROS /HISTORY /INSERT /OVERSTRIKE
```

Following are explanations of the components of this command:

- /REINSTALL installs another copy of Doskey and clears the command-history buffer. This command does not, however, remove existing copies of Doskey that already are in memory.
- /BUFSIZE sets the size of the command buffer. The size parameter represents the number of bytes that the buffer occupies in memory. The default size is 512 bytes; the minimum size is 256 bytes.
- /MACROS displays a list of the currently defined Doskey macros.
- /HISTORY displays the contents of the command-history buffer.
- /INSERT instructs DOS to insert new text into the existing text at the cursor position. (You cannot use this switch with /OVERSTRIKE.)
- /OVERSTRIKE, the default condition, instructs DOS to insert new text in place of existing text at the cursor position. (You cannot use this switch with /INSERT.)

Editing the Command Line

Even before you load Doskey, DOS provides some command-line editing capability. Table 17.1 lists the normal DOS command-line editing keys, which are available if Doskey is not memory-resident.

Table 17.1 DOS Command-Line Editing Keys

Key	Action
Tab	Moves the cursor to the following tab stop
Esc	Cancels the current line and does not change the buffer
Ins	Enables you to insert characters into the preceding command line
Del	Deletes a character from the preceding command line
F1 or right arrow	Copies one character from the preceding command line
F2	Copies all characters from the preceding command line up to, but not including, the next character you type
F3	Copies all remaining characters from the preceding command line
F4	Deletes all characters from the preceding command line up to, but not including, the next character typed (opposite of F2)
F5	Moves the current line into the buffer but prevents DOS from executing the line
F6	Produces an end-of-file marker (^Z) when you copy from the console to a disk file

A primary purpose of Doskey is to facilitate editing of DOS commands. If you are a typical PC user, you issue the same or similar commands frequently, and you don't always type each command correctly the first time. Doskey can save you typing by enabling you to edit commands without typing them from scratch every time you notice an error.

Suppose that you want to see a directory listing of all files with the .WQ1 extension in the \SPREADSH\QPRO2DAT directory in drive C. In haste, however, you type the DIR command as follows:

```
DOR C:\SPREADSH\QPRO2DAT\*.WQ1
```

Before you press Enter, you realize that you mistyped the DIR command, but you don't want to retype it. When Doskey is loaded, you can use the following procedure to correct the mistake:

1. Press the Home key to move the cursor to the left end of the command line.
2. Use the right-arrow key to move the cursor to the `O` in the word `DOR`.
3. Type **I** to correct the error.
4. Press Enter.

DOS displays the directory listing as you requested.

The keys listed in table 17.2 supplement the normal Doskey command-line editing keys.

Table 17.2 Additional Doskey Command-Line Editing Keys

Key	Action
Left arrow	Moves the cursor one character to the left
Right arrow	Moves the cursor one character to the right
Backspace	Moves the cursor one character to the left; erases character to the left
Ctrl-left arrow	Moves the cursor one word to the left
Ctrl-right arrow	Moves the cursor one word to the right
Ins	Toggles between Replace mode (the default) and Insert mode
Home	Moves the cursor to the left end of the command line
End	Moves the cursor to the space after the last character in the command line
Esc	Erases the command line

Reusing Commands

In addition to enhancing DOS's command-line editing capabilities, Doskey adds a capability that was not previously available in DOS: you can redisplay a command that you issued earlier during the current DOS session. You then can execute the command without changing it, or you can use the DOS and Doskey editing keys to make modifications before executing the command.

After you load Doskey into memory, the program maintains a buffer in memory that contains a history of DOS commands issued at the command prompt during the current DOS session. Doskey enables you to reuse the commands in this command-history buffer.

Suppose that earlier during the current DOS session, you issued the following COPY command:

```
COPY C:\DATABASE\FOXPRO\MAIL.DBF C:\WORD_PRO\WP
```

Now you want to issue the following similar command without retyping the entire command:

```
COPY C:\DATABASE\DBASE\MAIL.DBF C:\WORD_PRO\WP
```

To edit the earlier command, follow these steps:

1. Press the up-arrow key repeatedly until the original COPY command appears on the command line.
2. Use the DOS and Doskey editing keys to change the command.
3. Press Enter.

In addition to the up-arrow key, Doskey provides the keys listed in table 17.3 for use in retrieving commands from the command-history buffer.

Table 17.3 Doskey Command-History Buffer Keys

Key	Action
Up arrow	Displays the preceding DOS command
Down arrow	Displays the DOS command issued after the one currently displayed, or displays a blank line when you are at the end of the list
Alt-F7	Clears the command-history buffer
Alt-F10	Clears all macro definitions
F7	Displays the contents of the command-history buffer in a numbered list
F8	Searches for the command that most closely matches the characters typed at the command line

(continues)

Table 17.3 Continued

Key	Action
F9	Prompts for a line number, where line number refers to the number displayed next to a command in the command-history listing generated by pressing F7 (Type the number to display the corresponding command)
PgDn	Displays the last command stored in the Doskey command buffer
PgUp	Displays the earliest command issued that still is stored in the Doskey command buffer

To view the entire list of commands currently stored in the command-history buffer, press F7. Doskey lists all commands contained in the buffer, one on each line, with a number at the left end of each line. The oldest command—the command issued earliest in the current DOS session—is number 1. Subsequent commands are listed in the order in which you issued them.

Doskey provides another way for you to see the entire list of commands in the command-history buffer. Type the following command, and then press Enter:

```
DOSKEY /HISTORY
```

Doskey generates the same list of commands as the F7 command, but without line numbers.

To create a batch file that contains all the commands in the current command-history buffer, use the following command syntax:

```
DOSKEY /HISTORY > filename.BAT
```

Substitute for *filename* the name that you want to give the batch file. After you issue this command, the new batch file contains all the commands from the command-history buffer, including the command that created the batch file itself. Use the DOS Editor, Edlin, or some other text editor to delete the last command and any other commands you don't want to include in the batch file.

You can use the up-arrow key to display previously issued commands. Each time you press the up-arrow key, Doskey displays the preceding command. After you display one or more previous commands by pressing the up-arrow key, you can use the down-arrow key to move back down through the commands to the most recent command. Sometimes, however, selecting a command from the list generated by pressing F7 is easier. To use this method, press F9. Doskey displays the following message:

```
Line number:
```

Type the number that corresponds to the desired command in the list of commands generated by pressing F7. Doskey displays the selected command in the command line for you to edit or execute.

When you want to move quickly to the first command in the buffer, press PgUp. To go to the last command in the buffer, press PgDn.

If you want to clear the command-history buffer, press Alt-F7. Doskey abandons the contents of the command-history buffer.

Doskey also can help you locate a command quickly. Type the first several characters of the command you need to find, and then press F8. Suppose that you want to locate the following command:

```
COPY C:\DATABASE\FOXPRO\MAIL.DBF C:\WORD_PRO\WP
```

Type COPY and press F8. Each time you press F8, Doskey shows you the next command that contains the COPY command. When the desired command is displayed, you easily can edit and reuse the command with minimal typing.

Creating and Using Macros

In addition to providing command-line editing capabilities and the command-history buffer, Doskey enables you to create your own DOS commands, referred to as macros. A Doskey macro is similar to a batch file, but is contained in memory rather than on disk. Each macro can contain one or more DOS commands, up to a maximum of 127 characters.

Doskey macros are similar to batch files in the following ways:

- Macros can contain multiple DOS commands.
- You invoke macros by typing a name at the DOS prompt.
- Macros can use replaceable parameters.

Macros differ from batch files in the following ways:

- Macros are stored in memory (RAM); batch files are stored on disk.
- Macros are limited to 127 characters; batch files have unlimited maximum length.
- Ctrl-C or Ctrl-Break stops a single command in a Doskey macro; Ctrl-C or Ctrl-Break stops an entire batch file.
- The GOTO command is not available in macros.
- One macro cannot call another macro, and you cannot call a macro from within a batch file.
- Macros can define environment variables but cannot use them.

The following sections explain how to create and run Doskey macros.

Creating Macros

Doskey enables you to create macros at the command line or through a batch file. The syntax for creating a macro is as follows:

```
DOSKEY macroname=command(s)
```

The *macroname* parameter is the name that you want to give the macro. Use any keyboard characters in the name except <, >, ¦, or =. Do not include a space in the macro name; use an underscore or hyphen instead if you want the macro name to have the appearance of two words.

The *command* parameter can include any number of DOS commands, subject to the following rules:

- The entire command cannot exceed 127 characters (the DOS command-line limit).
- Each pair of commands must be separated by the characters $t.
- Instead of using the redirection and piping operators <, >, and ¦, use $l, $g, and $b, respectively.
- The ECHO OFF command is not effective in macros. Commands always appear on-screen.

Caution

If you use a macro name that is the same as an existing DOS command, you effectively replace the DOS command with the macro. Make sure you want to do this before you actually make the macro definition. To regain use of the original DOS command, see the section later in this chapter entitled "Deleting Macros."

There are several special characters you can use when defining your macros. These are shown in Table 17.4.

Table 17.4 Special Characters for Use in Doskey Macros

Character	Meaning
$G or $g	Redirects output; used in place of the greater-than sign (>)
GG or gg	Redirects and appends output; used in place of the double greater-than sign (>>)
$L or $l	Redirects input; used in place of the less-than sign (<)
$B or $b	Uses output from one command as input to another; used in place of the vertical bar (¦)
$T or $t	Used to separate commands on the Doskey command line
$$	The dollar sign character
$1 through $9	Individual replaceable parameters
$*	All parameters

Notice that when you want to use replaceable parameters in a macro, you use the codes $1 through $9 rather than %1 through %9. Suppose, for example, that you often use the REPLACE command to keep current copies of particular subdirectory files on floppy disks so that you can take the files with you. To do this, however, you must issue the REPLACE command twice for each subdirectory you want to keep current. An easier method is to create the following macro called UPD:

```
DOSKEY UPD=REPLACE \C:$1\$2 A:\$1 /U $T REPLACE C:\$1\$2 A:\$1 /A
```

In this example, you also see how the $T (or $t) special characters are used to separate commands on the command line.

Doskey has a special type of replaceable parameter that is not available in batch files. The characters $* represent not just one parameter, but all the characters you type in the command line to the right of the macro name. This type of replaceable parameter is useful when you don't know ahead of time how many parameters or switches you might type when you execute the macro.

For example, suppose that you want to create a macro to help you format floppy disks in drive A, a 3 1/2-inch, high-density drive. You want to be able to type FA 720 to format a 720K disk and FA 1.44 to format a 1.44M disk. Occasionally, however, you may want to use one or more of FORMAT's switches, such as the /S switch to create a system disk, the /Q Quick Format switch, or the /U unconditional format switch. To create the FA macro, you type the following command:

```
DOSKEY FA=FORMAT A: /F:$*
```

To confirm that Doskey has stored the macros you defined, you type the following command and then press Enter:

```
DOSKEY /MACROS
```

Doskey lists all macros currently stored in the Doskey macro buffer. Assuming you defined the UPD and FA macros, the preceding command displays the following lines:

```
UPD=REPLACE \C:$1\$2 A:\$1 /U $T REPLACE C:\$1\$2 A:\$1 /A
FA=FORMAT A: /F:$*
```

You easily can save a copy of the entire contents of the macro buffer by using redirection. To create a file named MACROS.BAT that contains all the current macros, you type the following command and press Enter:

```
DOSKEY /MACROS > MACROS.BAT
```

If you want to use this batch file later to re-create the macros during a future session, edit the file, adding DOSKEY to the beginning of each line.

Because Doskey macros reside in memory rather than on disk, all macros are erased when you turn off or reboot the computer. One disadvantage of using Doskey macros is that you need to reenter commonly used macros each time you turn on your computer. You can overcome this drawback, however, by using AUTOEXEC.BAT to define the macros that you use most often. To make the UPD and FA macros routinely available, for example, include the following commands in AUTOEXEC.BAT:

```
DOSKEY UPD=REPLACE \C:$1\$2 A:\$1 /U $T REPLACE C:\$1\$2 A:\$1 /A
DOSKEY FA=FORMAT A: /F:$*
```

Every time you turn on or reboot your computer, the preceding commands create the UPD and FA macros in the Doskey macro buffer.

Note

The first DOSKEY command in AUTOEXEC.BAT loads the program as memory-resident, even if the command also is defining a macro.

Running Macros

Using a Doskey macro is as easy as using any other DOS command. Simply type the macro name at the command line, and then press Enter. If the macro has any replaceable parameters, include appropriate values in the command line. For instance, suppose that you want to use the UPD macro to maintain current copies of files. Simply type the following:

```
UPD dirname filespec
```

As with a batch file, *dirname* is the first replaceable parameter, $1, and *filespec* is the second, $2. To keep current all files in C:\PROJECT1, you type the following at the DOS prompt:

```
UPD PROJECT1 *.*
```

Perhaps you want to use the FA macro created in the preceding section to format a 1.44M disk. You want to use Quick Format, make this disk bootable, and assign the volume label BOOT_DISK. You type the following command at the DOS prompt, and then press Enter:

```
FA 1.44 /Q /S /V:BOOT_DISK
```

DOS first displays the command in the following format:

```
FORMAT A: /F:1.44 /Q /S /V:BOOT_DISK
```

Then DOS prompts you as follows:

```
Insert new diskette for drive A:
and press ENTER when ready_
```

Press Enter to proceed with the formatting operation. DOS displays messages indicating the progress and successful completion of the procedure. Finally, DOS displays the following message:

```
QuickFormat another (Y/N)?
```

Press **Y** if you want to use the same switch settings to format another disk, or press **N** to return to the DOS prompt.

Deleting Macros

You can remove a macro from memory simply by putting nothing to the right of the equal sign when you define a macro. For instance, assume that you no longer needed the FA macro defined earlier. To remove it from memory (thereby freeing more space for other macros), you would type the following at the DOS prompt:

```
DOSKEY FA=
```

Summary

Doskey and macros can make your computer do the hard work for you, replacing repetitive typing with commands that execute automatically. As you work with Doskey, remember the following key points:

- Doskey enables you to redisplay a command that you issued earlier during the current DOS session.
- Doskey macros are stored in memory (RAM).
- Macros can contain multiple DOS commands, but are limited to 127 characters.
- The GOTO command is not available in macros.

Chapter 18

Configuring Your Computer

Computers on the market today have many similarities—they are based on the same family of computer chips, and they have similar components, such as memory, hard disks, and power supplies. Still, the differences between various makes and models of personal computers are greater today than ever before. DOS gives you the tools to fine-tune the operation of every element of your computer system, an exercise often called *configuring* your system. You can adjust a bewildering number of settings; how you manipulate these settings greatly affects how efficiently your PC works. Sadly, the people who do not understand how to configure their PCs greatly outnumber the people who do. By reading this chapter, you can become one who understands how to configure a computer.

Fortunately, the folks at Microsoft realize that configuring a modern PC can be challenging for most users, and perhaps the most important tool that Microsoft includes with DOS is MemMaker, a tool that performs the hardest part of the configuration automatically. If you want to call yourself a PC guru, you should understand the configuration process; but if you're a novice user, the worst part of working with MS-DOS just disappeared.

The default configuration of DOS, which may be adequate for many users, is designed as a "lowest common denominator," intended to work with the greatest number of systems. As PC technology advances, DOS also must allow users of the most up-to-date systems to take full advantage of their computers' most powerful features. This chapter describes how to use DOS to create the optimum configuration for your computer system, whether your system is a plain-vanilla PC or a banana split with all the toppings.

In this chapter, you learn how to use the files CONFIG.SYS and AUTOEXEC.BAT to configure your system. This chapter gives you an overview of how to customize your system configuration. The remainder of the chapter explains how to optimize your system's memory resources, enhance disk performance, and use several other configuration commands and techniques. After you master the information presented in this chapter, you can fine-tune your PC so that it provides all the power you expected when you bought it.

Getting the Most from Your Computer Resources

Whether you use your own computer or a computer owned by your employer, someone has invested a significant sum of money in the system. This chapter helps you discover how to configure your computer to operate most efficiently—how to get the "most bang for the buck." You generally can improve the performance of software running on your PC in two ways: you can increase the amount of memory available to the software, and you can increase the speed at which your system or its components operate. You can tackle these efficiency-oriented goals in two general ways:

- Add or replace hardware
- Use software to attain an optimal configuration for your existing hardware resources

DOS fits into the software category. This chapter teaches you how to use DOS to increase the amount of memory available to applications. The chapter also explains how to use special device drivers and utility programs to enhance the performance of your hard disk, which in turn enhances software performance.

Understanding Device Drivers

MS-DOS provides certain features that every DOS user needs. Regardless of the type of computer you use or the software you run, you must be able to create directories, access files, and print to your printer. Many other features, however, may not be important to you, depending on the type of computer you have and how you use it. For example, DOS can work with a mouse, but this capability is not important to you if you don't own a mouse. If you plan to use a mouse with DOS, DOS must load the mouse-handling functions when your computer boots. If you don't plan to use a mouse, loading the mouse-handling functions ties up valuable memory, a sacrifice you don't want to make.

In order to give you the flexibility of using only the parts of DOS that you need, DOS consists of a base portion (which contains the features that everybody needs) and a series of what you might think of as "plug-in modules" (pieces of programs that give DOS the instructions it needs to perform certain tasks). Because you can decide which of the optional modules to use, you don't waste memory-loading features you don't need.

These plug-in modules are called *device drivers* because they generally give DOS the information needed to access various types of hardware devices. In addition to the device drivers that come with DOS, some add-on hardware comes with a device driver that enables your system to recognize and use the hardware. If, for example, you buy a mouse to use with your computer, you also must load the appropriate device driver so that DOS knows how to control the mouse.

Most device drivers are loaded in your CONFIG.SYS file. One of the most important tasks this file performs is to tell DOS which device drivers to load when the computer boots. The DEVICE command tells DOS to load a device driver and uses the following syntax:

```
DEVICE = filespec /switches
```

where *filespec* is the complete file name (and optional disk and path) for the device driver file, and */switches* are any switches the device driver software needs.

If you buy a Microsoft mouse, for example, you also get a device driver called MOUSE.SYS that tells DOS how to use the mouse. If you place MOUSE.SYS in the root directory of your C drive, you can load MOUSE.SYS by adding the following command to CONFIG.SYS:

```
DEVICE = C:\MOUSE.SYS
```

(The spaces around the equal sign in this syntax are optional.)

You can load as many device drivers as you need, but you must use a separate DEVICE command for each driver you install.

Most users create a special subdirectory called \DRIVERS or \SYS and put the driver files in this directory so that they are out of the way of daily files. If you put the driver files in a separate subdirectory, you must specify the path name as part of the name of the device driver, as shown in the following examples:

```
DEVICE = C:\DRIVERS\MOUSE.SYS
```

or

```
DEVICE = C:\SYS\MOUSE.SYS
```

Table 18.1 lists the device driver files included with DOS 6.2.

Table 18.1 DOS 6.2 Device Drivers

Device Driver	Description
ANSI.SYS	Enables control of display by using ANSI control sequences
CHKSTATE.SYS	Used by MemMaker when optimizing your system
DBLSPACE.BIN	Enables disk compression, greatly increasing the amount of data you can store on your hard disk. The DBLSPACE.SYS file loads this driver in your CONFIG.SYS file.
DISPLAY.SYS	Provides support for code-page switching to the screen
DMDRVR.BIN	Provides support for Ontrack Disk Manager
DRIVER.SYS	Sets parameters for physical and logical disk drives
EGA.SYS	Saves and restores an EGA screen when using DOSSHELL and the task swapper
EMM386.EXE	Uses XMS memory in an 80386 or 80486 computer to emulate EMS memory and provide upper memory blocks
HIMEM.SYS	Manages extended memory
INTERLNK.EXE	Interlnk network client control program and device driver
MONOUMB.386	Device driver used by Windows which allows EMM386 access to the monochrome video region, treating it as a UMB area

Device Driver	Description
MOUSE.COM	Support for a Microsoft mouse
POWER.EXE	Support for computers utilizing APM (advanced power management) hardware
PRINTER.SYS	Support for international characters and code page switching on certain printers
RAMDRIVE.SYS	Uses a portion of random-access memory (RAM) to simulate a hard disk—often called a RAM disk
SETVER.EXE	Establishes a version table that lists the version number DOS reports to named programs
SMARTDRV.EXE	Uses extended or expanded memory to buffer disk reads
SSTOR.SYS	Support for SpeedStor hard disk compression
VFINTD.386	Used by Windows to give MWBACKUP access to tape drives

The most commonly used device drivers are discussed in this chapter. Refer to the Command Reference for the syntax of the drivers not covered here.

Note

When you install DOS, you may notice that DOS installs two files that appear to be device drivers because they end in the .SYS extension: COUNTRY.SYS and KEYBOARD.SYS. Despite their extension, these files are not device drivers; they are used internally by other DOS commands, and you cannot use them in your CONFIG.SYS file.

For Related Information

■ "CONFIG.SYS" p. 33

Optimizing Your Computer's Memory

In Chapter 1, "DOS and the Personal Computer," you learned about memory and how it relates to your PC. With that understanding in mind, you are ready to learn how you can make the most of your PC's memory.

Using Extended Memory and HIMEM.SYS

Most computers today are sold with at least some extended memory. The most significant feature offered by DOS, in terms of optimizing the use of your computer, is the capability to load most of the operating system software into extended memory. By doing this, DOS provides more conventional memory for applications, ultimately improving the performance of your system.

Understanding HIMEM.SYS. Before DOS or applications software can use extended memory, you must add to your CONFIG.SYS file a command to load an extended memory manager—a driver that provides a standard way for applications to address extended memory so that no two programs use the same portion of extended memory at the same time. DOS 4.0 and later versions include the extended memory manager HIMEM.SYS.

HIMEM.SYS manages memory according to the rules set out in the Extended Memory Specification (XMS) Version 2.0. According to this specification, three areas of memory above the conventional 640K barrier can be made available for programs to use:

- *Upper memory area (UMA).* This consists of the 384K of memory above 640K up to 1M and is divided into many different sized blocks, called upper memory blocks (UMBs).
- *High memory area (HMA).* This is a single block of memory essentially consisting of the first 64K of extended memory. However, the HMA slightly overlaps the upper memory area—the last 16 bytes of the upper memory area are the first 16 bytes of the high memory area. (Most people are not aware of this slight overlap, and it can be a good way to win bar bets.)
- *Extended memory blocks (XMS memory).* This portion of memory includes all memory above 1,024K. When extended memory is managed by an extended memory manager, you refer to the memory as XMS memory.

Note

The terms used to describe DOS memory can be maddening. Try not to confuse high memory with upper memory.

When used on an 80286, 80386, or 80486 PC, HIMEM.SYS provides HMA and XMS memory to programs that "know" how to use it. To access upper memory, however, the PC must contain an 80386 or 80486 CPU, and you must include one of the following device driver commands in CONFIG.SYS after HIMEM.SYS is loaded:

```
DEVICE=EMM386.EXE RAM
```

or

```
DEVICE=EMM386.EXE NOEMS
```

Refer to the next section for a full discussion of EMM386.EXE.

Invoking HIMEM.SYS. The syntax for using HIMEM.SYS is shown in the following:

```
DEVICE=d:path\HIMEM.SYS /A20CONTROL:ON¦OFF /NUMHANDLES=n /EISA
   /HMAMIN=m/INT15=xxxx /MACHINE:xx /SHADOWRAM:ON¦OFF
   /CPUCLOCK:ON¦OFF /QUIET
```

d: is the disk drive where the HIMEM.SYS resides, and *path* is the directory containing the device driver file. If HIMEM.SYS is contained in the \DOS directory on your C drive, for example, you include the following command in CONFIG.SYS:

```
DEVICE=C:\DOS\HIMEM.SYS
```

In most cases, you need only this command to activate the extended memory manager. In special cases, however, you may need to use one of the available switches described in the following paragraphs. The next section continues the discussion of loading DOS into upper memory.

According to the XMS specification, only one program at a time can use the high memory area. The switch /HMAMIN=*n* sets the minimum amount of memory that must be requested by an application before the application is permitted to use HMA. If you load DOS into HMA, you can omit this switch, as explained in the section "Loading DOS into High Memory" later in this chapter.

When the extended memory manager assigns memory to a particular program, the extended memory manager assigns one or more extended memory block handles to the program. The /NUMHANDLES=*n* switch indicates the maximum number of handles available. The number *n* must be from 1 through 128. The default is 32 handles, usually a sufficient number. Each reserved handle requires an additional 6 bytes of memory. Unless you are running software that complains about not having enough extended memory handles, you probably do not need this option.

Most current versions of commercial software support the XMS specification for addressing extended memory. Some older versions of programs, however, use a different method of addressing extended memory, known as the Interrupt 15h (INT15h) interface. If you work with software that uses the INT15h interface and you want to load DOS into HMA, add the /INT15=*xxxx* switch. The number *xxxx* indicates the amount of extended memory you want HIMEM.SYS to assign to the INT15h interface. This number must be from 64 to 65,535 (kilobytes), and the default is 0. If you assign some of your extended memory to the Int15 interface, that memory is not available to programs that expect the XMS interface.

Internally, DOS uses a wire called the A20 memory address line to access the high memory area. Explaining what the A20 address line is and how DOS uses it is not important here, but not all brands of PCs handle the A20 line in the same way. Normally, HIMEM.SYS can detect how your computer uses its A20 line, but if it is incorrect, HIMEM.SYS displays the following error message:

```
Unable to control A20
```

If you see this message, use the /MACHINE:*xx* switch in the HIMEM.SYS command to specify which type of A20 handler your machine uses. Insert for *xx* in the /MACHINE switch the code that matches your computer. You can find the text codes in the Code column and the number codes in the Number column in table 18.2. If you see the error message but your computer is not listed in table 18.2, try the switch /MACHINE:1.

Table 18.2 A20 Handler Codes

Code	Number	Computer
at	1	IBM PC/AT
ps2	2	IBM PS/2
pt1cascade	3	Phoenix Cascade BIOS
hpvectra	4	HP Vectra (A and A+)

Code	Number	Computer
att6300plus	5	AT&T 6300 Plus
acer1100	6	Acer 1100
toshiba	7	Toshiba 1600 and 1200XE
wyse	8	Wyse 12.5 MHz 286
tulip	9	Tulip SX
zenith	10	Zenith ZBIOS
at1	11	IBM PC/AT (alternative delay)
at2	12	IBM PC/AT (alternative delay)
css	12	CSS Labs
at3	13	IBM PC/AT (alternative delay)
philips	13	Philips
fasthp	14	HP Vectra
IBM 7552	15	IBM 7552 Industrial Computer
Bull Mioral	16	Bull Mioral 60
DELL	17	DELL XBios

Before DEVICE=HIMEM.SYS in CONFIG.SYS, you may have listed a device driver that also uses the A20 line. By default, HIMEM.SYS takes control of A20 even though the line is turned on when HIMEM.SYS loads. HIMEM.SYS warns you when this condition occurs by displaying the following message:

```
Warning: The A20 Line was already enabled!
```

Determine whether you really intend to have both drivers installed at one time. If so, you can prevent HIMEM.SYS from taking control of A20 by adding the switch /A20CONTROL:OFF (the default setting is /A20CONTROL:ON).

All PCs store some of their basic operating instructions in read-only memory (ROM); however, computers usually cannot access instructions from ROM as fast as they can access instructions from RAM. If you have plenty of memory and an 80386 (or better) computer, you usually can increase the performance of your computer by asking the computer to copy the instructions from ROM into an upper memory block (which is RAM). This technique is known as shadow RAM.

Shadow RAM uses some of your upper memory blocks. If you prefer to increase the amount of upper memory available for device drivers and memory-resident programs, use the /SHADOWRAM:OFF switch. As HIMEM.SYS loads, the following message appears:

```
Shadow RAM disabled.
```

In some cases, DOS cannot turn off shadow RAM. Instead, DOS displays a message telling you that Shadow RAM is in use and cannot be disabled. (Check your hardware documentation for other methods of disabling shadow RAM.)

The /CPUCLOCK:ON switch ensures that HIMEM.SYS does not slow your computer's clock speed, the speed at which your computer processes instructions. (Any change in clock speed does not affect your computer's real-time clock, which keeps time of day.) On the front panel of many PCs is an LED or other indicator that indicates the current clock speed. To prevent the clock speed from slowing, add the /CPUCLOCK:ON switch to the DEVICE=HIMEM.SYS command in CONFIG.SYS.

If you are using a machine that uses an EISA (Extended Industry Standard Architecture) bus with more than 16M of memory, HIMEM does not normally allocate all the extended memory. Use the /EISA switch to tell HIMEM to automatically allocate all available extended memory.

Note

EISA buses are found mostly on high-end systems and cost several hundred dollars more than the older and more common ISA bus systems. If you don't know which bus you have, it's probably ISA.

When HIMEM.SYS loads, it usually prints status messages. If you want HIMEM.SYS to load without the usual status messages, add the /QUIET switch.

Loading DOS into High Memory

DOS enables you to load most of the operating system into an area of extended memory known as the *high memory area* (HMA), the first 64K of extended memory (except the first 16 bytes, which overlap the upper memory area). After the device driver HIMEM.SYS is loaded into the computer's memory, the command DOS=HIGH in CONFIG.SYS loads DOS into high memory.

The next time you boot the computer, DOS uses about 14K of space in conventional memory and loads the remainder of the operating system into the HMA. If, however, you don't use this command in CONFIG.SYS or don't have extended memory installed in your computer, DOS occupies more than 62K of memory. By loading the operating system into high memory, DOS 6.2 can free about 47K of conventional memory.

Using Expanded Memory and EMM386.EXE

Because expanded memory was introduced before extended memory, many PC applications were written to take advantage of expanded memory, not extended memory. Today, however, extended memory is far less expensive and much more common. The DOS device driver EMM386.EXE enables applications to use extended memory as though it were expanded memory, freeing you from the need for the special memory boards and device drivers that expanded memory requires. Thus EMM386.EXE emulates expanded memory by using extended memory.

Note

The device driver HIMEM.SYS, discussed earlier, must be loaded before EMM386.EXE. HIMEM.SYS makes extended memory available, and EMM386.EXE enables you to use some or all extended memory as though it were expanded memory. Do not use EMM386.EXE if you are using another driver from a third-party software vendor as an expanded memory manager.

Some applications today can use either expanded memory or extended memory by accessing whichever is available. If you have a choice, use extended memory, which is faster.

In addition to its role as an expanded memory emulator, EMM386.EXE also is a UMB provider, working with HIMEM.SYS to provide upper memory blocks (UMBs) into which you can load device drivers and memory-resident programs. See the next section, "Loading Device Drivers and TSRs into Upper Memory," for further discussion of providing UMBs.

The syntax of the command for EMM386.EXE, used as a device driver, is shown in the following:

```
DEVICE=EMM386.EXE ON¦OFF¦AUTO memory W=ON¦OFF
   Mx¦FRAME=address /Pmmmm Pn=address X=mmmm-nnn
   I=mmmm-nnn B=address L=minxms A=altregs H=handles
   D=nnn RAM NOEMS MIN=n /VERBOSE ROM=mmmm-nnnn NOVCPI
   WIN=mmmm-nnnn NOMOVEXBDA NOHIGHSCAN ALTBOOT NOHI
```

In most cases, one of the following commands is sufficient:

```
DEVICE=EMM386.EXE RAM
```

or

```
DEVICE=EMM386.EXE NOEMS
```

The first command loads the expanded memory emulator and allocates 256K of extended memory to be used as expanded memory. The RAM switch enables upper memory. The second command also enables upper memory but tells EMM386 not to allocate extended memory for use as expanded memory.

Sometimes, you may need the remaining switches for the EMM386.EXE device driver to customize your computer for use with particularly demanding software or hardware. You can specify ON, OFF, or AUTO in the EMM386.EXE device driver command to indicate whether your computer starts in the EMM386.EXE active, inactive, or automatic mode, respectively. By default, the device driver is active, and EMM386.EXE makes extended memory available. However, some applications programs may not run properly when EMM386.EXE is active because EMM386.EXE places the computer in a mode known as *Virtual 8086 mode*. When you use EMM386.EXE as a device driver, the driver loads in memory and remains active (ON) unless you specify otherwise with the OFF switch.

The OFF switch starts the computer with EMM386.EXE loaded in memory but inactive. The XMS memory allocated as EMS memory is unavailable for any purpose. You can activate the driver with the following command at the DOS command prompt:

```
EMM386 ON
```

The OFF switch is not compatible, however, with the RAM or NOEMS switches, discussed later in this section.

Use AUTO if you want EMM386.EXE to activate only when an application requests EMS memory. This setting provides maximum compatibility with software that may not work properly in Virtual 8086 mode. Like the OFF switch, AUTO is not compatible with the RAM or NOEMS switches.

Note

Even though EMM386.EXE activates when an applications program requests EMS memory, the driver does not automatically deactivate when the applications program terminates. To turn off the driver, you must issue the following command at the command prompt:

```
EMM386 OFF
```

The *memory* parameter enables you to specify the amount of XMS memory you want EMM386.EXE to allocate as EMS memory. Type the number of kilobytes in the range 16 through 32,768. EMM386.EXE rounds any number you type down to the nearest multiple of 16. All unallocated memory remains available as XMS memory. The default EMS memory allocated is 256K.

As a general rule, allocate only as much EMS memory as is required by your applications programs. Any memory allocated as EMS memory is no longer available as XMS memory. Some of the most powerful applications programs currently available, such as Microsoft Windows 3.1, work best with the maximum amount of XMS memory available. If none of your applications need expanded memory, use the NOEMS option so that no memory is allocated as expanded memory.

Use the L=*minxms* switch, in which *minxms* is the number of kilobytes, to indicate the minimum XMS memory that EMM386.EXE should allocate. This parameter overrides the *memory* parameter.

If you installed a Weitek math coprocessor chip—a special computer chip that improves the performance of computation-intensive software, such as computer-aided design (CAD) software—use the W=ON switch. By default, the device driver does not support this type of coprocessor. You also can turn on or off support for the Weitek coprocessor with one of the following commands at the DOS prompt:

```
EMM386 W=ON
```

or

```
EMM386 W=OFF
```

In some circumstances, you may want to use upper memory for device drivers and memory-resident programs, but you don't need EMS memory. Use the NOEMS switch with the EMM386.EXE driver to free the maximum amount of upper memory and to provide no EMS memory. For example, you may intend to run Windows 3.1 on your computer. Because Windows can use all your XMS memory, this software doesn't need EMS memory.

The /VERBOSE switch causes EMM386 to print status and error messages when it loads. Normally EMM386 suppresses these messages. You can abbreviate /VERBOSE as /V.

EMM386 scans the upper memory area (UMA) for all available free memory. Unusual architectures may confuse EMM386, causing trouble when your computer boots or while you use the computer. The NOHIGHSCAN parameter limits EMM386's scanning of the UMA. If you experience problems when you use EMM386, adding the NOHIGHSCAN parameter may solve the problem.

EMM386 loads part of itself into the upper memory area. If one of your programs needs extra upper memory blocks, and you're willing to give up some of your conventional memory, the NOHI parameter causes EMM386 to load all of itself into conventional memory, and does not use any UMA.

The remaining switches available for use with EMM386.EXE are highly technical and beyond the scope of this book. Refer to your DOS User's Guide or the Technical Reference manual for more information.

Loading Device Drivers and TSRs into Upper Memory

In addition to allowing you to run DOS in high memory, DOS provides the capability of loading memory-resident programs and device drivers into upper memory blocks, freeing more conventional memory for other applications programs. DOS can access this area of memory in 80386 and 80486 PCs (including SXs) that have 1M or more of memory.

To load device drivers or memory-resident programs, also called terminate-and-stay-resident (TSR) programs, into upper memory, the following conditions must be met:

- Your computer has an 80386 or 80486 CPU.
- HIMEM.SYS is loaded as a device driver.
- EMM386.EXE is loaded as a device driver with the RAM or NOEMS switch.
- The command DOS=UMB appears in the CONFIG.SYS file.

If you also want to use the command DOS=HIGH to load DOS into high memory, you can combine the two commands as shown in the following:

```
DOS=HIGH, UMB
```

You can load two types of programs into upper memory: device drivers and memory-resident programs (TSRs). You already know that device drivers normally are loaded using the DEVICE command. When you want to load a device driver into upper memory, however, use the DEVICEHIGH command. The syntax for this configuration command is shown in the following:

```
DEVICEHIGH=filename.ext /switches
```

Note

The switches in the syntax for the preceding command are any switches you use for the file that you are loading, not for the DEVICEHIGH command itself.

To load into upper memory the screen driver ANSI.SYS, for example, you need the following command in CONFIG.SYS:

```
DEVICEHIGH=C:\DOS\ANSI.SYS
```

When you boot the computer, DOS attempts to load ANSI.SYS into the upper memory area.

Note

DEVICEHIGH and LOADHIGH recognize two switches, /L and /S. When you use MemMaker to automatically configure your PC, MemMaker may use these switches in the commands it generates. These switches are not intended for use by users.

To load a memory-resident program into upper memory, precede the program's start-up command with LOADHIGH. (You can use the abbreviation LH in place of LOADHIGH.) The syntax for the command for LOADHIGH is shown in the following:

```
LOADHIGH programname /switches
```

As an example, assume that you want to load DOSKEY (discussed in Chapter 17, "Mastering Doskey and Macros") into upper memory each time you start your computer. To do this, you add the following command to your AUTOEXEC.BAT file:

```
LOADHIGH DOSKEY
```

The next time you reboot the computer, DOS attempts to load Doskey into upper memory. DOS does not load a program into upper memory if the program requests that DOS allocate more memory during initialization than is available in the largest available upper memory block. If DOS is not successful when it tries to load device drivers or TSRs into the upper memory area, DOS loads the program into conventional memory instead.

Use the MEM command to determine whether a driver or program has loaded into upper memory.

Displaying the Amount of Free and Used Memory

To enable you to make the most efficient use of DOS' memory management utilities, DOS also enables you to display the amount of free and used memory at any point during a DOS session. Use the MEM command for this purpose.

The syntax for the MEM command is shown in the following:

```
MEM /CLASSIFY /DEBUG /FREE /MODULE modulename /PAGE
```

Most of these options (/DEBUG, /FREE, and /MODULE) are primarily of interest to programmers. For any option, you can specify just the first letter, such as /C in place of /CLASSIFY, for example.

With no switches, MEM gives a basic report of how the memory on your machine is being used. The following provides a sample of a basic MEM report from a typical computer with 8M of memory:

```
Memory Type        Total  =   Used  +   Free
----------------   ------    ------    ------
Conventional         640K       79K      562K
Upper                 71K       33K       38K
Reserved             384K      384K        0K
Extended (XMS)*    7,097K    2,537K    4,560K
----------------   ------    ------    ------
Total memory       8,192K    3,033K    5,159K

Total under 1 MB     711K      112K      599K

Total Expanded (EMS)                7,488K (7,667,712 bytes)
Free Expanded (EMS)*                4,800K (4,915,200 bytes)
```

```
* EMM386 is using XMS memory to simulate EMS memory as needed.
  Free EMS memory may change as free XMS memory changes.

Largest executable program size       561K (574,752 bytes)
Largest free upper memory block        22K  (22,016 bytes)
MS-DOS is resident in the high memory area.
```

Even this most basic report includes a wealth of information:

- This computer has 640K of conventional memory, of which 79K is currently in use, leaving 562K free.
- This computer loaded EMM386, which found 71K available in upper memory blocks. 33K of the 71K is currently in use.
- This computer has 7,097K of extended memory, 2,537K of which is in use.
- The computer has 599K of memory available below 1M, representing the memory available for loading programs and device drivers on this machine.
- The largest program you can load into conventional memory is 561K.
- The largest free upper memory block is 22K. Consequently, you cannot load "high" any program or device driver that requires more memory than 22K.
- Most of DOS has been loaded into the high memory area because the command DOS=HIGH appeared in the CONFIG.SYS file.

With the /CLASSIFY switch, MEM lists all DOS programs and device drivers currently loaded. Along with the information shown above, MEM lists this additional information if you use /CLASSIFY:

```
Modules using memory below 1 MB:

  Name          Total        =   Conventional   +   Upper Memory
  --------  ----------------   ----------------   ----------------
  MSDOS       18,029    (18K)     18,029    (18K)          0    (0K)
  HIMEM        1,168     (1K)      1,168     (1K)          0    (0K)
  EMM386       3,120     (3K)      3,120     (3K)          0    (0K)
  DBLSPACE    37,664    (37K)     37,664    (37K)          0    (0K)
  COMMAND      3,184     (3K)      3,184     (3K)          0    (0K)
  MOUSE       17,088    (17K)     17,088    (17K)          0    (0K)
  SETVER         816     (1K)          0     (0K)        816    (1K)
  ANSI         4,240     (4K)          0     (0K)      4,240    (4K)
  SMARTDRV    29,024    (28K)          0     (0K)     29,024   (28K)
  Free       613,472   (599K)    574,976   (562K)     38,496   (38K)
```

This sample report shows six programs and device drivers currently loaded and displays the amount of conventional and upper memory used by each:

- MSDOS is the portion of MS-DOS that did not get loaded into the high memory area.
- HIMEM is the HIMEM.SYS device driver.
- EMM386 is the EMM386.EXE device driver.
- DBLSPACE is the DoubleSpace device driver.
- COMMAND is the DOS command interpreter.
- MOUSE is the mouse device driver.
- SETVER is the device driver used to modify how DOS reports version information.
- ANSI is the ANSI.SYS device driver, which this computer loads.
- SMARTDRV is the device driver for caching information going to and from disk drives.

MEM /C often displays more than a screenful of information. The /P option tells MEM to pause after each screenful of data and wait for you to press a key before continuing.

After you identify a driver or memory-resident program that appears to be the right size to fit in the available UMB, edit CONFIG.SYS or AUTOEXEC.BAT to add DEVICEHIGH or LOADHIGH to the appropriate command. Reboot your computer, and issue the MEM /C command again to see whether the driver or program loaded.

Arriving at the optimal combination of device drivers and memory-resident programs loaded into upper memory may require some experimentation. DOS loads programs in the largest available UMB first, so try loading the largest drivers and programs first by placing their start-up commands earliest in CONFIG.SYS or AUTOEXEC.BAT. To alleviate some of the trial-and-error necessary in arriving at the optimal memory arrangement, DOS now provides the MemMaker utility, which is described in the following section.

General Tips for Optimizing Memory

Most computers sold today have at least a 386 microprocessor and come with some extended memory. If your computer meets these criteria, following these tips can enable you to use your memory most efficiently:

- Your CONFIG.SYS file should load HIMEM.SYS first and then EMM386.EXE. Together these two drivers allow access to extended memory and upper memory blocks.
- Unless you are running applications that need expanded memory, use the NOEMS option for EMM386.EXE so that all extended memory is available as XMS memory.
- Load DOS into the high memory area and make upper memory available to DOS with the command DOS=HIGH,UMB.
- Use the DEVICEHIGH command for as many drivers as possible in your CONFIG.SYS file. You cannot use DEVICEHIGH for HIMEM.SYS or EMM386.EXE, and some other device drivers may not load properly with DEVICEHIGH. Experiment, and use MEM/C to determine whether the drivers loaded properly.
- Use LOADHIGH for any TSRs you load in your AUTOEXEC.BAT. Because some TSRs may not work correctly when loaded high, experiment until you determine what TSR you can load high.
- If you own a 386 computer or better, your CONFIG.SYS should begin with the following:

```
DEVICE=C:\DOS\HIMEM.SYS
DEVICE=C:\DOS\EMM386.EXE NOEMS
DOS=HIGH,UMB
```

Configuring Memory with MemMaker

Understanding and configuring a PC's memory is one of the most challenging activities most users face. Because most users usually configure their computer's memory once, they never really get a chance to build any experience fiddling with the configuration. After nearly a dozen years of watching users stumble at configuring their PCs, Microsoft finally offers help. DOS includes MemMaker, a utility that analyzes your PC and makes the appropriate changes to your CONFIG.SYS and AUTOEXEC.BAT so that your computer uses its memory most effectively.

Tip
If you start an application such as Windows from your AUTOEXEC.BAT file, place the word REM in front of the start-up command (in this case, in front of WIN) before using MemMaker. REM causes DOS to ignore the rest of the command so that you don't have to exit your application during each MemMaker phase. When MemMaker has completed its work, remove REM so that your application again starts automatically each time you boot.

MemMaker and Applications That Start Automatically

Some people use Windows or a particular application so often that they add a command to the end of their AUTOEXEC.BAT file to start the application automatically every time they boot. If you have added such a command that takes you automatically into Windows or any other program, read this warning carefully. If, on the other hand, you find yourself at the DOS prompt when your computer boots, you can skip this warning.

MemMaker does its work in three phases; between each phase, it reboots your computer. Each time MemMaker causes your computer to reboot, your AUTOEXEC.BAT starts your application as usual, preventing MemMaker from continuing its work. You must exit these programs for MemMaker to perform the next phase.

You can take two different paths to configure your memory with MemMaker. One is to follow the Express Setup. The other path you can choose is the Custom Setup.

Express Setup is the easier path to choose. You have little interaction with Express Setup, other than pressing Enter when MemMaker prompts you to do so. MemMaker searches through the upper memory area to find open memory addresses. MemMaker sorts device drivers and TSRs that you load in memory to see the optimum loading order. Finally, MemMaker updates your CONFIG.SYS and AUTOEXEC.BAT files for two reasons. MemMaker ensures that HIMEM.SYS and EMM386.EXE load to manage memory and that the DOS=UMB directive is in CONFIG.SYS to provide the link to upper memory blocks. In addition, MemMaker inserts DEVICEHIGH and LOADHIGH before the device drivers and TSRs that load in upper memory.

Note

Although MemMaker adds the device drivers HIMEM.SYS and EMM386.EXE and the upper memory block directive HIGH=UMB, it does not ensure that DOS loads into upper memory with the directive DOS=HIGH. Before using MemMaker, ensure that your system loads DOS in the high memory area by inserting DOS=HIGH in your CONFIG.SYS file and rebooting your computer. After you are running DOS in the high memory area (the MEM command tells you that DOS is in the high memory area), run MemMaker.

Custom Setup is very similar to Express Setup in that it scans the upper memory area for open address space, sorts device drivers and TSRs for optimum order, and updates your AUTOEXEC.BAT and CONFIG.SYS files.

As you might expect, however, you may customize how MemMaker performs these tasks. The following list shows the elements you can customize using Custom Setup:

- Specify any TSRs that should not be included in optimization
- Aggressively scan the upper memory area
- Set aside upper memory for Windows use
- Use an area of upper memory set aside for the Monochrome Display Adapter (MDA) if you are using only an EGA or VGA display (but not SuperVGA)
- Keep any special memory inclusions or exclusions that you specified with EMM386.EXE
- Move the Extended BIOS data area in upper memory blocks

Now that you understand what MemMaker can do to optimize your computer's memory, you are ready to use MemMaker. The following two sections explain how to use MemMaker with Express Setup and with Custom Setup.

Using Express Setup. Follow these steps to run MemMaker using Express Setup:

1. At the DOS prompt, type **MEMMAKER** and press Enter.
2. MemMaker asks whether you want to continue. Press Enter to continue.
3. MemMaker asks whether you want Express or Custom Setup, as shown in figure 18.1. For most users, an Express setup does an excellent job. Unless you are very knowledgeable about PCs and want to guide MemMaker's every step, press Enter to select an Express setup.
4. MemMaker asks whether you intend to use EMS (expanded) memory, as shown in figure 18.2. Answer Y or N, and press Enter. (If the answer you want is already showing, just press Enter.)
5. Next, you see a screen indicating that MemMaker must reboot the computer, as shown in figure 18.3. Press Enter, and MemMaker reboots your computer. (If your computer does not start correctly, turning it off and back on reboots it.)

Tip
An easy way to run MemMaker is to use the /BATCH switch. From the command line, type **MEMMAKER /BATCH**. This command runs MemMaker in automatic mode, accepting all the default answers.

Fig. 18.1
The MemMaker setup selection screen. From this screen you select the type of setup you want performed.

```
Microsoft MemMaker

There are two ways to run MemMaker:

Express Setup optimizes your computer's memory automatically.

Custom Setup gives you more control over the changes that
MemMaker makes to your system files. Choose Custom Setup
if you are an experienced user.

          Use Express or Custom Setup? Express Setup

ENTER=Accept Selection  SPACEBAR=Change Selection  F1=Help  F3=Exit
```

Fig. 18.2
The MemMaker EMS selection. This is where you specify whether you will be using expanded memory in your system.

```
Microsoft MemMaker

If you use any programs that require expanded memory (EMS), answer
Yes to the following question.  Answering Yes makes expanded memory
available, but might not free as much conventional memory.

If none of your programs need expanded memory, answer No to the
following question.  Answering No makes expanded memory unavailable,
but can free more conventional memory.

If you are not sure whether your programs require expanded memory,
answer No.  If you later discover that a program needs expanded
memory, run MemMaker again and answer Yes to this question.

Do you use any programs that need expanded memory (EMS)? No

ENTER=Accept Selection  SPACEBAR=Change Selection  F1=Help  F3=Exit
```

Fig. 18.3
The first MemMaker reboot notice. Notice that if your system does not reboot automatically, you can turn your computer off and back on.

```
MemMaker will now restart your computer.

If your computer doesn't start properly, just turn it off
and on again, and MemMaker will recover automatically.

If a program other than MemMaker starts after your computer
restarts, exit the program so that MemMaker can continue.

     * Remove any disks from your floppy-disk drives and
       then press ENTER. Your computer will restart.
```

6. When your computer reboots, MemMaker automatically begins the next phase of its work, telling you that it has calculated the optimal configuration for your computer. MemMaker displays another screen, as shown in figure 18.4, that asks you to press Enter so that MemMaker can reboot again. Press Enter to continue.

```
MemMaker will now restart your computer to test the new memory
configuration.

While your computer is restarting, watch your screen carefully.
Note any unusual messages or problems. If your computer doesn't
start properly, just turn it off and on again, and MemMaker
will recover automatically.

If a program other than MemMaker starts after your computer
restarts, exit the program so that MemMaker can continue.

     * Remove any disks from your floppy-disk drives and
       then press ENTER. Your computer will restart.
```

Fig. 18.4
The second MemMaker reboot notice. After this reboot, your new memory configuration should be complete.

7. During the reboot, your computer executes the CONFIG.SYS and AUTOEXEC.BAT files that MemMaker created. Although MemMaker should do an excellent job of configuring your computer for peak performance, there is always a chance that it can make a mistake. As your computer boots, watch carefully for any errors produced by the device drivers and programs that you load from your CONFIG.SYS and AUTOEXEC.BAT files.

After your computer completes its reboot, MemMaker begins its last phase. MemMaker displays the message shown in figure 18.5, asking whether you saw any errors during boot. If your computer booted without errors, press Enter.

```
Microsoft MemMaker
------------------------------------------------------------------------

Your computer has just restarted with its new memory configuration.
Some or all of your device drivers and memory-resident programs
are now running in upper memory.

If your system appears to be working properly, choose "Yes."
If you noticed any unusual messages when your computer started,
or if your system is not working properly, choose "No."

Does your system appear to be working properly? Yes

ENTER=Accept Selection  SPACEBAR=Change Selection  F1=Help  F3=Exit
```

Fig. 18.5
MemMaker asking about boot errors. You should observe your boot process to see whether it appears normal; if it does, MemMaker is finished.

8. MemMaker displays a table showing how the changes affected your available memory. A sample is shown in figure 18.6. This report tells you how much of each type of memory you had available before and after MemMaker made its changes. In this example, MemMaker adjusts commands in the AUTOEXEC.BAT and CONFIG.SYS so that several device drivers and TSR programs are loaded into upper memory, freeing up about 114K of conventional memory. MemMaker also tells you that it has saved your original AUTOEXEC.BAT and CONFIG.SYS as AUTOEXEC.UMB and CONFIG.UMB in case you later discover a problem and want to return to using your original files.

Fig. 18.6
A summary report from MemMaker. The third column indicates how much conventional memory you have saved.

```
Microsoft MemMaker

MemMaker has finished optimizing your system's memory. The following
table summarizes the memory use (in bytes) on your system:

                                Before      After
  Memory Type                   MemMaker    MemMaker    Change
  ---------------------------   ---------   ---------   ---------
  Free conventional memory:     416,432     530,576     114,144

  Upper memory:
     Used by programs                 0     114,160     114,160
     Reserved for Windows             0           0           0
     Reserved for EMS                 0           0           0
     Free                       142,400      28,224

  Expanded memory:              Disabled    Disabled

Your original CONFIG.SYS and AUTOEXEC.BAT files have been saved
as CONFIG.UMB and AUTOEXEC.UMB.  If MemMaker changed your Windows
SYSTEM.INI file, the original file was saved as SYSTEM.UMB.

ENTER=Exit  ESC=Undo changes
```

9. When you finish examining this report, press Enter to exit MemMaker.

Tip
After running MemMaker, if you experience problems with any of your programs that you did not have before, issue the MEMMAKER /UNDO command to remove any changes that MemMaker made.

Using Custom Setup. Follow these steps to run MemMaker using Custom Setup:

1. At the DOS Prompt, type **MEMMAKER** and press Enter.
2. MemMaker asks whether you want to continue. Press Enter.
3. MemMaker asks whether you want Express or Custom Setup (refer to figure 18.1). Press the space bar to select Custom Setup, and then press Enter to continue.
4. MemMaker asks whether you intend to use EMS memory (refer to figure 18.2). Press the space bar to choose No or Yes. When you have made the desired selection, press Enter.
5. MemMaker now displays Advanced Options that enable you to customize the settings used when optimizing memory. Each advanced option

requires a Yes or No answer. Use the space bar to answer. Use the down- and up-arrow keys to move from one option to the next. The following list explains the options that you have to set:

- *Specify which drivers and TSRs to include in optimization?* Answering Yes enables you to leave TSRs out of optimization that must be loaded into memory in a specific sequence or that give MemMaker trouble during optimization.
- *Scan the upper memory area aggressively?* If you answer Yes, MemMaker includes the HIGHSCAN parameter in the EMM386.EXE line of CONFIG.SYS. Although EMM386.EXE normally scans the address range C600-EFFF for available upper memory, adding HIGHSCAN instructs EMM386.EXE to scan the address range C600F7FF.
- *Optimize upper memory for use with Windows?* If you answer Yes, EMM386.EXE sets aside upper memory for use by Windows. This provides more memory for DOS programs that you run from Windows. If you do not run DOS programs from Windows, choose No.
- *Use monochrome region (B000-BFFF) for running programs?* Answer Yes if you have installed an EGA or VGA display adapter but not a monochrome or SuperVGA display adapter. The address range B000-BFFF can be used as upper memory if you have an EGA or VGA display adapter installed.
- *Keep current EMM386 memory exclusions and inclusions?* If you currently are using EMM386.EXE and have specific addresses specified to include or exclude, answer Yes to this question.
- *Move Extended BIOS Data Area from conventional to upper memory?* Normally, EMM386.EXE moves the Extended Bios Data Area (EBDA) to upper memory. However, if any unusual problems occur while running MemMaker, answer No to this option.

6. After you answer all the Advanced Options correctly, press Enter to continue with MemMaker.
7. MemMaker searches your hard disk for a copy of Windows. If it finds Windows, MemMaker displays the directory in which the copy of Windows resides. If this directory is incorrect, type the correct directory. Press Enter to continue.

From this point, MemMaker behaves exactly as in the Express setup. Refer to the previous section, picking up with step 5.

Increasing Hard Disk Performance

If your computer is typical, it spends a lot of its time accessing data and programs on hard disk. Speeding up your hard disk is probably the single most significant thing you can do to increase the overall speed of your system. Although you can increase the speed of your system by buying a faster hard disk, DOS gives you facilities to make better use of the disk you have.

The BUFFERS command in CONFIG.SYS tells DOS how much memory to reserve for file transfers. DOS sets aside an area of RAM called a buffer for temporary storage of data being transferred between the disk and an applications program.

When DOS is asked to retrieve information from a disk, it reads the information in increments of whole sectors (512 bytes). Excess data not required from that sector is left in the buffer. If this data is needed later, DOS does not need to perform another disk access to retrieve the data. Similarly, DOS tries to reduce disk activity when it writes information to the disk. If less than a full sector is to be written to the disk, DOS accumulates the information in a disk buffer. When the buffer is full, DOS writes the information to the disk. This action is called *flushing the buffer*. To make sure that all pertinent information is placed into a file, DOS also flushes the buffers when a program closes a disk file.

Whenever a disk buffer is used, DOS marks it to indicate that it has been used recently. When DOS needs to reuse buffers for new information, it takes the buffer that has not been used for the longest time.

The net effect of DOS's use of buffers is to reduce the number of disk accesses by reading and writing only full sectors. By reusing the least-recently used buffers, DOS retains information more likely to be needed next. Your programs and DOS therefore run faster.

You can control the number of buffers available for DOS to use. Each buffer uses up some of your memory but results in faster disk access. The syntax for the BUFFERS command is shown in the following:

```
BUFFERS = n, m
```

The *n* parameter is the number of disk buffers you want DOS to allocate. A single buffer is about 512 bytes long (plus 16 bytes used by DOS). Use a number from 1 through 99. If you do not give the BUFFERS command, DOS uses a default value from 2 through 15, depending on the size of your disk drives, the amount of memory in your system, and the version of DOS you are using. Table 18.3 lists the different default buffer configurations.

Table 18.3 Default Number of Disk Buffers

Buffers	Hardware
2	360K floppy disk drive
3	Any other hard or floppy disk drive
5	More than 128K of RAM
10	More than 256K of RAM
15	More than 512K of RAM

The *m* parameter is a number in the range 1 through 8, that specifies the number of sectors DOS reads each time it is instructed to read a file. This feature is sometimes called a *secondary cache* or a *look-ahead buffer*. When files most often are read sequentially, this type of buffer increases performance. Do not use this secondary cache feature if you are using or plan to use a disk caching program such as SMARTDRV.SYS, discussed in Chapter 19, "Getting the Most from Your Hard Drive."

Increasing the number of buffers generally improves disk performance, up to a point. The recommended number of buffers increases with the size of your hard disk. Consider the suggested buffer numbers listed in table 18.4 when adding a BUFFERS command to CONFIG.EXE. Using a number higher than the recommended number of buffers probably uses more memory without further improving speed.

Table 18.4 Suggested Number of Disk Buffers

Hard Disk Size	Buffers
Less than 40M	20
40M to 79M	30

(continues)

For Related Information

- "Using a Disk Cache (SMARTDrive)," p. 492
- "Using FASTOPEN," p. 497
- "Using a RAM Disk," p. 498

Table 18.4 Continued

Hard Disk Size	Buffers
80M to 119M	40
120M or more	50

If you have an 85M hard disk and are not using a hard disk caching program, for example, you may include the following BUFFERS command in CONFIG.SYS:

```
BUFFERS=40,8
```

Fine-Tuning Your Computer with CONFIG.SYS and AUTOEXEC.BAT

In addition to the commands covered earlier in this chapter, you can use many other commands in CONFIG.SYS or AUTOEXEC.BAT to customize your computer configuration. The following sections discuss other useful commands: FCBS, FILES, LASTDRIVE, SHELL, INSTALL, REM, and SWITCHES.

Accessing Files through FCBS

The FCBS configuration command enables you to use programs written for DOS 1.1; some DOS users find FCBs indispensable. FCB is an acronym for *file control block*. FCBs serve as one way a program can access a file. This method of file access was used by DOS 1.1 to communicate with programs. Later versions of DOS borrow a UNIX-like method for controlling files, called *handles* (discussed in "Using the FILES Command" in this chapter). Although FCBs can be used with any version of DOS, only DOS 2.0 and higher can use handles.

The syntax for the FCBS command in the CONFIG.SYS file is as follows:

```
FCBS = maxopen
```

The *maxopen* parameter is a number from 1 through 255 which sets the maximum number of unique FCBs that programs can open at one time. The default number is 4. You don't need to use this command in CONFIG.SYS unless you have a program that was designed to work with DOS 1.1 and the program cannot open all the required files (a message to this effect appears). In that case, use the FCBS command to increase the number of FCBs that can be open at one time.

You pay a small price in RAM to use the FCBS command. For each number above 4 that *maxopen* exceeds, DOS uses about 40 bytes.

Using the FILES Command

FILES is the configuration command used in DOS 2.0 and higher to allow for UNIX-like file handling. UNIX and later versions of DOS use a file handle (a number corresponding to the file name) instead of file control blocks to access files. You never have to deal with file handles directly. Each application program gives the operating system the name of the file or device you want to use. The operating system gives the program a handle, and the program uses that handle to manipulate the file or device.

Tip

If you are still using the FCBS command, it's time to wake up and smell the coffee. It has been over ten years since DOS 2.0 (and file handles) were introduced. If your software does not yet support file handles, you are living in the past and should strongly consider different software.

To include the FILES command in CONFIG.SYS, use the following syntax:

```
FILES = n
```

The *n* parameter is a number (8, which is the default, through 255) that determines the number of files that can be open at one time during a DOS session. Each additional file over 8 increases the size of DOS by 39 bytes.

If you do not specify the FILES command, DOS starts with eight file handles and immediately takes five handles for the standard devices, leaving only three handles for your programs. This number is almost never large enough for applications you are likely to run. On most systems, increase the number of handles to 20 or 30.

Note

Many installation programs for full-featured applications edit CONFIG.SYS for you and increase the number of files when necessary to run the software efficiently.

Using LASTDRIVE to Change the Number of Disk Drives

The LASTDRIVE configuration command informs DOS of the maximum number of disk drives on your system. Generally, LASTDRIVE is a command used with networked computers or with the pretender commands (such as SUBST).

If you do not use the LASTDRIVE command, DOS assumes that the last disk drive on your system is one more than the number of physical drives and RAM disks you are using. If your LASTDRIVE command specifies a letter corresponding to fewer drives than the number physically attached to your computer or created as RAM disks, DOS ignores the command. The LASTDRIVE command enables you to tell DOS how many disk drives, real or apparent, are on your system, including network drives and directories (if any) and drives created with the SUBST command.

If you want to use the LASTDRIVE command in CONFIG.SYS, use the following syntax:

```
LASTDRIVE = x
```

The *x* parameter is the letter for the last disk drive on your system. The letters *A* through *Z* in upper- or lowercase are acceptable.

Using the SHELL Command

The SHELL command was originally implemented to enable programmers to replace the DOS command interpreter (COMMAND.COM) with other command interpreters. The SHELL command is more commonly used, however, to perform the following two functions:

- Inform DOS that the command interpreter is in another directory, not in the boot disk's root directory.
- Expand the size of the environment—an area of RAM that stores named variables used by DOS and applications programs. Commands such as PATH and PROMPT store their current settings as environment variables. To display the contents of the environment, type **SET** at the command prompt, and press Enter.

Caution

SHELL is a tricky command; use it with caution. If used incorrectly, the SHELL command can lock up your system. Keep a bootable floppy disk handy for restarting your computer in case you run into a problem.

The syntax for the SHELL command is shown in the following:

```
SHELL = filespec parameters
```

The *filespec* parameter is the path and file name of the command processor and should be COMMAND.COM if you are using the standard DOS command processor. The SHELL command doesn't take any other parameters or switches, but you can add command-line parameters or switches available for use with the command processor. The parameters for COMMAND.COM are explained in the next few paragraphs.

When used from the command line, COMMAND loads a copy of the command processor into memory. A common use of COMMAND is as a parameter of the SHELL command. The syntax for COMMAND is shown in the following:

```
COMMAND d:path\ device /E:size /P /C string /K:filename /MSG
```

The *d:path* parameter specifies the disk drive and path that contain the command processor if it is not located in the root directory. Always use this parameter when including COMMAND in the SHELL configuration command. This parameter has the additional effect of setting an environment variable named COMSPEC, which informs DOS and other programs of the location and name of the current command processor.

/E:*size* is an optional switch that sets the environment space. The *size* parameter is a number from 160 through 32,768 that denotes the amount of memory reserved for the environment. (If you do not specify a multiple of 16, DOS rounds the size parameter up to the next highest multiple of 16.) By default, DOS reserves 256 bytes for the environment.

The /P switch instructs DOS to load the command processor permanently. Without the /P switch, DOS loads COMMAND.COM only temporarily into memory. When you are using COMMAND with the SHELL command in CONFIG.SYS, be sure to use the /P switch.

The /C switch and string parameter work together. This combination causes DOS to load the command processor, execute any command represented by string, and then unload the command processor.

The /MSG switch tells DOS to store all its error messages in memory rather than read them from the disk. This feature can speed operation. More importantly, if you are running a system that only has floppy disks, you sometimes remove from the disk drive the disk that contains COMMAND.COM. Without the /MSG switch, DOS cannot access error messages contained on disk within the COMMAND.COM file itself. Use this switch only if you are running DOS from floppy disks. You also must use the /P switch any time you use the /MSG switch.

The /K parameter tells DOS to run a program or batch file. Use this switch only when running COMMAND from the DOS prompt and not as part of the SHELL command in CONFIG.SYS.

The DOS Setup program adds the following command to the default CONFIG.SYS file:

```
SHELL=C:\DOS\COMMAND.COM C:\DOS\ /P
```

This configuration command tells DOS that COMMAND.COM is the command interpreter and that it is located in the \DOS directory on the C drive. The /P switch causes the command interpreter to be loaded permanently, not temporarily, in memory.

The preceding SHELL command enables you to place a copy of COMMAND.COM in C:\DOS and delete the copy in the root directory. This practice helps you maintain a clean root directory and protects COMMAND.COM from being replaced by an older version that may be on a floppy disk you are copying. If you accidentally copy the disk to the root directory, you don't overwrite the current version of COMMAND.COM.

Occasionally, you create such a long PATH command in AUTOEXEC.BAT that you fill the available environment space, causing DOS to display the message

```
Out of environment space
```

If this message appears, use COMMAND with the SHELL command and the /E switch to specify a larger environment space. The following command used in CONFIG.SYS, for example, increases the environment to 384 bytes:

```
SHELL=C:\DOS\COMMAND.COM /E:384
```

If you already have a SHELL command in CONFIG.SYS, you can add the /E switch. Combining the two preceding SHELL commands, for example, you can include the following command in CONFIG.SYS:

```
SHELL=C:\DOS\COMMAND.COM C:\DOS\ /P /E:384
```

Note

The SHELL command itself doesn't use any memory, but by increasing the environment space, you can reduce the amount of free conventional memory by an equal amount. In other words, increasing the environment space from 256 bytes to 384 bytes reduces free memory by 128 bytes.

Using the INSTALL Command

The INSTALL configuration command enables you to load memory-resident programs from within CONFIG.SYS. In versions of DOS before 4.0, you had to load these programs from the DOS prompt or through a batch file, such as AUTOEXEC.BAT. You can save several kilobytes of memory by loading a program from CONFIG.SYS with INSTALL rather than from the command line or a batch file as an executable program. DOS 4.0 and later versions support loading any of the following programs by using INSTALL:

FASTOPEN.EXE

KEYB.COM

NLSFUNC.EXE

SHARE.EXE

(The Command Reference provides more information about these programs.)

The syntax for using INSTALL in CONFIG.SYS is shown in the following:

```
INSTALL = filespec parameters
```

The *filespec* parameter is the path and file name information of the utility you want to load, while *parameters* is used to specify any parameters or switches required by the utility you want DOS to load.

You may be able to use INSTALL with some memory-resident non-DOS programs. Do not use INSTALL to load a memory-resident program that uses environment variables or shortcut keys or that uses COMMAND.COM. The program you install with this command must have the extension .COM or .EXE.

Using the REM Command

The REM configuration command is equivalent to the REM batch file command. This command enables you to insert remarks into your CONFIG.SYS file. You can leave notes to yourself (or others) explaining what particular lines do. Such documentation in a CONFIG.SYS file is especially helpful if you use non-DOS device drivers for your hardware. You also can temporarily remove a CONFIG.SYS statement by prefacing the statement with a REM command. After you test the new configuration, you can return easily to the old configuration by simply removing the REM command.

The syntax for the REM command is shown in the following:

```
REM remarks
```

The *remarks* parameter can be any string of characters that fits on a single line in the CONFIG.SYS file.

Using the SWITCHES Command

The SWITCHES configuration command enables you to set any of four options that control how four of DOS's features operate. The syntax of the SWITCHES command is shown in the following:

```
SWITCHES = /K /W /N /F
```

You can specify one or more of these four switches in a single SWITCHES command.

The /K switch turns off the enhanced keyboard functions. This command works like the ANSI.SYS /K switch. Some software cannot work with the enhanced keyboard. Use this command to disable the enhanced keyboard so that the software functions properly. If you use the SWITCHES=/K command in CONFIG.SYS and also install ANSI.SYS as a device driver, add the /K switch to the DEVICE=ANSI.SYS line as well.

The /W switch specifies that the WINA20.386 file has been moved to a directory other than the root directory. Use this switch if you moved WINA20.386 to another directory and are using Windows in enhanced mode.

Normally, you can use the F5 or F8 keys during the first two seconds of booting to bypass some or all of the commands in CONFIG.SYS or AUTOEXEC.BAT. The /N switch tells DOS to ignore F5 or F8 during boot.

Normally DOS displays the message

```
Starting MS-DOS
```

at the beginning of the boot process and then pauses for two seconds before continuing. The /F switch tells DOS to skip the two-second pause.

Telling DOS When to Break

As you already know, Ctrl-Break and Ctrl-C are helpful but not foolproof panic buttons you can use to stop commands. The response to a Ctrl-Break or Ctrl-C is not instantaneous. Although only an "Oh, no" second may pass from the time you press the panic button until DOS responds, you still have time to wonder why DOS takes so long to respond. The reason is that DOS is busy doing other things most of the time and looks for Ctrl-Break only at intervals. You can use the BREAK command in CONFIG.SYS to tell DOS when to check for this key sequence. BREAK does not enable or disable the Break key; the BREAK command only controls when DOS checks for the Break key.

The syntax for the BREAK command is shown in the following:

```
BREAK=ON
```

or

```
BREAK=OFF
```

The default setting for this command is OFF.

If you use the command BREAK=ON in CONFIG.SYS, DOS checks to see whether you pressed Ctrl-Break whenever a program requests some activity from DOS (performs a DOS function call). If you use the command BREAK=OFF, DOS checks for a Ctrl-Break only when DOS is working with the video display, keyboard, printer, or asynchronous serial adapters (the ports at the back of the computer).

If you use programs that do a great deal of disk accessing but little keyboard or screen work, you may want to set BREAK=ON. This setting enables you to break out of the program quicker when something goes awry or when you simply want to stop DOS.

Using the DOS Pretender Commands

Because DOS manages disks in a logical rather than a strictly physical way, DOS can "pretend" that a disk's identity is different from the disk's name. DOS provides the following three commands that pretend that a disk's identity has changed:

- ASSIGN redirects disk operations from one disk to another.
- JOIN attaches an entire disk as a subdirectory to the directory structure of another disk.
- SUBST makes a directory of a disk appear to commands as a separate disk.

Detailed information on these commands is provided in Chapter 13, "Controlling Your Environment."

Using Other Device Control Commands

DOS provides other commands to control devices and report system information, which are briefly discussed in this section. These commands are explained in greater detail in the Command Reference.

For Related Information

- "The SUBST Command," p. 343
- "Expanding the File System through Subdirectories," p. 131
- "Changing the Command Prompt with PROMPT," p. 334
- "Changing Disk Drives," p. 342

The SET command displays the current environment settings and enables you to make new variable assignments.

The PRINT command enables you to print text files on your printer while you continue to do other PC work. This "background" printing can be a great time-saver if your applications programs don't have a similar feature.

The MODE command is a multifaceted device-control command. MODE can establish the height and width of your screen's lines and characters and control the speed of your serial ports. MODE can redirect the output from a parallel printer port to a serial port. You also can use MODE in association with code page support for international character sets on the PC. You may want to browse through the MODE section of the Command Reference.

Summary

In this chapter, you learned the following important points:

- DOS can alter your system's configuration through instructions in the CONFIG.SYS and AUTOEXEC.BAT files.
- The CONFIG.SYS file must be in the root directory of the boot disk. When you alter CONFIG.SYS, configuration changes do not occur until DOS is rebooted.
- Disk buffers make DOS work faster by placing requested information in RAM.
- DOS provides several memory management features that can free significant portions of conventional memory as well as speed the operation of your system.
- The FILES command sets the number of files DOS can open at any one time.
- The LASTDRIVE command specifies the last disk drive letter you want to use in your system.
- You can tell DOS when to look for the Ctrl-Break key sequence.

In the next chapter, you discover additional ways to wring the greatest capabilities out of your hard disk.

Chapter 19

Getting the Most from Your Hard Drive

Your hard disk just may be the most important component of your computer. Many aspects of your computer's performance are strongly influenced by the characteristics of your disk. These characteristics include the following:

- *Speed.* The speed of your hard disk influences the speed of your system. Even if your computer's processor is super-fast, a slow disk can make your computer perform like a snail.
- *Space.* The amount of space on your disk determines what you can do with your computer. No matter how fast and powerful your processor is, if you have only 20M of space on your disk, you cannot run much Windows software.
- *Safety.* The safety of your disk plays a large role in the amount of confidence you have in your system. If you are afraid that you may lose important data at any time because of mistakes or viruses, you cannot think kindly of your computer.

The most dramatic way to increase your computer's performance is to purchase a larger, faster hard disk. Large, fast hard disks are expensive, however. As an alternative to buying another hard disk, you often can increase your computer's performance simply by making the best use of your current hard disk. In this chapter, you learn how to get the most speed and the most space from your hard disk. The safety issue is covered thoroughly in Chapter 10, "Protecting Your Data," and Chapter 11, "Emergency Procedures."

Getting the Most Speed from Your Hard Disk

The programs you use on your computer frequently must access data on disk. The speed at which your computer can retrieve that information is one of the most significant factors that determine how fast the computer operates. You can buy faster disk drives (which are expensive), or you can use DOS, which provides several techniques that you can use to increase the speed at which your programs access information without actually increasing the speed of your disk. The following sections explain those techniques.

Using a Disk Cache (SMARTDrive)

Perhaps the most significant way to enhance the performance of your hard disk is to use a disk-caching program. Disk caching takes advantage of the fact that during the course of normal work, most users access the same programs and data repeatedly within a short period. You might list the contents of a file, and then edit the file, and then print it; or you might run the same program several times in a row. Even if you don't access programs or data repeatedly, the programs you use probably do.

If you have a disk-caching program installed, that program allocates some of your memory for temporary data storage on disk. When you access data, the disk-caching program saves that data in its memory area, on the assumption that you are likely to use the same data—or related data stored with it—in the near future (within a few seconds, perhaps). If you or your program do try to read the same data again soon, the disk-caching program intercepts the disk access and gives the program the data stored in memory. You (or your program) receive the data immediately because DOS doesn't actually read the data from disk; instead, the disk-caching program finds the data in its cache buffer. If your program never requests the same information again, the caching program eventually realizes that you are not likely to use that data soon and deletes the data from memory.

The disk-caching program that comes with DOS is named SMARTDRV.EXE, or simply *SMARTDrive*. SMARTDrive builds its buffer area in XMS or EMS memory, using very little conventional memory. When DOS reads information from the disk, it places that information in the cache and sends specifically requested information to the program that requested it. SMARTDrive, however, reads more information than the program requests and stores this information in memory. If the program later requests information that already is in memory, the cache can supply the information faster than DOS could if DOS had to read the disk again.

SMARTDrive eliminates redundant disk writing by putting information on disk only when the data differs from data already stored. The program also accumulates information, writing out data only when a certain amount has accumulated. Write-caching operations decrease the amount of time that your programs spend writing to disk, but write-caching also forces you to shut your computer down by issuing a special SMARTDrive command (explained later in this section), or by making sure you return to the DOS prompt.

Caution

You may not want to use write-caching in an area with unreliable electrical power. If the power fails while SMARTDrive is accumulating data, you lose the data that it has not yet written to disk. This risk of data loss is of little concern if you own an uninterruptable power supply (UPS) which keeps your computer running during a power failure. There is no equivalent danger in the case of read cache.

A disk-caching program like SMARTDrive remembers which sections of the disk you have used most frequently. When the cache must be recycled, the program retains the data in the most frequently used areas and discards the data in the less frequently used areas. In a random disk-access operation in which program and data files are scattered uniformly across the disk, the cache method of recycling the least frequently used area is more efficient than the buffer method of recycling the oldest area. A cache tends to keep in memory the most heavily used areas of the disk.

To start SMARTDrive, enter a command in your AUTOEXEC.BAT file that has the following syntax:

```
SMARTDRV drive+ ¦ drive-... /E:elementsize initcachesize
wincachesize
     /B:buffersize  /C /R /F /N /L /Q /S /U /V /X
```

The SMARTDRV command is followed by the drives for which you want caching used. This notation takes the form of a drive letter, followed optionally by a plus (+) or minus (–) sign, as in the following examples:

C	Specifies that drive C will be cached for reads but not for writes
C+	Specifies that drive C will be cached for reads and writes
C–	Specifies that drive C will not be cached

If you don't specify any drive letters in your SMARTDRV command, floppy disk drives are read-cached but not write-cached, and hard disks are read-cached and write-cached. If you are using the version of SMARTDrive supplied with DOS 6.2, you also can cache your CD-ROM drives. Other kinds of drives—such as network drives and compressed drives—are not cached.

As an alternative to specifying every drive you want read-cached, but not write-cached, you can use the /X switch. SMARTDrive then enables only read-caching; write-caching for all drives is automatically disabled. The /X switch is used automatically when you install DOS 6.2 (unless you were using SMARTDrive with different switches in an existing AUTOEXEC.BAT file).

The /E:*elementsize* parameter specifies the number of bytes that SMARTDrive reads or writes at a time: 1024, 2048, 4096, or 8192 (the default value). The larger the value, the more conventional memory SMARTDrive uses, but the fewer disk accesses you are likely to need.

The *initcachesize* parameter is a number that specifies the size (in kilobytes) of the cache when SMARTDrive starts. The larger the cache, the more likely that SMARTDrive can find information required by programs in the cache. The larger the cache, however, the more memory SMARTDrive requires. If you do not specify *initcachesize*, SMARTDrive selects a value based on the amount of memory in your system.

The *wincachesize* parameter specifies the size (in kilobytes) to which DOS can reduce the cache when you start Windows so that Windows can use the memory for other purposes. The philosophy behind this parameter is that if SMARTDrive uses too much of your memory, Windows runs too slowly. Therefore, even though SMARTDrive becomes less efficient by giving up some of its memory, Windows can run faster. When you exit Windows, SMARTDrive recovers the memory it gave up for Windows. (Table 19.1 shows the default values for *initcachesize* and *wincachesize*.)

Table 19.1 Default SMARTDrive Memory Values

Size of Extended Memory	Default Value for *Initcachesize*	Default Value for *Wincachesize*
Up to 1M	All XMS	Zero (no caching)
Up to 2M	1M	256K
Up to 4M	1M	512K
Up to 6M	2M	1M
6M or more	2M	2M

The /B:*buffersize* parameter tells SMARTDrive how much additional information to read when DOS executes a disk read. Because programs often read sequentially through files, SMARTDrive anticipates that the next data request will be for the area following the current area. The default size of the read-ahead buffer is 16K; this value can be any multiple of *elementsize*. The larger the value of *buffersize*, the more conventional memory SMARTDrive uses.

The /L switch prevents SMARTDrive from loading into your upper-memory area (UMA). This option may be useful if other programs need to use the UMA.

Normally, the DOS 6.2 version of SMARTDrive enables read-caching for CD-ROM drives. If you do not want this enabled, you can use the /U switch.

The /Q switch tells SMARTDrive to be "quiet" while installing itself rather than displaying the usual status messages. This is the opposite of the /V switch, which turns on "verbose" mode and shows the status messages.

You also can run SMARTDrive as a command from the DOS prompt. Several special switches are available from the command line which provide important features. The first of these is the /S switch. You determine the status of SMARTDrive by using the /S switch. Following is an example of typical output:

```
Microsoft SMARTDrive Disk Cache version 5.0
Copyright 1991,1993 Microsoft Corp.
```

```
Room for    256 elements of   8,192 bytes each
There have been   3,251 cache hits
    and    524 cache misses

Cache size:  2,097,152 bytes
Cache size while running Windows:  2,097,152 bytes

             Disk Caching Status
drive   read cache   write cache   buffering
-------------------------------------------
  A:        yes           no           no
  B:        yes           no           no
  C:        yes           yes          no
  D         yes           yes          no
  I*        yes           yes          no

* DoubleSpace drive cached via host drive.
Write behind data will be committed before command prompt returns.


For help, type "Smartdrv /?".
```

Perhaps the most interesting information in this output is the speed that SMARTDrive achieves. In the preceding example (which was generated after a session with a word processing program), for 3,251 disk accesses, SMARTDrive already had the data in its cache. For only 524 attempted disk accesses did SMARTDrive actually have to access the disk. In other words, because of SMARTDrive, the computer didn't have to perform 80 percent of attempted disk accesses.

The /C switch is important if you use write-caching. Remember that write-caching causes SMARTDrive to accumulate data that is destined for the disk until a certain amount accumulates. If you are getting ready to turn your computer off, you must tell SMARTDrive that no more data will be written to disk and instruct the program to finish writing whatever data it has accumulated. You can perform this operation (called *flushing* in technical circles) by typing the following command:

```
SMARTDRV /C
```

You do not need to execute this command if you are rebooting by pressing Ctrl-Alt-Del. But if you have enabled write-caching, use this command when you reset or turn off your computer.

If you are using DOS 6.2, you the precaution of using the /C switch is not necessary. Instead, SMARTDrive automatically flushes the write buffer to disk whenever you return to the DOS prompt. This assumes, of course, that you have not disabled the feature by using the /N switch. (Typically, you would disable this feature only if you were doing extensive batch file operations and didn't want the continual buffer flushing to degrade the performance of your batch files.) If you turn off this feature, using the /N switch, you can later turn it on using the /F switch.

Using FASTOPEN

Another way to improve hard disk performance is to use the FASTOPEN program. FASTOPEN is not a device driver per se, but an executable program that you can include in AUTOEXEC.BAT. You also can load the program through CONFIG.SYS, using the special INSTALL command (as covered in Chapter 18, "Configuring Your Computer").

You can use FASTOPEN only with hard drives. FASTOPEN caches directory information, holding in memory the locations of frequently used files and directories.

Directories are a type of file that users cannot access through regular means. DOS reads and writes directories in a manner similar to the way it handles other files. Part of the directory entry for a file or subdirectory holds the starting point for the file in the file allocation table (FAT). Because DOS typically holds the FAT in the disk buffers, FASTOPEN was developed to hold directory entries in memory.

FASTOPEN is not a complex command, but you must do a little work before you can use it effectively. FASTOPEN's syntax is as follows:

```
FASTOPEN.EXE d: = n /X
```

The *d:* parameter is the name of the first hard drive that you want FASTOPEN to track. (You can specify up to 24 hard disks or hard disk partitions at one time.) The /X switch, which is similar to the /X switches of other commands, enables FASTOPEN information to reside in EMS. By default, FASTOPEN uses conventional memory.

The *n* parameter is the number of directory entries that FASTOPEN should cache. Each file or subdirectory requires one directory entry. You can enter a value ranging from 10 through 999. If you do not specify a value for *n*, DOS uses a default value of 48.

You can use FASTOPEN on as many disks as you want. Be aware, however, that the total number of directory entries or fragmented entries FASTOPEN can handle is 999. If you issue the command for several disk drives, the sum of the *n* values cannot exceed 999. The practical limit of *n* is between 100 and 200 per disk. If you specify a value much higher, DOS wades through the internal directory entries more slowly than it reads information from disk.

Additionally, each directory entry stored in memory takes 48 bytes. Considering this trade-off of speed and memory, the 100-to-200-disks limit yields adequate performance.

Using too small a number for *n* also can be a disadvantage. When directory entries are recycled, FASTOPEN discards the least recently used entry when it needs space for a new entry. If the *n* value is too small, DOS discards entries that it still may need. The objective is to have enough entries in memory so that FASTOPEN operates efficiently, but not so many entries that FASTOPEN wastes time wading through directory entries.

To load FASTOPEN as part of your regular configuration, use the INSTALL command in your CONFIG.SYS file, as in the following:

```
INSTALL = FASTOPEN.EXE C:
```

To load FASTOPEN into upper memory, use LOADHIGH in AUTOEXEC.BAT. The following command, for example, loads FASTOPEN into upper memory and tracks file names and directories on drive C:

```
LOADHIGH C:\DOS\FASTOPEN C:
```

Note

Keep in mind the following points regarding the use of FASTOPEN:

- Do not use FASTOPEN if you are using Windows.
- Do not run a disk defragmenting program, such as DEFRAG, while FASTOPEN is running.

Using a RAM Disk

Another way to speed disk operation doesn't involve a disk at all. A RAM disk is a device driver that uses a portion of your computer's memory to emulate a disk drive. You use a RAM drive as you use any other disk drive. Because this "imitation," or virtual, disk is located in RAM, a RAM disk is extremely fast compared with a real disk drive. You must, however, give up a significant amount of memory to create a useful RAM disk. Worse, you cannot store anything in that disk permanently—the contents of the RAM disk disappear when you turn off or reboot your computer.

As a general rule, a disk-caching program such as SMARTDrive provides better overall performance gains than a RAM disk. You generally use RAM disks to enhance the performance of one or two specific programs that read and write to the disk frequently or that use overlays. A disk cache, on the other hand, improves the performance of all programs that read and write to disk. If your computer's memory resources are limited, give more consideration to a disk cache than to a RAM disk.

Overlays and RAM Disks

Some programs are too large to fit in your PC's memory. These programs load a core part into memory and access additional parts from overlay files as necessary. When a new section of the program is needed, the appropriate overlay for that section is read from the disk into the area occupied by the current overlay.

The term *overlay* comes from this process of overlaying sections of program space in memory with new sections. RAM disks facilitate rapid switching of active overlays because the overlay disk files actually are in memory, not on disk. You must copy any needed overlay files to the RAM disk before starting the program. You also must configure the program to look for its overlays on the RAM disk.

The RAM disk driver that comes with DOS is named RAMDRIVE.SYS. To install RAMDRIVE and create a virtual disk, include RAMDRIVE.SYS as a device driver in CONFIG.SYS. The syntax for including RAMDRIVE.SYS is shown in the following:

```
DEVICE = RAMDRIVE.SYS disksize sectorsize entries  /E /A
```

The *disksize* parameter indicates the size of the RAM disk (in kilobytes). This number can range from 16 to 32,767 (equivalent to 32M). The default value is 64.

The *sectorsize* parameter represents the size of the sectors used in the virtual disk. You can specify one of three sector sizes: 128, 256, or 512 (the default) bytes. Normally, you do not change this parameter; if you do, however, you also must specify the *disksize* parameter.

The *entries* parameter determines the maximum number of directory entries permitted in the RAM disk's root directory. This parameter can be a value ranging from 2 through 1,024. The default value is 64. You normally don't need to change this parameter. If you do specify the entries parameter, you also must enter the *disksize* and *sectorsize* parameters. Set the number of directories based on the size of the RAM disk and the number of files you are storing.

By default, DOS creates a RAM disk in conventional memory. You can, however, include the /E switch to cause the RAM disk to be created in XMS memory. Even with this switch, however, RAMDRIVE uses some conventional memory, so you may want to try loading the RAMDRIVE.SYS device driver into upper memory. The following command creates a 1,024K RAM disk in XMS memory and loads the device driver into upper memory:

```
DEVICEHIGH=C:\DOS\RAMDRIVE.SYS 1024 /E
```

Caution

If you want your RAM disk to use extended memory, it must follow the CONFIG.SYS commands that load HIMEM.SYS or a different memory manager.

The /A switch creates the RAM disk in EMS memory. To use this switch, you must load an expanded memory manager (such as EMM386.EXE) before loading RAMDRIVE.SYS. You cannot use the /A and /E switches for the same RAM disk. You can create different RAM disks, however, some using EMS memory and others using XMS memory. Given a choice, use XMS memory.

After you insert the DEVICE=RAMDRIVE.SYS command into CONFIG.SYS and reboot your computer, DOS displays a message similar to the following during initialization of your computer:

```
Microsoft RAMDrive version 3.07 virtual disk D:
  Disk size: 64k
  Sector size: 512 bytes
  Allocation unit: 1 sectors
  Directory entries: 64
```

Most importantly, this message tells you that this RAM disk is accessed as drive D. The message also shows the disk size, sector size, allocation-unit (cluster) size, and maximum number of root-directory entries.

The amount of RAM in your computer, the programs you use, and the convenience of a RAM disk help determine what size RAM disk you use and even whether you should use a RAM disk.

Drive Letters and Block Devices

The logical disk drive names (the drive letters) that DOS assigns to disks created by RAMDRIVE.SYS and DRIVER.SYS (see the Command Reference) depend on the placement of the commands in the CONFIG.SYS file. You may try to use the wrong disk drive name if you do not know how DOS assigns drive names. When DOS encounters a block device driver (that is, any device that transfers data in blocks rather than in bytes), DOS assigns the next highest drive letter to that device. The order is first come, first assigned.

The potential for confusion comes when several block device drivers are loaded. The order of loading, based on the order of the commands in the CONFIG.SYS file, determines the names assigned by DOS. If you load RAMDRIVE.SYS first and DRIVER.SYS second, the RAM disk may be named D and the DRIVER.SYS disk one letter higher. If you switch the lines so that DRIVER.SYS loads first, the disk drive names also switch; the DRIVER.SYS disk is D, and the RAM disk is E.

Caution

Because RAM disks are memory-based devices, you lose their contents when you reboot or turn off your PC. To prevent data loss, you must copy the contents of a RAM disk to a conventional disk file before rebooting or turning off the power. If you (or your program) are creating or modifying RAM disk files, copy the files to an actual disk regularly in case a power failure occurs.

One excellent way to use a RAM disk is to assign the TEMP environment variable to this virtual drive. Certain programs use an environment variable named TEMP to determine where to create various temporary files. These temporary files usually are written and read frequently during the operation of the program; their temporary nature makes them good candidates for storage in a RAM disk.

To assign TEMP to a RAM disk, you first have to determine a name for the virtual disk and then use the SET command (see the Command Reference). Assign the TEMP variable to a subdirectory rather than to the RAM disk's root directory to avoid the 64 file name limit. Assuming that the RAM disk becomes drive D, use the following commands in AUTOEXEC.BAT to create a directory on the virtual disk and to cause temporary files to be written to that directory:

```
MD D:\TEMPDATA
SET TEMP = D:\TEMPDATA
```

Some programs use an environment variable named TMP instead of TEMP for the same purpose. In such a case, substitute TMP for TEMP in the preceding command.

Defragmenting Your Disk

If all you ever did with your hard disk was add files, the space available on your disk would be used very efficiently. DOS would add one file and then another to your disk, with each file being stored entirely within a contiguous area, followed by another contiguous file, an arrangement that enables DOS to access your files very efficiently.

Nobody, however, only adds new files to a disk. As you use your disk, you add new files, delete existing files, and add new data to existing files. Over time, data becomes scattered over the disk, and even the data within a single file may reside in chunks throughout the disk. This scattering of data is called *fragmentation*. The following sections discuss fragmentation in detail.

Understanding the Effects of Fragmentation. The more fragmented your disk, the slower your computer runs. Suppose that a third of your hard disk currently is full and that all the used space is at the front of the disk so that you have no fragmentation. Whenever you request data from the disk, the disk heads do not have to move very far and can access your data quickly.

If the same data is spread across the disk, however, the disk heads may have to move across the entire disk to access data. The longer movement requires more time, and you may notice the difference. Moreover, the disk may require more time to access each individual file. When you run a program (at least, a program that doesn't use overlays), DOS must read the program from disk into memory. That operation is much faster if the entire program is in successive locations on the disk and much slower if the disk heads must move to widely separated locations on the disk.

Fragmentation, which is almost inevitable, tends to increase the longer you use your disk. Programs that defragment your disk—that is, move all the data to the beginning of the disk and store each file's data in the same place—have long been available from third-party software vendors. The following section discusses DOS's built-in defragmentation program.

Understanding the Basic Operation of DEFRAG. DOS 6.0 was the first version of DOS to come with a defragmentation program, called DEFRAG. You execute DEFRAG by typing

```
DEFRAG
```

at the DOS prompt. A dialog box appears, asking which drive you want to defragment (see fig. 19.1).

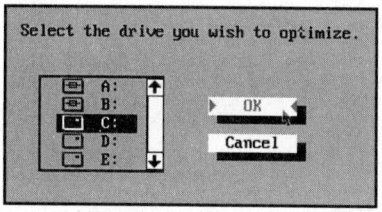

Fig. 19.1
The DEFRAG disk selection dialog box.

Select a drive by clicking a drive letter. Alternatively, use the arrow keys to move to the desired drive, and then press Enter. DEFRAG scans the selected drive and displays a map of the used and unused portions. You need not understand the map to use DEFRAG effectively, but if you're interested in understanding DEFRAG's analysis of your disk, study the legend at the bottom right corner of the screen, which explains the symbols in the disk map.

After displaying the map, DEFRAG suggests one of the following courses of action:

- *Do nothing.* If the disk is not fragmented, DEFRAG tells you that you don't need to perform any operation.
- *Unfragment files only.* If most of the data in the used area of the disk is stored together but the individual files are scattered throughout that area, DEFRAG recommends that you defragment the files. After DEFRAG completes this operation, the same area of the disk will be in use, but the data in that area is rearranged so that the data for each file is stored together. DEFRAG usually recommends this operation for disks that are mostly full.
- *Full optimization.* If the used area of the disk is scattered across the disk, DEFRAG recommends that you perform a full optimization, meaning that you defragment the entire disk. DEFRAG rearranges the used areas on the disk so that all the used portion of the disk is at the beginning of the disk and the data for each file is stored contiguously.

Figure 19.2 shows a typical recommendation from DEFRAG.

If you choose Optimize, DEFRAG reorganizes your disk, using the suggested method. Be prepared to wait. Although DEFRAG does its work quickly, it still may take a long time on a large, heavily fragmented disk.

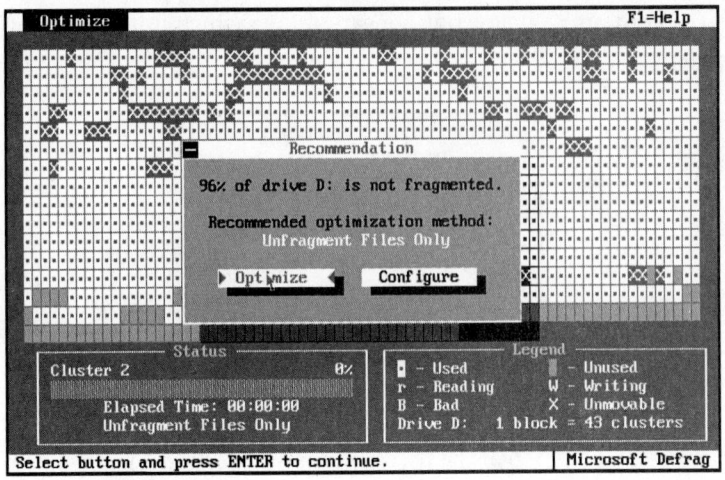

Fig. 19.2
DEFRAG analysis and recommendation.

When DEFRAG suggests a particular type of defragmentation, you do not have to accept its recommendation. When DEFRAG recommends that only the files be defragmented, for example, it is telling you that the extra efficiency you would gain by performing a disk defragmentation is not worth the time required by DEFRAG. However, you may be willing to let DEFRAG take the extra time to do the more complete disk defragmentation.

As figure 19.2 shows, when DEFRAG makes a recommendation, you can click Configure to select various options that control how DEFRAG works. When you click Configure, DEFRAG presents the Optimize menu, which includes more operations than just configuration—the first item tells DEFRAG to begin the defragmentation procedure. Table 19.2 lists the functions available in the Optimize menu.

Table 19.2 The DEFRAG Optimize (Configuration) Menu

Selection	Meaning
Begin Optimization	Begins optimization of your hard disk, using any configuration options you have selected
Drive	Enables you to choose the drive you want to optimize
Optimization Method	Enables you to choose full optimization or file only (may leave empty space between files)

Selection	Meaning
File Sort	Enables you to choose how files will be sorted within directories, if at all
Map Legend	Displays a legend of the symbols DEFRAG uses to show disk usage
About Defrag	Displays information about the DEFRAG program
Exit	Exits DEFRAG

If you want to change the type of defragmentation that DEFRAG performs, choose Optimization Method. This option presents a dialog box that enables you to specify whether DEFRAG defragments only files or completely defragments the disk. After you make a selection, you can choose Begin Optimization from the Optimize menu; DEFRAG performs the optimization you selected.

Sorting Directories. Normally DOS doesn't store file names in a directory in any particular order. As you create and delete files, DOS removes old names and inserts new names wherever empty space occurs. The result is that when you use DIR to list the contents of a directory, often the files appear to be listed in random order. You can overcome this disorganized appearance by using the sorting switches available with the DIR command or by using some application programs, such as WordPerfect, which sort a directory each time they display it. This is not a permanent solution, however. The directory information is still stored on disk in a disorganized manner.

While DEFRAG reorganizes your disk, you can tell it to organize the names of the files within the directories in one of five ways:

- *Unsorted.* This option, which is the default, tells DEFRAG to leave the names in their current order.
- *Name.* DEFRAG organizes the directory alphabetically by file name. This option is probably the one you find most useful.
- *Extension.* DEFRAG organizes the directory by extension name; for example, all the .COM files appear together, all the .EXE files together, and so on.

- *Date & Time.* DEFRAG sorts the directory by the time and date the files were last modified. This option enables you to tell at a glance which files have and have not been modified recently.
- *Size.* DEFRAG organizes files by the amount of disk space they consume.

You also can specify that the sort be in ascending or descending order—that is, that values get larger or smaller as the directory listing proceeds. Usually you want an ascending sort for names so that the list starts with the beginning of the alphabet and proceeds through the end of the alphabet. If you're sorting by size, however, you may want a descending sort so that the biggest files are listed first and the smallest files last.

You can specify how DEFRAG sorts directories from the DEFRAG Optimize menu by choosing File Sort. Figure 19.3 shows the File Sort menu. Alternatively, you can provide command line arguments, discussed in the next section, to specify file sort type.

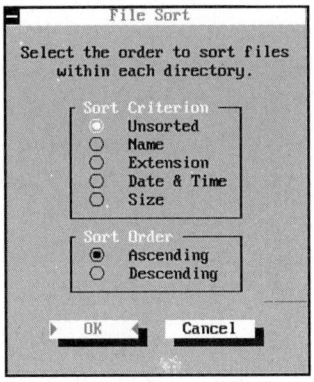

Fig. 19.3
The DEFRAG File Sort menu.

DEFRAG Startup Options. When you use DEFRAG, you usually start it simply by typing DEFRAG. Like most DOS commands, however, DEFRAG has a number of startup options available. The complete syntax for DEFRAG is shown in the following:

```
DEFRAG d:  /F /U /S:order  /B /SKIPHIGH /LCD /BW /G0 /H
```

Normally DEFRAG asks you which drive you want to defragment. If you specify the *d:* parameter, DEFRAG uses that as the drive you want to defragment.

Normally DEFRAG recommends the type of defragmentation you should perform. The /F parameter tells DEFRAG to defragment the disk (leaving no empty spaces between files); the /U parameter tells DEFRAG to defragment files (possibly leaving empty space between files). If you specify one of these parameters, DEFRAG does not make a recommendation, but immediately carries out the type of defragmentation you specify.

You can control whether DEFRAG sorts directory entries by using the /S switch. /S is optionally followed by a colon and one or more characters that specify how you want the entries sorted within each directory. Valid letters are listed in the following:

N	Alphabetical order by name
E	Alphabetical order by extension
D	By time and date, with the oldest dates (that is, files that were last modified farthest in the past) listed first
S	By size, with the smallest files listed first

For example, the following command defragments drive C and sorts files in alphabetical order by name:

```
DEFRAG C: /SN
```

You can also place a minus sign (–) after a sort letter to specify a descending sort instead of ascending. Consider these two commands:

```
DEFRAG C: /SS
DEFRAG C: /SS-
```

The first (without the minus) lists the smallest files first; the second (with the minus) lists the largest files first.

The /B switch tells DEFRAG to reboot your computer after the defragmentation process is complete.

The /SKIPHIGH switch tells DEFRAG to load itself into conventional memory. Otherwise DEFRAG uses upper memory, if available.

The /LCD switch uses a color scheme that is likely to be more readable if you are using a laptop or notebook computer with an LCD screen.

The /BW switch tells DEFRAG to use a black-and-white color scheme, which is likely to be more pleasing if you have a monochrome monitor.

The /G0 switch disables the mouse and graphic character set. Use this switch if DEFRAG displays strange characters on your monitor.

Normally DEFRAG does not reorganize hidden files. Use the /H switch to tell DEFRAG to move hidden files.

Note

When you use DEFRAG, keep in mind the following restrictions:

- You cannot use DEFRAG to defragment drives over a network.
- You cannot run DEFRAG from Windows.
- Disk statistics reported by DEFRAG and CHKDSK or SCANDISK differ slightly. When listing the number of directories, for example, DEFRAG counts the root directory, but CHKDSK does not.

Getting the Most Space from Your Hard Disk

For Related Information

- "Using the INSTALL Command," p. 486

Since the introduction of PCs in 1981, the amount of disk storage space available to the average user has increased steadily. The original PCs used cassette tapes for mass storage and offered, as an option, floppy disks with only 160K of storage space. Today, many PCs are sold with hard disks that have several thousand times that amount of space; 100M and 200M hard disks are common.

You might think that if people managed to get by with less than 1M, they should be perfectly content with 200M or more. As when you buy a bigger briefcase, however, you simply find more things to put in it. This is true of hard disks. As disk capacity has increased, so has the need for space.

A decade ago, few software vendors wrote software that required several megabytes of disk storage because they knew that few of their potential customers' systems had that kind of storage capability. Now vendors rarely think twice about releasing software that requires 5M or 10M of disk storage; they expect that most people have that much space to spare.

Although you cannot increase the physical capacity of your disk without buying a larger disk, you may be able to increase the amount of data you can store on your disk by using the techniques discussed in the next couple of sections. First you learn about manual methods of freeing disk space, and then you learn about DoubleSpace, which provides full-time disk compression.

Freeing Up Disk Space

The two most popular methods of freeing disk space are to delete files you no longer need and to compress computer files. You also can archive files that you no longer need on floppy disks or tape backup.

Deleting Unnecessary Files

Much of the software available today is very complex, offering many features that you probably will never use. As a result, many of the files that are copied to your hard disk when you install a software program are files that you never open. You may be able to find and delete some of these files, thereby freeing some of your hard disk space.

Some programs, such as Microsoft Word for Windows, ask which features you expect to use and install only the files that are appropriate for you. If you later change your mind, you can install the missing pieces then.

When you install DOS, dozens of programs are installed on your hard disk. If you are short on disk space, you may want to browse through these programs and delete those that are not important to you. Consider the following examples:

- DOS includes many files that enable it to work with foreign-language character sets, including German, Swedish, and French. If you expect to use your computer only in the United States, you can delete these files to free disk space.
- Some DOS utilities may duplicate functions that are available in other programs installed in your system. If you use a backup program (such as Norton Backup or FastBack), for example, you can delete the DOS backup program, MSBACKUP.

If you are considering deleting any of the files supplied with DOS, refer to the Command Reference to determine which files you can safely remove.

Another side effect of upgrading your version of DOS is that the old DOS files (from the previous version) are stored in a directory that begins with the letters OLD_DOS. After the upgrade is complete, and you are sure you want to continue using the new version of DOS, you can safely delete this directory and everything within it. The program DELOLDDOS, provided with DOS, can take care of this deletion for you.

Using File Compression

If you were to examine the file that contains the text for this chapter, you would find that many words—such as *DOS* and *the*—are repeated frequently. Most data includes such repetition—patterns that occur over and over within a file, whether the file contains text, customer data, or machine instructions.

Many programmers have written programs that analyze these patterns and squeeze a file's data into a smaller space by converting the data to a kind of shorthand notation. (PKZip and LHArc are examples of such programs.) This process is known as *compression*. In special cases, the compressed data may require as little as 10 percent of the original space, although 50 percent is more typical.

If you are interested in acquiring a good compression program, you should check out an on-line service such as CompuServe or your local BBS. File compression software is used extensively in telecommunications because the smaller files transfer faster and with less cost.

Archiving Files

Over time, you probably use your computer to perform many different tasks and complete a multitude of projects. When you complete a project, a good plan of action is to compress the files using compression software discussed in the previous section.

You can easily move compressed files to high-density floppy disks or to a backup tape. You then can store these disks or tapes for long periods of time in case you need the information again.

Take a look at your hard drive and the dates of the data files contained on it. You may find that you have many files that you have not accessed for a long time. Such files are prime candidates for archiving.

Understanding DoubleSpace

Beginning with DOS 6.0, Microsoft decided to include a disk-compression program called DoubleSpace. The decision to include this was apparently prompted by the popularity and success of third-party disk compression programs such as Stacker. Microsoft has refined and improved DoubleSpace in DOS 6.2.

DoubleSpace enables DOS to compress data automatically when you store the data on disk and to uncompress the data when you use it. DoubleSpace works transparently—you have no indication that the program is compressing your files, except that your disk can hold more data than before. You can select which drives use compression and which do not. You might decide, for example, to compress drive C, but not drive D, which contains OS/2.

Caution

Only if the DoubleSpace driver is loaded can you read a compressed drive. If you use another operating system in addition to DOS—such as OS/2, UNIX, Xenix, or Windows NT—you cannot access a compressed drive while you are running that other system.

Using DoubleSpace provides one major advantage: the amount of data you can store on your hard disk is roughly doubled because DoubleSpace is analyzing your data and squeezing more information into less space. DoubleSpace uses a compression algorithm similar to that used in the compression programs discussed earlier (PKZip and LHArc). The exact amount of additional data you can store varies, depending on the characteristics of the data itself. This is because different data can be compressed different amounts. For instance, text files and some graphic files (such as .TIF files) can be compressed quite a bit. Other files, such as .WAV files (used for sound) or .GIF files (used for graphics) are already compressed and do not benefit from DoubleSpace.

Using DoubleSpace also has the following minor disadvantages:

- DoubleSpace must perform extra work to compress and uncompress data each time you access your disk. This extra work takes time and slows your computer slightly. If you have a fast computer, such as a 386 or 486, the slowdown is so insignificant that you almost certainly will never notice the difference. On slower computers, however, you may notice that operations involving a lot of disk access seem to run a bit more slowly than before.

- DoubleSpace requires some conventional memory—about 50K if you load DoubleSpace high (into upper memory) by using DEVICEHIGH.
- Without the DoubleSpace device driver, a system cannot access a hard disk on which the files are compressed with DoubleSpace. This restriction is not likely to cause problems, but if your computer breaks, you cannot remove your hard disk and use it in a computer that has an earlier version of DOS.
- You cannot use DoubleSpace with some disk-intensive programs. This is primarily evident with some game programs that swap screens and sound between memory and disk.

Tip
If you have programs that will not work with DoubleSpace, but you still want to enjoy the benefits of disk compression, place the programs on an uncompressed volume. Then, when you need to use those programs, reboot your computer and use the Ctrl-F5 or Ctrl-F8 keys to control whether DoubleSpace capability is loaded. See Chapter 2, "Starting DOS," for more information.

Caution

A drive may contain files that cannot or should not be compressed. The Windows swap file, for example, must remain uncompressed.

When you apply compression to a drive, DoubleSpace makes the drive appear as though it were two drives, with two distinct drive letters. DoubleSpace divides the disk into a compressed drive and an uncompressed drive so that you still can store some of your files in an uncompressed format.

You can decide how much of the disk to allocate for each area. If you don't expect to store any files in an uncompressed format, make the uncompressed drive small (a fraction of a megabyte) and allocate the rest to the compressed drive. Conversely, if you expect to store the Windows swap file on the uncompressed drive, allocate several megabytes to that drive.

DOS assigns a new drive letter to one of the areas so that you can access either area by using the appropriate drive letter. If you apply compression to drive C, for example, DoubleSpace might tell you that from now on, C refers to the uncompressed portion of the disk and J refers to the compressed portion.

Installing DoubleSpace

To install DoubleSpace, type the following command at the DOS prompt:

DBLSPACE

You must not have any other programs running when you first issue this command. In particular, you must not be running Windows or the DOS Shell.

DoubleSpace first asks whether you want an Express or Custom Setup; the default is Express. If you choose Express, DoubleSpace compresses the existing files on drive C. Choose Custom setup if you want to select the drive to compress. DBLSPACE then installs the DoubleSpace driver in the DOS kernel and reboots your machine.

DoubleSpace also may add a line to your CONFIG.SYS file, such as the following:

```
DEVICEHIGH=C:\DOS\DBLSPACE.SYS /MOVE
```

This line does not load the DoubleSpace device driver; the DOS kernel loads the driver automatically when you install DoubleSpace. Instead, the line moves the driver into upper memory (if you have upper memory blocks available). If you remove this line from your CONFIG.SYS, you still load the DoubleSpace driver, just not into upper memory.

Controlling the Operation of DoubleSpace

You can run DoubleSpace at any time to get information about compression on your disks or to control various facets of DoubleSpace's operation. You run DoubleSpace simply by typing the following command:

DBLSPACE

When DoubleSpace starts, it lists all the available drives that employ compression. For each drive, DoubleSpace shows the total amount of space and the current free space available.

Many DoubleSpace operations require you to select a drive, either by using the arrow keys to position the selection bar on one of the drives or by clicking a drive.

Displaying Compressed Drive Information

To display information about a compressed drive, select the compressed drive, choose Drive from the menu bar, and then choose Info from the resulting menu. (If you do not have a mouse, press Alt-D, and then position the cursor on Info and press Enter.) For a shortcut, you can also double-click or simply press Enter when the drive is first selected.

Figure 19.4 shows the information display for a small compressed drive. Notice that in this example, most of the disk is allocated for compressed files and is accessed as drive I; about 2M is uncompressed and is accessed as drive D.

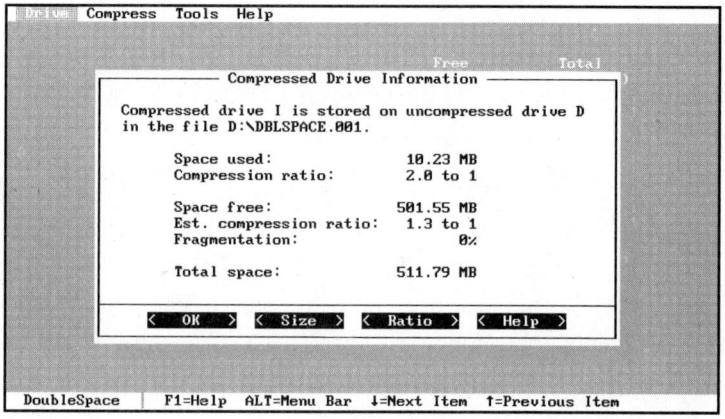

Fig. 19.4
The DoubleSpace Compressed Drive Information dialog box.

This figure also tells you that the estimate of 501.55M free is based on a compression ratio of 1.3-to-1, but the compression ratio that DoubleSpace actually has achieved on the data stored so far is only 2-to-1. Therefore, if the rest of the drive is used for the same type of data, you will be able to actually store more data than DoubleSpace's estimate of 501M leads you to expect.

Clicking the Size and Ratio buttons enables you to change the size of the compressed area and the estimating ratio, respectively. The following sections discuss both methods.

Changing the Size of a Compressed Drive

On each compressed disk, DoubleSpace reserves some room for uncompressed files. To change the size of the uncompressed area (thereby changing the size of the compressed area correspondingly), perform one of the following actions:

- While displaying the Compressed Drive Information dialog box click the Size button.
- In the main screen, select Drive, then Change Size.

When you perform either action, the Change Size dialog box appears (see fig. 19.5).

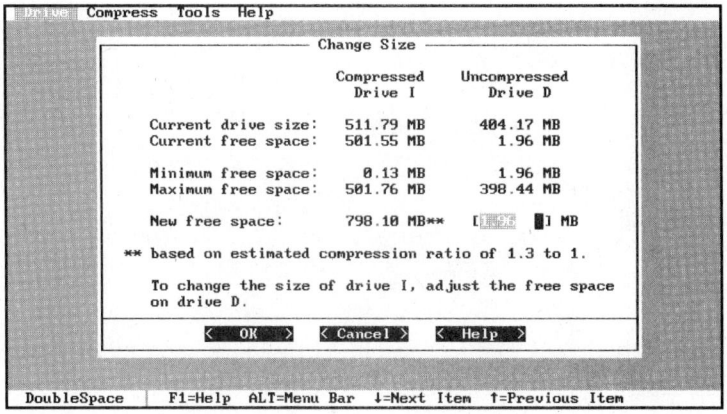

Fig. 19.5
The Change Size dialog box.

You can change the amount of space that DoubleSpace reserves for the uncompressed area.

Changing the Compression Ratio

After you use a compressed drive for a time, you may discover that the actual compression ratio achieved by DoubleSpace is different from the ratio it uses to predict free space. You can ask DoubleSpace to use a different ratio to estimate free space by performing one of the following:

- While displaying the Compressed Drive Information dialog box, click the Ratio button.
- In the main screen, choose Drive and then Change Ratio.

DoubleSpace displays the current ratio that it is using for estimates and the actual ratio that it has been able to achieve in compressing your files so far. If the files you previously stored in this drive are typical of the files that you expect to store in the future, you will want to change the new ratio to match the ratio for stored files.

In the Change Compression Ratio dialog box shown in figure 19.6, DoubleSpace is using a 1.3-to-1 ratio to estimate free space, but has achieved a 2-to-1 ratio for existing files.

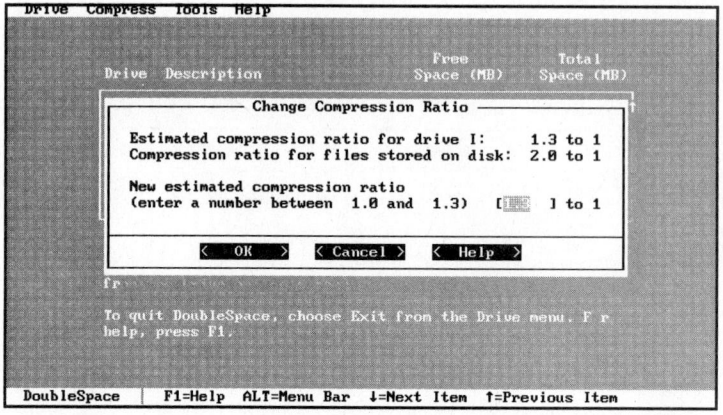

Fig. 19.6
The Change Compression Ratio dialog box.

The amount of total space and free space that DoubleSpace displays are estimates that depend on the type of data you store on the disk. In predicting free space, DoubleSpace takes into account the size and actual free space of the compressed volume and then determines an estimated compression ratio. The general rule of thumb is that the larger the amount of free space on your compressed volume, the lower the compression ratio used by DoubleSpace. Thus, the large compressed volume used as an example in this chapter has a low 1.3-to-1 compression ratio.

If you have a smaller compressed volume, DoubleSpace uses a higher compression ratio, closer to 2-to-1, which is to say that if DoubleSpace has 10M of physical disk space free, the program predicts that it can compress 20M of your data into that space.

It should go without saying that the estimates used by DoubleSpace will necessarily be off—sometimes way off. As you work with your compressed volume, adjust the compression ratio used by DoubleSpace for its estimates.

Note

Changing the compression ratio does not change the amount of compression that DoubleSpace can squeeze out of any specific file, only the ratio that DoubleSpace uses to estimate future compression.

Formatting a Compressed Drive

You do not need to format a compressed drive in the same sense that you format other drives to prepare them for use. When you use DoubleSpace to create a compressed drive, you must have already formatted that drive in the usual way. On the other hand, people often format an existing drive as a simple way of erasing all data on a drive, and you can format a compressed drive if you want to erase all the data stored on that drive. However, you cannot use the standard DOS format on a compressed drive.

To format a compressed drive, select the drive you want to format from the list of compressed drives, and then choose Drive and Format. DoubleSpace displays an alert box that asks whether you're sure you want to format the drive. If you click OK, DoubleSpace erases all data stored in that drive.

Caution

You cannot unformat a compressed drive. After you choose Format and click OK, your data is gone forever.

Deleting a Compressed Drive

If you no longer want to use a compressed drive, you can delete that drive. Select the drive that you want to delete from the list of compressed drives. Choose Drive and Delete. DoubleSpace displays a dialog box warning you that you will permanently destroy the contents of the compressed drive and asks you for confirmation. If you click OK, DoubleSpace deletes the drive and all the data in the drive. The space that was allocated to the compressed drive returns to the corresponding uncompressed drive.

Caution

Make sure you copy all the data from your compressed drive to a backup device or to an uncompressed drive before you delete a compressed drive. You can also use the Uncompress feature, discussed later in this chapter.

Creating a New Uncompressed Drive

You can create a new compressed drive by choosing the Compress menu. DoubleSpace displays a menu from which you can select either of two ways of compressing the disk.

To compress an existing disk and all the data stored on it, follow this procedure:

1. From the Compress menu, choose Existing drive. DoubleSpace displays a dialog box listing existing uncompressed drives, along with their current free space and projected free space.

2. Select the drive to which you want to apply compression. DoubleSpace displays a dialog box showing the drive letter that it will assign to the uncompressed drive and the amount of space it will allocate to that drive. DoubleSpace allocates the rest of the space to the compressed drive.

   You must allocate at least 0.14M to the uncompressed drive; use this value if you do not expect to need any uncompressed space. If you want to change either of these values, select the value that you want to change.

   When you are ready to proceed, choose Continue or press Enter.

3. DoubleSpace displays a screen informing you that it is ready to compress the drive. DoubleSpace then prompts you to press C. If you press C, the program creates the compressed drive and compresses existing files in that drive. The new compressed drive uses the original drive letter, and the uncompressed drive receives the new drive letter.

If you want to leave existing files in the uncompressed drive and create a new compressed drive from the free portion of the existing drive, follow this procedure:

1. From the Compress menu, choose Create new drive. DoubleSpace displays a dialog box listing existing uncompressed drives, along with their current free space and projected free space.

2. Select the drive to which you want to apply compression. DoubleSpace displays the drive letter it will assign to the compressed drive, the compression ratio it will use to estimate free space, and the amount of free space it will leave in the uncompressed drive, in addition to the space already used by existing files. The program allocates the rest of the space to the compressed drive.

You must leave at least 0.14M of free space in the uncompressed drive; use this value if you do not expect to need any more uncompressed space. If you want to change any of these values, click the value you want to change.

When you are ready to proceed, click Continue or press Enter.

3. DoubleSpace tells you how much time the program requires to create the drive and prompts you to press C to continue. The program then creates the compressed drive, which will be empty. All existing files remain in the uncompressed drive. The uncompressed drive retains the original drive letter, and the compressed drive receives the new drive letter.

Using Other DoubleSpace Features

You can choose two other useful features from the Tools menu: Defragment and Uncompress. There is also a Chkdsk option from the Tools menu, but all it does is display information indicating that the Chkdsk function has been replaced by the SCANFIX command (as covered in Chapter 7, "Preparing and Maintaining Disks").

The Defragment option allows you to defragment a compressed volume. You can use either this option or the standard DEFRAG command (from the DOS prompt). If you choose to use this option, DoubleSpace displays a dialog box asking whether you want to defragment the disk. If you choose Yes, DoubleSpace performs the defragmentation. Note that defragmenting a compressed disk does not significantly increase the speed with which you can access the disk (as DEFRAG does for a regular disk), but it does sometimes enable you to store a bit more data on the compressed disk.

Beginning with DOS 6.2, DoubleSpace allows you to uncompress a previously compressed drive. This is done by copying the data on a compressed portion of a drive to the uncompressed portion. Before you choose this option, you should do the following:

- Make sure that you reduce the size of the compressed drive as far as possible by using the Size feature previously discussed. Conversely, this increases the size of the uncompressed portion of the disk.
- Make a backup of your compressed volume. This is done using the MSBACKUP program discussed in Chapter 10, "Protecting Your Data."

Caution

Uncompressing a DoubleSpace volume can take up to several hours. Make sure you allocate enough free time to complete the procedure.

After reducing the size of the compressed drive and backing it up, choose Uncompress from the Tools menu. DoubleSpace displays a dialog box indicating that it is going to uncompress files and copy them to the uncompressed portion of the hard drive and reminding you to make a backup of your compressed data. When you choose Yes, the drive uncompression begins. DoubleSpace then does the following steps:

1. Performs a surface scan using SCANFIX to determine the reliability of the destination (uncompressed) disk drive.
2. Performs other SCANFIX tests to verify the integrity of the compressed volume.
3. Performs another surface scan, this time on the source (compressed) disk drive.
4. Uncompresses the files on the source drive, moving them to the destination drive.
5. Deletes the compressed drive.
6. If the compressed drive being deleted is the last one in your system, removes all references to DoubleSpace from CONFIG.SYS and marks the DoubleSpace kernel so it doesn't load when DOS is booted.
7. Reboots the computer.

After the computer reboots, the uncompression is complete. You should check your data to make sure it all appears intact, and then you can use your system as normal.

Summary

In this chapter, you discovered the utility programs that DOS provides to enable you to use your hard disk most efficiently. You also learned the following:

- You can increase the effective speed with which you can access data on your hard disk by creating a disk cache with SMARTDrive.
- A RAM disk, created with RAMDRIVE, can help improve program speed for programs using many temporary files.
- Defragmenting your disk regularly with DEFRAG improves disk access and loading times.
- You can increase the amount of space available to you by using disk compression with DBLSPACE.

The next chapter, "Understanding ANSI.SYS," begins Part V, "Customizing DOS," where you learn how to get the most out of DOS.

Part V

Customizing DOS

20 Understanding ANSI.SYS

21 Understanding the International Features of DOS

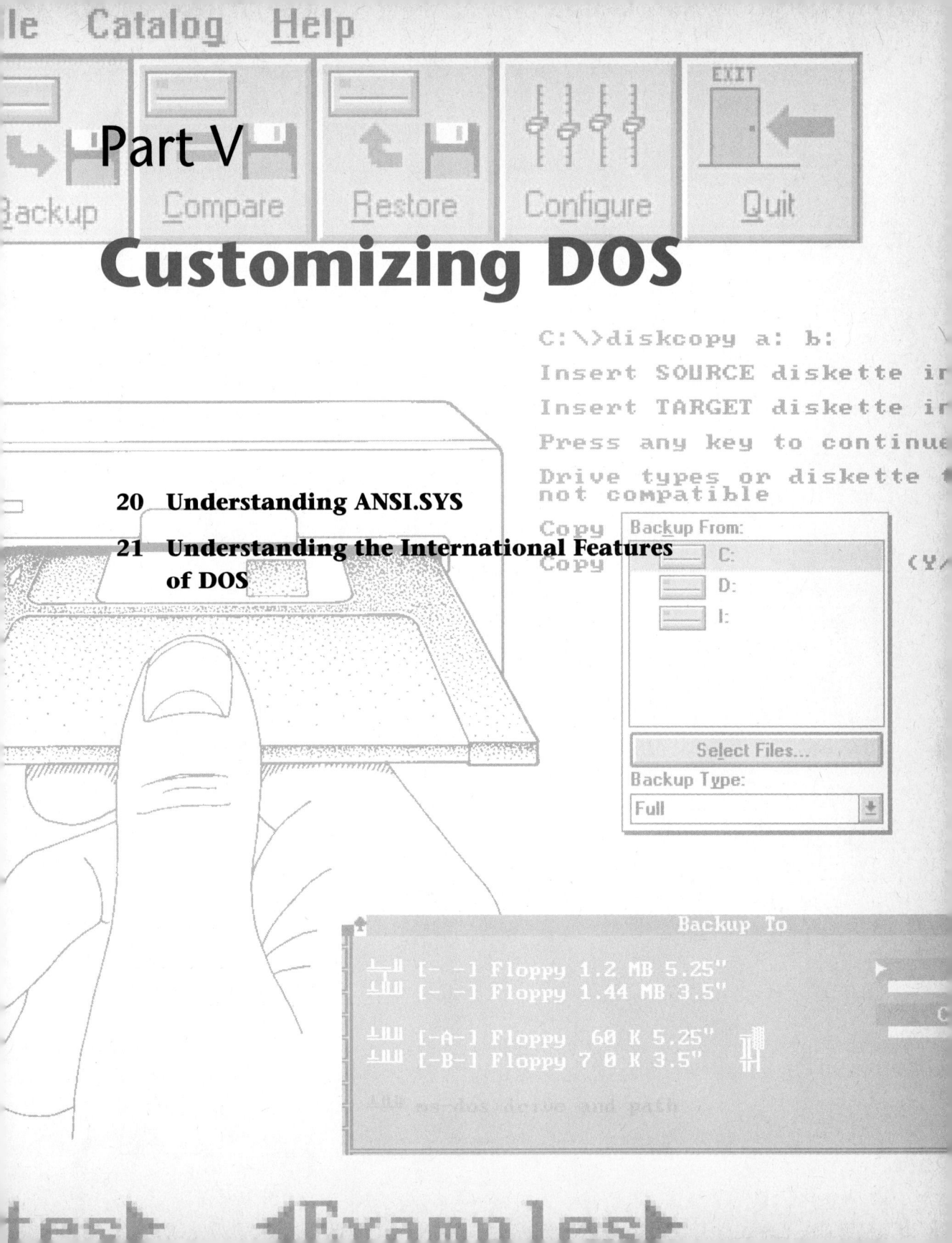

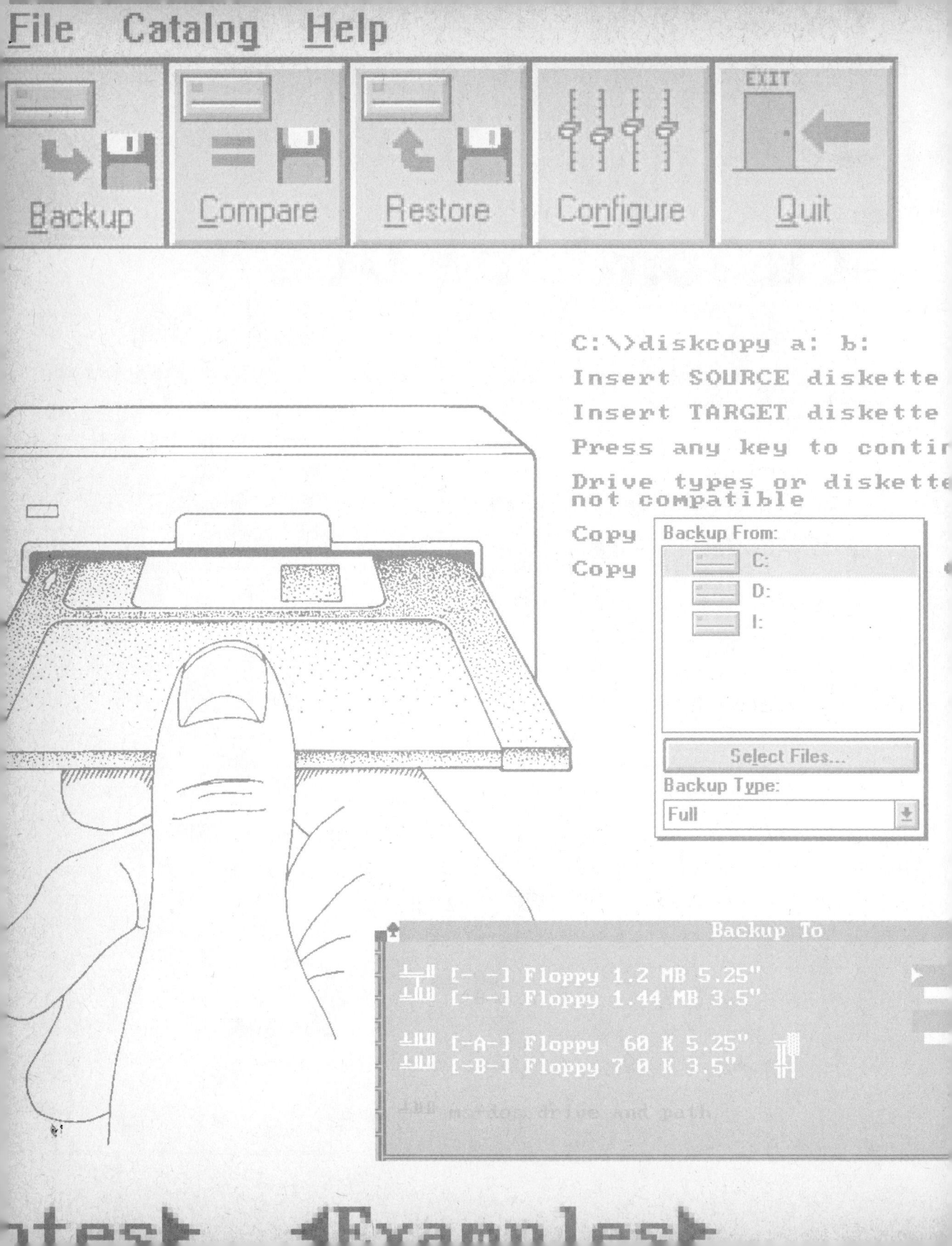
File Catalog Help
Backup
Compare
Restore
Configure
EXIT
Quit
C:\>diskcopy a: b:
Insert SOURCE diskette
Insert TARGET diskette
Press any key to contir
Drive types or diskette
not compatible
Copy
Copy
Backup From:
C:
D:
I:
Select Files...
Backup Type:
Full
Backup To
[- -] Floppy 1.2 MB 5.25"
[- -] Floppy 1.44 MB 3.5"
[-A-] Floppy 60 K 5.25"
[-B-] Floppy 7 0 K 3.5"

Chapter 20

Understanding ANSI.SYS

The term *ANSI* refers to the American National Standards Institute. ANSI is one of several sets of computer standards established by the institute to specify the codes that computer manufacturers can use to control video displays and keyboard mapping.

ANSI.SYS is a device driver, which means that it gives DOS additional control of the screen and keyboard devices beyond the control features built into the operating system. You use ANSI.SYS to enhance the functions of your video screen and keyboard. With ANSI.SYS, you can set screen colors, use graphics, and specify other video attributes. You can provide that personal touch to your DOS prompt. You even can change the assignments of keys on your keyboard.

The ANSI.SYS file supplied with MS-DOS contains a subset of the ANSI standards. Third-party suppliers of other ANSI.SYS files may include more features in their versions of this file, but those features are not necessary for most users.

Installing ANSI.SYS

The only way you can install the ANSI.SYS driver is to include it in your CONFIG.SYS file. The format of the line must be as follows:

```
DEVICE = C:\DOS\ANSI.SYS /X /K /R
```

or

```
DEVICEHIGH = C:\DOS\ANSI.SYS /X /K /R
```

The /X option enables you to remap extended keys if you are using a 101-key keyboard. The /K option treats 101-key keyboards as if they were 84-key keyboards, ignoring extended keys. The /R option slows screen scrolling for improved readability.

Note

The /X and /K switches are mutually exclusive. You can use one of them, but you cannot use both.

When you install MS-DOS on your computer, DOS places the ANSI.SYS file in the \DOS subdirectory. If ANSI.SYS is located in the root directory of your boot drive, you don't have to include its drive and directory name in the command line. If you placed the ANSI.SYS file in another directory or on another drive, however, make sure that you specify in the CONFIG.SYS statement the exact location of ANSI.SYS.

After you add ANSI.SYS to your CONFIG.SYS file, reboot your computer. DOS includes the ANSI.SYS driver in the operating system configuration. In the following sections, you learn how to use this driver and take advantage of its features.

Using ANSI.SYS

After you place the ANSI.SYS command in the CONFIG.SYS file and reboot the system so that the new configuration takes effect, you must issue commands that tell DOS to use the ANSI features.

Because some software is written to use ANSI codes, one or more of your software programs may require that ANSI.SYS be loaded. The installation procedure for this type of software notifies you of this requirement. (The program may even install the command in the CONFIG.SYS file for you.)

You can activate ANSI.SYS features also by issuing the ANSI commands yourself. However, you cannot simply type the commands at the DOS prompt; you must enter an Escape sequence. All ANSI.SYS sequences begin with the Escape character (ASCII value 27), followed by a left bracket ([). If you type this sequence at the prompt, DOS understands the Escape character to be a command to cancel the current operation; DOS cancels the operation, displays a backslash (\), and moves the cursor down to the next line.

If ANSI.SYS codes are not included in a program, you can send these codes to DOS in three ways: by executing a batch file, by typing a text file (that is, by using the DOS TYPE command), or by including the codes in a PROMPT command. When you embed ANSI codes in Escape sequences, the ANSI.SYS device driver intercepts the codes and executes the appropriate commands, ignoring any characters that are not preceded by the proper codes.

You can create a text file or a batch file or set up your PROMPT format in the AUTOEXEC.BAT file by using the MS-DOS editor (EDIT) or another text editor. Whatever utility you use must be capable of entering the Escape character, which is beyond the capability of many word processing programs and older text editors.

For information on using EDIT, see Chapter 15, "Using the DOS Editor." To enter the Escape character while using EDIT, hold down the Ctrl key, press P, and then press Esc.

Note

Some text editors display the Escape character as ^[. Because the ANSI code sequence requires a left bracket after the Escape character, the ANSI sequence may appear as ^[[.

Issuing ANSI.SYS Codes in Batch Files

The key to using ANSI.SYS is to have the Escape sequences sent to the display screen. This procedure is the only way to ensure that the device driver properly intercepts and executes the commands. Batch files send these sequences to the screen through the ECHO command, which tells DOS to display all commands on the screen. (For more information on batch files, see Chapter 16, "Understanding Batch Files.")

Note

By default, ECHO is set ON unless you explicitly issue an ECHO OFF command. If you do use ECHO OFF, any ANSI code line you enter thereafter must begin with the ECHO command.

Suppose that you want to use a batch file to set up formatting for a double-density disk (360K) in a 5 1/4-inch high-density (1.2M) drive. Use EDIT to create the batch file containing the instruction for the special effect, such as changing the color of the screen. If you enter the following batch file, giving it the name NEWDISK.BAT, it will do the trick:

```
@ECHO OFF
ECHO <Esc>[37;41m
ECHO THIS FUNCTION FORMATS DOUBLE DENSITY DISKETTES (360K) IN DRIVE A:
FORMAT A: /F:360
ECHO <Esc>[37;40m
```

The first line in the batch file tells DOS not to display any of the commands in the batch file unless specifically instructed to do so through the ECHO command. The leading character (@) instructs DOS not to display the ECHO OFF command.

The second line is an ANSI.SYS code sequence that sets the color of the screen (red, with white characters). *<Esc>* should be replaced with the actual Escape code (ASCII value 27). The ANSI code 37 produces a white foreground; 41 is the ANSI code for a red background. The character *m* indicates that screen attribute codes are being issued. The last line of the batch file resets the screen to white on black—the default setting. (Make sure that you use the lowercase character *m* in the ANSI.SYS Escape sequences.)

Note

If you have a monochrome monitor, you can substitute 7m for 35;41m in the second line of the batch file. The code 7 tells ANSI.SYS to set reverse video. If you use 7m instead of 35;41m, substitute 0m for 37;40m in the last line to set the screen back to normal.

To see why you must use the ECHO command in the ANSI Escape sequence, remove the ECHO command from the last line of the batch file and then run the file again. DOS informs you that it received a bad command or file name, and the screen color does not change to normal.

Issuing ANSI.SYS Codes in Text Files

Issuing ANSI codes in text files is similar to using the codes in batch files, except that you do not use an ECHO command in a text file. Also, for the commands to take effect, you must use the TYPE command to pass the codes to the display for DOS to execute. To create an example text file, create a SCREEN.TXT file that contains the following line:

```
<Esc>[37;41m
```

After you create and save this file, you can change the screen to red with white characters by entering the following command at the DOS prompt:

```
TYPE SCREEN.TXT
```

ANSI.SYS intercepts the characters of the file when being sent to the screen with the TYPE command. The Escape sequence, followed by the bracket, causes the device driver to execute the ANSI commands instead of passing the characters through to DOS. Your screen is now red with white characters.

You can return your screen to normal as follows. In the same way that you created SCREEN.TXT, create NORMAL.TXT with the following single line:

```
<Esc>[37;40M
```

After you enter this line, save the file. At the DOS prompt, enter the following to return your screen to normal:

```
TYPE NORMAL.TXT
```

Issuing ANSI.SYS Codes with the PROMPT Command

The third way to issue ANSI.SYS instructions is to include these instructions in a PROMPT command. You learned about the PROMPT command in Chapter 13, "Controlling Your Environment." In short, the PROMPT command alters the way that the DOS prompt appears. The normal syntax of the command follows:

```
PROMPT string
```

The *string* consists of a set of characters that may or may not include an ANSI Escape sequence. The characters you enter tell DOS how you want the DOS prompt to look. For full information on the characters you can use with the command, refer to Chapter 13. This section focuses on using the ANSI sequences with the PROMPT command.

To add more pizzazz to your DOS prompt, you can add color, as outlined in the following examples. If you have a color monitor, enter the following command, using nine spaces for the nine periods:

```
PROMPT $E[1;37;44mTime:
   $T$H$H$H$H$H$H.........$E[40m$E[K$_$E[1;44mDate:
   $D$E[0;40m$E[K$_[DOS 6.2] $P$G
```

The display shows the time and date in bright white text on a blue background, returning to normal white on black for the prompt.

If you have a monochrome monitor, enter the following command, using nine spaces for the nine periods:

```
PROMPT $E[7mTime: $T$H$H$H$H$H$H.........$E[0m$E[K$_$E[7mDate:
   $D$E[0m$E[K$_[DOS 6.2] $P$G
```

For Related Information

- "Mastering Fundamental Editing Techniques," p. 385
- "Learning Special Editing Techniques," p. 388
- "Using Batch-File Commands," p. 421
- "Changing the Command Prompt with PROMPT," p. 334

The display now shows the time and date in black characters on a white background, returning to normal white on black for the prompt.

As the inclusion of [DOS 6.2] in these two examples indicates, you also can display a message in the DOS prompt. (The brackets are included for cosmetic purposes only. They are not required.) Be creative. *Beam me up, Scotty; The BRAIN; USA Forever;* and *BOOM!* are a few examples of DOS users' humor and imagination.

Controlling Your Screen with ANSI.SYS

Now that you understand how to issue ANSI.SYS commands in batch files, in text files, and as part of a PROMPT command, you're ready to use ANSI.SYS commands to control and customize your screen display.

All ANSI screen commands begin with the normal Escape code and a left bracket ([) and end with a letter of the alphabet. The letter depends on the type of command you are asking ANSI.SYS to execute. In all instances, the capitalization of the ending letter is important. As you are working through the examples in this chapter, pay strict attention to the capitalization.

You can use as many ANSI control codes as you require on the same line, as long as the codes are separated by semicolons (;) and no code contradicts another code. The order of the codes is not important.

The following sections detail the general functions that can be performed with ANSI.SYS.

Cursor Movement

If you end the Escape sequence with the uppercase letter *A*, ANSI.SYS assumes you want to move the cursor up a given number of lines on the screen. For instance, the following will move the cursor up four lines on the screen:

```
<Esc>[4A
```

The horizontal position of the cursor is not affected; it only moves up. If the cursor is already at the top of the screen, the Escape code is ignored.

If you end the Escape sequence with a *B* (instead of an *A*), the cursor is moved down on the screen. Again, if the cursor is already at the bottom of the screen, the sequence is ignored.

Ending the Escape sequence with a *C* moves the cursor to the right by the number of indicated spaces; a *D* moves the cursor left. For example, the following line moves the cursor 23 spaces to the right:

```
<Esc>[23C
```

Cursor Positioning

To position the cursor at a given character location on the screen, you can use either the *H* or *f* codes. For instance, either of the following will move the cursor to line 10, column 32:

```
<Esc>[10;32H
<Esc>[10;23f
```

Note that the upper-left corner of the screen is considered position 0,0.

To save the current cursor position (in preparation for moving it and later restoring it), you use the *s* code, as shown here:

```
<Esc>[s
```

There are no other parameters; the cursor position is immediately saved. When you want to restore the cursor to the saved position, use the *u* command:

```
<Esc>[u
```

Setting the Screen Mode

You can use ANSI.SYS to change the display mode of your system. This is accomplished by providing a screen code and ending the sequence with the *h* code. The screen codes are listed in table 20.1.

Table 20.1 ANSI Screen Display Codes

Code	Screen Type
0	40 x 25 characters, monochrome
1	40 x 25 characters, color
2	80 x 25 characters, monochrome
3	80 x 25 characters, color
4	320 x 200 pixels, monochrome
5	320 x 200 pixels, color
6	640 x 200 pixels, monochrome

(continues)

Table 20.1 Continued

Code	Screen Type
7	Turns word wrap on and off
14	640 X 200 pixels, color
15	640 X 350 pixels, monochrome
16	640 X 360 pixels, color
17	640 X 480 pixels, monochrome
18	640 X 480 pixels, color
19	320 X 200 pixels, color

For example, the following line sets the screen mode to 80 x 25 color text:

```
<Esc>[3h
```

You can end the sequence also with the lowercase *l*; the only difference is in how screen code 7 is handled. With the *h* code, line wrap is turned on; with *l*, it is turned off. For instance, the following turns on 80 x 25 monochrome text with screen wrapping disabled:

```
<Esc>[2;7l
```

Setting the Text Attributes

Text attributes include color, bold, or reversed video. To set these, you list the desired attribute codes, separated by semicolons, and then terminate the Escape sequence with the *m* code. Table 20.2 lists the ANSI codes for setting the character attributes.

Table 20.2 ANSI Character Attribute Codes

Code	Effect
0	Normal display (the default)
1	High-intensity text
4	Underlined text (monochrome)
5	Blinking text
7	Reverse video (black on white)
8	Hidden text (black on black)

Code	Effect
30	Black foreground (character) color
31	Red foreground (character) color
32	Green foreground (character) color
33	Yellow foreground (character) color
34	Blue foreground (character) color
35	Magenta foreground (character) color
36	Cyan foreground (character) color
37	White foreground (character) color
40	Black background color
41	Red background color
42	Green background color
43	Yellow background color
44	Blue background color
45	Magenta background color
46	Cyan background color
47	White background color

Note

Some screen effects depend on the hardware. Underlined text, for example, cannot be displayed on all monitors.

You can use the codes in table 20.2 to customize your system. You may, for example, use ANSI codes to set the default screen colors to bright green on black:

```
<Esc>1;32;40m
```

Screen Control

Besides the functions discussed so far, ANSI.SYS also provides functions that you can use to control your screen. You can use the following ANSI code to clear the screen. It is the equivalent of the CLS command:

```
<Esc>[2J
```

If you want to erase only to the end of the current line, the following will do the trick:

```
<Esc>[K
```

Customizing Your Keyboard with ANSI.SYS

Computers use a set of 256 codes to indicate specific characters. These codes make up the *ASCII character set.* (ASCII is an acronym for the American Standard Code for Information Interchange.) A space, for example, is ASCII code 48; the uppercase *A* is ASCII code 65; and the lowercase *a* is ASCII code 97. You already know that the Escape code used in an ANSI control sequence has an ASCII value of 27. (See Appendix E, "ASCII and Extended ASCII Codes," for a list of ASCII codes.)

Every time you press a key on your keyboard, the system's circuits send a code to DOS. This code interprets the keystroke and displays the appropriate character. Not every code in the ASCII set, however, has a corresponding keyboard key. Moreover, some keys represent more than one character.

Keyboards actually send individual codes to DOS for each key or key combination you press on the keyboard. These codes are known as *scan codes.* Many scan codes correspond to ASCII codes. With the key combinations that involve the Ctrl, Alt, Shift, and Num Lock keys, however, more than 256 keystrokes (the ASCII code limit) are possible. This problem is solved by preceding some scan codes with a 0 entry.

When DOS receives a scan code from the keyboard, the program uses a built-in table to ascertain the proper character. When the ANSI.SYS device driver has been loaded through the CONFIG.SYS file, the ANSI driver takes over this chore. The driver also enables you to modify the table and to assign different characters to the scan codes.

Suppose that you must prepare documents or data files that include fractions. You can assign ASCII codes for some fractions to keys that you normally don't use. ASCII code 171, for example, stands for 1/2, and code 172 stands for 1/4. (See Appendix E for a complete list of ASCII codes.) Using ANSI.SYS makes key reassignments easy.

To assign the 1/2 fraction (ASCII 171) to the Shift-6 key combination, which produces the character ^ (ASCII 94), you can use either of the following commands:

```
<Esc>["^";"1/2"p
<Esc>[94;171p
```

The ANSI.SYS keyboard-assignment Escape sequence starts with the standard Escape character, followed by a left bracket ([). The next character is the ASCII code, the scan code, or the key representation in quotation marks. Then you specify the new ASCII code or the key representation in quotation marks. The two characters are separated by a semicolon. The sequence ends with the lowercase *p* code. Thus, in the first example, the key representation ^ is entered with quotation marks ("^") and is changed to "1/2". In the second example, scan code 171 replaces scan code 94.

Caution

Do not use spaces in the ANSI.SYS code sequence. If you use spaces, DOS may not interpret the sequence properly.

Remember that the first specification is for the key to be assigned. To restore the original key assignment, enter the code twice, for example:

```
<Esc>[94;94p
```

A key assignment does not need to be a single character. You also can assign a text message to a keystroke. This process is referred to as a *macro substitution*. If you often need to type the same sequence of characters, you can easily set up a macro substitution that enters those characters for you. Don't confuse this with the macro capability of DosKey, however. Macros that can be created with DosKey are much more powerful than those created with ANSI.SYS.

In the following example, the words *Heigh-Ho, Silver!* are assigned to the F7 key, which has the scan code 0;65:

```
<Esc>[0;65;"Heigh-Ho, Silver!"p
```

After you issue this ANSI.SYS instruction, either in a text file that you TYPE or in a batch file, DOS (through ANSI.SYS) displays the message *Heigh-Ho, Silver!* whenever you press F7.

Because no scan code or ASCII code of 0 exists, ANSI.SYS understands that the second number indicates the extended scan code for the F7 key instead of the ASCII code for the uppercase *A*, which is 65. If you want to add a carriage return (ASCII code 13) after the message, include that code in the Escape sequence as follows:

```
<Esc>[0;65;"Heigh-Ho, Silver!";13p
```

Caution

ANSI.SYS reassignment of normal character keys on your keyboard is not a good idea. Such a reassignment interferes with the normal operation of DOS and with many, if not all, of your software programs.

You can enter many of the ASCII character codes on your keyboard by holding down the Alt key while you type the ASCII code for the character you want to display. If you reassign keys, however, you no longer can enter certain key characters in this manner. Further, reassigned keys no longer function the same way. If you reassign the backslash key (\), for example, you no longer can use the backslash character to access subdirectories.

Refer to the "ANSI Keyboard Layout Control Codes" section in Appendix F for a list of scan codes for the function keys and other keys you may want to reassign.

Caution

When you use ANSI.SYS to reassign keys, keep in mind that DOS allows a total of 200 characters. If your key reassignments take more than 200 bytes, you overwrite part of the command processor in memory and your system may lock up.

Summary

In this chapter, you learned that ANSI.SYS is a device driver that gives DOS increased screen- and keyboard-handling capability. You load the driver through a statement in the CONFIG.SYS file.

The key points covered in this chapter include the following:

- You communicate with ANSI.SYS by issuing Escape sequences.
- You cannot issue an Escape sequence from the command line.
- You can issue an Escape sequence in a batch file, a prompt command, and a text file that you TYPE to the display.
- You use MS-DOS EDIT to create the batch and text files for ANSI.SYS commands.
- You can change screen attributes and colors with the ANSI.SYS commands.
- You can change key definitions with the ANSI.SYS commands.

In the next chapter, you learn another method of changing the characters on your screen display. The chapter discusses DOS support for international languages and for alternative time and date stamping.

Chapter 21

Understanding the International Features of DOS

Communication is making the world appear progressively smaller and smaller. Frequent contact among people from many different countries is not unusual. You can use computers to prepare documents and other files to send to all parts of the world.

Anything you work on that has international implications can cause you inconvenience if you do not adapt your computer to handle various languages and national customs. Presumably, most people reading this book, and using DOS as their operating system, live in the United States and have computers built to operate in the United States. Fortunately, however, Microsoft has built in to DOS the capability to internationalize your computer.

DOS provides three levels of internationalization. These levels involve the use of COUNTRY.SYS, KEYB.COM, and code page switching.

You may consider your standard version of DOS as perfect for most uses. Suppose, however, that you must use a certain national format for expressing the time, the date, and currency symbols. You can learn how to access these formats by reading this chapter and understanding the use of the COUNTRY.SYS configuration driver.

In Chapter 20, "Understanding ANSI.SYS," you learned how to reassign keyboard characters to any of the 256 available ASCII characters. In this chapter, you learn how to use the KEYB command to change keyboard-produced characters to those for another country or language.

You also learn how to change your system's default character set to that of another country. This procedure is called code page switching. (A code page is a complete national language character set.) With this feature of DOS, you can type on your keyboard, display on the screen, and print (with the proper printer) characters from other languages.

DOS supports 24 national languages or country customs. Each country or language is identified by a country code that corresponds to the country's international telephone code. Appendix G, "International Country Codes," lists the countries and languages supported by DOS and their country codes. These country codes are referenced throughout this chapter.

Note

When you use the country code or the code page number, you must use all three digits, including any leading zeros.

In addition to the American standard version that you can customize for the supported country codes, Microsoft produces special language versions in Arabic, Chinese, Israeli, Japanese, Korean, and Taiwanese.

Understanding COUNTRY.SYS

COUNTRY.SYS is a configuration file that you can use to display alternate currency, date, and time formats on your system without using other language characters. This file contains all the conventions for the supported countries and national formats. Of course, if you have no need to change the default formats for your version of DOS, you have no need to use COUNTRY.SYS.

When you perform a disk directory command (DIR), the date and time stamps for disk files are displayed in the current national format. In the United States, the system date is normally displayed and stamped on files as MM-DD-YY. You can use alternate methods such as YY-MM-DD (French Canadian) or DD/MM/YY (United Kingdom).

Time formats separate hours, minutes, seconds, and hundredths of a second using colons (HH:MM:SS:HS), periods (HH.MM.SS.HS), or colons and a comma (HH:MM:SS,HS).

In addition to the variety of currency symbols, such as $, and £, differing customs dictate whether the decimal characters are periods or commas—likewise for the thousands separator. The placement of the currency symbol also can vary. In the United States, the dollar sign precedes the amount, but some currency symbols are placed after the amount.

Note

COUNTRY.SYS contains information only for the video display, not for keyboards. To provide keyboard support, you must use the KEYB command in your AUTOEXEC.BAT file or from the DOS prompt. For more information, see the next section, "Understanding KEYB.COM."

You load COUNTRY.SYS by entering the COUNTRY command in the CONFIG.SYS file. Use EDIT to enter a statement into the file. Enter the command in the following format:

```
COUNTRY=xxx,yyy,C:\DOS\COUNTRY.SYS
```

You must place the three-character numeric country code as the first parameter, as indicated by *xxx*. You cannot omit this code. The second parameter is the code page number for the country, as represented by *yyy*. If you omit this code, DOS uses the default code page number for the country specified by the country code. See Appendix G, "International Country Codes," for country codes and country code page numbers.

Note

The inclusion of the code page in the COUNTRY command is optional, even if you install code page switching. Make sure to include the code page, however, if you want an alternate code page—rather than the default code page—to be installed for the indicated country.

If you do not specify the second parameter (*yyy*), you still must include the second comma when you include the file specification:

```
COUNTRY=xxx,,C:\DOS\COUNTRY.SYS
```

The default statement for the United States version is shown in the following:

```
COUNTRY=001
```

or

```
COUNTRY=001,,C:\DOS\COUNTRY.SYS
```

Figure 21.1 shows a standard directory listing that uses the United States country code formats for the date (MM-DD-YY) and time (12-hour format with A.M. or P.M. indicator).

Fig. 21.1
A directory in the United States country code format.

```
 Volume in drive C is DSK1_DRVC
 Volume Serial Number is 11DA-3B69
 Directory of C:\

C-ROOT        <DIR>      02-10-93   2:52p
CHAMPION      <DIR>      02-10-93   3:09p
CHAMPSTA      <DIR>      02-10-93   3:09p
COLLAGE       <DIR>      02-11-93   6:46p
DBASE         <DIR>      02-10-93   3:09p
DOS           <DIR>      02-10-93   1:58p
JOBCST        <DIR>      02-10-93   3:09p
TAPE          <DIR>      02-10-93   2:44p
TEMP          <DIR>      02-10-93   1:58p
UTILS         <DIR>      02-11-93   1:50p
WINA20   386      9349 01-28-93   6:00a
AUTOEXEC BAT        58 02-11-93   1:47p
DATA     BAT        16 01-27-93   1:39p
NEWDISK  BAT       111 02-10-93   8:33p
COMMAND  COM     52841 01-28-93   6:00a
BEFSETUP MSD     13996 02-10-93   5:28p
CONFIG   SYS       207 02-11-93   1:51p
        17 file(s)      76578 bytes
                   179462144 bytes free

C:\>
```

For Related Information

- "CONFIG.SYS," p. 33
- "Understanding Device Drivers," p. 456

If you want to use the United Kingdom currency, date, and time formats, use the following statement in your CONFIG.SYS:

```
COUNTRY=044,,C:\DOS\COUNTRY.SYS
```

After you use EDIT to modify your CONFIG.SYS file to contain this statement, save the file to disk and exit the Editor. Then reboot your computer so that your change takes effect. When you next execute the DIR command, a directory listing shows the new format (see fig. 21.2).

Fig. 21.2
A directory in the country code format for the United Kingdom.

```
 Volume in drive C is DSK1_DRVC
 Volume Serial Number is 11DA-3B69
 Directory of C:\

C-ROOT        <DIR>      10/02/93   14:52
CHAMPION      <DIR>      10/02/93   15:09
CHAMPSTA      <DIR>      10/02/93   15:09
COLLAGE       <DIR>      11/02/93   18:46
DBASE         <DIR>      10/02/93   15:09
DOS           <DIR>      10/02/93   13:58
JOBCST        <DIR>      10/02/93   15:09
TAPE          <DIR>      10/02/93   14:44
TEMP          <DIR>      10/02/93   13:58
UTILS         <DIR>      11/02/93   13:50
WINA20   386      9349 28/01/93    6:00
AUTOEXEC BAT        58 11/02/93   13:47
DATA     BAT        16 27/01/93   13:39
NEWDISK  BAT       111 10/02/93   20:33
COMMAND  COM     52841 28/01/93    6:00
BEFSETUP MSD     13996 10/02/93   17:28
CONFIG   SYS       203 11/02/93   18:53
        17 file(s)      76574 bytes
                   179445760 bytes free

C:\>
```

Notice that the date format has changed to DD/MM/YY, and the time is displayed in 24-hour format.

Understanding KEYB.COM

Whereas the COUNTRY.SYS driver provides nondefault formats on the display screen, KEYB.COM provides compatible keyboard characters for the selected nationality. For a list of international keyboard codes, refer to Appendix G, "International Country Codes."

You normally place KEYB.COM in the AUTOEXEC.BAT file, although you can type the command at the DOS prompt. You also can load KEYB.COM through the CONFIG.SYS file when you use the INSTALL= command.

Note

You can use the KEYB command even if you have not installed any country codes through COUNTRY.SYS.

Make sure your DOS subdirectory (normally C:\DOS) is in your system's search path. Then you do not need to specify the location of KEYB.COM unless you install the utility in the CONFIG.SYS file. The format of this command follows:

```
KEYB xx,yyy,C:\DOS\KEYBOARD.SYS /E /ID:nnn
```

The *xx* parameter is the two-letter code for the country or language. The *yyy* parameter is the code page number, if used. (Refer to Appendix G for country codes and code page numbers.)

You also can add two options to the KEYB command: /E and /ID. Use /E to tell DOS that you are using an enhanced keyboard (101- or 102-key style) on a computer with an Intel 8086 or compatible processor. The second switch, /ID, tells DOS which keyboard you are using. You can use one of 20 keyboards specially designed for the supported countries. France, Italy, and the United Kingdom have two keyboard layouts available. For a list of countries with the alternate keyboards and the ID numbers you can use with KEYB, refer to Appendix G, "International Country Codes."

If you set your system to one of these three countries with COUNTRY.SYS and KEYB.COM and you use an alternate keyboard, you may find it useful to add the /ID:*nnn* switch to the KEYB command line (where *nnn* is one of the three-digit ID numbers) to make your keyboard work properly.

If you want to specify the code page to be used, you include it in the command line for KEYB. If the KEYBOARD.SYS file is not in the root directory of the boot drive, you must include that file specification together with its path. The path is normally C:\DOS. If you include the location and name of KEYBOARD.SYS, you must include the second comma, as follows, to hold the place for the code page parameter, even if you do not include the code page number:

```
KEYB xx,,C:\DOS\KEYBOARD.SYS
```

If you enter the KEYB command without any parameters or switches and you have not yet installed the keyboard utility, DOS responds with the following message:

```
KEYB has not been installed
Active code page not available from CON device
```

At the DOS prompt, type **KEYB UK** and press Enter to load KEYB with the character set used for the United Kingdom. Then type **KEYB** and press Enter. DOS displays the following message:

```
Current keyboard code: UK  code page: 437
Active code page not available from CON device
```

As you can see, DOS assumes the default code page number for the United Kingdom, 437. Because at this point you are not concerned with code page switching, you can ignore the code page message. This subject is discussed later in this chapter (in the section "Understanding Code Page Switching").

To install KEYB when MS-DOS boots and processes the CONFIG.SYS file, use the following format:

```
INSTALL=C:\DOS\KEYB.COM xx,yyy,C:\DOS\KEYBOARD.SYS
```

Because your system search path has not yet been set, you must include the location of the utility. You must include also the full name and extension of the program (C:\DOS\KEYB.COM) before continuing with the parameters for KEYB.

DOS provides a way of switching between your hardware default keyboard layout and the layout you loaded with KEYB.COM. Press Ctrl-Alt-F1 (hold down the Ctrl and Alt keys while pressing F1) to switch to the United States keyboard layout. Press Ctrl-Alt-F2 to return to the keyboard layout installed with KEYB.

For Related Information
■ "AUTOEXEC.BAT," p. 36

Considering Keyboard Remappings

When you change the default country and keyboard codes on your computer system, you find that certain keys no longer work as labeled. The following information pertains to standard United States keyboards, but changing the country code also may affect systems with national keyboards.

Continuing with the previous examples for COUNTRY.SYS and KEYB.COM, set the country and keyboard codes to 044 and UK for the United Kingdom. Your CONFIG.SYS file should contain the following statement:

```
COUNTRY=044,,C:\DOS\COUNTRY.SYS
```

If necessary, reboot your computer so that this command takes effect. Then in your AUTOEXEC.BAT file or at the DOS prompt, type the following command and press Enter:

```
KEYB UK,,C:\DOS\KEYBOARD.SYS
```

After your system reboots and KEYB is installed, press the backslash key (\). Notice that instead of displaying the backslash character, your system displays a pound sign, #. Pressing the pound sign key (Shift-3) produces the British currency symbol £. A few other key remappings occur when you use the United Kingdom country and keyboard codes on a standard American keyboard with the American default version of MS-DOS. Table 21.1 lists the remappings for this configuration.

Table 21.1 Remappings for the United Kingdom on a United States Keyboard

Standard Character	Remapped Character
~	/
@	"

(continues)

Table 21.1 Continued

Standard Character	Remapped Character
#	£
¦	~
\	#
"	@

If you require extensive use of an alternate language keyboard, you can save yourself the problem of remembering the key changes. Print the changed characters on address or disk labels, cut out the characters, and paste them to your keyboard in the remapped positions.

Because you lose the backslash key (\) with this remapping of your keyboard, you may have trouble working with subdirectories. To enter the backslash character, hold down the Alt key and, using the numeric keypad on the right side of your keyboard, type the numbers 9 and 2. You also can press Ctrl-Alt-F1 to switch to the Unites States layout and Ctrl-Alt-F2 to return to the country format you installed.

Understanding Code Page Switching

Certain areas of memory in your system store the character tables for your video screen and your keyboard. By switching tables, you can configure MS-DOS to use alternate character tables to suit your national language and customs. These tables are called code pages.

Note

Changing the character set used in your computer to support another language through code page switching does not change the language that DOS uses. All messages are displayed in the default (English) language in which DOS was written. No translation is made.

You can set your system to use an alternate code page permanently, or you can enable several code pages in memory and switch between them from the command line. These code pages are software prepared; your system's hardware is not changed. Your system already has a built-in hardware code page.

In the previous section that discussed COUNTRY.SYS, you learned that each country or area of the world has a unique country code number borrowed from the international telephone convention. Each country or group of countries also has a code page number. (Many countries share a code page number with another country.) See Appendix G, "International Country Codes," for a list of code pages supported by DOS.

Each DOS-supported code page includes support for several languages. This feature may simplify international communications so that documents prepared with the same character table may be processed by people in different countries using different languages, with all characters appearing the same to all concerned.

The international code page, code 850, has some graphic limitations to provide room for additional language characters required by some countries. A total of only 256 codes are available. If you normally use the United States code page (437), for example, you may find that boxes under 850 lose their graphic corners and are replaced with other characters.

Note

When you install alternate code pages in your computer, the normal typewriter keys and their ASCII display characters do not change. Symbol keys are remapped, and by using special keystrokes, you can enter national language characters.

Checking Your Hardware for Code Page Switching

You do need the proper hardware to use software code page switching. All code page information required for loading alternate character sets is contained in disk files with the extension CPI. Two screen device code page information files are supplied with DOS. EGA.CPI provides support for EGA and VGA displays, and LCD.CPI provides support for LCD screens. You must have an EGA, VGA, or LCD video display. Hercules-type monographic and CGA screens do not support this feature.

Note

The LCD.CPI, 4201.CPI, 4208.CPI, 5202.CPI, and EGA2.CPI files as well as PRINTER.SYS are no longer automatically supplied as part of DOS. However, these files and others are available from Microsoft on a Supplemental Disk. Call or write Microsoft to request this disk or download the information from the CompuServe MSDOS6 forum.

If you have an EGA or a VGA screen, you can have up to six software code pages. If you have an LCD display, you can have only one software code page. If you have a monographic or CGA video adapter and monitor, you can use only the built-in hardware code page.

Certain printers, along with others that are 100-percent compatible with them, also support code page switching. Three code page information files are provided with DOS: 4201.CPI, 4208.CPI, and 5202.CPI. Table 21.2 lists the printers supported by these files. Even if your printer emulates one of these printers, it also must have the capability to accept code page switching. (Some printers provide emulation but not code page support.)

Table 21.2 National Code Page Printer Files

Printer	Code Page File
IBM Proprinter II, III	4201.CPI
IBM Proprinter XL	4201.CPI
IBM Proprinter X24E	4208.CPI
IBM Proprinter XL24E	4208.CPI
IBM Quietwriter III	5202.CPI

Installing Code Page Switching

Assuming that you have the appropriate hardware, you must take a number of steps and load certain programs to enable code page switching, both for your video screen and for your printer. (Use MS-DOS EDIT to make the necessary changes to the CONFIG.SYS file and the AUTOEXEC.BAT file.)

To enable code page switching for your video display, you add to the CONFIG.SYS file a statement for the DISPLAY.SYS device driver. To enable code page switching for your printer, you add a statement for the

PRINTER.SYS device driver. If you want code page switching enabled for both devices, you simply include both statements. (You also must use the COUNTRY.SYS device driver to handle the screen formats for currency, the date, and the time.) Then, to provide the national language support, you add the NLSFUNC.EXE command to your AUTOEXEC.BAT file.

The following sections explain how you set up code page switching on your system, including how to use DISPLAY.SYS, PRINTER.SYS, and NLSFUNC.EXE to enable the feature; how to use MODE PREPARE to load the code page tables; and how to use CHCP and MODE SELECT to switch the code page.

Using DISPLAY.SYS. Use the DISPLAY.SYS device driver to enable code page switching for your video display. You can use DISPLAY.SYS only if you have an EGA, VGA, or LCD monitor and adapter.

The format of the command follows:

```
DEVICE=C:\DOS\DISPLAY.SYS CON=(monitor,hardware,xx)
```

or

```
DEVICE=C:\DOS\DISPLAY.SYS CON=(monitor,hardware,(xx,yy))
```

Unless you move the DISPLAY.SYS file to the root directory of your boot drive, you must specify the location of the file (normally C:\DOS). Enter the *monitor* type as the first parameter for the CONsole device (monitor). EGA is the typical *monitor* entry and stands for both EGA and VGA monitors. Use LCD for LCD screens. No other values are possible.

The second parameter, *hardware,* refers to the built-in hardware code page. In the United States, this code page is 437; if you are not certain of your system's built-in hardware code page, however, do not specify it.

The *xx* variable refers to the number of code pages you want enabled in your system. This parameter tells DOS to set aside memory for the number of additional character tables to be installed in the AUTOEXEC.BAT file or at the DOS prompt.

Enter a number for the *yy* variable to represent the number of subfonts you want. You can specify the number of fonts that DOS should store in memory. Two subfonts are available for EGA/VGA displays, and only one is available for LCD displays. Normally all are stored; however, you can lower the number stored to reduce the amount of memory used. If you use this variable, you must place a pair of parentheses around the number of code pages and the number of fonts, as shown in the second example.

Suppose that you want to enable code page switching for your display for French Canada and also to allow for the use of the international code. You would enter the following statement in your CONFIG.SYS file:

```
DEVICE=C:\DOS\DISPLAY.SYS CON=(EGA,,2)
```

No default hardware code page is declared, and DOS is instructed to set aside memory for two code pages for an EGA or VGA adapter and monitor. Do not omit the commas.

You can specify up to six code page tables to be prepared in memory in addition to the hardware code page. Just remember that each code page takes up RAM (about 5632 bytes for EGA and VGA) and may lower the amount of conventional memory available for your applications. Do not set aside more memory than is required.

Using PRINTER.SYS. Use the PRINTER.SYS device driver to enable code page switching for your printer if you have one of the supported printers or a compatible. Supported printers can be attached to any or all of the three allowed parallel printer ports: LPT1, LPT2, and LPT3.

The format of the command follows:

```
DEVICE=C:\DOS\PRINTER.SYS LPTx=(printer,hardware,yy)
```

Unless you move the PRINTER.SYS file to the root directory of your boot drive, you must specify the location of the file (normally C:\DOS). Replace *x* with the proper parallel port number: 1, 2, or 3.

Replace *printer* with 4201, 4208, or 5202, whichever is appropriate for your printer. The next parameter, *hardware,* refers to the built-in hardware code page. In the United States, this code page is 437, but do not specify it if you are not certain of your printer type.

The variable *yy* refers to the number of additional code pages that your hardware can support and you want prepared. This parameter tells DOS to set aside memory for the number of additional character tables to be installed in the AUTOEXEC.BAT file or at the DOS prompt.

To instruct DOS to set aside memory for two code pages for an IBM Quietwriter III or compatible printer attached to LPT1, for example, enter the following statement in your CONFIG.SYS file:

```
DEVICE=C:\DOS\PRINTER.SYS LPT1=(5202,,2)
```

No default hardware code page is declared.

You can specify up to six code page tables to be prepared in memory. The maximum, however, depends on the printer you are using. Do not set aside more memory than is required because these tables consume memory.

Note

To enable code page switching on your printer, make sure that your printer is turned on and is on-line when your system is booted. Otherwise, the control signals cannot be downloaded to the printer.

Using NLSFUNC.EXE. After you take care of the required statements in your CONFIG.SYS file for COUNTRY.SYS and DISPLAY.SYS, move your attention to the AUTOEXEC.BAT file. As discussed in this chapter's "Understanding KEYB.COM" section, make sure that your keyboard is specified for the appropriate national keyboard and code page number. The following command, for example, specifies code page 863 for French Canada:

```
KEYB cf,863,C:\DOS\KEYBOARD.SYS
```

You then must include NLSFUNC as the next command to provide the National Language Support (NLS) for code page switching. You can type this command at the DOS prompt or place the command in your AUTOEXEC.BAT or CONFIG.SYS file for automatic loading whenever you boot your computer. To enter the NLSFUNC command in your CONFIG.SYS file, use the following format:

```
INSTALL=C:\DOS\NLSFUNC.EXE
```

Because a path has not yet been established when the command is in your CONFIG.SYS file, you must specify the location of the NLSFUNC file.

Up to this point, you have specified your country code of choice and have prepared your system to use code page switching. The following sections explain how to use the commands that load the specified code pages into the prepared memory areas.

Loading the Code Page Tables

You include the MODE command in the AUTOEXEC.BAT file to load code page information, specifying the code pages to be prepared and the code page file to use for the tables. Use MODE CON: to load the code page information for your video display (the console). Use MODE LPT1: to load the code page information for your printer and to download the information to the printer. (Make sure that your printer is turned on and is on-line to receive the downloaded data.)

In the command, you can list as many code pages as you specified in the CONFIG.SYS file. Do not specify the hardware default code page number because this table is already built in. The format of the command is shown in the following (the parentheses are required):

```
MODE device CP PREPARE=((xxx,yyy) filename)
```

The *device* indicates that you want to load a character set into your console, keyboard, or parallel printers. The *xxx* and *yyy* parameters indicate the code page numbers to be prepared, and *filename* refers to the CPI file where the table is stored on disk for the device.

Consider the following example:

```
MODE CON: CP PREPARE=((863,850) C:\DOS\EGA.CPI)
```

In this command, MODE is used to PREPARE (or PREP) the console (CON:) for code pages (CP), with code pages 863 for French Canada and 850 for International. EGA.CPI is listed as the table file for EGA and VGA monitors. The location of this file is the C:\DOS subdirectory.

For your printer, use the MODE command for each parallel printer port listed in the CONFIG.SYS file's PRINTER.SYS statement. The following examples prepare the printers at the LPT1 and LPT2 ports:

```
MODE LPT1: CP PREP=((863,850) C:\DOS\5202.CPI)
MODE LPT2: CP PREP=((863,850) C:\DOS\4201.CPI)
```

As with the other AUTOEXEC.BAT commands for code page switching, you also can enter the MODE commands at the DOS prompt.

Switching the Code Page

After you complete all the preparation work—specifying the nationality and code page codes to be used, setting aside the memory for the language tables, and loading the character tables—you are ready to use the new code pages.

In the previous examples, you prepared your system to use the French Canada character set. To have this character set take effect, you must issue the CHCP command, for *CH*anging the *C*ode *P*age. Use the CHCP command, along with the code page number, as shown in the following:

```
CHCP 863
```

Enter this command in your AUTOEXEC.BAT file or at the DOS prompt. The instruction tells DOS to change the current code page to the new code page specified in the command on all devices prepared, including the printer if you have included it in the CONFIG.SYS and AUTOEXEC.BAT files. Make certain that the printer is turned on and is on-line so that the new code page can take effect.

You also can selectively change code pages of individual devices by using the MODE SELECT command and pressing Enter. The full format of the command follows:

```
MODE device CODEPAGE SELECT = xxx
```

For *device*, use CON for console or use PRN (which is the same as LPT1), LPT1, LPT2, or LPT3 for the printer ports. After the equal sign (=), enter the code page number (*xxx*).

Suppose, for example, that you want to change the code page in your IBM Quietwriter III printer, but you don't want to affect the monitor display. If your printer is attached to LPT1 and you want to print with the French Canada character set, issue the following command and press Enter:

```
MODE LPT1 CP SEL=863
```

Tip
You can abbreviate CODEPAGE as CP and SELECT as SEL.

Exploring More Uses for MODE and CODEPAGE

To ascertain the currently active code page for any device, issue the following command and press Enter:

```
MODE device CODEPAGE /STATUS
```

This command works the same with or without the `/STATUS` option. DOS returns the status of the active code page and all prepared code pages for the specified device, including the hardware code page, as shown in figure 21.3.

To check the code page for the display monitor, for example, type this command at the DOS prompt and press Enter:

```
MODE CON CP
```

At times, you may need to refresh the code page for a particular device, especially code page printers. The printers do not store the code page fonts when they are turned off and on again. Also, use the following command if the printer was not turned on and on-line when you enabled code page switching on the printer:

```
MODE device CODEPAGE REFRESH
```

Tip
You can abbreviate CODEPAGE as CP and REFRESH as REF.

Fig 21.3
Viewing the code page status.

```
C:\>MODE CON CODEPAGE /STATUS

Active code page for device CON is 863
Hardware code pages:
  code page 437
Prepared code pages:
  code page 863
  code page 850

MODE status code page function completed

C:\>
```

To refresh the code page for the printer hooked up to LPT1, for example, type the following command at the DOS prompt and press Enter:

```
MODE LPT1 CP REF
```

If you issue a code page command for your printer through CHCP, MODE SELECT, or MODE REFRESH, and your printer does not accept code pages or is not turned on and on-line, an error message appears when you try to print. You may notice a delay before receiving the error message, depending on the length of the time-out period.

Using Dead Keys to Cope with the Changed Keyboard

When you tell DOS to use a different keyboard or character set, your keyboard keys produce different results. In addition to the remapped keyboard, a new device called a *dead key* enables you to enter special language characters.

Normally when you type an alphabetic character on your keyboard, the letter appears without any accents. The use of a dead key enables you to enter an acute accent (´), a grave accent (`), or a circumflex accent (^) with certain vowels and other keys. These marks are used in some languages but are not provided on a standard American keyboard.

When you press the dead key, nothing appears on the screen. When you press the next appropriate letter key, the accented character appears. If you press an inappropriate key, DOS beeps and displays nothing.

Table 21.3 lists the keys on the United States keyboard that are remapped when you enable code page 863 (for French Canada).

Table 21.3 Language Support for French Canada on United States Keyboard

Standard Character	Remapped Character
'	#
~	¦
@	"
#	/
^	?
\	<
¦	>
/	e´
?	E´

Table 21.4 lists the dead key keyboard mappings for French Canada.

Table 21.4 French Canada Language Support Using Dead Keys

Dead Key	Standard Character	Remapped Character
]	c	ç
Shift-]	C	Ç
Shift-]	e	ë
Shift-]	i	ï
Shift-]	u	ü
Shift-]	E	Ë
Shift-]	I	Ï
Shift-]	U	Ü
[	a	â
[	e	ê
[	i	î

(continues)

Table 21.4 Continued

Dead Key	Standard Character	Remapped Character
[	o	ô
[	u	û
Shift-[	A	Â
Shift-[	E	Ê
Shift-[	I	Î
Shift-[	O	Ô
Shift-[	U	Û
'	a	à
'	e	è
'	u	ù
'	A	À
'	E	È
'	U	Ù
'	'	`

For other national languages on a U.S. or other keyboard, a little testing should give you the ability to use the language-specific characters you require. The four keys you should test as dead keys are the apostrophe ('), question mark (?), left square bracket ([), and right square bracket (]).

For Related Information

- "Optimizing Your Computer's Memory," p. 459

As an alternative to using code page switching to access special language-specific characters, you can load the support for the required language table with the KEYB command and then use the Alt-*nnn* technique. The *nnn* stands for the ASCII code for the specific character and is typed on the numeric keypad of your keyboard (not on the numbers above the typewriter keys of your keyboard).

Summary

In this chapter, you learned how you can customize your computer system with national language support. This chapter included the following important points:

- You use COUNTRY.SYS to provide national formats for currency, the date, and the time.
- You use KEYB.COM to nationalize your keyboard for certain characters. You can load this command in the AUTOEXEC.BAT file, the CONFIG.SYS file, or at the DOS prompt.
- You enable code page switching to use foreign language character sets on your EGA, VGA, or LCD monitor, your keyboard, and a supported printer.
- You can place the COUNTRY.SYS device driver in your CONFIG.SYS file with the international country code and an optional code page number.
- To enable code page switching, you first must set aside memory for the language tables by using DISPLAY.SYS and PRINTER.SYS statements in the CONFIG.SYS file. Then you enter the command to enable national language support, NLSFUNC, specifying the COUNTRY.SYS file.
- To load the code page tables, you use the MODE device CODEPAGE PREPARE command, one time for your video display and once for your printer.
- You use the new language character set by issuing the CHCP command for the appropriate code page number or by selectively using the MODE device CODEPAGE SELECT command.

MS-DOS 6 Command Reference

With every new release, Microsoft has added features to MS-DOS. MS-DOS 6 now contains well over one hundred commands, providing configuration support and utilities for the large variety of computers that run MS-DOS. Many commands help you organize the files and subdirectories on your hard disk or enable you to configure your computer system to run more efficiently. Other commands let you automate routine tasks that you perform with your computer every day. MS-DOS has become the most popular operating system in the world for microcomputers; and now DOS includes commands that provide support for the various characters and conventions used in many countries other than the United States.

This Command Reference describes all the commands that Microsoft provides in the standard MS-DOS 6 package. Each command entry includes a description of the command's purpose, its syntax, notes and rules on how to use it, examples of its use, error messages and exit codes when applicable, and a "See Also" section that points you to additional information about using a particular command.

DOS Commands by Function

In order to help you to find the command you're looking for, the following lists group the various DOS commands by their functions and contain short descriptions of each command. Many commands have more than one function, so they may appear in more than one group. When you locate the command you want in these function lists, turn to the reference section for much more detailed information about a particular command. The reference section lists the commands in alphabetical order.

In the following function lists, the commands are divided into these categories:

Batch File Commands

CONFIG.SYS Commands

CONFIG.SYS Device Drivers

Directory Commands

Disk Commands

File Commands

Full-Screen DOS Applications

Help Commands

International Commands and Device Drivers

Memory and System Performance Commands

Miscellaneous Commands

Windows Applications

Batch File Commands

CALL	Executes a batch file from within another batch file.
CHOICE	Accepts a single keystroke from the keyboard.
COMMAND	Runs a second copy of the MS-DOS command interpreter.
ECHO	Echoes text to the screen from a batch file.
FOR	FOR-IN-DO loop for batch files.
GOTO	Jumps to a labeled line in a batch file.
IF	IF-THEN decision structure for a batch file.
PAUSE	Waits for a keystroke before continuing.
REM	Inserts a remark into a batch file.
SHIFT	Shifts batch file parameters down one place.

CONFIG.SYS Commands

BREAK=	Turns on or off extended Ctrl-Break checking.
BUFFERS=	Sets the number of disk buffers used by DOS.
COUNTRY=	Sets country information.
DEVICE=	Loads an installable device driver.
DEVICEHIGH=	Loads an installable device driver into high (UMB) memory.
DOS=	Sets whether DOS will use the High Memory Area (HMA) and Upper Memory Blocks (UMB).
DRIVPARM=	Redefines the physical characteristics of an existing disk drive.
FCBS=	Sets the maximum number of open File Control Blocks (FCBs) that DOS will allow.
FILES=	Sets the maximum number of open files that DOS will allow.
INCLUDE=	Includes the commands from one CONFIG.SYS block within another.
INSTALL=	Loads TSR programs into memory from CONFIG.SYS.
LASTDRIVE=	Sets the maximum number of drive letters available to DOS.
MENUCOLOR=	Sets the color of the screen for the CONFIG.SYS start-up menu.
MENUDEFAULT=	Sets the default menu choice in a CONFIG.SYS menu block.
MENUITEM=	Sets the text and configuration block associated with menu items in CONFIG.SYS.
NUMLOCK=	Sets the state of the NumLock key when the computer starts up.
REM	Inserts a remark into CONFIG.SYS.

SET	Sets environment variables.
SHELL=	Sets the name of the program used as a command-line shell by MS-DOS.
STACKS=	Sets the number of stacks set aside for hardware interrupts.
SUBMENU=	Defines a submenu in CONFIG.SYS.
SWITCHES=	Sets miscellaneous control options for MS-DOS.

CONFIG.SYS DEVICE= Drivers

ANSI.SYS	Alternates console driver, which provides ANSI standard control of the display and keyboard.
DBLSPACE.SYS	Dummy drivers that can relocate DBLSPACE.BIN in memory.
DISPLAY.SYS	Device driver for the display with international code page support.
DRIVER.SYS	Sets the DOS drive letter for an existing disk drive or creates an additional drive letter for a disk drive.
EMM386.EXE	Expanded (EMS) Memory Manager with Upper Memory Block (UMB) support.
HIMEM.SYS	Extended (XMS) Memory Manager.
INTERLNK.EXE	Client device driver for an InterLnk network.
POWER.EXE	Advanced Power Management (APM) device driver for portable computers.
RAMDRIVE.SYS	Driver that sets up a disk drive in RAM memory.
SETVER.EXE	DOS version control program that can fool certain programs into running with the "incorrect" version of MS-DOS.
SMARTDRV.EXE	Installs double-buffering to make SMARTDrive compatible with certain hard disk drives.

Directory Commands

CD or CHDIR	Changes the current directory of a disk drive.
DELTREE	Deletes a directory, including all the files and subdirectories it may contain.
MD or MKDIR	Creates a new subdirectory on a disk.
RD or RMDIR	Deletes an empty subdirectory on a disk.
TREE	Displays the subdirectory structure present on a disk.

Disk Commands

CHKDSK	Checks a disk for errors and provides information on the amount of space in use.
DEFRAG	Defragments the files on a disk. This can cut down on the time it takes your computer to find files on your hard disk.
DISKCOMP	Compares two floppy disks to see if they are identical.
DISKCOPY	Makes an exact copy of a floppy disk.
FDISK	Hard disk partitioning program. Prepares a new hard disk to accept DOS or partitions a single drive into two or more logical drives.
FORMAT	Formats a hard or floppy disk for MS-DOS.
LABEL	Creates, edits, or deletes the volume label on a disk.
SCANDISK	Analyzes disks and repairs errors. The ScanDisk utility can repair DoubleSpace compressed drives as well as normal disks.
SUBST	Creates a disk drive letter that refers to a subdirectory of another drive.
SYS	Installs the MS-DOS system files on another disk.
UNFORMAT	Returns a disk to the state it was in before FORMAT was run.
VERIFY	Controls whether DOS will read everything written to disk to ensure that no errors occurred.
VOL	Displays the volume label of a disk.

File Commands

ATTRIB	Views or changes file attributes.
COPY	Copies or concatenates a file or group of files.
DEL or ERASE	Deletes a file or group of files.
DIR	Displays a listing of the files in a subdirectory.
EXPAND	Expands (uncompresses) files on the MS-DOS 6 distribution disks.
FC	Compares two files for differences.
FIND	Finds matching text in a file.
MOVE	Moves a file from one subdirectory to another or renames a subdirectory.
REN or RENAME	Renames a file or group of files.
REPLACE	Replaces or adds files to a subdirectory.
SHARE	Provides file sharing and locking capabilities for DOS.
TYPE	Displays the contents of a file on-screen.
UNDELETE	Undeletes a file or group of files.
XCOPY	Copies files and subdirectories.

Full-Screen DOS Applications

DBLSPACE	Program that compresses information on a disk, providing up to twice the amount of space you previously had.
DEBUG	Programmer's debugger.
DEFRAG	Defragments the files on a disk. Running this program can cut down on the time it takes your computer to find files on your hard disk.
DOSSHELL	Graphical shell program for DOS.
EDIT	A full-screen ASCII text file editor.

FDISK	Hard disk partitioning program. Prepares a new hard disk to accept DOS, or partitions a single drive into two or more logical drives.
HELP	An online help system that provides descriptions and examples for every DOS command.
MSAV	The Microsoft Anti-Virus program. Checks your computer for viruses.
MSBACKUP	The Microsoft Backup program. Backs up files on your hard disk to a series of floppy disks.
MSD	The Microsoft System Diagnostics program. Provides information about the configuration of your computer system.
QBASIC	Provides access to the Microsoft QuickBASIC development environment, which enables users to write and run programs written in the QuickBASIC language.

Help Commands

FASTHELP	Displays a short description of what each DOS command is for and the correct syntax for its use.
HELP	A full-screen, on-line help system that provides descriptions and examples for every DOS command.
/?	Not an actual command; if you include a **/?** on the command line with a DOS command, a short description is displayed of what the command does and how you can use it.

International Commands and Device Drivers

CHCP	Changes the active country code page.
COUNTRY=	Sets country information.
DISPLAY.SYS	Device driver for the display with international code page support.
KEYB	Sets the active keyboard layout.

MODE	Configures standard DOS devices, including changing the active code page for the keyboard, display, and printer.
NLSFUNC	Contains code page switching support required by CHCP and MODE.

Memory and System Performance Commands

BUFFERS=	Sets the number of disk buffers used by DOS.
DEFRAG	Defragments the files on a disk. This can cut down on the time it takes your computer to find files on your hard disk.
DEVICEHIGH=	Loads an installable device driver into high (UMB) memory.
DOS=	Determines whether DOS loads itself into conventional memory or into the High Memory Area (HMA).
EMM386.EXE	Expanded (EMS) Memory Manager with Upper Memory Block (UMB) support.
HIMEM.SYS	Extended (XMS) Memory Manager.
LH or LOADHIGH	Loads a TSR program into high (UMB) memory.
MEM	Displays how memory in your computer system is being used.
MEMMAKER	Utility to optimize memory usage on your computer.
SMARTDRV	Disk cache program that can speed up disk access time.

Miscellaneous Commands

APPEND	Establishes a DOS search path for data files.
BREAK	Turns on or off extended Ctrl-Break checking.
CLS	Clears the screen.
CTTY	Changes the device used for standard input and output.
DATE	Sets or views the system date.

DOSKEY	Provides enhanced command-line editing and macros capability.
EXIT	Exits (terminates) a temporary copy of COMMAND.COM.
GRAPHICS	Provides support for a graphics mode Print Screen function.
INTERLNK	Controls the client device driver in an InterLnk network.
INTERSVR	Server program for an Interlnk network.
LOADFIX	Forces a program to load into the second 64K of memory.
MODE	Configures standard DOS devices such as serial ports, parallel ports, the display, and the keyboard.
MORE	Pauses display output when the screen is full.
PATH	Establishes a DOS search path for executable files.
PRINT	Print spooler for ASCII text files.
PROMPT	Customizes the prompt used by DOS at the command line.
RESTORE	Restores files backed up with the DOS 5 version of BACKUP.
SET	Sets, clears, or displays environment variables.
SORT	Sorts ASCII text lines into alphabetical order.
TIME	Sets or views the system time.
VER	Displays the version of DOS running on the computer.
VSAFE	Resident program that watches for viruses.

Windows Applications

MWAV	The Microsoft Anti-Virus for Windows program. Checks your computer for viruses.
MWAVTSR	A Windows program that enables VSAFE to alert you to trouble when you are running Windows.

MWBACKUP	The Microsoft Backup for Windows program. Backs up files on your hard disk to a series of floppy disks.
MWUNDEL	The Microsoft Undelete for Windows program. Undeletes a file or group of files.
SMARTMON	The SMARTDrive monitoring and configuration program for Windows.

Conventions Used in This Command Reference

In order to make the command descriptions clear and accurate, the following conventions have been used throughout this reference:

Bold	Required literal. Indicates an argument that is required and must be typed as part of the command. For example, the command name always appears in bold because it must be included when you issue the command.
Italics	Optional placeholder. The *placeholder* holds the place for the actual name or value that you would type when you issue the command. In other words, you don't type the word *filename*, you replace *filename* with the actual name of a file.
Bold italics	Required placeholder. Indicates a placeholder argument that is required. When you issue the command, you *must* substitute an appropriate value for an argument that appears in bold italics.
Regular type	Optional literal. Indicates an optional argument that, if included, must be typed as shown. Switch parameters often are optional literal arguments.

The COPY command, for example, uses all four types of arguments in its syntax.

COPY ***source*** *destination* /V

COPY is a required literal, so it appears in bold. The command name always has to be typed exactly as it is shown, although you can add a drive and subdirectory path before the command when necessary.

source is a required placeholder, so it appears in bold italics. In this case, you would enter the name of the file or files that you wanted to copy.

destination is an optional placeholder, so it appears in regular italics. If you choose to omit this argument, a default value is assumed. As with all placeholders, if you include this argument, you replace the word *destination* with the file name and path where you want to copy the files.

/V is an optional literal, so it appears in regular text. Most switch parameters are optional. If you want to include one, you must type it exactly as it is shown.

DOS is not usually sensitive to the case of the characters you use. Normally, you can type command lines in any mixture of upper- or lowercase characters. Some third party-utilities and a few DOS commands, however, do use case-sensitive parameters. When upper- or lowercase is significant in a command's syntax, it is noted in the text.

Pay particular attention to the punctuation used in syntax lines. DOS is often very picky about punctuation; if a semicolon is shown, a comma rarely will do the trick. Spaces are an exception: where one space is shown, more than one space or tab usually is acceptable. The order of command arguments is usually somewhat flexible, with switches allowed either before or after file name arguments. Exceptions to this are noted in the text.

Every command line begins the same way—with the name of the command you want to run. *Internal* commands are located inside COMMAND.COM and are always available at the DOS prompt. *External* commands are files with .COM or .EXE extensions that are located on your disk. In order to run an external command, COMMAND.COM must be able to find the corresponding file on disk. The Setup program for DOS 6 places all the external commands in the C:\DOS subdirectory by default. To help COMMAND.COM find external commands, Setup also adds or edits the PATH statement in your AUTOEXEC.BAT file to include the C:\DOS subdirectory. As long as the subdirectory in which the command is located is included in your DOS PATH, you can simply type the name of the command at the command line and COMMAND.COM finds the executable file. If you move any of the files, or if you remove the C:\DOS subdirectory from your DOS PATH, you will have to specify the location of external commands by including the subdirectory in which they are located as part of the name of the command.

Icons Used in This Command Reference

To help you quickly identify the function of a particular command, this Command Reference uses the following icons:

Avoid using this command unless absolutely necessary.

This command frequently is used in batch files.

Issue this command from the DOS prompt.

You can choose to include this command in your CONFIG.SYS file.

This is a dangerous command; use with extreme caution.

This command is used as a device driver and normally is loaded through your CONFIG.SYS file.

Use this command to access a full-blown DOS utility.

This command enables you to configure your system for use outside the U.S.

This command is new in MS-DOS 6.2.

This command is included on the MS-DOS 6.0 or 6.2 Supplemental Disk.

You can choose to include this command in your SYSTEM.INI file.

A terminate-and-stay-resident command; this command loads into memory and may be accessed anytime thereafter.

You can use this command with Microsoft Windows.

File Names and Path Names

File names and path names for MS-DOS consist of a series of standard parts, and DOS makes certain assumptions when these parts are omitted. A fully qualified path name consists of the following parts:

drive:\path1\path2\ ... \filename.ext

drive:	Represents the disk drive letter.
path1, path2	Represent the subdirectories.
filename	Represents the one- to eight-character name of the file.
.ext	Represents the optional extension to the file name. When included, the extension can be up to three characters in length.
...	An ellipsis in a syntax line indicates that the preceding argument can be repeated one or more times. The spaces around the ellipsis are added here only for clarity. An actual path name can never include any spaces.

Note that a disk drive letter, when present, is always followed by a colon. The drive (with colon), all path names, and the file name are separated from each other by backslash characters (\). The file name extension, when present, is always separated from the file name by a period.

If no drive is specified, the current disk drive is assumed. If no path is specified, the current subdirectory of that disk drive is used. Typically, commands that accept wildcard characters in their file name arguments default to "all files" if no file name is specified. Otherwise, no defaults are assumed for the file name portion.

In this command reference, the term *filename* refers to the one- to eight-character name of a file, either with or without a one- to three-character extension. The term *pathname* refers to the complete path to a file (the drive, subdirectory path, and file name).

Legal File Name Characters

DOS only allows certain characters to be included in the name of a file or subdirectory. All the letters *A* to *Z*, either uppercase or lowercase, and the numbers *0* to *9* are allowed. In addition, the following punctuation characters are acceptable:

& ' @ ^ _ { } $! - # ( ) % ' ~

No other punctuation or special characters are permissible in a file name. (If you are using a non-USA code page, you may have additional legal file name characters, such as accented characters.)

Most of the illegal file name characters have a special meaning on the command line. Spaces, tabs, commas, and semicolons are typically used to separate arguments. The colon (:) is used to indicate a disk drive letter, and the backslash (\) separates subdirectories or indicates the root directory. The greater than (>), less than (<), and vertical bar (¦) characters are used for redirection and piping. Although legal, you should avoid using percent signs (%) in your file names, because this character is used to indicate replaceable parameters and can lead to some confusing errors in batch files.

Tip
Consider using an underscore (_) or a hyphen (–) in file or subdirectory names in which you normally would use a space. This can help make your file names more readable, as in MY_FILE.TXT.

DOS converts all path name characters to uppercase before searching for the file, so you can enter path names in any combination of upper- and lowercase letters that suits you. MYFILE.TXT, myfile.txt, and MyFiLe.TxT all refer to the same file as far as DOS is concerned.

DOS Reserved Names

Although you are free to name your files anything you would like, there are a few file names that have special meaning to MS-DOS. They refer to specific devices attached to your computer system; when you use them on the command line in place of a file name, they always refer to that device, not a file on the disk.

Name	Device That Name Refers To
NUL	The null device. This is your computer's equivalent of the Black Hole, which accepts (and ignores) anything written to it.
CON	The standard device for input and output. CON normally refers to the keyboard for input and the video display for output.
LPT*x*	The printer (parallel) ports. The *x* represents the port number, as in LPT1.
PRN	The primary printer port, normally the same as LPT1.

Name	Device That Name Refers To
COM*x*	The serial ports. The *x* represents the port number, as in COM1.
AUX	The primary serial port, normally the same as COM1.

In some cases you are required to enter these names followed by a colon (:), as if you were referring to a disk drive. Normally, however, you just use them as if they referred to a file in the current directory. No matter what drive, path, or extension you include with these reserved names, they always refer to that device and never to a file on your disk. (In other words, you cannot have a file named PRN.TXT on your disk, because this name always refers to the printer and not to a disk file.) However, if you specify a drive or path that doesn't exist, you do receive an error message.

?, *

1.0 and later—Internal

Certain commands let you use wildcard characters in the file name portion of a path name argument to specify more than one file at a time. You can use the question mark (?) to match any single character and the asterisk (*) to match multiple characters. Wildcards are never allowed in the drive or subdirectory portions of a path name.

Using the ? Wildcard Character in a File Name or Extension

A question mark (?) can be used to match any single character in a file name or extension. For example, typing MYFILE.T?T matches files named MYFILE.TXT and MYFILE.TOT but not MYFILE.TT or MYFILE.TXB. To match the latter, you have to specify MYFILE.T??. Notice that a question mark placed in the middle of the file name or extension matches any *single* character in that position, whereas a question mark placed at the end also matches zero characters.

Using the * Wildcard Character in a File Name or Extension

An asterisk (*) matches zero or more characters from the position in which it is placed to the end of the file name or extension. For example, MY*.TXT matches MYFILE.TXT and MYHOUSE.TXT but not MYFILE.DOC or YOURFILE.TXT. Any characters following an asterisk in the file name, or following an asterisk in the extension, are ignored. In other words, typing MY*.TXT or MY*FILE.TXT gives you exactly the same result.

For most commands that accept wildcards, if you enter a file name with no extension, all extensions are matched. For example, MYFILE matches MYFILE, MYFILE.TXT, and MYFILE.DOC, whereas MY* matches MYHOUSE.TXT as well. If you type a period after the file name (for example, MYFILE. or MY*.), only files with no extension are matched.

Examples

.	Match any file name.
*	Same as *.* in most cases.
????????.???	Same as *.*
*.	Match any file name that has no extension.
*.??	Match any file that has a zero- to two-letter extension
?.*	Match any file that has a one-letter file name.
*.BAK	Match all files with a .BAK extension.
MYFILE	Match all files with the file name *MYFILE* with any (or no) extension.
MY*.*	Match all files that begin with *MY*.
M?F*.?XT	Match any file that begins with the letter *M*, has an *F* as the third character in the file name, and has a three-letter extension that ends in *XT*.

See Also

"Introducing the DOS File System" in Chapter 5

> and >> 2.0 and later—Internal

BATCH FILE

You can use the greater than redirection symbols (> and >>) on the command line to instruct DOS to take any output that normally would be written to the screen and send it somewhere else. These symbols are handy for sending the output of a command, such as DIR, to the printer (DIR > PRN) or to a file on disk (DIR > MYFILE.TXT). Using two greater than signs (>>) tells DOS to append the output to the file specified (if it already exists) instead of overwriting the file as it normally would. For example,

```
DIR C:\DOS > DIR_LIST.TXT
```

creates (or overwrites if it already exists) the file DIR_LIST.TXT in the current directory and fills it with a list of all the files in the C:\DOS subdirectory. However, the command

```
DIR C:\WIN >> DIR_LIST.TXT
```

appends (adds) a list of all the files in the C:\WIN subdirectory to the end of the DIR_LIST.TXT file.

Notice that only the program output normally written to the screen is redirected. For example, the command

```
COPY MYFILE.TXT YOURFILE.TXT > COPYMSG.TXT
```

still copies MYFILE.TXT to YOURFILE.TXT, but the message `1 file(s) copied` is written to the file COPYMSG.TXT.

In batch files, it is fairly common to redirect messages from commands like COPY to the NUL device, as in the following:

```
COPY MYFILE.TXT YOURFILE.TXT > NUL
```

This technique can keep the on-screen clutter generated by a batch file to a minimum, because anything written to the NUL device is essentially thrown away.

See Also

<, ¦, FIND, MORE, and SORT

"The Redirection Commands" in Chapter 14

< 2.0 and later—Internal

Programs normally expect input from the user to come from the keyboard. If you want to provide this input from a file instead of the keyboard, you can use the less than redirection symbol (<) to redirect that program's input. DOS includes three commands specifically designed to use with input redirection: MORE, SORT, and FIND.

One common use for input redirection is with the MORE filter program. To display the contents of the file README.TXT one screen at a time, you type the following command:

```
MORE < README.TXT
```

To sort all the lines in a text file, you might use the SORT command like this:

```
SORT < UNSORTED.TXT > SORTED.TXT
```

This command sorts all the lines in UNSORTED.TXT into alphabetical order and writes the sorted output to SORTED.TXT. If you did not include the > SORTED.TXT argument, SORT would write the sorted lines to the display (standard output). If you forgot to redirect the input to the SORT command (that is, if you did not include the < UNSORTED.TXT argument), DOS would wait for you to type the input at the keyboard.

Occasionally you find a use for input redirection when you are automating the input to a program. Many software patches distributed as batch files use this technique to redirect DEBUG's input to a text file, in order to make changes to a program file. (Indeed, this is just what the SPATCH.BAT file on the DOS 6 distribution disk does.) Just remember that after the input to a program is redirected, control does not return to the keyboard until the program terminates. If you forget to put the keystrokes that exit the program at the end of your input file, you have to reboot your computer in order to regain control.

See Also

> and >>, ¦, FIND, MORE, and SORT

"The Redirection Commands" in Chapter 14

¦ — 2.0 and later—Internal

You can use the *pipe* character (¦) on the command line to tell DOS to use the screen output from one program as the keyboard input to another. (The term *pipe* comes from the UNIX operating system, which often uses this method to string together several programs to perform a particular job.) For the pipe character to work, the first program must write output to the screen that the second program expects to get from the keyboard.

In DOS, pipe characters are most often used with the TYPE and MORE commands to display a text file one screen at a time, as in the following:

```
TYPE README.TXT ¦ MORE
```

You also can combine MORE with FIND to look at the results of a text search one screen at a time.

```
FIND "Mr. Merryweather" BIGTEXT.TXT ¦ MORE
```

DOS actually accomplishes piping by writing the output from the first program to a temporary file, and then redirecting the input for the second program from that file. When the second program terminates, DOS deletes the temporary file. So, the preceding command accomplishes the same thing as the following three commands:

```
FIND "Mr. Merryweather" BIGTEXT.TXT > TEMP.TXT
MORE < TEMP.TXT
DEL TEMP.TXT
```

Using the pipe character saves you from having to type all three of these commands.

See Also

> and >>, <, FIND, MORE, and SORT

"The Redirection Commands" in Chapter 14

:label

1.0 and later—Internal

In a batch file, you can type a colon (:) in the first column of any line to indicate that the next eight characters on that line should be interpreted as a label. Any additional characters on the line after the label are ignored. Labels are used as the destination for GOTO statements in batch files.

Syntax

:label

Notes

1. To define a label, a colon must be the first character on the line. Not even a space or a tab character can precede it.
2. Only the first eight characters of a label are significant, although the label can be as long as you like. Everything on the line after the eighth character of the label is ignored.
3. Although you can define the same label in more than one place in a batch file, the GOTO command always jumps to the first occurrence.

4. Labels and file names share the same legal characters with the exception that labels cannot include percent signs (%) or hyphens (–). Batch file labels can be typed in any mixture of upper- and lowercase characters.

Examples

```
GOTO SKIP_DEL
DEL *.BAK
:SKIP_DEL   This text will be ignored
```

In this example, when DOS executes the line containing the GOTO SKIP_DEL command, DOS searches for the :SKIP_DEL label and continues execution with the line that follows it. The DEL *.BAK command is never executed.

Messages

`Label not found`

Error: The label specified in a GOTO statement was not found. After displaying this message the batch file terminates.

See Also

GOTO

"Branching with GOTO" in Chapter 16

%*n* 1.0 and later—Internal

You can use *replaceable parameters* to represent command-line arguments from within a batch file. DOS replaces these markers with their corresponding command-line arguments when the batch file is executed.

Syntax

%*n*

Notes

1. Ten replaceable parameters are available, %0 through %9.

2. %0 returns the name of the batch file as it was entered on the command line, %1 returns the first argument on the command line, %2 returns the second, and so on. Spaces, tabs, commas, and semicolons all are considered valid argument delimiter. To include a delimiter in a command-line argument, enclose the argument in double quotation marks.

3. DOS can find replaceable parameters almost anywhere in a batch file, including within double quotation marks and embedded in words. For example, the file name MY%1FILE.TXT is a perfectly legal file name for

DOS; in a batch file, however, the %1 embedded in the name is replaced with the first argument to the batch file. This can lead to some strange errors.

4. If you want to include a percent sign in a batch file, write it twice. When DOS is parsing the file it sees the two percent signs (%%) and replaces it with a single one (%). For example, %1 is replaced with the first argument to the batch file, whereas %%1 simply becomes %1.

   This explains why the variable markers in a FOR loop must be written as %%a in a batch file, but as %a from the command line. In a batch file, DOS removes the doubled %% signs and replaces them with a single % before the FOR command gets to see it. If you forget and use a single percent sign, DOS removes it and leaves only the *a*, which results in a syntax error.

5. If you require more than nine arguments in your batch file, you can use the SHIFT command to gain access to them.

6. An empty parameter is replaced with nothing at all. In other words, if you enter MY%2.TXT in your batch file and then forget to enter a second parameter when you run the batch file, DOS looks for the file MY.TXT.

Examples

The following batch file displays a series of files one screen at a time.

```
:START
IF "%1"=="" GOTO END
IF NOT EXIST %1 GOTO END
TYPE %1 ¦ MORE
SHIFT
GOTO START
:END
```

In the first IF statement, the %1 is replaced with the first argument to the batch file. As long as the argument exists, the statement is false and execution continues on the next line. The second IF statement checks to see if this argument is a valid path name. If the argument passes this check, execution finally passes to the TYPE command, which types the file to the screen through the MORE filter program. When TYPE finishes, SHIFT moves the arguments down one place, and the next line transfers execution back to the first line in the batch file. The loop continues until the batch file runs out of arguments or finds an invalid path name.

Note

The preceding example isn't quite bulletproof. If wildcards are included in the first argument to this batch file, it easily could pass both of the tests we perform with the IF commands. TYPE, however, cannot handle wildcards and would display the message `Invalid filename or file not found` rather than the files you specified.

See Also

%name%, IF, FOR, and SHIFT

"Understanding Replaceable Parameters" in Chapter 16

%envir% 4.0 and later—Internal

With the addition of the *%envir%* syntax in MS-DOS 4.0, users finally had access to variables in batch files. Before executing a line in a batch file, DOS replaces every occurrence of *%envir%* with the contents of the corresponding environment variable. When combined with the ability of the SET command to create and destroy environment variables, this can be a very powerful feature.

Syntax

%envir%

Notes

1. The name of the environment variable can be entered in upper- or lowercase characters, but it must be surrounded by percent signs (%) to be recognized by DOS.

2. DOS can find the variable placeholder almost anywhere in a batch file, including enclosed in double quotation marks or embedded within words. Any pair of percent signs enclosing characters is assumed to be an environment variable. (If the first character following the percent sign is a digit, DOS assumes you are referring to a replaceable parameter, not an environment variable.) The string "with values between 7% and 15% annually" would tell DOS to search for an environment variable named " and 15". When DOS failed to find one, it would change the string to read "with values between 7 annually".

3. If you want to include a percent sign in a batch file, write it twice. When DOS is parsing the file it sees the two percent signs (%%) and replaces them with a single one (%). For example, %PATH% is replaced with the contents of the PATH environment variable, whereas %%PATH%% becomes %PATH%.

4. If no environment variable with that name exists, the %*envir*% placeholder is replaced with an empty string.

Examples

To add a subdirectory to your PATH, execute a particular program, and then restore your original PATH, you might use a batch file like this:

```
SET OLDPATH=%PATH%
PATH C:\CADD;%PATH%
C:\CADD\CADD.EXE %1
PATH %OLDPATH%
SET OLDPATH=
```

The first line saves the current PATH setting in an environment variable named OLDPATH. Next, the subdirectory C:\CADD is added to the PATH. In the third line, the program is executed and a single command-line argument is passed to it if one exists. Finally, when the program terminates, PATH is set equal to OLDPATH and the OLDPATH variable is deleted.

You can easily run out of space in the environment while manipulating variables in batch files, especially if you are running them from a Shell program like DOSSHELL. When this happens, DOS displays the message `Out of environment space` and then continues executing the batch file. To make the preceding example abort if there isn't enough environment space available, add an IF statement to check whether OLDPATH was successfully created.

```
SET OLDPATH=%PATH%
IF "%OLDPATH%"=="" GOTO ERROR
PATH C:\CADD;%PATH%
C:\CADD\CADD.EXE %1
PATH %OLDPATH%
SET OLDPATH=
GOTO END
:ERROR
ECHO Can't start CADD - not enough environment space
:END
```

Now CADD won't execute if there isn't enough environment space to save OLDPATH. To increase the size of the environment, increase the size of the /E:*size* parameter specified in the SHELL= command in your CONFIG.SYS file.

If you are running batch files from within a Shell program such as DOSSHELL, increasing the /E:*size* parameter may not help. When DOS runs a program, it gives the program access to a copy of the current environment. This copy is only big enough to hold the environment variables that are currently defined and has very little free space in it. When you run a batch file from within a Shell program, a temporary copy of COMMAND.COM is loaded into memory, and a copy of the shrunken environment the Shell program was using is passed to it. With so little available space in the current environment, batch files often run out of environment space.

One technique to avoid `Out of environment space` error messages when you run batch files from a Shell program is to define a dummy variable in your AUTOEXEC.BAT file that simply takes up space.

```
SET DUMMY=XXXXXXXXXXXXXXXXXXXXXXXXXXXXXXXXXXXXX
```

When you need space in the environment, simply delete the DUMMY variable before you define any new variables that your batch file needs.

```
SET DUMMY=
SET OLDPATH=%PATH%
```

When your batch file terminates, you return to your Shell program, and the copy of the environment that the batch file was using will be discarded. Because it is being thrown away, there is no reason to restore the DUMMY variable before the batch file exits.

If there is a chance you will run this batch file from the DOS prompt when your Shell program isn't running, include a SET statement, such as the following, that restores your DUMMY variable after you delete OLDPATH.

```
SET OLDPATH=
SET DUMMY=XXXXXXXXXXXXXXXXXXXXXXXXXXXXXXXXXXXXX
GOTO END
```

See Also

%n, IF, SET, and SHELL=

Chapter 16, "Understanding Batch Files"

@ 4.0 and later—Internal

Normally, DOS echoes to the screen every line in a batch file before executing it. Although this can be handy when you are testing a new batch file, you usually want to use ECHO OFF to turn off the echo feature in a batch file you use everyday. With the "at" sign (@), you can turn echo off for each line individually if you want to.

Syntax

@command_line

Notes

1. The @ symbol must be the first character on the line. Don't insert any spaces before or after it.

2. The most common use of the @ symbol is with the ECHO OFF command that begins most batch files. Because the echo feature is on when this command is executed, the ECHO OFF command is echoed to the screen—unless you precede the ECHO OFF command with an @ symbol.

3. Only the display of the command line that DOS executes is suppressed, not screen output generated by a command, which can be rather confusing to some users. To suppress the output generated by a command, you have to redirect the output of the command to the NUL device. For example

   @COPY MYFILE.TXT YOURFILE.TXT

   does not echo the command line itself (COPY MYFILE.TXT, and so on) to the screen, but still displays the message `1 file(s) copied` that is generated by COPY. If, in addition, you redirected the screen output of the COPY command to the NUL device

   @COPY MYFILE.TXT YOURFILE.TXT > NUL

   then nothing would be displayed on the screen at all.

See Also

> and >>, and ECHO

"Using Batch File Commands" in Chapter 16

; 6.0 and later—Internal

When DOS encounters a semicolon as the first character on a line in your CONFIG.SYS file, it ignores the contents of the rest of the line. Using a semicolon in this way is exactly the same as using the REM command. Inserting comments into your CONFIG.SYS file can help you remember what each line is for.

Syntax

;comment text

Notes

1. To mark a line in CONFIG.SYS as a comment, the semicolon (;) must be the first character on the line. Do not precede it with any spaces.
2. Note that this technique for creating a comment line only works in CONFIG.SYS. To insert a comment in a batch file, you either have to use REM or define a dummy label line with a colon.
3. If you find yourself continually commenting and uncommenting DEVICE= lines in your CONFIG.SYS, consider using the question mark (?) instead, so that you can enable or disable that driver interactively each time you boot up. If you insert a question mark (?) between the command name and the equal sign, DOS will ask you before it executes a command in your CONFIG.SYS file.

Tip

The configuration lines necessary for many devices are quite complicated, so using a semicolon to "comment them out" can be a handy way to turn features on and off in your CONFIG.SYS file.

Examples

Comments can help you keep track of what each line in your CONFIG.SYS file is for, as shown in the following:

```
; The old SCSI drive requires double buffering.
; Remember to remove this line when the new drive gets installed!!!
DEVICE=C:\DOS\SMARTDRV.EXE /DOUBLE_BUFFER
```

DOS skips over all lines that start with a semicolon and only executes the DEVICE= line that loads SMARTDrive's double buffering feature.

See Also

?, REM

Chapter 2, "Starting DOS"

? 6.0 and later—Internal

In CONFIG.SYS, if you put a question mark (?) between a command and the equal sign (=), DOS prompts you for confirmation before executing that command. This works for all CONFIG.SYS commands that use the *command=* form, including the SET command.

Syntax

command?=settings

Parameters and Switches

command This parameter can be any CONFIG.SYS command that uses the *command*= format.

settings The settings used with the ***command*** specified (when you allow it to be run).

Notes

1. Use the question mark (?) for individual features you want to control. If you find yourself using more than one or two question marks in your CONFIG.SYS file, however, you may want to consider setting up a menu instead. It is very easy to get confused and select the wrong combination of drivers when you're enabling each line individually.

2. The question mark (?) must come between the command and the equal sign, with no spaces between it and the command name.

3. Each line you have marked for confirmation will be displayed followed by `[Y,N]?`. Enter `Y` to execute the line and `N` to skip it.

4. Pressing the F8 key when DOS displays the `Starting MS-DOS...` message causes DOS to prompt you for confirmation of every line in your CONFIG.SYS file, whether or not the line includes a question mark.

5. DOS doesn't necessarily process the lines in your CONFIG.SYS in the order they appear in the file, which can be confusing when you receive a prompt for a line near the end of the file before being prompted for a line at the beginning. In general, DOS processes commands like DOS=, FILES=, and BUFFERS= before it begins to load any of your device drivers. However, once DOS begins processing the DEVICE= (and DEVICEHIGH=) lines, it loads them in the order they appear in the file.

Examples

To instruct DOS to prompt you before setting up a 1.4M RAM disk in extended memory, place a question mark in the line that loads the RAMDRIVE.SYS driver.

```
DEVICEHIGH?=C:\DOS\RAMDRIVE.SYS 1450 512 224 /E
```

If MemMaker has optimized your CONFIG.SYS, there may be /L and /S switches on the DEVICEHIGH line. Make sure you place the ? directly after the command name, not before the equal sign.

```
DEVICEHIGH? /L:1,1200 /S =C:\DOS\RAMDRIVE.SYS 1450 512 224 /E
```

Messages

If you place the ? incorrectly in a CONFIG.SYS command, you will receive one of the following error messages when you reboot:

```
Bad command or parameter - ?=
Error in CONFIG.SYS line #
```

or

```
Bad or Missing ?
Error in CONFIG.SYS line #
```

Edit your CONFIG.SYS file, and make sure that all your question marks (?) are placed directly after the name of the command, with no intervening spaces.

See Also

;, [*blockname*], and MENUITEM=

Chapter 2, "Starting DOS"

[*blockname*] 6.0 and later—Internal

Defining blocks in CONFIG.SYS is part of the multiple configuration feature in DOS 6. By naming blocks of commands, you can choose which blocks to execute from a menu when you start your computer.

Syntax

[*blockname*]

Notes

1. The name for a block can be up to 70 characters long and contain any legal file name characters. You cannot use spaces in block names, so you may want to consider using underscores (_) or hyphens (-) to separate words and make your block names more readable. Upper- and lowercase characters are considered the same. The name must be surrounded by square brackets ([and]) and appear on a line by itself. Any commands that follow the block name are considered to be part of that block until the next [*blockname*] is encountered in the file.

2. Blocks cannot be embedded inside each other. When DOS encounters another block name in the CONFIG.SYS file, it considers the preceding block to be complete.

3. Any block never referred to by a MENUITEM= line is never executed by DOS. Exceptions to this are the predefined block names [MENU] and [COMMON].

4. The [MENU] block defines entries for the main start-up menu and should contain the configuration menu that you want DOS to display when the computer starts up. DOS always executes this block.

5. Commands in a [COMMON] block are always executed by DOS. [COMMON] is also the only block that you are allowed to define more than once in your CONFIG.SYS file. A [COMMON] block located before the [MENU] block is run before the start-up menu is displayed. Similarly, a [COMMON] block located at the end of your CONFIG.SYS file is executed after all other blocks.

6. Any commands that you include in your CONFIG.SYS before the first block name are considered to be part of a [COMMON] block. As far as DOS is concerned, CONFIG.SYS files that don't use any multiple configuration features are simply one big [COMMON] block.

7. Microsoft recommends that you include a [COMMON] block command at the end of your CONFIG.SYS file, even if you don't need to place any commands in it. Many software installation programs modify your CONFIG.SYS file by adding to the end of the file the settings the software requires. With a [COMMON] block defined at the end, these added commands are run when you start your system; without [COMMONBLOCK], these added commands might never run at all.

Examples

Suppose that you wanted to set up a menu that let you choose between three basic configurations for your computer: Windows, DOS, and Maintenance. Begin by adding a menu block at the beginning of your CONFIG.SYS file with the predefined block name [MENU].

```
[MENU]
MENUITEM=WIN, Configure for Windows (Default)
MENUITEM=DOS, Configure for MS-DOS
MENUITEM=MAINT, Configure for File & Disk Maintenance
```

When these lines are included in your CONFIG.SYS file, DOS will search for blocks named [WIN], [DOS], and [MAINT]. You also may want to include a [COMMON] block that contains any commands that you always want executed.

```
[COMMON]
DEVICE=C:\DOS\SETVER.EXE
DEVICE=C:\DOS\HIMEM.SYS
DEVICE=C:\DOS\EMM386.EXE RAM MIN=0
DOS=HIGH,UMB
```

```
BREAK=ON
FILES=50
DEVICE=C:\DOS\ANSI.SYS
SHELL=C:\DOS\COMMAND.COM C:\DOS\ /P /E:512

[WIN]
BUFFERS=10

[DOS]
BUFFERS=10
DEVICE=C:\DOS\RAMDRIVE.SYS 1450 512 224 /E

[MAINT]
BUFFERS=30
DEVICE=C:\DOS\RAMDRIVE.SYS 1450 512 224 /E

[COMMON]
```

Include a [COMMON] block at the end of your CONFIG.SYS file. That way, any commands added to the file by software installation programs will be executed, no matter what configuration you choose. Without the final [COMMON] block, any commands that are added to the end of the file are only executed when you choose the maintenance configuration, because they will be part of the [MAINT] block.

The start-up menu DOS displays looks something like this:

```
MS-DOS 6 Startup Menu
=====================

1. Configure for Windows (Default)
2. Configure for MS-DOS
3. Configure for File & Disk Maintenance

Enter a choice: 1
```

Entering 1, 2, or 3 at this menu tells DOS to select the [WIN], [DOS], and [MAINT] blocks, respectively. DOS will set the CONFIG environment variable equal to the name of the configuration block you selected from the start-up menu.

In this example, you might be able to better understand the small differences between these three configurations if you look at a few lines from the AUTOEXEC.BAT file:

```
IF "%CONFIG%"=="MAINT" GOTO SET_TEMP
C:\DOS\SMARTDRV

:SET_TEMP
SET TEMP=C:\TEMP
SET TMP=C:\TEMP
```

```
IF NOT "%CONFIG%"=="WIN" GOTO THE_REST
MD D:\TEMP
SET TEMP=D:\TEMP
SET TMP=D:\TEMP

:THE_REST
```

The SMARTDrive disk cache is loaded if you are using the DOS or Windows configurations, which is why so few DOS buffers are needed (BUFFERS=10). In the Maintenance configuration, there is no disk cache, and so the number of DOS buffers is set to 30.

Similarly, the Windows configuration doesn't use a RAM drive; therefore, the TEMP (and TMP) environment variables are set pointing to the C:\TEMP subdirectory, instructing programs to create any temporary files they require in that subdirectory. When a RAM drive is present, temporary files are written to the RAM drive instead.

See Also

? and MENUITEM=

"Creating Multiple Configurations" in Chapter 2

ANSI.SYS (device driver)

2.0 and later—External

ANSI.SYS is a device driver that provides a subset of the commands defined by the American National Standards Institute (ANSI) for controlling video displays and keyboards. ANSI.SYS enables you to control cursor positioning, display colors, video modes, and keyboard mapping. To use it, you must load ANSI.SYS with a DEVICE= command in your CONFIG.SYS file. ANSI.SYS replaces the default CON driver provided by the MS-DOS kernel.

Syntax

DEVICE=*drive:\path***ANSI.SYS** /X /K /R

or

DEVICEHIGH=*drive:\path***ANSI.SYS** /X /K /R

Parameters and Switches

drive:\path — The full path to the ANSI.SYS file on your system. Setup places the ANSI.SYS file in the C:\DOS subdirectory by default. If the full path to ANSI.SYS isn't specified, DOS looks for the file in the root directory of the start-up drive.

/X — Enables you to remap extended keys if you are using a 101-key keyboard.

/K — Forces ANSI.SYS to treat a 101-key keyboard as if it were an 84-key keyboard, which is a handy feature with older TSR programs that don't recognize the new keycodes properly. Using this switch is the same as specifying SWITCHES=/K. If you are using the SWITCHES=/K switch already, you should also include the /K option in the DEVICE= line that loads ANSI.SYS.

/R — Slows down the line scrolling rate so that lines on the display are more readable. Chances are you won't be able to notice any difference when you use this switch, because the scrolling rate doesn't change that much. Microsoft claims this switch can aid screen-reading programs that make computers more accessible to people with disabilities.

Notes

1. You can load ANSI.SYS with either the /X or the /R switch, but not both. These two functions are mutually exclusive.
2. ANSI.SYS occupies about 4K of memory in your computer and can be loaded into upper memory with the DEVICEHIGH command.
3. Note that all ANSI commands begin with the Escape character and are case sensitive. After it is loaded, ANSI.SYS scans all text that is written to the screen, looking for commands.
4. The MODE command requires ANSI.SYS to be loaded in order to change the number of text lines displayed on your screen. MODE can switch between color and monochrome adapters, however, without ANSI.SYS.

5. When it's loaded, ANSI.SYS resets your screen colors to the default (white on black). If you've set screen colors with the MENUCOLOR= command, they are reset when ANSI.SYS loads into memory. If this is a problem, either insert an ANSI command into your AUTOEXEC.BAT file to reset your screen colors, or load ANSI.SYS from a [COMMON] block located before your [MENU] block in CONFIG.SYS.

6. All ANSI commands begin with an Escape character (ASCII 27). When you press the Esc key at the DOS prompt, DOS interprets that as a request to cancel the current command line, so you cannot simply send ANSI commands from the command line by typing them. To get around this, people often use PROMPT to send ANSI commands. Another alternative is to place the ANSI commands in a file and then copy the file to the console like this:

```
COPY ANSI_CMD.TXT CON
```

7. Appendix F, "ANSI Control Codes," provides a list of all the ANSI commands supported by ANSI.SYS.

Examples

To use the PROMPT command to set your screen colors to blue on white, you would enter the following command:

```
PROMPT $e[34;47m$p$g
```

Some people like to create very elaborate DOS prompts with ANSI.SYS. For example, entering the command

```
PROMPT $e[s$e[H$d$e[0;68H$t$e[u"Good morning Mr. Phelps"$_$p$g
```

changes the DOS prompt to display the current date in the upper-left corner of the screen, the time in the upper-right corner, and creates a two-line prompt that starts with `Good morning Mr. Phelps` and then has the familiar C:\> on the following line. Notice that case is significant in ANSI commands, and the above command will not work if, for example, you type `E` rather than `e`.

See Also

DEVICE= and PROMPT

Chapter 20, "Understanding ANSI.SYS," and Appendix F, "ANSI Control Codes"

APPEND

3.3 and later—External

You can use the APPEND command to set up a search path that enables DOS to find data files even if they're not in the current directory. The subdirectories in the APPEND path are appended to the current directory when DOS searches for data files. APPEND was developed so that programs requiring you to make their program directories current can be run from the subdirectory which contains their data files, rather than the one that contains their program files.

Syntax

To load APPEND into memory:

APPEND /X:*onoff* /E

or

APPEND *path1;path2;...* /X:*onoff* /PATH:*onoff*

To replace and/or set the appended directory search path:

APPEND *path1;path2;...* /X:*onoff* /PATH:*onoff*

To clear the appended directory search path:

APPEND ;

To display the current appended directory search path:

APPEND

Parameters and Switches

path1;path2;... Each *path* specifies a valid subdirectory that exists on your system. Use full, absolute path names that include drive letters for each subdirectory included in your appended directory search path; the current subdirectory and disk drive often change. Separate each subdirectory from the previous one with a semicolon (;).

/E — Stores the appended directory search path in an environment variable named APPEND rather than internally. With this switch specified, you can use SET to view or change the appended directory search path. You can only specify this option when you first load APPEND into memory.

/X:*onoff* — Specifies whether DOS is to search appended directories (/X or /X:ON) or not (/X:OFF) when executing programs. Directories on the APPEND path are searched before those specified with the PATH command. To use this feature you must specify it when you load APPEND into memory, after which you can toggle it on (/X or /X:ON) and off (/X:OFF).

/PATH:*onoff* — Normally, if you specify a full path name for a file, DOS only searches that directory. /PATH:ON instructs DOS to search the appended directories even if the full path name of the file is given. /PATH:OFF turns off this feature.

Notes

1. The first time you run APPEND, it loads itself into memory as a TSR program, occupying about 5K of memory. APPEND does not remove itself from memory until you restart DOS.

2. After loading APPEND into memory, do not specify the .EXE file extension. At this point, APPEND is resident in memory and will not load more than once.

3. You can use the /E switches only when you first load APPEND into memory, and you cannot specify any search paths on the same line. In other words, if you want the APPEND path to be stored in the environment, you have to run the command twice: once with /E and then again to set your appended directory search path.

4. To use the /X switch, you must specify it in the line that loads APPEND into memory. After APPEND is loaded with this feature enabled, you can toggle it on and off with /X:ON and /X:OFF.

5. Each path you specify in the appended directory search path must be separated by a semicolon. Don't include any spaces between paths. The total length of the appended directory search path cannot exceed 127 characters.

6. When DOS looks for a data file, it first searches the current directory and then the appended directories in the order you specified them. If DOS encounters an invalid path it skips it without displaying any error messages.

7. Do not use APPEND when running Microsoft Windows or Windows Setup.

8. APPEND can't change the environment being used by running applications, so the /E switch does not work with shell programs, such as DOSSHELL, XTree, or Norton Commander. To work with these types of programs, APPEND must store the appended directory search path internally (that is, don't specify /E).

9. The DIR command ignores the appended directory search path and never displays files from appended directories.

10. APPEND ignores any drive assignments made with the ASSIGN command. To use both utilities, you must load APPEND into memory before using ASSIGN or an error message appears.

11. DOS searches the appended directories when it opens files requested through Interrupt 21h functions 0Fh (Open File), 3Dh (Open File Handle), and 23h (Get File Size). When /X or /X:ON is specified, functions 11h (Find First Entry), 4Eh (Find First File), and 4Bh (Execute Program) search the appended directories as well.

Trap

APPEND is intended for locating and reading files, but not for writing them. Any files written to disk are placed in the current subdirectory, no matter what subdirectory they originally were read from. This works out well for program overlay and help files, which are rarely written to, but can be very frustrating if APPEND starts scattering data files all over your hard disk.

Examples

The following line loads APPEND into memory, enables searching for executable files in appended directories, and stores the active APPEND path in the environment. This line assumes that the file APPEND.EXE is located in the C:\DOS subdirectory:

```
C:\DOS\APPEND /X /E
```

To instruct DOS to search the current directory, C:\BIN, and C:\BIN\OVR when opening data files, enter the following command:

```
APPEND C:\BIN;C:\BIN\OVR
```

When the program that needed data file path support terminates, disable APPEND with the following command.

```
APPEND ;
```

To reactivate APPEND, simply specify a new APPEND path.

Messages

`APPEND/ASSIGN conflict`

Error: You tried to load APPEND after reassigning disk drives with ASSIGN. Break any disk drive reassignments you may have set, load APPEND, and then reset your ASSIGN settings.

`APPEND already installed`

Warning: You attempted to load APPEND a second time. Try running the command again, making sure to enter APPEND and not APPEND.EXE on the command line.

`Incorrect APPEND version`

Error: You used a version of APPEND from a different version of DOS. Make sure that you do not use an APPEND version from the IBM Local Area Network (LAN) program. The problem may be that the wrong version of APPEND is loading first from a subdirectory included in your DOS PATH.

`No Append`

Information: You typed APPEND, to display the current appended directory path, and APPEND currently is inactive.

See Also

PATH

ASSIGN

2.0 to 5.0—External

ASSIGN was a utility that enabled you to attach an alias drive letter to an existing drive. Microsoft no longer distributes ASSIGN in the standard DOS package and is encouraging everyone to begin using SUBST instead. ASSIGN is included on the DOS 6 Supplemental Disk.

Using SUBST instead of ASSIGN

You can use ASSIGN to create an alias of A: for your B: drive if you want to fool an installation program that only runs from drive A: To accomplish this task with ASSIGN, you use the following command:

```
ASSIGN B = A
```

To do the same thing with SUBST, you enter the following command:

```
SUBST A: B:\
```

See Also

SUBST

"Changing Disk Drives" in Chapter 13

ATTRIB

3.0 and later—External

In a file's directory entry on disk, DOS stores information about the file's size, the date and time the file was last modified, and any attributes associated with that file. File attributes are used to flag files that have to be backed up, to control whether a file can be written to, and to hide files from view. With ATTRIB you can view or change the attributes associated with a particular file.

Syntax

Use this syntax to display the attributes currently set for a file or group of files:

ATTRIB *pathname* /S

Use this syntax to set or clear attributes for a file or group of files:

ATTRIB ±A ±R ±S ±H *pathname* /S

Parameters and Switches

±A — Sets (+A) or clears (–A) the archive attribute for all files matching the path name specified. By default, new files always have their archive attribute turned on. DOS sets this attribute each time a file is written to.

±R — Sets (+R) or clears (–R) the read-only attribute for all files matching the path name specified. Marking a file as read-only can prevent COPY from overwriting it, but many programs can override this flag.

±S — Sets (+S) or clears (–S) the system attribute for all files matching the path name specified. Few files use this attribute. It is used to flag the hidden MS-DOS system files that are in the root directory of your start-up disk drive.

±H — Sets (+H) or clears (–H) the hidden attribute for all files matching the path name specified. A file with the hidden attribute normally does not show up in a listing of the files in a directory. ATTRIB lets you set the hidden flag for subdirectories as well as for files.

pathname — The file or files that you want ATTRIB to display information about. Wildcards are allowed in the file name portion. If no path name is specified, all files (*.*) in the current directory are displayed. If no file name is specified, ATTRIB displays or changes the attributes of that subdirectory. Notice that the root directory has no attributes, and therefore cannot be changed.

/S — Searches for files in the specified subdirectory and all subdirectories below it.

Notes

1. If a file has either the hidden or the system attribute set, you must clear that attribute before you can change any other attributes for the file. Otherwise, you will be denied access to the file (see the following "Messages" section). If a single file has both the system and hidden attributes set, you must clear both attributes with a single ATTRIB command to avoid being denied access to the file.

2. Normally ATTRIB only displays or alters the attributes of files. To change the attributes of a subdirectory, enter the full path name for that subdirectory on the command line with ATTRIB. You cannot use wildcards when you are specifying subdirectories.

Trap

Commas can make strange things happen with ATTRIB. If you include a comma in an ATTRIB command, ATTRIB clears all the attributes for all the files in the current directory.

```
ATTRIB ,
```

If you also include the /S switch, ATTRIB clears the attributes of all the files on your hard disk, not just the ones below the current directory.

```
ATTRIB , /S
```

This problem has been confirmed by Microsoft and is present in DOS 5 versions of ATTRIB as well.

Examples

To display the attributes of all the .TXT files in the C:\MYWORK subdirectory, you would enter the following:

```
ATTRIB C:\MYWORK\*.TXT
```

If you wanted to extend the search to include any subdirectories under the C:\MYWORK subdirectory, you would include the /S switch, as in the following:

```
ATTRIB C:\MYWORK\*.TXT /S
```

To set the archive bit on for all the files you found so that MSBACKUP would be sure to back them up the next time you ran it, enter the following:

```
ATTRIB +A C:\MYWORK\*.TXT /S
```

To clear all the attributes of all the files in the root directory of drive C:, including the MS-DOS system files, enter the following:

```
ATTRIB -A -R -H -S C:\*.*
```

To hide the C:\SECRET subdirectory so that it no longer shows up in directory listings, enter the following:

```
ATTRIB +H C:\SECRET
```

Messages

```
Not resetting hidden file
Not resetting system file
```

Error: ATTRIB is unable to set or clear the attributes you've requested because the file has either the hidden or the system attribute set. To get around this, clear the hidden or system attributes for that file first (for example, ATTRIB -H -S); then retry the command.

See Also

XCOPY

"Understanding File Attributes" in Chapter 5

BACKUP

2.0 to 5.0—External

The BACKUP utility has been around for quite a while. You could use it to back up files from your hard disk drive to a series of floppy disks. It created a special file on each backup disk, a file that could only be read by the RESTORE utility. RESTORE, however, would often refuse to restore files if anything went wrong with your disks. With MS-DOS 6.0, Microsoft began distributing the new MSBACKUP program. For those who still want to use the old BACKUP utility, Microsoft has included it on the DOS 6 Supplemental Disk.

See Also

MSBACKUP and RESTORE

BREAK 2.0 and later—Internal
BREAK= 2.0 and later—Internal

When DOS detects a Ctrl-Break (or Ctrl-C), it attempts to stop the program that is currently running. DOS checks for a Ctrl-Break after performing any screen, keyboard, or printer I/O operation. Turning BREAK ON or setting BREAK=ON in your CONFIG.SYS file instructs DOS to check for Ctrl-Break after performing disk I/O operations as well. This enables you to regain control more quickly when you are trying to stop disk-oriented DOS commands.

Syntax

In CONFIG.SYS, to set extended Ctrl-Break checking on or off, use the following format:

BREAK=*onoff*

To turn extended Ctrl-Break checking on or off from the command line, use the following format:

BREAK *onoff*

Parameters and Switches

onoff Specifies whether you want extended Ctrl-Break checking to be turned ON or OFF. The only legal values for the *onoff* parameter are ON and OFF. In the CONFIG.SYS form of this command, this parameter is required. If you omit the *onoff* parameter when you run BREAK from the command line, the current state of extended Ctrl-Break checking will be displayed.

Notes

1. When DOS starts up, it sets extended Ctrl-Break checking OFF by default.

2. Set BREAK=ON in your CONFIG.SYS file. The speed penalty is negligible, and if it saves just one file from a mistyped COPY command, it is well worth it. Most long operations involve reading or writing to disk. If BREAK is off you may be unable to stop a lengthy process you would rather not wait for.

3. In most cases, pressing Ctrl-C produces the same effect as pressing Ctrl-Break, but there is a subtle difference. The Ctrl-C key combination is

passed through the keyboard buffer. If any other key is pressed before Ctrl-C, it is ignored until the program reads the keyboard. For example, DIR stops if you press Ctrl-C, but not if you press the space bar and then Ctrl-C. Ctrl-Break is passed directly to DOS without buffering and often gets a quicker response.

4. In theory, turning on extended Ctrl-Break checking should slow down your system. In practice, any slow down is so insignificant that you probably will never notice it.

5. Programs have complete control over what happens when a Ctrl-Break is detected. The default action is for the running program to be halted; but applications often disable Ctrl-Break so that you can save your work before exiting. Typically, short command-line utilities respond to Ctrl-Break, whereas most full-screen applications do not.

6. The state of the BREAK flag can be changed by a running program. Programming etiquette dictates that when an application finishes running, it should reset all flags to their original states. Still, you may run across applications that forget to reset BREAK. If this causes problems, you can run the application from a batch file that restores the BREAK flag setting when the program terminates.

See Also

VERIFY

"Telling DOS When to Break" in Chapter 18

BUFFERS= 2.0 and later—Internal

DOS stores any information read from or written to disk in memory buffers. With more buffers available, it is more likely that DOS already has in memory the data requested by a program. The BUFFERS= command enables you to fine tune your system so that DOS can perform disk I/O as efficiently as possible. BUFFERS= can only be used in your CONFIG.SYS file.

Syntax

BUFFERS=*number*,*read_ahead*

Parameters and Switches

number The number of disk buffers DOS should use, from 1 to 99. The default value varies depending on the amount of memory in your computer. Normally, 15 is used for a computer with at least 512K of RAM.

read_ahead The number of buffers in the secondary, read-ahead cache. For DOS 5.0 this value could be from 1 to 8, with a default value of 1. In DOS 6.0, you can specify 0 secondary cache buffers, and 0 is the default value.

Notes

Tip
Make sure that you explicitly set the number of DOS buffers in your CONFIG.SYS file. If you aren't using disk-caching software, the default for BUFFERS (usually 15) is too low. You may be slowing down your computer by not requesting more.

1. Each disk buffer uses approximately 532 bytes of memory. If DOS is loaded HIGH, it attempts to locate these buffers in the HMA as well. About 48 buffers can fit in the HMA with DOS 6. If you have specified more buffers than can fit in the HMA, DOS loads them all into conventional memory.

2. If you are using disk-caching software, such as SMARTDRV.EXE, you may want to decrease the number of buffers that DOS uses. A dedicated disk cache is much more efficient at optimizing disk access time than the simple memory buffers that DOS uses, and having a lot of DOS buffers can slow your system. In this situation, set the number of buffers fairly low—using only 15 or 20.

3. Although the perfect setting for buffers can only be found through trial and error, a good place to start is half the size of your hard disk (in megabytes) divided by two, adjusted to be in the range of 15 to 55. For example, if you have an 80M drive, a good setting might by 40. With large drives, you may be tempted to specify a higher number of buffers; but under normal circumstances, using a number higher than 50 hurts, rather than helps, performance.

4. The secondary, read-ahead buffer setting can give you a performance boost if you aren't running any other caching software. Because many programs read files sequentially, DOS can perform fewer disk accesses by reading in more information than was requested. The number of read-ahead buffers you specify is the amount of data that DOS reads from disk in addition to the data requested by a program.

   Cache software, such as SMARTDRV.EXE, usually includes much more sophisticated read-ahead capabilities than DOS can provide. If you are using any cache software, you should turn off this feature by letting DOS default to 0 read-ahead buffers.

See Also

DOS=HIGH, FASTOPEN, FILES, HIMEM.SYS, and SMARTDRV.EXE

Chapter 18, "Configuring Your Computer"

CALL

3.3 and later—Internal

You can use the CALL command to execute a second batch file and return control to the first batch file. CALL normally is used to replace the awkward COMMAND /C syntax that was required before DOS 3.3. CALL can be used to run any executable file, but there is no reason to use it for .COM or .EXE files because they return control automatically. If you execute a batch file from a batch file without using CALL, control is never returned.

Syntax

CALL *drive:\path**filename** parameters*

Parameters and Switches

drive:\path	The drive and/or path to the batch file you want to execute. If no drive or path is specified, the DOS PATH is searched for ***filename***.
filename	The file name of the batch file you want to execute. This argument is required and wildcards cannot be used. You are not required to enter the .BAT extension, but you can include it if you want to ensure that a batch file, rather than an executable file, is found.
parameters	Any parameters that you want passed to the batch file you are executing.

Notes

1. When you use the CALL command to execute a batch file from within a batch file, control returns to the first batch file when the second one terminates. If you execute a batch file from within a batch file without the CALL command, control never returns to the first batch file.

2. Any *parameters* specified are passed to the called batch file. You can access these *parameters* from within the called batch file with replaceable parameters (for example, %1) as usual.

3. Avoid using redirection symbols (<, >, and >>) or the pipe character (¦) in the *parameters* you pass to the batch file with the CALL command. DOS ignores any redirection operations you specify, which might cause some programs (like MORE) to lock up or crash.

4. Although the CALL command is very similar to the COMMAND /C command, there is one significant difference: CALL doesn't execute a temporary copy of the command interpreter, whereas COMMAND /C does. For this reason, CALL requires less memory to use.

5. If you CALL a program that returns an exit code, that exit code value will be available after CALL returns. Unfortunately, you can't set the exit code for a batch file, so CALL can't return an exit code from a batch file you have executed. To return status information from a batch file executed with the CALL command, create an environment variable and set it equal to your return status. You can then test this environment variable in the calling batch file.

6. A batch file executed with the CALL command uses the same copy of the command interpreter that its parent is using; therefore, they share access to the same environment area. Any environment variables you set in the called batch file can be read by the parent batch file when it regains control. This is not true when you use COMMAND /C. The environment of a batch file executed with COMMAND /C disappears when the temporary copy of the command interpreter it is running under is removed from memory.

7. If you are going to load any resident software from a called batch file, make sure you use CALL rather than COMMAND /C. When you return from COMMAND /C, the temporary copy of the command interpreter is unloaded from memory. If you load any resident software while this temporary copy is running, the memory occupied by the temporary command interpreter remains unavailable until you reboot your computer. This "memory loss" doesn't happen with the CALL command, because no temporary copy of the command interpreter is loaded.

8. A batch file can CALL itself, but you must be careful to explicitly terminate the batch file at some point to avoid an endless loop. A batch file

can be terminated by instructing the user to press Ctrl-Break at a PAUSE or by executing another batch file (without CALL) at some point.

9. Note that while it's perfectly legal to execute a .COM or .EXE file with the CALL command, there is little reason to do so. After executing a .COM or .EXE file, control returns to the batch file with or without using the CALL command. Executing the CALL command from the DOS prompt, although legal, is fairly useless unless it is part of a FOR-IN-DO loop.

Examples

To call a batch file from another batch file, simply include the name of the batch file in a CALL command, as shown in the following:

```
CALL OTHER.BAT
```

Note that you can omit the .BAT extension; but if DOS locates an .EXE or .COM file named OTHER, it will execute that program rather than your batch file. DOS will search the current directory as well as any subdirectories listed in your DOS PATH looking for OTHER.BAT. To save time by limiting DOS's search, specify the full path name of the batch file.

Arguments can be passed to the called batch file. Suppose that you had previously written a batch file named COPYDOC.BAT, which would copy all the .DOC files in a subdirectory (%1) to a floppy disk (%2). The project you are working on is stored in five separate subdirectories, and you want to write a batch file, as shown in the following example, that runs COPYDOC once for each subdirectory:

```
@ECHO OFF
CALL COPYDOC.BAT C:\PROJECT\WORK B:
CALL COPYDOC.BAT C:\PROJECT\LTR B:
CALL COPYDOC.BAT C:\PROJECT\EXPN B:
CALL COPYDOC.BAT C:\PROJECT\RES B:
CALL COPYDOC.BAT C:\PROJECT\OLD B:
ECHO *** All Done ***
```

Each CALL command would execute COPYDOC with different parameters, backing up all five of the C:\PROJECT subdirectories. When all the copy commands had been executed, the message `*** All Done ***` would be displayed on-screen. If you had executed the COPYDOC.BAT file without using CALL, the batch file would have terminated after backing up one subdirectory because control would never return to this batch file from COPYDOC.BAT.

To eliminate the repetition in the example above, you could combine all five CALL commands into a single FOR-IN-DO loop, as shown in the following:

```
@ECHO OFF
FOR %%A IN (WORK LTR EXPN RES OLD) DO CALL COPYDOC.BAT
C:\PROJECT\%%A B:
ECHO *** All Done ***
```

Note that you could execute this FOR command from the command line, as long as you remembered to substitute single percent signs for the double ones that are required in batch files, like this:

```
FOR %A IN (WORK LTR EXPN RES OLD) DO CALL COPYDOC.BAT C:\PROJECT\%A B:
```

Messages

`Batch file missing`

Error: DOS attempted to read the next line from the batch file it was executing and was unable to find the file. This can happen if you execute a batch file from a floppy disk and change disks before the batch file has finished. It also is possible that the batch file has renamed or deleted itself, in which case you will have to edit it to avoid this behavior.

See Also

COMMAND

"Running Batch Files from Other Batch Files" in Chapter 16

CD or CHDIR

2.0 and later—Internal

BATCH FILE

Each disk drive has one subdirectory that is referred to as the *current* directory. When a path name contains no subdirectories, DOS assumes the current directory for that drive is being referenced. The CD (or CHDIR) command enables you to display or change the current directory for a disk drive.

Syntax

CD *drive:\path*

or

CHDIR *drive:\path*

Parameters and Switches

drive:\path — The subdirectory (*path*) on a particular *drive:* that you want to make current. If only a *path* is specified, it becomes the current directory on the current drive.

If only a *drive:* is specified, the name of the current subdirectory on that drive is displayed. If this parameter is omitted, the name of the current directory of the current drive is displayed.

Notes

1. If a backslash (\) is the first (or only) character in a subdirectory path, it is considered an *absolute* path and is specified starting from the root directory. If the subdirectory path begins with a subdirectory name, it is considered a *relative* path, and the current directory is used as the starting point. A drive letter, followed by a colon, can precede either an absolute or relative path.

2. Two periods (..) represent the parent of the current directory. A very common shorthand with the CD command is to switch to the parent directory with a CD .. command. The "double-dot" can be used in any path name, but it is more useful in relative path names than in absolute ones. Notice that the root directory has no parent; attempting to switch to the parent of the root directory (for example, CD \..) causes an error message to be displayed. (See the first item in the following "Messages" section.)

3. Do not specify a file name with the CD (or CHDIR) command, or DOS interprets the file name as a subdirectory name and displays an error message. (See the first item in the following "Messages" section.)

4. You must include a colon after the drive letter, or DOS interprets the drive letter as a subdirectory name and displays an error message. (See the first item in the following "Messages" section.)

Examples

To change to the root directory of the current drive, enter CD (or CHDIR) followed by a backslash.

```
CD \
```

To change to the parent or the current directory, enter CD followed by two periods.

```
CD ..
```

If the current directory was the root directory, switching to the parent directory with the preceding command causes an `Invalid directory` message to be displayed (because the root directory has no parent). (See the first item in the following "Messages" section.)

For the next set of examples, assume the following directory tree:

```
C:\
        DOS
        TEMP
        WIN
                SYSTEM
        WORK
                STEVE
                ALICE
```

Enter the following command to display the current directory on drive C:.

```
CD C:
```

If you omit the C:, the current directory of the current drive is displayed. Assuming that drive C is the current drive, you enter the following command to change to the C:\WORK\STEVE subdirectory:

```
CD \WORK\STEVE
```

Then, if you want to change to the C:\WORK\ALICE subdirectory, you can use either of the following two commands:

```
CD \WORK\ALICE
```

or

```
CD ..\ALICE
```

The second line uses the "double-dot" directory to specify a relative path to the new subdirectory. It is interpreted as "the subdirectory ALICE of the parent of the current directory."

Relative path names can get very convoluted. If the current drive and directory is C:\WORK\ALICE, and you want to change to the C:\WIN\SYSTEM subdirectory, enter one of the following commands:

CD ..\..\WIN\SYSTEM

or

CD ..\STEVE\..\..\DOS\..\WIN\SYSTEM

The preceding examples can help you understand how DOS interprets relative path names, but it is much easier to use absolute path names when you want to move to a remote part of the subdirectory structure.

Messages

`Invalid directory`

Error: You have used the *path* argument to specify a directory that doesn't exist. Make sure that you entered the subdirectory path correctly and that you did not include a file name at the end of the *path*.

`Invalid drive specified`

Error: You have specified an invalid drive letter.

See Also

DELTREE, MD (or MKDIR), MOVE, RD (or RMDIR), and TREE

"Changing the Current Directory with CHDIR (CD)" in Chapter 5

CHCP

3.3 and later—Internal

The CHCP command is a system-wide, code-page (character-set) changer. CHCP simultaneously resets all affected devices to the changed font. MODE works in a similar manner but changes only one device at a time.

Syntax

To change the current code page, use the following format:

CHCP *codepage*

To display the current code page, use the following format:

CHCP

Parameters and Switches

codepage A valid three-digit code-page number. See Appendix G for a list of the code pages that MS-DOS supports.

Notes

1. Before using CHCP, you must use the COUNTRY command (to specify the location of the country-information file, normally COUNTRY.SYS), use the NLSFUNC command (to specify a location that overrides that of the COUNTRY command), or place COUNTRY.SYS in the root directory of the current disk. Otherwise, DOS returns the message `Cannot open specified country information file.`

2. Before using CHCP, you must use the NLSFUNC command.

3. When you select a code page, the new code page becomes the specified code page. If you include CONFIG.SYS directives for devices that use code pages, such as DEVICE=DISPLAY.SYS, CHCP loads the correct code pages for the devices.

4. You can access the COUNTRY.SYS file to get country information. If you do not specify the location of COUNTRY.SYS when you invoke NLSFUNC, COUNTRY.SYS must exist in the current disk's root directory. Otherwise, DOS returns the message `Cannot open specified country information file.`

Messages

`Code page` *`nnn`* `not prepared for device` *`ddd`*

Error: CHCP could not select the code page *nnn* because of one of the following errors:

- You did not use MODE to prepare a code page for this device.
- An I/O error occurred while DOS was sending the new font information to the device.
- The device is busy (for example, a printer is in use or off-line).
- The device does not support code-page switching.

Check to make sure that the command MODE CODEPAGE PREPARE was issued for the appropriate devices and the devices are on-line and ready. Then try CHCP again.

`Invalid code page`

Error: CHCP could not select the code page because of one of the following errors:

- You specified an invalid code page for the country.
- You did not use the MODE command to prepare a code page.

Be sure that you run NLSFUNC and use the command MODE CODEPAGE PREPARE to prepare the code page for the appropriate devices.

`NLSFUNC not installed`

Error: You attempted to change the code page but did not initiate NLSFUNC before using CHCP. If you plan to use code pages and have the correct directives in CONFIG.SYS, add NLSFUNC to your AUTOEXEC.BAT file so that the command is executed when you boot the computer.

See Also

COUNTRY=, MODE device CP, and NLSFUNC

Chapter 21, "Understanding the International Features of DOS" and Appendix G, "International Country Codes"

CHDIR (see CD)

CHDIR is an alternate name for the CD command. For information on using the CD or CHDIR command, see the entry for CD earlier in this Command Reference.

CHKDSK 1.0 and later—External

The CHKDSK command checks the directory and File Allocation Table (FAT) of the disk and reports disk and memory status. CHKDSK also can repair errors in the directories or the FAT.

Syntax

CHKDSK *drive:\path\filename.ext* /F /V

Parameters and Switches

drive:	The disk drive to be analyzed.
\path	The directory path to the files to be analyzed.
filename.ext	A valid DOS file name. Wildcards are permitted.

/F — Fixes the FAT and other problems if errors are found. (Do not use this switch when you are running under Microsoft Windows or the DOS Task Swapper.)

/V — Shows CHKDSK's progress and displays more detailed information about the errors that the program finds. (This switch is known as the *verbose switch*.)

Exit Codes

ERRORLEVEL Value	Meaning
0	No errors found
255	Errors were found

Rules

1. You must direct CHKDSK to repair the disk by using the /F switch. CHKDSK asks you to confirm that you want the repairs made before it proceeds.
2. CHKDSK cannot process a directory in which you used the JOIN command—that is, a second disk joined to a subdirectory.
3. CHKDSK does not process a disk on which you used a SUBST command.
4. CHKDSK cannot process a disk drive on which you used the ASSIGN command.
5. CHKDSK cannot process a networked (shared) disk.
6. Do not use CHKDSK on disks that contain open files, or have another program running that may access the disk drive while CHKDSK is running.
7. (Not MS-DOS 6.2) After completing its normal checks on a DoubleSpace drive, CHKDSK automatically runs DBLSPACE /CHKDSK on the drive.

Notes

1. In MS-DOS 6.2, CHKDSK now displays numbers with embedded commas, making them much easier to read.

2. CHKDSK displays the following information:
   - Volume name and creation date (only disks with volume labels)
   - Volume serial number (if it exists)
   - Total disk space
   - Number of files and bytes used for hidden or system files
   - Number of files and bytes used for directories
   - Number of files and bytes used for user (normal) files
   - Bytes used by bad sectors (flawed disk space)
   - Bytes available on disk (free space)
   - Bytes of total conventional memory (RAM)
   - Bytes of available conventional memory
3. In DOS 4.0 and later, CHKDSK also reports the following information:
   - Total bytes in each allocation unit
   - Total allocation units on the disk
   - Available allocation units on the disk (An allocation unit equates to a cluster)
4. CHKDSK checks the directories and the FAT of a disk. The command also checks the amount of memory in the system and determines how much of that memory is free. If errors are found, CHKDSK reports them on-screen before making a status report.
5. If lost clusters are found, CHKDSK asks whether you want to repair them. You must type **Y** or **N**. If you type **Y**, CHKDSK shows a report on-screen as if the lost clusters were repaired. This report is only a simulation, however. To actually reclaim the lost clusters, you must issue a second command: CHKDSK /F.
6. The CHKDSK file name checks to see whether the specified files are stored contiguously on the disk. DOS reports any noncontiguously stored files and how many different sections store the files. If CHKDSK

Tip

If you are using MS-DOS 6.2, Microsoft advises you stop using the CHKDSK command and use the new ScanDisk program instead. ScanDisk can identify and fix many more types of errors than CHKDSK. If you use DoubleSpace, ScanDisk will identify and fix any errors it finds on your compressed drives as well.

reports many noncontiguous files, you may want to run DEFRAG on the disk.

7. CHKDSK does not check to see whether your files can be read. Neither does CHKDSK test your disk to determine whether new bad spots have appeared.

Messages

`All specified file(s) are contiguous`

Information: The files you specified are stored in contiguous sectors on the disk. Disk performance for the files should be optimal.

filename
`Allocation error, size adjusted`

Warning: The file name has an invalid sector number in the FAT. The file was truncated by CHKDSK at the end of the last valid sector.

Check this file to verify that all information in the file is correct. If you find a problem, use your backup copy of the file. This message usually appears when the problem is in the FAT, not in the file. Your file probably is still good.

filename
`Contains` *xxx* `non-contiguous blocks`

Information: filename is not stored contiguously on the disk but in *xxx* number of pieces. This arrangement can decrease the performance of the disk. If you find that many files on a disk are stored in noncontiguous pieces, you may want to run DEFRAG.

directoryname
`Convert directory to file (Y/N)?`

Warning: directoryname contains so much bad information that the directory no longer is usable. If you type **Y**, CHKDSK converts the directory into a file so that you can use DEBUG or another tool to repair the directory. If you type **N**, no action is taken.

The first time you see this message, type **N**. Try to copy files from this directory to another disk, and check the copied files to see whether they are usable. Then rerun CHKDSK to convert the directory into a file and try to recover the rest of the files.

```
Errors found, F parameter not specified
Corrections will not be written to the disk
```

Information: CHDSK found an error. This message tells you that CHKDSK will go through the motions of repairing the disk but will not actually change the file because you did not use the /F switch.

```
filename
First allocation unit is invalid, entry truncated
```

Warning: filename's first entry in the FAT refers to a nonexistent portion of the disk. If you used the /F switch, the file becomes a zero-length file (truncated).

Try to copy this file to another floppy disk before CHKDSK truncates the file. You may not get a useful copy, however, and the original file will be lost.

```
. or ..
Entry has a bad attribute
or Entry has a bad size or
Entry has a bad link
```

Warning: The link to the parent directory (..) or the current directory (.) has a problem. If you used the /F switch, CHKDSK attempts to repair the problem. Normally this procedure is safe, and you do not risk losing files.

```
filename
Has invalid allocation unit, file truncated
```

Information and warning: Part of the chain of FAT entries for *filename* points to a nonexistent part of the disk. The /F switch truncates the file at its last valid sector. If you did not use the /F switch, DOS takes no corrective action. Try to copy this file to a different disk, and then rerun CHKDSK with the /F switch. (You may lose part of the file.)

```
filename1
Is cross linked on allocation unit x
filename2
Is cross linked on allocation unit x
```

Warning: Two files—*filename1* and *filename2*—had entries in the FAT that point to the same area (cluster) of the disk. In other words, the two files believe that they own the same piece of the disk.

CHKDSK takes no action. To handle the problem, copy both files to another floppy disk, delete the files from the original disk, and edit the files as necessary. (The files may contain garbage.)

```
Insufficient room in root directory
Erase files from root and repeat CHKDSK
```

Error: CHKDSK recovered so many "lost" clusters from the disk that the root directory is full. CHKDSK aborts at this point.

Examine the FILE*xxxx*.CHK files. If you find nothing useful, delete them. Rerun CHKDSK with the /F switch to continue recovering lost clusters.

```
xxxxxxxxxx bytes disk space freed
```

Information: CHKDSK regained some disk space that was improperly marked as "in use." *xxxxxxxxxx* tells you how many additional bytes are now available. To free this disk space, review and delete any FILE*xxxx*.CHK file that does not contain useful information.

```
xxx lost allocation units found in yyy chains
Convert lost chains to files (Y/N)?
```

Information: Although CHKDSK found *xxx* blocks of data allocated in the FAT, no file on the disk is using these blocks. The blocks are lost clusters, which CHKDSK normally can free if no other error or warning message appears.

If you use the /F switch and type **Y**, CHKDSK joins each set of lost chains into a file placed in the root directory of the disk. That file is called FILE*xxxx*.CHK, in which *xxxx* is a consecutive number between 0000 and 9999. Examine this file, and delete any clusters that contain no useful information.

If you use the /F switch and type **N**, CHKDSK simply frees the lost chains so that other files can reuse the disk space. No files are created. If you type **Y** and omit /F, CHKDSK displays the actions that you can take but takes no action itself.

See Also

DEFRAG, DOUBLESPACE /CHKDSK, and SCANFIX

"Analyzing a Disk with CHKDSK" in Chapter 7

CHKSTATE.SYS (see MEMMAKER)

The CHKSTATE.SYS device driver helps MemMaker optimize memory use on your computer. MemMaker only requires this driver while optimizing your system; it's not needed at any other time. You should not attempt to use this device driver yourself.

Very few details about CHKSTATE.SYS's operation are documented. It's loaded into memory by MemMaker with a DEVICE= line in your CONFIG.SYS file during the optimization process. Presumably, CHKSTATE.SYS communicates with MEMMAKER about the state of your computer, verifying that system integrity is not violated as different combinations of drivers are loaded. When optimization is complete, MemMaker removes this driver from the CONFIG.SYS file.

See Also

MEMMAKER and SIZER

CHOICE

6.0 and later—External

The CHOICE command suspends batch-file processing and prompts the user to make a choice before processing resumes. You can specify which keystrokes are accepted and what default choices are made if no keys are pressed.

Syntax

CHOICE /C:*keys* /N /S /T:*choice,seconds* *prompt*

Parameters and Switches

/C:*keys*	Specifies which keys are displayed in the prompt. The colon (:) is optional. If /C is not specified, CHOICE acts as though you specified /C:YN.
/N	Suppresses the key list and question mark that DOS normally adds to the *prompt* (see the first item in the following "Notes" section).
/S	Enables case sensitivity for the *keys*. That is, if /S is specified, the uppercase key represents a different response from the lowercase key. If /S is not specified, the uppercase key is the same as the lowercase key.
/T:*choice,seconds*	Specifies a default key and the number of seconds to wait for the user to press a key before the default is used. The colon (:) is optional. *choice* must be one of the keys specified by /C:*keys*, and *seconds* must be from 0 to 99 (0 means no pause before *choice* is used).
prompt	The prompt line that is displayed to inform the user about the choice that has to be made. To the end of the *prompt* you specify, DOS adds a bracketed list of allowable keys and a question mark. Quotation marks (") can be used around *text*, but you don't have to use

them unless the *prompt* contains a switch character (/), redirection symbols, or trailing blank spaces. If no *prompt* is specified, DOS does not display any prompt at all.

Exit Codes

ERRORLEVEL Value	Meaning
0	CHOICE terminated by user (Ctrl-Break or Ctrl-C)
1	User picked first key in /C:*keys* parameter
2	User picked second key in /C:*keys* parameter
3	User picked third key in /C:*keys* parameter
4 up	... and so on ...
255	Terminated by illegal syntax or other error conditions.

Notes

1. When a CHOICE command is executed, the user sees the command's *prompt*, followed by a prompt. The prompt is a left bracket ([), followed by the first key in /C:*keys*, followed by a comma, followed by any other keys in *keys* (separated by commas), followed by a right bracket (]), followed by a question mark (?). /C:YN, for example, produces the prompt `[Y,N]?`

2. CHOICE returns different exit code values to the batch file, depending on which of the keys in /C:*keys* is pressed in response to the prompt. Pressing the first key returns 1, pressing the second returns 2, and so on.

3. If the user presses Ctrl-Break and then does not terminate the batch job, a value of 0 is returned. If DOS detects an error, a value of 255 is returned.

4. If the user presses a key that is not one of the keys in /C:*keys*, the computer beeps.

Examples

To ask the user whether to continue with the batch file, issue the following commands:

```
CHOICE /C:YN "Yes to continue and No to exit "
IF ERRORLEVEL 2 GOTO EXIT
```

You then see the following line:

```
Yes to continue and No to exit [Y,N]?
```

Notice the trailing space at the end of the prompt text specified in the CHOICE command. CHOICE adds the `[Y,N]?` text to the end of the prompt you specify. Adding a trailing space to your *prompt* text can make the final prompt more readable on-screen.

To load the mouse driver from your AUTOEXEC.BAT file unless told otherwise within three seconds, issue the following commands:

```
CHOICE /C:YN /T:3,Y "Load the mouse driver "
IF ERRORLEVEL 2 GOTO NOMOUSE
```

To provide a menu of choices:

```
@ECHO OFF
CLS
ECHO.
ECHO F First action
ECHO S Second action
ECHO T Third action
ECHO.
CHOICE /C:FST "Choose an action "
IF ERRORLEVEL 255 GOTO ERROR
IF ERRORLEVEL 3 GOTO THIRD
IF ERRORLEVEL 2 GOTO SECOND
IF ERRORLEVEL 1 GOTO FIRST

:ERROR
ECHO GOT AN ERROR OR BREAK
GOTO END

:THIRD
ECHO PRESSED T
GOTO END

:SECOND
ECHO PRESSED S
GOTO END

:FIRST
ECHO PRESSED F
GOTO END

:END
```

See Also

IF

"Making a Two-Way Choice" in Chapter 16

CLS

2.0 and later—Internal

The CLS command clears a text screen and returns the cursor to the upper-left corner. It's very useful for clearing away messages left by other commands or batch files. Normally, CLS is limited to clearing 25-line text mode screens, but if ANSI.SYS is loaded, CLS clears 43- and 50-line text modes as well.

Syntax

CLS

Notes

1. This command clears all information from the screen and places the cursor at the home position in the upper-left corner.
2. This command affects only the active video display, not memory.
3. If you used the ANSI control codes to set the foreground and background, the color settings remain in effect.
4. If you did not set the foreground/background color, the screen reverts to light characters on a dark background.

See Also

ANSI.SYS

"The CLS Command" in Chapter 14

COMMAND

2.0 and later—External

COMMAND invokes another copy of COMMAND.COM, the command processor. If you write complicated batch files, this command may be useful. Normally, a user gets involved with this command when setting up the SHELL= line in the CONFIG.SYS file.

Syntax

COMMAND *path\ cttydevice* /E:*size* /K *filename* /P /MSG /C *string*

In your CONFIG.SYS, use the following format:

SHELL=*drive:\path***COMMAND.COM** *path\ condevice* /E:*size* /P /MSG

Parameters and Switches

drive:\path	The DOS drive and path to the copy of COMMAND.COM that the SHELL= command should load.
path	The drive and directory location of COMMAND.COM. This path is assigned to the COMSPEC environment variable.
condevice	The device used for input and output. The default is CON:. The colon is optional. This parameter rarely is used.
/E:*size*	Sets the *size* of the environment. Size is a decimal number from 160 to 32,768 bytes, rounded up to the nearest multiple of 16 (refer to the SHELL command). The default is 256.
/K *filename*	Runs *filename* (a program or batch file) and then displays the DOS command prompt.
/P	Keeps this copy permanently in memory (until the next system reset). Generally used only as part of the SHELL command. Do not use the /P parameter from a batch file.
/MSG	Loads all error messages into memory. Must be used with /P. Generally useful only if you are running DOS from floppy disks.
/C *string*	Passes the command and parameters represented by *string* to the new copy of COMMAND.COM and returns to the primary command processor.

Rules

1. The string in the /C option is interpreted by the additional copy of COMMAND.COM, just as though you typed the string at the system level. /C must be the last switch used in the line. Do not use the form COMMAND/C *string* /P.

2. You can exit from the second copy of the command processor by issuing the command EXIT, unless you used the /P option (permanent).

3. If you issue the /P and /C switches together, /P is ignored.

4. Do not use the /K switch in the SHELL command line in your CONFIG.SYS. This switch can cause problems with applications and installation programs that alter your AUTOEXEC.BAT file.

Notes

1. COMMAND often is used with the SHELL directive to enable COMMAND.COM to reside in a subdirectory, rather than in the root directory.

2. You can use COMMAND with all versions of DOS to call a second batch file from an originating batch file. Suppose that a batch file named BATCH1.BAT contains the following line:

   ```
   COMMAND /C BATCH2
   ```

   BATCH1 calls BATCH2.BAT. BATCH2.BAT executes and, after completing the last line of the batch file, returns to BATCH1 to complete the originating batch file. This method of calling a batch file is similar to the CALL batch subcommand available in DOS Version 3.3 and later.

3. If you use DOS 5.0 or 6.0 with a floppy-disk-only system, you can specify the /MSG switch in the SHELL directive of CONFIG.SYS. This switch loads all error messages in memory. If an error occurs, you do not need a disk with COMMAND.COM in the drive. (The switch uses an additional 1K of RAM.)

4. You can use the /K *filename* switch to specify that the DOS prompt in Microsoft Windows should use a start-up file other than AUTOEXEC.BAT. Open the DOSPRMPT.PIF file (using the PIF Editor) and type /K *filename* in the Optional Parameters box.

See Also

CALL and SHELL=

"Loading a Secondary Command Processor" in Chapter 12

COMP

1.0 to 5.0—External

You can use COMP to compare two sets of disk files of the same name and length. The FC command, which is discussed later in this Command Reference, provides many of the same capabilities as COMP. COMP is included on the DOS 6 Supplemental Disk, not in the standard DOS 6.0 package.

Syntax

COMP *pathname1 pathname2* /D /A /L /N=*num* /C

Parameters and Switches

pathname1	The drive, path, and file name for the primary set of files. Wildcards are allowed. If no file name is specified, all files (*.*) are assumed.
pathname2	The drive, path, and file name for the secondary set of files. Wildcards are allowed. If no file name is specified, all files (*.*) are assumed.
/D	Displays differences in hex format.
/A	Displays differences as alphanumeric characters.
/L	Displays the line number in which the difference occurred.
/N=*x*	Compares the first *x* number of lines of a file.
/C	Performs a non-case sensitive comparison of files.

Notes

1. If you do not enter a file name, all files for that set, whether primary or secondary, are compared (which is the same as typing ***.***). However, only the files in the secondary set with names that match file names in the primary set are compared.

2. If you do not enter a drive, path, or file name, COMP prompts you for the primary and secondary file sets to compare. Otherwise, the correct disks must be in the correct drive if you are comparing files on disks. COMP does not wait for you to insert disks if you use both primary and secondary file names.

3. After 10 mismatches (unequal comparisons) between the contents of two compared files, COMP ends the comparison and aborts.

4. A more versatile utility for file comparison is FC, discussed later in this Command Reference. COMP no longer is distributed with the standard DOS package.

Messages

`Compare error at offset xxxxxxxx`

Information: The files that you are comparing are not the same. The difference occurs at *xxxxxxxx* bytes from the start of the file. The number provided is in hexadecimal format, base 16. The values of the differing bytes in the files also are displayed in hexadecimal format.

`Files are different sizes`

Warning: You asked COMP to compare two files of different lengths. Because COMP compares only files of the same size, COMP skips the comparison.

`10 Mismatches - ending compare`

Warning: COMP found 10 mismatches between the two files you compared. COMP, therefore, assumes that no reason exists to continue, and the comparison is aborted.

See Also

FC

COPY

1.0 and later—Internal

Use the COPY command to copy files between disk drives or between drives and devices. COPY enables you to keep or change the file names and also enables you to combine (concatenate) files.

Syntax

The syntax used to copy files from one place to another is very simple:

COPY ***source*** *destination* /V /Y /Y–

You can tell DOS what kind of files you are copying with the /A (ASCII) and /B (BINARY) parameters.

COPY /A /B ***source*** /A /B *destination* /A /B /V /Y /Y–

By adding plus signs, you can specify more than one source file, and have them all combined (concatenated) into one destination file.

COPY /A /B ***source*** /A /B *+source2* /A /B +... /A /B *destination* /A /B /V /Y /Y–

Parameters and Switches

source — The file or files that you want to copy. A full path name (for example, *drive:\path\ ... \filename.ext*) can be specified, and wildcards are allowed. This parameter is required, and must include a file name (*.* is not assumed). To combine files, specify more than one *source* path name and separate them with plus signs (+).

destination — The location, and optionally, the file name you want to copy to. A full path name can be specified, although normally only a drive and/or path is included. Wildcards are allowed when a file name is specified. If this parameter is omitted, the current drive and subdirectory are used as the destination.

/V — Verifies that the copy was recorded correctly. Similar to setting VERIFY ON for this COPY operation.

/Y — Specifies that you want COPY to overwrite files without prompting you for confirmation. Including this parameter overrides any setting specified with the COPYCMD environment variable.

/–Y — Specifies that you want COPY to prompt you for confirmation before overwriting any files, even if the command is run from within a batch file. Including this parameter overrides any setting specified with the COPYCMD environment variable.

The /A and /B switches create different effects on the source and the destination files. Normally, you don't have to specify these switches, because DOS's default assumptions are correct.

For the source file:

/A — Treats the file as an ASCII (text) file. The command copies all the information in the file up to, but not including, the end-of-file marker (Ctrl-Z). Data after the end-of-file marker is ignored. This is the default for copy operations that combine multiple files.

/B — Copies the entire file (based on size, as listed in the directory) as if the file were a program file *(binary1)*. All end-of-file markers (Ctrl-Z) are treated as normal characters, and EOF characters are copied. This is the default for copy operations that do not combine multiple files.

For the destination file:

/A — Adds an end-of-file marker (Ctrl-Z) to the end of the ASCII text file at the conclusion of the copying process. This is the default for copy operations that combine multiple files.

/B — Does not add the end-of-file marker to this binary file. This is the default for copy operations that do not combine multiple files.

Rules

Adhere to the following rules when you are copying files for which both the source and the destination are given.

1. The following rules apply to the file name:
   - You must provide either a path name or a file name. Wildcards are allowed in the source file name. If you do not provide a file name but provide a path name for the source, DOS assumes *.*.
   - If you do not provide a destination file name, the copied file has the same name, creation date, and creation time as the source file.
2. You can substitute a device name for the complete source or destination name.
3. When you copy between disk drives, COPY assumes that binary files are copied (as though you used the /B switch).

4. When you copy to or from a device other than a disk drive, COPY assumes that ASCII files are copied (as though you used the /A switch).
5. An /A or /B switch overrides the default settings for COPY.

Adhere to the following rules when you are copying files and only one file is specified.

1. The file specification you use (*d1:path1***filename1.ext1*) is the source. This specification must have one or both of the following items:
   - A valid file name. Wildcards are allowed.
   - A drive name, a path name, or both. If you provide only one name, that name must differ from the current drive name or path name. If you provide both names, at least one name must differ from the current drive name or path name.
2. The source cannot be a device name.
3. The destination is the current drive and current directory.
4. The copied files use the same names as the source files.
5. COPY assumes that binary files are copied (as though you used the /B switch).

Adhere to these rules when you concatenate files:

1. The destination file is the last file in the list unless you add a plus sign (+) before that file name. If you do not specify a destination file name, the first source name becomes the destination name.
2. If you do not provide a drive name, DOS uses the current drive.
3. If you do not provide a path, DOS uses the current directory.
4. The following rules apply to source files:
   - You must provide a valid file name. Wildcards are allowed, but using them can be dangerous. If you do not provide a destination file name, DOS uses the first file name as the destination file name.
   - After the first file name, any additional source file specifications must be preceded by a plus sign (+).

5. The following rules apply to the destination file:

   - You can use only one destination file specification. If you provide a destination without wildcards, DOS uses that name for the destination file. If you provide a destination file name with wildcards, DOS uses the first source file name for the destination file.

   - If you do not provide a destination, DOS uses the first source file as the destination. The first file that matches the wildcard file name is used as the destination file if you used a wildcard as part of the first source file name, and the files to be joined are appended to the first source file.

Notes

1. The COPY command, when run from the command line, now prompts you for confirmation before overwriting files. However, in order to avoid forcing people to rewrite all their batch files, COPY does not prompt you before overwriting a file when it is run from a batch file.

   If you don't like the way COPY now behaves, you can change it by defining an environment variable named COPYCMD. Setting COPYCMD equal to /Y forces COPY to act as it has in all previous versions of DOS, never prompting for confirmation before overwriting a file. If you set COPYCMD equal to /–Y, COPY always prompts for confirmation—even when it is run from within a batch file.

2. The meanings of the /A and /B switches depend on their positions in the line. The /A or /B switch affects the file that immediately precedes the switch and all files that follow the switch until DOS encounters another /A or /B switch. When you use one of these switches before a file name, the switch affects all following files until DOS encounters another /A or /B that contradicts the earlier switch.

3. Use XCOPY to copy zero-length files and all of a directory's files and subdirectories.

4. To change the time and date of a file to the current time and date:

   COPY /B *filename.ext*+,,

5. You can create a text file by copying what you type to a file. Use the following format:

   COPY CON *filename.ext*

Everything you type is then copied to *filename.ext* until you press Ctrl-Z or F6.

Messages

`Cannot do binary reads from a device`

Error: If you specify a device name such as CON or COM1 as the *source* in a COPY command, you cannot include the /B switch parameter. These devices operate in character mode only. Try the command again without specifying the /B switch parameter.

`Content of destination lost before copy`

Error: You may see this message when you are combining files with the COPY command. If the *destination* file has the same name as any of the *source* files (except the first) that you've specified, COPY will overwrite that *source* file before it has a chance to read it. When this message appears, at least one of your source files has been overwritten, and the file is gone for good. Be very careful combining files with the COPY command, especially if you are using wildcards in the *source* or *destination* parameters.

`File cannot be copied onto itself`

Error: COPY tried to copy a file onto itself. The *destination* file must have a different file name or be in a different subdirectory than the *source* file. Change the *destination* you specified and try the COPY command again.

See Also

MOVE, REN or RENAME, and VERIFY

"Copying Files" in Chapter 9

COUNTRY= 3.0 and later—Internal

You can use the COUNTRY= command to instruct DOS to use certain country-specific conventions when it displays or accepts dates, times, numbers, currency, sort ordering, and case conversions. So that transitions from one set of conventions to another can be as painless for the user as possible, application programs are encouraged to use this country-specific information. COUNTRY= can be used only in your CONFIG.SYS file.

Syntax

COUNTRY=*country_code*,*code_page,path\filename*

Parameters and Switches

country_code — A three-digit number that indicates the country whose conventions you want to use. Typically, the number is the international long-distance telephone code for that country. (See Appendix G.)

code_page — The code page (character set) to use for the country that you are specifying. If no code page is specified, the default code page for that country is used. You can switch between the default and the alternate code pages with MODE or CHCP.

path\filename — The full path and file name of the file that contains country-specific information, which is usually COUNTRY.SYS. If no file name is specified, COUNTRY= will look for COUNTRY.SYS in the root directory of the start-up drive.

Notes

Tip
Always include the full path to the COUNTRY.SYS file when you use the COUNTRY= command. In this way, you can keep the COUNTRY.SYS file in a more logical place, such as in your C:\DOS directory (which is where Setup puts it anyway).

1. COUNTRY= affects the following items:
   - Date and time formats, both for display and input. DOS commands that use the country setting for date and time include DATE, TIME, RESTORE, DIR, PROMPT, and XCOPY.
   - The thousands separator and the decimal character used in numbers. In the U.S., these are a comma and a period respectively (for example, 1,024.45).
   - The location and symbol used for currency.
   - Upper- to lowercase conversions. For each character set (code page), a table of case conversions is maintained by DOS.
   - Alphabetical sorting order for characters in the set. This allows accented characters to sort into their proper places.
2. The default country code is 001 (United States), code page 437, for versions of MS-DOS sold in the U.S.
3. Not all application programs are written to support the international features of DOS, and many ignore the COUNTRY= settings.

4. The MS-DOS distribution disks include a special version of COUNTRY.SYS named COUNTRY.ICE (COUNTRY.IC_ in its compressed form) that contains information supporting an Icelandic keyboard and character set. For details, see the README.TXT file distributed with DOS 6.

5. Microsoft has special versions of MS-DOS available for other languages and countries not listed in the country codes table, such as Arabic, Israel, Japan, Korea, the People's Republic of China, and Taiwan.

6. It is often best to leave out the code page argument in the COUNTRY= line and let DOS use the default code page. To do so, just type two commas before you enter the location and name of the COUNTRY.SYS file. (See the first example that follows.)

Examples

To set the country to France, insert the following line in your CONFIG.SYS file:

```
COUNTRY=033,,C:\DOS\COUNTRY.SYS
```

Notice that two commas are used so that DOS selects the default code page, which in this case is code page 850. Later, you could change to code page 437 by using the CHCP command.

The following line sets the country to the United States with code page 437 active:

```
COUNTRY=001,437,C:\DOS\COUNTRY.SYS
```

In the U.S., this example is almost the same as not using the COUNTRY= command at all, except that you now have the ability to switch to code page 850 if you want to.

See Also

MODE device CP, CHCP, NLSFUNC, and KEYB

Chapter 21, "Understanding the International Features of DOS," and Appendix G, "International Country Codes"

COUNTRY.SYS (see COUNTRY=)

Despite the .SYS extension, COUNTRY.SYS is not a device driver. COUNTRY.SYS is a file that contains country information—such as code page symbol sets—used by the COUNTRY= command. A similar file, containing information needed for an Icelandic configuration, is found in the file COUNTRY.ICE on the MS-DOS 6 distribution disks. (For details on setting up an Icelandic configuration, see the README.TXT file distributed with DOS 6.)

Trap

Do not attempt to load CONTRY.SYS into memory by placing it in a DEVICE= or DEVICEHIGH= command in your CONFIG.SYS file. Your computer will lock up, and you will have to reboot from a floppy disk.

See Also

COUNTRY= and NLSFUNC

Chapter 21, "Understanding the International Features of DOS"

CTTY 2.0 and later—Internal

You can use the CTTY command to change the standard input and output devices to an auxiliary console or to change the input and output devices back from an auxiliary console to the keyboard and video display.

Syntax

CTTY ***device***

Parameters and Switches

device The device you want to use as the new standard input and output device. This name must refer to a valid DOS character device. Normally, CON is the standard input and output device, which allows you to enter standard input from the keyboard and view standard output on the display. This parameter is required.

Notes

1. The device must be a character-oriented device capable of both input and output. DOS supplies several such devices, including AUX, COM1, COM2, COM3, COM4, CON, LPT1, LPT2, LPT3, and PRN.

2. Typing a colon (:) after the device name is optional. If you don't include a *device* in the command line for CTTY, an `Invalid device` message is displayed.

3. CTTY does not affect any other form of redirected I/O or piping. For example, the < (redirect input symbol), > (redirect output symbol), and ¦ (pipe between programs character) work as usual.

4. The CTTY command is designed so that you can use a terminal or teleprinter—rather than the normal keyboard and video display—for console input and output. This versatility has little effect on most PC users.

5. To return control to the standard console, type **CTTY CON** on the auxiliary console. If the auxiliary console isn't working, or you don't have one connected to your computer, you must reboot to re-enable the standard console.

6. The CTTY command does not affect programs that input and output directly to hardware. Most major software applications fall into this category, so the CTTY command is rarely useful with them.

7. COMMAND can also be used to change the device that DOS uses for standard input and output.

8. Do not attempt to reconfigure Windows with the CTTY command. Windows can be configured to use devices other than the keyboard and video display, but not with the CTTY command.

See Also

COMMAND

"The CTTY Command" in Chapter 14

DATE

1.0 and later—Internal

The DATE command can display and set the current date for your computer. Normally, DOS and your computer's hardware keep the date set properly for you. If you have no AUTOEXEC.BAT file, DOS prompts you to enter the current date each time your computer reboots.

Syntax

DATE *mon-day-year*

Parameters and Switches

mon-day-year The current date in a format consistent with the COUNTRY= setting in your CONFIG.SYS file. *mon* can be any number from 1 to 12. *day* can be any number from 1 to 31. *year* can be any number from 80 to 99 or from 1980 to 2099. In the United States, legal delimiters are the hyphen, the period, or the slash (/). If this parameter is omitted, the current date is displayed, and you are prompted to enter a new date.

Notes

1. The date entry and display correspond to the COUNTRY setting in your CONFIG.SYS file. If you are unsure of what format to use for the date, enter the DATE command with no parameters. DOS displays the current date in an appropriate format, and you can use that as a guide when entering a new date at the prompt.

2. When you boot the computer, DOS issues the DATE and TIME commands to set the system clock. If you placed an AUTOEXEC.BAT file on the boot disk, DOS does not display a prompt for the date or time. You can include the DATE or TIME commands in the AUTOEXEC.BAT file to have these functions set when DOS boots.

3. Most computers contain a real-time clock running on a battery. The date should stay set properly as you turn your computer on and off, but it's a good idea to check the date occasionally.

4. When you create or update a file, DOS updates the directory using the current date in the computer. This date shows which copy is the latest revision of the file. Several DOS commands (such as XCOPY) can use the date in selecting files.

5. The day-of-year calendar uses the time-of-day clock. If you leave your system on overnight, the day advances by one at midnight. DOS makes appropriate calendar adjustments for leap years.

See Also

COUNTRY= and TIME

"Changing the Date and Time" in Chapter 12

DBLSPACE

6.0 and later—External

DBLSPACE starts the full-screen interface to the DoubleSpace disk-compression utility. DoubleSpace automatically compresses information on hard disks or floppy disks and configures many aspects of the compression process. Compression enables you to put more programs and information on a disk.

With switches and parameters, you can control each aspect of DoubleSpace from the DOS command line. The many combinations are covered in the sections that deal with specific DoubleSpace commands.

MS-DOS 6.2 has brought a number of new features to DoubleSpace. DoubleSpace can now share the HMA with MS-DOS, thereby decreasing DoubleSpace's size in memory from 43K to 33K (or 37K if the new automount feature is enabled). A DoubleGuard feature verifies the integrity of your data before writing it to disk. Also added is the Uncompress command, which enables you to uncompress a DoubleSpace drive easily. Finally, removable disks can now be automounted, making it possible to work with compressed floppy and cartridge disks from Windows.

Syntax

DBLSPACE

Notes

1. The first time you use the DBLSPACE command, DoubleSpace Setup starts. The setup program enables you to compress one or more hard disks and loads DBLSPACE.BIN into memory. (DBLSPACE.BIN is the device driver that provides access to compressed drives.) Subsequent uses of the DBLSPACE command start the full-screen interface. The full-screen interface and the DBLSPACE switches and parameters give you control of all DoubleSpace operations.

2. DoubleSpace creates a large hidden file, called a compressed volume file (CVF), on one of your drives, called the *host drive*, and presents that drive as a new drive, called a *compressed drive*. For example, you might make a CVF on your drive D that results in a compressed drive E; you and your programs then can use the files on the compressed drive without taking any special action.

3. CVF names use the format DBLSPACE.*xxx*, where *xxx* is a number (such as 000 or 001).

4. Normally, after you have started using DoubleSpace on your computer, it automatically loads into memory every time you start your computer. To start your computer without loading DoubleSpace into memory, press Ctrl-F5 (Clean) or Ctrl-F8 (Interactive) when the `Starting MS-DOS...` message appears on your screen. Because DBLSPACE.BIN will not be loaded, you may not be able to access any of your compressed drives. For more information, see Appendix D, "DOS and DOS Utility Programs' Keyboard Commands."

See Also

"Understanding DoubleSpace" in Chapter 19

DBLSPACE /AUTOMOUNT 6.2—External

BATCH FILE

The DBLSPACE /AUTOMOUNT command enables or disables automatic mounting of removable drives such as floppy and cartridge disks. This command changes the automount settings saved in the DBLSPACE.INI file. The default setting is for DoubleSpace to automatically mount removable drives.

Automounting makes it possible for you to change compressed floppy and cartridge disks from Microsoft Windows. You cannot use the DBLSPACE /AUTOMOUNT command while Windows is running.

Syntax

DBLSPACE /AUTOMOUNT=*drives*

Parameters and Switches

drives The removable drives that you want DoubleSpace to automatically mount. Enter each drive letter—without a colon—and with no spaces in between. You can also specify 0 to disable automatic mounting or 1 to automatically mount all removable drives. The default setting is 1.

Notes

1. For the automount setting to take effect, you must restart your computer.
2. Specifying 0 decreases the size of DoubleSpace in memory by approximately 4K.
3. The parameters you specify are written to the DBLSPACE.INI file in the AUTOMOUNT= line.

Examples

To enable automounting of only two floppy drives A and B, enter the following command:

```
DBLSPACE /AUTOMOUNT=AB
```

To disable automounting of all removable drives (and save a little memory), enter the following command:

```
DBLSPACE /AUTOMOUNT=0
```

See Also

"Understanding DoubleSpace" in Chapter 19

DBLSPACE /CHKDSK 6.0 only—External

DBLSPACE /CHKDSK checks the structure of a compressed drive. The command reports errors (such as lost clusters and cross-linked files) and can correct some errors. If you are running DOS 6.2, this command is not available; you should use the SCANDISK utility instead.

Syntax

DBLSPACE /CHKDSK /F *drive:*

or

DBLSPACE /CHK /F *drive:*

Parameters and Switches

/F DoubleSpace attempts to repair any errors it finds rather than simply report them.

drive: The letter of the compressed drive you want to check. The default is the current drive.

Notes

If you run CHKDSK on a compressed drive, DBLSPACE /CHKDSK is invoked automatically after CHKDSK finishes checking the integrity of the drive's file allocation table (FAT).

See Also

CHKDSK and SCANDISK

"Understanding DoubleSpace" in Chapter 19

DBLSPACE /COMPRESS

6.0 and later—External

DBLSPACE /COMPRESS compresses the files on an existing hard disk, floppy disk, or other removable disk, making more space available.

Syntax

DBLSPACE /COMPRESS *drive:* /NEWDRIVE=*host:* /RESERVE=*size* /F

or

DBLSPACE /COM *drive:* /NEW=*host:* /RES=*size* /F

Parameters and Switches

drive: The uncompressed (host) drive that you want to compress.

/NEWDRIVE=*host:* The uncompressed (host) drive after compression. This parameter can be abbreviated to /NEW=*host:*. If you omit the /NEWDRIVE=*host:* parameter, DoubleSpace uses the next available drive letter. Enter DBLSPACE /LIST to see a list of drive assignments.

/RESERVE=*size* The amount of space (in megabytes) to be left uncompressed on the host drive. This parameter can be abbreviated to /RES=*size*. The default is 2M for hard disks and 0 for floppy disks.

/F DoubleSpace doesn't display the compression statistics screen when compression is complete, but simply returns to the DOS command prompt. Use this switch when you are running DBLSPACE /COMPRESS from a batch file.

Notes

1. A drive must contain some free space before DoubleSpace can compress it. If you want to compress your boot drive, for example, it must have at least 1.2M of free space. Other hard disks and floppy disks must have at least 1.1M of free space (650K for DOS 6.0).
2. DoubleSpace cannot compress 360K floppy disks because they do not have enough free space.
3. A compressed floppy disk must be mounted before you can use it. (For more information, see the DBLSPACE /MOUNT command.)
4. If you want to read a compressed floppy disk on another computer, that computer must be running DoubleSpace as well.
5. Your system probably needs some uncompressed disk space because some files (such as Windows permanent swap files) do not work properly if you store them on a compressed drive.

Examples

To compress drive D so that the compressed part is known as D and the uncompressed (host) part, known as E, contains 3M of uncompressed free space, use the following:

```
DBLSPACE /COMPRESS D: /NEWDRIVE=E: /RESERVE=3
```

See Also

DBLSPACE /CREATE, DBLSPACE /LIST, and DBLSPACE /MOUNT

"Understanding DoubleSpace" in Chapter 19

DBLSPACE /CREATE 6.0 and later—External

DBLSPACE /CREATE creates a new compressed drive by using free space on an uncompressed drive. DBLSPACE /CREATE can be used on only nonremovable media, such as a hard drive.

Syntax

DBLSPACE /CREATE *drive:* /NEWDRIVE=*host:* /RESERVE=*size* /SIZE=*size*

or

DBLSPACE /CR *drive:* /N=*host:* /RE=*size* /SI=*size*

Parameters and Switches

drive: The uncompressed (host) drive that contains the free space from which the new compressed drive will be created.

/NEWDRIVE=*host:* The new compressed drive. The default is the next available drive letter. This parameter can be abbreviated to /N=*host:*.

/RESERVE=*size* The amount of space (in megabytes) to be left uncompressed on the host drive. This parameter can be abbreviated to /RE=*size*. To make the compressed drive as large as possible, specify a *size* of 0. If you omit both the /RESERVE and /SIZE parameters, DoubleSpace reserves 1M of uncompressed space on your disk. You cannot specify /RESERVE if you specify /SIZE.

/SIZE=*size* The size (in megabytes) of the compressed volume file (CVF) that will be created on the host drive. This parameter can be abbreviated to /SI=*size*. Depending on how well your files compress, the CVF will hold approximately twice as much information as you specify for *size*. You cannot specify /SIZE if you specify /RESERVE.

Notes

1. The DBLSPACE /CREATE command creates a compressed volume file (CVF) with the name DBLSPACE.001 on the drive specified with the ***drive:*** parameter. If this file already exists, the 002 extension is added, and then the 003 extension is added, and so on.

2. When you use the DBLSPACE /CREATE command, unlike the DBLSPACE /COMPRESS command, the letter with which you refer to the host drive will not change.

3. You can use the DBLSPACE /CREATE command to create additional CVF files on the host drive of a disk compressed with the DBLSPACE /COMPRESS command. However, after you have created a CVF on a disk drive with the DBLSPACE /CREATE command, you cannot use the DBLSPACE /COMPRESS command on that drive without first deleting the existing CVF files. DBLSPACE /COMPRESS reassigns the drive letter you will use when accessing the host drive; it cannot do this if the host drive contains compressed drives.

4. You cannot use DBLSPACE /CREATE on removable media such as floppy disk drives or cartridge hard drives. To compress a floppy disk or cartridge hard disk, use the DBLSPACE /COMPRESS command.

5. Microsoft recommends that you use DBLSPACE /CREATE rather than DBLSPACE /COMPRESS to create a compressed drive on a RAM disk.

6. Your system probably needs some uncompressed disk space because some files (such as Windows permanent swap files) do not work properly when you store them on a compressed drive.

Examples

To create a compressed drive that has the next available drive letter as its name and uses all the available free space on the uncompressed drive D:

```
DBLSPACE /CREATE D: /RESERVE=0
```

To create a new compressed drive F that uses 20M of free space on the uncompressed drive D:

```
DBLSPACE /CREATE D: /NEWDRIVE=F: /SIZE=20
```

See Also

DBLSPACE /COMPRESS, DBLSPACE /LIST, and DBLSPACE /MOUNT

"Understanding DoubleSpace" in Chapter 19

DBLSPACE /DEFRAGMENT

6.0 and later—External

DBLSPACE /DEFRAGMENT defragments a compressed drive by moving all the drive's free space to the end of the drive. This command enables you to get the maximum reduction in the size of the drive when you issue the DBLSPACE /SIZE command.

Syntax

DBLSPACE /DEFRAGMENT *drive:* /F

or

DBLSPACE /DEF *drive:* /F

Parameters and Switches

drive: The compressed drive that you want to defragment. The default is the current drive.

/F Specifies that you would like the DoubleSpace drive defragmented more fully.

Notes

1. Unlike defragmenting an uncompressed hard disk, defragmenting a DoubleSpace disk does not improve the disk's performance. Defragmenting only moves the free space to the end of the compressed drive so that DBLSPACE /SIZE can be most effective.

2. You cannot tell how badly fragmented a compressed drive is before you decide to defragment it.

3. How long defragmenting takes depends on many factors, including the speed of your computer, the size of your compressed drive, and the speed of your disk drive. The process can take a long time—perhaps several hours.

4. You can stop the defragmentation process at any time by pressing Esc.

5. To thoroughly defragment a compressed drive, perform the following steps. First, correct any errors on the host and compressed drives with the ScanDisk utility. Next, defragment the host drive with the DEFRAG command. Then defragment the compressed drive with the DBLSPACE /DEFRAGMENT /F command. Finally, collect all the free space at the end of the compressed drive with the DBLSPACE /DEFRAGMENT command. (Don't specify the /F switch.)

See Also

CHKDSK and SCANDISK

"Understanding DoubleSpace" in Chapter 19

DBLSPACE /DELETE 6.0 and later—External

The DBLSPACE /DELETE command unmounts a compressed drive and deletes its compressed volume file (CVF) from the host drive. If you simply want to delete all the files on a compressed drive, use the DBLSPACE /FORMAT command.

Syntax

DBLSPACE /DELETE *drive:*

or

DBLSPACE /DEL *drive:*

Parameters and Switches

drive: The compressed drive that you want to delete. Note that you should specify the compressed drive, not the host drive.

Notes

1. Deleting a compressed drive deletes all the files in that drive.
2. If you accidentally delete a compressed drive, you may be able to restore it with UNDELETE, because a compressed drive is a file on one of your uncompressed disks (its host drive). The files corresponding to compressed drives are hidden and have names in the format DBLSPACE.*xxx*, where *xxx* is a number such as 000 or 001. If you can undelete the associated file, you can remount it with DBLSPACE /MOUNT.
3. DoubleSpace will not allow you to delete a compressed drive C.

See Also

DBLSPACE /FORMAT and UNDELETE

"Understanding DoubleSpace" in Chapter 19

DBLSPACE /DOUBLEGUARD 6.2—External

DoubleGuard is a safety feature that monitors the integrity of the memory that DoubleSpace is using to minimize damage by a runaway program. This setting is stored in the DBLSPACE.INI file on the DOUBLEGUARD= line.

Syntax

DBLSPACE /DOUBLEGUARD=*zero_one*

Parameters and Switches

zero_one Enables (1) or disables (0) the DoubleGuard feature.

Notes

1. If DoubleGuard is enabled and memory corruption is detected, DoubleSpace halts your computer to minimize damage to data on the disk. DoubleGuard is enabled by default.
2. Disabling DoubleGuard (/DOUBLEGUARD=0) may speed up your system a little, but could lead to a loss of data if an errant program overwrites DoubleSpace's memory.
3. You must restart your computer for this setting to take effect.

Examples

To turn on DoubleGuard integrity checking, enter the following command and reboot your computer:

```
DBLSPACE /DOUBLEGUARD=0
```

To turn on DoubleGuard integrity checking again, enter the following command and reboot your computer:

```
DBLSPACE /DOUBLEGUARD=1
```

See Also

"Understanding DoubleSpace" in Chapter 19

DBLSPACE /FORMAT 6.0 and later—External

The DBLSPACE /FORMAT command deletes all the files and subdirectories on a compressed drive, but leaves the drive itself intact. UNFORMAT cannot restore the files deleted with this command, so be careful when you use it. To delete the drive as well, use the DBLSPACE /DELETE command.

Note

DBLSPACE /FORMAT is a dangerous command. Formatting a compressed drive is a quick operation, and after you have given DoubleSpace the go-ahead, there is no turning back. The UNFORMAT command cannot be used to recover a formatted compressed drive. Make absolutely sure you don't need anything on the drive before formatting it.

Syntax

DBLSPACE /FORMAT *drive:*

or

DBLSPACE /F *drive:*

Parameters and Switches

drive: The compressed drive that you want to format. Note that you should specify the compressed drive, not the host drive.

Notes

1. Formatting a compressed drive deletes all the files on that drive.
2. You cannot unformat a compressed drive after performing a /FORMAT operation on it.
3. DoubleSpace does not allow you to format drive C.

See Also

DBLSPACE /DELETE

"Understanding DoubleSpace" in Chapter 19

DBLSPACE /INFO 6.0 and later—External

The DBLSPACE /INFO command displays the following information about the specified compressed drive: its host drive, used and free space, actual and estimated compression ratio, and total size. DBLSPACE /INFO can be handy for monitoring the compression ratio on the drive.

Syntax

DBLSPACE /INFO *drive:*

Parameters and Switches

/INFO — This parameter can be omitted. If /INFO is included and *drive:* is omitted, information about the current drive is displayed. If both /INFO and *drive:* are omitted, the full-screen DoubleSpace program is run.

drive: — The compressed drive that you want information about. Note that you should specify the compressed drive, not the host drive. If *drive:* is omitted and /INFO is specified, information about the current drive is displayed.

See Also

DBLSPACE /LIST

"Understanding DoubleSpace" in Chapter 19

DBLSPACE /LIST — 6.0 and later—External

The DBLSPACE /LIST command displays information about all the local drives connected to your computer, whether or not they are compressed drives. For each drive, the letter, type, free space, total size, and CVF file name are displayed. DBLSPACE /LIST can be handy for finding out the host drive for a compressed drive, because the host drive is included in the CVF file name. DBLSPACE /LIST cannot display information about network or CD-ROM drives attached to your computer.

Syntax

DBLSPACE /LIST

or

DBLSPACE /L

See Also

DBLSPACE /INFO

"Understanding DoubleSpace" in Chapter 19

DBLSPACE /MOUNT 6.0 and later—External

The DBLSPACE /MOUNT command associates a drive letter with a compressed volume file (CVF) so that you can access the files in the CVF as though they were on a disk. Normally, DoubleSpace mounts CVFs for you, so you must mount a CVF only if you have explicitly unmounted it or if the CVF is on a removable (floppy) disk.

Syntax

DBLSPACE /MOUNT=*nnn* ***host:*** /NEWDRIVE=*drive:*

or

DBLSPACE /MO=*nnn* ***host:*** /NEW=*drive:*

Parameters and Switches

=*nnn* — Mounts the CVF named DBLSPACE.*nnn* on *host:*. This parameter can be abbreviated to /MO=*nnn*. If *nnn* is not specified, DBLSPACE.000 is assumed.

host: — The uncompressed (host) drive containing the CVF that you want mounted.

/NEWDRIVE=*drive:* — If you are mounting a CVF file created with the /COMPRESS parameter (*nnn*=000), *drive:* specifies the drive letter you want to use for the host drive after the CVF is mounted. If you are mounting a CVF file created with the /CREATE parameter (*nnn*>000), *drive:* specifies the drive letter you want to use for the compressed drive after the CVF is mounted. This parameter can be abbreviated to /NEW=*drive:*. The default is the next available drive letter.

Notes

You cannot mount a compressed drive from Microsoft Windows. If you are running MS-DOS 6.2, you can get around this with the new automount feature, which will work while Windows is running. If you are using MS-DOS 6.0, you must exit Windows before mounting a compressed floppy or removable cartridge disk.

Examples

To mount CVF D:\DBLSPACE.001 as the next available drive letter:

```
DBLSPACE /MOUNT=001 D:
```

To mount a DoubleSpace compressed floppy disk in A as the next available drive letter:

DBLSPACE /MOUNT A:

See Also

DBLSPACE /UNMOUNT

"Understanding DoubleSpace" in Chapter 19

DBLSPACE /RATIO 6.0 and later—External

BATCH FILE

DoubleSpace uses the estimated compression ratio to estimate how much free space a compressed drive contains. With the DBLSPACE /RATIO command you can change the estimated compression ratio that DoubleSpace is using for a compressed drive. You may want to change the estimated ratio if you are about to copy to the compressed drive files that differ significantly from those that already are on the drive.

Syntax

DBLSPACE /RATIO=*ratio drive:* /ALL

or

DBLSPACE /RA=*ratio drive:* /ALL

Parameters and Switches

=*ratio*	The new estimated compression ratio from 1.0 to 16.0. *ratio* must be entered with one decimal place (for example, 2.0, not 2). The default is the actual compression ratio for the drive.
drive:	The compressed drive for which you want to change the estimated compression ratio. DOS uses the current drive unless you specify /ALL. You cannot specify both *drive:* and /ALL.
/ALL	Changes the estimated compression ratios for all mounted compressed drives. You cannot specify both *drive:* and /ALL.

Notes

To view the actual compression ratio for a compressed drive, use the DBLSPACE /INFO command.

Examples

To change all your mounted compressed drives so that their estimated compression ratios equal their actual compression ratios:

```
DBLSPACE /RATIO D: /ALL
```

To change the estimated compression ratio of compressed drive E to 1.7:

```
DBLSPACE /RATIO=1.7 E:
```

See Also

DBLSPACE /INFO

"Understanding DoubleSpace" in Chapter 19

DBLSPACE /SIZE 6.0 and later—External

The DBLSPACE /SIZE COMMAND changes the size of a compressed drive. You may want to make a compressed drive smaller if you need more free space on its host drive. You may want to make a compressed drive larger if its host drive has a great deal of free space.

Syntax

DBLSPACE /SIZE=*size* /RESERVE=*size* ***drive:***

or

DBLSPACE /SI=*size* /RES=*size* ***drive:***

Parameters and Switches

=*size*	The space (in megabytes) that the CVF on *drive:* should take up on its host (uncompressed) drive. You cannot specify both =*size* and /RESERVE=*size*. The default is to make the host drive as small as possible.
/RESERVE=*size*	The space (in megabytes) to be left free on the host (uncompressed) drive after *drive:* is resized. This parameter can be abbreviated to /RES=*size*. You cannot specify both =*size* and /RESERVE=*size*. The default is to make the host drive as small as possible.
drive:	The compressed drive that you want to make larger or smaller.

Examples

To change the size of compressed drive E so its CVF takes up 30M on its host (uncompressed) drive:

```
DBLSPACE /SIZE=30 E:
```

To make compressed drive E as large as possible so that its host drive contains no uncompressed free space:

```
DBLSPACE /SIZE /RESERVE=0 E:
```

Notice that when you specify the amount of space to reserve with the /RESERVE=0 parameter, you cannot specify a *size* with the /SIZE parameter.

See Also

"Understanding DoubleSpace" in Chapter 19

DBLSPACE /UNCOMPRESS 6.2—External

The DBLSPACE /UNCOMPRESS command uncompresses a compressed DoubleSpace drive. If you uncompress all the compressed drives in your system, DoubleSpace removes itself from memory.

Syntax

DBLSPACE /UNCOMPRESS *drive:*

Parameters and Switches

drive: The compressed drive that you want to uncompress.

Notes

1. You should always back up all the files on a compressed drive before uncompresssing it. (If anything can go wrong, it will.)
2. You can uncompress a drive only if the files in the compressed drive will fit on the host drive in their uncompressed state.
3. If files in the root directories of both the host and the compressed drive have the same names, DoubleSpace cannot uncompress the drive. When this happens, DoubleSpace displays an error message and saves to the DBLSPACE.LOG file a list of the duplicate files involved.

When you have resolved all the duplicate root directory file names by renaming, moving, or deleting the files listed in DBLSPACE.LOG, you can try to uncompress the drive again.

4. After the last compressed drive in your system has been uncompressed, DoubleSpace removes DBLSPACE.BIN from memory. This can free 40K to 50K of memory in your system. The next time you mount a compressed volume file, DBLSPACE.BIN must be loaded back into memory before you can access the compressed drive.

See Also

DBLSPACE /COMPRESS and DBLSPACE /CREATE

"Understanding DoubleSpace" in Chapter 19

DBLSPACE /UNMOUNT

6.0 and later—External

The DBLSPACE /UNMOUNT command breaks the association between a drive letter and a compressed volume file (CVF), temporarily making a compressed drive unavailable.

Syntax

DBLSPACE /UNMOUNT *drive:*

or

DBLSPACE /U *drive:*

Parameters and Switches

drive: The compressed drive that you want to unmount. The default is the current drive.

Notes

1. You cannot unmount drive C.
2. Use DBLSPACE /MOUNT to regain access to the compressed drive.

See Also

DBLSPACE /MOUNT

"Understanding DoubleSpace" in Chapter 19

DBLSPACE.SYS (device driver)

6.0 and later—External

To allow DoubleSpace to perform its compression magic, DOS loads the DBLSPACE.BIN file into memory very early in the boot process. Initially, DBLSPACE.BIN is placed at the top of conventional memory. The DBLSPACE.SYS device driver enables you to move DBLSPACE.BIN to its final location in conventional or upper memory. Moving DBLSPACE.BIN to upper memory can save as much as 43K of conventional memory for your DOS programs to use. To move DBLSPACE.BIN, DBLSPACE.SYS must be loaded in a DEVICE= or DEVICEHIGH= statement in your CONFIG.SYS file.

In MS-DOS 6.2, DoubleSpace can share the HMA (high memory area) with DOS, decreasing the size of DoubleSpace in upper or lower memory to 33K or to 37K if the automounting feature is enabled.

Syntax

To relocate the DBLSPACE.BIN driver to the bottom of conventional memory, load the DBLSPACE.SYS device driver with the DEVICE= command.

DEVICE=*drive:\path***DBLSPACE.SYS /MOVE** /NOHMA

To relocate the DBLSPACE.BIN driver into upper memory, load the DBLSPACE.SYS device driver with the DEVICEHIGH= command.

DEVICEHIGH=*drive:\path***DBLSPACE.SYS /MOVE** /NOHMA

Parameters and Switches

drive:\path	Enter the full path to the DBLSPACE.SYS file on your system. Setup places the DBLSPACE.SYS file in the C:\DOS subdirectory by default. If the full path to DBLSPACE.SYS isn't specified, DOS will look for the file in the root directory of the start-up drive.
/MOVE	DBLSPACE.SYS moves the DBLSPACE.BIN driver in memory. This parameter is required.
/NOHMA	Prevents DoubleSpace from locating a portion of itself in the HMA with DOS.

Notes

1. When DBLSPACE.BIN is first loaded into memory, it locates itself at the top of conventional memory. If you let DBLSPACE.BIN remain in that

position, a device driver that requires access to this area in memory may overwrite it, crashing your computer. If you are using DoubleSpace, you should always use the DBLSPACE.SYS device driver to relocate DBLSPACE.BIN to a more permanent, safe location.

2. To relocate DBLSPACE.BIN to the bottom of conventional memory, load DBLSPACE.SYS with the DEVICE= command. To relocate DBLSPACE.BIN to upper memory, load DBLSPACE.SYS with the DEVICEHIGH= command. Note that you must specify the /MOVE parameter either way. If you do not load the DBLSPACE.SYS driver, DBLSPACE.BIN is moved to the bottom of conventional memory after all other CONFIG.SYS processing is complete.

3. Moving DBLSPACE.BIN to upper memory with DEVICEHIGH= will free approximately 43K of conventional memory. If there isn't enough room in upper memory, DBLSPACE.BIN is moved to the bottom of conventional memory instead.

4. (DOS 6.2 only) DoubleSpace can share the HMA with DOS, thereby decreasing the amount of upper or lower memory it requires to 33K or to 37K if the automounting feature is enabled. You can prevent DoubleSpace from loading into the HMA with the /NOHMA parameter.

5. If DOS and DoubleSpace are sharing space in the HMA and you are using a disk cache (for example, SMARTDrive), you may want to decrease the BUFFERS= setting to 10. With DoubleSpace in the HMA, there is room for about 10 buffers, so specifying more than this may cause DOS to locate all its buffers in conventional memory instead.

6. MemMaker optimizes the placement of DBLSPACE.BIN in memory if it finds the DBLSPACE.SYS driver being loaded in CONFIG.SYS. Specifying the /L and /S options with DEVICEHIGH= causes DBLSPACE.SYS to move DBLSPACE.BIN to the specified region(s). Therefore, to MemMaker, optimization for this device driver works just like any other.

7. Unlike most device drivers, DBLSPACE.SYS doesn't remain in memory. After it has moved DBLSPACE.BIN into upper or lower memory, it unloads itself. Therefore, you can install DBLSPACE.SYS more than once in your CONFIG.SYS file without wasting memory. DoubleSpace may insert more than one DEVICE=DBLSPACE.SYS statement in your CONFIG.SYS file to avoid certain problems with network device drivers.

8. You should load DBLSPACE.SYS before loading INTERLNK.EXE in your CONFIG.SYS file. If you load INTERLNK.EXE first, you may not be able to access all the drives on the client computer. In general, INTERLNK.EXE should be the last block device driver loaded in CONFIG.SYS.

9. If DBLSPACE.BIN is relocated after certain network drivers are loaded in memory, your system may begin rebooting when certain DBLSPACE commands are run. If this happens, make sure that the device line for DBLSPACE.SYS comes before all network drivers loaded from CONFIG.SYS.

10. The placement of the DEVICE=DBLSPACE.SYS line in your CONFIG.SYS file may affect the drive letters used in your system. In general, to allow device drivers to allocate letters that follow the physical drives in the system, load them before the DBLSPACE.SYS driver. After DBLSPACE.BIN has been moved, it allocates extra drive letters for host drives. Any device drivers loaded after this are assigned drive letters that follow DoubleSpace's drive letters.

Trap

Having drive letters change simply because you added a device driver to your CONFIG.SYS file can result in time-consuming chores. Batch files often have to be edited to reflect the new drive letters. All references to drives that have changed must be corrected in your CONFIG.SYS and AUTOEXEC.BAT files. Microsoft Windows is sensitive to drive letter changes, and some Windows applications will fail if they are suddenly located on a different drive.

Before you add or rearrange DEVICE= lines in your CONFIG.SYS, think through the changes you may be making to drive letter assignments. You often can accomplish what you need without changing drive letter assignments.

Examples

The following lines install a RAM disk and relocate the DBLSPACE.BIN driver in upper memory if enough space is available:

```
DEVICEHIGH=C:\DOS\RAMDRIVE.SYS  1450  512  224  /E
DEVICEHIGH=C:\DOS\DBLSPACE.SYS  /MOVE
```

Because the RAM drive was loaded before DBLSPACE.BIN was moved, RAMDRIVE.SYS allocates drive letters before DoubleSpace. In a typical system with one or two floppy drives and a hard disk (with a CVF), the RAM drive would be D, and DoubleSpace, which normally saves four letters for later use, would use I as the host drive for C.

In the next example, the order is reversed, and the DEVICE= command is used to relocate DBLSPACE.BIN to the bottom of conventional memory instead of upper memory:

```
DEVICE=C:\DOS\DBLSPACE.SYS  /MOVE
DEVICEHIGH=C:\DOS\RAMDRIVE.SYS  1450  512  224  /E
```

This time, DoubleSpace uses H for the host drive, and the RAM drive will become drive I.

See Also

DBLSPACE, DEVICE=, and DEVICEHIGH=

"Understanding DoubleSpace" in Chapter 19

DEBUG

1.0 and later—External

The DEBUG utility tests and edits programs. You can use DEBUG to view and change the state of your computer at the hardware level. Be very careful when using DEBUG, because with just a few keystrokes you can wipe out your hard drive, destroy files, disable your mouse, lock up the keyboard, and cause all sorts of nasty things. However, you can also learn a lot about your computer by poking around with DEBUG. This program is a programmer's tool and is rarely used by anyone else.

Syntax

DEBUG *pathname parameters*

Parameters and Switches

pathname — The program file that you would like DEBUG to load into memory. If this parameter is omitted, DEBUG will start with no file loaded.

parameters — Any parameters that you want to pass to the program file you specified with the *pathname* parameter. You cannot specify *parameters* if you do not specify *pathname*. This parameter is useful only if you are loading program files that accept arguments on their command line.

Notes

1. The DEBUG utility enables you to load a program into memory and then edit, test, and save the edited program back to the disk. You also can use DEBUG to create small assembly language programs.

2. Most people come in contact with DEBUG only when they are given explicit instructions on patching a particular file. In most cases, this will involve creating a text file, and then redirecting the input to DEBUG. The SPATCH.BAT file on the DOS 6 distribution disks uses this technique to patch (change) the Windows SWAPFILE.EXE program.

3. Details on using the DEBUG program are beyond the scope of this book. If you want to learn about using DEBUG, check the MS-DOS online help system or the *DOS 6 Technical Reference* manual.

Examples

To start DEBUG, simply enter the following:

```
DEBUG
```

To start DEBUG and load PROGRAM.EXE from C:\UTILS for editing, enter this:

```
DEBUG C:\UTILS\PROGRAM.EXE
```

After you have started the DEBUG program, it displays its prompt (the hyphen) and waits for you to enter commands. To quit DEBUG, enter the Q (quit) command.

DEFRAG

6.0 and later—External

Files become fragmented due to the way MS-DOS stores them on the disk. If parts of a single file are scattered over the disk, it takes more time for your disk drive to find and load all the pieces into memory. DEFRAG rearranges the files on your disk so that each is located in a series of contiguous clusters. This makes file access more efficient.

Syntax

DEFRAG *drive:* /F /Q /U /S:*order* /B /H /SKIPHIGH /LCD /BW /G0

Parameters and Switches

drive: The drive to be optimized. If omitted, DEFRAG assumes that you want to defragment the current drive.

/F The full optimization method. This provides the best optimization but takes the most time. It defragments all your files, moves them to the front of the disk, and puts all the empty space at the end of the disk. You cannot specify the /U or /Q parameters with /F.

/Q (Undocumented) The quick optimization method. This method moves all your files to the beginning of the disk and maximizes the amount of contiguous free space on the disk, buy your files are still fragmented. You cannot specify the /F, /U, or /S parameters with /Q. This parameter is not documented by Microsoft, and may not be available in all versions.

/U The unfragment only optimization method. This method defragments all your files but does not rearrange them on the disk. The empty space is left spread over the disk. You cannot specify the /F, /Q, or /S parameters with /U.

/S:*order* Controls the order of files in their directories. If you omit this switch, the current order of files on your disk is unchanged. The colon (:) is optional. Use any combination of the following values for *order*, without separating them with spaces:

- N Sorts in alphabetical order by name (A to Z)
- N– Sorts in reverse alphabetical order by name (Z to A)
- E Sorts in alphabetical order by extension (A to Z)
- E– Sorts in reverse alphabetical order by extension (Z to A)
- D Sorts by date and time (newest to oldest)

D– Sorts by date and time (oldest to newest)

S Sorts by size (smallest to largest)

S– Sorts by size (largest to smallest)

/B Restarts (reboots) your computer after the files have been reorganized. Make sure you use this switch if you use the FASTOPEN utility.

/H Allows DEFRAG to move a file even if it has the hidden attribute set. (Normally, DEFRAG will not move files with hidden attributes.) Note that even when /H is specified, DEFRAG still does not move files with the system attribute.

/SKIPHIGH Normally, DEFRAG uses upper memory if it is available. Specifying the /SKIPHIGH switch forces DEFRAG not to use any upper memory.

/LCD Uses screen colors suited to a liquid crystal display. You cannot specify the /BW parameter with /LCD.

/BW Uses screen colors suited to a monochrome display. You cannot specify the /LCD parameter with /BW.

/G0 Disables the graphic mouse and graphic character set on EGA and VGA screens. (Note that this is G and a zero.) By combining /G0 with the /BW or /LCD parameter, you should be able to run DEFRAG on any DOS display.

Exit Codes

ERRORLEVEL Value	Meaning
0	Disk was defragmented successfully
1	An internal error occurred
2	No free clusters (DEFRAG requires at least one)
3	Operation halted by the user (Ctrl-C)
4	Operation halted by a general error
5	Operation halted by a disk read error

ERRORLEVEL Value	Meaning
6	Operation halted by a disk write error
7	Operation halted by an error in the FAT; use CHKDSK /F
8	Operation halted by a memory allocation error
9	Not enough free memory to defragment this disk

Notes

1. DOS starts DEFRAG in interactive mode if you omit one or more required parameters from the command line.
2. DEFRAG takes over the entire screen to show what it is doing.
3. By default, DEFRAG is loaded into upper memory if enough memory is free.
4. Do not use DEFRAG to optimize network drives or drives created with INTERLNK.
5. If you are using FASTOPEN when you defragment, specify DEFRAG /B so that out-of-date buffers kept by FASTOPEN are not used after the defragmenting operation.
6. Do not run DEFRAG when any other program is running, including Microsoft Windows. If you have any programs resident in memory that might try to access the disk being defragmented, you should disable or remove them from memory before running DEFRAG. An exception to this is the SMARTDRV disk cache. (You don't have to remove it because DEFRAG disables it for you automatically.) If a program accesses a disk while it is being defragmented, data may be lost.
7. It is a good idea to run a utility such as CHKDSK or SCANDISK before running DEFRAG to correct any logical errors on the drive before defragmenting its files.

See Also

CHKDSK and SCANDISK

"Defragmenting Your Disk" in Chapter 19

DEL or ERASE

1.0 and later—Internal

BATCH FILE

The DEL command deletes one or more files from the drive and directory you specify. ERASE is an alternate name for this command. Many times, you can restore an accidentally deleted file with the UNDELETE command—if you use the command soon enough.

Syntax

DEL ***pathname*** /P

or

ERASE ***pathname*** /P

Parameters and Switches

pathname The file or files that you want to delete. If no drive is specified, the current drive is used. If no subdirectory path is specified, the current subdirectory is used. If only a path (with or without a drive) is specified, all files (*.*) are assumed. Wildcards are allowed.

/P DOS prompts you before deleting each file. This can make it easier to delete a group of files that are difficult to specify with wildcards.

Notes

1. If you provide a drive name, a path name, or both, and specify either *.* or no name for the file name, the DEL command prepares to delete all the files in the specified directory. Before it deletes them, DOS displays the following message:

   ```
   All files in directory will be deleted
   Are you sure (Y/N)?
   ```

   If you type **Y**, DOS erases all files in the specified directory (but not in the subdirectories). If you type **N**, no files are erased.

2. If you specify the /P parameter, DEL prompts you before deleting each file by displaying a line such as the following:

   ```
   MYFILE.TXT     Delete (Y/N)?
   ```

   If you type **Y**, DOS erases the file. If you type **N**, the file is skipped.

3. You may be able to recover an erased file by using the special DOS 5.0 and 6.0 UNDELETE utility program. Use UNDELETE immediately after accidentally erasing a file.

4. The DOS RECOVER utility does not recover erased files. RECOVER is designed only to repair a file that contains bad sectors or that has a bad directory entry.

Messages

`Access denied`

Error: You attempted to erase a file that is marked as read-only or that is being used by another program or computer and is temporarily marked as read-only. If the file that you intend to erase has the read-only, system, or hidden attributes set, use the ATTRIB command to turn off those attributes before attempting to erase the file again.

See Also

DELTREE and UNDELETE

"Deleting Files" in Chapter 8

DELOLDOS

5.0 and later—External

DELOLDOS deletes from the hard disk all files from a previous version of DOS after a DOS 5.0 or 6.0 installation.

Syntax

DELOLDOS /B

Parameters and Switches

/B	Forces DELOLDOS to use black-and-white screen mode. You may want to use this switch if you have an LCD display screen or a one-color monitor attached to a CGA adapter.

Notes

1. When you upgrade to DOS 5.0 or 6.0, the old version of DOS is preserved in part on your hard disk in the directory OLD_DOS.1 and on the Uninstall disks that the DOS Setup program creates. After you are

sure that the upgrade works correctly and is compatible with the programs that you normally use, you can delete the old DOS from the hard disk, thereby freeing additional storage space.

2. After you start DELOLDOS, you can exit without deleting the old version of DOS by pressing any key except Y.
3. Be sure that all your programs are compatible with the new DOS before you delete the old version.
4. After doing a DELOLDOS, you cannot use the Uninstall disks created by DOS 5.0 or 6.0 Setup to restore your previous DOS version.
5. After DELOLDOS has deleted the previous version of DOS from your disk, it will delete itself. This really is a one-shot utility.

See Also

SETUP

DELTREE

6.0 and later—External

With DELTREE, you can delete an entire branch of your subdirectory tree. Unlike RD (or RMDIR), DELTREE deletes subdirectories that contain files. Because you can delete so many files so quickly with this command, you should always be careful when using it.

Syntax

DELTREE *drive:**path* /Y

Parameters and Switches

drive:	The drive that contains the subdirectory you want to delete.
path	The subdirectory that will be deleted. All subdirectories and files contained in the specified subdirectory are deleted as well. You are allowed to use wildcards in the path parameter; but use extreme caution if you do.
/Y	Suppresses prompting for permission to delete each directory specified by *path*. Do not use this switch. A typographical error could wipe out too many files.

Exit Codes

ERRORLEVEL Value	Meaning
0	Subdirectory was successfully deleted

Notes

1. This command deletes all files, including hidden, read-only, and system files.
2. DOS prompts you for permission to delete each directory specified by *path*, unless you specify /Y.

Trap

Use great care with the DELTREE command, particularly if you specify wildcards. You easily can delete more files than you intend.

See Also

DEL or DELETE, and RD or RMDIR

"Using DELTREE to Delete Directories" in Chapter 7

DEVICE= 2.0 and later—Internal

The DEVICE= command is used to load device drivers into conventional memory. Through the use of installable device drivers, DOS can be expanded to support many features and devices that aren't supported in the DOS kernel. Installation programs often add device drivers to your CONFIG.SYS file for you. DEVICE= can be used in only your CONFIG.SYS file.

Syntax

DEVICE=*drive:\path**filename*** *parameters*

Parameters and Switches

drive:\path Although optional, you should always include the full drive and path to the device driver file. If this is omitted, the device driver file is assumed to be in the root directory of the start-up drive.

filename The full file name, with extension, of the device driver to be loaded. Although many device drivers use a SYS extension, this isn't assumed, and the driver file's extension must always be specified. No wildcards are allowed. This parameter is required.

parameters Any parameters that the device driver may require are included after its name. DOS passes these parameters directly to the driver when it is loaded into memory. Some device drivers use case-sensitive or position-sensitive parameters. See the instructions provided with the device driver for details.

Notes

1. If MS-DOS cannot find the specified device driver file, it displays a `Bad or missing filename` message and continues processing CONFIG.SYS. (See the first message in the "Messages" section for the DEVICE= command.)

2. Device drivers are often sensitive to the order in which they are loaded. DOS executes each DEVICE= or DEVICEHIGH= command in the order in which it appears in CONFIG.SYS.

3. The following device drivers are provided with MS-DOS:

   ANSI.SYS
   CHKSTATE.SYS*
   DBLSPACE.SYS
   DISPLAY.SYS
   DRIVER.SYS
   EGA.SYS
   EMM386.EXE
   HIMEM.SYS
   INTERLNK.EXE
   POWER.EXE
   PRINTER.SYS**
   RAMDRIVE.SYS
   SETVER.EXE
   SMARTDRV.EXE
   SMARTDRV.SYS***

* CHKSTATE.SYS is used by MemMaker and shouldn't be installed in your CONFIG.SYS file.

** PRINTER.SYS is not distributed with DOS 6 but is available on the supplemental disk.

*** SMARTDRV.SYS was replaced by SMARTDRV.EXE in MS-DOS version 6.

All of the device drivers in this list can be installed with the DEVICE= command.

Trap

DOS 6 includes two files with the SYS extension that are not device drivers: COUNTRY.SYS and KEYBOARD.SYS. If you attempt to load these files with the DEVICE= or DEVICEHIGH= commands, your computer may lock up, forcing you to reboot. COUNTRY.SYS and KEYBOARD.SYS are data files used by COUNTRY= and KEYB, respectively.

4. You cannot load normal, executable files into memory with the DEVICE= command. Entering CHKDSK.EXE or even DOSKEY.COM on a DEVICE= line will generate an error message (see the first message in the "Messages" section) or lock up your computer. Device drivers are in a special format, and only files conforming to that format can be successfully loaded with the DEVICE= command. If an executable program is capable of being loaded during the processing of the CONFIG.SYS file (not all are), it can be placed in memory by the INSTALL= command.

External commands that load in a DEVICE= command line and run from the DOS prompt as well (such as EMM386, INTERLNK, POWER, and SETVER) are hybrid files that conform to both formats. When loaded from a DEVICE= command in CONFIG.SYS, the device driver portion of the file is loaded into memory. Executing the same command from the DOS prompt runs the executable portion of the file, which typically sets operating parameters or displays the status of the device driver already in memory.

Examples

Normally, the following two DEVICE= lines appear in CONFIG.SYS somewhere near the beginning of the file:

```
DEVICE=C:\DOS\HIMEM.SYS
DEVICE=C:\DOS\EMM386.EXE  RAM  MIN=0
DOS=HIGH,UMB
```

The DEVICE= lines load HIMEM.SYS and EMM386.EXE into memory, and provide the services necessary for DOS to load into the HMA with the DOS=HIGH,UMB command. Note that the DEVICE= line for HIMEM.SYS must be before the line for EMM386.EXE because EMM386 requires memory provided by HIMEM to operate.

Messages

`Bad or missing filename`
`Error in CONFIG.SYS line number`

Warning: DOS displays this message if it can't find the file you specified in the DEVICE=, DEVICEHIGH=, or INSTALL= command in your CONFIG.SYS file. *filename* is the name of the file that DOS was looking for, and *number* is the line in CONFIG.SYS where the command is located. Edit the line so that the path and file name are correct, then restart your computer.

`Unrecognized command in CONFIG.SYS`
`Error in CONFIG.SYS line number`

Warning: A line in your CONFIG.SYS file contains an illegal command. Usually, this indicates that you have mistyped the name of a CONFIG.SYS command or have placed the ? in an illegal position.

See Also

DEVICEHIGH= and INSTALL=

Chapter 18, "Configuring Your Computer"

DEVICEHIGH= 5.0 and later—Internal

With the DEVICEHIGH= command, DOS can load device drivers into upper memory space, saving conventional memory for your application programs. To do this, DOS must have a UMB provider, such as EMM386, available. Also, the driver must be small enough to fit into the available UMB space. If DOS cannot load a driver specified with the DEVICEHIGH= command into upper memory, it loads the driver into conventional memory instead. Not all device drivers can run in upper memory. DEVICEHIGH= can be used only in your CONFIG.SYS file.

Trap

Before you begin inserting DEVICEHIGH= commands in CONFIG.SYS, you should have a bootable floppy disk available. That way, you can always start DOS from a floppy disk if changes you make in CONFIG.SYS prevent DOS from booting. Alternatively, with DOS 6 you can use the F5 (Clean boot) key to bypass CONFIG.SYS completely or use F8 (Interactive) to choose which lines in your CONFIG.SYS to execute when problems arise.

Syntax

In its simplest form, the DEVICEHIGH= command works just like the DEVICE= command.

DEVICEHIGH=*drive:\path**filename*** *parameters*

(DOS 6 only) DEVICEHIGH= has two additional switches that MemMaker uses to specify the placement and size of the device driver in memory.

DEVICE /L:*region,min;region,min;...* /S =*drive:\path**filename*** *parameters*

The following alternate syntax is used with DOS 5. Although it is supported under DOS 6, you are advised to switch to the new syntax whenever possible.

DEVICE SIZE=*hexsize drive:\path**filename*** *parameters*

Parameters and Switches

drive:\path — Although optional, you should always include the full drive and path to the device driver file. If this is omitted, the device driver file is assumed to be in the root directory of the start-up drive.

filename — The full file name, with extension, of the device driver to be loaded. Although many device drivers use a SYS extension, this isn't assumed, and the driver file's extension must always be specified. No wildcards are allowed. This parameter is required.

parameters Any parameters that the device driver may need are included after its name. DOS passes these parameters directly to the driver when it is loaded into memory. Some device drivers use case-sensitive or position-sensitive parameters. See the instructions provided with the device driver for details.

/L:*region,min* (DOS 6 only) The region in upper memory, and optionally the minimum size in bytes, that the device driver should be loaded into. More than one region can be specified by separating each region from the previous one with a semicolon. For instance, /L:1;2 allows the driver access to UMB regions 1 and 2. /L:1,4096;2,512 further specifies that the minimum size of regions 1 and 2 should be 4096 bytes and 512 bytes, respectively. This parameter must precede the device driver *filename*. MemMaker sets these values for you.

/S (DOS 6 only) If the /L parameter is specified with a minimum size, /S instructs DOS to shrink the UMB to the specified size and create a new UMB from the remainder. /S must precede the device driver *filename*. This switch is best left to MemMaker's use.

SIZE=*hexsize* (DOS 5) The minimum size block, in hexadecimal notation, into which DOS should attempt to load the driver. (MEM /D can provide the hexadecimal value needed for this syntax.) This parameter must precede the device driver *filename*.

Notes

1. Before using the DEVICEHIGH= command, you must install a UMB provider and then execute a DOS=UMB command. Typically, this means that you must load HIMEM.SYS and EMM386.EXE with UMB support enabled and then specify DOS=UMB (or DOS=HIGH,UMB), before using the DEVICEHIGH= command.

Trap

You must install a UMB provider and the DOS=UMB command before using the DEVICEHIGH= command in your CONFIG.SYS file. That way, you can always start DOS from a floppy disk if changes you make in CONFIG.SYS prevent DOS from booting. Alternatively, with DOS 6 you can use the F5 (Clean) and F8 (Interactive) boot keys to bypass completely or choose which lines in your CONFIG.SYS to execute when problems arise.

Trap

If you use other memory managers, such as 386MAX, BLUEMAX, QEMM, or CEMM, it may be better to use their versions of DEVICEHIGH= and LOADHIGH rather than the ones DOS provides. Sometimes, simply specifying DOS=UMB is a mistake. Follow the instructions and recommendations that came with the product you purchased.

2. If DOS is unable to load the device driver into upper memory, it loads it into conventional memory instead. No error messages are displayed when this happens. To see what device drivers have been loaded into upper memory, use the MEM /C command.

3. If MS-DOS cannot find the specified device driver file, it displays a `Bad or missing` *`filename`* message and continues processing CONFIG.SYS. (See the first message in the DEVICEHIGH= command's "Messages" section.)

4. Device drivers are often sensitive to the order in which they are loaded. DOS executes each DEVICE= or DEVICEHIGH= command in the order in which it appears in CONFIG.SYS.

5. The following device drivers provided with MS-DOS can be loaded into UMB space with the DEVICEHIGH= command:

   ANSI.SYS
   DBLSPACE.SYS
   DISPLAY.SYS
   DRIVER.SYS
   EGA.SYS
   PRINTER.SYS*
   RAMDRIVE.SYS
   SETVER.EXE

*PRINTER.SYS is not distributed with DOS 6 but is available on the supplemental disk.

INTERLNK.EXE, POWER.EXE, and SMARTDRV.EXE all use UMB space automatically if it is available, so there's no need to load them with a DEVICEHIGH= command. CHKSTATE.SYS is best left for MemMaker to handle. HIMEM.SYS and EMM386.EXE minimize their use of conventional memory when they load.

Trap

DOS 6 includes two files with the SYS extension that are not device drivers: COUNTRY.SYS and KEYBOARD.SYS. If you attempt to load these files with the DEVICE= or DEVICEHIGH= command, your computer may lock up, forcing you to reboot. COUNTRY.SYS and KEYBOARD.SYS are data files used by COUNTRY= and KEYB, respectively.

6. MemMaker can optimize your CONFIG.SYS file for you, inserting DEVICEHIGH= and LOADHIGH commands as needed to load as many device drivers and resident programs into upper memory space as possible. MemMaker also takes care of specifying the correct parameters for EMM386.EXE, ensuring that you have the maximum amount of UMB space available. This can be a big timesaver.

7. Before you start optimizing memory in your system, look at the resident software you're loading to see if you need it all. For instance, the setup program for DOS 6 installs SETVER.EXE whether or not you use any software that needs to be fooled into working with DOS 6. The cardinal rule is, Less is more. Fewer drivers and TSRs mean fewer complicated interactions and less problems with load orders and "RAM cram." Look for the balance of features and free memory that lets you use your system efficiently. Trim your system to the essentials, and then let MemMaker optimize it.

8. By default, DOS loads a driver into the largest free UMB and makes the other UMBs available to that driver. The /L switch can be used to fine-tune your configuration by forcing small drivers to be loaded into small UMBs. However, loading a driver with the /L switch gives the driver access to only the UMB specified. Therefore, if the driver requires more than one UMB, you must specify multiple regions with the /L switch

(for example, /L:1;2). To see how a driver uses memory and get a better idea of what values to use with the /L switch, use the MEM /M *driver_name* command.

9. MEM can be an enormous help in understanding memory usage in your computer. If you redirect the output of MEM to a file with the line

   /C > MEM_USE.TXT

   and then load that file into EDIT, you can page back and forth through MEM's report. With the information MEM supplies, it's easy to see how your computer's memory has been divided, and which drivers and TSRs are responsible for your "RAM cram" problems.

10. DOS doesn't load a driver in a UMB if the UMB is smaller than the driver's load size. (Usually the device driver's file size is equal to its load size.) If the driver requires more memory to run, you must specify one or more *min* parameters, which are the sizes of the UMBs that the driver requires when it runs. This procedure forces DOS to load the driver into a larger than normal UMB. Specify *min* in bytes after the corresponding *region* parameter, with a comma between (for example, /L:1,4096;2,512).

Examples

Before you can use the DEVICEHIGH= command to load device drivers into upper memory, UMB space must be available to DOS. The following lines set the stage for using DEVICEHIGH= on a typical 80386 or 80486 computer system:

```
DEVICE=C:\DOS\HIMEM.SYS
DEVICE=C:\DOS\EMM386.EXE  RAM
DOS=HIGH,UMB
```

First, the DEVICE= lines load HIMEM.SYS and EMM386.EXE into memory. These drivers provide the services necessary for the DOS=HIGH,UMB command, which comes next. Without these three lines at the beginning of your CONFIG.SYS file, the DEVICEHIGH= and LOADHIGH commands cannot access upper memory and use conventional memory instead. Note that the DEVICE= line for HIMEM.SYS must come before the line for EMM386.EXE, because EMM386 requires memory provided by HIMEM. Neither of these device drivers can be loaded with the DEVICEHIGH= command, but both drivers do attempt to minimize their impact on conventional memory when they load.

Now that everything is ready, use the DEVICEHIGH= command to load device drivers into upper memory just as you would use the DEVICE= command to load them into conventional memory. For instance, the following lines will load the ANSI.SYS and SETVER.EXE device drivers into UMBs:

```
DEVICEHIGH=C:\DOS\ANSI.SYS
DEVICEHIGH=C:\DOS\SETVER.EXE
```

When MemMaker optimizes your CONFIG.SYS for you, the DEVICEHIGH= command lines start looking more complicated with the inclusion of the /L and /S switches:

```
DEVICEHIGH  /L:1,4096  /S=C:\DOS\ANSI.SYS
DEVICEHIGH  /L:1,1024  /S=C:\DOS\SETVER.EXE
```

At this point, if you want DOS to prompt you before loading ANSI.SYS and SETVER.EXE, add question marks directly after DEVICEHIGH on each command lines:

```
DEVICEHIGH?  /L:1,4096  /S=C:\DOS\ANSI.SYS
DEVICEHIGH?  /L:1,1024  /S=C:\DOS\SETVER.EXE
```

Note that making these drivers optional defeats the purpose of optimizing their placement in memory, but it does clearly show that the question mark must be placed directly after the command name, not with the equal sign.

Messages

`Bad or missing filename`
`Error in CONFIG.SYS line number`

Warning: DOS displays this message if it can't find the file you specified in a DEVICE=, DEVICEHIGH=, or INSTALL= command in your CONFIG.SYS file. *filename* is the name of the file that DOS is looking for, and *number* is the line in CONFIG.SYS where the command is located. Edit the line so that the path and filename are correct, and then restart your computer.

`Unrecognized command in CONFIG.SYS`
`Error in CONFIG.SYS line number`

Warning: A line in your CONFIG.SYS file contains an illegal command. Usually this indicates that you have mistyped the name of a CONFIG.SYS command or have placed ? in an illegal position.

See Also

DEVICE=, DOS=, EMM386.EXE, HIMEM.SYS, LH or LOADHIGH, MEM, and MEMMAKER

"Loading Device Drivers and TSRs into Upper Memory" in Chapter 18

DIR

1.0 and later—Internal

The DIR command displays information about files on your disks. It is one of the most commonly used DOS commands. DIR is very handy for trying out complicated path names with wildcards to see if they match the files you wanted.

Syntax

DIR *pathname* /P /W /A:*attributes* /O:*sortorder* /S /B /L /C /CH

Parameters and Switches

pathname — The file or group of files that you want to display information about. Wildcards are permitted in the file name portion. If no drive is specified, the current drive is used. If no subdirectory path is specified, the current subdirectory is used. If no file name is specified, all files (*.*) are assumed.

/P — Pauses when the screen is full and waits for you to press any key.

/W — Generates a wide (80-column) display of the file names; the file size, date, and time are not displayed.

/A:*attributes* — (DOS 5 and later) Displays only files with the attributes you specify. If the /A:*attributes* parameter is omitted, DOS displays all files except hidden and system files. The colon is optional. *attributes* can be any combination of the following, but do not separate them with spaces:

- A — Displays files that are ready for archiving (backup)

–A Displays files that have not changed since the last backup

D Displays only directories (no files)

–D Displays only files (no directories)

H Displays hidden files

–H Displays all files that are not hidden

R Displays read-only files

–R Displays files that are not read-only

S Displays only system files

–S Displays all files except system files

/O:*sortorder* (DOS 5 and later) Controls the order in which DOS displays the information about the files and directories. If you omit the /O:*sortorder* parameter, DOS displays directories and files in the order in which they occur on the disk. The colon is optional. *sortorder* can be any combination of the following, but do not separate them with any spaces:

N Sorts alphabetically by name (A to Z)

–N Sorts by name in reverse alphabetical order (Z to A)

E Sorts alphabetically by extension (A to Z)

–E Sorts by extension in reverse alphabetical order (Z to A)

D Sorts by date and time (earliest to latest)

–D Sorts by date and time in reverse order (latest to earliest)

S Sorts by size (smallest to largest)

–S Sorts by size (largest to smallest)

C (DOS 6.0 only) Sorts by DoubleSpace compression ratio (lowest to highest)

–C (DOS 6.0 only) Sorts by DoubleSpace compression ratio (highest to lowest)

G Groups directories before files

–G Groups directories after files

/S (DOS 5 and later) Lists all the specified files in the specified directory and any subdirectories below it.

/B (DOS 5 and later) Lists only file names with no header or trailer information. This switch overrides /W. When combined with /S, the drive and path are included with each file name, but no date, time, or size information is displayed.

/L (DOS 5 and later) Displays directory names and file names in lowercase.

/C (DOS 6.0 and later) Displays the compression ratios of files on a DoubleSpace volume, assuming an 8K cluster size. /C is suppressed by /W or /B. This parameter cannot be combined with the /CH parameter.

/CH (DOS 6.0 and later) Displays the compression ratios of files on a DoubleSpace volume, assuming the cluster size of the host drive. /CH is suppressed by /W or /B. This parameter cannot be combined with the /C parameter.

Notes

1. DIR now displays numbers with embedded commas, making them much easier to read.

2. By default, the list displayed the DIR command includes the following information:

   Volume label and serial number

   One directory or file name per line

   File size (in bytes)

   Date and time of the last modification

Number of files listed

Total bytes listed

Number of available bytes remaining on the disk

3. When more than one *sortorder* value is specified, the file names are sorted from the left value to the right value.

4. You cannot use the DIR command for a drive in which you used the ASSIGN or JOIN command. You must break the assignment before you view the directory for a drive in which you used ASSIGN. You cannot use the DIR command on the guest disk drive involved in a JOIN command.

5. DIR does not report statistics for disk drives in which you used the ASSIGN or JOIN command. For disk drives in which you used JOIN, DIR reports the free space of the host disk drive (the disk drive to which the second disk drive is joined) but does not report the total of the two disk drives. First remove ASSIGN or JOIN from the drive to find its amount of free space.

6. In DOS 5.0 or 6.0, you can use SET DIRCMD to set DIR switches in the AUTOEXEC.BAT file. If you want DIR to display files and directories a page at a time, enter the following command in your AUTOEXEC.BAT file:

```
SET DIRCMD=/P
```

To override the preset switch, use the following format:

```
DIR /-P
```

To view the options set with the DIRCMD variable, type the following command:

```
SET
```

See Also

SET

Appendix B, "DOS Environment Variables," and "Searching for Files with the DIR Command" in Chapter 8

DISKCOMP

1.0 and later—External

BATCH FILE

DISKCOMP compares two floppy disks on a track-for-track, sector-for-sector basis to see whether their contents are identical.

Syntax

DISKCOMP *source: destination:* /1 /8

Parameters and Switches

source: The source drive to use for the comparison. If this parameter is omitted, the current drive is used. The *source* drive must be a DOS floppy disk drive.

destination: The destination drive to use for the comparison. If this parameter is omitted, the current drive is used. The *destination* drive must be a DOS floppy disk drive and can be the same as the *source* drive.

/1 Compares only the first side of the floppy disk, even if the disk or disk drive is double-sided.

/8 Compares only eight sectors per track, even if the first disk has a different number of sectors per track.

Exit Codes

ERRORLEVEL Value	Meaning
0	Disks are the same (success)
1	Disks are not the same
2	Operation halted by the user (Ctrl-C)
3	Operation halted by a fatal disk error
4	Operation halted by an internal error

Notes

1. If you provide only one valid floppy-drive name, DOS uses the current drive for the comparison.
2. If *source:* and *destination:* are the same, DISKCOMP prompts you when diskettes must be swapped.

3. Compare only compatible floppy disks formatted with the same number of tracks, sectors, and sides. Other types of comparisons will fail or give misleading results.

4. Do not use DISKCOMP for a network drive or a drive in which you used the ASSIGN, JOIN, or SUBST command.

5. Two disks containing the same files will not compare the same with DISKCOMP if the information in the files is arranged differently. For that reason, DISKCOMP is only useful when comparing floppy disks that were duplicated with the DISKCOPY command.

Messages

`Compare error on`
`Track` *`track`*`, side` *`side`*

Warning: The disks you are comparing are different at the indicated track and side. DISKCOMP does not specify which sectors are different. If you just used DISKCOPY on these disks and DOS reported no problem, the second disk probably has a flaw. Reformat the disk and try DISKCOPY again. Otherwise, assume that the disks are different.

`Compare OK`

Information: DISKCOMP compared the two floppy disks and found that they match.

`Drive types or diskette types not compatible`

or

`Incompatible disks`

Error: The disk drives are of different types (3 1/2- or 5 1/4-inch disks) or the floppy disks are different. The first disk was successfully read on both sides. DOS noticed the discrepancy when it tried to read the second disk.

`Unrecoverable read error on drive` *`x`*
`Track` *`track`*`, side` *`side`*

Warning: DOS made four attempts to read the data from the floppy disk in the specified drive. The error is on the indicated track and side. If drive *x* is the disk that holds the destination (copied) disk, the copy probably is bad. (The disk has a hard, or unrecoverable, read error.) If drive *x* holds the original disk, a flaw existed when the disk was formatted, or a flaw developed during use.

Run CHKDSK on the original disk and look for the line `bytes in bad sectors`. Even if this line is displayed, the original disk and the copy may be good. (The bad sectors may not be used by any of the files on the disk.) When you format a disk, FORMAT detects bad sectors and "hides" them. DISKCOMP, however, does not check for bad sectors; it tries to compare the tracks, even if bad sectors exist. For safety's sake, retire the original disk soon.

```
Invalid drive specification
Specified drive does not exist or is non-removable
```

Error: One (or both) of the specified drives does not exist or is a hard disk. This can result if you specify only one drive to DISKCOMP and the current drive is a hard disk.

See Also

DISKCOPY

"Comparing Disks with DISKCOMP" in Chapter 9

DISKCOPY

1.0 and later—External

DISKCOPY copies the contents of one floppy disk to another on a track-for-track basis, making an exact copy. DISKCOPY works only with floppy disks.

Syntax

DISKCOPY *source: destination:* /1 /8 /V

Parameters and Switches

source: The source drive to use for the copy. If this parameter is omitted, the current drive is used. The *source* drive must be a DOS floppy disk drive.

destination: The destination drive on which the copy will be made. If this parameter is omitted, the current drive is used. The *destination* drive must be a DOS floppy disk drive and can be the same as the *source* drive.

/1 Compares only the first side of the floppy disk, even if the disk or disk drive is double-sided.

/8 (DOS 1.0 to 5.0 only) Compares only eight sectors per track, even if the first disk has a different number of sectors per track.

/V Verifies that the copy is correct by reading back all information written to the destination disk. This slows the copy process. The /V switch is similar to VERIFY set ON.

Exit Codes

ERRORLEVEL Value	Meaning
0	Diskcopy operation successful
1	Operation halted by a non-fatal disk read/write error
2	Operation halted by the user (Ctrl-C)
3	Operation halted by a fatal disk error
4	Operation halted by an internal error

Notes

1. DISKCOPY now uses the directory pointed to by the TEMP environment variable if it runs out of memory while reading the source disk. Therefore, if you make single drive copies (for example, DISKCOPY A: A:), you no longer have to swap disks two or three times to make a copy of a disk. As long as there is enough space on your hard drive, DISKCOPY reads the entire source disk before asking for the destination disk.

2. The source and destination disk drives must be floppy disk drives—not hard or networked disk drives, RAM disks, or disk drives in which you used the JOIN or SUBST command. Defaulting to or specifying a nonreal source or destination disk drive causes DOS to return an error message and abort the copy operation.

3. If you do not provide a source disk drive name, DISKCOPY uses the default disk drive. If you provide an improper source disk drive, DISKCOPY issues an error message and aborts.

4. If your system has a single floppy disk drive and you provide only one valid floppy disk drive name, DOS uses that drive as both the source and destination disk drive for the copy. If your system uses two floppy disk drives and you provide only one valid disk drive name, DOS displays the `Invalid drive specification error` message.

5. DISKCOPY destroys any information recorded on the destination disk. Do not use as the destination disk one that contains information you want to keep.

6. To ensure that the copy is correct, run DISKCOMP on the two disks.

7. DISKCOPY ignores the effects of an ASSIGN command.

8. DISKCOPY recognizes unformatted destination disks and automatically formats them as part of the copying process.

9. Write-protecting the source disk is important when you use only one floppy disk drive to make a copy of a disk. DOS periodically prompts you to change the disk. You cannot damage a write-protected source disk if you inadvertently insert that disk when DOS asks for the destination disk.

10. When you use DISKCOPY, DOS reads into memory as much information as possible from the source disk. DOS then copies this information to the destination disk and reads the next batch of information from the source disk. The more free memory is available, the less time you need to copy a disk.

11. DISKCOPY copies whatever level of file fragmentation is on the source disk to the destination disk. To avert this problem, you may want to DEFRAG the source disk before copying it or FORMAT the destination disk and then XCOPY files to it.

Messages

`Drive types or diskette types not compatible`

Error: The drive types or disk capacities that you tried to use are different and cannot handle the operation, or the destination disk is the wrong capacity. DOS read the first disk, but the drive specified as the destination is not the right type. DISKCOPY cannot create a high-density copy in a double- or single-density disk drive, or a double-sided copy in a single-sided disk drive. Additionally, most high-density drives cannot make a high-density copy using double-density disks.

`Read error on drive d:`
`Write error on drive d:`

Warning: DISKCOPY cannot accurately read or write the disk in drive *d*. The disk is not properly inserted, the source disk is not formatted (or is a non-DOS disk), or the drive door is open. Check these possibilities.

```
SOURCE diskette bad or incompatible
TARGET diskette bad or incompatible
```

Warning: DISKCOPY detected errors while reading the source disk (first message) or writing to the destination, or target, disk (second message). Bad sectors may exist on either disk, or the disk may be in the wrong type of drive.

Determine whether either floppy disk has bad sectors. If so, do not use DISKCOPY on either disk. If the source disk is bad, use COPY *.* to copy files from the source disk. If the destination disk is bad, try a different disk or try to reformat the disk and then use DISKCOPY.

```
Invalid drive specification
Specified drive does not exist or is non-removable
```

Error: One or both of the two specified drives do not exist or are hard disks.

See Also

DISKCOMP and VERIFY

"Copying an Entire Disk with DISKCOPY" in Chapter 9

DISPLAY.SYS (device driver)

3.3 and later—External

The DISPLAY.SYS device driver adds international code page switching to the DOS console device. When combined with the other international utilities that DOS provides, it enables you to display one of six international character sets (code pages) on your EGA, VGA, or LCD screen. DISPLAY.SYS must be loaded in a DEVICE= or DEVICEHIGH= statement in your CONFIG.SYS file.

Syntax

DEVICE=*drive:\path***DISPLAY.SYS CON:=(*type*,***hard_cp,num_cp*)

DEVICEHIGH=*drive:\path***DISPLAY.SY CON:=(*type*,***hard_cp,num_cp*)

To specify the number of subfonts that the display hardware can support, use the following format:

DEVICE=*drive:\path***DISPLAY.SYS**
CON:=(*type*,*hard_cp*,(*num_cp*,*subfonts*))

DEVICEHIGH=*drive:\path***DISPLAY.SYS**
CON:=(*type*,*hard_cp*,(*num_cp*,*subfonts*))

Parameters and Switches

drive:\path Enter the full path to the DISPLAY.SYS file on your system. Setup places the DISPLAY.SYS file in the C:\DOS subdirectory by default. If the full path to DISPLAY.SYS isn't specified, DOS looks for the file in the root directory of the start-up drive.

CON:= Specifies that the CON device is being described. The colon is optional, but the parameter itself is required.

type The type of display that is being used. It must be one of the type codes from the display type table below. This parameter must be enclosed in parentheses.

Display Type	*type*	*num_cp*	*subfonts*
Color Graphics Adapter	CGA	0	0
Monochrome Display Adapter	MONO	0	0
EGA, VGA, or Super VGA	EGA	0 to 6	2
IBM PC Convertible LCD	LCD	0 to 1	1

Note that although CGA and MONO display types are allowed, neither of these displays supports code page switching. Loading DISPLAY.SYS for a CGA or MDA display is a waste of memory.

hard_cp The hardware code page built into the display, normally 437 in the United States. As long as you specify this parameter, you can always switch back to the default hardware code page built into your display adapter. See Appendix G for a list of the code pages that MS-DOS supports.

num_cp The number of software code pages to allow space for in memory. Valid values for *num_cp* are shown in the previous display type table. If this parameter is omitted, a default value of 1 is used. Specifying 0 reserves no memory for display code pages, which effectively disables code page switching.

subfonts The number of subfonts that your display hardware supports for each code page. The default values for this parameter are shown in the previous display type table. If *subfonts* is specified, it and the *num_cp* parameter must be enclosed in a second set of parentheses.

Notes

1. Load the DISPLAY.SYS driver after any other device drivers that affect the DOS console device. For instance, you should load DISPLAY.SYS after you load ANSI.SYS in your CONFIG.SYS file. Otherwise, the other console driver is likely to disable DISPLAY.SYS.

2. When DISPLAY.SYS is loaded, it reserves memory for itself and for *num_cp* code pages. DISPLAY.SYS itself uses about 5K of memory, the first code page adds 13K, and each additional code page requires about another 10K. Adding it up, DISPLAY.SYS needs 18K of RAM for one code page, 28K of RAM for two code pages, and so on.

3. If you do not specify the hardware code page that the display supports, you will not be able to switch back to it after you activate an alternate software code page. For this reason, you should always specify a value for *hard_cp*.

4. Although you are allowed to specify *num_cp* equal to zero, doing so defeats the purpose of loading DISPLAY.SYS. With no additional code pages in memory, you can't switch to a different one, which is the only reason for using DISPLAY.SYS in the first place. CGA and MDA displays do not support code page switching, so the maximum *num_cp* you can specify for these displays is zero, which once again is a pointless configuration.

5. To display a software code page, you'll need to perform a number of additional steps. The MODE command is used to prepare and load the code page information into the memory set aside by DISPLAY.SYS. Then MODE can be used to select the display code page, or you can load NLSFUNC and use the CHCP command to change the active code page for all of your devices at once. Additionally, you may want to add

the COUNTRY= command to your CONFIG.SYS file to make case conversion and sort order information available.

6. The KEYB utility provides code page support for the input side of the DOS console device. With KEYB, you can remap your keyboard to conform with various international conventions.

7. PRINTER.SYS performs a similar function for certain IBM printers that support code page switching. It is available on the DOS 6 Supplemental disk.

Examples

The following line enables an EGA or a VGA display, which use hardware code page 437, to load and switch to an alternate code page:

```
DEVICE=C:\DOS\DISPLAY.SYS  CON:=(EGA,437,1)
```

If you want to load DISPLAY.SYS into upper memory with room for two code pages, use the following line:

```
DEVICEHIGH=C:\DOS\DISPLAY.SYS  CON=(EGA,437,2)
```

Notice that you can use the CON= or the CON:= format. Two subfonts are available in both of the examples because a display type of EGA defaults to two subfonts.

If you have an IBM Convertible LCD display that uses hardware code page 865 (Nordic) and you want to enable code page switching on it, add the following line to your CONFIG.SYS file:

```
DEVICE=C:\DOS\DISPLAY.SYS  CON=(LCD,865,1)
```

Only one subfont is because that is the default (and maximum) for LCD displays.

See Also

CHCP, COUNTRY=, MODE device CP, NLSFUNC, and PRINTER.SYS

Chapter 21, "Understanding the International Features of DOS"

DOS= 5.0 and later—Internal

The DOS= command has two options that allow you to adjust the way DOS loads and uses upper memory. By specifying DOS=HIGH, DOS attempts to load itself into the high memory area (HMA). The DOS=UMB command allows DOS to load resident programs into upper memory blocks (UMBs) with the DEVICEHIGH= and LOADHIGH commands. DOS= can be used only in your CONFIG.SYS file.

Syntax

DOS=*high_low,umb_noumb*

Parameters and Switches

high_low Specifies whether DOS should attempt to load itself in the high memory area (DOS=HIGH) or in conventional memory (DOS=LOW). To load HIGH, DOS requires an extended memory (XMS) manager such as HIMEM.SYS. The default value is LOW.

umb_noumb Specifies whether DOS should manage upper memory blocks created by a UMB provider such as EMM386.EXE (DOS=UMB) or not (DOS=NOUMB). The default value is NOUMB.

Tip

Always specify DOS=HIGH in CONFIG.SYS if your computer supports it. Few programs use the HMA, and loading DOS high can easily free 45K to 55K of conventional memory. This is a rare opportunity to get something valuable without losing anything.

Notes

1. If you include a DOS= command in your CONFIG.SYS, you must include at least one parameter with it. To include more than one parameter, separate them with commas (for example, DOS=HIGH,UMB).

2. Although you can enter more than one DOS= line in your CONFIG.SYS file, it's better not to do so. In general, if the combination of parameters specified with more than one DOS= line would be legal on the first DOS= line in the file, you'll be okay. Sometimes you can specify DOS=UMB after using the DEVICEHIGH= command, but avoid this when possible. All the load order interactions are too confusing and aren't guaranteed to remain the same from one version of DOS to the next. Use one DOS= line, located directly after the line that loads your memory manager software.

3. You must load HIMEM.SYS (or another extended memory manager) before specifying DOS=HIGH in your CONFIG.SYS. DOS will load itself into the HMA after all other CONFIG.SYS processing is complete. If the HMA is unavailable or in use at that time, DOS displays an error message (see the first message in the "Messages" section) and loads itself into conventional memory. The HMA is not available on 8088 and

8086 processors, but is available on 80286 computers with A20 line support and at least 1M of RAM.

4. To allow DOS to load resident programs into upper memory blocks, you must load a UMB provider (such as EMM386.EXE) and specify DOS=UMB in your CONFIG.SYS. No error message is displayed if DOS is unable to access the upper memory blocks.

Examples

A typical entry for DOS= in your CONFIG.SYS follows:

```
DEVICE=C:\DOS\HIMEM.SYS
DEVICE=C:\DOS\EMM386.EXE  RAM
DOS=HIGH,UMB
```

This loads DOS into the HMA and enables the use of the LOADHIGH and DEVICEHIGH= commands. Note that HIMEM.SYS and EMM386.EXE must be loaded before the DOS=HIGH,UMB command. The following series of commands uses an alternate syntax to do the same thing:

```
DEVICE=C:\DOS\HIMEM.SYS
DEVICE=C:\DOS\EMM386.EXE  RAM
DOS=HIGH
DOS=UMB
```

Because you can split the DOS=HIGH and DOS=UMB commands, you may be tempted to add other commands between them. The following series of commands is legal, but you should avoid chaotic arrangements like this in your CONFIG.SYS file:

```
DEVICE=C:\DOS\HIMEM.SYS
DOS=HIGH
FILES=50
BUFFERS=20
DEVICE=C:\DOS\EMM386.EXE  RAM
LASTDRIVE=Z
SWITCHES=/W
DEVICEHIGH=C:\DOS\ANSI.SYS
DEVICEHIGH=C:\DOS\RAMDRIVE.SYS
DOS=UMB
```

The use of DEVICEHIGH= before the DOS=UMB command is misleading. Also, if a future version of DOS executes the UMB portion of the DOS= command with the first DOS=HIGH line, UMB support may not be present yet, and the command could fail without displaying an error message. Although this particular series of commands seems to work, other arrangements and commands may cause problems. Because there is nothing to gain from this type of arrangement, avoid it. Use one DOS= line in your CONFIG.SYS, located directly after the lines that load HIMEM.SYS and EMM386.EXE, and insert blank lines to make logical groups of commands stand out.

```
DEVICE=C:\DOS\HIMEM.SYS
DEVICE=C:\DOS\EMM386.EXE  RAM
DOS=HIGH,UMB

BUFFERS=20
FILES=50
LASTDRIVE=Z
SWITCHES=/W

DEVICEHIGH=C:\DOS\ANSI.SYS
DEVICEHIGH=C:\DOS\RAMDRIVE.SYS
```

You probably will agree that this example is much easier to read and understand than the one before it.

Messages

`HMA not available: Loading DOS low`

Warning: You specified DOS=HIGH, but DOS was unable to load into the HMA. Typically, this is because the DEVICE=C:\DOS\HIMEM.SYS line in your CONFIG.SYS is not present or is after the DOS=HIGH line. Less likely causes are that the HMA is already in use or that HIMEM was unable to gain control of the A20 line.

See Also

DEVICEHIGH=, EMM386.EXE, HIMEM.SYS, and LH (or LOADHIGH)

Chapter 18, "Configuring Your Computer"

DOSKEY

5.0 and later—External

DOSKEY enhances the usability of the DOS command line. It adds standard editing capabilities and the capability to recall recently used command lines. Finally, it has fairly extensive macro capabilities, with which you can create command aliases or fast batch files. When DOSKEY is first run, it loads itself into memory and remains there until you reboot your computer.

Syntax

DOSKEY /REINSTALL /BUFSIZE=*size* /MACROS /HISTORY /INSERT /OVERSTRIKE *macroname=text ...*

or

DOSKEY /REINSTALL /BUFSIZE=*size* /M /H /INSERT /OVERSTRIKE *macroname=text ...*

Parameters and Switches

/REINSTALL — Installs a new copy of Doskey even if a copy already is installed. This is the only way to resize the Doskey buffer without restarting your computer, but the memory used by the previous copy of Doskey will be wasted. This clears the Doskey buffer.

/BUFSIZE=*size* — The size of the buffer, in bytes, that Doskey uses to store macros and command lines. The default is 512, and the minimum is 256. Increasing or decreasing the buffer size affects how much memory Doskey requires when loaded.

/MACROS — Displays a list of the Doskey macros you have defined. You can redirect output by using the redirection symbol, >. This switch can be abbreviated as /M.

/HISTORY — Displays a list of all commands currently stored by Doskey. You can redirect output by using the redirection symbol, >. This switch can be abbreviated as /H.

/INSERT — Inserts new text into the command line (insert mode on). The default is /OVERSTRIKE. Pressing the Insert key toggles between insert and overstrike modes.

/OVERSTRIKE	New text overwrites old text on the command line (overstrike mode on). This is the default setting. Pressing the Insert key toggles between insert and overstrike modes.
macroname	The name of the macro that you want to define.
text	The commands that you want DOS to execute when you type *macroname* at a DOS command prompt. If *text* is null, the definition of *macroname* is deleted.
...	Indicates that you can enter as many *macroname=text* definitions as will fit into the current command line. (DOS is limited to 127 characters in a single command line.)

Notes

1. Ordinarily, DOS remembers the last command you typed at the command line. With Doskey, however, DOS can store a history of commands in memory. The number of commands retained in memory depends on the size of the buffer (normally 512 bytes). When the buffer is full, Doskey eliminates the oldest command to make room for the new command. The buffer contains macros and the history of commands.

2. You can press several keys to recall a command in the history. In addition, there are many keys and key combinations for editing a command on the command line. These keys and their functions are listed in Appendix D, "DOS and DOS Utility Programs' Keyboard Commands."

3. Doskey enables you to create macros. A macro, like a batch file, performs one or more DOS commands assigned to a specific name. After you type the name of a macro and press Enter, the macro executes the commands assigned to the macro name. When you create a macro, you can use the following special symbols:

Code	Description
$g or $G	Redirects output; use instead of >
gg or GG	Adds to an output file; use instead of >>

Code	Description
$l or $L	Redirects input; use instead of <
$b or $B	For piping; use instead of ¦
$t or $T	Separates macro commands
$$	Places the dollar sign in the command line
$1 through $9	Replaceable parameters; same as %1 through %9 in a batch file
$*	Replaceable parameter that represents everything typed in the command line after the macro name

When you create a macro, you can include any valid DOS command, including the name of a batch file. You can start a batch file from a macro, but you cannot start a macro from a batch file.

Examples

With Doskey installed, you can easily turn the last few DOS commands that you typed into a batch file. Simply ask Doskey to display the contents of the command-line history buffer and redirect the output to a file as follows:

```
DOSKEY /HISTORY > MYHIST.BAT
```

Next, load MYHIST.BAT into an ASCII editor such as EDIT, and remove any command lines that you don't need.

To define a macro, enter the name of the macro followed by the commands you want executed. Separate the macro name from the commands with an equal sign. For example, the following creates a macro named CDD that changes the current drive and the current directory:

```
DOSKEY CDD=$1: $T CD $2
```

After the CDD macro is defined, you could enter the following command at the DOS prompt to make drive D the current drive and \MYSTUFF the current directory on drive D:

```
C:\>CDD D \MYSTUFF
```

When the preceding command is executed, the CDD macro runs and executes the following DOS commands:

```
C:\>D:
D:\>CD \MYSTUFF
D:\MYSTUFF>
```

Messages

`Cannot change BUFSIZE`

Error: You cannot change the Doskey buffer unless you also use the REINSTALL switch, which clears the buffer.

`Insufficient memory to store macro.`
`Use the DOSKEY command with the /BUFSIZE switch to increase available memory.`

Warning: Your Doskey macros have filled the total space set aside for them. You must enlarge the memory area for macros (the default is 512 bytes) by using the BUFSIZE switch (and the REINSTALL switch) before you can enter any new macros. Using REINSTALL clears the buffer.

`Invalid macro definition`

Error: You entered an illegal character or command with Doskey or attempted to create a Doskey macro with an illegal definition. This message appears, for example, if you use a GOTO command in a DOSKey macro. Correct any errors and carefully retype the macro.

See Also

Chapter 17, "Mastering Doskey and Macros" and Appendix D, "DOS and DOS Utility Programs' Keyboard Commands"

DOSSHELL — 4.0 to 6.0—External

The DOSSHELL command starts the DOSShell program, which is a full-screen graphical shell program that provides an alternative to using the traditional DOS command line. DOSShell is not included in the standard DOS 6.2 package, but is available on the DOS 6.2 Supplemental disk.

Syntax

DOSSHELL /B /T:*screen* /G:*screen*

Parameters and Switches

/B — Starts the DOS Shell in black-and-white mode rather than in color.

/T:*screen* — Displays the DOS Shell in text mode, using the resolution described by *screen*. (See the screen table below.) You cannot specify /T:*screen* with /G:*screen*.

/G:*screen* — Displays the DOS Shell in graphics mode, using the resolution described by *screen*. (See the following table.) You cannot specify /G:*screen* with /T:*screen*.

Switch	Monochrome or CGA	EGA	VGA
/T:L	25 lines	25 lines	25 lines
/T:M		43 lines	43 lines
/T:M1		43 lines	43 lines
/T:M2		43 lines	50 lines
/T:H		43 lines	43 lines
/T:H1		43 lines	43 lines
/T:H2		43 lines	50 lines
/G:L	25 lines	25 lines	25 lines
/G:M		43 lines	30 lines
/G:M1		43 lines	30 lines
/G:M2		43 lines	34 lines
/G:H		43 lines	43 lines
/G:H1		43 lines	43 lines
/G:H2		43 lines	60 lines

Notes

1. When you start the DOS Shell without parameters, it uses the display and color settings from the last time DOSSHELL was run. To use a different display mode, specify a /T:*screen* or /G:*screen* parameter when you start the program. DOS Shell records these settings in the DOSSHELL.INI file.

2. At least 384K of free conventional memory are required to start the DOS Shell.

3. Each time you start the DOS Shell, it searches the disk for directories and files in order to display up-to-date listings in file and tree windows. If you have a large hard disk or a complicated directory structure, this may take a few seconds.

4. Do not start Microsoft Windows from the DOS Shell. If you need to run both programs, start Microsoft Windows first, and then run the DOS Shell from Windows.

5. Your DOSSHELL settings are preserved in your DOSSHELL.INI file. The DOS 6.0 installation does not overwrite or modify this file if it exists, which may produce inconsistencies on your system (references to BACKUP rather than to MSBACKUP, for example). You can avoid these inconsistencies by renaming DOSSHELL.INI before you install DOS 6.0 and then manually editing changes from your renamed DOSSHELL.INI into your new DOSSHELL.INI.

   When the DOS 6.0 Setup program installs DOSSHELL, it expands one of three files (CGA.IN_ for CGA monitors, EGA.IN_ for EGA and VGA monitors, or MONO.IN_ for monochrome monitors) from the DOS 6.0 distribution disks and renames it DOSSHELL.INI. To restore your DOS Shell configuration to its defaults, you can expand one of these three files (with EXPAND) and replace your present copy of DOSSHELL.INI with it.

6. By defining an environment variable named DOSSHELL, you can specify where you would like DOSSHELL.INI to be located. For instance, to store the DOSSHELL.INI file in the C:\DOS\MSDOSDATA subdirectory, you could add the following SET command to your AUTOEXEC.BAT file.

   ```
   SET DOSSHELL=C:\DOS\MSDOSDATA
   ```

   If no environment variable named DOSSHELL is defined, DOS Shell searches for its settings file in the directory that contains DOSSHELL.EXE. If DOSSHELL.INI cannot be found, a new one is created.

7. DOS Shell creates any temporary files, including task swapping files, in the subdirectory pointed to by the TEMP environment variable if it is

defined. If TEMP isn't defined, temporary files are created in the subdirectory that contains DOSSHELL.EXE.

8. If you are running POWER, the clock displayed in the DOS Shell program may slow down or stop completely. DOS Shell uses a timer to update the onscreen clock, and POWER slows the timer down. Note that only the onscreen clock displayed by DOS Shell is affected. The MS-DOS system clock continues to reflect the correct time.

9. In DOS 4.0, DOS Shell was started by a batch file that recorded all the configuration information needed to run DOS Shell on your system. This version of the DOS Shell was very different from later versions, and most of the information presented here doesn't apply to it.

Examples

To start the DOS Shell in the default screen mode, enter the following:

```
DOSSHELL
```

To start the DOS Shell in black-and-white mode, enter the following:

```
DOSSHELL /B
```

Use this command if you have a black-and-white monitor or a laptop or notebook computer with an LCD screen.

Messages

`Not enough memory to run DOSSHELL`

Error: Not enough conventional memory is available to start DOSSHELL. The DOS Shell program requires 384K of free conventional RAM to load into memory. You may have too many resident programs (TSRs) loaded into memory, in which case you should attempt to remove any that you don't need. You may be trying to start DOSSHELL from a secondary copy of the command processor launched from another program, in which case you should type EXIT to return to your program, quit the program, and then
run DOSSHELL.

`Not enough free conventional memory to run program`

or

`Not enough free extended memory to run program`

Either of these messages can appear when you try to start a program from the DOS Shell without sufficient available memory. Remove TSRs from memory to free conventional memory. If you are short of extended memory, use MEM /C to see what programs are using extended memory in your computer. Often you can make more extended memory available by decreasing the size of your SMARTDRV disk cache or by allocating less to use as expanded memory with EMM386.

```
Unable to run specified program.
Too many tasks running.
```

Error: You have already opened the maximum number of tasks for your configuration. Close one or more of open tasks.

```
Unable to run specified program.
```

Error: The program that you tried to start cannot be started correctly. You may have specified the program name incorrectly.

```
You cannot quit MS-DOS Shell with programs in the Active Task List; quit
those programs first.
```

Error: You tried to exit the DOS Shell while at least one program was switched. Exit the switched program, and then quit the DOS Shell.

See Also

Chapter 4, "Using the DOS Shell"

DRIVER.SYS (device driver)

3.2 and later—External

The DRIVER.SYS device driver can be used to create an additional drive letter for a floppy disk drive or set the characteristics of a floppy disk drive. For instance, if an external floppy drive is attached to your computer, you can use DRIVER.SYS (or DRIVPARM=) to tell DOS to assign a drive letter to the drive. A more common use is to create a new drive letter—perhaps one with different characteristics—for a drive.

Syntax

DEVICE=*drive:\path***DRIVER.SYS** **/D:*num*** /C /F:*type* /H:*heads* /S:*sectors* /T:*tracks*

or

DEVICEHIGH=*drive:\path***DRIVER.SYS** **/D:*num*** /C /F:*type* /H:*heads* /S:*sectors* /T:*tracks*

Parameters and Switches

drive:\path Enter the full path to the DRIVER.SYS file on your system. Setup places the DRIVER.SYS file in the C:\DOS subdirectory by default. If the full path to DRIVER.SYS isn't specified, DOS looks for the file in the root directory of the start-up drive.

/D:*num* The physical drive number (*num*). Valid numbers are 0 to 127. DOS assigns floppy drive numbers sequentially, with the first floppy drive as 0, the second as 1, the third as 2, and so on. Note that if you have only one floppy disk drive installed, DOS assigns it both letters A and B, but it is still drive 0, not drive 1. This parameter is required, and must be the first parameter specified after the name and location of the DRIVER.SYS file.

/C Specifies that the drive has change line support. This means that the drive can signal DOS that the media in it may have been changed. Most newer floppy disk drives have change line support built in. Specifying the /C parameter can speed up access to your floppy drive.

/F:*type* The type of drive that is being accessed, where *type* is one of the values in the following table. If you omit this value, a default value of 2 (720K 3 1/2-inch) is assumed.

type	Floppy Drive Specifications	Heads (Sides)	Sectors per Track	Tracks per Head (Side)
0	Double-density 360K 5 1/4-inch floppy disk drive; includes 160K, 180K, 320K, and 360K formatted media sizes	2	9	40
1	High-density 1.2M 5 1/4-inch floppy disk drive	2	15	80
2	Double-density 720K 3 1/2-inch floppy disk drive	2	9	80
7	High-density 1.44M 3 1/2-inch floppy disk drive	2	18	80

(continues)

type	Floppy Drive Specifications	Heads (Sides)	Sectors per Track	Tracks per Head (Side)
9	Super high-density 2.88M 3 1/2-inch floppy disk drive	2	36	80

/H:*heads* The number of read/write heads (sides) that the drive has. Valid values are 1 to 99. The default value is 2.

/S:*sectors* The number of sectors per track for the drive's media. Valid values are 1 to 99. The default value depends on /F:*type* setting, or is 9 if /F:*type* is omitted. See the preceding table.

/T:*tracks* The number of tracks per side (head) for the drive's media. Valid values are 1 to 999. The default value depends on the /F:*type* setting, or is 80 if /F:*type* is omitted. See the preceding table.

Notes

1. DOS assigns drive letters in a specific order. A and B always refer to the first one or two floppy drives in the system. If the system has a hard disk, the primary partition is assigned the letter C. Next, any remaining hard disk partitions are assigned letters. After that, each DOS accessible block device driver listed in CONFIG.SYS is assigned a letter on a first come, first served basis. (If DoubleSpace is loaded, it modifies this assignment order by skipping four letters and then working backward. See DBLSPACE for more information.)

   For instance, if you have two floppy drives and one hard disk (with a single partition) and you include a single DRIVER.SYS line in your CONFIG.SYS, the letter D would be assigned. DRIVER.SYS displays a message informing you of the letter assigned when it is installed. (See the first message in the "Messages" section.)

2. Most newer floppy disk drives can signal the computer when their drive door has been opened. Because opening the door implies that the disk in the drive may have been changed, this feature is referred to as *change line support*. Unless you are installing a 360K 5 1/4-inch disk drive, the chances are good that your new floppy drive has change line support built in. Specifying the /C parameter can speed up DOS access to the drive.

3. MS-DOS 6 seems to have problems recognizing that the media in a drive has changed when the media does not have a volume serial number. Disks most likely to not have serial numbers are ones formatted by DOS versions before 4.0, preformatted disks, and disks formatted with some third-party utilities. This is a good reason to make sure that the hardware change line is working for your disk drive. If DOS is unaware that you have changed the disk in a floppy disk drive, it may write the wrong file allocation table (FAT) to the disk, destroying any data that was previously on it.

4. If you specify the /F:*type* parameter, you can omit the /H:*heads*, /S:*sectors*, and /T:*tracks* parameters, and vice versa. You may use any combination of these parameters; the last ones entered have precedence.

5. Many times, the DRIVER.SYS device driver is simpler and more flexible to use than DRIVPARM=, although both often achieve the same results. They can both configure logical drives, but only DRIVER.SYS can create a new one. DRIVPARM=, however, uses no additional memory in your system.

6. You cannot use DRIVER.SYS to reconfigure an existing drive to support a format it was not made for. For instance, DRIVER.SYS cannot be used to allow an older 360K 5 1/2-inch disk drive to read the newer 1.2M disks. DRIVER.SYS can instruct DOS to make use of only the capabilities that both DOS and the drive support.

Examples

Suppose that your system has two 5 1/4-inch disk drives and a hard disk. To configure an external 1.44M 3 1/2-inch floppy disk drive that you have attached to your system, enter a line such as the following in your CONFIG.SYS file:

```
DEVICE=C:\DOS\DRIVER.SYS  /D:2  /F:7
```

After loading, DRIVER.SYS displays the following message: `Loaded External Disk Driver for Drive D.`

Or, if your system has a single 1.44M 3 1/2-inch floppy and a hard drive, you might want to create an alias for the floppy drive so that you can format

720K disks without specifying any switches for FORMAT. To create a 720K alias for it, you might enter the following line in your CONFIG.SYS file:

```
DEVICEHIGH=C:\DOS\DRIVER.SYS /D:0 /F:2
```

As far as DOS is concerned, drive D refers to a 720K 3 1/2-inch floppy drive. Drives A and B are unchanged and refer to a 1.44M 3 1/2-inch floppy drive. All three drive letters refer to the same physical drive, but D has different characteristics than A and B.

Messages

`Loaded External Disk Driver for Drive` *`letter`*

Information: After installing DRIVER.SYS, DOS displays this message to tell you which drive letter has been assigned.

See Also

DRIVPARM=

DRIVPARM= 3.2 and later—Internal

DRIVPARM is an advanced command that defines the characteristics of an existing block device, such as a disk drive, and associates a drive letter with it. Normally, you use this command only when instructed to do so by the manufacturer of the drive you are installing. DRIVPARM= can be used only in your CONFIG.SYS file.

Syntax

DRIVPARM=/D:*num* /C /F:*type* /H:*heads* /I /N /S:*sectors* /T:*tracks*

Parameters and Switches

/D:*num*	The physical drive number (*num*). Valid numbers are 0 to 255, where drive A=0, drive B=1, drive C=2, and so on. This parameter is required and must be the first parameter on the command line.
/C	Specifies that the drive has change line support. This means that the drive can signal DOS that the media in it may have been changed. Most newer floppy disk drives have change line support built in. Specifying the /C parameter can speed up access to your floppy drive.

/F:*type*

The type of drive that is being accessed, where *type* is one of the values in the following table. If you omit this value, a default value of 2 (720K 3 1/2-inch) is used.

type	Drive Specifications
0	A double-density 360K 5 1/4-inch floppy disk drive; includes 160K, 180K, 320K, and 360K formatted media sized
1	A high-density 1.2M 5 1/4-inch floppy disk drive
2	A double-density 720K 3 1/2-inch floppy disk drive
5	A hard disk
6	A tape drive
7	A high-density 1.44M 3 1/2-inch floppy disk drive
8	A read-write optical disk drive
9	A super high-density 2.88M 3 1/2-inch floppy disk drive

Note that types 3 and 4, which formerly specified single-density and double-density 8-inch floppy disk drives, respectively, are no longer supported by MS-DOS.

/H:*heads*

The number of read/write heads (sides) that the drive has. Valid values are 1 to 99. The default value depends on the /F:*type* setting.

/I

Indicates that a 3 1/2-inch disk drive, which the ROM BIOS doesn't support, is attached to a standard floppy disk drive controller.

/N

Indicates that this drive uses nonremovable media. This switch is assumed if /F:5 (hard disk) is specified.

/S:*sectors*

The number of sectors per track for the drive's media. Valid values are 1 to 99. The default value depends on the /F:*type* setting.

/T:*tracks* The number of tracks per side (head) for the drive's media. Valid values are 1 to 999. The default value depends on the /F:*type* setting.

Notes

1. In many cases, the DRIVER.SYS device driver is simpler and more flexible to use than DRIVPARM=, although both often achieve the same results. They can both configure logical drives, but only DRIVER.SYS can create a new one. However, DRIVPARM= uses no additional memory in your system.

2. In most cases, the DRIVPARM= line should come immediately after the line that loads the device driver for the drive you are configuring. Normally, the instructions for installing the drive's device driver tell you which parameters to use with DRIVPARM=. An exception is when you are adding support for a 3 1/2-inch floppy drive attached to a standard floppy controller, which requires no device driver.

3. Most newer floppy disk drives can signal the computer when their drive door has been opened. Because opening the door implies that the disk in the drive may have been changed, this feature is referred to as *change line support.* Unless you are installing a 360K 5 1/4-inch disk drive, the chances are good that your new floppy drive has change line support built in. Specifying the /C parameter can speed up DOS access to the drive.

4. MS-DOS 6 seems to have problems recognizing that the media in a drive has changed when the media does not have a volume serial number. Disks most likely to not have serial numbers are ones formatted by DOS versions before 4.0, preformatted disks, and disks formatted with some third-party utilities. This is a good reason to make sure that the hardware change line is working for your disk drive. If DOS is unaware that you have changed the disk in a floppy disk drive, it may write the wrong file allocation table (FAT) to the disk, destroying any data that was previously on it.

5. Do not use DRIVPARM= unless the installation instructions for the hardware or software you are installing in your system tells you to do so. Normally, DRIVPARM= can be used to only support additions to your system rather than reconfigure existing hardware or software.

6. You cannot use DRIVER.SYS to reconfigure an existing drive to support a format it was not made for. For instance, DRIVER.SYS cannot be used to allow an older 360K 5 1/2-inch disk drive to read the newer 1.2M disks. DRIVER.SYS can instruct DOS to make use of only the capabilities that both DOS and the drive support.

Examples

Probably the most common use of the DRIVPARM= command is to create a drive letter for a 3 1/2-inch floppy disk drive that is not supported by the ROM BIOS in that computer. The following line defines the 3 1/2-inch 1.44M floppy disk drive as drive D (3), using the default values for heads, sectors, and tracks:

```
DRIVPARM=/D:3 /F:7 /I
```

If the floppy disk drive was the second one in your system and only supported 720K media, you would use the following line:

```
DRIVPARM=/D:1 /I
```

Note that you can omit the /F:2 because, in this case, the default value is correct. If you ran the preceding command on a system in which the second floppy drive was a 1.44M 3 1/2-inch drive, you could read only 720K disks; you could not read 1.44M disks.

See Also

DRIVER.SYS

ECHO

2.0 and later—Internal

The ECHO command has two functions. First, you can use it to display messages on-screen from a batch file. Second, you can use ECHO to control whether DOS displays on-screen each command line from the batch file before executing the command line.

Syntax

To display a message, use the following format:

ECHO message

To turn on or off the display of commands and other batch-command messages, use the following format:

ECHO *onoff*

To see the status of ECHO, use the following format:

ECHO

Parameters and Switches

message The text of the message to be displayed on-screen.

onoff Specifies whether or not each command line in the batch file is displayed before being executed. ECHO ON turns on the display of command lines. ECHO OFF turns off the display of command lines. Note that this has no effect on the output generated by a command, only on the display of the command line that DOS is about to execute.

Notes

1. Setting ECHO ON or OFF only controls the display of command lines from the batch file before they are executed. It has no effect on the output generated by a DOS command. The message generated by the PAUSE command, `Press any key to continue...`, and the message generated by the COPY command, `1 file(s) copied`, are examples of output generated by a command. They are not suppressed by ECHO OFF.

2. When ECHO is ON, DOS displays each command line before executing it. This can be handy when you are debugging a batch file. After the batch file is working correctly, you generally want to include an ECHO OFF command at the beginning of the batch file to suppress echoing command lines. Turning ECHO OFF can speed up the batch file a little as well.

3. You can suppress the display of a single batch file line by typing **@** as the first character in the line. The command itself is executed, but the command line is not displayed. For example, when you type the line **@ECHO OFF**, the command line ECHO OFF is not displayed, but the ECHO flag is set to OFF.

4. To display a blank line on-screen, enter the command ECHO followed by a period (with no intervening spaces) in your batch file. This is a

special use for the ECHO command and can make your batch file screen output more attractive and readable.

5. You cannot display pipe characters (¦) or redirection symbols (< or >) in an ECHO message. Redirection symbols are intercepted by the parser and are acted on.

6. DOS starts every batch file with ECHO ON. The ECHO setting (ON or OFF) remains in effect until DOS completes batch processing or encounters another ECHO ON or ECHO OFF command. If one batch file invokes another, the ECHO setting from the first batch file remains in effect. When DOS returns control to the command line, ECHO is restored to the ON state.

7. If you issue an ECHO OFF command at the DOS prompt, the DOS prompt will not be displayed. You can still see the commands you are entering, however. To restore the DOS prompt, enter ECHO ON.

8. You can use ECHO to send ANSI commands to your screen. If ANSI.SYS is active in memory, and the message displayed by ECHO contains legal ANSI commands, they will be acted on rather than displayed. You can use this technique to display very complex, multicolored screens from a batch file. To enter ANSI commands into your batch file, you need an editor that allows you to enter Escape characters (ASCII 27) into the text.

9. To suppress the output of a command, use I/O redirection to the null device (NUL). For example, to suppress the `1 file(s) copied` message generated by the COPY command, use the following format:

   COPY file1.ext file2.ext > NUL

   The command output is sent to the null device instead of to the console, so it is not displayed on-screen.

Trap

If you redirect the output of a program that is going to remain resident in memory (TSR), you may waste one of the file handles that DOS has available for programs to use. When you redirect the output of a program to the NUL device, the NUL device is assigned a file handle that isn't released until the program terminates. In the case of resident programs, this file handle often remains unavailable until you restart DOS. This can cause problems if you are in the habit of suppressing the output of resident programs loaded in your AUTOEXEC.BAT file.

Examples

It is very common for a batch file to begin with the following line:

```
@ECHO OFF
```

This command turns ECHO OFF at the beginning of the batch file, and the at sign (@) tells DOS not to display the ECHO OFF command line itself. By starting a batch file with this command, no unnecessary screen output is displayed.

Another very common use for ECHO is to explain the inclusion of a PAUSE command in a batch file. For example, to instruct the user to insert a particular floppy disk in drive B, include the following lines in a batch file:

```
ECHO Insert the Working Backup disk in drive B:
ECHO.
ECHO Press Ctrl-Break to abort the backup, or
PAUSE
```

Assuming that ECHO is OFF when these commands are executed, the following messages are displayed:

```
Insert the Working Backup disk in drive B:

Press Ctrl-Break to abort the backup, or
Press any key to continue...
```

Note that the PAUSE message is anticipated in the ECHO messages. If you use the CHOICE command instead, you can control all the text that is displayed on-screen.

To display a menu, you can use ECHO to display a screenful of messages. Then you can let the user pick an item from the list with the CHOICE command, as the following lines demonstrate:

```
@ECHO OFF
CLS
ECHO.
ECHO F  First action
ECHO S  Second action
ECHO T  Third action
ECHO.
CHOICE /C:FST "Choose an action "
```

The CLS command is often used with ECHO to control the amount of distracting information that is left behind on the screen by other commands. Note that the `ECHO.` (ECHO period) command is used to display blank lines.

(Blank lines included in a batch file are ignored by DOS and will not be displayed on-screen.)

See Also

@, ANSI.SYS, CHOICE, CLS, and PAUSE

Chapter 16, "Understanding Batch Files"

EDIT

5.0 and later—External

The EDIT command activates the DOS full-screen ASCII text-file editor. EDIT is very handy for writing batch files or making changes to your AUTOEXEC.BAT or CONFIG.SYS file. Although limited to working on one file at a time, EDIT offers block copy and move operations as well as search and replace features. EDIT uses the editor built into QBASIC.EXE; so to use EDIT, QBASIC.EXE must be in one of the subdirectories listed in your PATH variable.

Syntax

EDIT *pathname* /B /G /H /NOHI

Parameters and Switches

pathname	The file you want EDIT to load. If no drive is specified, the current drive is assumed. If no subdirectory path is specified, the current directory is assumed. Wildcards are not allowed.
/B	Specifies that EDIT should use colors more appropriate for a black-and-white (monochrome) or LCD display.
/G	Specifies that EDIT should use the fastest screen-updating method for a CGA monitor. Don't specify the /G switch if you see "snow" on your monitor.
/H	Specifies that EDIT should display 43 lines on an EGA monitor or 50 lines on a VGA monitor.
/NOHI	Specifies that EDIT should limit itself to 8 colors rather than 16.

See Also

Chapter 15, "Using the DOS Editor"

EDLIN

1.0 to 5.0—External

Edit an ASCII text file

EDLIN is an old-fashioned, line-oriented text editor that is much more awkward to use than EDIT. If you have anything else to use for editing text files, you probably want to avoid using EDLIN. The only good thing about EDLIN is that the program file is small. EDLIN is no longer distributed with the standard DOS package, but is available on the DOS 6 Supplemental Disk. Instructions for using EDLIN are in the COMMANDS.TXT file included on the Supplemental Disk.

See Also

EDIT

EGA.SYS (device driver)

5.0 and later—External

Because of the way EGA display adapters are made, they present certain problems for task switching software. EGA.SYS attempts to solve these problems. If you have an EGA display and use the task switching functions of the DOS Shell program, you need to load EGA.SYS. You must load EGA.SYS in either a DEVICE= or DEVICEHIGH= statement in your CONFIG.SYS file.

Syntax

DEVICE=*drive:\path***EGA.SYS**

or

DEVICEHIGH=*drive:\path***EGA.SYS**

Parameters and Switches

drive:\path — The full path to the EGA.SYS file on your system. Setup places the EGA.SYS file in the C:\DOS subdirectory by default. If the full path to EGA.SYS isn't specified, DOS looks for the file in the root directory of the start-up drive.

Notes

1. You can use EGA.SYS only if your system uses an EGA display. With any other type of display, EGA.SYS will not load into memory.

2. In addition to being required by the task swapper in DOS Shell, EGA.SYS may be required by Microsoft Windows. Third-party task switching software often requires the assistance of EGA.SYS or a similar driver that it provides. You can have (and need) only one EGA.SYS type driver loaded at a time.

3. If you have an EGA display and you use the Microsoft Mouse driver, you may be able to save some memory by loading EGA.SYS before loading your mouse driver into memory. Many of the functions in EGA.SYS are duplicated in the Microsoft Mouse driver, and if it finds EGA support already in place, the mouse driver won't load those functions.

Examples

To load the EGA.SYS device driver into upper memory, you might add the following line to your CONFIG.SYS file.

```
DEVICEHIGH=C:\DOS\EGA.SYS
```

See Also

DOSSHELL and MOUSE

EMM386

5.0 and later—External

The EMM386 command allows you to control the use of expanded memory (EMS) and upper memory blocks (UMBs) in a computer with an 80386SX or higher CPU. Before you can run EMM386 from the DOS command line, you must load the EMM386.EXE device driver into memory with a DEVICE= statement in your CONFIG.SYS file. After the EMM386.EXE device driver is loaded into memory, you can use EMM386 from the DOS command line to view the status of EMS and UMB memory and turn various features on and off.

Syntax

EMM386 *onoffauto* W=*onoff*

Parameters and Switches

onoffauto Enables EMM386.EXE (ON), disables it (OFF), or enables it to provide expanded memory and upper memory block support only when a program requests it (AUTO). The default is ON.

W=*onoff* Enables (W=ON) or disables (W=OFF) support for the Weitek coprocessor. The default is *W=OFF*.

Notes

1. Before you can use EMM386.EXE from the command line, you must install EMM386 as a device driver in CONFIG.SYS.
2. Entering EMM386 with no parameters causes a status report of EMS and UMB memory use to display.
3. EMM386 only honors a request to turn off when no EMS or UMB memory is in use. In other words, you can't use the OFF parameter if you are loading any programs into upper memory.
4. The high memory area (HMA) must be available to enable a Weitek coprocessor. If DOS is loaded into HMA by a DOS=HIGH in your CONFIG.SYS file, you may not be able to enable the Weitek coprocessor.

See Also

EMM386.EXE

"Using Expanded Memory and EMM386.EXE" in Chapter 18

EMM386.EXE (device driver)

5.0 and later—External

The EMM386.EXE device driver can convert extended memory (XMS) into LIM 4.0-compatible expanded memory (EMS) on a computer with an 80386SX or higher CPU. EMM386.EXE can also create upper memory blocks (UMBs), which DOS can use to load other device drivers and programs into with the DEVICEHIGH= and LOADHIGH commands, respectively. EMM386.EXE requires that an XMS-compatible memory manager, such as HIMEM.SYS, be present before EMM386.EXE will load into memory. EMM386.EXE must be loaded in a DEVICE= statement in your CONFIG.SYS file.

Syntax

DEVICE=*drive:\path***EMM386.EXE** *onoffauto ramval* MIN=*size* W=*onoff* M*s* FRAME=*xxxx* /P*yyyy* /P*n*=*yyyy* X=*mmmm-nnnn* I=*mmmm-nnnn* B=*zzzz* L=*xmsmem* A=*regs* H=*hhh* D=*nnn* RAM=*mmmm-nnnn* NOEMS NOVCPI HIGHSCAN VERBOSE WIN=*mmmm-nnnn* NOHI ROM=*mmmm-nnnn* NOMOVEXBDA ALTBOOT

Parameters and Switches

drive:\path
: The full path to the EMM386.EXE file on your system. By default, Setup places the EMM386.EXE file in the C:\DOS subdirectory. If the full path to EMM386.EXE isn't specified, DOS looks for the file in the root directory of the start-up drive.

onoffauto
: Enables EMM386.EXE (ON), disables it (OFF), or enables it to provide expanded memory and upper memory block support only when a program requests it (AUTO). The default is ON.

ramval
: Represents the maximum amount of RAM, in kilobytes, to be assigned as EMS 4.0/Virtual Control Program Interface (VCPI) memory. Enter a value ranging from 64, to the smaller of 32768 or the amount of extended memory available when EMM386.EXE is loaded. Any number that you enter is rounded down to the nearest multiple of 16. The default is 0 if NOEMS is specified. Otherwise, all available extended memory is used as EMS/VCPI memory.

MIN=*size*
: (DOS 6 and later) The minimum amount of RAM (in kilobytes) that EMM386 is guaranteed to provide. Enter a value ranging from 0 to the value of *ramval*. The default is 0 if *NOEMS* is specified; otherwise it is 256. If *size* is greater than *ramval*, *size* is used.

W=*onoff*
: Enables (W=ON) or disables (W=OFF) support for the Weitek coprocessor. The default is *W=OFF*.

M*s*
: The beginning address of the EMS page frame. *s* is a number that represents the beginning address. You cannot combine the M*s* parameter with the

/FRAME=*xxxx* or the /P*yyyy* parameters. The numbers and associated hexadecimal addresses are as follows:

Ms	Memory Address	Ms	Memory Address
M1	C000	M8	DC00
M2	C400	M9	E000
M3	C800	M10*	8000
M4	CC00	M11*	8400
M5	D000	M12*	8800
M6	D400	M13*	8C00

**Use only in computers with at least 512K of memory.*

FRAME=*xxxx*

A hexadecimal address from 8000 through 9000, and C000 through E000 in increments of 400 hexadecimal or *NONE*. The latter disables the page frame and may cause programs that require expanded memory to fail. You cannot combine the FRAME=*xxxx* parameter with the M*s* or /P*yyyy* parameters.

/P*yyyy*

A hexadecimal address from 8000 through 9000, and C000 through E000 in increments of 400 hexadecimal. You cannot combine the /P*yyyy* parameter with the M*s* or FRAME=*xxxx* parameters.

P*n*=*yyyy*

Defines an address for a page segment. *n* represents the page and can have a value of 0 through 255. *yyyy* is a hexadecimal address from 8000 through 9000, and C000 through E000 in increments of 400 hexadecimal. To remain compatible with EMS 3.2, P0 through P3 must be contiguous addresses. You cannot specify P0 through P3 with this option if you use the M*s*, FRAME=*xxxx*, or /P*yyyy* parameters.

X=*mmmm-nnnn*

A range of memory that should not be used for an EMS page frame or UMB space. *mmmm* and *nnnn* can have values ranging from A000H through FFFFH and are rounded down to the nearest 4K boundary. The X switch overrides the I switch if their ranges overlap.

I=*mmmm-nnnn* A range of memory that can be used for an EMS page frame or UMB space. *mmmm* and *nnnn* can have values ranging from A000H through FFFFH and are rounded down to the nearest 4K boundary. The X switch overrides the I switch if their ranges overlap.

B=*zzzz* The lowest address to use for bank switching (swapping of 16K pages). *zzzz* can have a value from 1000H through 4000H. The default is 4000H.

L=*xmsmem* The number of kilobytes that must remain as extended memory instead of being converted to EMS memory. The default is 0. For one megabyte of memory to remain as extended memory, use L=1024.

A=*regs* Allocates the number of fast alternative register sets that EMM386.EXE may use (for multitasking). *regs* can have a value from 0 through 254. The default is 7. Each alternative register set adds about 200 bytes to the size of EMM386.EXE in memory.

H=*hhh* Enables you to change the number of handles EMM386.EXE can use. *hhh* can have a value from 2 to 255. The default is 64.

D=*nnn* The amount of memory (in kilobytes) reserved for DMA (buffered direct-memory access). This value should cover the largest non-floppy transfer. *nnn* can have a value from 16 through 256. The default is 32.

RAM=*mmmm-nnnn* A range of memory to be used for UMBs. If you specify RAM without a value, EMM386.EXE allocates all available extended memory, an EMS page frame is established in upper memory, and all remaining upper memory space is converted to UMBs.

NOEMS Specifies that access to UMBs be provided, but not for expanded memory; that is, an EMS page frame is prohibited.

NOVCPI	(DOS 6.0 and later) Disables support for VCPI applications. Must be used with NOEMS, in which case *ramval* and MIN are ignored.
HIGHSCAN	(DOS 6.0 and later) Causes EMM386.EXE to be more aggressive in scanning upper memory for UMBs. Your computer may stop responding if you use this switch.
VERBOSE	(DOS 6.0 and later) Directs EMM386.EXE to display status and error messages when DOS boots. This switch can be abbreviated as V. (You can also get status and error messages by holding down the Alt key while DOS boots.)
V	(DOS 6.0 and later) Same as VERBOSE (see preceding entry).
WIN=*mmmm-nnnn*	(DOS 6.0 and later) Reserves the specified memory address range for Microsoft Windows, and prevents EMM386.EXE from using that area of memory. *mmmm* and *nnnn* can have values ranging from A000H through FFFFH and are rounded down to the nearest 4K boundary. The X switch overrides the WIN switch if their ranges overlap. The WIN switch overrides the RAM, ROM, and I switches if their ranges overlap.
NOHI	(DOS 6.0 and later) Prevents EMM386.EXE from loading any part of itself into upper memory. Normally, EMM386.EXE uses about 5K of upper memory for itself. Specifying this switch makes more UMB space available but increases the size of EMM386.EXE in conventional memory.
ROM=*mmmm-nnnn*	(DOS 6.0 and later) A range of memory for shadow RAM, which is read-only memory (ROM) copied into faster RAM. *mmmm* and *nnnn* can have values ranging from A000H through FFFFH and are rounded down to the nearest 4K boundary.
NOMOVEXBDA	(DOS 6.0 and later) Prevents EMM386.EXE from moving the extended BIOS data from conventional memory to upper memory.

ALTBOOT (DOS 6 and later) Directs EMM386.EXE to use a different method of restarting your computer when you press Ctrl-Alt-Del. Specify this parameter only if your computer stops responding or exhibits other unusual behavior when EMM386.EXE is loaded into memory and you press Ctrl-Alt-Del.

Notes

1. EMM386.EXE works only on 80386, 80386SX, and higher systems.
2. HIMEM.SYS must be installed as a device driver in CONFIG.SYS before EMM386.EXE.
3. You cannot use the DEVICEHIGH= command to load EMM386.EXE into memory. EMM386.EXE is required to provide the UMBs that the DEVICEHIGH= command loads device drivers into. EMM386.EXE does attempt to minimize its impact on conventional memory when it loads, using only about 3K in most cases. To prevent EMM386.EXE from loading parts of itself into upper memory, specify the NOHI parameter.
4. To create UMBs, you must include the RAM or NOEMS parameters, and you must include at least DOS=UMB in CONFIG.SYS.
5. Before you can use EMM386 from the command line, you must install EMM386.EXE as a device driver in CONFIG.SYS.
6. Any DEVICEHIGH= commands in CONFIG.SYS must come after the DEVICE=HIMEM.SYS and DEVICE=EMM386.EXE RAM (or NOEMS) commands.
7. When EMM386.EXE is used with Microsoft Windows 3.1, the I, X, NOEMS, M*s*, FRAME, and P*yyyy* switches override the EMMINCLUDE, EMMEXCLUDE, and EMMPAGEFRAME settings in the Windows SYSTEM.INI file.
8. SMARTDRV double-buffering may be required before DEVICEHIGH= commands which load installable device drivers that use expanded memory.
9. When EMM386.EXE is not supplying expanded memory, non-VCPI-compliant programs can run (for example, Microsoft Windows 3.0 in Standard mode).

10. The high memory area (HMA) must be available to enable a Weitek coprocessor. If DOS is loaded into HMA by a DOS=HIGH in your CONFIG.SYS file, you may not be able to enable the Weitek coprocessor.

See Also

DEVICE= and HIMEM.SYS

"Using Expanded Memory and EMM386.EXE" in Chapter 18

ERASE (see DEL)

ERASE is an alternate name for the DEL command. For information on using the DEL or ERASE command, see the entry for DEL in this command reference.

EXE2BIN

1.1 to 5.0—External

The EXE2BIN command changes appropriately formatted .EXE files to .BIN or .COM files. EXE2BIN is a programmer's utility; it is provided as a courtesy for those who have compilers that cannot create a memory-image file directly. Most people never find an occasion to use this program. EXE2BIN is included with the DOS 6.0 Supplemental Disk, not in the standard DOS 6.0 package.

Syntax

EXE2BIN ***exe_file*** *binary_file*

Parameters and Switches

exe_file The .EXE file to be converted into a memory-image file. If no drive is specified, the current drive is assumed. If no subdirectory path is specified, the current subdirectory is assumed. A file name is required, but if you don't specify an extension, .EXE is assumed. Wildcards are not allowed.

binary_file The name of the memory-image file that will be created. If no drive is specified, the current drive is assumed. If no subdirectory path is specified, the current subdirectory is assumed. If no file name is specified, the file name designated in ***exe_file*** is used. If no extension is specified, a BIN extension is added.

Notes

1. EXE2BIN is a programming utility that converts .EXE (executable) program files to .COM or .BIN (memory-image) files. The resulting program consumes less disk space and loads slightly faster. Unless you use a compiler-based programming language, you probably will never use this command.

2. Before EXE2BIN converts an .EXE file to memory-image format, a number of requirements have to be met. In most cases, a program has to be written with this transformation in mind. You cannot convert the typical .EXE program file using EXE2BIN.

EXIT

2.0 and later—Internal

You can use EXIT to remove a temporary copy of COMMAND.COM from memory. Typically, you use this command to return to an application program that allows you access to the DOS prompt while it's running. EXIT can only remove temporary copies of COMMAND.COM; it cannot accidentally remove the permanent copy that is loaded when your computer starts up.

Syntax

EXIT

Notes

1. EXIT has no effect on a copy of COMMAND.COM loaded with the /P switch. Normally, you load COMMAND.COM with the /P switch only in the SHELL= command in your CONFIG.SYS file. Any additional copies that you run (from a batch file, for example) can be removed from memory with the EXIT command.

2. EXIT is used to close a DOS window in Microsoft Windows. It terminates the temporary copy of COMMAND.COM that Windows launched in order to create the DOS window.

See Also

COMMAND

"Using EXIT to Leave the Current Copy of the Command Processor" in Chapter 12

EXPAND

5.0 and later—External

You can use the EXPAND command to copy a compressed, unusable file from the DOS distribution disks to an uncompressed, usable form.

Syntax

EXPAND *source1 source2 ... destination*

Parameters and Switches

source1 — The name of the compressed source file. If no drive is provided, the current drive is assumed. If no subdirectory path is provided, the current subdirectory is assumed. If this parameter is omitted, you are prompted for the source and destination. Wildcards are not allowed.

source2 — Additional compressed source files. You can designate as many as can fit in the 127-character limit for a DOS command line. You cannot specify additional *source* parameters without also specifying a *destination* parameter.

destination — If only one source file is specified, *destination* can be the full name and location of the destination file, with normal default assumptions. If more than one source file is specified, only a drive and/or a path can be specified for the destination. If *destination* is omitted, DOS prompts you for the name and location to use for expanded files.

Rules

1. You can use EXPAND to decompress files from the DOS distribution disks only.
2. If you specify more than one compressed file, you can only specify a destination drive or path (not a file name).
3. If you don't specify a compressed file or a destination, EXPAND prompts you for the missing information.
4. If you use EXPAND on a file that is not compressed, an error message appears (see the first item in the following "Messages" section.) Despite the error message, the file is still copied to the destination, it just isn't expanded.

Notes

1. Files stored on the original DOS 5.0 and 6.0 disks are compressed files. This compression enables more data to be stored on fewer disks. Before you can use a file on these disks, however, you must decompress the file.

2. When you use SETUP to install DOS, the files are decompressed as they are transferred to the subdirectory you chose to install DOS into. If you delete a file accidentally, or if a file becomes corrupted, you must retrieve the file again from the original DOS disk. EXPAND transfers the file and decompresses it in the process. Consider EXPAND to be a kind of "one-way" COPY command.

3. Refer to the file PACKING.LST for a list of which files are included on each of the DOS distribution disks. Microsoft marks the compressed files by replacing the last letter of the extension with an underscore (_). Setup copies the PACKING.LST file into your DOS subdirectory when it installs MS-DOS 6.

Examples

To expand MOVE.EXE from DOS distribution disk #1 to the C:\DOS subdirectory, enter the following line:

```
EXPAND A:MOVE.EX_ C:\DOS\MOVE.EXE
```

Messages

`Input file 'filename' already in expanded format`

Error: You attempted to expand an uncompressed file. Verify that you specified the correct compressed file.

`Error in compressed input file format: filename`

Error: The compressed file was corrupted. Use a different copy of the compressed file.

See Also

SETUP

FASTHELP

6.0 and later—External

The FASTHELP command provides a brief description and the syntax of a DOS command. This is the same help you get by including the /? switch when you issue a DOS command.

Syntax

FASTHELP *command*

Parameters and Switches

command The DOS command for which you want help. If you do not provide a command name, DOS provides short, one-line descriptions of all DOS commands.

Notes

The information FASTHELP provides about a command is the same as that provided by the following:

command **/?**

For more extensive information on DOS commands, type **HELP *command***.

See Also

HELP

"Getting Help" in Chapter 3

FASTOPEN 3.3 and later—External

FASTOPEN keeps directory information in memory so that DOS can quickly find and open the files you use most. FASTOPEN remains in memory (TSR), so be careful not to run it more than once. If you use FASTOPEN, you should add it to your AUTOEXEC.BAT file.

Syntax

FASTOPEN ***drive:***=*num* ... /X

Parameters and Switches

drive: The name of the drive for which directory information should be held in memory.

=*num* The number of directory entries to be held in memory (10 to 999). The default is 48. The equal sign is optional.

... You can specify as many additional ***drive***:=*num* parameters as you need.

/X Tells DOS to use expanded memory to store the information buffered by FASTOPEN.

Rules

1. You must specify the name of at least one drive for which entries are to be kept in memory. The drive cannot be a floppy drive.

2. You can use FASTOPEN for up to 24 nonfloppy drives for a total of 999 files. In the command line, simply type the additional drives, separated by spaces.

3. Do not use FASTOPEN from the DOS Shell or when you are running Windows or a disk defragmentation program, such as DEFRAG.

4. If you provide *nnn*, the value must be between 10 and 999, inclusive. The minimum value for FASTOPEN is 10, or the maximum level of your deepest directory plus 1—whichever is greater.

5. You cannot run more than one copy of FASTOPEN. If you want to change FASTOPEN settings, you must reboot your computer.

6. Each FASTOPEN entry you specify increases the size of FASTOPEN by approximately 48 bytes.

Notes

1. FASTOPEN works by keeping directory information in memory. Because disk buffers already hold FAT information, FASTOPEN enables DOS to search memory for a file or a subdirectory entry, to locate the corresponding FAT entry quickly, and to open the file. If you have many files and use FASTOPEN effectively, you can increase DOS's performance.

2. As is true of BUFFERS, no predetermined best number exists. The default value of 48 works well in many installations. If your subdirectories run many levels deep, or if you use many files, specifying a larger number can improve performance. Using too large a value for *nnn* (greater than 200), however, slows the system. DOS spends more time examining in-memory directory entries than rereading the entries from the disk.

3. Alternatively, FASTOPEN can be loaded from your CONFIG.SYS file with the INSTALL= command rather than in your AUTOEXEC.BAT file. With DOS 6, there is no advantage to either placement. Just make sure that you do not attempt to load FASTOPEN from both your CONFIG.SYS file and your AUTOEXEC.BAT file.

4. In most cases, you should use the SMARTDRV disk cache instead of FASTOPEN. SMARTDRV has fewer dangerous interactions with other programs and can speed up your computer even more than FASTOPEN. If you don't have enough memory to use SMARTDRV effectively, consider using the BUFFERS= command to optimize disk-access time.

See Also

BUFFERS= and SMARTDRV

"Using FASTOPEN" in Chapter 19

FC

3.3 and later—External

The FC command allows you to compare files for differences. FC has switches that enable it to be configured to do a strict byte-for-byte comparison (as COMP does) or to attempt to resynchronize after differences are detected.

Syntax

For ASCII text files, use the following syntax:

FC ***pathname1 pathname2*** /A /C /L /LB*buffer* /N /T /W /*resync*

For binary files, use the following syntax:

FC ***pathname1 pathname2*** /B

Parameters and Switches

pathname1 A file or group of files to compare. Normal drive and subdirectory defaults apply, and wildcards are permitted. This parameter must match at least one existing file.

pathname2 The file or group of files that should be compared to ***pathname1***. Normal drive and subdirectory defaults apply, and wildcards are permitted. Wildcards used with FC are interpreted the same way they are with COPY and REN: missing characters in the file name are replaced with the corresponding characters in ***pathname1***. If this file isn't found, FC moves on to the next set of files.

/A Abbreviates the display of an ASCII comparison to the first and last lines of each group of differences.

/B	Forces a binary file comparison, which involves a byte-by-byte comparison with no synchronization after a mismatch. This switch is the default for files with .EXE, .COM, .SYS, .OBJ, .LIB, and .BIN extensions.
/C	Causes DOS to ignore the case of letters.
/L	Compares files in ASCII mode, which involves a line-by-line comparison with resynchronization attempted after a mismatch. This switch is the default for files without .EXE, .COM, .SYS, .OBJ, .LIB, and .BIN extensions.
/LB*buffer*	Sets the internal buffer to the number of lines specified by *buffer*. A comparison is terminated if the files have more than this number of consecutive differing lines.
/N	Displays line numbers for ASCII comparisons.
/T	Suppresses expansion of tabs to spaces.
/W	Compresses tabs and spaces to a single space and causes tabs and spaces to be ignored if those characters are at the beginning or end of a line.
/*resync*	Sets the number of lines (1 through 9) that must match before the files are considered to be resynchronized. The default is 2.

Notes

1. A difference in a binary file comparison is displayed as follows:

   aaaaaaaa: *xx yy*

   aaaaaaaa represents the hexadecimal address of a mismatching pair of bytes; *xx* is the mismatching hexadecimal byte from the first file; and *yy* is the mismatching hexadecimal byte from the second file.

2. If you use a wildcard in the first file name, DOS compares all the specified files with the second file name. If you use a wildcard in the second file name, DOS uses the corresponding value from the first file name in the second file name.

Examples

To compare every text file in the current directory with C:\README.TXT:

```
FC *.TXT C:\README.TXT
```

To compare README.TXT in the current directory with C:\README.TXT:

```
FC README.TXT C:\*.TXT
```

To compare every text file in the current directory with the file of the same name in C:\:

```
FC *.TXT C:\*.TXT
```

See Also

DISKCOMP

"Comparing Files with FC" in Chapter 9

FCBS= 3.1 and later—Internal

File handles were added in DOS 2.0. Most programs written since that time use file handles, not file control blocks (FCBs), to open files. The FCBS= command sets the maximum number of open files a program using DOS 1.0 FCBs can have. With newer programs, you usually don't need this command. FCBS= can only be used in your CONFIG.SYS file.

Syntax

FCBS=*maxopen*

Parameters and Switches

maxopen The maximum number of open FCBs that a program can use. Any value in the range of 1 to 255 is allowed. The default value is 4.

Notes

1. Not many programs use FCBs anymore. Include the FCBS= command in your CONFIG.SYS only if a program asks you to, or if an old utility starts mysteriously failing. Otherwise, accept DOS's default setting of four FCBs. If you set *maxopen* less than two, however, you may find that certain small command-line utilities begin to fail.

2. Be aware that FCBs are ancient history. If you depend on any programs that require them you are living on borrowed time, and you should start looking for replacements. If you receive a new program that asks you to use the FCBS= command, complain (loudly) to the manufacturer. Microsoft has carried this legacy from CP/M for 10 years now, and with every release of DOS comes the chance that FCBs will no longer be supported.

3. If a program attempts to open more than *maxopen* FCBs, DOS automatically closes some of them.

4. Each FCB that is available to programs increases the size of DOS by approximately 60 bytes.

5. For newer programs, set the maximum number of open files with the FILES= command.

6. Some older versions of DOS supported a second argument, *neverclose*, for FCBS=. DOS 5 and 6 have no need for the *neverclose* argument and will ignore it.

See Also

FILES=

"Accessing Files through FCBS" in Chapter 18

FDISK

2.0 and later—External

FDISK is a full-screen program that prepares a hard disk to accept an operating system, such as DOS. It sets up partitions on a hard disk as well as designates which partitions are used to start-up the computer if no floppy disk is in drive A. On a new hard drive, you must run FDISK before you can use the FORMAT command on the drive.

Caution

FDISK is an extremely dangerous command. Making any changes with FDISK effectively deletes all the information on your hard drive. MS-DOS 6 does not include any utilities with which you can recover information lost through the use of FDISK.

Syntax

FDISK /STATUS

Parameters and Switches

/STATUS	(DOS 6.0 and later) Displays some partition information without starting FDISK.

Rules

1. You must use FDISK to create a partition on a hard disk before you can use FORMAT to format the hard disk.

2. You may change the size of a partition only by deleting existing partitions and creating new ones. This procedure deletes all data in the partitions.

3. FDISK does not work with SUBST aliases, Interlnk drives, network drives, CD-ROM drives, or with removable drives of any kind. FDISK works only with hard drives that are supported by the ROM BIOS in your computer. FDISK does not work with hard drives that require you to load a device driver in your CONFIG.SYS file to operate.

Notes

1. Although Setup places FDISK in the C:\DOS subdirectory by default, consider copying FDISK.EXE to a floppy disk and deleting it from your hard drive. If FDISK.EXE isn't on your hard disk no one can run it, avoiding the possible data loss that could result from somcone's curiosity.

2. If you need to use FDISK, back up your hard disk; make sure that you have a bootable floppy disk with at least the FORMAT command and your backup software on it. After FDISK has finished with your hard drive, you will not be able to boot from it (or even read it) until you have reformatted the drive.

3. The MIRROR command has the ability to save partition information into a file, which can be used by the UNFORMAT command to restore a damaged partition table. Although this capability is still a part of UNFORMAT, the MIRROR command is no longer distributed with DOS and is only available on the Supplemental Disk. Before you use FDISK, you may want to get a copy of MIRROR and save your partition information so that you can restore it if things go wrong.

4. Starting with DOS 3.3, FDISK was given the ability to create multiple logical partitions on a single drive. In DOS 4.0, FDISK and DOS were upgraded to handle partitions larger than 32M. The maximum size of a single partition for the DOS 6 version of FDISK is 2 gigabytes.

5. If you plan to use more than one operating system, use FDISK to partition part of the hard disk for DOS and another part of the hard disk for the other operating system.

See Also

MIRROR, UNDELETE, and UNFORMAT

"Dividing a Hard Disk with FDISK" in Chapter 7

FILES= 2.0 and later—Internal

When a program wants to open a file, DOS assigns that file a handle, which is just a fancy name for an ID number. The FILES= command sets the maximum number of file handles that DOS has available for programs to use. FILES= can only be used in your CONFIG.SYS file.

Syntax

FILES=*maxopen*

Parameters and Switches

maxopen The maximum number of open file handles that DOS allows. Any value in the range of 8 to 255 is allowed. The default value is 8.

Notes

1. Always specify a value for FILE= in your CONFIG.SYS file. DOS's default value of 8 is much too low for today's software programs. You typically need around 30 to 40 file handles, perhaps more if you are running programs like Microsoft Windows. A good minimum setting is 20.

2. If a program attempts to open a file when DOS has no more file handles available, it is denied access to the file. Unlike FCBs, DOS does not close open file handles while a program is running.

3. Each file handle available to programs increases the size of DOS by approximately 60 bytes.

Tip

If, when you load resident software in your AUTOEXEC.BAT file, you are in the habit of redirecting the output to the NUL device, you may be wasting file handles. Each such redirection unnecessarily ties up one file handle until you restart your computer.

4. Most programs display a meaningful message if they run out of file handles. If this happens, increase the FILES= setting in your CONFIG.SYS by five and restart your computer.

5. Many software installation programs inspect the setting you are using for FILES=, and may even increase it without telling you. Always look through your CONFIG.SYS and AUTOEXEC.BAT files after installing new software, and make sure that any modifications they've made are acceptable to you.

Examples

The following line sets the maximum number of open file handles to 30.

```
FILES=30
```

See Also

FCBS=

"Using the FILES Command" in Chapter 18

FIND — 2.0 and later—External

The FIND command displays all the lines of the designated files that match (or do not match, depending on the switches used) the specified string.

Syntax

FIND /V /C /N /I ***"string"*** *pathname* ...

Parameters and Switches

"string"	Represents the characters you want to find. The characters must be enclosed in quotation marks.
pathname	The file that you want to search. All the normal drive and subdirectory defaults apply, but you cannot use wildcards. If you omit *pathname*, FIND acts as a filter, searching input that has been redirected to it.
...	The ellipsis indicates that you can enter as many *pathname* parameters as necessary.
/C	Displays a count of the total number of lines that contain ***"string"***.

/I Specifies that the search is case-insensitive (DOS 5.0 and later versions).

/N Displays lines that contain "***string***", preceded by the file line number.

/V Displays lines that do not contain "***string***".

Exit Codes

ERRORLEVEL Value	Meaning
0	FIND completed successfully and found at least one match.
1	FIND completed successfully but found no matches.
2	FIND aborted due to an error and cannot report whether any matches were found.

Rules

1. You can use more than one file specification. All file specifications must appear after the string and must be separated by spaces.
2. If you do not provide any file specifications, FIND expects information from the keyboard (standard input).
3. If you use switches with FIND, you must place them between FIND and the string. Most DOS commands require that you place switches at the end of the command line.
4. You must enclose the string in double quotation marks. To use the double-quote character itself in the string, use two double quotation marks in a row.
5. Wildcards are not allowed in file specifications. You can get the effect of wildcards by using FIND in a FOR command.

Notes

1. FIND is one of several filters provided with DOS 3.0 and later versions. The command can find lines that contain strings and those that do not. FIND also can number and count lines of text, instead of simply displaying them.
2. This filter is useful when it is combined with DOS I/O redirection. You can redirect FIND's output to a file by using the > redirection symbol.

Because FIND accepts a sequence of files to search, you do not have to redirect the input to FIND.

Examples

To search README.TXT for "Microsoft":

```
FIND "Microsoft" C:\DOS\README.TXT
```

To search all batch files in the current directory for "default":

```
FOR %%A IN (*.BAT) DO FIND "default" %%A
```

To determine the path and file names for all batch files on the current disk:

```
DIR \ /S /B ¦ FIND ".BAT"
```

See Also

MORE and SORT

"The FIND Filter" in Chapter 14

FOR

2.0 and later—Internal

You can use the FOR command to repeat a single command, executing it once for each member of a list or group of files. Unlike most of the other batch commands, FOR can be very useful from both the command line as well as in a batch file.

Syntax

When used in a batch file, the syntax is as follows:

FOR %%*variable* IN (*set*) DO *command* *parameters*

When used on the DOS command line, the syntax is as follows:

FOR %*variable* IN (*set*) DO *command* *parameters*

Parameters and Switches

variable A single character DOS uses to represent the current value of **set**. Any character can be used for ***variable*** except the digits 0 through 9, the redirection symbols (<, >, and ¦), and the slash (/). In a batch file, ***variable*** must be preceded by two percent signs, but on the DOS command line only one is used.

set One or more words or path names separated by spaces or commas. Wildcards are allowed in the *filename.ext* portion of any pathname specified. None of the members of ***set*** can include embedded spaces. The enclosing parentheses are required.

command Represents the DOS command to be executed for each word or file in the ***set***. Almost all DOS internal or external commands can be used, with the notable exception of the FOR command itself.

parameters Represents any parameters you would like to pass to the ***command*** being executed. Normally, one or more occurrences of ***variable*** are used in the command parameters to pass the current value of ***set*** to the ***command***.

Notes

1. You can use more than one word or file path name in the *set*. Use spaces or commas to separate each word or file path name from the next. Any or all parts of a path name may be used, but wildcards are only allowed in the file name and extension portions.

2. No member of the *set* can include embedded spaces. In other words, you can't use *variable* to replace more than a single "word".

3. You must precede every occurrence of *variable* with two percent signs in a batch file and one percent sign at the DOS prompt. The reason for this difference is that each line in a batch file is passed through a routine called a parser, which fills in any replaceable parameters before DOS executes each command. The parser removes any single percent signs it finds; if two percent signs in a row are encountered, however, one will remain after the parser is finished. By the time DOS executes the command, only one of the two percent signs you typed remains. When you execute the FOR command from the DOS prompt, the line isn't parsed, and no percent signs are removed.

4. *variable* becomes each literal word or file name in *set*. If wildcards are used, then each file matched becomes a member of the set. The DO command executes once for each value in the set.

5. *variable* can be used in the *command* portion of the FOR command as well as in the *parameters* portion. This can be useful if you want to execute a series of commands. You can use the *variable* as many times as you need to after the DO keyword. It will be replaced with the current member of *set* every time it appears.

6. You cannot nest FOR..IN..DO commands. That is, you cannot use FOR as the command executed in the DO portion of a FOR..IN..DO loop. All other DOS internal and external commands are legal.

7. If you execute a batch file directly in the DO portion of the FOR loop, batch file processing ends when that batch file terminates, and control never is returned to the FOR loop. To avoid this situation, use the CALL or COMMAND /C commands to execute batch files in FOR..IN..DO loops.

8. If you use a variable name that is more than one character long, or if you omit IN, the parentheses around *set*, or DO, DOS displays a syntax error message.

9. Avoid using redirection symbols (<, >, and ¦) with the FOR command. In general, DOS ignores output redirection, and most redirected input will fail.

10. Do not attempt to use the "at" sign (@) to suppress the display of the command in the DO loop. DOS does not interpret the @ correctly, and searches for an executable file that begins with an "at" sign. To accomplish the same thing, turn ECHO OFF before executing the FOR command.

11. Although legal, you can't use the GOTO command to jump to a series of labels in a batch file from the DO portion of a FOR command. The GOTO command works just fine, but there is no mechanism available that allows you to return to the FOR loop when the section of the batch file that you jumped to is finished. To accomplish this, you have to use the CALL command to call separate batch files instead of jumping to sections in the same batch file.

12. Be very careful if you are using destructive commands like DEL or DELTREE in a FOR loop. Although you are debugging the FOR command, you may want to substitute the DIR command, which will not do any harm if anything goes wrong. Make sure that you think through

every possible situation. Also make sure that the wrong files won't be deleted before putting any batch file with a destructive FOR loop into use.

Examples

Suppose that you wanted to back up all settings files that Windows uses from a batch file. By combining the COPY command with FOR, you could accomplish this with the following line in your batch file:

```
FOR %%A IN (INI GRP PAR DAT) DO COPY
   C:\WINDOWS\*.%%A A:\
```

Assuming that you had previously prompted to insert the backup disk in drive A, the FOR command would execute the COPY command once for each type of file (.INI, .GRP, .PAR, and .DAT) in which Windows typically saves configuration information.

To execute the same command from the DOS prompt, use single percent signs rather than double ones.

```
FOR %A IN (INI GRP PAR DAT) DO COPY C:\WINDOWS\*.%A A:\
```

You can use the FOR command to execute a command a specific number of times. For example, to display five blank lines from a batch file, you could include the following command:

```
FOR %%A IN (1 2 3 4 5) DO ECHO.
```

After all, there is no rule that says you have to use the %%A variable in the DO portion of the command. The preceding FOR loop repeats the ECHO. (ECHO period) command once for each member in the set, displaying five blank lines on-screen.

You can use FOR to enable a command that doesn't support wildcards to process a path name specified with wildcards. A classic example of this technique involves the TYPE command. To display multiple files with TYPE, you could enter the following command in a batch file:

```
FOR %%A IN (%1) DO TYPE %%A
```

If you specified a path name that included wildcards as the first parameter to the batch file, TYPE would be executed once for each file that matched the path name. The only thing wrong with this is that TYPE would display all the files without pausing; so, to see a particular file, you would have to hover over the pause key. Despite this drawback, this example illustrates how the FOR command can be used to overcome this limitation in a command.

See Also

"Using FOR..IN..DO" in Chapter 16

FORMAT

1.0 and later—External

The FORMAT command initializes a disk to accept DOS information and files. FORMAT also checks the disk for defective tracks and (optionally) places DOS on the floppy disk or hard disk.

Syntax

FORMAT ***drive*:** /V /V:*label* /Q /U /F:*size* /N:*sectors* /T:*tracks* /S /B /1 /4 /8

Parameters and Switches

***drive*:**	A valid drive letter to be formatted, followed by a colon (:).
/V	Prompts for a volume label for the disk.
/V:*label*	Makes *label* (which can be up to 11 characters long) the disk's volume label.
/Q	FORMAT performs a *quick* format by clearing only the FAT and the root directory on the disk; this switch does not check the disk for bad sectors.
/U	An *unconditional* format for a floppy disk. Unconditional formatting destroys all data on a floppy disk, which means that you cannot unformat the disk. (For more information on unformatting, see UNFORMAT later in this command reference.)
/F:*size*	The size to which a disk should be formatted, which can be less than the drive's maximum. Generally, use this switch in preference to a combination of /N and /T. The following table lists the possible values for *size*:

Drive Capacity	Allowable Values for *size*
160K, 180K	160, 160K, 160KB, 180, 180K, and 180KB
320K, 360K	All of preceding, plus 320, 320K, 320KB, 360, 360K, and 360KB
1.2M	All of preceding, plus 1200, 1200K, 1200KB, 1.2, 1.2M, and 1.2MB
720K	720, 720K, and 720KB
1.44M	All for 720K, plus 1440, 1440K, 1440KB, 1.44, 1.44M, and 1.44MB
2.88M	All for 1.44M, plus 2880, 2880K, 2880KB, 2.88, 2.88M, and 2.88MB

/N:*sectors* Formats the disk with the number of sectors (*sectors* ranges from 1 to 99). Must be used with /T. Generally, use /F instead of this switch.

/T:*tracks* Formats the disk with the number of tracks per side (*tracks* ranges from 1 to 999). Must be used with /N. Generally, use /F instead of this switch.

/S Places copies of the operating-system files on the disk so that DOS can boot from the disk. For MS-DOS, those files are the command-line interpreter pointed to by the environment variable COMSPEC (generally COMMAND.COM), the hidden files IO.SYS and MSDOS.SYS, and, if necessary, DBLSPACE.BIN.

/B Leaves space for the system version, but does not place the operating-system files on the disk. (See the section on the SYS command later in this command reference.) This switch is not necessary in DOS 6.0.

/1 Formats only the first side of the floppy disk.

/4 Formats a floppy disk in a 1.2M drive for double-density (320K/360K) use. Some systems, however, cannot reliably read the resulting disk.

/8 Formats an eight-sector 5 1/4-inch floppy disk (for compatibility with DOS 1.0).

Exit Codes

ERRORLEVEL Value	Meaning
0	Format operation successful
3	Halted by user (Ctrl-C)
4	Halted by a fatal disk error
5	Halted by user at the Proceed with Format (Y/N)? prompt

Rules

1. If you do not provide a drive name, DOS uses the current drive.
2. Unless otherwise directed through a switch, DOS formats the disk to the DOS maximum capacity for the drive.
3. Some switches do not work together. For example, you cannot use the following switch combinations:
   - /V with /8
   - /1, /4, /8, or /B with the hard disk
   - /F with /N and /T
4. In DOS 5.0 and later versions, if you do not specify /U, FORMAT performs a "safe" format. DOS creates a file containing file information and saves the file to a safe place on disk where the UNFORMAT command can find it if you need to unformat the disk. FORMAT then clears the FAT and root directory of the disk but does not erase any data. Therefore, the UNFORMAT command enables you to restore a disk if you did not intend to format the disk.
5. If you are formatting a hard disk, FORMAT displays the following message:

```
WARNING, ALL DATA ON NON-REMOVABLE DISK
DRIVE d: WILL BE LOST!
Proceed with Format (Y/N)?
```

   Type **Y** to format the hard disk or **N** to abort the formatting operation.

Notes

1. FORMAT now displays numbers with embedded commas, making them much easier to read.

2. Do not try to format any type of virtual disk; a disk that is part of an ASSIGN, SUBST, or JOIN command; or a networked or Interlnk disk.

3. Never try to format a RAM disk. Under some circumstances, FORMAT acts erratically when you use it to format a RAM disk, particularly RAMDRIVE (the DOS RAM disk program). The responses can range from a `Divide overflow` message to a lockup of your computer. If the computer locks up, turn the system off and then turn it on again. Obviously, you lose the RAM disk's contents, but no hard or floppy disks are damaged.

4. In pre-5.0 versions of DOS, FORMAT destroys the information recorded on a floppy or hard disk. Do not use the command on any disk—floppy or hard—that contains useful information.

5. In DOS 5.0 and later versions, FORMAT performs a safe format. When you use the command to format a previously formatted disk, DOS copies the FAT and root directory before clearing them and then checks the disk. The existing data is not cleared. If you accidentally format a safely formatted disk, you can unformat the disk. To erase all data from a previously used floppy disk, use the /U switch. An unconditional format takes about 27 percent longer than the default safe format.

6. The /Q switch, another feature of DOS 5.0 and later, enables you to format a disk quickly. The /Q switch clears the FAT and root directory but does not check the disk for bad sectors. To reuse a disk that you know is good, use the /Q switch. The quick format is nearly 80 percent faster than the default safe format.

7. 160K and 180K disks are known as single-sided, double-density, 5 1/4-inch disks.

   320K and 360K disks are known as double-sided, double-density, 5 1/4-inch disks.

   1.2M disks are known as double-sided, quadruple or high-density, 5 1/4-inch disks.

   720K disks are known as double-sided, double-density, 3 1/2-inch disks.

   1.44M disks are known as double-sided, quadruple or high-density, 3 1/2-inch disks.

   2.88M disks are known as double-sided, extra-high-density, 3 1/2-inch disks.

Messages

`Checking existing disk format`

Information: FORMAT is checking the disk to see whether it has been formatted previously.

`Saving UNFORMAT information`

Information: If the disk has been formatted, the directory and FAT are saved on the disk, and a safe format is performed. A safely formatted disk can be unformatted.

`Drive A error. Insufficient space for the MIRROR image file.`

`There was an error creating the format recovery file.`

Warning: The previously formatted disk doesn't have room for the mirror-image file (the file that contains a copy of the FAT and root directory). The disk doesn't have enough room to save a copy of the root directory and FAT. Be sure that you want to format the disk that is located in the drive.

`This disk cannot be unformatted.`

Warning: FORMAT displays this message when it is prevented from saving information on the disk for UNFORMAT to use. You most likely will see this message when the disk is too full and not enough free space exists for the UNFORMAT information to be saved.

`Invalid media or track 0 bad`

`disk unusable`

Warning: Track 0 holds the boot record, the FAT, and the directory. This track is bad, and the floppy disk is unusable. Try reformatting the floppy disk. If the error reoccurs, you cannot use the floppy disk.

This error can occur when you format 720K floppy disks as 1.44M floppy disks (if you forget to use the /N:9 or /F:720 switch when you format the disk in a 1.44M drive), or when you format 360K floppy disks as 1.2M floppy disks (if you forget the /4 or /F:360 switch).

This error also can occur when you format 1.2M floppy disks at lower capacities (such as 360K) and use the /4 switch. In this case, try using a floppy disk rated for double-sided, double-density use.

`WARNING, ALL DATA ON NON-REMOVABLE DISK`

`DRIVE d: WILL BE LOST!`

```
Proceed with Format (Y/N)?
```

Warning: FORMAT is warning you that you are about to format a hard disk. To format the hard disk, type **Y** and press Enter. If you do not want to format the hard disk, type **N** and press Enter.

See Also

SYS and UNFORMAT

Chapter 6, "Understanding Disks and Disk Drives"

GOTO

2.0 and later—Internal

GOTO transfers control to the line following a labeled line in the batch file and continues executing the batch file from that line. GOTO is an unconditional jump and always transfers control whenever the command is encountered.

Syntax

GOTO *label*

Parameters and Switches

label The label that DOS should jump to. ***label*** transfers execution to the batch file line following ***label***.

Notes

1. To define a label, enter it at the beginning of a line, preceded by a colon (:). Only the first eight characters of a label are significant, although you can enter as many characters as you want without generating an error. All characters on a line past the eighth character of a label are ignored. Spaces are not allowed in labels.

2. When the command GOTO *label* is executed, DOS jumps to the line following the label and continues executing the batch file. The label can be placed before or after the GOTO statement in the batch file.

3. If a batch file does not contain the label specified by a GOTO, the batch file stops and DOS displays a `Label not found` error message.

4. Adding a colon as the first character of a line in a batch file effectively "comments out" the line by causing DOS to treat it as a label rather than as a line to be executed. DOS interprets it as a label, however, so using REM is safer.

5. Although GOTO doesn't generate an error message when you use it from the DOS command line, neither does it serve any purpose. Labels have no meaning on the command line, so the GOTO command has no place to jump to.

See Also

:label and REM

"Branching with GOTO" in Chapter 16

GRAFTABL

3.0 to 5.0—External

GRAFTABL loads into memory the tables of additional character sets to be displayed on the Color Graphics Adapter (CGA). GRAFTABL is included on the DOS 6.0 Supplemental Disk, not in the standard DOS 6.0 package.

Syntax

GRAFTABL *codepage* /STATUS

Parameters and Switches

codepage Represents the three-digit number of the code page for the display. The default value is 437, the code page for the USA. See Appendix G for a list of the code pages that DOS supports.

/STATUS Displays the code page selected for use by GRAFTABL. You cannot specify a *codepage* and request /STATUS information in the same command. This parameter can be abbreviated as /STA.

Exit Codes

ERRORLEVEL Value	Meaning
0	New character set loaded—no set was loaded previously
1	New character set loaded—previous set replaced
2	Disk error prevented loading new character set
3	Command line invalid—no action taken
4	Incorrect DOS version running

Notes

1. Load GRAFTABL to display legible characters in the ASCII range 128 to 255 when you are in graphics mode on the Color Graphics Adapter (CGA).
2. GRAFTABL increases the size of DOS by 1,360 bytes.
3. If you do not specify a *codepage*, DOS uses code page 437 in the USA.
4. After you invoke GRAFTABL, the only way to deactivate the command is to restart DOS.
5. The IBM CGA in graphics mode produces low-quality ASCII characters in the 128-to-255 range.
6. GRAFTABL is useful only when your system is equipped with the CGA and when you use the CGA in medium- or high-resolution graphics mode.

See Also

DISPLAY.SYS and CHCP

GRAPHICS

2.0 and later—External

GRAPHICS enables the Print Screen key to print the contents of a graphics screen on a suitable printer. When you first run GRAPHICS it loads itself into memory and remains there until you restart your computer.

Syntax

GRAPHICS *printer pathname.pro* /R /B /PRINTBOX:STD /PRINTBOX:LCD /LCD

Parameters and Switches

printer The type of printer you are using. *printer* can be one of the following values:

Printer	Description
COLOR1	IBM Personal Color Printer with a black ribbon
COLOR4	IBM Personal Color Printer with an RGB (red, green, blue, and black) ribbon, which produces four colors

(continues)

Printer	Description
COLOR8	IBM Personal Color Printer with a CMY (cyan, magenta, yellow, and black) ribbon, which produces eight colors
GRAPHICS	IBM Personal Graphics Printer, IBM ProPrinter, or IBMQuietwriter
THERMAL	IBM PC-Convertible thermal printer
GRAPHICSWIDE	IBM Personal Graphics Printer with an 11 inch wide carriage
HPDEFAULT	Any Hewlett-Packard PCL printer
DESKJET	A Hewlett-Packard DeskJet printer
LASERJET	A Hewlett-Packard LaserJet printer
LASERJETII	A Hewlett-Packard LaserJet II printer
PAINTJET	A Hewlett-Packard PaintJet printer
QUIETJET	A Hewlett-Packard QuietJet printer
QUIETJETPLUS	A Hewlett-Packard QuietJet Plus printer
RUGGEDWRITER	A Hewlett-Packard RuggedWriter printer
RUGGEDWRITERWIDE	A Hewlett-Packard RuggedWriterwide printer
THINKJET	A Hewlett-Packard ThinkJet printer

pathname.pro The file that contains printer information. Normal drive and subdirectory defaults apply, but wildcards are not allowed. If you do not specify a printer information file, DOS looks for the file GRAPHICS.PRO in the current directory or the directory containing the GRAPHICS.COM program file (normally C:\DOS).

/R Reverses the colors so that the image on the paper matches the image on-screen (a white image on a black background).

/B Prints the background in the color displayed on-screen. You can use this switch only when the printer type is COLOR4 or COLOR8.

/PRINTBOX:STD or /PRINTBOX:LCD The printbox size, or aspect ratio, to use when converting the image on-screen. This parameter must match the first Printbox statement in the printer profile. You can abbreviate /PRINTBOX as /PB.

/LCD Prints the image as displayed on the PC Convertible's LCD display. This switch is the equivalent of /PRINTBOX:LCD.

See Also

"The GRAPHICS Command" in Chapter 14

HELP

5.0 and later—External

HELP is a full screen, on-line help system that includes information about every DOS command. HELP contains the entire text of the "MS-DOS 6 Command Reference" section from the Technical Reference manual published by Microsoft. In addition, there are hypertext links and a searchable index that can help you move quickly from one topic to the next. DOS version 5.0 included a HELP command as well, but it bore more resemblance to the DOS 6 FASTHELP command than to the DOS 6 on-line help system.

Syntax

HELP *command* /B /G /H /NOHI

Parameters and Switches

command	The command that you want information about. If this parameter is omitted, HELP displays its table of contents screen.
/B	Specifies that HELP should use colors more appropriate for a black-and-white (monochrome) or LCD display.
/G	Specifies that HELP should use the fastest screen-updating method for a CGA monitor. Don't specify the /G switch if you see "snow" on your monitor.
/H	Specifies that HELP should display 43 lines on an EGA monitor or 50 lines on a VGA monitor.
/NOHI	Specifies that HELP should limit itself to 8 colors rather than 16.

Notes

1. For HELP to work, QBASIC.EXE must be in the current directory, in your search path, or in the same directory as HELP.COM.
2. Help is available for many topics other than DOS commands (for example, CONFIG.SYS commands). See Help's table of contents for a complete list.
3. In addition to extensive syntax help, Help displays usage notes and examples, and links related material by hypertext links.
4. Simple syntax help for DOS commands is available from FASTHELP or by typing the following command:

   command **/?**

See Also

FASTHELP

"Getting Help" in Chapter 3

HIMEM.SYS (device driver)

4.0 and later—External

If your computer has more than 1M of RAM installed, you should load HIMEM.SYS in your CONFIG.SYS file. HIMEM.SYS is an XMS v3.0-compatible extended memory manager. Its services are required in order for DOS to use the extended memory your computer has installed. HIMEM.SYS should be one of the first device drivers loaded with the DEVICE= command in your CONFIG.SYS file.

Syntax

For most people, the DEVICE= line that loads HIMEM.SYS can be very simple.

DEVICE=*drive:\path***HIMEM.SYS**

The full syntax for HIMEM.SYS can seem intimidating, but all the optional parameters have appropriate defaults.

DEVICE=*drive:\path***HIMEM.SYS** /A20CONTROL:*onoff* /CPUCLOCK:*onoff* /EISA /HMAMIN=*min* /INT15=*size* /NOTEST /NUMHANDLES=*num* /MACHINE:*machcode* /SHADOWRAM:*onoff* /VERBOSE /V

Parameters and Switches

drive:\path — The full path to the HIMEM.SYS file on your system. Setup places the HIMEM.SYS file in the C:\DOS subdirectory by default. If the full path to HIMEM.SYS isn't specified, DOS looks for the file in the root directory of the start-up drive.

/A20CONTROL:*onoff* — The A20 line is the address line that controls access to extended memory, including the high memory area (HMA). Specifying /A20CONTROL:OFF instructs HIMEM.SYS to take control of the A20 line only if it's off when HIMEM.SYS loads into memory. The default value is /A20CONTROL:ON, which allows HIMEM.SYS to take control of the A20 address line no matter what state it is in. As long as HIMEM.SYS is the first program to access extended memory when you reboot your computer, you should never need this parameter.

/CPUCLOCK:*onoff*

On certain computers, HIMEM.SYS may change the CPU clock speed when it loads. If this happens to you, specify the /CPUCLOCK:ON parameter to prevent HIMEM.SYS from changing the CPU clock speed. The default value is /CPUCLOCK:OFF, which allows HIMEM.SYS to load a little faster on most computers.

/EISA

You only need to include this parameter if you have an EISA (Extended Industry Standard Architecture) computer with more than 16M of RAM installed. Including this parameter allows HIMEM.SYS to control all the available extended memory in such a system.

Note

HIMEM.SYS versions 3.07 through 3.09 (v3.09 is distributed with DOS 6) may fail to recognize more than 64M of memory on an EISA computer even with the /EISA parameter specified. If you have this problem, contact Microsoft and ask for document number Q98111 as well as any other material they have available that can help you get around this limitation.

/HMAMIN=*min*

Only one application can use the HMA at a time. The /HMAMIN=*min* parameter specifies the minimum amount of RAM (in kilobytes) that an application must request in order to be granted access to the HMA. Valid values for *min* are in the range 0 through 63. If this parameter is omitted, a value of 0 is assumed, and the HMA is granted to the first program that requests it.

Normally, you will want to load DOS into the HMA in order to save 43K of conventional memory. However, DOS does not allocate the HMA until after all other device drivers and programs in your CONFIG.SYS file are loaded. To prevent them from allocating the HMA before DOS can get to it, try specifying /HMAMIN=40 in the line that loads HIMEM.SYS.

/INT15=*size*

Certain older applications use the Interrupt 15h interface to allocate extended memory. If you are using a program that requires this type of memory, you can set some aside for it with the /INT15=*size* parameter. *size* is specified in kilobytes, and can be any value in the range 64 to 65535, or the amount of extended memory you have in your system—whichever is lower. Note that you should specify 64K more than your application requires, since the HMA is allocated from this memory as well. Any memory you set aside with the /INT15 parameter is unavailable to programs using the standard XMS interface. If you do not specify the /INT15 parameter, no memory is set aside (except the HMA).

/NOTEST

Specifies that you do not want HIMEM.SYS to scan extended memory when it loads. Normally, HIMEM.SYS attempts to identify weak and unreliable RAM chips by scanning all extended memory.

/NUMHANDLES=*num* When programs request extended memory, they are given a handle to an extended-memory block by HIMEM.SYS. The /NUMHANDLES=*num* parameter specifies how many handles HIMEM.SYS should have available. *num* can be any value in the range 1 to 128. If this parameter is omitted, 32 handles will be available. Each handle increases the size of HIMEM in memory by approximately 6 bytes. If the /VERBOSE (or /V) parameter is specified, HIMEM.SYS displays the number of handles available when it finishes loading into memory. (See the message `num extended memory handles available` in the following "Messages" section.)

/MACHINE:*machcode* This parameter is only required if HIMEM.SYS is unable to gain control of the A20 address line for your computer. When this happens, HIMEM.SYS stops loading and displays an error message. (See the message `ERROR: Unable to control A20 line!` in the following "Messages" section.) To enable HIMEM.SYS to work with your computer, you may have to specify one of the machine codes from the following table.

The default value for this parameter is /MACHINE:1 or /MACHINE:AT.

machcode can be the number in the code column or the abbreviation shown, whichever you find easier to type and remember. Note that more than one computer type may use the same code number.

Computer type	Code	Abbreviation
IBM AT or 100% compatible	1	AT
CompuAdd 386 systems	1 or 8	AT or
JDR 386/33	1	AT
Phoenix BIOS	1 or 8	AT or WYSE
IBM PS/2	2	PS2
Datamedia 386/486	2	PS2
UNISYS PowerPort	2	PS2
Phoenix Cascade BIOS	3	PTLCASCADE
HP Vectra (A and A+)	4	HPVECTRA
AT&T 6300 Plus	5	ATT6300PLUS
Acer 1100	6	ACER1100
Toshiba 1600, 1200XE, and 5100	7	TOSHIBA
Wyse 12.5 MHz 286	8	WYSE
Hitachi HL500C	8	WYSE
Intel 301z or 302	8	WYSE
Tulip SX	9	TULIP
Zenith ZBIOS	10	ZENITH
IBM PC / AT (alternative delay)	11	AT1
IBM PC / AT (alternative delay)	12	AT2
CSS Labs	12	CSS
IBM PC / AT (alternative delay)	13	AT3
Philips	13	PHILIPS

Computer type	Code	Abbreviation
HP Vectra	14	FASTHP
IBM 7552 Industrial Computer *	15	IBM7552
Bull Micral 60 *	16	BULLMICRAL
Dell XBIOS *	17	DELL

**Not available in the version of HIMEM.SYS distributed with DOS 5.*

It is possible that you may have to specify 1 or AT as the machine type for your computer, despite the fact that 1 is the default value for the /MACHINE parameter. HIMEM.SYS tries to determine what type of computer you have when it loads into memory; if it gets confused, it may select the wrong method for controlling the A20 line. In these cases, you may have to explicitly set the machine type to 1.

For the version of HIMEM.SYS that is distributed with DOS 6 (v3.09), the only systems that should require the use of the /MACHINE parameter to operate are the Acer 1100 (code 6), the Wyse 12.5 MHz 286 (code 8), and the IBM 7552 Industrial Computer (code 15). Systems that have the same code value as these systems are likely to require this parameter as well.

/SHADOWRAM:*onoff* This parameter is only useful on computer systems with less than 2M of RAM. On such systems, if HIMEM.SYS detects that the ROM BIOS is running from shadow RAM, it attempts to reclaim that memory and turn it into available XMS memory. If you don't want HIMEM.SYS to do this, specify the /SHADOWRAM:ON parameter.

Note that specifying /SHADOWRAM:ON only allows the ROM BIOS to continue to run from RAM. HIMEM.SYS cannot set up shadow RAM on a system that doesn't already have it.

/VERBOSE Specifies that HIMEM.SYS should display status messages while it loads. By default, HIMEM.SYS won't display any messages unless an error occurs. You also can turn on the display of messages while HIMEM.SYS is loading by pressing the Alt key.

/V — Abbreviated form of the /VERBOSE parameter.

Notes

1. HIMEM.SYS now automatically performs a memory scan to identify RAM chips which are becoming unreliable. An unreliable RAM chip can halt your computer in the middle of a critical operation and could lead to a serious loss of data. If you don't want HIMEM.SYS to perform this memory scan, include the new /NOTEST switch.

2. HIMEM.SYS requires at least a 80286-based computer with more than 1M of RAM installed in order to run. Computers with less than 1M of RAM have no extended memory to manage.

3. You cannot load HIMEM.SYS with a DEVICEHIGH= command. HIMEM.SYS is one of the programs that enables you to load other device drivers or programs into upper memory with the DEVICEHIGH= or LOADHIGH commands. HIMEM.SYS does attempt to minimize its use of conventional memory; after HIMEM.SYS is loaded, it uses only about 1K of conventional memory.

4. The line that loads HIMEM.SYS should be one of the very first DEVICE= lines in your CONFIG.SYS file. If any other driver using extended memory is loaded before HIMEM.SYS, the chances are very good that HIMEM.SYS will refuse to load.

5. The DOS 6 Setup program inserts the DEVICE= line, which loads SETVER.EXE before the line for HIMEM.SYS. This doesn't cause any problems, but it does prevent you from loading SETVER.EXE into upper memory with the DEVICEHIGH= command. To gain a little conventional memory, move the DEVICE= line for SETVER.EXE after the lines that load HIMEM.SYS and EMM386.EXE and change the DEVICE= command into a DEVICEHIGH= command.

6. HIMEM.SYS (or another XMS-compatible memory manager) must be loaded before you can use any of the following commands or drivers in your CONFIG.SYS file.

```
DEVICEHIGH=
DOS=HIGH
DOS=UMB
EMM386.EXE
```

The DOS=UMB and the DEVICEHIGH= commands actually depend on a UMB provider such as EMM386.EXE. Because most UMB providers require the use of XMS memory, however, they are all indirectly dependent on HIMEM.SYS.

7. If HIMEM.SYS is unable to gain control of the A20 address line, it aborts with an error message. (See the message `ERROR: Unable to control A20 line!` in the following "Messages" section.) Unless your computer's hardware is incompatible, HIMEM.SYS should be able to gain control; its failure to do so usually means that another program is preventing HIMEM.SYS from doing its job. Two programs cannot share control of extended memory, so you have to remove one of them from your CONFIG.SYS file. Check to see if you are loading any third-party memory managers before the line that loads HIMEM.SYS. (If HIMEM.SYS was loading first, your third-party memory manager would be the one displaying the error message, probably telling you to remove HIMEM.SYS.)

   If no other memory managers are loading before HIMEM.SYS, it might be baffled by the method used to control the A20 address line in your computer. In these cases, you have to specify a /MACHINE:*machcode* parameter to tell HIMEM how to control the A20 address line. Look for your computer in the table of machine codes. (See the table of machine codes in the preceding "Parameters and Switches" section.) If you find your computer listed, add a /MACHINE:*machcode* parameter to the line that loads HIMEM.SYS in your CONFIG.SYS file.

Examples

The first few lines in most people's CONFIG.SYS files look something like this:

```
DEVICE=C:\DOS\HIMEM.SYS
DEVICE=C:\DOS\EMM386.EXE RAM MIN=0
DOS=HIGH,UMB
```

First, HIMEM.SYS is loaded into memory to provide access to the HMA and XMS-compatible memory. Then EMM386.EXE is loaded, which provides upper memory block (UMB) support for DOS as well as EMS-compatible memory for those programs that use it. (The RAM switch enables UMB and EMS support, and the MIN=0 lets EMM386.EXE release back into the memory pool EMS memory that's not in use.) Finally, DOS is instructed to load itself into the high memory area (HMA) provided by HIMEM.SYS, and to establish connections with the UMBs provided by EMM386.EXE.

If you own an Acer 1100 computer, you might have to include a /MACHINE parameter to let HIMEM.SYS know how to control the A20 line in your computer, as shown in the following example:

```
DEVICE=C:\DOS\HIMEM.SYS /MACHINE:ACER1100 /V
```

By including the /V (or /VERBOSE) parameter, HIMEM.SYS displays all messages while it loads into memory, so you can keep track of how it is doing. Notice that you can enter the machine code parameter as /MACHINE:ACER1100 or /MACHINE:6, but not as /ACER1100.

Messages

`64K High Memory Area is available`

Information: If you have specified the /VERBOSE parameter, HIMEM.SYS displays this message after successfully gaining control of the A20 line.

`ERROR: An Extended Memory Manager is already installed`

Error: Another XMS memory manager was installed before HIMEM.SYS. If you are using a third-party memory manager, remove the line that loads HIMEM.SYS from your CONFIG.SYS file. If you want to use HIMEM.SYS, remove the other memory manager instead.

`ERROR: HIMEM.SYS requires an 80x86-based machine`

Error: HIMEM.SYS can't run on 8088- and 8086-based computers. The only function of HIMEM.SYS is to control and regulate the use of extended memory, and these types of computers don't have any.

`ERROR: HIMEM.SYS requires DOS 3.00 or higher`

Error: Version 3.09 of HIMEM.SYS, which is the version distributed with MS-DOS 6.0, requires at least DOS 3 to run. If you know that you're running DOS 5 or 6 (to find out, use the VER command), check your SETVER.EVE version table to make sure that no one has entered HIMEM.SYS into it as a practical joke.

`ERROR: No available extended memory was found`

Error: HIMEM.SYS can't find any extended memory in your system. You may not have enough RAM installed to run HIMEM.SYS.

`ERROR: Unable to control A20 line!`

Error: HIMEM.SYS displays this message if it is unable to gain control of the A20 line in your computer. Normally, this message means that you must specify a /MACHINE:*machcode* parameter on the line that loads HIMEM.SYS in your CONFIG.SYS file.

`ERROR: VDISK memory allocator already installed`

`XMS Driver not installed`

Error: A device driver that loaded before HIMEM.SYS allocated some extended memory with the Interrupt 15h interface. To get HIMEM.SYS to load, make sure that the DEVICE= line for HIMEM.SYS precedes the driver using Interrupt 15h. To reserve memory for this other driver, specify an /INT15=*size* parameter on the line for HIMEM.SYS.

`Installed A20 handler number num`

Information: HIMEM.SYS has gained control of the A20 line using machine handler number *num*. Check the table shown earlier in the "Parameters and Switches" section to see what computer system *num* corresponds to.

`Minimum HMA size set to minK`

Information: Programs that attempt to allocate less than *min*K RAM in the HMA are denied. If *min* is greater than zero, you've probably set the /HMAMIN=*min* parameter to prevent another program from grabbing the HMA before DOS can get to it.

`num extended memory handles available`

Information: HIMEM.SYS has created *num* extended memory-block handles, either by default or through the use of the /NUMHANDLES=*num* parameter.

`Shadow RAM disabled`

Information: On computers with less than 2M of RAM, HIMEM.SYS often disables shadow RAM to make more extended memory available. If you don't want HIMEM.SYS to disable shadow RAM, specify the /SHADOWRAM:ON parameter.

`WARNING: Invalid parameter ignored`

Warning: An invalid parameter was specified on the line that loaded HIMEM.SYS. Check the line in CONFIG.SYS carefully, and look any for mistyped options.

`WARNING: Shadow RAM disable not supported on this system`

Warning: HIMEM.SYS is unable to disable shadow RAM for your computer. If you want to turn shadow RAM off, you have to use your computer's CMOS Setup program or set jumpers on the motherboard.

```
WARNING: Shadow RAM is in use and can't be disabled
```

Warning: You have specified /SHADOWRAM:OFF, but it's already in use and HIMEM.SYS can't disable it. You may have to use your CMOS Setup program if you want to turn shadow RAM off on your computer.

```
WARNING: The A20 Line was already enabled
```

Warning: Another program has enabled your computer's A20 line, and HIMEM.SYS is unsure what to make of it. Usually, HIMEM.SYS still assumes control of extended memory. To avoid this warning, make sure that HIMEM.SYS is loaded before any other drivers that use extended memory. If you have another device driver that needs to control the A20 line, you may have to specify the /A20CONTROL:OFF parameter to get HIMEM.SYS to cooperate with the other device driver.

```
WARNING: The High Memory Area is unavailable
```

Warning: This message may appear if you have only 1M of RAM, or if another program has taken over the HMA. Make sure that HIMEM.SYS is loaded before any other drivers that use extended memory.

See Also

DEVICE=, DOS=, and EMM386.EXE

"Using Extended Memory and HIMEM.SYS" in Chapter 18

IF

2.0 and later—Internal

You can use the IF command to add conditional execution of a DOS command to your batch files. You can test for three types of conditions with the IF command: the value of an exit code returned by a program, the equivalence of two alphanumeric strings, and the existence of a file or subdirectory.

Syntax

To test the exit code returned by a program, use the following form of the IF command:

IF NOT **ERRORLEVEL** ***number command*** *parameters*

To compare two alphanumeric strings, use the following form of the IF command:

IF NOT ***string1==string2 command*** *parameters*

To check for the existence of a file or files, use the following form of the IF command:

IF NOT EXIST ***pathname command*** *parameters*

Parameters and Switches

NOT	Tests for the opposite of the condition. In other words, IF NOT executes the ***command*** if the condition is false.
ERRORLEVEL ***number***	Tests the exit code (0 to 255) that a program returns when it terminates. If the exit code is greater than or equal to the ***number***, the condition is true.
string1==string2	Compares two alphanumeric strings to determine whether they are identical. This comparison is case sensitive, so upper- and lowercase characters are not considered equal. The strings can include literals, batch file replaceable parameters (such as %1), environment variables (such as %COMSPEC%), or any combination of the three.
EXIST ***pathname***	Tests whether the file specified by ***pathname*** exists. If no drive or path is included in ***pathnam***, the current drive or directory is assumed. The file name portion is required. Wildcards are allowed in the filename and extension portions of ***pathnam***.
command	Represents the DOS command that is executed if the condition is true (or false if NOT is specified). If you want to run a batch file, use the CALL or COMMAND /C command instead of executing the batch file directly.
parameters	Represents any parameters you want to pass to the ***command*** being executed.

Notes

1. For the IF command, if *condition* is true, *command* is executed. If *condition* is false, DOS skips *command* and immediately executes the next line of the batch file.

2. For the IF NOT subcommand, if *condition* is false, *command* is executed. If *condition* is true, DOS skips *command* and immediately executes the next line of the batch file.

3. If you want to run a batch file from the *command* portion of an IF command, use the CALL or COMMAND /C command instead of executing it directly. Without CALL or COMMAND /C, control never returns to your batch file.

4. IF commands can be nested. That is, you can use the IF command in the *command* portion of an IF command. This can be a handy way to test for a range of exit code values, freeing you from the tyranny of descending order IF ERRORLEVEL statements. (See the following "Examples" section.)

5. Do not attempt to use the "at" sign (@) to suppress the display of the command specified in the *command* portion of an IF command. DOS will not interpret the @ correctly, and will search for an executable file that begins with an "at" sign. To accomplish the same thing, turn ECHO OFF before executing the IF statement.

6. IF ERRORLEVEL *number* returns true if the number you specified is less than or equal to the exit code returned by the previous program. For this reason, IF ERRORLEVEL commands usually have to be arranged in descending order to get the desired results. You must test for this value immediately after the program terminates. Executing any other command, even if it doesn't return an exit code, may clear the previous exit code from memory.

7. Not all programs return exit codes. If a program doesn't return an exit code, an IF ERRORLEVEL 0 command will evaluate to true, but any other *number* will cause the IF statement to be false. Presently, no DOS internal commands return exit codes, and, unfortunately, you can't set the exit code for a batch file either. (Maybe if we all complain....) The following DOS external commands return exit codes:

BACKUP	DISKCOPY	MSAV
CHKDSK	FIND	REPLACE
CHOICE	FORMAT	RESTORE
DEFRAG	GRAFTABL	SCANDISK
DELTREE	KEYB	SETVER
DISKCOMP	MOVE	XCOPY

8. If you CALL a program which returns an exit code, that exit code value is available after CALL returns. Unfortunately, you can't set the exit code for a batch file, so CALL can't return an exit code from a batch file you have executed. To return status information from a batch file executed with the CALL command, create an environment variable and set it equal to your return status. Then you can test this environment variable in the calling batch file.

9. For *string1==string2*, DOS makes a literal, character-by-character comparison of the two strings. Neither string can contain embedded spaces or equal signs. If you want to include a percent sign (%) in either string, include it twice if this IF command is executed from a batch file. The comparison IF performs is case sensitive, that is, uppercase and lowercase characters are considered to be different.

10. When you include environment variables (such as %COMSPEC%) or replaceable parameters (such as %0 through %9) in either string argument in a batch file, they are replaced with the value of the environment variable or replaceable parameter when DOS parses the line. DOS does not parse commands you enter at the DOS prompt, so you can't include either type of variable in a command that you execute from the DOS prompt.

11. When IF is performing *string1==string2* comparisons, each string must have at least one character in it or a syntax error will result, and DOS will abort the batch file. In DOS 6 and later, *string2* can be empty without causing an error. This problem often happens in IF statements that test replaceable parameters or environment variables and typically is solved by adding dummy characters to both strings. For instance, test %1x==ERNIEx or "%1"=="ERNIE" instead of %1==ERNIE.

12. Including less than two equal signs in an IF string comparison results in a syntax error. Interestingly enough, you can use more than two equal signs without causing an error.

13. The EXIST *pathname* form of the IF command returns true if at least one file matches the *pathname* specified. If an invalid subdirectory or drive is specified, the condition is false. DOS does not search the DOS PATH for *pathname*; DOS only searches the drive and subdirectory specified. If *pathname* is omitted, DOS searches the current drive and directory.

14. Although the EXIST *pathname* form of the IF command is intended to test for the existence of files, you can use it to test for the existence of a subdirectory by specifying the NUL device as the file name. The NUL device (or any other valid DOS device) exists in every subdirectory; so if the subdirectory specified exists, then the IF EXIST *path*\NUL command will be true.

Examples

Notice that because of the way the IF ERRORLEVEL command works—testing whether an exit code is greater than or equal to the number specified—the following statement always executes the GOTO statement:

```
IF ERRORLEVEL 0 GOTO ALWAYS_JUMP
```

When testing an ERRORLEVEL number, be sure to test for the highest possible number first. Consider the following example:

```
IF ERRORLEVEL 1 GOTO ONE_OR_GREATER
IF ERRORLEVEL 2 GOTO TWO_OR_GREATER
```

The preceding example always goes to ONE_OR_GREATER, even if an ERRORLEVEL of 2 is returned, because 2 is greater than or equal to 1. Make sure that when you use IF ERRORLEVEL commands, you include them in descending order.

You can get around the limitation just noted by nesting IF ERRORLEVEL commands, checking for ranges of values with upper and lower bounds. Test for the lowest value; then test for NOT the highest value plus one in an embedded IF command. For example, consider the following IF commands:

```
IF ERRORLEVEL 1 IF NOT ERRORLEVEL 4 GOTO ONE_TO_THREE
```

In English, if the exit code returned by the program is greater than or equal to the first value (1) and less than the second value (not greater than or equal to 4), execute the command. Notice that this form of the IF ERRORLEVEL command will execute the proper GOTO command, no matter what order they are executed in. To test for a single value, simply embed a negative test for one more than the value you want, like this:

```
IF ERRORLEVEL 2 IF NOT ERRORLEVEL 3 GOTO ONLY_TWO
```

IF string comparisons are often used to make sure that at least one parameter is specified when the batch file is executed.

```
IF "%1"=="" GOTO HELP_MESSAGE
IF "%1"=="/?" GOTO HELP_MESSAGE
```

If no parameters to the batch file are specified, the first IF condition is true, and the GOTO command jumps to a section of the batch file where you can display a help message. The second IF statement tests for the /? help switch, enabling this batch file to honor a request for help from the user as well.

Sometimes this technique is combined with the SHIFT command to allow a batch file to loop through a variable number of parameters, as shown in the following:

```
:LOOP
IF "%1"==""  GOTO  END
TYPE  %1  |  MORE
SHIFT
GOTO  LOOP

:END
```

You could specify as many text files as you wanted to when executing this batch file, and the TYPE command would display each one in turn. After the last file had been displayed, the IF command would execute the GOTO END command, and the batch file would terminate. By combining IF and GOTO in this way, a multiline loop can be created in a batch file.

To jump around part of a batch file if the network menu choice was not chosen from a DOS 6.0 start-up menu, use the following line:

```
IF NOT "%CONFIG%"=="NETWORK" GOTO FINISH
```

Notice that in all the examples above, quotation marks are used to ensure that the string comparisons never try to evaluate a null string. For example, in the preceding command, if the CONFIG environment variable turns out to be undefined, DOS evaluates the following statement after the parser makes substitutions:

```
IF NOT ""=="NETWORK" GOTO FINISH
```

Without the quotation marks, one side of the comparison would be empty, and the batch file would be aborted with a syntax error message. With the quotation marks included, DOS simply finds "" not equal to "NETWORK".

Suppose that you want to copy all the .DOC files in your C:\WORK subdirectory to a backup disk. You could use the IF EXIST command to make sure that at least one .DOC file existed before executing the COPY command.

```
IF EXIST C:\WORK\*.DOC COPY C:\WORK\*.DOC A:
```

The IF EXIST command can be used to check for the existence of a subdirectory, by specifying the NUL device as the file name. You can use this technique to create a subdirectory if it doesn't already exist:

```
IF NOT EXIST C:\WORK\NUL MD C:\WORK
```

By nesting IF EXIST commands, you can also check to make sure that a file doesn't exist:

```
IF EXIST C:\WORK\NUL IF NOT EXIST C:\WORK\MYFILE.TXT
GOTO NOFILE
```

Notice that simply checking for the file with IF NOT EXIST can return true if the subdirectory or drive is invalid, which might lead to errors later in your batch file. By testing for the existence of the path and then checking that the file doesn't exist, you can be sure that creating MYFILE.TXT in the C:\WORK subdirectory will succeed without overwriting another file.

See Also

:label, %environ%, %n, and GOTO

"Using the IF Command" in Chapter 16

CONFIG SYS

INCLUDE= 6.0 and later—Internal

After you have set up a start-up menu, you may find that in certain configuration blocks, you are entering the same commands over and over. Instead of retyping them, you can gather them all together in a block of their own and use the INCLUDE= command to include that block within the others. The [COMMON] block performs a similar function for commands that you want to include in all your configuration blocks. INCLUDE= can only be used in your CONFIG.SYS file.

Syntax

INCLUDE=*blockname*

Parameters and Switches

blockname The name of the configuration block that you want to include when the active configuration block is processed. ***blockname*** must match a configuration block you have defined elsewhere in your CONFIG.SYS file, and it also may contain INCLUDE= commands. This argument is required.

Notes

1. The INCLUDE= command can only appear inside configuration blocks in CONFIG.SYS and can only refer to another configuration block. You cannot use INCLUDE= to include the selections from one menu block within another.

2. CONFIG.SYS allows two types of blocks: menu blocks and configuration blocks. Each block begins with a [*blockname*] and includes all the lines that follow—up to the next [*blockname*]. Menu blocks, which are blocks named [MENU] or defined with a SUBMENU= command, can include only menu-related commands. All other CONFIG.SYS commands belong in configuration blocks.

   The [COMMON] block is a special kind of configuration block, and certain special rules apply to it. It is the only block name that you can have more than once in your CONFIG.SYS file. All commands included in a [COMMON] block are always executed. Any commands in CONFIG.SYS that are not included in any block (that is, they appear before the first [*blockname*]) are assumed to be in a [COMMON] block.

   [COMMON] blocks are an alternative to using the INCLUDE= command. If you are using INCLUDE= to include a single block of commands in all your configuration blocks, consider using a [COMMON] block instead.

3. You are allowed to nest INCLUDE= commands. That is, a block included with the INCLUDE= command can have another INCLUDE= command within it. Although there is no clear limit to how deep this nesting can go, for the sake of clarity, you should limit yourself to no more than one or two levels of INCLUDE= commands.

Trap

Because nesting is allowed, there is the possibility of creating an endless loop. Make sure that an included block never includes any block that included it (that is, A includes B, which includes A).

4. The INCLUDE command is meant to help you eliminate repetition in your CONFIG.SYS file. Its use, however, often makes your CONFIG.SYS file harder to understand. Weigh these factors carefully when you decide whether to use an INCLUDE block. When software you are installing makes a mess of your menu system, a clear, simple CONFIG.SYS file is easier to repair than a complicated one.

Examples

The following sample CONFIG.SYS file is meant to illustrate the use of INCLUDE= blocks and [COMMON] blocks.

```
[MENU]
MENUITEM=MINIMUM, Minimal Configuration
MENUITEM=NORMAL, Normal Configuration (Default)
MENUITEM=NORM_EMS, Normal Configuration with EMS Available
MENUITEM=MAXIMUM, All the Bells and Whistles
MENUDEFAULT=NORMAL, 30

[COMMON]
DEVICE=C:\DOS\HIMEM.SYS
DOS=HIGH
BREAK=ON
NUMLOCK=OFF

[MINIMUM]
BUFFERS=30
LASTDRIVE=H
STACKS=9,256

[NORMAL]
INCLUDE=MINIMUM
DEVICE=C:\DOS\EMM386.EXE NOEMS
DOS=UMB

[NORM_EMS]
INCLUDE=MINIMUM
DEVICE=C:\DOS\EMM386.EXE RAM
DOS=UMB

[MAXIMUM]
INCLUDE=NORM_EMS
DEVICEHIGH=C:\DOS\RAMDRIVE.SYS 1450 512 224 /E
DEVICEHIGH=C:\DOS\ANSI.SYS
```

```
[COMMON]
SHELL=C:\DOS\COMMAND.COM C:\DOS\ /P /E:512
```

Notice that the MAXIMUM configuration includes the NORM_EMS configuration, which in turn includes the MINIMUM configuration. All the configuration choices automatically "include" the commands in the two COMMON blocks. As you can see, this kind of nesting can quickly become confusing. Don't use this example as a model for your own CONFIG.SYS file; it is only meant to illustrate the use of the INCLUDE= command and is much more complicated than it needs to be.

As it turns out, all the commands in the MINIMUM block could be placed in the COMMON block preceding it, leaving the MINIMUM block empty. (No matter what configuration you choose, the MINIMUM block is included.) However, if you removed the MINIMUM block completely, the corresponding menu line would not display, and you would need to remove the INCLUDE=MINIMUM commands from the other blocks as well.

See Also

[*blockname*] and MENUITEM=

"Creating Multiple Configurations" in Chapter 2

INSTALL= 4.0 and later—Internal

INSTALL= can load resident software (TSRs) from your CONFIG.SYS file into conventional memory. Programs loaded with INSTALL= are executed after all other CONFIG.SYS lines have been processed, and just before the command-line interpreter (COMMAND.COM) is loaded into memory. INSTALL= can be used only in your CONFIG.SYS file.

Syntax

INSTALL=*drive:\path***filename** *parameters*

Parameters and Switches

drive:\path — Although optional, you should always include the full drive and path to the resident program file. If this is omitted, the file is assumed to be in the root directory of the start-up drive.

filename — The full file name, with extension, of the resident program to be loaded. No extension is assumed, and wildcards are not allowed. This parameter is required.

parameters Any parameters that the resident program requires are included after its name. DOS passes these parameters directly to the program when it's loaded into memory. For more information, see the instructions for loading the resident program.

Notes

1. If MS-DOS cannot find the program file you have specified, it displays a `Bad or missing filename` message and continues processing CONFIG.SYS. (See the first item in the following "Messages" section.)

2. Resident programs included with DOS that can be safely loaded with the INSTALL= command include FASTOPEN.EXE, KEYB.COM, NLSFUNC.EXE, and SHARE.EXE.

3. In versions of DOS prior to DOS 6, many resident programs could not be loaded with INSTALL= because no environment was available to them. Starting with DOS 6, an environment is available to installed programs, and most resident software can now be successfully loaded this way.

4. With DOS 6, there is little reason to use INSTALL= anymore. In the past, one of the main reasons to use INSTALL= was to save the small amount of memory wasted on environments for resident software. But with DOS 6, you save little or nothing. Also, INSTALL= is limited to loading software into conventional memory, and you can't include LOADHIGH in an INSTALL= command to get around this. All in all, you usually are better off avoiding INSTALL= entirely; instead, load your resident software from your AUTOEXEC.BAT file.

5. DOS executes all other lines in CONFIG.SYS, including any SET commands, before executing any INSTALL= lines. When all the INSTALL= lines have been processed, the command interpreter (COMMAND.COM) is loaded and begins to process your AUTOEXEC.BAT file.

6. Only resident software should be loaded with an INSTALL= command. DOS waits until the program terminates before continuing, and if a normal program is run, neither COMMAND.COM nor your AUTOEXEC.BAT file is loaded until you quit the program. Although this might be interesting, it could make your system very unstable and should be avoided.

Examples

To load SHARE.EXE from your CONFIG.SYS file, you would include the following line:

```
INCLUDE=C:\DOS\SHARE.EXE  /L:50
```

This line assumes that SHARE.EXE is located in the C:\DOS subdirectory and sets the number of file locks to 50. For DOS to find SHARE.EXE, the file extension must always be included with the file name, because no default extensions are assumed with INSTALL=.

Messages

`Bad or missing filename`

`Error in CONFIG.SYS line number`

Warning: DOS displays this message if it can't find the file you specified in a DEVICE=, DEVICEHIGH=, or INSTALL= command in your CONFIG.SYS file. *filename* is the name of the file that DOS was looking for, and number is the line in CONFIG.SYS where the command is located. Edit the line so that the path and file name are correct, and then restart your computer.

See Also

DEVICE= and LOADHIGH

"Using the INSTALL Command" in Chapter 18

INTERLNK

6.0 and later—External

When you run INTERLNK from the DOS command-line, it communicates with the INTERLNK.EXE device driver in memory, allowing you to view or change the server drives you have access to. If the connection to the server hasn't been established, INTERLNK attempts to connect with the server, using the parameters you specified when you loaded the INTERLNK.EXE device driver. Before you can run INTERLNK from the DOS command line, you must load the INTERLNK.EXE device driver into memory with a DEVICE= statement in your CONFIG.SYS file.

Syntax

INTERLNK *client:=server: ...*

Parameters and Switches

client: The client drive letter that you want to use to access a disk drive on the Interlnk server. *client:* must be one of the drive letters that the INTERLNK.EXE device driver reserved when it loaded into memory. The trailing colon is optional.

server: The server drive that you want *client:* to refer to. *server:* must be a drive on the Interlnk server that is available for redirection. The trailing colon is optional. If this parameter is omitted, the *client:* drive letter is disconnected from the Interlnk server.

Notes

1. The INTERLNK.EXE device driver must be installed before you can run INTERLNK from the command line. If you try to run INTERLNK without installing the device driver, an error message is displayed. (See the following "Messages" section.)

2. INTERLNK.EXE actually is two files: a device driver and an executable program. The device driver portion does all the real work and has to be loaded into memory with a DEVICE= command in your CONFIG.SYS file. After this device driver has been loaded into memory, the executable portion of the file communicates with the device driver to reassign drive letters and display status information.

3. To display Interlnk's status, type **INTERLNK** at the DOS prompt. Interlnk displays a list of client drive letters on the left, with the server drives they are connected to on the right. If any of the server drives have volume labels, they are displayed as well.

4. You can include as many *client:=server:* parameters as you need in a single INTERLNK command. Separate each *client:=server:* assignment with spaces.

5. To disconnect an Interlnk drive, specify the *client:=* parameter but omit the *server:* drive letter. A disconnected *client:* drive letter is immediately available for use connecting to another server drive. You can perform a mixture of drive assignments and disconnections in a single INTERLNK command by separating each one with spaces.

6. The drives that INTERLNK.EXE reserves when it loads into memory are private; they can't be used by other programs even if Interlnk isn't using them. For example, you cannot use an inactive Interlnk drive letter as a network drive or a SUBST alias. INTERLNK.EXE displays the drive letters it has reserved when it is loading into memory.

7. To use a printer on an Interlnk server from within Windows, you first have to access the Printer dialog box in Control Panel. Next, click the Connect... button. In the Connect dialog box, either clear the Fast Printing Direct To Port check box, or specify the port as LPT1.DOS or LPT2.DOS rather than LPT1 or LPT2. Normally, Windows prints directly to the hardware and bypasses Interlnk's printer redirection. However, when you disable Fast Printing or print to a file name rather than the port name, Windows prints through DOS, and Interlnk can redirect the data to the server's printer port.

8. All disk drives redirected by Interlnk are considered removable drives because the connection to them can be lost at any time. DoubleSpace refers to Interlnk drives as normal, removable local drives. MSD reports that Interlnk drives are floppy drives with one cylinder. SMARTDrive defaults to read-caching Interlnk drives, as it does with local floppy disk drives. Windows File Manager represents Interlnk drives with a "floppy icon."

9. An Interlnk client cannot access CD-ROM drives on the server. Interlnk can only recognize standard DOS drives, not network drives. CD-ROM drives use the network interface, so Interlnk cannot be used to give the client computer access to CD-ROM drives on the server.

10. Redirected Interlnk drives do not support disk-level operations, and the following DOS commands should not be used on redirected drives:

    CHKDSK, DEFRAG, DEBUG, DISKCOMP, DISKCOPY, FDISK, FORMAT, MIRROR, SCANDISK, SYS, UNDELETE, UNFORMAT

    Third-party utilities that require low-level disk access should also be avoided.

11. In order to run, INTERLNK requires DOS 3.0 or later. You can run different versions of DOS on the client and server computers, although the limitations of each version must be respected. For example, disk partitions greater than 32M on an Interlnk server are not accessible on an

Interlnk client running DOS 3.0. (The Microsoft MS-DOS 6 license agreement requires at least one of the two computers involved to be running a licensed copy of MS-DOS 6.)

12. An appropriate cable is required to connect two computers with Interlnk. If you are using serial ports for the Interlnk connection, a 3-wire or 7-wire null-modem serial cable is required. If you are using parallel ports, an 11-wire parallel cable is required. These cables are often referred to as LapLink cables, in honor of the product that popularized this simple type of network. Check the two computers to see what type of connectors you need. Microsoft includes detailed wiring charts for these cables in the entry for INTERLNK in the DOS 6 on-line help system (that is, type **HELP INTERLNK** at the DOS prompt and click the Notes entry).

Examples

Assuming that Interlnk is running and you have successfully connected with the server, redirect the client drive letter D: to access drive C: on the server by entering the following command.

```
INTERLNK D=C
```

Notice that you are not required to enter colons with the drive letters, although colons are acceptable.

To break the relationship (cancel the redirection) between the client's D drive and the server drive, enter this command:

```
INTERLNK D=
```

You can make more than one assignment in a single command by separating them with spaces like this:

```
INTERLNK D=A E=B F=C
```

This command would connect you to three server drives. Drive D on the client computer would refer to drive A on the server, drive E to drive B on the server, and drive F to drive C on the server.

If you ever get lost and want to see what assignments you have, type the INTERLNK command with no parameters.

```
INTERLNK
```

INTERLNK displays a status screen that looks something like this:

```
This Computer        Other Computer
  (Client)              (Server)
------------   -----------------------
  D:    equals    A:
  E:    equals    B:
  F:    equals    C: (120Mb)  CONNER 120
  LPT2: equals    LPT1:
```

This screen reflects the assignments made earlier with the INTERLNK D=A E=B F=C command. You can't control the assignment of printer ports from the command line, but the display does show you what drive assignments Interlnk has made. To print to the server's printer, you would print to LPT2 on the client computer.

Interlnk shows the size of any server hard drives in parentheses after the drive letter in the right-hand column. Notice that if any of the server drives have volume labels, they're displayed as well (`CONNER 120` is the volume label for the server's C: drive in the example). Volume labels can make a confusing assignment display a bit easier to understand.

Messages

```
Connection NOT Established
Make sure that a serial or parallel canble connects the server and
client computers, and that INTERSVR.EXE is running on the server
computer.
```

Error: Interlnk was unable to establish a connection with the server program. Before trying to establish this connection from the client computer, make sure that the cable is connected at both ends and that INTERSVR is running on the server computer.

```
Drive assignment syntax error.
```

Error: You have made a syntax error while attempting to assign drive letters to remote drives on the Interlnk server. This message is often caused by trying to assign drive letters which weren't reserved by INTERLNK.EXE. The only drive letters you can use to access drives on the Interlnk server are the ones that INTERLNK.EXE displays when it is loaded into memory from your CONFIG.SYS file.

```
Driver NOT installed
To install Interlnk, add the following line to your CONFIG.SYS file
and reboot:
    DEVICE=drive:\path\INTERLNK.EXE
```

Information: You have attempted to run the INTERLNK program without first installing the INTERLNK.EXE device driver. *drive:\path* in the preceding message reflects the current location of INTERLNK.EXE on your system. You can only run INTERLNK from the command line when the client device driver is in memory, so you must load INTERLNK.EXE from your CONFIG.SYS before you can access the executable portion of the program.

```
Invalid unit reading drive drive
Abort, Retry, Fail
```

Error: You've tried to access an Interlnk drive that isn't assigned to a drive on the Interlnk server. Press A to abort, R to Retry, and F to Fail. The safest choice is to Fail the operation by pressing F. In most cases, Retry simply redisplays the error message. After you have cleared the error message, you can assign this drive letter to a server drive by using the INTERLNK *client:=server:* command.

```
Not ready reading drive drive
Abort, Retry, Fail
```

Error: You have tried to access an Interlnk drive (or another reserved drive letter), but the connection to the Interlnk server hasn't been made yet. Press A to abort, R to Retry, and F to Fail. Normally, you should Fail the operation by pressing F. You can establish the connection to the server by running INTERLNK from the command line.

```
The version number of Interlnk in memory does not match the version
number in the file: pathname
```

Error: The version of Interlnk you ran from the DOS command line doesn't match the version of the device driver that is being loaded in your CONFIG.SYS file. Somehow, you have ended up with two different copies of INTERLNK.EXE on your disk. Locate the newer copy of INTERLNK.EXE, and make sure that you are loading that copy in your CONFIG.SYS file. You may want to remove the old copy of INTERLNK.EXE from your disk so that you do not run it by accident.

See Also

INTERLNK.EXE and INTERSVR

"Using Interlnk to Share Another Computer's Resources" in Chapter 8

INTERLNK.EXE (device driver)

6.0 and later—External

The INTERLNK.EXE device driver establishes a link by way of a serial or parallel cable with another computer that is running the INTERSVR program. INTERLNK.EXE provides the client side of this relationship and usually is installed on a laptop computer (the client) from which you want to access files or printers on a desktop computer (the server). INTERLNK.EXE must be loaded in a DEVICE= statement in your CONFIG.SYS file.

Syntax

DEVICE=*drive:\path***INTERLNK.EXE** /DRIVES:*num* /NOPRINTER /COM /COM:*num* /COM:*addr* /LPT /LPT:*num* /LPT:*addr* /AUTO /NOSCAN /LOW /BAUD:*rate* /V

Parameters and Switches

drive:\path
: The full path to the INTERLNK.EXE file on your system. Setup places the INTERLNK.EXE file in the C:\DOS subdirectory by default. If the full path to INTERLNK.EXE isn't specified, DOS looks for the file in the root directory of the start-up drive.

/DRIVES:*num*
: The number of drive letters to reserve for redirected drives on the client computer. *Num* can be any value from 0 to the number of drive letters still available when INTERLNK.EXE is loaded. (DOS can allocate 26 drive letters, from A to Z.) If this parameter is omitted, 3 drive letters are reserved. Specifying /DRIVES:0 disables drive redirection, and only printers will be redirected.

/NOPRINTER
: Specifies that no printers should be redirected. Normally, Interlnk redirects all available printers. Specifying this parameter can reduce the size of INTERLNK.EXE in memory.

/COM
: Specifies that Interlnk should scan all serial ports when it's looking for a connection with the server. This is the default setting. If you have a serial mouse, you may want to use a /COM:*num* or /LPT:*num* parameter to specify the port that Interlnk should use.

/COM:*num*

The serial port (by DOS number) that Interlnk should use to connect with the server. This parameter can be entered as /COM:1 or as /COM1, the colon is optional. Typical values are /COM1, /COM2, /COM3, and /COM4.

/COM:*addr*

The serial port (by hexadecimal port address) that Interlnk should use to connect with the server. Typical addresses for serial ports are 3F8 and 2F8. Unless you have a particular reason to specify the serial port by address, you should use the more familiar port numbers.

/LPT

Specifies that Interlnk should scan all parallel ports when it's looking for a connection with the server. This is the default setting.

/LPT:*num*

The parallel port (by DOS number) that Interlnk should use to connect with the server. This parameter can be entered as /LPT:1 or as /LPT1—the colon is optional. Typical values are /LPT1, /LPT2, and /LPT3. This parameter has nothing to do with redirected printers. It specifies the port being used to connect the two computers together.

/LPT:*addr*

The parallel port (by hexadecimal port address) that Interlnk should use to connect with the server. Typical addresses for parallel ports are 3BC, 378, and 278. Unless you have a particular reason to specify the parallel port by address, you should use the more familiar port numbers instead.

/AUTO

Specifying this parameter instructs INTERLNK.EXE not to remain in memory if the server is unavailable. By using this parameter, you can leave in your CONFIG.SYS file the DEVICE= line that loads INTERLNK.EXE. With /AUTO specified, Interlnk only loads into memory if you are connected to a server when you start up your computer.

/NOSCAN

Specifying this parameter stops INTERLNK.EXE from trying to establish a connection with the server when

INTERLNK.EXE loads into memory. You have to establish the connection later by running INTERLNK from the DOS command line.

/LOW — If upper memory is available, INTERLNK.EXE normally tries to load itself high. If you want to make sure that INTERLNK.EXE loads into conventional memory instead, specify the /LOW parameter.

/BAUD:*rate* — The maximum baud rate you want Interlnk to use for serial communications. *rate* can be one of the following values: 9600, 19200, 38400, 57600, and 115200. If no maximum rate is specified, 115200 is assumed.

Note that *rate* only limits the maximum data transfer rate that can be used between the client and the server for a serial connection. If you are using a parallel connection, the /BAUD:*rate* parameter has no effect.

/V — If either the client or the server computer freezes while accessing Interlnk drives, try specifying the /V parameter on one or both computers. This parameter attempts to correct problems that arise from conflicts with the system timers on connected computers.

Notes

1. The INTERLNK.EXE device driver must be installed before you can run INTERLNK from the command line. If you try to run INTERLNK without installing the device driver, an error message is displayed. (See the first item in the following "Messages" section.)

Trap

When Interlnk scans serial ports looking for a server connection, it interferes with the operation of any mouse drivers that are servicing those ports. If your mouse is attached to a serial port, be sure to use a */COM:num* or */LPT:num* parameter to specify the port that Interlnk should use.

2. INTERLNK.EXE actually is two files: a device driver and an executable program. The device driver portion does all the real work and has to be loaded into memory with a DEVICE= command in your CONFIG.SYS

file. After this device driver is loaded into memory, the executable portion of the file communicates with the device driver to reassign drive letters and display status information.

3. If you regularly use Interlnk to connect your laptop to a desktop computer, make sure that you specify the /AUTO parameter. Then, when you're on the road, INTERLNK.EXE will fail to find the server and not waste memory by loading anyway. Whenever you want to use Interlnk, simply connect the cable to a server and reboot the laptop.

4. INTERLNK.EXE automatically loads into upper memory if it's available. It's not necessary to use the DEVICEHIGH= command with INTERLNK.EXE.

5. By default, all of the client's serial ports and then all of the client's parallel ports are scanned when Interlnk looks for a connection with the server. As soon as the server is found, scanning stops. If /COM is specified without /LPT, only the client's serial ports are scanned. Similarly, if /LPT is specified without /COM, only the client's parallel ports are scanned. Interlnk's default behavior is equivalent to specifying both the /COM and /LPT parameters.

6. Under normal circumstances, INTERLNK.EXE requires about 15K of memory. You can decrease this amount by specifying certain parameters. When you specify the /NOPRINTER parameter, Interlnk does not load the routines required to redirect printer output. If you specify the /DRIVES:0 parameter, Interlnk does not load the routines required to redirect disk drives. If you specify either the /COM or the /LPT parameter (but not both), Interlnk does not load the routines required to access the type of port you are not using. Depending on what combination of Interlnk services you need, you may be able to slim Interlnk's memory use significantly.

7. The drives that INTERLNK.EXE reserves when it loads into memory are private and can't be claimed by other programs even if Interlnk isn't using them. For example, you cannot use an inactive Interlnk drive letter as a network drive or a SUBST alias.

8. If INTERLNK.EXE fails to connect with a server when it loads, or is prevented from connecting by the /NOSCAN parameter, the drives it reserves will be empty. To establish a connection with the server you will

have to run INTERLNK from the command line and redirect the server drives manually.

9. Because INTERLNK.EXE allocates drive letters, you should be very careful about where you locate it in your CONFIG.SYS file. In most cases, you will want to load INTERLNK.EXE last so that any drives it allocates leave other drive assignments in CONFIG.SYS unchanged.

Trap

It can be a painful chore having your drive letters change simply because you added a device driver to your CONFIG.SYS file. Batch files often have to be edited to reflect the new drive letters. All references to drives that have changed have to be corrected in your CONFIG.SYS and AUTOEXEC.BAT files. Microsoft Windows is very sensitive to drive letter changes, and some Windows' applications fail if they are suddenly located on a different drive.

Before you add or rearrange DEVICE= lines in your CONFIG.SYS, think through the changes you may be making to drive letter assignments and the impact the changes will have on your system. If you are careful, you can often accomplish your task without changing any drive letter assignments, or at least keep the changes to a minimum. Doing so can save you a great deal of work.

10. If you use DoubleSpace, always load the DBLSPACE.SYS driver before you load INTERLNK.EXE. If you load INTERLNK.EXE first, the DoubleSpace host (uncompressed) drives may become unavailable on the client computer.

11. To use a printer on an Interlnk server from within Windows, you first have to access the Printer dialog box in Control Panel. Next, click the Connect... button. In the Connect dialog box, either clear the Fast Printing Direct To Port check box, or specify the port as LPT1.DOS or LPT2.DOS rather than LPT1 or LPT2. Normally, Windows prints directly to the hardware and bypasses Interlnk's printer redirection. However, when you disable Fast Printing or print to a file name instead of the port name, Windows prints through DOS, and Interlnk can redirect the data to the server's printer port.

12. All disk drives redirected by Interlnk are considered removable drives, because the connection to them can be lost at any time. DoubleSpace refers to Interlnk drives as normal, removable local drives. MSD reports that Interlnk drives are floppy drives with one cylinder. SMARTDrive

defaults to read-caching Interlnk drives, as it does with local floppy disk drives. Windows File Manager represents Interlnk drives with a "floppy icon."

13. An Interlnk client cannot access CD-ROM drives on the server. Interlnk can only recognize standard DOS drives, not network drives. Because CD-ROM drives use the network interface, Interlnk cannot be used to give the client computer access to CD-ROM drives on the server.

14. Redirected Interlnk drives do not support disk-level operations, and the following DOS commands should not be used on redirected drives:

    CHKDSK, DEFRAG, DEBUG, DISKCOMP, DISKCOPY, FDISK, FORMAT, MIRROR, SCANDISK, SYS, UNDELETE, UNFORMAT

    Third-party utilities that require low-level disk access should also be avoided.

15. INTERLNK.EXE requires DOS 3.0 or later in order to run. You can run different versions of DOS on the client and server computers, although the limitations of each version must be respected. For example, disk partitions greater than 32M on an Interlnk server are not accessible on an Interlnk client running DOS 3.0. (The Microsoft MS-DOS 6 license agreement requires at least one of the two computers involved to be running a licensed copy of MS-DOS 6.)

16. An appropriate cable is required to connect two computers with Interlnk. If you are using serial ports for the Interlnk connection, a 3-wire or 7-wire null-modem serial cable is required. If you are using parallel ports, an 11-wire parallel cable is required. These cables are often referred to as LapLink cables, in honor of the product that popularized this simple type of network. Check the two computers to see what type of connectors you need. Microsoft includes detailed wiring charts for these cables in the entry for INTERLNK in the DOS 6 on-line help system (that is, type HELP INTERLNK at the DOS prompt and click the Notes entry).

Examples

A typical line that loads INTERLNK.EXE in the CONFIG.SYS file of your Laptop computer might look like this:

```
DEVICE=C:\DOS\INTERLNK.EXE /COM2 /AUTO
```

As long as the connection with the Interlnk server is established (on COM2), the Interlnk client device driver will load into memory and reserve three drive letters (the default is three) with which it can access drives on the server. Any printers attached to the server will be available on the client computer as well. Because of the /AUTO parameter, if INTERSVR isn't running on the server when this DEVICE= line is executed, INTERLNK.EXE won't load into memory.

If memory is tight, and you don't need access to more than one disk drive or any printers on the Interlnk server, you could add the /NOPRINTER parameter, like this:

```
DEVICE=C:\DOS\INTERLNK.EXE /COM2 /AUTO /DRIVES:1
  /NOPRINTER
```

Note that in both examples above, INTERLNK.EXE loads into upper memory if it's available. To force INTERLNK.EXE to load into conventional memory, specify the /LOW parameter, as in the following:

```
DEVICE=C:\DOS\INTERLNK.EXE /COM2 /AUTO /LOW
```

If you used a parallel cable to connect the two computers instead of a serial cable, you would specify a parallel port rather than a serial port.

```
DEVICE=C:\DOS\INTERLNK.EXE /LPT1 /AUTO
```

Note that you must use the same type of port on both computers. You can't use a serial port on one computer and a parallel port on the other. The cables you need aren't interchangeable, either.

After INTERLNK.EXE has successfully established a connection with the Interlnk server, it automatically assigns the drive letters it has reserved to disk drives on the Interlnk server. To see what assignments have been made, run INTERLNK from the DOS command line.

Messages

`*** Bad /COM argument` *`parameter`*

Error: Interlnk was unable to initialize the serial port you specified with a */COM:num* parameter. Check to make sure that you specified /COM1, /COM2, /COM3, or /COM4, and that your computer has that port installed. If you can't get this parameter to work, you may be forced to use the */COM:addr* parameter.

```
*** Bad /DRIVES parameter ignored (/DRIVES:n, n = 0 - 24).
```

Error: You have specified an invalid */DRIVES:num* parameter. Legal values for *num* are in the range 0 to 24, as indicated in the message. You may get this message if you have embedded any spaces in the parameter or if you have specified a letter instead of a digit.

```
*** Bad /LPT argument parameter
```

Error: Interlnk was unable to initialize the parallel port you specified with a */LPT:num* parameter. Check to make sure that you specified /LPT1, /LPT2, or /LPT3, and that your computer has that port installed. If you can't get this parameter to work, you may be forced to use the */LPT:addr* parameter.

```
*** Bad parallel port address: addr
```

or

```
*** Bad serial port address: addr
```

Error: Interlnk was unable to initialize the parallel or serial port you specified with a */LPT:num* or */COM:num* parameter. Make sure that you are specifying the correct value for *addr* and that the value is entered in hexadecimal notation.

```
*** Invalid /BAUD parameter ignored.
```

Warning: You have specified an invalid */BAUD:rate* parameter, and Interlnk has used the default value of 115200. Check to make sure that the value you specified for *rate* is 9600, 19200, 38400, 57600, or 115200. You can't embed commas in these values.

```
*** Specified COM port number not recognized by BIOS: COM#
```

or

```
*** Specified LPT port number not recognized by BIOS: LPT#
```

Error: You have specified a port with the */LPT:num* or */COM:num* parameter, which isn't supported by the ROM BIOS in your computer. You may get this message if you specify a port that doesn't exist in your computer, or if your ports are using non-standard port addresses. If the problem is non-standard port addresses, you still may be able to use this port by specifying its address with a */LPT:addr* or */COM:addr* parameter.

```
Connection NOT Established
Make sure that a serial or parallel cable connects the server and client
computers, and that INTERSVR.EXE is running on the server computer.
```

Error: Interlnk was unable to establish a connection with the server program. Before trying to establish this connection from the client computer, make sure that the cable is connected at both ends and that INTERSVR is running on the server computer.

```
Drive letters redirected: num (drive: through drive:)
```

Information: INTERLNK.EXE displays this message when it loads into memory. You may want to write down the drive letters that the INTERLNK.EXE device driver has reserved. These are the only letters you can use to access drives on the Interlnk server.

```
Driver NOT installed
To install Interlnk, add the following line to your CONFIG.SYS file
and reboot:
    DEVICE=drive:\path\INTERLNK.EXE
```

Information: You have attempted to run the INTERLNK program without first installing the INTERLNK.EXE device driver. The *drive:\path* in the preceding message reflects the current location of INTERLNK.EXE on your system. You can run INTERLNK only from the command line when the client device driver is in memory; therefore, you must load INTERLNK.EXE from your CONFIG.SYS before you can access the executable portion of the program.

```
Invalid switch - parameter
```

Error: You have specified an invalid parameter on the DEVICE= line for INTERLNK.EXE in your CONFIG.SYS file. The *parameter* displayed in the message is the one that's confusing INTERLNK.EXE. Correct this entry and try the command again.

```
No drive letters redirected
```

Information: You have loaded the INTERLNK.EXE device driver with a */DRIVES:0* parameter. You will not be able to access any disk drives on the Interlnk server.

```
No printer ports redirected
```

Information: You have loaded the INTERLNK.EXE device driver with a */NOPRINTER* parameter. You will not be able to access any printers on the Interlnk server.

```
The Interlnk device driver requires version 3.0 or later of DOS.
```

Error: INTERLNK.EXE requires that you be running at least DOS 3.0. If you know that the computer is running a later version of DOS than 3.0 (type VER), you may have a bad entry for INTERLNK.EXE in your SETVER table.

`Too many block devices`

Warning: DOS has run out of drive letters and cannot load any more block devices from your CONFIG.SYS file. DOS will continue to start up, but some of your device drivers may not be loaded. DOS can handle up to 26 accessible block devices.

Certain device drivers allocate more than one letter when they are loaded. DoubleSpace allocates at least one letter for each compressed drive you have in your system, plus some spares. INTERLNK.EXE allocates the number requested with the /DRIVES:*num* parameter, or 3 if a number isn't specified. RAMDRIVE.SYS and DRIVER.SYS allocate one letter each time they are loaded. Check your CONFIG.SYS file and eliminate any DEVICE= lines you don't need, or decrease the number of drives set aside for Interlnk.

See Also

DEVICE=, INTERLNK, and INTERSVR

"Using Interlnk to Share Another Computer's Resources" in Chapter 8

INTERSVR

6.0 and later—External

INTERSVR provides server services for an Interlnk network. The server in an Interlnk network is the computer that is making its drives and printers available for use on another computer (the client). INTERSVR monopolizes the server computer while it is running, preventing you from using the server computer for anything else. You have to have an appropriate serial or parallel cable to connect the two computers.

Syntax

INTERSVR *drive:* ... /X=*drive:* ... /COM /COM:*num* /COM:*addr* /LPT /LPT:*num* /LPT:*addr* /BAUD:*rate* /V /B

To copy the Interlnk files to a connected computer that is not running Interlnk, use the following format:

INTERSVR /RCOPY

Parameters and Switches

drive: ... The letter of a drive that can be redirected. The ellipsis (...) indicates that more than one drive can be redirected by a single INTERSVR command. By default, all drives are available for redirection.

/X=*drive: ...* The letter of a drive that will not be redirected. The ellipsis (...) indicates that more than one drive can be excluded by a single INTERSVR command. By default, no drives are excluded.

/COM Specifies that INTERSVR should scan all serial ports when it's looking for a connection with the client. This is the default setting. If you have a serial mouse, you may want to use a */COM:num* or */LPT:num* parameter to specify the port Interlnk should use.

/COM:*num* The serial port (by DOS number) that INTERSVR should use to connect with the client. This parameter can be entered as /COM:1 or as /COM1—the colon is optional. Typical values are /COM1, /COM2, /COM3, and /COM4.

/COM:*addr* The serial port (by hexadecimal port address) that INTERSVR should use to connect with the client. Typical addresses for serial ports are 3F8 and 2F8. Unless you have a particular reason to specify the serial port by address, you should use the more familiar port numbers instead.

/LPT Specifies that INTERSVR should scan all parallel ports when it's looking for a connection with the client. This is the default setting.

/LPT:*num* The parallel port (by DOS number) that INTERSVR should use to connect with the client. This parameter can be entered as /LPT:1 or as /LPT1—the colon is optional. Typical values are /LPT1, /LPT2, and /LPT3. Note that this parameter has nothing to do with redirected printers; it specifies the port being used to connect the two computers together.

/LPT:*addr* — The parallel port (by hexadecimal port address) that INTERSVR should use to connect with the client. Typical addresses for parallel ports are 3BC, 378 and 278. Unless you have a particular reason to specify the parallel port by address, you should use the more familiar port numbers instead.

/BAUD:*rate* — The maximum baud rate you want Interlnk to use for serial communications. *rate* can be one of the following values: 9600, 19200, 38400, 57600, and 115200. If no maximum rate is specified, 115200 is assumed.

rate only limits the maximum data transfer rate that can be used between the client and the server for a serial connection. If you are using a parallel connection, the */BAUD:rate* parameter has no effect.

/V — If either the client or the server computer freezes while accessing Interlnk drives, try specifying the /V parameter on one or both computers. This parameter attempts to correct problems that arise from conflicts with the system timers on connected computers.

/B — Forces the use of a color scheme appropriate for a black-and-white (monochrome) monitor or LCD display.

/RCOPY — Copies the Interlnk files INTERLNK.EXE and INTERSVR.EXE to another computer. If your Laptop computer doesn't have a floppy disk drive, use this parameter to set up an Interlnk connection. The two computers must be connected by a seven-wire, null-modem serial cable (sometimes referred to as a LapLink cable). The MODE command must be available on the target computer for this transfer to work. You can't specify any other parameters when you're using the /RCOPY feature.

Notes

1. When INTERSVR scans serial ports looking for a client connection, it interferes with the operation of any mouse drivers that are servicing those ports. If your mouse is attached to a serial port, be sure to use a

/COM:num or */LPT:num* parameter to specify the port that Interlnk should use.

2. By default, all of the server's serial ports, and then all of the server's parallel ports are scanned when Interlnk searches for a connection with the client computer. As soon as the client is found, scanning stops. If /COM is specified without /LPT, only the server's serial ports are scanned. Similarly, if /LPT is specified without /COM, only the server's parallel ports are scanned. INTERSVR's default behavior is equivalent to specifying both the /COM and /LPT parameters.

3. INTERSVR is unable to make network or CD-ROM drives available to the client computer. Network and CD-ROM drives are not considered local drives because DOS uses the network redirector interface to access them.

4. While INTERSVR is running, it displays a list of redirected drives and printers on-screen. The left-hand column lists the disk drives and printers on the server that are being shared, and the right-hand column lists the letters and/or ports that are being used on the client computer to access the server drives. To exit INTERSVR and disconnect the Interlnk network, press Alt-F4.

5. You can't use the computer for anything else while INTERSVR is running. If you start INTERSVR in a task-switching environment such as Windows, it won't allow you to switch to another task without first exiting the INTERSVR program. Don't try to access any memory-resident programs; serious data loss could result. To be safe, you may want to disable or remove memory-resident programs before running INTERSVR.

6. Redirected Interlnk drives do not support disk-level operations, and the following DOS commands should not be used on redirected drives:

   CHKDSK, DEFRAG, DEBUG, DISKCOMP, DISKCOPY, FDISK, FORMAT, MIRROR, SCANDISK, SYS, UNDELETE, UNFORMAT

   Third-party utilities that require low-level disk access should also be avoided.

7. INTERSVR.EXE requires DOS 3.0 or later in order to run. You can run different versions of DOS on the client and server computers, although the limitations of each version must be respected. For example, disk

partitions greater than 32M on an Interlnk server are accessible on an Interlnk client running DOS 3.0. (The Microsoft MS-DOS 6 license agreement requires at least one of the two computers involved to be running a licensed copy of MS-DOS 6.)

8. An appropriate cable is required to connect two computers with Interlnk. If you're using serial ports for the Interlnk connection, a 3-wire or 7-wire null-modem serial cable is required. If you are using parallel ports, an 11-wire parallel cable is required. These cables are often referred to as LapLink cables in honor of the product that popularized this simple type of network. Check the two computers to see what type of connectors you need. Microsoft includes detailed wiring charts for these cables in the entry for INTERLNK in the DOS 6 on-line help system (that is, type HELP INTERLNK at the DOS prompt and click the Notes entry).

Examples

Before you start the Interlnk server program, connect with an appropriate serial or parallel cable the two computers you want to link. You also may want to remove or disable any resident programs you are running. You don't have to quit Windows or the DOS Shell, but you will be unable to switch to another task while the Interlnk server program is running.

To start the Interlnk server program, type the following command:

```
INTERSVR
```

INTERSVR scans your ports looking for an Interlnk connection. After it finds one, INTERSVR makes all local drives and printers on the server computer available to the Interlnk client.

If you are using a serial mouse, you should specify the port Interlnk should use. For example, if your mouse is attached to COM1 and you want to use COM2 on the server for the Interlnk connection, add the /COM2 parameter.

```
INTERSVR /COM2
```

If you don't need access to either of the server's floppy disk drives (A: and B:, in this example) from the client computer, you can exclude them by adding a /X=drive: parameter.

```
INTERSVR /COM2 /X=A: B:
```

If either computer stops responding when you access a remote drive or printer, you may have to specify the /V parameter for INTERSVR.

INTERSVR /COM2 /V

To use the remote copy feature, you must first connect the two computers with a 7-wire null-modem serial cable. (These cables are often referred to as LapLink cables, in honor of the company which made this sort of connection popular.) You cannot use parallel ports for this operation. Next, make sure that the computer which is to receive the Interlnk files is running DOS 3.0 or later and that the MODE command is available. Finally, on the computer containing the Interlnk files, start the Interlnk server with the /RCOPY parameter.

INTERSVR /RCOPY

INTERSVR will lead you through the copy operation, prompting you at each step. After the files INTERLNK.EXE and INTERSVR.EXE have been successfully transferred, you can start up the Interlnk network by running INTERSVR on the server computer, adding the INTERLNK.EXE device driver to the CONFIG.SYS file on the client computer, and rebooting the client computer.

Messages

`Error initializing port port at address addr`

Error: INTERSVR found your Interlnk port but was unable to initialize it. This error can be caused by INTERSVR finding the wrong port when it scans your system. Specify the port that you want to use with the /COM:*num* or /LPT:*num* parameter and try the command again.

`File allocation error in: pathname, run chkdsk /f to correct.`

Error: INTERSVR encountered a problem in the file allocation table (FAT) while it was accessing the file *pathname*. Quit INTERSVR, and run SCANDISK or CHKDSK /F to identify and fix the problem.

`If SHARE.EXE is loaded on the remote computer the remote install cannot be performed on COM2. Please use COM1 or insure that SHARE.EXE is not loaded on the remote computer before attempting a remote install.`

Warning: You are performing a remote copy operation using COM2 on the remote computer. Interlnk is warning you that the operation may fail if SHARE.EXE is running on the remote computer. If SHARE.EXE is running on the remote computer, you may want to choose a different serial port or restart the remote computer without loading SHARE.EXE.

`Invalid /BAUD parameter - rate`

Error: You have specified an invalid /BAUD:*rate* parameter. Check to make sure that the value you specified for *rate* is 9600, 19200, 38400, 57600, or 115200. You can't embed commas in these values.

`Invalid parallel port address LPT#: addr`

Error: You have specified a parallel port address with the /LPT:*addr* parameter, but Interlnk is unable to communicate with it. Make sure that you are specifying the correct value for *addr* and that the value is entered in hexadecimal notation.

`Invalid serial port address COM#: addr`

Error: You have specified a serial port address with the /COM:*addr* parameter, but Interlnk is unable to communicate with it. Make sure that you are specifying the correct value for *addr*, and that the value is entered in hexadecimal notation.

`Invalid server drive letter - drive`

Error: You have specified a server drive letter which either doesn't exist or Interlnk is unable to redirect. You cannot redirect any network or CD-ROM drives connected to the server computer. Check your entry to make sure that all the drive letters you have specified are valid, local disk drives.

`Invalid switch  parameter`

Error: You have specified an invalid parameter on the command line for INTERSVR. The *parameter* displayed in the message is the one that is confusing INTERSVR. Correct this entry and try the command again.

`There are no serial or parallel ports available for communication.`

Error: When INTERSVR scanned your computer's ports, it couldn't find the port you are using for the Interlnk connection. Specify the port that you want to use with the /COM:*num* or /LPT:*num* parameter and try the command again.

`Unable to initialize serial port COM#`

Error: INTERSVR found your Interlnk port but was unable to initialize it. This error can be caused by specifying the wrong port. Correct your entry for the
/COM:*num* or /LPT:*num* parameter and try the command again.

```
Unrecoverable transmission error, maximum retries exceeded.
```

Error: Your Interlnk connection has failed. Make sure that the cable you are using hasn't become unplugged at one or both ends. If you continue to see this error message, you may have to purchase a new cable.

```
You have started the Interlnk server in a task-switching environment.
Task-switching, key combinations, and some disk-writing operations are
disabled. To restore these functions, exit the server.
```

Information: INTERSVR displays this message if you start the server program while a task-switching environment like Windows is active. You will not be able to switch tasks until you exit INTERSVR with the Alt-F4 command.

See Also

INTERLNK and INTERLNK.EXE

"Using Interlnk to Share Another Computer's Resources" in Chapter 8

JOIN

3.1 to 5.0—External

The JOIN command produces a directory structure by connecting one drive to a subdirectory of another drive. JOIN is included on the DOS 6.0 Supplemental Disk, not in the standard DOS 6.0 package.

Syntax

To connect disk drives, use the following format:

JOIN ***drive***: *drive2:***dirname*

To disconnect disk drives, use the following format:

JOIN ***drive***: /D

To show currently connected drives, use the following format:

JOIN

Parameters and Switches

drive: The drive that you want to refer to as a subdirectory on another drive. DOS calls ***drive:*** the *guest disk drive.*

drive2: The drive to which ***drive:*** is to be connected. DOS calls *drive2:* the *host disk drive.* If *drive2:* isn't specified, the current drive is assumed.

\dirname	A subdirectory on *drive2:* (the host drive). DOS calls ***\dirname*** the *host subdirectory*. ***\dirname*** holds the connection to ***drive:*** (the guest drive), and should be empty. If ***\dirname*** doesn't exist, DOS creates it.
/D	Disconnects the specified guest drive from the host drive.

Rules

1. You must specify the guest drive when you make or change assignments.
2. If you do not name a host drive, DOS uses the current drive.
3. You must specify the host subdirectory. The host subdirectory cannot be the root directory of any drive.
4. The host and guest drives must not be network or CD-ROM drives.
5. The host and guest drives must not be part of a SUBST or ASSIGN command.
6. You cannot use the current drive as the guest drive.
7. If the host subdirectory does not exist, JOIN creates one. The subdirectory, if it exists, must be empty (DIR must show only the . and .. entries).
8. When the drives are joined, the guest drive's root directory and entire directory tree are added to the host subdirectory. All subdirectories of the guest's root directory become subdirectories of the host subdirectory.
9. A guest drive, when joined to the host drive, appears to be part of the host subdirectory. You can access this drive only through the host drive and subdirectory.
10. To break the connection, specify the guest drive's normal name with the /D switch. You can use the guest drive's normal name only when you disconnect the drives.
11. To see all the current drive connections, type **JOIN** with no parameters. If no connections exist, JOIN does not display any message, and the system prompt appears.

12. Do not use the BACKUP, CHKDSK, DISKCOMP, DISKCOPY, FDISK, RESTORE, or FORMAT command in the guest or host drive.

13. When JOIN is in effect, the DIR command works normally but reports the bytes free only for the host drive.

14. While JOIN is in effect, CHKDSK processes the host drive but does not process or report information on the guest portion of the drive. To run CHKDSK on the guest drive, you first must disconnect the guest drive from the host drive.

Notes

1. You can use JOIN to connect a RAM disk to a real disk so that you can use the RAM disk as though it were part of a floppy disk or hard disk drive. You also can use JOIN to connect two hard drives.

2. Some programs allow only one drive to hold data or certain parts of the program. Programs written for DOS 2.0 and later, however, enable you to specify subdirectory names. If you use such a program, you can invoke the JOIN command to trick the program into using multiple drives as though the drives were one large drive.

3. JOIN does not affect the guest drive. Rather, JOIN affects only the way you access the files in that drive. You cannot exceed the maximum number of files in the guest drive's root directory. In the host subdirectory, a file's size cannot exceed the guest drive's size.

Messages

`Directory not empty`

Error: You tried to use a host subdirectory that is not empty; the subdirectory contains files other than the . and .. entries. Perform any one of the following actions before you try the command again:

- Delete all files in the host subdirectory.
- Specify an empty subdirectory.
- Create a new subdirectory.
- Name a nonexistent host subdirectory.

See Also

ASSIGN and SUBST

"The JOIN Command" in Chapter 13

CONFIG SYS

DEVICE =

KBDBUF.SYS (device driver) External

The keyboard buffer set aside by the ROM BIOS is normally 16 bytes long. If a program fails to read the keyboard before the 17th character arrives, characters are lost. If you're a fast typist, you may want to increase the size of the keyboard buffer with KBDBUF.SYS to avoid losing keystrokes. KBDBUF.SYS isn't distributed with the standard DOS 6 package, but is available from Microsoft on the MS-DOS 6 Supplemental Disk. You must load KBDBUF.SYS in a DEVICE= statement in your CONFIG.SYS file.

Syntax

DEVICE=*drive:\path***KBDBUF.SYS** ***bufsize***

Parameters and Switches

drive:\path — Enter the full path to the KBDBUF.SYS file on your system. KBDBUF.SYS is available on the DOS 6 Supplemental Disk. If you do not specify the full path to KBDBUF.SYS, DOS looks for the file in the root directory of the start-up drive. The KBDBUF.SYS file is included on the MS-DOS 6.x Supplemental Disk.

bufsize — The new keyboard buffer size, in bytes. Acceptable values are in the range of 16 to 1024. This parameter is required.

Notes

1. Some programs read keystrokes directly from the keyboard, bypassing the keyboard buffer that the ROM BIOS maintains. KBDBUF.SYS does not affect programs that read the keyboard directly.
2. Do not attempt to load KBDBUF.SYS into upper memory with the DEVICEHIGH= command. The ROM BIOS can't use a keyboard buffer located in upper memory.
3. You should load the KBDBUF.SYS device driver as early as you can in CONFIG.SYS to avoid troublesome interactions with other device drivers and resident programs.
4. Requesting a very large keyboard buffer is not normally a very good idea. If you have increased it to 50 or 100 characters and your software is still losing keystrokes, the program is probably not using the keyboard buffer at all. The only time a large keyboard buffer might be useful is if you were injecting keystrokes into it from another source that can't wait when the buffer is full.

Examples

To increase the size of the keyboard buffer to 32 characters, enter the following line in your CONFIG.SYS file:

DEVICE=C:\DOS\KBDBUF.SYS 32

This assumes that you have copied the KBDBUF.SYS file from the DOS 6 Supplemental Disk to your C:\DOS subdirectory.

Messages

```
Part of the new keyboard buffer is beyond the range of the ROM BIOS data
segment. Load this driver earlier in CONFIG.SYS, do not load it into
high memory, or decrease the size of the buffer.
```

Error: KBDBUF.SYS couldn't create the keyboard buffer you requested, usually because you tried to load it with the DEVICEHIGH= command. Use the DEVICE= command to load KBDBUF.SYS into conventional memory instead.

```
Requested buffer size is too large.
```

Error: You have specified a keyboard buffer size larger than 1024 characters, which is the maximum size allowed by KBDBUF.SYS.

```
Requested buffer size is too small.
```

Error: You have specified a keyboard buffer size of under 16 characters, which is the minimum size allowed by KBDBUF.SYS.

See Also

DEVICE=

KEYB

3.3 and later—External

Changes the keyboard layout and characters from American English to another language/country.

Syntax

To change the current keyboard layout, use the following format:

KEYB ***keycode***, *codepage, drive:\path*\KEYBOARD.SYS /ID:*code* /E

To display the current values for KEYB, use the following format:

KEYB

Parameters and Switches

keycode
The two character keyboard code for the keyboard layout that you want to use. See Appendix G for a list of keyboard codes that MS-DOS supports.

codepage
The three-digit code page that you want to use. *codepage* must be one of the code pages available for use with the ***keycode*** specified. If you omit *codepage*, DOS assumes the default code page for the ***keycode*** specified. See Appendix G for a list of the code pages that MS-DOS supports.

drive:\path\KEYBOARD.SYS
The drive and path to KEYBOARD.SYS or an equivalent file which contains keyboard layout information. Setup places this file in the C:\DOS subdirectory by default.

/E
Informs KEYB that an enhanced keyboard is being used. This switch is necessary only on 8088- and 8086-based systems that use enhanced keyboards.

/ID:*code*
Specifies the type of enhanced keyboard that you want to use. This switch is only for countries that have more than one keyboard for the same language (for example, France, Italy, and the United Kingdom). See Appendix G for a list of the keyboard ID codes that MS-DOS supports.

Exit Codes

ERRORLEVEL Value	Meaning
0	New keyboard template loaded successfully
1	Invalid keyboard code, code page, or command line syntax
2	Keyboard definition file is bad or missing

ERRORLEVEL Value	Meaning
4	Halted by console (CON) error
5	Requested code page not prepared

Notes

1. To use one of the foreign-language character sets, load the KEYB program and type the appropriate two-letter code for your country.
2. If you do not specify a code page, DOS uses the default code page for your country. The default code page is established by the COUNTRY directive in CONFIG.SYS, or by the DOS default code page if the COUNTRY directive is not used.
3. You must specify a code page that is compatible with your keyboard code selection.
4. If you do not specify the keyboard definition file, it defaults to KEYBOARD.SYS. DOS looks for this file in the current disk's root directory. Otherwise, DOS uses the full file name to search for the file. If you do not specify a disk drive, DOS searches the current disk drive. If you do not specify a path, DOS searches the current directory.
5. After loading, the program reconfigures the keyboard into the appropriate layout for the specified language.
6. To use the American English layout after you issue the KEYB command, press Ctrl-Alt-F1. To return to the foreign-language layout, press Ctrl-Alt-F2. To switch to "typewriter mode," press Ctrl-Alt-F7.
7. When you use it for the first time, the KEYB command increases the size of DOS by approximately 10K. After that, you can use KEYB as often as you want without further enlarging DOS. You can load KEYB into upper memory with the LOADHIGH command.
8. To display the active keyboard and the code pages, type **KEYB** without any parameters.
9. You can use KEYB with INSTALL in your CONFIG.SYS file.

Messages

`Active code page not available from CON device`

Information: You issued the KEYB command to display the current setting, but the command could not determine what code page was in use. The DEVICE=DISPLAY.SYS directive is not in CONFIG.SYS, or no currently loaded CON code page is active.

If the DISPLAY.SYS line was included in your CONFIG.SYS file, you must give the MODE CON CODEPAGE PREPARE command to load the font files into memory.

`Bad or missing Keyboard Definition File`

Error: The keyboard definition file (usually KEYBOARD.SYS) is corrupted, or KEYB cannot find the file. If you did not specify a drive and path name, KEYB looks for the file in the current drive's root directory.

Copy the file to the root directory, or provide the full drive and path name for the file to KEYB.

`Code page requested (codepage) is not valid for given keyboard code`

Error: You provided a keyboard code but not a code page, or the specified keyboard code does not match the currently active code page for the console. KEYB does not alter the current keyboard or code page. Choose a new console code page that matches the keyboard code (by using the MODE CON CODEPAGE SELECT command), or specify the appropriate matching code page when you reissue the KEYB command.

`Code page specified is inconsistent with the selected code page`

Warning: You specified a keyboard code and a code page, but a different code page is active for the console (CON). The code page specified to KEYB is now active for the keyboard but not for the video display.

Use the MODE CON CODEPAGE SELECT command to activate the correct code page (the one specified to KEYB) for the video screen.

`Code page specified has not been prepared`

Error: The DEVICE=DISPLAY.SYS directive was included in your CONFIG.SYS file, but your KEYB command specified a keyboard code that needs a code page that is not prepared. Use the MODE CON CODEPAGE PREPARE command to prepare the code page for the keyboard code that you want to use.

`Current CON code page: codepage`

Information: The console's current code page is designated by the number *codepage*.

```
Current keyboard code: keycode
code page: codepage
```

Information: The current keyboard code is a two-character *keycode*, and the code page used by the keyboard is a three-digit *codepage*. A list of the legal keyboard codes and their corresponding code pages is included in Appendix G.

```
One or more CON code pages invalid for given keyboard code
```

Warning: You used the MODE command to prepare several code pages for the console (CON), but you specified a keyboard code that is not compatible with one or more console code pages. KEYB creates the necessary information to work with those keyboard and code pages that are compatible. DOS ignores the incompatible keyboard and code page combinations.

See Also

CHCP, COUNTRY=, DISPLAY.SYS, MODE *device* CP, and NLSFUNC

"Understanding KEYB.COM" in Chapter 21 and Appendix G, "International Country Codes"

KEYBOARD.SYS

(see KEYB)

Despite the .SYS extension, KEYBOARD.SYS is not a device driver. KEYBOARD.SYS is a data file that contains information about the various keyboard layouts that are used in different countries. The KEYB command uses this file.

Trap

Do not attempt to load KEYBOARD.SYS (or DVORAK.SYS) into memory with a DEVICE= or DEVICEHIGH= command in CONFIG.SYS. If you do, your computer will lock up, and you will need to reboot from a floppy disk.

A similar file, containing information needed for an Icelandic keyboard layout, is in the file KEYBOARD.ICE on the MS-DOS 6 distribution disks. (For details on setting up an Icelandic configuration see the README.TXT file distributed with DOS 6.) For people who prefer a Dvorak keyboard, there is a

DVORAK.SYS file on the DOS 6 Supplemental Disk which supports two-handed, left-handed, and right-handed Dvorak layouts.

DOS 6.2 includes an alternate keyboard layout information file named KEYBRD2.SYS which contains a few additional keyboard layouts. For details, see Appendix G, "International Country Codes" or the README.TXT file included with MS-DOS 6.2.

See Also

KEYB

"Understanding KEYB.COM" in Chapter 21 and Appendix G, "International Country Codes"

LABEL

3.0 and later—Internal

Each disk can have a volume label as well as a volume serial number. The volume label is text and can be up to 11 characters long. The LABEL command allows you to display, add, delete, or change the volume label for a disk.

Syntax

LABEL *drive:volume_label*

Parameters and Switches

drive:	The disk whose label you want to change or display. (The colon is required.)
volume_label	The disk's new volume label.

Rules

1. A valid volume label immediately becomes the volume label for the specified drive.
2. If you do not specify a volume label, DOS prompts you to enter a new volume label. You can perform one of the following actions:
   - Type a valid volume name, and then press Enter. DOS makes this name the new volume label. If a volume label already exists, DOS replaces the old volume label with the new.
   - Press Enter to delete the current label without specifying a replacement label. DOS asks you to confirm the deletion.

3. If you enter an invalid volume label, DOS responds with a warning message and asks again for the new volume label.

4. Do not use LABEL in a networked disk drive (one that belongs to another computer). If you try to label a networked drive, DOS displays an error message and ignores the command.

5. Do not use LABEL on a disk in any drive that is affected by the SUBST, JOIN, or ASSIGN commands, because DOS labels the "real" disk in the drive instead.

   Suppose that you use the command ASSIGN A=C. If you then enter the command LABEL A:, DOS actually changes the volume label of the disk in drive C.

6. A label consists of up to 11 printing characters and may include spaces but not tabs or any of the following characters:

   * ? / \ | . , ; : + = [ ] ( ) & ^ < >

   Lowercase ASCII characters are mapped to uppercase.

Notes

1. When you format a disk in DOS 4.0 and later versions, DOS prompts you to enter a volume label. Whether or not you assign a label, DOS gives the disk a serial number. The serial number is not part of the volume label. Remember that a space is a valid character in a volume label.

2. Spaces and underscores can increase the readability of a volume label. DOS 3.0 and 3.1, however, reject a space in a volume name when the name is typed in the command line (for example, LABEL MY DISK). To put a space in a volume label, type LABEL, press the space bar, type the drive name (if needed), and then press Enter. Do not type a volume label in the command line. When LABEL asks for a new volume label, you can type the label with spaces.

Messages

```
Delete current volume label (Y/N)?
```

Information and Warning: You did not enter a volume label when DOS prompted you. DOS is asking whether to delete the current label or to leave it unaltered. To delete the current label, press **Y**; to keep the label intact, press **N**.

See Also

FORMAT and VOL

"Naming Disks with LABEL" in Chapter 7

LASTDRIVE= 3.0 and later—Internal

If you're connected to a network, running MSCDEX for access to a CD-ROM drive, or using the SUBST command to create drive aliases, you may need the LASTDRIVE= command to tell DOS to save space for the additional drive letters you'll need. You can use LASTDRIVE= only in your CONFIG.SYS file.

Syntax

LASTDRIVE=*drive*

Parameters and Switches

drive The letter of the last disk drive that you want to have available. Note that ***drive*** is entered without a trailing colon. Valid letters are A to Z. The default value is either E or the last drive letter allocated during the processing of your CONFIG.SYS file, whichever is higher.

Notes

1. If you specify a letter lower than the number of letters needed for your system, DOS overrides it and allocates space for the drives your system has. For instance, if you have one floppy and one hard drive and you specify LASTDRIVE=A, DOS allocates space in the current directory data structure for drives A, B, and C (as if you'd specified LASTDRIVE=C). DOS does not display an error message if it overrides your LASTDRIVE= parameter. Notice that DOS allocates two floppy drive letters (A and B) even if you have only one floppy disk drive installed in the system.

2. Each additional drive letter (above E) you have available increases the size of DOS in memory. If you aren't attached to a network, running a CD-ROM drive, or using SUBST drive aliases, there's little reason for you to waste memory on extra drive letters.

3. You never need LASTDRIVE= for a device that is assigned a drive letter when its driver is loaded in CONFIG.SYS. This includes drives assigned by DoubleSpace, RAMDRIVE.SYS, INTERLNK.EXE, or DRIVER.SYS.

LASTDRIVE= is only needed to reserve space for drive letters created after the processing of your CONFIG.SYS file is complete.

Examples

If you are attached to a network, you will usually want the following line in your CONFIG.SYS:

```
LASTDRIVE=Z
```

This allows room for the maximum number of drive letters, leaving plenty of room to attach network drives. On the other hand, if you have two floppy drives (A and B), a hard disk with two partitions (C and D), a RAM disk (E), and have run DBLSPACE to compress both hard drives (hosts assigned to I and J), your highest drive letter will be J. To leave room for two additional drives after J, you enter the following command:

```
LASTDRIVE=L
```

Notice that in the preceding example, drive letters F, G, H, K, and L would be available for network, CD-ROM, or SUBST drives. If you had included no LASTDRIVE= command, drive letters F, G, and H would still be available.

Messages

```
Bad command or parameters
Error in CONFIG.SYS line number
```

Warning: If you specify an invalid parameter for LASTDRIVE=, you get this error message. A very common mistake is to enter a colon after the drive letter in the LASTDRIVE= command.

See Also

SUBST

"Using LASTDRIVE to Change the Available Disk Drives" in Chapter 18

LH (see LOADHIGH)

LH is an alternative name for the LOADHIGH command. For information on using the LOADHIGH or LH command, see the entry for LOADHIGH in this Command Reference.

LOADFIX

5.0 and later—External

Some programs may have trouble running if they are loaded in the first segment of memory. Often when this happens, they display a `Packed file corrupt` message and abort. LOADFIX can help a program with this problem to run by making sure that it's loaded in the second 64K segment of memory.

Syntax

LOADFIX ***program*** *parameters*

Parameters and Switches

program The program file which you would like to load into the second 64K segment of memory. A drive and path can be specified. If they are omitted the current directory and all directories on the DOS PATH will be searched for the executable file. This parameter is required.

parameters The parameters you want passed to ***program*** when it's loaded into memory.

Notes

If you are using DOS 5.0 or a later version to load DOS into the high memory area (HMA), a packed file may be loaded into the first 64K of RAM and may fail to work. In such a case, DOS may display the error message `Packed file corrupt`, and the computer then returns to the DOS prompt.

Use LOADFIX only to start a program when DOS displays the message `Packed file corrupt`.

LOADHIGH or LH

5.0 and later—Internal

You can use the LOADHIGH command to load programs into upper memory. By loading resident software into upper memory, you can leave more conventional memory available for application programs to use. LOADHIGH is typically used in your AUTOEXEC.BAT file.

Syntax

LOADHIGH ***program*** *parameters*

or

LH ***program*** *parameters*

LOADHIGH has two additional switches that MemMaker uses to specify the placement and size of the program in memory. (DOS 6)

LOADHIGH /L:*region,min;region,min;...* /S ***program*** *parameters*

or

LH /L:*region,min;region,min;...* /S ***program*** *parameters*

Parameters and Switches

program The program file that you want to load into upper memory. You can specify a drive and path. If you omit them, DOS searches the current directory and all directories on the DOS PATH for the executable file. This parameter is required.

parameters Any parameters you want passed to ***program*** when it's loaded into memory.

/L:*region,min* (DOS 6) Specifies the region in upper memory, and optionally the minimum size in bytes, into which the program should be loaded. You can specify more than one region by separating each region from the preceding one with a semicolon. For instance, /L:1;2 allows the program access to UMB regions 1 and 2, and /L:1,4096;2,512 further specifies that the minimum size of regions 1 and 2 should be 4096 and 512 bytes, respectively. This parameter must precede the program's file name on the line. MemMaker sets these values for you.

/S (DOS 6) If you specify the /L parameter with a minimum size, /S instructs DOS to shrink the UMB to the specified size and create a new UMB from the remainder. /S must precede the program's file name on the line. This switch is best left to MemMaker's use.

Rules

1. You must use an upper memory manager. For a computer equipped with an 80386SX or higher microprocessor and at least one megabyte of RAM, DOS provides EMM386.EXE.

2. Your CONFIG.SYS file must contain at least the following statements (or the equivalent third-party memory-management routines):

```
DEVICE=HIMEM.SYS
DEVICE=EMM386.EXE  RAM  (or NOEMS)
DOS=UMB
```

3. If enough upper memory is not available to accommodate a program, DOS loads the program into conventional memory without warning.

4. When a program is loaded by default into the largest free UMB, that program automatically gains access to all other UMBs. If you use /L, you have to explicitly grant the program access to other upper-memory regions by specifying other /L parameters.

5. /S normally is used only by MemMaker, which analyzes a program's memory usage to determine whether /S is safe.

6. You can use /S only when you also include an /L switch that specifies a minimum size.

7. Use *min* when a program is larger when it runs than when it loads.

8. Use MEM /F to determine the size of free regions.

Examples

To load the driver MYDRV.COM into upper-memory regions 1 and 3:

```
LOADHIGH /L:1;3 C:\BIN\MYDRV.COM
```

See Also

DEVICEHIGH=, MEM, and MEMMAKER

"Loading Device Drivers and TSRs into Upper Memory" in Chapter 18

MD or MKDIR

2.0 and later—Internal

The MD (or MKDIR) command can create new subdirectories on your disks. Storing files in various subdirectories helps you to keep them organized, and with MD you can create as many as you need.

Syntax

MD *drive:**path***

MKDIR *drive:**path***

Parameters and Switches

drive: The *drive:* on which you want to create a new subdirectory. If you omit *drive:*, DOS assumes the current drive.

path The subdirectory on *drive:* that you want to create. ***path*** can be either absolute or relative—that is, specified from the root directory or specified from the current directory (see Note 7 in the following section). If you specify only the name, DOS creates the new subdirectory in the current directory. You cannot create a subdirectory with the same name as a file in its parent directory.

Notes

1. Separate each subdirectory in ***path*** with a backslash (\) character. The last subdirectory name in ***path*** is the subdirectory created.
2. You must specify the new subdirectory name (1 to 8 characters); specifying an extension is optional. The name must conform to the rules for creating directory names.
3. You cannot use a directory name that is identical to a file name in the parent directory. If you have a file named MYFILE in the current directory, for example, you cannot create the subdirectory MYFILE in this directory. If the file is named MYFILE.TXT, however, the names do not conflict, and you can create the MYFILE subdirectory.
4. The maximum length of a path (from the root directory to the final directory) is 63 characters, including the backslashes.
5. You are not restricted to creating subdirectories in the current directory. If you add a path name, DOS establishes a new subdirectory in the directory that you specify.
6. You must put a colon after the drive letter if it is included. If you don't include the colon, DOS will interpret the drive letter as a subdirectory name, which is probably not what you wanted.
7. If a backslash (\) is the first (or only) character in a subdirectory path, it's considered absolute and specified starting from the root directory. If the subdirectory path begins with a subdirectory name, it's considered relative, and the current directory will be used as it's starting point.

Tip

Avoid using extensions with subdirectory names. Although it's perfectly legal to do so, having them "extensionless" makes them easier to pick out from the file names in a directory listing. This practice has become so pervasive that certain programs have difficulties using subdirectories with extensions because they are rather uncommon and rarely tested for in new software.

Tip

Keep your subdirectory names as short as you can. This can help with DOS's 63-character path name limit and the 127-character command- line limit, and saves typing as well.

A drive letter, followed by a colon, can precede either an absolute or a relative path.

Messages

`Unable to create directory`

Error: One of the following errors occurred:

- You tried to create a directory that already exists.
- You provided an incorrect path name.
- The disk's directory is full.
- The disk is full.
- A file with the same name already exists.

Check the directory in which the new subdirectory was to be created. If a conflicting name exists, either change the file name or use a new directory name. If the disk or the root directory is full, delete some files, create the subdirectory in a different directory, or use a different disk.

`Invalid drive specified`

Error: You have specified an invalid drive letter.

See Also

CD or CHDIR, MOVE, and RD or RMDIR

"Creating Directories with MKDIR (MD)" in Chapter 5

MEM

4.0 and later—External

MEM is a utility that displays the amount of used and unused memory, allocated and open memory areas, and all programs currently in the system. MEM can be enormously useful when you want to see just how your memory is being used, and whether you have enough space left for another resident program to be loaded high.

Syntax

For DOS 6, the following parameters is available for MEM:

MEM /CLASSIFY /DEBUG /FREE /MODULE *name* /PAGE

or

MEM /C /D /F /M *name* /P

For DOS 5.0, the following parameters are available for MEM:

MEM /CLASSIFY /DEBUG /PROGRAM

or

MEM /C /D /P

Parameters and Switches

/CLASSIFY or /C	Displays programs that are in conventional and upper memory, their location in memory, and their size. Also displays a summary of the total free bytes of conventional and upper memory and the size of the largest executable program. You cannot use this switch with /DEBUG, /FREE, or /MODULE *name*.
/DEBUG or /D	Displays detailed information about the programs and driver in memory, including the address, name, size, and type of each segment for every program. Also displays a summary of the total free bytes of conventional and upper memory and the size of the largest executable program. You cannot use this switch with /CLASSIFY, /FREE, or /MODULE *name*.
/FREE or /F	(DOS 6) Displays the free areas of conventional and upper memory in decimal and hexadecimal format. You cannot use this switch with /CLASSIFY, /DEBUG, or /MODULE *name*.
/MODULE *name* or /M *name*	(DOS 6) Displays the memory usage of the *name* program or driver, including the segment address, UMB region number, name, and type of each segment. You cannot use this switch with /CLASSIFY, /DEBUG, or /FREE.
/PAGE or /P	(DOS 6) Pauses after each screen of output. You can use this switch with any of the other switches.
/PROGRAM or /P	(DOS 4.0 and 5.0 only) Displays the status of programs that are loaded into memory. You cannot use this switch with /CLASSIFY or /DEBUG.

Rules

1. You can specify /CLASSIFY, /DEBUG, /FREE, and /MODULE one at a time. You cannot combine any of these parameters. You can combine the /PAGE parameter with any of them, however.

2. MEM displays the status of extended memory only if you have more than one megabyte of memory in your computer. If you have only one megabyte or less, you don't have any extended memory.

3. The status of expanded memory displays only if you have expanded memory that conforms to Version 4.0 of the Lotus/Intel/Microsoft Expanded Memory Specification (LIM EMS). Loading EMM386.EXE in your CONFIG.SYS can provide expanded memory for 80386 or better computer systems with more than one megabyte of memory installed.

4. MEM displays the status of upper memory only if a UMB provider (for example, EMM386) is installed and DOS=UMB is included in your CONFIG.SYS file.

5. MEM does not display the status of upper memory if you are running DOS under Microsoft Windows 3.0.

Notes

1. Starting with DOS 6.2, MEM displays numbers with embedded commas, making them much easier to read.

2. A good way to determine a module name for MEM /MODULE *name* is first to issue the command MEM /C.

3. If your PC has UMBs, you can use MEM /C or MEM /D extensively as you begin to load device drivers and TSRs into upper memory. MEM displays the location and size of each program in memory. This information can help you determine the order in which device drivers and TSRs load so that you can determine how best to use UMBs.

See Also

DEVICEHIGH=, EMM386.EXE, HIMEM.SYS, LOADHIGH or LH, and MEMMAKER

"Displaying the Amount of Free and Used Memory" in Chapter 12

MEMMAKER

6.0 and later—External

MemMaker is a full-screen program that attempts to maximize the amount of free conventional memory you have in your computer by moving device drivers and memory-resident programs (TSRs) into upper memory blocks (UMBs). To use MemMaker, you must have an 80386SX or above computer with more than one megabyte of memory installed. MemMaker relies on the services provided by HIMEM.SYS, EMM386.EXE and DOS. (If you are using third-party memory management software, you should use its memory optimization program instead of MemMaker.)

Syntax

MEMMAKER /B /BATCH /SESSION /SWAP:*drive* /T /UNDO /W:*size1,size2*

Parameters and Switches

/B	Causes MemMaker to display correctly on a monochrome (black-and-white) monitor or LCD screen.
/BATCH	Runs MemMaker in batch (unattended) mode. When you use this switch, DOS takes only the default actions and, if an error occurs, restores your CONFIG.SYS, AUTOEXEC.BAT, and (if necessary) Microsoft Windows SYSTEM.INI files. You can determine what was done by looking in the MEMMAKER.STS file.
/SESSION	Used only by MemMaker during its optimization process. Do not specify this parameter.
/SWAP:*drive*	Specifies your boot drive's original disk letter, the one that refers to the drive when your CONFIG.SYS file begins. You need this switch only in rare cases (for example, when disk-compression software, such as Stacker 1.0, swaps drive letters.) Unless MemMaker knows your boot disk drive, it cannot find your start-up files. You do not need this switch if you are using DoubleSpace, Stacker 2.0 or later, or SuperStor.
/T	Disables IBM Token Ring detection. Use this switch only if you are connected to a Token Ring network and have trouble running MemMaker.

/UNDO — Undoes changes in the CONFIG.SYS, AUTOEXEC.BAT, and (if necessary) Microsoft Windows SYSTEM.INI files from a previous use of MemMaker. Use this switch if your system does not work after you run MemMaker or if you are dissatisfied with the new configuration.

/W:*size1,size2* — Specifies how much upper memory (in kilobytes) to reserve for Microsoft Windows translation buffers. Windows needs two such buffers in either upper or conventional memory. *size1* is the size of the first, and *size2* is the size of the second. You may need to increase these values if Windows begins to run slowly after optimizing with MemMaker. The default is /W:0,0—MemMaker reserves no upper memory for Windows translation buffers.

See Also

DEVICEHIGH=, EMM386.EXE, HIMEM.SYS, LOADHIGH or LH, and MEM

"Configuring Memory with MEMMAKER" in Chapter 18

MENUCOLOR= 6.0 and later—Internal

Normally, DOS displays a start-up menu in white text on a black background. With the MENUCOLOR= command, you can choose the screen colors that DOS uses. This command affects all text that DOS displays on-screen, not just the start-up menu. You can use MENUCOLOR= only inside a menu block in your CONFIG.SYS file.

Syntax

MENUCOLOR=*textcolor*,*background*

Parameters and Switches

textcolor — The color to use for foreground text. Legal values are 0 through 15 (see the table of color values below). This parameter is required.

background The color to use for the background. Legal values are 0 through 15 (see the table of color numbers below). On some displays, using background colors above 7 causes the screen to blink. Do not include a space after the comma, or DOS ignores the entire MENUCOLOR= command. If no value is entered, DOS assumes Black (0).

Value	Color	Value	Color
0	Black	8	Gray
1	Blue	9	Bright Blue
2	Green	10	Bright Green
3	Cyan	11	Bright Cyan
4	Red	12	Bright Red
5	Magenta	13	Bright Magenta
6	Brown	14	Yellow
7	White	15	Bright White

Notes

1. The MENUCOLOR= command can appear only once inside each menu block in CONFIG.SYS.

2. CONFIG.SYS allows two types of blocks—*menu blocks* and *configuration blocks*. Each block begins with a [blockname] and includes all the lines that follow, up to the next [blockname]. Menu blocks, which are blocks named [MENU] or defined with a SUBMENU= command, can include only menu-related commands. All other CONFIG.SYS commands belong in configuration blocks.

3. If you do not specify a MENUCOLOR= command, the menu displays in white (7) on black (0). If only a foreground text color is specified, the background remains black (0). You cannot set the background color without also setting the foreground text color.

4. Color choices set with this command remain in effect until another command or program resets them. Running CLS, or loading the ANSI.SYS device driver, resets the screen to its default colors.

Trap

Unlike many other commands, the MENUCOLOR= command does not allow a space after the comma between its parameters. If you include a space, DOS ignores the MENUCOLOR= command and does not set your color choices.

5. If you select a bright background color (values above 7), some displays set the blink attribute for the foreground text, and all the text on-screen starts to blink. Although this may be annoying, it does no harm, and can be turned off with the CLS or the MODE CO80 command. To fix the problem, choose a background color between 0 and 7, and restart your computer.

6. A really nasty mistake is to set the foreground color the same as the background color. Since you can't read any of the prompts when this happens, you may need to reboot and use the F5 Clean key to bypass your CONFIG.SYS file. Alternatively, you can select a menu choice blind (press 1 and then press Enter), wait for all the drive activity to stop, and then type CLS and press Enter.

Examples

Suppose that you had set up a menu that let you choose between three basic configurations for your computer; Windows, DOS, and Maintenance. To jazz it up a bit, you wanted to set the screen colors to bright blue text on a white background.

```
[MENU]
MENUITEM=WIN, Configure for Windows (Default)
MENUITEM=DOS, Configure for MS-DOS
MENUITEM=MAINT, Configure for File & Disk Maintenance
MENUDEFAULT=WIN, 30
MENUCOLOR=9,7
```

The MENUCOLOR= command sets the foreground color to bright blue (9) and the background color to white (7). These colors remain in effect until another program resets them.

See Also

[blockname], MENUDEFAULT=, MENUITEM=, and SUBMENU=

"Creating Multiple Configurations" in Chapter 2

MENUDEFAULT= 6.0 and later—Internal

With the MENUDEFAULT= command, you can select which start-up configuration DOS executes if no keys are pressed within the timeout period you specify. Without this command, DOS chooses menu item #1 and waits for you to press the Enter key. If you specify a default configuration and a timeout period, DOS can continue booting without you. You can use MENUDEFAULT= only inside a menu block in your CONFIG.SYS file.

Syntax

MENUDEFAULT=*blockname*, *timeout*

Parameters and Switches

blockname The menu line that DOS should highlight when the menu displays. If you specify a *timeout* value, DOS executes this configuration block automatically after *timeout* seconds. ***Blockname*** must match the corresponding entry in a MENUITEM= or SUBMENU= command. This argument is required.

timeout The number of seconds, from 0 to 90, that DOS should wait before executing the ***blockname*** configuration block. If you do not specify a *timeout* value, DOS waits until you press the Enter key before executing the selected configuration. A *timeout* value of 0 executes the ***blockname*** configuration block without displaying the menu on-screen at all.

Notes

1. The MENUDEFAULT= command can appear only once inside each menu block in CONFIG.SYS.

2. CONFIG.SYS allows two types of blocks—*menu blocks* and *configuration blocks*. Each block begins with a [blockname] and includes all the lines that follow, up to the next [blockname]. Menu blocks, which are blocks

named [MENU] or defined with a SUBMENU= command, can include only menu-related commands. All other CONFIG.SYS commands belong in configuration blocks.

3. The menu item selected with the MENUDEFAULT= command displays highlighted on-screen. You can move the highlight with the arrow keys or type the line number to select a different menu line. The `Enter a Choice:` prompt displays the number of the selected menu item.

4. When a you specify a *timeout* value, DOS displays a countdown on-screen as it waits for you to override the default choice. If you press any key before the *timeout* period has elapsed, the timer stops and DOS waits for you to make a menu selection and press the Enter key.

Trap

If the *timeout* parameter contains an illegal value, DOS assigns a timeout of zero, and the menu doesn't display at all. This can be troublesome when you are debugging a new menu. To determine whether an incorrectly set *timeout* value is causing the problem, press the F8 Interactive key when the `Starting MS-DOS...` message appears on-screen. If the menu appears, the *timeout* value is defaulting to zero. If the menu still doesn't display, look for undefined or misspelled blocknames.

Examples

Suppose that you had set up a menu that let you choose between three basic configurations for your computer; Windows, DOS, and Maintenance. Because you normally worked with Windows programs, you wanted the default choice to be the WIN configuration.

```
[MENU]
MENUITEM=WIN, Configure for Windows (Default)
MENUITEM=DOS, Configure for MS-DOS
MENUITEM=MAINT, Configure for File & Disk Maintenance
MENUDEFAULT=WIN, 30
```

When you include these lines in your CONFIG.SYS file, DOS searches for blocks named [WIN], [DOS], and [MAINT]. As long as those blocks exist in the file, the menu that DOS displays looks something like this:

```
MS-DOS 6 Startup Menu
=====================

1. Configure for Windows (Default)
2. Configure for MS-DOS
3. Configure for File & Disk Maintenance

Enter a choice: 1
```

Entering 1, 2, or 3 at this menu instructs DOS to select the [WIN], [DOS], or [MAINT] block, respectively. If you don't make an entry within about 30 seconds, DOS chooses the [WIN] configuration by default.

See Also

[blockname], MENUCOLOR=, MENUITEM=, and SUBMENU=

"Creating Multiple Configurations" in Chapter 2

MENUITEM= 6.0 and later—Internal

New with DOS 6 is the capability to define a start-up menu from which you can choose the group of CONFIG.SYS commands to process when you reboot. You use the MENUITEM= command to define the text of a menu line, as well as the configuration block that DOS should process when that menu line is chosen. You can use MENUITEM= only inside a menu block in your CONFIG.SYS file.

Syntax

MENUITEM=*blockname*, *menutext*

Parameters and Switches

blockname The name of the configuration block that you want to execute when this menu item is chosen. ***blockname*** can be up to 70 characters long, but it can't contain any spaces or the following special characters:

```
\ / , ; = [ ]
```

(For more details, see [blockname] in this reference.) The CONFIG environment variable is set to the value of the ***blockname*** selected. This argument is required.

menutext The text you want DOS to display for this menu line. *menutext* can be up to 70 characters long and contain any text you want, including spaces. Separate *menutext* from ***blockname*** with a comma. If you do not provide *menutext*, DOS displays the ***blockname*** in the menu.

Notes

1. The MENUITEM= command can appear only inside menu blocks in CONFIG.SYS.

2. CONFIG.SYS allows two types of blocks—*menu blocks* and *configuration blocks*. Each block begins with a [blockname], and includes all the lines that follow, up to the next [blockname]. Menu blocks, which are blocks named [MENU] or defined with a SUBMENU= command, can include only menu-related commands. All other CONFIG.SYS commands belong in configuration blocks.

3. The top level (first) menu block must be named [MENU] so that DOS can recognize it. You can name additional menu blocks that you define with the SUBMENU= command anything you like.

4. Up to nine choices can be displayed in a menu, so you are limited to nine MENUITEM= and/or SUBMENU= commands in a menu block. The menu items display on-screen in the order that they appear in the menu block, numbered from 1–9.

5. If DOS cannot find the block referred to by a MENUITEM= command in your CONFIG.SYS file, it doesn't display that choice in the menu. To get around this limitation, add a [blockname] line to your CONFIG.SYS file, but don't include any commands in it.

6. DOS sets the CONFIG environment variable equal to the name of the configuration block selected from the start-up menu. You can use the CONFIG variable in your AUTOEXEC.BAT file to continue customizing your system's configuration based on the choice you made at the start-up menu.

Trap

If you intend on using the CONFIG variable in GOTO statements in your AUTOEXEC.BAT file, try to keep your blocknames short. Only the first eight characters in a batch file label are significant, so if any of your blocknames start with the same eight characters, one or more of the GOTO labels you set up will never be reached. You can get around this limitation by using the IF command to make comparisons, or simply using shorter blocknames.

Examples

Suppose that you want to set up a menu that lets you choose between three basic configurations for your computer: Windows, DOS, and Maintenance. To do so, add the following lines to your CONFIG.SYS file:

```
[MENU]

MENUITEM=WIN, Configure for Windows (Default)
MENUITEM=DOS, Configure for MS-DOS
MENUITEM=MAINT, Configure for File & Disk Maintenance
MENUDEFAULT=WIN, 30
```

When you include these lines in your CONFIG.SYS file, DOS searches for blocks named [WIN], [DOS], and [MAINT]. As long as those blocks exist in the file, the menu that DOS displays looks something like this:

```
MS-DOS 6 Startup Menu
=====================

1. Configure for Windows (Default)
2. Configure for MS-DOS
3. Configure for File & Disk Maintenance

Enter a choice: 1
```

Entering 1, 2, or 3 at this menu instructs DOS to select the [WIN], [DOS], or [MAINT] block, respectively. If you don't make an entry within about 30 seconds, DOS chooses the [WIN] configuration by default.

See Also

[blockname], MENUCOLOR=, MENUDEFAULT=, and SUBMENU=

"Creating Multiple Configurations" in Chapter 2

MIRROR

5.0—External

MIRROR is a utility that can record information about the file allocation table (FAT) and the root directory to enable you to use the UNFORMAT and UNDELETE commands. MIRROR can also save partition table information to a file that UNFORMAT can use if your partition table becomes corrupted.

MIRROR is included on the DOS 6.0 Supplemental Disk, but not in the standard DOS 6 package. For information about similar capabilities in DOS 6, see the section on the UNDELETE command later in this Command Reference.

Syntax

MIRROR *drive: ... /Tdrive-entries* /1

To save information about a drive partition, use the following format:

MIRROR /PARTN

To quit tracking deleted files, use the following format:

MIRROR /U

Parameters and Switches

drive: ...	The drive(s) for which you want MIRROR to record FAT and root directory information. You can specify as many drive letters (with colons) as you want, just separate each one from the others with a space.
/T*drive-entries*	Loads a memory-resident tracking program that records information about deleted files. The *drive* specifies the drive where MIRROR saves information about deleted files. *-entries* is an optional value (ranging from 1 to 999) that specifies the maximum number of deleted files to be tracked. Default values are listed in the table in the Notes section below.
/1	Keeps MIRROR from creating a backup of the mirror file when the FAT and root directory information are updated.
/PARTN	Makes a copy of the drive's partition table.
/U	Removes the deleted file tracking program from memory. You may not be able to unload MIRROR if you've loaded other resident software into memory after MIRROR.

Rules

1. Do not use the /T switch with drives that use JOIN or SUBST.
2. If you use ASSIGN, you must place this command before the MIRROR command. If possible, don't use any "pretender" programs while Mirror's deleted-file tracking program is active.
3. DOS saves information about deleted files in the file PCTRACKR.DEL. The UNDELETE command uses this file. With DOS 6, UNDELETE has

Delete Tracker and Delete Sentry options of its own, and you should use them in preference to Mirror's deleted file tracking features.

4. DOS saves system information, the FAT, and the root directory in the file MIRROR.FIL. The UNFORMAT command uses this file. FORMAT saves information for UNFORMAT as well.

5. DOS saves information about the hard-drive partition in the file PARTNSAV.FIL. The UNFORMAT command uses this file. DOS 6 provides no utility in the standard package which can save this information for UNFORMAT to use.

Notes

Caution

The MIRROR and UNFORMAT commands are not replacements for proper backups of your hard disk. While the information that MIRROR saves can be very handy, full and regular backups are a much safer and more reliable means of ensuring that you do not lose data.

1. When you track deleted files, you can specify how many files are contained in the PCTRACKR.DEL file (1 to 999) with the /T*drive-entries* parameter. The default values, however, probably are satisfactory. Those values are as follows:

Size of disk	Entries stored
360K	25
720K	50
1.2M/1.44M	75
20M	101
32M	202
Larger than 32M	303

2. Using the /PARTN switch with MIRROR creates the file PARTNSAV.FIL. This file contains information from the drive's partition table.

The partition initially is created with FDISK. You are instructed to place a floppy disk in drive A, rather than save PARTNSAV.FIL on the hard disk. The file is saved on the disk. Label and store the disk in a safe place.

3. UNFORMAT, a companion command to MIRROR, uses these files. If you lose information, if you accidentally format a disk, or if the partition table is damaged, you can recover the lost information by using UNFORMAT if you previously used MIRROR.

Messages

```
Creates an image of the system area.
Drive C being processed.
The MIRROR process was successful.
```

Information: These messages appear when you issue the command MIRROR while drive C is the current drive. The messages indicate that MIRROR performed successfully.

```
Deletion-tracking software being installed.
The following drives are supported:

Drive C - Default files saved.
Installation complete.
```

Information: These messages appear when you install MIRROR with delete tracking. The messages indicate that delete tracking for drive C is installed correctly.

```
WARNING! Unrecognized DOS INT 25h/26h handler. Some other TSR
programs may behave erratically while deletion-tracking software is resident
Try installing MIRROR program before your other resident programs.
```

Warning: Some other TSR conflicted with delete tracking. Experiment with loading TSRs and delete tracking in a different order. As suggested in the message, you may have to install MIRROR before any other resident software you use. When you find the correct order, modify AUTOEXEC.BAT so that the TSRs and delete tracking are loaded in the correct sequence.

See Also

FDISK, UNDELETE, and UNFORMAT

MKDIR (see MD)

MKDIR is an alternate name for the MD command. For information on using the MD or MKDIR command, see the entry for MD in this Command Reference.

MODE 1.1 and later—External

The MODE command generally configures system devices. The details of the command's functions, however, are so varied that the syntax quickly becomes quite complex. Therefore, the following sections cover each of the MODE command's functions separately:

To set serial ports, see the entry for MODE COM#.

To configure the keyboard and display, see the entry for MODE CON.

To use MODE's code page functions, see the entry for MODE *device* CP.

To set the display device and mode, see the entry for MODE display.

To set parallel (printer) ports, see the entry for MODE LPT#.

Display Device Status Information

To display the status of any or all the devices that MODE can control, use the following command format:

MODE *device* /STATUS

Parameters and Switches

device The DOS device for which you want to see status information. *device* can be any one of the following:

Device Name	Description
COM1 through COM4	Serial communication ports
CON	The console, which is your keyboard and display
LPT1 through LPT3	Parallel printer ports
PRN	The primary printer port, normally LPT1

If you omit this parameter, MODE displays information about the status of all the devices attached to your system.

/STATUS — Including this parameter requests the status of any redirected parallel ports you may have set without cancelling the redirection. If you omit the /STATUS parameter and you are redirecting any parallel ports, the redirection is canceled when the information about that port displays. You can abbreviate /STATUS as /STA.

Notes

1. If you ask for the status of the PRN device (for example, MODE PRN), MODE displays information about the code page status of the primary printer port. If you ask for the status of LPT1 however, it reports on the retry setting currently in effect.
2. You can include a colon after the device name or leave it off; its use is optional.
3. The AUX device, which is normally the same as COM1, is not recognized by the MODE command.
4. Status information has been available from the MODE command since DOS 4.0.

Messages

`Illegal device name - device`

Error: You have specified a device name that is not present in your computer. *device* is the name of the device that you entered in the MODE command.

`Invalid parameter - parameter`

Error: You have specified the name of a device that MODE doesn't recognize, or have included an unsupported parameter. Check the command to make sure that you have entered it correctly.

See Also

ANSI.SYS, CHCP, COUNTRY=, DISPLAY.SYS, KEYB, and NLSFUNC

"Altering the Look of the Screen with MODE" in Chapter 13, "The MODE Command" in Chapter 14, and "Understanding Code Page Switching" in Chapter 21

MODE COM# 1.1 and later—External

You use this form of the MODE command to initialize serial ports connected to your computer. Many programs do this themselves, but in case they don't, DOS provides this functionality in the MODE COM# command. The INTERSVR /RCOPY remote copy operation depends on the services of MODE COM# to make the remote copy operation succeed, for instance.

Syntax

This is the old syntax, which is simple but not very intuitive:

MODE COM#: *baud, parity, databits, stopbits, retry*

If you are running DOS 4.0 or later, you can use the following format:

MODE COM#: BAUD=*baud* PARITY=*parity* DATA=*databits* STOP=*stopbits* RETRY=*retry*

Parameters and Switches

#: The serial port that you want to initialize. DOS supports COM ports 1, 2, 3, and 4, but they may not all be installed in your computer. The colon after the number is optional.

baud The baud rate to use. Legal values for *baud* are 110, 150, 300, 600, 1200, 2400, 4800, 9600, or 19200. You need to enter only the first two digits, for instance, 24 instead of 2400. (Baud equals bits per second for rates higher than 300.) Not all computers can support 19200-baud serial transmissions.

parity The parity checking setting. Legal values are N for None, O for Odd, E for Even, M for Mark, or S for Space. Not all computers support the Mark and Space parity settings. The default setting is E.

databits The number of data bits. Legal values are 5 through 8. The default value is 7. Not all computers support 5 and 6 data bits.

stopbits Specifies the number of stop bits. Legal values are 1, 1.5, and 2. If *baud* is 110, the default is 2; otherwise, the default is 1. Not all computers support 1.5 stop bits.

retry Instructs DOS about how to handle timeout errors. Using this parameter causes part of MODE to remain resident in memory. You can choose one of the following options:

retry	Action
B	Return busy when the port is busy
E	Return error when the port is busy
P	Retry until output is accepted
R	Return ready when the port is busy (infinite retry)
N or NONE	Take no action (the default)

Notes

1. For DOS versions before 5.0, you must enter the adapter's number, followed by a space and a baud rate. If you type the optional colon, you must type the adapter number immediately before the colon. All other parameters are optional.

2. Note that with the older, unlabeled syntax, MODE interprets each parameter by position alone, and you must enter them in the order shown. If you do not want to enter a value for a particular parameter, enter a comma for that value, or use the newer syntax where relative position on the command line is unimportant.

3. If you enter an invalid parameter, DOS responds with an invalid-parameter message and takes no further action.

4. You can abbreviate the baud rate parameter by using only the first two digits of the baud rate. For example, you can specify 11 for 110 baud, or 96 for 9600 baud.

5. If you want continuous retries after a timeout, you must enter RETRY=B (or P for versions of DOS before 5.0) every time you use the MODE COM#: command. Other settings remain in effect if you do not specify new values for them.

6. If the adapter is set for continuous retries (RETRY=B) and the device is not ready, the computer may appear to hang up when it's really just waiting for the port. You can abort this loop by pressing Ctrl-Break.

7. If you use a networked printer, do not specify any of the RETRY values.

8. To display the current status of a serial port, enter the MODE COM# command without any parameters. To display the status of all the DOS devices attached to your computer, enter the MODE command alone.

See Also

MODE LPT# and MODE *device* /STATUS

"Using MODE to Change Serial Port Settings" in Chapter 14

MODE CON

4.0 and later—External

BATCH FILE

MODE can configure various aspects of the console device, which refers to your keyboard and display. For the keyboard, MODE can set the keyboard repeat rate and delay. For the monitor, MODE can, with the help of the ANSI.SYS device driver, control the number of lines and columns displayed in text mode.

Syntax

To configure the keyboard, use the following format:

MODE CON: **RATE=*rate* DELAY=*delay***

To configure the monitor, use the following format:

MODE CON: COLS=*columns* LINES=*lines*

Parameters and Switches

CON: Specifies the console device. The colon is optional.

rate The rate at which a character repeats when you hold down a key. Legal values are in the range of 1 to 32, which represents approximately 2 to 30 characters per second. The default is 20 for most keyboard and 21 for IBM PS/2 keyboards. To set the ***rate***, you must also set the ***delay***.

delay The length of the delay between the initial pressing of the key and the start of automatic character repetition. This value can be 1, 2, 3, or 4, which represent delays of 1/4 second, 1/2 second, 3/4 second, and one full second, respectively. The default is 2. To set the ***delay***, you must also set the ***rate***.

columns The number of columns to display on-screen. Legal values are 40 and 80. Most computers start up in an 80-column screen mode. If you omit this parameter, the display keeps its present column setting.

lines The number of lines to display on-screen. Legal values are different for different types of monitors. CGA and MDA monitors support 25-line text modes only. EGA monitors support 25- and 43-line text modes. VGA monitors support 25-, 43-, and 50-line text modes. Most computers start up in a 25-line screen mode. If you omit this parameter, the display keeps its present lines setting.

Notes

1. To set the keyboard repeat rate, you must specify both a *rate* and a *delay* setting. You cannot use these parameters individually.
2. The CapsLock, ScrollLock, NumLock, and Insert keys never repeat, no matter how long you hold them down.
3. Only enhanced keyboards support having their repeat rate changed. The original 84-key keyboards supplied with the IBM PC use a fixed repeat rate and ignore the MODE CON command.
4. Using the MODE CON command to change the number of lines and columns displayed on your screen requires the assistance of the ANSI.SYS device driver. If ANSI.SYS isn't in memory when the command executes, an error message displays, and the requested screen mode change does not take place. (See the first message in the "Messages" section.)

Examples

To set the keyboard to repeat as quickly as possible, but increase the delay before repeating to 3/4 of a second, you enter the following command:

```
MODE COM RATE=32 DELAY=3
```

To reset the keyboard to its default values, you enter the following command:

```
MODE COM RATE=20 DELAY=2
```

To set an EGA or VGA monitor to a 43-line text mode, you enter the following command:

```
MODE CON LINES=43
```

Messages

`ANSI.SYS must be installed to perform requested function`

Error: MODE requires the assistance of the ANSI.SYS device driver to perform the requested operation, but it isn't loaded. To use this MODE command, you have to add a DEVICE= line loading the ANSI.SYS device driver to your CONFIG.SYS file and restart your computer.

`Rate and delay must be specified together`

Error: MODE CON requires that you specify both the rate and the delay in order to change the keyboard setting for these parameters. Make sure that you specified both parameters on the command line.

See Also

ANSI.SYS and MODE display

"Using MODE to Change the Typematic Rate" in Chapter 14

MODE *device* CP — 3.3 and later—External

The MODE command offers four subfunctions that you can use to prepare and manipulate code pages on your computer. You use these commands in conjunction with the other international commands to configure your computer to use standards popular in various countries.

Syntax

To prepare and load a code page into the DISPLAY.SYS and/or PRINTER.SYS device drivers, use the following format:

MODE *device* CODEPAGE PREPARE=((*codepage*...) *cpi_file*)

or

MODE *device* CP PREP=((*codepage*...) *cpi_file*)

To switch to a code page that has been previously prepared, use the following format:

MODE *device* CODEPAGE SELECT=*codepage*

or

MODE *device* CP SEL=*codepage*

To reload the current code page into the hardware, use the following format:

MODE *device* CODEPAGE REFRESH

or

MODE *device* CP REF

To display code page status information, use the following format:

MODE *device* CODEPAGE /STATUS

or

MODE *device* CP /STA

Parameters and Switches

device The DOS device that you want to use. This parameter is required. ***device*** can be any one of the following:

Device Name	Description
CON	The console, which is your keyboard and display
LPT1 through LPT3	Parallel printer ports
PRN	The primary printer port, normally LPT1

CODEPAGE PREPARE or **CP PREP**

Prepares code pages (character sets), which simply means that it loads the specified code page into the device driver in memory (DISPLAY.SYS or PRINTER.SYS). You must **PREPARE** a code page be fore you can use it with the CHCP or the MODE *device* CODEPAGE SELECT commands. **CODEPAGE** can be abbreviated as **CP**, and **PREPARE** can be abbreviated as **PREP**.

CODEPAGE SELECT or **CP SEL**

Switches the current code page to the one specified. The code page you switch to must have been previously loaded with the MODE *device* CODEPAGE PREPARE command, or be permanently available from the hardware. **CODEPAGE** can be abbreviated as **CP**, and **SELECT** can be abbreviated as **SEL**.

CODEPAGE REFRESH or **CP REF**

Reloads the current code page. You need to use this command if your printer loses the code page information loaded into it by being turned off. The code page you refresh must have been previously loaded with the MODE *device* CODEPAGE PREPARE command. **CODEPAGE** can be abbreviated as **CP**, and **REFRESH** can be abbreviated as **REF**.

codepage

The code page (character set) that you want to prepare or select. You can enter more than one *codepage* in the prepare command. For a list of the code pages supported by MS-DOS, see Appendix G.

cpi_file

The name and location of the file that contains code page information for the specified device. If you don't specify a drive, DOS assumes the current drive. If you don't specify a subdirectory path, DOS assumes the current directory. The file name is required. MS-DOS 6 provides the following code page information files for use with DISPLAY.SYS and PRINTER.SYS.

CPI File	Description
EGA.CPI	Code pages for EGA and VGA displays

PI File	Description
EGA.ICE	(DOS 6.0 only) Icelandic code pages for EGA and VGA displays
EGA2.CPI	An alternative set of code pages for EGA and VGA displays
LCD.CPI	(Supplemental Disk) Code pages for an IBM Convertible's LCD display
4201.CPI	(Supplemental Disk) Code pages for IBM Proprinters II and III Model 4201 and IBM Proprinters II and III XL Model 4202
4208.CPI	(Supplemental Disk) Code pages for IBM Proprinters X24E Model 4207 and IBM Proprinters XL24E Model 4208
5202.CPI	(Supplemental Disk) Code pages for IBM Quietwriter III printer

Setup places these files in the C:\DOS subdirectory by default.

/STATUS

Displays the number of code pages prepared or selected for the specified ***device***. You can include this parameter or leave it out, it makes no difference. Microsoft states that you can abbreviate it as /STA, but since you can abbreviate it to nothing it hardly matters.

Notes

1. You must specify a valid device. The options are CON:, PRN:, LPT1:, LPT2:, and LPT3:. The colon after the device name is optional.

2. MODE *device* CODEPAGE PREPARE is used to prepare code pages (character sets) for the console (keyboard and display) and printers. Issue this

subcommand before issuing the MODE *device* CODEPAGE SELECT subcommand, unless you use the IBM Quietwriter III printer, whose font information is contained in cartridges. If the code page that you need is in a cartridge, you do not need to use the PREPARE command.

3. For the PREPARE command, you must specify one or more code pages. You can use commas or spaces to separate the numbers if you specify more than one. You must enclose the entire list of code pages in parentheses.

4. When you add or replace code pages with a PREPARE command, enter a comma for any code page that you do not want to change.

5. For the SELECT command, you must specify a single code page. The code page must be either part of a MODE *device* CODEPAGE PREPARE command for the device or the hardware code page specified to the appropriate device driver.

6. MODE *device* CODEPAGE SELECT activates a currently prepared code page or reactivates a hardware code page. You can use MODE device CODEPAGE SELECT only on these two types of code pages.

7. MODE *device* CODEPAGE SELECT usually completes a downloading of any software font to the device, except for the Quietwriter III printer, which uses cartridges.

8. MODE *device* CODEPAGE SELECT activates code pages for individual devices. You can use the CHCP command to activate the code pages for all available devices.

9. MODE *device* CODEPAGE REFRESH downloads, if necessary, and reactivates the currently selected code page on a device. Use this command after you turn on your printer, or after a program changes the video display and leaves the console code page in ruins.

10. MODE *device* CODEPAGE /STATUS displays the following information about the device:

    - The selected (active) code page, if one is selected
    - The hardware code page(s)

- Any prepared code page(s)
- Any available positions for additional prepared code pages

Examples

To prepare the first parallel port with the multilingual (Latin 1) code page found in the file C:\DOS\4201.CPI:

```
MODE LPT1 CP PREP=((850) C:\DOS\4201.CPI)
```

See Also

CHCP, COUNTRY=, DISPLAY.SYS, KEYB, NLSFUNC, and PRINTER.SYS

"Understanding Code Page Switching" in Chapter 21 and Appendix G, "International Country Codes"

MODE *display* — 2.0 and later—External

BATCH FILE

This form of the MODE command can switch the active display adapter between the monochrome display (MDA) and a graphics display adapter (Color Graphics Adapter (CGA), Enhanced Color Graphics Adapter (EGA), or Video Graphics Array (VGA)) on a two-display system.

Syntax

MODE ***display_mode***, *lines*

For systems with CGA monitors, you can use the following syntax to shift the display on your screen:

MODE *display_mode*, ***shift***, T

Parameters and Switches

display_mode — The display adapter to activate if you have more than one installed in your computer. This also specifies the text mode to be used, so it's handy even with only one monitor installed. Legal values for *display_mode* are listed in the following table.

Display Mode	Description
40	Sets the graphics display to 40 characters per line

Display Mode	Description
80	Sets the graphics display to 80 characters per line
BW40	Makes the graphics display the active display and sets the mode to 40 characters per line, black and white (color disabled)
BW80	Makes the graphics display the active display and sets the mode to 80 characters per line, black and white (color disabled)
CO40	Makes the graphics display the active display and sets the mode to 40 characters per line (color enabled)
CO80	Makes the graphics display the active display and sets the mode to 80 characters per line (color enabled)
MONO	Makes the monochrome display the active display

If your computer has an MDA adapter (monochrome or Hercules Mono), it starts up in MONO mode. All other display adapters start up in CO80 mode.

lines

The number of lines to display on-screen. Legal values are different for different types of monitors. CGA and MDA monitors support 25-line text modes only. EGA monitors support 25- and 43-line text modes. VGA monitors support 25-, 43-, and 50-line text modes. Most computers start up in a 25-line screen mode. If you omit this parameter, the display keeps its current lines setting.

shift

(CGA displays only) Allows you to shift the on-screen image left or right. Legal values are L to shift left and R to shift right. In an 80-column mode, the screen shifts two characters at a time, and in a 40-column mode, 1 character at a time.

T (CGA displays only) Displays a test pattern. This parameter can help you when you are using the left and right shift parameter to get the screen centered.

Notes

1. The MODE CO80 command can be very handy for resetting your screen when it's left in an unknown state by an inconsiderate program. It will also restore the cursor to its normal size and position. If your screen goes black when you exit the new graphics utility program you picked up, try typing in this command, even if you can't see what you're typing.

2. For the first form of the command, you must enter the ***display_mode***. All other parameters are optional.

3. The second form of this command is only legal to use with displays which use a Color Graphics Adapter (CGA). On any other type of display, this form of the command does nothing. To adjust a CGA display, you must enter the ***shift*** parameter (L or R), but you can avoid resetting the *display_mode* by typing a comma before the ***shift*** parameter. Depending on whether you are in a 40- or an 80-column screen mode, the screen shifts 1 or 2 characters to the right or left. Including the T parameter displays a test pattern on-screen and prompts you to press **Y** if the screen is centered or **N** to shift the display further left or right.

4. Using the MODE CON command to change the number of *lines* displayed on your screen requires the assistance of the ANSI.SYS device driver. (You can change the *display_mode* without ANSI.SYS, however.) If ANSI.SYS isn't in memory when the command executes, an error message displays, and the requested screen mode change does not take place. (See the first message in the "Messages" section.)

Examples

If you have a CGA, EGA, or VGA display and you want to reset the screen to normal, including the shape of the cursor, enter the following command:

```
MODE CO80
```

MODE CO80 can be a lifesaver when a program leaves your screen in limbo. Even if you can't see what you're typing, DOS resets the screen mode to its normal mode when you enter these commands.

Messages

`ANSI.SYS must be installed to perform requested function`

Error: MODE requires the assistance of the ANSI.SYS device driver to perform the requested operation, but it isn't loaded. To use this MODE command, you have to add a DEVICE= line that loads the ANSI.SYS device driver to your CONFIG.SYS file and restart your computer.

See Also

CLS and MODE CON

"Altering the Look of the Screen with MODE" in Chapter 13

MODE LPT# 3.2 and later—External

You can use this form of the MODE command to set the operating characteristics of your printer, or to redirect printer output to a serial port. You can only set the lines and columns for IBM- and Epson-compatible printers.

Syntax

MODE LPT#: *columns, lines, retry*

or

MODE LPT#: COLS=*columns* LINES=*lines* RETRY=*retry*

To force DOS to print to a serial printer instead of a parallel printer, use the following format:

MODE LPT#:=COM#

Parameters and Switches

LPT#: The parallel printer port you want to configure. DOS supports LPT ports 1, 2, and 3, but they may not all be installed in your computer. The colon after the number is optional.

COM#: The serial port to which you want to redirect printer output. DOS supports COM ports 1, 2, 3, and 4, but they may not all be installed in your computer. The colon after the number is optional.

columns (IBM- and Epson-compatible printers only) The number of characters per line to print on the printer. Legal values are 80 and 132. Most printers start up in an 80-column mode. If you omit this parameter, the printer keeps its current characters-per-line setting.

lines (IBM- and Epson-compatible printers only) The number of lines per inch to print on the printer. Legal values are 6 and 8. Most printers start up in a 6-line-per-inch mode. If you omit this parameter, the printer keeps its current lines-per-inch setting.

retry Instructs DOS about how to handle timeout errors. Using this parameter causes part of MODE to remain resident in memory. You can choose one of the following options:

retry	Action
B	Return busy when the port is busy
E	Return error when the port is busy
P	Retry until output is accepted
R	Return ready when the port is busy (infinite retry)
N or NONE	Take no action (the default)

Rules

1. When configuring a parallel port, you must specify a printer number, but all other parameters are optional, including the colon after the printer number.
2. If you do not want to change a configuration parameter, enter a comma for that parameter.
3. The MODE LPT#:=COM#: command cancels the effect of the MODE LPT#: command.
4. A parameter does not change if you skip that parameter or use an invalid parameter. The printer number, however, must be entered correctly.

5. In DOS 3.3 and earlier versions, if you specify P for continuous retries, you can cancel P only by reentering the MODE command without P. In later versions of DOS, the RETRY=B option has the same effect as the P option of previous DOS versions.

6. If you use a networked printer, do not use any of the RETRY values.

7. The characters-per-line and lines-per-inch portions of the command affect only IBM printers, Epson printers, and other printers that use Epson-compatible control codes.

8. When you are redirecting printer output, the port you specify for both the parallel printer port and the serial printer port must be valid. In other words, you cannot redirect printer output to a serial printer if you don't have a parallel port, and you can't use a nonexistent parallel port to get around this.

9. After you issue the redirection command, all printing that normally goes to the parallel printer goes to the designated serial printer. Programs that write directly to the hardware, such as Microsoft Windows, are not affected by this redirection. For programs like this, try printing to a file named LPT1.TXT, substituting whatever parallel port you've redirected.

10. If you are using a serial printer, you usually have to use the MODE COM# command to set the parameters on your serial port to match the printer. Check your printer's documentation to find out the correct settings to use.

11. You can cancel or undo the redirection command by issuing the MODE LPT#: command.

Notes

This command controls IBM matrix and graphics printers, all Epson printers, and Epson-compatible printers. The command may work partially or not at all on other printers.

When you change the column width, MODE sends the special printer-control code that specifies the normal font (80) or the condensed font (132). When you change the lines-per-inch setting, MODE sends the correct printer-control code for printing 6 or 8 lines per inch. MODE also sets the printer to 88 lines per page for an 8-lines-per-inch setting and to 66 lines per page for a 6-lines-per-inch setting.

If you use the P option of DOS 3.3 or earlier versions or the B retry option of later versions of DOS and attempt to print on a deselected printer, the computer does not issue a timeout error. Rather, the computer internally loops until the printer is ready (turned on, connected to the PC, and selected). For about a minute, the computer appears to be locked up. To abort the continuous retry, press Ctrl-Break.

The redirection capabilities of MODE are useful for systems that are connected to a serial printer. When you type the following command, the serial printer receives all the output that usually is sent to the system printer (assuming that the serial printer is connected to the first Asynchronous Communications Adapter):

```
MODE LPT1: = COM1:
```

This output includes the print-screen (Shift-PrtSc) function. Before you issue the MODE LPT=COMy command, use the MODE COMn: command to set up the serial adapter used for the serial printer.

See Also

MODE COM#

"Using MODE to Change Parallel Port Settings" and "Using MODE to Redirect a Parallel to a Serial Port" in Chapter 14

MONOUMB.386 — 6.0 and later—Windows

If you have a VGA display, you may be able to increase the amount of upper memory space by instructing MemMaker to include the monochrome display region (B000h to B7FFh) in its search for available UMB space. If you run Windows, and you're using this region as UMB space, you need to add a device line for the MONOUMB.386 driver to the [386Enh] section of SYSTEM.INI so that Windows knows what you're up to.

Syntax

To use the monochrome region as UMB space, include the following line in the [386Enh] section of SYSTEM.INI.

DEVICE=*drive:\path***MONOUMB.386**

Parameters and Switches

drive:\path Include the full path to the MONOUMB.386 file on your system. The setup program for DOS 6 places this file in the C:\DOS subdirectory by default.

Notes

1. There are a few good reasons why you may not want to use the monochrome region as upper memory space on a VGA system. If you or one of your software programs switches the VGA to monochrome mode (perhaps with the MODE MONO command), the display overwrites whatever resident software you have loaded there. Also, some Super VGA adapters use this memory region when they are in high-resolution graphics modes.

2. To instruct MemMaker to include this region in its search for upper memory space, choose Custom Setup and answer yes to the question
`Use monochrome region (B000-B7FF) for running programs?`

See Also

MEMMAKER

MORE

2.0 and later—External

MORE displays one screen of information from the standard input device, pauses, and then displays the message `--More--`. When you press any key, MORE displays the next screen of information. MORE is one of the filter programs that MS-DOS provides and is normally used with input redirection or pipes from the command line.

Syntax

MORE < ***pathname***

or

command ¦ **MORE**

Parameters and Switches

< ***pathname*** The name of a file that you want MORE to display one page at a time on your screen. All the normal defaults for drives and subdirectories apply. Wildcards are not allowed.

command ¦ Pipes the screen output from a command into the MORE program, which displays it one screen at a time. ***command*** can be any legal DOS command that writes its output to the standard output device (normally the screen).

Rules

1. MORE displays one screen of information on a standard screen.
2. After displaying a screen of information, MORE waits for a keystroke before filling the screen with new information. This process repeats until all output has displayed.
3. MORE is useful with input and output redirection and piping.

Notes

1. MORE is a DOS filter that enables you to display information without manually pausing the screen.
2. MORE, when used with redirection or piping, is similar to the TYPE command, but MORE pauses after each screen of information.
3. MORE intelligently handles two aspects of displaying text. The command pauses after displaying a screenful of lines, as defined by you with the MODE command. The command also wraps lines that are longer than the width of your screen and reduces the number of lines that display so that unread lines do not scroll off the screen.

See Also

FIND and SORT

"The MORE Filter" in Chapter 14

MOVE

6.0 and later—External

BATCH FILE

You can use MOVE to move a file or group of files from one location to another or to rename subdirectories.

Syntax

To move a file or group of files, use the following format:

MOVE ***source***, *source*, ... ***destination*** /Y /–Y

To rename a subdirectory, use the following format:

MOVE *old_dirname new_dirname*

Parameters and Switches

source The file or files that you want to move. You can specify a full path name that is *drive:\path\...\filename.ext*), and wildcards are allowed. You can enter additional *source* parameters by separating them with commas. This parameter is required and must include a file name (*.* is not assumed).

destination The location to which you want to move the ***source*** file(s). Normally just a drive and/or path is included, although you can enter a destination file name (to rename it) if you are moving only one file. If you omit parts of this parameter, DOS assumes the current drive and subdirectory as necessary.

old_dirname The name of the subdirectory that you want to rename. You can include a disk drive and subdirectory path if you want. If ***old_dirname*** refers to a file, DOS moves the file instead.

new_dirname The new name that you want to give the ***old_dirname*** subdirectory. If ***new_dirname*** isn't in the current directory, you must specify the same drive and/or path you specified with ***old_dirname***; otherwise, DOS thinks you are trying to move the subdirectory, which isn't allowed.

/Y Specifies that you want MOVE to overwrite files without prompting you for confirmation. Including this parameter overrides any setting specified with the COPYCMD environment variable.

/–Y Specifies that you want MOVE to prompt you for confirmation before overwriting any files, even if the command is run from within a batch file. Including this parameter overrides any setting specified with the COPYCMD environment variable.

Exit Codes

ERRORLEVEL Value	Meaning
0	Files were moved successfully.
1	Files weren't moved due to errors or user abort.

Notes

1. Starting with DOS 6.2, the MOVE command, when run from the command line, prompts you for confirmation before overwriting files. However, in order to avoid forcing people to rewrite all their batch files, when run from a batch file, MOVE does not prompt you before overwriting a file.

   If you don't like MOVE's new behavior you can change it by defining an environment variable named COPYCMD. Setting COPYCMD equal to /Y forces MOVE to act as it had in all previous versions of DOS, never prompting for confirmation before overwriting a file. If you set COPYCMD equal to /–Y, MOVE always prompts for confirmation, even when it's run from within a batch file.

2. If you move a file to a directory that already includes a file with that name, DOS overwrites the file in the destination directory without warning.

3. You cannot rename a directory that you are moving to a different disk or to a different relative position on a disk. The disk and path in front of both ***old_dirname*** and ***new_dirname*** have to be the same.

4. If the destination directory does not exist, DOS can create it automatically.

5. If you specify several files to be moved and a file name, rather than a directory, as the destination, DOS displays the message `Cannot move multiple files to a single file.`

6. If a MOVE operation is successful, DOS returns an ERRORLEVEL of 0. If an error occurs, DOS returns a value of 1.

Examples

To move the file README.TXT in the current directory and the file C:\BIN\SETUP.EXE to the directory C:\TEMP (the files are not renamed):

MOVE README.TXT, C:\BIN\SETUP.EXE C:\TEMP

To change the name of the file README.TXT in the current directory to README.1ST:

MOVE README.TXT README.1ST

To move and rename C:\INFO\README.TXT to C:\TEMP\README.BAK:

MOVE C:\INFO\README.TXT C:\TEMP\README.BAK

To change the name of the directory C:\BIN to C:\OLDBIN:

MOVE C:\BIN C:\OLDBIN

See Also
COPY, REN or RENAME, and XCOPY

"Using the MOVE Command" in Chapter 9

MSAV

6.0 and later—External

Microsoft Anti-Virus (MSAV) is a full-screen program that can help you to detect and clean any computer viruses found in your system. It can be adapted to run from a batch file, so you can automate routine scans of your system or floppy disk drives.

Syntax
To interact with MSAV's full-screen interface, use the following format:

MSAV /R */video /mouse*

To immediately start scanning one or more disks, directories, and/or files using MSAV's full-screen interface to show progress, use the following format:

MSAV *pathname drive: ...* /S /C /R /A /L */video /mouse*

To immediately start scanning one or more disks, directories, and/or files using a command-line interface to show progress, include the /N or the /P switch:

MSAV *pathname drive: ...* /S /C /R /A /L /N /P /F */video /mouse*

To get on-line help for MSAV's video and mouse options, use the following format:

MSAV /VIDEO

Parameters and Switches

pathname The drive, subdirectory, or file to limit the virus scan to. All normal drive and subdirectory defaults apply. If you specify a subdirectory, Anti-Virus also scans all subdirectories below the one specified. Do not specify additional drives when you are specifying a path name as the scan target.

drive: ... One or more drives that you want MSAV to scan.

/S Specifies that you want to scan for viruses but not remove any that are found. This is the default setting. Using this switch causes MSAV to start scanning immediately.

/C Specifies that you want MSAV to remove (Clean) any viruses it finds. Using this switch causes MSAV to start scanning immediately.

/R Specifies that MSAV should record the results of each scan in a file (MSAV.RPT) that is created in the root directory of each drive scanned.

/A Specifying this switch causes MSAV to scan all your drives. This includes network and CD-ROM drives, but not floppy disk drives. If you have a CD-ROM drive or are connected to a network, you should probably avoid this switch.

/L Specifying this switch causes MSAV to scan all your local drives. This includes any floppy disk drives, but not network and CD-ROM drives.

/N Specifies that MSAV should not display anything at all while it's working. It displays the contents of the MSAV.TXT file if it exists in the same subdirectory as MSAV.EXE (normally C:\DOS). If a virus is found, an exit code of 86 is returned instead of a warning message. When the specified scanning operation is completed, MSAV terminates automatically, making it suitable for use in a batch file. You cannot specify both the /P and the /N switches.

/P

Specifying this switch activates MSAV's command-line interface instead of the full-screen interface it normally uses. When the specified scanning operation is completed, MSAV terminates automatically, making it suitable for use in a batch file. You cannot specify both the /P and the /N switches.

/F

Specifies that you do not want MSAV to display a list of the files it's scanning. You can use this switch only with the /N or /P switch.

/video

MSAV provides quite a few video-related options. Legal values for *video* are listed in the following table.

video	**Description**
25	Sets the display to 25 lines (the default)
28	Sets the display to 28 lines (VGA only)
43	Sets the display to 43 lines (EGA and VGA)
50	Sets the display to 50 lines (VGA only)
60	Sets the display to 60 lines (Video 7 video adapters only)
IN	Forces the display to use color
BW	Forces the display to use shades of gray
MONO	Forces the display to use black and white only (monochrome)
LCD	Forces the display to use a liquid-crystal-display (LCD) color scheme

video	**Description**
FF	Uses the fastest screen updating for CGA (may cause "snow")
BF	Uses your computer's BIOS fonts (use only if the default graphics characters in the full-screen display do not display properly)
NF	No fonts (no graphics characters should be used in the full-screen display)
BT	Allows the use of a graphics mouse in Microsoft Windows and graphics fonts in DESQview and Ultravision

/mouse

MSAV provides three mouse-related options. Legal values for *mouse* are listed in the following table.

mouse	**Description**
NGM	No graphics mouse; uses the default mouse character rather than a graphics cursor in the full-screen display
LE	Switches the left and right mouse buttons
PS2	Resets the mouse if the cursor disappears or freezes

/VIDEO

Specifying this option alone on the command line requests MSAV to display a list of the available video and mouse options.

Exit Codes

When you run MSAV with the /N switch, it generates the following exit codes, which can be read by the IF ERRORLEVEL command in a batch file.

ERRORLEVEL Value	**Meaning**
0	No viruses were detected.
86	One or more viruses were found.

Notes

1. Different options are available from the full-screen display and from the command line.
2. The options you choose while in full-screen mode are recorded in the file MSAV.INI.

See Also

MWAV and VSAFE

"Understanding Computer Viruses" in Chapter 10

MSBACKUP

6.0 and later—External

Microsoft Backup (MSBACKUP) is a full-screen program that can back up the contents of your hard disk to a series of floppy disks (or another DOS-accessible drive). You can define setup files that record your preferences and allow you to quickly perform different backup chores. No matter how careful you are, you should periodically back up the contents of your hard disk.

Syntax

MSBACKUP *setupfile* /BW /LCD /MDA

Parameters and Switches

setupfile — The file that holds your saved settings, the names of the files to be backed up, and the type of backup you want. This file must have a .SET extension. The default is DEFAULT.SET. DOS searches for this file in the subdirectory pointed to by the MSDOSDATA environment variable if you do not specify drive or subdirectory information in the path name.

/BW — Specifies that MSBACKUP should use colors appropriate for a black-and-white display.

/LCD — Specifies that MSBACKUP should use colors appropriate for a liquid-crystal display.

/MDA — Specifies that MSBACKUP should use colors appropriate for a monochrome display adapter.

Rules

1. You do not explicitly create a setup file. MSBACKUP creates a setup file (or updates it, if you specified one in the MSBACKUP command line) when you save your program settings and file selections.

2. You cannot start MSBACKUP from a floppy disk. This utility and its other program files must be on your hard disk.

3. When looking for its configuration information, backup sets, and catalogs, MSBACKUP first looks in the directory specified by the MSDOSDATA environment variable, then in the directory from which it was started, and then in the current directory. You can use MSDOSDATA to point at your own configuration if you share MSBACKUP with other people.

4. DOS 6.0 includes a Microsoft Windows version of MSBACKUP.

Notes

1. When it performs a backup, MSBACKUP creates a catalog file that contains information about the files that it backs up. When you need to restore a file, you can search the catalog files to determine which one contains the files you want.

   Catalog files encode information in their names. Decoding CD30401A.FUL, for example, yields the following characters:

Character	Meaning
C	The first drive backed up in this set.
D	The last drive backed up in this set. (Had C been the only drive, the catalog file's name would have been CC30401A.FUL.)
3	The last digit of the year of the backup (here, 1993).
04	The month of the backup (here, April).
01	The day of the backup (here, the first).
A	The ID of the backup on that day. If more than one backup of the same drive(s) is performed on the same day and the Keep Old Backup Catalogs options is set, MSBACKUP assigns a letter, from A through Z, to indicate the order in which the otherwise identically named catalog files were created. A is the first, B is the second, and so on. If the Keep Old Backup Catalogs option is not set, the ID alternates between A and B.

Character	Meaning
FUL	The backup type (here, FULL). The other possibilities are INC (incremental) and DIF (differential).

2. When you perform a full backup, MSBACKUP creates a master catalog file, which keeps track of all the backup catalogs that are made during a backup cycle. When you need to restore a file, loading the master catalog automatically merges all the catalogs of the backup cycle, so you can select the latest version of a file easily (although you can choose to restore an earlier version).

   MSBACKUP puts one copy of the backup catalog on your hard disk and a second copy on the disk or network drive that contains your backup set.

3. If DOS displays the message `Insufficient memory` while you are using MSBACKUP, follow these steps:

   a. Make sure that your computer has at least 512K of conventional memory.

   b. Quit MSBACKUP, remove all memory-resident programs (TSRs) from memory, and try again.

   c. In MSBACKUP, turn off the Compress Backup Data option (in the Disk Backup Options dialog box).

See Also

MWBACKUP

"Understanding Microsoft Backup" in Chapter 10

MSCDEX

6.0 and later—External

MSCDEX provides DOS access to CD-ROM drives. CD-ROM drives usually have their own device drivers, but these drivers aren't directly accessible to DOS. MSCDEX uses the network redirector interface to assign a drive letter to a CD-ROM drive. In order to use MSCDEX you must have one or more drive letters available and often have to include the LASTDRIVE= command in your CONFIG.SYS file to set them aside.

Syntax

MSCDEX /D:*driversig* ... /E /K /S /V /L:*letter* /M:*number*

Parameters and Switches

/D:*driversig* ...
For each CD-ROM drive to which you want to assign a drive letter, you need to specify the driver signature (***driversig***) that you assigned to its device driver with the /D switch when you loaded it in your CONFIG.SYS file. You must specify at least one driver signature.

/E
Enables the CD-ROM driver to use available expanded memory to store its sector buffers. This can conserve conventional memory for application programs.

/K
Enables recognition of Kanji (Japanese) CD-ROM labels. Normally MSCDEX cannot recognize Japanese CD-ROM disks.

/S
Enables sharing of CD-ROM drives on an MS-NET or Windows for Workgroups network server.

/V
Displays memory statistics when MSCDEX starts (Verbose).

/L:*letter*
Specifies the drive letter to be assigned to the first CD-ROM. Additional CD-ROMs are assigned letters in sequence. These drive letters must be available for use. The default is to use the next available drive letter(s).

/M:*number*
Specifies the number of sector buffers MSCDEX should use to buffer CD-ROM reads. More buffers can increase the speed of your CD-ROM drive, but they also use more memory. These buffers can be put in expanded memory with the /E switch.

Notes

1. Your CD-ROM's device driver must be loaded by your CONFIG.SYS file. It should include a /D parameter to assign a driver signature (also called a *driver name*) to the driver.

2. Your CONFIG.SYS file must include a LASTDRIVE command that provides enough device letters for your network, SUBST, and MSCDEX needs.

3. MSCDEX can be invoked by your AUTOEXEC.BAT file or from the DOS command line.

4. Invoke MSCDEX before you start Microsoft Windows.

Examples

Following is a typical CONFIG.SYS line which loads a device driver to access a CD-ROM drive. Notice that the driver signature is assigned with the /D switch:

```
DEVICE=C:\DEVICES\CDROMDRV.SYS  /D:MSCD000
```

The following line would most likely be included in your AUTOEXEC.BAT file, and would enable the MSCD000 CD-ROM drive as drive E:

```
C:\DOS\MSCDEX  /D:MSCD000  /L:E
```

See Also

LASTDRIVE=

MSD

6.0 and later—External

MSD stands for Microsoft System Diagnostics and is a handy tool for checking what is going on in a computer system. Via certain command-line options, you can instruct MSD to generate text files that record the state of your computer. These reports can be very useful when you are troubleshooting.

Syntax

To use MSD interactively with a full-screen display, use the following format:

MSD /B /I

To use MSD to generate a report to a file, use the following format:

MSD /I /F*pathname* /P*pathname* /S*pathname*

Parameters and Switches

/B	Forces the display to black and white for monochrome or LCD displays.
/I	Prevents MSD from detecting hardware when it starts. Use this switch if MSD does not start or run properly on your computer.

/F*pathname* Specifies that you want a full report generated. MSD prompts you for certain information (your name, company, address, country, telephone number, and comments) and then incorporates that information into a report that it writes to the specified file. You can specify a full path name with drive and/or path information, but wildcards are not allowed. If you do not include *pathname*, MSD writes the report to the screen.

/P*pathname* Specifies that you want a partial report generated. A partial report contains all of the detailed system information, but none of the identifying information that /F prompts you for. You can specify a full path name with drive and/or path information, but wildcards are not allowed. If you do not include *pathname*, MSD writes the report to the screen.

/S*pathname* Specifies that you want a summary report generated. A summary report provides a shorter listing that highlights the key features of your computers configuration. You can specify a full path name with drive and/or path information, but wildcards are not allowed. If you do not include *pathname*, MSD writes the report to the screen.

Notes

MSD provides information about your computer (for example, its manufacturer, bus type, and ROM BIOS manufacturer) and about its upper memory use, video display, network, operating system, mouse, other adapters, disk drives, LPT ports, COM ports, IRQ stations, TSR programs, and device drivers. This information can be valuable when you are correcting problems or installing new hardware.

See Also

MEM

MSHERC

5.0—External

Since the Hercules Monochrome Graphics Adapter had no support built into the ROM BIOS of the computer, to use the display, programmers had to write their own drivers. The MSHERC program, when run, installs itself in memory and provides BIOS-like services for a Hercules Graphics Adapter. Certain QBasic programs require the use of this program to run. If you do not use a Hercules Graphics Adapter, you will have no use for this command. MSHERC is not distributed in the standard DOS 6 package, but is available on the DOS 6 Supplemental Disk.

Syntax

MSHERC /HALF

Parameters and Switches

/HALF — Specifying this parameter allows you to use a Hercules Graphics Adapter and a Color Graphics Adapter (CGA) in the same system. It limits the driver to using only the memory on the Hercules card, which does not conflict with standard CGA memory space.

Notes

Hercules has stopped making these graphics cards for sale. If you need to set up a two-monitor system and need both monitors to be graphics capable, look into setting up two VGA monitors or a VGA monitor with an 8514 display.

MWAV

6.0 and later—Windows

Microsoft Anti-Virus for Windows (MWAV) is a Windows program that can help you to detect and clean any computer viruses found in your system. This program is the Windows counterpart to the MSAV program.

You cannot run MWAV from the DOS command line; you need to start it from within Windows with, for example, Program Manager's File Run command. For instruction on using the program, run MWAV and press F1, or choose HELP from the menu.

MWAV keeps its settings information in a separate file from MSAV, so the settings you make in one program are not honored in the other program.

MWAV stores its settings in the MWAV.INI file that it creates in the main Windows directory. MSAV stores its settings in the MSAV.INI file that it creates in either the subdirectory that contains MSAV.EXE or the one pointed to by the MSDOSDATA environment variable.

See Also

MSAV, MWAVTSR, and VSAFE

"Using the Windows Version of Microsoft Anti-Virus" in Chapter 10

MWAVTSR — 6.0 and later—Windows

When Windows is running, VSAFE cannot display its messages when a forbidden system activity arises. MWAVTSR provides a channel through which VSAFE can contact you if it needs your attention while Windows is running. If you are using both Windows and VSAFE, you should add MWAVTSR to your start-up group or include it in the LOAD= line in WIN.INI so that it starts up automatically every time you start Windows.

You cannot run MWAVTSR from the DOS command line; you need to start it from within Windows with, for example, Program Manager's File Run command.

See Also

MSAV, MWAV, and VSAFE

"Guarding against Infection" in Chapter 10

MWBACKUP — 6.0 and later—Windows

Microsoft Backup for Windows (MWBACKUP) is a Windows program that can back up the contents of your hard disk to a series of floppy disks (or another DOS-accessible drive). You can define setup files that record your preferences and allow you to quickly perform different backup chores. No matter how careful you are, you should periodically back up the contents of your hard disk. This program is the Windows counterpart to the MSBACKUP program.

You cannot run MWBACKUP from the DOS command line; you need to start it from within Windows with, for example, Program Manager's File Run command. For instruction on using the program, run MWBACKUP and press F1 or choose HELP from the menu.

MWBACKUP keeps its settings information in a separate file from MSBACKUP, so the settings you make in one program are not honored in the other program. MWBACKUP stores its settings in the MWBACKUP.INI file that it creates in the main Windows directory. MSBACKUP stores its settings in the MSBACKUP.INI file that it creates in either the subdirectory that contains MSBACKUP.EXE or the one pointed to by the MSDOSDATA environment variable.

MWBACKUP and MSBACKUP can share catalog files and backup set files. If the MSDOSDATA environment variable is defined, both programs look for these files in the subdirectory it points to. If MSDOSDATA is not defined, they create and look for these files in the subdirectory where the corresponding executable file is located.

See Also

MSBACKUP

"Understanding Microsoft Backup" in Chapter 10

MWUNDEL

6.0 and later—Windows

Microsoft Undelete for Windows (MWUNDEL) is a Windows program that allows you to recover files that you have deleted accidentally. This program is the Windows counterpart to the UNDELETE program. If you are running Windows, you should use this program in preference to the DOS version. You can control various aspects of the "tracking" and "sentry" options of UNDELETE from within Windows with MWUNDEL, but the resident portions of UNDELETE need to be loaded into memory before Windows is started.

You cannot run MWUNDEL from the DOS command line; you need to start it from within Windows with, for example, Program Manager's File Run command. For instruction on using the program, run MWUNDEL and press F1 or choose HELP from the menu.

MWUNDEL share's its settings file with UNDELETE. Both programs look for the UNDELETE.INI file in the subdirectory pointed to by the MSDOSDATA environment variable. If MSDOSDATA is not defined, they create and look for UNDELETE.INI in the subdirectory where their executable files are located, which is C:\DOS by default.

See Also

UNDELETE

"Using the Microsoft Undelete Program for Windows" in Chapter 11

NLSFUNC

3.3 and later—External

NLSFUNC is a resident program that provides support for code page switching on your computer. If you use code pages, you usually have to load NLSFUNC. You can load NLSFUNC from your CONFIG.SYS file with the INSTALL= command. Do not attempt to load NLSFUNC if Windows is running on your computer.

Syntax

NLSFUNC *drive:\path\COUNTRY.SYS*

Parameters and Switches

drive:\path\COUNTRY.SYS The name and location of the country information file you want to use. This normally is COUNTRY.SYS, which Setup places in the C:\DOS subdirectory by default. You don't have to include this parameter if you have included the full path name of the country file in the COUNTRY= command in your CONFIG.SYS file. If you don't specify this parameter, either here or in the COUNTRY= command, DOS searches for COUNTRY.SYS in the root directory of the start-up drive.

Notes

1. If you provide a drive or path name, you also must provide the name of the information file (usually COUNTRY.SYS).
2. If you omit the full file name, DOS searches for the file COUNTRY.SYS in the root directory of the current disk.
3. After it is loaded, NLSFUNC remains active until you restart DOS.
4. You can load NLSFUNC into upper memory with the LOADHIGH command if you have upper memory available on your computer.
5. NLSFUNC can be loaded from you CONFIG.SYS file with the INSTALL= command. If you use INSTALL=, remember that you must include the full path name (with the extension) of the NLSFUNC.EXE file on your system. Setup places the NLSFUNC.EXE file in the C:\DOS subdirectory by default.

See Also

CHCP, COUNTRY=, DISPLAY.SYS, KEYB, MODE *device* CP, and PRINTER.SYS

Chapter 21, "Understanding the International Features of DOS"

NUMLOCK= 6.0 and later—Internal

NUMLOCK= is new with DOS 6. It enables you to choose the state of NumLock key (ON or OFF) when the system starts up. If you are among those who have been cursed with a computer that toggles the NumLock key the "wrong" way when you reboot, the NUMLOCK= command is just what you have been looking for. NUMLOCK= can only be used in your CONFIG.SYS file.

Syntax

To have NumLock turned on (numbers on keypad active) when you reboot your computer, include the following line in your CONFIG.SYS:

NUMLOCK=ON

To have NumLock turned off (cursor keys on keypad active) when you reboot your computer, include the following line in your CONFIG.SYS:

NUMLOCK=OFF

Notes

1. Although you may read information to the contrary, NUMLOCK= can be used anywhere in your CONFIG.SYS file. You don't have to set up menus in your CONFIG.SYS to use the NUMLOCK= command. In its documentation, Microsoft erroneously implied that NUMLOCK= could only be used in a menu block, and this mistake has been duplicated in virtually every description of this command since.

2. The CMOS Setup program in certain computers has a setting for controlling the state of NumLock as well. If your computer has such a setting, you can either use it to set NumLock or use the NUMLOCK= command. If the settings disagree, no harm is done, but the setting in CONFIG.SYS will override the CMOS Setup, because it is executed after the ROM BIOS start-up routines are complete.

3. If you are using an older computer, you may find that using the NUMLOCK= command causes the NumLock light on your keyboard to

get out of sync with the state the key is in. In the design of the original IBM PC, there was no way for the computer to tell the keyboard to toggle the lights. IBM fixed this when it introduced the enhanced 101-key keyboard with the IBM AT. If your computer still uses the old-style interface, however, you may have to either ignore the light or avoid using the NUMLOCK= command.

Examples

If your computer normally sets the NumLock key on at start-up, and you want it turned off, include the following line anywhere in your CONFIG.SYS file:

```
NUMLOCK=OFF
```

If you want DOS to ask you whether to turn the NumLock key off at start-up, insert a ? into the NUMLOCK= command, like this:

```
NUMLOCK?=OFF
```

When DOS processes your CONFIG.SYS file, it prompts you with `NUMLOCK=OFF [Y,N]?` before executing the NUMLOCK= command. Press **Y** to turn off the NumLock key or **N** to leave it on.

PATH

2.0 and later—Internal

The PATH command can be used to change or display the PATH environment variable. When DOS cannot find an executable program in the current directory, it searches through each directory listed in the PATH environment variable. Executable programs are files that end in .COM, .EXE, or .BAT, and DOS searches each directory on the search path, in that order, for each type. By specifying a PATH, you can save yourself from having to enter the full path name for each command you want to execute. The Setup program for DOS 6 places a PATH command in your AUTOEXEC.BAT file that places the C:\DOS subdirectory (or whatever install directory you specified) on your search path.

Syntax

To specify an executable file search path, use the following format:

PATH *path1;path2;path3;...*

To display the current PATH, use the following format:

PATH

To clear the current PATH, use the following format:

PATH ;

Parameters and Switches

path1;path2;path3;... Each path listed must specify a valid subdirectory that exists on your system. The current subdirectory often changes, so it is a good idea to use full, absolute path names—including drive letters—for each subdirectory included in your PATH statement. Separate each subdirectory from the previous one with a semicolon (;).

Notes

1. If you specify more than one set of paths, the following rules apply:
   - The path sets must be separated by semicolons.
   - The order in which you list the path sets is the order DOS looks for the programs or batch files. First, DOS searches the current directory; then DOS searches the first *path* specified, then the second *path* specified, and so on, until the command or batch file is found.
2. The maximum length of PATH is 127 characters. This is one of the most compelling reasons to use short subdirectory names whenever you can.
3. The PATH command establishes the value of an environment variable named PATH. You can view, set, or delete the PATH with the SET command, as well as with the PATH command. The PATH command is simply shorthand for SET PATH=.
4. When you type the name of a program or batch file, DOS searches the current directory. If the program or batch file is not found, DOS searches each path in sequence. If the program or batch file is not found in any of the paths, DOS displays the error message `Bad command or filename.`
5. You can shorten PATH by using the SUBST command to substitute drive letters for deeply nested paths. Another technique is to remove a path that is included only to start one program. Then, make a batch file that

performs a CD to that path and invokes the program, and place the batch file in a directory that is still included in PATH.

Messages

`Invalid drive in search path`

Warning: You specified a nonexistent drive name in one of the paths. This message appears when DOS searches for a program or batch file, not when you give the PATH command.

Use PATH or SET to see the current path. If the drive temporarily is invalid because of a JOIN or SUBST command, you can ignore this message. If you specified the wrong disk drive, issue the PATH command again and provide the complete set of directory paths that you want to use.

See Also

SET

"Helping DOS Find Files with PATH" in Chapter 5

PAUSE — 1.0 and later—Internal

The PAUSE command displays a `Press any key to continue...` message and waits for the user before continuing to execute the batch file. This command is useful if you want the user to be able to abort a batch file, using Ctrl-C or Ctrl-Break, before some action is taken. You can also use PAUSE to give the reader time to read a screen of messages displayed with the ECHO command.

Syntax

PAUSE

Notes

1. The PAUSE command simply displays the `Press any key to continue...` message when it is executed. The next key you press (except Ctrl-C or Ctrl-Break, see Note #2) releases the pause, and execution of the batch file continues.

2. Pressing Ctrl-C or Ctrl-Break in response to the `Press any key to continue...` message displays the `Terminate batch job (Y/N)?` message. Pressing **Y** aborts the batch file, returning you to the DOS prompt. Pressing **N** skips the line that was executing and continues with the next line in the batch file.

3. If you are running the batch file from within a Shell program, such as DOS Shell, the `Terminate batch job (Y/N)?` message is not displayed. When you press Ctrl-C or Ctrl-Break in these circumstances, the batch file is always aborted.

4. If you want to wait for a keypress, but you don't want PAUSE to display the `Press any key to continue...` message, redirect the output of the PAUSE command to the NUL device. DOS still waits for a keypress, but no message is displayed.

5. The CHOICE command included with DOS 6 gives you much more flexibility in choosing allowable keys and making decisions than PAUSE. If you are using DOS 6, consider using CHOICE instead of PAUSE in your batch files.

Examples

One very common use for PAUSE is to give the user time to do something. For example, if you wanted to make certain that a floppy disk had been placed in drive B, you might include the following lines in a batch file:

```
ECHO Insert the Working Backup disk in drive B:
ECHO.
ECHO Press Ctrl-Break to abort the backup, or
PAUSE
```

When these commands are executed, the following messages are displayed:

```
Insert the Working Backup disk in drive B:

Press Ctrl-Break to abort the backup, or
Press any key to continue...
```

Note that the PAUSE message is anticipated in the ECHO messages. If you redirect the output from PAUSE to the NUL device, you can control all of the text that's displayed on-screen, as shown in the following:

```
ECHO  Insert the Working Backup disk in drive B:
ECHO.
ECHO  Press Ctrl-Break to abort the backup, or any
ECHO  other key to update the Working Backup disk.
PAUSE  >  NUL
```

When these commands are executed, the following messages are displayed:

```
Insert the Working Backup disk in drive B:

Press Ctrl-Break to abort the backup, or any
other key to update the Working Backup disk.
```

If you press Ctrl-C or Ctrl-Break at the pause, the following message is displayed (as long as you aren't running this batch file from within a Shell program):

```
Terminate batch job (Y/N)?
```

Type **Y** to abort the batch file; type **N** to continue with the next line.

Messages

```
Press any key to continue...
```

Prompt: PAUSE displays this message any time it is executed. DOS waits for a key to be pressed before continuing execution of the batch file. Entering Ctrl-C or Ctrl-Break when this message is displayed enables you to terminate the batch file rather than continuing.

```
Terminate Batch Job (Y/N)?
```

Prompt: When you press Ctrl-C or Ctrl-Break while a batch file is running, DOS displays this message. Typing **Y** aborts the batch file, returning you to the DOS prompt. Typing **N** skips the line that was executing and continues with the next line in the batch file. Note that if the batch file was run from within a Shell program, such as DOS Shell, this message won't be displayed, and the batch file will be aborted.

See Also

CHOICE and ECHO

"Pausing for Input in a Batch File" in Chapter 16

POWER

6.0 and later—External

BATCH FILE

For laptop computers that conform to the Advanced Power Management (APM) specification, the POWER command enables you to control the trade-off between extended battery life and maximum performance from your computer. You can also use POWER to switch back and forth between the power-management system built into your laptop and the APM-style idle detection methods. Before you can run POWER from the command line, you must use a DEVICE= command to load the POWER.EXE device driver into memory from your CONFIG.SYS file.

Syntax

POWER *setting*

Parameters and Switches

setting

This value determines how agressive you want the power-management features to be. *setting* can be one of the values listed in the following table. You can only specify one setting at a time. If no value is included for *setting*, POWER displays a short report on the current power settings in your computer. (See item #2 in the following "Notes" section.)

***setting* Value**	**Description**
ADV:MAX	The most aggressive power setting. Power savings can be as much as 25%, but performance may suffer.
ADV:REG	The default setting.
ADV:MIN	The most conservative power setting. Use this setting when you are running programs that slow down too much when the ADV:REG setting is used.
ADV	The same as specifying ADV:REG.
STD	For computers that conform to the APM specification, this setting uses the computer's built-in power-management features. For computers that don't support the APM specification, this setting is the same as OFF.
OFF	Disables the power-management features. You may want to use this setting (or STD) when you are running communications software.

Notes

1. The POWER.EXE device driver must be installed before you can run POWER from the command line. If you try to run POWER without installing the device driver, an error message appears. (See the following "Messages" section.)

2. POWER.EXE is actually two files: a device driver and an executable program. The device driver portion does all the real work. You have to load it into memory with a DEVICE= command in your CONFIG.SYS file in order for the DOS power-management features to be enabled.

After this device driver has been loaded into memory, the executable portion of POWER.EXE communicates with the device driver to adjust settings and display status information.

3. If you enter the POWER command without specifying a new setting, a status report is displayed that summarizes the active settings and the current power use in your system. On non-APM-compliant systems, POWER displays the following report:

```
Power Management Status
-----------------------
Setting = ADV:REG
CPU: idle 75% of the time
```

If your system supports the APM specification, a more detailed report, like the following, is displayed:

```
Power Management Status
-----------------------
Setting = ADV:REG
CPU: idle 75% of time
AC Line Status : OFFLINE
Battery status : High
Battery life (%) : 90
```

The computer's ROM BIOS provides the additional information in this report. This information is not displayed on non-APM-compliant computers.

4. When you are running communications software, CPU-intensive applications, or other applications that don't access your hard disk very often, you may want to turn off power-management features. With an ADV:MAX setting, POWER may think your computer was idle when it was actually busy handling serial communications or recalculating a large spreadsheet. To minimize the possibility of false idle-time detection but still keep power-management features active, use a setting of ADV:MIN. To disable APM features and regain maximum performance from your computer, use a setting of OFF or STD.

5. POWER.EXE detects idle time with a variety of methods. It monitors hard disk activity, video functions, and MS-DOS service requests to determine if your system is busy. In addition, POWER.EXE monitors the keyboard polling and application-idle interrupts to sense idle time in active programs. When idle time is detected, a CPU HALT instruction is executed, causing the CPU to sleep until the next hardware interrupt arrives. (The timer interrupt occurs 18.2 times per second, so the CPU only sleeps for 55 milliseconds or less.)

If a busy program routinely polls the keyboard, such as communication programs often do, POWER.EXE may think your computer is idle when it isn't. False idle detection can interfere with a program's operation, unnecessarily slowing it down. The ADV:MAX, REG, and MIN settings control the level of keyboard polling detection that POWER.EXE uses. If you are having performance problems with an application, try turning down keyboard polling detection with an ADV:REG setting, or disabling it with ADV:MIN.

6. Even if your system doesn't support the APM specification, you still may get some benefit from POWER.EXE. Microsoft's testing indicates that, on the average, a 5% reduction in power consumption can be realized by using POWER.EXE on non-APM-compliant computers. Of course, the power-management features built into your laptop might surpass this savings, in which case you are better off not using POWER.EXE at all.

Examples

Assuming the POWER.EXE device driver has been loaded from your CONFIG.SYS file, entering the following command requests maximum power savings:

```
POWER ADV:MAX
```

If you were about to fax some work back to the office, you might want to turn down your power-management features to avoid interfering with your communications software. You could enter the following line:

```
POWER ADV:MIN
```

Back in your hotel room, working on deadline, you want to disable the power-management system entirely so you can get maximum performance out of your laptop computer. After all, there's no need to extend battery life when you are plugged into an AC outlet.

```
POWER OFF
```

Messages

`Power Manager (POWER.EXE) not installed`

Information: You have attempted to run the POWER program without first installing the POWER.EXE device driver. POWER can only adjust the settings of the device driver in memory, so you must load

POWER.EXE with a DEVICE= command in your CONFIG.SYS file before you can use any of its features.

See Also

POWER.EXE

POWER.EXE (device driver)

6.0 and later—External

For laptop computers that conform to the Advanced Power Management (APM) specification, POWER.EXE enables you to control the trade-off between extended battery life and maximum performance from your computer. POWER.EXE must be loaded with a DEVICE= statement in your CONFIG.SYS file before you can use it from the command line.

Syntax

DEVICE=*drive:\path***POWER.EXE** *setting* /LOW

Parameters and Switches

drive:\path — The full path to the POWER.EXE file on your system. Setup places the POWER.EXE file in the C:\DOS subdirectory by default. If the full path to POWER.EXE isn't specified, DOS looks for the file in the root directory of the start-up drive.

setting — This value determines how agressive you want the power-management features to be. *Setting* can be one of the values listed in the table below. You cannot specify more than one setting at a time. If no value is included, the ADV:REG setting is assumed.

Value	Description
ADV:MAX	The most aggressive power setting. Power savings can be as much as 25%, but performance may suffer.
ADV:REG	The default setting.
ADV:MIN	The most conservative power setting. Use this setting when you are running programs that slow down too much when the ADV:REG setting is used.

Value	Description
ADV	The same as specifying ADV:REG.
STD	For computers that conform to the APM specification, this setting uses your computer's built-in power-management features. For computers that don't support the APM specification, this setting is the same as OFF.
OFF	Disables the power-management features. You may want to use this setting (or STD) when you are running communications software.
/LOW	Instructs POWER.EXE to load itself into conventional memory. Normally, POWER.EXE loads into upper memory if it is available.

Notes

1. The POWER.EXE device driver must be installed before you can run POWER from the command line. If you try to run POWER without installing the device driver, an error message appears. (See the following "Messages" section.)

2. POWER.EXE is actually two files: a device driver and an executable program. The device driver portion does all the real work. You have to load it into memory with a DEVICE= command in your CONFIG.SYS file in order for the DOS power-management features to be enabled. After this device driver has been loaded into memory, the executable portion of POWER.EXE communicates with the device driver to adjust settings and display status information.

3. POWER.EXE automatically loads into upper memory if it is available. It is not necessary to use the DEVICEHIGH= command with POWER.EXE.

4. When you are running communications software, CPU-intensive applications, or other applications that don't access your hard disk very often, you may want to turn off the power-management features. With an ADV:MAX setting, POWER might think your computer was idle when it was actually busy handling serial communications or recalculating a large spreadsheet. To minimize the chance of false idle-time detection but keep power-management features active, use a setting of ADV:MIN. To disable APM features and regain maximum performance from your computer, use a setting of OFF or STD.

5. POWER.EXE detects idle time with a variety of methods. It monitors hard disk activity, video functions, and MS-DOS service requests to determine if your system is busy. In addition, POWER.EXE monitors the keyboard polling and application-idle interrupts to sense idle time in active programs. When idle time is detected, a CPU HALT instruction is executed, causing the CPU to sleep until the next hardware interrupt arrives. (The timer interrupt occurs 18.2 times per second, so the CPU sleeps for only for 55 milliseconds or less.)

   If a busy program routinely polls the keyboard, as communications programs often do, POWER.EXE may think your computer is idle when it isn't. False idle detection can interfere with a program's operation, unnecessarily slowing it down. The ADV:MAX, REG, and MIN settings control the level of keyboard polling detection that POWER.EXE uses. If you are having performance problems with an application, try turning down keyboard polling detection with an ADV:REG setting, or disabling it with ADV:MIN.

6. Even if your system doesn't support the APM specification, you still may get some benefit from POWER.EXE. Microsoft's testing indicates that, on the average, a 5% reduction in power consumption can be realized by using POWER.EXE on non-APM-compliant computers. Of course, the power-management features built into your laptop might surpass this savings, in which case you are better off not using POWER.EXE at all.

7. POWER.EXE is fully compatible with Windows. If you are running Windows 3.1 on a system with an APM-compliant ROM BIOS, you should select `MS-DOS System With APM` in Window's Setup as the type of computer you are using. By doing so, Windows can cooperate and control the power-management features supplied by POWER.EXE. On non-APM-compliant computer systems, you can use POWER.EXE without selecting a special computer type.

Examples

To load the POWER.EXE device driver and enable the ADV:REG (default) level of power management, you could add the following line to your CONFIG.SYS file:

```
DEVICE=C:\DOS\POWER.EXE
```

If you wanted to enable the maximum level of power management, specify the ADV:MAX setting instead of using the default, as shown in the following line:

```
DEVICE=C:\DOS\POWER.EXE  ADV:MAX
```

As long as there is enough upper memory available, POWER.EXE loads high without using the DEVICEHIGH= command. If you wanted to force it to load into conventional memory instead, add the /LOW parameter, as shown here:

```
DEVICE=C:\DOS\POWER.EXE  /LOW
```

Messages

`Power Manager (POWER.EXE) not installed`

Information: You have attempted to run the POWER program without first installing the POWER.EXE device driver. POWER can only adjust the settings of the device driver in memory, so you must load POWER.EXE from your CONFIG.SYS before you can use any of its features.

See Also

POWER

PRINT

2.0 and later—External

The PRINT command is a memory-resident utility that enables you to print files in the background on your computer. Unfortunately, PRINT is limited to printing text files; you can't use it as a general-purpose print spooler.

Syntax

To load PRINT into memory, use the following format:

PRINT /D:*device* /B:*bufsiz* /M:*maxticks* /Q:*maxfiles* /S:*timeslice* /U:*busyticks* /T *textfile* /P /C

To add or delete files in the queue, use the following format:

PRINT /T /P /C *textfile1* /P /C *textfile2* /P /C ...

Parameters and Switches

When you first use the PRINT command after turning on or rebooting your computer, you can specify any of the following switches:

/B:*bufsiz* — The size (in bytes) of the memory buffer to be used while the files are printing. *bufsiz* can be any number from 512 to 16,384. The default is 512 bytes. You won't have to increase this value unless you have a very fast printer.

/D:*device* — The device to be used for printing. Legal values are PRN, LPT1, LPT2, LPT3, COM1, COM2, COM3, or COM4. The default is PRN. This parameter must precede any *textfile* included on the command line.

/M:*maxticks* — The maximum amount of time (in clock ticks) that PRINT uses to send characters to the printer every time PRINT gets a turn. *maxtick* can be any number from 1 to 255. The default is 2.

/Q:*maxfiles* — The number of files that can be held in the queue for printing. *maxfiles* can be any number from 4 to 32. The default is 10.

/S:*timeslice* — The number of clock ticks allocated for PRINT. *timeslice* can be a number from 1 to 255. The default is 8. Increasing *timeslice* speeds printing and slows other tasks.

/U:*busyticks* — The maximum amount of time (in clock ticks) PRINT should wait for a busy or unavailable printer before releasing its timeslice. PRINT tries again the next time it gets control. *busytick* can be any number from 1 to 255. The default is 1.

You can specify any of these switches whenever you use PRINT:

/C — Cancels the background printing of files. (See item #3 in the following "Notes" section.)

/P — Queues up files for printing. (See item #3 in the following "Notes" section.)

/T — Terminates the background printing of all files, including any file that currently is printing (clears the queue).

Rules

1. If you do not provide a file name, DOS displays the background printing status.

2. You can specify the switches /B, /D, /M, /Q, /S, and /U only when you first use PRINT. If you use the /D switch, you must type this switch first in the line. You can list the remaining five switches in any order before you specify a file name.

3. The /D switch specifies the print device that you want to use (LPT1, LPT2, LPT3, COM1, COM2, COM3, or COM4). If you omit /D the first time you use PRINT, DOS displays the following prompt:

   ```
   Name of list device [PRN]:
   ```

   You can respond in either of two ways:

   - Press Enter to send the files to PRN (normally LPT1:). If LPT1: is redirected (refer to the MODE command entry earlier in this command reference), the files are rerouted.

   - Enter a valid DOS device name. Printing is directed to this device. If you enter a device that is not connected to your system, PRINT accepts files in the queue. The files are not processed, however, and you lose processing speed.

   After you have chosen the print device that you want PRINT to use, you cannot change it without restarting DOS.

4. If you name a file with no switch, DOS assumes that you want to use the /P (print) switch.

5. Files print in the order in which you list their names. If you use wild cards, files are printed in the order in which they are listed in the directory.

6. The command PRINT /C has no effect if you do not specify a file name.

7. The first time you invoke PRINT, DOS increases in size by approximately 5,500 bytes. When you increase or decrease certain default settings, you proportionally change the size of DOS. To regain this memory space, however, you must restart DOS.

8. If you use PRINT to print files to a serial printer, you may need to configure the serial port with the MODE COM# command.

9. PRINT expands tab characters in the files it prints the same way the TYPE command does. Also, PRINT stops printing a file when it encounters an end-of-file marker (Ctrl-Z). For these two reasons, you should print only straight ASCII files with PRINT. Any other type of file is likely to be garbled by tab expansion and truncated when it encounters a Ctrl-Z character and terminates prematurely.

Notes

1. The /B switch acts like a disk buffer. PRINT reads into memory a portion of the document to be printed. As you increase the value of *bufsiz*, you decrease the number of times PRINT must read the file from the disk, thereby increasing printing speed. Always use a multiple of 512 (1,024, 2,048, and so on) as the value of *bufsiz*. The default size (512 bytes) is adequate for most printers.

2. When the default values are assumed, PRINT gets 22 percent of the computer's time.

3. The positions of the /P, /C, and /T switches in the command line are important. Each switch affects the file immediately preceding it in the command line, and all subsequent files, until DOS encounters another switch. The following command, for example, uses the /P switch to place the files LETTER.TXT and PROGRAM.DOC in the queue to be printed. The /C switch cancels the background printing of MYFILE.TXT and TEST.DOC.

```
PRINT LETTER.TXT /P PROGRAM.DOC MYFILE.TXT
/C TEST.DOC
```

   In this example, the /P switch affects the preceding file (LETTER.TXT) and the following file (PROGRAM.DOC). Similarly, the /C switch affects the preceding file (MYFILE.TXT) and the following file (TEXT.DOC).

4. If you use the /T switch, background printing is canceled for all files in the queue, including the file that is currently printing, and any files listed in the command line.

5. If a disk error occurs during background printing, DOS cancels the current print job and places a disk-error message on the printout. The printer then performs a form feed, the bell rings, and DOS prints all remaining files in the queue.

Messages

```
filename is currently being printed
filename is in queue
```

Information: This message tells you which file is printing and names the files that are in line to be printed. This message appears when you use PRINT with no parameters or when you queue additional files.

```
PRINT queue is empty
```

Information: No files are in line to be printed by PRINT.

```
PRINT queue is full
```

Warning: You attempted to place too many files in the PRINT queue. The request to add more files fails for each file past the limit. You must wait until PRINT processes a file before you can add another file to the queue.

```
Resident part of PRINT installed
```

Information: The first time you use PRINT, this message indicates that PRINT installed itself in DOS and increased the size of DOS by about 5,500 bytes.

See Also

MODE COM#

"The PRINT Command" in Chapter 14

PRINTER.SYS (device driver)

3.3 to 5.0—External

The PRINTER.SYS device driver provides international code page support for certain IBM printers or close compatibles. When combined with the other international utilities DOS provides, PRINTER.SYS enables you to use various international character sets with your printer. You must load PRINTER.SYS by using a DEVICE= or DEVICEHIGH= statement in your CONFIG.SYS file. Microsoft no longer distributes PRINTER.SYS with MS-DOS, but it is available on the MS-DOS 6 Supplemental Disk.

Syntax

DEVICE=*drive:\path***PRINTER.SYS LPT***x***=(*_type_*,***hard_cp,num_cp***)**

DEVICEHIGH=*drive:\path***PRINTER.SYS LPT***x***=(*_type_*,***hard_cp,num_cp***)**

Parameters and Switches

drive:\path

The full path to the PRINTER.SYS file on your system. If the full path to PRINTER.SYS isn't specified, DOS looks for the file in the root directory of the start-up drive. The PRINTER.SYS file is included on the MS-DOS 6 Supplemental Disk.

LPT*x*=

The printer port (LPT1=, LPT2=, or LPT3=) your printer is attached to. You can enter a colon between the port name and the equals sign (for example, LPT1:=). This parameter is required.

type

The type code for the printer being used. The type code must be listed in the following table, and the parameter must be enclosed in parentheses.

***type* Code**	**Printer**
4201	IBM Proprinters II and III, Model 4201 IBM Proprinters II XL and III XL, Model 4202
4208	IBM Proprinter X24E, Model 4207 IBM Proprinter XL24E, Model 4208
5202	IBM Quietwriter III, Model 5202

hard_cp

The hardware code page built into the printer. See Appendix G for a list of the code pages that MS-DOS supports.

num_cp

The number of software code pages you want to use with the printer. Valid entries for *num_cp* are 1 or 2.

Notes

1. PRINTER.SYS no longer is distributed with MS-DOS, but it is available on the MS-DOS 6 Supplemental Disk. Three printer code page information files are included as well (4201.CPI, 4208.CPI, and 5202.CPI). The MODE command requires these files when it is preparing to download code page information to your printer.

2. When PRINTER.SYS is loaded, it uses about 11K of memory.

3. Although you can have up to three printers attached to your computer, PRINTER.SYS can only support international code pages on one of them at a time. To change to a different printer or printer port, you have to edit the DEVICE= line for PRINTER.SYS and reboot your computer.

4. You should always specify a value for *hard_cp*. IBM printers often use a hardware code page of 850, but check your printer manual to be sure.

5. Even if you don't own one of the printers listed in the table, your printer may be compatible with one of them. To find out whether you can use PRINTER.SYS, check your printer's documentation or call the manufacturer.

6. In order to print with a software code page, you must perform a number of additional steps. The MODE command is used to prepare and download code page information to your printer. After this is done, you can use MODE to select the downloaded code page, or you can load NLSFUNC and use the CHCP command to change the active code page for all your devices at once. Additionally, you may want to add the COUNTRY= command to your CONFIG.SYS file to make case conversion and sort order information available.

7. DISPLAY.SYS performs a similar function for EGA, VGA, Super VGA, and LCD screens.

Examples

The following line added to your CONFIG.SYS file would set up an IBM Proprinter X24E, attached to LPT1, for use with two additional code pages. The hardware code page for the X24E is 850, Multilingual (Latin I).

```
DEVICE=C:\DOS\PRINTER.SYS  LPT1=(4208,850,2)
```

If an IBM Quietwriter was attached to LPT2, and you wanted to load PRINTER.SYS into upper memory, you would use the following command:

```
DEVICEHIGH=C:\DOS\PRINTER.SYS  LPT2=(5202,850,2)
```

See Also

CHCP, COUNTRY=, DISPLAY.SYS, MODE device CP, and NLSFUNC

Chapter 21, "Understanding the International Features of DOS"

PROMPT

2.0 and later—Internal

The prompt that MS-DOS displays can be customized with the PROMPT command. PROMPT, like PATH, saves its settings in the DOS environment. People often use ANSI control codes in their prompt strings, in which case ANSI.SYS has to be loaded into memory from your CONFIG.SYS file.

Syntax

PROMPT *promptstring*

Parameters and Switches

promptstring The text of the DOS command-line prompt. It can include any of the meta-strings defined for use in the PROMPT command (see the following table).

Notes

1. If you do not enter the *promptstring*, the standard system prompt reappears, which is equivalent to PROMPT NG (`C>`).

2. A very popular prompt string, and the one that the Setup program for MS-DOS 6 inserts into your AUTOEXEC.BAT file, is PROMPT PG (`C:\DOS>`). Beginning with DOS 6.0, COMMAND.COM inserts the value PG in PROMPT if it finds the PROMPT environment variable undefined when the system starts up.

3. The new system prompt stays in effect until you restart DOS or reissue the PROMPT command.

4. The PROMPT command establishes the value of an environment variable named PROMPT. You can view, set, or delete the PROMPT environment variable with the SET command, as well as with the PROMPT command. The PROMPT command is simply shorthand for SET PROMPT=.

5. Any text you type for *promptstring* becomes the new system prompt. You can include special characters by using the meta-strings.

   A *meta-string* is a group of characters that is transformed into another character or group of characters. All meta-strings begin with the dollar-sign symbol ($) and have two characters, including the $. The case of the characters isn't significant in a prompt meta-string, but it is significant in ANSI commands. The following table contains the meta-string characters and their meanings:

Meta-string	Example	Description
$$	$	Dollar sign
$B	¦	Vertical bar (pipe) character
$D	Tue 09-14-1993	The current date
$G	>	Greater-than symbol
$L	<	Less-than symbol
$N	C	The current drive letter
$P	C:\DOS	The current drive and path, including the current directory
$Q	=	Equals sign
$T	12:19:12.45	The current time (Note that the time will not be updated as the time changes, only when a new prompt line is displayed.)
$V	MS-DOS Version 6.0	The DOS version number

The following meta-strings do not display characters on-screen, but they are useful when you want to make a fancier DOS prompt.

Meta-string	Description
$_ (underscore)	Carriage return and line feed—moves the cursor to the first position of the following line
$E	The Escape character (ASCII 27)—useful for sending ANSI control codes
$H	The Backspace character (ASCII 8)—erases the preceding character
$(any other)	Nothing or null character—DOS ignores

Note

To include a dollar sign in a prompt string you have to enter it twice.

6. When you open a DOS window within Windows, the prompt is changed to the value of the WINPMT environment variable if it has

been defined. If you want to have a different prompt under Windows, use the SET command to define an environment variable named WINPMT, and set it equal to the prompt you want to use. For example, the line

```
SET WINPMT=**Windows** $P$G
```

gives you the following prompt in a DOS window within Windows:

```
**Windows** C:\DOS>
```

This is a handy prompt to remind you that Windows is running.

Examples

To make the prompt be the current drive and path, followed by >, use this command:

```
PROMPT $P$G
```

Assuming that your CONFIG.SYS loads ANSI.SYS and that you have white text (foreground) on a blue background, the following command changes the prompt to a blinking red `HI`, followed by >:

```
PROMPT &E[5; 3/mHI$E[0; 37; 44m$G
```

See Also

ANSI.SYS and SET

"Changing the Command Prompt with PROMPT" in Chapter 13 and Appendix F, "ANSI Control Codes"

QBASIC — 5.0 and later—External

QBasic is the Microsoft QuickBASIC programming environment, a full-screen, interactive programming tool for writing programs in BASIC. Traditionally, all operating system software came with a simple set of programming tools. Few microcomputer users have an interest in these programs anymore, but it is nice that Microsoft keeps providing them free for those who want them. QBasic also is the "behind the scenes" program that EDIT and HELP require; so whether or not you actually write any BASIC programs, it's likely that you will be running QBasic on your computer.

Syntax

QBASIC /RUN *pathname* /EDITOR *pathname* /B /G /H /NOHI /MBF

Parameters and Switches

/RUN *pathname*	The BASIC file that you want QBASIC to load into memory and run. If no drive is specified, the current drive is assumed. If no subdirectory path is specified, the current directory is assumed. Wildcards are not allowed. You cannot specify the /EDITOR parameter with the /RUN parameter.
/EDITOR *pathname*	The ASCII file that you want QBASIC to load into the full-screen text editor (EDIT). If no drive is specified, the current drive is assumed. If no subdirectory path is specified, the current directory is assumed. Wildcards are not allowed. If you don't specify a *pathname*, the editor starts without a file. You cannot specify the /RUN parameter with the /EDITOR parameter.
/B	Specifies that QBASIC should use colors more appropriate for a black-and-white (monochrome) or LCD screen.
/G	Specifies that QBASIC should use the fastest screen-updating method for a CGA monitor. Don't specify the /G switch if you see "snow" on your monitor.
/H	Specifies that QBASIC should display 43 lines on an EGA monitor or 50 lines on a VGA monitor.
/NOHI	Specifies that QBASIC should limit itself to 8 colors rather than 16.
/MBF	Specifies that QBASIC should use the Microsoft Binary Format for floating-point numbers. Specifically, the /MBF switch converts CVS, CVD, MKS$, and MKD$ so that they act like CVSMBF, CVDMBF, MKSMBF$, and MKDMBF$, respectively.

Notes

1. QBasic is a comprehensive development environment for interpreted BASIC and a subset of Microsoft QuickBASIC. BASIC, BASICA, and GWBASIC are no longer provided with MS-DOS.

2. QBASIC.EXE is required to run EDIT and HELP.

3. The use and operation of QBasic is beyond the scope of this book. If you want to learn to write BASIC programs with QBasic, you can either try to find your way with the QBasic help system, or you can get a book on programming with QBasic.

RAMDRIVE.SYS (device driver)

3.2 and later—External

A RAM disk is a simulated drive that uses RAM, rather than a magnetic disk, to store files. Because it has no moving parts, a RAM disk is much faster than a hard drive or floppy disk. Unfortunately, whenever you shut down or restart your computer, the contents of a RAM disk are lost. With RAMDRIVE.SYS, you can create a RAM disk in extended, expanded, or conventional memory. You must load RAMDRIVE.SYS with a DEVICE= or DEVICEHIGH= statement in your CONFIG.SYS file.

Syntax

DEVICE=*drive:\path***RAMDRIVE.SYS** *disksize sectorsize dir_entries* /E /A

To load the RAMDRIVE.SYS device driver into upper memory, use the DEVICEHIGH= command. This specifies the placement in memory of the driver, not the RAM disk.

DEVICEHIGH=*drive:\path***RAMDRIVE.SYS** *disksize sectorsize dir_entries* /E /A

Parameters and Switches

drive:\path — The full path to the RAMDRIVE.SYS file on your system. Setup places the RAMDRIVE.SYS file in the C:\DOS subdirectory by default. If the full path to RAMDRIVE.SYS isn't specified, DOS looks for the file in the root directory of the start-up drive.

disksize — The size, in kilobytes, of the RAM disk you want to create. *disksize* can be from 4K to 32767K. (For DOS 5, the limits were 16K to 4096K.) If no *disksize* is specified, a 64K RAM disk is created.

sectorsize The sector size the RAM disk should use. *sectorsize* can be 128, 256, or 512. If this parameter is omitted, a *sectorsize* of 512 is assumed. (You should have a very good reason before setting *sectorsize* to a different value. All DOS disks use a sector size of 512, and many disk utilities will fail if a different sector size is used.) To specify *sectorsize*, you must also specify *disksize*.

dir_entries The maximum number of root directory entries that the RAM disk can hold (in other words, the size of the root directory). *Dir_entries* can be in the range 2 to 1024 and are rounded up to the nearest multiple that fits evenly in *sectorsize*. Each directory entry takes 32 bytes of disk space. If this parameter is omitted, a root directory with room for 64 entries is created (four 512-byte sectors in size). To specify *dir_entries*, you must also specify *disksize* and *sectorsize*.

dir_entries limits only the size of the root directory, not any subdirectories you create on the RAM disk. Subdirectories grow as needed to accommodate an unlimited number of directory entries.

/E Creates the RAM disk in extended memory. An XMS-compatible memory manager, such as HIMEM.SYS, must be available.

/A Creates the RAM disk in expanded memory. A LIM EMS-compatible memory manager, such as EMM386.EXE, must be available.

Notes

1. DEVICEHIGH= loads the RAMDRIVE.SYS device driver into upper memory, but the RAM disk still is created in the memory area you have specified with the command's parameters. RAMDRIVE.SYS uses about 1K of memory for the device driver.

2. If there isn't room in memory for the RAM disk you have specified, RAMDRIVE.SYS decreases the size of the root directory to 16 entries and tries again. If the RAM disk still doesn't fit, the driver aborts with an error message. (See the third item in the following "Messages" section.)

3. A RAM disk runs more efficiently from extended memory than from the simulated expanded memory provided by EMM386.EXE. Unless you have a hardware EMS board in your computer, always create RAM disks in extended memory.

4. Normally, you won't want to create RAM disks in conventional memory. Although they run efficiently there, they also use up memory that is required to run your application programs. The only time this memory trade off might be worthwhile is when you are working on a floppy-disk-only system. The increased speed from a RAM disk could be worth the loss of memory for certain operations.

5. Although RAM disks are very fast, SMARTDrive can provide similar speed increases for all your programs—not just those that use the RAM disk. For many people, committing memory into a disk cache such as SMARTDRV.EXE makes more sense than creating a RAM drive. Of course, if you have a lot of RAM that you don't use, you can always do both.

Trap

If you use a RAM disk to store data files, remember to copy them to your hard drive before shutting off your system or rebooting. Whenever you restart your computer, everything on a RAM disk is lost.

6. One popular use of a RAM disk is to store temporary files generated by programs. By setting the TEMP and TMP environment variables to point to a RAM disk, many programs will create their temporary files on the RAM disk. (See Appendix B for a description of the DOS programs that use the TEMP environment variable.) Not only can this technique speed up your applications, but it also can eliminate the need to periodically delete temporary files which, for one reason or another, have escaped automatic deletion by their parent programs.

7. If you run Windows and set the TEMP variable to point to a RAM disk, Microsoft advises that the RAM disk be at least 2M (2048K) in size to avoid possible printing problems.

8. You can load RAMDRIVE.SYS as many times as memory allows from CONFIG.SYS. Each time you load it, another RAM disk is created. When created, a RAM disk is assigned the next available drive letter by DOS.

9. If RAMDRIVE.SYS is loaded after DBLSPACE.SYS, it receives a drive letter that follows the letters allocated by DoubleSpace. To avoid having your RAM disk drive letter change as you create and destroy DoubleSpace drives, always place the DEVICE= line for RAMDRIVE.SYS before the line for DBLSPACE.SYS in your CONFIG.SYS file.

10. You can use DoubleSpace to compress a RAM disk, but the Compressed Volume File (CVF) that DoubleSpace creates is lost each time you reboot your computer. To keep from having to create a new CVF file each time you start up, you could clear its attributes with the ATTRIB command and copy it from the RAM disk to your hard disk. Your AUTOEXEC.BAT file could then copy the CVF file back to the RAM disk; restore the system, hidden, and read-only attributes; and mount it for you each time you reboot.

Examples

For the following examples, let's assume that the computer you are using has 8M of RAM, HIMEM.SYS loaded, EMM386.EXE loaded, and UMB support enabled. To create a 64K RAM disk in conventional memory, you can load RAMDRIVE.SYS with no parameters, as shown here:

```
DEVICEHIGH=C:\DOS\RAMDRIVE.SYS
```

The DEVICEHIGH= command locates the RAMDRIVE.SYS driver in upper memory, but the RAM disk itself still is created in conventional memory. To increase the size of the RAM disk to 1M (1024K) and place it in extended memory, you add the *disksize* and /E parameters, as the following line shows:

```
DEVICEHIGH=C:\DOS\RAMDRIVE.SYS  1024  /E
```

Because other values were not specified, the sector size would be 512 and the root directory would have room for 64 directory entries. If you wanted to create a RAM disk that was about the same size as a 1.44M 3 1/2-inch floppy disk, you might use the following line in your CONFIG.SYS file:

```
DEVICEHIGH=C:\DOS\RAMDRIVE.SYS  1450  512  224  /E
```

To increase the number of root directory entries to 224, a sector size of 512 had to be specified, despite the fact that 512 is the default value for sector size.

Messages

Messages from the RAMDRIVE.SYS device driver all begin with the word RAMDrive:. Here are the ones you are most likely to encounter.

`RAMDrive: Expanded memory manager not present`

Error: You have specified the /A switch to create a RAM drive in expanded memory; however, expanded memory is not available, and the RAM disk was not created. Make sure that you have loaded EMM386.EXE (or another EMS provider), with EMS enabled, before the DEVICE= line in your CONFIG.SYS file that loads RAMDRIVE.SYS.

`RAMDrive: Extended memory manager not present`

Error: You have specified the /E switch to create a RAM drive in extended memory; however, extended memory is not available, and the RAM disk was not created. Make sure that you have loaded HIMEM.SYS (or another XMS provider) before the DEVICE= line in your CONFIG.SYS file that loads RAMDRIVE.SYS.

`RAMDrive: Insufficient memory`

Error: Not enough memory was available to create the RAM drive you specified. Typically, this is caused by forgetting to specify the /E or /A switch, in which case RAMDRIVE.SYS attempts to create the RAM disk in conventional memory. You may also receive this message if you specify the *disksize* in bytes rather than kilobytes. Edit the DEVICE= line for RAMDRIVE.SYS in your CONFIG.SYS file to correct any errors; then restart your computer.

`RAMDrive: No extended memory available`

Error: You have specified the /E switch to create a RAM drive in extended memory, but no extended memory is available. Usually this error is caused when EMM386.EXE claims all available XMS memory to use for EMS memory. With the DOS 6 version of EMM386.EXE, you can include a MIN parameter so that EMM386.EXE returns unused EMS memory to the memory pool when another program, such as RAMDRIVE.SYS, requests extended memory.

See Also

DEVICE=, DEVICEHIGH=, DBLSPACE.SYS, and SMARTDRV.EXE

"Using a RAM Disk" in Chapter 19 and Appendix B, "DOS Environment Variables"

RD or RMDIR

2.0 and later—Internal

You can use the RD (or RMDIR) command to delete empty subdirectories. If the subdirectory still contains any files, RD aborts and displays an error message. To delete a subdirectory and all its files, use the DELTREE command.

Syntax

RD *drive:**path***

RMDIR *drive:**path***

Parameters and Switches

drive: The drive containing the subdirectory you want to delete. If *drive:* is omitted, the current drive is assumed.

path The subdirectory you want to delete on *drive:*. ***path*** can either be absolute or relative—that is, specified from the root directory or specified from the current directory (see item #4 in the following "Notes" section). If only the subdirectory name is specified with no path information, the subdirectory in the current directory with that name is deleted. You cannot delete the current directory.

Notes

1. You must explicitly name the subdirectory you want to delete.
2. The subdirectory you want to delete must be empty of all files, including hidden files.
3. You cannot delete the current directory of any drive.
4. If a backslash (\) is the first (or only) character in a subdirectory path, it is considered absolute and is specified starting from the root directory. If the subdirectory path begins with a subdirectory name, it is considered relative, and the current directory is used as its starting point. A drive letter, followed by a colon, can precede either an absolute or a relative path.

Messages

```
Invalid path, not directory
or directory not empty
```

Error: RMDIR did not remove the specified directory because one of the following errors occurred:

- You listed an invalid directory in the path.
- Files other than the . and .. entries still exist.
- You misspelled the path or directory name.

Check each possibility and try again.

You can delete all the files in a directory and remove the directory in one step with DELTREE.

```
Attempt to remove current directory - drive:path
```

Error: RMDIR did not remove the specified directory for one of the following reasons:

- The directory is the current directory of the current drive.
- The directory was the current directory of another drive.
- The directory was redirected with the SUBST command.

In the first two cases, perform a CHDIR operation on a directory that is not a subdirectory of the directory that you want to delete, and then attempt the RMDIR operation again. In the third case, perform a RMDIR operation on the actual directory affected by the SUBST command.

See Also

CD (or CHDIR), DELTREE, and MD (or MKDIR)

"Deleting Directories with RMDIR (RD)" in Chapter 5

RECOVER

2.0-5.0—External

RECOVER is a dangerous utility that can do more harm than good. If a disk develops a bad sector within a file, DOS is unable to copy any part of the file. If the root directory of a disk becomes damaged, DOS may not be able to read the disk at all. RECOVER is supposed to help you in these situations, but at times it is a case of a little help being worse than no help at all. With DOS 6,

Microsoft stopped distributing RECOVER, and it's not even available on the Supplemental Disk. If you have a copy of RECOVER on your disk, you may want to delete it to keep from running it accidentally.

Situations like the ones that RECOVER was supposed to address do arise. DOS 6.2 includes the ScanDisk utility, which can repair many of the problems that can arise on your disks. If ScanDisk can't fix the problem, or if you aren't running DOS 6.2 when disaster strikes, reach for a good third-party utility package. The Norton Utilities, PC Tools, and the Mace Utilities, are just a few of the packages that offer excellent tools to help you recover damaged files and disks. Any one of these packages will pay for itself many times over the first time you lose access to your hard disk due to a runaway program overwriting your root directory.

See Also

SCANDISK

"Analyzing a Disk with SCANDISK" in Chapter 7

REM

1.0 and later—Internal

You can use the REM command to insert comments into batch files or your CONFIG.SYS file. Any text on the line after REM (with a few exceptions in batch files) is ignored when DOS is processing that line in the file. This can be extremely handy for documenting or temporarily "commenting out" lines in the file.

Syntax

REM *comment*

Parameters and Switches

comment Can be any text. DOS truncates any line longer than 127 characters, but this usually won't matter in a comment line. In batch files, comments are read by the parser, so the pipe character (¦) and redirection symbols (< and >) should be avoided.

Notes

1. REM should to be placed at the beginning of a line, with only spaces or tabs preceding it. A legal delimeter of some sort (for example, a space) needs to follow the REM so that DOS can recognize it.

2. In batch files, the pipe (¦) and redirection symbols (< and >) should be avoided in comments, because the parser may see and act on them. Including a greater-than sign in a comment line may cause an empty file to be created with the next eight characters as its name.

3. DOS has a maximum line length of 127 characters; any line longer than that will be truncated. Still, as long as you are not depending on the comment line being displayed, it really doesn't matter if DOS cuts it off. Comments are for you to read when you are working on the file, and the length of the line is really limited by your editing software, not DOS.

4. In CONFIG.SYS, you can use a semicolon rather than REM as an easier and somewhat cleaner way to mark comments. The semicolon comment isn't valid in batch files or versions of DOS before MS-DOS 6.

5. Blank lines can make your batch files and CONFIG.SYS file much easier to understand. DOS ignores any blank lines in these files, so there is no need to mark them as comments with REM.

6. Although REM is legal at the DOS prompt, it serves no purpose. REM is only useful for inserting comments in batch files and CONFIG.SYS.

Examples

If you wanted to document why a particular environment variable was being created in your AUTOEXEC.BAT file, you might include something like this:

```
REM  I set DIRCMD here to avoid always telling DIR that I prefer my
REM  filenames in lowercase letters with screen pauses.
SET  DIRCMD=/L /P
```

Or perhaps you want to "comment out" the line that loads the driver for your tape drive until the replacement driver arrives in the mail.

```
REM  DEVICE=C:\DOS\TAPE\SQ55.SYS
```

You also could use a semicolon to comment out the preceding line, like this:

```
;DEVICE=C:\DOS\TAPE\SQ55.SYS
```

See Also

;

Chapter 16, "Understanding Batch Files," and Chapter 18, "Configuring Your Computer"

REN or RENAME

1.0 and later—Internal

REN (or RENAME) is a utility you can use to rename files. Unlike many third-party utilities, REN cannot move files from one subdirectory to another, and it cannot rename subdirectories. To rename subdirectories, see the MOVE command.

Syntax

REN *old_name new_name*

or

RENAME *old_name new_name*

Parameters and Switches

old_name The file, or files, that you want to rename. A full path name (such as drive:\path\...\filename.ext) can be specified, and wildcards are allowed. This parameter is required and must include a file name (*.* is not assumed).

new_name The new file name, or names, you want to use. Only a file name and extension can be specified, you can't include any drive or path information. Wildcards are allowed; if they are used, they are filled in with the corresponding characters from ***old_name***. This parameter is required.

Notes

1. REN (or the long form, RENAME) changes the name of a file on the disk. The command does not rename directories. You can use the MOVE command to rename a directory.
2. Because you are renaming an established disk file, the file's drive or path designation goes with the old name so that DOS knows which file to rename.
3. Wildcard characters are acceptable in either the old or the new name.

Messages

`Duplicate filename or File not found`

Error: You attempted to change a file name to a name that already exists, or you asked DOS to rename a file that does not exist in the directory. Check the directory for conflicting names, make sure that the file name exists and that you spelled the name correctly, and then reissue the command.

See Also

MOVE

"Renaming Files" in Chapter 9

REPLACE

3.2 and later—External

The REPLACE command enables you to selectively update files on one disk from matching files on another disk, thereby overwriting old copies of files. REPLACE has other options that can help you maintain backup floppy disks, such as adding new files only or prompting you for confirmation before copying each file.

Syntax

REPLACE ***source_files*** *destination_path* /A /S /U /P /R /W

Parameters and Switches

source_files The file, or files, that you want to selectively copy. A full path name (such as drive:\path\...\filename.ext) can be specified, and wildcards are allowed. The file name portion of this parameter is required.

destination_path The location you want to selectively copy the ***source_files*** to. You can include a drive and a path, but you cannot specify a file name. If this parameter is omitted, the current drive and subdirectory are used as the destination.

/A Adds all the files specified by ***source_files*** that do not exist on the *destination_path*. You cannot combine the /A switch with the /S or /U switches.

/S Replaces all the files specified by ***source_files*** that are found in *destination_path* or any subdirectories below it. You can't combine the /S switch with the /A switch.

/U Updates (replaces) all the files specified by ***source_files*** that are found in *destination_path* with dates and times preceding the source file's date and time. You can't combine the /U switch with the /A switch.

/P — Prompts you as each file is replaced or added to *destination_path*.

/R — Enables REPLACE to overwrite read-only files on the *destination_path*. Normally, REPLACE terminates with an error if it attempts to overwrite a read-only file.

/W — Tells REPLACE to display the `Press any key to continue...` message and wait for a keystroke before beginning the replace operation. Using this switch gives you time to switch floppy disks if necessary.

Exit Codes

ERRORLEVEL Value	Meaning
0	Replace operation successful
1	Incorrect DOS version running (6.0 and later)
1	Invalid command-line syntax (3.2 and v3.3)
2	Source file(s) not found
3	Source or destination path not found
5	Unable to replace files—access denied
8	Insufficient memory to complete replace operation
11	Invalid command-line syntax (4.0 and later)
15	Source or destination drive invalid (undocumented)

Rules

1. If you do not name the source drive, DOS uses the current drive.
2. If you do not name the source path, DOS uses the current directory.
3. You must specify a source file name. Wildcards are allowed.
4. If you do not name the destination drive, DOS adds files to, or replaces files in, the current drive.
5. If you do not name the destination path, DOS adds files to, or replaces files in, the current directory.

Notes

1. Use REPLACE with caution, or this command's speedy find-and-replace capability can have the effect of an unrelenting search-and-destroy mission on your data. Be careful when you unleash REPLACE on several subdirectories at a time, particularly when you use REPLACE /S on the entire disk. Because REPLACE updates a file based only on the file name, you could accidentally replace a file somewhere on the disk that you intended to save.

2. To prevent such unwanted replacements, limit the destination path name to cover only the directories that hold the files you want replaced. Check the source and destination directories for matching file names. If you find conflicts or have doubts, use the /P switch; REPLACE asks for approval before replacing files.

3. If you use DOS 4.0 or later, the /U switch can help you avoid replacing wrong files. /U compares the files' date and time stamps. The destination file is replaced only if the file is older than the source file.

Messages

`File cannot be copied onto itself filename`

Warning: The source and destination disk and directories are identical. You probably did not specify a destination, so the source disk and directory are the current disk and directory. Otherwise, you specified the same drive and directory twice. REPLACE does not process filename.

Check the command line to ensure that you specified the correct source and destination for REPLACE, and then try the command again.

`nnn file(s) added`

or

`nnn file(s) replaced`

Information: REPLACE indicates how many files are added or replaced. The first message appears when you use the /A switch; the second message appears if you do not use the /A switch. The message does not indicate that potential files are added or replaced; rather, the message appears when at least one file is added or replaced, regardless of errors that occur later.

`No files found filename`

Error: REPLACE could not find any files that matched the source file name. One of the following errors probably occurred:

- You misspelled the source file name.
- You provided the drive and directory names but omitted the file name.
- You provided the wrong drive or directory name for the source.
- You inserted the wrong floppy disk into the drive.

Check the command line to ensure that the correct disk is in the drive, and then retry the command.

`Invalid parameter combination`

Error: You used both the /A and /S switches or the /A and /U switches, which you cannot use together in a REPLACE command. To replace files, omit /A. Because you cannot add files to more than one directory at a time, you cannot use /S with /A. To add files to more than one directory, issue separate REPLACE commands, each time specifying a different directory to which files are to be added.

See Also

COPY and XCOPY

"Combining Copying and Directory Management with XCOPY" and "Using the COPY Command" in Chapter 9

RESTORE

2.0 and later—External

You can use the RESTORE command to restore from one disk to another disk, one or more backup files created with the BACKUP command. If your backup file was created by MSBACKUP, you must use MSBACKUP to restore data from that file.

Syntax

RESTORE ***drive1:*** *drive2:path****filename.ext*** /S /P /M /N /B:*date* /A:*date* /L:*time* /E:*time* /D

Parameters and Switches

drive1:	The drive that holds the backup files.
drive2:	The drive that is to receive the restored files.
path\	The path to the directory that is to receive the restored files. This parameter must be the same as the directory from which the files were backed up.
filename.ext	The file, or files, that you want to restore. Wildcards are allowed.
/A:*date*	Restores all files that were created or modified on or after the date you specify. The format of *date* depends on the COUNTRY in your CONFIG.SYS file.
/B:*date*	Restores all files that were created or modified on or before the date you specify. The format of *date* depends on the COUNTRY in your CONFIG.SYS file.
/D	(DOS 5.0 and later) Lists files to be restored without actually performing the restoration. You must specify *drive2:*.
/E:*time*	Restores all files that were created or modified either at the time or earlier than the time you specify. The format of *time* depends on the COUNTRY in your CONFIG.SYS file.
/L:*time*	Restores all files that were created or modified either at the time or later than the time you specify. The format of *time* depends on the COUNTRY in your CONFIG.SYS file.
/M	Restores all files that were modified or deleted since the backup set was made.
/N	Restores all files that no longer exist in the destination directory.
/P	Prompts you before restoring a file that was changed since the last backup or before restoring a file marked as read-only.

/S Restores files in the current directory and all subdirectories. When you use this switch, RESTORE re-creates all necessary subdirectories that were removed and then restores the files in the re-created subdirectories.

Exit Codes

ERRORLEVEL Value	Meaning
0	Restore operation successful
1	No files found to restore
2	Halted by file-sharing violation (undocumented)
3	Halted by user (Ctrl-C)
4	Halted by fatal disk error

Rules

1. You must provide the name of the drive that holds the backup files. If the current disk is to receive the restored files, you do not have to specify the destination drive.
2. If you do not name a path, RESTORE uses the current directory of the receiving disk.
3. If you do not provide a file name, RESTORE restores all backup files from the directory. Omitting the file name is the same as using *.*.
4. RESTORE prompts you to insert the backup disks in order. If you insert a disk out of order, RESTORE prompts you to insert the correct disk.
5. Do not combine the /B, /A, and /N switches in the same RESTORE command.
6. Be cautious when you restore files that were backed up while an ASSIGN, SUBST, or JOIN command was in effect. When you use RESTORE, clear any existing APPEND, ASSIGN, SUBST, or JOIN commands. Do not use RESTORE /M or RESTORE /N while APPEND /X is in effect. RESTORE attempts to search the directories for modified or missing files. APPEND tricks RESTORE into finding files in the paths specified to the APPEND command. RESTORE may then restore files that should not be restored, and not restore files that should be restored. To disable APPEND, issue the APPEND ; command.

7. RESTORE cannot restore DOS system files (for example, IO.SYS and MSDOS.SYS) to the appropriate positions in the file structure so that the disk is bootable.

Notes

BACKUP and RESTORE in DOS 3.3 and later are radically different from the corresponding commands in previous versions. These commands place all backed-up files in one larger file and maintain a separate information file on the same disk. In DOS 3.3 and later, RESTORE handles the new and old backup-file formats, which means that these newer versions of RESTORE can restore backups created by any version of BACKUP.

Messages

```
Insert backup diskette nn in drive d:
Strike any key when ready
```

Information: RESTORE wants the next disk in sequence. This message appears when you are restoring files that were backed up onto floppy disks. Insert the next floppy disk (in the proper sequence) into drive *d:*, and then press any key.

```
Insert restore target in drive d:
Strike any key when ready
```

Information: RESTORE is asking you to insert the floppy disk that is to receive the restored files. This message appears only when you restore files onto floppy disks. Insert the target disk into drive *d:*, and then press any key.

```
*** Listing files on drive A: ***
```

Information: You used the /D switch with RESTORE, and the files that *would be* restored are displayed. The listed files follow the file specification that you used for restoration.

```
Source does not contain backup files
```

Error: RESTORE found no files that were backed up with the BACKUP command. BACKUP may have malfunctioned when backing up files, or you may have inserted the wrong disk.

```
Source and target drives are the same
```

Error: RESTORE determined that the drive that holds the backup files is the same as the drive that you designated to receive the restored files. You may have forgotten to specify the drive that holds the backup files or the target disk. If your system has one floppy drive and you tried to restore files onto a floppy disk, specify drives A and B.

```
System files restored
Target disk may not be bootable
```

Warning: You restored the three system files (IO.SYS, MSDOS.SYS, and COMMAND.COM) from the backup floppy disks. These files may not have been restored to the proper location on the disk, and you cannot use them to start DOS.

```
Warning! Diskette is out of sequence
Replace the diskette or continue if okay
Strike any key when ready
```

Warning: You inserted a backup floppy disk out of order. Place the correct disk in the drive and continue.

```
Warning! File filename
was changed after it was backed up
or is a read-only file
Replace the file (Y/N)?
```

Warning: This message appears when you use the /P switch. Either the file *filename* already exists on the hard disk and is marked as read-only, or the date of the file on the target disk is more recent than that of the backup copy (which may mean that the backup copy is obsolete). Press **Y** to replace the existing file with the backup copy or **N** to skip the file.

```
Warning! No files were found to restore
```

Warning: The files you wanted to restore are not on the disk from which you tried to restore them. Try again with another disk or another file specification. If you did not create a log file when you created the BACKUP floppy disk, you can determine which directories and files are on the floppy disk by using the TYPE command to display the floppy disk's binary CONTROL.*xxx* file, and then interpreting what you see. The *xxx* in the file name will reflect the backup disk's number. For example, the first disk in the backup set would have the file CONTROL.001 on it.

RMDIR (see RD)

RMDIR is the alternate name for the RD command. For information on using the RD or RMDIR command, see the entry for RD in this command reference.

SCANDISK

6.2—External

BATCH FILE

The ScanDisk program can locate and fix errors on disks. It works on most local drives, including DoubleSpace compresssed drives. ScanDisk also can perform a surface scan, which reads every sector on the disk to make sure that it is error free and readable.

Syntax

To check one or more disk drives for errors, use the following format:

> **SCANDISK** *drive: ...* /ALL /CHECKONLY /AUTOFIX /NOSAVE /CUSTOM /SURFACE /MONO /NOSUMMARY

To check an unmounted DoubleSpace volume file for errors, use the following format:

> SCANDISK *cvf_file* /CHECKONLY /AUTOFIX /NOSAVE /CUSTOM /MONO /NOSUMMARY

To check the degree of fragmentation in a group of files, use the following format:

> **SCANDISK** /FRAGMENT *pathname*

To undo the changes ScanDisk previously made fixing files, use the following format:

> **SCANDISK** /UNDO *undo:* /MONO

Parameters and Switches

drive: ... — The disk drive, or drives, you want to scan for errors. You can specify as many drive letters as you want. If *drive:* is omitted, the current drive is assumed. The colon following the drive letter is optional. You can't combine this parameter with the /ALL parameter.

cvf_file — The name of an unmounted DoubleSpace volume file you want to scan for errors. You should include the drive letter and the full name of the Compressed Volume File (CVF), such as C:\DBLSPACE.000.

pathname — The file, or files, you want to check for fragmentation. A full path name is allowed, and all the normal defaults for drive and/or path apply. Wildcards are allowed in the file name portion of the path name.

undo: The disk drive containing the undo disk that ScanDisk previously created. The colon following the drive letter is optional.

/ALL Requests that ScanDisk check all local disk drives. If you specify this switch, you should not include any *drive:* parameters.

/CHECKONLY Requests that ScanDisk check the drive for errors but not to repair any errors it finds. You must specify this parameter if you want to run ScanDisk while other programs are running, such as Windows. You can't combine this parameter with the /AUTOFIX, /NOSAVE, or /CUSTOM parameters.

/AUTOFIX Requests that ScanDisk fix any errors it finds without prompting you first. Any lost clusters that are found are saved as files in the root directory of the drive. If you specify the /NOSAVE parameter with /AUTOFIX, any lost clusters are deleted. You can't combine this parameter with the /CHECKONLY or /CUSTOM parameters.

/NOSAVE Requests that ScanDisk delete any lost clusters it finds on the disk. You can only use this parameter if you also specify the /AUTOFIX parameter.

/CUSTOM Requests that ScanDisk follow the settings in the [CUSTOM] section of the SCANDISK.INI file. If you intend to run ScanDisk from a batch file, you may want to use this parameter. For information about setting options in the SCANDISK.INI file, read the comments included in the file itself. You can't combine this parameter with the /AUTOFIX, /NOSAVE, or /CHECKONLY parameters.

/SURFACE Requests that ScanDisk automatically perform a surface scan after checking the disk for errors. Surface scans can take time, but they do verify that all the data on your disk is error free and readable.

/MONO Configures ScanDisk to use display colors more appropriate for a monochrome monitor or LCD screen.

/NOSUMMARY — Prevents ScanDisk from displaying a full-screen summary after scanning each drive.

/FRAGMENT — Requests that ScanDisk check all files specified with the *pathname* parameter to see how fragmented they are. You can't specify any other parameters except *pathname* when you are requesting a fragmentation report.

/UNDO — Requests that ScanDisk reverse the changes it made to your disk. The drive specified with this parameter must be the drive containing the undo disk that ScanDisk created. Note that you should not undo the changes ScanDisk made if you have made any changes to the disk since fixing the errors.

Exit Codes

ERRORLEVEL Value	Meaning
0	ScanDisk found no errors
1	Command-line syntax error
2	Terminated due to an internal error or lack of memory
3	ScanDisk halted by user during integrity checks
4	ScanDisk halted by user during surface scan
254	ScanDisk found errors, but they were all corrected
255	ScanDisk found errors, and they were not all corrected

Notes

1. If you enter SCANDISK with no parameters, ScanDisk scans the current drive.
2. Normally, if any errors are found, a dialog box appears that explains what the error is. You can choose to have ScanDisk fix the error or leave it alone. If you have specified the /AUTOFIX parameter, these dialog boxes are skipped.
3. After the disk has been checked for errors in its logical structure, ScanDisk asks if you want to perform a surface scan. If you have specified the /SURFACE parameter, the surface scan takes place

automatically. If you have specified the /CHECKONLY parameter, no surface scan is done.

4. ScanDisk can find and repair errors on most hard disk drives, floppy disk drives, DoubleSpace drives, RAM disk drives, and memory card drives.

5. ScanDisk can only check local disk drives. Do not attempt to run ScanDisk on any network, CD-ROM, or Interlnk drives attached to your system. You also shouldn't run ScanDisk on any alias drives created by the ASSIGN, JOIN, or SUBST commands.

6. If you try to run ScanDisk when other programs are running, ScanDisk refuses to fix any problems it encounters because the other programs might try to access the disk while ScanDisk is working, and more serious problems could be created. If Windows is running and you try to start ScanDisk, you will see the message shown in the third item in the following "Messages" section.

   If you run ScanDisk with the /CHECKONLY parameter, it checks your disks for errors while other software, such as Windows, is running. If ScanDisk finds any errors, quit all your active programs, including Windows, and run ScanDisk again. In multitasking situations, it is possible that ScanDisk will find errors when none really exist. By running ScanDisk again with no outside interference, you can find out for sure.

7. If you ask ScanDisk to check a mounted or unmounted DoubleSpace drive, it asks if it should first check the host drive for errors. Normally, you should answer *Yes*. It is best to fix the host drive and then the DoubleSpace volume if errors exist in either of them. Answer *No* only if you have just finished checking the host drive and are sure that no errors exist.

8. After ScanDisk repairs errors on a drive, it asks if you want to create an undo disk. It is usually a good idea to make an undo disk. You must have a blank, formatted floppy disk that you can place in drive A or B for the undo information to be written to. After you have exited ScanDisk, try not to write anything to the disk until you are sure that you don't want to undo the changes ScanDisk has made. Do not undo changes after writing to the disk or serious damage could result.

9. ScanDisk can find and repair the following types of problems on your drives:
   - Bad sectors on the disk
   - Boot sector errors
   - Crosslinked files
   - Directory tree structural errors
   - DoubleSpace compression structure errors
   - DoubleSpace volume file allocation errors
   - DoubleSpace volume header structure errors
   - DoubleSpace volume signature errors
   - File allocation table (FAT) errors
   - Lost clusters
10. You can customise many of ScanDisk's settings by editing the SCANDISK.INI file. Setup places this file in the C:\DOS subdirectory by default. By setting the features you want to use in SCANDISK.INI and using the /CUSTOM parameter, you can automate a ScanDisk session and run it all from a batch file. For instructions on editing the SCANDISK.INI file, see the comments included in the SCANDISK.INI file itself.

Examples

To scan drives C and D for errors, you enter the following command:

```
SCANDISK C: D:
```

If you want to perform a surface scan as well, and not be prompted about fixing errors, you include the /SURFACE and /AUTOFIX options, as follows:

```
SCANDISK C: D: /AUTOFIX /SURFACE
```

If Windows is running, you have to do the surface scan later and for now specify the /CHECKONLY parameter, as in the following:

```
SCANDISK C: D: /CHECKONLY
```

To find out if it is time to run DEFRAG, you can check on the fragmentation level of the files in your correspondence subdirectory, like this:

```
SCANDISK C:\LETTERS\*.* /FRAGMENT
```

Messages

`Invalid switch: parameter`

Error: The *parameter* you specified is unknown to ScanDisk. Check the command line for typing errors. To see a list of legal parameters for ScanDisk, enter the SCANDISK /? command.

`parameter is not a valid name for a DoubleSpace volume file`

Error: You have entered an incorrect parameter for ScanDisk. You will see this message if you omit one of the slashes (/), which begin most of ScanDisk's parameters. Of course, you may have mistyped the name of a DoubleSpace CVF file as well.

`You cannot use ScanDisk to fix problems while Windows is running.`

`To check for disk problems without fixing them, type SCANDISK /CHECKONLY at the command prompt.`

Error: You have attempted to run ScanDisk without the /CHECKONLY parameter while Microsoft Windows is running. Specify the /CHECKONLY parameter and try again.

See Also

CHKDSK and DEFRAG

SET

2.0 and later—Internal

The SET command enables you to view, add, delete, or change variables contained in the DOS environment. Starting with DOS 6.0, you can use the SET command in your CONFIG.SYS file. MS-DOS uses quite a few environment variables to control different aspects of its operation.

Syntax

To display all the variables defined in the environment, use the following format:

```
SET
```

To add or replace an environment variable, use the following format:

SET *name*=*string*

Parameters and Switches

name The string that you want to add to the environment. DOS converts these characters to uppercase before storing the variable in the environment.

string The text that you want associated with ***name***. *string* is stored in the environment exactly as you enter it—with upper- and lowercase characters and including any spaces you specify.

Notes

1. The environment is an area of memory that DOS sets aside to store a series of text strings in the form ***name***=*string*. The ***name*** portion is converted to uppercase before being stored in memory, but the *string* portion is stored as is.

2. If SET is executed with no parameters, the current contents of the DOS environment is displayed. (Don't use this form of the SET command in your CONFIG.SYS file.) To display the value of a single environment variable, pipe the output from SET through the FIND filter. (See the following "Examples" section.)

3. Entering SET with the ***name*** of the variable and an equals sign but no *string* deletes the specified variable from the environment. Note that if no variable with the ***name*** you've specified is found, nothing happens, and no error message is displayed.

4. When SET is executed with both a ***name*** and a *string* parameter, DOS searches the current environment looking for a variable that matches ***name***. If a match is found, DOS replaces the variable with the new value specified in *string*. If no match is found, a new variable is defined in the current environment.

5. The total length of an environment variable, including the name and equals sign, cannot exceed the DOS 127-character limit. When you use SET to create environment variables, the limit is actually 123 because the SET command itself uses 3 characters and a space.

6. Spaces are legal in both the ***name*** and the *string* portion of an environment variable. In fact, spaces are not ignored when searching for

environment variables; so any trailing spaces you include after the ***name***, but before the equal sign, become a significant portion of that variable's name. Keep this in mind when you define new environment variables.

7. Avoid using redirection symbols (<, >, and ¦) and equal signs (=) in environment variables. Although you can use them in some cases, they can cause strange, hard-to-predict side effects when you use these variables in a batch file.

8. The DOS environment is limited to the size specified by the /E:*size* parameter specified in the SHELL= statement that names the command interpreter (usually COMMAND.COM) in your CONFIG.SYS file. If you haven't specified an /E:*size* parameter, it defaults to 256 characters. When a program is run, it is passed a copy of the current environment that has been shrunk to the smallest multiple of 16, which is big enough to hold all the variables currently defined.

   One annoying side effect of this behavior is that, if you normally run DOS from a Shell program, you will never have much environment space available no matter how big you make it in your CONFIG.SYS file. To avoid the `Out of environment space` error messages, you may have to define a DUMMY variable that you can delete from a batch file whenever you need more environment space. (See the following "Examples" section.)

9. Several DOS commands make use of the environment to store their current values. PATH and PROMPT both store their settings in the environment. If you are running APPEND with the /E parameter, it stores its settings in the environment as well.

10. DOS defines a number of environment variables when you start up your computer, and certain commands modify their behavior if certain variables are defined. For more information about the environment variables DOS uses, refer to Appendix B.

Examples

To display the contents of the current DOS environment, enter SET with no parameters, as shown here:

```
SET
```

A series of definitions similar to the following will then be displayed on your screen:

```
CONFIG=WIN
COMSPEC=C:\DOS\COMMAND.COM
MOUSE=C:\DOS
TEMP=C:\TEMP
TMP=C:\TEMP
DIRCMD=/L
PATH=C:\BAT;C:\NORTON;C:\DOS;C:\UTIL
PROMPT=*Windows* $p$g
windir=d:\win
```

There are a number of interesting things that you can tell from this list. First of all, the computer uses a start-up menu, and the configuration that was chosen is named WIN (CONFIG=WIN). Also, notice that the WINDIR environment variable is shown in lowercase. Microsoft Windows inserts this variable into the environment as a flag to indicate that it is active. Inserting it in lowercase is a trick that prevents you from changing or deleting it with the SET command.

If you wanted to see how a particular environment variable was defined, pipe the output of the SET command through the FIND filter, like this:

```
SET ¦ FIND "COMSPEC"
```

Only the lines that contain "COMSPEC" will be displayed. Note that FIND is case sensitive by default, so make sure that you enter the name of the variable you are loooking for in all uppercase (or specify the /I switch).

To change the defaults for the DIR command to lowercase file names (/L) five columns wide (/W), sorted by date with directories first (/OGD), you can define (or replace) the DIRCMD environment variable with the following SET command:

```
SET DIRCMD=/L /W /OGD
```

Note that you can't include any spaces before the equals sign or a new variable (DIRCMD<space>) will be defined that the DIR command will not recognize. To delete the DIRCMD variable entirely and let DIR use its built in defaults, use the following command.

```
SET DIRCMD=
```

If you want to make sure that an environment variable you define in a batch file was successfully created, add an IF command after the SET command that defines the new variable.

```
SET NEWVAR=Do we have space for this?

IF "%NEWVAR%"==""  GOTO OUT_OF_SPACE
```

One technique to help you avoid `Out of environment space` error messages when you run batch files from a Shell program is to define a DUMMY variable in your AUTOEXEC.BAT file that simply takes up space:

```
SET
DUMMY=XXXXXXXXXXXXXXXXXXXXXXXXXXXXXXXXXXXXX
```

When you need space in the environment, simply delete the DUMMY variable before you define any new variables that your batch file needs.

```
SET DUMMY=

SET NEWVAR=Now we have space for this
```

When your batch file terminates, returning you to your Shell program, the copy of the environment that the batch file was using is discarded. Because it is being thrown away, there is no reason to restore the DUMMY variable before the batch file ends.

If you might run this batch file when your Shell program is not running, you should reset the DUMMY variable and delete the NEWVAR variable before exiting the batch filem like this:

```
SET NEWVAR=

SET
DUMMY=XXXXXXXXXXXXXXXXXXXXXXXXXXXXXXXXXXXXX
```

Otherwise, the next time you need the DUMMY variable, it might not be there.

Messages

`Out of environment space`

Error: You will see this message if the environment is not large enough to hold the string you want to add with the PATH, PROMPT, or SET command. To increase the size of the environment, use the /E:*size* parameter in the SHELL= statement in your CONFIG.SYS file.

```
Syntax error
```

Error: SET displays a syntax error message if you forget to include the equal sign. This most often happens after you have been using the PATH and PROMPT commands, which get you out of the habit of including an equals sign between the variable name and its value.

See Also

COMMAND, PATH, PROMPT, and SHELL=

"Changing DOS Variables" in Chapter 13 and Appendix B, "DOS Environment Variables"

SETVER

5.0 and later—External

When programmers write software, they often add code to check the version of DOS that is running. To be on the safe side, they may prevent their program from running if the preliminary check reveals the presence of a version of DOS that they didn't test. In many cases, this paranoia is unnecessary, and lying to the program about which version of DOS is running enables the software to operate safely. The SETVER.EXE device driver maintains in memory a version table that tells it exactly which programs to lie to and what version of DOS to tell the program it is running. When you run SETVER from the command line, you can view, add, change, or delete entries in SETVER.EXE's version table. These changes take effect the next time SETVER.EXE is loaded into memory.

Syntax

SETVER *drive:\path filename n.nn*

SETVER *drive:\path filename* /DELETE /D /QUIET

Parameters and Switches

drive:\path — The drive and path to the SETVER.EXE file. Setup places the SETVER.EXE file in the C:\DOS subdirectory by default. If *drive:\path* is not specified, SETVER searches the current directory and along the DOS PATH to find the SETVER.EXE file. You can usually omit this parameter.

filename — The full name of the program you want SETVER to locate in the version table. Include the file name and extension, but do not include any path information. No default extensions are assumed, and wildcards are not allowed. If you include this parameter, you also must include either an *n.nn*, /DELETE, or /D parameter.

n.nn — The DOS version number that SETVER.EXE reports to the program specified by the *filename* parameter. Valid entries are in the range 2.11 to 9.99. You are required to enter the period delimiting the major and minor version numbers, and you should always enter the value with two decimal places (that is, 2.00, not 2.0 or 2). If this parameter is specified, you cannot specify the /DELETE, /D, or /QUIET parameters.

/DELETE — Delete the version table entry for the program file specified by *filename*. If /DELETE is specified, you cannot specify the *n.nn* parameter.

/D — Same as /DELETE.

/QUIET — Suppresses the two-line successful update message that appears after an entry is deleted from the version table. (Refer to the actual message in the following "Messages" section.) You can only specify /QUIET with /DELETE or /D.

Exit Codes

ERRORLEVEL Value	Meaning
0	SETVER operation successful
1	Invalid command-line switch specified
2	Invalid file name specified
3	Insufficient memory to complete the requested operation
4	Invalid version number format used
5	Entry not found in the version table
6	SETVER.EXE not found
7	Invalid drive letter specified

(continues)

ERRORLEVEL Value	Meaning
8	Too many command-line parameters specified
9	Required command-line parameter missing
10	Error reading from SETVER.EXE
11	Version table in SETVER.EXE is corrupt
12	SETVER.EXE file specified doesn't support a version table
13	Version table full
14	Error writing to SETVER.EXE

Notes

1. If you enter SETVER without any parameters, DOS displays all entries from the version table contained in the first copy of SETVER.EXE it comes across. DOS searches the current directory for the SETVER.EXE file, followed by all the subdirectories specified in your DOS PATH. If you enter SETVER *drive:\path*, the entries in the version table contained in the *drive:\path*\SETVER.EXE file are displayed. In this case, no other directories are searched if SETVER.EXE isn't found in the *drive:\path* subdirectory.

2. Microsoft ships SETVER.EXE with a version table that lists programs known to work safely with MS-DOS 6, but which have to be fooled in order to run.

Microsoft's SETVER.EXE Version Table for MS-DOS 6

filename	n.nn	filename	n.nn
KERNEL.EXE	5.00	JOIN.EXE	5.00
NETX.COM	5.00	RECOVER.EXE	5.00
NETX.EXE	5.00*	GRAFTABL.COM	5.00
NET5.COM	5.00	LMSETUP.EXE	5.00
BNETX.COM	5.00	STACKER.COM	5.00
BNETX.EXE	5.00*	NCACHE.EXE	5.00
EMSNETX.EXE	5.00*	NCACHE2.EXE	5.00

filename	n.nn	filename	n.nn
EMSNET5.EXE	5.00	IBMCACHE.SYS	5.00
XMSNETX.EXE	5.00*	XTRADRV.SYS	5.00
XMSNET5.EXE	5.00	2XON.COM	5.00
DOSOAD.SYS	5.00	WINWORD.EXE	4.10
REDIR50.EXE	5.00	EXCEL.EXE	4.10
REDIR5.EXE	5.00	LL3.EXE	4.01
REDIRALL.EXE	5.00	REDIR4.EXE	4.00
REDIRNP4.EXE	5.00	REDIR40.EXE	4.00
EDLIN.EXE	5.00	MSREDIR.EXE	4.00
BACKUP.EXE	5.00	WIN200.BIN	3.40
ASSIGN.COM	5.00	METRO.EXE	3.31
EXE2BIN.EXE	5.00		

* The ***n.nn*** entry for these files was changed to 6.00 in MS-DOS 6.2.

Note

If you look through the version table provided by Microsoft, you see that WINWORD.EXE and EXCEL.EXE are listed as requiring DOS version 4.10. However, Word for Windows 2.0 and Excel 4.0 will run under DOS 6 without SETVER. These entries are for older versions of these programs. If your Windows software is up to date, you don't have to worry about using SETVER to fool these two programs.

In the version table, you also see entries for the DOS utilities that were not distributed with DOS 6. When you use the DOS 5 versions of these utilities, they have to be included in the version table for SETVER or they will not run. Instead, an `Incorrect DOS version` message is displayed. If you install updated versions of these utilities with the DOS 6 Supplemental Disk Setup program, their version table entries are deleted.

3. Do not specify the DOS version number with the file name if you are trying to delete an entry in the version table. Doing so causes this error message to be displayed: `Too many command line parameters`. (Read more about this message in the following "Messages" section.)

4. Don't add a program to the SETVER.EXE version table unless you are sure that it can safely run with DOS 6. There is a chance that an incompatible program might appear to run and still cause system instabilities or data loss. This is the reason Microsoft displays the `WARNING` paragraph whenever you add or update an entry in the version table. (Read more about this message in the following "Messages" section.) To be safe, contact the manufacturer of the software program in question to find out if the version you have can be run safely under DOS 6.

5. Any changes you make to the version table with SETVER are written to the SETVER.EXE file on disk, not to the device driver in memory. These changes do not take effect until you reload the SETVER.EXE device driver into memory by restarting your computer.

6. Specify the drive and path to the SETVER.EXE file you want to update and not the drive and path to the program you are looking for in the version table. If you don't specify the drive and path correctly, SETVER usually fails to find SETVER.EXE and an error message is displayed (see the second item in the following "Messages" section). Normally, SETVER.EXE is located on your DOS PATH, and you can omit the *drive:\path* parameter to avoid this confusing syntax.

7. Remember to specify only the file name (with extension) of the program file you want to add, update, or delete from the SETVER version table. No path information is stored in the table, so only the file name is needed to locate the entry. The extension is included in the table, so you must specify it as well. No default extensions are assumed, and wildcards are not allowed.

8. Device drivers, as well as executable programs, can be included in the version table. If SETVER.EXE is already in memory when the device driver loads in your CONFIG.SYS file, SETVER.EXE can lie to it about the version of DOS that is running.

Examples

To display the contents of the version table in the SETVER.EXE file located on your DOS PATH, enter SETVER on the command line:

```
SETVER
```

You don't use the METRO.EXE program, and you want to delete the entry from the version table. To do so, enter the following command:

```
SETVER METRO.EXE /DELETE
```

You can abbreviate the /DELETE switch as /D if you want to. To add METRO.EXE back into the version table and restore its setting to DOS 3.31, you enter the following command:

```
SETVER METRO.EXE 3.31
```

If all goes well, you will see the WARNING paragraph. (See the last item in the following "Messages" section.)

Messages

`An invalid path to SETVER.EXE was specified`

Error: A subdirectory you specified in the path to SETVER.EXE is invalid.

`Could not find the file SETVER.EXE`

Error: SETVER.EXE was not found along the DOS search path or in the subdirectory you specified. (ERRORLEVEL value 6 returned)

`ERROR: Reading SETVER.EXE file`

Error: A disk error occurred while the SETVER.EXE file was being read. This could be due to file sharing violations, errors in the disk's FAT, corrupted formatting information, or bad sectors on the disk. The SETVER.EXE file may be corrupted. (ERRORLEVEL value 10 returned)

`ERROR: Writing SETVER.EXE file`

Error: A disk error occurred while the SETVER.EXE file was being written to. This can happen if the disk fills up or a bad sector is encountered. The SETVER.EXE file may be corrupted. (ERRORLEVEL value 14 returned)

`Insuffient memory`

Error: There isn't enough memory available to run SETVER. (*Note*: The spelling error is Microsoft's, not ours.) (ERRORLEVEL value 3 returned)

`Invalid drive specifier`

Error: The disk drive you specifed in the path to SETVER.EXE isn't a valid DOS drive. (ERRORLEVEL value 7 returned)

`Invalid filename`

Error: An invalid file name was specified on the command line, or the specified file doesn't exist. (ERRORLEVEL value 2 returned)

`Invalid switch`

Error: You have specified a switch on the command line that SETVER doesn't understand. (ERRORLEVEL value 1 returned)

`Invalid version number, format must be 2.11 - 9.99`

Error: The version number you specifed is invalid. You can report DOS versions 2.11 through 9.99 only. You may also see this message if you specify DELETE or D without the slash (/R). (ERRORLEVEL value 4 returned)

`Missing parameter`

Error: You specified a file name, but you have not included either a version number (to add or update an entry) or /D (to delete an entry). (ERRORLEVEL value 9 returned)

`No entries found in version table`

Information: You asked SETVER to display the version table, but the copy of SETVER.EXE it found has no entries in the version table. This can happen if you delete all the entries (one by one) in SETVER.EXE with the SETVER /D command.

`NOTE: SETVER device not loaded. To activate SETVER version reporting you must load the SETVER.EXE device in your CONFIG.SYS.`

Warning: When you use SETVER without loading the SETVER.EXE device, it displays this message to remind you that the version table is only active when the SETVER.EXE device driver is loaded.

`Specified entry was not found in the version table`

Warning: You have tried to delete an entry that is not in the version table. Check to see if you mistyped the name of the program or included the wrong extension. If everything looks correct, type SETVER and take another look at the current version table to make sure that the program you are trying to delete is indeed included in it. (ERRORLEVEL value 5 returned)

`There is no more space in version table new entries`

Error: The version table in SETVER.EXE is full. You must delete one or two entries before you can add any more. (Microsoft seems to have misplaced the *for* in this message.) (ERRORLEVEL value 13 returned)

```
Too many command line parameters
```

Error: Too many command line parameters were specified, and SETVER doesn't know what to do with them all. (ERRORLEVEL value 8 returned)

```
Version table is corrupt
```

Error: The version table stored within SETVER.EXE has become damaged. You will have to delete the damaged file and replace it with a fresh copy from your MS-DOS 6 distribution disks. SETVER.EXE is compressed on the distribution disks, and you must use the EXPAND command to expand it you can use it. (ERRORLEVEL value 11 returned)

```
Version table successfully updated
The version change will take effect the next time you restart your
system
```

Information: You have successfully deleted an entry in the version table. This is the message you can suppress with the /QUIET parameter. (ERRORLEVEL value 0 returned)

```
WARNING - Contact your software vendor for information about whether a
specific program works with MS-DOS version 6.0. It is possible that
Microsoft has not verified whether the program will successfully run if
you use the SETVER command to change the program version number and
version table. If you run the program after changing the version table
in MS-DOS version 6.0, you may lose or corrupt data or introduce system
instabilities. Microsoft is not responsible for any loss or damage, or
for lost or corrupted data.

Version table successfully updated
The version change will take effect the next time you restart your system
```

Information: You have successfully updated the version table. The warning paragraph is a reminder that lying to software programs can be a risky business, and you do so at your own risk. To be safe, contact the manufacturer of the program you are trying to fool, and ask them if it's safe to run their software under DOS 6. (ERRORLEVEL value 0 returned)

See Also

SETVER.EXE

"Setting the Version with SETVER" in Chapter 12

SETVER.EXE (device driver)

5.0 and later—External

When programmers write software, they often add code to check the version of DOS that is running. To be on the safe side, they may prevent their program from running if the preliminary check reveals the presence of a version of DOS that they didn't test. In many cases, this paranoia is unnecessary, and lying to the program about which version of DOS is running enables the software to operate safely. The SETVER.EXE device driver maintains in memory a version table that tells it exactly which programs to lie to and what version of DOS to tell the program it is running. SETVER.EXE must be loaded in a DEVICE= or DEVICEHIGH= statement in your CONFIG.SYS file.

Syntax

DEVICE=*drive:\path***SETVER.EXE**

or

DEVICEHIGH=*drive:\path***SETVER.EXE**

Parameters and Switches

drive:\path The drive and path to the SETVER.EXE file on your system. Setup places the SETVER.EXE file in the C:\DOS subdirectory by default. If the full path to SETVER.EXE isn't specified, DOS looks for the file in the root directory of the start-up drive.

Notes

1. Microsoft ships SETVER.EXE with a version table that lists programs known to work safely with MS-DOS 6, but which need to be fooled in order to run. You can add or subtract programs from the version table by running SETVER from the command line. To activate any changes you make, you must reboot your computer.

Microsoft's SETVER.EXE Version Table for MS-DOS 6

filename	n.nn	filename	n.nn
KERNEL.EXE	5.00	JOIN.EXE	5.00
NETX.COM	5.00	RECOVER.EXE	5.00
NETX.EXE	5.00*	GRAFTABL.COM	5.00

filename	n.nn	filename	n.nn
NET5.COM	5.00	LMSETUP.EXE	5.00
BNETX.COM	5.00	STACKER.COM	5.00
BNETX.EXE	5.00*	NCACHE.EXE	5.00
EMSNETX.EXE	5.00*	NCACHE2.EXE	5.00
EMSNET5.EXE	5.00	IBMCACHE.SYS	5.00
XMSNETX.EXE	5.00*	XTRADRV.SYS	5.00
XMSNET5.EXE	5.00	2XON.COM	5.00
DOSOAD.SYS	5.00	WINWORD.EXE	4.10
REDIR50.EXE	5.00	EXCEL.EXE	4.10
REDIR5.EXE	5.00	LL3.EXE	4.01
REDIRALL.EXE	5.00	REDIR4.EXE	4.00
REDIRNP4.EXE	5.00	REDIR40.EXE	4.00
EDLIN.EXE	5.00	MSREDIR.EXE	4.00
BACKUP.EXE	5.00	WIN200.BIN	3.40
ASSIGN.COM	5.00	METRO.EXE	3.31
EXE2BIN.EXE	5.00		

* The ***n.nn*** entry for these files was changed to 6.00 in MS-DOS 6.2.

Note

If you look through the version table provided by Microsoft, you see that WINWORD.EXE and EXCEL.EXE are listed as requiring DOS version 4.10. However, Word for Windows 2.0 and Excel 4.0 will run under DOS 6 without SETVER. These entries are for older versions of these programs. If your Windows software is up to date, you don't have to worry about using SETVER to fool these two programs.

In the version table, you also see entries for the DOS utilities that were not distributed with DOS 6. When you use the DOS 5 versions of these utilities, they have to be included in the version table for SETVER or they will not run. Instead, an `Incorrect DOS version` message is displayed. If you install updated versions of these utilities with the DOS 6 Supplemental Disk Setup program, their version table entries are deleted.

2. If upper memory is available on your computer, SETVER.EXE can be loaded there with the DEVICEHIGH= command. SETVER.EXE requires about 500 bytes of memory with its original version table.

3. The Setup program for DOS 6 automatically includes a DEVICE= line loading SETVER.EXE in your CONFIG.SYS file. You may want to look over the contents of the version table to see if you are using any of the programs listed in it. If you are not using any of the programs and the rest of your software is happy running under DOS 6, you can safely delete the SETVER.EXE device driver from your CONFIG.SYS file.

4. Besides lying to programs, SETVER.EXE can also lie to device drivers. Just make sure that SETVER.EXE is loaded before the device driver loads, and that the name of that device driver is included in the version table.

Examples

To load the DOS version table driver into memory, include the following line in your CONFIG.SYS file:

```
DEVICE=C:\DOS\SETVER.EXE
```

This line assumes that the SETVER.EXE file is in the C:\DOS subdirectory. If your computer has upper memory available, you may want to load SETVER.EXE into upper memory with the following command:

```
DEVICEHIGH=C:\DOS\SETVER.EXE
```

Messages

`Version table is corrupt`

Error: The version table stored within SETVER.EXE has become damaged. You must delete the damaged file and replace it with a fresh copy from your MS-DOS 6 distribution disks. SETVER.EXE is compressed on the distribution disks, and you must use the EXPAND command to expand it before you can use it.

See Also

DEVICE=, DEVICEHIGH=, and SETVER

"Setting the Version with SETVER" in Chapter 12

SHARE

3.0 and later—External

The SHARE program enables DOS support for file and record locking. When you run SHARE, it remains resident in memory, becoming a part of DOS. If you use any multitasking software, such as Microsoft Windows, you should run SHARE in your AUTOEXEC.BAT file. You can load SHARE into upper memory with the LOADHIGH command on systems that have upper memory available.

Syntax

SHARE /F:*name_space* /L:*numlocks*

Parameters and Switches

/F:*name_space*	The amount of memory space in bytes to use for file sharing. The default is 2,048.
/L:*numlocks*	The maximum number of file/record locks that are available to programs. The default is 20.

Rules

1. When SHARE is loaded, DOS checks for file and record locks as each file is opened, read, and written.
2. SHARE normally enlarges DOS by approximately 6,192 bytes in DOS 5.0, and approximately 5,248 bytes in DOS 6.0. If the number of locks (/L switch) or memory space (/F switch) increases or decreases, DOS also increases or decreases proportionately. SHARE can be loaded into upper memory with the LOADHIGH command.
3. The only way to remove SHARE is to restart DOS.
4. In DOS 4.0, use SHARE if your hard disk is formatted with partitions larger than 32M. SHARE is not required to use large partitions in DOS 5.0 and later versions.
5. You can load SHARE with INSTALL= in your CONFIG.SYS file (DOS 4.0 and later versions).
6. You should be running SHARE if you use any multitasking software on your computer. In a multitasking environment, the possibility exists that two programs will attempt to update the same file. If that happens, data can be lost. Examples of multitasking environments include the DOSShell's Task Swapper, Microsoft Windows, and DesqView.

Notes

1. Use SHARE when two or more programs or processes share a computer's files. After SHARE is loaded, DOS checks each file for locks whenever the file is opened, read, or written. If a file is open for exclusive use, an error message results from subsequent attempts to open the file. If one program locks a portion of a file, an error message results if another program tries to read or write the locked portion.

2. SHARE is most effective when all file-sharing programs can handle the DOS functions for locking files and records (DOS 3.0 and later versions). SHARE is either partially or completely ineffective with programs that do not use the DOS file- and record-locking features.

3. SHARE affects two or more programs running on the same computer, not two or more computers using the same file (networked computers). For networks, record- and file-locking are made possible by software provided with the network.

4. You must use SHARE if you use DOS 4.0 or 4.01 and if your hard disk is formatted larger than 32M. For convenience, you can use INSTALL= in the CONFIG.SYS file to activate SHARE. In the CONFIG.SYS file, for example, the following command activates SHARE if SHARE.EXE is located in the \DOS subdirectory of drive C:

```
INSTALL=C:\DOS\SHARE.EXE
```

See Also

INSTALL= and LOADHIGH

SHELL= 2.0 and later—Internal

SHELL= is used to specify the name and location of the command interpreter that MS-DOS should use. Normally, this is COMMAND.COM, but other third-party shells, such as 4DOS and NDOS, can use SHELL= to gain control of the command line. Another common use of the SHELL= command is to change the size of the environment. SHELL= can only be used in your CONFIG.SYS file.

Syntax

SHELL=*drive:\path***filename** *parameters*

Parameters and Switches

drive:\path — The drive and path to the command interpreter must be specified here if the command interpreter isn't located in the root directory of the start-up drive.

filename — The name of the program to use as the command interpreter for DOS. Normally this is COMMAND.COM.

parameters — Any parameters or switches that the specified command interpreter requires. (For the parameters and switches that COMMAND.COM uses, see the description for COMMAND earlier in this Command Reference.)

Notes

1. Be careful when you experiment with the SHELL= command, and be sure that you have a bootable floppy disk handy. If you set something incorrectly, chances are you either will have to reboot from a floppy disk or perform a "clean boot" with F5.

2. If no SHELL= command exists in CONFIG.SYS, DOS will attempt to load COMMAND.COM from the root directory of the start-up drive. If COMMAND.COM cannot be found, or is from a different version of DOS, an error message is displayed (see the following "Messages" section). When you receive this error message, you must either enter the full path name of a valid copy of COMMAND.COM or reboot the computer from a bootable floppy disk.

3. Do not confuse the SHELL= command with the DOSSHELL program. SHELL= is a CONFIG.SYS command that designates the program to be used as the command-line interface to MS-DOS. DOSSHELL is a program that provides a graphical interface from which you can operate your computer if you choose. The DOSSHELL program and the SHELL= command have nothing to do with each other.

4. MemMaker "comments out" the SHELL= line in your CONFIG.SYS file if the SHELL= line specifies a command interpreter other than COMMAND.COM. If you are using a third-party shell program, be sure that COMMAND.COM is in the root directory of the start-up drive before you run MemMaker. After MemMaker is done, you must

manually "uncomment" the SHELL= line that loads your command line-interpreter to restore the use of your third-party shell.

5. Many third-party shell programs do not require the /P switch to tell them that they should install themselves permanently in memory. Instead, they look for a valid environment. If one is present, they assume that they have already been run, do not install themselves permanently, and do not execute the AUTOEXEC.BAT file. In DOS 6, an environment already may be present when the shell programs are loaded from the SHELL= line in CONFIG.SYS, which can lead to problems.

   If you find yourself in the situation just described, try including the /P switch on the SHELL= line that loads your command-line interpreter. Also, you should contact the manufacturer of your shell program to see if an upgrade is available that is more compatible with MS-DOS 6.

Examples

The setup program for DOS 6 may insert a SHELL= line in your CONFIG.SYS file that looks something like this:

```
SHELL=C:\DOS\COMMAND.COM  C:\DOS\  /E:512  /P
```

It sets the command interpreter to COMMAND.COM, located in the C:\DOS subdirectory, with a reload path of C:\DOS, and an environment size of 512 bytes. The final /P switch tells COMMAND.COM to remain in memory permanently. Never specify the /P switch for COMMAND.COM except in the SHELL= line in your CONFIG.SYS file.

Messages

```
Bad or missing Command Interpreter
Enter correct name of Command Interpreter (eg, C:\COMMAND.COM)
```

Error: If the SHELL= command in your CONFIG.SYS file does not point to a valid command interpreter, and the copy of COMMAND.COM in the root directory of your start-up drive is missing or invalid, this message is displayed. To continue, you have to enter the full path to a valid (DOS 6) copy of COMMAND.COM so that DOS can load it into memory. DOS has already checked the copy of COMMAND.COM in your root directory, so entering C:\COMMAND.COM as suggested in the error message usually does not work. You can try entering C:\DOS\COMMAND.COM, because Setup places a copy of COMMAND.COM in the subdirectory in which DOS was installed. If a valid copy of COMMAND.COM can't be found, you must reboot from a floppy disk.

Even if you locate a valid copy of COMMAND.COM and load it into memory, this copy of COMMAND.COM is only temporary; so typing EXIT will bring this error message right back on-screen. Also, your AUTOEXEC.BAT file is not executed by temporary copies of COMMAND.COM, so none of the settings or resident software you typically use will be available. Use the COPY command to transfer a new copy of COMMAND.COM to the root directory of your start-up disk (usually C:\), and reboot with Ctrl-Alt-Del to set things back to the way they should be.

See Also

COMMAND

"Using the SHELL Command" in Chapter 18

SHIFT

2.0 and later—Internal

The SHIFT command shifts a batch file's command-line parameters one position to the left. You have to use the SHIFT command if your batch file requires more than 9 parameters. SHIFT also is handy for batch files that repeat an operation for each command-line parameter. SHIFT is only useful when used in a batch file.

Syntax

SHIFT

Notes

1. When you use SHIFT, DOS moves the command-line parameters one position to the left. That is, the parameter %1 becomes $0, %2 becomes %1, %3 becomes %2, and so on.

2. DOS discards the former first parameter (%0). Any parameter shifted off the left end is gone for good.

3. DOS shifts parameter 10, if it exists, into %9, parameter 11 into parameter 10, and so on. SHIFT is the only way to access more than 9 command-line parameters from within a batch file.

See Also

"Moving Parameters with SHIFT" in Chapter 16

SIZER (see MEMMAKER)

MemMaker uses the SIZER program to help it optimize memory use on your computer. MemMaker requires this program while optimizing your system, but it is not necessary at any other time. You cannot use this program yourself. SIZER aborts if MemMaker (and possibly CHKSTATE.SYS) is not in control when it is run, displaying the following message:

```
SIZER.EXE is used by MemMaker during the memory-optimization process
and is not intended to be started from the command prompt.
```

Very few details about SIZER's operation are documented. When MemMaker is optimizing, it adds a SIZER.EXE command to the beginning of every command that loads device drivers or resident programs in your CONFIG.SYS and AUTOEXEC.BAT files. Load size information about these drivers and programs is written to the MEMMAKER.STS file by SIZER. When optimization is complete, MemMaker removes all references to the SIZER program from your start-up files.

See Also

CHKSTATE.SYS and MEMMAKER

SMARTDRV 6.0 and later—External

When used from the command line, SMARTDRV loads or configures SMARTDrive, a disk-caching utility that can speed disk operations significantly. The first time you run SMARTDRV, it loads itself into memory (upper memory if space is available) and establishes the disk cache. To unload SMARTDRV from memory, you have to reboot your computer.

Syntax

To start SMARTDrive from your AUTOEXEC.BAT file or from a command prompt, use the following format:

SMARTDRV /X *drive* ± ... *initsize winsize* /U /C /R /F /N /V /Q /S /L /E:*esize* /B:*bsize*

After SMARTDrive is running, use the following format:

SMARTDRV *drive* ± ... /C /R /Q /S

With DOS version 6.2, you can also use the /X, /F, and /N parameters after SMARTDrive is running:

SMARTDRV /X *drive* ± ... /C /R /F /N /Q /S

Parameters and Switches

/X

Specifies that you want to disable write-behind caching for all drives by default. You can then enable or disable individual drives with the *drive* ± parameter.

drive ± ...

One or more drives for which you want to enable or disable disk caching. *drive*— enables read caching and disables write caching. *drive*+ enables read and write caching. *drive*–disables caching.

If you start SMARTDrive but do not specify a drive, floppy and Interlnk drives are read-cached only; hard drives are read and write cached; and CD-ROM, network, compressed, and Microsoft Flash memory card drives are not cached.

CD-ROM drives are read-cached by default.

initsize

The size (in kilobytes) of the cache when SMARTDrive starts. The following table shows the default values for this parameter:

Extended memory	*initsize*	*winsize*
Up to 1M	All	0 (no caching)
Up to 2M	1024K	256K
Up to 4M	1024K	512K
Up to 6M	2048K	1024K
More than 6M	2048K	2048K

winsize

The size (in kilobytes) by which SMARTDrive reduces its cache when Microsoft Windows starts, freeing that memory for Windows to use. When you quit Windows, that memory is returned to SMARTDrive and defaults to the values listed in the preceding table.

If *winsize* is larger than *initsize*, SMARTDrive acts as though the two parameters were the same.

/U — Specifies that you do not want SMARTDrive to load the CD-ROM caching module. If you specify this switch, SMARTDrive cannot cache any CD-ROM drives. If you don't specify /U, you can enable or disable CD-ROM caching at any time with the *drive* ± parameter.

/C — Clears SMARTDrive by writing all write buffers to disk.

/R — Resets SMARTDrive by clearing all caches and restarting SMARTDrive.

/F — Writes cached data to the disk after each command finishes, before the DOS command prompt reappears. This is the default behavior.

/N — Writes cached data to the disk whenever the system is idle. To ensure that all data is written to disk, use the /C (Clear) switch.

/N — (Not DOS 6.2) Forces "verbose" mode, so status messages appear when SMARTDrive starts. In DOS 6.2, this switch has been renamed to /V. You cannot use this switch with /Q.

/V — Forces "verbose" mode, so status messages appear when SMARTDrive starts. You cannot use this switch with /Q.

/Q — Forces "quiet" mode, so status messages do not appear when SMARTDrive starts. (Error messages always appear.) /Q is the default. You cannot use this switch with /N.

/S — Displays SMARTDrive's status, including what and how drives are cached and a cache hit statistic.

/L — Forces SMARTDrive to load into low (conventional) memory even if room exists in upper memory.

/E:*esize* — The element size (in bytes), which is the amount of cache data that SMARTDrive moves in one operation.

Values can be 1024, 2048, 4096, and 8192. The default is 8192. The smaller the number, the less memory SMARTDrive takes and the slower the performance.

/B:*bsize* — The size of the read-ahead buffer (in bytes that are a multiple of *esize*), which is how much SMARTDrive reads beyond a disk request. The default is 16384. The smaller the number, the less memory SMARTDrive takes and the slower the performance.

Notes

1. Before you turn off or reset your computer, you must perform a SMARTDRV /C operation to guarantee that no data is lost from SMARTDrive's write buffers. SMARTDrive performs the operation automatically if you press Ctrl-Alt-Del.

   SMARTDrive now flushes all write buffers to disk before allowing COMMAND.COM to display the DOS command-line prompt. As long as you haven't turned off this option, you can safely turn off your computer as soon as you see the DOS prompt.

2. For SMARTDrive to use extended memory, you must load HIMEM.SYS or some other extended-memory manager.

3. By default, SMARTDRV.EXE tries to load into upper memory. You do not need to use the LOADHIGH command.

4. If you are using double-buffering and your system runs slowly, try loading SMARTDrive with the /L switch.

5. Double buffering is required only by some ESDI and SCSI hard-disk interfaces.

6. If you have a compressed disk drive, use SMARTDrive on the underlying uncompressed (host) drive.

7. If you want SMARTDrive to cache a CD-ROM drive, you have to load MSCDEX into memory before SMARTDrive. MSCDEX creates the link that DOS needs to access a CD-ROM drive. If SMARTDrive is loaded before the drive letter is allocated, it will never know that the drive exists. You can enable or disable CD-ROM read-caching with the *drive* ± parameter, or you can disable it completely with the /U switch. Using the /U switch decreases SMARTDrive's memory use a little.

8. If you are using a third-party CONFIG.SYS and AUTOEXEC.BAT file manager, that utility needs to be set up to perform a SMARTDRV /C operation before it reboots your computer.

9. DOS 6.0 comes with SMARTMON.EXE, a Windows program for monitoring and adjusting SMARTDrive.

Examples

To start SMARTDrive with all the defaults (a good fit for most systems):

```
C:\DOS\SMARTDRV
```

To enable read-caching for drive C, read- and write-caching for drive D, and using a 4M cache for DOS that can get no smaller than 2M when Microsoft Windows is running, issue the following command:

```
C:\DOS\SMARTDRV  C  D+ 4096 2048
```

See Also

BUFFERS=, EMM386.EXE, HIMEM.SYS, SMARTDRV.EXE, and SMARTMON

"Using a Disk Cache (SMARTDrive)" in Chapter 19

SMARTDRV.EXE (device driver)

6.0 and later—External

When used as a device driver, SMARTDRV.EXE enables double buffering, which is required by certain types of hard-disk controllers that cannot work with the memory provided by EMM386.EXE.

Syntax

DEVICE=*drive:\path***SMARTDRV.EXE** /DOUBLE_BUFFER

Parameters and Switches

drive:\path — The full path to the SMARTDRV.EXE file on your system. Setup places the SMARTDRV.EXE file in the C:\DOS subdirectory by default. If the full path to SMARTDRV.EXE isn't specified, DOS looks for the file in the root directory of the start-up drive.

/DOUBLE_BUFFER Enables double buffering. Inserting this switch into your CONFIG.SYS file does not hurt if your system does not need it, but it does take up memory. You can remove the switch if all the entries in the buffering column of the SMARTDRV /S display are no. (It may take a while for – entries to turn into no entries.)

Notes

1. Double buffering is required only by some ESDI and SCSI hard-disk interfaces when used on a computer that provides upper-memory blocks for DOS to use.
2. If you are using double-buffering and your system runs slowly, try loading SMARTDrive with the /L switch.

Examples

To load the SMARTDrive double-buffering feature, add the following line to your CONFIG.SYS file.

```
DEVICE=C:\DOS\SMARTDRV.EXE /DOUBLE_BUFFER
```

See Also

DEVICE= and SMARTDRV

"Using a Disk Cache (SMARTDrive)" in Chapter 19

SMARTMON 6.0 and later—Windows

The SMARTDrive Monitor (SMARTMON) is a Windows program that can display the status of the SMARTDrive disk cache and adjust its settings. SMARTMON can even help you update the setting you use to load SMARTDRV in your AUTOEXEC.BAT file. For SMARTMON to be useful, you must be running the SMARTDrive disk cache on your computer.

SMARTMON cannot be run from the DOS command line. SMARTMON must be started from within Windows with, for example, Program Manager's File Run command. For instructions on using the program, run SMARTMON and press F1 or choose HELP from the menu.

See Also

SMARTDRV

SORT

2.0 and later—External

SORT is a program that reads lines from the standard input device, performs an ASCII sort on those lines, and then writes them to the standard output device. The sort can be in ascending or descending order and can start at any column in the line. SORT is one of the filter programs provided by MS-DOS for use with redirection symbols from the command line.

Syntax

SORT /R /+*column* < ***source_file*** > *dest_file*

or

command ¦ **SORT** /R /+*column*

Parameters and Switches

< ***source_file*** — The name of a file that you want SORT to sort. All the normal defaults for drives and subdirectories apply. Wildcards are not allowed.

> *dest_file* — The name of a file that you want SORT to write the sorted output to. All the normal defaults for drives and subdirectories apply. Wildcards are not allowed. If the output of SORT is not redirected, it is written to the screen.

command ¦ — Pipes the screen output from a command into the SORT program, which displays it sorted. ***command*** can be any legal DOS command that writes its output to the standard output device (normally the screen).

/+*column* — Starts sorting with the characters in column number *column*. *column* needs to be a positive integer. The default is 1.

/R — Sorts in descending order. Thus, the letter Z comes first and the letter A comes last, followed by the numbers 9 to 0. The default sort order is ascending.

Notes

1. If you do not redirect the input or output, all input is from the keyboard (standard input), and all output is to the video display (standard output). If you redirect input and output, use different names for the input and output files.
2. SORT can handle a maximum file size of 64K (65,535 characters).
3. SORT sorts text files and discards any information after, and including, the end-of-file marker (Ctrl-Z).
4. SORT uses the collating sequence appropriate to your country code and code-page settings if you are using them.
5. SORT is case-insensitive—that is, the command treats *b* and *B* alike.
6. You cannot set the maximum column that SORT can use to resolve equalities. SORT starts at the /+*column* specified and continues the comparison until the lines are proven unequal or the end of the line is reached. Because of this, you cannot use SORT to perform a multikey sort by sorting the file more than once.

Examples

To sort the lines in the file WORDS.TXT and display the sorted lines on-screen:

```
SORT < WORDS.TXT
```

To sort, in reverse order, the lines in the file WORDS.TXT and display the lines on-screen:

```
SORT < WORDS.TXT /R
```

To start sorting at the eighth character of each line in WORDS.TXT and display the output on-screen:

```
SORT /+8 < WORDS.TXT
```

To display directory information, sorted by file size:

```
DIR | SORT /+14
```

(The file size starts in the 14th column.) Unfortunately, other lines, such as the volume label, also are sorted, starting in the 14th column. DIR /O provides a more direct and elaborate way of sorting directory information.

See Also

FIND and MORE

"The SORT Filter" in Chapter 14

STACKS= 3.2 and later—Internal

Whenever a device needs the computer's attention, it generates an interrupt. Before switching to the appropriate interrupt service routine, DOS stores the information it needs to resume the interrupted task in an area called a *stack*. You can use the STACKS= command to determine how many stacks DOS sets aside for this purpose and how big each stack is. You can use STACKS= only in your CONFIG.SYS file.

Syntax

STACKS=*numstacks,size*

Parameters and Switches

numstacks The number of stacks to set aside for hardware interrupts. Legal values are 0 and 8 through 64. The default value is 0 for 8088- and 8086-based computers and 9 for all others.

size The size of each stack in bytes. Legal values are 0 (only if you specify 0 stacks as well) and 32 through 512. The default value is 0 for 8088- and 8086-based computers and 128 for all others.

Notes

1. Both parameters for the STACKS= command are required. Note that a ***size*** of 0 is only allowed if you are using 0 ***numstacks*** as well.

2. There is considerable controversy over whether separate hardware stacks are needed for the average computer system, but in general, using at least MS-DOS's default values is a good idea. This uses some memory, but if it saves you from losing your work, it's worth it. Almost all the devices attached to your computer generate interrupts, and if they all want attention at once, they can quickly exhaust a low STACKS= setting. When the internal DOS stacks overflow, an error message displays (see the first item, `Internal Stack Overflow`, in the following Message section), and the system halts. MemMaker often increases the STACKS= setting to 9,256.

STACKS=0,0 forces DOS to use the active program's stack space when servicing hardware interrupts. Many people run their computers with this setting and never experience any problems. But be warned that STACKS=0,0 may work for months and then, without warning, overflow a program's stack space, crashing your computer. If you are using this setting and see a `Stack Overflow` error message, increase the STACKS= setting to at least 9,128 or 9,256.

3. If you are not using the STACKS=0,0 setting, try to limit your choices for the ***size*** parameter to 128, 256, or 512. This isn't required, but specifying a ***size*** which is an even power of two makes the stacks easier for DOS to manage. Also, except when using the STACKS=0,0 setting, avoid ***size*** values less than 128. A small stack is much more likely to overflow, and you are just asking for trouble setting the size of DOS's hardware stacks to anything less than 128.

Examples

To use the default number of stacks, but increase their size to 256 bytes each, use the following line in your CONFIG.SYS file. (This setting has virtually become the standard for people who are not disabling internal stacks in their computers.)

```
STACKS=9,256
```

To instruct DOS not to set up any internal stacks, and use the active program's stack space for servicing interrupts, include the following line in your CONFIG.SYS file:

```
STACKS=0,0
```

Messages

```
Internal stack overflow
System halted
```

Error: The stack that MS-DOS was using to service interrupts has overflowed, and the system has been halted. You need to restart your computer. If this happens, increase the *numstacks* and/or *size* setting for the STACKS= command in your CONFIG.SYS file.

`Exception Error 12`

Error: Same as the preceding message, except this is the message displayed when you are running in protected mode (for example, under Windows).

`Invalid STACK parameters`

Warning: You have specified an invalid parameter on the STACKS= line in your CONFIG.SYS. Check the entry to make sure that you have specified values for both *numstacks* and *size* and that these values are within the legal range for the STACKS= command.

SUBMENU= 6.0 and later—Internal

SUBMENU= is one of the new CONFIG.SYS menu commands. With it, you can create a multilevel menu from which to choose your start-up configuration. You can use SUBMENU= only inside a menu block in your CONFIG.SYS file.

Syntax

SUBMENU=*blockname*, *menutext*

Parameters and Switches

blockname The name of the menu block that you want to display when this menu item is chosen. ***blockname*** can be up to 70 characters long, but it can't contain any spaces or the following special characters:

```
\ / , ; = [ ]
```

(For more details, see the entry for [blockname] in this Command Reference.) This argument is required.

menutext The text you want DOS to display for this menu line. *menutext* can be up to 70 characters long and contain any text you want, including spaces. Separate *menutext* from ***blockname*** with a comma. If no *menutext* is provided, DOS displays the ***blockname*** in the menu.

Notes

1. The SUBMENU= command can appear only inside menu blocks in CONFIG.SYS.

> **Note**
>
> CONFIG.SYS allows two types of blocks—menu blocks and configuration blocks. Each block begins with a [blockname], and includes all the lines that follow, up to the next [blockname]. Menu blocks, which are blocks named [MENU] or defined with a SUBMENU= command, can include only menu-related commands. All other CONFIG.SYS commands belong in configuration blocks.

2. Up to nine choices can be displayed in a menu, so you are limited to nine MENUITEM= and SUBMENU= commands in each menu block. Each menu item appears on-screen in the order that it appears in the menu block, numbered from 1 to 9.

3. If DOS cannot find the block referred to by a SUBMENU= command in your CONFIG.SYS file, it doesn't display that choice in the menu. Your start-up menu may fail if SUBMENU= doesn't refer to a valid menu block.

4. In a multi-configuration submenu, you can return to the previous menu by pressing the Backspace key.

Tip
Before you construct an extensive menu system in CONFIG.SYS, remember that you will have to wade through it each time you reboot your computer. A simple start-up menu, with a handful of options and perhaps one submenu, works best.

Examples

Suppose that you're using a main menu that lets you choose between three basic configurations for your computer; Windows, DOS, and Maintenance. For the DOS configuration, you want to add a submenu with two variations: one configures memory for normal DOS programs, and the other provides your CADD program with the special memory interface it requires.

```
[MENU]
MENUITEM=WIN, Configure for Windows (Default)
SUBMENU=DOS, Configure for MS-DOS
MENUITEM=MAINT, Configure for File & Disk Maintenance
MENUDEFAULT=WIN, 30

[DOS]
MENUITEM=NORMAL, Configure for Normal MS-DOS Programs
MENUITEM=CADD, Configure for CADD with INT15 Interface
MENUDEFAULT=NORMAL, 30
```

When you include these lines in your CONFIG.SYS file, DOS searches for blocks named [WIN], [DOS], and [MAINT]. If those blocks exist in the file, the main menu that DOS displays looks something like the following:

```
MS-DOS 6 Startup Menu
=====================

1. Configure for Windows (Default)
2. Configure for MS-DOS
3. Configure for File & Disk Maintenance

Enter a choice: 1
```

Entering 1, 2, or 3 at this menu instructs DOS to execute the [WIN], [DOS], or [MAINT] block, respectively. If no entry is made within about 30 seconds, DOS chooses the [WIN] configuration by default. As long as the [NORMAL] and [CADD] blocks exist in CONFIG.SYS, choosing 2 brings up the following submenu.

```
MS-DOS 6 Startup Menu
=====================

1. Configure for Normal MS-DOS Programs
2. Configure for CADD with INT15 Interface

Enter a choice: 1
```

Entering 1 or 2 at this menu instructs DOS to execute the [NORMAL] or [CADD] configuration block, respectively. If you do not make an entry within about 30 seconds, DOS chooses the [NORMAL] configuration by default. To return to the first menu, press the Backspace key.

See Also

[blockname], MENUCOLOR=, MENUDEFAULT= and MENUITEM=

"Creating Multiple Configurations" in Chapter 2

SUBST

3.1 and later—External

SUBST is one of the pretender commands. It can create a drive alias for a subdirectory and fool many (but not all) programs. You may need to use SUBST in order to get older programs that don't understand subdirectories to run. Unless you have a specific use for SUBST, however, avoid it. It's too easy to make a mistake and lose data when you are pretending.

Syntax

SUBST *alias: drive:path* /D

Parameters and Switches

alias: A valid drive name that becomes the alias, or nickname. *alias:* may be a nonexistent drive, but it must be available for use and less than or equal to the value specified by the LASTDRIVE= command in your CONFIG.SYS file.

drive:path The drive name and directory path to be nicknamed *alias:*. The default for *drive:* is the current drive. You cannot specify the /D parameter when you create an alias with *drive:path*.

/D Deletes the alias drive. Do not specify a *drive:path* parameter when you are deleting an alias drive.

Notes

1. Entering SUBST with no parameters displays a list of all the drive substitutions currently defined.

2. The drive letter you use as the alias drive must be available and within the range specified with the LASTDRIVE= command in your CONFIG.SYS file. You cannot use drive letters reserved by Interlnk as SUBST drive aliases. If a drive letter is already in use as a SUBST drive alias, you must delete the previous assignment before assigning that drive letter to another *drive:path*.

3. You cannot create SUBST alias drives that refer to subdirectories on a drive that is not local to your computer. Network drives, CD-ROM drives, and Interlnk drives are all redirected drives and cannot be used with SUBST.

4. When you delete an alias drive created by the SUBST command, include the drive letter of the alias drive, not the subdirectory that the alias refers to. For example, to delete the alias drive E, enter the following line at the DOS prompt:

   ```
   SUBST E: /D
   ```

5. You can't use any of the following DOS commands on an alias drive created by the SUBST command:

ASSIGN, BACKUP, CHKDSK, DEFRAG, DISKCOMP, DISKCOPY, FDISK, FORMAT, JOIN, LABEL, MIRROR, RECOVER, RESTORE, SYS

The above commands refuse to work on an alias drive created by SUBST, so if you do try to use them no harm will be done.

6. Do not create or delete any SUBST alias drives while Microsoft Windows is running. If you create the SUBST aliases before starting Microsoft Windows, you can use the alias drives from within a DOS session in Windows.

Messages

`Cannot SUBST a network drive`

Error: You tried to use a nonlocal drive as the alias drive. You cannot use network drives, Interlnk drives, or CD-ROM drives with SUBST.

`Drive already SUBSTed`

Error: You are trying to create a new SUBST drive alias using a drive letter which is a SUBST drive alias. Delete the previous assignment with SUBST *drive:* /D and try again.

`Invalid parameter`

Error: The value that you specified for the alias drive (*alias:*) is invalid. You may need to increase the value specified by the LASTDRIVE= command in your CONFIG.SYS file. This message is also displayed if you try to create an alias for a subdirectory on an alias drive. The *drive:path* parameter for the SUBST command must refer to a real local disk drive.

See Also

ASSIGN and JOIN

"The SUBST Command" in Chapter 13

CONFIG SYS

SWITCHES= 5.0 and later—Internal

The SWITCHES= command is a collection of options that configure DOS for certain circumstances. Options allow the WINA20.386 file to be moved out of the root directory, cause an enhanced keyboard to behave like a standard keyboard, and allow you to disable DOS 6's new start-up keys. You can use SWITCHES= only in your CONFIG.SYS file.

Syntax

SWITCHES=/K /F /N /W

Parameters and Switches

/K	The /K switch forces an enhanced keyboard to behave as though it were an older, standard keyboard.
/F	(DOS 6 only) The /F switch eliminates the two-second pause that occurs when the `Starting MS-DOS...` message appears on-screen.
/N	(DOS 6 only) The /N switch disables the F5 Clean and F8 Interactive boot keys.
/W	The /W switch allows you to move the WINA20.386 file out of the root directory of your start-up drive.

Notes

1. The SWITCHES= command can be located anywhere in your CONFIG.SYS file. DOS scans the file looking for it before displaying the `Starting MS-DOS...` message.

2. If you are having problems with an older application incorrectly interpreting your enhanced keyboard, the /K switch might solve your problems. Enhanced keyboards normally generate certain key codes that were not available on the older, 84-key keyboards. Specifying /K forces DOS to translate these new key codes into their equivalent 84-key keyboard codes.

   The /K switch only affects programs that get their keyboard input from DOS. Many programs bypass DOS, getting keyboard input from the BIOS or, in some cases, directly from the keyboard. For these programs, the /K switch has no effect.

3. If you are using both the /K switch and the ANSI.SYS device driver, make sure to include a /K switch on the line that loads ANSI.SYS as well.

4. By disabling DOS 6's F5 Clean and F8 Interactive boot keys with the /N switch, you force your computer to always start up with the CONFIG.SYS and AUTOEXEC.BAT files that are present in your root directory. If security is a concern, and you load security features in

these files, you may want to specify this switch. To truly secure your computer, however, you may need to lock your floppy drives, protect your start-up files, and take other precautions, as well. This switch is only a minor obstacle to a determined user and is meant as a simple means to perhaps "user-proof" a menu system.

Trap

Before you specify the /N switch, be sure that you have a bootable floppy disk that starts up your system in a usable condition. (You need access to your hard drive and at least a text editor such as EDIT to fix your start-up files.) Never specify this switch until you have completely debugged your CONFIG.SYS and AUTOEXEC.BAT files.

5. The /F switch is intended to be used with the /N switch. After you have disabled the F5 and F8 keys, there is no need for a two-second pause at start up that waits for you to press them.

6. Windows 3.0 in enhanced mode requires the WINA20.386 driver file to be available before it loads. (See the first message in the following "Messages" section.) If you want to move the WINA20.386 file out of your root directory, you need to specify the /W switch in CONFIG.SYS and add the following line to the [386Enh] section of your SYSTEM.INI file:

   DEVICE=*drive:\path*\WINA20.386

   You should specify the full drive and path to WINA20.386 in the device line in SYSTEM.INI.

Trap

Windows 3.1 can load successfully in enhanced mode without access to the WINA20.386 driver, but any version 3.0 drivers that you're using may still require the services of the WINA20.386 driver. If they do, and that driver is unavailable, Windows may become unstable or crash. Because enhanced-mode drivers for Windows are distributed with many software packages, most people are running Windows 3.1 with Windows 3.0 drivers without knowing it. To be safe, be sure that the WINA20.386 driver is available, either in the root directory or through the /W switch and a device line in SYSTEM.INI.

Examples

You depend on an older application that doesn't respond to the right-hand Shift and Ctrl keys properly. To force your enhanced keyboard to return the same keycodes for both the left and right Shift and Ctrl keys, you include the following line in your CONFIG.SYS file.

```
SWITCHES=/K
```

If you use ANSI.SYS, remember to add the /K switch to the DEVICE= line that loads ANSI.SYS, as well.

Perhaps you have a menu system set up that you want everyone who uses your computer to use. To avoid having people bypass it, you might want to disable the new DOS 6 interactive start-up features with the following line in your CONFIG.SYS file:

```
SWITCHES=/F /N
```

Although you use Windows 3.1, you're not sure whether all your Windows enhanced-mode drivers have been updated yet and want to make sure that the WINA20.386 driver is available, just in case. Because you've moved the WINA20.386 file into the C:\DOS subdirectory with your other DOS 6.x files, you need to include the following line in your CONFIG.SYS file:

```
SWITCHES=/W
```

Now that DOS knows you've moved WINA20.386, you need to tell Windows where you put it. To do so, add the following line to the [386Enh] section of your SYSTEM.INI file, which is located in your main Windows subdirectory:

```
DEVICE=C:\DOS\WINA20.386
```

Messages

`You must have the file WINA20.386 in the root directory of your boot drive to run Windows in Enhanced Mode`

Error: This message displays only if you are running Windows 3.0 in enhanced mode and the WINA20.386 file is not present in your root directory. To allow Windows 3.0 to run in enhanced mode with the WINA20.386 driver located somewhere else, specify the SWITCHES=/W command in your CONFIG.SYS and enter a DEVICE=*drive:\path*\WINA20.386 line in the [386Enh] section of SYSTEM.INI.

See Also

ANSI.SYS and WINA20.386

"Using the SWITCHES Command" in Chapter 18

SYS

1.0 and later—External

SYS can make a floppy disk bootable without reformatting the disk. It places a copy of DOS (the hidden system files IO.SYS, MSDOS.SYS, and COMMAND.COM for MS-DOS; the files IBMBIO.COM, IBMDOS.COM, and COMMAND.COM for IBM DOS) on the specified disk. In DOS 6, DBLSPACE.BIN also can be copied.

Syntax

SYS *source* ***drive:***

Parameters and Switches

source — The source drive and path for the system files. This parameter defaults to the root directory of the current drive for the system files and to the file pointed to by the environment variable COMSPEC for the command-line interpreter (generally, COMMAND.COM).

drive: — The drive that is to receive the copies of the DOS files from the root directory of the current drive. The trailing colon (:) is required.

Notes

1. You must specify the drive that will receive a copy of DOS.
2. In pre-4.0 versions of DOS, the disk that was to receive the DOS operating-system files was required to have sufficient contiguous free space for the files IO.SYS and MSDOS.SYS (IBMBIO.COM and IBMDOS.COM in IBM DOS). Subsequent versions of DOS require only that enough free space exist, not that the space be contiguous.
3. SYS copies the DOS system files from the root directory of the current disk (or *source* if it was specified) to the destination ***drive:***. If the DOS system files (IO.SYS and MSDOS.SYS) are not found and the source drive is a floppy disk drive, you are prompted to insert a system disk

into the drive. If the source disk is a hard drive, reenter the SYS command and specify where the DOS system files are located with the *source* parameter.

4. You cannot use SYS in a networked drive; in a drive formed by ASSIGN, JOIN, or SUBST; or in an Interlnk drive.

5. In pre-5.0 versions of DOS, you have to copy COMMAND.COM to the target disk in a separate step.

6. SYS looks for a copy of COMMAND.COM either in the root directory of the current drive or in the subdirectory specified by the *source* parameter if one is specified. If COMMAND.COM is not found, a warning message displays. When this happens, use the COPY command to add a copy of COMMAND.COM to the disk.

7. With DOS 6, SYS copies the DBLSPACE.BIN file to the system disk you are creating even if you do not use DoubleSpace. If SYS is unable to find the DBLSPACE.BIN file, no error message displays. SYS searches the DOS PATH for DBLSPACE.BIN if the file isn't found in the same location as the other system files.

Messages

`Could not copy COMMAND.COM onto target disk`

Warning: SYS was unable to find the file COMMAND.COM in the root directory of the current drive or, if you specified a *source* parameter, in the *source* subdirectory. To make the disk bootable, use the COPY command to copy COMMAND.COM to the disk.

```
Insert system disk in drive d:
and strike any key when ready
```

Prompt: SYS cannot find the DOS system files (IO.SYS and MSDOS.SYS) on the floppy drive that you specified with the *source* parameter (or the root directory of the current drive if you didn't specify a *source* parameter). Insert a floppy disk that contains the DOS system files.

`Invalid path or System files not found`

Error: You executed the SYS command with a *source* parameter, but SYS cannot find the DOS system files in the subdirectory you specified. This message displays if the *source* subdirectory is invalid or does not contain the files IO.SYS and MSDOS.SYS. Correct your *source* parameter entry and retry the command.

`No room for system on destination disk`

Error: The disk you are trying to make bootable with SYS doesn't have enough free space for the system files. Delete some of the files on the disk and try the SYS command again.

`No system on default disk drive`

Error: You executed the SYS command without specifying a *source* parameter, but SYS cannot find the DOS system files (IO.SYS and MSDOS.SYS) on the current hard drive. Reenter the SYS command, specifying the location of the DOS system files with the *source* parameter.

`SYS cannot operate on target drive`

Error: SYS cannot transfer the system files (IO.SYS and MSDOS.SYS) to the target drive. You may get this message if you try to use SYS to make a DoubleSpace-compressed drive bootable. SYS can transfer the DOS system files to the host drive, but not to the DoubleSpace-compressed drive. SYS is unable to transfer the DOS system files to network and Interlnk drives as well.

`System transferred`

Information: SYS has placed the files IO.SYS, MSDOS.SYS, COMMAND.COM, and possibly DBLSPACE.BIN on the target disk.

See Also

FORMAT

TIME

1.0 and later—Internal

BATCH FILE

The TIME command can display and set the current time for your computer. Normally, DOS and your computer's hardware attempt to keep the time set properly. If you have no AUTOEXEC.BAT file, DOS prompts you to enter the current date each time your computer reboots.

Syntax

TIME ***hh***:*mm:ss.xx* A|P

To display the time and have DOS prompt you to enter a new time, use the following format:

TIME

Parameters and Switches

hh The one or two digit number that represents hours (0 to 23). To set the time, this parameter is required.

mm The one or two digit number that represents minutes (0 to 59). This parameter is optional.

ss The one or two digit number that represents seconds (0 to 59). This parameter is optional.

xx The one or two digit number that represents hundredths of a second (0 to 99). This parameter is optional.

A|P Entering an A or a P can designate a.m. or p.m., respectively. You can use upper- or lowercase letters. If you do not use A or P, you must enter the time in 24-hour (military) format.

Notes

1. Depending on the country-code setting in your CONFIG.SYS file, a comma may be the separator between seconds and hundredths of seconds. (Refer to the section on the COUNTRY command earlier in this Command Reference.)

2. The TIME command sets the computer's internal 24-hour clock. The time and date are recorded in the directory when you create or change a file. This information can help you find the most recent version of a file when you check your directory.

3. Most PCs use an internal clock, backed up by a battery, that is accurate to about one minute a month, so you rarely have to set the time after you set it initially. If your system does not retain the time after you turn off your computer, however, put TIME and DATE commands in your AUTOEXEC.BAT file so that DOS does not default to a nonsense time and date when you turn on your computer.

4. If you press Enter after the time prompt, DOS does not change the current time.

See Also

COUNTRY= and DATE

"Issuing the TIME Command" in Chapter 12

TREE

2.0 and later—External

The TREE command displays a visual representation of the subdirectory structure on your disk, which is often referred to as the *directory tree*. TREE can be useful for printing a map of your hard drive if you redirect its output to your printer.

Syntax

TREE *drive:path* /F /A

Parameters and Switches

drive:	The drive that holds the disk for which you want to display the directory structure. If you omit *drive:*, DOS assumes the current drive.
path	The subdirectory in which you want the examination to start. If you omit *path*, DOS displays a directory tree that starts with the current directory.
/F	Displays all files in each directory. Using the /F switch can make the output generated by TREE rather lengthy.
/A	Uses ASCII characters to display the connection of subdirectories, rather than the default graphics characters. If you are redirecting the output of TREE to your printer, you may want to use this switch. Not all printers can print the block graphics characters that TREE uses in its display.

See Also

CD or CHDIR, DELTREE, MD or MKDIR, MOVE, RD or RMDIR

"Listing Directories with TREE" in Chapter 5

TYPE

1.0 and later—Internal

The TYPE command displays the contents of a file on-screen. If the file is an ASCII text file, you are able to read it. If it's a binary file, however, the screen may seem to fill up with gibberish while beeping, and you may think you've broken your computer. No harm has been done, but displaying binary files on-screen is a fairly useless operation. The CLS command cleans up the mess for you.

Syntax

TYPE *pathname*

Parameters and Switches

pathname The file that you want TYPE to display. If you do not specify a drive, DOS assumes the current drive. If you do not specify a subdirectory path, DOS assumes the current directory. The file name portion of this parameter is required. Wildcards are not allowed.

Notes

1. The TYPE command displays a file's characters on-screen. You can use TYPE to see a file's contents.
2. Strange characters appear on-screen when you use TYPE for some data files and most program files, because TYPE tries to display the machine-language instructions as ASCII characters.
3. As you can with most other DOS commands, you can redirect the output of TYPE to the printer by adding "> PRN" to the command line or by pressing Ctrl-PrtSc. Don't forget to press Ctrl-PrtSc again to turn off the printing instruction.
4. To keep the contents of a long file from scrolling off the screen before you can read them, you can pipe the output of TYPE through MORE. Alternatively, you can press Ctrl-S to stop the display and Ctrl-Q to restart it.

Examples

To display the contents of the DOS README.TXT file one screen at a time:

```
TYPE C:\DOS\README.TXT | MORE
```

See Also
MORE

"Viewing Files" in Chapter 8

UNDELETE

5.0 and later—External

Recovers files that were deleted with the DEL command. In DOS 5.0, UNDELETE uses MIRROR's delete-tracking file (if available) to restore a deleted file. In DOS 6, UNDELETE uses a delete-sentry file or a delete-tracking file (if either exists) to restore a deleted file. Either version may be able to restore a deleted file without any special files if the file was deleted recently and little disk activity has occurred since the deletion.

Syntax
In DOS 5.0, use the following format:

UNDELETE *pathname* /LIST /DT /DOS /ALL

In DOS 6, to load the memory-resident program that UNDELETE uses for delete sentry and delete tracking protection, use the following format:

UNDELETE /LOAD /S*drive* /T*drive-entries*

In DOS 6, to manipulate UNDELETE, use the following format:

UNDELETE /LIST /ALL /PURGE*drive* /STATUS /UNLOAD

In DOS 6, to undelete one or more files, use the following format:

UNDELETE *pathname* /DT /DS /DOS /LIST /ALL

Parameters and Switches

pathname The file or files that you want to undelete. If you do not specify a drive, DOS assumes the current drive. If you do not specify a subdirectory path, DOS assumes the current directory. Wildcards are allowed. If you omit this parameter, DOS undeletes all deleted files in the current directory.

/ALL — Restores files without prompting. The Delete Sentry method is used if it is available. Otherwise, the Delete Tracker method is used, if it is available. If neither method is available, the normal DOS directory method is used (see the "Notes" section for this command). You can use /ALL with any of the other switches.

/DOS — Restores files that DOS lists as deleted. UNDELETE prompts you before each file is restored.

/DS — Recovers only the files listed in the SENTRY directory. UNDELETE prompts you before each file is restored.

/DT — Restores only the files listed in the delete-tracking file. UNDELETE prompts you before each file is restored.

/LIST — Provides a list of deleted files but does not undelete them. The type of list produced varies with the use of the /DT, /DS, and /DOS switches.

/LOAD — Loads the Undelete memory-resident program into conventional memory, using the UNDELETE.INI file. If that file does not exist, UNDELETE creates a default UNDELETE.INI file.

/PURGE*drive* — Deletes the contents of the SENTRY directory created by Delete Sentry protection. *drive* defaults to the current drive.

/S*drive* — Enables Delete Sentry protection and loads the Undelete memory-resident program into memory, using the UNDELETE.INI file. *drive* defaults to the current drive.

/STATUS — Displays the type of protection in effect for each drive.

/T*drive-entries* — Enables Delete Tracker protection and loads the Undelete memory-resident program into memory, using the UNDELETE.INI file. The *drive* parameter is the drive for which you want Delete Tracker protection. *entries* is a number (ranging from 1 through 999) that specifies the maximum number of entries in the delete-tracking file, PCTRACKR.DEL. DOS determines the default value by the factors in the following list:

Disk Size	Entries	PCTRACKR.DEL Size
360K	25	5K
720K	50	9K
1.2M	75	14K
1.44M	75	14K
20M	101	18K
32M	202	36K
Larger than 32M	303	55K

/UNLOAD

Unloads the Undelete memory-resident program from memory, disabling Delete Tracker or Delete Sentry protection if either was active. Undelete is unable to release the memory it was using if any other memory-resident software has been loaded after it.

Rules

1. UNDELETE cannot restore deleted subdirectories.
2. UNDELETE cannot restore a file if you deleted the subdirectory that contained the file.
3. Do not use Delete Tracker for any drive that has been redirected with JOIN or SUBST.

Notes

1. UNDELETE restores deleted files, using the delete-tracking or delete-sentry file (if either exists), or the standard DOS directory.
2. Delete Sentry provides the highest level of protection by saving deleted files in a SENTRY directory. The size of the SENTRY directory (including the files that it contains) is limited to approximately 7 percent of your disk. DOS purges old files to make room for new ones.
3. Delete Tracker provides an intermediate level of protection by maintaining a hidden file called PCTRACKR.DEL that records the locations of a file's allocation units (clusters). You can recover a deleted file until its freed allocation units are allocated to a new file. Delete Tracker takes the same amount of memory as Delete Sentry.

4. When you delete a file, DOS removes the first character in the file name. If you use UNDELETE with the /DOS switch, you are prompted for a character to replace the missing first character. If you use the /ALL switch, and if a delete-tracking or delete-sentry file does not exist, UNDELETE restores each deleted file without prompts, using the character # as the first character of the file name. A deleted file named BETTER.TXT, for example, is undeleted as #ETTER.TXT.

   If BETTER.TXT and LETTER.TXT are deleted, DOS restores BETTER.TXT as #ETTER.TXT and LETTER.TXT as %ETTER.TXT. UNDELETE tries the following replacement characters for the first letter of the file name, in the order shown, until a unique file name is found:

   The pound sign (#)

   The percentage sign (%)

   The ampersand (&)

   The digits 0 through 9

   The characters A through Z

5. Although UNDELETE enables you to recover files that you deleted accidentally, do not use this command as a substitute for backing up data. Be sure to keep up-to-date backups of your data.

Examples

For the following examples, assume that the DOS commands are stored in a directory that is in your PATH.

To restore all deleted files in the root directory of drive C without prompting for confirmation on each file:

```
C:\UNDELETE /ALL
```

To provide a list of all currently deleted files:

```
UNDELETE /LIST
```

To create C:\PCTRACKR.DEL to track up to 200 deleted files on drive C and load the memory-resident portion of UNDELETE:

```
UNDELETE /TC-200
```

See Also

MWUNDEL and UNFORMAT

"Recovering Deleted Files with UNDELETE" in Chapter 11

UNFORMAT 5.0 and later—External

The UNFORMAT utility can recover a disk that was inadvertently reformatted. In DOS 5.0, UNFORMAT uses the files produced by the MIRROR command (if those files are available) to restore the disk to its condition before reformatting. In DOS 5.0 and 6, you probably can unformat disks if they were not formatted with FORMAT /U. The UNFORMAT command works on both hard disks and floppy disks.

Syntax

UNFORMAT ***drive*:** /J /P /L /U /TEST /PARTN

Parameters and Switches

***drive*:**	The drive where the deleted file resides. This parameter is required.
/J	Confirms that the MIRROR command contains the necessary information to restore the disk. This switch does not unformat the disk.
/L	Lists all files and directory names found. If used with the /PARTN switch, /L displays current partition tables. The default (no /L) is to list only subdirectories and fragmented files.
/P	Directs all output to the printer connected to LPT1.
/PARTN	Restores the partition table of a hard disk. You must use the PARTNSAV.FIL file created by the MIRROR /PARTN command.
/TEST	Shows how UNFORMAT will re-create the information on the disk. Like the /J switch, this switch does not actually unformat the disk.
/U	Unformats without using the MIRROR files.

Rules

1. To unformat your hard disk, you first must reboot from drive A, using a specially prepared floppy disk (see the Notes section for this command).
2. If you format a floppy disk by using the FORMAT /U switch, UNFORMAT cannot restore the disk.
3. UNFORMAT works only on disks that use sector sizes of 512, 1024, or 2048 bytes.
4. The /J, /U, and /PARTN parameters for UNFORMAT were omitted from the documentation for MS-DOS 6, but UNFORMAT still supports them. They are included in the FASTHELP that you display by entering UNDELETE /? at the DOS command prompt.

Notes

1. UNFORMAT attempts to recover a formatted disk by using the MIRROR.FIL and MIRORSAV.FIL files created by the MIRROR command or by using information in the disk's root directory and file-allocation table. The second process is slower and less reliable than the first.
2. To prepare for the eventuality that you may need to use UNFORMAT, format a floppy disk (using the /S switch to make the disk bootable) and then transfer the UNFORMAT.EXE file to that disk. Also transfer the CONFIG.SYS files, the AUTOEXEC.BAT files, and any device drivers needed for the computer's operation. Thereafter, if you accidentally format the hard disk, you can boot from the floppy disk and perform an UNFORMAT operation.

   Before you use UNFORMAT to recover the disk, use the command with the /J or /TEST switches to determine whether your MIRROR files are up-to-date or whether the UNFORMAT command can recover files in the way that you want.
3. In DOS 6, UNFORMAT cannot recover fragmented files. DOS asks you whether you want to recover such files by truncating them at the end of their contiguous sectors.

See Also

MIRROR and UNDELETE

"Unformatting a Disk" in Chapter 11

VER

2.0 and later—Internal

VER is a very simple command that displays the version number of MS-DOS on-screen. If you are ever wondering what version of DOS is running on the computer you are using, type **VER** at the DOS command prompt.

Syntax

VER

Notes

1. The VER command displays a one-digit DOS version number, followed by a two-digit revision number, reminding you which DOS version the computer is using.
2. If a computer is running a customized OEM version of MS-DOS, the name of that company is normally included in the line that VER displays. For instance, Compaq computers usually display the name COMPAQ along with the DOS version number. IBM versions normally display PC-DOS instead of MS-DOS.
3. VER is unaffected by the SETVER program. VER always displays the actual version of DOS that the computer is running.

Examples

To display the version of MS-DOS that's running on a computer, enter the VER command at the DOS prompt.

```
VER
```

For MS-DOS 6.2, the following line displays on-screen:

```
MS-DOS Version 6.20
```

See Also

"Displaying the Version with VER" in Chapter 12

VERIFY

2.0 and later—Internal

Normally, when DOS writes information to a disk, it trusts the disk hardware to make sure that the data was stored safely. If you want to be absolutely sure, you can turn VERIFY ON; DOS then reads back all the data written to disk and compares it to make sure that it was stored safely. Turning VERIFY ON, however, slows down disk-write operations substantially, so this additional level of protection doesn't come without a price.

Syntax

VERIFY *onoff*

Parameters and Switches

onoff Specifies whether you want to turn VERIFY ON or OFF. If you omit this parameter, the current state of the verify flag displays.

Notes

1. By default, when DOS starts up, VERIFY is OFF.
2. VERIFY accepts only the parameters ON and OFF.
3. VERIFY works by instructing the disk controller to read back all data written to disk, calculate a new CRC (error checking) value from the data read, and compare it to the CRC value stored on the disk. (The disk controller normally does this every time data is read from the disk, which is how DOS discovers bad sectors when copying files.) Any differences between the two CRC values indicates that an error has occurred. Setting VERIFY ON doesn't compare the data on disk to the data that DOS was requested to write, it only makes sure that the data written to the disk is readable.
4. If VERIFY is set ON, you have more assurance that your data is being safely stored on disk. If VERIFY is OFF, writing data to disk takes less time. When deciding which setting to use, you have to choose between data integrity and speed.
5. Specifying the /V parameter for COPY, DISKCOPY, or XCOPY sets VERIFY ON for the duration of the command. When the copy operation is finished, they set VERIFY back to the state it was in before the command executed.
6. The VERIFY state can be changed by a running program. Programming etiquette dictates that, when done, an application reset any flag, such as VERIFY, to the state in which it was found. Still, you may run across applications that forget to reset VERIFY. If this causes problems, run the application from a batch file, which restores the VERIFY state when the program terminates.

Examples

If you were about to update your company's accounts receivables, you might want to turn the verify flag on before starting your accounting software:

```
VERIFY ON
```

After you are finished, you might set the verify flag back off so that your routine computer tasks aren't unnecessarily slowed down:

```
VERIFY OFF
```

If you ever want to know whether the verify flag is off or on, enter the VERIFY command with no parameters at the DOS prompt:

```
VERIFY
```

Messages

`Must specify ON or OFF`

Error: The only parameters that the VERIFY command accepts are ON or OFF. Entering anything else displays the error message above.

`VERIFY is on`

or

`VERIFY is off`

Information: If you enter VERIFY with no parameters, one of the preceding messages displays, informing you of the current state of the verify flag.

See Also

"Turning on Verification with VERIFY" Chapter 8

VFINTD.386 — 6.0 and later—Windows

Setup installs this device driver in the [386Enh] section of SYSTEM.INI to allow Microsoft Backup for Windows access to your floppy disk drives. If you have any other Windows backup software installed, this driver often conflicts with the drivers installed for that software.

Syntax

To use Microsoft Backup for Windows, you must include the following line in the [386Enh] section of the SYSTEM.INI file.

DEVICE=*drive:\path***VFINTD.386**

Parameters and Switches

drive:\path The full path to the VFINTD.386 file on your system. The setup program for DOS 6 places this file in the C:\DOS subdirectory by default.

Notes

1. Almost all backup software for Windows adds a device driver to SYSTEM.INI that allows access to your tape drives and floppy disk drives. Unfortunately, few of these drivers can get along with each other, and you're usually forced to remove all but one driver before any of them will work. The following list includes some of the more common third-party drivers to look for in SYSTEM.INI:

Driver File Name	Backup Program
VFINTD.386	Microsoft Backup for Windows (with DOS 6) and Norton Backup for Windows
CMSDTAPE.386	Colorado Tape Backup
MYABU.386	My Advanced Backup
FASTBACK.386	Fastback for Windows
VFD.386	Central Point Backup for Windows
CPBVXD.386	Central Point Backup for Windows

2. Microsoft suggests that you disable any third-party drivers you find in SYSTEM.INI by adding a semicolon to the front of the DEVICE= line that loads them. Be aware that doing this may cause your other backup software to stop working.

3. If your computer fails the compatibility test that Microsoft Backup for Windows runs, you are probably having a driver conflict in SYSTEM.INI. If this happens, quit Windows, "comment out" any lines in SYSTEM.INI that load third-party backup drivers (see the Driver table above), restart windows, and try the test again. As long as you comment

out the driver lines (by placing a semicolon at the beginning of the line) instead of deleting them, you can easily restore them when you want to use your other backup software.

4. Be aware that Windows does not recognize any changes you make in SYSTEM.INI until you quit Windows completely and restart it from the DOS prompt.

Examples

Setup for DOS 6 adds the following line to the [386Enh] section of your SYSTEM.INI file when it installs Microsoft Backup for Windows on your computer.

```
DEVICE=C:\DOS\VFINTD.386
```

Setup does not, however, comment out third-party drivers in SYSTEM.INI that are known to cause conflicts with the VFINTD.386 driver.

VOL — 2.0 and later—Internal

VOL displays the volume label and serial number of a disk if they exist. The volume label is simply a name that you can assign when you format a disk, or later with the LABEL command. DOS began adding serial numbers to disks with DOS 4.0.

Syntax

VOL *drive:*

Parameters and Switches

drive: The drive whose label and serial number you want to display. If you omit this parameter, DOS assumes the current drive.

Notes

1. You can add a label to a disk when you format it with the FORMAT /V command, or later with the LABEL command.

2. The serial number is meant to be a unique identifier assigned to the disk when it's formatted. DOS uses the serial number to verify that a disk hasn't been changed in disk drives that don't have change line support. Preformatted disks often do not have serial numbers on them,

and some third-party formatting utilities neglect to add them, as well. DOS may be unable to tell whether you have changed a floppy disk if it has no serial number and your drive doesn't have change line support.

3. DOS can only assign serial numbers to a disk with the FORMAT command. You can't add or change the serial number of a disk without reformatting it.

Examples

To display the volume label of a floppy disk in drive B:, enter the following command at the DOS prompt.

```
VOL B:
```

If you omit the *drive:* parameter (B:), DOS assumes the current disk.

VOL displays the following messages if the disk specified has both a volume label and a serial number.

```
Volume in drive B: is NEW WORK
Volume Serial Number is 4EF7-9C30
```

If the disk has no serial number, the second line is omitted. If the disk has no volume label, the following message displays.

```
Volume in drive B: has no label
```

Messages

`Invalid drive specification`

Error: You specified an invalid drive letter in the *drive:* parameter.

`Invalid switch - switch`

Error: You specified an invalid switch parameter. The only parameter that VOL accepts is a single disk drive.

`Too many parameters - parameter`

Error: You've specified more than one parameter on the command line. The only parameter that VOL accepts is a single disk drive.

See Also

FORMAT and LABEL

"Examining Volume Labels with VOL" in Chapter 6

VSAFE

6.0 and later—External

VSAFE is a memory-resident utility that can monitor the activity in your computer. If any program is acting suspiciously, VSAFE can halt the process and request guidance from you as to what to do about it.

Syntax

VSAFE */option±* ... /NE /NX /A*key* /C*key* /N /D /U

Parameters and Switches

/A*key*	Sets the hot key as Alt plus the key specified by *key*.
/C*key*	Sets the hot key as Ctrl plus the key specified by *key*.
/D	Turns off checksumming.
/N	Instructs VSAFE to monitor network drives.
/NE	Prevents VSAFE from loading into expanded memory.
/NX	Prevents VSAFE from loading into extended memory.
/option± ...	Specifies how VSAFE checks for viruses. Use a plus sign (+) after *option* to enable the switch; use a minus sign (–) after *option* to disable it. Choose *option* from the following list:

1 Warns of low level formatting that could erase your hard disk (default: on)

2 Warns of a program's attempt to stay resident in memory (default: off)

3 Prevents programs from writing to any of your disks (default: off)

4 Checks executable files that DOS opens for viruses (default: on)

5 Checks all disks for boot sector viruses (default: on)

6 Warns of attempts to write to the boot sector or to the partition table of the hard disk (default: on)

7 Warns of attempts to write to the boot sector of a floppy disk (default: off)

8 Warns of attempts to modify executable files (default: on)

/U Disables and unloads VSAFE from memory. If VSAFE wasn't the last resident program loaded, the memory it was using will not be released.

Rules

1. Turn off VSAFE before you install Microsoft Windows.
2. Do not use VSAFE after you start Microsoft Windows.
3. If you use VSAFE with Microsoft Windows, run the MWAVTSR.EXE memory-resident program by adding the following line to your WIN.INI file:

   LOAD=C:\DOS\MWAVTSR.EXE

   MWAVTSR.EXE enables VSAFE messages to be displayed in Windows.
4. The default hot key is Alt-V.

Notes

VSAFE is a memory-resident program that takes up a varying amount of conventional, extended, and expanded memory. In DOS 6.0 and 6.2, VSAFE takes up 44K of conventional memory, 23K of conventional and 23K of extended memory, or 7K of conventional and 64K of expanded memory.

Examples

To turn on warnings about programs' attempts to stay in memory, to turn off checks for boot-sector viruses, and to make Alt-Q the hot key:

```
VSAFE /2+ /5- /AQ
```

See Also

MSAV, MWAV, and MWAVTSR

"Guarding against Infection" in Chapter 10

SYSTEM INI

WINA20.386

5.0 and later—Windows

Windows 3.0 enhanced-mode drivers often require the help of the WINA20.386 driver to perform their duties. Setup for MS-DOS 6 places this driver in the root directory if it finds Windows installed on your system. If you move the WINA20.386 file to another subdirectory, you need to tell Windows where it is and add a SWITCHES=/W line to your CONFIG.SYS file.

Syntax

To tell Windows where you have located the WINA20.386 driver, include the following line in the [386Enh] section of SYSTEM.INI.

DEVICE=*drive:\path***WINA20.386**

Parameters and Switches

drive:\path — The full path to the WINA20.386 file on your system. The setup program for DOS 6 places this file in the root directory of the start-up drive by default.

Notes

Windows 3.0 in enhanced mode requires the WINA20.386 driver file to be available before it can load. (See the first message in the following "Messages" section.) If you want to move the WINA20.386 file out of your root directory, you need to specify the /W switch in CONFIG.SYS and add a DEVICE=*drive:\path*\WINA20.386 line to the [386Enh] section of your SYSTEM.INI file. You should specify the full drive and path to WINA20.386 in the device line in SYSTEM.INI.

Trap

Windows 3.1 will load successfully in enhanced mode without access to the WINA20.386 driver, but any version 3.0 drivers that you're using may still require the services of the WINA20.386 driver. If they do, and that driver is unavailable, Windows may become unstable or crash. Since enhanced-mode drivers for Windows are distributed with many software packages, most people are running Windows 3.1 with Windows 3.0 drivers without knowing it. To be safe, be sure that the WINA20.386 driver is available, either in the root directory or through the /W switch and a device line in SYSTEM.INI.

Examples

Although you use Windows version 3.1, you're not sure if all of your Windows enhanced-mode drivers have been updated yet and want to make sure that the WINA20.386 driver is available, just in case. Because you've moved the WINA20.386 file into the C:\DOS subdirectory with your other DOS 6 files, you need to include the following line in your CONFIG.SYS file:

```
SWITCHES=/W
```

Now that DOS knows you've moved WINA20.386, you need to tell Windows where you put it. To do so, add the following line to the [386Enh] section of your SYSTEM.INI file, which is in your main Windows subdirectory:

```
DEVICE=C:\DOS\WINA20.386
```

Messages

```
You must have the file WINA20.386 in the root directory of your
boot drive to run Windows in Enhanced Mode
```

Error: This message displays only if you are running Windows 3.0 in enhanced mode and the WINA20.386 file is not present in your root directory. To allow Windows 3.0 to run in enhanced mode with the WINA20.386 driver located somewhere else, specify the SWITCHES=/W command in your CONFIG.SYS and enter a DEVICE=*drive:\path*\WINA20.386 line in the [386Enh] section of SYSTEM.INI.

See Also

SWITCHES=

XCOPY

3.2 and later—External

XCOPY can copy groups of files and subdirectories from one disk to another. When copying large groups of files, XCOPY is somewhat faster than COPY since it reads more than one file at a time into memory.

Syntax

XCOPY ***source*** *destination* /A /D:*date* /E /M /P /S /V /W /Y /-Y

Parameters and Switches

source The file(s) that you want to copy. You can specify a full path name (that is *drive:\path\...\filename.ext*), and wildcards are allowed. This parameter is required. If you include a drive and/or path but no file name, DOS assumes all files (*.*).

destination The location and optionally the file name(s) to which you want to copy. You can specify a full path name, although normally just a drive and/or path is included. Wildcards are allowed when a file name is specified. If you omit this parameter, DOS uses the current drive and subdirectory as the destination.

/A Copies only files whose archive attribute is on (modified files), but doesn't turn off the archive attribute. /A is similar to /M, except that /A does not reset the archive attribute.

/D:*date* Copies only files that were changed or created on or after the date you specify. The date's form depends on the setting of the COUNTRY= command in CONFIG.SYS.

/E Creates parallel subdirectories on the destination disk, even if the original subdirectory is empty.

/M Copies only files whose archive attribute is on (modified files), and turns off the archive attribute. /M is similar to /A, except /M resets the archive attribute.

/P Causes XCOPY to prompt you for approval before copying each file.

/S Copies all directories and subdirectories below ***source*** that contain files.

/V Verifies that the copy was written correctly.

/W Causes XCOPY to prompt you and wait for your response before starting the copy operation. You can use this switch to give yourself time to insert the source floppy disk, for example.

/Y

Specifies that you want XCOPY to overwrite files without prompting you for confirmation. Including this parameter overrides any setting specified with the COPYCMD environment variable.

/-Y

Specifies that you want XCOPY to prompt you for confirmation before overwriting any files, even it the command is run from within a batch file. Including this parameter overrides any setting specified with the COPYCMD environment variable.

Exit Codes

ERRORLEVEL Value	Meaning
0	Extended copy operation successful
1	No files found to copy
2	Halted by user (Ctrl-C)
4	Copy operation failed—Invalid drive letter, invalid switches or parameters, not enough memory, or not enough disk space
5	Halted by fatal error writing to disk

Rules

1. You must specify the source drive, path, and file name first, and then the destination drive, path, and file name.
2. Do not use a device name other than a drive for the *source* or *destination*. For example, you cannot use LPT1: or COM1:.
3. The *source* file specified must include one or both of the following:
   - A valid file name. Wildcards are permitted.
   - A drive name, a path name, or both.
4. If you do not specify the source drive name, DOS uses the current drive.
5. If you do not specify the source path, DOS uses the drive's current directory.
6. If you specify a drive or path for the source but do not specify a source file name, DOS assumes all files (*.*).

7. If you omit a new name for the destination file, the copied file has the same name as the source file.

8. If you do not specify a *destination* parameter, the ***source*** parameter must include one or both of the following:

   - A drive name other than the current drive.
   - A path name other than the current disk's current directory.

9. XCOPY sets the archive bit on for the files it creates.

Notes

1. Starting with DOS 6.2, the XCOPY command, when run from the command line, prompts you for confirmation before overwriting files. However, in order to avoid forcing people to rewrite all their batch files, XCOPY does not prompt you before overwriting a file when run from a batch file.

   If you don't like XCOPY's new behavior, you can change it by defining an environment variable named COPYCMD. Setting COPYCMD equal to /Y forces XCOPY to act as it has in all previous versions of DOS, never prompting for confirmation before overwriting a file. If you set COPYCMD equal to /-Y, XCOPY always prompts for confirmation, even when it's run from within a batch file.

2. To use XCOPY to copy more files than fit on one destination disk, make sure that the files' archive attribute is on. You can use the ATTRIB command to perform this step. Then use the XCOPY command repeatedly with the /M or /M /S switches.

   When the destination floppy disk is full, change floppy disks and reissue the command. The files that were copied now have their archive attribute turned off, so XCOPY skips these files. XCOPY copies the files not already copied—those files that have the archive attribute turned on.

3. XCOPY and APPEND /X are a troublesome combination. To use XCOPY on a disk that is involved in an APPEND command, disconnect APPEND before you execute the XCOPY command.

4. Use XCOPY, rather than DISKCOPY, to copy files to a device that is not the same format as the source.

Messages

`Cannot perform a cyclic copy`

Error: You used the /S switch, and at least one of the destination directories is a subdirectory of the source directories. When you use /S, XCOPY cannot copy files to destination directories that are part of the source directories. If you must copy files from more than one directory, issue individual XCOPY commands to copy the directories one at a time.

`Cannot XCOPY from a reserved device`

Error: You specified one of DOS's reserved device names (for example, LPT1) as the source of the files to be copied. Reissue XCOPY, using a disk path and directory.

`Does pathname specify a file name or directory name on the target (F = file, D = directory)?`

Information: You specified a destination file name in which the final name does not exist as a directory. XCOPY does not know whether the final name in the destination is a file name or a directory.

If the destination name is a directory name, press **D**. XCOPY creates the needed directory and begins copying files. If the destination name is a file name, press **F**. XCOPY copies files to this file.

`nnn File(s) copied`

Information: XCOPY copied *nnn* files to the destination disk. This message appears regardless of any errors that occur.

`Insufficient disk space`

Error: The destination disk ran out of space. The file that you were copying when the error occurred was erased from the destination. Delete any unneeded files from the destination disk, or use a different disk and then retry the command.

`Reading source file(s)...`

Information: XCOPY is reading the source directories for file names.

`Unable to create directory`

Error: XCOPY cannot create a subdirectory on the destination disk for one of the following reasons:

- Part of the destination path name is wrong or misspelled.
- The disk's root directory is full.
- The disk is full.
- A file with the same name as the created directory already exists.
- You used a directory name that actually is a device name.

Be sure that the destination name is correct. Use the DIR command to check the destination disk. If the disk or the root directory is full, erase files or use another destination disk. If a file exists that uses the same name as the intended directory, rename the file or change the directory's name when you reissue the XCOPY command.

See Also
COPY and REPLACE

"Management with XCOPY" in Chapter 9

Appendix A

Files Supplied with MS-DOS 6

Microsoft supplies MS-DOS 6 in two forms. Your local software vendor sells the Microsoft MS-DOS 6 Upgrade package, which can be installed on a computer running only a previous version of DOS. When you buy a new computer, you receive the OEM version, which may (or may not) include additional utilities specific to your computer system. In either case, most of the files you receive remain the same, and the descriptions in this appendix apply to either version.

Microsoft is offering a new type of upgrade for MS-DOS 6.2 called StepUp. The StepUp version of MS-DOS 6.2 can be used only by people who are running MS-DOS 6.0 now, because it simply makes changes to the MS-DOS 6.0 files on your disk. A full upgrade version of MS-DOS 6.2, similar to the upgrade packages offered for previous versions of DOS, is available as well.

Although full details about the contents of the release version of MS-DOS 6.2 are not available at the time of this writing, most of the information in the following list will apply to MS-DOS 6.2 as well as 6.0. To help keep things straight, files that were added or removed in 6.2 are marked. In the text, MS-DOS 6 is used to refer to both version 6.0 and version 6.2 of MS-DOS.

The following list of MS-DOS 6 files is arranged alphabetically, with support files grouped under the associated main file. Each is accompanied by a short description of how the file is used. Knowing the purpose of each file makes it easier to decide which files to delete when your hard disk space runs low. Microsoft datestamps DOS 6.0 files 3/10/93 6:00AM.

The files are marked with the following designations:

Vital	Files that are required to run MS-DOS
Keep	Files everyone should keep handy
Danger!	Dangerous files you may want to move off the path
Remove?	Files few people use or need
International	Files you need only if you use the international features of DOS
80286	Files that require an 80286 or higher processor to use
80386	Files that require an 80386 or higher processor to use
Windows	Files that are useful only if you are running Microsoft Windows

If you decide to remove any of these files from your hard disk, play it safe and copy them to a floppy disk first. That way, you can get them back easily if you make a mistake. Most of these files are placed by Setup in the subdirectory you choose, normally C:\DOS. Exceptions to this are noted.

Most of these files are distributed in a compressed form. Microsoft indicates this by replacing the last character of the file name extension with an underscore (_). When Setup installs these files on your system, they are expanded and renamed automatically. If you copy the files from the distribution disks, however, you'll need to use the Expand utility (located on Setup Disk 1) to make the files usable.

MS-DOS 6 Files

ANSI.SYS	Keep. ANSI display (CON) device driver. Provides enhanced control of the display, as well as keyboard redefinition support. Used by MODE and certain application programs.
APPEND.EXE	Append utility (TSR). Defines a search path for data.

ATTRIB.EXE	File attribute utility. Views or changes file attributes.
CHKDSK.EXE	Keep. Check-disk utility. Checks a disk's logical file structure for errors and displays useful information about available disk space.
CHOICE.COM	Command-line choice utility. Displays a prompt and then waits for you to press a key.
COMMAND.COM	Vital. MS-DOS command-line shell. Normally located in the root directory of the boot disk drive.
COUNTRY.ICE	International. (DOS 6.0 only) Code page symbol set support for Icelandic keyboards. See the README.TXT file for details.
COUNTRY.SYS	International. Code page symbol set support file. Loaded with the COUNTRY= command in CONFIG.SYS.
DBLSPACE.EXE	DoubleSpace disk compression utility program.
DBLSPACE.BIN	DoubleSpace device driver loaded into memory by MS-DOS (before CONFIG.SYS processing). Located in the root directory of the startup drive, DBLSPACE.BIN is marked with system, hidden, and read-only attributes.
DBLSPACE.HLP	DoubleSpace on-line help file.
DBLSPACE.INF	DoubleSpace setup information file.
DBLSPACE.INI	DoubleSpace configuration information file. Created by DBLSPACE.EXE.

DBLSPACE.SYS	CONFIG.SYS utility that allows the DBLSPACE.BIN driver to be moved into high memory.
DBLSPACE.WIN	DoubleSpace uses this file to keep track of Windows during the installation of a CVF (compressed volume file).
DBLSPACE.00x	DoubleSpace CVF created by DBLSPACE.EXE. You normally won't see these files because they are hidden, but they're your DoubleSpace compressed disk drives.
DBLWIN.HLP	Windows. Help for the DoubleSpace Info Box in Windows File Manager Tools menu.
DEBUG.EXE	Danger! Programmer's debugging utility. A low-level programmer's tool that has almost unrestricted access to your computer. Debug can erase your hard disk with just a few keystrokes. Don't run Debug in a Windows DOS box.
DEFRAG.EXE	Keep. Disk defragmenting program. Rearranges files to eliminate fragmentation on your disk.
DEFRAG.HLP	DEFRAG on-line help file.
DELOLDOS.EXE	Remove? Deletes OLD_DOS.x subdirectories from your hard disk and then deletes itself. Feel free to delete this file if you've already removed the old DOS files from your system.
DELTREE.EXE	Delete directory branch utility.
DISKCOMP.COM	Disk compare utility. Makes an exact comparison of two floppy disks.

DISKCOPY.COM	Keep. Disk copy utility. Makes a copy of a floppy disk. Use this to make backup copies of the MS-DOS distribution disks.
DISPLAY.SYS	International. Display device driver with code page symbol set support.
EGA.CPI	International. Code page information file for EGA and VGA video displays.
EGA.ICE	International. (DOS 6.0 only) Code page information file for EGA and VGA video displays using an Icelandic symbol set. See the README.TXT file for details.
EGA2.CPI	International. (DOS 6.2 only) Alternate code page information file for EGA and VGA video displays. See the README.TXT file for details.
DMDRVR.BIN	Ontrack disk manager version 5.0 device driver upgrade. Installed by Setup only if an older version is on the disk.
XBIOS.OVL	Ontrack disk manager overlay file (AT Software BIOS Extended v1.3). Installed by Setup only if an older version is present on the disk.
DOSKEY.COM	DOS command-line editing and macro utility (TSR).
DOSSHELL.COM	(Not DOS 6.2) DOS Shell loader program.
DOSSHELL.EXE	(Not DOS 6.2) DOS Shell executable program file.
DOSSHELL.HLP	(Not DOS 6.2) DOS Shell on-line help file.
DOSSHELL.INI	(Not DOS 6.2) DOS Shell configuration file (ASCII text). DOSSHELL.INI is updated as you make changes to the way the DOS Shell is configured on your computer.

CGA.INI EGA.INI MONO.INI	(Not DOS 6.2) When Setup installs DOS Shell it renames one of these files and copies it to the install directory.
DOSSHELL.GRB	(Not DOS 6.2) DOS Shell video grabber file.
CGA.GRB EGA.GRB EGAMONO.GRB HERC.GRB MONO.GRB VGA.GRB VGAMONO.GRB	(Not DOS 6.2) When Setup installs DOS Shell it renames one of these files DOSSHELL.GRB and copies it to the install directory.
DOSSHELL.VID	(Not DOS 6.2) DOS Shell video driver file.
8514.VID CGA.VID EGA.VID HERC.VID VGA.VID	(Not DOS 6.2) When Setup installs the DOS Shell, it renames one of these files DOSSHELL.VID and copies it to the install directory.
DOSSWAP.EXE	(Not DOS 6.2) DOS Shell task swapper. Used internally by the DOS Shell. Cannot be run from the command line.
DRIVER.SYS	Remove? Device driver that can assign drive letters to an existing floppy drive or create an alias for a floppy disk drive.
EDIT.COM	Keep. ASCII text file editor. This file is actually a loader that runs the editor included in QBASIC.EXE. If you delete QBASIC.EXE, you can't use EDIT.
EDIT.HLP	ASCII text file editor on-line help file.
EGA.SYS	Remove? Device driver that is required by the DOS Shell (and other task swapping software) when running on an EGA display. Without an EGA display this driver is useless.

EMM386.EXE	80386 expanded (EMS) and upper (UMB) memory manager. Requires an XMS provider, such as HIMEM, to run. Required by MS-DOS for loadhigh functions.
EXPAND.EXE	Keep. Utility that must be used when you want to expand the files supplied on the MS-DOS distribution disks into a usable form.
FASTHELP.EXE	Displays syntax help for DOS commands. This is the same help you get when you type the /? switch.
DOSHELP.HLP	Fasthelp help text file (ASCII text). You can add or edit entries in this file, as long as the entries remain properly formatted in alphabetical order. This file is handy for the shareware utilities you can never remember how to use.
FASTOPEN.EXE	Danger! Remove? Directory information cache (TSR). FASTOPEN is slower and more dangerous than SMARTDRV. If you can't use SMARTDRV, use the BUFFERS command to optimize disk access on your computer.
FC.EXE	File compare utility. Useful for both binary and ASCII text files.
FDISK.EXE	Danger! Disk partitioning utility. Prepares a new hard drive and optionally creates one or more logical drives on it. However, one wrong keystroke can wipe out all the information on your hard disk! Get this program off your path. We strongly advise removing it from your hard disk. Keep it on a bootable floppy disk with other disaster recovery tools.

FIND.EXE	Find text filter utility. Useful in batch files.
FORMAT.COM	Keep. Format disk utility.
GRAPHICS.COM	Enable graphics mode print screen utility (TSR).
GRAPHICS.PRO	Printer information file used by GRAPHICS.COM (ASCII text).
HELP.COM	Keep. MS-DOS on-line hypertext help system. This file is actually a loader that runs QBASIC.EXE. If you delete QBASIC.EXE, you can't use Help.
HELP.HLP	Keep. MS-DOS on-line help system data file.
HIMEM.SYS	80286. Extended memory (XMS) manager. Required by EMM386 and by MS-DOS for loadhigh support. Required by Windows.
INTERLNK.EXE	Interlnk network client control program/ device driver.
INTERSVR.EXE	Interlnk network server control program.
IO.SYS	Vital. One of two files that form the core of the MS-DOS operating system. (The other is MSDOS.SYS.) It must be present in the root directory of the startup drive.
KEYB.COM	International. Keyboard remapping utility with code page support. Uses the KEYBOARD.SYS file by default.
KEYBOARD.ICE	International. (DOS 6.0 only) Code page information file for Icelandic keyboards. Loaded by KEYB.COM. See the README.TXT file for details.
KEYBOARD.SYS	International. Code page information keyboard file. Loaded by KEYB.COM.

KEYBRD2.SYS	International. (DOS 6.2 only) Alternate code page information keyboard file. Loaded by KEYB.COM. See the README.TXT file for details.
LABEL.EXE	Disk volume label utility.
LOADFIX.COM	80286. Patch that fills the first 64K segment so that programs loaded after it will be in the second 64K segment of memory. Some programs display a `Packed file corrupt` message if they are run in the first 64K segment of RAM.
MEM.EXE	Keep. Display information on memory usage utility.
MEMMAKER.EXE	80386. Optimize RAM memory usage program.
MEMMAKER.HLP	80386. MemMaker help file.
MEMMAKER.INF	80386. MemMaker configuration file (ASCII text).
MEMMAKER.STS	80386. MemMaker statistics file (ASCII text). This file is created by MemMaker and can provide insight into how your system is configured.
CHKSTATE.SYS	80386. Device driver used by MemMaker to monitor and help optimize memory usage on your system.
SIZER.EXE 80386.	Utility to help MemMaker determine how much memory each device driver and TSR requires.
MODE.COM	Utility program that can control the settings for a variety of standard ports and devices. In some cases, MODE remains resident in memory.

MONOUMB.386	Windows. Device driver for Windows (SYSTEM.INI) that allows EMM386 to use the B000–B7FFh region of VGA memory as UMB space. See the README.TXT file for details.
MORE.COM	MS-DOS. Filter (pipe) that enables you to view a text file or the screen output of a program, one page at a time.
MOUSE.COM	Microsoft Mouse Driver version 8.20. Installed by Setup only if an older version is present on the disk. If you use a Microsoft mouse, keep a close watch on the version you are using. Microsoft distributes updated drivers with most of its software packages, and it's easy to end up using an older driver by mistake.
MOUSE.INI	Microsoft Mouse configuration file (ASCII text). This file is created by MOUSE.COM in the subdirectory pointed to by the MOUSE environment variable if it is defined.
MOVE.EXE	Keep. Move files or rename directories utility program.
MSAV.EXE	Microsoft Anti-Virus program.
MSAV.HLP	Microsoft Anti-Virus on-line help file.
MSAV.INI	Microsoft Anti-Virus configuration file (ASCII text). This file is created by MSAV in the same subdirectory as MSAV.EXE or in the subdirectory pointed to by the MSDOSDATA environment variable if it is defined.
MSAVHELP.OVL	Microsoft Anti-Virus overlay file.
MSAVIRUS.LST	Microsoft Anti-Virus file that contains the list of known virus signatures that MSAV uses when scanning your disks.

CHKLST.MS	Microsoft Anti-Virus checksum files. MSAV creates these files in every subdirectory it scans, unless you turn this feature off.
MSBACKUP.EXE	Microsoft Backup program.
MSBACKUP.LOG	Microsoft Backup log file. This file is created by MSBACKUP or MWBACKUP in the same subdirectory as the corresponding executable file or in the subdirectory pointed to by the MSDOSDATA environment variable if it is defined. The Windows and DOS versions of Microsoft Backup share this file.
MSBACKDB.OVL	Microsoft Backup overlay file.
MSBACKDR.OVL	Microsoft Backup overlay file.
MSBACKFB.OVL	Microsoft Backup overlay file.
MSBACKFR.OVL	Microsoft Backup overlay file.
MSBACKUP.HLP	Microsoft Backup configuration file (ASCII text). This file is created by MSBACKUP in the same subdirectory as MSBACKUP.EXE or in the subdirectory pointed to by the MSDOSDATA environment variable if it's defined. The Windows version of MS Backup keeps a separate INI file in the Windows directory.
MSBACKUP.INI	Microsoft Backup on-line help file.
MSBACKUP.OVL	Microsoft Backup overlay file.
MSBCONFG.HLP	Microsoft Backup configuration on-line help file.
MSBCONFG.OVL	Microsoft Backup configuration overlay file.

DEFAULT.SET	Microsoft Backup default setup file (ASCII text). This file is created by MSBACKUP or MWBACKUP in the same subdirectory as the corresponding executable file or in the subdirectory pointed to by the MSDOSDATA environment variable if it is defined. The Windows and DOS versions of Microsoft Backup share this file.
DEFAULT.SLT	Microsoft Backup default selection file. This file is created by MSBACKUP or MWBACKUP in the same subdirectory as the corresponding executable file or in the subdirectory pointed to by the MSDOSDATA environment variable if it is defined. The Windows and DOS versions of Microsoft Backup share this file.
*.SET	Microsoft Backup setup files (ASCII text). You create and name these files to save preferred settings for backup sets. This file is created by MSBACKUP or MWBACKUP in the same subdirectory as the corresponding executable file or in the subdirectory pointed to by the MSDOSDATA environment variable if it is defined. The Windows and DOS versions of Microsoft Backup share these files.
*.SLT	Microsoft Backup selection files. These files contain the file selection information that you've chosen for a particular backup set. This file is created by MSBACKUP or MWBACKUP in the same subdirectory as the corresponding executable file or in the subdirectory pointed to by the MSDOSDATA environment variable if it is defined. The Windows and DOS versions of Microsoft Backup share these files.

*.FUL *.INC *.DIF	Full, incremental, and differential backup catalog files. This file is created by MSBACKUP or MWBACKUP in the same subdirectory as the corresponding executable file or in the subdirectory pointed to by the MSDOSDATA environment variable if it is defined. The Windows and DOS versions of Microsoft Backup share this file.
MSCDEX.EXE	Utility that assigns drive letters to CD-ROM drives. Installed by Setup only if an older version is present on the disk.
MSD.EXE	Keep. Microsoft system diagnostics. A handy utility that can tell you how your system is configured. Used by Microsoft Product Support when troubleshooting.
MSDOS.SYS	Vital. One of two files that form the core of the MS-DOS operating system. (The other is IO.SYS.) It must be present in the root directory of the start-up drive.
MSTOOLS.DLL	Windows. Windows File Manager extension DLL. Provides the File Manager Tools menu.
MWAV.EXE	Windows. Microsoft Anti-Virus for Windows program.
MWAV.HLP	Windows. Microsoft Anti-Virus for Windows on-line help file.
MWAV.INI	Windows. Microsoft Anti-Virus for Windows configuration file (ASCII text). It is created by MWAV in the same subdirectory as MWAV.EXE or in the subdirectory pointed to by the MSDOSDATA environment variable if it's defined. MSAV and MWAV keep separate configuration files so options set in one will not affect the other.

MWAVABSI.DLL	Windows. Microsoft Anti-Virus for Windows absolute disk I/O library.
MWAVDLG.DLL	Windows. Microsoft Anti-Virus for Windows dialogs library.
MWAVDOSL.DLL	Windows. Microsoft Anti-Virus for Windows operating system library.
MWAVDRVL.DLL	Windows. Microsoft Anti-Virus for Windows drive list custom control library.
MWAVMGR.DLL	Windows. Microsoft Anti-Virus for Windows TSR manager library.
MWAVSCAN.DLL	Windows. Microsoft Anti-Virus for Windows virus scanning support library.
MWAVSOS.DLL	Windows. Microsoft Anti-Virus for Windows context-sensitive help library.
MWGRAFIC.DLL	Windows. Microsoft Anti-Virus for Windows graphics control library.
MWAVTSR.EXE	Windows. VSAFE manager program for Windows. Enables VSAFE to display warning messages when Windows is running.
MWBACKUP.EXE	Windows. Microsoft Backup for Windows program.
MWBACKF.DLL	Windows. Microsoft Backup for Windows DLL.
MWBACKR.DLL	Windows. Microsoft Backup for Windows DLL.
MWBACKUP.HLP	Windows. Microsoft Backup for Windows on-line help file.

MWBACKUP.INI	Windows. Microsoft Backup for Windows configuration file (ASCII text). This file is created by MWBACKUP in the subdirectory pointed to by the WINDIR environment variable. MSBACKUP and MWBACKUP keep separate configuration files so options set in one are set in the other.
VFINTD.386	Windows. Windows device driver (SYSTEM.INI) that allows MWBACKUP to access your tape drive. Setup doesn't check for conflicts with other drivers in your SYSTEM.INI file when installing this file. See the README.TXT file for details.
MWUNDEL.EXE	Windows. Microsoft Undelete for Windows program.
MWUNDEL.HLP	Windows. Microsoft Undelete for Windows on-line help file.
NETWORKS.TXT	Remove? ASCII text file containing information about installing and using MS-DOS 6 on various networks.
NLSFUNC.EXE	International. National language support program (TSR). Required to enable code page switching functions in MODE and CHCP.
OS2.TXT	Remove? ASCII text file describing how to install MS-DOS 6 if you are running OS/2.
PACKING.LST	Remove? ASCII text file listing the contents of the MS-DOS 6 distribution disks. Each file's full name and compressed name are listed.
POWER.EXE	Remove? Power management utility/device driver, with support for Advanced Power Management (APM) hardware.

PRINT.EXE	MS-DOS background print spooler utility (TSR).
QBASIC.EXE	Keep. QuickBASIC programming environment. QBASIC.EXE is used by EDIT.COM and HELP.COM, so even if you never plan to do any BASIC programming, you will probably want to keep this file.
QBASIC.HLP	QuickBASIC on-line help file.
QBASIC.INI	QuickBASIC configuration file. QBASIC.INI is updated when you make changes to the way QuickBASIC is configured on your computer.
RAMDRIVE.SYS	RAM disk device driver.
README.TXT	Remove? ASCII text file containing last minute information about MS-DOS 6. It's a good idea to look for this file in every software package you get and read it before you install the software.
REPLACE.EXE	Update files utility. With this utility you can keep two disks or directories full of files in sync.
RESTORE.EXE	Remove? Restores backup disks created with the old BACKUP utility. If possible, make new backups with MSBACKUP, move RESTORE.EXE to a floppy disk, and forget that the old backup program ever existed.
NEW MS-DOS 6.2 SCANDISK.EXE	Keep. (DOS 6.2 only) ScanDisk disk analysis and repair program. Checks a disk's logical and physical integrity and repairs any errors.
NEW MS-DOS 6.2 SCANDISK.INI	Keep. (DOS 6.2 only) ScanDisk settings information file (ASCII text). Many ScanDisk settings can be customized and controlled from this file.

SETUP.EXE	MS-DOS installation program.
BUSETUP.EXE	Bootable upgrade setup utility program. If you reboot your computer with distribution disk #1 in drive A, BUSETUP will start, check whether your computer has an operating system installed, and refuse to continue if it doesn't. This is Microsoft's way of including a bootable disk in an upgrade-only package. BUSETUP can be run from drive A only .
DOSSETUP.INI	DOS setup information file (binary).
SETUP.MSG	DOS setup messages file (ASCII text).
AUTOEXEC.BAT	DOS setup disk AUTOEXEC.BAT file. Runs BUSETUP.
CONFIG.SYS	DOS setup disk CONFIG.SYS file.
UNINSTALL.EXE	Uninstall utility program. Placed on the UNINSTALL disk created by Setup during installation of MS-DOS 6.
SETVER.EXE	DOS version alias program/device driver. This utility will fool certain programs into believing they are running under a different version of MS-DOS. Setup installs this program on almost every computer; if you don't need this file, it's a waste of memory.
SHARE.EXE	Keep. Utility that provides file sharing and locking support for MS-DOS (TSR). Most people should be running SHARE, especially if they use Microsoft Windows. It can save you from some nasty disk errors.
SMARTDRV.EXE	80286. Disk cache utility program (TSR). SMARTDRV can provide a dramatic speedup for your computer.

SMARTMON.EXE	Windows. Smart monitor, a control program for SMARTDRV that runs under MS Windows. Strangely, there is no DOS counterpart to this program.
SMARTMON.HLP	Windows. Smart monitor on-line help file.
SMARTMON.LOG	Windows. Smart monitor cache hit log file (ASCII text).
SORT.EXE	Sort text filter utility. Useful in batch files.
SPATCH.BAT	Batch file that can patch the Windows 3.0 SWAPFILE.EXE file to make it compatible with DOS 6. Not required if you are running Windows 3.1. You'll find this file on distribution disk #3. See the README.TXT file for details.
SSTOR.SYS	SpeedStor hard disk device driver version 6.3.1. Installed by Setup only if an older version is on the disk.
SUBST.EXE	Remove? Assign drive alias to a subdirectory utility. Use this utility only when you have to, and turn it off when you're finished.
SYS.COM	Keep. Transfer system files utility. Handy for making preformatted disks bootable.
TREE.COM	Display directory structure utility.
UNDELETE.EXE	Keep. Recover deleted files utility. Using the sentry or tracker modes of protection causes UNDELETE to stay resident in memory.
UNDELETE.INI	UNDELETE and MWUNDEL configuration file (ASCII text). It should be located in either the same subdirectory as UNDELETE.EXE or the subdirectory pointed to by the MSDOSDATA environment variable.

UNFORMAT.COM	Utility for restoring an accidentally formatted disk. Uses the information saved on the disk by FORMAT or MIRROR.
VSAFE.COM	Memory resident virus protection program.
WINA20.386	Windows. Windows A20 line support driver. Setup places this file in the root directory. You can move it, but you must update SYSTEM.INI and your CONFIG.SYS file if you do so. Required if you are running Windows in enhanced mode and use any Windows 3.0 device drivers. (This includes most people running Windows 3.1.)
WNTOOLS.GRP	Windows. Windows Program Manager group file. Installed by Setup into the Program Manager if you select to install any Windows version of DOS utilities.
AV.GRP BK.GRP BKAV.GRP BKUD.GRP BKUDAV.GRP UD.GRP UDAV.GRP UDAV.GRP	Depending on which Windows utilities you ask Setup to install, one of these group files is copies and renamed WNTOOLS.GRP.
XCOPY.EXE	Keep. Extended copy utility. Copies files and subdirectories.

MS-DOS 6 Supplemental Disk Files

Microsoft will send you the MS-DOS 6 Supplemental Disk if you request it. It contains utilities that provide enhanced support for people with disabilities, updated copies of commands no longer distributed with the standard MS-DOS package, updated drivers for certain networks, and some example BASIC programs. A batch file is provided (SETUP.BAT) that expands the groups of files you select, as well as updates SETVER. The contents of the Supplemental Disk often change, so what you receive may be different from the following list. This list is for the DOS 6.0 Supplemental Disk with files dated 4/5/93, 6:00 a.m.

Note

In addition to other files listed in this section, the DOS 6.2 Supplemental Disk includes the DOSSHELL program and its related files. DOSSHELL does not come in the MS-DOS 6.2 package.

ADOS.COM	Access DOS program. Provides various utilities designed to assist people with disabilities in using a computer.
ADOS.CFG	Access DOS configuration file.
ADOS.OVL	Access DOS overlay file.
ADOS.TXT	Access DOS instruction manual (ASCII text).
AREADME.TXT	Access DOS last minute information (ASCII text).
FAKEMOUS.COM	IBM PS/2 "No Mouse" utility. See the description of usage in ADOS.TXT.
ASSIGN.COM	DOS 5 disk alias utility program. Assigns an alias drive letter to an existing disk drive. Microsoft is encouraging people to use SUBST instead, but ASSIGN is still the best choice for fooling certain older programs.

BACKUP.EXE	DOS 5 backup utility. Backs up files on your hard disk to a set of floppy disks. This old utility was replaced by the MSBACKUP utility. The continued use of BACKUP should be avoided because it is not reliable.
COMMANDS.TXT	Instructions on how to use the utilities on the DOS 6 Supplemental Disk (ASCII text). This is the manual for this Supplemental Disk.
COMP.EXE	DOS 5 file compare utility. FC, which is distributed with DOS 6, is easier to use and more flexible than COMP.
CV.COM	Replacement loader for Codeview versions 3.0 to 3.13. Using Codeview versions 3.0 to 3.13 without CV.COM may cause data loss if you are using an 80386 memory manager such as EMM386. See COMMANDS.TXT for details.
DBLBOOT.BAT	Batch file to aid in creating a bootable DoubleSpace floppy disk.
DBLBOOT.INI	Prototype INI file used by DBLBOOT.BAT (ASCII text).
DVORAK.SYS	Alternate keyboard layout. Use with KEYB.COM.
DVORAK.TXT	Instructions for using DVORAK.SYS (ASCII text).
EDLIN.EXE	DOS 5 line-oriented text editor. This is an old-fashioned and awkward line editor. Instructions on using EDLIN are included in the COMMANDS.TXT file.

EXE2BIN.EXE	Converts EXE files to binary format. Useful only to programmers who are writing device drivers or COM format utilities and cannot get this service directly from their linker.
GRAFTABL.COM	Supports international characters and code page switching on a CGA video adapter. Not needed for EGA or VGA.
JOIN.EXE	DOS 5 utility that makes a disk drive appear to be a subdirectory of another drive. Many DOS commands will fail, destroy data, or both when used on a joined drive, so run this utility only if you must.
KBDBUF.SYS	A device driver that enables you to specify the size of the keyboard typeahead buffer. Cannot be run in high memory.
LCD.CPI	Code page information file for the IBM PC Convertible's LCD display. Use with DISPLAY.SYS.
MIRROR.COM	DOS 5 utility that saves information UNDELETE and UNFORMAT use when recovering files. Very useful, but it may interfere with creating DoubleSpace drives.
MSHERC.COM	TSR that installs support for a Hercules graphics card. Required by some QBasic programs.
NET.TXT	Supplemental network drivers instruction file (ASCII text). Contains information on when and how to use the following drivers provided on the DOS 6 Supplemental Disk. Note that some files must be renamed before they can be used. Their "real" names

	(which are what you must rename them to before you can use them) are shown in parentheses.
NET.1XE	LAN Manager 2.0 basic version (NET.EXE).
NETBEUI.DOS	LAN Manager 2.0 basic and enhanced version driver.
NETWKSTA.1XE	LAN Manager 1.x enhanced version (NETWKSTA.EXE).
NETWKSTA.2EX	LAN Manager 2.0 enhanced version (NETWKSTA.EXE).
REDIR.1XE	LAN Manager 1.x basic version (REDIR.EXE).
REDIR.2XE	LAN Manager 2.0 basic version (REDIR.EXE). Microsoft MS-NET (REDIR.EXE). 3COM 3+ Share version 1.6 (MSREDIR.EXE).
SETNAME.EXE	Microsoft MS-NET utility.
PRINTER.SYS	Device driver that provides support for international characters and code page switching on certain printers.
4201.CPI	Code page information file for IBM Proprinter II and III model 4201 and XL model 4202.
4208.CPI	Code page information file for IBM Proprinter X24E model 4207 and XL24E model 4208.
5202.CPI	Code page information file for IBM Quietwriter III printer.
PRINTFIX.COM	Utility that prevents MS-DOS from checking the status of your printer. Use only if problems have developed with your printer since installing MS-DOS 6.

QBASIC

GORILLA.BAS	QuickBASIC example program (game).
MONEY.BAS	QuickBASIC example program (personal finance manager).
NIBBLES.BAS	QuickBASIC example program (game).
REMLINE.BAS	QuickBASIC example program (remove line numbers).

MS-DOS Utility File Extensions by Version

Over the years Microsoft has changed the name, the extension, or both of many DOS external utility programs. Table A.1 lists these changes. The blank entries indicate when Microsoft started or stopped distributing a particular utility. If you are in the habit of entering full path names for programs in your batch files, a quick glance at the last few rows will show you which of your batch files you must edit.

Table A.1 File Name Extension by Version

File	1.x	2.0	2.1	3.0 3.1	3.2	3.3	4.0	5.0	6.0	6.2
APPEND						EXE	EXE	EXE	EXE	EXE
ASSIGN		COM	COM	COM	COM	COM	COM	COM		
ATTRIB				EXE	EXE	EXE	EXE	EXE	EXE	EXE
BACKUP		COM	COM	COM	COM	COM	COM	EXE		
BASIC*	COM	COM	COM	COM	COM					
BASICA*	EXE	EXE	EXE	EXE	EXE					
CHKDSK	COM	COM	COM	COM	COM	COM	COM	EXE	EXE	EXE
CHOICE									COM	COM
COMMAND	COM	COM	COM	COM	COM	COM	COM	COM	COM	COM

File	1.x	2.0	2.1	3.0 3.1	3.2	3.3	4.0	5.0	6.0	6.2
COMP**	COM	COM	COM	COM	COM	COM	COM	EXE		
DBLSPACE									EXE	EXE
DEBUG	COM	COM	COM	COM	COM	COM	COM	EXE	EXE	EXE
DEFRAG									EXE	EXE
DELTREE									EXE	EXE
DELOLDDOS								EXE	EXE	EXE
DISKCOMP	COM	COM	COM	COM	COM	COM	COM	COM	COM	COM
DISKCOPY	COM	COM	COM	COM	COM	COM	COM	COM	COM	COM
DOSKEY								COM	COM	COM
DOSSHELL							BAT	COM	COM	
EDIT								COM	COM	COM
EDLIN	COM	COM	COM	COM	COM	COM	COM	EXE		
EMM386								EXE	EXE	EXE
EXE2BIN	EXE	EXE	EXE	EXE	EXE	EXE	EXE	EXE		
EXPAND								EXE	EXE	EXE
FASTHELP									EXE	EXE
FASTOPEN						EXE	EXE	EXE	EXE	EXE
FC**						EXE	EXE	EXE	EXE	EXE
FDISK		COM	COM	COM	COM	COM	EXE	EXE	EXE	EXE
FILESYS							EXE			
FIND		EXE	EXE	EXE	EXE	EXE	EXE	EXE	EXE	EXE
FORMAT	COM	COM	COM	COM	COM	COM	COM	COM	COM	COM
GRAFTABL				COM	COM	COM	COM	COM		
GRAPHICS		COM		COM	COM	COM	COM	COM	COM	COM
GWBASIC*						EXE	EXE			

(continues)

Table A.1 Continued

File	1.x	2.0	2.1	3.0 3.1	3.2	3.3	4.0	5.0	6.0	6.2
IFSFUNC							EXE			
INTERLNK									EXE	EXE
INTERSVR									EXE	EXE
HELP								EXE	EXE	EXE
JOIN					EXE	EXE	EXE	EXE		
KEYB						COM	COM	COM	COM	COM
KEYBFR				COM	COM					
KEYBGR				COM	COM					
KEYBIT				COM	COM					
KEYBSP				COM	COM					
KEYBUK				COM	COM					
LABEL				COM	COM	COM	COM	EXE	EXE	EXE
LINK	EXE	EXE	EXE	EXE	EXE	EXE	EXE			
LOADFIX								COM	COM	COM
MEM							EXE	EXE	EXE	EXE
MEMMAKER									EXE	EXE
MIRROR								COM		
MODE	COM	COM	COM	COM	COM	COM	COM	COM	COM	COM
MORE		COM	COM	COM	COM	COM	COM	COM	COM	COM
MOVE									EXE	EXE
MSAV									EXE	EXE
MSBACKUP									EXE	EXE
MSD									EXE	EXE
MWAV									EXE	EXE
MWAVTSR									EXE	EXE

File	1.x	2.0	2.1	3.0 3.1	3.2	3.3	4.0	5.0	6.0	6.2
MWBACKUP									EXE	EXE
MWUNDEL									EXE	EXE
NLSFUNC						EXE	EXE	EXE	EXE	EXE
POWER									EXE	EXE
PRINT		COM	COM	COM	COM	COM	COM	EXE	EXE	EXE
QBASIC								EXE	EXE	EXE
RECOVER		COM	COM	COM	COM	COM	COM	EXE		
REPLACE				EXE		EXE	EXE	EXE	EXE	EXE
RESTORE		COM	COM	COM	COM	COM	COM	EXE	EXE	EXE
SCANDISK										EXE
SELECT				COM	COM	COM	COM			
SETVER								EXE	EXE	EXE
SHARE				EXE	EXE	EXE	EXE	EXE	EXE	EXE
SMARTDRV							SYS	SYS	EXE	EXE
SMARTMON									EXE	EXE
SORT		EXE	EXE	EXE	EXE	EXE	EXE	EXE	EXE	EXE
SUBST					EXE	EXE	EXE	EXE	EXE	EXE
SYS	COM	COM	COM	COM	COM	COM	COM	COM	COM	COM
TREE		COM	COM	COM	COM	COM	COM	COM	COM	COM
UNDELETE								EXE	EXE	EXE
UNFORMAT								COM	COM	COM
VSAFE									COM	COM
XCOPY						EXE	EXE	EXE	EXE	EXE

* *BASICA (Advanced BASIC) was often distributed as both an EXE file and a small COM loader program. Also, some OEMs used the GWBASIC name long before Microsoft started calling it that, often including BASIC.COM and BASICA.COM loader files so users could type the same command to start BASIC on any computer. (Industry legend has it that the* GW *in GWBASIC stands for* gee whiz.*)*

** *FC and COMP have had a confusing journey through the various DOS versions. COMP was originally included by IBM with PC DOS 1.0 and then disappeared in subsequent IBM releases, reappearing officially in MS-DOS 3.3. During this period many OEMs added utilities to their versions of MS-DOS. A popular add-on was COMP, often under a different name (such as FILCOM, FC, or COMPARE). Even the generic Microsoft MS-DOS often included some type of file compare utility. Mapping all these variations would be overly complicated, so the table just indicates that COMP has been with DOS since the beginning.*

Appendix B

DOS Environment Variables

The *environment* is a small area in memory that DOS sets aside for storing text variables. Normally, you set the size of the master environment area with a SHELL= statement in your CONFIG.SYS file. The default size of the environment is 256 bytes, but you almost certainly will want to increase this as you begin to use environment variables to automate your daily tasks.

Each variable in the environment consists of two parts: the name of the variable, which DOS stores in uppercase characters, and the contents of the variable, which is the text associated with the variable. Normally, you view, create, and replace environment variables with the SET command. The PATH and PROMPT commands store their settings in the environment. MS-DOS automatically creates certain environment variables, such as COMSPEC and CONFIG, when you start up your computer.

Whenever DOS loads a program into memory, it makes a copy of the current environment and passes this copy to the program. This copy is only big enough to include the variables currently defined in the environment, rounded up to an even multiple of 16 bytes. Although this is an efficient use of memory, it is inconvenient for people who normally operate from a shell program such as DOSShell, Norton Commander, or XTree because there isn't much environment space available no matter how large an environment area you set aside. If you get an `Out of environment space` message while you are running a shell program, quit the shell and try the operation again. If you still receive an error message, you must increase the size of the master environment with the SHELL= statement in your CONFIG.SYS file.

The following sections list the standard environment variables used by MS-DOS. Also noted is the version of DOS in which the variable first appeared as well as the creator of the variable. An *MS-DOS* label indicates that this variable is created automatically when your computer starts up. A *User* label indicates that you must create it with the SET command or, for certain variables, with the PATH, PROMPT, or APPEND command. A *Windows* label indicates that the environment variable is created by Microsoft Windows.

APPEND — 3.3 and later—User

The APPEND environment variable is created by DOS if you specify the /E parameter when loading APPEND into memory. With the /E parameter, APPEND stores the appended directory search path in the environment instead of internally.

This variable is stored much like the PATH variable. It is a list of subdirectories to be searched, separated by semicolons. If the APPEND environment variable is created with the SET command, it might appear like this:

```
SET APPEND=C:\DOS;C:\WS
```

When you instruct APPEND to store the appended directory search path in the environment, you can change or replace the search path with the SET command as well as with the APPEND command.

Note that APPEND /E will not work if you are launching programs that must search the appended directory search path from a shell program such as DOSShell, Norton Commander, or XTree. In such cases, APPEND must store the appended directory search path internally.

COMSPEC — 2.0 and later—MS-DOS

The COMSPEC variable points to the active copy of the command interpreter shell loaded with the SHELL= command in your CONFIG.SYS file. All of COMMAND.COM isn't in memory all the time; when parts of it must be reloaded, the COMSPEC variable is used to find the COMMAND.COM file on disk.

In the following SHELL= command, COMMAND.COM sets the COMSPEC variable using the C:\DOS\ parameter that follows the command interpreter's name:

```
SHELL=C:\DOS\COMMAND.COM C:\DOS\ /E:512 /P
```

DOS executes the SHELL= command at the end of CONFIG.SYS processing. When it does, COMMAND.COM sets the COMSPEC variable in the environment as if it had executed SET COMSPEC=C:\DOS\COMMAND.COM. (Note that COMMAND.COM doesn't actually use the SET command.)

Many programs search the environment for the COMSPEC variable when they must locate COMMAND.COM. If you have trouble shelling to a DOS prompt from one of your application programs, check the COMSPEC environment variable and make sure that it's pointing to a valid copy of COMMAND.COM.

CONFIG — 6.0 and later—MS-DOS

When MS-DOS processes a startup menu in CONFIG.SYS, it defines the CONFIG environment variable, setting it equal to the block name of the menu item you selected. You can use the CONFIG environment variable with GOTO and IF in your AUTOEXEC.BAT file to continue making choices based on the configuration chosen in the start-up menu.

For example, assume that your CONFIG.SYS file includes the following start-up menu.

```
[MENU]
MENUITEM=WIN, Configure for Windows (default)
MENUITEM=DOS, Configure for MS-DOS
MENUITEM=MAINT, Configure for file & disk maintenance
MENUDEFAULT=WIN, 10
```

The CONFIG environment variable is set equal to WIN, DOS, or MAINT, depending on which configuration you select when your computer displays the start-up menu. In your AUTOEXEC.BAT file, you can check this value and process different commands for each configuration. For example, you might set up separate sections for each start-up configuration, and label them with the block names you used in your CONFIG.SYS file, which in this case would be :WIN, :DOS, and :MAINT. (For more information on block names, see the [blockname] entry in the Command Reference section.) Then a simple GOTO statement like the following might be all you need to jump to the correct section of your AUTOEXEC.BAT file:

```
GOTO %CONFIG%
```

A slightly safer method is to check each value with an IF statement, and report an error if an unexpected value for CONFIG is encountered:

```
IF %CONFIG%x==WINx GOTO WIN
IF %CONFIG%x==DOSx GOTO DOS
IF %CONFIG%x==MAINTx GOTO MAINT
GOTO ERROR
```

The use of x prevents the generation of an error message if the CONFIG environment variable is null or undefined. When using an IF comparison, always include a character (any character will do) that prevents one side of the equation from being empty.

COPYCMD — 6.2 and later—User

Starting with MS-DOS 6.2, COPY, MOVE, and XCOPY all prompt for confirmation before overwriting a file. Because this behavior might wreak havoc with your old batch files, this is the default behavior only when these commands are run from the command line. If COPY, MOVE, or XCOPY is run from a batch file, it overwrites files without warning, which is its behavior in previous versions of DOS.

You can change the new default behavior by defining an environment variable named COPYCMD. To force COPY, MOVE, and XCOPY to prompt you before overwriting a file in all cases, even from a batch file, add the following line to your AUTOEXEC.BAT file:

```
SET COPYCMD=/-Y
```

To prevent COPY, MOVE, and XCOPY from prompting before overwriting a file, add the following line to your AUTOEXEC.BAT file:

```
SET COPYCMD=/Y
```

DIRCMD 5.0 and later—User

You use the DIRCMD environment variable to customize the default options the DIR command will use. When you run the DIR command, the contents of the DIRCMD environment variable—if it exists—are added invisibly to what you type on the command line.

Suppose that you prefer file names in lowercase letters, sorted by directories and then sorted by date and time. You also want the screen to pause after each page of files is displayed. You could define the DIRCMD variable in your AUTOEXEC.BAT file as follows:

```
SET DIRCMD=/L /O:GD /P
```

Now you don't have to enter those options every time you want to use them. To override these options, specify the switch with a hyphen added before the letter. For example, to turn off the pause option in your customized DIR command, enter the following command:

```
DIR /-P
```

Note that overriding options this way is temporary, and only changes the behavior of the command in which the override switch appears.

MSDOSDATA 6.0 and later—User

The MSDOSDATA environment variable defines where certain DOS utility programs look for their data files. Defining this variable can make it easier to keep programs and data separate on your hard disk. It can make it easier also to run these utility programs from a network using individual configuration files.

The most convenient place to define the MSDOSDATA variable is in your AUTOEXEC.BAT file with a SET command. For example:

```
SET MSDOSDATA=C:\DOS\DATA
```

This sets MSDOSDATA to point to the C:\DOS\DATA subdirectory on your hard drive. Note that this subdirectory has to exist first; the SET command will not create it for you.

Table B.1 is a list of the MS-DOS programs that create data files as well as the locations where the programs look for the data files.

Table B.1 Data File Search Paths

Program	Data File	Primary Location	Secondary Location
DBLSPACE	DBLSPACE.INF	Program directory	
	DBLSPACE.INI	Program directory	
DOSSHELL	DOSSHELL.INI	DOSSHELL	Program directory
MEMMAKER	MEMMAKER.INI	Program directory	
	MEMMAKER.STS	Program directory	
MSAV	CHKLST.MS	All directories	
	MSAV.INI	MSDOSDATA	Program directory
MSBACKUP	MSBACKUP.INI	MSDOSDATA	Program directory
	*.DIF	MSDOSDATA	Program directory
	*.FUL	MSDOSDATA	Program directory
	*.INC	MSDOSDATA	Program directory
	*.SET	MSDOSDATA	Program directory
	*.SLT	MSDOSDATA	Program directory
MWAV	MWAV.INI	MSDOSDATA	Program directory
MWBACKUP	MWBACKUP.INI	Windows directory	
	*.DIF	MSDOSDATA	Program directory
	*.FUL	MSDOSDATA	Program directory
	*.INC	MSDOSDATA	Program directory
	*.SET	MSDOSDATA	Program directory
	*.SLT	MSDOSDATA	Program directory
MWUNDEL	UNDELETE.INI	MSDOSDATA	Program directory
SCANDISK	SCANDISK.INI	MSDOSDATA	Program directory
UNDELETE	UNDELETE.INI	MSDOSDATA	Program directory

In table B.1, *program directory* refers to the directory that the executable program file is located in. Locations shown in all caps are environment variables that point to subdirectories. Programs that list both a primary and secondary location search for the data file in the primary location first.

If you set up a separate data subdirectory for MS-DOS, you may need to move some of these data files from your DOS subdirectory to that subdirectory. See the MOVE command in the command reference section for details about how to move a file.

PATH 2.0 and later—User

The PATH command stores its settings in the DOS environment under the PATH variable name. (You can set the path with either the PATH command or the SET command.) You probably will want to set the initial DOS search path in your AUTOEXEC.BAT file. DOS does not define a default PATH automatically, although the Setup program for DOS 6 does insert the PATH command in your AUTOEXEC.BAT file if you don't have one there already.

DOS uses the PATH environment variable to find executable files. Whenever a command is executed, DOS searches for the first "word" on the command line in

- The DOSKey macro list, if DOSKey is loaded
- The COMMAND.COM internal command list
- Files with an extension of .COM, then .EXE, then .BAT in the current directory
- Files with an extension of .COM, then .EXE, then .BAT in the first directory listed in the PATH variable
- Files with an extension of .COM, then .EXE, then .BAT in the second directory listed in the PATH variable
- Files with an extension of .COM, then .EXE, then .BAT in the next directory listed in the PATH variable, and so on until the last subdirectory in the PATH variable has been searched

This order can be modified depending on what parts of the full path name you enter with the command name. If you specify a drive or path with the file name, only that drive and path are searched. If you specify an extension, the other extensions are not searched for. The DOSKey macro and internal command search are skipped if you include a disk drive or a path that includes a backslash in the name of the command, but not if you include only an extension.

Other programs may search the PATH variable as well. Programs that require the addition of their subdirectory to the PATH often use the PATH environment variable to find overlay and help files.

PROMPT — 2.0 and later—User

The PROMPT environment variable describes the type of command-line prompt you want DOS to use. It is set by the user with either the PROMPT command or the SET PROMPT= command. The default command-line prompt that DOS uses if the PROMPT environment variable is undefined is the letter of the current drive and >; for example, C>.

If the PROMPT environment variable doesn't exist, the DOS 6.0 and 6.2 versions of COMMAND.COM create it automatically with a value of PG. This prompt shows the current directory as well as the current drive; for example, C:\DOS>. The only way to have the PROMPT environment variable undefined is to delete it.

The PROMPT environment variable uses meta-strings to include system information in the command prompt. For a description of which meta-strings are available and how they can be used, see the entry for PROMPT in the Command Reference.

TEMP and TMP — 5.0 and later—User

Many programs use the TEMP environment variable as the preferred place to create and delete temporary files. This environment variable evolved somewhat informally, which is why there are two popular spellings: TEMP and TMP. TEMP is the more common variation and is the one DOS uses. Typically, if the TEMP environment variable isn't defined, the program creates its temporary files in the root directory of the current drive (or sometimes the start-up drive).

DOS creates the following types of files in the directory pointed to by the TEMP environment variable:

- Files required by the use of redirection (< and >) or piping (¦)
- Swap files created by the DOSShell Task Swapper
- Temporary files created by any full-screen application program, such as MSAV, MSBACKUP, and QBASIC

- (DOS 6.2 only) Temporary disk data storage for DISKCOPY
- Microsoft Windows Print Manager spooling files
- Microsoft Windows swapping files (standard mode only)

Many programs use the TEMP environment variable if it is defined. Temporary files that escape deletion by their parent program are easier to delete when they are gathered in their own subdirectory. Windows recommends at least 2M in the subdirectory pointed to by the TEMP environment variable. (If you point TEMP to a RAM disk, you'll never have to worry about deleting leftover temporary files. They will all disappear whenever you reboot or turn off your computer.)

windir

Windows

Microsoft Windows adds the windir environment variable whenever you open a DOS window. The windir environment variable always points to the main Windows directory, which is normally C:\WINDOWS. If you issue the SET command to view the variables defined in a DOS window launched from Windows, the list might look like the following:

```
COMSPEC=C:\DOS\COMMAND.COM
PROMPT=$P$G
PATH=C:\BAT;C:\DOS;C:\WINDOWS;C:\UTIL
TEMP=C:\TEMP
TMP=C:\TEMP
windir=C:\WINDOWS
```

Windows adds the windir variable to the environment in lowercase letters to keep you from modifying or deleting it. If you issue a SET windir= command, SET capitalizes the variable name before searching for it, and a new variable named WINDIR is created.

WINPMT

User

If the WINPMT variable is defined, Microsoft Windows uses it to format the DOS prompt displayed in a DOS window. Using a different DOS prompt from Windows can help you remember that Windows is running and that you should type EXIT and quit Windows with Alt-F4 before shutting off your computer.

To use the WINPMT environment variable, define WINPMT with the SET command (perhaps in your AUTOEXEC.BAT file) before you start Microsoft Windows. Set WINPMT equal to the prompt you want to use from Windows, using the same formatting you would use with the PROMPT command.

For example, you could define the Windows prompt as a simple reminder:

```
SET WINPMT=**Windows** $P$G
```

This results in the following prompt in a DOS window:

```
**Windows** C:\DOS>
```

Use the following if you prefer a more direct reminder of how to close a DOS window:

```
SET  WINPMT=**Type EXIT to return to Windows** $P$G
```

This results in the following prompt in a DOS window:

```
**Type EXIT to return to Windows** C:\DOS>
```

Appendix C

DOS Messages

DOS messages can be divided into two groups: general error messages and device error messages. This appendix first lists general messages, which are the larger group, and then lists device error messages. Both lists are organized alphabetically.

General DOS Messages

There are three groups of general DOS messages: error messages, warning messages, and information messages. *Error messages* indicate that DOS has encountered a problem with a command or with the syntax you used. Execution stops when DOS displays an error message. *Warning messages* tell you that the next action you take may cause unwanted changes to files or to your system and often include a prompt, which enables you to select an action. *Information messages* display needed information about your system's operation or your DOS version's performance. Like warning messages, these messages also often include a prompt.

The messages in this section may appear any time during a work session. Messages that can occur when you start DOS are indicated by "(start-up)". With most start-up errors, DOS does not start and you must reboot the system.

`d contains n non-contiguous blocks`

Warning: CHKDSK found noncontiguous blocks on drive *d*. If you like, you can use a defragmenter to eliminate the fragmentation, or use COPY or XCOPY to transfer the fragmented files to a freshly formatted floppy disk in a sequential form.

`A BAD UMB number has been specified`

Error: You have attempted a LOADHIGH (or LH) with the /L parameter referring to a nonexistent UMB area. The best way to correct this is to rerun MEMMAKER.

```
A program was run that took memory that Backup requires
The program must be removed from memory before Backup can continue
```

Error: You have installed a TSR (terminate-and-stay resident program) that leaves insufficient memory for BACKUP. Examples of this are PRINT or some forms of MODE. The resident program must be unloaded before you can continue the backup. Use MEM /C to see which TSR was loaded last.

`Access denied`

Error: You or a program attempted to change or erase a file that is in use or marked as read-only. You can change the read-only attribute with the ATTRIB command.

`Active code page: xxx`

Information: You issued CHCP, which displayed the code page currently in use by the system (represented by *xxx*).

`Active code page for device ddd is xxx`

Information: You issued MODE, which lists the code page (*xxx*) currently in use for the device (*ddd*). To display a single screen at a time, pipe this command into MORE (MODE¦MORE).

`Active code page not available from CON device`

Error: You used KEYB with a code page not supported on the CON device (screen).

`Add filename? (Y/N)`

Prompt: You issued REPLACE /P. DOS asks whether you want to add the file to the disk.

`Adding filename`

Information: REPLACE displays this message while adding *filename* to your disk.

`All available space in the Extended DOS Partition is assigned to logical drives`

Error: No room remains for logical drives in the extended partition. Use FDISK to change the size of the extended partition.

`All files canceled by operator`

Information: You issued PRINT /T, which removes all files from the print queue.

```
All files in directory will be deleted!
Are you sure (Y/N)?
```

Warning: You issued DEL or ERASE with the *.* wildcard. To continue, press Y; to cancel, press N. Then press the Enter key.

`All logical drives deleted in the Extended DOS Partition`

Information: While using FDISK, you removed all logical drives associated with the extended DOS partition.

`All specified file(s) are contiguous`

Information: None of the files you specified (to CHKDSK) are fragmented.

`Allocation error, size adjusted`

Warning: The contents of a file have been truncated because the size indicated in the directory is inconsistent with the amount of data allocated to the file. Use SCANDISK or CHKDSK /F to correct the discrepancy.

`An incompatible DOSKey is already installed`

Error: The version of DOSKey you are trying to run is incompatible with the one in memory. Make sure you don't mix the DOSKEY.COM that comes with DOS 6.0 with the version that comes with DOS 6.2 or another vendor's command-line editor.

`ANSI.SYS must be installed to perform requested function`

Warning: While using MODE, you requested a screen function that cannot be performed until you load ANSI.SYS.

`APPEND already installed`

Information: You tried to issue APPEND with /X or /E after previously using APPEND. You can use the /E switch only the first time you type APPEND after starting your system. You can use the /X switch only if it was used during initialization.

`APPEND/ASSIGN conflict`

Warning: You cannot use APPEND on an assigned drive. Cancel the drive assignment before using APPEND with this drive.

`ATTENTION: A serious disk error has occurred while writing to drive`

Error: SMARTDRV has detected a hard disk error when write caching was enabled. Because the application may have already continued with something else, the usual corrections don't apply. Write caching must be enabled for only reliable media.

`/B invalid with a black and white printer`

Error: You tried to print the background color by using GRAPHICS /B, but you do not have a color printer connected to your computer.

`***Backing up files to drive x:***`

Information: This message appears while you back up files to the specified drive.

`Bad command or file name`

Error: You entered an invalid name for invoking a command, program, or batch file. The most frequent causes are misspelling a name, omitting a required disk drive or path name, or omitting the command name when giving parameters (for example, omitting the WordStar command, WS, by typing MYFILE instead of WS MYFILE).

Check the spelling on the command line and make sure that the command, program, or batch file is in the location specified. Then try the command again.

`Bad or missing command interpreter`

Error (start-up): DOS does not start because it cannot find COMMAND.COM, the command interpreter.

If this message appears during start-up, COMMAND.COM is not on the start-up disk or a COMMAND.COM file from a previous version of DOS is on the disk. If you used the SHELL command in CONFIG.SYS, the message means that the SHELL command is improperly phrased or that COMMAND.COM is not where you specified.

With DOS 6.0 or 6.2 you can override CONFIG.SYS using the F8 or F5 key while booting. This solution works if the correct COMMAND.COM is in the root directory. Otherwise, place another disk that contains the operating system (IO.SYS, MSDOS.SYS, and COMMAND.COM) in the floppy disk drive and reset the system. After DOS starts, copy COMMAND.COM to the original start-up disk so that you can boot DOS in the future.

Error: If this message appears while you are running DOS, there are several possibilities: COMMAND.COM has been erased from the disk and directory you used when starting DOS, a version of COMMAND.COM from a previous version of DOS has overwritten the good version, or the COMSPEC entry in the environment has been changed. You must restart DOS by resetting the system.

If resetting the system does not solve your problem, restart the computer from a copy of your DOS master disk. Copy COMMAND.COM from this disk to the offending disk.

`Bad or missing filename`

Warning (start-up): The device driver file name was not found, an error occurred when the device driver was loaded, a break address for the device driver was beyond the RAM available to the computer, or DOS detected an error while loading the driver into memory. DOS continues booting without the device driver file name.

If DOS loads, check your CONFIG.SYS file for the line DEVICE=filename. Make sure that the line is typed correctly and that the device driver is at the specified location; then reboot the system. If the message reappears, copy the file from its original disk to the boot disk and try starting DOS again. If the error persists, the device driver is bad; contact the dealer or publisher who sold you the driver.

`Bad or missing keyboard definition file`

Warning: DOS cannot find KEYBOARD.SYS as specified by the KEYB command. Solving this problem may take several steps. First, check to make sure that KEYBOARD.SYS exists and is in the correct path; then retype the KEYB command. If you get the same message, KEYB.COM or KEYBOARD.SYS may be corrupted.

`Bad partition table`

Error: While using FORMAT, DOS was unable to find a DOS partition on the fixed disk you specified. Run FDISK and create a DOS partition on this fixed-disk drive.

`Batch file missing`

Error: DOS could not find the batch file it was processing. The batch file may have been erased or renamed. With DOS 3.0 only, the disk containing the batch file may have been changed, causing DOS to abort processing of the batch file.

If you are using DOS 3.0 and you changed the disk that contains the batch file, restart the batch file without changing the disk. You may need to edit the batch file so that you do not need to change disks. This procedure applies only to DOS 3.0.

If the batch file includes a RENAME command that causes the originating batch file name to change, edit the batch file to prevent renaming when the batch file is processed again. If the file was erased, re-create the batch file from its backup file if possible. Edit the file to ensure that the batch file does not erase itself.

`Baud rate required`

Error: When using MODE COM*x* commands to set any COM port parameters, you must at least indicate the baud rate.

`BREAK is off`

`BREAK is on`

Information: When you use BREAK by itself, one of these messages displays the current BREAK setting. You can set BREAK at the command line or in CONFIG.SYS.

`Cannot change BUFSIZE`

Error: When DOSKey has been loaded into memory, you cannot change the buffer size.

`Cannot CHDIR to path - tree past this point not processed`

Error: CHKDSK was unable to go to the specified directory. No subdirectories below this directory are verified. Run SCANDISK or CHKDSK /F to correct this error.

`Cannot CHDIR to root`

Error: CHKDSK was checking the tree structure of the directory and was unable to return to the root directory. Remaining subdirectories were not checked. Restart DOS. If the message continues to display, the disk is unusable and must be reformatted.

`Cannot CHKDSK a network drive`

Warning: You cannot use CHKDSK to check drives redirected over the network.

`Cannot CHKDSK a SUBSTed or ASSIGNed drive`

Warning: You cannot use CHKDSK to check substituted or assigned drives.

`Cannot create a zero size partition`

Error: While using FDISK, you tried to create a partition of zero percent (0 megabytes). To correct this error, you must allocate one percent (or a minimum of 1M) of hard disk space to any partition you create.

`Cannot create extended DOS partition without primary DOS partition on disk x`

Error: While using FDISK, you tried to create an extended DOS partition before giving your first fixed-disk drive a primary DOS partition. To correct this problem, simply create a DOS partition on your first fixed-disk drive. When this operation is complete, you can create an extended DOS partition if you have room on this disk or if you have a second fixed disk.

`Cannot create logical DOS drive without an Extended DOS Partition on the current drive`

Error: When using FDISK, you must create an extended DOS partition before you can create a logical drive.

`Cannot DISKCOMP to or from a network drive`

Error: You cannot compare disks on any disk drive that has been reassigned to a network.

`Cannot delete Extended DOS Partition while logical drives exist`

Error: When using FDISK to delete an extended DOS partition, you first must remove any logical drives.

`Cannot DISKCOPY to or from a network drive`

Error: You attempted to copy a floppy disk to a drive that was redirected to a computer network. DISKCOPY does not copy disks directly to a networked disk drive. Use COPY to copy the disk.

`Cannot do binary reads from a device`

Error: You tried to copy from a device by using the /B switch. To complete the copy process, use the ASCII (/A) switch to create an ASCII copy. You can also use the COPY command without the /B switch.

`Cannot find file QBASIC.EXE`

Error: EDIT.COM or HELP.COM cannot find the QBASIC.EXE program file. QBASIC must be available to EDIT a file or access the MS-DOS online HELP system.

`Cannot find GRAPHICS profile`

Error: You did not give the path of the GRAPHICS.PRO file; DOS could not find it in the current directory.

`Cannot find System files`

Error: While running FORMAT, you specified a drive that did not have the system files in the root directory.

`Cannot FORMAT a network drive`

Error: You tried to format a disk in a drive being used by a network.

`Cannot FORMAT an ASSIGNed or SUBSTed drive`

Error: You attempted to format a drive that was mapped to another drive with ASSIGN or SUBST. To perform a successful format, you must run ASSIGN or SUBST again to clear the drive assignments.

`Cannot LABEL a JOINed, SUBSTed or ASSIGNed drive`

Error: You attempted to label a drive created with JOIN, SUBST, or ASSIGN.

`Cannot LABEL a network drive`

Error: You cannot use LABEL with drives redirected over the network.

`Cannot load COMMAND, system halted`

Error: DOS attempted to reload COMMAND.COM, but the area where DOS keeps track of memory was destroyed or the command processor was not found in the directory specified by the COMSPEC= entry. The system halts.

This message may indicate that COMMAND.COM was erased from the disk and directory you used when starting DOS, or that the COMSPEC= entry in the environment has been changed. Restart DOS from your usual start-up disk. If DOS does not start, the copy of COMMAND.COM has been erased. Restart DOS from the DOS start-up or master disk, and copy COMMAND.COM to your usual start-up disk.

Alternatively, an errant program may have corrupted the memory allocation table where DOS tracks available memory. Try running the same program that was in the computer when the system halted. If the problem occurs again, the program is defective. Contact the dealer or publisher who sold you the program.

`Cannot loadhigh batch file`

Warning: The LOADHIGH (or LH) command is used only for TSR programs. Batch files may not be run this way.

`Cannot move multiple files to a single file`

Error: When using MOVE with wildcards for the source file specification, you must specify a directory for the destination. The most common cause of this error is a misspelled name.

```
Cannot perform a cyclic copy
```

Error: When using XCOPY /S, you cannot specify a target that is a subdirectory of the source. You may use a temporary disk or file to bypass this limitation if the directory tree structure allows a temporary disk or file.

```
Cannot recover .. entry
Entry has a bad attribute (or link or size)
```

Error, Warning: The .. entry (the parent directory) is defective and cannot be recovered. If you have specified the /F switch, CHKDSK tries to correct the error.

```
Cannot set up expanded memory
```

Error: FASTOPEN cannot correctly access expanded memory (EMS).

```
Cannot specify default drive
```

Error: You specified the default drive as a SYS destination. Switch to another drive before issuing the SYS command.

```
Cannot start COMMAND, exiting
```

Error: You or one of your programs directed DOS to load another copy of COMMAND.COM, but DOS could not load it. Your CONFIG.SYS FILES command is set too low, or you do not have enough free memory for another copy of COMMAND.COM.

If your system has 256K or more and FILES is less than 10, edit the CONFIG.SYS file on your start-up disk, using FILES=15 or FILES=20. Then restart DOS.

If the problem recurs, you do not have enough memory in your computer, or you have too many resident or background programs competing for memory space. Restart DOS, loading only the essential programs. If necessary, eliminate unneeded device drivers or RAM disk software. You also can obtain additional RAM for your system.

```
Cannot SUBST a network drive
```

Error: You cannot substitute drives redirected over the network.

`Cannot SYS a network drive`

Error: You cannot transfer system files to drives redirected over the network.

`Cannot use FASTOPEN for drive x`

Error: You attempted to use FASTOPEN over a network, with a floppy disk drive, or with more than four disks at one time.

`Cannot use PRINT - Use NET PRINT`

Error: You tried to use PRINT over the network. Use NET PRINT, or consult your system administrator for the correct procedure for printing files over the network.

`Cannot XCOPY from a reserved device`

`Cannot XCOPY to a reserved device`

Error: The specified XCOPY source or target is a character device (printer), an asynchronous communication device, or NULL. You must specify a file or block device as your source and your target.

`CHDIR .. failed, trying alternate method`

Warning: CHKDSK was unable to return to a parent directory while checking the tree structure. CHKDSK attempts to return to the parent directory by starting over at the root and repeating the search.

`Code page not prepared`

Error: While using MODE, you selected a code page not yet prepared for the system or without the correct font to support the current video mode. To correct this error, prepare a code page using the MODE PREPARE command. If you have installed the DISPLAY.SYS installable device driver, make sure that the DEVICE command line in your CONFIG.SYS file allows additional subfonts.

`Code page xxx`

Information: This message displays the code page currently in use by the specified device. If you type MODE CON, for example, the message returns the code page in use for your screen.

`Code page xxx not prepared for all devices`

Error: While using CHCP, you selected a code page not currently supported by a device. To correct this error, first make sure that your device supports code-page switching and that it is on-line. Then issue the MODE PREPARE command to ready the device for the code page. You are ready to retry CHCP.

`Code page xxx not prepared for system`

Error: CHCP is unable to select a code page for the system. If NLSFUNC is installed and your CONFIG.SYS file does not install device drivers, you can retry CHCP. If CONFIG.SYS installs device drivers, you must issue the MODE PREPARE command to prepare the specific code page for each device before retrying the CHCP command.

`Code page operation not supported on this device`

Error: While using MODE, you selected a device and code page combination not recognized by DOS. Make sure that you specified a valid device and code page and that the code page you selected is supported on the device.

`Code page requested (xxx) is not valid for given keyboard code`

Error: You selected an incompatible keyboard code and code page combination. Reenter the KEYB command with a valid keyboard code and code page.

`Code page specified has not been prepared`

Error: You issued the KEYB command with an unrecognized code page. Prepare the code page for your CON (console screen device) by using the MODE PREPARE command; then retry KEYB.

`Code page specified is inconsistent with selected code page`

Warning: You used KEYB with an option incompatible with the code page for your console screen device. Specify a compatible option, or issue the MODE select command to change the code page for your console screen device.

`Code pages cannot be prepared`

Error: You attempted to use a duplicate code page for the specified device; or with MODE PREPARE, you specified more code pages than DOS supports for that device. Check CONFIG.SYS to see how many prepared code pages your device command line allows, or issue MODE /STATUS at the command line to view the code pages already prepared for the device (for example, MODE /STATUS CON).

`Compare error at offset xxxxxxxx`

Information: The files you are comparing are not the same. The difference occurs *xxxxxxxx* bytes from the beginning of the file. The number of bytes as well as the values for the differing bytes are given in hexadecimal format (base 16).

`Compare error on side s, track t`

Information: DISKCOMP has located a difference on the disk in the specified drive on side *s* at track *t*.

`Compare process ended`

Error: A fatal error occurred during the comparison operation.

`Comparing t tracks n sectors per track, s side(s)`

Information: This message confirms the format of the disks you are comparing.

`Configuration too large for memory`

Error (start-up): DOS could not load because you set too many files or buffers in your CONFIG.SYS file or specified too large an environment area (/E) with the SHELL command. This problem occurs only on systems with less than 256K.

Restart DOS with a different configuration; then edit the CONFIG.SYS file on your boot disk, lowering the number of files, or buffers, or both. You also can edit CONFIG.SYS to reduce the size of the environment in addition to or as an alternative to lowering the number of files and buffers. Restart DOS with the edited disk.

Another alternative is to increase the RAM in your system.

`Content of destination lost before copy`

Error: The original contents of the destination file for the COPY (concatenation) operation were overwritten because the destination and one of the source files had the same name. You may be able to recover the file with UNDELETE; if not, you can restore the destination file from your backup disk.

`Copy process ended`

Error: The DISKCOPY process ended before completion. Test with SCANDISK or CHKDSK, and then copy the remaining files onto the disk with COPY or XCOPY.

`Current code page settings:`

Information: You issued the MODE command and specified a device with code page support. MODE displays the active code page, the hardware code page, other prepared code pages, and the space available for additional code pages on the lines that follow the message. If you want to see status information for all devices, type MODE without listing a device.

`Current CON code page: xxx`

Information: This message displays the current keyboard code and code page along with the current code page used by the console screen device (CON).

`Current drive is no longer valid`

Warning: The system prompt includes the meta-symbol $p, to display the current directory, or $n, to display the current drive. You tried to change the default drive to an invalid drive. (For example, you tried to make a floppy drive current without a floppy present.) DOS presented the `Abort, Retry, Fail?` prompt. When you responded by pressing F, DOS temporarily changed the prompt to the `Current drive is no longer valid` message.

The invalid drive error also occurs when a current networked or SUBST disk drive is deleted or disconnected. Simply change the current drive to a valid disk drive.

`Current keyboard does not support this code page`

Error: You selected a code page incompatible with the current keyboard code. First, check the selected code page. If the code page is correct, change the keyboard code with KEYB.

`Device ddd not prepared`

Error: No code page is present for this device.

`Disk boot failure`

Error (start-up): An error occurred when DOS tried to load into memory. The disk contained IO.SYS and MSDOS.SYS, but one of the two files could not be loaded.

Try starting DOS from the disk again. If the error recurs, try starting DOS from a disk you know is good, such as a copy of your DOS start-up or master disk. If DOS still fails to boot, you have a disk drive problem. Contact your dealer.

`Disk full. Edits lost.`

Error: EDLIN cannot save your work to disk because the designated disk is full. Always make sure that you have a disk with plenty of room to save your files.

`Disk unsuitable for system disk`

Warning: FORMAT detected one or more bad sectors on the floppy disk in the area where DOS normally resides. Because the portion of the disk where DOS must reside is unusable, you cannot boot DOS from this disk.

Try reformatting the disk. Some floppy disks format successfully the second time. If FORMAT gives this message again, you cannot boot from the disk.

```
Divide overflow
```

Error: DOS aborted a program that attempted to divide by zero. The program was incorrectly entered or contains a logic flaw. If you wrote the program, correct the error and try the program again. If you purchased the program, report the problem to the dealer or publisher.

This message also may appear when you attempt to format a RAM disk with DOS 3.0 or 3.1. Make sure that you are formatting the correct disk and try again.

```
Do not specify filename(s)
Command format: DISKCOMP [drive1: [drive2:]] [/1] [/8]
```

Error: You typed an incorrect switch or added one or more file names with the DISKCOMP command. DISKCOMP syntax does not accept file names on the command line.

```
Do not specify filename(s)
Command Format: DISKCOPY [drive1: [drive2:]] [/1] [/V]
```

Error: You added an incorrect switch to the command or placed a file name in the command string. Retype the command and press Enter.

```
DOS is in HMA
```

```
DOS is in low memory
```

Information: Most of the DOS system can be optionally loaded above the first megabyte in the HMA (high-memory area), if you have at least a 286, have some available extended memory, and use the DOS=HIGH parameter in CONFIG.SYS. These messages tell you whether or not DOS is in HMA.

```
DOS memory-arena error
```

Error: When you are using the DOS editor, this message indicates a serious memory error. If possible, save your work to a different file and reboot your computer.

```
Drive assignment syntax error
```

Error: INTERLNK found a syntax error in its command line. Double-check the syntax with HELP INTERLNK.

`Drive types or diskette types not compatible`

Error: When using DISKCOMP or DISKCOPY, you specified two drives of different capacities. You cannot DISKCOMP or DISKCOPY, for example, from a 1.2M drive to a 360K drive. Retype the command using compatible drives.

`Duplicate filename or file not found`

Error: While using RENAME (or REN), you attempted to change a file name to a name that already exists, or the file to be renamed did not exist in the directory. Check the directory to make sure that the file name exists and that you have spelled it correctly. Then try again.

`Enter current volume label for drive d:`

Warning: You are attempting to format a hard disk that has a volume label. Enter the exact volume label to proceed with the format; if you do not want to enter a volume label, press Enter and FORMAT will quit.

`Error in COUNTRY command`

Warning (start-up): The COUNTRY command in CONFIG.SYS is improperly phrased or has an incorrect country code or code page number. DOS continues to load but uses the default information for the COUNTRY command.

After DOS has started, check the COUNTRY line in your CONFIG.SYS file. Make sure that the command is correctly phrased (with commas between the country code, code page, and COUNTRY.SYS file) and that any given information is correct. If you detect an error in the line, edit the line, save the file, and restart DOS.

If you do not find an error, restart DOS. If the same message appears, edit CONFIG.SYS. Reenter the COUNTRY command and delete the old COUNTRY line. The old line may contain some nonsense characters that DOS can see but that are not apparent to your text-editing program.

`Error in EXE file`

Error: DOS detected an error while attempting to load a program stored in an EXE file. The problem, which is in the relocation information DOS needs to load the program, may occur if the EXE file has been altered.

Restart DOS and try the program again, this time using a backup copy of the program. If the message appears again, the program is flawed. If you are using a purchased program, contact the dealer or publisher. If you wrote the program, issue LINK to produce another copy of the program.

`Error loading operating system`

Error (start-up): A disk error occurred when DOS was loading from the hard disk. DOS does not start.

Restart the computer. If the error occurs after several tries, restart DOS from the floppy disk drive. If the hard disk does not respond (that is, you cannot run DIR or CHKDSK without getting an error), you have a problem with the hard disk. Contact your dealer. If the hard disk does respond, place another copy of DOS on your hard disk by using SYS. You also may need to copy COMMAND.COM to the hard disk.

Increase to 15 or 20 the number of FILES in the CONFIG.SYS file of your start-up disk. Restart DOS. If the error recurs, you may have a problem with the disk. Try a backup copy of the program. If the backup works, copy the backup over the offending file.

If an error occurs in the copying process, you have a flawed disk. If the problem is a floppy disk, copy the files from the flawed disk to another disk and reformat or discard the original disk. If the problem is the hard disk, immediately back up your files and run RECOVER on the offending file. If the problem persists, your hard disk may be damaged.

`Error reading directory`

Error: During a FORMAT procedure, DOS was unable to read the directory; bad sectors may have developed in the file allocation table (FAT) structure.

If the message occurs when DOS is reading a floppy disk, the disk is unusable and should be thrown away. If DOS cannot read your hard disk, however, the problem is more serious, and you may have to reformat your disk. Remember to back up your data files regularly to prevent major losses.

`Error reading (or writing) partition table`

Error: DOS could not read from (or write to) the disk's partition table during the FORMAT operation because the partition table is corrupted. Run FDISK on the disk and reformat the disk.

`Error writing to file on remote system`

Error: INTERSVR has detected that the remote system (the one running INTERLNK) has a write error. The most likely reason is that the remote disk is full.

`Extended error`

Error: COMMAND.COM has detected an error but cannot tell you the normal error message because the diskette containing COMMAND.COM is missing. (This error doesn't generally occur on a hard disk system.) To avoid these "anonymous" errors, use the /MSG switch on the SHELL= line of CONFIG.SYS.

`File allocation table bad, drive d`
`Abort, Retry, Fail?`

Warning: DOS encountered a problem in the file allocation table of the disk in drive *d*. Press R to retry several times; if the message recurs, press A to abort.

CHKDSK can't repair this type of error in the file allocation table. If you have DOS 6.2, SCANDISK may be able to correct this problem for you. Commercial third-party utility packages often include tools that can repair this problem as well. Otherwise, you will be forced to back up as many files as you can, and then reformat the disk. If FORMAT finds no errors, you can safely go back to using the disk.

`File cannot be copied onto itself`

Error: You attempted to copy a file to a disk and directory containing the same file name. This error often occurs when you misspell or omit parts of the source or destination drive, path, or file name. This error may occur also when you are using wildcard characters for file names or when you used SUBST. Check your spelling and the source and destination names, and then try the command again.

`File creation error`

Error: A program or DOS failed to add a new file to the directory or to replace an existing file.

If the file already exists, issue the ATTRIB command to check whether the file is marked as read-only. If the read-only flag is set and you want to change or erase the file, remove the read-only flag with ATTRIB; then try again. If the problem occurs when the read-only flag is not set, run SCANDISK or CHKDSK without the /F switch to determine whether the directory is full, the disk is full, or some other problem exists with the disk.

`File not found`

Error: DOS could not find the specified file. The file is not on the current disk or directory, or you specified the disk drive name, path name, or file name incorrectly. Check these possibilities and try the command again.

`Filename device driver cannot be initialized`

Warning (start-up): In CONFIG.SYS, the parameters in the device driver file name or the syntax of the DEVICE line is incorrect. Check for incorrect parameters and phrasing errors in the DEVICE line. Edit the DEVICE line in the CONFIG.SYS file, save the file, and restart DOS.

`FIRST diskette bad or incompatible`

`SECOND diskette bad or incompatible`

Error: One of these messages may appear when you issue DISKCOMP. The messages indicate that the FIRST (source) or the SECOND (target) floppy disk is unreadable, or that the disks you are attempting to compare have different format densities.

`Format not supported on drive x:`

Error: You cannot use the FORMAT command on the specified drive. If you entered device driver parameters that your computer cannot support, DOS displays this message. Check CONFIG.SYS for bad DEVICE or DRIVPARM commands.

`Formatting while copying`

Information: DISKCOPY displays this message as it copies data to an unformatted disk.

`Illegal device name`

Error: DOS does not recognize the device name you entered with the MODE command.

`Incorrect DOS version`

Error: The copy of the file holding the command you just entered is from a different version of DOS.

Get a copy of the command from the correct version of DOS (usually from your copy of the DOS start-up or master disk), and try the command again. If the disk you are using has been updated to hold new versions of DOS, copy the new versions over the old ones.

`Insert disk with batch file`
`and strike any key when ready`

Prompt: DOS attempted to execute the next command from a batch file, but the disk holding the batch file is not in the disk drive. This message occurs for DOS 3.1 and later versions. DOS 3.0 gives a fatal error when the disk is changed.

`Insert disk with batch file into disk drive, and press a key to continue`

`Insert disk with \COMMAND.COM in drive d and strike any key when ready`

Prompt: DOS needs to reload COMMAND.COM but cannot find it on the start-up disk. If you are using floppy disks, the disk in drive *d* (usually A) has probably been changed. Place a disk with a good copy of COMMAND.COM in drive *d*, and press a key.

`Insert diskette for drive x and press any key when ready`

Prompt: On a system with one floppy disk drive or a system in which DRIVER.SYS creates more than one logical disk drive from a physical disk drive, you or one of your programs specified a tandem disk drive *x* (such as A or B) that is different from the current disk drive.

If the correct disk is in the disk drive, press a key. Otherwise, insert the correct disk into the floppy disk drive, and then press a key.

`Insufficient disk space`

Warning, Error: The disk does not have enough free space to hold the file being written. All DOS programs terminate when this problem occurs, but some non-DOS programs continue.

If you think that the disk should have enough room to hold the file, run SCANDISK or CHKDSK to determine whether the disk has a problem. When you terminate programs early by pressing Ctrl-Break, DOS may not be able to do the necessary clean-up work, leaving some disk space temporarily trapped. SCANDISK or CHKDSK can free these areas.

If you have simply run out of disk space, free some disk space or insert a different disk; then try the command again.

`Insufficient memory to store macro. Use the DOSKEY command with the /BUFSIZE switch to increase available memory.`

Warning: Your DOSKey macros have filled the total space set aside for them. You must enlarge the memory area for macros (the default is 512 bytes) by using the BUFSIZE switch before you can enter any new macros.

`Intermediate file error during pipe`

Error: DOS cannot create or write to one or both of the intermediate files it uses when piping information between programs because the disk is full, the root directory of the current disk is full, or the TEMP environment variable points to an illegal path. The most frequent cause is insufficient disk space.

Run DIR on the root directory of the current disk drive to make sure that you have enough room in the root directory for two additional files. If you do not have enough room, make room by deleting or copying and deleting files. You also can copy the necessary files to a different disk that has sufficient room.

This error also may occur if a program is deleting files, including the temporary files DOS creates. In this case, correct the program, contact the dealer or program publisher, or avoid using the program with piping.

```
Internal stack overflow
System halted
```

Error: Your programs and DOS have exhausted the stack, which is the memory space reserved for temporary use. This problem is usually caused by a rapid succession of hardware devices demanding attention. DOS stops, and the system must be turned off and on again to restart DOS.

The circumstances that cause this message are generally infrequent and erratic, and they may not recur. If you want to prevent this error from occurring, add the STACKS command to your CONFIG.SYS file. If the command is already in your CONFIG.SYS file, increase the number of stacks specified.

```
Invalid /BAUD parameter
```

Warning: You have selected an illegal baud rate for either INTERLNK or INTERSVR. For example, you have /BAUD:9200 instead of /BAUD:9600.

```
Invalid characters in volume label
```

Error: You attempted to enter more than 11 alphanumeric characters, or you entered illegal characters (+, =, /, \ , and ¦, for example) when you typed the disk's volume label (the disk name). Retype the volume label with valid characters.

Invalid COMMAND.COM in drive *d*:

Warning: DOS tried to reload COMMAND.COM from the disk in drive *d* and found that the file was from a different version of DOS. Follow the instructions for inserting a disk with the correct version.

If you frequently use the disk that generated this warning message, copy the correct version of COMMAND.COM to that disk.

`Invalid COMMAND.COM, system halted`

Error: DOS could not find COMMAND.COM on the hard disk. DOS halts and must be restarted.

COMMAND.COM may have been erased, or the COMSPEC variable in the environment may have been changed. Restart the computer from the hard disk. If a message indicates that COMMAND.COM is missing, the file was erased. Restart DOS from a floppy disk, and copy COMMAND.COM to the root directory of the hard disk or to the location your SHELL command indicates, if you have placed this command in your CONFIG.SYS file.

If you restart DOS and this message appears later, a program or batch file is erasing COMMAND.COM or altering the COMSPEC variable. If a program is erasing COMMAND.COM, contact the dealer or publisher who sold you the program. If a batch file is erasing COMMAND.COM, edit the batch file. If COMSPEC is being altered, edit the offending batch file or program, or place COMMAND.COM in the subdirectory your program or batch file expects.

`Invalid COUNTRY code or code page`

Warning (start-up): The COUNTRY code number or the code page number given to the COUNTRY command in CONFIG.SYS is incorrect or incompatible. DOS ignores the COUNTRY command and continues the start-up process.

Check the COUNTRY command in your CONFIG.SYS file (see Chapter 21, "Understanding the International Features of DOS") to determine whether the correct and compatible country code and code page numbers are specified. If you detect an error, edit and save the file. Then restart DOS.

`Invalid date`

Error: You gave an impossible date or an invalid character to separate the month, day, and year. This message also appears if you enter the date from the keypad when it is not in numeric mode.

`Invalid device parameters from device driver`

Error: The partition did not fall on a track boundary. You may have set the DEVICE drivers incorrectly in CONFIG.SYS or attempted to format a hard disk formatted with DOS 2.x so that the total number of hidden sectors is not evenly divisible by the number of sectors on a track. Therefore, the partition may not start on a track boundary.

To correct the error, run FDISK before performing a format, or check CONFIG.SYS for a bad DEVICE or DRIVPARM command.

`Invalid directory`

Error: You specified a directory name that does not exist, you misspelled the directory name, the directory path is on a different disk, you did not give the path character (\) at the beginning of the name, or you did not separate the directory names with the path character. Check your directory names to make sure that the directory exists, and try the command again.

```
Invalid disk change
Abort, Retry, Fail?
```

Warning: A floppy disk was changed while a program had open files to be written to the floppy disk. Place the correct disk in the disk drive, and press R to retry. Typically this check is supported on drives bigger than 360K.

`Invalid drive in search path`

Warning: You specified an invalid disk drive name in the PATH command, or a disk drive you named is nonexistent or hidden temporarily by a SUBST or JOIN command.

Use PATH to check the paths you instructed DOS to search. If you gave a nonexistent disk drive name, issue the PATH command again with the correct search paths. If the problem is temporary because of a SUBST or JOIN command, you can run PATH, leaving out or correcting the wrong entry. Or you can just ignore the warning message.

`Invalid drive or file name`

Error: You gave the name of a nonexistent disk drive, or you mistyped the disk drive or file name.

Remember that certain DOS commands (such as SUBST and JOIN) temporarily hide disk drive names while the command is in effect. Check the disk drive name you gave, and try the command again.

`Invalid drive specification`

Error: You entered an invalid or nonexistent disk drive as a parameter to a command; you specified the same disk drive for the source and destination; or by not giving a parameter, you defaulted to the same disk drive for the source and the destination.

Remember that some DOS commands (such as SUBST and JOIN) temporarily hide disk drive names while the command is in effect. Check the disk drive names. If the command is objecting to a missing parameter and defaulting to the wrong disk drive, name the correct disk drive explicitly.

```
Invalid drive specification
Specified drive does not exist or is non-removable
```

Error: You gave the name of a nonexistent disk drive, you named the hard disk drive when using commands for only floppy disks, you did not give a disk drive name and defaulted to the hard disk when using commands for only floppy disks, or you named or defaulted to a RAM disk drive when using commands for a floppy disk.

Remember that certain DOS commands (such as SUBST and JOIN) temporarily hide disk drive names while the command is in effect. Check the disk drive name you gave, and try the command again.

`Invalid keyboard code specified`

Error: You selected an invalid code. Enter the KEYB command again with the correct keyboard code.

`Invalid macro definition`

Error: You entered an illegal character or command with DOSKey or attempted to create a DOSKey macro with an illegal definition. This message appears, for example, if you use a GOTO command in a DOSKey macro. Correct any errors, and carefully retype the macro.

`Invalid media or Track 0 bad - disk unusable`

Error: A disk you are trying to format may be damaged. A disk may not format the first time. Try to format again; if the same message appears, the disk is bad and should be discarded. With some versions of FORMAT, this same symptom can be caused by memory boundary problems. If the symptom occurs for multiple floppy disks, try changing the number or sizes of TSRs to see whether the symptoms change.

`Invalid number of parameters`

Error: You have given too few or too many parameters to a command. One of the following occurred: you omitted required information, you omitted a colon immediately after the disk drive name, you inserted an extra space, you omitted a required space, or you omitted a slash (/) in front of a switch.

`Invalid parameter`

Error: At least one parameter you entered for the command is not valid. One of the following occurred: you omitted required information, you omitted a colon immediately after the disk drive name, you inserted an extra space, you omitted a required space, you omitted a slash (/) in front of a switch, or you used a switch the command does not recognize. For more information, check the explanation of this message in the Command Reference for the command you issued.

`Invalid parameter combination`

You typed conflicting parameters with a DOS command. Retype the command with only one of the conflicting switches.

`Invalid partition table`

Error (start-up): DOS has detected a problem in the hard disk's partition information. Restart DOS from a floppy disk. Back up all files from the hard disk, if possible, and run FDISK to correct the problem. If you change the partition information, you must reformat the hard disk and restore all its files.

`Invalid path`

Error: The path name contains illegal characters, the path name has more than 63 characters, or a directory name within the path is misspelled or does not exist.

Check the spelling of the path name. If necessary, check the disk directory with DIR to make sure that the directory you have specified exists and that you have specified the correct path name. Make sure that the path name contains no more than 63 characters. If necessary, change the current directory to a directory "closer" to the file to shorten the path name.

`Invalid path or file name`

Error: You gave a directory name or file name that does not exist, specified the wrong directory name (a directory not on the path), or mistyped a name. COPY aborts when it encounters an invalid path or file name. If you specified a wildcard for a file name, COPY transfers all valid files before it issues the error message.

Check to see which files have been transferred. Determine whether the directory and file names are spelled correctly and whether the path is correct. Then try again.

`Invalid STACK parameters`

Warning (start-up): One of the following problems exists with the STACKS command in your CONFIG.SYS file. A comma is missing between the number of stacks and the size of the stack, the number of stack frames is not in the range of 8 through 64, the stack size is not in the range of 32 through 512, you have omitted the number of stack frames or the stack size, or the stack frame or the stack size (but not both) is 0. DOS continues to start but ignores the STACKS command.

Check the STACKS command in your CONFIG.SYS file. Edit and save the file; then restart DOS.

`Invalid time`

Error: You gave an impossible time or invalid character to separate the hour, minute, and second. This message also appears if you enter the time from the keypad when it is not in numeric mode.

```
Invalid volume ID
```

Error: When formatting a fixed (or hard) disk, you entered an incorrect volume label, and DOS aborted the format attempt. Type VOL at the DOS prompt and press Enter to view the volume label of the disk, and try the command again.

```
Memory allocation error
Cannot load COMMAND, system halted
```

Error: A program destroyed the area where DOS keeps track of memory. You must restart DOS. If this error occurs again with the same program, the program has a flaw. Try a backup copy of the program. If the problem persists, contact the dealer or program publisher.

```
Missing operating system
```

Error (start-up): The DOS hard disk partition entry is marked as bootable (capable of starting DOS), but the DOS partition does not contain a copy of DOS. DOS does not start.

Start DOS from a floppy disk. Issue the SYS C: command to place DOS on the hard disk, and then copy COMMAND.COM to the disk. If this command fails to solve the problem, you must back up the existing files, if any, from the hard disk; then issue FORMAT /S to place a copy of the operating system on the hard disk. If necessary, restore the files you backed up.

```
MSBACKUP program files must be located on your hard disk
You cannot start MSBACKUP from a floppy disk
```

Error: MSBACKUP relies on repeated access to its program files during the backup operation. You must start it from a hard disk so that the program files will be available throughout the process. Change the default drive to the hard disk before starting MSBACKUP.

```
Must enter both /T and /N parameters
```

Error: On FORMAT, you must specify /T (number of tracks per side) and /N (number of sectors per disk) on the same command line. If you include the one, you must include the other.

```
Must specify COM1, COM2, COM3, or COM4
```

Error: You must specify COM1, COM2, COM3, or COM4 when using this form of the MODE command.

```
No drive letters redirected
```

Information: INTERLNK isn't currently redirecting any drive letters to the remote system.

```
No free file handles
Cannot start COMMAND, exiting
```

Error: DOS could not load an additional copy of COMMAND.COM because no file handles were available. Edit the CONFIG.SYS file on your start-up disk to increase by five the number of file handles (using the FILES command). Restart DOS, and try the command again.

```
No printer ports redirected
```

Information: INTERLNK isn't currently redirecting any printer ports to the remote system.

```
No room for system on destination disk
```

Error: This error isn't nearly so prevalent in DOS 6.0 or 6.2. SYS rearranges the files as needed to make a system bootable, but issues this error if there is insufficient room or if the root directory is full.

```
No serial ports were found
```

Error: You specified the /COM switch on INTERSVR, but no serial ports are available. This could happen if a TSR program has taken control of the available port or if the hardware is configured to an invalid address.

```
No system on default drive
```

Error: SYS cannot find the system files. Insert a disk containing the system files, such as the DOS disk, and type the command again. If the system files are available on another drive, issue the other form of the SYS command, indicating the location of the system files.

```
Non-System disk or disk error
Replace and strike any key when ready
```

Error (start-up): Your disk does not contain IO.SYS and MSDOS.SYS, or a read error occurred when you started the system. DOS does not start.

If you are using a floppy disk system, insert a bootable disk into drive A, and press a key. The most frequent cause of this message on hard disk systems is leaving a nonbootable disk in drive A with the door closed. Open the door to disk drive A, and press a key. DOS boots from the hard disk.

`Not enough memory`

`Insufficient memory`

Error: The computer does not have enough free RAM to execute the program or command. If you loaded a resident program, such as PRINT, GRAPHICS, SideKick, or ProKey, restart DOS, and try the command again before loading any resident programs. If this method fails to solve the problem, remove any nonessential device drivers or RAM disk software from CONFIG.SYS and restart DOS. If this option also fails, your computer does not have enough memory for this command. You must increase the amount of RAM installed in your computer to run the command.

`Out of environment space`

Warning: There isn't enough room in the current environment to add (or change) the variables you have specified with the SET, PATH, or PROMPT command. If you are running SET, PATH, or PROMPT from a shell program such as DOS Shell, quit the shell program and try the command again. If the command still fails, you can increase the size of the environment by increasing the /E:*size* parameter for the SHELL= command in your CONFIG.SYS file and restarting your computer.

For more information about using the DOS environment, see the "Changing DOS Variables" section in Chapter 13.

`Out of memory`

Error: The amount of memory is insufficient to perform the operation you requested. This error occurs in the DOS 5.0 Editor.

`Packed file corrupt`

Error: The program appears to be damaged. A common cause of this symptom is older format-packed executables, which could not load into the first 64K of conventional memory. With older operating system versions, the resident portion of the system generally used enough memory that this wasn't a problem. In DOS 5.0, 6.0, and 6.2, the DOS=HIGH, DEVICEHIGH, and LOADHIGH features can reduce memory usage enough that this problem occurs with certain programs. Use the LOADFIX command to temporarily use up enough memory so that the program is loaded at a location it can manage.

`Parameters not supported`

`Parameters not supported by drive`

Error: You entered parameters that do not exist, that are not supported by the DOS version you are running, or that are incompatible with the specified disk drive. Run VER to determine whether the current DOS version supports the parameters (or switches) you specified.

`Parameters not compatible with fixed disk`

Error: A device driver for a hard disk does not support generic IOCtl functions.

`Parse Error`

Error: COMMAND.COM has detected an error but cannot tell you the normal error message because the floppy disk containing COMMAND.COM is missing. (This error doesn't generally occur on a hard disk system.) To avoid these "anonymous" errors, use the /MSG switch on the SHELL= line of CONFIG.SYS.

`Path not found`

Error: A specified file or directory path does not exist. You may have misspelled the file name or directory name, or you may have omitted a path character (\) between directory names or between the final directory name and the file name. Another possibility is that the file or directory does not exist in the place specified. Check these possibilities, and try again.

`Path too long`

Error: You have given a path name that exceeds the DOS 64-character limit or you omitted a space between file name parameters. Check the command line. If the phrasing is correct, you must change to a directory "closer" to the file you want and try the command again.

`Program too big to fit in memory`

Error: The computer does not have enough memory to load the program or the command you invoked. If you have any resident programs loaded (such as PRINT, GRAPHICS, or SideKick), restart DOS, and try the command again without loading the resident programs. If this message appears again, reduce the number of buffers (BUFFERS) in the

CONFIG.SYS file, eliminate nonessential device drivers or RAM disk software, and restart DOS. If the problem persists, your computer does not have enough RAM for the program or command. You must increase the amount of RAM in your computer to run the program.

`Required parameter missing`

Error: Many DOS commands give this error when you omit part of the parameter list. You may have specified only a single name with the MOVE command, for example.

`Same parameter entered twice`

Error: You duplicated a switch when you typed a command. Retype the command using the parameter only once.

`Sector size too large in file filename`

Error: The device driver *filename* that you are loading in your CONFIG.SYS file with a DEVICE= or DEVICEHIGH= command uses a sector size that is too large. You will not be able to use this device driver.

`SOURCE diskette bad or incompatible`

Error: The disk you attempted to read during a copy process was damaged or in the wrong format (for example, a high-density disk in a double-density disk drive). DOS cannot read the disk.

`Specified COM port number not recognized by BIOS`

Error: The port number is legal, but your ROM BIOS doesn't support it. Generally, this can happen with an older BIOS that only supports two COM ports. Either replace the computer's ROM BIOS or specify COM1 or COM2.

`Syntax error`

Error: You phrased a command improperly by omitting needed information, giving extraneous information, inserting an extra space into a file or path name, or using an incorrect switch. Check the command line for these possibilities, and try the command again.

```
Target diskette bad or incompatible
```

```
Target diskette may be unusable
```

```
Target diskette unusable
```

Error: A problem exists with the target disk. DOS does not recognize the format of the target disk in the drive, or the disk is defective. Make sure that the target disk is the same density as the source disk, run SCANDISK or CHKDSK on the target disk to determine the problem, or try to reformat the disk before proceeding with the disk copy operation.

```
Target media has lower capacity than Source
Continue anyway (Y/N)?
```

Warning: The target disk can hold fewer bytes of data than the source disk. The most likely cause is bad sectors on the target disk. If you press Y, some data on the source disk may not fit on the target disk.

To avoid the possibility of an incomplete transfer of data, press N, and insert a disk with the same capacity as the source disk. If you are not copying "hidden" files, you also can issue the COPY *.* command to transfer files.

```
There are no serial ports or parallel ports available for communication
```

Error: INTRSVR cannot find any serial ports or any parallel ports that are not already in use. Without such a port, INTRSVR cannot communicate with INTRLNK.

```
There is not enough room to create a restore file
You will not be able to use the unformat utility
Proceed with Format (Y/N)?
```

Warning: The disk lacks sufficient room to create a restore file. Without this file, you cannot use UNFORMAT to reverse the format you are attempting.

```
This program requires Microsoft Windows
```

Error: You tried to run a program at the DOS prompt that needs Microsoft Windows to execute. If you're already running Windows, use Alt-Tab to switch to the Program Manager, and start it from there. If you haven't started Windows, use WIN to do so.

`Too many block devices`

Warning (start-up): Your CONFIG.SYS file contains too many DEVICE commands. DOS continues to start but does not install additional device drivers.

DOS can handle only 26 block devices. The block devices created by the DEVICE commands plus the number of block devices automatically created by DOS exceed this number. Remove any unnecessary DEVICE commands from your CONFIG.SYS file and restart DOS.

`Too many parallel ports, port ignored`

Warning: INTERLNK cannot automatically scan this many parallel ports. The earlier ones will be used.

`Too many serial ports, port ignored`

Warning: INTERLNK cannot automatically scan this many serial ports. The earlier ones will be used.

`Top level process aborted, cannot continue`

Error (start-up): COMMAND.COM or another DOS command detected a disk error, and you chose the A (abort) option. DOS cannot finish starting itself, and the system halts.

Try to start DOS again. If the error recurs, start DOS from a floppy disk (if starting from the hard disk) or from a different floppy disk (if starting from a floppy disk). After DOS has started, issue the SYS command to place another copy of the operating system on the disk, and copy COMMAND.COM to the disk. If DOS reports an error while copying, the disk is bad. Reformat or discard the floppy disk or back up and reformat the hard disk.

`Trying to recover allocation unit` *`nnn`*

Information, Warning: A bad allocation unit was found when the FORMAT command executed.

`Unable to create destination`

Error: MOVE was unable to create the destination file. Possible reasons are that the destination drive is full or that the destination is the root directory, which lacks room.

`Unable to create directory`

Error: You or a program could not create a directory for one of the following reasons. A directory by the same name already exists; a file by the same name already exists; you are adding a directory to the root directory, and the root directory is full; or the directory name has illegal characters or is a device name.

Issue DIR to make sure that no file or directory already exists with the same name. If you are adding the directory to the root directory, remove or move (copy and then erase) any nonessential files or directories. Check the spelling of the directory name, and make sure that the command is properly phrased.

`Unable to initialize serial port COM`*n*

Error: INTRSVR was unable to initialize the specified serial port. The most common reason is that two devices in the system have the same port address.

`Unable to load MS-DOS Shell, Retry (y/n)?`

Error, Prompt: DOSSHELL.COM could not load DOSSHELL.EXE. Normally, this error is caused by not having enough conventional memory. If you are attempting to run DOSSHELL from another program, quit the program and try again.

A less likely cause for this error message is that the DOSSHELL.EXE file is corrupted. If you have plenty of conventional memory available (MEM /FREE), get a fresh copy of DOSSHELL.EXE from a backup disk.

`[Unable to open source]`

Error: MOVE was unable to open the specified source file. This could be due to an illegal character in the file name, but the more common cause is trying to move a directory to a different place in the disk hierarchy. You may rename a directory with the MOVE command but not actually move it.

`Unable to read source`

Error: A disk problem occurred while transferring the data from the source file to the destination. Use COPY to copy the file, compare it, and then delete the original.

`Unable to write BOOT`

Error: FORMAT cannot write to the BOOT track or DOS partition of the disk that is being formatted because one of these areas is bad. Discard the bad disk, insert another unformatted disk, and try the FORMAT command again.

`Unable to write destination`

Error: A disk problem occurred while transferring the data from the source file to the destination. Double-check that the destination disk has sufficient room for the file. If the error still occurs, use COPY.

`Unrecognized command in CONFIG.SYS`

`Error in CONFIG.SYS line nnn`

Warning (start-up): DOS detected an improperly phrased command in CONFIG.SYS. The command is ignored, and DOS continues to start. Examine the indicated line in the CONFIG.SYS file, looking for an improperly phrased or incorrect command. Edit the line, save the file, and restart DOS.

`Unrecognized switch`

Error: You tried to use a switch that was illegal for the particular internal command. Type the command followed by /? to find out what options are permitted.

`Unrecoverable read error on drive x side n, track n`

Error: DOS was unable to read the data at the specified location on the disk. DOS makes four attempts before generating this message. Copy all files on the questionable disk to another disk, and try the command again, first with a new disk and then with the backup disk. If the original disk cannot be reformatted, discard it.

`Unrecoverable transmission errors, maximum retries exceeded`

Error: INTRSVR is getting excessive errors on the communications cable to INTERLNK. Check that the connections are screwed in tightly and that the cable is not routed too close to electrical interference, such as an arc welder.

`Unrecoverable write error on drive x side n, track n`

Error: DOS was unable to write to a disk at the location specified. Try the command again; if the error recurs, the target disk is damaged at that location. If the damaged disk contains important data, copy the files to an empty, freshly formatted disk, and try to reformat the damaged disk. If the disk is bad, discard it.

`WARNING: Unable to use a disk cache on the specified drive`

Warning: You specified a drive that SMARTDRV cannot cache, such as a network drive. The version of SMARTDRV distributed with DOS 6.2 can cache CD-ROM drives, but previous versions cannot. SMARTDRV ignores this drive letter.

`Write failure, diskette unusable`

Error: The disk you are writing to has bad sectors in the boot sector or file allocation table (FAT). Run SCANDISK if you have DOS 6.2 to see if the error can be corrected. If the disk is a floppy, you should probably discard it.

```
You have started the Interlnk server in a task-switching environment.
Task-switching, key combinations, and some disk-writing operations are
➥disabled
To restore these functions, exit the server
```

Warning: INTERLNK cannot permit certain things to happen while it is in control. One of these is the DOSSHELL capability to switch tasks. If INTERLNK was swapped while communicating with the INTERSVR, it could mean loss of data. Therefore, INTERLNK inhibits these operations until it completes.

`You must specify the host drive for a DoubleSpace drive`

Error: SMARTDRV must be given the host drive letter to cache. The compressed drive will also be cached, and the effective cache size is increased because of the compression. You cannot separately cache the compressed drive.

DOS Device Error Messages

When DOS detects an error reading or writing to a disk drive or device, one of the error messages in this section is displayed. Most of these messages are followed by this prompt:

```
Abort, Ignore, Retry, Fail?
```

You can enter one of the following characters to indicate the action that you would like DOS to take:

A *Abort*. This option terminates the currently running program and returns you to the DOS prompt. Any unsaved data in an application program is lost.

I *Ignore*. This option pretends that the error hasn't occurred and returns (successfully) to the program that was running. If you are reading from a file, nonsensical data may be returned to your application program. If you are writing to a file, the application won't know that the data hasn't been written to disk, and this message may reappear many times as it keeps writing more data. In most cases, you should avoid choosing Ignore. For most floppy disk errors, the Ignore option is not displayed.

R *Retry*. This is the safest option to choose. If you can correct the problem (by turning on the printer or closing the disk drive door, for example), do so and then choose Retry. Even if you can't correct the problem, choose Retry a few times and see if the error message goes away. Bad sectors can often be read if you Retry a few times.

F *Fail*. This option fails the operation and returns to the program that was running. Not all programs will notice that the operation they requested has failed, in which case Fail has the same problems as Ignore. Use this option in preference to Ignore, but try Retry first. Versions of DOS before 3.3 never display the Fail option.

Many of the error messages have a similar format, as follows:

```
error_type reading¦writing drive¦device
```

error_type Indicates the type of disk or device error that has occurred. *drive* indicates the disk drive where the error occurred. *device* indicates the device (AUX, CON, PRN, and so on) where the error occurred.

Each type of error can occur when either reading or writing to a disk or device. Rather than list all four possibilities for each error message, only the most common ones are shown in the text.

`Invalid device request reading drive x:`

`Invalid device request writing drive x:`

Error: This is an uncommon error message. A software program has issued an invalid or unsupported command to the drive or device indicated. The problem may be with the device driver or with the software program. If either of them is new to your system, contact the manufacturer of the software to see if an upgrade is available.

`Invalid device request parameters reading drive x:`

`Invalid device request parameters writing drive x:`

Error: This is an uncommon error message. A software program has issued a command to the indicated drive or device, but the command contains an invalid request header. The problem is usually with the software program. Contact the manufacturer of the software to see if an upgrade is available.

`Invalid unit reading drive x:`

Error: An invalid subunit number was passed to the device driver. This error is displayed if you try to access one of Interlnk's drives when the drive letter isn't currently redirected to the Interlnk server. Use the INTERLNK command to link the drive letter to a drive on the server and try again.

`Data error reading drive x:`

Error: DOS was unable to read some of the data on the disk. When this message appears, choose Retry at least two or three times before giving up. Quit the application you are using, and run SCANDISK or CHKDSK to see if they can locate and correct the problem on the disk.

`Not ready reading drive x:`

`Not ready writing drive x:`

Error: An error occurred when DOS tried to read or write to the disk drive. For floppy disk drives, the drive door may be open, the floppy disk may not be fully inserted, or the disk may not be formatted. Correct the situation and choose Retry. For hard disk drives, this error may indicate a hardware problem. If you get this error for a device rather than a disk drive, check to see that the device is turned on and ready to read or write.

`FCB unavailable reading drive x:`

`FCB unavailable writing drive x:`

Error: A program using file control blocks (FCBs) attempted to open more file control blocks than were specified with the FCBS= command. Usually you will have to choose the Abort option and terminate the program you are using. Increase the value of the FCBS= command in your CONFIG.SYS file by four or five, and reboot the system. If the message appears again, increase the value again and reboot.

This method of opening files dates back to DOS 1 and CP/M, and should not be used by any current programs that you work with. Chances are very good that FCBs won't be supported much longer by MS-DOS. If this error message occurs while running any new software you purchase, complain (loudly) to the software manufacturer, and demand your money back.

`General failure reading drive x:`

`General failure writing drive x:`

`General failure reading device dev`

`General failure writing device dev`

Error: This message is a catchall for errors not covered elsewhere, and can occur with disk drives or other devices. Whenever a device driver is unsure of what to call the error it has just received, it calls it a general failure. Reading disks formatted for operating systems other than DOS can often result in a general failure message.

If you load the file-sharing SHARE.EXE program into memory, you may see this message more often. SHARE prevents two programs from opening the same file at the same time. Newer programs recognize that SHARE is denying them access, but others may return general failure messages. If you are running Windows and receive this message in a DOS program, don't panic. It probably means that another application has a file open, and you are being denied access.

`Lock violation reading drive x:`

`Lock violation writing drive x:`

Error: With a file-sharing program such as SHARE.EXE or network software loaded, a program attempted to access a locked file. Your best choice is Retry. If you are on a network, get a cup of coffee and try Retry again to see if the other user has released the lock yet. If you just can't seem to get access to the file, choose Fail. The program you are using may notice the failure and ask you what to do about it. The last resort is to choose Abort, but be aware that any unsaved data in memory will be lost when the program is terminated.

`Sharing violation reading drive x:`

`Sharing violation writing drive x:`

Error: With a file-sharing program such as SHARE.EXE or network software loaded, a program attempted to access a file that is in use by another program. Your best choice is Retry. If you are on a network, get a cup of coffee and then try Retry again to see if the file is available yet. If you can't get access to the file, choose Fail. The program you are using may notice the failure and ask you what to do about it. The last resort is to choose Abort, but be aware that any unsaved data in memory will be lost when the program is terminated.

`Printer out of paper error writing device dev`

Error: The printer is out of paper (or not turned on). Check your printer, add paper, make sure the printer is on-line, and choose Retry. The message DOS displays will stay on the screen waiting for you to make a choice, so you could go across town and buy paper if you need to.

`Invalid media type reading drive x:`

`Invalid media type writing drive x:`

Error: The boot sector or the file allocation table (FAT) of the disk contains invalid information, making the disk unusable. If you come into contact with computers using operating systems other than DOS, you may be trying to read one of their disks.

When you are sure that the disk is a DOS disk, run SCANDISK or CHKDSK to see if it can be repaired. Even if the repair is successful, you should back up all the files on the disk and reformat it. If FORMAT finds no errors, you can safely begin using the disk again.

`Not ready reading drive x:`

`Not ready writing drive x:`

Error: This is a common error message. It usually means that you've left the door to your floppy disk drive open. Other common causes are that the drive is empty or the disk isn't seated properly. Check the drive or reinsert the disk, and then choose Retry. If you can't get a floppy disk drive to read any disks that you put in it, it may be a hardware problem.

`Read fault error reading drive x:`

Error: DOS was unable to read data from the drive. Often this is caused by a floppy disk that isn't seated properly in the drive, or you may have a bad spot on the disk. Reinsert the disk and choose Retry. Usually, the read operation succeeds after you choose Retry a few times. Check the disk with SCANDISK to make sure that there are no errors on it, or back up any files and reformat the disk.

If you begin to get a lot of these errors, your floppy disk drive may be out of alignment. When this happens, people typically start complaining that they can't read your disks. If your drive is out of alignment, your only options is either to repair or replace the drive.

`Sector not found reading drive x:`

`Sector not found writing drive x:`

Error: The disk drive was unable to find the requested sector on the disk. This error is usually the result of a defective spot on the disk. Choose Retry quite a few times before you give up; often the sector will be found if you're persistent. Check the disk with SCANDISK to make sure that there are no errors on it, or back up any files and reformat the disk.

Some copy-protection schemes use a defective spot to prevent unauthorized duplication of the disk. If you have reason to believe that the disk you are reading or writing to is copy-protected, do not correct the disk with SCANDISK. Contact the manufacturer of the copy-protected software and ask for a replacement disk.

`Seek error reading drive x:`

`Seek error writing drive x:`

Error: The disk drive could not find the proper track on the disk. Seek errors are often the result of failing drive electronics. If, however, the disk is not properly seated in the drive, reseating it will correct the problem. Choose Retry a few times, and see if the problem goes away. If it is a hardware problem, you will get more of these errors as time goes on and will eventually have to repair or replace your disk drive.

`Write fault error writing drive x:`

Error: DOS was unable to write data to the drive. Often this is caused by a floppy disk that isn't seated properly in the drive, or you may have a bad spot on the disk. Reinsert the disk and choose Retry. The write operation usually succeeds after you choose Retry a few times. Check the disk with SCANDISK to make sure that there are no errors on it, or back up any files and reformat the disk.

If you begin to get a lot of these errors, your floppy disk drive may be out of alignment. When this happens, people typically start complaining that they can't read your disks. If your drive is out of alignment, repair or replacement are your only options.

`Write fault error writing device dev`

Error: DOS could not write the data to this device. This error is typically caused by not having your printer turned on or on-line, although the same thing can happen with an external modem. Check the device and choose Retry. If the problem persists, you may have a faulty cable.

`Write protect error writing drive x:`

Error: DOS attempted to write to a disk that is write-protected. If the disk is a floppy and the write operation is intentional, remove the disk, adjust the write-protect tab, and reinsert the disk. Don't switch floppy disks at this prompt. To allow the write operation to proceed, make sure that the disk is no longer write-protected and choose Retry. If you don't want to allow the program to write to the disk, choose Fail or, as a last resort, Abort. Remember that if you choose Abort, any unsaved data in memory is lost.

`Invalid disk change reading drive x:`

`Invalid disk change writing drive x:`

Error: You have removed a disk that DOS needs access to. This message can occur only with removable media, such as floppy disks . Unfortunately, DOS doesn't tell you what disk it needs; it tells you only the drive. Think back, put the previous disk back in the drive, and choose Retry. Choosing any other option may mean that the disk that was prematurely removed may be damaged or incomplete. Never choose Fail or Abort at this message without first removing all media from the disk drive, because DOS could write the wrong file allocation table (FAT) to that disk and destroy all the data on it.

Appendix D

DOS and DOS Utility Programs' Keyboard Commands

This appendix lists keyboard commands available from DOS and certain DOS-supplied utility programs.

DOS Start-Up Control Keys

When you start your computer and the `Starting MS-DOS...` message appears on-screen, you have about 5 seconds to press a few special keys to bypass some or all of the commands in your CONFIG.SYS and AUTOEXEC.BAT files. These keys are available only in MS-DOS 6.0 and later.

F5	Clean boot. MS-DOS performs a minimal start up, ignoring any CONFIG.SYS and AUTOEXEC.BAT files in the root directory of the start-up drive. DBLSPACE.BIN is still loaded into memory if your system uses compressed drives.
Ctrl-F5	Clean boot. Just like F5, except DBLSPACE.BIN is not loaded into memory. Any compressed drives are inaccessible.

F8

Interactive boot. MS-DOS prompts you for every line in your CONFIG.SYS file, enabling you to selectively execute or skip each line. To execute the remaining commands without being prompted, press the Esc key. When the CONFIG.SYS file is complete, DOS asks whether you want to execute your AUTOEXEC.BAT file.

Note that DBLSPACE.BIN is still loaded into memory if your system uses compressed drives. With F8 (Interactive Boot), you cannot choose whether to load DBLSPACE.BIN into memory.

For MS-DOS 6.2, Microsoft has changed the behavior of the F8 key, and you are now prompted for each line in your AUTOEXEC.BAT file as well as in your CONFIG.SYS file. To stop being prompted for each line, press the Esc key to execute or press the F5 key to bypass all the remaining lines in your start-up files.

Ctrl-F8

Interactive boot. Just like F8, except DBLSPACE.BIN is not loaded into memory. Any compressed drives are inaccessible.

ROM BIOS Control Keys

ROM BIOS commands are available at all times, although an application program can prevent them from working. (All are eliminated or changed when Microsoft Windows is active.) Break and Reboot should be avoided if possible, because terminating a program in this way can damage open files, causing lost clusters or data loss. Your computer's ROM BIOS may provide other key combinations as well, such as commands to change processor speed, enter sleep mode, or access the CMOS Setup screen. Some keyboards provide a single key for these services.

Ctrl-Alt-Del

Reboot. Requests the BIOS to perform a system reset (warm boot). Use only at the DOS prompt or when the computer stops responding to normal commands.

Ctrl-Break	Break. Stops (exits) a command or software application program. Use with caution.
Shift-PrtSc	Print screen. Prints the contents of the video display (text only). Check that your printer is turned on before requesting this service.
SysReq	System request. Requests system services. Does nothing on most PC systems. Not available on older 83-key keyboards.

DOS Control Keys

DOS provides the following functions, although application programs often prevent them from working. (All are eliminated or changed when Microsoft Windows is active.)

Ctrl-C	Break. Stops (exits) a command or software application program. Very useful for halting DOS commands. This DOS-provided Break command is somewhat safer than the Break command provided by the ROM BIOS.
Ctrl-S	Pause. Pauses the system until the next key is pressed. Identical to the ROM BIOS provided service.
Ctrl-P	Echo to PRN. Echoes all characters to the printer (LPT1) as well as to the screen. Press Ctrl-P a second time to turn off.

Command-Line Editing Keys without Doskey

The following keys enable you to edit text on the command line when Doskey is *not* loaded. When you press Enter, the command line is placed in a template buffer, and then executed by DOS. By pressing certain function keys you can reuse characters from the template buffer in the next command line.

A cursor (current position) is maintained for both the template buffer off-screen and the command line on-screen. Normally, both cursors track each other, but certain function keys can alter this tracking. All actions are performed on the character at the cursor.

Enter	Execute. Executes the current command line and places a copy of it in the template buffer.
Esc	Cancel. Cancels the current command line without changing the template buffer. Resets the template cursor to the beginning of the line.
Backspace or left arrow	Delete. Moves left and deletes one character from the command line. Leaves the template buffer unchanged.
F1 or right arrow	Copy one. Copies one character from the template to the command line.
F2	Copy up to. Copies all remaining characters from the template up to, but not including, the next character you type.
F3	Copy all. Copies all remaining characters from the template to the command line.
Del	Skip one. Skips (deletes) one character in the template buffer. (Complement of F1.)
F4	Skip up to. Skips (deletes) all remaining characters from the template up to, but not including, the next character you type. (Complement of F2.)
Ins	Add in. Toggles insert mode. In insert mode, characters you type at the command line do not cause the template cursor to move. Note that this doesn't enable you to insert characters on the command line by moving the cursor and typing. It enables you to only type without moving the template cursor at the same time.

F5	New template. Copies the current command line into the template buffer, but doesn't execute the command line.
F6	EOF. Inserts an end-of-file (EOF) marker (Ctrl-Z) into the command line.

When the console is used like an input file in certain commands (for example, COPY CON *filename*), some of the previous keystrokes become very useful. Pressing F6 will insert an end-of-file marker (Ctrl-Z) into the file and terminate the copy operation when you press Enter. (Anything you type after the Ctrl-Z is discarded.) Ctrl-Break or Ctrl-C abort the copy operation.

Command-Line Editing Keys with Doskey

If you have Doskey loaded, the following keys are available:

Enter	Executes the current command line.
Esc	Clears the current command line.
Left arrow	Moves left one character.
Right arrow	Moves right one character.
Ctrl-left arrow	Moves left one word.
Ctrl-right arrow	Moves right one word.
Home	Moves to the beginning of the command line.
End	Moves to the end of the command line.
Backspace	Moves left one character and deletes that character.
Del	Deletes the character at the cursor.
Ctrl-Home	Deletes all characters from the cursor to the beginning of the command line.
Ctrl-End	Deletes all characters from the cursor to the end of the command line.

Up arrow	Displays the previous DOS command.
Down arrow	Displays the next DOS command; displays a blank line if you are at the end of the list.
PgUp	Displays the first (earliest) command in the command-history buffer.
PgDn	Displays the last command in the command-history buffer.
F7	Displays the contents of the command-history buffer in a numbered list.
Alt-F7	Clears the command-history buffer.
F8	Searches for the command or commands that most closely match the characters on the command line.
F9	Prompts you for the line number of the stored command you want to display. Use F7 to see a numbered list of the commands in the command-history buffer.
Alt-F10	Clears all macro definitions from memory.
Ins	Toggles between overwrite mode (the default) and insert mode. (Note that the cursor changes shape.)
Ctrl-T	Inserts a paragraph mark in the command line. Use Ctrl-T to separate multiple commands typed on one line.

Edit Keystroke Commands

When you are using the DOS editor (Edit), the following keystroke commands are available. If you are familiar with WordStar, you will recognize many of the Ctrl key combinations.

Alt	Accesses menus.
Esc	Cancels a menu choice or a dialog box; exits Help.

F1		Opens context-sensitive help.
Shift-F1		Opens the "Getting Started" section of Help.
Left arrow	Ctrl-S	Moves left one character.
Right arrow	Ctrl-D	Moves right one character.
Ctrl-left arrow	Ctrl-A	Moves left one word.
Ctrl-right arrow	Ctrl-F	Moves right one word.
Up arrow	Ctrl-E	Moves up one line.
Down arrow	Ctrl-X	Moves down one line.
	Ctrl-Q,S	Moves to the beginning of the current line.
Home		Moves to the first indent level on the line.
End	Ctrl-Q,D	Moves to the end of the current line.
Ctrl-Enter	Ctrl-J	Moves to the beginning of the next line.
	Ctrl-Q,E	Moves to the top of the window.
	Ctrl-Q,X	Moves to the bottom of the window.
F6		Toggles between the Help window and the Editing window when both are open.
Ctrl-up arrow	Ctrl-W	Scrolls up one line.
Ctrl-down arrow	Ctrl-Z	Scrolls down one line.
PgUp	Ctrl-R	Scrolls up one screen.
PgDn	Ctrl-C	Scrolls down one screen.
Ctrl-PgUp		Scrolls left one window.
Ctrl-PgDn		Scrolls right one window.

Shift-left arrow		Selects the character to the left.
Shift-right arrow		Selects the character to the right.
Ctrl-Shift-left arrow		Selects the word to the left.
Ctrl-Shift-right arrow		Selects the word to the right.
Shift-up arrow		Selects the line above.
Shift-down arrow		Selects one current line.
Shift-PgUp		Selects one screen up.
Shift-PgDn		Selects one screen down.
Ctrl-Shift-Home		Selects to the beginning of the file.
Ctrl-Shift-End		Selects to the end of the file.
Ctrl-Ins		Copies selected text to the Clipboard.
Shift-Ins		Pastes (inserts) text from the Clipboard.
Shift-Del		Cuts selected text to the Clipboard.
	Ctrl-Y	Cuts the current line to the Clipboard.
	Ctrl-Q,Y	Cuts to the end of the line to the Clipboard.
Backspace	Ctrl-H	Deletes the character to the left.
Del	Ctrl-G	Deletes the current character.
Del	Ctrl-G	Deletes the selected text.
	Ctrl-T	Deletes to the end of the current word.
Shift-Tab		Deletes leading spaces from selected lines.
	Home,Ctrl-N	Inserts a line above the cursor.

End-Enter		Inserts a line below the cursor.
	Ctrl-Q,F	Searches for text.
F3	Ctrl-L	Repeats the search.
	Ctrl-Q,A	Changes text (search and replace).
Ins	Ctrl-V	Toggles between insert mode (the default) and overwrite mode.
Ctrl-P, Ctrl-*key*		Inserts a control character into the text.

DOS Shell Keystroke Commands

DOS 6.0 assigns special functions to some keys when you use them in the DOS Shell.

Enter	Executes a command or operation.
Esc	Cancels a command or operation; exits Help.
F1	Displays context-sensitive Help.
F3 or Alt-F4	Exits the MS-DOS Shell.
Shift-F5	Repaints the screen.
Shift-F9	Goes to the DOS command prompt; type **EXIT** to return to the MS-DOS Shell.
F10 or Alt	Accesses the menu bar.
Up arrow	Scrolls up one line.
Down arrow	Scrolls down one line.
PgUp	Scrolls up one screen.
PgDn	Scrolls down one screen.
letter key	Moves to (finds) the next line in a list that begins with the letter entered.
Home	Moves to the beginning of a line or a list.
End	Moves to the end of a line or a list.

Ctrl-Home	Moves to the beginning of a list.
Ctrl-End	Moves to the end of a list.
Tab	Moves to the next area or window.
Shift-Tab	Moves to the previous area or window.
F5	Updates (refreshes) the directory tree and file list.
Ctrl-F5	Updates the file list for the current directory.
Ctrl-*drive*	Selects the specified disk drive and display its directories and files.
F7	Moves the selected files.
F8	Copies the selected files.
F9	Views the contents of the selected file; use F9 to toggle between an ASCII view and a hexadecimal view of the file.
Del	Deletes the selected files.
Space bar	Selects the current file (Add mode).
Shift-up arrow	Selects the previous file.
Shift-down arrow	Selects the next file.
Shift-PgUp	Selects the previous screen of files.
Shift-PgDn	Selects the next screen of files.
Shift-space bar	Selects all files from the previously selected file to the cursor (Add mode).
Ctrl-/	Selects all files in the list.
Ctrl-\	Deselects all files in the list.
Shift-F8	Toggles Add mode on and off.
Minus (-)	Collapses (hides) the current branch of the directory tree.

Plus (+)	Expands (displays) the current branch of the directory tree one level.
Asterisk (*)	Expands (displays) the current branch of the directory tree completely.
Ctrl-*	Expands (displays) all directories in the tree.

When the task list is activated, the following functions are available:

Shift-Enter	Adds a program to the active task list.
Ctrl-Shift-Enter	Adds a program to the active task list; when you run the program, it opens the file specified in the Properties dialog box automatically.
Ctrl-Esc	Suspends a program and returns to the MS-DOS Shell.
Alt-Esc	Switches to the next program in the task list.
Shift-Alt-Esc	Switches to the previous program in the task list.
Alt-Tab	Cycles forward through the active task list.
Ctrl-Alt-Tab	Cycles backward through the active task list.

Appendix E

ASCII and Extended ASCII Codes

ASCII (American Standard Code for Information Interchange) is a widely used standard that defines numeric values for a common set of alphabetic characters. The first 32 characters are reserved for formatting and hardware control codes. Following these codes are 96 "printable" characters. IBM defined symbols for the final 128 ASCII values when it released the IBM PC, and referred to the additional characters as *Extended ASCII codes*. This entire set of 256 characters is often referred to as the PC-8 character set, or code page 437.

Dec X_{10}	Hex X_{16}	Binary X_2	ASCII Character	Ctrl	Key
000	00	0000 0000	null	NUL	^@
001	01	0000 0001	☺	SOH	^A
002	02	0000 0010	☻	STX	^B
003	03	0000 0011	♥	ETX	^C
004	04	0000 0100	♦	EOT	^D
005	05	0000 0101	♣	ENQ	^E
006	06	0000 0110	♠	ACK	^F
007	07	0000 0111	●	BEL	^G
008	08	0000 1000	■	BS	^H
009	09	0000 1001	○	HT	^I

Dec X_{10}	Hex X_{16}	Binary X_2	ASCII Character	Ctrl	Key
010	0A	0000 1010	■	LF	^J
011	0B	0000 1011	♂	VT	^K
012	0C	0000 1100	♀	FF	^L
013	0D	0000 1101	♪	CR	^M
014	0E	0000 1110	♪♪	SO	^N
015	0F	0000 1111	☼	SI	^O
016	10	0001 0000	►	DLE	^P
017	11	0001 0001	◄	DC1	^Q
018	12	0001 0010	↕	DC2	^R
019	13	0001 0011	!!	DC3	^S
020	14	0001 0100	¶	DC4	^T
021	15	0001 0101	§	NAK	^U
022	16	0001 0110	–	SYN	^V
023	17	0001 0111	↨	ETB	^W
024	18	0001 1000	↑	CAN	^X
025	19	0001 1001	↓	EM	^Y
026	1A	0001 1010	→	SUB	^Z
027	1B	0001 1011	←	ESC	^[
028	1C	0001 1100	∟	FS	^\
029	1D	0001 1101	↔	GS	^]
030	1E	0001 1110	▲	RS	^^
031	1F	0001 1111	▼	US	^_
032	20	0010 0000	Space		
033	21	0010 0001	!		
034	22	0010 0010	"		
035	23	0010 0011	#		
036	24	0010 0100	$		
037	25	0010 0101	%		
038	26	0010 0110	&		
039	27	0010 0111	'		
040	28	0010 1000	(		

Dec X_{10}	Hex X_{16}	Binary X_2	ASCII Character
041	29	0010 1001	)
042	2A	0010 1010	*
043	2B	0010 1011	+
044	2C	0010 1100	'
045	2D	0010 1101	-
046	2E	0010 1110	.
047	2F	0010 1111	/
048	30	0011 0000	0
049	31	0011 0001	1
050	32	0011 0010	2
051	33	0011 0011	3
052	34	0011 0100	4
053	35	0011 0101	5
054	36	0011 0110	6
055	37	0011 0111	7
056	38	0011 1000	8
057	39	0011 1001	9
058	3A	0011 1010	:
059	3B	0011 1011	;
060	3C	0011 1100	<
061	3D	0011 1101	=
062	3E	0011 1110	>
063	3F	0011 1111	?
064	40	0100 0000	@
065	41	0100 0001	A
066	42	0100 0010	B
067	43	0100 0011	C
068	44	0100 0100	D
069	45	0100 0101	E
070	46	0100 0110	F
071	47	0100 0111	G
072	48	0100 1000	H
073	49	0100 1001	I

Dec X_{10}	Hex X_{16}	Binary X_2	ASCII Character
074	4A	0100 1010	J
075	4B	0100 1011	K
076	4C	0100 1100	L
077	4D	0100 1101	M
078	4E	0100 1110	N
079	4F	0100 1111	O
080	50	0101 0000	P
081	51	0101 0001	Q
082	52	0101 0010	R
083	53	0101 0011	S
084	54	0101 0100	T
085	55	0101 0101	U
086	56	0101 0110	V
087	57	0101 0111	W
088	58	0101 1000	X
089	59	0101 1001	Y
090	5A	0101 1010	Z
091	5B	0101 1011	[
092	5C	0101 1100	\
093	5D	0101 1101	]
094	5E	0101 1110	^
095	5F	0101 1111	–
096	60	0110 0000	`
097	61	0110 0001	a
098	62	0110 0010	b
099	63	0110 0011	c
100	64	0110 0100	d
101	65	0110 0101	e
102	66	0110 0110	f
103	67	0110 0111	g
104	68	0110 1000	h
105	69	0110 1001	i

Dec X_{10}	Hex X_{16}	Binary X_2	ASCII Character
106	6A	0110 1010	j
107	6B	0110 1011	k
108	6C	0110 1100	l
109	6D	0110 1101	m
110	6E	0110 1110	n
111	6F	0110 1111	o
112	70	0111 0000	p
113	71	0111 0001	q
114	72	0111 0010	r
115	73	0111 0011	s
116	74	0111 0100	t
117	75	0111 0101	u
118	76	0111 0110	v
119	77	0111 0111	w
120	78	0111 1000	x
121	79	0111 1001	y
122	7A	0111 1010	z
123	7B	0111 1011	{
124	7C	0111 1100	¦
125	7D	0111 1101	}
126	7E	0111 1110	~
127	7F	0111 1111	Delete
128	80	1000 0000	Ç
129	81	1000 0001	ü
130	82	1000 0010	é
131	83	1000 0011	â
132	84	1000 0100	ä
133	85	1000 0101	à
134	86	1000 0110	å
135	87	1000 0111	ç
136	88	1000 1000	ê
137	89	1000 1001	ë

Dec X_{10}	Hex X_{16}	Binary X_2	ASCII Character
138	8A	1000 1010	è
139	8B	1000 1011	ï
140	8C	1000 1100	î
141	8D	1000 1101	ì
142	8E	1000 1110	Ä
143	8F	1000 1111	Å
144	90	1001 0000	É
145	91	1001 0001	æ
146	92	1001 0010	Æ
147	93	1001 0011	ô
148	94	1001 0100	ö
149	95	1001 0101	ò
150	96	1001 0110	û
151	97	1001 0111	ù
152	98	1001 1000	ÿ
153	99	1001 1001	Ö
154	9A	1001 1010	Ü
155	9B	1001 1011	¢
156	9C	1001 1100	£
157	9D	1001 1101	¥
158	9E	1001 1110	Pt
159	9F	1001 1111	*f*
160	A0	1010 0000	á
161	A1	1010 0001	í
162	A2	1010 0010	ó
163	A3	1010 0011	ú
164	A4	1010 0100	ñ
165	A5	1010 0101	Ñ
166	A6	1010 0110	a̲
167	A7	1010 0111	o̲
168	A8	1010 1000	¿
169	A9	1010 1001	⌐

Dec X_{10}	Hex X_{16}	Binary X_2	ASCII Character
170	AA	1010 1010	┐
171	AB	1010 1011	½
172	AC	1010 1100	¼
173	AD	1010 1101	¡
174	AE	1010 1110	«
175	AF	1010 1111	»
176	B0	1011 0000	░
177	B1	1011 0001	▒
178	B2	1011 0010	▓
179	B3	1011 0011	│
180	B4	1011 0100	┤
181	B5	1011 0101	╡
182	B6	1011 0110	╢
183	B7	1011 0111	╖
184	B8	1011 1000	╕
185	B9	1011 1001	╣
186	BA	1011 1010	║
187	BB	1011 1011	╗
188	BC	1011 1100	╝
189	BD	1011 1101	╜
190	BE	1011 1110	╛
191	BF	1011 1111	┐
192	C0	1100 0000	└
193	C1	1100 0001	┴
194	C2	1100 0010	┬
195	C3	1100 0011	├
196	C4	1100 0100	─
197	C5	1100 0101	┼
198	C6	1100 0110	╞
199	C7	1100 0111	╟
200	C8	1100 1000	╚
201	C9	1100 1001	╔

Dec X_{10}	Hex X_{16}	Binary X_2	ASCII Character
202	CA	1100 1010	╩
203	CB	1100 1011	╦
204	CC	1100 1100	╠
205	CD	1100 1101	═
206	CE	1100 1110	╬
207	CF	1100 1111	╧
208	D0	1101 0000	╨
209	D1	1101 0001	╤
210	D2	1101 0010	╥
211	D3	1101 0011	╙
212	D4	1101 0100	╘
213	D5	1101 0101	╒
214	D6	1101 0110	╓
215	D7	1101 0111	╫
216	D8	1101 1000	╪
217	D9	1101 1001	┘
218	DA	1101 1010	┌
219	DB	1101 1011	╗
220	DC	1101 1100	▄
221	DD	1101 1101	▌
222	DE	1101 1110	▐
223	DF	1101 1111	▀
224	E0	1110 0000	α
225	E1	1110 0001	β
226	E2	1110 0010	Γ
227	E3	1110 0011	π
228	E4	1110 0100	Σ
229	E5	1110 0101	σ
230	E6	1110 0110	μ

Dec X_{10}	Hex X_{16}	Binary X_2	ASCII Character
231	E7	1110 0111	τ
232	E8	1110 1000	Φ
233	E9	1110 1001	θ
234	EA	1110 1010	Ω
235	EB	1110 1011	δ
236	EC	1110 1100	∞
237	ED	1110 1101	ø
238	EE	1110 1110	∈
239	EF	1110 1111	∩
240	F0	1111 0000	≡
241	F1	1111 0001	±
242	F2	1111 0010	≥
243	F3	1111 0011	≤
244	F4	1111 0100	⌠
245	F5	1111 0101	⌡
246	F6	1111 0110	÷
247	F7	1111 0111	≈
248	F8	1111 1000	°
249	F9	1111 1001	•
250	FA	1111 1010	·
251	FB	1111 1011	√
252	FC	1111 1100	η
253	FD	1111 1101	2
254	FE	1111 1110	■
255	FF	1111 1111	

Appendix F

ANSI Control Codes

ANSI.SYS is an alternate console (CON) driver that provides more control over the display and keyboard than the built-in MS-DOS console driver. This appendix provides a summary of ANSI commands for controlling display appearance, cursor placement, and keyboard layout.

All ANSI commands are prefixed by two characters: the Escape character (ASCII 27) and the left square bracket (ASCII 91). Because the Escape keypress usually is interpreted as a command, inserting it in a text file may require you to enter a special command, such as Ctrl-P, before your text editor will accept it as text.

Uppercase and lowercase are significant in these commands, so you must type them exactly as indicated. In commands that allow a variable number of codes, separate each code with a semicolon.

ANSI Set and Reset Display Mode Control Codes

Set mode codes end in a lowercase h as shown. Reset mode codes substitute a lowercase l for the h. Not all displays support all screen modes, and other modes may be available for your display.

<*Esc*>[=0h	Text mode	40 x 25	Monochrome
<*Esc*>[=1h	Text mode	40 x 25	Color
<*Esc*>[=2h	Text mode	80 x 25	Monochrome

<*Esc*>[=3h	Text mode	80 x 25	Color
<*Esc*>[=4h	Graphics mode	320 x 200	4 color
<*Esc*>[=5h	Graphics mode	320 x 200	Monochrome
<*Esc*>[=6h	Graphics mode	640 x 200	Monochrome
<*Esc*>[=13h	Graphics mode	320 x 200	Color
<*Esc*>[=14h	Graphics mode	640 x 200	16 color
<*Esc*>[=15h	Graphics mode	640 x 350	2 color
<*Esc*>[=16h	Graphics mode	640 x 350	16 color
<*Esc*>[=17h	Graphics mode	640 x 480	2 color
<*Esc*>[=18h	Graphics mode	640 x 480	16 color
<*Esc*>[=19h	Graphics mode	320 x 200	256 color

ANSI Display Color and Attribute Control Codes

Background color, foreground color, and screen attribute codes may be combined in a single command. If any of the choices conflict, the rightmost color or attribute in the command is set. Not all colors or attributes are available on all displays.

<*Esc*>[*code;...;code*m	**Set Display Color/Attribute**
0	All attributes off
1	Bold or bright characters
4	Underlined characters (monochrome display adapter only)
5	Blinking characters
7	Reverse video characters
8	Hidden or invisible characters
30	Foreground color: black
31	Foreground color: red
32	Foreground color: green

<Esc>[*code;...;code*m	Set Display Color/Attribute
33	Foreground color: yellow
34	Foreground color: blue
35	Foreground color: magenta
36	Foreground color: cyan
37	Foreground color: white
40	Background color: black
41	Background color: red
42	Background color: green
43	Background color: yellow
44	Background color: blue
45	Background color: magenta
46	Background color: cyan
47	Background color: white

ANSI Cursor Control Codes

***<Esc>*[*row;col*H** Cursor position. Moves the cursor to the specified *row* and *col* or to home (0;0) if no position is specified

***<Esc>*[*row;col*f** Cursor position. Same as *<Esc>*[*row;col*H

***<Esc>*[*num*A** Cursor up. Moves the cursor up the specified number of rows or to the first row on the screen

***<Esc>*[*num*B** Cursor down. Moves the cursor down the specified number of rows or to the last row on the screen

***<Esc>*[*num*C** Cursor right. Moves the cursor right the specified number of columns or to the right side on the screen

<*Esc*>[*num*D	Cursor left. Moves the cursor left the specified number of columns or to the left side on the screen
<*Esc*>[s	Saves current cursor position
<*Esc*>[u	Returns cursor to saved position

ANSI Miscellaneous Display Control Codes

<*Esc*>[2J	Clears the entire screen
<*Esc*>[K	Clears from the cursor to the end of the line
<*Esc*>[=7h	Enables line wrapping
<*Esc*>[=7l	Disables line wrapping

ANSI Keyboard Layout Control Codes

By using the following ANSI command, the entire keyboard can be redefined or simple text macros can be set for use at the command line. Some software application programs ignore keyboard reassignments set this way.

<Esc>[keycode;keytext;...p	**Set Keyboard Text**
keycode	One of the key codes listed in the following table. Some keys use two codes, in which case both must be entered, separated by a semicolon as shown. Keycodes that are shown in parentheses may not be available on all keyboards. (Do not include the parentheses.) Also, some keyboards use different codes for certain keys. Check your computer's documentation.
keytext	Either the ASCII code for a single character or text enclosed in double quotation marks. For example, both 83 and "S" can be used to represent an uppercase *S*. "Hello" also is allowed; it would return the full word when the key was pressed.

Keys indicated as (gray) refer to the gray-colored cursor pad area of the keyboard. Keys indicated as (keypad) refer to the numeric keypad area. Key codes shown in parentheses are not available on all keyboards, and ANSI.SYS may not interpret them if the /X switch was not specified in the device command that loaded it. A blank entry indicates that this keyboard combination doesn't return a valid code.

Key	Alone	Shift-Key	Ctrl-Key	Alt-Key
F1	0;59	0;84	0;94	0;104
F2	0;60	0;85	0;95	0;105
F3	0;61	0;86	0;96	0;106
F4	0;62	0;87	0;97	0;107
F5	0;63	0;88	0;98	0;108
F6	0;64	0;89	0;99	0;109
F7	0;65	0;90	0;100	0;110
F8	0;66	0;91	0;101	0;111
F9	0;67	0;92	0;102	0;112
F10	0;68	0;93	0;103	0;113
F11	0;133	0;135	0;137	0;139
F12	0;134	0;136	0;138	0;140
Home	0;71	55	0;119	
Up arrow	0;72	56	(0;141)	
PgUp	0;73	57	0;132	
Left arrow	0;75	52	0;115	
Right arrow	0;77	54	0;116	
End	0;79	49	0;117	
Down arrow	0;80	50	(0;145)	
PgDn	0;81	51	0;118	
Ins	0;82	48	(0;146)	
Del	0;83	46	(0;147)	

(continues)

Key	Alone	Shift-Key	Ctrl-Key	Alt-Key
PrtSc			0;114	
Pause/Break			0;0	
Backspace	8	8	127	(0)
Enter	13		10	(0;28)
Tab	9	0;15	(0;148)	(0;165)
Home (gray)	(224;71)	(224;71)	(224;119)	(224;151)
Up arrow (gray)	(224;72)	(224;72)	(224;141)	(224;152)
PgUp (gray)	(224;73)	(224;73)	(224;132)	(224;153)
Left arrow (gray)	(224;75)	(224;75)	(224;115)	(224;155)
Right arrow (gray)	(224;77)	(224;77)	(224;116)	(224;157)
End (gray)	(224;79)	(224;79)	(224;117)	(224;159)
Down arrow (gray)	(224;80)	(224;80)	(224;145)	(224;154)
PgDn (gray)	(224;81)	(224;81)	(224;118)	(224;161)
Ins (gray)	(224;82)	(224;82)	(224;146)	(224;162)
Del (gray)	(224;83)	(224;83)	(224;147)	(224;163)
Enter (keypad)	13		10	(0;166)
/ (keypad)	47	47	(0;142)	(0;74)
* (keypad)	42	(0;144)	(0;78)	
–(keypad)	45	45	(0;149)	(0;164)
+ (keypad)	43	43	(0;150)	(0;55)
5 (keypad)	(0;76)	53	(0;143)	
A	97	65	1	0;30
B	98	66	2	0;48
C	99	67	3	0;46
D	100	68	4	0;32
E	101	69	5	0;18
F	102	70	6	0;33

Key	Alone	Shift-Key	Ctrl-Key	Alt-Key
G	103	71	7	0;34
H	104	72	8	0;35
I	105	73	9	0;23
J	106	74	10	0;36
K	107	75	11	0;37
L	108	76	12	0;38
M	109	77	13	0;50
N	110	78	14	0;49
O	111	79	15	0;24
P	112	80	16	0;25
Q	113	81	17	0;16
R	114	82	18	0;19
S	115	83	19	0;31
T	116	84	20	0;20
U	117	85	21	0;22
V	118	86	22	0;47
W	119	87	23	0;17
X	120	88	24	0;45
Y	121	89	25	0;21
Z	122	90	26	0;44
0	48	41		0;129
1	49	33		0;120
2	50	64	(0) Null	0;121
3	51	35		0;122
4	52	36		0;123
5	53	37		0;124
6	54	94	30	0;125

(continues)

Key	Alone	Shift-Key	Ctrl-Key	Alt-Key
7	55	38		0;126
8	56	42		0;127
9	57	40		0;128
Spacebar	32	32		
' (single quote)	39	34		0;40
, (comma)	44	60		0;51
–(hyphen)	45	95	31	0;130
. (period)	46	62		0;52
/ (slash)	47	63		0;53
; (semicolon)	59	58		0;39
= (equal)	61	43		0;131
[	91	123	27	0;26
\ (backslash)	92	124	28	0;43
]	93	125	29	0;27
` (accent)	96	126		(0;41)

Appendix G

International Country Codes

MS-DOS provides support for a number of different international code pages, which are simply character sets which facilitate the needs of a particular language. The lower ASCII characters (0 to 127) always remain the same, but the characters available in the upper ASCII set (128 to 255) are changed to make certain special characters available. The code page information file included with DOS 6 (EGA.CPI) includes displayable character sets for the following international code pages.

Code Page	Country or Language
437	United States
860	Portuguese
850	Multilingual (Latin I)
863	Canadian-French
852	Slavic (Latin II)
865	Nordic

MS-DOS 6.2 provides an additional file (EGA2.CPI) that supports the following international code pages.

Code Page	Country or Language
437	United States
857	Turkish
850	Multilingual (Latin I)
861	Icelandic
852	Slavic (Latin II)
869	Greek

In the following table, you can find the countries or languages supported by the international features of MS-DOS 6. The country code and the default and alternate code pages (character sets) are specified for each country. DOS's international commands, such as COUNTRY=, CHCP, KEYB, and MODE, use country codes, keyboard codes, and code pages. See Chapter 21, "Understanding the International Features of DOS," or the Command Reference for more information on using these codes.

Country or Language	Country Code	Default Code Page	Alternate Code Page	1st DOS Version
Belgium	032	850	437	2.1
Brazil	055	850	437	5.0
Canada (French)	002	863	850	3.3
Croatia	038	852	850	6.0
Czech Republic	042	852	850	6.0
Denmark	045	850	865	2.1
Finland	358	850	437	2.1
France	033	850	437	2.1
Germany	049	850	437	2.1
Hungary	036	852	850	5.0
International English	061	437	850	2.1
Italy	039	850	437	2.1

Country or Language	Country Code	Default Code Page	Alternate Code Page	1st DOS Version
Latin America	003	850	437	3.3
Netherlands	031	850	437	2.1
Norway	047	850	865	2.1
Poland	048	852	850	5.0
Portugal	351	850	860	3.3
Serbia/Yugoslavia	038	852	850	6.0
Slovakia	042	852	850	6.0
Slovenia	038	852	850	6.0
Spain	034	850	437	2.1
Sweden	046	850	437	2.1
Switzerland (French)	041	850	437	2.1
Switzerland (German)	041	850	437	2.1
United Kingdom	044	437	850	2.1
United States	001	437	850	2.1

There are also special versions of MS-DOS available that support the following countries and languages: Arabic, Israel, Japan, Korea, People's Republic of China, and Taiwan. Contact Microsoft for more information about these versions of MS-DOS. (See the Introduction for information on contacting Microsoft.)

Each country code has a specific date and time format associated with it. The following table lists those international date and time formats, with an example shown for August 23, 1993 at 2:42 p.m., 10 seconds, 20 hundredths of a second.

Country	Country Code	Date Format	Date Example	Time Format	Time Example
Belgium	032	dd/mm/yyyy	23/08/1993	hh:mm:ss	14:42:10
Brazil	055	dd/mm/yyyy	23/08/1993	hh:mm:ss	14:42:10

(continues)

Country	Country Code	Date Format	Date Example	Time Format	Time Example
Canada (French)	002	yyyy-mm-dd	1993-08-23	hh:mm:ss	14:42:10
Croatia	038	yyyy-mm-dd	1993-08-23	hh:mm:ss	14:42:10
Czech Republic	042	yyyy-mm-dd	1993-08-23	hh:mm:ss	14:42:10
Denmark	045	dd-mm-yyyy	23-08-1993	hh.mm.ss	14.42.10
Finland	358	dd.mm.yyyy	23.08.1993	hh.mm.ss	14.42.10
France	033	dd.mm.yyyy	23.08.1993	hh:mm:ss	14:42:10
Germany	049	dd.mm.yyyy	23.08.1993	hh:mm:ss	14:42:10
Hungary	036	yyyy-mm-dd	1993-08-23	hh:mm:ss	14:42:10
International English	061	dd-mm-yyyy	23-08-1993	hh:mm:ss.00p	2:42:10.20p
Italy	039	dd/mm/yyyy	23/08/1993	hh.mm.ss	14.42.10
Latin America	003	dd/mm/yyyy	23/08/1993	hh:mm:ss.00p	2:42:10.20p
Netherlands	031	dd-mm-yyyy	23-08-1993	hh:mm:ss	14:42:10
Norway	047	dd.mm.yyyy	23.08.1993	hh:mm:ss	14:42:10
Poland	048	yyyy-mm-dd	1993-08-23	hh:mm:ss	14:42:10
Portugal	351	dd-mm-yyyy	23-08-1993	hh:mm:ss	14:42:10
Slovakia	042	yyyy-mm-dd	1993-08-23	hh:mm:ss	14:42:10
Serbia/Yugoslavia	038	yyyy-mm-dd	1993-08-23	hh:mm:ss	14:42:10
Slovenia	038	yyyy-mm-dd	1993-08-23	hh:mm:ss	14:42:10
Spain	034	dd/mm/yyyy	23/08/1993	hh:mm:ss	14:42:10
Sweden	046	yyyy-mm-dd	1993-08-23	hh.mm.ss	14.42.10
Switzerland (French)	041	dd.mm.yyyy	23.08.1993	hh,mm,ss	14,42,10
Switzerland (German)	041	dd.mm.yyyy	23.08.1993	hh,mm,ss	14,42,10
United Kingdom	044	dd/mm/yyyy	23/08/1993	hh:mm:ss.00	14:42:10.20
United States	001	mm-dd-yyyy	08-23-1993	hh:mm:ss.00p	2:42:10.20p

Microsoft added and/or changed the names for several of the countries in the preceding list for MS-DOS 6.0. In particular, the entry for Yugoslavia has been changed to three separate entries: Serbia/Yugoslavia, Slovenia, and Croatia. Also, the entry for Czechoslovakia is now two separate entries: Czech Republic and Slovakia. These are name changes only—none of the country codes assignments have been changed.

MS-DOS 6 supports various alternate keyboard layouts. The following table lists the code(s) and code pages for each country or language. The KEYB command supports international keyboard layouts through the use of the KEYBOARD.SYS information file.

Country or Language	Keyboard Code	Default Code Page	Alternate Code Page	Keyboard ID Code(s)
Belgium	be	850	437	
Brazil	br	850	437	
Canada (French)	cf	863	850	
Croatia	yu	852	850	
Czech Republic	cz	852	850	
Denmark	dk	850	865	
Finland	su	850	437	
France	fr	850	437	120, 189
Germany	gr	850	437	
Hungary	hu	852	850	
Italy	it	850	437	141, 142
Latin America	la	850	437	
Netherlands	nl	850	437	
Norway	no	850	865	
Poland	pl	852	850	
Portugal	po	850	860	
Serbia/Yugoslavia	yu	852	850	
Slovakia	sl	852	850	
Slovenia	yu	852	850	
Spain	sp	850	437	
Sweden	sv	850	437	
Switzerland (French)	sf	850	437	

(continues)

Country or Language	Keyboard Code	Default Code Page	Alternate Code Page	Keyboard ID Code(s)
Switzerland (German)	sg	850	437	
United Kingdom	uk	437	850	166, 168
United States	us	437	85	

MS-DOS 6.2 includes an alternate keyboard layout file, KEYBRD2.SYS, that KEYB can use. KEYBRD2.SYS doesn't support either Switzerland layout, but it adds alternate keyboard layouts for Brazil, Canada, Greece, Iceland, Romania, and Turkey. For information on using the layouts available in KEYBRD2.SYS, see the README.TXT file distributed with MS-DOS 6.2.

Glossary

This glossary provides short definitions of some of the more common terms used in this book. If you require more in-depth information, refer to a computing dictionary such as *Que's Computer User's Dictionary*.

Absolute path The path named from the root directory, including all intervening subdirectories.

Attribute A directory-based indicator of a file's status. Attributes include read only, archive, system, hidden, and volume label.

AUTOEXEC.BAT A special batch file that DOS automatically executes during the booting process. This file, usually placed in the root directory, is an ideal place to include commands that initialize the operation of a PC.

Batch file A text file containing commands that DOS executes as though the commands were entered at the DOS prompt. Batch files always have the .BAT extension.

Binary file A file containing instructions or data that has meaning to the PC but that cannot be displayed or printed as ASCII characters.

Boot sector A special area in track 0 of each DOS disk. DOS uses this area to record important information about a disk's format to reference later when working with the disk.

Buffer A portion of memory reserved for storing data.

Character string A series of ASCII characters.

Clipboard An area of memory where text can be stored temporarily.

Cluster A unit of one, four, or eight sectors. This is the smallest amount of disk space that DOS allocates to a file.

Cold boot To start a PC from a power-off condition.

Command A directive you type at the DOS prompt or include in a batch file that instructs DOS to perform an action.

Compare To make a byte-by-byte comparison of the contents of a file or an entire disk to ensure that they are accurate copies of each other.

CONFIG.SYS A special text file that DOS reads during booting to find and execute configuration commands.

Cylinder The logical alignment of heads on the same track on different sides (and platters) of the same disk.

Default A condition or value that is used when you do not supply one.

Delimiter A character that separates the "words" in a command. Common delimiters are the space and the slash (/).

Device driver A special program file, usually with a .SYS extension, that DOS can load through a configuration command. Device drivers control how DOS and applications programs interact with specific items of hardware.

Dialog box A window that pops open when a program needs more information before executing a command.

Directory A disk-based table of file names and other file-related information that DOS uses with the file allocation table (FAT) to access a file's data content.

Disk A magnetic storage medium and the predominant means of file storage for DOS.

Disk drive The electromechanical components that record data to and play back data from the magnetic surfaces of a disk.

Disk partition A division of a hard disk that DOS views as a separate disk.

Diskette Another term for a 5 1/4-inch or 3 1/2-inch disk.

DOS prompt The characters that COMMAND.COM displays to inform you that you can enter a DOS command.

End-of-file (EOF) marker In a text file, a Ctrl-Z (^Z) ASCII character, which tells DOS that the end of the usable portion of a file has been reached.

Expanded memory Also referred to as EMS-Expanded Memory Specification. Special RAM that DOS accesses as a device. Expanded memory conforms to the Lotus/Intel/Microsoft (LIM) EMS 3.2 or 4.0 standards.

Extended memory Memory at addresses above 1M on 80286, 80386, and 80486 PCs. DOS can load most of the operating system into the first 64K of extended memory.

Extension A file name suffix, which can include a period and up to three characters. It usually describes the type of file.

External command A DOS command whose instructions are stored in a file other than COMMAND.COM.

File A variable-length collection of related information referenced by a name.

File system The predefined organization method that a disk operating system uses to read and write to data files on disks.

Filter A program that modifies information coming from a program before the information reaches the screen or is piped to another program.

Floppy disk Any disk with a lower capacity than the hard drive that you can remove from your PC's drive.

Flow control The capability to control the order in which DOS processes lines of a batch file.

Format The initial preparation of a disk for data storage.

Full backup A special series of disks containing all the data stored on a hard disk, along with information about the previous location of the data files.

Graphics mode A screen mode available to users of PCs equipped with graphics adapters. In graphics mode, screen presentation uses bit-mapped graphics.

Ground An electrical path directly to earth. Grounds can dissipate static discharges safely. A PC chassis normally is grounded, but this grounding is not always adequate to stop a static discharge.

Hard disk A high-capacity, typically nonremovable disk drive.

High memory area *(HMA)* The first 64K of extended memory. DOS can load part of the operating system files into this area of memory.

Highlighted option A command or option that appears in reverse video. The highlighted option executes when you press Enter.

Insert mode The editing mode in which a typed character is inserted into the existing text at the current cursor position.

Intermediate backup A series of disks containing copies of all files modified since the most recent full backup.

Internal command A DOS command built into COMMAND.COM.

Keyword A word that specifically identifies the action you want DOS to perform.

LCD A liquid-crystal display. This is the type of screen found on most laptop and notebook computers.

Location counter The two numbers at the right end of the status bar that indicate the cursor's current row and column.

Logical drive A partitioned section of a hard disk that DOS views as an additional hard disk.

Macro A series of DOS commands stored in memory under a single name. You execute a macro by typing its name.

Meta-string A series of characters that in DOS takes on a meaning different from the string's literal meaning. DOS displays substitute text when the program finds meta-strings in the PROMPT command.

Mouse pointer The block- or arrow-shaped screen icon that indicates where the mouse action occurs.

Name The first portion of a file name, consisting of up to eight characters. It usually describes the contents of a file.

Overtype mode The editing mode in which a typed character replaces the character at the current cursor position.

Parameter Additional information given with a command to more precisely control its actions.

Parser A portion of a computer program that translates a command line into tokens that the computer can act on.

Pipe To send information that normally goes to the screen to another program by using the pipe symbol (¦).

Platter A disk contained in a hard disk drive. Most hard disk drives contain two or more platters.

Prompt A symbol, character, or group of characters displayed by DOS or a program, indicating that you must enter information.

Pull-down menu A menu interface used in many programs that is characterized by a vertical list of main menu choices. When you use a mouse to select one of the choices, additional choices appear below the main menu choice.

Queue A list of files to be printed.

Redirection Sending the output from a command or program to a device other than the one expected (usually the screen); sending input to a command or program from a point other than the one expected (usually the keyboard).

Relative path A path specified with the current directory—as opposed to the root directory—as the starting point.

Root directory A master directory created on each disk by FORMAT.

Scroll bar An area of the screen containing arrows and icons that move (or scroll) text or graphics through the window.

Sector A section of a track that is the disk's smallest possible storage unit.

Selected text A block of text you highlight with various Shift-key combinations. Selected text can be deleted, moved, and edited as a single block.

Selection cursor An area of highlighted text that shows where the selected action occurs.

Shell A program that is a user interface to the features and capabilities of an operating system.

Shortcut key A keystroke combination that immediately activates an editing command, bypassing the menu system.

Sorting To order a list of items.

Source A file name expression that identifies the file(s) to be copied, or the device that will serve as the source for a copy operation.

Static electricity A high-voltage charge that builds on objects (including people) and can be discharged when another object is touched. Static electricity discharges can damage electronic circuits.

Subdirectory A directory within another directory.

Surge protector A protective device inserted between a power outlet and a computer's power plug. By acting as a circuit breaker, a surge protector helps block power surges that can damage the computer's circuits.

Switch A slash followed by one or more characters that are used to enable a command's optional functions. (Similar to a parameter.)

Syntax A specific set of rules you follow when issuing commands.

Target A file name expression that identifies the disk location of the file(s) to be created as a result of the copy operation. A target also can be a DOS device other than a file.

Task A program that DOS has loaded into memory.

Text file A file that contains only ASCII text characters (without special formatting characters). The DOS Editor works only with text files.

Text mode The screen mode available to all PC users. In text mode, all screen presentation is composed of ASCII characters.

Track A circular section of a disk's surface that holds data.

Undelete To restore the FAT and directory entries of a file in order to undo a deletion.

Upper memory area A 384K area of memory between 640K and 1M, usually reserved for use by certain system devices, such as your monitor. DOS can use a portion of this upper memory area, referred to as upper memory blocks, for memory-resident programs and device drivers.

Voltage regulator An electrical device that keeps voltage fluctuations from reaching an electrical device. Regulators usually don't stop all power surges.

Volume label A name that identifies a particular disk.

Warm boot To restart a PC while the power is on.

Wildcard A character in a command that represents one or more characters. In DOS, the ? wildcard represents any single character. The * wildcard represents any remaining characters in a "word" in the command.

XMS The Lotus/Intel/Microsoft/AST Extended Memory Specification. This standard specifies a set of rules by which several programs can use extended memory cooperatively by means of a device driver.

Index

Symbols

/? (Help) switch, 53-60
¦ (pipe character), 213
4201.CPI file, 989
4208.CPI file, 989
5202.CPI file, 989
80386 chips, 21
80486 chips, 21
8088 chips, 21
8514.VID file, 972

A

absolute paths, 1087
accessing
  CVFs (compressed volume files), 647-648
  files, 482-483
  servers, 765-770
active display, 338
active task list area, 72
adapters, 708-709
Add Group dialog box, 92, 94
Add Program dialog box, 95
ADOS.CFG file, 986
ADOS.COM file, 986
ADOS.OVL file, 986
ADOS.TXT file, 986
Advanced Power Management (APM), 860-867
aliases, 596
All Files command (DOS Shell View menu), 86
American National Standards Institute, *see* ANSI
analyzing
  disks with CHKDSK command, 192-196
  hard disks with SCANDISK command, 196-198
ANSI (American National Standards Institute), 525, 589
  Character Attribute Codes, 532-533
  control codes, 1073-1080
ANSI.SYS file, 41, 458, 968
  customizing keyboards, 534-536
  installing, 525-526
  issuing codes
    batch files, 527-528
    PROMPT command, 529-530
    text files, 528-529
ANSI.SYS command, 589-591
APM (Advanced Power Management), 860-867
APPEND command, 592-595
APPEND environment variable, 996
APPEND.EXE file, 968
applications, *see* programs
ARC (Archive) file name extension, 121
Archive file attribute, 125
archiving files, 510
area title bar, 72
AREADME.TXT file, 986
arrow keys, 386
ASC (ASCII text) file name extension, 121
ASCII (American Standard Code for Information Interchange)
  chart, 16, 1063-1071
  extended character set, 1063
  mode comparison, 242
  text characters in batch files, 413
  text files
    combining with COPY command, 228-229
    editing, 707
    viewing with TYPE command, 211-214
ASM (Assembler source file) file name extension, 121
ASSIGN command, 342-345, 596
ASSIGN.COM file, 986
Associate command (DOS Shell File menu), 105
Associate File dialog box, 105
AST Research Enhanced Expanded Memory Specification (EEMS), 23
ATTRIB command, 125-128, 596-599
ATTRIB.EXE file, 969
attribute bits, 125
Attribute control codes (ANSI), 1074-1075
attributes, 1087
  files, 124-128, 596-599
AUTOEXEC.BAT file, 20, 30-32, 36-46, 983, 1087
  dates/times, 311
  defining macros from bootup, 453
  UNDELETE command, 297-300

auxiliary consoles (I/O devices), 632-633
AV.GRP file, 985

B

/B:*buffersize* parameter disk caching, 495
background printing, 352-356, 867-871
backslashes (\), 52
Backspace key, 1054
BACKUP command, 275, 599
Backup Options dialog box, 274-275
BACKUP.EXE file, 987
backups, 599
  differential, 268
  full, 264-267, 1089
  hard disks, 845-847, 852-853
  incremental, 267, 268
  intermediate, 1090
  policies, 262-263
  restoring, 275-280, 891-895
  special-purpose, 268-273
BAK (Backup) file name extension, 121
BAS (BASIC program file) file name extension, 121
BAT (Batch) file name extension, 121, 412
batch file commands, 421-422, 560
batch files, 377, 411, 603-606, 1087
  as templates, 420
  calling, 438-441
  CHOICE command, 430-433
  command line parameters, 921
  command-history (Doskey program), 448
  components, 413-414
  conditional execution, 754-760
  COPYCOMP, 415
  creating, 414-416
  DCOPY.BAT, 426
  displaying contents with TYPE command, 420
  executing, 441
  FOR..IN..DO command, 434-435
  guidelines for creation, 413-414
  IF command, 424-430
  inserting comments, 422
  installation, 420
  issuing ANSI.SYS codes, 527-528
  on-screen messages, 703-707
  pausing for input, 430-433
  remarks, 885-886
  replaceable parameters, 416-421
  returning, 438-441
  running other batch files, 437-441
  suspending, 617-619
  using GOTO command, 423-424
batch processing, 411
BGI (Borland Graphics Interface) file name extension,121
BIN (Binary program) file, 121
  converting .EXE files, 716-717
binary mode comparison, 242
binary files, 211-212, 1087
bits, 16
BK.GRP file, 985
BKAV.GRP file, 985
BKUD.GRP file, 985
BKUDAV.GRP file, 985
blocks of text, 390-393
BMP (Windows bitmap) file name extension, 121
boot disks, 30-32
boot sector, 1087
booting, 18-20, 29-32, 38-40
  cold, 1087
  reboot commands, 813-815
  warm, 1093
BREAK command, 33, 488, 600-601
BREAK= command, 600-601
buffers, 1087
  keyboard, 790-791
BUFFERS command, 33, 480-482, 601-603
bugs, 254
BUSETUP.EXE file, 983

C

C (C source file) file name extension, 121
/C switch (disk caching), 496
cables, configuration with Interlnk, 216-217
caching hard disks, 492-497
CALL command, 438-441, 603-606
calling batch files, 438-441
Canadian-French code page, 1081
canceling commands, 61-63
CBL (COBOL source file) file name extension, 121
CD command, 606-609
CD ROMs, 27, 847-849
central processing units, *see* CPUs
CFG (program configuration information) file name extension, 121
CGA display adapters, 349
CGA.GRB file, 972
CGA.INI file, 972
CGA.VID file, 972
Change command (DOS Editor Search menu), 394, 396-397
Change Compression Ratio dialog box, 516
Change Size dialog box, 515
Character Attribute Codes (ANSI), 532-533
character sets
  ASCII Extended, 16
  changing, 609-611
  international, 871
character strings, 1087
characters
  ANSI Character Attribute Codes, 532-533
  ASCII extended character set, 1063
  changing keyboards to other languages, 791-795
  file names, 571-572
  wildcards, 573-574
characters per line in video display, 337-341
CHCP command, 552, 609-611
CHDIR command, 138-140, 606-609
check boxes, 80
CHKDSK command, 126, 192-196, 611-616
CHKDSK.EXE file, 969
CHKLST.MS file, 977
CHKSTATE.SYS command, 458, 616-617, 975
CHOICE command, 617-619
  batch files, 425, 430-433
  creating menus, 431-432
  display menus, 432-433
  syntax, 430

CHOICE.COM file, 969
CHP (Chapter) file name extension, 121
CHR (Character) file name extension, 121
Clean boot (Ctrl-F5) key, 1051
Clean boot (F5) key, 1051
cleaning floppy drive read/write heads, 176
Clear command (DOS Editor Edit menu), 392
clearing command-history buffer with Doskey program, 449
clients, 780-787
Clipboard, 1087
clipboard (DOS Editor), 391-392
CLS command, 348-349, 620
clusters, 169, 175, 194, 1087
CMOS (Complimentary Metal Oxide Semiconductor), 18
CNF (Program configuration information) file name extension, 121
code pages, 609-611, 825-830
  international, 871-873, 1081-1086
  switching, 539-540, 546-556, 854-855
    dead keys, 554-556
    hardware checks, 547-548
    installing, 548-551
    international, 682-685
    loading tables, 551-552
    MODE command, 553-554
    page switches, 552-553
    printer support, 548
cold boot, 29, 1087
Collapse Branch command (DOS Shell Tree menu), 99
Color Graphics Adapter (CGA), 740-741
colors
  menus, 42-44
  screen (DOS Editor), 404-406
  video adapters, 808-811
COM (Program) files, 121
  converting .EXE files, 716-717
command buttons, 81
COMMAND command, 325-329, 484-486, 620-622
command interpreter, 918-921
command keys
  Contents (Alt-C), 57-58
  File menu (Alt-F), 58
  Last Topic (Alt-B), 58
  Next (Alt-N), 57
  Next Topic (Alt-N), 58
  on-line help, 58
  Search (Alt-S), 58
command line
  deleting files, 250
  editing capabilities, 689-692
  editing keys, 62, 444-445, 1053-1055
    Doskey program, 446
  switches, 53-60
command-history buffer (Doskey program), 447-449
COMMAND.COM file, 20, 30, 47-49, 71, 969
  batch file execution, 441
  copying, 620-622
  deleting temporary copy, 717
  exiting, 328
  second copy, 325-329
commands, 1088
  ANSI.SYS, 589-591
  APPEND, 592-595
  ASSIGN, 342-345, 596
  ATTRIB, 125-128, 596-599
  BACKUP, 275, 599
  batch file, 421-422, 560
  BREAK, 33, 488, 600-601
  BUFFERS, 33, 480-482, 601-603
  CALL, 438-441, 603-606
  canceling, 61-63
  CD, 606-609
  CHCP, 552, 609-611
  CHDIR, 138-140, 606-609
  CHKDSK, 126, 192-196, 611-616
  CHKSTATE.SYS, 616-617
  CHOICE, 617-619
    batch files, 425
    creating menus, 431-432
    syntax, 430
  CLS, 348-349, 620
  COMMAND, 325-329, 484-486, 620-622
  COMP, 623-624
  CONFIG.SYS, 561-562
  CONFIG.SYS DEVICE, 562
  contents, 57
  COPY, 225-230, 255, 624-629
    defaults, 239-240
    redirecting input to COPYCOMP.BAT file, 415
  COUNTRY, 33, 541-542
  COUNTRY.SYS, 632
  COUNTRY=, 629-631
  Ctrl-Break key combination, 488-489
  Ctrl-C key combination, 488-489
  CTTY, 357-358, 632-633
  DATE, 311-312, 634-635
  DBLSPACE, 635-636
    /AUTOMOUNT, 636-637
    /CHKDSK, 637-638
    /COMPRESS, 638-639
    /CREATE, 639-641
    /DEFRAGMENT, 641-642
    /DELETE, 643
    /DOUBLEGUARD, 643-644
    /FORMAT, 644-645
    /INFO, 645-646
    /LIST, 646
    /MOUNT, 647-648
    /RATIO, 648-649
    /SIZE, 649-650
    /UNCOMPRESS, 650-651
    /UNMOUNT, 651
  DBLSPACE.SYS, 652-655
  DEBUG, 212, 655-656
  DEFRAG, 656-659
  DEL, 160
  delimiters, 1088
  DELOLDOS, 661-662
  DELTREE, 140-142, 662-663
  DEVICE, 34-36, 215, 457, 469, 663-666
  device control commands, 489-490
  device drivers, 565-566
  DEVICEHIGH, 22, 34, 36, 469, 666-673
  DIR, 129, 203-210, 673-676
  directory, 563
  DISKCOMP, 247-248, 677-679
  DISKCOPY, 245-246, 425, 681-682
  DISPLAY.SYS, 684-685
  DOS, 34, 49-50, 687-688
    parameters, 52
    switches, 52-53
    syntax, 50-52
  DOSKEY, 62, 444, 690-692
  DOSSHELL, 694-696
  DRIVER.SYS, 698-700
  DRIVPARM, 34, 702-703
  ECHO, 421, 703-707
  ECHO OFF, 37

EDIT, 36, 38, 196, 403-404, 707
Edit menu (DOS Editor)
Clear, 392
Copy, 392
Cut, 392
Paste, 392
editing, 61-63
editing with Doskey program, 447
EDLIN, 708
EGA.SYS, 708-709
EMM386, 709-710
EMM386.EXE, 710-716
ERASE, 248-251, 255, 660-661, 716
EXE2BIN, 716-717
EXIT, 328-329, 717
EXPAND, 718-719
external, 48-49, 1089
FASTHELP, 719-720
FASTOPEN, 720-722
FC, 240-245, 722-724
FCBS, 34, 482-483, 724-725
FDISK, 180-188, 725-727
FILE, 34
file, 564
File menu (DOS Editor)
Exit, 398, 403
New, 398
Open, 398
Print, 398, 402
Save, 398
Save As, 399-400
File menu (DOS Shell)
Associate, 105
Copy, 109
Create Directory, 100
Delete, 94, 96
Move, 109
New, 92, 95
Properties, 93, 96
Reorder, 94
Select All, 103
View File Contents, 104
FILES, 483, 727-728
FIND, 214, 369-371, 728-730
FOR, 730-734
FOR..IN..DO, 433-436
batch file use, 434-435
from DOS prompt, 435
interactive usage, 435-436
FORMAT, 30-32, 129, 168-179, 188-189, 255, 291, 734-739
GOTO, 45, 423-424, 739-740
GRAFTABL, 740-741
GRAPHICS, 349-352, 741-743
grouping in blocks, 760-763
HELP, 55, 743-744
help, 719-720
HIMEM.SYS, 745-754
hot key, 77-78
IF, 754-760
batch files, 424-430
comparing strings, 427-429
searching for files, 429-430
improving efficiency with Doskey program, 443-449
INCLUDE=, 760-763
INSTALL, 34, 486-487
INSTALL=, 763-765
INTERLNK, 765-770
INTERLNK.EXE, 771-780
internal, 48, 1090
international, 565-566
INTERSVR, 780-787
JOIN, 342-345, 789
KBDBUF.SYS, 790
KEYB, 541, 791-795
KEYBOARD.SYS, 795-796
LABEL, 796-798
LASTDRIVE, 34-35, 483-484, 798-799
LH, 38, 800-802
LOADFIX, 800
LOADHIGH, 22, 38, 469, 800-802
locating with Doskey program, 449
MD, 802-804
MEM, 319-325, 470, 804-806
MEMMAKER, 807
memory, 566
MENUCOLOR=, 808
MENUDEFAULT=, 811
MENUITEM=, 813
MIRROR, 815
MKDIR, 137-138, 802-804
MODE, 337-341, 358-365, 490, 553-554, 819, 825, 830
MODE COM#, 821
MODE CON, 340, 823
MODE LPT#, 833-836
MONOUMB.386, 836
MORE, 367-369, 837
MOVE, 142, 231-233, 239-240, 838
MSAV, 841
MSBACKUP, 263-264, 845
MSCDEX, 847-849
MSD, 849
MSHERC, 851
MWA, 851
MWAVTSR, 852
MWBACKUP, 852-853
Next, 57
NLSFUNC, 854-855
NUMLOCK, 34, 855-856
Optimize menu (DEFRAG program), 504
Options menu (DOS Editor), 404
Options menu (DOS Shell)
Display, 88
Enable Task Swapper, 106
parameters, 1090
PATH, 37, 48, 143-144, 856-858
PAUSE, 422, 858-860
POWER, 860-864
pretender commands, 489
PRINT, 352-356, 490, 867-871
processing when rebooting, 813-815
PROMPT, 37, 334-337, 529-530, 874-876
RD, 883-884
RECOVER, 291, 884-885
redirecting, 342
REM, 34, 487, 885-886
in batch files, 422
REN, 233-234, 887-888
repeating for group of files, 730-734
REPLACE, 888-891
RESTORE, 275, 891-895
reusing with Doskey program, 446-449
RMDIR, 140, 883-884
SCANDISK, 196-198, 896-901
Search menu (DOS Editor)
Change, 394, 396-397
Find, 59, 394-395
Repeat Last Find, 394-395
SET, 34, 36, 332-334, 490, 901-906
SETVER, 315-319, 906-913
SHARE, 917-918
SHELL, 34-36, 484-486, 918-921
SHIFT, 921
moving with SHIFT command, 436-437

SMARTDRV, 922-926
SMARTMON, 927
SORT, 371-373, 928-930
STACKS, 34-35
STACKS=, 930-932
SUBMENU=, 932-934
SUBST, 343-345, 934-936
SWITCHES, 34-35, 488, 936-940
switches, 1092
syntax, 1092
SYS, 30-31, 190-192, 940-942
system, 566
TIME, 313-314, 942-944
TREE, 145, 944
Tree menu (DOS Shell)
Collapse Branch, 99
Expand All, 99
Expand One Level, 98
TYPE, 196, 212-214, 945-946
displaying batch file contents, 420
UNDELETE, 249, 256, 295-301, 946-950
UNFORMAT, 289-295, 950-951
used in batch files, 412
VER, 314-315, 952
VERIFY, 952-954
View menu (DOS Shell)
All Files, 86
Dual File Lists, 84, 107
Program List, 86
Program/File Lists, 72, 86
Refresh, 82
Single File List, 84-85
VOL, 190, 956-957
VSAFE, 958-959
wildcards, 63-64
XCOPY, 234-240, 961-966
COMMANDS.TXT file, 987
comments in batch files, 422
COMP command, 623-624
COMP.EXE file, 987
comparing, 1088
disks
floppy, 677-679
with DISKCOMP command, 247-248
files, 623-624
with FC command, 240-245, 722-724
strings with IF command, 427-429
Complimentary Metal Oxide Semiconductor (CMOS), 18
compressed disk drives, 637-638
Compressed Drive Information dialog box, 515
compressing
disk drives, 638-639
changing sizes, 649-650
defragmenting, 641-642
deleting files and subdirectories, 644-645
free space, 639-641, 648-649
information, 645-646
uncompressing, 650-651
unmounting, 643
disks, 517-519, 635-636
files, 510
copying, 718-719
compression ratio, 648-649
(DoubleSpace), 515-516
computer viruses, *see* viruses
computers, linking, 771-787
with Interlnk, 215-223
COMSPEC environment variable, 996-997
COMSPEC settings, 326, 333
CONFIG environment variable, 997-998
CONFIG.SYS file, 19, 30-46, 482-490, 983, 1088
commands, 561-562
configuration, 455
AUTOEXEC.BAT file, 482-490
CONFIG.SYS file, 482-490
device drivers, 456-459
hard disks, 480-482
memory, 473-480
memory optimization, 459-480
menu, 44-46
Microsoft Backup/Backup for Windows, 258-260
system, 33-38, 40-46
system devices, 819-853
Undelete program (Windows), 301-302
consoles, 338
configuring, 823-825
copying files from, 229-230
input/output devices, 356-358
redirection operators, 365-367
Contents (Alt-C) command key, 57, 58
Contents command, 57
control keys, 1053
Control Program for Microcomputers (CP/M), 17
controlling
cursor, 530-531
DoubleSpace, 513
screen display, 530-534
conventional memory, 21-23, 320-325, 807-808
loading device drivers, 663-666
loading TSRs, 763-765
conventions
command reference, 568-573
country-specific, 629-631
file-naming, 120-124
COPY command, 225-230, 255, 624-629
defaults, 239-240
redirecting input to COPYCOMP.BAT file, 415
Copy command
DOS Editor Edit menu, 392
DOS Shell File menu, 109
Copy File dialog box, 109
COPYCMD environment variable, 998
COPYCOMP.BAT file, redirecting input, 415
copying
directories
branches, 238-239
with XCOPY command, 234-238
disks
floppy, 679-682
with DISKCOPY command, 245-246
with XCOPY command, 234-238
files, 225-230, 624-629
COMMAND.COM, 620-622
compressed, 718-719
DOS Shell, 107-109
with batch files, 419
COUNTRY command, 33, 541-542
COUNTRY.ICE file, 969
COUNTRY.SYS file, 539-542, 632, 969
COUNTRY= command, 629-631
CP/M (Control Program for Microcomputers), 17
CPI (code page information), 121
CPP (C++ source file) file name extension, 121

CPUs (central processing units), 14-17
Create Directory command (DOS Shell File menu), 100
Create Directory dialog box, 101
Ctrl-Alt-Del (reboot) key combination, 1052
Ctrl-Break (break) key combination, 488-489, 1053
Ctrl-C key (break) combination, 488-489, 1053
Ctrl-F5 (Clean boot) key, 1051
Ctrl-F8 (Interactive boot) key, 1052
Ctrl-key interface (DOS Editor), 385
Ctrl-P (Echo to PRN) key combination, 1053
Ctrl-S (pause) key combination, 1053
CTTY command, 357-358, 632-633
current directory, 606-609
cursor control codes (ANSI), 1075-1076
cursors
  movement, 530-531
    DOS Editor, 385-386
  positioning, 531
Custom setup
  DoubleSpace, 513
  MemMaker, 474, 478-479
customizing
  cursor, 530-531
  DIR command, 210
  keyboards, 534-536
  prompt, 874-876
  screen display, 530-534
Cut command (DOS Editor Edit menu), 392
CV.COM file, 987
CVFs (compressed volume files)
  accessing, 647-648
  deleting, 643
  unmounting, 651
cylinders (disks), 158-160, 169, 1088

D

DAT (Data) file name extension, 121
DATE command, 311-312, 634-635
date/time formats, 1083-1084
dates, 310-314, 634-703
DAYBACK.BAT file, 427
DB (Database, Paradox) file name extension, 121
DBF (Database, dBASE) file name extension, 121
DBLBOOT.BAT file, 987
DBLBOOT.INI file, 987
DBLSPACE commands, 635-636
  /AUTOMOUNT, 636-637
  /CHKDSK, 637-638
  /COMPRESS, 638-639
  /CREATE, 639-641
  /DEFRAGMENT, 641-642
  /DELETE, 643
  /DOUBLEGUARD, 643-644
  /FORMAT, 644-645
  /INFO, 645-646
  /LIST, 646
  /MOUNT, 647-648
  /RATIO, 648-649
  /SIZE, 649-650
  /UNCOMPRESS, 650-651
  /UNMOUNT, 651
DBLSPACE.00x file, 970
DBLSPACE.BIN file, 458, 969
DBLSPACE.EXE file, 969
DBLSPACE.HLP file, 969
DBLSPACE.INF file, 969
DBLSPACE.INI file, 969
DBLSPACE.SYS command, 652-655
DBLSPACE.SYS file, 970
DBLSPACE.WIN file, 970
DBLWIN.HLP file, 970
DCOPY.BAT file, 426
DCT (Dictionary) file name extension, 121
dead keys, 554-556
DEBUG command, 212, 655-656
DEBUG.EXE file, 970
default, 1088
default configurations, 42, 455
DEFAULT.SET file, 978
DEFAULT.SLT file, 978
DEFRAG program (Optimize Menu commands), 502-508, 656-659
DEFRAG.EXE file, 970
Defragment option (DoubleSpace), 519
defragmenting
  compressed disk drives, 641-642
  files, 656-659
  hard disks, 502-508
DEL command, 160
Delete command (DOS Shell File menu), 94, 96
Delete Item dialog box, 94, 96
delete sentry, 295
delete tracker, 296
deleting
  compressed drives, 517
  CVFs (compressed volume files), 643
  directories, 883-884
    branches, 662-663
    DELTREE command, 140-142
    RMDIR command, 140
  files, 305, 509-510
    from drives and directories, 660-661
    on compressed drives, 644-645
    prior to DOS 5.0, 661-662
    with ERASE command, 248-251
  lines of text in DOS Editor, 388
  macros, 454
  program groups, 94
  program items, 96
  subdirectories
    branches, 662-663
    on compressed drives, 644-645
  temporary copy of COMMAND.COM file, 717
deletion-tracking files, 300
delimiters, 52, 1088
DELOLDOS command, 661-662
DELOLDOS.EXE file, 970
DELTREE command, 140-142, 662-663
DELTREE.EXE file, 970
DEV (Program device driver) file name extension, 121
DEVICE command, 34-36, 215, 457, 469, 663-666
device control commands, 489-490
device drivers, 456-459, 589-591, 1088
  commands, 565-566
  DBLSPACE.SYS, 652-655

floppy disk drives, 696-700
INTERLNK.EXE, 765-780
loading
into conventional memory, 663-666
into upper memory, 807-808
into upper memory area, 666-673
loading into upper memory, 468-470
MOUSE.COM, 69
POWER.EXE, 864-867
PRINTER.SYS, 871
RAMDRIVE.SYS, 878-882
SETVER.EXE, 914-916
SMARTDRV.EXE, 926-927
VFINTD.386, 954-956
WINA20.386, 960-961
DEVICEHIGH command, 22, 34, 36, 469, 666-673
dialog boxes, 78-81, 1088
Add Group, 92, 94
Add Program, 95
Associate File, 105
Backup Options, 274-275
Change Compression Ratio, 516
Change Size, 515
Compressed Drive Information, 515
Copy File, 109
Create Directory, 101
Delete Item, 94, 96
DOS Editor, 380, 381-382
Find, 59, 394
Find Deleted Files, 303
Move File, 109
New Program Object, 92
Print, 59
Program Group Properties, 93
Program Item Properties, 96
Screen Display Mode, 88
DIF (Data Interchange Format) files, 121, 979
differential backups, 268
DIR command, 129, 203-210, 673-676
DIR (program data file, directory) file name extension, 121
DIRCMD environment variable, 999
directories, 81-87, 97, 116, 128-131, 497, 611, 802-804, 1088
adding disk drives, 342-343
changing, 138-140, 606-609
CHKDSK command, 192
commands, 563
copying
branches, 238-239
with XCOPY command, 234-238
creating, 100-101, 137-138
deleting, 883-884
branches, 662-663
DELTREE command, 140-142
RMDIR command, 140
entries, 124
expanding/collapsing branches, 98-100
files
deleting, 660-661
information, 673-676
selecting, 101-104
listing
with DIR command, 205
with TREE command, 145
moving with MOVE command, 232-233
PATH command, 856-858
path name expressions, 133-137
paths
absolute, 1087
relative, 1091
renaming, 142
with MOVE command, 233
root, 1091
sorting, 505-506
splitting, 343-345
subdirectories, 1092
temporary, 145-147
disk caching (hard disks), 492-497, 922-926
disk drives, 1088
adding to directory of other disks, 342-343
aliases, 596
commands, 342
compressed, 637-638
changing size, 649-650
defragmenting, 641-642
deleting files and subdirectories, 644-645
free space, 648-649
information, 645-646
uncompressing, 650-651
unmounting, 643
cylinders, 158-160
directories, splitting, 343-345
free space, 639-641
information, 646
installing, 700-703
mounting removable, 636-637
networks, 798-799
read/write heads, 157
sectors, 160-162
tracks, 157-158
disk-compression programs, 635-636, 638-639
DISKCOMP command, 247-248, 677-679
DISKCOMP.COM file, 970
DISKCOPY command, 245-246, 425, 679-682
DISKCOPY.COM file, 971
disks, 26-27, 167-170, 1088
boot, 30-32
boot sectors, 1087
clusters, 1087
comparing
floppy, 677-679
with DISKCOMP command, 247-248
copying
floppy, 679-682
with DISKCOPY command, 245-246
with XCOPY command, 234-238
cylinders, 1088
diskettes, 1088
errors, 896-901
floppy, 1089
formatting, 160
hard, 1090
magnetic storage, 150-151
partitions, 1088
platters, 1091
RAM disks, 498-502
sectors, 1091
storage memory, 17
tracks, 1092
unformatting, 289-295
rebuilding partition tables, 294-295
recovering from accidental formats, 291-294
volume labels, 796-798, 1093
see also floppy disks; hard disks

display adapters
Color Graphics Adapter (CGA), 740-741
EGA, 708-709
Display color codes (ANSI), 1074-1075
Display command
DOS Editor Options menu, 404
DOS Shell Options menu, 88
display control codes (ANSI), 1076
display menus, 432-433
DISPLAY.SYS command, 458, 684-685
DISPLAY.SYS file, 549, 971
displaying
compressed information (DoubleSpace), 514
free/used memory, 470-473
file information, 304
DLL (Windows Dynamic Link Library) file name extension, 121
DMDRVR.BIN file, 458, 971
DOC (Document) file name extension, 122
documents, *see* files
DOS
commands, 49-50
parameters, 52
switches, 52-53
syntax, 50-52
programs, 564-565
starting, 811-813
versions, 314-319
DOS command, 34, 687-688
DOS Editor, 377-378
clipboard, 391-392
cursor movement, 385-386
dialog boxes, 381-382
exiting, 403
files, 378
creating, 402
loading at start, 401-402
opening, 400-401
printing, 402-403
saving, 398-400
menus, 380-381
File, 397-398
Help, 406-408
mouse, 383-385
Overtype mode, 388
screen, 379-380
customizing, 404-406
shortcut keys, 382-383
starting, 378
with optional switches, 403-404
text
blocks, 392-393
deleting lines, 388
finding/replacing, 393-397
indents, 388
inserting, 387
inserting lines, 388
place markers, 390
scrolling, 386-387
selecting, 390-391
splitting/joining lines, 388
tabs, 389-390
DOS prompt, 1088
DOS Shell, 67-69
areas
navigating, 73-74
selecting, 72-73
directories, 97
creating, 100-101
expanding/collapsing branches, 98-100
files, 97, 101
associating with programs, 105-106
copying, 107-109
deselecting, 103-104
moving, 109
selecting, 101-104
viewing, 104-105
help system, 88-89
interface, 70-72
menus
dialog boxes, 78-81
hot keys, 77-78
pull-down, 75-76
selecting options, 74-75
program groups, 90-95
program items, 95-97
starting, 69-70
task swapping, 106-107
video modes, 87-88
views, 81-87
DOSHELP.HLP file, 973
Doskey program, 62, 444, 690-692
command-history buffer keys, 447-448
command-line editing keys, 446, 1055-1056
editing commands, 447
loading, 443-444
macros, *see* macros
reusing commands, 446-449
syntax, 444
DOSKEY.COM file, 971
DOSSETUP.INI file, 983
DOSSHELL command, 694-696
DOSSHELL.COM file, 971
DOSSHELL.EXE file, 971
DOSSHELL.GRB file, 972
DOSSHELL.HLP file, 971
DOSSHELL.INI file, 971
DOSSHELL.VID file, 972
DOSSWAP.EXE file, 972
DOT (Word for Windows template) file name extension, 122
double-density disks, 173
double-density formats, 162
DoubleSpace program, 32, 511-520, 635-655
compressing drives, 517-519
compression ratio, 515-516
controlling, 513
Defragment option, 519
deleting compressed drives, 517
displaying compressed information, 514
drive size, 514-515
formatting compressed drives, 517
installing, 513
uncompressing disks, 520
DRIVER.SYS command, 458, 698-700, 972
drivers
device drivers, 589-591
commands, 565-566
DBLSPACE.SYS, 652-655
floppy disk drives, 696-700
INTERLNK.EXE, 765-770
loading, 663-673
INTERLNK.EXE, 771-780
MOUSE.COM, 69
drives
CD-ROM, 847-849
floppy disk, 151, 154-155
hard disk, 152-153
logical, 1090
mounting removable, 636-637
path name expressions, 133-137
subdirectories, 787-789
see also disk drives

DRIVPARM command, 34, 702-703
DRV (program device driver) file name extension, 122
DTA (Data) file name extension, 122
dual file list, 84
Dual File Lists command (DOS Shell View menu), 84, 107
DVORAK.SYS file, 987
DVORAK.TXT file, 987

E

/E parameter (KEYB command), 543
/E:elementsize parameter (disk caching), 494
ECHO command, 421, 703-707
ECHO OFF command, 37
Edit keystroke commands, 1056-1059
EDIT command, 36, 38, 196, 403-404, 707
Edit menu commands (DOS Editor)
  Clear, 392
  Copy, 392
  Cut, 392
  Paste, 392
EDIT.COM file, 972
EDIT.HLP file, 972
editing
  command-line, 444-446
  commands, 61-63
    Doskey program, 447
  files (ASCII text), 707
  programs, 655-656
  text, 708
EDLIN command, 708
EDLIN.EXE file, 987
EEMS (Enhanced Expanded Memory Specification), 23
EGA display adapters, 349, 708-709
EGA.CPI file, 547, 971
EGA.GRB file, 972
EGA.ICE file, 971
EGA.INI file, 972
EGA.SYS command, 458, 708-709, 972
EGA.VID file, 972
EGA2.CPI file, 971
EGAMONO.GRB file, 972
EISA (Extended Industry Standard Architecture) buses, 464
electricity
  static, 1092
  surge protectors, 1092
  voltage regulators, 1092
EMM 386 (Expanded Memory Manager), 24
EMM386 command, 709-710
EMM386.EXE, 22, 35, 458, 465-468, 710-716, 973
EMS (Expanded Memory Specification), 23-26, 320-325, 709-716
emulating expanded memory, 465-468
Enable Task Swapper (DOS Shell Options menu), 106
:END label in batch files, 428
end-of-file (EOF) marker, 1088
Enhanced Color Graphics Adapter (EGA), 830-833
Enhanced Expanded Memory Specification (EEMS), 23
Enter key, 1054
environment, 33, 326
environment variables, 332-334, 995
  APPEND environment variable, 996
  COMSPEC, 996-997
  CONFIG, 997-998
  COPYCMD, 998
  DIRCMD, 999
  MSDOSDATA, 999-1001
  PATH, 1001-1002
  PROMPT, 1002
  TEMP/TMP, 1002-1003
  windir WINDOWS, 1003
  WINPMT, 1003-1004
EPS (Encapsulated PostScript) file name extension, 122
ERASE command, 248-251, 255, 660-661, 716
error messages, 1005
ERRORLEVEL, testing with IF command, 424-427
Esc key, 1054
EXE (executable program) files, 122, 716-717
EXE2BIN command, 716-717
EXE2BIN.EXE file, 988
executing batch files, 441
exit codes
  DISKCOPY command, 425
  programs, 425
EXIT command, 328-329, 717
Exit command (DOS Editor File menu), 398, 403
exiting
  command processor, 328
  DOS Editor, 403
Expand All command (DOS Shell Tree menu), 99
EXPAND command, 718-719
Expand One Level command (DOS Shell Tree menu), 98
EXPAND.EXE file, 973
expanded memory (EMS), 21-25, 465-468, 709-716, 1089
Expanded Memory Manager (EMM386), 24, 35
Expanded Memory Specification (EMS), 23-26
Express setup
  DoubleSpace, 513
  MemMaker, 474-478
extended memory (XMS), 460-464, 1089
  converting to LIM expanded memory (EMS), 710-716
extended memory blocks (XMS memory), 460
Extended Memory Specification (XMS), 25-26
extended-memory managers, 35, 745-754
extensions, 1089
  file names, 116, 120
  program utilities, 990-994
external commands, 48-49, 1089

F

/F switch
  FORMAT command, 172
  SWITCHES command, 35
F5 (Clean boot) key, 1051
F8 (Interactive boot) key, 1052
FAKEMOUS.COM file, 986
FASTHELP command, 719-720
FASTHELP.EXE file, 973
FASTOPEN program, 720-722
  hard disks, 497-498
FASTOPEN.EXE file, 973
FATs (File Allocation Tables), 116, 159, 168, 611-616
  CHKDSK command, 192, 195
  information, 815-818
FC command, 240-245, 722-724

FC.EXE file, 973
FCBS command, 34, 482-483, 724-725
FDISK command, 180-188, 725-727
FDISK.EXE file, 973
fields file attribute, 125
File Allocation Tables, *see* FATs
FILE command, 34
file control blocks (FCBs), 724
File menu (Alt-F) command key, 58
File menu commands (DOS Editor)
  Exit, 398, 403
  New, 398
  Open, 398
  Print, 398, 402
  Save, 398
  Save As, 399-400
File menu commands (DOS Shell)
  Associate, 105
  Copy, 109
  Create Directory, 100
  Delete, 94, 96
  Move, 109
  New, 92, 95
  Properties, 93, 96
  Reorder, 94
  Select All, 103
  View File Contents, 104
file names, 115-120, 124, 571
  conventions, 120-124
  extensions, 26, 990-994
file systems, 113-128, 1089
files, 26, 81-87, 97, 114-116, 201-202, 1089
  4201.CPI, 989
  4208.CPI, 989
  5202.CPI, 989
  8514.VID, 972
  accessing, 482-483
    CVFs (compressed volume files), 647-648
  ADOS.CFG, 986
  ADOS.COM, 986
  ADOS.OVL, 986
  ADOS.TXT, 986
  ANSI.SYS, 41, 968
  APPEND.EXE, 968
  archiving, 510
  AREADME.TXT, 986
  ASCII text, 707
  ASSIGN.COM, 986
  ATTRIB.EXE, 969
  attributes, 124-128, 596-599, 1087
  AUTOEXEC.BAT, 20, 30-32, 36-46, 983, 1087
    dates/times, 311
    defining macros from bootup, 453
  AV.GRP, 985
  backups, 599, 845-847
    differential, 268
    full, 264-267
    incremental, 267-268
    policies, 262-263
    restoring, 275-280
    special-purpose, 268-273
  BACKUP.EXE, 987
  batch files, 377, 603-606, 1087
    conditional execution, 754-760
    on-screen messages, 703-707
    running other batch files, 437-441
  binary, 1087
  BK.GRP, 985
  BKAV.GRP, 985
  BKUD.GRP, 985
  BKUDAV.GRP, 985
  BUSETUP.EXE, 983
  CFFs (compressed volume files), 651
  CGA.GRB, 972
  CGA.INI, 972
  CGA.VID, 972
  CHKDSK.EXE, 969
  CHKLST.MS, 977
  CHKSTATE.SYS, 975
  CHOICE.COM, 969
  COMMAND.COM, 20, 30, 47-49, 71, 969
    deleting temporary copy, 717
    exiting, 328
    second copy, 325-329
  commands, 564
  COMMANDS.TXT, 987
  COMP.EXE, 987
  comparing, 623-624
    with FC command, 240-245, 722-724
  compressing, 510, 638-639
  CONFIG.SYS, 19, 30-36, 38-46, 983, 1088
  converting .EXE to .BIN or .COM files, 716-717
  COPYCOMP.BAT, 415
  copying, 225-230, 624-629
    COMMAND.COM, 620-622
    compressed, 718-719
    with batch files, 419
  COUNTRY.ICE, 969
  COUNTRY.SYS, 540-542, 969
  creating with DOS Editor, 402
  CV.COM, 987
  date and time stamp, 310-314
  DAYBACK.BAT, 427
  DBLBOOT.BAT, 987
  DBLBOOT.INI, 987
  DBLSPACE.00x, 970
  DBLSPACE.BIN, 969
  DBLSPACE.EXE, 969
  DBLSPACE.HLP, 969
  DBLSPACE.INF, 969
  DBLSPACE.INI, 969
  DBLSPACE.SYS, 970
  DBLSPACE.WIN, 970
  DBLWIN.HLP, 970
  DCOPY.BAT, 426
  DEBUG.EXE, 970
  DEFAULT.SET, 978
  DEFAULT.SLT, 978
  DEFRAG.EXE, 970
  defragmenting, 656-659
  delete sentry, 295
  delete tracker, 296
  deleting, 305, 509-510
    from drives and directories, 660-661
    prior to DOS 5.0, 661-662
    with ERASE command, 248-251
  deletion-tracking, 300
  DELOLDOS.EXE, 970
  DELTREE.EXE, 970
  directories, 497
  DISKCOMP.COM, 970
  DISKCOPY.COM, 971
  DISPLAY.SYS, 549, 971
  displaying information, 304, 673-676
  DMDRVR.BIN, 971
  DOS Editor, 378
  DOS Shell, 101
    associating with programs, 105-106
    copying, 107-109
    deselecting, 103-104
    moving, 109
    selecting, 101-104
    viewing, 104-105

DOSHELP.HLP, 973
DOSKEY.COM, 971
DOSSETUP.INI, 983
DOSSHELL.COM, 971
DOSSHELL.EXE, 971
DOSSHELL.GRB, 972
DOSSHELL.HLP, 971
DOSSHELL.INI, 971
DOSSHELL.VID, 972
DOSSWAP.EXE, 972
DRIVER.SYS, 972
DVORAK.SYS, 987
DVORAK.TXT, 987
EDIT.COM, 972
EDIT.HLP, 972
EDLIN.EXE, 987
EGA.CPI, 547, 971
EGA.GRB, 972
EGA.ICE, 971
EGA.INI, 972
EGA.SYS, 972
EGA.VID, 972
EGA2.CPI, 971
EGAMONO.GRB, 972
EMM386.EXE, 35, 973
EXE2BIN.EXE, 988
EXPAND.EXE, 973
extensions, 1089
  .DIF, 979
  .FUL, 979
  .INC, 979
  .SET, 978
  .SLT, 978
FAKEMOUS.COM, 986
FASTHELP.EXE, 973
FASTOPEN.EXE, 973
FC.EXE, 973
FDISK.EXE, 973
FIND.EXE, 974
finding, 143-144, 592-595, 728-730
  text, 369-371
  with DIR command, 209-210
  with FIND command, 214
FORMAT.COM, 974
fragmentation, 160
GORILLA.BAS, 990
GRAFTABL.COM, 988
GRAPHICS.COM, 974
GRAPHICS.PRO, 974
handles, 483, 727-728
HELP.COM, 974
HELP.HLP, 974
HERC.GRB, 972
HERC.VID, 972
HIMEM.SYS, 35, 974
information, 815-818
INTERLNK.EXE, 215-218, 974
INTERSVR, 219
INTERSVR.EXE, 974
IO.SYS, 19, 30-31, 974
JOIN.EXE, 988
KBDBUF.SYS, 988
KEYB.COM, 543-545, 974
KEYBOARD.ICE, 974
KEYBOARD.SYS, 974
KEYBRD2.SYS, 975
LABEL.EXE, 975
LCD.CPI, 547, 988
listing with DIR command, 205-206
LOADFIX.COM, 975
loading at DOS Editor start-up, 401-402
locking, 917-918
MACROS.BAT, 452
MEM.EXE, 975
MEMMAKER.EXE, 975
MEMMAKER.HLP, 975
MEMMAKER.INF, 975
MEMMAKER.STS, 975
MIRROR image files, 290
MIRROR.COM, 988
MODE.COM, 975
MONEY.BAS, 990
MONO.GRB, 972
MONO.INI, 972
MONOUMB.386, 976
MORE.COM, 976
MOUSE.COM, 976
MOUSE.INI, 976
MOVE.EXE, 976
moving, 232-233, 838-841
MSAV.EXE, 976
MSAV.HLP, 976
MSAV.INI, 976
MSAVHELP.OVL, 976
MSAVIRUS.LST, 976
MSBACKDB.OVL, 977
MSBACKDR.OVL, 977
MSBACKFB.OVL, 977
MSBACKFR.OVL, 977
MSBACKUP.EXE, 977
MSBACKUP.HLP, 977
MSBACKUP.INI, 977
MSBACKUP.LOG, 977
MSBACKUP.OVL, 977
MSBCONFG.HLP, 977
MSBCONFG.OVL, 977
MSCDEX.EXE, 979
MSD.EXE, 979
MSDOS.SYS, 19, 30-31, 979
MSHERC.COM, 988
MSTOOLS.DLL, 979
MWAV.EXE, 979
MWAV.HLP, 979
MWAV.INI, 979
MWAVABSI.DLL, 980
MWAVDLG.DLL, 980
MWAVDOSL.DLL, 980
MWAVDRVL.DLL, 980
MWAVMGR.DLL, 980
MWAVSCAN.DLL, 980
MWAVSOS.DLL, 980
MWAVTSR.EXE, 980
MWBACKF.DLL, 980
MWBACKR.DLL, 980
MWBACKUP.EXE, 980
MWBACKUP.HLP, 980
MWBACKUP.INI, 981
MWGRAFIC.DLL, 980
MWUNDEL.EXE, 981
MWUNDEL.HLP, 981
names, 120-124, 1090
NET.1XE, 989
NET.TXT, 988
NETBEUI.DOS, 989
NETWKSTA.1XE, 989
NETWKSTA.2EX, 989
NETWORKS.TXT, 981
NIBBLES.BAS, 990
NLSFUNC.EXE, 549, 551, 981
opening, 720-722
  DOS Editor, 400-401
OS2.TXT, 981
PACKING.LST, 981
path name expressions, 133-137
POWER.EXE, 981
PRINT.EXE, 982
PRINTER.SYS, 549-550, 989
PRINTFIX.COM, 989
printing, 304, 352-356
  DOS Editor, 402-403
  with MODE command, 359-363
QBASIC.EXE, 982
QBASIC.HLP, 982
QBASIC.INI, 982
RAMDRIVE.SYS, 982
README, 378
README.TXT, 982
recovering, 295-301
  DOS directory method, 300-301

from command line, 297-300
UNDELETE command, 295-297
Undelete program (Windows), 303-304
REDIR.1XE, 989
REDIR.2XE, 989
REMLINE.BAS, 990
renaming, 887-888
with COPY command, 229
with REN command, 233-234
REPLACE.EXE, 982
replacing, 888-891
RESTORE.EXE, 982
restoring backup files, 891-895
saving in DOS Editor, 398-400
SCANDISK.EXE, 982
SCANDISK.INI, 982
scratchpad, 145-147
searching for with IF command, 429-430
selecting, 305
SETNAME.EXE, 989
SETUP.EXE, 983
SETUP.MSG, 983
SETVER.EXE, 983
SHARE.EXE, 983
SIZER.EXE, 975
SMARTDRV.EXE, 983
SMARTMON.EXE, 984
SMARTMON.HLP, 984
SMARTMON.LOG, 984
SORT.EXE, 984
sorting, 304
SPATCH.BAT, 984
SSTOR.SYS, 984
SUBST.EXE, 984
SYS.COM, 984
system, 190
text, 1092
transferring with Interlnk, 220-221
TREE.COM, 984
UD.GRP, 985
UDAV.GRP, 985
UNDELETE.EXE, 984
UNDELETE.INI, 984
undeleting, 301-305
UNFORMAT.COM, 985
UNINSTALL.EXE, 983
VFINTD.386, 981
VGA.GRB, 972
VGA.VID, 972
VGAMONO.GRB, 972
viewing, 211-214
VSAFE.COM, 985
WINA20.386, 985
WNTOOLS.GRP, 985
XCOPY.EXE, 985
see also batch files
FILES command, 483, 727-728
filter programs, 837-838
filters, 1089
FIND, 369-371
MORE, 367-369
SORT, 371-373
FIND command, 214, 369-371, 728-730
Find command
DOS Editor Search menu, 394-395
Search menu, 59
Find Deleted Files dialog box, 303
Find dialog box, 59, 394
FIND.EXE file, 974
finding
files, 143-144, 592-595, 728-730
with DIR command, 209-210
with FIND command, 214
text, 369-371
DOS Editor, 393-395
fixed disks, *see* hard disks
floppy disks, 26, 1089
analyzing with CHKDSK command, 192-196
booting PCs, 31-32
comparing, 677-679
compressing files, 638-639
copying, 679-682
drives, 151, 154-155, 696-700
formats, 162-164
formatting, 170-179, 734-739
magnetic storage, 150-151
raw/usable capacity, 164-165
viruses, 281, 286-287
volume labels, 190
write-protecting, 155-156
flow control, 1089
FNT (Font) file name extension, 122
FOR command, 730-734
FOR..IN..DO command, 433-436
batch file use, 434-435
from DOS prompt, 435
interactive usage, 435-436
FORMAT command, 30-32, 129, 168-179, 188-189, 255, 291, 734-739
FORMAT.COM file, 974
formatting, 1089
compressed drives, 517
disks, 160
floppy, 162-164, 170-179, 734-739
hard, 165-166, 188-189, 734-739
fragmentation (disks), 502-508
free memory, displaying, 470-473
FUL file name extension, 979
full backups, 264-267, 1089
functions in Microsoft Backup/Backup for Windows, 260-262

G

German code page, 1082
GIF (Graphics Interchange Format) file name extension, 122
GORILLA.BAS file, 990
GOTO command, 45, 423-424, 739-740
GRAFTABL command, 740-741
GRAFTABL.COM file, 988
graphical user interface (GUI), 67, 87
graphics, printing, 741-743
GRAPHICS command, 349-352, 741-743
graphics display adapter (Color Graphics Adapter), 830-833
graphics mode, 87, 1089
GRAPHICS.COM file, 974
GRAPHICS.PRO file, 974
grayed commands, 381
Greek code page, 1082
groups of files, copying, 228
GRP (Windows Program Group) file name extension, 122
GUI (graphical user interface), 67, 87
guidelines for batch files creation, 413-414

H

H (Header files, C program) file name extension, 122
handler codes (memory), 462-463
handles (file handles), 483
hard disks, 27, 152-153, 1090
  analyzing
    with CHKDSK command, 192-196
    with SCANDISK command, 196-198
  backing up, 599, 845-847, 852-853
  booting PCs, 31-32
  buffers, 601-603
  compressing, 638-639
  defragmenting, 502-508
  disk caching, 492-497
  disk errors, 896-901
  DoubleSpace program, 511-520
    compressing drives, 517-519
    compression ratio, 515-516
    controlling, 513
    Defragment option, 519
    deleting compressed drives, 517
    displaying compressed information, 514
    drive size, 514-515
    formatting compressed drives, 517
    installing, 513
    uncompressing disks, 520
  FASTOPEN program, 497-498
  files
    deleting prior to DOS 5.0, 661-662
    information, 673-676
  formats, 165-166, 188-189, 734-739
  maximizing space, 509-510
    archiving, 510
    compression, 510
    deleting files, 509-510
  optimizing, 503-508
  partitioning, 180-188, 725-727
  performance, 480-482, 491-521
    RAM disks, 498-502
    RECOVER command, 884-885
    speed, 492-508
    splitting directories, 343-345
    status, 611-616
    subdirectories, 802-804
    system configuration, 482-490
    volume labels, 190
hardware, 13-14
  checking for code page switching, 547-548
  problems/prevention, 254
hardwired CPUs, 14
Help, 53-60
  commands, 719-720
  DOS Shell, 88-89
  on-line, 406-408, 743-744
Help (F1) hot key, 88
HELP command, 55, 743-744
HELP.COM file, 974
HELP.HLP file, 974
HERC.GRB file, 972
HERC.VID file, 972
Hercules Monochrome Graphics Adapter, 851
Hewlett-Packard printers, 350
Hidden file attribute, 125
high memory area (HMA), 22, 460, 686-688, 1090
  loading DOS, 464-465
high-density disks, 173
highlighted options, 1090
HIMEM.SYS, 22, 35, 458, 460-464, 745-754, 974
HLP (Help) file name extension, 122
HMA (high-memory area), 1090
hot keys, 77-78, 88

I

I/O (input/output) devices, 632-633
IBM printers, 349
Icelandic code page, 1082
icons in command reference, 570
/ID parameter (KEYB command), 543
IDX (Index file), 122
IF command, 754-760
  batch files, 424-430
  comparing strings, 427-429
  searching for files, 429-430
IMG (GEM image) file name extension, 122
INC file name extension, 979
INCLUDE= command, 760-763
incremental backups, 267-268
indents, 388
INF (Information) file name extension, 122
infinite loops, 424
information messages, 1005
INI (Initialization) file name extension, 122
initcachesize parameter in disk caching, 494
INKEY( ) values, 1064-1071
input devices, 356
insert mode, 1090
inserting text in DOS Editor, 387-388
INSTALL command, 34, 486-487, 763-765
installation
  ANSI.SYS, 525-526
  batch files, 420
  code page switching, 548-551
  disk drives, 700-703
  DoubleSpace, 513
  Interlnk remotely, 221-222
  UNDELETE command in AUTOEXEC.BAT, 297-300
Intel
  chips, 21
  EMS (Expanded Memory Specification), 23-26
  expanded memory, 21
Interactive boot (Ctrl-F5) key, 1052
Interactive boot (F5) key, 1052
interfaces
  COMMAND.COM, 20
  DOS Shell, 70-72
Interlnk, 215
  installing remotely, 221-222
  loading, 217-219
  remote printing, 221
  running programs remotely, 222-223
  setup, 215-217
  transferring files, 220-221
INTERLNK command, 765-770
INTERLNK.EXE, 215-218, 458, 771-780, 974
intermediate backups, 1090
internal commands, 48, 1090

international features, 539-557
character sets, 871
code pages, 546-556, 682-685, 871-873, 1081-1086
commands, 565-566
country codes, 1081-1086
COUNTRY.SYS, 540-542
date/time formats, 1083-1084
KEYB.COM, 543-545
keyboards, 545-546, 1085-1086
interrupts, 47
INTERSVR program, 219, 771-787
INTERSVR.EXE file, 974
IO.SYS file, 19, 30-31, 974

J–K

JOIN command, 342-345, 787-789
JOIN.EXE file, 988
joining lines of text (DOS Editor), 388
jumps, 56

/K switch (SWITCH command), 35
KBDBUF.SYS command, 790, 988
KEYB command, 541, 791-795
KEYB.COM, 539, 543-545, 974
KEYBOARD.ICE file, 974
KEYBOARD.SYS command, 795-796, 974
keyboards
ANSI Keyboard Layout Control Codes, 1076-1080
buffers, 790-791
changing layout/characters to other languages, 791-795
configuring, 823-825
copying files from, 229-230
customizing ANSI.SYS, 534-536
dead keys, 554-556
input/output devices, 356-358
international, 541 795-796, 1085-1086
keystroke commands, 1051-1061
remapping, 545-546
typematic rates, 364-365
KEYBRD2.SYS file, 975
keypad interface (DOS Editor), 385
keystroke command shortcuts, *see* hot keys
keywords, 50, 1090

L

/L switch in disk caching, 495
LABEL command, 796-798
LABEL.EXE file, 975
labels
:END (batch files), 428
GOTO command, 423
TRY_AGAIN (batch files), 428
volume, 1093
laptop computers
POWER command, 860-864
POWER.EXE device driver, 864-867
Last Topic (Alt-B) command key, 58
LASTDRIVE command, 34-35, 483-484, 798-799
layouts (keyboard), 791-795
LCD (liquid-crystal display), 1090
LCD.CPI file, 547, 988
Left Arrow key, 1054
LET (Letter) file name extension, 122
LH command, 38, 800-802
LHA (compressed) file name extension, 122
LIB (program library) file name extension, 122
LIM 3.2 specification, 23-26
linking computers, 215-223, 771-787
liquid-crystal display (LCD), 1090
list boxes, 80
listing
directories with TREE command, 145
files with DIR command, 205-206
LOADFIX command, 800
LOADFIX.COM file, 975
LOADHIGH command, 22, 38, 469
loading
code page tables, 551-552
DOS, 461-465
Doskey program, 443-444
files at DOS Editor startup, 401-402
programs into upper memory, 800-802
TSRs into conventional memory, 763-765
locating commands with Doskey program, 449
location counter, 1090
locking files/records, 917-918
LOG (file logging actions) file name extension, 122
logical devices, 118
logical drives, 1090
look-ahead buffers, 481
Lotus
EMS (Expanded Memory Specification), 23-26
expanded memory, 21
Lotus/Intel/Microsoft/AST Extended Memory Specification (XMS), 1093
low-level formats, 166
LST (program listing) file name extension, 122

M

macros, 443, 449-454, 1090
activating, 453-454
creating, 450-453
defining from bootup, 453
deleting, 454
naming, 451
special characters, 451
syntax, 450
MACROS.BAT file, 452
magnetic storage, 150-151
MAK (Programmer's make file) file name extension, 122
MAP (Linker map) file name extension, 122
maximizing hard disks, 509-510
MD or MKDIR command, 802-804
MEM command, 319-325, 470, 804-806
MEM reports, 470-472
MEM.EXE file, 975

MemMaker, 455, 473-480
Custom Setup, 474, 478-479
Express Setup, 474-478
MEMMAKER command, 807
MEMMAKER.EXE file, 975
MEMMAKER.HLP file, 975
MEMMAKER.INF file, 975
MEMMAKER.STS file, 975
memory, 15, 319-325
allocating, 804-806
buffers, 601-603, 1087
commands, 566
configuring, 473-480
conventional, 21-23, 807-808
loading TSRs, 763-765
disk storage, 17
displaying free/used, 470-473
EMS (expanded), 709-710
expanded, 21, 23-25, 1089
expanded memory manager, 35
extended, 1089
extended memory manager, 35, 745-754
handler codes, 462-463
HMA (high memory area), 22, 1090
loading device drivers
into conventional, 663-666
into upper area, 666-673
monitoring integrity by DoubleGuard, 643
optimizing, 459-480, 616-617
EMM386.EXE, 465-468
expanded memory, 465-468
extended memory, 460-464
HIMEM.SYS, 460-464
upper memory, 468-470
overlays, 499
programs loaded in first segment, 800
RAM (random-access memory), 16-17, 20-21
disks, 498-502
drives, 878-882
ROM (read-only memory), 16-17
shadow RAM, 464
status, 611-616
UMBs (upper memory blocks), 22, 709-716, 1092
loading programs, 800-802
XMS (Extended Memory Specification), 25-26, 710-716
menu bars, 70
DOS Editor, 379
MENUCOLOR= command, 808
MENUDEFAULT= command, 811
menuing programs, 90
MENUITEM= command, 813
menus
color, 42-44
configuration, 44-46
creating with CHOICE command, 431-432
display menus, 432-433
DOS Editor, 380-381
DOS Shell
dialog boxes, 78-81
hot keys, 77-78
pull-down, 75-76
selecting options, 74-75
pull-down, 1091
system, 44-46
messages, 1005-1042
meta-strings, 335, 1090
PROMPT command, 335-337
microprocessor chips, *see* CPUs
Microsoft Anti-Virus, 255, 281-286, 841-845, 851-852
Microsoft Backup/Backup for Windows, 256-258, 852-853
configuring, 258-260
differential backups, 268
full backups, 264-267
functions, 260-262
incremental backups, 267-268
special-purpose backups, 268-273
Microsoft System Diagnostics, 849-850
MIRROR command, 815
MIRROR image files, 290-292
MIRROR.COM file, 988
MKDIR command, 137-138
MODE COM# command, 821
MODE command, 337-341, 358-365, 490, 553-554, 819, 825, 830
MODE CON command, 340, 823
MODE LPT# command, 833
MODE.COM file, 975
modes
graphics, 87, 1089
insert, 1090
Overtype, 388, 1090
protected, 20-21
real, 20-21
text, 1092
video (DOS Shell), 87-88
MONEY.BAS file, 990
MONO.GRB file, 972
MONO.INI file, 972
monochrome display adapters (MDA), 830-833, 836-837
MONOUMB.386 command, 458, 836, 976
MORE command, 367-369, 837
MORE.COM file, 976
motherboard, 14
mounting removable drives, 636-703
mouse
DOS Editor, 383-385
DOS Shell, 69
pointer, 1090
MOUSE.COM device driver, 69, 459, 976
MOUSE.INI file, 976
MOVE command, 142, 231-233, 239-240, 838
Move command (DOS Shell File menu), 109
Move File dialog box, 109
MOVE.EXE file, 976
moving
directories, 232-233
files, 232-233
DOS Shell, 109
MS-DOS 6
files included with, 967-985
Supplemental Disk files, 985-990
upgrade versions, 967
MSAV command, 841
MSAV, *see* Microsoft Anti-Virus
MSAV.EXE file, 976
MSAV.HLP file, 976
MSAV.INI file, 976
MSAVHELP.OVL file, 976
MSAVIRUS.LST file, 976
MSBACKDB.OVL file, 977
MSBACKDR.OVL file, 977
MSBACKFB.OVL file, 977
MSBACKFR.OVL file, 977
MSBACKUP command, 263-264, 845

MSBACKUP.EXE file, 977
MSBACKUP.HLP file, 977
MSBACKUP.INI file, 977
MSBACKUP.LOG file, 977
MSBACKUP.OVL file, 977
MSBCONFG.HLP file, 977
MSBCONFG.OVL file, 977
MSCDEX command, 847-849
MSCDEX.EXE file, 979
MSD command, 849
MSD.EXE file, 979
MSDOS.SYS file, 19, 30-31, 979
MSDOSDATA environment variable, 999-1001
MSG (program message) file name extension, 122
MSHERC command, 851
MSHERC.COM file, 988
MSTOOLS.DLL file, 979
Multilingual (Latin I) code page, 1081-1082
MWA command, 851
MWAV.EXE file, 979
MWAV.HLP file, 979
MWAV.INI file, 979
MWAVABSI.DLL file, 980
MWAVDLG.DLL file, 980
MWAVDOSL.DLL file, 980
MWAVDRVL.DLL file, 980
MWAVMGR.DLL file, 980
MWAVSCAN.DLL file, 980
MWAVSOS.DLL file, 980
MWAVTSR command, 852
MWAVTSR.EXE file, 980
MWBACKF.DLL file, 980
MWBACKR.DLL file, 980
MWBACKUP command, 852-853
MWBACKUP.EXE file, 980
MWBACKUP.HLP file, 980
MWBACKUP.INI file, 981
MWGRAFIC.DLL file, 980
MWUNDEL.EXE file, 981
MWUNDEL.HLP file, 981

N

names, 1090
  files, 116-120, 571-573
  macros, 451
national language support, 540
navigating
  DOS Shell areas, 73-74
  help system, 55-60
NDX (Index) file name extension, 122
NET.1XE file, 989
NET.TXT file, 988
NETBEUI.DOS file, 989
NETWKSTA.1XE file, 989
NETWKSTA.2EX file, 989
networks, 798-799
NETWORKS.TXT file, 981
New command
  DOS Editor File menu, 398
  DOS Shell File menu, 92, 95
New Program Object dialog box, 92
Next (Alt-N) command key, 57
Next command, 57
Next Topic (Alt-N) command key, 58
NIBBLES.BAS file, 990
NLSFUNC command, 854-855
NLSFUNC.EXE file, 549, 551, 981
NUMLOCK command, 34, 855-856

O

OBJ (Intermediate object code) file name extension, 122
OLD (Backup) file name extension, 122
on-line help, 53-60, 406-408, 743-744
Open command (DOS Editor File menu), 398
opening files, 720-722
  DOS Editor, 400-401
operators, 365-367
optical disks, 27
Optimize Menu commands (DEFRAG program), 504
optimizing
  hard disks, 503-508
  memory, 459-480, 616-617
option buttons, 80
option check boxes, 80
Options menu commands (DOS Editor)
  Display, 404
Options menu commands (DOS Shell)
  Display, 88
  Enable Task Swapper, 106
OS2.TXT file, 981
output devices, 356
overlays, 499
Overtype mode (DOS Editor), 388
overtype mode, 1090
OVL (Program overlay) file name extension, 123
OVR (Program overlay) file name extension, 123

P

/P switch (DIR command), 206
PACKING.LST file, 981
page switches (code page tables), 552-553
PAK (Packed archive) file name extension, 123
parallel ports
  redirecting to serial ports, 363-364
  settings, 358-360
parameters, 52, 1090
  moving with SHIFT command, 436-437
  replaceable, in batch files, 416-421
parsers, 1091
partition tables
  information, 815-818
  rebuilding, 294-295
partitioning hard disks, 725-727, 1088
  FDISK command, 180-188
PAS (Pascal source) file name extension, 123
Paste command (DOS Editor Edit menu), 392
PATH command, 37, 48, 143-144, 856-858
PATH environment variable, 1001-1002
PATH settings, 326
paths
  absolute, 1087
  names, 133-137, 571
  relative, 1091
PAUSE command, 422, 858-860
pausing batch files for input, 430-433
PC AT computer, 21
PCs (personal computers)
  booting, 18-20, 29-32, 38-40, 813-815
  hardware, 13-14
  memory
    conventional, 21-23
    expanded, 23-25
    RAM, 20-21

XMS (Extended Memory Specification), 25-26
peripherals, 17-18
troubleshooting, 849-850
PCX (Picture, PC Paintbrush) file name extension, 123
peripherals, 14, 17-18
PIF (Program Information File) file name extension, 123
piping commands, 367-369, 1091
place markers, 390
platters, 152, 1091
PM4 (PageMaker 4 data) file name extension, 123
PM5 (PageMaker 5 data) file name extension, 123
point-and-shoot method, selecting menu options, 75
ports
parallel
redirecting to serial ports, 363-364
settings, 358-360
serial
initializing, 821-823
settings, 360-363
Portuguese code page, 1081
power
surge protectors, 1092
voltage regulators, 1092
POWER command, 860-864
Power On Self Test (POST), 18
POWER.EXE device driver, 459, 864-867, 981
pretender commands, 489
PRINT command, 352-356, 490, 867-871
Print command
DOS Editor File menu, 398, 402
File menu, 59
Print dialog box, 59
Print Screen key, 349, 741-743
PRINT.EXE file, 982
PRINTER.SYS device driver, 459, 549-550, 871, 989
printers, 833-836
national code page printer files, 548
settings, 349-350
PRINTFIX.COM file, 989
printing
background printing, 867-871
files, 304, 352-356
DOS Editor, 402-403
with MODE command, 359-363
graphics, 741-743
remote, 221
screen contents, 349-352
PRN (program listing, printing) file name extension, 123
PRO (Profile) file name extension, 123
Program Group Properties dialog box, 93
program groups, 72, 90-95
Program Item Properties dialog box, 96
program items, 95-97
Program List command (DOS Shell View menu), 86
Program/File Lists command (DOS Shell View menu), 72, 86
programming utilities (EXE2BIN), 716-717
programs, 851-852
associating with files in DOS Shell, 105-106
BACKUP, 599
DEBUG, 655-656
DEFRAG, 502-508
disk-compression, 635-636, 638-639
DOS, 564-565
DOS Shell, 67-74
Doskey, 443-449
DOSSHELL, 692-696
DoubleSpace program, 32, 511-520, 635-655
compressing drives, 517-519
compression ratio, 515-516
controlling, 513
Defragment option, 519
deleting compressed drives, 517
displaying compressed information, 514
drive size, 514-515
formatting compressed drives, 517
installing, 513
uncompressing disks, 520
EXE2BIN, 716-717
FASTOPEN, 497-498
filter, 837-838
INTERSVR, 771-787
loaded, 800-802
Microsoft Anti-Virus, 255, 281-286, 841-845
Microsoft Backup/Backup for Windows, 256-258, 845-847, 852-853
configuring, 258-260
differential backups, 268
full backups, 264-267
functions, 260-262
incremental backups, 267-268
special-purpose backups, 268-273
MSHERC, 851
MWAVTSR, 852
Power On Self Test (POST), 18
QBASIC, 876-878
running remotely with Interlnk, 222-223
ScanDisk, 896-901
SIZER, 922
SMARTDRV (disk caching), 492
SpinRite II, 166
stopping, 600-601
TSRs
FASTOPEN, 720-722
Interlnk, 215
Undelete (Windows), 304-305
utilities, 201-202, 990-994
VSAFE, 852
Windows Anti-Virus, 255
PROMPT command, 37, 334-337, 874-876
issuing ANSI.SYS codes, 529-530
PROMPT environment variable, 1002
PROMPT settings, 326
prompts, 1091
DOS, 1088
FOR..IN..DO command, 435
properties of program groups, 93
Properties command (DOS Shell File menu), 93, 96
protected mode, 20-21
PS (PostScript program) file name extension, 123
pull-down menus, 75-76, 1091
DOS Editor, 381

Q

/Q switch (disk caching), 495
QBASIC, 876-878
  Supplemental Disk (MS-DOS 6) files, 990
QBASIC.EXE file, 982
QBASIC.HLP file, 982
QBASIC.INI file, 982
queues, 1091
quick formatting, 178

R

RAM (random-access memory), 16, 20-21
  disks, 498-502
    TEMP environment variable, 501
  shadow RAM, 464
RAMDRIVE.SYS device driver, 459, 499, 878-882, 982
random-access memory, *see* RAM
RD command, 883-884
read-caching, 494
Read-only file attribute, 125, 127
read-only memory (ROM), 17
read/write heads, 157, 176
README files, 378, 982
real mode, 20-21
rebooting (Ctrl-Alt-Delete key combination), 1052
rebuilding partition tables, 294-295
records, locking, 917-918
RECOVER command, 291, 884-885
recovering
  data, 291-292
    MIRROR image files, 291-292
    rebuilding partition tables, 294-295
    without Mirror Image files, 292-294
  files, 295-301
    DOS directory method, 300-301
    from command line, 297-300
    UNDELETE command, 295-297
    Undelete program (Windows), 303-304
REDIR.1XE file, 989
REDIR.2XE file, 989
redirection operators, 365-367, 1091
Refresh command (DOS Shell View menu), 82
relative paths, 1091
REM command, 34, 422, 487, 885-886
remapping keyboards, 545-546
REMLINE.BAS file, 990
REN command, 233-234, 887-888
renaming
  directories, 142, 233
  files, 887-888
    with COPY command, 229
    with REN command, 233-234
  subdirectories, 838-841
Reorder command (DOS Shell File menu), 94
Repeat Last Find command (DOS Editor Search menu), 394-395
REPLACE command, 888-891
REPLACE.EXE file, 982
replaceable parameters
  in batch files, 416-421
  macros, 451
replacing text with DOS Editor, 393-397
reserved names, 118, 572-573
Reset mode codes (ANSI), 1073-1074
RESTORE command, 275, 891-895
RESTORE.EXE file, 982
restoring backup files, 275-280, 891-895
returning batch files, 438-441
reusing commands with Doskey program, 446-449
RFT (Revisable Form Text) file name extension, 123
Right Arrow key, 1054
RMDIR command, 140, 883-884
ROM (read-only memory), 17
ROM BIOS command keys, 1052-1053
root directory, 98, 129, 132, 1091
RPT (Report) file name extension, 123
RTF (Rich Text Format, Microsoft) file name extension, 123
running batch files from batch files, 437-441

S

/S switch
  disk caching, 495
  FORMAT command, 32
SAM (Ami-Pro) file name extension, 123
SAV (Backup) file name extension, 123
Save As command (DOS Editor File menu), 399-400
Save command (DOS Editor File menu), 398
saving files (DOS Editor), 398-400
ScanDisk utility, 885, 896-901
SCANDISK.EXE file, 982
SCANDISK.INI file, 982
SCANFIX command, 196-198
scanning disks for viruses, 286-287
scratchpad files, 145-147
Screen Display Mode dialog box, 88
screens
  clearing of text, 348-349
  controlling/customizing, 530-534
    cursors, 530-531
    DOS Editor, 404-406
    screen mode, 531-532
    screens, 533-534
    text attributes, 532-533
  DOS Editor, 379-380
  input/output devices, 356-358
  LCD (liquid-crystal display), 1090
  mode, setting, 531-532
  pausing, 368
  printing contents, 349-352, 1053
  text, clearing, 620

scroll bars, 63, 72-73, 1091
DOS Editor, 379, 386-387, 404-406
Search (Alt-S) command key, 58
Search menu commands (Find), 59
Search menu commands (DOS Editor)
Change, 394, 396-397
Find, 394-395
Repeat Last Find, 394, 395
searching for files with IF command, 429-430
secondary caches, 481
sector interleaving, 159
sectors, 160-162, 168-169, 1091
boot sectors, 1087
Select All command (DOS Shell File menu), 103
selecting
files, 305
text, 1091
DOS Editor, 390-391
selection cursor, 73, 1091
Serbian code page, 1083
serial numbers (floppy disks), 174-176
serial ports
initializing, 821-823
settings, 360-363
servers, 780-787
accessing, 765-770
Interlnk, 219
SET command, 34, 36, 332-334, 490, 901-906
SET file name extension, 978
Set mode codes (ANSI), 1073-1074
SETNAME.EXE file, 989
setting
screen mode, 531-532
text attributes, 532-533
SETUP.EXE file, 983
SETUP.MSG file, 983
SETVER command, 315-319, 906-913
SETVER.EXE device driver, 459, 914-916, 983
shadow RAM, 464
SHARE command, 917-918
SHARE.EXE file, 983
SHELL command, 34-36, 484-486, 918-921
Shell, *see* DOS Shell
SHIFT command, 921
moving with SHIFT command, 436-437
Shift-PrtSc (Print Screen) key combination, 1053
shortcut keys, 1091
DOS Editor, 382-383
shortcut keys, *see* hot keys
single file list, 85
Single File List command (DOS Shell View menu), 84-85
SIZER program, 922, 975
slashes (/), 52
Slavic (Latin II) code page, 1081-1082
SLT file extension, 978
SMARTDrive program (disk caching), 492, 922-926
SMARTDRV.EXE device driver, 459, 926-927, 983
SMARTMON command, 927
SMARTMON.EXE file, 984
SMARTMON.HLP file, 984
SMARTMON.LOG file, 984
software problems/prevention, 254-256
see also programs
SORT command, 371-373, 928-930
SORT.EXE file, 984
sorting, 1092
directories, 505-506
files, 304
sources, 1092
SPATCH.BAT file, 984
special characters (macros), 451
specifying command interpreter, 918-921
speed of hard disks, 492-508
SpinRite II program, 166
splitting lines of text (DOS Editor), 388
SSTOR.SYS file, 459, 984
STACKS command, 34, 35, 930-932
Start-up control keys, 1051-1052
start-up menus, 813-815
starting
DEFRAG program, 506-508
DOS timeout periods, 811-813
DOS Editor, 378
loading files, 401-402
with optional switches, 403-404
DOS Shell, 69-70
Doskey program, 443-444
static electricity, 1092
/STATUS switch (FDISK command), 186
status bar (DOS Editor), 379
status line (DOS Shell), 70
StepUp version of MS-DOS 6.2, 967
stopping programs, 600-601
strings
character, 1087
comparing with IF command, 427-429
meta-strings, 1090
STY (Stylesheet) file name extension, 123
subdirectories, 131-133, 802-804, 1092
deleting branches, 662-663
joining to other drives, 787-789
listing with DIR command, 205
renaming, 838-841
sorting, 372-373
Subdirectory file attribute, 125
SUBMENU= command, 932-934
SUBST command, 343-345, 934-936
SUBST.EXE file, 984
Supplemental Disk (MS-DOS 6) files, 985-990
surge protectors, 1092
Survival Guide, 378
switches, 52-53, 1092
/? (Help), 53-60
command-line, 53-60
commands
COPY, 227-228
DIR, 203, 205-206
DISKCOPY, 245-246
EDIT, 403-404
FC, 241-242
FDISK command, 186
FORMAT, 32, 172, 177-178
MODE, 359-363
MOVE, 231
PRINT, 353-354
SCANDISK, 197, 198
SWITCHES, 35
XCOPY, 235-236
SWITCHES command, 34-35, 488, 936-940

switching code pages, 854-855
syntax, 1092
commands, 50-52
DOSKEY command, 444
macros, 450
SYS (System or device driver) file name extension, 123
SYS command, 30-31, 190-192, 940-942
SYS.COM file, 984
system
commands, 566
configuring, 33-46, 455, 819-853
AUTOEXEC.BAT, 482-490
CONFIG.SYS, 482-490
device drivers, 456-459
hard disks, 480-482
memory optimization, 459-480
files
formatting disks, 179
transferring with SYS command, 190
System file attribute, 125
system memu, 44-46
system performance (hard disks), 491-521
system requests, 1053
system variables, 333

T

tabs, 389-390
targets, 1092
task list area, 72
task swapping, 106-107
tasks, 1092
TEMP environment variable, 1002-1003
RAM disks, 501
templates, batch files as, 420
temporary directories, 145-147
terminate-and-stay-ready (TSR) programs, Interlnk, 215
terminating commands (Ctrl-Break key combination), 1053
testing ERRORLEVEL with IF command, 424-427
text
attributes, 532-533
clearing from screens, 348-349
DOS Editor
blocks, 392-393
deleting lines, 388
finding/replacing, 393-397
indents, 388
inserting, 387
inserting lines, 388
place markers, 390
scrolling, 386-387
selecting, 390-391
splitting/joining lines, 388
tabs, 389-390
editing, 708
finding, 214, 369-371
selected, 1091
text boxes, 79
text editors, 377
text files, 1092
ASCII
combining with COPY command, 228-229
editing, 707
viewing with TYPE command, 211-214
comparing, 243-245
issuing ANSI.SYS codes, 528-529
text mode, 1092
text screens, clearing, 620
text strings, 394
text-based user interface, 334-341
TIF (Tagged Image File Format) file name extension, 123
TIME command, 313-314, 942-944
timeout periods (start-up configuration), 811-813
times, 310-314
title bars, 70
TMP (Temporary) file name extension, 123
TMP environment variable, 1002-1003
tracks, disk drives, 157-158, 1092
transferring files with Interlnk, 220-221
TREE command, 145, 944
Tree menu commands (DOS Shell)
Collapse Branch, 99
Expand All, 99
Expand One Level, 98
TREE.COM file, 984
TRY_AGAIN label (batch files), 428
TSRs (terminate-and-stay-resident) programs, 468
FASTOPEN, 720-722
Interlnk, 215
loading into upper memory, 468-470, 807-808
loading into conventional memory, 763-765
TST (Test) file name extension, 123
Turkish code page, 1082
TXT (Text) file name extension, 123
TYPE command, 196, 212-214, 420, 945-946
typematic rate, 364-365

U

/U switch in disk caching, 495
UD.GRP file, 985
UDAV.GRP file, 985
UMBs (upper memory blocks), 709-716
uncompressing disks, 520
unconditional formatting, 179
UNDELETE command, 249, 256, 295-301, 946-950
Undelete program (Windows), 301-305
configuring, 301-302
file selection, 302-303
recovering files, 303-304
UNDELETE.EXE file, 984
UNDELETE.INI file, 984
undeleting, 301-305, 1092
UNFORMAT command, 289-295, 950-951
UNFORMAT.COM file, 985
unformatting disks, 289-295
rebuilding partition tables, 294-295
recovering from accidental formats, 291-294
UNINSTALL.EXE file, 983
United Kingdom code page, 1083
United States code page, 1081
updating files, 888-891
upgrading MS-DOS 6, 967
upper memory area (UMA), 22, 460, 468-470, 685-688, 1092
loading device drivers, 666-673
loading DOS, 461-464
loading programs, 800-802